Contemporary
Literary Criticism

Guide to Gale Literary Criticism Series

For criticism on	Consult these Gale series
Authors now living or who died after December 31, 1959	*CONTEMPORARY LITERARY CRITICISM (CLC)*
Authors who died between 1900 and 1959	*TWENTIETH-CENTURY LITERARY CRITICISM (TCLC)*
Authors who died between 1800 and 1899	*NINETEENTH-CENTURY LITERATURE CRITICISM (NCLC)*
Authors who died between 1400 and 1799	*LITERATURE CRITICISM FROM 1400 TO 1800 (LC)* *SHAKESPEAREAN CRITICISM (SC)*
Authors who died before 1400	*CLASSICAL AND MEDIEVAL LITERATURE CRITICISM (CMLC)*
Authors of books for children and young adults	*CHILDREN'S LITERATURE REVIEW (CLR)*
Black writers of the past two hundred years	*BLACK LITERATURE CRITICISM (BLC)*
Short story writers	*SHORT STORY CRITICISM (SSC)*
Poets	*POETRY CRITICISM (PC)*
Dramatists	*DRAMA CRITICISM (DC)*
Major authors from the Renaissance to the present	*WORLD LITERATURE CRITICISM, 1500 TO THE PRESENT (WLC)*

For criticism on visual artists since 1850, see
MODERN ARTS CRITICISM (MAC)

ISSN 0091-3421

Volume 79

Contemporary Literary Criticism

Excerpts from Criticism of the Works
of Today's Novelists, Poets, Playwrights,
Short Story Writers, Scriptwriters, and
Other Creative Writers

James P. Draper
EDITOR

Jennifer Brostrom
Jeffery Chapman
Jennifer Gariepy
Christopher Giroux
Drew Kalasky
Marie Lazzari
Thomas Ligotti
Brigham Narins
Sean René Pollock
David Segal
Janet Witalec
ASSOCIATE EDITORS

Gale Research Inc. • *DETROIT* • *WASHINGTON, D.C.* • *LONDON*

STAFF

James P. Draper, *Editor*

Library of Congress Catalog Card Number 76-46132
ISBN 0-8103-4987-6
ISSN 0091-3421

Printed in the United States of America
Published simultaneously in the United Kingdom
by Gale Research International Limited
(An affiliated company of Gale Research Inc.)
10 9 8 7 6 5 4 3 2 1

The trademark **ITP** is used under license.

Contents

Preface vii

Acknowledgments xi

Preface

A Comprehensive Information Source
on Contemporary Literature

Named "one of the twenty-five most distinguished reference titles published during the past twenty-five years" by *Reference Quarterly*, the *Contemporary Literary Criticism (CLC)* series provides readers with critical commentary and general information on more than 2,000 authors now living or who died after December 31, 1959. Previous to the publication of the first volume of *CLC* in 1973, there was no ongoing digest monitoring scholarly and popular sources of critical opinion and explication of modern literature. *CLC*, therefore, has fulfilled an essential need, particularly since the complexity and variety of contemporary literature makes the function of criticism especially important to today's reader.

Scope of the Series

CLC presents significant passages from published criticism of works by creative writers. Since many of the authors covered by *CLC* inspire continual critical commentary, writers are often represented in more than one volume. There is, of course, no duplication of reprinted criticism.

Authors are selected for inclusion for a variety of reasons, among them the publication or dramatic production of a critically acclaimed new work, the reception of a major literary award, revival of interest in past writings, or the adaptation of a literary work to film or television.

Attention is also given to several other groups of writers—authors of considerable public interest—about whose work criticism is often difficult to locate. These include mystery and science fiction writers, literary and social critics, foreign writers, and authors who represent particular ethnic groups within the United States.

Format of the Book

Each *CLC* volume contains about 500 individual excerpts taken from hundreds of book review periodicals, general magazines, scholarly journals, monographs, and books. Entries include critical evaluations spanning from the beginning of an author's career to the most current commentary. Interviews, feature articles, and other published writings that offer insight into the author's works are also presented. Students, teachers, librarians, and researchers will find that the generous excerpts and supplementary material in *CLC* provide them with vital information required to write a term paper, analyze a poem, or lead a book discussion group. In addition, complete bibliographical citations note the original source and all of the information necessary for a term paper footnote or bibliography.

Features

A *CLC* author entry consists of the following elements:

- The **Author Heading** cites the author's name in the form under which the author has most commonly published, followed by birth date, and death date when applicable. Uncertainty as to a birth or death date is indicated by a question mark.

- A **Portrait** of the author is included when available.

- A brief **Biographical and Critical Introduction** to the author and his or her work precedes the excerpted criticism. The first line of the introduction provides the author's full name, pseudonyms (if applicable), nationality, and a listing of genres in which the author has written. Previous volumes of *CLC* in which the author has been featured are also listed in the introduction.

- A list of **Principal Works** notes the most important works by the author.

- The **Excerpted Criticism** represents various kinds of critical writing, ranging in form from the brief review to the scholarly exegesis. Essays are selected by the editors to reflect the spectrum of opinion about a specific work or about an author's literary career in general. The excerpts are presented chronologically, adding a useful perspective to the entry. All titles by the author featured in the entry are printed in boldface type, which enables the reader to easily identify the works being discussed. Publication information (such as publisher names and book prices) and parenthetical numerical references (such as footnotes or page and line references to specific editions of a work) have been deleted at the editor's discretion to provide smoother reading of the text.

- Critical essays are prefaced by **Explanatory Notes** as an additional aid to readers. These notes may provide several types of valuable information, including: the reputation of the critic, the importance of the work of criticism, the commentator's approach to the author's work, the purpose of the criticism, and changes in critical trends regarding the author.

- A complete **Bibliographical Citation** designed to help the user find the original essay or book follows each excerpt.

- A concise **Further Reading** section appears at the end of entries on authors for whom a significant amount of criticism exists in addition to the pieces reprinted in *CLC*. Cross-references to other useful sources published by Gale Research in which the author has appeared are also included: *Children's Literature Review, Contemporary Authors, Something about the Author, Dictionary of Literary Biography, Drama Criticism, Poetry Criticism, Short Story Criticism, Contemporary Authors Autobiography Series,* and *Something about the Author Autobiography Series*.

Other Features

CLC also includes the following features:

- An **Acknowledgments** section lists the copyright holders who have granted permission to reprint material in this volume of *CLC*. It does not, however, list every book or periodical reprinted or consulted during the preparation of the volume.

- A **Cumulative Author Index** lists all the authors who have appeared in the various literary criticism series published by Gale Research, with cross-references to Gale's biographical and autobiographical series. A full listing of the series referenced there appears on the first page of the indexes of this volume. Readers will welcome this cumulated author index as a useful tool for locating an author within the various series. The index, which lists birth and death dates when available, will be particularly valuable for those authors who are identified with a certain period but whose death dates cause them to be placed in another, or for those authors whose careers span two periods. For example, Ernest Hemingway is found in *CLC,* yet a writer often associated with him, F. Scott Fitzgerald, is found in *Twentieth-Century Literary Criticism.*

■ A **Cumulative Nationality Index** alphabetically lists all authors featured in *CLC* by nationality, followed by numbers corresponding to the volumes in which the authors appear.

■ A **Title Index** alphabetically lists all titles reviewed in the current volume of *CLC.* Listings are followed by the author's name and the corresponding page numbers where the titles are discussed. English translations of foreign titles and variations of titles are cross-referenced to the title under which a work was originally published. Titles of novels, novellas, dramas, films, record albums, and poetry, short story, and essay collections are printed in italics, while all individual poems, short stories, essays, and songs are printed in roman type within quotation marks; when published separately (e.g., T. S. Eliot's poem *The Waste Land*), the titles of long poems are printed in italics.

■ In response to numerous suggestions from librarians, Gale has also produced a **Special Paperbound Edition** of the *CLC* title index. This annual cumulation, which alphabetically lists all titles reviewed in the series, is available to all customers and is published with the first volume of *CLC* issued in each calendar year. Additional copies of the index are available upon request. Librarians and patrons will welcome this separate index: it saves shelf space, is easy to use, and is recyclable upon receipt of the following year's cumulation.

Citing *Contemporary Literary Criticism*

When writing papers, students who quote directly from any volume in the Literary Criticism Series may use the following general forms to footnote reprinted criticism. The first example pertains to material drawn from periodicals, the second to material reprinted in books:

[1]Anne Tyler, "Manic Monologue," *The New Republic* 200 (April 17, 1989), 44-6; excerpted and reprinted in *Contemporary Literary Criticism,* Vol. 58, ed. Roger Matuz (Detroit: Gale Research Inc., 1990), p. 325.

[2]Patrick Reilly, *The Literature of Guilt: From 'Gulliver' to Golding* (University of Iowa Press, 1988); excerpted and reprinted in *Contemporary Literary Criticism,* Vol. 58, ed. Roger Matuz (Detroit: Gale Research Inc., 1990), pp. 206-12.

Suggestions Are Welcome

The editor hopes that readers will find *CLC* a useful reference tool and welcomes comments about the work. Send comments and suggestions to: Editor, *Contemporary Literary Criticism,* Gale Research Inc., Penobscot Building, Detroit, MI 48226-4094.

Acknowledgments

The editors wish to thank the copyright holders of the excerpted criticism included in this volume, the permissions managers of many book and magazine publishing companies for assisting us in securing reprint rights, and Anthony Bogucki for assistance with copyright research. We are also grateful to the staffs of the Detroit Public Library, the Library of Congress, the University of Detroit Library, Wayne State University Purdy/Kresge Library Complex, and the University of Michigan Libraries for making their resources available to us. Following is a list of the copyright holders who have granted us permission to reprint material in this volume of *CLC*. Every effort has been made to trace copyright, but if omissions have been made, please let us know.

COPYRIGHTED EXCERPTS IN *CLC*, VOLUME 79, WERE REPRINTED FROM THE FOLLOWING PERIODICALS:

America, v. 110, February 22, 1964. © 1964, renewed 1992. All rights reserved. Reprinted with permission of America Press, Inc., 106 West 56th Street, New York, NY 10019.—*The Bloomsbury Review,* v. 8, March-April, 1988 by "Writers on Writing" by Ed Quillen; v. 11, April-May, 1991 for an interview by Rick Bass and John Murray; v. 11, April-May, 1991 for a review of "Winter: Notes form Montana" by John Murray. Copyright © by Owaissa Communications Company, Inc. 1988, 1991. All reprinted by the respective authors.—*Book World—The Washington Post,* April 20, 1980. © 1980, *The Washington Post.* Reprinted with permission of the publisher.—*Books in Canada,* v. XX, September, 1991./ v. 8, May, 1970 for "Short Day's Journey into Night" by George Woodcock. Reprinted by permission of the author.—*Callaloo,* v. 10, Spring, 1987. Copyright © 1987 by Charles H. Rowell. All rights reserved. Reprinted by permission of the publisher.—*The Canadian Fiction Magazine,* n. 47, 1983. Copyright © 1983 by *The Canadian Fiction Magazine.* Reprinted by permission of the publisher.—*Canadian Forum,* v. 63, October, 1983 for "Warts, Reticences and All" by Jon Peirce. Reprinted by permission of the author.—*Canadian Literature,* n. 47, Winter, 1971 for "Dorothy Livesay: 'The Love Poetry' " by Peter Stevens. Reprinted by permission of the author.—*Chicago Tribune—Books,* February 17, 1991 for "Rick Bass Seeks Solace in Snowland" by Lee K. Abbott. © 1991, Chicago Tribune Company. All rights reserved. Reprinted by permission of the author./ February 14, 1988; December 11, 1988; July 23, 1989. © 1988, 1989, Chicago Tribune Company. All rights reserved. All used with permission.—*Children's Literature: Annual of The Modern Language Association Group on Children's Literature and The Children's Literature Association,* v. 6, 1977. © 1977 by Francelia Butler. All rights reserved. Reprinted by permission of the publisher.—*Classical and Modern Literature,* v. 10, Fall, 1989. © 1989 CML, Inc. Reprinted by permission of the publisher.—*College English,* v. 39, November, 1977 for "Authority, 'Cognitive Atheism', and the Aims of Interpretation: The Literary Theory of E.D. Hirsch" by William E. Cain./ v. 40, November, 1978 for "On 'Atlas Shrugged'" by Judith Wilt. Copyright © 1977, 1978 by the National Council of Teachers of English. Both reprinted by permission of the publisher and the respective authors.—*Comparative Literature,* v. 31, Fall, 1979 for a review of "The Aims of Interpretation" by John M. Ellis. © copyright 1979 by University of Oregon. Reprinted by permission of the author.—*Critique: Studies in Modern Fiction,* v. IX, 1967. Copyright © 1967 Helen Dwight Reid Educational Foundation. Reprinted with permission of the Helen Dwight Reid Educational Foundation, published by Heldref Publications, 1319 18th Street, N.W., Washington, DC 20036-1802.—*Essays on Canadian Writing,* n. 37, Spring, 1989. © 1989 Essays on Canadian Writing Ltd. Reprinted by permission of the publisher.—*Essays in Literature,* v. XIV, Spring, 1987. Copyright 1987 by Western Illinois University. Reprinted by permission of the publisher.—*Essays and Studies,* n.s. v. 24, 1971. © The English Association 1971. All rights reserved. Reprinted by permission of the publisher.—*The Explicator,* v. 41, Spring, 1983. Copyright 1983 by Helen Dwight Reid Educational Foundation. Reprinted with permission of the Helen Dwight Reid Educational Foundation, published by Heldref Publications, 1319 18th Street, NW, Washington DC 20036-1802.—*The French Review,* v. LVI, February, 1983; v. LVI, March, 1983. Copyright 1983 by the American Association of Teachers of French. Both reprinted by permission of the publisher.—*The Humanities Association Bulletin,* v. XXI, Spring, 1970 for

Reprinted by permission of *Quill and Quire* and the author./v. 57, February, 1991. Reprinted by permission of *Quill and Quire.—Revue des langues vivantes*, v. XXXVI, 1970 for "Ayn Rand's Neurotic Personalities of Our Times" by Paul Deane. Reprinted by permission of the author.—*Rooms of One's Own*, v. 5, 1979. © 1979 by the Growing Room Collective. Reprinted by permission of the publisher.—*Salmagundi*, v. 72, Fall, 1986. Copyright © 1986 by Skidmore College. Both reprinted by permission of the publisher.—*The Saturday Review of Literature*, v. XXX, February 1, 1947. Copyright 1947, renewed 1975, *Saturday Review* magazine. Reprinted by permission of the publisher.—*South Atlantic Quarterly*, v. 89, Winter, 1990. Copyright © 1990 by Duke University Press, Durham, NC. Reprinted with permission of the publisher.—*The Southern Quarterly*, v. XXII, Fall, 1983. Copyright © 1983 by the University of Southern Mississippi. Reprinted by permission of the publisher.—*The Spectator*, v. 259, September 12, 1987. © 1987 by *The Spectator*. Reprinted by permission of *The Spectator.—The Theatre Book of the Year, 1944 & 1945*. Copyright 1945 by George Jean Nathan. Renewed 1972 by Mrs. George Jean Nathan. Reprinted by permission of Associated University Presses, Inc., for the Estate of George Jean Nathan.—*Time,* New York, v. 130, July 20, 1987; v. 134, July 14, 1989. Copyright 1987, 1989 The Time Inc. Magazine Company. All rights reserved. Both reprinted by permission of *Time.—The Times Literary Supplement*, n. 3911, February 25, 1977; n. 4521, November 24, 1989; n. 4618, October 4, 1991. © The Times Supplements Limited 1977, 1989, 1991. All reproduced from *The Times Literary Supplement* by permission.—*The Twentieth Century*, v. 175, First quarter, 1967. © *The Twentieth Century* 1967.—*Twentieth Century Literature*, v. 25, Spring, 1979. Copyright 1979, Hofstra University Press. Reprinted by permission of the publisher.—*Western American Literature*, v. XXI, May, 1986; v. XXV, November, 1990. Copyright, 1986, 1990, by the Western Literature Association. Both reprinted by permission of the publisher.—*Wilderness*, v. 51, Summer, 1988; v. 54, Summer, 1991. © 1988, 1991 by The Wilderness Society. Both reprinted by permission of the publisher.

COPYRIGHTED EXCERPTS IN *CLC*, VOLUME 79, WERE REPRINTED FROM THE FOLLOWING BOOKS:

Adorno, Theodor W. From *Prisms*. Spearman, 1967. Copyright © Theodor W. Adorno 1967. All rights reserved. Reprinted by permission of the publisher.—Baker, James T. From *Ayn Rand*. Twayne, 1987. Copyright © 1987 by G. K. Hall & Co. All rights reserved. Reprinted with the permission of Twayne Publishers, an imprint of Macmillan Publishing Company.—Bellow, Saul. From *Seize the Day*. The Viking Press, 1956. Copyright © Saul Bellow, 1956, 1974. All rights reserved.—Bettelheim, Bruno. From *A Good Enough Parent: A Book on Childbearing*. Random House, Inc., 1987. Copyright © 1987 by Bruno Bettelheim. All rights reserved.—Bigsby, C. W. E. From *Confrontation and Commitment: A Study of Contemporary American Drama, 1959-66*. University of Missouri Press, 1968. © 1967 and 1968 by C. W. E. Bigsby. Reprinted by permission of the author.—Boyers, Robert. From "Politics & History: Pathways in European Film," in *The Salmagundi Reader*. Edited by Robert Boyers and Peggy Boyers. Indiana University Press, 1983. Copyright © 1983 by Robert Boyers and Peggy Boyers. All rights reserved. Reprinted by permission of the publisher.—Branden, Nathaniel. From *Judgment Day: My Years with Ayn Rand*. Houghton Mifflin Company, 1989. Copyright © 1989 by Nathaniel Branden. All rights reserved. Reprinted by permission of Houghton Mifflin Company.—Brustein, Robert. From *Seasons of Discontent: Dramatic Opinions, 1959-1965*. Simon & Schuster, 1965. Copyright © 1959, 1960, 1961, 1962, 1963, 1964, 1965 by Robert Brustein. All rights reserved. Reprinted by permission of Simon & Schuster, Inc.—Ciancio, Ralph. From "The Achievement of Saul Bellow's 'Seize the Day'," in *Literature and Theology*. Edited by Thomas F. Staley and Lester F. Zimmerman. University of Tulsa, 1969. Copyright 1969 by The University of Tulsa. All rights reserved. Reprinted by permission of the publisher.—Clayton, John Jacob. From *Saul Bellow: In Defense of Man*. Indiana University Press, 1968. Copyright © 1968 by Indiana University Press. All rights reserved. Reprinted by permission of the publisher.—Colmer, John. From *Coleridge to Catch-22: Images of Society*. St. Martin's Press, 1978. © John Colmer 1978. All rights reserved. Reprinted with permission of St. Martin's Press, Incorporated.—Costello, Peter. From *The Heart Grown Brutal: The Irish Revolution in Literature, from Parnell to the Death of Yeats, 1891-1939*. Gill and Macmillan, 1977. © Peter Costello 1977. Reprinted by permission of the publisher.—Dahl, Roald. From *Going Solo*. Johnathan Cape, 1986. Copyright © 1986 by Roald Dahl.—Dodson, Owen, and John O'Brien. From an interview in *Interviews with Black Writers*.

Edited by John O'Brien. Liveright, 1973. Copyright © 1973 by Liveright. Reprinted by permission of Liveright Publishing Corporation.—Firchow, Peter Edgerly. From *The End of Utopia: A Study of Aldous Huxley's "Brave New World."* Bucknell University Press, 1984. Reprinted by permission of the publisher.—Gladstein, Mimi Reisel. From *The Ayn Rand Companion.* Greenwood Press, 1984. Copyright © 1984 by Mimi Reisel Gladstein. All rights reserved. Reprinted by permission of Greenwood Publishing Group, Inc., Westport, CT.—Greenblatt, Stephen. From *Three Modern Satirists: Waugh, Orwell, and Huxley.* Yale University Press, 1965. Copyright © 1965 by Yale University. All rights reserved. Reprinted by permission of the author.—Hess, Hermann. From an extract translated by G. Wallis Field in *Aldous Huxley: The Critical Heritage.* Edited by Donald Watt. Routledge & Kegan Paul Ltd., 1975. Reprinted by permission of the publisher.—Hirsch, E. D., Jr. From *Cultural Literary: What Every American Needs to Know.* Houghton Mifflin Company, 1987. Copyright © 1987 by Houghton Mifflin Company. All rights reserved.—Jeffs, Rae. From *Brendan Behan: Man and Showman.* Hutchinson, 1966. Copyright © 1966 by Rae Jeffs. All rights reserved.—Kearney, Colbert. From *The Writings of Brendan Behan.* St. Martin's Press, 1977. © Colbert Kearney, 1977. All rights reserved. Reprinted with permission of St. Martin's Press, Incorporated.—Krause, David. From *The Profane Book of Irish Comedy.* Cornell, 1982. Copyright © 1982 by Cornell University Press. All rights reserved. Used by permission of the publisher, Cornell University Press.—Twigg, Alan. From an interview in *For Openers: Conversations with 24 Canadian Writers.* Harbour Publishing, 1981. Copyright © 1981 Alan Twigg. All rights reserved. Reprinted by permission of the publisher.—Márquez, Robert, and David Arthur McMurray. From an introduction to *Man-Making Words: Selected Poems of Nicolás Guillén.* Translated by Robert Márquez and David Arthur McMurray. University of Massachusetts Press, 1972. Translations copyright © 1972 by Robert Márquez and David Arthur McMurray. All rights reserved. Reprinted by permission of the publisher.—Maxwell, Desmond. From "Brendan Behan's Theatre," in *Irish Writers and The Theatre.* Edited by Masaru Sekine. Colin Smythe, 1986. Copyright © 1986 Desmond Maxwell. All rights reserved. Reprinted by permission of the publisher.—Merrill, Ronald E. From *The Ideas of Ayn Rand.* Open Court, 1991. Copyright 1991 by Ronald E. Merrill. All rights reserved. Reprinted by permission of Open Court Publishing Company, La Salle, Illinois.—Mitcham, Allison. From *The Northern Imagination: A Study of Northern Canadian Literature.* Penumbra Press, 1983. © Allison Mitcham and Penumbra Press, 1983. Reprinted by permission of the publisher.—Porter, M. Gilbert. From *Whence the Power?: The Artistry and Humanity of Saul Bellow.* University of Missouri Press, 1974. Copyright © 1974 by The Curators of the University of Missouri. All rights reserved. Reprinted by permission of the publisher.—Shek, Ben-Zion. From *Social Realism in the French-Canadian Novel.* Harvest House, 1977. Copyright 1977 by Harvest House Ltd. All rights reserved. Reprinted by permission of the publisher.—Smart, Ian Isidore. From *Nicolás Guillén: Popular Poet of the Caribbean.* University of Missouri Press, 1990. Copyright © 1990 by The Curators of the University of Missouri. All rights reserved. Reprinted by permission of the publisher.—Smith, George H. From *Atheism, Ayn Rand, and Other Heresies.* Prometheus Books, 1991. Copyright © 1991 by George H. Smith. All rights reserved. Reprinted by permission the publisher.—Thériault, Yves. From *Agaguk.* Translated by Miriam Chapin. McGraw-Hill Ryerson. English Translation © The Ryerson Press 1963.—Tougas, Gerard. From *History of French-Canadian Literature.* Translated by Alta Lind Cook. Second edition. Ryerson Press, 1966. © The Ryerson Press, 1966. Reprinted by permission of the publisher.

PHOTOGRAPHS AND ILLUSTRATIONS APPEARING IN *CLC*, VOLUME 79, WERE RECEIVED FROM THE FOLLOWING SOURCES:

L.L. Griffin © 1992: **p. 1;** Photograph by Tony Armstrong Jones: **p. 23;** Drawing by Liam Martin: **p. 46;** © Thomas Victor: **p. 60;** AP/Wide World Photos: **pp. 105, 173, 283;** © 1993 Sigrid Estrada: **p. 152;** UPI/Bettmann: **pp. 185, 356;** Photograph by Arthur Kopit: **p. 201;** © Lütfi Özkök: **p. 226;** Reproduced by permission of the Estate of Carl Van Vechten, Joseph Solomon Executor: **p. 237;** Editorial La Muralla: **p. 245;** Photograph by Vaughn Winchell: **p. 253;** Photograph by Janosz Meissner: **p. 331;** Courtesy of Dorothy Livesay: **p. 346;** Photograph by Kéro: **p. 398.**

Rick Bass

1958-

American nonfiction writer, essayist, and short story writer.

The following entry provides an overview of Bass's career and works through 1992.

INTRODUCTION

Best known for his treatment of the connection between man and nature, Bass is widely regarded as an innovative contributor to contemporary American literature. While he often writes in a journal form sometimes termed "creative nonfiction," combining observations of the natural world with personal reflections, Bass is also considered a gifted fiction writer whose short stories feature realistic characters placed in bizarre situations. Critics have consistently emphasized Bass's unique perspective on environmental topics and praised his use of a vernacular idiom.

Bass was born in Fort Worth, Texas. As a child he frequently listened to the tall tales and stories told by his grandfather and older relatives during family hunting expeditions—experiences which later influenced his use of an informal, colloquial prose style in his fiction. John Murray commented: "As a result of this unique apprenticeship, there is a strong oral quality to Bass' nonfiction and fiction narratives. . . . In this orality, he comes straight out of a southwestern literary line that runs back through Edward Abbey and Mark Twain to Thomas Trapp and James Pattie." In 1976 Bass began studies at Utah State University, where he majored in wildlife sciences and later specialized in geology. After graduating, he moved to Mississippi, where he was employed as a petroleum geologist. During this time Bass began writing essays and fiction about hunting and camping. In 1987 he left his position in the petroleum industry and moved to Yaak, Montana, a remote community where he began writing full-time while serving as the caretaker of a ranch.

Bass's enchantment with nature informs each of his works. In his first book, a collection of essays entitled *The Deer Pasture,* Bass recalls the hunting expeditions of his childhood, providing painstaking descriptions of the people, activities, and sensations associated with the trips. Included in this collection is "Why We Do It," an essay in which Bass describes the thrill, challenge, and tradition often associated with hunting. In praising *The Deer Pasture,* critics noted Bass's unapologetic enthusiasm for the sport and his defense of his seemingly contradictory position as an environmentalist and hunter. Bass incorporates similar subjects in *Wild to the Heart,* his second collection of wilderness essays. In this volume Bass provides first-person narratives of his camping and fishing expeditions

and emphasizes the bond that exists among outdoor sport enthusiasts.

Bass turned to fiction with his next book, *The Watch,* for which he received a PEN/Nelson Algren Award Special Citation in 1988. A collection of short stories, *The Watch* displays the same minimalist style and preoccupation with nature found in Bass's earlier works. The stories feature unconventional characters and situations; in "Mexico," for example, the narrator and his wife become obsessed with raising a record-breaking bass in their swimming pool, but their hopes are dashed when a group of teenagers sneak into their yard and steal the fish. The title story of the collection, anthologized in the 1989 *O. Henry Awards* volume, concerns a man's search for his father who has abandoned the ghost town where the two had been living alone. This story was applauded by such critics as Peter S. Prescott, who commented that "The Watch"—"which proceeds imperceptibly from country realism to wild fantasy, has the look of an American classic." Bass also garnered high praise for the other stories in *The Watch;* he received the 1987 General Electric Younger Writers Award for "Wild Horses," and "Cats and Students, Bubbles and Abysses" was anthologized in *Best American Short Stories of 1988*.

Oil Notes is a loosely constructed journal of Bass's experiences as a petroleum geologist and a record of his personal philosophies. In this work Bass provides various accounts of oil prospecting and drilling, but the majority of his entries detail such private topics as his mishaps with a company car; his love for his girlfriend, Elizabeth Hughes, whose illustrations appear in the text; and his reflections on his career and the natural world. Bass employs a similar journal style in *Winter: Notes from Montana,* which chronicles the harsh winter he endured while living in Yaak, Montana. Bass details Yaak's landscape, its people, and such area establishments as the Dirty Shame Saloon, where people gather to watch "Monday Night Football." Many critics extolled Bass's character sketches and his meticulous attention to detail in *Winter: Notes from Montana,* but some faulted what they perceived to be a lack of introspection and self-analysis.

In his book-length essay *The Ninemile Wolves* Bass addresses the controversy associated with the reappearance of a wolf pack in Montana. Having neared extinction, the wolves have been a source of much debate: wildlife conservationists argue that the animals are an integral part of the ecosystem while ranchers and hunters view the species as a threat to livestock and game. Bass acknowledges both viewpoints in the essay, but by illustrating the nobility and beauty of the wolves, he implicitly presents an argument for the preservation of American wolf packs. Several commentators characterized Bass's arguments in *The Ninemile Wolves* as forceful and moving, and his images as striking. Christopher Lehmann-Haupt commented: "At the best places in *The Ninemile Wolves,* it is as if the reader too were one of the pack."

Bass has established himself as an important figure in contemporary fiction and nonfiction with his conversational style and his trenchant perspectives on environmental topics. While some commentators characterize Bass's prose style as overly simplistic, many praise his personal honesty and commend his skill in creating vivid, lasting images. John Murray commented: "Rick Bass is one of the most gifted young writers to appear in quite a few years. . . . [A] truly significant writer is emerging here."

PRINCIPAL WORKS

The Deer Pasture (essays) 1985
Wild to the Heart (essays) 1987
The Watch (short stories) 1988
Oil Notes (nonfiction) 1989
Winter: Notes from Montana (nonfiction) 1991
The Ninemile Wolves (essay) 1992

CRITICISM

Nancy Williams   **(review date May 1986)**

[*In the following excerpt, Williams praises Bass's complex and paradoxical depiction of deer hunting in* The Deer Pasture.]

The mystique of the annual deer hunt is assumed by many nonhunters to consist of the thrill of shooting, boozing it up under starry skies around a campfire, and generally escaping from civilized life with a few days of primitive stench and sweat. Rick Bass, in [*The Deer Pasture*], puts the lie to this popular myth—but gently. Deer stalkers will find plenty to enjoy in this volume, even while confirmed bambi-lovers gasp in recognition, realizing that they finally understand why their friends and loved ones venture forth each autumn with guns. Turns out it's not just blood lust that propels them; it's not even purely escapism. According to Bass, it's also tradition, memories, and storytelling. It's Cousin Randy, and the way the armadillos that also populate the Texas woods leap straight into the air and bolt when you surprise them; it's the smell of hickory trees turning gold in Gillespie County, and the taste of Bass Wonder Biscuits and Dr. Pepper bread.

The author and his family have made pilgrimages each November for 50 years to this "deer pasture," a hunting lease in the Texas Hill Country. This collection of stories is as much about that family and its lore as it is about hunting, although Bass includes a piece called **"Why We Do It"** that begins thus:

> By now you may be beginning to suspect that we go to the deer pasture each November for reasons other than hunting deer, and it's true, but for a fact there is essentially one and only one thing that is thought about during the daylight hours, from first grey light to too-dark-to-see-through-the-scope dusk, or at least until we each have a deer in the freezer, and the thought is exactly that: getting one. Challenging. Winning. Making the kill, to put it bluntly. Harvesting, to put it to people who do not understand.

And there you have the paradox that Bass has spun his book around, the reason to keep turning pages.

Rick Bass's life is a study in more paradoxes: employed as a petroleum geologist, he is also an active environmentalist and Sierra Club member. He's a regular contributor of articles to *Field and Stream, Sports Afield, Gray's Sporting Journal, Outdoor Life*—but yearns to publish his fiction. He's an alumnus of the Breadloaf Writer's Workshop and has won several awards for his stories.

This is Bass's first book. I hope there will be more. (pp. 72-3)

> *Nancy Williams, in a review of "The Deer Pasture," in* Western American Literature, *Vol. XXI, No. 1, May, 1986, pp. 72-3.*

Charles E. Little   **(review date Summer 1988)**

[*Little is an American critic whose book review column*

appears regularly in the periodical Wilderness. *In the following excerpt, he applauds Bass's wit and depth of emotion in* Wild to the Heart.]

[In **Wild to the Heart,** Bass] juxtaposes tales of mad-dash weekend journeys to old western wilderness haunts, and local forays down southern rivers and into southern swamps. Bass writes vividly and with great wit. Concerning a wilderness trek into the Northern Rockies, for example: "The closer you get to Canada, the more things'll eat your horse." Or, concerning a white-water trip down a nasty patch of wild southern river: "Bull Sluice is to solo canoeists what the Hindenberg was to aviation safety."

But he writes with great tenderness, too. This is about Lolo Pass, in Utah:

> There's got to be a strange and long-lost history about the place; sometimes, working my way through a narrow niche in a sheer cliff wall between two wild and empty valleys, threading my way down a talus slope as a snow-dusting August storm comes rolling in low and foggy, rolling in to meet me, then sometimes I will begin crying for no reason. A terrible sadness wrenches from me, and I have to get away from the place and down to one of the meadows below me before the feeling is gone.

Here is a fresh new voice, from a writer not yet thirty, a marvel in a way, as surprising (though quite differently) as Edward Abbey was a generation ago. (pp. 60-1)

> *Charles E. Little, "We Salute New Advocates for Wilderness," in* Wilderness, *Vol. 51, No. 181, Summer, 1988, pp. 60-1.*

Joseph Coates (review date 11 December 1988)

[*In the following excerpt, Coates praises several aspects of Bass's writing style but faults the lack of conceptual thought in his fiction.*]

Fiction by Rick Bass probably ought to be a controlled substance, but thank God it isn't—yet. In fact, one way of describing his work [in **The Watch**] (and it won't be easy) is to say that it seems to have been written by someone who expects to be arrested any minute.

Its salient feature is a kind of headlong, defiant intoxication that quickly hooks the reader into its subversive message, which is one of rebellion against all the paltry but overpowering forces in modern America that combine to squeeze the sweetness out of life.

His protagonists are the last cowboys, Huck Finns who lit out for what's left of the Territory only to find it full of Tom Sawyers selling quiche or playing some other stupid game that mortgages their own freedom and threatens to destroy ours.

His men get high on lots of things, but the intoxicant of choice is the high country itself, as in **"Choteau"**:

> We'll sit here, so high in the Canadian Rockies, and watch clouds pass over the moon, feel the bite of what feels like the edges of eternity, a certain forever-aspect to things, as if this is the way

it should always be up in this country—frigid, locked-in and cold, with springtime and yellow-flowered summer only an accident, which will, one year, not even bother happening.

In the PEN/Nelson Algren Award Special Citation that Bass received this year, the judges singled out his "magic realism." But that quality, if it exists in his work, appears not in the kind of surreal events or atmosphere that we see in García Márquez but in the arbitrary strangeness of Bass' situations, which he somehow makes plausible. Each story [in **The Watch**] sets things up with broad brush-strokes of primary color, as in a kindergarten.

"Kirby's faithful," the first one begins.

> He's loyal: Kirby has fidelity. He has one wife, Tricia. The bass's name is Shack. The fish is not in an aquarium. It's in the swimming pool that Kirby built, out in his and Tricia's front yard. It's a big pool. I believe it can hold a twenty-three-pounder. When we're drunk, I'm sure of it.

The story then proceeds to make us believe (I swear) in this extended family of man, wife, fish and buddy-narrator, and in the worthiness of their preposterous undertaking, which is to grow Shack to record size.

That, minus the fish, is the essential constellation in the basic Bass story, which could be described as a buddy movie taken to mystical extremes: Two good guys, plus a girl who belongs to one of them, opposed by a foil whose villainy consists of money-grubbing and inability to love. Resistance to growing up is how Bass defines the goodness of this primitive "community of saints," as Lionel Trilling described Huck and Jim on their raft.

What's exhilarating about Bass' stories is that they show every hallmark of "the natural"—that lucid, free-flowing, particularly American talent whose voice we can hear in Twain, Fitzgerald and Hemingway, one especially suited to the American scene.

—Joseph Coates

"Galena Tom [the good guy in **'Choteau'**] is the last tough man there is, for a fact—but it's because he's still got that boy in him, some part he flat-out refuses to let go of." And the narrator of another Kirby story, **"Juggernaut,"** admits frankly that "we were frightened of growing up."

Take the watch apart and what have you got? In this case, the theme of Leslie Fiedler's *Love and Death in the American Novel:* "The failure of the American fictionist to deal with adult heterosexual love and his consequent obsession with death, incest and innocent homosexuality." Which is to say, the more we try to analyze Bass' stories, the farther we get from their magical, evocative essence.

That essence is in riffs like this, from **"Mississippi"**:

> There are wild turkeys in the woods. When it rains it smells like orchids out here. None of the preachers have any spit or love to them but they can be avoided. Tornadoes are exciting. They said the governor was a homosexual but he got elected anyway. When you are canoeing at night and the paddle first goes into the water it sounds like God is talking to you.

This might seem to have been taken out of context, but in fact it *is* the context; the story is built on blocks of lyrical description from which the basic Bass fable gradually emerges. This technique is reminiscent of Renata Adler's *Speedboat* or Rilke's *Notebooks of Malte Laurids Brigge*. Although those are very urban books, Bass seems to have applied their method to the American Outback.

What's exhilarating about Bass' stories is that they show every hallmark of "the natural"—that lucid, free-flowing, particularly American talent whose voice we can hear in Twain, Fitzgerald and Hemingway, one especially suited to the American scene. It's also what is depressing about Bass: There is no sign he has any conceptual awareness of what might be done with such a stunning instrument, though that might be too much to expect from an initial book of short stories.

That lack is an especially American failing, as Wright Morris says in "The Territory Ahead": ". . . the labyrinthine reminiscence of Proust is . . . *consciously* conceptual, in contrast to the highly unconscious reminiscence in 'Huckleberry Finn.' Not *knowing* what he was doing, Mark Twain was under no compulsion to do it again."

And with no more conceptual baggage than the values of a buddy movie, not even a peckerwood Rilke can get very far. (pp. 1, 12)

> *Joseph Coates, "A 'Natural' Writer Who Won't Grow Up," in* Chicago Tribune—Books, *December 11, 1988, pp. 1, 12.*

Peter S. Prescott   (review date 9 January 1989)

[*Prescott is an American educator and critic. In the following review, he provides a positive assessment of* The Watch.]

Rick Bass's **The Watch** conveys some of the excitement that Richard Ford's *Rock Springs* provoked two years ago: a sense that a potentially significant writer of short stories has emerged. Like Ford, Bass has lived in both the South and the mountainous West; like Ford, he writes eloquently about marginally articulate men. Women appear in Bass's stories, and they are attractive, but they're usually attached to the narrator's buddy—and they can prove at times superfluous. So, in the great tradition of American fiction, the men break away to act boyishly again, and in the tradition of American fiction since World War I, a sense of loss invades their antics. Bass's aging boys share premonitions that they can't recapture what they had; they haven't even a sense of a firm future before them. One says: "It seems that we've already died . . . and everything is over."

Bass sets his stories in Houston, the bayous of the Mississippi, the Texas coast, a county in Montana so cold that deer and elk freeze in their tracks upright. One man dreams that a hybrid bass he shelters in his swimming pool will grow to record weight; another, a retired rodeo hand, rides a moose "in a land where no one else can get to." In **"The Watch,"** an altogether remarkable story of "poisoned loneliness," a man lives alone in a ghost town with his father—until his father escapes to a new life in the yellow-fever swamplands. In an attempt to recover the past, the son hunts the old man down. This story, which proceeds imperceptibly from country realism to wild fantasy, has the look of an American classic. The others are of uneven merit, but never less than interesting. Bass will soon learn that his readers can grasp a metaphor before it is explicitly defined; in the meantime, he is always an elegant writer.

> *Peter S. Prescott, "Old Witchery, New Elegance: Unusually Fine Stories," in* Newsweek, *Vol. CXIII, No. 2, January 9, 1989, p. 57.*

Mark Kamine   (review date 6 February 1989)

[*In the following review, Kamine applauds Bass's characterizations in* The Watch.]

Over the past two years Rick Bass has published short fiction in the *Paris Review, Esquire, GQ,* and the *Quarterly.* His work has been anthologized in *Best American Short Stories* and *New Writing from the South,* and his was the opening story in *The Pushcart Prize XIII.* **"The Watch,"** the title piece of this first collection, will appear in the upcoming *O'Henry Awards* volume. All told, as impressive a record as any young writer of the '80s has compiled—and these have been boom years for young writers.

The book is equally impressive. Bass gives us more than well-crafted prose and the glimmerings of a voice; several of the stories are fully achieved, free from all residue of apprenticeship.

The 10 stories in **The Watch** are set in the heart of the country: Texas, Utah, the woods of Mississippi and the hills of Montana. They are dominated by their male figures, and thus full of fishing and hunting and drinking. But Bass does not glamorize these American male pastimes, he realizes how easy it is to hide behind them, to use them to avoid confronting the more substantial challenges presented to us in living with ourselves and among others.

In **"Choteau,"** the chief figure is Galena Jim Ontz, a man with "two girlfriends and a key to Canada." He's one of those fearless, hard-drinking, hard-driving frontiersmen out of America's legendary past, and the nameless first-person narrator follows wherever Galena Jim leads. The narrator understands Jim better than he understands himself, however, as we soon learn:

> [Jim]'s got black hair, an old lined-looking face—he's forty—and light blue eyes, a kid's grin. . . . He loves to hunt. I do not know how he got the key [to the gate leading to Canada]. Some sort of charm or guile somewhere, I'm

sure. People only see that side of him. Though surely Patsy, who has been his girlfriend ever since she left Oklahoma with him, sees the other part. I do, too. He is still a boy, still learning to be a man, this is the fortieth year of his life.

Jim's nickname harks back to the night he stole a cement-mixer, filled it with the luminous blue ore called galena, then poured the mixture of ore and cement onto the streets and sidewalks and main plaza of his town, creating galena-speckled surfaces: "Your car or truck headlights will pick up sudden, flashing blue-bolt chunks and swatches in the road, blazing like blue eyes, sunk down in the road—the whole road glittering and bouncing with that weird blue galena light, if you are driving fast." It's the kind of mythic incident Bass' characters seem to exist for. (In **"Mexico,"** the protagonist is trying to raise the world's largest bass—in his swimming pool.)

But by the end of **"Choteau"** the myth is shattered, the vulnerability of the legendary figure is revealed. On a hunting trip, Galena Jim tries to ride a moose. He's thrown, the moose comes after him, and he is reduced to "running and scrambling, diving around rocks and rolling under logs, clutching his heart." Jim has what appears to be a mild stroke, and suddenly the mask falls away:

> He didn't have any color, and for a moment, broken and hurt like that, almost helpless, he seemed like my friend rather than a teacher of any sort; and he seemed young, too, like he could have been just anybody, instead of Galena Jim Ontz, who had been thrown by a moose; and we sat there all afternoon, he with his eyes closed, resting, saving up, breathing slowly with cracked ribs.

There is always, in these stories, a moment when the hero is brought low, when the dream is surrendered and all that's left is the memory of glory. In **"Mexico,"** the bass in the swimming pool is caught by high-school kids who have snuck into the yard. The rugged, alligator-wrestling Buzbee of **"The Watch"** ends up chained to the porch of the general store run by his bachelor son, who only wants someone to talk to. Women leave the odd, stubborn, obsessed narrators of **"Mississippi"** and **"In Ruth's Country"** for safer, more conventional alternatives.

Yet despite the consistency of theme, the stories sometimes fail to hit their marks because Bass' influences overwhelm him. Barry Hannah is a kind of presiding deity here—a brave choice for a mentor in these days when the goal of many young writers seems to be a muting of voice, but a dangerous one, too.

Two of the stories disappear under Hannah's weight. **"Mississippi"** and **"Cats and Students, Bubbles and Abysses"** are too full of the kind of extended nominative groupings he has perfected—"the wild big fairway of pumping and producing oil wells" is an example from **"Mississippi."** Other Hannahisms compound the problem, including frequent interjections of commentary on the narrative ("That is what my state is about"; "Another desperate Southerner, done escaped at his first chance") and a similar narrative pointing used to introduce an episode or a descriptive passage ("This is how we discovered

Robby"; "Summers in Mississippi are like this"). Although Bass does Hannah well, he is better when he eases up on the verbal accelerator and moves us along at a pace more in line with the secret yearnings of his characters who, for all of their exploits with cars and trucks and horses, with guns and fishing poles, are less after perfect sporting moments than a little bit of human contact.

We know we are a long way from the manly heroics of a character out of Hemingway when we find that the narrator and his friend Kirby in **"Redfish"** have gotten what little knowledge they have about fishing from their reading, and even their drinks are new to them. "It was our first time to drink Cuba Libres, and we liked them even better than margaritas. We had never caught redfish before either, but had read about it in a book." Given the newness of it all to them, there is just the right amount of clumsiness in those sentences—the awkward use of the infinitive in the first, the not quite secure antecedent of the "it" in the second. And the more we learn about the narrator and his friend, the more apt these effects become. (Bass excels at subtly adjusting syntax to aid his characterizations.)

Before long we see what's at stake here, what in essence has been at stake throughout. The narrator and Kirby wander along the beach. It's windy and cold and they haven't caught any fish. When they decide to drag a lifeguard tower back to their camp but can't get it to budge, their hopes for living out even one successful night of mythic American malehood begin to crumble. Kirby admits he misses his wife.

> We were a long way from our fire, and it looked a lot smaller, from where we were. . . . Kirby started crying and said he was going home to Tricia but I told him to buck up and be a man. I didn't know what that meant or even what I meant by saying that, but I knew I did not want him to leave.

The narrator is lonely, and his friend Kirby is lost. The fishing trip—and the whole macho ethos, it seems—is only their excuse to stay close, to comfort each other (they never do catch any fish, though when Bass leaves them, they are still trying).

Throughout **The Watch** Bass' characters have a yearning for the old achievements. They want to catch the biggest fish, make the fastest time, regain their youth, their lovers, their belief in legends. Yet only when they give up these pursuits, or at least gain some perspective on them, do they achieve something important: intimacy, recovery, wisdom.

At the end of **"Wild Horses,"** one of the longer, more powerful stories in the book, Bass leaves us with the image of a boy training a horse to pull a sled. "The egrets hopped and danced, following at a slight distance, but neither the boy nor the horse seemed to notice. They kept their heads down, and moved forward." It's an image of dedication and progress, both in abundant evidence in **The Watch**. (pp. 19-20)

Mark Kamine, "The Macho Myth Unmasked," in The New Leader, *Vol. LXXII, No. 3, February 6, 1989, pp. 19-20.*

Christopher Zenowich   (review date 12 February 1989)

[*Zenowich is an American novelist, educator, and critic. In the following excerpt, he commends Bass's ability to create engaging, memorable characters and comments on the author's use of two opposing narrative styles.*]

Rick Bass' debut work of fiction, **The Watch,** is a collection of stories notable in their oddly beautiful description of characters struggling with loneliness, loss, and diminished expectations. Bass, a petroleum geologist rather than a workshop refugee, has already published two books of nonfiction, and attracted wide attention as a story writer. He received the 1987 General Electric Younger Writers Award for **"Wild Horses"** and his **"Cats and Students, Bubbles and Abysses"** appears in *Best American Stories 1988.* **"The Watch"** was anthologized in *New Stories from the South 1988.* These three stories stand out from the collection—the first two by virtue of the control Bass maintains in creating characters who overcome the loss of loved ones or a sudden awareness of limitations without giving in to despair; the third, by far the longest, by virtue of its Gothic quirkiness as it depicts the tensions among an aging father, a son 14 years his junior, and an overweight cyclist transfixed by the son.

These are stories . . . in which landscape, most often in the South, figures importantly—it is larger and more powerful than the characters who own or use it, and their interactions with the land and its animals often take Bass' fiction beyond the confines of ordinary existence.

Three of the stories in this collection are set in Texas, and of these, **"Mexico"** best conveys the vision Bass has of Houston as an oil boom-and-bust wasteland. In describing a stag party stunt, the unnamed first-person narrator states:

> Mostly it's just drinking. Driving cars into each other, head-on . . . on empty lamplit Main Street: the gold light coming down past the oaks, twinkling, like haze at a football stadium. The crunch and tear of metal, the tinkle of glass, the laughs and the cheers. Seeing who can make the biggest noise.

The art of Bass' writing is found in a passage like this, in which an incident becomes emblematic of the whole. Although the story drifts into a situation all too reminiscent of *The Sun Also Rises,* its evocation of excessive wealth and individual impotence layered over a swampy, sweltering landscape makes it the best of Bass' triad of Houston stories.

In **"Wild Horses,"** a man who sat still as his best friend jumped to his death off a high bridge forms a sadomasochistic relationship with the dead friend's fiancé. Their mutual efforts to assuage their suffering and guilt lead them to steal a yearling black Angus and throw it off the same bridge. It is a story in which suffering and beauty are artfully melded without ever suggesting a simple resolution to the tragedy experienced by its two main characters.

In **"Cats and Students, Bubbles and Abysses,"** the narrator states:

> In the noble West, where I used to live before I

reached puberty, it was manly and virtuous not to tell people about yourself. . . . But not in Mississippi. In the South, you were supposed to tell them. They held it against you if you didn't, because it meant you were trying to hide something.

This passage suggests competing aesthetic credos for Rick Bass—and the tensions in his work could be seen as the result of attempting to resolve the difference between these two styles of presentation. Bass' narrators most often are first person, and to the extent he can maintain the verve and jazz of Barry Hannah's narrators, as in **"Cats and Students, Bubbles and Abysses,"** he succeeds as Hannah does. There is an explosive, unconventional syntax to the voice of such narrators that spawns descriptions of great beauty and propels the story onward with delightful unpredictability. But it's a high-risk narrative strategy that does occasionally send his stories swerving into sentimentality. When Bass adopts the Western mode of presentation, as he does—despite the story's setting—in **"Wild Horses,"** narrated in a limited third person through the two principal characters, he succeeds again, unforgettably. In either style, Bass has the power to create fictions that reverberate long after they have been read. (p. 9)

> Christopher Zenowich, "Watchers in an Unquiet Country," in Los Angeles Times Book Review, February 12, 1989, pp. 1, 9.

Susan Lowell   (review date 5 March 1989)

[*Lowell is an American short story writer, journalist, educator, and critic. In the following review, she provides a positive assessment of* The Watch, *discussing structural elements and symbolism in the stories.*]

Rick Bass is a petroleum geologist by trade, a writer by nature. Geology is a ticket to exotic and isolated places, hidden ways of life and natural beauty. Its history—maps and mines, dreams and exploitation—is bound up in the history of human migration, and especially in the history of the American West. Probably every geologist is at heart a treasure hunter, a detective; it's surprising that this richness has produced so few nontechnical writers. Mr. Bass is an exception. **The Watch,** his first collection of short stories, shows an impressive command of the devices of contemporary fiction.

He can start a story with a bang: "Galena Jim Ontz has two girlfriends and a key to Canada." (Galena Jim, in **"Choteau,"** takes his nickname from a mineral, "pure glittering space-blue slick and shiny heavy-as-lead galena," which adds an eerie glow and dimension of meaning to the story.) Elsewhere, memorable voices speak up, as in **"The Government Bears"**: "My family's snake-bit. Since I got struck by the pipe wrench and blew up the rig in anger, this state's never given me any trouble directly but it's sure taken it out on my kin." And in the story called **"Mexico"** (one of a triptych of stories that sets the end of the Texas oil boom against the end of youth and innocence for two young men), a pet fish in a Houston swimming pool becomes a symbol of a peculiarly Texas condition.

In **"Cats and Students, Bubbles and Abysses,"** Mr. Bass

also writes about writing: "It's like there's this shell over Robby, this confining, restricting, elastic-like bubble; it's like he's got to write his way out of it." This sometimes self-conscious story is packed with literary allusions; when Robby, the embryo author, and his two mentors, both failed writers, set out to visit Faulkner's old house, they end up lost and stuck in the mud. The bad angel here—the character contrasted with the poor, pure writer—is a crass geologist.

Plotted on a map, the settings of the stories in *The Watch* form an arc from Mississippi through Texas and Utah to Montana, where Mr. Bass now lives as the caretaker of a remote ranch. The influences on his work also run in a similar course, from Faulkner's Southern tradition to the modern Montana school of Thomas McGuane and Richard Ford. There is also perhaps a dash of the young D. H. Lawrence, especially in a story called **"Wild Horses,"** which, like Lawrence's "Horse Dealer's Daughter," presents a country love affair as a desperate struggle, with elements of both drowning and redemption.

Although Mr. Bass is essentially a romantic, he balances humor against pathos and relieves the lyricism in his prose with an occasional gritty touch. While he is only 30, he has already won a number of honors, including a General Electric Younger Writers Award and a PEN/Nelson Algren Award Special Citation. And a number of the stories in *The Watch* have appeared in anthologies of the best short fiction published in the past few years.

Not every geologist makes good maps, finds ore, strikes oil. That requires the gift of imagining what lies beneath the ground—and perhaps a certain magic. As the narrator of **"Mississippi"** puts it:

> Her father was in oil, oil was in her father. He used to say: "Finding oil is not so complex. It is really nothing more than deciding what you like. Everyone, all geologists, have access to pretty much the same set of facts. You just have to decide which ones you like in order to get to what it is you are looking for."

When Mr. Bass gets to what he's looking for, he goes past technical excellence to his best work, which is fresh and strange. He likes triangles (usually an active man, a passive man and a woman) and animals. A cat, a moose, a mule, bears, cattle, horses, reptiles and fish all become symbolic.

The title story concerns an old man who has escaped from his mad son, a boring nonstop storyteller, to camp in a fever-infested swamp with a harem of naked runaway laundresses. The third main character here is a man, a bicycle racer who gets fat and builds himself a go-cart. Possibly all the characters are insane. But the tale is told so candidly that nothing within it seems even improbable. The old man catches big fish with his bare hands and wrestles alligators, hanging them, in an extraordinary image, "like villains, all around in his small clearing, like the most ancient of burial grounds . . . mouths gaping in silent death, as if preparing to ascend: they were all pointing up." This piece of fiction is fantastic, larger than life, won-

derful; but like the old man, it is also hard to bring to a satisfactory end.

Mr. Bass's women are somewhat shadowy, often viewed as distant icons or puzzles, while his young men in their quest for adult experience can seem simply callow. However, these are gaps that experience should fill, as Mr. Bass does more prospecting, away from contemporary fiction's mined-out places, down deep.

> *Susan Lowell, "Country Love and Naked Laundresses," in* The New York Times Book Review, *March 5, 1989, p. 11.*

Robert Kanigel   **(review date 9 July 1989)**

[*Kanigel is an American nonfiction writer, educator, and critic. In the following review, he presents a negative assessment of* Oil Notes.]

Great idea: Who better to tell of the rousing, romantic world of oil discovery, of wildcats and roustabouts and instant millionaires, of the black science of finding liquid gold trapped underground for a hundred million years, than a petroleum geologist who can write? No need to confine himself to geology and drilling rigs, either. Include personal stuff too—*humanize* it. The geologist at home, as it were—off with his artist girlfriend, driving down the back roads of the rural South. . . .

Great idea. And now, Rick Bass' *Oil Notes* in hand, we can weigh the results of the experiment: It didn't work.

Bass *could* have brought it off. A real working geologist, like his father, he knows his oil; he hunts it for a living. And he's surely got the writerly gifts to tell about it, as we see, for example, in his account of core point: "While drilling, the bit grinds up underground rock into flake-shaped pieces brought to the surface by circulating mud. Analyzed, these often suffice to tell the geologist what he's encountered a mile down."

But sometimes, as when near the oil, the geologist needs a closer reading. So he orders his men to take up the drill bit and replace it with a hollow tube perhaps 30 feet long laced with diamonds at one end; back underground, it cuts out a neat core of earth, the way a cookie cutter punches out cookie dough.

"They bring the barrel up . . . and knock the core out by banging on the side of the barrel with hammers," writes Bass. "The core slides out like a skinny pole, wet and steaming, broken in places, but they piece it back together and wrap it quickly in foil to keep all the oils and gases and fluids trapped in it from escaping." These are then analyzed.

But it's a big step to do all this—and expensive. Ten thousand bucks for the diamond-studded barrel alone—which you use only once. And the drilling has to stop. And you have to make sure you've got people on hand ready to rush off and analyze the samples. So picking the right time to do it—establishing the core point—is crucial. "Drilling, drilling, drilling, watching, and then knowing, or thinking you know, that you are right on top of the formation you're interested in: a foot above it or less. Son, you had better be right."

Well, all this is great. Why, then, isn't there more of it? And that's just the problem: *Oil Notes* hasn't enough oil.

What it has instead is the author's loose-fitting white T-shirt, his girlfriend Elizabeth, the big-antlered deer he sees, the biscuits and milk gravy he eats, his pet likes and dislikes. "I love sitting on tractors and smelling their old oil smell," he tells us. "It sounds as if I'm drinking beer but I'm not; it's really an orange soda, and the March sun going down is still warm on my left elbow."

There's a merciless self-indulgence at work here, pumping out "telling details" not telling at all, but merely details. We care about the contents of the author's office in Jackson, Miss., not nearly as much as he thinks we should. He concludes his six-page inventory of erasers, newspaper clippings, oil exploration magazines, maps, arrowheads and bottles of antacid with the throwaway line: "It is a good place to work"—as if that justifies subjecting the reader to it. A paragraph or two, maybe. But six pages? He prefaces it all with a question: "Do you want to know what my office looks like?"—but, of course, never offers the opportunity to say, "No."

It's not just that the personal details fail to enhance the book; they detract from it. At one point, the author starts to tell how some geologists, charged with eking out all they can from existing fields, seek never to drill a dry hole; while others, who hunt new fields and know they'll often come up dry, "don't especially care about being right or not, and don't particularly mind being less than careful with people's hopes. We're leaving the realm of geology here and going into the abrasions of sociology."

Then, abruptly: " . . . wind on my porch this morning, and a mockingbird fighting something—John Prine spinning on my turntable . . . " followed by his half-hearted return to a distinction that could have been developed, but now winds down to nothing within the space of a paragraph.

We are supposed to experience links between the seeming trifles of Bass' personal life and the profundities of oil. Too often, though, the links are feeble, or non-existent, forged from air: "We lay in the hammock together today. Her yellow shirt was the color of a banana. I didn't go to work until 10. I was burned out. I didn't lie, didn't call in sick. Just told them I'd be in around 10."

"You can't find oil if you're not honest," he decides.

Occasionally, while off with Bass, we are seduced into appreciating some lovely little scene, as when he finds two scraggly, worm-ridden, flea-tortured, abandoned puppies in the weeds, and drives them to Elizabeth's house. "We gave them milk. They paused before the bowl, then leapt upon it like hockey players in a face-off."

And sometimes, he does link his life to the oil fields. At one point, he tells how, when Coca-Cola changed its formula, he and Elizabeth had driven all over the country stocking up on old-formula Coke—800 cans of it. Then,

20 pages later, he argues that any oil gluts you see mask ever-smaller oil reserves, adding:

> When they did away with the old Cokes, the day they stopped producing them, there were plenty of Cokes on the shelf, were there not? Perhaps even a glut, to someone interested in buying a lot of them? Hell, I bought a thousand, no sweat, and at a good price.

Point made. But such revealing linkages come too rarely. And often we're driving to ask, "Where's the oil?"

Astonishingly, for a book called *Oil Notes,* there's far too little of it. How do you prepare the drill site? How do you control a drill bit two miles underground? What powers it? How long does a bit last? What does it look like? How do you know when it's hit something new?

You won't find out here.

Repeatedly, the author stops short of delivering the goods. To "log" a hole means to lower into it an electronic gizmo that emits signals and picks up others that together tell the geologist about underground formations. "I know what to look for," Bass writes, "and if I see the things I want to see—good high resistivity, good porosity and good permeability, like the three cherries spinning into view at the end of a slot machine play—then we've got a well, a producer."

But what's "resistivity"? Or, for that matter, the others? And what makes them "good"? For the reader, they're just three more polysyllabic words, with no inkling as to what they mean, and making no contribution to his appreciation of the underground world. Bass knows what they mean. But it's as if the novelist in him secretly doubts that anyone cares about oil that much and so feels the need to cuteify it with his girlfriend and his vagrant puppies.

But if it's not oil that justifies this book—as its title seems to suggest it should—then what does? The sun on the author's left elbow?

"Occasionally," writes Bass, "you will meet a geologist with an ego, who acts as if every lift of his eyebrows should be chronicled in a little black book." *Oil Notes* has too many eyebrow lifts.

> *Robert Kanigel, "Oil Drilling with a Human Face," in* Los Angeles Times Book Review, *July 9, 1989, p. 2.*

Rhoda Koenig (review date 17 July 1989)

[*In the following favorable review of* Oil Notes, *Koenig commends Bass's honesty and sensitivity.*]

Rick Bass says that oilmen can be of either sex, but the terms in which he describes his occupation, right on page one of *Oil Notes,* sound anything but gender-neutral.

> You're drilling through a hard formation, bearing down; then the drill bit pierces a softer formation . . . the pipe shifts, sinking down into this softer formation, going faster, and it makes a barking, torquing, squealing sound. It sounds exactly like beagles.

Bass, who describes himself as a hunter and a game player, is a 31-year-old development geologist; after a new source of oil has been discovered,

> I've got to figure out how much oil is there, where it is, how many wells to drill to get it out, and where and when to drill them. The oil's existence has been proven; now I've got to learn that particular reservoir's nature . . . and the lightning-bolt atrocities of its own underground existence.

As you can see, Bass might also fairly be described as a romantic. The secrets hidden in the earth, the fortunes and tragedies of those who would prize them out are to him a metaphor for life, and the qualities he demands of a successful oilman—honesty, modesty, chivalry—are those of a knight-errant. Yet Bass admits that the mysterious earth sometimes couldn't care less about the qualities of the men who try to conquer her, and willfully splashes her favors around.

> The truth is that there have been giant oil and gas fields found by men in plain, white, sterile laboratory offices, and there have been giant oil and gas fields found by men in offices full of duck decoys and shotgun shells and aspen leaves and canoe paddles, and there have also been fields found by crazy men drilling for water, digging for gold, or shooting at deer. Just like in *The Beverly Hillbillies.*

Bass's journal is a little text in how oil is created, found, and produced, a friendly introduction to the subject for those intimidated by earth science. Along with discussing anticlines and igneous rock, Bass outlines the economics of oil, beginning with the acquisition of a lease.

> The man who owns the land where you want to drill does not necessarily own the rights to the minerals beneath the land. They may still belong, in entirety or in part, to some old bearded pioneer who lives out in California in a tent with no address. . . . Occasionally there are disputes in which several oil companies each believe they have the lease. Oh, wily landowner! Or the landowner (rather, mineral rights owner) simply might not want to lease; it's certainly his or her prerogative. Some people like being poor; that's fine.

As well as being a portrait of the industry and the ideal driller, *Oil Notes* gives a picture of Bass as a very gentle, indeed mild-mannered knight, someone whom homeless and repulsive dogs know as a soft touch, and someone who is rather worryingly accident-prone for a man whose occupation is dealing with flammable substances.

> I used to have a company car, but too many things kept happening to it (them). The insurance company that covers all of [my employer's] businesses said that they had to cut me out of their coverage, like the soft part of an apple.

Two of the things that happened were his crashing into a truck being driven by a dog and sinking a car in a swamp. On the latter occasion, Bass went home, changed, and took the oil rig's logs to his boss. "We spread them out on the table in the kitchen, discussed the different formations, and decided to run pipe on it, to attempt to make a well. I forgot to tell him about the car." The forgetting sums up the message of his appealing little book:

> Everything is so much smaller than the act of finding oil that it must be like belonging to a cult, I would think. It takes you over. It gets in you. You feel as if it is *you* and not the oil or gas that is trapped down there, being pressured down.

(pp. 49-50)

Rhoda Koenig, "The Long and Winding Road," in New York *Magazine, Vol. 22, No. 28, July 17, 1989, pp. 49-50.*

Martha Duffy   (review date 17 July 1989)

[*In the following review of* Oil Notes, *Duffy praises Bass's candid and descriptive prose style.*]

Rick Bass was a fence post in his third-grade play. His father still calls him "Animal." As a petroleum geologist around Jackson, Miss., he drove a lot but was hard on automobiles. After he steered one company car into shallow water, the boss sent him a 20-ft. length of chain for Christmas. Bass acknowledges his clumsiness: "Sometimes I feel almost out of control." But he glories in a rare natural gift: "I know how to find oil."

As readers of Bass's stories (collected . . . in **The Watch**) can attest, he also knows how to write; and like his oil witchery, this gift is extravagant and natural. His new book is based on notebook jottings he kept for about three years, 1984-87, chasing a quarry that was "shy here, coy there, blatant elsewhere." His father, another petroleum geologist, complained after reading **Oil Notes** that he didn't learn much from it about finding oil, but to the uninitiated it richly reveals just what that line of work involves. There is no better conversation, spoken or written, than good shop talk, and this is superb—direct, expert and reeling with the joys of outdoor adventure.

Bass, 31, has likened his job to that of a field-goal kicker, a man whose calculations must be exactly right ("You can't even look relieved"). But he revels in the pressure and fevered pace.

> Sometimes day, as opposed to night, loses significance, and also you feel like you're being washed down a mad stream somewhere. Fatigue becomes the currency with which you pay. It makes sense though. It is energy, after all, that you are looking for: buried.

He recalls the mineral's origin, millions of years ago, in ancient seashores, and feels that there is a "frozen sea in me." Describing the geology of Alabama and Mississippi, he writes, "The old sea retreated two hundred and fifty million years ago . . . the sands, five and six thousand feet down, like plunging porpoises, sounding, headed back to the deep."

The author, who now lives in rural Montana and is a consulting geologist, says little about his writing career. He reveals that he is a poetic observer of the earth's surface as well as its depths, ever alert to the sounds of silence—a cricket, a katydid, a car passing in the distance, the hum of a freezer. Crisp winter walks during his college days at Utah State made him feel like "the president of snow."

Oil Notes has many such phrases, evocative, amusing, but also a little silly. Bass writes that "all geologists are hyperbolic"; he certainly is. At one point he suggests putting a small bottle of oil to the ear, the better to hear the ancient waters. At another he intones, "You can't find oil if you are not honest; I'm not sure I know how to explain this." The rueful part, after the semicolon, redeems the rest. He natters on about his girlfriend, Elizabeth Hughes, whose mild, pleasant drawings accompany the text. Is he happy with her? Without her? Will they marry? One wonders whether, as a suitor, he will ever top an early gambit, when he invited her to a park to share a bacon-lettuce-and-tomato sandwich, then showed up with the ingredients and a portable microwave oven.

Bass can laugh at himself. His linking of oil with eons-old oceans may be the stuff of poetry, but how about oil and Coke? The author, preoccupied with the earth's dwindling oil reserves, was aghast to learn four years ago that his personal fuel was also in peril. When the Coca-Cola Co. announced a new formula for Coke, he began buying up crates of the old stuff. "The world is so thirsty for oil, uses so, so much. We are down to the last thousand Cokes," he mourned. Of course, Coke got a reprieve. That seems unlikely in the case of oil, but if vast new fields are discovered, Bass and his notebook will probably be there.

> *Martha Duffy, "At Play in Fields of Energy," in* Time, *New York, Vol. 134, No. 3, July 17, 1989, p. 84.*

Stephen Jones   (review date 23 July 1989)

[*Jones is an American nonfiction writer, novelist, and critic. In the following excerpt, he comments on the eclectic compositional style of* Oil Notes *and characterizes the work as occasionally shallow but unpretentious.*]

In America the trouble with writing about work is that the better you write, the less it seems as if it's work you're talking about. If, as Wallace Stevens said, "money is a kind of poetry," then the labor by which the money is gotten may be tainted with literary intent. Chasing a buck in the whale-oil business may become a yarn about the pursuit of God; hoeing beans by a pond can be a polemic to awaken your otherwise undeliberative neighbor; the ascending lisp of your saw is the poem that loves all mankind. Here, finding oil becomes "notes" on making love, eating food, art and "everything," while building a stone wall leads to reflections on finding a kind of secular salvation.

Rick Bass' book [*Oil Notes*] is "about" locating oil, but he is in a hurry to tell you that it also is about finding himself. To help you, his publisher says that Bass "writes about oil the way Thoreau wrote about Walden Pond." If this is so, it is the Thoreau who craved to eat the woodchuck raw, the Thoreau who was mocked by the loon, the Thoreau who once set the woods on fire to see the show. "(Oil) has taught me not to apologize for anything I am,"

says Bass, who adds that eating food is a lot like finding oil.

> I try to figure this out, and all I can come up with are the words 'lust,' 'passion' and 'gluttony'. . . . If life and living are not like oil, then I do not know what is.

Early in *Oil Notes,* in an aside on baseball, Bass renders a paradigm for his compositional method. He recalls a youthful mound stint in which he was "all over the place," throwing the ball in the dugout, over the backstop and bouncing it up to the plate. His enemy, the neighborhood bully, temporarily on his side, enters from third base to show him how to control the ball.

Unfortunately, there is no persistent guru here, There are vague bosses, most always deferred to, and a shadowy girl, Elizabeth, who has about the same role as "Betty" in the old Jack Armstrong radio show. The 28-year-old Bass makes references to when he was "young," adding meditations on maturity. Once in a while, he wildcats into emotional complexity ("I don't know why some people get sad in the fall, even while claiming paradoxically that is their favorite time of year.")

Readers hot on the evils of oil companies will find only occasional lunges at the petroleum industry's moral difficulties. He jury-rigs a comparison likening the oil crises to that in the distribution of Classic Coke, an analogy that might possibly be apt yet is almost Dan Quayle-like in its insensivity to resonance.

But Bass' bounding prose soon accustoms us not to expect any long thoughts from a youth bent on celebrating his lust for oil. We get scraps of genuine poetry, a few yarns from the field, lucid geology lessons, promises of eroticism, wisps of suspense. It's certainly more fun than John McPhee and full of attractive bravado. ("You can always find a reason not to do something, or to be skeptical, or frightened. There is no talent involved in not doing.") And we should be grateful that Bass did not lash-up these notes into a lite-beer novel/film or more ponderously apologize for Big Petro. (p. 7)

> *Stephen Jones, "Of Stone Walls, Oil Wells and Life Itself," in* Chicago Tribune—Books, *July 23, 1989, pp. 6-7, 9.*

Christopher Lehmann-Haupt   (review date 24 July 1989)

[*Lehmann-Haupt is an American critic. In the following excerpt, he faults* Oil Notes *as superficial and states that "there is a studied casualness to [Bass's] writing . . . that borders on affectation."*]

Oil Notes is a journal Mr. Bass kept while he went about his work of finding energy in the ground. It is his fourth book, his previous three having been a gifted collection of short stories called *The Watch* and two books about the outdoors titled *The Deer Pasture* and *Wild to the Heart.*

In his *Notes,* Mr. Bass explains what he does:

> I am given a producing well, a new discovery—a wildcat that has proven itself to be good, to be

a 'producer' ('making a well,' they call it: 'Did y'all make a well?')—and I must drill all the other wells in the area, or field, after that. I've got to figure out how much oil is there, where it is, how many wells to drill to get it out, and where and when to drill them.

And he relates his job to the other things in life he loves, which include the land, food and his friend Elizabeth.

> I am not going to apologize for it. You can't have a passion for one thing and not another. If you like to find oil, you like to eat. I'm not sure I understand it. Only that the feeling for food, oil and Elizabeth are so often so alike.

But there is a studied casualness to his writing, an "Aw, shucks" quality, that borders on affectation. "I don't know if I've told you about leases or not," he writes, as if he couldn't go back over his manuscript and see whether he has or not. "Don't you want to know what my office looks like?" he asks, as if the reader were free to answer.

Mr. Bass is out to charm us, it would seem. But charm is not enough. At the beginning of *Oil Notes,* he announces: "In the fall of 1985, my twenty-seventh year, I read in a work by the poet-novelist Jim Harrison a quote from Kafka about 'freeing the frozen sea within us.' " He can't be bothered to track down the source of that famous quotation, which, according to Bartlett's *Familiar Quotations,* is in a 1904 letter to Oskar Pollak in which Kafka wrote, "A book must be the ax for the frozen sea inside us."

Oil Notes is intermittently charming. But unfortunately, like its author's citation of Kafka, it is missing the ax's sharp edge.

> *Christopher Lehmann-Haupt, "The Lure of the Outdoors, Then and Now," in* The New York Times, *July 24, 1989, p. C16.*

Perry Glasser   (review date September 1989)

[*Glasser is an American critic, short story writer, novelist, and educator. In the following excerpt, he characterizes the stories in* The Watch *as the works of a talented amateur.*]

[Bass's collection *The Watch*] gives us an insight into the development of a young writer. Bass acknowledges "helpful advice" from Carol Houck Smith, Tom Jenks, Rust Hills and Gordon Lish, as well as James Linville and the staff of *The Paris Review.* The collection contains Houston stories, Mississippi stories and Utah/Montana stories. Not surprisingly, Rick Bass has lived in all of these places, but though many of these stories share locales and characters, they are separated from each other in the book. This seems less a collection than an aggregation of Bass's early work. Reading *The Watch,* we witness a young writer wrestling with his material, trying to order his experience, searching for his voice, and discovering what works and what does not.

When Bass's fiction works well, it works very well indeed—but a few of these stories seem generated by a young writer's desire to write well, rather than a young writer who urgently needs to tell a story. The former isn't

a *bad* point of generation, of course, but when unaccompanied by the latter, the consequent fiction falls flat. Reading Bass's first book is like watching a newborn thoroughbred learn to stand; you smile at the awkwardness, hoping that at some future date you'll see the awesome power and speed of a champion.

One has to hope Bass will resist any who'd urge him to publish too much too soon, to capitalize on the moment. They will necessarily move on to next season's discovery, discarding last year's writer like a pet rock or a hula hoop. It's possible to publish too early.

Take **"Mexico,"** for example, the first story in the collection. It is overworked, coy in its resolution and use of imagery. The same is true of **"Cats and Students, Bubbles and Abysses,"** which from the title down puts a reader on notice to prepare for work that will be profound and cute all at once, a regular *tour de force,* so you'd better sit up and pay attention. It's a student's work, a very good student, but still a student. Too much attention to craft overwhelms whatever story lurks behind the prose, and characters over-trimmed for the sake of linguistic dexterity and some trendy idea of art eventually are reduced to stereotypical caricatures. In **"Cats and Students,"** we read,

> I guess the most weight I've ever lifted is the back end of Slater's car. Robby and Slater and I took it up to Oxford to look at Faulkner's old house out in the country one Sunday. We got sort of lost and sort of stuck in the mud. We had a couple of dozen watermelons and a keg of beer in the back, and it was a hot Mississippi summer, and we were going to have a picnic, and the jack sank down in the mud and got lost, but I lifted the back end up anyway . . .

Familiar stuff. Good ol' boys on a muddy road, a six-pack of beer, watermelons, ingenuous language. The reference to Faulkner, of course, is supposed to make us know that the characters are a cut above the ordinary red-neck. Too many of Bass's southern grotesques or executives in the "awl bizness" are simply clichéd characters whose obsessions fill us with neither delight nor insight, but leave us wondering why we're reading about people habitually feeble-minded. And there isn't a single female character who serves as anything other than an ideal object for the males in the book.

In too many of the stories, Bass relies on the newest typographical boost to profundity, the isolated paragraph. Designed to make each paragraph seem chiseled and finely honed, a work of art in and of itself, the page design rivets our eyes to each block of narrative, and only incidentally fills a book with white space.

It's an illusion.

Seeing such paragraphs, we believe we are reading short fiction dedicated to compression. We can only pray such mannerisms soon go the way of dialogue introduced with dashes, poetry typed without employing the shift key. Trendy writing *looks* smart but says nothing special.

Bass constructs whole stories whose point is to equate a character with an animal, the hunter's mentality. We acquire the qualities of that which we stalk, capture, or kill. Wear the fetish, be the creature. Eat its heart. Beside each other, stories such as **"The Government Bears," "Redfish,"** and **"Wild Horses,"** become obvious as soon as we read their titles, though separately they read well, even brilliantly, especially **"Redfish."**

Once he gets out of his own way, Bass writes wonderfully lucidly, able to tell a sensitive, well-observed, moving tale that has at its core a mystery. **"Juggernaut"** is such a story. The middle-aged, slope-shouldered Mr. Odom, a high school teacher whose seeming only claim to fame is a forest green Corvette, is discovered to be Larry Loop, the "goon" for a Texas ice hockey team, the Juggernauts.

> You could tell he was not from the north. You could tell he had not grown up with the game, but had discovered it, late in life. He was big, and the oldest man on the ice, grey-headed, tufts of it sticking out from behind his savage, painted goalie's mask—though he was not a goalie—and more often than not when he bumped into people, they went over.

When the narrator and his friend see one of their high school classmates, Laura, waiting after a game in a parking lot for Mr. Odom, the rhapsodic Conrad-esque ending is completely earned.

> . . . in two months she would be graduating, and what she was doing would be okay then, . . . and for the first time we saw the thing, in its immensity, and it was like coming around a bend or trail in the woods and seeing the hugeness and emptiness of a great plowed pasture or field, when all one's life up to that point has been spent close to but never seeing a field of that size. . . . it was very clear to us that the whole rest of our lives would be spent in a field like that, and the look Laura gave us was sweet and kind, but also wise, and was like an old familiar welcome.

No gimmicks here. No elaborate gyrations to draw a simple equation between character and animal, just a story that is plainly felt and honestly told. As Rick Bass grows as a writer, and he clearly will, he will develop the authority that comes with trusting his material and his reader. Who knows? Maybe he'll stop taking so much advice from New York mandarins and listen more intently to his own very fine muse. (pp. 71-2)

> *Perry Glasser, "Purer Than Everything Else,"*
> *in* The North American Review, *Vol. 274, No. 3, September, 1989, pp. 69-72.*

Ronald Wright   (review date 24 November 1989)

[*In the following review, Wright responds positively to* Oil Notes, *focusing on Bass's portrayal of the relationship between his personal life and his career in the petroleum industry.*]

[In *Oil Notes*], Rick Bass, a young petroleum geologist and short-story writer from Texas, has accomplished the remarkable feat of doing for oil exploration what Isaak Walton did for fishing. With quirky charm and a chunky style, he conveys the fascination of the black, oozy life-essence waiting in the cracks and folds of the earth: "It is future, undrilled and I am present, knowing. . . . It is the frozen sea within me. I know how to find oil." He has also discovered the literary form of the fake notebook—long a preserve of the best travel-writers—and explored its possibilities as assiduously as he probes the earth. Information about geology, technology and oil sits easily beside musings on nature, on human nature, on the nature of his girlfriend and of himself. The very oddness and originality of Bass's book make one search for comparisons, none of which seems exactly right. His woodsy American vigour and idiosyncrasy derive from Thoreau (but what would Thoreau have made of a man who lives on pizza and Coke?) His blend of mechanics and mysticism is reminiscent of Pirsig's *Zen and the Art of Motorcycle Maintenance,* but mercifully, with the heavier fractions left behind in the refining tower. His gift for *non sequitur,* digression and sudden confidences reminds one of [Laurence] Sterne, but a Sterne who is brief. And his delight in a subterranean craft is reminiscent of *The Specialist,* the minor classic on the digging and building of what Americans call "outhouses". Only seldom is his whimsy too much and his style collapses in self-parody: "Elizabeth . . . is an artist, and plays tennis pretty well. She likes chocolate ice cream, and is pretty."

Elizabeth is Bass's other obsession. Digressions about her come easily after thoughts on the earth. Like oil, she is sometimes there, sometimes not. Bass implies that he might like marriage, children, commitment; Elizabeth, whose delightful drawings are scattered through the text like pressed leaves, is apparently too free a spirit. But this, one senses, is the source of her appeal. Bass worships the elusive and the uncertain; he is a collector of irreplaceable things. (When Coca-Cola changed its recipe, he hoarded a thousand bottles.) A large part of his fascination with oil lies in the fact that it will soon be gone: "It is not like gold, silver, trees. It disappears. It is here only once." He would like to hoard Elizabeth, but Elizabeth is wise enough to disappear from time to time.

There is of course a central contradiction to Bass's book and to his life. He loves nature and abhors pollution, but his job ineluctably contributes to the miasma that threatens the world. At first he extols oil and gas as better and kinder than their rivals such as coal. But later in the book, environmental worry undermines the breezy delight. Bass himself is changing from a Texas oilman to a pastoral author. He has moved to a ranch in the country; and he cites Senator J. Caleb Boggs:

> We vowed less than a decade ago that we would put a man on the moon and bring him back by the end of the 1960s. We met that deadline. Now maybe we should . . . do something really spectacular—like putting a man into Lake Erie and bringing him back out alive.

As his "notebook" ends, Rick Bass obliquely concludes that life is more precious and precarious than oil. This may be good news for readers; perhaps he will produce less oil and more prose.

> *Ronald Wright, "Dilemmas of a Gas Lover,"*

in The Times Literary Supplement, *No. 4521, November 24, 1989, p. 1297.*

Dick Kirkpatrick (review date November 1990)

[*In the following review of* Oil Notes, *Kirkpatrick applauds Bass's discussion of petroleum geology and evaluates his writing style.*]

> There are two ways to write: the way I do, and the way I want to. Sometimes people like what I write. The smartest readers know that I am saying nothing, but like a wild fighter, occasional punches slip through the defense: knockdown.

So says developmental geologist, writer, and sometimes philosopher Rick Bass in *Oil Notes,* a journal kept while developing petroleum holdings at Black Warrior Basin in the Mississippi Delta. Along the way he manages to tell the reader about his current romance, the disappearance of "classic" Coke, and learning to pitch a baseball from the school bully. I agree with the author's assessment of his own writing. Although elements of the book approach banality, sometimes I do like what he writes. Just when I'm ready to dismiss the book as trite, Bass sneaks in an observation, an image, a quick jab or a combination that may not be a knockout punch, but one that snaps my head back and gets my attention.

My primary complaint with *Oil Notes* is that Bass's spare writing often seems simplistic. About his girlfriend he says, "Elizabeth is my age, twenty-seven, and has long brown hair. She is an artist and plays tennis pretty well. She likes chocolate ice cream, and is pretty." At times the simplicity of *Oil Notes* seems contrived to convince the reader that this really is a journal. In a three-page span the author manages to talk about how it feels to know oil is beneath the ground, a winter in Utah, and the global oil crisis. He then continues with, ". . . soft-shell crab. Key lime pie. Tomatoes." "Girls with big chests. . . . Calves that have been to aerobic class." "Shish kebob. Mediterranean beef. Melon balls." It's the sort of non-sequitur nonsense that one might have heard in a San Francisco coffee house during the late '50s.

Nonetheless, there are many elements, and I suspect these are not the lucky punches of a "wild fighter," to commend the book. For starters, anyone under thirty who sits on his porch in the morning and listens to a John Prine album can't be all bad. Also, as Bass tells the reader, "I know how to find oil." And in the process of relating this knowledge of "reverse history," he tells us many fascinating things about his craft. The history of oil exploration in Black Warrior Basin is brief and interesting. The discussion of geological mapping and drilling new holes is well wrought.

In addition, there are many fresh and delightful images that make *Oil Notes* worthwhile. Bass reflects on the slowness of changes, saying, "We do not see them, do not call them 'changes' at all, no more than we call a beach 'sandstone' or a jellyfish 'oil.'" Comparing keeping discovered oil samples in a frosted glass jar with an Olympic gold medal, or a photo of a home run hit in a World Series, Bass says, "But you can't hold those things and you can't

put them in a bottle and see them after they are gone. Immortal as these other things may sound, capturing energy is really the most magnificent experience."

So what is the final verdict on Rick Bass and *Oil Notes*? Is he, as Annie Dillard suggests on the book's jacket, "the best young writer to come along in years."? Probably not. Is good writing like finding oil, as Bass tells us, a combination of luck and skill? Probably. Am I impressed with *Oil Notes* enough to read more Rick Bass? You bet! (pp. 273-74)

Dick Kirkpatrick, in a review of "Oil Notes," in Western American Literature, *Vol. XXV, No. 3, November, 1990, pp. 273-74.*

Christopher Noxon (review date February 1991)

[*In the following review, Noxon praises Bass's narrative style in* Winter: Notes from Montana.]

It takes a while to discover that there will be no great epiphanies splitting the sky open in Rick Bass's book *Winter: Notes From Montana. Winter,* after all, is an eloquent isolation journal from a naturalist hermit. But this is not a collection of grand commentary or polemic insight (Thoreau he is not); it is simply a recounting of the daily routine in a remote Montana valley. Bass's greatest achievement is that he manages to create such an affecting book, one that leaves behind such a satisfying buzz of truth having been told, out of such plain and simple goings-on.

Bass's last book, the acclaimed *Oil Notes,* centred on the author's stint as a petroleum geologist for an oil company in Texas; it was about the poetry of geology and the financial and environmental risks of gambling for a pay-off that may or may not lie miles underfoot. Both *Oil Notes* and *Winter* are written in journal form and are marked by Bass's spare, minimal style. Most significantly, the narrative pull in the two books is the same: the author's desire to make peace with a natural force.

Winter chronicles a seven-month period as the author prepares for and then endures a bitter season in the valley of Yaak, a region with only a few phone lines and no electricity. Bass becomes immersed in the habits of life among Yaak's 30 inhabitants: operating a chainsaw, stringing fences in the fields, and eating burritos in the Dirty Shame Saloon.

Bass falls in love with the things of Yaak, and it is this love that carries the book. His attention stays fixed on the everyday—the smell of fresh hay in a snowstorm, the chime that comes when crystals of ice collide in mid-air—and he translates these small revelations with moving clarity.

Christopher Noxon, in a review of "Winter: Notes from Montana," in Quill and Quire, *Vol. 57, No. 2, February, 1991, p. 33.*

Ursula Hegi (review date 10 February 1991)

[*Hegi is a German-born American novelist, critic, and educator. In the following review of* Winter: Notes from

Montana, *she extols Bass's descriptions of nature as "powerful and lucid" and praises the insightful quality of his narrative.*]

After moving to the Yaak valley—a place without electricity in the northwest corner of Montana—Rick Bass admits to himself, "Everything I have learned so far has been wrong." In *Winter: Notes From Montana* he explores his attempt "to listen and feel for myself, and to learn rather than always having to be told."

An intensely private man, Mr. Bass, a petroleum geologist and environmentalist, shares only those aspects of his life that he wants to reveal. His relationship with his housemate, Elizabeth Hughes, the artist whose pen and ink sketches illustrate this book, is barely touched upon, and he discloses hardly anything about his work as a writer; yet, it is evident that he cares deeply about both. Although their inclusion would have offered a more complex picture of those first six months in the Yaak, it's not hard to respect the limits this insightful writer has set.

He focuses on his relationship with his surroundings and its impact on him as he yields to his vision and finds a validation of something he's always felt—that sense of being most true to himself when he is in the wilderness, separate from the rest of the human race. "It's as if you'd looked down at your hand and seen the beginnings of fur. It's not as bad as you might think."

Mr. Bass, who grew up in the South, hadn't experienced snow before moving to Montana, but he'd always felt drawn to the woods. As he observes the transformations in the landscape and in the animals—grizzly bears, elk, owls, bobcats, moose, wolves—he finds himself adapting to his new environment like the rabbits that change their color to white with the beginning of winter.

His description of the Yaak—of the wind and the quality of light and of a woman who weaves "dream hoops" that free people from nightmares—are as powerful and lucid as the details in the title story of his collection of short fiction, *The Watch.* In both, he creates moments that shimmer with an almost mystical quality.

He establishes a strong sense of place and of the splendid isolation in this valley that lies in the heart of two million acres of national forest and has its own myths and songs, its own stories. "You listen to ravens, and keep the fire going."

Only about 30 people live in the Yaak, leading simple and often strenuous lives, not much different from the way life there must have been a hundred years ago. They may visit one another or meet at the Dirty Shame Saloon for Monday night football, but their reasons for staying in the valley are the silence and the insulation from the artificial world outside their region.

Winter: Notes From Montana juxtaposes realistic accounts of ordinary chores—like chopping 40 cords of wood—with stunning insights into nature and self. To see—to see deeply and without sentimentality—becomes a way of being, of celebrating a landscape that claims lives, a landscape that many have romanticized and few have embraced.

Time takes on a character of its own, slowing to a pace that allows Mr. Bass to reflect on each moment:

> The danger in yielding to thoughts of spring . . . is that once these thoughts enter your mind, you can't get them out. Love the winter. Don't betray it. Be loyal. When the spring gets here, love it, too—and then the summer.

It's a privilege to follow Rick Bass on this personal journey through a landscape that proves to be right for him, and to share his wonder at the wisdom of an 80-year-old woman who has always lived in the Yaak. "Think of all the things she has missed. But think of all the things she has seen that the rest of the world has missed."

> *Ursula Hegi, "Splendid Isolation," in* The New York Times Book Review, *February 10, 1991, p. 19.*

Lee K. Abbott   (review date 17 February 1991)

[*Abbott is an American short story writer, educator, and critic. In the following review, he praises Bass's descriptions of his surroundings in* Winter: Notes from Montana, *but faults the absence of introspection in his narrative.*]

For one boy, me, growing up in the deserts of New Mexico, winter was more rumor than fact of life, a disaster of cold and ice and mukluks that befell the unfortunate folks of America's northernmost M-states (Maine, Michigan, Minnesota). But for Rick Bass, the much-acclaimed author of *The Watch,* a collection of stories, and of *Oil Notes,* a more deservedly celebrated series of observations about "black gold," winter is anything but a horror of howling winds and chattering teeth.

"Anything I'm guilty of is forgiven when the snow falls," Bass writes [in *Winter: Notes from Montana*].

> I feel powerful. In cities I feel weak and wasted away, but out in the field, in snow, I am like an animal—not in control of my emotions, my happiness and furies, but in charge of loving the snow. . . . I am never going to grow old. The more that comes down, the richer I am.

In the "horrible, heated summer of 1987," Bass and his girlfriend, Elizabeth, a painter, set out from Mississippi in search of "the ideal 'artist's retreat,' " a place of "ultimate wildness, with that first and last yardstick of privacy." It is a journey that hurries them throughout the Rocky Mountains and ends only at what a real estate agent describes as "the end of the world"—a forest in the Purcell Mountains outside Yaak, Mont., a "town" with a "mercantile" (i.e., a general store), the Dirty Shame Saloon and two "open-to-the-elements pay phones (with a stump beneath each phone, to use as a stool)."

For Bass, the house they rent, along with its acreage and outbuildings, is both refuge and outpost, a place to take the true measure of himself and a world he feels is too much with him:

> Perhaps all the snow in the world will fall, burying everything, such silence, and then I will

come out of it in the spring, different, cleaner, not born again so much as built up. I'll laugh at more things, and not get so angry at decadence, at laziness, at deceit and the theft of time, the theft of truth, starting with the President and going all the way down to the grocery store.

Naturally—and in ways central to self-inspection—it is a measure best taken one page at a time:

> I don't know how to write about this country in an orderly fashion, because I'm just finding out about it. If a path develops, I'll be glad to see it—as with math, chemistry, genetics, and electricity, things with rules and borders—but for now it is all loose events, great mystery, random lives.

The result is part journal, part memoir, part diary, part screed—a yearbook organized by two calendars, one that is winter and another that is the equally elemental force of self-discovery. The problem, however, is that after Bass has told us about the cold, the isolation, the creepy silence, the respect and caution and preparation that brutal weather demands, he has, finally, very little to reveal about the true subject of his narrative, himself.

"There are," he writes,

> two worlds for me—and for anybody, I think—and I do better in one than in the other. I used to be able to exist in both, but as I pay more and more attention to the one world, the world of the woods and of this valley, I find myself, each day, less and less able to operate in the other world.

As beguiling and compelling as his sketches of the land and its caretakers are, Bass denies his readers exactly what he says he came to "Paradise" for: the painstaking self-analysis that accounts for his wonder and his fear, his love and his dread. We know nothing of the novel he's writing, nor of the pictures Elizabeth is painting; we know next to nothing about their relationship, how it is changed or not by the actions of time and weather. To be sure, we learn that TV is "hideous" and that car dealers are cheats—insights as hackneyed as they are general—but we learn virtually nothing about the man before he chose to hunker down and hide out.

"Winter covers some things and reveals others," Bass tells us.

> I admire the weasels, the rabbits, and the other wild creatures that can change with the seasons, that can change almost overnight. It's taken me a long time to change completely—thirty-plus years—but now that I've changed, I don't have an interest in turning back.

Perhaps in his next book, from the retreat that is his greenhouse near the Canadian border in northwest Montana, Rick Bass will tell us what those forces are in the world that "lay claim to you, that lay a hand on your shoulder so gently that you do not even feel it." Until then, we'll just have to take his word for it, or wait again for the snow to fly.

Lee K. Abbott, "Rick Bass Seeks Solace in Snowland," in Chicago Tribune—Books, *February 17, 1991, p. 6.*

Rick Bass with John Murray　　(interview date April-May 1991)

[*Murray is an American nonfiction writer, educator, and critic whose works include* The Islands and the Sea: Five Centuries of Nature Writing in the Caribbean *(1991). In the following interview, Bass discusses his literary influences, his writing habits, and his concern for environmental issues.*]

Although Rick Bass now lives in the high, elk-filled mountains of northwestern Montana, just a short walk from the wilds of Canada, his personal and literary roots reach across the continent to the sunny, white-tailed deer country of south Texas where he was born and reared. It was in the Texas hill country, as a youngster, that Bass learned the art of storytelling from listening to his grandfather and older relatives recount adventures and spin yarns at the family hunting lodge. Bass' fond recollections of these early yearly expeditions are memorialized in his first book **The Deer Pasture** (1985).

As a result of this unique apprenticeship, there is a strong oral quality to Bass' nonfiction and fiction narratives, with a vernacular idiom; a digressive, rather than discursive mode; and the frequent use of the second person to engage the reader. In this orality, he comes straight out of a southwestern literary line that runs back through Edward Abbey and Mark Twain to Thomas Trapp and James Pattie. With respect to the contemporary scene, Rick Bass has more in common, stylistically, with southwestern writers like John Nichols and N. Scott Momaday than with writers of the northern Rockies such as William Kittredge and Tom McGuane. Bass is characteristically southwestern in his independence, his restlessness, his humor, his vitality, his sunny outlook, his distrust of unchallenged authority, and his disdain for affectation and pretense. All of Rick Bass' subsequent books—**Wild to the Heart,** (1988), **The Watch,** (1989), **Oil Notes,** (1989), **Winter** (1991)—have steadily built upon the promise of **The Deer Pasture** and have borne witness to the persistent influence of his home region.

I first met Rick Bass in late January 1990, when he came to the University of Alaska, Fairbanks, as a guest writer for the week. Unlike many authors who are often surprisingly different in person from the persona they project in print, Rick Bass the man was the same as Rick Bass the author—self-effacing, jocular, and charged with willfully restrained vigor. He exuded both good nature and good health. What impressed me most during his stay was that he went ice fishing one morning at 42 degrees below zero and actually swore he had a wonderful time. His craft lecture was favorably received. During the talk, Bass, who has taught at the University of Texas, Austin, emphasized some of the basics: the need for every narrative to have a beginning, middle, and end, and the importance of surprising the reader, of having the plot make some unexpected turns now and then. Toward the end of the hour, he spoke of the writer's obligation to tell the truth, but he also reminded the audience—graduate MFA students, creative writing faculty, and local writers—of the responsibility that every writer has to tell a good story. In this last point, he reminded me of the southwestern folklorist J. Frank Dobie, who once jokingly remarked that he would "never let the truth stand in the way of telling a good story."

Rick Bass felt the lure of the Rockies in his late teens and in 1976 matriculated at the Utah State University, where he played football—he still has the arms, shoulders, and neck to show for it—and majored in, of all things, petroleum geology. He also took some English courses from Thomas Lyon, who encouraged him to continue writing. After graduating, Bass worked in the oil industry in Mississippi, Louisiana, and Texas, but eventually—in 1987— moved with his companion Elizabeth Hughes, an accomplished artist, to a ranch in Montana, where he has since devoted himself to writing. Although Bass may continue to live in Montana and to write more about his experiences there than of his past in Texas, he will always be a citizen of the Southwest, in the same way that Joyce bore Dublin with him all over Europe and Hemingway lovingly carried his stories of Horton Bay from the Seine to the snows of Kilimanjaro to the big house overlooking the Gulf Stream.

One final note. Rick Bass spent four days with me this past September in Denali National Park, photographing grizzly bears. The weather could not have been worse. The Siberian front that pushed through on the second day— blowing down our tents, closing the park road, covering the highlands with snow—was so severe as to be reported in *The New York Times*. And yet through it all, Bass remained a tireless bon vivant and an absolute pleasure to have in camp and on the trail. Captain John Bourke once wrote, in the southwestern classic *On the Trail with Crook* (1887), that the truest test of man's character is to ride with him in bad weather. We saw some of the worst weather the subarctic can deliver on that trip, and yet I saw only the best in my companion

. . . . .

[Murray]: *What authors, dead or living, have influenced you the most in your nonfiction and secondly in the fiction?*

[Bass]: I've had that question asked many times, but I've never differentiated between nonfiction and fiction. That's a good idea. I guess I've separated the two less and less. But as far as nonfiction, certainly, Annie Dillard, Edward Abbey, Peter Matthiessen, and Barry Lopez. I guess I was in high school when I read *Pilgrim at Tinker Creek*. I read *The Monkey Wrench Gang* in college, quickly followed by *Desert Solitaire* and was immediately seduced by Abbey's values, his passion. I was thinking about this the other day. George Plimpton is nonfiction, where he would go and play football and write about the people in the various sports, or he'd play baseball or something. And I read that in high school. It was really funny and that really influenced me, how close he could get to these people. I like to do that in nonfiction, write about people's reactions in a certain place itself.

As far as fiction, that's a much longer list. Jim Harrison, I think, was the first writer I read who really knocked me out and made me think that I wanted to write fiction. And

after that it gets to be a real long list. All of the southern writers, Robert Penn Warren and William Faulkner and Eudora Welty. Wallace Stegner. Joy Williams. I love her stories. There's a writer in the South, Clyde Edgerton. I enjoy reading him. I haven't read much Hemingway, but I'm starting to now. I'm kind of rationing it because I enjoy it so much, he's only got so many books. I'm trying to read one or two a year to make them last. Other authors include a New England novelist, Craig Nova [*The Good Son*], and Raymond Carver and Tom McGuane and Richard Ford and John Irving's long novels. I also remember reading *To Kill a Mockingbird* several times.

What books did you read this winter?

A lot of galleys. I haven't been able to read many old books or books that are on my shelf and that list that everybody keeps by their bed. It seems like I just keep getting these galleys in the mail and reading them as quickly as they come in. Mark Reisner's book *Game Wars,* about the undercover pursuit of poachers, is tremendous. I read Peacock's *Grizzly Years* (1990) after it came out, and that was a marvelous book. Larry Brown had some short stories out that I read a while back. Those were very good. I think *Big Bad Love* was the title of it. Peter Matthiessen's *Killing Mr. Watson* (1990) I read this fall. Chris Spain's book, the one I talked about when I was up in Alaska. *Praying for Rain.* Such wonderful short stories. What with the Persian Gulf and all, I've been thinking about rereading *The Things They Carried* (1991) by Tim O'Brien. It talks about all of the supplies that are in the soldiers' backpacks: their little can openers and K rations and cooking utensils and pictures from home and stuff, talking about the great burden in the pack. It's a beautiful metaphor or a hideous one, whatever. I've also been reading Dan O'Brien's new galleys of *In the Center of the Nation (Atlantic Monthly,* 1991, June release) and Wallace Stegner's *Collected Stories* (1990), as well as *The Long Drive Home* (1990), poems by Nick Bozanic.

Now, the writing part of it. Do you use a computer or a typewriter? Or do you write it in longhand?

I write in spiral notebooks and just date them, like whatever month. I go through almost exactly one a month, so that's a good system. In the evenings, we turn the generator on for a couple hours, and I'll transcribe what I've written into a word processor I got this year. So it's stored on disk that way, so I can edit future copies.

I assume you do keep a journal, after having read **Winter.**

Yes, I do. That was the first time I had kept a journal. Since doing **Winter,** I've started keeping one. I love to go back and read it, even a few months ago, it surprises me, things I would have forgotten or just kind of settled in me as far as the different seasons and what all goes on at different times of the year.

Do you have a book of those that you've published to date, **The Watch, The Deer Pasture, Oil Notes,** *and* **Winter,** *that is a favorite? Or are they all similar in that respect? I asked Dave Brower that question, and he said, "Well, John, that would be like picking my favorite child, because they're all my kids in a way."*

Well, they are, of course. You're very fond of each book for different reasons. I was writing some friends in Arizona, and I guess I got to sounding kind of windy about **Winter.** I must have just gone on and on about it, how pleased I was with it, and they say, "I didn't know it was out yet." Like surely it must have been out for me to be talking about it at such length, which embarrassed me. But right now, **Winter** has a very special . . . I feel good about it. I think it's the first book I wrote just for myself and not to tell a story, not for anybody else. It was just written for me and my new life up here in the valley. And once we decided to publish it, we had to go back in and spend a couple years rewriting it and making it more like a novel with a beginning, middle, and end, inviting other people for readers, but without compromising some of the information I had put down for myself. It's not a collection of short stories, it's not a novel, it's not trying to explain what it feels like to find oil, it's not trying to explain what it feels like to hunt.

It would have been very easy for me discipline-wise to not take the time to record the new things I was seeing and was feeling up here in this valley and instead just go out and run up and down the mountains all day. For a couple hours each day I worked hard at crafting the journal and working on the writing in it and putting down those things perfectly that happened to me or that happened to other people up here.

Do you plan to stay permanently in Montana?

Yes, for now. I think about that an awful lot. I thought about it a lot today, actually, because it makes me so happy up here in this valley. I'm fond of pretty much every place in the country, but Yaak is the best place for me to live, just to hole up. So as long as it stays unspoiled and kind of hidden, I'll stay up here. If it changes, then I'll have to find some other place. That's all there is to it.

You've written about a lot of different parts of the country. I was rereading the essays in **Wild to the Heart,** *and I'm thinking of* "River People," *which is set in North Carolina, and* "Grizzly Cowboys," *which is in Montana, and* "Magic at Ruth Lake," *which is in the Utah high country, and* "Sispsy in the Rain," *which is in the southern hardwood forest.*

In *Hayduke Lives,* Abbey calls Hayduke "the world's greatest misanthrope." It could just be that I'm so misanthropic that I love the land so much more than all the populations on that land. I just fall in love with any land wherever I am. And if you're in love with something, you're going to write about it.

With reference to "River People," *which is about running some rivers back East, I was wondering if you have run any western rivers?*

No, I haven't. That's kind of along the lines of **Winter.** It seems to have been a part of my life, something I did pretty regularly for a good period of time, and then moved on. We've still got our canoe up here. There's just so little time. And any time we've got now, we spend just hiking, exploring the valley up here.

I'm curious about the genesis of **The Deer Pasture.** *Did*

that book grow out of an article or journal or just a general love for the place and a compelling need to share it and your love for it with others?

It was the latter, the need to share it and write about it, which is what writers do. I guess I was twenty-three or so when I started writing **The Deer Pasture.** It was the first thing I started writing about because it was the thing I could remember the best about being young. It's been in our family for, I guess, over sixty years now. It's kind of the cornerstone of our family, that piece of land up in the hill country. It's certainly the cornerstone of the men's side of the family, so that was the first thing I started writing about. In that same manner, I'm glad I did, because I couldn't write that book now. I think it's very important to write about certain things as you're living them, as you're learning about them.

When did you first start writing?

I did a little bit at Utah State University, just a couple of undergraduate classes to fulfill the electives for my major, which was at first wildlife science. Then I got out of school and ended up getting my degree in geology and went to work down in Mississippi. That's kind of when I started, on my lunch breaks there at my job. I'd walk over to the little city park and just write. And a lot of the writing then was about hunting and fishing and about the deer pasture, and just things I knew—or thought I knew.

Do you want to talk about your current fiction project at all? You had mentioned this summer that you were working on a longer narrative.

Sure. It's a novel, and it is longer, indeed. I've got more than 1,500 pages on it. It's called *Where the Sea Used to Be.* It's about things I know, about oil and gas geology. It takes place in Alabama and Texas and then up here in Montana. It's about wolves and a wolf biologist. She's central to the story or at least to the middle part of the story. I've been having a lot of fun with it for a long time now, just working along on and off since 1985. I'm just now starting to really, really enjoy it. But I don't think it was worth all the time I spent on it to get to this point where I'm enjoying it. I think as far as gratification, short stories may be the way to go. It's true what they say about novels: You put everything you know into it.

Speaking of your short stories, I reread "Choteau" *from* **The Watch,** *and I was curious as to whether the characters like Galena Jim Ontz and Patsy came from people who you really knew in Montana, or whether they're composites of various people, or just purely imaginative creations.*

I've heard that word used a lot about other writers' characters as composites. These guys were not composites. They sprang out of real people, and then my imagination altered them beyond that genesis. I rarely mix people to form what they call a composite. I take something I like or dislike in somebody I've seen or even something I think I've seen, and then the story is going to alter it. The flow and force of the story is going to change that character anyway. It would be very hard to maintain someone's true identity for me through a story. But those characters did have their genesis, however brief, in real people.

Getting back to **Winter,** *one of the things I found very interesting is that there used to be woodland caribou in the mountains where you now live. Are those now completely extirpated from northwestern Montana?*

There is one herd in the lower forty-eight that has come back into northern Idaho. Every now and then, every three or four years, one of the bulls which roam more will cross the line and come over into the valley, and then cut back over to Idaho. So they're not a viable breeding population. It's interesting that in Montana they're not listed as an endangered species, just because of the politics that would be involved, because they're dependent on old growth, on the lichen that grow on the old trees in the deep forest. And it would really shut down a lot more logging than has already been stopped if they were even to be acknowledged, so they pretend they're not even on the face of the earth. But they are.

So many of the western writers—Dan O'Brien and Bill Kittredge and Barry Lopez—seem to be deeply concerned with environmental issues. And I know you and Peter Matthiessen participated in the environmental writing conference last May in Missoula. Are you active in any particular groups or causes? I know you're very much interested in the valley there and protecting it. But are you involved in any particular groups?

No, I just belong to all the clubs, the Montana Wilderness Association and the Sierra Club, and groups like that. And I do all my letter-writing when they tell me to. If something comes up, they say this senator needs this letter about this issue. But I don't go to the meetings and don't go on the hikes. Again, there's just so much time. The only real activism I do is with a law firm over in Kalispell. I was introduced to them once when they were looking for testimony against an oil and gas well on the west flank of the glacier. So I went over there and met with them and just fell in love with this law firm, because they're working for free. They're real heroes, so whenever they have a big trial I'll go over there and sit with them and write about what's going on and learn some of what they're doing. But as far as being internally in some community of environmentalists, I'm not. I would like to, but I'd rather be off hiking.

It seemed like the three major areas of concern in the valley—from reading **Winter**—*were the mining and increased summer home development and logging—clearcutting—blitzkriegs in the forest. Is that correct?*

Well, it is. The logging is probably not even so bad up here as much as the road-building that's associated with it. But they're silting up all the streams. They cut down all over northwestern Montana. They don't have a streamside management act. They can cut right down to the water, and often do, and on too steep a slope. It's the old story. It's not different, it's just our particular story. I mean, Arizona has the same list of grievances with grazing, and Wyoming with water usage. In northwest Montana, it's logging, clearcutting, and the road-building associated with it. They're burning a lot of wood down in the little cities, the little towns, Libby and Missoula. These are just our

problems that we need to fix locally. There's not a place in the West that doesn't have a crisis. (pp. 9-10)

Rick Bass and John Murray, in an interview in The Bloomsbury Review, *Vol. 11, No. 3, April-May, 1991, pp. 9-10.*

John Murray (review date April-May 1991)

[*In the following positive assessment of* Winter: Notes from Montana, *Murray characterizes Bass as "a truly significant writer."*]

Rick Bass is well known to readers of nature literature from his previous books *Wild to the Heart,* (1987), *The Deer Pasture,* (1988), and *Oil Notes,* (1989). In this new volume, [*Winter: Notes from Montana*],—literally a journal of his activities on a remote Montana ranch through one winter—Bass provides a very personal look at his life as a writer and as a resident of the rural West. Bass was born and reared in Houston, Texas—where outdoor vegetable gardens flourish during the winter—and, as a result, has a fascination with the cold, snowy north. Although he has written passionately in earlier books about his cherished deer-hunting grounds in Texas, his favorite backpacking haunts in Utah, and his beloved northern New Mexico, one has the sense in reading this journal that he means to stay in Montana for good. The place has seeped into his blood, and, despite the bitter-cold temperatures of January and the various perils of living in an isolated mountain valley, Bass seems to be—like so many other major writers of our time who have settled in the northern Rockies—hopelessly in love with the place and willing to accept its challenges in order to savor its beauties.

One of the most enjoyable qualities of Rick Bass' prose is its warm, conversational voice. One can almost hear his soft Texas drawl:

> On up toward Missoula . . . and then farther north, toward Glacier National Park and the little ski town of Whitefish. . . . We went in to see a realtor on the little main street. It was a slow day, a slow town. . . . Ross, who was delighted with our plight, our search, began telling us about a wild, magical valley right up on the Canadian line over near Idaho . . . a handful of people lived there year around, sprinkled back in the woods and along the Yaak River. Ross said it was hard to get to, that you needed four-wheel drive, which we had, and that he had a property for sale there. . . . It was the end of the world, Ross said. Beautiful, but just too hard to get to. The only way to get in touch with the ranch was by mail or, lacking phones, by shortwave radio. . . . Heading northwest, we drove without seeing any sign of human life—deeper and deeper into the last and largest spot of unroaded green on our highway map.

It is on this ranch that Bass and his wife Elizabeth, an artist who has illustrated all of his books, decide to settle.

Bass finds loveliness and tranquility in Yaak Valley, but he also finds trouble in paradise, in the form of development, both private and public. For example, the woodland caribou were once abundant in his mountains, but now, because the old-growth forest has been so decimated by clear-cutting, the species is virtually extirpated. Bass observes:

> It's time to stop cutting old-growth forests. We'll cut them all, and then the same cries of more jobs, more money, will go up, and where'll we be then? I don't mean to rant. I'm trying to keep this polite, low-key, respectful. Quiet. Falling snow. But inside, I rage. Sure, cut lodgepoles selectively. But the big larches, the last giant cedars? When there are so few left, and when they're so important to wild nature? Some people want money, other people want caribou. You have to draw a line and stand on one side or the other.

Even more menacing clouds are gathering on the horizon—a silver mine, increased summer home development, new logging blitzkriegs—and Bass emerges in this book like Richard Nelson with Baranof Island, Alaska (*The Island Within,* 1989) or Chuck Bowden with the Santa Catalina Mountains of Arizona (*Frog Mountain Blues,* 1989), as a spokesperson and defender of his home range.

There are dangers in Yaak Valley that are much closer to home. Rick Bass almost amputates his foot one day while cutting wood:

> Splitting logs with the maul, I was dressed for safety, wearing boots, goggles, and ankle guards for when the quarter-and-half pieces kick back and hit me occasionally. I hadn't thought about the drawstring of the sweatshirt I was wearing, however, and when I was raising the maul over my shoulders for the swing, I got the drawstring wrapped around my waist, which distracted me on the downswing, and I almost missed the log and cut my foot off.

Later in the winter, when the snows are deep on the valley, his wife Elizabeth has an equally frightening experience, as her heavy flannel nightgown catches fire as she stands beside the fireplace:

> Elizabeth happened to see a reflection in the front window, which she thought at first was a car driving up with its headlights on, but which she then saw was the reflection of the flames . . . she slapped the flames out with her hands, and has blisters on her palms to prove it.

Bass concludes: "Everything is another world up here in winter . . . There are no rules. Anything can happen. You can't take anything for granted."

Rick Bass is one of the most gifted young writers to appear in quite a few years. Although only thirty-two years old, he has already published three impressive works of nonfiction and one critically acclaimed collection of short stories, *The Watch.* It is sobering to consider that, for example, when Edward Abbey was thirty-two, he was still a full eight years from the publication of his first work of nonfiction, *Desert Solitaire.* The publication of *Winter* merely confirms the judgment that a truly significant writer is emerging here, and that readers have much to look forward to in the decades to come from this strong new voice (there are rumors of a first novel to be published within

a year or so). For now, he has found a source of inspiration as well as a home, and makes fitting tribute to the Yaak Valley in this fine book:

> This valley shakes with mystery, with beauty, with secrets—and yet it gives up no answers. I sometimes believe that this valley—so high in the mountains, and in such heavy woods—is like a step up to heaven, the last place you go before the real thing.

(pp. 9, 14)

John Murray, in a review of "Winter: Notes from Montana," in The Bloomsbury Review, *Vol. 11, No. 3, April-May, 1991, pp. 9, 14.*

Charles E. Little (review date Summer 1991)

[*In the following favorable assessment of* Winter: Notes from Montana, *Little emphasizes the influence of the American South on Bass's writing.*]

It has long been my view that the best writing about the natural landscape takes the form of what is now called "creative nonfiction"—personal essays, usually in narrative form, that can vividly convey a combination of fact and impression to make our wild places real and meaningful. Let me now propose a corollary to this dictum: that a disproportionate number of the practitioners of this form have hailed from or lived in the South—Harry Caudill, John Graves, and Sue Hubble, for example, to name some favorites of mine. Even though the landscape described by many of these writers is not always in the South, a southern sensibility seems to shine through nevertheless. An historic agrarian economy doubtless accounts for some of this, where lives are lived out of doors for perfectly practical reasons. And mild climate, too, which can greatly increase the potential for time afield in the good ol' boy seasonal round. And then there is that wonderfully rich literary tradition of Edgar Allen Poe and George W. Cable and Thomas Wolfe and William Faulkner and Tennessee Williams.

But whatever the provenance of the impress, when books of the genre—creative land-essays by southern writers—are published, attention must be paid. . . .

Bass deals with place in a quintessentially southern way. By this I mean that he does not separate land from people, but integrates them into an organic whole.

—*Charles E. Little*

Rick Bass hails from east Texas. Child of an oil-patch family, he dutifully took a job as a petroleum geologist after college, working out of Jackson, Mississippi. A number of his books were written during that time, including two I enthusiastically reviewed here, *Wild to the Heart* (essays) and *The Watch* (short stories), and one I did not, *Oil Notes* (it was as good as the others, but a bit off the topic for [*Wilderness*]). Having demonstrated to critics, publishers, and himself that he was a writer in for the distance, Bass removed to northern Montana a few years ago to ply the writing trade full-time.

The Yaak Valley of Montana—for it was there that he and his friend Elizabeth Hughes took on the job of ranch caretakers—is a geography about as antithetical to that of Bass's birth as any place could be. And this plain fact provides the organizing idea for *Winter: Notes from Montana.* The basic conceit is that as a thin-blooded southerner if he can manage a Montana winter, then by God he can manage, period—his life, his writing, his relation to the power of the land. Along the way in this book, which is written in diary form with entries starting in mid-September and ending in mid-March, Bass deals with place in a quintessentially southern way. By this I mean that he does not separate land from people (in the manner of the eremitic Thoreau, for example), but integrates them into an organic whole. To a southerner, land *is* people, and vice versa. In *Winter,* the result is an impression of the Montana Rockies that is extraordinarily fresh and compellingly readable. "It looked so easy," Bass writes of "Don T.," a woods worker who agreed to help the newcomer sharpen his chainsaw in zero-degree weather.

> I was humbled that he'd take so much time out from his own woodcutting that I said, 'Let me try, I think I've got it now.' He grinned and his face split into a thousand wrinkles. Then he laughed, saying, 'No, you don't *got* it,' and kept filing gently, laughing, watching the snow above coming down, as if expecting someone.

Such effortless prose conceals a hard-won craft, yet reveals the soul of a true artist—and as likable a writer as you're ever going to meet on the printed page. (p. 34)

> *Charles E. Little, in a review of "Winter: Notes from Montana," in* Wilderness, *Vol. 54, No. 193, Summer, 1991, pp. 34, 36.*

Chris Goodrich   (review date 19 July 1992)

[*Goodrich is an American nonfiction writer and critic. Below, he presents a negative assessment of* The Ninemile Wolves.]

Rick Bass writes in the appendix to [*The Ninemile Wolves*], right after saying that wolves and men are brothers in the soul as well as in the hunt, that "You've come too far in this story to turn away now, when I start talking crazy like this. You can't turn away. We have to follow." In fact, of course, we don't, and in *The Ninemile Wolves,* which traces the story of a Montana wolf pack, Bass gives us many reasons not to: his superior attitude, his routine romanticization of wolves, his failure to shape his notes into book form. A good idea lies at the heart of *The Ninemile Wolves*—What does the wolf's return to the continental U.S. signify? Why does the animal evoke such strong reactions?—but Bass (perhaps best known for *Oil Notes*) doesn't do his subject justice. Had he gone more deeply into the lives and interests of the wolves' support-

ers—Mike Jimenez, a devoted Department of Fish and Wildlife biologist, or ranchers Ralph and Bruce Thisted, who loved watching the Ninemile pups grow up on their land—Bass might have created a book of lasting value, but this one simply makes the reader yearn for Barry Lopez or Edward Abbey.

> *Chris Goodrich, in a review of "The Ninemile Wolves," in* Los Angeles Times Book Review, *July 19, 1992, p. 6.*

Christopher Lehmann-Haupt   (review date 30 July 1992)

[*In the following review of* The Ninemile Wolves, *Lehmann-Haupt commends Bass for building a convincing argument for preserving wolf packs in the United States.*]

> They say not to anthropomorphize—not to think of them as having feelings, not to think of them as being able to think—but late at night I like to imagine that they are killing: that another deer has gone down in a tangle of legs, tackled in deep snow; and that, once again, the wolves are feeding. That they have saved themselves, once again.

So writes Rick Bass—a nature writer, novelist and unabashed admirer of wolves—at the opening of *The Ninemile Wolves* about the return of the wolf to the state of Montana after an absence of some 60 years.

What inspired Mr. Bass's eloquent book-length essay was the appearance in Marion, Mont., in early 1989 of a black, green-eyed female that was captured, collared and released in Glacier National Park. From there she fled and somehow made her way south a hundred miles to the Ninemile Valley, near Interstate 90 and the Idaho border, where she mated and had a litter of six pups in early 1990. The pack thus formed was watched closely by ranchers, hunters, environmentalists, politicians and bureaucrats, and became the object of the passionate hopes and fears that wolves had inspired in humans ever since the first one was kept away from the door.

Unfortunately for these creatures that are officially listed as endangered, many people hate them as much as Mr. Bass admires them. Ranchers consider them a threat to their livestock. Hunters find them competitors for such favorite prey as deer, elk and moose. Although the penalty for killing a wolf is a fine of $100,000 and a year in prison, people continue to gun them down, even when they have been collared by biologists for tracking purposes. And in the mythic role that the wolf plays in the human imagination and you get a sense of why the attitude of people toward the animals is as complex as a strand of DNA.

In tracking the adventures of the Ninemile wolf pack, Mr. Bass, whose previous books include *The Watch, Oil Notes* and *Winter: Notes From Montana,* struggles gamely to treat the wolf's enemies evenhandedly. Wolves do kill livestock, he admits, although there is evidence that they have to be trained to do so, and the mortality rate where wolves have been present in recent years has amounted to less than 1 percent of the herds annually.

One must not think of hunters in stereotypes, he urges, for polls have shown that "71.5 percent of residents in northwestern Montana were in favor of natural wolf recovery, as were nearly 60 percent of the hunters polled, as long as no restrictions were placed on hunters' limits of deer." Still, hardly has he entered this plea when he offers a description of the

> slob hunters who take poor, unsporting shots or who are poor marksmen—bellies heaving perhaps as they labor to aim the rifle, jerking the barrel off target in their fat-tremors so that the shot blows out the deer's stomach, or hind leg.

Struggle as he may for objectivity, it is wolves that Mr. Bass is clearly devoted to: their physical beauty; their remarkable intelligence despite having such "tiny" brains; their complex social patterns; their devotion to their mates and offspring; their extraordinary capacity to travel great distances, and the out-and-out passion with which they carry out their lives.

With his own passion, Mr. Bass makes a powerful case for reviving wolf packs in the United States.

> I have come away from following the Ninemile wolves convinced that to diminish their lives would be wicked; that it would involve a diminishing of a significant force in the world, that it would slow the earth's potential and cripple our own species' ability to live with force; that without the Ninemile wolves, and other wolves in the Rockies . . . the bright lights of potential—of strength in the world—would grow dimmer.

This sort of prose is inspiring if you happen to share Mr. Bass's feelings about wolves, though it is probably highly irritating to people who consider wolves their blood enemies.

At the end of this report, both sides get their ways. The members of the pack that the author has been watching have to be tranquilized with darts and removed from Ninemile Valley "following livestock depredation." Some of them die, others escape and disappear. Bad news for the pack, but as if to balance it, there are reports of new sightings all over the state. At least the wolf 's existence is not likely to revert to what it was in the 1870's, when some 700,000 animals were killed in Montana between 1870 and 1877.

The ambiguity of this news is neatly captured in the book's closing account of a dentist from Anchorage, Alaska, boasting how he and some friends had hunted wolves from the air. Although Mr. Bass is disgusted by the wrongness of doing this ("he was signing wolves' death warrant, humans' souls' death warrant, the death warrant of the earth, of our respect for our place on it, and for respect in all forms and fashions"), he is also awed by how close that dentist came to understanding: "I tell you, Joe," Mr. Bass quotes him as saying in the book's final passage,

> it was like nothing I've ever seen or done—Joe, for a few seconds there, we were right in with them, following right behind them—and the big

leader looked back, and for a minute, Joe, following along behind them like that, it was like we were one of the pack.

At the best places in *The Ninemile Wolves,* it is as if the reader too were one of the pack.

> *Christopher Lehmann-Haupt, "Who's Afraid of the Big, Bad Wolves?" in* The New York Times, *July 30, 1992, p. C17.*

FURTHER READING

Begley, Adam. Review of *The Watch,* by Rick Bass. *Boston Review* XIV, No. 3 (June 1989): 25.

> Praises Bass's ability to create authentic stories that explore "the verge of the recognizably real and believable, and [point] to what lies beyond, to a realm of danger, mystery, and wonder."

"Cry Wolf!" *The Economist* 323, No. 7764 (20 June 1992): 91-2.

> Negative assessment of *The Ninemile Wolves* in which the critic outlines the Montana wolf controversy.

Little, Charles E. Review of *The Watch,* by Rick Bass. *Wilderness* 52, No. 185 (Summer 1989): 59-60.

> Positive assessment of *The Watch.*

——. Review of *The Ninemile Wolves,* by Rick Bass. *Wilderness* 56, No. 198 (Fall 1992): 34.

> Applauds Bass's portrayal of wolf extirpation and endangered species preservation in *The Ninemile Wolves.*

Miller, David. "Slices of Wildlife." *The Sewanee Review* XCIX, No. 2 (Spring 1991): 319-27.

> Evaluates *The Deer Pasture* and *Oil Notes,* praising Bass's "cocky, energetic, tumbleweed prose."

Sanders, Joan. Review of *The Watch,* by Rick Bass. *Western American Literature* XXV, No. 1 (May 1990): 72.

> Positive assessment of *The Watch.* Sanders characterizes the stories as "compelling" and Bass's prose style as poetic and humorous.

Solomon, Charles. Review of *Wild to the Heart,* by Rick Bass. *Los Angeles Times Book Review* (18 March 1990): 10.

> Favorable review of *Wild to the Heart.* Solomon comments: "Bass' spare prose has a studied artlessness reminiscent of Japanese brush painting."

Stabiner, Karen. Review of *Winter: Notes from Montana,* by Rick Bass. *Los Angeles Times Book Review* (10 February 1991): 6.

> Positive assessment of *Winter: Notes from Montana.*

Stuewe, Paul. Review of *The Watch,* by Rick Bass. *Quill & Quire* 55, No. 3 (March 1989): 83.

Stuewe provides a positive assessment, commenting: "*The Watch* is an extraordinarily impressive début that vaults Bass into the front rank of American short-story writers."

Additional coverage of Bass's life and career is contained in the following source published by Gale Research: *Contemporary Authors,* Vol. 126.

Brendan Behan

1923-1964

(Full name Brendan Francis Behan; also wrote under the pseudonym Emmet Street) Irish playwright, memoirist, novelist, poet, and journalist.

The following entry provides an overview of Behan's complete career. For further information on Behan's life and works, see *CLC,* Volumes 1, 8, 11, and 15.

INTRODUCTION

Often considered one of the most important Irish writers of the post-World War II era, Behan is best known for works noted for their obscenities, humorous dialogue, and realistic depiction of topical and daily aspects of Irish life. As a journalist he commonly wrote about the Irish working class, but also focused on his experiences as a member of the Irish Republican Army (IRA) and the troubled relations between the Irish and the English. According to Alfred Kazin, Behan has identified himself "not with the abstract cause of art but with the profane and explosive speech of the streets, the saloons, the prisons."

Born in Dublin, Behan attended Irish-Catholic schools and later worked as an apprentice house painter. His working-class family was intensely patriotic, and the family's Irish Republican sympathies shaped Behan's life and career. In 1939 he was apprehended in England for possession of explosives and imprisoned for two years in a reformatory in Borstal, England. Throughout the course of his life, Behan would spend over six years in various prisons. Drawing from his early experiences in Borstal, Behan wrote his memoir *Borstal Boy,* perhaps his best-known work. Describing his arrest and subsequent incarceration, *Borstal Boy* relates the difficulties endured by Irish rebels in the English prison system. When *Borstal Boy* was published in 1958, Behan had already garnered considerable attention for his plays *The Quare Fellow* and *The Hostage.* Set in the death row of an Irish prison, *The Quare Fellow* ostensibly focuses on a man who is to be executed the following morning for murdering his brother. *The Hostage* portrays the kidnapping and killing of a British soldier by members of the IRA. The popular success of Behan's plays allowed him to lead a carefree and indulgent lifestyle. Notorious for his socializing and drinking, Behan died at the age of forty-one due to complications resulting from alcohol abuse.

Critical reaction to Behan's work has been mixed. Many commentators have commended his narrative style for its enthusiasm and wit, citing the dialogues of *The Quare Fellow* and *The Hostage* as examples of his ability as a storyteller. Others who consider Behan's works to be sensationalist and profane cite the coarse language and sometimes violent subject matter of his works. Considering Behan's

position among Irish dramatists of the twentieth century, Patrick A. McCarthy stated: "Behan's iconoclastic interpretation of the modern Irish scene, related in the tough language of the Dublin slums yet informed by a warm human vision, represents a substantial addition to the modern Irish theater."

PRINCIPAL WORKS

The Quare Fellow (drama) 1956
An giall (drama) 1958
  [*The Hostage,* 1958]
Borstal Boy (memoir) 1958
Brendan Behan's Island (sketches) 1962
Hold Your Hour and Have Another (sketches) 1963
Brendan Behan's New York (sketches) 1964
The Scarperer (novel) 1964
Confessions of an Irish Rebel (monologue) 1965
Richard's Cork Leg (drama) 1974
After the Wake (sketches) 1981

The Times Literary Supplement (review date 24 October 1958)

[*In the following review of* Borstal Boy, *the critic praises Behan's insight into prison life and "virtuoso understanding of accent and rhythm" in language.*]

The name of a village in Kent has by now become synonymous with a system of training young offenders which, in spite of many failures, has proved the most imaginative achievement of British penology. Based, perhaps too naively, on the traditions of the English public school, with its houses and captains and assumptions of "honour," Borstal became an easy target for the music-hall, though the spectacular increase in crime among boys and young men has of recent years made the jokes uncertain. And it may be that an optimism about the effect on young criminals of conditions of comparative freedom, with an emphasis on training rather than on punishment as such, has by this time been often sadly disappointed. Certainly—if statistics are a valuable guide—success, in terms of a subsequent law-abiding life, has latterly been less encouraging.

Mr. Behan, who was sentenced to Borstal training for I.R.A. activities during the war (he was too young for imprisonment), is not at all concerned with abstract considerations of penal reform. His book [***Borstal Boy***] is a brilliantly evocative account of the effect of Borstal on a group of youths who bring to the enforced community life of such a place all their awkward individuations of upbringing and confirmed habits of violence and vice. They can seem to conform, and indeed they have their own loyalties and moments of generosity. But the impression is of a jungle that is only temporarily cleared, and at any moment the tigers will take over and the law of the forest will be supreme.

Mr. Behan can afford to stand outside, for his offence, in his own conscience, has nothing in common with the dismal catalogue of grievous bodily harm and robbery and rape which are the credentials of his fellows. He is not at all censorious, but he exposes the rather pitiful helplessness of authority in the face of this troubled and treacherous world. And his stupendous gift of language, exuberant, ungoverned and indeed ungovernable, creates the very image of the rackety, reeking life of his wide boys, ponces, and screws.

But beneath the surface of this lewd and riotous book lies an essential charity which is altogether moving and memorable. Thus his picture of Charlie, the sailor who was his "china." (Mr. Behan's use of rhyming slang is throughout remarkable, and has for the first time given a literary stature to this acrobatic use of language.) Or, again, his deep understanding of Tom, the murderer of impeccable industry, the model prisoner who is essentially alone. These are more than the shrewd portraits, achieved by artifice, of the writer of imagination. They reflect, as does every page of the book, the capacity to see beyond the superficial level of bawdy talk and wicked deeds. Mr. Behan—and he will no doubt be surprised to hear it—in fact shares a quality which the best Borstal governors have: namely, a sense of justice that does not excuse, that is never surprised, and

always remembers that, in the final analysis, society gets the crime it deserves.

Much in Mr. Behan's book is disturbing. Much of the picture he draws is a judgment on ourselves: on the values of a society which has created an army of psychopathic offenders which shows no signs of growing less. And the dilemma of Mr. Behan and of all other Irish rebels against English rule is clearly revealed, not least in the account of his difficulties with the priests who excommunicated him. But ***Borstal Boy,*** whatever one's judgment of crime or punishment or the ethics of rebellion, remains a work of unique authority in its confident evocation of the very breath and being of life under captivity. And scarcely ever can dialogue have been handled with such a virtuoso understanding of accent and rhythm, the very vocabulary of the world of the condemned.

> *"Rebel for a Cause," in* The Times Literary Supplement, *No. 2956, October 24, 1958, p. 606.*

Paul Gavaghan (review date 22 February 1964)

[*In the following review of* Hold Your Hour and Have Another, *Gavaghan finds freshness and wit in Behan's barroom dialogues and discussions of everyday life.*]

The poet laureate of Irish pubdom, Brendan Behan, is represented [in ***Hold Your Hour and Have Another***] with a collection of diverting pieces culled from columns he wrote for the *Irish Press* between 1954 and 1956. This book will hardly add to the stature he gained with his play, ***The Quare Fellow,*** and his prolonged memoir, ***Borstal Boy.*** In fact, at times it is pointless and banal. . . . And still, the man is worth reading; he brings a witty, fresh point of view to bear on subjects as diverse as Great Britain and widowhood.

Most of his columns in this volume are taproom conversations involving the author and three antic characters: Mrs. Brennan, Mr. Crippen and Maria Concepta. The two ladies are widows with bottomless thirsts and merry memories of their late husbands, while Crippen serves as a tart-tongued opponent to Behan in some madcap exchanges. Their talk is thronged with allusions to politics, horse-racing, hurling, poverty and popular ballads. It is easy to detect the materials and the perspective that enabled Behan to fashion his more familiar works.

Behan cheerfully recounts varied opinions concerning his own worth: he is "a liar and a hack," "odious from educayshing," a writer who cannot read because he missed half his education, and "a lovely voice to scream the readers."

It is only in a few places that the house painter turned author chooses to voice his own strongly held opinions. As a tribune of the poor, he favors better housing, air and light for Dubliners over stately architecture. He points out the historic irony that Irish soil, so painfully regained through rebellion, is largely in alien hands today. And he closes with a charming little sermon on cats and how they helped the "tenement Irish" survive in their teeming ratholes.

There is a persistent consciousness of war permeating most of this talk in a "snug pub." Anecdotes of the Black and Tans, the Civil War, De Valera's economic war of the 1930's against Britain, and colonial service with Victoria's army are related with an eye for the comic or ludicrous. One reminiscence zestfully tells of the ragtag musicians parading behind British troops in 1913 to the tune of "Here's the Robbers Passing By."

If the reader is willing to surmount such initial obstacles as a Joycean style of dialogue, he will be rewarded with brilliant, terse descriptions: the sergeant with a face like a "plateful of mortal sins," the man who wasn't "tall enough to pick shamrock," London as "the second biggest suburb in the world," and Maria Concepta crying like "an out-of-work banshee."

While a hasty perusal of these sketches tends to strengthen Behan's reputation as a braggart and tippler, closer inspection affirms that this is a man with a peculiarly pungent style and breadth of view. We admire his admission: "I, however, have never in my travels met anything worse than myself," and hope that in the future he will give ampler expression to his rare gift of humor. (pp. 261-62)

Paul Gavaghan, in a review of "Hold Your Hour and Have Another", in America, *Vol. 110, No. 8, February 22, 1964, pp. 261-62.*

Anne O'Neill-Barna   (review date 21 June 1964)

[*In the following review of* The Scarperer, *O'Neill-Barna applauds Behan's ability as a storyteller and his use of vernacular language.*]

On the galleys [of **The Scarperer**] sent for advance review: "In quoting . . . it is essential that the final printed book be referred to, since the author may make changes on these proofs before the book goes to press." The fact that Brendan Behan can make no changes now fixes all this not only with irony—but with a finality beyond the cares of publisher and printer. In any case, trivial differences would not matter, for this is a most entertaining story.

"The Scarperer isn't the Scarlet Bloody Pimpernel, you know. He doesn't pull these strokes from the goodness of his heart." The Scarperer is one who assists escapes from jail for pay. The story, naturally, is told from the jail's-eye view. Its best scenes are the ones in the Dublin Bridewell. Reminiscent of **The Quare Fellow,** they show jailers and jailbirds enjoying mutually tolerant, humane relations. This attitude is so typical as to be almost symbolic of Behan. It is also typical of Ireland, where the distinction between the two sides of the law has long been transcended by a broader view.

The essence of Behan, his famous lack of inhibition, his being himself at all times, is part and parcel of this intimate Irish realism—which, on the basis of a long memory, sees law as an instrument of conquest and sees justice as something quite different, as the starving child fed, whether or not the food is "stolen." The contrast between Irish jails here and English jails as described in **Borstal Boy** is striking. In **The Scarperer,** Behan's tenderness toward the weak and beaten, and toward their rather innocent captors

as well, gets full scope. It enriches the characters, gives them a Shakespearean comic warmth. And it touches with Shakespearean pathos their unconsciousness of the treachery of the big-time criminals on the outside.

The story moves fast—from The Shakey Man's (and none better than Behan on Dublin pubs, his major field), to jail, to escape hide-outs, to sea, to Paris pubs, which Behan clearly minored in. Taken merely as a thriller in a literary climate of spies coming in from the cold, *The Scarperer* rates as excellent value. But it is different. No sex. No single point-of-view. Instead, good old-fashioned adventure, omniscient author, suspense, poetic justice—the classic recipe refreshed by what is practically a new language.

Behan retained an engaging sense of amazement at his literary career. As far as he was concerned, he wanted only to entertain—that is, to talk. And to be allowed to talk in Dublin (where all are talkers), to be given the floor, to be acknowledged as the most entertaining by the Irish, who are not only the father and mother but the connoisseurs of English wit, was a gigantic achievement.

This book is a suitable last testament for him. It is a talkative story, a compendium of Dublin speech such as we are not likely to get soon again. He had a formidable intelligence and a grace of expression which were his own. But he also reproduced authentically and at its most colorful the idiom of the people. The shades are not only of O'Casey but also of Synge. City folk, too, use constructions borrowed from the Gaelic, and they still have a clink of freshness which 60-odd years of literary familiarity have not dulled. Behan himself spoke Irish and translated from it. His first big success, **The Quare Fellow,** was originally written in Irish.

Before that, **Borstal Boy** had been published. Chapters of it ran in *The Bell*—which Sean O'Faolain was then editing. He recognized Behan's ability and edited the work, which appeared in book form in 1958. It covers the eight years Behan spent in English jails and borstals. It begins in 1939—when, at the age of 16, he arrived in England to fight on the part of the I.R.A. "for the Irish Workers' and Small Farmers' Republic, for a full and free life for his countrymen, North and South, and for the removal of British imperialism from Irish affairs." Later he was jailed in Ireland when the I.R.A. was declared illegal there. It is a fact which may account for the mixed reverence and contempt for the past which he shared with other unreconstructed patriots.

His plays, **The Quare Fellow** (an Irish prison on the eve of a hanging) and **The Hostage** (a Cockney soldier held in a Dublin brothel), came in 1956 and 1959, both edited and produced by Joan Littlewood, both hits and both already permanent parts of English theater. **The Big House,** a short comedy, played briefly in 1963. Meanwhile **Brendan Behan's Island** (1962) and **Hold Your Hour and Have Another** (1963) have also been published. These are collections of previously written pieces. Parts of another collection to be called **Brendan Behan's New York** have been printed in an English newspaper and there are two plays as yet unproduced.

The rumor circulated briefly that Behan might have

pulled out of his last illness had a "friend" not smuggled a bottle of whisky to him in the hospital. Others recollected his reply when someone remarked that success had spoiled him. "Spoiled me? It's damn near killed me." But surely his own nature made his destiny. He was too big-minded, too idealistic and too generous to "reckon costs," even that of his own existence, against the need to assert and demonstrate among the Irish "a full and free life."

> Anne O'Neill-Barna, in a review of "The Scar-perer", in The New York Times Book Review, *June 21, 1964, p. 5.*

Christopher Ricks   (essay date 30 July 1964)

[*Ricks is a highly respected English literary critic and educator who specializes in the study of poetry. In the following overview of Behan's works, he discusses the author's repetition of themes and anecdotes, judging this unoriginality to be the result of a lack of imagination.*]

The name Behan is said to mean beekeeper, but the good thing about Brendan Behan was that he didn't keep them in his bonnet. Not that it would have been surprising if he had turned into a crank—after all, he was involved in a fatiguing series of balancing-acts, and it would have been easy to totter. An Irishman all right, but stingingly critical of blarney and Irishness, and using them in his books only to ridicule them or to outwit his persecutors. A *New Statesman* reader, but half-afraid of and half-contemptuous of intellectuals. A Roman Catholic, but scornful of the Church for its loving support of all the wrong political causes—and moreover a man who took the line, still dangerously bizarre in Ireland, of being as much against anti-Protestant vindictiveness as against anti-Catholic ditto. A leftist with a long memory but no rancor, who ringingly announced that his ambition was to be a rich Red. A card-carrying, indeed bomb-carrying, member of the Irish Republican Army, who spent the best years of his life (in more senses than just the schooldays one) behind bars, but who was later to find himself sentenced to death by the I.R.A. for removing his toes from the party line. (Fortunately the sentence was passed in his absence, so he was able to send a courteous note suggesting that it be executed in the same manner.) Such self-warring loyalties and likings would be enough to drive a man to drink. Not, apparently, that Behan needed much driving.

It would be good if one could think of his passionate boozing as nothing more than a plain man's delight in good fellowship. But it does look more obsessive than that, and Behan's death in March of this year has, as everyone has pointed out, a great deal in common with Dylan Thomas's. With both, there was a willed thoroughness about seeming hard-drinkingly normal that itself ended up not normal. With both, there was the fatal fact that the modern publicity industry prefers its celebrities drunk. The appeal now is from Philip sober to Philip drunk. There was no intrinsic reason why Behan's famous insobriety in 1956 alongside Malcolm Muggeridge on B.B.C. television, or later under Ed Murrow, should ever have done him any harm. In fact it must have, and just because it was in a

worldly sense the making of him. Drinking became, perilously, part of making money rather than spending it, and Behan, like Thomas, now had a reputation to keep down. Again like Thomas, there is one's nagging feeling that he drank because he didn't really want to write, was perhaps dismayed at how quickly he had run through what he had to say, and so was trying to stave off a sense of bankruptcy. The force of these pressures on Behan and the force with which his witty courage withstood them can both be seen in that extraordinary face, so photogenic and so exuberantly ugly, with the rubbery dimpled gentleness of a baby and yet the strength of "a hillocky bull in the swelter of summer."

Any reader of *Borstal Boy* or of *Brendan Behan's Island* will feel that with the death of Behan we lost a very unusual man, notable for a fairmindedness and a generous humanity that never became theoretical or tepid. How unusual he was as a writer is another matter. *Borstal Boy* is sure to last because of its sufficiently unusual warmth, knowledge, and detail—far from being flamboyant or outrageous, it is by and large a work of considerable quiet dignity. Behan doesn't rant during "God Save the King" or even remain seated—he slips out with a warm tact as if going to the lavatory: "I did not want to insult my friends and I did not want to stand for 'God Save the King'." But both *The Quare Fellow* and *The Hostage* will be seen as having been overrated—understandably overrated, because of the dreary poverty of contemporary drama, a poverty which leads to an excessive gratitude for any work of sense, observation, or humanity. Behan's plays are not inferior to, say, John Osborne's; that is, they make a real and pleasant change from the usual vapidities, but if the same material, informed with the same degree of understanding, had been presented in the form of a novel, critics would hardly have been prostrate with admiration. That a play turns out to be not execrable now elicits a natural but dangerous warmth. In the case of Behan, the point matters, because so much of the tone, the stuff, and the sympathy of the plays is indeed to be found, often verbatim, in his other writing.

He was born in 1923 in Dublin, the son of a house-painter. He was apprenticed to the trade himself, and his respect for such skills comes out in some oddly touching episodes in *Borstal Boy.* At the age of sixteen he was arrested in Liverpool for possessing I.R.A. explosives:

> My name is Brendan Behan. I came over here to fight for the Irish Workers' and Small Farmers' Republic, for a full and free life, for my countrymen, North and South, and for the removal of the baneful influence of British Imperialism from Irish affairs. God save Ireland.

Too young for the heavy sentence he would otherwise have received, he was given three years in Borstal. (He was eventually to spend eight years locked up.) He had written and published pieces in verse and prose since he was twelve, in various Republican and Left-wing magazines, and in Borstal he won an essay competition. But it was not until the 1950s that there was a real breakthrough. He was liked as a writer by the Dublin intelligentsia—according to him, because he had hardly published anything. But the intelligentsia was not too keen on some pieces of pornography which he had written, in English, for French magazines. Short of money, he wrote a serial about Dublin's underworld, *The Scarperer,* which ran for thirty days in the *Irish Times.* He took the precaution of using a pseudonym ("Emmet Street"), and he drew on his prison experiences. The result, now republished, is lightweight but enjoyable. Behan was still feeling his way towards his own characteristic form, but the story (of a man who is helped to "scarper" from prison only to find that he is to be murdered) has a genuine suspense. But what mattered to Behan was that the *Irish Times* believed in his abilities, even to the extent of sending him ninety pounds to live on while he completed the story.

Then from 1954 to 1956 he wrote weekly articles for the *Irish Press,* some of which have now been collected as *Hold Your Hour and Have Another.* A somewhat ingratiating use of charm, an uneasiness about looking like a high-brow, and a feeble use of malapropisms—these are real faults, and such a book does Behan no service. But then whose weekly pieces would be worth reprinting? And even here there is evidence of Behan's extraordinary gifts as an anecdotalist. The thing about the anecdote is that it so totally doesn't need any gifts of characterization; Behan seems to have been as completely without such gifts as a writer could possibly be, and yet he was saved by anecdotes. The British officer loftily murmuring "I see they have cripples in their army"—to be met by the Irish retort "We have, but no conscripts." Or, "at one of the street battles in Cathal Brugha Street that helped to pass the depression for the people," Paddins shouting "You have the best of men in your jails, and I dare you to take me now"—only to be softly undone by the public speaker: "I am not," he said, "a collector of curios." Or the old lady who does nothing but embroider notices which say "Beware!" This is Behan's world, and he sees it with an unsentimental sanity and optimism. As an anecdotalist he may have embroidered, but not at any rate "Beware!"

What is worrying about *Hold Your Hour,* though, is that it already shows that for all his energy and width of sympathy he was dangerously short of material. Mainly this was because of his dilemma as a no-nonsense ordinary man who happened also to be rather a reader. *Borstal Boy* shows that Dickens, Hardy, Dostoievsky, and of course *The Ragged Trousered Philanthropists* all meant a lot to Behan, and the book even had the courage to offer an epigraph from Virginia Woolf. But the *Irish Press* was afraid of Virginia Woolf—or perhaps Behan was afraid it might be. So he tended to neglect, as sources of inspiration or information, much that past literature makes available. History, yes—Behan like all Irishmen knew a lot of history and deployed it brilliantly. As he said in *Borstal Boy,* "I was never short of an answer, historically informed and obscene." But literature he seems to have found a bit suspect, going along with snobbery and effeminacy. So despite the strength of history and of his pub-taking oral traditions, Behan found himself cut off from an important and reinvigorating source of creativity. Clearly he knew about this; one of his sketches about "Brending Behing" ends: " 'Sad case,' said Crippen, looking at me with commiseration. 'Only went to school half the time, when they

were teaching the writing—can't read.' " Behan coped with the problem with dignity but also with some embarrassment. And sometimes he fell back on an amiable but unconvincing pretense, as when he praised Sean O'Casey: "All I can say is that O'Casey's like champagne, one's wedding night, or the Aurora Borealis or whatever you call them—all them lights." See that tell-tale shift from *one's* to *you;* Behan, blunt man, doth protest too much. Likewise when he beautifully quotes Keats as at last the Borstal boys reach the sea, only to retreat from a feared sentimentality with "By Jasus, this equals any fughing Darien." In fact Behan's dedication to the drama is related to this dilemma—it offered the appearance of a way out, since of all the literary forms it is the one which can apparently go furthest in dispensing with literature.

It was his macabre comedy of prison life, *The Quare Fellow,* which in 1956 made Behan. He had written it as a radio-script, *The Twisting of Another Rope:* then it became a one-act play, and finally three acts. *The Hostage* was commissioned by Gael Linn, the organization for reviving the Irish language. It took Behan a fortnight. Applauded in Irish, it was disliked in English; Behan's friend Alan Simpson has suggested that the worthy Irish patrons didn't understand the obscenities when in their "native language." Possibly too the pitying humor with which Behan now regarded the I.R.A.'s religiosity seemed renegade. But in England both the plays, with their music-hall mixture of comedy and tragedy, song and dance, were the successes that Behan deserved and needed. 1958 was a good year for him; not only *The Hostage* but also *Borstal Boy* (banned in the Republic of Ireland and in Australia). But since then the stream was running dry. There was a radio play, *The Big House,* set in the early Twenties, which was adapted for the stage in 1963. (It is printed in *Brendan Behan's Island,* a delightfully reminiscential scrapbook that shows Behan at his best.) But *The Big House* is like second-rate Dylan Thomas, "Under Milk and Water Wood." There were a couple of radio sketches; there was the jazz revue, *Impulse,* with Behan as compère, which petered out in Toronto in 1961; there were two new plays which came to nothing and were at last shelved, *Richard's Cork Leg* and *Checkmate.* But something was going badly wrong. To look back now over Behan's work is to see how terribly repetitive he was. Three times he used the anecdote about Queen Victoria giving five pounds to the Battersea Dogs' Home at the same time as to the Irish famine fund, so as not to seem to be encouraging rebels. The jokes, the songs, the historical incidents—all return word for word again and again and again. Not because they are obsessions, but because Behan was short of material.

> "Where the hell were you in nineteen-sixteen
> when the real fighting was going on?" "I wasn't
> born yet." "You're full of excuses."

A good old joke, and worth using once. But only once. There could be a very long list indeed of these verbatim repetitions. There is nothing immoral about them, but they make very sad reading because, in its sheer mass of detail, such a list would be clear proof that Behan's undeniable vigor was not correspondingly matched by fertility of imagination. As a writer he was unlikely to have had much more to give the world. Which is not to deny that as a man he still had a shrewd compassion. (pp. 8-9)

Christopher Ricks, "Bee-Keeper," in The New York Review of Books, Vol. II, No. 12, July 30, 1964, pp. 8-9.

Rae Jeffs, on working with Behan during the recording of *Brendan Behan's Island*:

As soon as we had breakfasted the next morning, Brendan moved into the front room and asked me to set up the machine. His large face radiated activity without the slightest sign of fatigue and although by now I was getting used to the incredible, his limitless stamina astounded me. Prodding myself into action, I gave him the list of Paul Hogarth's illustrations [for *Brendan Behan's Island*], and allowing himself the customary moments in which to collect his thoughts, he indicated that he was ready to record.

It would always have been an experience to listen to Brendan talking about the city that cradled him, for his family and families before them came from Dublin, and his fantastic memory and passionate interest enabled him to remember in minute detail every story handed down from generation to generation. Added to which, he had an extraordinary gift for words and was happy to have the opportunity to use it. For myself, I truthfully forgot that the purpose of the operation was to produce a book and I became immersed in the history of Dublin, in her splendour and her poverty in past and present days. In a way, it was the ideal set-up for Brendan because he enjoyed monopolising the stage and his role as entertainer was an essential and delightful part of his character when he was not cocooned in worthless adulation. At the same time he was fulfilling a commitment and functioning as a writer, for the use of the tape-recorder is not uncommon by even less eccentric authors. Brendan knew that I regarded his work seriously and although the sessions were conducted in a free-and-easy atmosphere and his uninhibited singing punctuated most of the facts that he was relating, his approach was always professional without a trace of the clown. In my delight I moved to play back the tape, but Brendan would have none of it.

'Much as I like the sound of my own voice,' he chuckled, 'I'll stand no competition from it.' Nor did he ever. Throughout the morning there had again been a stream of callers to the house; people wanting to meet him; cadgers, journalists and others eager to take him out for a drink; and I realised more clearly the difficulties he was facing as a gregarious man and the strain he was under for having become a world-famous character. As long as he could work, he would be able to resist the temptations.

Rae Jeffs, in her Brendan Behan: Man and Showman, 1966.

Sean O'Faolain   (review date 26 June 1966)

[*Considered a master of the short story, O'Faolain has documented—in both his fiction and his nonfiction—much of the history of twentieth-century Ireland, often basing his works on his own role in important events. Al-* *though he has been one of Ireland's most outspoken advocates of reform, his love for his country and admiration for its people are evident throughout his work. In the following review of* Confessions of an Irish Rebel, *O'Faolain recalls Behan's exuberance, gregariousness, and vulnerability as an author and individual, citing these qualities as causes of Behan's early death.*]

Everybody says Brendan Behan loved life. If he did he did not dominate it; it dominated him. He loved it so much that it slew him. He gave himself no time to tame it or to write it. He did not write [his last book, *Confessions of an Irish Rebel*]; it was recorded on tape, transcribed and edited by Rae Jeffs, a proper English lady whom he enchanted into nonconformity; "once-proper" is her own word today. I am not sure that it is right even to call this record a book, if that word conveys at least a beginning, middle and end—temporalities that no more existed in Brendan's being than they do in eternity.

Who recorded it anyway? Brendan, or Life pouring over him and out of him in song, verse, drink, passion, guff, rude jokes and flat statements (such as that Lord Carson's real name was Carsoni, or that London is named after a Celtic god), blasphemy (he says he always liked it and most Catholics do—who else *can* blaspheme?), cursing, praise of the Lord, lots of F-words, S-words, and other such explosives, but all too rarely that priceless stuff that ends up as unforgettable print. How lamentably the good Lord distributes talent! I could name offhand 10 Irish writers with 10 times Brendan's talents who would give their eyeteeth for a hundredth part of his amazing vitality and combustibility, and a thousandth part of his experience.

What a man! And then one pauses, and asks the chilling question: What kind of a writer? Did he really and truly ever want to be a writer at all? Or did he belong to that type of writer, something on the order of Thomas Wolfe, who acts as if he believes that if you live hard enough, and emotionally enough, literature will follow as a matter of course—the eye in a fine frenzy rolling? I do not know if Brendan ever read Thomas Mann's "Tonio Kröger," with its dismaying if salutary description of how an artist really works, moving from primal, hot excitement into coldly deliberate creation. It could hardly have been Brendan's cup of tea, or glass of malt.

Rae Jeffs, in her highly percipient Foreword, sees the fundamental truth about him: childlike in his frankness and candor, full of innocence, tenderness and sensitivity behind all his outward ferocity, the prisoner and victim of a fatal persona or role, a man who did not want to die, only to stop living the self-destructive life that he had concocted for himself. All this is made perfectly clear in these *Confessions*, where his reactions to life are sometimes deep but mostly very simple, and utterly spontaneous— always provided one agrees that every Irishman is conditioned from birth by the immemorial and inescapable Irish myth and tradition.

From boyhood his love for Ireland was not merely all-embracing but all-devouring. The record here of his experiences with the latter-day I.R.A. is the first thing I have ever read that gives the full blast of the pride, passion and sincerity of those doomed young idealists, as when he writes of the burial of a young man whom Mr. de Valera's Government deliberately allowed to die of a hunger-and-thirst strike in May, 1946:

> The firing party . . . was held in Dublin and the Guard of Honor fired revolvers over his coffin.
>
> 'From your holster, withdraw. Fire! fire! fire!'
>
> Funnily enough, the Guard of Honor in the Free State Army only use rifles, but in the I.R.A. we never use anything but revolvers. There are six men in our Guard of Honor and eight in the Free State Army who, strangely, give their shooting orders in Irish whereas ours are given in English. We also have the distinction of using live ammunition.

It might be written by the colonel of some crack regiment in the French, British or American army. "In the I.R.A. *we never* use . . ." This burning pride of the dedicated patriot runs all through his last testament. It comes out of an emotion and a devotion as simple as a hand grenade.

Such a man had no defenses against the complexities of life. He just waded into them; and so into jail after jail, as here recorded—Mountjoy, Arbour Hill, the Curragh Internment Camp, Strangeways, Lewes. And, once again as in **Borstal Boy,** however much he blasphemes, curses or uses all the usual four-letter words *ad nauseam,* he never once whines or complains, a slim, handsome, curly-headed youth, who, once the jail-diet days ended, was to finish as an obese and sodden boaster, possibly, quite probably, with a breaking heart for the days when he had more to die for as a failure than he ever got from the harlequinade of success.

This record is full of good humor: from the islets of Dublin's wild life that rise and fall like atolls, to his days in Paris as pimp, pornographer and sign-painter; his first efforts at writing, when, as editor of *The Bell,* I had the honor of printing his first paid-for article (a section of what later became **Borstal Boy**), to his great success with **The Hostage,** first directed and brilliantly produced by Joan Littlewood (without whom it would never have reached the stage) in London, and later at the Théâtre des Nations in Paris, representing, of all countries, Great Britain's contribution to contemporary drama. The record ends with Brendan's marriage to the girl who played the heroine in **The Hostage,** Beatrice ffrench Salkeld, in 1955. Somebody else may record his last nine years, largely unfruitful, mainly frightening.

Do those whom the gods love die young? Or is this one of the smug phrases of old age? When he was dying, his constitution undermined by liquor, he said, more persuasively, "I don't like this dying lark, at all." When I heard that he was dead, being then over 20 years his senior, and acutely aware how valuable twenty years of maturity might have been to him, I did not think much of this alleged love of the benignant gods. Only a few artists have been able to cope with the *vita brevis,* all men of genius: Mozart, Marlowe, Keats, Alain-Fournier. Brendan was no genius.

And even if he were! Had Villon died at his age, what would remain of him? Or of Yeats? I once said to Brendan, "If you don't live to be an old man I'll kill you!" He preferred countless hours of glorious life and a worthwhile output in print that you could count on three fingers—and this last, gay, sad, earthy thumb to Charon: "Going my way?" It is a book that makes me want, all over again, to embrace and throttle his endearing, feckless shade.

But there is, of course, another possible thought about his all-too-early death, a thought too depressing to be called a consolation: he might have lived on to become another garrulous old Dublin bore. For such passionate men as he, there is such a thing as the fatality of too-long life. The rest of us, less warm, less talented, less fated, have to trudge along under the whip of the will. He, being what he here calls a Daylight Catholic, shivering at night in fear of the gods, believed in Fate—and surrendered to it. At the end his love of Life was the kiss of Death.

Any writer who ends by talking to a machine instead of whispering to his page must have begun to lose a considerable part of his faith in art, life and himself. He was a very gallant youth. "From your holsters, withdraw. Fire! fire! fire!" God be good to him. He used live ammunition. And though most of it goes wild in this machine-made book, the real whiff of the Behan cordite emerges from time to time from the silently turning wheel.

> *Sean O'Faolain, "Love of Life was the Kiss of Death," in* The New York Times Book Review, *June 26, 1966, p. 7.*

Johannes Kleinstück   (essay date 1971)

[*In the essay below, Kleinstück considers the plot and style of* The Hostage, *judging the work to be written in the vein of Shakespearean drama.*]

Brendan Behan did not leave any extensive work behind him: two plays, one novel, some books of sketches and memories. His relatively small productivity as an artist is not to be explained by the fact that he died too early; he was not, in himself, immature, nor did he suffer from what we sometimes call a loss of words, for this disease is not prevalent in Ireland. Indeed, according to his companion and biographer Rae Jeffs, Behan was full of stories, easily understood by the uninitiated, particularly those stories and songs which so frequently interrupt his narratives and of which he mastered an immense amount. It was his way of living which prevented his writing. Of the forty years of his life (from 1923 to 1964) even Behan might not have been able to reckon how much time was spent in taverns. Moreover, he spent about eight years behind bars, for while he was still an adolescent he entangled himself in the muddle of Irish politics—not as a politician but as a fighter for the unity and liberty of his native island. He became a member of the I.R.A., long an illegal organization in Eire; and it was his intention to blow up a warship in Liverpool docks which first brought him to trial and to subsequent imprisonment in a Borstal (that prison without real bars). Yet even after his return to his birthplace, Dublin, he did not cease rebelling, as he describes for us in **Borstal Boy** (1958). For there he came into conflict with the law again, and even when he was finally released he rarely practised his occupation as a painter, but roamed about Ireland France and England (where he was once again imprisoned).

Behan wrote only in order to make money, as he himself asserted. Nevertheless he enjoyed his fame as a writer and liked to pose as the wild Irishman. This aspect of him is appreciated by the English, while the Irish disapprove of it. (If I may be allowed a personal comment—I was told in Ireland in 1962 that he was by no means considered a national hero, rather a 'villain', a word which seems archaic to us but which is well known there—yet I have heard other opinions too.)

Brendan Behan played a part, that of the rebel, of the outsider who despises laws and conventions. He played, one might say, the stage Irishman, and, according to report, he played the role well. He did not consider himself to be an artist. Joyce, whom Behan seems to have revered, wrote a book on the experience of becoming an artist, in which he became tenderly engrossed in his own youthful portrait, enjoying and conveying the melody of his own early verse. Behan abstained from that kind of self-glorification. When he talks about himself he is interested in Guinness and whiskey, abundant food, splendid talk with farmers on the West Coast, and his own proud past as a defender of Irish liberty, or the impertinent answers that he gave his judges and jailors. He is not interested, however, in how his own books came about, what he felt, or what he wanted to say in them. He talks of experience, of what is around him, of what is going on inside him, just as Yeats (in his *Autobiographies*) abstains from the interpretation of himself or his works.

Behan might have rejected, perhaps angrily, such comparison with Yeats. For Behan's origins were in the proletariat, whereas Yeats admired the society of the Great House and aspired to be an aristocrat—but even Yeats was often accused of posing, so that Lennox Robinson, in defence of him, said:

> [H]is pose would have been to try and pass himself off as an ordinary man.

Behan, at least partially, may be likened to that ideal writer addressed by Yeats in his valedictory poem ["Under Ben Bulben"]:

> Sing the peasantry, and then
> Hard-riding country gentlemen,
> The holiness of monks, and after
> Porter-drinkers' ready laughter;
> Cast your mind on other days
> That we in coming days may be
> Still the indomitable Irishry.

Behan belongs to the 'indomitable Irishry', though he did not want to have anything to do with country gentlemen. However, he did not move only within the circle of the proletariat but also within that which is called, in French, *le milieu*. Both had strong associations for him; for he grew up in a flat adjacent to a kind of brothel:

> It wasn't much of a brothel, God knows, but the inhabitants enjoyed themselves or seemed so, I think they did more drinking there than anything else; it was more a shebeen than a kip, kip

being the Dublin word for a brothel and shebeen the Irish for a place where people are able to drink after hours.

To this milieu Behan transferred the plot of his play *The Hostage*. First written in Irish, as he tells us in his *Irish Sketch Book,* it was performed, as *An Giall,* at the Damer Hall, St. Stephen's Green, Dublin in 1957. The first English production followed on 14 October, 1958 at Joan Littlewood's Theatre Royal, Stratford, London E.15. The play's location, according to the text, is 'an old house in Dublin'; the *Sketch Book* tells us that we should envisage this house to be in Nelson Street, near to Nelson's Pillar—since then, of course, blown up by the still active I.R.A. The house is built in Georgian style and has seen better times, so, it is said, have its present occupants. Pat, the manager, had earlier fought for Ireland's liberty, and having lost a leg in the process is only too ready to talk about his heroic past. His former superior and brother in arms lives solely in the past, devises imaginary battle plans, wears a kilt, makes a bagpipe resound now and then, and, if he could have his way, would dispense with the use of English and speak nothing but Irish—but which Irishmen would understand him? Thus, in order to avoid the English and unpatriotic Mister he calls himself Monsewer. We are not surprised to learn that he is English on his father's side, and that he is the only member of this circle of aristocratic descent; but he ignores his origin in the same way that he ignores the present time. We live in the age of the atom bomb, and in Pat's opinion this makes the I.R.A., or any other force, useless, whether they are 'the Coldstream Guards, the Scots Guards, the Welsh Guards, the Grenadier Guards and the bloody fire guards'. Yet the I.R.A. is not diverted in its activity by such realization. In Belfast one of their soldiers (whom some would call a terrorist) has been imprisoned and sentenced to death by hanging on the following morning. As a counter-move the I.R.A. have abducted a young English soldier, Leslie Williams, holding him as a hostage, to be shot in reprisal if the sentence is not amended. To Pat's great annoyance two I.R.A. volunteers quarter the hostage in the house which Pat manages, and keep a close guard on their captive.

From this situation the plot of the play is developed, and occupies the few hours of the prisoner's detention. The inhabitants of the house receive Leslie in a friendly fashion, provide him with cigarettes, beer (Guinness, of course), tea, and readings from the Bible: Teresa, the country-bred, convent-educated, maid-servant even offers him her love. But Leslie is killed when the house is besieged by the Irish police, tipped off by an informer. No one knows whose bullet killed him. It is not even clear if he is dead, in one sense, since he stands up, enveloped in a ghostly green light, and sings:

> The bells of hell,
> Go ting-a-ling-a-ling
> For you but not for me,
> O death, where is thy sting-a-ling-a-ling,
> Or grave thy victory?

At the close of the play all sing together; indeed, the audience has joined in on several occasions.

Many an English audience will have felt this play to be 'very mad and very Irish'; indeed, it is only comprehensible from the standpoint of a knowledge of Irish history. For one needs to recall that the Anglo-Irish conflict began in the twelfth century, when the English—or more strictly, the Normans—began their settlement on Irish shores before gradually extending their rule over the whole island. The struggle seemed over in 1921. Michael Collins, the leader of the Irish rebels, signed a treaty which left the six northern counties, most of them predominantly Protestant, still within the British Commonwealth, while the rest, mainly Catholic, achieved independence. This seemed a reasonable solution to many people—to many, but not to all. The radicals continued to fight, and Michael Collins, more than anyone else a national hero, was ambushed and killed. The I.R.A., an illegal and underground organization, still fights today for the liberation of the six counties, whose inhabitants—and not only the Protestants among them—resist such liberation strongly.

This extraordinarily complex situation must be understood as the necessary basis for an understanding of Behan's play, whose author found it necessary to expound upon the problem through dramatic dialogues. Pat, the former hero, who belongs with those unable to accept the treaty, is the play's spokesman: Meg, 'his consort', Colette, the young whore, and Ropeen, the old, listen to him, and let fall their remarks:

Pat: Five years' hard fighting.

Colette: Ah, God help us.

Ropeen: Heavy and many is the good man that was killed.

Pat: We had the victory—till they signed that curse-of-God treaty in London. They sold the six counties to England and Irishmen were forced to swear an oath of allegiance to the British Crown.

Meg: I don't know about the counties, but the swearing wouldn't come so hard on you.

Ropeen: Whatever made them do it, Mr. Pat?

Pat: Well, I'll tell you, Ropeen. It was Lloyd George and Birkenhead made a fool of Michael Collins and he signed an agreement to have no more fighting with England.

Meg: Then he should have been shot.

Pat: He was.

Meg: Ah, the poor man.

And then Pat is asked to sing the song of Michael Collins, the 'Laughing Boy', and he willingly does so.

No mention is made of the fact that the Six Counties did not want to become a part of the Irish Free State; that they were not sold, as Pat says. It is a matter of fact that the majority of Northern Irishmen remains faithful to the Union Jack. Diehards, if at all, recognize this very unhappily, and Brendan Behan does not go into the matter deeply. Perhaps this does not surprise us. It is, however, strange that in this dialogue he turns such events into comedy, thereby ridiculing his own I.R.A. activities as well. He has gained a different point of view, yet without wholly rejecting his own patriotism.

In the *Sketch Book* he writes about the famine of 1847, for which he holds the English responsible:

> The greatest disaster to happen to any one nation in Europe, until the murder of six million Jews in the last war, was the Irish famine of 1847. Eight million people lived in Ireland at the time, but when the famine ended there were only four million left.

Behan accuses the English of mass murder, comparable in scale with the German one, and he continues, with bitter sarcasm:

> Queen Victoria was very distressed at the famine among her loyal subjects and she sent £5 to the Famine Relief Fund; then in case she might be thought to be showing open sympathies with a crowd of rebels, she sent £5 to the Battersea Dogs' Home.

In *The Hostage* the English soldier, Leslie Williams, asks for what crime he is to be shot, and Pat explains:

> I'll tell you what you've done. Some time ago there was a famine in this country and people were dying all over the place. Well, your Queen Victoria, or whatever her bloody name was, sent five pounds to the famine fund and at the same time she sent five pounds to the Battersea Dogs' Home so no one could accuse her of rebel sympathies.

The same story, in almost the same words, but their meaning is different. In order to ensure that the tale is not taken too seriously the dramatist makes Meg comment:

> Good God, Pat, that was when Moses was in the Fire Brigade.

Since the play was written before the *Sketch Book* we cannot say that the author has changed his mind. He was, however, capable of revising his opinions in the light of facts, and could look ironically at convictions which had compelled him to fight. In this play Behan faced his own past, and with it part of his nature; and he found both were comic.

Throughout the play the plot is controlled by a distancing irony, already perceptible in the description of the scene:

> Since the action of the play runs throughout the whole house and it isn't feasible to build it on stage, the setting is designed to represent one room of the house with a window overlooking the street. Leading off from this room are two doors and a staircase leading to the upper part. Between the room and the audience is an area that represents a corridor, a landing, or another room in the house and also serves as an extension of the room when the characters need room to dance and fight in.

No attempt is made to create illusions; from the start we know that this is no drama of naturalism, no drama, that is, concerned to give the appearance of reality. Consequently, the action does not aim at illusions either; obviously the characters speak colloquialisms, but one might take this opportunity of remarking that the playwright controls this manner of speech; moreover, the characters do not hesitate to do what a theorist of the classic theatre would censure, that is, they play outside their rôles, they address the audience, break into song and dance; yet, despite all this, they do not forget themselves, because it has been made clear from the beginning that they are playing a rôle, and do not intend to try to persuade an audience that they are doing otherwise.

Shall we then add this play to those categorized as epic theatre, acknowledge in it the 'alienation' effect, and assume the influence of Brecht? This would be wrong, for Behan does not use the theatre as a means to an end, however much he shares with Brecht certain formal elements in their use of theatre. Behan does not wish to teach an ideology, nor call upon the world to change in the cause of socialism. Therefore, he neither sums up morally nor requires his audience to reflect in any dogmatic way; he does not show how, ideally, things might be improved, but presents what he observes; he is interested in human events, not in theoretical inferences or conclusions.

Behan thus continues the tradition of the Irish Theatre movement in the way in which it was founded and practised by Yeats and Synge, though he is, perhaps, unaware of this. His final song celebrates the triumph of life over death, in which the Christian belief in salvation is partly parodied, partly affirmed. It would have been very easy indeed to have provided elevating songs of mutual understanding and peace among the peoples instead! This would have been not only easy but even obvious, because the play moves towards such a message and seems to contain it. The English soldier is not presented as a stranger, or an enemy, within the Irish environment, but seems to belong to it at once. At the end of the first Act he is pushed on to the stage where communal dancing is taking place, and with his very first words he adapts himself:

> Don't stop. I like dancing.

He feels at home immediately. So much so that when the I.R.A. officer orders him to be silent he pays no attention but sings:

> There's no place on earth like the world,
> There's no place wherever you be.

All join in with him. The community of feeling is established without questioning. Why should a young Englishman have objections against the Irish, and vice versa? It is ridiculous to reproach him with wrongs committed in earlier times by his fellow-countrymen. For, on the one hand, the past has gone for ever, and on the other hand, it was the English landlords who were guilty of causing the misery of the Irish in the nineteenth century; and though they were his fellow-countrymen, they were members of a different caste, of a ruling class by which he is still ruled. He is an underdog, every bit as much as are the inhabitants of this house in Dublin. Among simple people of all nations mutual understanding should not be difficult to achieve.

The proletarian Brendan Behan sympathizes with the labouring class, whom he called 'the only real people'—in Dublin at least; and he even went so far as to assert that only 'the generals and the politicians' are interested in warfare, though this is difficult to accept in the light of his own activity in the I.R.A. Obviously, in some respects, Behan is again close in outlook to Brecht; but Behan does not believe in the doctrine of the 'election' of the working class: above all, he is indifferent to notions of class-consciousness. He likes labourers because he can talk and drink with them easily. Similarly, he also likes farmers, and British soldiers, above all the brave, and he even feels benevolence towards the 'Earl of Birkenhead, who by all accounts was a very charming man and an alcoholic like myself'; Behan's humanity is not dictated by abstract principles. Thus the girl, Teresa, a devout Catholic, falls in love with the English soldier, Leslie, a Protestant. She puts a medal with the image of the Virgin round his neck, which he will carry for love of her. Love and sympathy do not obey either frontiers or principles, and therefore the common people are not, in principle, philanthropic in general terms. Leslie sings:

> I love my dear old Notting Hill, wherever I may
> roam,
> But I wish the Irish and the niggers and the
> wogs,
> Were kicked out and sent back home.

Behan sees no reason why Leslie's wishes should be corrected, as if they represented a false ideology. He accepts men, even the mad Monsewer, and only the fanatical I.R.A. officer cuts a bad figure, perhaps the worst in the whole play.

Men, and the world, are accepted. This is what marks the difference between the radical Behan and Brecht and all other Marxists, who had to condemn the play as pessimistic and defeatist. The threat of the atom bomb is ever-present, yet nobody complains, nobody expects, hopefully, a disarmament conference. The fate of the young rebel in Belfast is sealed from the start, as Pat acknowledges steadfastly:

> Tomorrow morning at the hour of eight,
> He'll hang as high as Killymanjaro.

Such will be Leslie's fate whatever friendship he is offered, and he knows that nobody can save him:

> You're as barmy as him if you think what's happening to me is upsetting the British Government. I suppose you think they're all sitting round in their West End clubs with handkerchiefs over their eyes, dropping tears into their double whiskies.

The fatalistic consciousness of the unavoidable gives the play a tragic tone which pierces the grotesque and comic formulation of its detail. Leslie is given the tragic status of a hero who atones for a guilt which is not of his making but which he bears on behalf of a remote, scarcely probable, past. For a moment the tragic form gains the upper hand. Leslie lies there shot; Teresa bends over him, and says:

He died in a strange land, and at home he had
   no one.
I'll never forget you, Leslie, till the end of time.

And then, all of a sudden, the appropriate requiem turns
into a celebration of life. Comedy overcomes tragedy; the
'play' its seriousness. And looking back we recognize, retrospectively, that the tragic tone was never more than an
overtone, that the fatalism always dissolved into comedy,
and that all the burden, the pressure, of the past evanesced
in a prevailing irony. The playful character of the work is
due to the fact that even our existence is conceived of as
a game: 'All the world's a stage'—Behan is nearer to
Shakespeare than to Brecht.

[In *Das Drama Shakespeares, Ausgewählte Vorträge und
Aufsätze,*] Wolfgang Clemen has written:

> In Shakespeare's last plays, his so-called fairy
> plays or romances, among them *The Tempest,
> Cymbeline,* and *The Winter's Tale,* we find in-
> creasingly the impression that reality, in the
> main, is to be understood as appearance; a world
> of dreams, in which fantasy and spells are pow-
> erful, begins to supersede reality.

Obviously in **The Hostage** there are no dreams or spells,
but the presented appearance of life is fantastical and theatrical. Monsewer, with kilt and bagpipe, presents an Irishness larger than life; the two I.R.A. men play the parts
of soldiers at war, though one is a teacher and the other
a railwayman. One wants to laugh at them, but their playing at warfare leads to a sanguinary end, which, moreover,
if forced still further, leads into the realm of fantasy. For
the pandemonium which breaks out at the end of the play
seems to be a parody of a battle, as if to provide the actors
with an opportunity to rage to the full, shooting, shouting
and running, while Leslie performs a kind of dance before
he dies:

> The soldier makes a break for it, zig-zagging
> across the stage, but every door is blocked. The
> drum echoes his runs with short rolls. As he
> makes his last run there is a deafening blast of
> gunfire and he drops.

In this world of play-acting everyone is aware that the
dead man will rise again in order to sing; everyone knows
that he has only pretended to be afraid before he fell; and
even then, we all know that soldiers must die, for truth
flashes momentarily in appearance. It is in accord with
this author's temperament that appearance and reality, or
truth, are so closely interwoven.

Behan's biographer called him both 'man and showman',
one who played both the Irishman and the rebel, and yet
was both. This post was not only forced upon him, it was
also closely related to his nature. Again one finds a similarity with Yeats, who, when talking of poets [in *Essays
and Introductions*], thought of his nature in the following
terms:

> He is Lear, Romeo, Oedipus, Tiresias; he has
> stepped out of a play . . . He is part of his own
> phantasmagoria.

Differences apart, in **The Hostage** Behan makes himself
part of his own phantasmagoria, for he allows Leslie to de-

scribe the author of the play as 'too anti-British', to which
the I.R.A. officer replies:

> Too anti-Irish, you mean. Bejasus, wait till we
> get him back home. We'll give him what-for for
> making fun of the Movement.

And Leslie turns to the audience:

> He doesn't mind coming over here and taking
> your money.

Pat explains:

> He'd sell his country for a pint.

This kind of irony—which we often call romantic—can be
found wherever drama is not considered to be a copy of
life, of nature, or of reality, but where a play establishes
its own laws. Brendan Behan is working in a long-
established tradition, reaching back to the time of the Elizabethan drama.

To what extent Behan was aware of this tradition cannot
be ascertained; what is certain, however, is that **The Hostage** could scarcely have been conceived without Shakespeare's example. The common people whom Behan depicts with sympathy, raise their voice with similar power,
for the first time, in Shakespeare's history play of *Henry
IV.*

In that play the lives of the unimportant merge with the
lives of the important. In **The Hostage** Behan has created
for himself a part of the Shakespearian cosmos, comparable to that represented in the Dublin-based plays of Sean
O'Casey. Politicians and other important persons remain
outside this world; they work upon it unseen; but even
with Shakespeare there is already a recognition of those
who must resign themselves for the present but who will
not always do so, since they have their own problems and
concerns. As early as Shakespeare (and, as is acknowledged, his work was the first of this kind) comedy and
tragedy are intermingled on the stage, leading to brute dis-
sonances; think of the death of Hotspur, followed by the
grotesque epilogue of Falstaff, and compare with this the
death of the English soldier, where the grave mourning of
the girl is literally outplayed by a wild and gay song.
Behan follows in the tracks of Shakespeare. And presumably he would have been a good Elizabethan. The Mer-
maid tavern would have been as pleasant to him in the way
that Leslie found congenial company in the old Dublin
house. (pp. 69-82)

> *Johannes Kleinstück, "Brendan Behan's 'The
> Hostage',"* translated by R. Hausen, in Essays
> and Studies, *n.s. Vol. 24, 1971, pp. 69-82.*

Peter Costello   (essay date 1977)

[*Costello is an Irish critic and author of nonfiction. In
the following excerpt, he discusses political aspects of
Behan's works.*]

[The] real laureate of the [Irish Republican Army] is Brendan Behan. Behan was born and bred a Republican, his
family having been involved in the national struggle for
decades: his uncle Peadar Kearney is the author of the Na-

tional Anthem. At the age of sixteen Behan was arrested in Liverpool carrying a caseful of bombs for blowing-up letter boxes. Typically, the mission to England was his own idea, unauthorised by the I.R.A. His experiences at Hollesley Bay gave him the material for *Borstal Boy.* Released from there, he was arrested again in Dublin after trying to kill a policeman at Sean McCaughty's funeral. Jailed, he was released under an amnesty for political offences. He then turned to writing seriously, his first stories being published in *The Bell* by Sean O'Faolain.

We are still too close to Behan to measure his full worth, but *Borstal Boy* and *The Quare Fellow* are among the best things in modern Irish writing. His other books are, as they say, of interest. The celebrated *Hostage,* however, gets carried away in its Theatre Workshop version by the music-hall elements which swamp the delicate love story of the soldier and the girl.

The plot of *The Hostage* was derived directly from the kidnapping of a young British soldier in Northern Ireland who was brought down to Dublin and kept prisoner in a Nelson Street brothel. This incident from the same campaign in the fifties in which Sean South and Fergal O'Hanlon were killed, provided the immediate idea. But in Behan's imagination it fused with a story he had been told about from the Troubles [in Northern Ireland]. An old IRA man had once described to him how he had waited in ambush for a British troop train. The train came around a bend with the soldiers, some scarcely more than boys, singing happily. The next moment the shooting started. Behan could never forget that image of happy song obliterated by machine-gun fire.

His politics—the politics of machine-gun fire—clashed with his writing, his kind of happy song. He was intensely loyal to the family tradition of Republicanism—he often boasted how his father had snubbed [Irish political leader Eamon de Valera] at his uncle's funeral. But the artist had seen enough of life in jail and out to know that human beings were difficult characters, good enough in themselves, but often led by duty to awful deeds. If *The Quare Fellow* unleashes its jovial scorn on capital punishment, *The Hostage* is equally hard on the Organisation and its pietistic career rebels. Yet in the end it is the mad pride in the IRA—almost the pride of a St Cyr officer, Sean O'Faolain once observed—that comes through.

When Behan died, his old comrades in the IRA covered the coffin with the tricolour and fired over the Glasnevin grave a parting salute. Some of those in that crowd must have remembered a passage in his last book:

> The firing party for Sean McCaughty was held in Dublin and the Guard of Honour fired revolvers over his coffin.
>
> 'From your holster, withdraw.
> Fire. Fire. Fire.'
>
> Funnily enough, the Guard of Honour in the Free State Army only use rifles, *but in the IRA we never use anything but revolvers.* There are six men in our Guard of Honour and eight in the Free State Army who, strangely, give their shooting orders in Irish, whereas ours are given

in English. *We also have the distinction of using live ammunition* (added emphasis). [*Confessions of an Irish Rebel*]

It is exactly this distinction of using live ammunition, of being an active force, that keeps the tradition of the IRA alive among young people. They have their traditions: for the rest of us the songs and the poetry are enough.

But it is through the songs and the poetry, for good or evil, that the Fenian tradition of this country, the memory of the dead, lingers on. Because of them that live ammunition modifies the guts of the living. In memory of those two boys, South and O'Hanlon, killed in raiding an Ulster barracks in 1956, Dominic Behan wrote a fierce song that should have been the last word:

> Come all you young fellows,
> Stay here while I sing,
> For the love of one's country
> Is a terrible thing.
> It banishes feeling
> At the spurt of a flame,
> And it makes you a part
> Of the Patriot Game.

True and terrible words, if only the gunmen would listen to them. But they do not. They have the distinction of using live ammunition. And here as in so many things, the poet makes his way into those minds and finds the final words, where tradition and imagination become one. (pp. 294-96)

Peter Costello, *"Epilogue: Live Ammunition,"* in his The Heart Grown Brutal: The Irish Revolution in Literature, from Parnell to the Death of Yeats, 1891-1939, *Gill and Macmillan, 1977, pp. 291-98.*

Colbert Kearney   (essay date 1977)

[*In the following excerpt from his* The Writings of Brendan Behan, *Kearney discusses the significance of Behan's Irish-language poetry.*]

Behan after the publication of Borstal Boy.

Behan first achieved literary prominence as a poet in Irish: he was the youngest author represented in *Nuabhéar-saíocht,* a collection of modern Irish poetry edited by Seén Ō Tuama in 1950. Máirtín Ō Cadhain, arguably the greatest writer of Irish in this century, reckoned that among those whose work was included in *Nuabhéarsaíocht* there were two genuine poets, one of whom was Behan. Within two years of this recognition he had written his last poem.

His output was small—a dozen short lyrics—but sufficiently strong to merit reassessment today. Nor is it only the intrinsic merit of the verse which engages attention. His career as an Irish poet prompts two questions. Why did he write poetry in a language which was not his vernacular? And why, having done so well, did he stop? It must have been obvious to one of his upbringing that a poet in Irish wrote for a tiny fraction of the population, and that a national revival of the language was, despite the optimism of enthusiasts, a dim prospect. The native speaker may argue that Irish is the only medium for him, and others, less plausibly, that though it be a secondary and acquired language for them, it is, for historical reasons, the one best equipped to express the imagination of an Irish writer. Some writers have sought in the Irish language and tradition an alternative to what they saw as the sterility of mid-Atlantic English culture, and it is fashionable today to translate from the Irish, partly, no doubt, in search of technical novelty, partly in reaction to loss of identity in the contemporary world. One fact is undeniable. The writer who chooses to work in Irish rather than in English is seeking something other than popularity: he may write great verse, but must leave it to a little clan.

Neither of Behan's parents knew more than a few words of Irish but they used them with pride, teaching their children to respect the language as an aspect of that national independence to which they were committed. The gifts which people noticed in the young Brendan were those which would have facilitated language-learning: a fine ear, a prodigious memory and a talent for mimicry. He was probably being falsely modest when he alluded to 'the bit of Irish' he knew as a result of his formal schooling. As he graduated from the Fianna to the IRA he had ample opportunity to meet fluent Irish speakers. Although not all members of the IRA could speak Irish, the movement gave it unqualified support and there were close links and overlapping membership between the IRA and organisations more specifically dedicated to cultural affairs. In republican circles Behan encountered native speakers, musicians, and storytellers. His higher education in Irish took place during his imprisonment from 1942 to 1946, his studies directed by teachers who knew by heart an amount of poetry and poetic lore which seems incredibly extensive to those whose education has been through books rather than through oral transmission. Almost as important as the availability of teachers was the special atmosphere among republican prisoners and internees. IRA men maintained some sense of discipline and community while confined: in the classes which they organised themselves, many read at least as rewardingly as they would have in an educational institution.

Behan was particularly fortunate to find among his fellow-prisoners in Mountjoy Seán Ō Briain, a schoolteacher from Ballyferriter in the Irish-speaking part of County Kerry. It was in Seán Ō Briain's company that he acquired the ability to converse in Irish with something of the ease and copiousness of a native speaker. He also learned a lot of the poetry and social history of Gaelic Ireland. In describing his own birthplace for Behan, Ō Briain conjured up an Ireland worth fighting for. The barrier of language had enabled the people of the Kerry *Gaeltacht* to preserve a cultural continuity of which the greater part of the country had been deprived. Successive waves of invaders had been absorbed and had become as Irish as the original inhabitants. In this close-knit community Behan could see a Gaelic version of his own area in northside Dublin. The people were proud of themselves and their descent, of the history in song and story which they handed from generation to generation. Behan was attracted to the apparent classlessness and the absence in Irish of a system of accents denoting social status which a working-class Dubliner could not fail to notice in English. These people had produced and treasured the princely Piaras Feiritéir and the rakish Eoghan Rua Ō Súilleabháin. Ō Briain's picture enchanted Behan: it epitomised with a new clarity the ideal to which he had dedicated himself from childhood, an Irish society which had proudly maintained a cultural identity impervious to British colonial abuse.

Behan's immersion in the Irish language coincided with the beginning of his adult career as a writer. There were growing-pains. He was uncomfortably aware of contradictions within himself, between his republican idealism and his own experiences in England, between his duties as a soldier and his ambitions as a writer. The Irish language offered a possible resolution: were he to write in Irish he could follow his own private inclinations while at the same time continuing his part in the struggle against British imperialism. It is interesting to consider to what extent did his commitment to Irish influence his writings as a whole. During these years he acquired a discipline which never came easily to him, the ability to transmute into quiet industry those elements of his personality which craved public performance; between 1942 and 1946 he began to work towards his two masterpieces, ***The Quare Fellow*** and ***Borstal Boy.*** To a great extent the cell in Mountjoy facilitated this, but perhaps even more influential was the focusing of aim and energy on the demands of Irish literature.

Early in 1944 Behan was transferred to the Curragh where he encountered Máirtín Ō Cadhain who used his period of internment to read, write, study and teach. Ō Cadhain was concerned with the feasibility of a modern Irish literature. A brilliant control of language was not enough, he argued; unless there was creative talent nobody would read simply for the sake of the language. He was aware of the revival of interest in Irish writing but was sceptical: 'Those who begin to write in a language they don't know and which they do not try to learn properly have an awful cheek. I myself could write English better than most of them—most of this crowd who are writing in Irish without knowing it' [*As an nGéibheann,* 1973]. The revival was not confined to republican prisoners but was a national phenomenon. In his introduction to *Nuabhéarsáiocht,* Seán Ō Tuama was to write:

In future when people try to establish when the development of modern Irish poetry began, they will probably settle for 1939. In that year, Conradh na Gaeilge resumed the Oireachtas competitions in Dublin; at the same time the second world war began. It would be difficult to decide if those events had a greater influence than the founding of the universities' magazine, *Comhar,* three years later; yet this much is certain: the resurgence of national feeling in this country during the war brought a proportionate reawakening of interest in writing; and in the case of poetry, this revival was developed and assisted to a considerable extent by the Oireachtas competitions and by the Irish-language periodicals, especially *Comhar.*

The writers involved saw that their basic problem was that of using the resources of Irish to create a medium which would suit modern poetry, increasingly urban in its preoccupations. Yet most of the writers—and all of those who were native speakers—came from rural backgrounds and inherited a poetic tradition which was untouched by the twentieth-century city. All poets must to some extent expand language to embrace their imaginative discoveries but the problem was unusually pressing for the Irish poet. For the non-native speaker the need for expansion was coupled with that of acquisition, while in all cases there was some element of doubt as to the survival of the language as a modern tongue. After three years of writing in English and learning Irish, Behan took the obvious first step towards writing in Irish, translation. He sent a version of **The Landlady** and an early draft of **The Quare Fellow** to the Abbey Theatre.

Towards the end of Behan's time in the Curragh, Seán McCaughey, an IRA leader, died on hunger-strike in Portlaoise. The December issue of *Comhar* contained a poem by Behan which commemorated McCaughey's self-sacrifice. Entitled **'The Return of McCaughey',** it concentrates not on the physical death but on the spiritual triumph as seen in the return of the remains to Belfast. The ballad captures the victory of mind over matter. The second stanza:

> I had expected to witness a funeral
> With pipes of condolence droning their keen,
> Had thought that the sound of guns would be
>   mournful,
> But, like the victorious host of O'Neill,
> Come from the Pale having crushed the invader,
> The Gaels are delighted to carry their trophy,
> To welcome McCaughey back home to Ulster,
> For pride is eventually stronger than woe.

Taken on its own terms—as a celebration of glorious death—it is quite successful, full of zest and colour. There are loosenesses of expression which might have been tidied up, and the three and a half stanzas would suggest that the author ran out of steam and did not bother to reorganise what he had written, but the poem is essentially rhetorical and is more concerned with atmosphere than with argument. As the work of a beginner it is remarkably fluent in movement and sound-pattern, an *amhrán* [based on a pattern of vowel-rhyme which includes both end-line and mid-line consonance] rather than a translation.

In January 1947 Behan walked in the funeral of Jim Larkin, champion of the Dublin workers, and two months later a poem appeared in *Comhar* which is rather similar in theme to the McCaughey ballad. It is at first sight surprising that Behan should not think it more apt to honour Larkin in the language of the Dublin worker; a poem in Irish meant nothing to most of those with whom Behan had followed the coffin. The Larkin verses show how committed Behan was at the time to Irish. They are not particularly good, having the weaknesses of the previous effort without its strength. The structural looseness emphasises the lack of direction.

> He was me—he was every mother's son of us,
> Ourselves alone—strong as we wished to be,
>   As we knew how to be.
> He threatening fight and bringing freedom,
> We following his coffin through the jaws of the
>   city,
>   Amid great bellows of rage.
> Following his coffin through the jaws of the city
>   last night,
> Were we ourselves in the coffin?
> No. We were marching in the street,
> Alive—grateful to the dead one.

This is the assertion of emotion rather than the imaginative expression of emotion: there is no living sense of Larkin's greatness or of 'our' loss. As a socialist and an aspiring poet, Behan felt obliged to mark the occasion but the command performance lacks depth.

In 1947 Behan found himself in prison again for IRA activities. In Strangeways Jail, Manchester, it struck him that this was the same old story: that he would never achieve his literary ambitions but would be carried around the vicious circle of hope, political action, arrest and despair. With a mail-bag needle he began to scratch out his troubled thoughts in a poem, **'Repentance'**. This was a standard topic for Irish poets, and Behan wrote that the first stanza was a translation of an English verse which had come down from his maternal grandmother, but this poem as a whole achieves a life of its own and writhes with deep feeling. It is, in contrast with the earlier efforts, a private poem, unhindered by political abstractions. Far from being an assertion of emotions, the communication of the poem is in the expression, the sound, rhythm and syntax revealing the theme. The struggle between hope and despair, between faith in the Virgin and the masochistic orgy of self-accusation, emerges in the musical pattern of lingering supplicatory vowels and the harsh clamour of consonants and images of pursuit. The final stanza may be translated as follows:

> Recollection hoots like a hunting-horn
> Calling my sins like a ravenous pack;
> To the end of my trail comes death on a horse,
> Each year a jump behind his back;
> As I wait for the kill, cornered and panting,
> The bloodsweat breaking on my face,
> As I tremble before their red-eyed howling,
> Virgin, don't grudge me your merciful grace.

Here is a tone of voice which is rare in Behan's writings other than his Irish poems. Generally, in and out of his works, he projected himself as larger-than-life; the tough, cocky, jovial veneer covered more uncertainty than he cared to reveal and was, in biographical terms, self-defensive. In **'Repentance'** and in many of the subsequent poems, the protective devices are dropped and it is possible to detect a direct honesty which is latent in his other works. The *persona* of the Irish poems would seem to be the closest approximation to his basic personality. Perhaps, because the language was so closely associated with his sense of literary vocation, writing in Irish enabled him to subject himself to confessional scrutiny; certainly, the monastic tenor of the life of the writer in Irish (especially when compared with the clamour of his public performances) allowed him to express himself with a minimum of self-consciousness. **'Repentance'** describes the death-bed of a guilt-stricken sinner, but the temptation is strong to see the imagined death as a correlative of another doom which haunted him at the time—the death of the writer within him, dissipated in the aimlessness of his life.

He returned to Dublin but was unable to establish a productive routine: in 1948, after a bout of drinking, he ended up in Mountjoy. He recalled the vision he had had there six years previously: his lack of progress towards it worried him and inspired him to poetry. Superficially, the poem is an expression of nostalgia for life on the Blasket Islands; by 1948 almost all the inhabitants had removed to the mainland. Given what is known of Behan's attitude to the Blaskets and of his situation at the time of composition, the poem becomes more complex. The Blaskets were part of Seán Ō Briain's Gaelic Kerry, an ideal Ireland.

'I thought of the wonderful kind people [*the islanders*] were and the free and independent, if frugal lives they and their ancestors had on these islands, their eras of quiet happiness there on the uttermost fringe of Europe' [*Brendan Behan's Island*]. The loss of the Blasket community was the loss of a symbol which he had hoped would help him integrate his political and cultural hopes. The islands had fallen, not to a foreign invader but to modern times. Similarly, the IRA had apparently been outmanoeuvred, not by an alien but by an Irish government. Was his hope of becoming an Irish writer to fail also? In such grey moments on the brink of despair he could imagine so. What was he but a Dublin house-painter imprisoned for drunken brawling?

The title, **'A Jackeen cries at the loss of the Blaskets'**, is interesting. 'Jackeen' is the non-Dubliner's term for the Dubliner: it is never intended as a compliment—implying as it does that the Dubliner has turned his back on his Irishness to ape English ways—yet Dubliners usually welcome it as a means of differentiating between themselves and others. There is an element of aggressive pride in Behan's usage here, in the idea of a 'jackeen' paying his respects in Irish. Behan's biographer rendered the title 'A Jackeen says goodbye to the Blaskets', and suggested that the poem was Behan's unconscious farewell to Irish poetry. This is possible but doubtful. 'Says goodbye' is not a good translation of 'ag caoineadh' in the context: it is final and resolved whereas the poem itself is full of fear and uncertainty and love.

> In the sun the ocean will lie like a glass,
> No human sign, no boat to pass,

Only, at the world's end, the last
Golden eagle over the lonely Blasket.

Sunset, nightshadow spreading,
The climbing moon through cold cloud stretch-
    ing
Her bare fingers down, descending
On empty homes, crumbling, wretched.

Silent, except for birds flying low
Grateful to return once more;
The soft wind swinging a half-door
Of a fireless cottage, cold, wet, exposed.

This is a version of the nightmare which others have described as a waste land, a deserted village, a dark night of the soul: it is essentially an insight into Behan's own situation. The tears are not only for the islands but for all they meant to him. To take the conclusion as one of renunciation would be to over-emphasise the negative aspects and miss some of the complexity. The poem, dedicated to Seán Ō Briain, is an effort to hold on to something of value at a time when his life seems to be slipping away.

It was not long after this sentence in Mountjoy that he headed for Paris. Two lyrics date from this period. Behan was sometimes bought drink by people wishing to learn about Joyce's Dublin; he showed his gratitude in **'Thanks to Joyce'**, a casual *jeu d'esprit.*

Here in Rue St Andre des Arts,
In an Arab tavern, drunk,
I explain you to an inquisitive Frenchman,
Some ex-GIs and a Russian, drunk.
I praise every single work of yours
And as a result, in France, I drink liqueurs.
You're the *conteur* we value the most
And thanks, by the way, for the Calvados.

If I was you
And you were me,
On the way from Les Halles
With this load of cognac
Full of grub and booze and glee
You'd write a verse or two in praise of me.

The use of Irish in the context of cosmopolitan Paris complements the confidentiality of this grateful nudge. There were many such taverns in Paris and Behan's life developed into a series of sprees, but no amount of acting could disguise his frightened reaction to the house in which Oscar Wilde had died in 1900. He sought to exorcise the ghost by writing a poem. Short lines sketch the grim scene: once the prince of elegance, the scandal of high society, he now lies stretched out in a dingy Paris room, watched by guttering candles and a landlady who feels cheated of her rent. Towards the end, the immoralist had sought the consolation of the Church; Narcissus turned to holy water.

Priestless death is risky
Even for the happy sinner;
More power to you, Oscar—
Either way a winner.

This finale tries to laugh away a poem which was no laughing matter: the image of an Irish writer reduced to a neglected 'foreign boozer' in the squalor of a cheap Paris room was not lost on Behan at the time.

All but one of his poems to date—the exception, if it is an exception, is **'Thanks to Joyce'**—dealt with death. Those on McCaughey and Larkin avoided the physical fact by celebrating a metaphysical resurrection. In **'Repentance'** the poet turned to heaven; in the case of Wilde, Behan escaped from the morbid spectacle by means of a humour which is slightly forced. Only in the Blasket verses is the vision presented and accepted without recourse to any comfort, but then the subject was not the death of a person but that of a community. Two other poems from 1949 are built on a triangle of love, life and death; though related in theme, they differ in tone and treatment.

'Grafton Street' is a night-poem, obscure in style and dark in intention. The obscurity is due to the distance between the poet's vantage-point and position of the people he is contemplating. The opening stanza establishes the hostility between them and their environment:

> Saw last night the living
> On death's island,
> Heard talk in a place
> Devoted to the silent.

In this same manner, rather like that of a hand-held camera, the next two stanzas focus on a girl. Details of her appearance—false shoulders, shampoo, Max Factor cosmetics—and her youthful laugh are set against the fact that she is tubercular. The fourth and final stanza tells how the pleasure of a brief physical love must be partially repressed, how even the doomed laughter must be muted:

> Whisper, as one must,
> Of love in this sour land
> Before they go in
> To dance in the Classic.

This little piece is Behan's most jaundiced vision of his native place and gives some idea of the difficulty he had in returning to live in Ireland in 1950.

The companion poem, **'To Bev'** is a hymn to a girl who has feathered a comfortable nest for herself by smashing her way through the repressive atmosphere of 'this sour land'. In golden contrast to the dark night of Grafton Street, it exudes the sunshine of the countryside around Cahirdaniel, County Kerry, where it was written. Basically a *chanson* on the marriage of a rich old man to a lively young girl, it is also something of a parody of a traditional Irish form, the *aisling.* In the *aisling,* the poet encounters a beautiful female whom he assumes to be a goddess or a mythological heroine; she, however, tells him she is Ireland, longing for the arrival of her true lover (the Stuart Pretender) who will free her from the tyranny of the English king. Behan's apparition is not likely to be mistaken for Diana or Deirdre of the Sorrows, and if in the end she turns out to be Ireland, things have changed a great deal since independence.

> One sunny day I saw a vision,
> Her cloak, hat and dress the newest of new,
> In all respects elegant, expensive, in fashion,
> From the feather in her hat to the buckle on her
>   shoe.
> More pleasing than her dress was the laugh on
>   her lips,
> Her satisfied manner, the glint of her smile:

> 'True love my arse,' said she to me sweetly,
> 'I'd sooner my old man, my wardrobe and style.'

> 'I know nothing of scarcity, waiting or wanting;
> I have all I desire and enjoy it in bliss.
> If my husband is old, there's no end to his boun-
>   ty
> Lest he forfeit his conjugal right to my kiss.'

> 'My blessing on greed and intelligent marriage,
> Bringing hundreds in banknotes and gold on re-
>   quest;
> Utterly free from the sharp taste of shortage,
> Of food and of drink I just order the best.'

> The height of my joy is that no one will live
> (Not the devil's own brother) to more than five
>   score,
> And so, in the meantime, what harm if the kitch-
>   en-
> Window is open and a string hold the door?

How very different from the tightlipped gloom of **'Grafton Street'**.

The Behan of sunny Cahirdaniel lingers in the public mind but the lines **'To Bev'** come between two poems which are anything but lighthearted, **'Grafton Street'** and **'Loneliness'**.

> The taste of blackberries
> After rain
> On top of the mountain
> In the silence of prison
> Cold whistle of the train.
> The lovers' whispered laugh
> To the lonely one.

In this impressionistic experiment, the paucity of disjunctive syntax allows the images to exist both in isolation and in various relationships to each other. One reading will suggest that the lonely person compares the bitter-sweet of the overheard laugh to the two earlier images of joy and isolation. Another will perhaps produce something like this: remembered confinement sweetens the blackberries, the sound of the train pains the prisoner all the more because it is travelling to where the blackberries grow, loneliness is worse for the person who has known love. The limpid melancholy seems to arise from the realisation that life has its Grafton Street as well as its Cahirdaniel.

In 1950 Behan wrote **'Guí an Rannaire'** which was included in *Nuabhéarsaíocht* along with the Blasket verses. **'Guí an Rannaire'** is, in the context of this study, the most interesting of his poems. The precise connotations of the title are important. It is doubtful if there is any current English equivalent of 'rannaire' which is less pejorative than its usual rendering 'versifier'. A 'rannaire' is (in this case) a writer of verse who is not a poet or 'file'. (The early modern English 'rimer' was very close in meaning.) The distinction may seem over-fine, but this is because English lacks some word to differentiate between the poetical practitioner and the poet. History is not so broadminded: precedent would suggest that of the legions of poets writing today, only one or two will continue to be considered poets in a few decades.

> If some grown-up guy, with fluent Irish,

Wrote of people and things in a civilised style,
Of moods and opinions in the words of today,
Impudent, easy, expansive, *au fait*—
I'd happily hear what he had to say.
A poet with punch, with power and plenty,
A burgeoning bard, blazing and brazen,
Pained, impassioned, paganpenned.

But Jesus wept! what's to be seen?
Civil servants come up from Dún Chaoin,
More gobdaws down from Donegal
And from Galway bogs—the worst of all,
The Dublin Gaels with their golden *fáinnes,*
Tea-totalling toddlers, turgid and torpid,
Maudlin maidens, morbid and mortal,
Each one of them careful, catholic, cautious.

If a poet came and inspired some spirit,
I'd go home, my job finished.

It is difficult to envisage a translation doing full justice to sound and sense. The gusto, the concatenations and the apt choice of key-consonants recall Merriman's *Midnight Court,* a legal saga of the battle between the love-hungry women and the repressed men of Ireland. Merriman's work was frowned on by some, but it circulated in manuscripts. Seán Ō Briain had a copy in Mountjoy and it was probably by means of this that Behan acquired something of Merriman's comic rhetoric. Later on he translated *The Midnight Court* into English and included the opening lines in **Borstal Boy**; it is said that he translated all one thousand lines of the work but lost the manuscript in a punch-up. Merriman does not use alliteration as a merely metrical device; he chooses and varies the key-consonants—ebullient plosives, sneering sibilants, vituperative fricatives and so on—to reinforce the narrative without ever becoming excessive. It is not difficult to imagine the appeal of his poem for a prisoner-student: it played physical deprivation against sensual abandon and surveyed love, lust, greed, marriage and the clergy with a verve which even today retains a *risqué* excitement. Behan's effort, another broadside against the prim and proper, resurrects Merriman's verbal power.

'Guí an Rannaire'—the prayer of the 'rannaire'—is aimed at the hyper-respectable element in the national movement, epitomised by the shrewd rustic who makes good in Dublin, where his knowledge of Irish is useful for state employment. The twin emblems of this group are the pioneer-pin, denoting their pledge to abstain from alcohol, and the *fáinne,* a ring worn on the lapel by those willing to converse in Irish. Brought up in a repressive form of Catholicism as puritan idealists, they are attracted to organisations of national renewal, including the IRA. As an intense and religious child, Behan had become involved with such people but he grew up to detest their bourgeois piousness. His own knowledge of the Gaelic tradition told him that such narrowmindedness was a recent innovation: the poets, even those who took the precaution of writing a *repentance,* were generally a wild lot. Behan resented the image of Gaelic Ireland which was held up by the language-enthusiasts of 1950. As a poet, he was in the forefront of the battle for revival, yet among those who shared this hope he found nothing else in common. His poem is really a prayer, an ejaculation in time of sore temptation

to give up, a prayer to Mother Ireland that this chalice might pass from him. Yet he will hope and hold on awhile.

Within this framework, another drama is enacted. Behan is not being falsely modest when he describes himself as a 'rannaire' rather than as a 'file'. He feels that he is not the great poet capable of igniting the ashes of Irish society; if such a poet were to come on the scene, Behan would withdraw, having carried out his rear-guard action. He lists the qualities which this messianic figure would need: a modern mature mind, capable of poetry which was passionate and radically exciting. Behan himself wrote very little poetry after 1950, but not because the 'file' had come. Towards the end of 1950 he began to create **Borstal Boy,** the main theme of which was the development of a modern Irish mind. It was both an account of his time in England and a compressed history of his life to date. In a less obvious way it was a history of Ireland in his own time. Was this the work to which the 'rannaire' had looked?

> . . . of people and things in a civilised style,
> Of moods and opinions in the words of today,
> Impudent, easy, expansive, *au fait* . . .

The novel was not in Irish, but it was in the language of Ireland. Behan had injected his poetry with the modernity of Dublin and Paris but it is unlikely that he could have written a sustained work in Irish which was up to the standards laid down by the 'rannaire'.

> . . . with punch, with power and plenty,
> . . . burgeoning . . . blazing and brazen,
> Pained, impassioned, paganpenned.

This energy appeared not in his poetry but in **Borstal Boy.**

'The Coming of Spring' was published in October 1951. It is a poem of wintering out: the poet prepares for the hardships of winter in confident expectation of a new year's growth. The title and the reference to St Brigid's Day recall Raftery's poem, but Behan's is more introverted and private. The taut lapidary style of the short Irish lyrics suits Behan's intentions better than Raftery's *amhrán.*

Harsh Irish winter
I loathe your face
The north wind comes
Strong shaken pained
No growth or good
No lift or life
Till bright St Brigid's Day
And joy's revival.
Comes the south wind
Pledge of sun for my frame
Exciting new life
The blood awakening.
Winter weather
Old men's time
Welcome and thousands
Spring of youth.

He had come back to Ireland to labour on his novel; the confidence of the working writer is reflected in the formal economy of the poem, in the tight lines and unstrained flow.

One more poem remains. 'L'Existentialisme' is really a

verse doodle, but is not without its own curious interest. Subtitled 'An Echo of St Germaine-de-Prés', the poem presents replies as ironic echoes of questions.

Watchman, walking the wall—
of an empty hall.
What is the chase after?
a grave matter.
A journey to hell?
Of course, but your mind as well?
What was before our time?
Dunno. I wasn't alive,
amn't yet.
Evil our fate?
too lazy
to say.
Virtue, not a gleaning,
nor pain, nor even meaning,
nor truth in what I posit—
nor in the opposite.

As a doodle, it succeeds in vanishing up its own question mark with a yawn; as a comment on the fashionable cult of existentialism, it is mildly amusing. Why write it in Irish? It has no apparent connection with Ireland. If the original impulse was satirical, would it not have been better served by parody which came so easily to him in English? What inspired the piece?

The watchman or sentry is on guard but it is possible that he is wasting his time. His assiduity on the wall is mocked by the sinister, dismissive antiphon:

of an empty building.

This is repeated, less specifically:

What is the course of the hunt?
a matter of the grave.

If all endeavour leads to the grave, is all effort futile? The interplay of endeavour and futility is not resolved and this seems due more to the poet's lassitude than to his existentialist principles. Huge abstractions are introduced and, too tired to ponder them, he allows them to drift away into careless negation. It would be dangerous to read too much into such a lightweight piece, but if this is, as it seems to be, Behan's last attempt at Irish verse, there is probably some relationship between the sentry and the *rannaire* of the rearguard. (There was an Old IRA periodical called *An Fear Faire*, the term Behan uses for sentry or watchman.) The *rannaire* knew that he was holding the fort only until relief came. Was he wasting his time? Was the hope of an Irish revival a hollow one? When dealing with Behan's poetry it is often useful to look at the poem in the light of his attitude to the language. **'L'Existentialisme'**, which opens with a suspicion of futility and fades away into vacuity, may well have arisen from a crisis of faith similar to that which inspired the *rannaire*—loss of confidence in the future of Irish and in his own ability as a poet. If so, it marks also the loss of that military resolve to remain at his post until replaced. (pp. 46-61)

Colbert Kearney, in his The Writings of Brendan Behan, *St. Martin's Press, 1977, 155 p.*

Beatrice Behan, on life in New York with her husband, Brendan Behan:

The Quare Fellow, The Hostage and *Borstal Boy* were known in New York and Brendan attempted to live up to his reputation as a writer who was larger than life.

One evening in the Algonquin, Celia, who was always observant about Brendan, said to me, 'I worry about his success, Beatsy. Don't you see he's oversensitive? He cares too much about people. He's giving too much of himself and he'll have to pay the price.'

I looked at her, not willing to accept the truth of what she was saying.

'Beatsy, he's an innocent. He's too sincere for this city.'

As Brendan and I lay in bed in the mornings, tired after a round of parties, I did not dare ask him if he thought the city was demanding too much of him. He always looked weary. I wanted to say, 'Slow down, love. You can't go on like this.' But Brendan was a man to whom you could not say 'don't'. With his love of life he delighted to roam New York, seeking new friends, talking incessantly to the friends he had made—Mailer, Ginsberg, Thurber, Kerouac— knowing they would reassure him of his gifts as a writer.

Beatrice Behan, in her My Life with Brendan, *1973.*

David Krause   (essay date 1982)

[*In the following excerpt, Krause examines aspects of traditional drama and humor in Behan's plays.*]

Brendan Behan was a radical anarchist in the theater who experimented freely and even recklessly with the episodic structure of drama, and who in the tradition of O'Casey's tragicomic knockabout concentrated on the barbarous rituals of political and comical rebellion in his plays. There is a rich texture of mythic profanation in Behan's uninhibited desecration of Ireland's household gods, for his comic characters abundantly illustrate in their fabulous posture the view held by Freud and Lévi-Strauss that "myths express unconscious wishes which are somehow inconsistent with conscious experience." In Behan's works the world of experience creates obstacles of restraint that must be mocked and undermined by his antic comedians, who are the self-appointed spokesmen for the unconscious wishes of the Irish folk imagination, an imagination that Yeats had described as "wild and ancient." Behan, in his own instinctive way, understood and dramatized the Freudian concept of comic circumvention: the sharp edge of his knockabout laughter represents "a rebellion against authority, a liberation from its pressure" [Sigmund Freud, *Jokes and Their Relation to the Unconscious*]. That wild act of comic liberation involves a structural as well as a thematic rebellion, for in **Borstal Boy** (1958), his unqualified masterpiece of autobiographical writing, as well as in his plays, **The Quare Fellow** (1954), **The Hostage** (1958), and the posthumous **Richard's Cork Leg** (1972), he circumvents and profanes all authority with an ironic technique that might be called the music-hall principle of comic diversion.

Music-hall comedy is a loosely organized catchall of knock-about routines composed of gags and pratfalls, parodies and burlesques, songs and dances, all of which are calculated to divert an audience from the serious business of life; and those routines often function as a profane commentary on the serious business. The ironic connection between the serious main plot and the farcical subplot was a popular device in many Elizabethan plays, as we know, for example, from the antics of Wagner in *Dr. Faustus* and the drunken Porter in *Macbeth*. But in Irish comedy, especially the plays of O'Casey, Beckett, and Behan, that Elizabethan structure is inverted because the farcical subplots, largely composed of episodic music-hall routines, dominate the stage, while the serious main plots, dealing with civil war, metaphysical speculation, and executions, run their secondary yet significant course offstage. This structural inversion defines the uniquely open and contingent form of *The Quare Fellow* and *The Hostage,* since Behan creates his music-hall diversions in order to entertain his audience while the serious business develops fitfully yet organically in the wings, until he gradually moves it to the center of the stage from time to time, finally allowing it to merge with the antic routines with a tragicomic jolt. And even that jolt is inverted and mocked by gallows humor when the prisoners argue and toss for the sacrificial quare fellow's letters, and when the dead hostage is resurrected and sings a jesting song. These comic diversions underscore the tragic horror, for Behan is of course on Christ's side even as he winks at the Passion with a last laugh.

In a reply to some critics who had objected to what they believed to be the gratuitous laughter and disjointed form of *The Hostage,* Behan defended his dramatic methods in a forthright statement that could be applied to all his works:

> I wrote the play very quickly—in about twelve days or so. I wrote it in Irish and it was first put on in Irish in Dublin. I saw the rehearsals of this version and while I admire the producer, Frank Dermody, tremendously, his idea of a play is not my idea of a play. I don't say that his is inferior to mine or that mine is inferior to his—it just so happens that I don't agree with him. He's of the school of Abbey Theatre naturalism of which I am not a pupil. Joan Littlewood, I found, suited my requirements exactly. She has the same views on the theatre that I have, which is that the music hall is the thing to aim at for to amuse people and any time they get bored, divert them with a song or a dance. I've always though T. S. Eliot wasn't far wrong when he said that the main problem of the dramatist today was to keep his audience amused; and that while they were laughing their heads off, you could be up to any bloody thing behind their backs; and it was what you were doing behind their bloody backs that made your play great.

So behind their backs and under their laughter Behan the jester was building up an indictment of the hypocrisy and fanaticism that warped people's minds, and the noble reasons they gave for the ignoble ways they exploited and killed each other. This was hardly a new indictment, since variations of it had long provided the main thesis of naturalistic literature since Zola. Behan, however, was in revolt against naturalism as well as society, and what made his plays "great" or memorable was not so much the unorthodox ingredients as the outrageous way they were mixed and measured out: take a superabundance of comic diversions well spiced with song and dance and a minimum of serious plot, add a ton of anarchic knockabout to an ounce of righteous indignation, a barrel of antic irreverence to a teaspoon of morality, then attach a slow farcical fuse, sit back, and wait, laughing. If most uninhibited audiences entered into the spirit and fun of Behan's revels more enthusiastically than some middle-class critics, part of the reason may be found in T. S. Eliot's observations [in "The Decay of the Music Hall"]:

> With the decay of the music-hall, with the encroachment of the cheap and rapid-breeding cinema, the lower classes will tend to drop into the same state of protoplasm as the bourgeoise. The working man who went to the music-hall and saw Marie Lloyd and joined in the chorus was himself performing part of the act; he was engaged in that collaboration of the audience with the artist which is necessary in all art and most obviously in dramatic art.

On some notorious occasions during performances of *The Hostage* in London and New York, Behan himself suddenly appeared on stage briefly and became part of the singing and dancing in an unprecedented collaboration between the dramatist, the actors, and the audience. The irrepressible Behan may have stepped over the line of artistic objectivity, but his merry indulgence must have been prompted by the music-hall spirit of fun, as well as the excess of spirits he had probably consumed, and this wild behavior should not prevent us from realizing that in his writing he was a serious comic artist with his own unique idea of a play.

When Behan's idea of a play led to his quarrel with Frank Dermody over the music-hall diversions in *The Hostage,* the dispute was somewhat similar to O'Casey's quarrel with Yeats over the experimental form of *The Silver Tassie*. Both dramatists were determined to break away from the structural stereotypes of Abbey Theatre naturalism, the predictable form of the well-made play, which O'Casey had already done in *The Plough and the Stars,* though Yeats and his directors could not see this, and which Behan had already done in *The Quare Fellow,* though Dermody and many critics could not see this. O'Casey was distressed by the dictatorial Yeats because he suspected that his new methods as well as his play had been rejected; but thirty years later Behan could be magnanimous with the powerless Dermody because he knew that his new methods and his play had been performed successfully. On both occasions, however, the limitations of middle-class naturalism had been exposed by two dramatists from the working-class north side of Dublin who had learned much of their craft from the free form of the music-hall theater, unorthodox dramatists who had their own ideas of a loosely structured play with song and dance and a wild mixture of comedy and tragedy. O'Casey later wrote *Purple Dust* (1940), *Cock-a-Doodle Dandy* (1949), and *The Drums of Father Ned* (1960), all of them antic comedies with dark overtones of satiric vision and pastoral symbolism in which he fully exploited the music-hall principle of high spirit and low comedy. Behan unfortunately died in 1964 at the age of forty-one, too soon to fulfill his dramatic genius, which nevertheless rests securely on the extraordinary achievements in *The Quare Fellow* and *The Hostage.*

Those achievements have often been questioned, representatively by two very intelligent Irish and American critics, Kevin Casey and Robert Brustein, who offer some concessions of praise but basically object to Behan's plays because he breaks the "rules" of drama. Perhaps too much intelligence can be a dangerous thing, especially if it interferes with the willing suspension of disbelief in the freewheeling form of music-hall-inspired drama. Like many critics, Casey prefers *The Quare Fellow* to *The Hostage,* though he rigorously measures both of these unconventional plays by what he calls the "conventional discipline" and conventional "machinery" of dramatic construction:

> In "The Quare Fellow" a maximum amount of bizarre comedy is extracted from a hauntingly tragic situation. In "The Hostage" a maximum of farce is loaded into a situation which, under the strain, collapses into something that is neither comic nor tragic. Although "The Quare Fellow" is entirely devoid of the machinery which is generally thought to be essential for dramatic construction, it does move, with a strong degree of inevitability, towards its climax. . . . They represent, of course, a perfectly valid approach to the theatre but if variety is to be the object of the exercise, it should be balanced by some degree of conventional discipline. Control, in "The Hostage" is hidden in the wings: irrelevancy is the key-note of the proceedings and the piece, although theatrically effective within its own limitations, is by no means as good as "The Quare Fellow." ["The Raw and the Honest: A Critical Look," in *The World of Brendan Behan,* edited by Sean McCann, 1965]

These comments are tainted by the sort of scholastic carping that demands that all plays must conform to a preconceived pattern of "control," a formal structure and discipline the precise nature of which Casey does not identify and few critics, from neo-Aristotelians to neo-Marxists and neutrals, can agree upon. It is safe to say only that historically all innovations in art have been criticized by precisely those formalistic old standards from which the new art seeks to liberate itself.

In a review of *The Hostage* Robert Brustein continued Casey's exercise in academic strictures by deducing that Behan's drama lacked an "organizing principle" as well as "dramatic logic," though of course he failed to identify which principles of dramatic organization and logic he had in mind. First Brustein tried to be fair by holding Behan up as "a welcome presence in our sanctimonious times," but then he put him down as an impure and totally disorganized example of what he called "the destructive Libido":

> Behan is waging total war on all social institutions excepting brothels and distilleries. But though destructive Libido can be the source of a lot of fun, it is hardly an organizing principle, so the author's assault on order leaves his play almost totally lacking in dramatic logic. Its substance is taped together with burlesque routines, Irish reels, barroom ballads, and outrageous gags (some old, some new, some borrowed, but all "blue"), while its scarecrow plot is just a convenient appendage on which to hang a string of blasphemous howlers. [*Seasons of Discontent,* 1965]

Some unenthusiastic Irish critics [according to Dominic Behan in his *My Brother Brendan,* 1965] had made the same complaint about *The Quare Fellow* when it was first produced by Alan Simpson and Carolyn Swift in Dublin at the Pike Theatre in 1954 and after its production by Joan Littlewood in London at the Theatre Royal in 1956, charging that it was only "a stringing together of music-hall sketches." The prim people who are unamused by "mere" farce usually complain about "mere" music hall. It is not a foregone conclusion that a dramatist who writes a farcical play in an episodic music-hall form is "merely" having fun—though he certainly is entertaining his audience with his wild antics as well as arranging some surprises and jolts behind their backs—or that in rejecting the structural proprieties of the well-made play he must end up with a badly made play. Farce is not formless, it only seems that way, for there is reason in mischief as well as madness, as Eric Bentley points out in his wise discussion on farce [*The Life of the Drama,* 1964]. Bentley insists that "every form of drama has its rendezvous with madness," and that "in farce chance ceases to seem chance, and mischief has method in its madness":

> Our colloquial use and abuse of words is always full of meaning, and what we mean when we say of some non-theatrical phenomenon, "It's a farce," or "It's absolutely farcical," throws light back on the theatrical phenomenon. We mean: farce is absurd; but not only that, farce is a veritable structure of absurdities. Here the operative word is *structure,* for normally we think of absurdities as amorphous. It is only in such a syndrome as paranoia that we find reason in the madness: the absurdities which we would be inclined to call stupid are connected in a way we cannot but consider the reverse of stupid. There is an ingenious and complex set of interrelationships.

It may therefore be possible to say that farce is controlled by an ingenious and complex structure of interrelated absurdities; and that the chain-reaction process that unites those absurdities functions like the cause-and-effect syndrome of paranoia, or comic reason in madness. Delusions of grandeur are of course endemic to farcical characters, as we know from the paranoiac fantasies of such diverse figures as the Chaplin and Buster Keaton tramps, Laurel and Hardy, W. C. Fields and Harpo Marx; Falstaff, Leopold Bloom, Christy Mahon, Roger Carmody, "Captain" Boyle, Dick Cartney, Gogo and Didi, Dunlavin and Monsewer: their delusions grow out of their insecurities, which create the need for mad dreams that tentatively protect them from the terrible constraints of the supposedly sane world. For all these reasons, and for what Freud called the psychic process by which tendentious or desecrating jokes allow people to circumvent the obstacles of society and achieve a gratification of forbidden wishes—for all these subversive games of laughter, the low comedy of farce is perhaps the most irresistible art form; it provides an open structure of compensatory absurdities, a mad fantasy of vicarious freedom for discredited or dispossessed clowns, for the tramps, prevaricators, cowards, parasites, cuckolds, and prisoners of antic Irish comedy.

Consider, for example, some of the compensatory absurdities of Dunlavin and Neighbour in **The Quare Fellow,** and the connections between their comic rituals of survival and the mad prison world that in the name of retributive sanity is about to execute the quare fellow. Dunlavin and Neighbour represent only one of many episodic subplots that rotate around and dominate the main plot of the execution, inverting and mocking that terrible deed because this is the only way people can go on living and waiting in the shadow of the gallows. It is the classic example of how gallows humor functions as the chief diversion in a play about gallows tragedy. Only the laughter makes the tragedy bearable. While they laugh and wait, then, Dunlavin and Neighbour and their cell mates conduct their absurd revels. At the beginning of the play Dunlavin is preparing a special sideshow, tidying up his cell, polishing his enamel chamber pot, and hanging up his holy pictures in the expectation of obtaining favors from "Holy" Healey, the official from the Department of Justice who always visits the prison before a hanging:

> I have to do me funny half-hour for Holy Healey. . . . I have to hang up my holy pictures and think up a few funny remarks for him. God, what Jimmie O'Dea is getting thousands for I've to do for a pair of old socks and a ticket for the Prisoners' Aid.

Dunlavin's continuous entertainment for everyone is indeed parallel to the jokes and antics of Jimmie O'Dea, Dublin's most popular music-hall comedian. When a sexual deviate is placed in an adjoining cell, Dunlavin's sense of propriety is outraged and he protests that he would rather be next to "a decent murderer" than "a bloody sex mechanic"; and when they have to fall in to see the doctor, Dunlavin calls to the deviate: "Hey, come out and get gelded." The sex jokes become blasphemous when everyone rushes to the windows to watch the female prisoners hanging up their laundry in the exercise yard, a spectacle that the men irreverently call "the May procession," an allusion to the annual devotion to the Virgin Mary. This prompts Dunlavin and Neighbour, dirty old men who are now beyond the sexual mechanics of any persuasion, to create their own procession of venerable prostitutes, a devotional roll call of fond memories of the women they have known: Meena La Bloom, May Oblong, Lottie L'Estrange, Cork Annie, Lady Limerick, Julia Rice, and the Goofy One. Some of the younger men boast about what they could do to the women prisoners, and, as they leave dancing the samba with their cleaning brushes, they mockingly condemn the old men to prayer and Bible reading. But this "disrespectful" attitude encourages Neighbour and Dunlavin to recall the many times they were comforted by the Bible:

> *Neighbour.* Many's the time the Bible was a consolation to a fellow all alone in the old cell. The lovely thin paper with a bit of mattress coir in it, if you could get a match or a bit of tinder or any class of light, was as good a smoke as ever I tasted. Am I right, Dunlavin?
>
> *Dunlavin.* Damn the lie, Neighbour. The first twelve months I done, I smoked my way halfway through the book of Genesis and three inches of my mattress. When the Free State came in we were afraid of our life they were going to change the mattresses for feather beds. And you couldn't smoke feathers, not, be God, if they were rolled in the Song of Solomon itself. But sure, thanks to God, the Free State didn't change anything more than the badge on the warders' caps.

This allusion to the Irish Free State government broadens the scope of the jest, for many people felt they would be living in clover and sleeping in fine feather beds once the Irish drove the British out and governed themselves. But Dunlavin's irony implies that the rosy promises of a changed life in Ireland amounted to nothing more than the change of the badge on the warders' caps; and the Irish government went about hanging its condemned prisoners as cheerfully as the British government had done when it was in power with a different badge on the caps. Dunlavin therefore has little faith in the Irish government and its civil service bureaucracy, of which "Holy" Healey exemplifies the educated and secret drinker who in his official piety is too close to God for God's good. As a result Dunlavin wants to protect God as well as himself from such hypocritical time servers who do the devil's work while they look condescendingly upon God as if He were a naive civil service department head fresh from the bog who needs the patronizing support of His allied departments. Dunlavin explains it to Neighbour:

> The likes of Healey would take a sup all right, but being a high-up civil servant, he wouldn't drink under his own name. You'd see the likes of Healey nourishing themselves with balls of malt, at eleven in the morning, in little back snugs round Merrion Row. The barman would lose his job if he so much as breathed their name. It'd be "Mr. H. wants a drop of water but not too much."
>
> "Yes, Mr. O." "No, sir, Mr. Mac wasn't in this morning." "Yes, Mr. D. Fine morning; it will be a lovely day if it doesn't snow." Educated drinking, you know. Even a bit of chat about God at an odd time, so as you'd think God was in another department, but not long off the Bog, and they was doing Him a good turn to be talking well about Him.

Immediately after this speech Dunlavin gives us a farcical example of the *uneducated* drinking habits reserved for the prisoners when he steals some swallows from the bottle of methylated spirits that Warder Regan is rubbing on Dunlavin's supposedly rheumatic leg. It is a game that Dunlavin and Neighbour play regularly, but this time the sly Dunlavin is too full of himself to share a drink with the miserable Neighbour as the two men go through their hilarious Boyle-and-Joxer routine. They are interrupted when "Holy" Healey finally appears to offer his officious bromides to the prisoners, and to check the details of the hanging with Regan. Here at the end of the first act the horror of the main plot breaks through the compensatory comedy as Regan, the only voice of conscience among the prison officials, assures Healey that the quare fellow's neck will be "properly broken in the morning," then shakes Healey with another twist of gallows humor:

> *Healey.* Well, we have one consolation, Regan, the condemned man gets the priest and the sacraments, more than his victim got maybe. I venture to suggest that some of them die holier deaths than if they had finished their natural span.

> *Warder Regan.* We can't advertise "Commit a murder and die a happy death," sir. We'd have them all at it. They take religion very seriously in this country.

But Healey with his characteristic misunderstanding of the religious attitudes of the prisoners gives his pious sermon and one of his holy pictures to Silvertop, the condemned man just reprieved from the gallows, who responds by trying unsuccessfully to hang himself at the end of the act. It is a grim rehearsal of what awaits the quare fellow. As the curtain falls, "the old triangle goes jingle jangle," and Regan tries to comfort the shaken Healey: "It's a soft job, sir, between hangings."

It's a soft play, between hangings, for this is Behan's characteristic method of entertaining and shaking his audience, using gallows humor to withhold the terror until the moment of truth draws near; and even then the violence of institutional killing is reflected through the subterfuge of comic irony. Since Behan was clearly determined not to allow his play to become a naturalistic debate on the transparent evil of capital punishment, it is pointless for some critics to object on the old naturalistic assumption that [according to Kevin Casey] "the first act was really nothing but an overblown exposition scene." The open and inverted structure of Act I does not develop through the expository machinery of the traditional play of ideas, but through a series of entertainments and delayed shocks, which continue in the remaining two acts.

In the second act, as a contrast to such hardened old comedians as Dunlavin and Neighbour, we find another subplot in the two young innocents with Kerry accents from the same island off the west coast of Ireland, the Irish-speaking Prisoner C, and a new warder named Crimmin, who have no humor or experience to protect them from the shadow of the gallows. While these new men worry about the execution for all of us, Neighbour bets Dunlavin his Sunday bacon that there will be no last-minute reprieve for the quare fellow; and Prisoner E, a bookie, "acts as if he were a tick-tack man at the races" by taking side bets on the bacon. As nerves become raw the comic contentiousness increases. All the prisoners argue about the quare fellow's fate, and in spelling out the gruesome details of his deed of fratricide they subvert Prisoner C's sen-

timental attitude toward the condemned man. Prisoner A, "a hard case," pointedly reminds everyone of the crime: "Begod, he's not being topped for nothing—to cut his own brother up and butcher him like a pig." But for the men this knowledge does not alter the fact that the government will now compound the crime by butchering the quare fellow. And Regan, who is sickened by both crimes, quietly tries to calm the trembling Crimmin by absolving the imported British Hangman, an amusing and impersonal publican who moonlights as an executioner: "Himself has no more to do with it than you or I or the people that pay us, and that's every man or woman that pays taxes or votes in elections. If they don't like it, they needn't have it."

This biting comment points the finger of guilt directly at the people in the audience, who gradually realize that the understated tragic theme has been breaking through the overstated comic subplots. In the third act even the warders become contentious when Regan gets into an argument with the Chief Warder and repeats the charge: "I think the whole show should be put on in Croke Park; after all, it's at the public expense and they let it go on. They should have something more for their money than a bit of paper stuck up on the gate." At this point a variety of "shows" are in progress as the world inside and outside the prison approaches knockabout hysteria: the pipe-tapping Morse code system has been increasing in volume and frenzy since the beginning of the last act; a riotous crowd outside the walls can be heard protesting and singing; the tipsy Hangman and his hymn-singing assistant are preparing the gallows in a mood of unconscious humor that qualifies their cockney reverence; Mickser gives a horse-race announcer's account of the final preparations as the clock strikes the fatal hour; the prisoners let loose a ferocious howling; Crimmin faints and is carried away as the deed is done; Neighbour reminds Dunlavin that he has lost his Sunday bacon, and Dunlavin cheerfully replies that he has lost nothing since his stomach is bad and the doctor has put him on a milk diet; and at the final curtain, to the accompaniment of the "old triangle" ballad, three prisoners toss for the right to sell the quare fellow's letters to the Sunday papers, in an ironic allusion to the soldiers who gambled for the seamless robe of Christ.

It is finished. The quare fellow dies for all of us, but if he is not a sacred figure, his life represents something sacred that is inhumanly violated. Behan has wisely understated this theme because his play is more than an indictment of capital punishment; it is a profane celebration of the sanctity of life. He has allowed a shocked audience to enjoy the spectacle they should despise because he felt that we could accommodate ourselves to the reality of such a terrible deed only through the antic rituals of low comedy. Cathartically as well as dramatically, such terror demands such comedy.

This extravagant exploitation of the music-hall principle of comic diversion is treated with even greater freedom, if less tension, in *The Hostage,* another open-structured gallows entertainment about waiting for an execution. Again the threat of violent death demands the compensation of wild laughter. Like all writers of profane Irish comedy, Behan understood the universal efficacy of Freud's comic circumvention strategy: "By making our enemy small, inferior, despicable or comic, we achieve in a roundabout way the enjoyment of overcoming him" [Freud, *Jokes and Their Relation to the Unconscious*]. This is of course one of the most enduring gratifications of comic desecration: he who laughs feels superior, he who is laughed at feels inferior. This time the sacred "enemies" are excessive Irish nationalism and religiosity, both of which created the repressive climate of fanatical patriotism and puritanism so prevalent in modern Ireland. In the broader sense, however, all the political and religious pieties associated with both side of the Anglo-Irish "troubles" are desecrated in the play, since the pompous John Bull is just as ridiculous as the sentimental Cathleen Ni Houlihan. Masters and martyrs are equally vulnerable to comic exposure, the pathetic Captains and Kings of England, the Holy Joes and Horse Protestants of Ireland— the RCs and the C of E, the I.R.A. and the R.A.F., and for good measure the F.B.I. and the perpetrators of the H-Bomb.

Some people in Ireland, such as Ulick O'Connor, feel that this play is a betrayal of Behan's republican as well as his artistic principles, since he was in his youth a member of the I.R.A. and served two prison terms for political offenses. But as a man and artist Behan was one of his own "laughing boys" whose sense of humor and humanity made it difficult for him to accept the fighting and dying for Ireland without a skeptical and profane point of view: "This is nineteen-fifty-eight, and the days of the heroes is over this thirty-five years past. Long over, finished and done with. The I.R.A. and the War of Independence are as dead—as dead as the Charleston." Behan identifies himself with the gallant old I.R.A. of Michael Collins, the original "Laughing Boy" of the War of Independence, in contrast to the new breed of fanatical puritan-patriots, such as the I.R.A. Officer in the play, the "Holy Joe" who is a total teetotaler: no drinking, no smoking, no sex, and above all no laughter. When the irreverent Pat, the sly caretaker of the brothel who claims he lost a leg fighting with the old I.R.A., confronts the officer of the new breed, the contentious issue becomes clear:

> *Officer.* This is no laughing matter, you idiot.
>
> *Pat* (to audience). You know, there are two sorts of gunmen, the earnest, religious-minded ones, like you, and the laughing boys.
>
> *Officer.* Like you.
>
> *Pat.* Well, you know in the time of the troubles it was always the laughing boys who were the most handy with a skit.
>
> *Officer.* Why?
>
> *Pat.* Because it's not a natural thing for a man with a sense of humour to be playing with firearms and fighting. There must be something the matter with him.

There must be something the matter with everyone in the play except Pat and Meg, Teresa and Leslie, the old and young couples of experience and innocence, who are the only characters that do not pretend to be anything other than what they are, a brothel caretaker and his madame

and two naive orphans. All the other characters are involved in political, religious, and sexual masquerades. The central metaphor of the play as a brothel world of illusions in a time of rebellion can be compared to Genet's "House of Illusions" in *The Balcony* (1956). The simulated masquerades that Irma, the madame in Genet's play, blasphemously calls "the liturgies of the brothel" have their parallels in Behan's play, although Behan has more comedy and compassion than Genet, and less Artaudian cruelty. Behan's blithely cracked Monsewer, the mad owner of the brothel who thinks all the girls and their clients are working for the nationalist cause, is an Irish-speaking Anglo-Irish Oxonian masquerading in kilts and playing the war pipes as a buffoon of a fanatical I.R.A. commander. The religious hypocrites and homosexuals, led by Mulleady, turn out to be secret police in disguise; and when the police raid the house at the end, the diehard patriots, led by the I.R.A. Officer and his men, disguise themselves as whores and flee ingloriously from the battle. Heroism and religion in Ireland are thoroughly discredited. In a world of such corrupted idealism, Meg and Pat speak the ironic language of reality:

> *Meg.* Pound notes is the best religion in the world.
>
> *Pat.* And the best politics.

The Irish Teresa and the cockney Leslie speak the ironic language of innocence on Anglo-Irish politics when they talk about Monsewer's decision to leave England and fight for Ireland:

> *Teresa.* Anyway, he left your lot and come over and fought for Ireland anyway.
>
> *Soldier.* What did he want to do that for? Was somebody doing something to Ireland?
>
> *Teresa.* Wasn't England, for hundreds of years?
>
> *Soldier.* That was donkeys years ago. Anyway, everybody was doing something to someone in those days.

and on Anglo-Irish religion when they talk about their childhood experiences in their orphanages:

> *Teresa.* We were not allowed to take off our clothes at all. You see, Leslie, even when we had our baths on Saturday nights they put shifts on the girls, even the little ones four or five years old.
>
> *Soldier.* Did they?
>
> *Teresa.* What did you have?
>
> *Soldier.* Oh no, we never had anything like that. I mean, in our place we had all showers and we were sloshing water over each other and blokes shouting and screeching and making a row—it was smashing. Best night of the week, it was.
>
> *Teresa.* Our best time was the procession we had for the Blessed Virgin on May Day—
>
> *Soldier.* Procession for who?
>
> *Teresa.* Shame on you, the Blessed Virgin. Anyone would think you were a Protestant.

Soldier. I am, girl.

Teresa. Oh, excuse me.

Soldier. That's all right. Never think about it myself.

This is an ingenuous account of the differences between Cathleen Ni Houlihan and John Bull, and Behan often hides his art in such innocent ironies. Meanwhile, as the suspense of imminent death mounts, he breaks the tension with irreverent songs and wild dances and asides to the audience, in a kind of Brechtian "alienation" process. Under these diversionary antics the suspense continues to build up gradually, almost leisurely but irrevocably to a jolt at the end of each act. And almost in spite of the alienating antics, or in effective contrast with them, the sympathy for Teresa and Leslie increases, just as it does for Grusha and Simon, the innocent young lovers in *The Caucasian Chalk Circle,* in spite of Brecht's alienating techniques. For both playwrights, laughter and song and love are enduring impulses in a brutalized world at war.

At the conclusion of their "mixed infants" scene Teresa and Leslie, who have only their love for comfort in this loveless world, get into bed together, after Teresa symbolically places her religious medal around his neck, to honor and protect him, as if he were King of the May, and after they ritualistically sing the Dublin children's street-rhyme ballad on marriage, "I Will Give You a Golden Ball," to sanctify their love. This was a very difficult episode for many Irishmen to accept, as Ulick O'Connor indicates in his objections to the play, on religious as well as political grounds. He is distressed by what he calls this cheap exploitation of "lust" and goes back to the earlier Irish version of the play for untainted innocence:

> Leslie the soldier and Teresa the maid know nothing of the world. They are both orphans. She has just left a convent where she had been reared by nuns. He has been brought up in an institution in Macclesfield. It is their innocence which produces the catharsis. In *An Giall* they are two flower children baffled by violence, understanding love but not lust. . . . The love treatment has been changed in the West End version so that the soldier has become a hardened sexual athlete, while Teresa is an experienced colleen who will hit the sack at the wink of an eyelid. They are no longer remote from what is going on about them. [*Brendan Behan,* 1970]

This rather moralistic objection overlooks Behan's basic point, that the Teresas and Leslies of the world cannot remain remote from the terrible things that are going on around them. Behind our backs this knockabout entertainment gradually concentrates on the loss of innocence, the loss of love, the loss of life. Teresa not only loves Leslie, she knows that he is a "quare fellow" doomed to die as an innocent hostage for the Belfast martyr, and she offers up her innocence for genuine love, for something that in her childlike mind is finally higher than narrow patriotism and repressive religion. How can she and Leslie remain pure "flower children" in that beleaguered brothel world of hypocrisies and imminent death? It is no "wink

of an eyelid" that brings Teresa to bed with Leslie; and since he has discovered he loves her, too, and only her, he can hardly be called "a hardened sexual athlete" when he accepts her sanctified medal and her love. If it is anything it is a profoundly moving as well as an amusing example of gallows love, deathbed love, not "lust." The profanation is blessed. And when the catharsis comes at the end, it is tragicomic, not sentimental, because Behan is wise enough to write a sharp entertainment, not a sermon on Irish purity. After Leslie is accidentally shot during the confusion of the police raid, after Teresa keens her poignant lament over his body, the dead Leslie suddenly comes back to life in a comic resurrection as he jumps up and sings a parody of the familiar passage in the First Epistle of St. Paul to the Corinthians, 15:55: "O death, where is thy sting? O grave, where is thy victory?" Just as John Gay rescues Macheath from the gallows with a laugh at the end of *The Beggar's Opera* (1728), Behan rescues the doomed Leslie with a comic flourish:

> The bells of hell
> Go ting-a-ling-a-ling
> For you but not for me.
> Oh death where is thy
> Sting-a-ling-a-ling
> Or grave thy victory?

So the art of gallows humor is an improvement on life, and the comic catharsis that accompanies this delightful shock is a Freudian victory of the psyche due to Leslie's miraculous circumvention of death. Suddenly the sorrow and pity that flooded the nervous system have been released

A drawing of Behan by Liam Martin, January, 1964.

and replaced by laughter and joy. [In his *Beyond Laughter,* 1957] Martin Grotjahn has appropriately described the psychological and dramatic pleasure that accompany such a curtain scene: "In humor, especially in Freud's favorite 'gallows' humor, energy is saved from the repressing emotions: I do not need to pity the condemned criminal because he is strong, he can take it, he does not need my pity. He is stronger than his fate and possibly stronger than reality."

In the light of this psychic victory it may be possible to say that the character who acts out of a profound or even capricious sense of comic profanation is temporarily stronger than his fate, whether he is a condemned criminal or hostage, or simply someone condemned to the repression of a living death: his desecrating laughter makes him stronger than the reality that might have subjugated or destroyed him. Freud himself once called this comic victory the "grandeur of humour" which results in a magnanimous conquest of despair. In a discussion of gallows humor he offers as an illustration the rogue who, while being led to his execution on a Monday morning, remarks ironically: "Well, this week's beginning nicely." Then Freud explains what he means by the "grandeur" of such humor:

> The case was the same when the rogue on his way to execution asked for a scarf for his bare throat so as not to catch cold—an otherwise laudable precaution but one which, in view of what lay in store so shortly for the neck, was remarkably superfluous and unimportant. It must be confessed that there is something like magnanimity in this *blague,* in the man's tenacious hold upon his customary self and his disregard of what might overthrow that self and drive it to despair. This kind of grandeur of humour appears unmistakably in cases in which our admiration is not inhibited by the circumstances of the humourous person. [*Jokes and Their Relation to the Unconscious*]

Dunlavin and Neighbour express this redemptive "grandeur of humour" for the doomed "quare fellow," for all the imprisoned or condemned men and women everywhere. Pat and Meg, Teresa and Leslie express it for themselves and for all the victims of "the terrible beauty" and the terrible reality of patriotic crusades. The bawdy and mock-heroic characters in Behan's fragmentary *Richard's Cork Leg* express it in all their graveyard profanations, which abound in such throwaway lines as the "Immaculate Contraception"; "Lourdes—Haemorrhage of Bad Taste"; "An honest God's the noblest work of man." Behan himself as the young delinquent narrator of *Borstal Boy* expresses it as effectively as any of his dramatic characters, that magnanimous gesture of comic grandeur which assures us that his literary *persona* is always stronger than his imprisoned fate. Only the real-life Behan, who impulsively burned himself out at the age of forty-one, was unable to achieve the comic grandeur and resurrection of Leslie and the Borstal boy.

In the end Behan's artistic role as a dramatist was more successful and more enduring that his public role as a playboy. The legend of his carousing life, which he invented and performed with such merry and self-destructive abandon, should not blind us to the fact that he was a deliberate and dedicated artist whose extravagant instincts for drama were incredibly moving and hilarious. As a man Behan was the ultimate "quare fellow," a great-hearted figure of a clown who was determined to laugh his way through a life that he sensed had to be lived magnanimously in the shadow of his premature death. (pp. 153-70)

> *David Krause, "The Comic Desecration of Ireland's Household Gods," in his* The Profane Book of Irish Comedy, *Cornell, 1982, pp. 105-170.*

Maureen Waters   (essay date 1984)

[*In the following excerpt from her study of Irish literature,* The Comic Irishman, *Waters examines the biographical nature of Behan's writings as evidenced in* The Quare Fellow, The Hostage, *and* Borstal Boy.]

"God help the poor Irish, if it was raining soup, we'd be out with forks." Like much of Brendan Behan's humor, this remark has personal relevance. Approximately seven years of his life were spent in prison for bungled attempts to carry out the revolutionary aims of the IRA. Those years had a profound effect on his emotional and intellectual development and provided him with material for his best work, *The Quare Fellow, The Hostage,* and *Borstal Boy.* Neither *The Quare Fellow* nor *The Hostage* has a well defined central comic character; however, I would like to briefly discuss these plays to illustrate Behan's major concerns as a writer as well as the nature of his comic talent.

The Quare Fellow takes place inside a Dublin prison, focusing on events leading up to the execution of a nameless criminal, the "quare fellow," who never actually appears on stage. The play strongly sympathizes with the prisoners, with their isolation and physical and emotional deprivation. Their suffering comes to represent the human condition while in the final scene the condemned man emerges as a kind of Christ figure, despite the fact that he brutally murdered his own brother.

Behan's unorthodox theme is developed through realistic detail. One sees the grim round of prison life from the inside as the convicts move back and forth between their cells and the prison yard, where a grave is being dug for the quare fellow. As they joke and quarrel among themselves, they seem much like ordinary men in their beliefs, prejudices, and fears. One significant difference is that the great majority are from working class backgrounds; the prison reflects a class system that protects and supports those with wealth and status, while the man at the bottom of the heap suffers, not only economic and social discrimination, but the full penalty of the law. Like O'Casey, Behan writes out of strong socialist and humanist sympathies, and he falters in the creation of middle-class characters who tend to be stereotypes like the convicted rapist, a religious hypocrite who quotes Carlyle. Beyond that, he has a distinctly Irish sense of death in the midst of life, a presence at once alluring and terrifying and therefore treated with barbed humor.

As the cold, monotonous, brutal quality of prison life is revealed, the crimes of the inmates are gradually outweighed by the calculated cruelty of the state which subjects them to a system which is wholly degrading and which, despite the profession of Christian principle, continues to execute men by hanging. The guards are not sadistic, but they also have been degraded by the prison system, and they routinely inform on one another and mete out punishment in hope of advancement. There are two remarkable exceptions. One is Crimmins, a romantic embodiment of Irish Ireland who has a natural purity and goodness (also characteristic of the Irish speaking prisoner C). The other is Regan, a blunt, compassionate, deeply religious man who, with Crimmins, offers emotional support to the quare fellow during his last few hours of life.

Although he has complete contempt for the social order which the prison system supports, as a moralist, Regan operates within that system to ameliorate its brutality. Outspoken in his opposition to capital punishment, he proposes that the quare fellow is a scapegoat figure, being executed by a "crowd of bigger bloody ruffians than himself. . . ." He believes that those in power, particularly the judges, are more guilty of vice than the prisoners, whom he regards as condemned to do penance for the rest of mankind. Thus Regan fuses Marxist and Catholic ideology, the ideology, in effect, of the left wing IRA, which had a strong influence on Brendan Behan.

The humor which permeates *The Quare Fellow* has the quality of an old fashioned Irish wake in its blend of mirth and melancholy. While the ritual knocking and screaming of the prisoners immediately preceding the execution suggest the keen, there is also a good deal of the burlesque, ranging from the con games played by the old alcoholics, Dunlavin and Neighbor, to the posturing of the guards. Even the hangman is a figure of fun—a British bartender who sings a sentimental ballad, "The Rose of Tralee," unintentionally punning on the "pure crystal fountain" ("poor Christian fountain"). Dialect is used as a source of humor and vitality; it is characteristically needling, aggressive, epigramatic, although Dunlavin, for one, can lapse into a maudlin stage Irish brogue when he's trying to wheedle a favor: "old and bet, sir, that's us. And the old pains is very bad with us these times, sir". . . . In the second act prisoners gamble on the possibility of the last minute reprieve, a grim game to disguise their fear of death as well as to break up the monotony. Here the focal point is the grave which the prisoners are forced to dig and around which they cavort and threaten one another. One old man scoffs: "We'll be eating the cabbages off that one in a month or two," and is himself tossed into the grave.

Death by hanging is grimly described by Warder Regan, who emphasizes the fact that it can be slow and torturous. His attitude cuts ironically through the orthodox Catholic position:

> HEALEY. Ah yes, you're helping the Canon at the execution tomorrow morning, I understand.
>
> WARDER REGAN. Well, I shall be with the condemned man sir, seeing that he doesn't do away with himself during the night and that he goes down the hole with his neck properly broken in the morning without making too much fuss about it.

Regan later suggests that the whole ritual should take place in Croke Park, a popular center for Gaelic sports, so that the taxpayers can get their money's worth. His outrage has a peculiar ironic and historic resonance because so many Irish political prisoners suffered death by hanging under an English penal code.

The theme of the condemned man is fundamental to the work of modern writers such as Kafka, Pinter, Ionesco, and Sartre, for whom man is the victim of powerful and deadly forces which he can neither understand nor resist. The institutions which formerly gave him a sense of identity and value—family, nationality, religion—have broken down in the face of continual war and genocide. Individual acts of heroism have come to seem futile against a technology capable of obliterating the entire human race. Until recently Irish writers, with the important exceptions of Samuel Beckett and Flann O'Brien, have not expressed any comparable sense of pessimism. In *Juno and the Paycock* and *The Plough and the Stars,* only the weak despair; Sean O'Casey, like Brendan Behan, believed that there were definable and hence remediable causes of human misery: The penal system can be reformed, the poor can be offered decent wages, the Irish and the English can learn to live with one another. This pronounced difference in attitude probably stems from the fact that, despite a history of oppression, the Irish people have retained Christian values and can still identify England as a cause of some of their internal problems. For all his irreverence and nonconformity Behan was a moralist, who believed in social and political reform and used an exuberant comic genius to gain sympathy for his point of view.

The Hostage also deals with the theme of the condemned man; it is allegedly based on an episode in which a British soldier captured by the IRA during the Suez crisis in 1955 was accidentally suffocated. The play was written originally in Irish for Gael Linn, an organization founded to promote Irish language and culture. In discussing his decision to use Irish, Behan indicated that he believed he could express certain moods in that language which he could not express in English, explaining that "Irish is more direct than English, more bitter." That bitterness is, however, charged with comic energy as melancholy and mirth again "flash together." The rapidly paced events that lead to the death of the hostage are interlaced with witty dialogue and the wildly burlesque antics of the characters. This might be termed gallows humor because of the centrifugal force of death, but it is not the *humour noir* of Beckett's *Watt,* the laugh that laughs at "that which is unhappy." It is too spirited a response, too alive to the pleasures of resistance.

After *An Giall,* as the original version of the play was called, received favorable notice, Joan Littlewood, the director of an avante garde theatre in London, offered to produce it if Behan would undertake the translation. As this proceeded rather slowly, Littlewood and her cast, who had staged *The Quare Fellow* in 1956, filled in some of the gaps themselves. Behan evidently gave them considerable freedom, and so topical allusions as well as camp humor were added, which were updated in later productions. The result was a free wheeling extravaganza and a smash hit.

Like *The Quare Fellow, The Hostage* is iconoclastic in temper, frequently and unabashedly outrageous in its ridicule of national pieties, a point which was immediately picked up by London critics.

In this play Behan provides us with the "buck lepper" version of the stage Irishman, a mad patriot who parades around in kilts, playing the bagpipes, believing he is in the thick of a revolution. "Monsewer" had been content with life as an English gentleman until, discovering his Irish heritage, he began to cultivate Irishness with a passion, learning the language at Oxford and ultimately fighting for the IRA during the Civil War. The peace treaty unhinged what remained of his wits; he clings to the romantic past ready to make the supreme sacrifice for the Republican cause. For the mad Monsewer, it would be "great happiness" to die for Ireland. Through Monsewer, Behan satirizes the Anglo-Irish who allied themselves with the Republican cause and became more Irish than the Irish in behalf of the cultural revival. Monsewer is so devoted to the concept of *fine Gael* that he has to be accompanied by a translator to get about in Dublin.

Sean O'Casey infuriated Dublin by bringing the Plough and the Stars, the flag of the Irish Citizen Army, into a pub where a prostitute is soliciting customers. Brendan Behan went a step further: the rooming house which Monsewer owns and which is run by a loyal subordinate from the old days, has been turned into a brothel, symbolizing the degradation of the old Republican ideal.

Held captive in the brothel is Leslie Williams, a young Englishman, who becomes a pawn in the continuing struggle of Irish nationalists to expel the English from Northern Ireland. He is taken hostage for another young man in Belfast, condemned to death for shooting a policeman. (It is worth noting that Behan himself served four years of a fourteen year sentence for firing at the Dublin police during an IRA memorial service.)

Most of the other characters in *The Hostage* are social outcasts of one kind or another, a scruffy, belligerent lot, the most outspoken of whom is Pat, an old IRA man. Witty and cynical, he ridicules the younger militants as mechanical fools, completely devoid of humor or common sense. Nonetheless, when the crisis comes he acts instinctively according to the revolutionary code, with tragic results for Leslie.

The central theme of the play is that nationalism is destructive, outdated, at the very least foolish because the world is changing too rapidly and is far too dangerous to accommodate cultural isolationism. Behan's sympathies are with the proletariat; like O'Casey's tenement dwellers, they have borne the heavist losses in the internal warfare that continues in Ireland.

Leslie, the hostage, and Theresa, the country girl who reaches out to him in a brief interlude of affection, are both orphans, symbolically placed outside the mainstream of English and Irish culture and thus a potential source of a new generation conceived without the blight of race ha-

tred. What further distinguishes them, particularly in the Irish version, is their innocence in contrast to the world around them in which love of God, country, or fellow human being has been thoroughly debased. Their relationship is unfortunately short-lived like most such love relationships—when they exist at all—in modern irish comedy. Their world is still in a "state of chassis." There is no immediate promise of peace or resolution; thus any commitment between lovers must be tenuous.

Behan's purpose, as in *The Quare Fellow,* is a humanitarian one. Underneath the joking is a serious statement about the futility of modern warfare and a conciliatory gesture from an old IRA man. [In *Brendan Behan,* 1970], Ulick O'Connor maintains, however, that Behan was uneasy with the Littlewood production, which was so emphatically an "entertainment" and so insistent in its ridicule of Irish types. With the exception of Leslie and Theresa, the characters are made ludicrous in their allegiance to a cause whose time has passed. The laughter is cathartic, but in a sense one has the spectacle of Handy Andy all over again. Everything that speaks of a peculiarly Irish mode of life—language, patriotism, religious beliefs—is being held up to laughter, and there is no balancing sense of cultural richness as there is in *Ulysses.* In the stage Irish tradition Behan's characters are boisterous drinkers and talkers, who sing and joke and dance to provide comic relief until the nightmarish scene in which Leslie is killed. At the final curtain he springs to life, a sentimental gesture tacked on to the English version.

Borstal Boy, an autobiographical account of Behan's own experience as a political prisoner in England, provides a real cultural context. The book also confirms the widely observed fact that the most compelling character he ever created was Brendan Behan. Long before the publication of *Borstal Boy,* Behan had attracted public attention because of his witty and rambunctious behavior. Within a month the autobiography sold twenty thousand copies and not only brought him literary fame but [according to O'Connor] "helped to fix his public image": a boy from the slums who liked to thumb his nose at the establishment, who had spent years in prison, but who finally won international acclaim because of his innate and untutored genius.

At the age of sixteen Behan was arrested in Liverpool with his "Sinn Fein conjuror's outfit"—explosives intended for the British shipyards. His arrest and internment are described in *Borstal Boy* through scenes which vividly express the fear, degradation, loneliness, and oddly humorous encounters of prison life. Behan provides a very open and frank account of the everyday routine, the threats of the guards, the complete lack of privacy, the physical attraction of other men, which make it clear how rooted in personal experience were the two major plays. He is adept at quickly and memorably characterizing a wide range of personalities as, for example, in this impression of the owner of the boardinghouse where he was captured:

> This landlady was mean and as barren as a bog.
> Her broken windows would be a judgement on
> her for the cheap sausages and margarine she
> poisoned her table with, for she was only gener-

ous with things that cost little in cash, locking hall doors at nighttime and kneeling down to say the Rosary with the lodger and her sister, who always added three Hail Marys for holy purity and the protection of her person and modesty, so that you would think half the men in Liverpool were running after her, panting for a lick of her big buck teeth.

And the chief administrator at Walton Jail where he was held for sentencing:

> The governor was a desiccated-looking man, in tweed clothes and wearing a cap, as befitted his rank of Englishman, and looking as if he would ride a horse if he had one. He spoke with some effort, and if you did not hear what he was saying you'd have thought from his tone, and the sympathetic, loving, and adoring looks of the screw, P.O., and Chief, that he was stating some new philosophical truth to save the suffering world from error.

Much of the dramatic tension in Part I of **Borstal Boy** derives from Behan's consciousness of being an Irish Revolutionary in an English jail. When first captured, he is determined to live up to the memory of men like Tom Clarke who, after fifteen years of penal servitude for planting explosives, took a leading role in the Easter Rising for which he was finally executed. In court he declares:

> My name is Brendan Behan, I came over here to fight for the Irish Workers and Small Farmers' Republic, for a full and free life, for my countrymen, North and South, and for the removal of the baneful influence of British Imperialism from Irish affairs. God save Ireland.

But under the conditions at Walton, he realizes that he could not withstand the punishment endured by earlier patriots.

To begin with he is excommunicated by an English priest when he refuses to repudiate the IRA. Although he remains a fundamentally religious person, this experience makes him skeptical of the institution of the Church. And when he is invited later on to serve Mass despite the fact that he may not receive the sacraments, he does so only in

> . . . memory of my ancestors standing around a rock, in a lonely glen, for fear of the landlords and their yesmen or sneaking through a backland in Dublin, and giving the password, to hear Mass in a slum public house, when a priest's head was worth five pounds and an Irish Catholic had no existence in law.

Behan seems as much outraged by the priest's insistence on his ignorance as a working class boy as by his use of religion as a political weapon. The autobiography may, in fact, be read as a rebuttal, demonstrating the rich heritage of history, legend, music, and conversation available to the ordinary Dubliner if, like Behan, he has the wit or the leisure to appreciate it. Unfortunately, his ferociously articulate response at this point precipitates a beating from the guards. Thereafter he is locked up in isolation, condemned to what he terms *"unaigneas gan cuineas,"* loneliness

without peace. He acknowledges his fear and determines to survive despite the hostility of many of the other prisoners and the guards who abuse him as an "Irish pig."

What is particularly strong and moving in Behan's memoir is his willingness to put aside the mask and speak openly of the difference between the "gallous story" and the "dirty deed," between songs and processions in memory of Irish heroes and the reality of an English jail: "I thought it better to survive my sentence and come out and strike a blow in vengeance for them, than be kicked to death or insanity here. And even that was not the truth. I only wanted to survive the night." The critical test comes with the approaching execution of two Irishmen condemned for the alleged murder of British civilians. Behan makes a devastating comedy out of his reaction to another Irishman, Callan, in jail for stealing an overcoat, but determined to prove his courage by staging a demonstration on the eve of the execution. As Callan roars out, "Up the Republic" to Behan's timid response, the latter comments: " . . . all honour to him, of course, I'll never deny it to him, but tell them at home how all alone he stood and shouted for the cause all on his own. If only he leaves me out of it."

Once he is remanded to the Borstal at Hollesley Bay, a detention center for juveniles, Behan is drawn into a new role, that of "Paddy," the comic Irishman. Relieved to find himself in a relatively humane institution, he becomes a genial performer sought after by the other prisoners whom he regales with Irish songs and obscene limericks and jokes. His memoir amply attests to his craving for companionship and his use of comedy to break out of isolation and surround himself with an admiring throng of friends. He warms to applause, enjoying the tone of friendly approval that he hears in the nickname "Paddy." Behan admits his willingness to stretch the truth and to suppress his own feelings in order to be accommodating, to avoid friction. In a curious way his career parallels the historical experience of the Irish in the nineteenth century, abused and ridiculed because of cultural differences and then applauded when those differences began to seem amusing, perceived through the distorting prism of a stereotype and often conforming to that stereotype.

In this section of the book there are many fine, dramatic scenes of life in the Borstal as well as splendid prose passages describing the natural landscape:

> The autumn got weaker and beaten, and the leaves all fell, and a bloody awful east wind that was up before us and we on our way to work in the morning, sweeping down off the top of the North Sea, which in the distance looked like a bitter band of deadly blue steel out along the length of the horizon, around the freezing marshes, the dirty grey shore, the gunmetal sea, and over us the sky, lead-colored for a few hours, till the dark fell and the wind rose, and we went down the road from work at five o'clock in the perishing night.

The dialogue, including Cockney, Welsh, rural English, and Northern Irish, attests to Behan's excellent ear for the nuances of the spoken word. It also demonstrates that he was becoming more tolerant of people regardless of racial, national, or religious background. He discovers that he has more in common with the English working class than with some of the Irish he encounters in prison: " . . . in Ireland, down the country anyway, if a girl got put up the pole she might as well leave the country or drown herself and have done with it—the people are so Christian and so easily shocked." He remains defensive toward the upper classes and the formally educated, presenting himself as a tough, blunt, street-wise Dubliner . . . : "I was no country Paddy from the middle of the Bog of Allen."

Nonetheless Sections II and III of **Borstal Boy** are inferior to the opening portion; they rarely attain the same level of intelligent introspection and one grows weary of Behan as a loveable character. The best part of the book remains his fine description of the loneliness and fear he experienced in Walton Jail, the racy dialogue and lyric prose passages and certain first-rate dramatic scenes like that of his capture in Liverpool. There are also many witty comments to liven up an otherwise ordinary page ("It's a queer world, God knows, but the best we have to be going on with.") For those interested in Irish culture, **Borstal Boy** remains a fascinating portrait of a quintessential Dubliner.

Brendan Behan's public career as a "broth of a bhoy" has been well chronicled. After the generally conservative mood of the fifties, his performance as "wild Irish" delighted a vast audience, particularly in England and America, where newsmen followed him around waiting for samples of the famous Irish wit. Ulick O'Connor emphasizes Behan's shrewdness at public relations; he was evidently quick to seize opportunities to bring himself to the attention of the media, frequently turning mischance—a drunken brawl or a night in jail—into a comic interlude. He created a legend by his escapades and by his superb gift as a story teller and mime, able to captivate listeners for hours at a time. He had a fine tenor voice and an excellent repertoire as well as a talent for parody and for composing limericks extemporaneously. Before he was well known he obviously relished the role of provocateur, of defeating the expectations of the intelligentsia and the middle class when he revealed his considerable knowledge and skill as a speaker in both English and Irish.

Behan became familiar with Irish through the help of his fellow IRA men during internment in Dublin and first attracted attention as a poet writing in this ancient tongue. He spoke of himself disparagingly as a *rannaire,* that is, a rimer, rather than a *fili;* but translations of his work, as for example **"A Jackeen cries at the loss of the Blaskets,"** suggest that he had talent as a poet. This particular poem confirms his affiliation with the stark simplicity of the old, vanished culture. It reveals an ascetic element in Behan's nature, linking him temperamentally to the islanders and further back in time to the solitary monks who wrote the first lyric poems in Irish. As a *jackeen* (a countryman's contemptuous term for a Dubliner), however, he would have been doubly removed, in culture as well as time, from the world of the Blaskets. By writing in Irish, Behan was apparently attempting to establish continuity with that remote world. After 1950 he wrote no further poetry; it is

believed that he lost faith in his own ability and in the future of Gaelic literature.

Reading through the work of contemporary poets, Thomas Kinsella, John Montague, Seamus Heaney, Seán Ó Tuama, and observing how they have burrowed into the substrata of history toward the sources of Irish culture, one cannot help thinking that Behan's career took a fatal turn in the fifties. This is not to say that his gifts were those of a poet rather than a dramatist, merely that he sacrificed the private to the public man. This conclusion is also suggested by Colbert Kearney who, in his analysis of Behan's work [*The Writings of Brendan Behan,* 1977], argues that "the persona of the Irish poems would seem to be the closest approximation to his basic personality."

In "North" Seamus Heaney speaks of composing like the *fili* in "darkness," of "keeping your eye clear, as the bleb of the icicle." History then becomes a source of renewal and strength, ensuring the writer a measure of perspective, not simply the makings of a good anecdote. Working at his craft in silence and darkness, keeping himself aloof, he sees with the inner eye of vision. The result is a distinctive voice and a new sense of authority in Irish literature.

The dramatist is necessarily a more public figure and his relation with his audience is a more precarious one. The

---

"The Ballad of Brendan Behan"

A Springtime day, yes, one of sorrow,
A day in March—1964
The Spotlights out, the curtain fallen,
The final bow, to his native shore.
This rebel artist, from down by Liffey,
Whose uncle gave us 'A Soldier's Song'
The grandson true, of a Fenian fighter.
Yes rebels all—in a day now gone.

At an early age he joined the Fianna,
And not—the Soldiers of Destiny,
Who still today, hold power and glory,
With a make believe of a nation free.
To serve old Ireland—the true ideals—
That was sealed in blood back in '16,
And for the truth, like others suffered,
For to Brendan Behan, 'twas no idle dream.

Afar from Ireland, her cause for freedom,
This Irish youth, got an English cell,
The Borstal boy, we know well the story,
Yes, all for Ireland, this goal of hell,
Then home deported and the specials waited
For this Irish rebel, with the determined will.
And once again Brendan Behan is prisoner,
In Mountjoy, the Curragh and Arbour Hill.

A bright spring morn, we laid him sleeping,
With a fond farewell from a soldier's pal,
And men of letters, his name saluted,
For his auld triangle, and the Royal Canal.

Jimmy Hiney, in Sean McCann's The World
of Brendan Behan, *1965.*

success of Behan's work depended in no small measure on the fact that he was often in the spotlight himself.

Onto the figure of the stage Irish bard, which infuriated Patrick Kavanagh and Flann O'Brien, he grafted that of the rebel, that is, the rebel as comedian, a bit of a turnabout for the defender of the Workers and Small Farmers' Republic, a bit of a throwback to the Shaughraun. By ridiculing Irish nationalism and turning his political past into grist for the publicity mill, he must have felt, at some level, that he was betraying his deepest roots.

It is hardly a new discovery that Behan was a stage Irishman, and it is a point that I do not wish to belabor considering his tragic early death from the combined ravages of diabetes and alcoholism. The general consensus is that he first created and then was trapped by his public image, by the expectations of the crowd. Toward the end of his life, the amiable witty surface cracked open under the pressure of what must have been extraordinary inner violence. He wrote less and less as his fame increased and he deteriorated physically, collapsing into drunken diabetic comas. His biographer has provided a sympathetic account of the contradictory elements of his personality with its shifting moods of savagery and kindness, of asceticism and drunken excess. What is germane to this study is the magnetism of the public mask, the appeal of the comic Irishman. (pp. 161-72)

> *Maureen Waters, "A Borstal Boy," in her* The Comic Irishman, *State University of New York Press, 1984, pp. 161-72.*

Desmond Maxwell   (essay date 1986)

[*Maxwell is a Northern Irish educator and critic. In the following essay, he examines the stage history and shared qualities of Behan's dramas.*]

> 'We're off, in this order: the Governor, the Chief, two screws Regan and Crimmin, the quare fellow between them, two more screws and three runners from across the Channel, getting well in front, now the Canon. He's making a big effort for the last two furlongs. He's got the white pudding bag on his head, just a short distance to go. He's in. [*A clock begins to chime the hour. Each quarter sounds louder.*] His feet to the chalk line. He'll be pinioned, his feet together. The bag will be pulled down over his face. The screws come off the trap and steady him. Himself goes to the lever and . . .
>
> *The hour strikes. The* WARDERS *cross themselves and put on their caps. From the* PRISONERS *comes a ferocious howling.*
>   —*The Quare Fellow*

This burlesque of a radio sports commentary, sardonically transferred to a condemned man's approaching the scaffold, had its first audience on 19 November 1954 at the Pike Theatre Club, Dublin. The next year the Pike presented Beckett's *Waiting for Godot,* a premiere shared with the production by the Arts Theatre Club, London. The work of Behan and Beckett was, of course, to become widely accessible. Still, there was at least a symbolic value in their Dublin presentation.

Both plays were directed by Alan Simpson, who with Carolyn Swift founded the Pike in 1953. Their intention [according to Alan Simpson, in his *Beckett and Behan and a Theatre in Dublin,* 1962], was 'to stir up the theatrical lethargy of post-war Ireland'. In that cause, if only for these two pioneering productions, the Pike has an importance out of proportion to its minute size. It represented an imaginative energy notably absent elsewhere in Dublin theatre. The established companies would have nothing to do with Behan, nor with Beckett. The former was disreputable, the latter riskily *avant-garde.*

Yet without making extravagant claims for Behan, it is fair to say that *The Quare Fellow* addressed its audiences with a good deal more urgency than the rather circumspect bill of fare then commonly on offer: Shaw (*St. Joan, The Doctor's Dilemma*), a Eugene O'Neill (*Anna Christie*), an Elmer Rice (*Not for Children*); from the home dramatists Lady Longford's *The Hill of Quirke,* Joseph Tomelty's *Is The Priest at Home?,* M. J. Molloy's *The Will and the Way,* and *Twenty Years A-Wooing* by John McCann, a prolific and popular writer of soap operas: revivals, safe new works, potboilers. Though Behan's career as a playwright was brief—he wrote only two considerable plays— it greatly enlivened this predictable scene; and was a harbinger of the revival of Irish theatre in the early sixties, when Behan was to make an unexpected posthumous appearance.

By way of comment on his own plays, Behan has had his word on Beckett. 'When Samuel Beckett', he said, 'was in Trinity College listening to lectures, I was in the Queen's Theatre, my uncle's music hall. That is why my plays are music hall and his are university lectures' [as recorded in Seamus de Burca's *Brendan Behan: A Memoir*]. It is a near-sighted view of Beckett, whose characters have a good deal of Laurel and Hardy in them. Applied to Behan's own plays it also calls for some reserve.

The Hostage is its obvious verification. It demonstrates Behan's affinity with—perhaps subservience to—Joan Littlewood's improvisational theatre, of which he said [in *Brendan Behan's Island*], 'the thing to aim . . . for [is] to amuse people and any time they get bored, divert them with a song or a dance'. Behan in the Littlewood orbit supplied *The Hostage* with an abundance of those vaudeville ingredients. Her 1958 production at Stratford East used the original script as a diagram for elaboration— spontaneous dance, the introduction of songs, of topical references—even of dialogue, an opportunity still embedded in the published text: 'The lines of this scene are largely improvised to suit the occasion'.

It was in a way a marriage of minds. The method suited Behan. Seated in a pub opposite the Theatre Royal during rehearsals, he was perfectly happy to supply a song, a scene, a snatch of dialogue on demand. The danger of the method is its potential for indiscipline, Behan's affliction. The authority of the playwright's words and design abates; parts acquire a momentum of their own. *The Hostage,* then, is not so much Behan as a joint Behan/Littlewood creation, and to the consequences of that relationship we shall return.

Behan's first play, **The Quare Fellow,** is a very different matter. It began as a one-act play in Gaelic, *Casadh Sugáin Eile* (*The Twisting of Another Rope*). The Abbey rejected it, and also its three-act version, as did Hilton Edwards for the Gate Theatre. When Alan Simpson finally took it up, he found Behan, like Joan Littlewood after him, an easygoing collaborator—'not', he says directorially, 'one of those playwrights who see everything differently to the director, or try to mess him around'. The manuscript was a mess, the play's structure sprawling and uneconomical, but Simpson had no doubt of its quality. His editorial intervention was much more modest than Joan Littlewood's, however. As he puts it:

> We re-arranged rather than re-wrote some of the play. I still have a copy of the original script, which is very rambling. A character would change subjects as though in a genuine conversation. We made Brendan sort it out so that one subject was dealt with at a time. We probably made cuts; in fact, I am sure we did, and we tied up loose ends such as curtain lines.

The play ran for a month and brought Behan forty or fifty pounds. None of the larger Dublin theatres would house it. **The Quare Fellow** went to Joan Littlewood at Stratford East.

The critics of the 1958 New York production responded without enthusiasm. *The New York Times* complained of Behan's 'uncertain command of the theatre medium' and of the play's looseness of design; the *Herald Tribune* of its triteness. These are curious opinions. The play is tightly knit and almost classically unified. Behan was perfectly capable, in 1954, of the kind of remaking suggested to him by Simpson.

Before curtain rise, the prisoner's sardonic lament, 'that old triangle', gives human voice to the stage set's images of confinement: the severe lines of metal cell doors and the administrative circle, the women's section visible but beyond reach, the notice in Victorian lettering which says, 'SILENCE'. All except the voice is institutional, correctional. The play, like the voice, challenges the restraints. Their physical duress—unsentimentally observed—represents the crude moral arbitrations of the prison. Sequences of action also dramatise the basic tension between the system and its creatures, routine and individuality, warders and prisoners:

> WARDER REGAN. Right, B. Wing, bang out your doors. B.I. get in off your steps and bang out your doors, into your cells and bang out your doors. Get locked up. BANG THEM DOORS! GET INSIDE AND BANG OUT THEM DOORS! [Stage directions as recorded in *The Complete Flap*, edited by Alan Simpson]

The scenes of morning stand-to, the line-up for inspection, the filing out to dig the grave should be played to suggest the prisoners' minimal obedience to the forms. These dreary rituals, paid mocking observance, stand against the antic caperings of the two Young Prisoners, who 'samba out with their brushes for partners humming the Wedding Samba': the play's only 'routine'. Like the choreographed coal-stealing in Wesker's *Chips With Everything* (1962),

the drill in McGrath's *Events While Guarding the Bofors Gun* (1966), **The Quare Fellow**'s chores and curbs evade the intention of their supervisors. 'By the left, laugh', as Dunlavin says. Elsewhere in the play, effects akin to those of music hall are immediately part of the action. As the quare fellow's last, superior meal is brought to him, the prisoners crowd round the yard with a kind of farewell, patter chorus:

PRISONER A:	Pork chops.
PRISONER B:	Pig's feet.
PRISONER A:	Salmon.
NEIGHBOUR:	Fish and chips.
MICKSER:	Jelly and custard.
NEIGHBOUR:	Roast lamb.
PRISONER A:	Plum pudding.
PRISONER B:	Turkey.
NEIGHBOUR:	Goose.
PRISONERS A, B, and	
NEIGHBOUR:	Rashers and eggs.
ALL:	Rashers and eggs; rashers and eggs, and eggs and rashers and eggs and rashers it is.

The Quare Fellow entirely avoids the pantomime extravagances of **The Hostage.** One song, 'that old triangle,' sounds the play's strict chronology, from 'To begin the morning/The warder bawling' through 'On a fine spring evening/The lag lay dreaming' to 'The day was dying and the wind was sighing'. Apart from that there are a few snatches only. Thus discreetly used, the harsh, haunting song generalises on the passage of time, which is the main 'action' of the play. The prison inmates return obsessively to it—particularly the coming hour of execution, but generally as the focus of their lives: 'Healy is coming up today', 'the small hours of this morning', 'long months here', 'out again this day week', 'three days of No. 1', 'the death watch coming on at twelve o'clock'. Hardly a page lacks such a confining definition by hours, days, years. Time and space impose their restrictions, brought together in the final song:

> In the female prison
> There are seventy women
> I wish it was with them that I did dwell,
> Then that old triangle
> Could jingle jangle
> Along the banks of the Royal Canal.

The crude song, in the diminuendo after the hanging, revives the sexual antithesis to death, with an artistic decorum which **The Hostage** vulgarises.

Behan was well aware from his own experience that these confinements neither eradicated individuality nor formed any liberal ethic in the prisoners. While he was in Mountjoy Jail after 1942 he worked on a play called **The Landlady,** which involved suicide and prostitution. It never had a chance to shock the bourgeois, as it certainly would have. It did shock a number of Behan's fellow-convicts, who forcibly prevented its staging in Mountjoy. The prisoners in **The Quare Fellow** are no more tolerant. Dunlavin is horrified that the cell next to him is to be occupied by a sexual offender, not the reprieved murderer: 'Killing your wife is a natural class of a thing could happen to the

best of us. But this other dirty animal on me left . . . '.
For the prisoners, the Quare Fellow is not a Cause. He is
a victim, a sacrifice, the ceremonies of his death detailed
in their minds. Through the prisoners the audience has entrance to the condemned cell and to knowledge of its occu-
pant, who is divested of the idiosyncrasies of self.

Much of the conversation about the Quare Fellow refers
to him only indirectly, through prison lore of the gruesome mechanics of hanging and the hours before it. He is
all the Quare Fellows who have met this death. Warders
and prisoners agree on, to put the matter mildly, its messiness. What do we learn of it? The duty warders make futile
attempts to conceal the passage of time. The washer is put
beneath the condemned man's ear, the hood is donned.
The prisoner's build may be wrongly estimated: decapita-
tion or strangulation—'his head was all twisted and his
face black, but the two eyes were the worst; like a rabbit's;
it was fear that had done it'.

The execution becomes an exercise in terror for almost all
concerned in it; that or a bureaucratic necessity. The prisoners' view of it is unsentimental, almost clinical, with a
colour of macabre fascination. Most feel some compassion, Prisoner C deeply. But the compassion is for a man
recognised, on the whole, as the agent of his own execution—'Begod, he's not being topped for nothing—to cut
his own brother up and butcher him like a pig'.

These responses are far from the absolutes of reformist
discourse. Their power is the greater for an anguish—and
an appetite—which does not come from a received Virtue
Crucified. The personification is not to suggest any symbolic association between the Quare Fellow and Christ.
Christ, however, did have to share his crucifixion with two
outcasts more of the Quare Fellow's persuasion. Without
urging an extension of that kind, Behan's play does inter-
polate exercises of observance which hint at the extension.

The prisoners' chorus makes a ceremony of the Quare Fellow's meal. The hangman, drunk, and his sober attendant
deliver a litany which tastelessly but formally solemnises
the soul and body of the Quare Fellow:

> JENKINSON [*sings*]: My brother, sit and think.
> While yet some time is left to thee
> Kneel to thy God who from thee does not
> shrink
> And lay thy sins on Him who died for thee.
>
> HANGMAN: Take a fourteen-stone man as a
> basis and giving him a drop of eight foot . . .

Finally, the prisoners enter the rite. Their wordless howling at the moment of execution, and Mickser's parody of
a race-course commentator, determine their presence at a
mystery, not a demonstration against capital punishment.
The play, for all its essentially naturalistic manner, invites
these larger understandings.

[In *The Writing of Brendan Behan*, 1977] Colbert Kearney
has remarked that *The Quare Fellow*

> is a play within a play, and structurally much
> more sophisticated than it is often thought.
> There are two audiences: those in the theatre
> watch those on the stage who witness the exter-

> nals of the closet-drama. . . . The theatre audi-
> ence cannot resist judging the behaviour of those
> on stage and invariably they laugh at the black
> humour of the prisoners and dissociate them-
> selves from the strict principles of the prison re-
> gime. At some point during or after the play the
> theatre-audience must realise that they have
> been tricked into a position which is critical of
> the very institution which they support outside
> the theatre.

The point about the play's structure is well taken, and as
Kearney argues, *The Quare Fellow* 'lacks the simplicity
of propaganda'. He rightly disputes the criticism that the
play is, a 'rather shallow bit of propaganda directed largely towards the evils of capital punishment'. Its effect
should be felt, Kearney argues, 'wherever there is an imperfect society which, in its desire to organise itself for the
good of the majority, makes imperfect laws which alienate
the exceptions, the unusual, the 'quare' fellows.'

The play reaches into the condition of the outcast and the
social defences erected against him. With considerable
perception it represents the psychological defences which
people set up against violent death, and at an even deeper
level its fascination. The emotions which welcome barbaric revenge in whatever form—execution, feud, assassina-
tion, war—enter the play's ambit, observed with a remarkable neutrality of tone. Even Warder Regan, who comes
closest to explicit condemnation of the whole process,
never fully interrogates its motives. One of his speeches,
towards the end, refers to the pandering to a lust for death
and spectacle, now hypocritically muted with the hanging
removed from public to private view, from mass audience
to secular and ecclesiastical representatives. Almost
shouting, Regan says, 'I think the whole show should be
put on in Croke Park; after all, it's at the public expense
and they let it go on. They should have something more
for their money than a bit of paper stuck up on the gate'.
But he continues in his office: '[The hangman] has no more
to do with it than you or I or the people that pay us, and
that's every man or woman that pays taxes or votes in elections. If they don't like it, they needn't have it'. Regan is
part of the 'they'. His dual position of critic and partici-
pant shades him away from a merely propagandist voice.

The Quare Fellow epitomises Behan's achievement in theatre. It is localised by language, through which it escapes
to its wider applications. The music-hall styles are there—
cross-talk, song, slapstick—but refined to subtler purpose.
The play has a message, but the message is not the play.
The play is entertainment, but entertainment is not its substance. *The Quare Fellow,* classically restricted to one
day's action, takes us into the presence of individuals who
merge into a voice beyond their individualities.

Unlike *The Hostage, The Quare Fellow* adroitly deploys
not intrusions but analogues of music-hall forms: of cross-
talk, 'routines', dance, patter. In *The Hostage,* Behan's
concern to avoid boredom interferes with muted effects.
He, or Joan Littlewood, will not leave alone the moving
conversation between Teresa and Meg about the young
boy who is to be hanged in Belfast. 'Come on, Kate', Meg
must say, 'give us a bit of music', and a wild dance takes
over. Some of the interference is less self-indulgent. The

song, 'I will give a golden ball' emerges congenially enough from Teresa's and Leslie's halting declarations of love. The song leads them to bed together, a bed for two individuals, not vaudeville turns. 'I know I wasn't much good to you', Leslie says later.

The Hostage has its points of control: the setting, an old house, once a Republican sanctuary, now a brothel, which has seen the Ascendancy days of Monsewer's,

> Tea and toast and muffin rings,
> Old ladies with stern faces,
> And the Captains and the Kings.

The location entertains the themes of internal Irish disputes, English/Irish antagonisms, and countering these the communion between Teresa and Leslie. The play's jumble of styles, however, confuses their presentation. Comedy and pathos never reach into each other. Behan manipulates his characters and situations to sudden reversals of effect as unfeelingly as Public Good, National Security, The Cause—his targets—manipulate their real-life counterparts.

The Hostage began as *An Giall* (The Hostage) a play in Irish commissioned by Gael-Linn and performed in 1958. Behan then wrote a translation for Joan Littlewood, which by the time it appeared in London had acquired another half-dozen characters and become 'a drastically modified version' [according to Richard Wall in "*An Giall* and *The Hostage* Compared," *Modern Drama* XVIII, No. 2 (June 1975)]. *An Giall*'s immediate origin was an incident during the British invasion of the Suez Canal Zone in 1956. A British officer captured by the Egyptians was later found dead, suffocated in a cupboard—Leslie's fate in *An Giall.*

The event fastened on Behan's imagination how large, public occasions reduce individuals to objects; and the imperative to resist this diminishment. His play, he said, 'is basically about the ordinariness of people—which is an extraordinary thing at such times . . . All that I am trying to show in my play is that one man's death can be more significant than the issues involved': sober thoughts, which *An Giall* embodies in its Irish setting. Richard Wall's examination of the two plays demonstrates conclusively that *The Hostage* vulgarises *An Giall*'s delicacies, achieving 'the destruction of [its] integrity, a drastic alteration of its tone, and a reduction of the impact of its most striking feature: the tender romance between Teresa . . . and Leslie . . . in a brutal world'.

Behan declared his approval of Joan Littlewood's rendering. He dismissed the original production as 'of the school of Abbey Theatre naturalism of which I'm not a pupil'. Whether this is genuine conviction or the self-deception of success it is impossible to say. Certainly, *The Hostage* is flawed; and *An Giall* is in the line of *The Quare Fellow*'s naturalism, which as in the Abbey tradition at its best pushes the convention beyond simply imitative designs.

In 1967, three years after Behan's death, the Abbey Theatre presented *Borstal Boy,* an adaptation of Behan's novel by Frank McMahon, directed by Tomás MacAnna. The transference from the one to the other form is a case history of the requirements imposed by the shift of medium. Changes in narrative tone, attitude, point of view in the novel must find equivalents on the stage among characters and settings literally present to the audience. The theatre demands a telescoping, a reduction, and in a sense a simplifying of the novel's expansiveness and its highly mobile chronology.

The dramatisation of *Borstal Boy* is remarkably coherent with both the quite complex scheme of the novel, and the style of Behan's theatre. It is lavish with song (as is the novel) and employs a good deal of intricately choreographed movement: much, one might think, like *The Hostage.* In *Borstal Boy,* however, these elements are not just beguiling interludes. They are translations from the language of the novel, they are under the authority of a clearly developed interpretation, and they are subject to MacAnna's belief in a final, inviolable script which embodies his view of the novel's statement.

Behan's novel—the most convenient term for it—is somewhat fictionalised autobiography, a kind of *Portrait of the Artist as a Young I.R.A. Man. Borstal Boy* is not only, in a documentary way, a classic of 'prison literature'. As Colbert Kearney remarks, Behan wrote 'an imaginative autobiography . . . just as Joyce did in the *Portrait*'. It is Behan's most controlled and most self-sustained work, a novel of adolescence, of experience finding a literary style for its meaning. Gradually, it unfolds a mutation in the author's view of himself, and of views outside him.

Despite its location in English jails (where Behan has a rough time) and for its greater part, the more humane Hollesley Bay Borstal, *Borstal Boy* never loses sight—or sound—of Ireland, Dublin particularly. The Irish past enters the present of the jails in reminiscence of a scene or an episode:

> The house we lived in was a great lord's town house before it was a tenement, and there was a big black Kilkenny marble fireplace before my bed. If the souls in Purgatory really came back, it was out of there they would come. A Hail Mary was all right, but there was more comfort in the sound of the trams. There were lights and people on them. Old fellows, a bit jarred and singing, and fellows leaving their mots home to Drumcondra after the pictures.
>
> There was a similar piece of sculpture over Kilmainham Prison. I had often passed it with my father, taking me for a walk on Sunday mornings. It was where he had first seen me, from his cell window, during the Civil War. I was born after he was captured, and when I was six weeks old my mother brought me up to the jail and held me up, on the road outside, for him to see from the cell window.
>
> . . . in Kerry, where the arbutus grows and the fuchsia glows on the dusty hedges in the soft light of the summer evening. '*Deorini De*'—'The Tears of God'—they called the fuchsia in Kerry, where it ran wild as a weed.

The recollections are of an experience and an inheritance which the alien scene is modifying. The reflexes of the rehearsed 'Irish rebel', without ever disappearing, adjust to new facts. Fresh experience re-directs the ingrained set of attitudes. ***Borstal Boy*** is about this interaction and its outcome. While political dogma softens, language in interesting ways acquires dominance.

The Irish earthing of the book is mainly in its language, in Behan's heightened Dublin idiom. Much of it is more or less transcription of authentic argot: ' "They said that", said I, "and they'd say Mass if they knew the Latin" '; ' "The blessings of God on you", said I, "and may the giving hand never falter".'; ' "You've a neck like a jockey's ballocks".' The same Dublin cant informs the language of narrative, meditation, judgement. It takes place—a recurrent phrase—'in my own mind'. Cant, however, in its extended periods ('in my own mind') ascends to High Cant, deriving recognisably still from a vernacular model, but transformed beyond its normal usages. As Behan is doing his 'Number One and solitary', his dinnertime frustration issues in a memorable, unspoken invocation to an Ireland that might do better by him:

> Oh, come up at once, the publican would say, what kind of men are you at all? Have you no decency of spirit about you, that wouldn't make way for one of the Felons of our Land? Come on, son, till herself gives you this plate of bacon and cabbage, and the blessings of Jasus on you, and on everyone like you. It's my own dinner I'm giving you, for you were not expected and you amongst that parcel of white-livered, thin-lipped, paper-waving, key-rattling hangmen. And, come on; after your dinner there's a pint to wash it down, aye, and a glass of malt if you fancy it. Give us up a song there. Yous have enough of songs out of yous about the boys that faced the Saxon foe, but, bejasus, when there's one of them here among you, the real Ally Dally, the real goat's genollickers, yous are silent as the tomb. Sing up, yous whores gets.

Unmistakably Dublin patter, the speech outsoars imitation to a Platonic Ideal. It assembles slang ('whores gets'), cliché ('Felons of our Land'), invention ('white-livered, thin-lipped, paper-waving, key-rattling hangmen'), formality ('the publican would say') into an individualised, breakneck rhetoric. It is a rhetoric which looks beyond its native origins, assimilating new possibilities. Behan has a curiosity about language and remarks his dealings with forms of it new to him.

Behan is very conscious of his ear for accent and idiom. He claims to speak English like a native ('Smashing, china') after two days and a bit in the country; his house master at Hollesley Bay compliments him on his command of rhyming slang. We see the process of acquisition at work. Behan notes: how Charlie says 'dawncing' and 'pipah'; the phrase, smoking 'as Charlie said, "like lords' bastards" ', an expression forty pages later appropriated into Behan's talk; the warders; 'Ill Kerr-ect, sir'; the Chief's 'chuckle, as it's called'; 'the Borstal Warders as 'better gentlemen, in the way that word is used'. A cohabitation of dialects comes about. Almost as a figure of the book's design, the English imitate Behan's accent, and he theirs. The absorption of each by the other, of all that language signifies of a way of life, reflects a mutation in the received sentiments of Behan's Republicanism: 'I was sav-

ing up to be a coward and if I'd fight for anyone it'd be for myself '.

Living within the essential vernaculars are passages in more formal style, dealing in mood and description, as in the evocation of the Kerry fuchsia. Their formality and heightened diction never bleach the colloquial pigment:

> The autumn got weaker and beaten, and the leaves all fell, and a bloody awful east wind that was up before us and we on our way to work in the morning, sweeping down off the top of the North Sea, which in the distance looked like a bitter band of deadly blue steel out along the length of the horizon, around the freezing marshes, the dirty grey shore, the gunmetal sea, and over us the sky, lead-coloured for a few hours, till the dark fell and the wind rose, and we went down the road from work at five o'clock in the perishing night.

The sense of cold and deprivation moves from 'bloody awful', in a sinewy sentence, to a sensuous elaboration of what constitutes 'bloody awful', making of it a fully articulated experience. ***Borstal Boy*** is a work of art whose language subtly enacts a development of feeling and imagination. Though it has not the complexity of manners of Joyce's *Portrait* it marks out a linguistic territory synonymous with the experiences that occupy it.

The reporting voice, manipulating its discourse, is an acquisition of the older Behan, a medium of retrospective judgment. The retrospective utterance gives experience a shape concealed in its past actuality. Underlying the whole book is the older Behan who has found the words that crystallise perceptions into meaning. The novel has a continuous double focus. That of the mature, sardonic, reflective Behan puts in perspective the events which for the sixteen-year old Behan are undergone, not fully apprehended and judged, a youth now regarded with amusement, irony, envy.

The adaptation of ***Borstal Boy*** had its genesis in Iceland where in 1962 MacAnna was directing ***The Hostage***. Its translator suggested that there might be dramatic value in ***Borstal Boy***. On his return to Dublin MacAnna asked Frank McMahon to prepare a script. According to MacAnna, this turned out to be a straight-forward working through the novel, employing flashbacks as the novel—frequently—has them. There was in consequence a multiplicity of short scenes, and the playing time would have been much too long. The final shape came out of a close collaboration between MacAnna and McMahon over the four-week rehearsal period.

There are three available texts. The Irish and American published versions are largely identical, the latter rather shorter and with a few Americanised idioms. The Abbey working typescript is the longest and technically the most interesting. Its stage directions are the amplest, and accompanied by extensive handwritten notes, the director's detailed instructions for the players' movements. Its fascination, not to the purpose here, is that from it we can anatomise the progress, by elisions and compoundings, to the final text, which most clearly shows the nature of the translation from the novel.

The most compelling effect in the adaptation is its transference of the older/younger duality in the novel. Both the younger self, as Brendan, and the older, as Behan, are represented on stage. Once seen, the device appears inevitable. In fact it came to MacAnna only gradually, from a feeling that some necessary depth in the novel, a distancing of the young Behan, was absent from the early drafts. The older Behan, as a voice over, the first solution, lacked substance.

Then serendipity played a part. The actor Niall Toibín happened to call in MacAnna's office and MacAnna, remembering him as a good friend of Behan, saw him in the play as the older man: as it turned out, an uncannily accurate stage resurrection of its subject. So the disembodied became the embodied, and the play found its point of control. Brendan as a separate character is freed to act throughout the play as a young boy, subject to extreme responses. The older Behan carries most of the tensions of the novel's narrator, recollecting with both irony and regret. The interactions between the two versions of self establish varied moods from which the audience views the action.

The flashbacks of the novel are absorbed into the interchanges between the two Behans. As the action moves forward for Brendan, these exchanges with his older self suggest a kind of timeless present. The present time that we see on stage is the young Behan's past, framed by his future, the elder Behan he will become, looking back. In the end, the effects are far from simple, and transfer perfectly the double focus of the novel.

As to construction, Brecht supplied MacAnna with, as he calls it, the strip-cartoon approach: a series of pictures in simple, or apparently simple, chronological order. But the scenes run so fluidly into each other that there is no sense of the 'real' time that has passed. The passage of time is subordinate to the passages of feeling, reflected in delicate gradations of lighting, where MacAnna's mentor was Adolphe Appia: 'the setting for a play is light and little else'. All these elements—the dual Behan, the Brechtian structure, the lighting—are the medium whose function is to accommodate on the stage the words of the novel.

The play's reliance on the words of the novel demonstrates its fidelity to its source. Of about 1100 lines of dialogue in Act I, just over two hundred are original to the play. The spare additional dialogue serves to conflate episodes separated in the novel. So two church scenes, one at Hollesley, one at Feltham jail—a location omitted from the play—become one, and the novel's dispersed comments on the various Borstal boys are unified into the single scene introducing them as they disembark at Hollesley.

The play bridges, associates, economises. An inventive care marks its editorial manoeuvrings within the novel. For example, on p. 107 of the play, Behan's comment on the boys' innocent appearance closes a scene taken from pp. 231-3 of the novel. 'Reposed and innocent', he says, 'they look now, every mother's son of them'. The sentiment is drawn partly from p. 200. 'Reposed and innocent,' however, comes from p. 349. So too the Assizes scene in Act I ranges over pp. 28, 41, 93, 124, 132, and 143-4 of the novel. All the exchanges in the court itself come in pp. 143-4, mostly in reported speech. The particular event is made, in a perfectly organic union, to entertain a synthesis of Brendan/Behan's attitudes to the law and to Ireland.

A simpler amalgamation illustrates the thoroughness of the editing. Brendan twice sings 'The sea, oh, the sea' in the novel, pp. 212 and 333. The play uses it once, during the gardening work-party. This scene takes its dialogue from pp. 212 and 333 to introduce and round off the song, and combines political deflation with it, a sardonic comment on romanticised Irish attitudes to the land—'our family's land was all in window boxes', lifted from p. 234. Enveloping that content is a brief surge of emotional release through the coastal vista, open fields and bright sunlight suggested by the stage lighting. Moving through these scenes, both immediate and remembered, like the two Gars of Brian Friel's *Philadelphia, Here I Come!*, Brendan and Behan are not merely in plain contrast. At various moments in the play they share a feeling, a memory, a judgment. As Brendan is going off to solitary they infect each other with enthusiastic defiance, and join in a union of abuse:

> BEHAN: Make way there, you with the face,
> and let in the man that's doing jail for Ireland,
> and suffering hunger and abuse amongst that
> parcel of white-livered—
> BRENDAN: —thin-lipped—
> BEHAN: —paper-waving—
> BRENDAN: —key-rattling hangmen.

As the play advances they reach towards identity, so that at the end, separating, they echo each other:

> IMMIGRATION MAN: It must be wonderful to
> be free.
> BRENDAN: It must.
>
> (*He goes.* BEHAN *is left alone, gazing after* BRENDAN.)
> BEHAN: It must indeed . . . (*Sings.*)
> Is go dteighidh tu, a mhuirnin slan

Critics now are looking at Behan with a colder eye than when his reputation for both work and riot was at its height, when he seemed, as according to Fintan O'Toole [in "The Laughing Boy," *Sunday Tribune*, 18 March 1984] he no longer seems, assured of a 'place in the automatic hierarchy of . . . Wilde, Shaw and O'Casey'. Behan left behind him, O'Toole concludes, 'a brilliant book of autobiography, two interesting but minor plays, a handful of fine short stories'. Beyond that, O'Toole associates Behan with 'a glow of life in the dullness of Dublin . . . an energy that was important to his times'.

However, the importance of **Borstal Boy,** novel and play, resides not so much in the flamboyant being whose creation it is as in the interplay which the work sustains between the man and the deliberating mask. The indiscipline of the life surrenders to an ordering vision. Part of its allure is that while it contains it does not muffle the disruptive impulse. Brendan Behan, the 'I' of the novel, Brendan/Behan the double 'I' of the play, is preserved in the one as a form of words, in the other as that form conveyed to the theatre.

Strictly speaking, of course, **Borstal Boy** is not part of Behan's dramatic work, and Alan Simpson rightly excludes it from the **Complete Plays.** But the Abbey's **Borstal Boy** renews the characteristics of Behan's own plays. Its dialogue is Behan's. It has as many songs as **The Hostage** but deploys them with the structural control of **The Quare Fellow.** It renders Behan's concern with individuals, not abstractions and causes—or with abstractions and causes implied in the individuals whose brief lives are paramount. **Borstal Boy,** like Behan's theatre, is densely populated, fluent in vernacular, fluid with movement, shifting in mood. It re-enters Behan's world of the outcast, with all its sardonic compassion.

As Behan in the mid-fifties enlivened a lethargic Irish theatre, in the mid-sixties he appropriately took posthumous part in an Irish dramatic revival. Tom Murphy's *A Whistle in the Dark* played in London in 1961; Brian Friel's *Philadelphia, Here I Come!* at the Dublin Theatre Festival of 1964, his *Lovers* at the Gate Theatre in 1967; Tom Kilroy's *The Death and Resurrection of Mr. Roche* at the 1968 Festival. The production of **Borstal Boy** signified, too, a revitalisation of the Abbey itself, a self-confidence in the potential of the manifold resources of its new theatre, which it occupied in 1966; and it honoured the harbinger of this renaissance, the dramatist who extended yet again the Abbey's tradition of imaginative excursions within an essentially realist style. (pp. 87-102)

> *Desmond Maxwell, "Brendan Behan's Theatre," in* Irish Writers and The Theatre, *edited by Masaru Sekine, 1986. Reprint by Barnes and Noble Books, 1987, pp. 87-102.*

FURTHER READING

Biography

Behan, Dominic. *My Brother Brendan.* New York: Simon and Schuster, 1965, 159 p.

Account of Behan's life by his brother Dominic, who states: "Nobody else could have written about him as he really was but Rory [Behan] or I. Because nobody else was a brother, a fellow worker, and a booser with him all three."

De Burca, Seamus. *Brendan Behan: A Memoir.* Newark, Delaware: Proscenium Press, 1971, 43 p.

A firsthand biographical sketch.

Muggeridge, Malcolm. "Brendan Behan at Lime Grove." *New Statesman* LXVII, No. 1724 (27 March 1964): 488.

Recollection of Behan's appearance—while intoxicated—on a BBC television program hosted by Muggeridge.

O'Connor, Ulick. *Brendan Behan.* London: Hamish Hamilton, 1970, 328 p.

An in-depth critical biography.

Criticism

Adams, Phoebe. "The Lord High Executioner." *The Atlantic Monthly* 200, No. 4 (October 1957): 180-81.

Comments favorably on the style and wit of Behan's dialogue in *The Quare Fellow.* According to Adams, the play—in part about a man sentenced to death—"makes a powerful case for human dignity."

Barrett, William. "Places and Pictures." *The Atlantic Monthly* 215, No. 1 (January 1961): 130-31.

Praises the representation of the people and places of New York City in *Brendan Behan's New York.*

Burgess, Anthony. "The Writer as Drunk." In his *Urgent Copy,* pp. 88-92. New York: W. W. Norton & Company, 1968.

Compares the creative abilities of alcoholic writers Behan and Dylan Thomas, and finds "little shape but immense vigour" in Behan's work.

Poore, Charles. "Books of the Times." *The New York Times* (23 October 1962): 35.

Praises *Brendan Behan's Island* for its lively anecdotes and colorful characterizations of Irish life.

Porter, Raymond J. *Brendan Behan.* New York: Columbia University Press, 1973, 48 p.

Assesses Behan's writings, considering *The Quare Fellow, The Hostage,* and *Borstal Boy* his best works.

Rosen, Carol. "Passing Time behind Bars." In her *Plays of Impasse: Contemporary Drama Set in Confining Situations,* pp. 165-89. Princeton, N.J.: Princeton University Press, 1983.

Contrasts stylistic and thematic aspects of *The Quare Fellow* and *The Hostage* with other examples of drama about prison life.

Seymour, Miranda. "Recent Fiction." *The Spectator* 250, No. 8067 (19 February 1983): 23-4.

Favorably judges Behan's posthumous short story collection *After the Wake.*

"Pen and Gab." *The Times Literary Supplement,* No. 3163 (12 October 1962): 291.

Assesses Behan's strengths and weaknesses as an observer of his native Ireland in *Brendan Behan's Island,* judging that "it is not for his political opinions . . . that one listens gladly to Mr. Behan, but for the fund of good anecdotes."

"Death and the Irish." *The Times Literary Supplement,* No. 3764 (26 April 1974): 440.

Discusses Behan's incomplete drama *Richard's Cork Leg,* which the critic describes as similar to *The Hostage* though more "mild" and "innocent." In addition the critic states that "the play is splendidly Behan, ribald and stuffed full of old jokes, new songs, bad puns and contagious irreverence."

Additional coverage of Behan's life and career is contained in the following sources published by Gale Research: *Concise Dictionary of British Literary Biography,* 1945-1960; *Contemporary Authors,* Vols. 73-76; *Contemporary Authors New Revision Series,* Vol. 33; *Contemporary Literary Criticism,* Vols. 1, 8, 11, 15; *Dictionary of Literary Biography,* Vol. 13; and *Major 20th-Century Writers.*

Seize the Day
Saul Bellow

The following entry presents criticism on Bellow's novella *Seize the Day* (1956). For further discussion of Bellow's life and career, see *CLC*, Volumes 1, 2, 3, 6, 8, 10, 13, 15, 25, 33, 34, and 63.

INTRODUCTION

Originally published with three short stories and a one-act play under the collective title *Seize the Day*, Bellow's novella has enjoyed strong critical approval since its initial publication in 1956. Considered his most effective work for its sustained unity of action and complexity of meaning, *Seize the Day* has been identified by several critics with the revolt against Modernism that took place after World War II, signaling a return to a more tenuous romanticism. Ralph Ciancio praised the novella as "a masterpiece of the first order. . . . [Its] content, enlarged as well as intensified by metaphor, is far-reaching indeed: ostensibly an indictment of contemporary urban society, the story also encompasses religious and, ultimately, metaphysical issues."

The son of Russian-born parents, Bellow was born in 1915 in a slum in Lachine, Quebec. While confined to a hospital for a year during his childhood, he developed an interest in literature. At seventeen, Bellow and his friend, the future newspaper columnist Sydney J. Harris, ran away to New York City, where they unsuccessfully attempted to sell their first novels. After briefly studying at the University of Chicago, Bellow graduated from Northwestern University in 1967 with honors in sociology and anthropology. He began graduate study in anthropology at the University of Wisconsin, but soon abandoned the field because "every time I worked on my thesis, it turned out to be a story." During World War II, Bellow tried to join the Canadian Army but was turned down for medical reasons; this experience provided the basis for his first published novel, *Dangling Man*. In 1943 Bellow worked on Mortimer Adler's "Great Books" project for the Encyclopedia Britannica. He then returned to New York, where he briefly contracted for freelance work before taking a teaching job at the University of Minnesota in 1946. In 1963 Bellow accepted a permanent position on the Committee on Social Thought at the University of Chicago.

Seize the Day, like many of Bellow's works, addresses questions of identity and lovelessness in contemporary America. The novella focuses on a single, disastrous day in the life of Tommy Wilhelm, a middle-aged, Jewish urbanite intellectual who quits his job out of pride and loses his life's savings in a risky speculation in the stock market. Scholars concur that Wilhelm exemplifies the typical Bellow anti-hero, which the Nobel Committee defined in 1976 as a man "who keeps trying to find a foothold during

his wanderings in our tottering world, one who can never relinquish his faith that the value of life depends on its dignity, not its success." A failure in his past personal and business relationships, Wilhelm displays a penchant for self-pity and suffering that has alienated him from his loved ones. For example, he maintains a bitter relationship with his estranged wife, Margaret, who makes excessive demands for child support because he deserted her. As a youth, Wilhelm also alienated his successful but unsympathetic father, a retired physician, by changing his Jewish patronymic from Adler to Wilhelm in an abortive attempt to become a Hollywood film star—"He had cast off his father's name, and with it his father's opinion of him."

Many critics, including Daniel Weiss and John Jacob Clayton, have analyzed the influence of psychoanalytic thought on Wilhelm's character in *Seize the Day*. Both view Wilhelm as a moral masochist who intentionally goes against his family's wishes out of spite and a desperate need for respect that he feels he has never received. As Weiss has noted, suffering enhances his sense of personal value in that it makes him worthy of love, although narcissism is the price he has had to pay. Psychoanalytic thought similarly pervades Wilhelm's relationship with

Dr. Tamkin, a surrogate father figure and semiliterate psychologist who serves as Wilhelm's destroyer as well as his savior. Although Tamkin urges Wilhelm to "seize the day," encouraging his risky investment in the stock market,—he also leads Wilhelm to distinguish between the "impostor soul" (his socially contrived self) and his real soul, and is responsible for Wilhelm's final enlightenment.

Seize the Day makes such sustained use of water imagery that some critics have placed the work within the Romantic tradition, which often emphasizes the link between water and the emotional life. Throughout the novella, Bellow employs the metaphor of Wilhelm drowning in a society that is already spiritually dead. For example, Wilhelm lives with his father in a hotel for retired people who are waiting to die, refers to himself as a floundering and ungraceful "hippopotamus," and is chronically short of breath when confronting his wife or father. According to Clinton W. Trowbridge, these details convey "an impression throughout the work of a man swimming for his life and, since he is largely unsuccessful, of a man slowly and painfully drowning." At several points in the text, Wilhelm recalls a line from Milton's poem "Lycidas"—"Sunk though he be beneath the wat'ry floor." Reflecting Wilhelm's willing acceptance of death as well as an opposing wish to return to the womb, this refrain culminates at the novel's conclusion in a tenuous sense of rebirth. After Dr. Adler rejects Wilhelm's final plea for financial assistance in a steam bath in the hotel's health club—"I want nobody on my back. Get off! And I give you the same advice, Wilky. Carry nobody on your back"—Wilhelm attends a stranger's funeral and finds himself grieving for the common lot of humanity, not out of choice but because he has been stripped of all material ties. At this point Bellow's water imagery intensifies. Imagining that the dead man has drowned, Wilhelm is finally able to breathe, having killed the impostor soul and achieved a sense of love and pity not just for himself but for humanity as a whole. The final scene, according to John Jacob Clayton, is "a symbolic rebirth out of water."

Critics generally concur that *Seize the Day* remains one of Bellow's principal achievements in the short fiction form. Due to its compressed imagery and density of meaning, the novella continues to evoke diverse critical readings, including analyses of the book's religious allusions and poetic aspects. Although some critics initially expressed disappointment at the apparent hopelessness of Wilhelm's situation at the end of *Seize the Day,* most have come to agree that Wilhelm gains a better understanding of himself and appreciation of others through his loss, and will go on to some sort of self-determined action. According to Clinton W. Trowbridge: "Bellow, far from having depicted the defeat of man, has given us one of his most moving accounts of the conditions under which he can hope to be victorious."

PRINCIPAL WORKS

Dangling Man (novel) 1944

The Victim (novel) 1947
The Adventures of Augie March (novel) 1953
*Seize the Day (short stories, novella, and play) 1956
Henderson the Rain King (novel) 1959
Recent American Fiction (lecture) 1963
Herzog (novel) 1964
The Last Analysis (play) 1964
The Last Analysis (novel) 1965
Like You're Nobody: The Letters of Louis Gallo to Bellow, 1961-1962, plus "Oedipus-Schmoedipus, the Story That Started It All" (letters and short story) 1966
**Under the Weather (plays) 1966; also produced as *The Bellow Plays,* 1966
Mosby's Memoirs, and Other Stories (stories) 1968
Mr. Sammler's Planet (novel) 1970
The Portable Bellow (miscellany) 1974
Humboldt's Gift (novel) 1975
Nobel Lecture (lecture) 1976
To Jerusalem and Back (memoir) 1976
The Dean's December (novel) 1982
Him with His Foot in His Mouth, and Other Stories (short stories) 1984
More Die of Heartbreak (novel) 1987
The Bellarosa Connection (novella) 1989
A Theft (novella) 1989
Something to Remember Me By (novellas) 1991

*Contains the one-act play *The Wrecker.*

**Includes the one-act plays *Out from Under, A Wen,* and *Orange Soufflé.*

CRITICISM

Herbert Gold   (essay date 17 November 1956)

[*Gold is an American novelist, short story writer, and critic noted for his sensitive treatment of modern American life and social problems. In the enthusiastic review below, Gold characterizes* Seize the Day *as "a story which will be explained, expounded, and argued."*]

For the best of all reasons, **Seize the Day,** a collection comprising a novella, three short stories and a one-act play, is not an interim book between Saul Bellow's **The Adventures of Augie March** and his next novel. The reason is this: the long title story is a great one.

Seize the Day presents the essence of the life of Tommy Wilhelm, a yearning, youngish, middle-aged flop, crowded by New York, stunned by his dead marriage, manipulated by a crazy, fraudulent psychologist, under attack from his sly and malevolent old father, grasping wildly for significant relationships with himself and with others. He needs money, he needs love, he needs his own strength, and he seems at first to be sinking hopelessly in retreat from himself within the dense sea of Manhattan. Then abruptly the action turns around, and with the surge of magic which occasionally happens both in real life and in fiction, Tommy Wilhelm moves that redeeming vital inch from pity of self to perception of self. He weeps for a stranger's death.

The story presents an extension of Bellow's view of contemporary life, integrated here in a desperately focussed action. We recognize his submissive, adaptable, strangely resilient hero; we find again the cagy, brilliant fraud who nuttily speaks the truth; the drama springs up within the blurring, blunting, bracing maelstrom of big-city life. Bellow is not much given to the besetting sin of American writers, a moral self-indulgence which we might call "Spokesmanship." Or when he falls, he falls with an indignant wit. Like Doctor Pep, Doctor Tamkin in this story is a stew of health and madness. As close to a spokesman as Bellow allows himself, Tamkin speaks from his own odd stance:

> Now, Wilhelm, I'm trying to do you some good. I want to tell you, don't marry suffering. Some people do. They get married to it, and sleep and eat together, just as husband and wife. If they go with joy they think it's adultery. . . .

The truth of Tamkin's rant is demonstrated by real action (not symbolic action) in the life of Tommy Wilhelm.

The story, though an exhausting one and as close as *The Death of Ivan Ilyitch* to our primary experience, like Tolstoy's story escapes self-pity by the triumph of perception. A superficial reading might stimulate self-pity; the deeper sense of the story lies in something indicated by the energy of Bellow's prose in addition to the climactic incident itself—there is a redeeming power in self-knowledge, and a redeeming pleasure.

Purged of hopelessness, Wilhelm can go on to some sort of self-determination in the world. A variety of stoicism seems to be emerging. A confrontation of the self can save us in a fragmented society—but this is an active, watchful stoicism which can do its part in putting the fragments back together.

> **Seize the Day** gives contemporary literature a story which will be explained, expounded, and argued, but about which a final reckoning can be made only after it ripples out in the imagination of the generations of readers to come. I suspect that it is one of the central stories of our day.
>
> —*Herbert Gold*

Seize the Day enables us to take another look at Bellow's career. It represents an important integration of the dense unity of *The Victim* and the wide-ranging playfulness and pathos of *The Adventures of Augie March.* Bellow is working now with the born storyteller's directness. Incident does not distract from the underlying action; Tommy

Wilhelm has the hallucinating fictional reality which Augie March sometimes sideslipped by irony. Irony is never used here to mask emotion; the humor bites without turning us away. The climactic scenes—with the father and at the end—are met climactically and feed each other. The value of Gertrude Stein's famous judgment, "Remarks are not literature," can be acknowledged in relation to the massive building, controlling and passion of this story. The rich play of incident and scene serves dramatic rather than symbolic purpose. The tale is of a magnificent piece. (pp. 435-36)

Seize the Day gives contemporary literature a story which will be explained, expounded, and argued, but about which a final reckoning can be made only after it ripples out in the imagination of the generations of readers to come. I suspect that it is one of the central stories of our day. (p. 436)

> *Herbert Gold, "The Discovered Self," in* The Nation, *New York, Vol. 183, No. 20, November 17, 1956, pp. 435-36.*

Brendan Gill   (essay date 5 January 1957)

[*Gill is an American film and drama critic who has reviewed books for* The New Yorker *since 1936. In the following review, Gill offers a mixed appraisal of* Seize the Day.]

Once upon a time, a lady showed a philosopher a pleated skirt, and he exclaimed with delight, "The things that could be more and are contented to be less!" In *The Adventures of Augie March,* Saul Bellow was busy being more; in the newly published *Seize the Day,* he is contented to be less. The book is made up of a novella, three short stories, and a one-act play. (p. 69)

The novella, from which the book takes its title, tells of a day in the life of middle-aged man named Tommy Wilhelm, who has not so much failed as never made good. Wilhelm is big, handsome, blowzy, and hollow. Son of a rich father, he is separated from his wife and children and is constantly being dunned for their support; is out of work; is without prospects; and is risking his last few hundred dollars in speculation on the commodities market. He has reached the point where he can do nothing but thrash about in his perplexity, try to borrow money from his irritated father, and pray. "Let me out of my trouble," he begs God. "Let me out of my thoughts, and let me do something better with myself. For all the time I have wasted I am very sorry. Let me out of this clutch and into a different life. For I am all balled up. Have mercy."

But God does not hear him and his father continues to rebuff him, and his speculation leads to disaster. We catch our final glimpse of Wilhelm at the coffin of a stranger, in a funeral home he has entered by accident, sobbing his heart out over his plight and yet feeling rather better than usual. For the truth is that Wilhelm is a slob and *Seize the Day* is that unlooked-for triumph, the portrait of a slob. It is a tribute to Mr. Bellow's genius that we consent to go trudging knee-deep through all the accumulated dreariness of Wilhelm's life to perceive this not very majestic truth. In *Seize the Day* Mr. Bellow has created a hell of gross, talkative, ill-dressed nonentities, offensive to look at; offensive to listen to, offensive to touch. But it is a true hell and its denizens are very much alive; against all our wishes, we look at them, listen to them, and reach out and touch them. Someday Mr. Bellow is going to tire of writing sentences like "He had Yankee pot roast, purple cabbage, potatoes, a big slice of watermelon, and two cups of coffee" and "The dead man was gray-haired. He had two large waves of gray hair at the front. But he was not old. His face was long, and he had a bony nose, slightly, delicately twisted. His brows were raised as though he had sunk into the final thought. Now at last he was with it." Someday Mr. Bellow is going to abandon his hell of odious and uninteresting people, and, oh, how willingly we are going to follow him! (pp. 69-70)

Brendan Gill, "Long and Short," in The New Yorker, *Vol. XXXII, No. 46, January 5, 1957, pp. 66, 69-70.*

Daniel Weiss   (essay date Fall 1962)

[*In the essay below, Weiss examines the influence of Freudian psychoanalysis on Bellow's novella.*]

Saul Bellow's novel *Seize the Day* represents, I believe, an extraordinary contribution to the relationship between father and son as a theme in fiction. The father-son relationship is an area of experience which the artist shares to a larger degree than he does any other kind of experience with the cultural historian, the moral philosopher, and more recently with the psychologist, particularly the psychoanalyst. (p. 277)

I should like to consider, with what I trust is neurotic sensibility, Saul Bellow's *Seize the Day* as a novel in which the character and the action of the central figure, Tommy Wilhelm, are determined by and represent the neurotic conflict between instinctual cravings and outwardly determined frustrations. The conflict between father and son is central to the novel, but its repressed content is latent throughout until the last moment, when, as Freud describes it, "the repression is shattered." The novel is interesting, too, in that without deserting the psychoanalytic point of view one can apprehend in the action certain cultural implications. When I finished reading *Seize the Day* I was struck by what appeared to me to be the premeditated delineations of the character and psychopathology of Tommy Wilhelm. But I was equally struck by the unpremeditated affinities of both Tommy Wilhelm and his father with Kafka father and son as they appear in Kafka's "Letter to his Father" [in *Dearest Father*]. It is this affinity that suggests an extension of the neurotic problem—the outwardly determined frustration which is the product not of a single cultural milieu, but of an encounter between two conflicting milieus.

Kafka, writing in the cosmopolitan city of Prague, lives, in the "Letter to his Father," in a psychological ghetto, stoning himself with marvellous, and I think semiconscious, irony, for the heresies of sensitivity, physical infirmity, and cultural breadth in the presence of the father whose insensitivity, brutality, and intolerance Kafka

praises as the virtues of a patriarch. In the "Letter" we see in its most acute form what must invariably take place within any cultural minority: the transitional generation arrested as Kafka says, "without forebears or progeny," between the microcosm and the macrocosm. In Kafka's case, because he was both a neurotic and an artist, we see him draining his genius white to justify his father's ways to himself, at the mercy of repressed infantile phantasies in which the father must be conciliated at all costs. The family situation which we can infer from Kafka's writings is typical of Jewish culture in its struggle to survive. The patriarch dies a hard death, adapting himself to the urban wilderness by shedding his Yahwistic dignity in favor of a religious concern for business. And the matriarch, whose only weapon against the hostile, un-Jewish environment, against perhaps the now predatory father, is tenderness and submission, teaches these questionable virtues to her over-protected, breast-loving children. Kafka himself describes it:

> Mother unconsciously played the part of a beater during a hunt. Even if your method of upbringing might in some unlikely case have set me on my own feet by means of producing defiance, dislike, or even hate in me, Mother cancelled that out again by kindness . . . and I was again driven back into your orbit . . . one could always get protection from her, but only in relation to you.

In *Seize the Day* when his father forgets the date of his wife's death, Tommy Wilhelm, who has asked the question disingenuously, thinks, bitterly, "what year was it! As though he didn't know the year, the month, the day, the very hour of his mother's death."

Kafka wrote to his father about his father's Judaism:

> Later, as a boy, I could not understand how with the insignificant scrap of Judaism you yourself possessed, you could reproach me for not (if for no more than the sake of piety, as you put it) making an effort to cling to a similar insignificant scrap. . . . And so there was the religious material that was handed on to me, to which may be added at most the outstretched hand pointing to "the sons of the millionaire Fuchs," who were in the synagogue with their father at the high holidays.

Tommy Wilhelm

> Often prayed in his own manner. He did not go to the synagogue but he would occasionally perform certain devotions, according to his feelings. Now he reflected, in Dad's eyes I am the wrong kind of Jew. He doesn't like the way I act. Only he is the right kind of Jew.

Kafka describes to his father the answer he gave him when the son asked his father for sexual advice.

> It is not easy to judge the answer you gave me then; on the one hand, there was after all, something staggeringly frank, in a manner of speaking, primeval about it. . . But its real meaning, which sank into my mind even then, but only much later came partly to the surface of my consciousness, was this: what you were advising me

to do was, after all, in your opinion at that time, the filthiest thing possible. . . . The main thing was . . . that you remained outside your own advice, a married man, a pure man, exalted above these things.

Similarly when Wilhelm asks his father for advice, the old man's impulse is to degrade the son in his own eyes. One of Wilhelm's numerous failures was in his job as a salesman. Dr. Adler asks him why he left the job.

"Since you have to talk and can't let it alone, tell the truth. Was there a scandal—a woman?"

Wilhelm fiercely defended himself. "No, Dad, there wasn't any woman. I told you how it was."

"Maybe it was a man, then," the old man said wickedly.

(pp. 280-83)

These are parallels only between Kafka's autobiographical letter and *Seize the Day,* and they exhibit a cultural frame of reference, dramatically abnormalized, within which one can consider the work of either writer. But when we turn to comparisons between *Seize the Day* and Kafka's fiction we are aware of only a pivotal connection—the mutilated relationship between sons and fathers. Kafka's grey Petrouchka-like protagonist and his two-dimensional, expressionistic backgrounds expand into the extremely dimensionalized Tommy Wilhelm and his crowded hour on upper Broadway. But the psychic conflict is identical, and the outcome, while it would not be one Kafka would have chosen, is at least Kafkan.

The desolation of Tommy Wilhelm is a very carefully determined event whose determinants are only explainable in psychoanalytic terms, and whose esthetic achievement is only valid if we accept the somewhat invidious precondition for enjoyment Freud proposes. In Kafka the neurotic is in the artist, not in the work. The work itself is delivered over, in a manner of speaking, to the controlled insanity of Kafka's world; the interpretive potential is manifold. In *Seize the Day* the neurotic is in the work—and the interpretive potential is singular, a matter of reconciling the events in the novel to the character of Tommy Wilhelm, of explaining the manifest in terms of the repressed.

The day Saul Bellow seizes on which to describe Tommy Wilhelm is the day of one of Wilhelm's many undoings, distinguished from the rest only by the lyric, and poetically desirable revelation purchased at the price of everything he owns.

On the day in question Wilhelm has been refused money and love by his father; his wife badgers him for more money; the bogus psychologist Dr. Tamkin has power of attorney over Wilhelm's remaining funds, which have presumably been invested in lard and rye futures. The lard and rye fall; Wilhelm is wiped out, and Tamkin disappears. Wilhelm's reaction to these mis-adventures is best described as despair, tempered at the very outset by resignation, neurotic fatalism.

But at the same time, since there were depths in Wilhelm not unsuspected by himself, he received

a suggestion from some remote element in his thoughts that the business of life, the real business—to carry his peculiar burden, to feel shame and impotence, to taste these quelled tears—the only important business, the highest business, was being done. Maybe the making of mistakes expressed the very purpose of his life and the essence of his being here. Maybe he was supposed to make them and suffer from them and suffer from them on this earth. . . .

How had this happened, but how had his Hollywood career begun? It was not because of Maurice Venice, who turned out to be a pimp. It was because Wilhelm himself was ripe for the mistake. His marriage too had been like that. Through such decisions somehow his life had taken form. And so, from the moment when he tasted the peculiar flavor of fatality in Dr. Tamkin, he could no longer keep back the money.

The broadest psychoanalytic category within which Tommy Wilhelm operates is that of the moral masochist, the victim, for whom suffering is a *modus vivendi,* a means of self-justification. This aspect of Tommy Wilhelm is the most explicitly realized level of his character. But it deserves closer study as the basis for other, more subtle elements in the novel. The person to whom Wilhelm is masochistically attached is, of course, his father, Dr. Adler, before whom he exhibits his helplessness. And it is equally apparent, even to Wilhelm, that, with individual differences, the other figures on whose mercy he throws himself, are in a declining series, fathers—Maurice Venice, the Rojax Corporation, Tamkin, Mr. Perls, and Mr. Rappaport. (pp. 283-85)

What determined Wilhelm's fixation on this all-powerful father in the past is supplied in the novel to the extent that we can reconstruct his childhood—the love and protection of his mother and the stern, sadistic disciplinarianism of his father—followed by his mother's death at the moment of his first failure in Hollywood. The death of one parent, in fact, any intimate bereavement induces a retreat from adult effectiveness toward dependence, and a heightened dependence on the surviving parent. Dr. Adler was pressed, willy nilly, into service as the mother in addition to his role as the father. But Dr. Adler's tyrannical, uncompromising character has anticipated what might in Wilhelm's life have been a momentary lapse from effectiveness into fixer regressive patterns, has rendered his son incapable of independence. In this sense, a psychoanalytic irony enters into the description of the relationship between father and son, in that the doctor's forthright disgust with his son's weaknesses is a disgust with a situation of which he himself is the author. There is more truth than Dr. Adler is aware of in his "What a Wilky he had given to the world!" But, we can reasonably argue, Wilhelm is not always unsuccessful. He has assumed adult responsibilities over twenty years of his life, and until the ultimate day of his latest failure, he has not invoked his father's help. However, we must consider that as a neurotic personality, Wilhelm is not completely *hors de combat;* he is crippled, not dead, and his ego, besieged from without and betrayed from within, is still in command. He knows a hawk from a handsaw.

What the day of the novel exhibits is the phenomenon known as traumatophilia. The neurotic calendar is crowded with grotesque anniversaries, the observance of which offer a certain relief to the mechanism of repression, worn out in the service of the ego. The consciousness must be allowed from time to time to participate in the unconscious strivings of the individual, as Ferenczi suggests, to "equalize" the effects of the original painful experience throughout the psyche. It is the return of the repressed. In Wilhelm it is the masochistic necessity to fail, to be destroyed at the hands of the punishing father, in order, under the terms of the moral masochistic commitment, to retain his love, and, in less obvious ways, to memorialize certain events in the past.

What might save Wilhelm from a complete debacle on this particular day would be his insistence that Tamkin withdraw from the market before the lard and rye drop. Tamkin agrees reluctantly to pull out, but Wilhelm then allows his money to ride. Certain fatalities intervene and paralyze his will. The first and most apparent is his father's cold, overt hostility, and the passionate review of the past that has taken place in Wilhelm's mind in the morning. A second recollection involves Wilhelm's distress that his mother's grave has been vandalized, and that his father cannot remember the date of her death. With this renewed grief over his mother's death Wilhelm's old dependence returns, displaced now to his dependence on Tamkin. "Poor Mother! How I disappointed her," he thinks, as he comes down for breakfast. And his next act unconsciously reveals the renewal of his own bereavement. He returns, as Otto Fenichel suggests that bereaved people return, to an oral phase of his development. Wilhelm must suckle. "He turned to the Coca-Cola machine. He swallowed hard at the Coke bottle and coughed over it, but he ignored his coughing, for he was still thinking, his eyes upcast and his lips closed behind his hand." It is a caricatured representation of the nursing child.

An external contribution to the significance of the day appears in the form of an actual anniversary. The month is late September, and it is, as old Rappaport reminds Wilhelm, the eve of *Yom Kippur,* the Jewish holiday immediately following the Jewish New Year. *Yom Kippur* is the Day of Atonement for the Jews, when one makes formal acknowledgment for one's sins. *Yiskor,* which falls on *Yom Kippur,* is the service at which one remembers and prays for the dead. "Well, you better hurry up if you expect to say *Yiskor* for your parents," old Rappaport tells Wilhelm. And Wilhelm remembers his mother's burial, and his father's indifference, and his having paid for having prayers sung for her. A moment later he allows Tamkin to let their combined investment ride to its loss.

I propose now to deal with Wilhelm's moral masochism, its causes and symptoms and contributions to his traits of character. Freud's first concept of the masochistic personality—the moral masochist specifically, to differentiate him from the sexual masochist, for whom sexual perversion is the outward enacting of his drive—was based on an intra-personal conflict. The original sadistic impulse directed at the parent, recoiled to become parentally derived super-ego, which commanded certain self-sacrifices as the penalty for aggressive phantasies. Thus Freud conceived of Dostoievsky's psychic epilepsy and gambling mania as a self-determined punishment for having willed the father's death. From this concept arises the accepted notion that self-degradation is simply the mirror image of hate. But though this concept falls short of explaining the dramatic conflict in Wilhelm's character, it requires coordination rather than replacement. Part of Wilhelm's character, (his gambling almost immediately suggests itself) is explained, but the concept does not completely explain his relationship with his father, although, as we shall see, it makes finally a major contribution to the end of the novel.

Bernhard Berliner in his essay, "On Some Psychodynamics of Masochism" [in *Psychoanalytic Quarterly* XVI, 1947], while accepting Freud's motivational basis for masochism (guilt, need for punishment) describes moral masochism, not as a pathological way of hating, but as a "pathological way of loving." It is not, as Freud described it, an intra-personal problem, but one involving an inter-personal relationship. "In all cases the disturbance of the interpersonal relationship leads to and is maintained by a peculiar character formation. Masochism is a character neurosis." The subject

> relives and re-enacts in interpersonal relations a submissive devotion to and need for love of a hating or rejecting love-object, . . . originally a parent or a preferred sibling or some other unfriendly person of his childhood, and who lives in his superego. It is the superego that keeps the original situation alive through transference to any suitable person or set of circumstances in later age.
>
> (pp. 285-88)

The ultimate sacrifice of the moral masochist to the love-object accounts for his greatest paradox, his perverse refusal to "please" the parent in any rational sense of the word. The masochist identifies himself with the hating love-object. He turns against himself, not his own sadism but the sadism of the parent. His guilt becomes the guilt the hating parent should feel if his cruelties are unjust. Since the parent cannot be wrong, the child must then feel guilty for him. He must be the bad child who deserves such chastisement. Turned against the world, these perversely "good" actions can be criminal, a psychopathic flouting of the law.

> To accommodate a hating person he may make himself as unlovable as he feels that parent wants him to be. He may deny his good qualities, or his intelligence, often to pseudo-imbecility . . . He is stigmatized with unwantedness and displays his stigma as his bid for affection.

As a person the moral masochist has a weak ego, is dependent and love seeking, and forms, because of his oral fixation, strong transferences. Unlike the anal-sadistic, compulsive neurotic, who punishes himself for hating, the masochist wants only to gain love. As Berliner differentiates between them, "The compulsive neurotic is paying imaginary debts, not knowing what the real debt was; the masochist is presenting an old, unpaid bill for affection."

Using this as our point of departure let us re-enter the world of Tommy Wilhelm. On this day of days his whole personality has been given over to an exhibition of his neurotic symptoms. And the external world obliges by offering him a realistic basis for such an exhibition. Systematically and seriatim the more-or-less loved objects from his present punish him—his father, his estranged wife, and Tamkin. Their betrayals evoke the memories of earlier betrayals and humiliations, finding their ultimate source in the original mistreatment by his father. To illustrate in a single example the relation between his masochistic submission to the father and the oral nature of the masochism I will take up one of the *leitmotifs* of Wilhelm's thoughts.

Thinking indignantly about his father's self-love, Wilhelm recalls from his college literature course the line from Shakespeare's sonnet 73—"love that well which thou must leave ere long."

> At first he thought it referred to his father, but then he understood that it was for himself, rather. *He* should love that well. "This thou perceivest, which makes thy love more strong."

The memory of this line reminds him of the anthology (Lieder and Lovett's *British Poetry and Prose*) and with it another poem he loved—"Lycidas," the line he remembers being "Sunk though he be beneath the wat'ry floor."

Later in the course of the morning, when, arising from his argument with his father, he has decided that it is his "peculiar burden to feel shame and impotence," the lines from "Lycidas" again return, this time coupled with a line from Shelley's "Ode to the West Wind," "that dirge of the dying year." The line is "I fall upon the thorns of life! I bleed!"

> And though he had raised himself above Mr. Perls and his father because they adored money, still they were called to act energetically and this was better than to yell and cry, pray and beg, poke and blunder and go by fits and starts and fall upon the thorns of life. And finally sink beneath that watery floor—would that be tough luck, or would it be good riddance?

The fourth poem comes to Wilhelm when Tamkin reminds him that he was an actor. Wilhelm remembers a job he had as a film extra. He had to blow a bagpipe. He "blew and blew and not a sound came out . . . He fell sick with the flu after that and still suffered sometimes from chest weakness."

Margaret nursed him.

> They had had two rooms of furniture which was later seized. She sat on the bed and read to him . . .
>
> > Come then, Sorrow!
> > Sweetest Sorrow!
> > Like an own babe I nurse thee on my breast!
>
> Why did he remember that? Why?

Of the four fragments the line from the sonnet is the one Wilhelm most immediately apprehends. Throughout the day Wilhelm's thoughts about his father's age and immi-

nent death undergo revealing vicissitudes. He excuses his father's self love as the fear of death. He reproaches his father, at the same time, for ignoring the fact that he himself must also die. But his most moving thought is what his father's death will mean for him.

"When he dies, I'll be robbed, like. I'll have no more father."

> "Of course, of course, I love him. My father. My mother—" As he said this there was a great pull at the very center of his soul. When a fish strikes the line you feel the live force in your hand.

His feelings about his father are in apposition to the sonnet in which the older man calls attention to his approaching death, not to arouse compassion, but to impress the younger man (presumably the sonnet is addressed to a young man) that he faces a great loss.

Even if we disallow the homoerotic nature of Shakespeare's sonnet and its bearing on Wilhelm's feeling about his father, we find, in the line from 'Lycidas,' an overdetermination of the homoerotic element, and in its combination with the line from Shelley's poem (the cruelty with which Shelley's father treated him, Shelley's doctrine of nonviolence, and his actual drowning reinforce the line of poetry) a willingness to be the sacrificial victim. Wilhelm has "fallen on the thorns of life," and the prospect of sinking beneath the ocean's watery floor is not such a distressing one. It is consistent with Wilhelm's masochistic character that the line has come to mean for him the return to the womb, the death instinct that is a component of masochism. Implicit, too, in the context of the novel, the lines suggest that achievement of superiority which is the bitter consolation of the victim, although Wilhelm makes an ironic distinction between his superiority to Mr. Perls and his father, and his abjection.

The fourth poem, the lullaby, and its autobiographical context, stands in relation to the first three as symptom stands to repressed aim. The sonnet names the object of Wilhelm's masochistic strivings; "Lycidas" and the "Ode to the West Wind" describe the wished for torment and oblivion, falling on the thorns and sinking. The lullaby and its context indicate the mental and physical character-components of the masochist.

The suckling dependence of the moral masochist is symbolically described here as well as the frustrations that accompany deprivation. Wilhelm's orality has expressed itself in character-formation in that he has been attracted to acting, speech being an acceptable oral survival. But his career as an actor was a failure, and the memory of Hollywood that returns to him returns him also to the roots of the failure. He is blowing a false bagpipe, "blew and blew, and not a sound came out." Bagpipe as breast and sound as milk are perfect correlatives. Wilhelm is "sucking a dry teat." He has lost his mother, who, because of his peculiar needs, epitomized the only generosity he can ever know. From his father, to whom he has attached himself, he can only draw the sour milk of sorrow, the masochistic substitute for real nourishment. His wife, Margaret, also figures here, nursing him, as Wilhelm's immediate substitute for his mother, but along with his father, equally unsatisfactory; Sorrow—"Like an own babe I nurse thee on my breast!"—is Wilhelm's baby. The thought of his mother drives him to the Coke machine; the ill-treatment of his father compels him to eat not only his own breakfast, but a large part of his father's. Denied any overt love on his father's part, Wilhelm works out a primitive solution; he eats from his father's plate.

> Wilhelm understood he was being put on notice and did not express his opinion. He ate and ate. He did not hurry but kept putting food on his plate until he had gone through the muffins and his father's strawberries and then some pieces of bacon that were left.

Another element remains to be explained in connection with the last poem Wilhelm remembers. It is his "chest weakness" which has never left him, the sense of suffocation he feels at critical moments during the day, especially at those moments when either his father or his wife is either rejecting him or making demands on him. Both are situations which cause anxiety connected with oral fixation. The one, the father's refusal, involves a denial of nourishment, a traumatic weaning; the other, Margaret's sadistic demands for money, is a projection of Wilhelm's own insistent need on to the woman. The flow is reversed; the woman drains the man. For the orally fixated man, orgastic discharge perverts the unconsciously infantile relationship between himself and the woman.

> Well, Dad, she hates me. I feel she's strangling me. I can't catch my breath. She just has fixed herself on me to kill me. She can do it at long distance. One of these days I'll be struck down by suffocation or apoplexy because of her. I just can't catch my breath.

Throughout the day Wilhelm suffocates in the presence of his tormentors. But this is not so much a "chest weakness" as it is a conversion hysteria, Wilhelm's repressed ideas expressing themselves in physical symptoms. Respiratory disorders are frequently associated with acute anxieties, centering mainly, according to Otto Fenichel, around "the repressed idea of castration," and the "reaction to separation from the mother." Wilhelm has reason to fear both; his sense of suffocation is induced by both. A further insight into the hysterical nature of his behaviour is afforded by the correlation of his dramatic acting out of the strangulation; and the phantasy he has woven about Margaret.

> "Strange, Father? I'll show you what she's like." Wilhelm took hold of his broad throat with brown-stained fingers and bitten nails and began to choke himself.

(Note even in the "brown-stained fingers" and the "bitten nails," the additional stigmata of Wilhelm's oral frustrations.) Fenichel identifies "irrational emotional reactions" as analogues to hysterical attacks. They serve to "reactivate infantile types of object relationships" when some associatively connected experience occurs. They involve an hysterical introversion, a turning from reality to phantasy.

> However, hysterical 'acting' is not only 'introversion' but is directed toward an audience. It is an attempt to induce others to participate in the daydreaming, probably to obtain some reassurance against anxiety and guilt feelings (or to evoke punishment for the same reason) . . . It is an attempt to return from introversion to reality, a kind of travesty of the process underlying artistic productivity.

When Wilhelm turns from his father to find a kinder father, his choice of object is determined for him by the same orality that governs his relations with his father. But with this difference, that as a singular individual his biological father must frustrate any preconceived phantasy on Wilhelm's part as to what his father should be to him. Wilhelm's masochistic submission to Dr. Adler represents the extent of his compromise. This is not so when he is free to exercise his phantasy and find in the real world the father who suits him. Dr. Tamkin (and Bellow invests him with a comic-grotesque unreality) is the answer to Wilhelm's dreams, and I will limit by discussion of him at this point to his appearance in Wilhelm's phantasy-life.

In his retreat to orality, Wilhelm returns to the infantile belief in the omnipotent parent, who grants in return for doglike trust and acceptance, full protection and endless beneficence. Wilhelm describes himself when he describes his beloved dog Scissors to his father,

> He's an Australian sheep dog. They usually have one blank or whitish eye which gives a misleading look, but they're the gentlest dogs and have unusual delicacy about eating or talking.

Tamkin is magic; he reads Wilhelm's mind. He is what [Otto Fenichel in his *Psychoanalytic Theory of Neurosis*, 1945] calls a "magic helper," whose relationship with Wilhelm, Karl Abraham describes [in *Selected Papers of Psychoanalysis*, 1954] in these terms.

> Some people [oral sucking types] are dominated by the belief that there will always be some kind person—a representative of the mother, of course—to care for them and to give them everything they need. This optimistic belief condemns them to inactivity.

As Wilhelm thinks about him, "That the doctor cared about him pleased him. This was what he craved, that someone should care about him, wish him well."

I have considered so far those qualities in Tommy Wilhelm which represent him as a willing sacrifice to fate, and indeed this would seem to be the only side of Tommy Wilhelm to consider. His last appearance, all alone beweeping his outcast state at the bier of a stranger, would seem to be his last and most satisfying submission to the austere, intractable father-image which dominates his being.

But in allowing this as the basis for **Seize the Day** we are ignoring an important portion of the statement I had considered axiomatic to the enjoyment of psychological literature: that the struggle within the soul of the hero "must end, not with the downfall of the hero, but with that of one of the contending impulses, in other words, with a renunciation."

Tommy Wilhelm's downfall, at the end of the novel, is not a downfall in the acute singular sense of the word as in classical tragedy. In the timeless world of Wilhelm's psyche the downfall has been a *fait accompli* almost from the beginning. The failure in the stock market is its latest and most vivid instance. Likewise the act of renunciation, the outcome of an inner conflict between opposing impulses, has taken place before, and now finds its perfect expression and, on an emotive level, recognizes itself beside the old man's coffin.

> Oh, Father, what do I ask of you? What'll I do about the kids—Tommy, Paul? My children. And Olive? My dear! Why, why, why—you must protect me against that devil, who wants my life. If you want it, then kill me. Take, take it, take it from me. . . .

> The flowers and lights fused ecstatically in Wilhelm's blind, wet eyes; the heavy, sea-like music came up to his ears. It poured into him where he had hidden himself in the center of the crowd by the great and happy oblivion of tears. He heard it, and sank deeper than sorrow, through torn sobs and cries toward the consummation of his heart's ultimate need.

The symphonic orchestration of such an ending must presuppose something beside an unchecked drift toward submission. There must be a crisis, a conflict, symphonic in its nature. At one point, before this resolution has been achieved, the brasses must have risen up against the violins and been, not without a struggle, silenced.

I have dealt thus far with the character of Tommy Wilhelm at its furthest remove from effective, mature activity. In doing so I have isolated the level of regression descriptive of such abject helplessness, the position of the infant at its mother's breast. But there are no "pure" strains of orality past actual infancy, while Wilhelm is denied, perhaps permanently, any successful adult accomplishment—the masculine self-sufficiency and self-esteem, the ability to have good relationships and pursue realistic rather than phantastic schemes for survival—his helplessness is more than the helplessness of a strong man caged than a weak man at liberty. To see him otherwise is to deny him his quality as a protagonist and to dismiss him as Freud dismisses the "full-blown and strange neurosis. . . . We call the physician and deem the person in question unsuitable as a stage figure."

What I must deal with now, are those traits of character and neurotic symptoms, which belong, in psychoanalysis, to the oral and anal-sadistic types of regression. To this aspect of Wilhelm's personality such concepts as Freud's original theory of masochism are more germane. We will deal with tendencies in which, although it is repressed, aggressive hostility takes the place of submissive exhibitions of suffering. Every phase of a child's development has its erotic and aggressive subdivisions. At the mother's breast the mouth is the pleasurable organ and suckling the means to that pleasure. With its first teeth, and the experience of weaning, come the first feelings of deprivation and frustration. The so-called biting stage sets in, in which the infant displays ambivalent feelings toward objects, compounded of aggressions against them and a wish to eat them. The withheld breast becomes an enemy to be taken by force. The old complicities of mother and child become a battle between the hungry infant and the alien world. At the same time another source of pleasure and aggression su-

pervene in the form of the anal period. The feces, the first objective products of the body, become a source of pleasure in their retention or elimination and, for the same reason, a source of power and aggression.

Because of the inauguration at a very early age of the discipline of bowel training and the overt disapproval of the infantile pleasure in fecal play, anal erotism is regularly repressed. In its place appear the aggressive qualities connected with bowel discipline—the "stool pedantry" Ferenczi describes. To these pregenital sources of pleasure and power, psychoanalysis attributes a whole system of orifice psychology. Good suckling and good weaning, good evacuation and good discipline are thought to constitute the basis for good work habits and good character traits in the mature human being. If, for a multiplicity of reasons, one or any of these stages is accompanied by a frustration or trauma, or if it offered a great deal of satisfaction, or if the stage following brought with it pain instead of pleasure, a fixation takes place. Anal-oral fixations survive in adult life as character traits and neurotic symptoms. But because the mouth can still retain its primacy as a pleasurable orifice—as in eating and speaking and kissing, these functions need not undergo repression to the same extent as the anal component of infantile sexuality. (pp. 289-98)

Tommy Wilhelm's aggressions are more inhibited, necessarily, than his masochistic bids for love. As distorted as they are, his gestures of submission achieve a certain level of completion. Hi aggressions are literally choked off, turned aside, or rendered as opposites of themselves.

Dr. Adler lives in his tight, tidy, old man's world of money saved. He has gone into his old age retaining everything, "a fine old scientist, clean and immaculate." His entire philosophy of life is costive, parsimonious. Love means expenditure and he cannot give it. His anal-sadism reveals itself in his cruelty to Wilhelm; his coarse suggestion that perhaps it was not a woman who caused Wilhelm's failure in his job, but a man, and his repeated injunction to his son, "I want nobody on my back. Get off!" are graphic revelations of the doctor's own anal preoccupations. "Concentrate on real troubles—fatal sicknesses, accidents."

Poor Wilhelm can only lumber after his father in an ape-like distortion of the thrifty anal character. He has accepted the economic objectives of society but he recognizes them as a form of cruelty, intimately connected in his case with his father. He is incapable of accomplishing the socially acceptable anal traits, the thrift and industry and self-discipline that distinguishes his father. He cannot "retain" money; his retentions, like so many of his other traits, are at an infantile level. His principal character trait is his messiness, his dirt, the barely acceptable substitute for feces.

> A faint grime was left by his fingers on the white of the egg after he had picked away the shell. Dr. Adler saw it with silent repugnance . . . The doctor couldn't bear Wilky's dirty habits. Only once,—and never again, he swore—had he visited his room. Wilhelm, in pajamas and stockings had sat on his bed, drinking gin from a coffee

mug and rooting for the Dodgers on television. . . . The smell of dirty clothes was outrageous.

His playing the stock market is, like his gin rummy, a form of gambling, in which he contrives to lose. Freud, in his "Dostoievsky and Parricide," describes the act of gambling as a compulsive, repetitive act, in which the anal-sadistic hostilities towards a parent are displaced to the gaming table. To make a "killing" at the table (or in the market) is to kill a hated object. But Wilhelm's aggressions are characterized by their abortive quality. He commits, instead, financial suicide.

> For the last few weeks Wilhelm had played gin almost nightly, but yesterday he had felt that he couldn't afford to lose any more. He had never won. Not once.

His pockets are full of "little packets of pills, and crushed cigarette butts and strings of cellophane," and pennies. His hatred of "the world's business" represents merely a diversion from aggressions directed against his father, for whom a large income is the mark of success. "Holy money! Beautiful money! It was getting so that people were feeble minded about everything except money. While if you didn't have it you were a dummy, a dummy!" Wilhelm's speech patterns are interesting as they reveal his oral-anal sadism. He is given to violent, explosive, scatological utterances, in which anal function has been displaced upward. "In certain neurotics," writes Karl Abraham, "speaking is used to express the entire range of instinctual trends . . . every kind of bodily evacuation, including fertilization."

> Too much of the world's business done. Too much falsity. He had various words to express the effect this had on him. Chicken! Unclean! Congestion! he exclaimed in his heart. Rat race! Phony! Murder! Play the game! Buggers!

But Wilhelm exhibits even more pronounced symptoms of repressed hostility, which translate themselves into tics, involuntary physical gestures, which reveal in an abstract movement of the body a repressed impulse. Rage, or sexual excitement, or grief are represented by a gesture. They are, says Fenichel, "an archaic means of communication."

> But Dr. Adler was thinking, why the devil can't he stand still when we're talking? He's either hoisting his pants up and down by the pockets or jittering with his feet. A regular mountain of tics he's getting to be. . .

> Unaware of anything odd in his doing it, for he did it all the time, Wilhelm had pinched out the coal of his cigarette and dropped the butt in his pocket, where there were many more. And as he gazed at his father the little finger of his right hand began to twitch and tremble.

Wilhelm also stammers, a "slight thickness in his speech," especially when he speaks to his father. In this too he reveals his concealed hostilities, the death wish. Stuttering is

> "exacerbated in the presence of prominent or authoritative persons, that is, of paternal figures

against whom the hostility is most intense. . . . Speaking means the uttering of obscene, especially anal words, and, second, an aggressive act directed against the listener."

The most direct form of aggression on Wilhelm's part appears as its opposite, as a reaction formation to Wilhelm's death-wish. It appears as Wilhelm's fear of giving pain and his preoccupation with his Father's death. He remembers explaining to his mother why he does not want to study medicine. "I can't bear hospitals," he tells her. "Besides, I might make a mistake and hurt someone or even kill a patient. I couldn't stand that." He is obsessed with the thought that all his father thinks about is his own death.

> And not only is death on his mind but through money he forces me to think about it, too. It gives him power over me. He forces me that way, he himself, and then he's sore. If he was poor, I could care for him and show it. The way I *could* care, too, if I only had a chance. He'd see how much love and respect I had in me. It would make him a different man too. He'd put his hands on me and give me his blessing.

"When he dies," Wilhelm tells Tamkin, "I'll be robbed, like. I'll have no more father."

It is out of these elements, which we have considered as being to the highest degree ambivalent expressions of love and hate—a wish to preserve, a wish for an omnipotent father and a paranoid fear of an omnipotent father—that we can construct the unconscious process by which Wilhelm comes to his act of renunciation.

When Wilhelm looks at the dead man he sees what his soul has wanted to see all during the terrible day; he sees his father dead. He sees, too, his own death, mirrored in the face of the grey-haired, "proper" looking, but not aged man before him. It is here that the renunciation proper to the psychological drama takes place. Wilhelm gives up his death wish against the father and accepts, but without the masochistic insistence that characterized his earlier courtship of paternal cruelty, his own role as victim.

A few minutes before this he has been standing over the body of his father stretched out on a table in the massage room of the hotel, "the thighs weak, the muscles of the arms had fallen, his throat was creased." He makes a last plea to his father for help, which will include not only money, but understanding. The father, as impatient with his suffering as he is with his dependence, sends him away with an old man's curse.

> "Go away from me now. It's torture for me to look at you, you slob!" cried Dr. Adler. Wilhelm's blood rose up madly, in anger equal to his father's, but then it sank down and left him helplessly captive to misery.

The dead man in his coffin is the symbolic fulfillment of two alternatives—the wish to destroy the hated father and the wish to be destroyed. In giving up his death-wish Wilhelm passes through what amounts to a phylogenetic process by which he is reconciled to his living father. The theme of *Totem and Taboo* is recapitulated here and extended beyond the suggestion that the only good fathers are dead fathers. Karl Abraham writes

> The results of psychoanalysis justify us in coming to the conclusion that it is only when he thinks of him as a dead person, or wishes him to be so, that the son elevates his father to the level of a sun-god. These death phantasies give expression to impulses of hate, hostility and jealousy on the part of the son. They rob the father of his power so that he is in reality helpless and harmless. An omniscient power is then subsequently granted him as a compensation.

But Wilhelm goes beyond this cycle of death and apotheosis. He has accepted Tamkin's existentialism; he no longer wishes for his father's death, can give up his helpless hatred, and with it, his equally hopeless love for this degraded, fragmented man of money.

The broadest cultural implications of *Seize the Day* involve the father's representing symbolically the sadistic, profit-seeking culture, and the son's willingness to be destroyed by it rather than share its heartless infamy, or fight against it.

That this cathartic experience will mark a new beginning for Wilhelm in a fatherless world would be a vain, Dickensian assumption. When we return *Seize the Day* to its coherences as art, its momentary solution is what must satisfy us. That moment of rest, like that moment in Joyce's *Ulysses* when Bloom and Stephen almost recognize their relationship, in which Tommy Wilhelm sees the futilities of his love-hate relationship with his father, is perhaps to be followed by the imperative *da capo* of his neurotic servitude.

Dr. Tamkin, the psychologist, is a problem.

He is a palpable fraud; the realistic hyperbole that envelopes him is hazardous to the realism of the novel. He abuses Wilhelm's confidence and loses his money for him, and yet he is wise, accurate psychologically, and responsible for Wilhelm's final enlightenment. He discusses the "guilt-aggression cycle," as if he had been reading Menninger's essay on character derivatives from the anal phase. He is aware of the relationship between counting as a sadistic activity and killing. He explains the market to Wilhelm in these terms. "You have an obsessed look on your face," he tells Wilhelm, who could easily have an obsessed look on his face, having immediately before been thinking about his father's death. "You have lots of guilt in you."

A transference appears to have been effected. Tamkin has been "treating" Wilhelm "secretly," and Wilhelm has responded to this paternal benevolence by finding himself able to remember his past with more clarity than ever before, "the poems he used to read." More significantly the sadistic homosexual phrase his father had used has shifted to Wilhelm's dependence on Tamkin.

> And Wilhelm realized that he was on Tamkin's back. It made him feel that he had virtually left the ground [a dream symbol for erection] and was riding upon the other man. He was in the air. It was for Tamkin to take the steps.

And Tamkin's advice is irreproachable; it enters the fabric of Wilhelm's mind as his vision of the authentic life. About his marriage Tamkin says.

> "Why do you let her make you suffer so? It defeats the original object in leaving her. Don't play her game. Now, Wilhelm, I'm trying to do you some good. I want to tell you, don't marry suffering. Some people do. They get married to it, and sleep and eat together, just as husband and wife. If they go with joy, they think it's adultery."

"This time," thinks Wilhelm, "the faker knows what he's talking about."

> "The real universe. That's the present moment. The past is no good to us. The future is full of anxiety. Only the present is real—the here and now. Seize the day."

I can only speculate on Tamkin's formal function in the novel, and my speculation leads me invariably beyond the bounds of the novel itself. I conceive of literary psychoanalysis as a truncated form of psychoanalysis. One does not willingly knock on the door of the artist's life. But I can only see in the character of Tamkin—beyond of course his simpler level of function in *Seize the Day*—an ironic portrait of a psychoanalyst and his patient, even to the fact that the patient gives all that he has in order to discover the unprofitable truth about himself. There is much to be said, if we accept this supposition, for the representation of the psychoanalyst as a figure of fun, whom even the patient can think of as being part faker. He combines areas of experience which have hitherto only been combined in comedy—the excremental with the spiritual (Freud's *ecclesia super cloacam*), the facts of life with the phantasies of love—his solemn and costly considerations of the trivial have added to the repertory of the *New Yorker* and *Punch* cartoonist what law and medicine added to the art of Hogarth and Daumier. But whatever Tamkin's extraordinary functions in *Seize the Day* may be, I cannot object to his presence. He is an accessory to the understanding of the novel. (pp. 298-304)

> *Daniel Weiss, "Caliban on Prospero: A Psychoanalytic Study on the Novel, 'Seize the Day', by Saul Bellow," in* American Imago, *Vol. 19, No. 3, Fall, 1962, pp. 277-306.*

Clinton W. Trowbridge   (essay date 1967)

[Trowbridge is an American critic and nonfiction writer. In the following essay, he examines Bellow's water imagery in Seize the Day.*]*

Saul Bellow's *Seize the Day* is one of the most profoundly sad novels to be written since *Tender is the Night*. On this day of reckoning, during the seven hours or so that comprise the action of the novel, all the troubles that constitute the present condition of Wilhelm Adler descend upon him and crush him, leaving him penniless, alone, and in such profound misery that one can hardly imagine his going on. He is, as he says, "at the end of his rope." "This has been one of those days," he says to his wife, "May I never live to go through another like it." We feel that he may not live at all, so great is his misery, so completely has he been destroyed.

Yet if we look more deeply, more accurately, we see that the meaning of the novel only begins here, that beneath this profound and moving sense of despair is the birth of a soul, Wilhelm's, and that Bellow, far from having depicted the defeat of man, has given us one of his most moving accounts of the conditions under which he can hope to be victorious. Wilhelm does not emerge triumphantly out of his troubles; but the very sufferings they cause him have brought his soul into being: Wilhelm's "pretender soul" has died, his "real soul" has been born. It may not live long. Although Bellow takes us no further than the birth, Marcus Klein [in *The Kenyon Review,* Spring 1962] has pointed out that "At the moment of death, his motion is toward existence, the vitality that defines and unites everyone, and his weeping is an acceptance of it and therefore an act of love toward life."

Yet this is by no means obvious. In fact, on a first or even a second reading, the opposite seems to be true. Wilhelm's seemingly deliberate attempts to ruin his own life, his own complete abandonment to tears at the end, both of these seem to point more to a love of death. Only after we have entered Bellow's world, after we have begun to grasp the craft with which this remarkable novel is written, can we understand the truth of Mr. Klein's statement. The concluding paragraph of the novel at first deceives but is finally the crucial one to our understanding of the work:

> The flowers and lights fused ecstatically in Wilhelm's wet eyes; the heavy sea-like music came up to his ears. It poured into him where he had hidden himself in the center of a crowd by the great and happy oblivion of tears. He heard it and sank deeper than sorrow, through torn sobs and cries toward the consummation of his heart's ultimate need.

"That need, the whole of the novel comes to reveal, is the need not to die," writes Marcus Klein. But Wilhelm is drowning. The repeated use of the image only intensifies the force of the metaphor, and it is not until we discover Bellow's attitude toward that state that we can accept Mr. Klein's statement. In fact, only by a study of how water imagery is employed in the whole novel can the paradox, life by drowning, be fully understood.

Human misery is generally the result of one of two things: being in a condition of life that is intolerable or being trapped within a self that creates its own hell. In the modern world the various social agencies aim at alleviating the former, the psychiatrist the latter. But when one is in need of both the social worker and the psychiatrist at the same time, the depths of human misery begin to be seen. Essentially this is Wilhelm's state, and what Bellow is saying is that under such conditions the self that feels these afflictions from within and without must be destroyed. Nothing can be done for it because it defeats its own good.

Wilhelm is a born loser: "After much thought and hesitation and debate he invariably took the course he had rejected innumerable times. Ten such decisions made up the history of his life." Although the conditions of his life are not those that would appeal to the sympathy of a social worker, he is none the less destitute: jobless, homeless, and penniless. On this final day in which his misery overwhelms him, he drowns; but he goes "deeper than sorrow" and out of this figurative death his soul is born.

Because Wilhelm is hardly aware of the new life he has entered, the whole action of the novel is ironic. What appeared to be the agonizing and increasingly fruitless efforts to escape destruction become the necessary contractions of birth. The escape turns out to be a pilgrimage, the victim a penitent, and the descent into hell the necessary suffering out of which the soul is born. Deep within himself Wilhelm *is* dimly aware of this. He curses himself for having fought with his father:

> But at the same time, since there were depths in Wilhelm not unsuspected by himself, he received a suggestion from some remote element in his thoughts that the business of life, the real business—to carry his peculiar burden, to feel shame and impotence, to taste those quelled tears—the only important business, the highest business was being done. Maybe the making of mistakes expressed the very purpose of his life and the essence of his being here. Maybe he was supposed to make them and suffer for them on this earth.

At moments he ceases from flight and pursues the good, his characteristic self-loathing falls away and he even feels within himself the powers of a savior. For instance, what really appeals to him about becoming an actor is that he believes that in this way he can be a lover to the whole world. The sense of a universal spirit that unites and blesses all mankind has recently come to him as he is walking through a dark tunnel beneath Times Square:

> A general love for all these imperfect and lurid-looking people burst out in Wilhelm's breast. He loved them. One and all, he passionately loved them. They were his brothers and sisters. He was imperfect and disfigured himself, but what difference did that make if he was united with them by this blaze of love? And as he walked he began to say, "Oh my brothers—my brothers and my sisters," blessing them all as well as himself.

Although such feelings never last long and are usually fled from rather than welcomed, on this day of reckoning he remembers this experience and thinks, "I must go back to that. That's the right clue and may do me the most good. Something very big. Truth, like."

This affirmation, feeble as it is, constitutes his own dim recognition of the saving end of what more often appears to him as a destructive element—his own intensely emotional nature. He continually blames his failures on his strong and often uncontrollable emotions; yet we are finally made aware that it is just this capacity to feel, more specifically this need to love and be loved, that makes possible the birth of Wilhelm's soul at the end of the novel. Ultimately, the clearest indication that the action of *Seize the Day* is ironic is found in Bellow's attitude toward man's emotional nature, not just as revealed in this novel but throughout his writing. That Bellow is in the tradition of the great English Romantic poets—Wordsworth in particular—in this respect has been brilliantly argued by Irvin Stock in [*The Southern Review,* Winter 1967].

Understanding the structure of Bellow's novel to be ironic, we are now able to state its major theme. Man's soul has existence only when it can love and feel love in return. Modern society, however, has no use for the soul. Kill or be killed is its law and that of material life. Most people learn this early and conform to it. They are not even aware that their souls have died in the process. Those few who refuse to abandon the life of the soul, who still yearn for its fruition, are punished through suffering and eventually destroyed, unable to fight against what appears to them to be the law of nature. Such destruction can only affect the "pretender soul," however. And the real soul is born as a result.

That Bellow should use water imagery more fully to render his theme is appropriate considering that water and the emotional life have been linked since ancient times and particularly so within the English Romantic tradition. What is striking, however, is the care he has taken to weave his imagery into so much of the novel, to illuminate it on so many different levels. Our understanding of how Bellow uses water imagery not only underlines for us his thematic intent, not only reveals to us the greater significance of details we might otherwise pass over, but dramatizes for us the workings of a subtle and profound creative imagination. The image, in fact, so powerfully is it used, takes on the radiance of the symbol; and like other great symbolist achievements, *Seize the Day* becomes richer with each re-reading. A short novel of just over a hundred pages, it is a marvelous compression, an artistic distillation of the kind that beautifully demonstrates the strengths of the symbolist technique used at its best, a technique that gives a particular kind of pleasurable intensity that is not found in novels that employ other methods.

[Like] other great symbolist achievements, *Seize the Day* becomes richer with each re-reading. A short novel of just over a hundred pages, it is a marvelous compression, an artistic distillation of the kind that beautifully demonstrates the strengths of the symbolist technique used at its best, a technique that gives a particular kind of pleasurable intensity that is not found in novels that employ other methods.

—*Clinton W. Trowbridge*

The image of the drowning Wilhelm is the controlling one, but because of the book's ironic structure it is an image that functions in two ways. On a first reading, and on each rereading on the surface of our experience, it intensifies our sympathy for Wilhelm's condition. Even when Wilhelm is being depicted least sympathetically, when he is most in the wrong, most the slob, we are continually made aware that we are witnessing the strugglings of a drowning man and we want to see him rescued. Thus our sympathy

is continual in a way that it is not, for instance, with Dostoevski's underground man. Once the ironic structure of the novel has been seen, however, this same image functions to bring us to an understanding of Bellow's real theme—the paradoxical life by drowning.

In the first part of the novel the image of the drowning Wilhelm is only barely suggested and in a way that would have little significance if it were not strengthened by the presence of other things: closely related water images and figures of speech linking his plight to that of a drowning man. At the end of the novel, however, we see him as almost literally drowning, unable to breath; then finally the suppressed tears rise to overflow his face; and then the sense of peace and the languorous movement of the drifting body toward its final resting place. Only after one has felt the full force of the image at the end can one go back and see where it lay, implicit but veiled in the story of Wilhelm's day. Only then can one appreciate the double significance the image holds.

The novel opens with Wilhelm's coming down in an elevator from the twenty-third floor of the Hotel Gloriana in New York City to the mezzanine to have breakfast with his father.

> The elevator sank and sank. Then the smooth door opened and the great dark red uneven carpet that covered the lobby billowed toward Wilhelm's feet. In the foreground the lobby was dark, sleepy. French drapes like sails kept out the sun, but three high, narrow windows were open, and in the blue air Wilhelm saw a pigeon about to light on the great chain that supported the marquee of the movie house directly underneath the lobby. For one moment he heard the wings beating strongly.

As we realize later, if we do not at the time, Wilhelm is here imagined as already drowned, under the water where all is still, dark, sleepy, merged with the other dead inhabitants of the earth. Only the pigeon is free, outside of this element, his wings "beating strongly." Because of Wilhelm's fear, because "he sensed that a huge trouble long presaged but till now formless was due," because of the symbolic kinship between the pigeon and the dove, and because to Wilhelm the bird is clearly thought of in contrast to himself; because of these things coupled with other similar suggestions in the whole passage, we see that the pigeon is meant to suggest Wilhelm's soul departing from him, that this is a scene foreshadowing the struggle to come. Other details indicate that the whole scene is to be imagined as taking place beneath the water. Rubin, the man at the newsstand, is staring dreamily out of the window as if he too were submerged. The Hotel Ansonia, at which he is gazing, "looked like the image of itself reflected in deep water, white and cumulous above, with cavernous distortions underneath." Both men are trapped in a mutual vision, as if they were actually aware of their metaphorical existence beneath the waters. The hotel itself is described as if it were beneath the waters and being viewed from them.

> The Ansonia, the neighborhood's great landmark, was built by Stanford White. It looks like a baroque palace from Prague or Munich en-

larged a hundred times, with towers, domes, huge swells and bubbles of metal gone green from exposure, iron fretwork and festoons. Black television antennae are densely planted on its round summits. Under the changes of weather it may look like marble or like sea water, black as slate in the fog, white as tufa in sunlight.

The Ansonia is significantly the neighborhood's great landmark. The area itself is a retired, elderly one and suggests in its own right the death of heart as well as the underwater world of spiritless existence.

The suggestions of the drowning Wilhelm amid a society that is already dead in its soul are far more obvious as the novel progresses, and they build toward the climactic final scene in which the sudden reversal of the image is felt. Appropriately, Wilhelm quotes several times from Milton's "Lycidas": "Sunk though he be beneath the wat'ry floor." Bellow even adds after one such reference, "such things had always swayed him." Wilhelm is chronically short of breath as he smokes too much, takes too many pills, and drinks too many Coca Colas; whenever he feels oppressed or even very stirred emotionally, he literally cannot catch his breath. Many references to his chest hurting him, along with the other details, give us the impression throughout the work of a man swimming for his life and, since he is largely unsuccessful, of a man slowly and painfully drowning. At the end of the novel the symbolic and the literal merge as he reaches what appears to be the point of death, struggling for air in a telephone booth. He shouts to his wife:

> "You've got to let up. I feel I'm about to burst." His face had expanded. He struck a blow upon the tin and wood and nails of the wall of the booth. "You've got to let me breathe . . . " He had scarcely enough air in his lungs to speak in a whisper, because his heart pushed upward with a frightful pressure . . . Wilhelm tried to tear the apparatus from the wall. He ground his teeth and seized the black box with insane digging fingers and made a stifled cry and pulled. Then he saw an elderly lady staring through the glass door, utterly appalled by him, and he ran from the booth, leaving a large amount of change on the shelf.

Every detail here functions perfectly, both symbolically and literally, especially, perhaps, the glass door of the booth which separates the element that is choking him from that which surrounds us. That element, on its deepest level, is the lack of love he feels so bitterly in his wife. Almost literally the very breath of his life is love, and when she hangs up on him it is as if she had cut the air hose.

Wilhelm feels suffocated, though to a lesser extent, simply by living in the city. The grabbing for money and especially the cynicism of the business world oppress him in a physical as well as mental way. Yet Bellow does not make him a complete victim, for clearly he is his own worst enemy, and in one beautiful simile Bellow links Wilhelm's self-destructiveness with these images of drowning: "Like a ball in the surf, washed beyond reach, his self-control was going out."

Only Professor Tamkin, one of Bellow's strangely ambivalent seers, offers to help him. Here most clearly salvation for Wilhelm is presented in terms of an ability to rise to the top of the waters, to ride the crest of the wave of life to victory and success; but here, also clearly, Tamkin is a destroyer of the soul, a false image of salvation. Wilhelm must be drowned, in other words, for his soul to swim, and this part at least of Tamkin's urging is aimed at a soulless success, an empty victory. Bellow calls Tamkin the great "confuser of the imagination," and although Bellow uses him to state many of the truths of the novel, Tamkin most ruthlessly preys upon Wilhelm. In the last words of section four Wilhelm imagines his own Lycidas-like end as he realizes how much he is now depending on Tamkin. "But what have I let myself in for? The waters of the earth are going to roll over me."

In connection with Tamkin, Bellow is most ironic in his use of water imagery. Tamkin is "the confuser of the imagination," but he also appears to be the great man of feeling and Wilhelm, whose deepest need is to live positively in his emotional life turns to him as a potential savior: "Secretly he prayed the doctor would give him some useful advice and transform his life." The doctor is the one who encourages Wilhelm to trust his emotions, who makes for Wilhelm the distinction between the "real" and "pretender" soul, and who apparently sees that Wilhelm is killing himself and being killed because he cannot release the deepest sources of his emotional being. He sees him as symbolic of "sick humanity" and offers to heal him. "My real calling is to be a healer," he tells Wilhelm: "I get wounded. I suffer from it. I would like to escape from the sicknesses of others, but I can't. I am only on loan to myself, so to speak. I belong to humanity." Just before this passage, however, he has told Wilhelm that his wife committed suicide, by drowning herself; and Tamkin is first mentioned in the novel in connection with his invention of an underwater suit in which one might escape from New York City by walking up the floor of the Hudson in case of an atomic attack. Increasingly we are made aware that Tamkin is using others rather than being used by them, that his is the touch of death, not life. Yet it is Bellow's genius to render him for us as both a savior and a destroyer, a fact which gives deeper meaning to Mr. Perls' statement about him: "He could be both sane and crazy. In these days nobody can tell for sure which is which."

The exact nature of Tamkin's dual role becomes clear when one compares the following passages, passages which are themselves contrasting water images. In the first Tamkin preaches to Wilhelm one of the fundamental doctrines of romanticism—union with nature through reliance on her goodness:

> If you could have confidence in nature you would not have to fear. It would keep you up. Creative is nature. Rapid. Lavish. Inspirational. It shapes leaves. It rolls the waters of the earth. Man is the chief of this. All creations are his just inheritance. You don't know what you've got within you. A person either creates or destroys. There is no neutrality. . . .

Making even more specific use of water imagery, he tells Wilhelm somewhat later in the novel:

Nature only knows one thing, and that's the present. Present, present, eternal present, like a big, huge, giant wave—colossal, bright and beautiful, full of life and death, climbing into the sky, standing in the seas. You must go along with the actual, the Here-and-Now, the glory. . . .

In the first passage Tamkin is telling Wilhelm not to fear, that if he relies on nature it will *keep him up.* Nature is like a great sea on which man can float. In the second passage, however, nature is a wave, man a surfer, and the feeling is desperate if also exhilarating. The first is passive and comforting, the second vital and rather terrifying. Within a broader literary tradition, the difference is roughly between the early Wordsworth and Nietzsche, and the difference is immense. Wilhelm feels incapable of the faith involved in accepting what is demanded in the first passage. Right after it, in fact, he says, "The waters of the earth are going to roll over me." But his reaction to the second is even stronger; it interrupts Tamkin's very words and is a memory, not a conscious thought:

> . . . chest weakness, Wilhelm's recollection went on. Margaret nursed him. They had two rooms of furniture, which was later seized. She sat on the bed and read to him. He made her read for days, and she read stories, poetry, everything in the house. He felt dizzy, stifled when he tried to smoke. They had him wear a flannel vest.
>
> Come then, Sorrow!
> Sweetest Sorrow!
> Like an own babe I nurse thee on my breast!
>
> Why did he remember that? Why?

In the sense that Tamkin drives Wilhelm further toward despair, he turns out to be his destroyer, not his savior, though ultimately, since Wilhelm must be destroyed in order to be saved, we see Tamkin as ironically a savior figure even here. To Wilhelm, however, Tamkin is at last recognized as the great betrayer. The final section of the novel opens with Wilhelm realizing, "I was the man beneath; Tamkin was on my back and I thought I was on his." While this specifically applies to the fact that Tamkin has lost Wilhelm's money for him in the stock exchange, it must also be read as a water image. Wilhelm has thought that Tamkin was supporting him in the waters of his troubles. It turns out that Wilhelm, struggling to swim himself, has been drowned by Tamkin who has been "supporting himself" on him. The beauty of the pun is that it also applies to Wilhelm's father whose real character is shown in the advice he gives his son earlier in the novel, advice which, because it is so cold-hearted, is what originally drove Wilhelm to seek help elsewhere: "I can't give you any money . . . You and your sister would take every last buck from me . . . And I want nobody on my back. Get off! And I give you the same advice, Wilky. Carry nobody on your back."

If Wilhelm is crushed by the Nietzschean, he finally discovers the true source of his being in something deeply Wordsworthean, for at the end of the novel it is the "still, sad music of humanity" that opens his heart, that "chas-

tens" and "subdues," and so gives birth to his real soul. Caught by the crowd on Broadway, he moves along within "the inexhaustible current of millions." A series of images bring Wilhelm to his vision and his birth in which he is imagined as a drowning body moving with the currents under the sea to its final resting place:

> It was he himself who was carried from the street into the chapel. The pressure ended inside, where it was dark and cool. The flow of fan-driven air dried his face, which he wiped hard with his handkerchief to stop the slight salt itch. He gave a sigh when he heard the organ notes that stirred and breathed from the pipes and he saw people in the pews.

He is caught in the line of mourners moving toward the coffin, and when he reaches it the meditative look on the face of the dead stranger forces him to step out of the procession. Here again Bellow uses water imagery to give us the deeper significance of the action, for suddenly it is the dead man who is imagined as having drowned, not Wilhelm. Wilhelm can finally breathe. He even wipes his face to rid himself of the "slight salt itch." All the imagery points to our seeing Wilhelm as suddenly saved from drowning, saved because he can now express his deepest emotions. He can love and pity mankind as a whole.

> The dead man was gray-haired. He had two large waves of gray hair at the front. But he was not old. His face was long, And he had a bony nose, slightly, delicately twisted, His brows were raised as though he had sunk into the final thought. Now at last he was with it, after the end of all distractions, and when his flesh was no longer flesh.

Wilhelm can at last cry. The seas of feeling, that have been welling up within him but have never found their natural outlet before, at last find their release. At the surface level of meaning he can now cry because the funeral is the one place where that is not only permissible but honorable. On a deeper level, however, he can be "drowned in tears" because these are the life-giving seas of feeling, not the terrifying Nietzschean wave of life and death.

> Soon he was past words, past reason, coherence. He could not stop. The source of all tears had suddenly sprung open within him, black, deep, and hot, and they were pouring out and convulsing his body, bending his stubborn head, bowing his shoulders, twisting his face, crippling the very hands with which he held the handkerchief. His efforts to collect himself were useless. The great knot of ill and grief in his throat swelled upward and he gave in utterly and held his face and wept. He cried with all his heart.

What is significant here is Wilhelm's change of character. He has abandoned himself to a despair which is not merely personal, though it includes himself. "A man—another human creature, was what first went through his thoughts." The fact of death, another's death, has brought him to a state in which he is utterly passive and completely dependent. He now exists wholly in his feelings, not because he has chosen to but because all else has been taken from him. He has been humbled by a great fact of nature.

His "stubborn head" is bowed. He has been forced into dependency on nature, but we see that this dependency brings him into union with her, for the important thing is that he is now afloat on a sea of feeling. In Bellow's own sense of the Wordsworthean vision, Wilhelm has "see[n] into the life of things" and become, at last, "a living soul." Moreover, there is hope that he will be buoyed up in this state and receive a return of feeling. His girl friend, Olive, loves him and will marry him if he can get a divorce, and it is to her that he gives himself at the end. In fact the implication is that his very life is now in her hands.

What makes this final scene so impressive as a literary achievement is just this sort of density of meaning. Wilhelm is the only person crying at the funeral, yet he is the only stranger. One of the suggestions here is that genuine sorrow is impersonal. Another is that only those in whom the soul is alive can truly mourn, for only they are capable of this intensity of feeling.

Many other examples of Bellow's use of water imagery to support and deepen his ironic vision of the drowning Wilhelm could be cited. The fluctuations of the stock market correspond to, and of course to a large extent determine, the alternations of hope and despair in Wilhelm's mind; and when the market crashes—when Wilhelm's stocks go down and he loses the last of his money—one can almost see Wilhelm crushed beneath Tamkin's "wave of life and death." You have to feel the "money flow" says Tamkin to Wilhelm when he promises him success in the market: "To know how it feels to be seaweed you have to get into the water." The stock market itself is symbolic of all the cold, impersonal forces that Wilhelm and Bellow regard as evil; and that Wilhelm is tempted by Tamkin to "take the plunge," that this crushes him but does no serious harm to Tamkin, emphasizes, among other things, the difference between their two natures. Wilhelm is instantly punished for his sin. He had betrayed his soul. Tamkin has no soul and so cannot be punished in this manner.

One of the ironies in the novel is that Wilhelm's father, who is the epitome of soulless success, is constantly bathing himself, recommends water and exercise as the cure for his son's miseries, and finally rejects him completely while in the steam baths of the hotel's health club. Wilhelm himself seldom bathes and refuses to use the hotel's swimming pool because he is offended by the smell of the chlorinated water. What is suggested here is that the waters of the earth can sustain the life of the body, can even be used to bring about that meditative calm that comes from complete detachment from the emotions; but to those whose souls are alive deeper waters are needed, and the waters of the earth are instinctively abhorrent.

Bellow's great achievement in *Seize the Day* is that he finally forces us to see Wilhelm as a kind of hero. It is easy to miss his intention and feel only sadness at the end of the novel. Wilhelm may there appear to us only as a poor slob who is weeping at what we dimly sense is really his own funeral. But Bellow can make beauty out of ugliness, not only out of what in the hands of a lesser artist might have been merely the sordidness of ordinary life but out of a character who even to himself seems detestable. Wilhelm refers to himself early in the novel as a "fair-haired

Hippopotamus," and this image is repeated many times. It is his characteristic way of seeing himself. Though Wilhelm is ugly to himself and a slob to others, his true element is, nevertheless, the waters of the spiritual life. The burden of this life, the suffering it contains, is suggested in the ugliness and massiveness of the hippo when out of water. The weight is removed, however, and the ugliness transformed into a sense of appropriateness that is the result of being powerfully in harmony with nature when the hippo is in the water. So it is with Wilhelm who at the end of the novel seizes the day of his soul's birth, a soul whose capacity is as unlimited as the hippo is large, and floats for the first time, buoyed up by the greater life into which he has finally entered. (pp. 62-73)

> *Clinton W. Trowbridge, "Water Imagery in 'Seize the Day',"* in Critique: Studies in Modern Fiction, *Vol. IX, No. 3, 1967, pp. 62-73.*

Alfred Kazin   (essay date 28 March 1968)

[*A highly respected American literary critic, Kazin is best known for his essay collections* The Inmost Leaf *(1955),* Contemporaries *(1962), and* On Native Grounds *(1942), a study of American prose writing since the era of William Dean Howells. Kazin has found that "criticism focused many—if by no means all—of my own urges as a writer: to show literature as a deed in human history, and to find in each writer the uniqueness of the gift, of the essential vision, through which I hoped to penetrate into the mystery and sacredness of the individual soul." In the essay excerpted below, Kazin praises Bellow's "little masterpiece"* Seize the Day *and examines the novella's portrayal of the forces that destroy individuality in modern life.*]

Just as many painters nowadays seem hung up on theory, are always trying to figure out some new bedazzlement to suit the "exhaustion of old forms," so many novelists have identified themselves with literary "progress." The marked academization of literary taste in our day has resulted in the idolatry of modernism. The novel, whose essential genius as a medium has always been the utter freedom it has given, since the eighteenth century, to individualizing and concretizing experience, has by its very freedom and plasticity in dealing with matter of fact become an embarrassment to those many over-impressionable intellectuals who no longer think of themselves as free men, who have no natural love for the unmediated facts of human existence, thus no longer think of the novel as the indispensable free form most bountifully expressive of life. "The novel," said D. H. Lawrence, "is the one bright book of life. . . . The novel as a tremulation can make the whole man tremble. . . . Only in the novel are *all* things given full play . . . when we realize that life itself, and not inert safety, is the reason for living."

The academicized novel became a marked feature of the 1940s, when Bellow began to publish, and is the necessary background to any real understanding of his counter-effort as a novelist and of his current favor with the common reader. "I rejoice to concur with the common reader," Dr. Johnson wrote, "for by the common sense of readers, uncorrupted by literary prejudices, after all the refinements of subtlety and the dogmatism of learning, must be generally decided all claim to poetical honours." In a period when young novelists frightened by the thought of being left behind were already doing their best to astonish, stupefy, and outwit the reader—if with nothing but typographical innovations—Bellow turned to fiction as a medium that would justify and support his devotion to the truth of experience—one might even say, to the truth of *his* experience. The most striking thing about his first novel *Dangling Man* (1944), was its somber lucidity, its straightforwardness, the hero's determination, in an era of "hard-boiled-dom, when emotions are at a discount," to talk openly about his troubles (a word that serves to introduce many of Bellow's stories, especially *Seize the Day*). The mid-Forties were a time when, to the sound of "the breaking of the nations," many Western traditions were coming to an end. In response to these dissolutions, when a visible panic came over the arts yet aestheticizing experience was proceeding happily under the aegis of the New Criticism, Bellow's first novel was marked by its open confrontation of human tragedy in a period of unprecedented destructiveness; the hero-narrator, in all the unease of youth, consciously tries not merely to save his life but to find some foundation for life itself.

In this first novel we see all the typical themes of Bellow's later fiction: the intellectual orientation of experience, the emphasis on *troubles,* the search for salvation. Above all—that which all his novels have now made his distinct signature—there is the contrast of this somber, often desperate *individual* world, a world deeply and engravedly personal, aggrieved, heavy, with an elegant intellectual wit, a consciously unavailing, rueful curiosity that may be useless in overcoming so much pressure, but which is sanctioned by some larger spiritual world, outside the narrow circle of the hero's own desperate existence. To this he seeks access.

In *Dangling Man* and in Bellow's second volume, *The Victim,* the protagonist seems constrained. He feels that he has been chosen by his mysterious destiny to be *in* trouble, to feel these vacancies—Joseph in *Dangling Man* is caught between civilian life and the army, Asa Leventhal in *The Victim* is inexplicably accused by a virtual stranger of ruining *his* life out of a Jew's hatred of non-Jews. Within this crisis of constraint the hero unsuccessfully pursues his speculations, trying to find the way to the source of all troubles, to lose himself in the larger whole from which he constantly feels himself deprived. He vaguely perceives that his suffering *is* the form that this deprivation takes. Life is a matter of destiny, thought is a matter of recognizing this destiny from inadequate signs; yet one reads one's own movements on the larger dial that shows all human destiny. There are typical sentiments of Jewish thought—fatalistic, yet without cynicism; preserving an aura of wonder at the providential, trans-human nature of a creation which yet has some mysterious bounty for the expectant spirit that knows how to distinguish between the ways of man and the ways of God. Though these deep-rooted convictions have up to the twentieth century been traditionally impervious to secular art, and have even been considered superior to art, not the least of Bellow's importance is that he has from the first made a bridge to modern literary forms. He has been able to personify the Jew in all his

mental existence, to fit ancient preconceptions to our urban landscape, to create the suffering, reaching, grasping, struggling mind of contemporary Jews.

Still, the constraint, the conscious somberness of Joseph and of Asa Leventhal, could not make the appeal to a wider current of feeling that Augie March did; Joseph and Asa, lost in their ghetto bleakness, as it were, have not been able to come up to the light. Augie is constructed entirely as a passageway to "America," is an attempt to break down all possible fences between the Jew and this larger country, so abundant and free in possibility that Augie is a conscious mythological creation—not only the messenger of the glad tidings that the long-awaited marriage between American and Jew has at last been accomplished, but also the rhetorically indomitable, unbuyable, American tough, from Huck Finn to James Cagney, who in Bellow's most abandoned free style has at last been balanced with a Jewish upbringing and the slums of Chicago.

If Bellow had not so urgently expanded and released himself in the early Fifties to complete *Augie March,* his "breakthrough" novel, he would never have been able to create his little masterpiece, *Seize the Day*—the short novel which even the most furious detractors of his larger and more self-assertive novels, *Augie March, Henderson the Rain King,* and *Herzog* admire as the painfully exact American tragedy of our affluent day. Bellow's progress as a novelist is clearly one of conscious personal development based on the value-system he ascribes to each of his protagonists in turn—Joseph, Leventhal, Augie. Tommy Wilhelm, Henderson, Herzog. His imaginative world is formed candidly and *submissively,* as if in homage to his own imagination, around some larger fictional self whose journeyings and afflictions and revelations are meticulously upheld as an allegory of Bellow's own strivings and revelations. The ground of this feeling is the romantic attachment to one's own experiences that Wordsworth in *The Prelude* and Keats in his letters established as the source of authentic growth. Along with the chastening and constraint that we see in *Dangling Man* and *The Victim* there is a constant release into the free upward movement that we see in *Augie March* and, later, in *Henderson.* But this pattern of constraint and expansion is actually the real inner life of Bellow's protagonists even when one may seem dominant over the other—Joseph's mind soars, if only in his journal; Asa Leventhal believes in happiness, and in his unwitting way will temporarily achieve it; Augie March and Henderson, despite their violent air of confidence, cannot be trusted to keep it up in solitude. The spirit of release and retreat, of up-and-down, hope and despair, marks Bellow's work from book to book, from character to character, often from line to line. It is vibrant with the moodiness of the Jew, the intellectual, the city man. But it is the expressive combination of these two faculties of the human heart so as to make them seem not merely "personal" but also the unwitting manifestations of our collective life under the rule of money that gives *Seize the Day* its subtle tension, its expression of the sinister fantasies at work on the city streets, its experiment in consciousness. The subject is the excruciatingly simultaneous pressures on a man not strong nor bright enough to bear them. The stage is the street of streets in the city of cities—Broadway.

The pattern of expansion and contraction is literally the situation itself in *Seize the Day.* Tommy Wilhelm, who is still "Wilky" Adler to his severely independent father, old Dr. Adler, is a salesman down on his luck, out of a job, separated from his wife and children, but still a dreamer for whom America The Rich, America The All-Powerful, America The Big Money, is still the most tempting of all delusions. He is not particularly intelligent, strong, or resourceful, is particularly given to self-deception and inaccurate reading of other people; so he easily identifies himself with every new promise and delusion on the wing. With his blond, deceptively non-Jewish good looks, the glib unthinking chatter that has made him a successful salesman in the past, Tommy looks and dresses a part that by now, the day through which the story takes place, he no longer has the spirit to sustain. Lost and dismayed, he begins his day by looking at his reflection in the glass surfaces of the Broadway hotel in the West Seventies where he now lives; he must reassure himself that the expansive image of the unreal Tommy Wilhelm which all the forces of his society have helped him to create is holding up. The money society has become Tommy Wilhelm's real self—everything must yet be expected of it, it will carry him (his father no longer will), surely nothing can go wrong for a man still in his early forties, with his blond good looks? Like other deluded, perpetually "young" men, Tommy cannot admit and address his own mediocrity until it is too late. By contrast with the expansive opulence of the American scene, where the money *seems* to pump through everybody like the bloodstream, Tommy Wilhelm himself is so constrained, brought down to his fundamental resources, that it is exactly his slow recognition that he can no longer make the effort, that he will fail to make himself equal to this society, which draws the story out to Tommy's one authentic and passionate emotion—he mourns himself as if he were dead. Tommy is finally doomed to be nothing and nobody but himself, and the deflation by which this is accomplished brings a matter-of-factness to the story that is the very taste of life on our own teeth—in this society where everything rises or falls on the rise or fall of our money.

Tommy Wilhelm is a weakling, a passive sufferer, a *nebbish* in the crowded storm of New York life. Only his illusions about "making it" have made him an interesting fabulist in the past—he even left college to take a screen test! But on this early summer day the fabulousness will vanish to the point where Tommy will stray into a stranger's funeral and mourn his own life. What, then, sustains our interest in this non-hero? What makes him an interesting contender with life? What lifts him for a moment above our thick urban swarm, so that we *can* identify with him and finally mourn him as he mourns himself? It is the fact that in this kind of urban, modern American fiction environment serves as meaning. "Society" has replaced nature, and the collaboration of so many souls, senses, eyes in the contemporary city becomes Bellow's opportunity. He shows with a peculiar vividness and sharpness that Tommy Wilhelm lives constantly with his mind pressing on other minds and other minds pressing on his. In the

city, where the triumph of numbers is complete, the technical collaboration between men persists in the midst of the greatest loneliness and destructiveness. There is a meticulous unending confrontation between man and other men, between man and his *things,* even between things and *their* things. In the city of cities, every mind has been so socialized that the whimper of loneliness deep inside Tommy's soul is, curiously, the last of his individuality. At the end, when Tommy has lost everything exactly on the day that the false messiah. Dr. Tamkin, has promised fulfillment (and profit on the commodities market), he identifies this individuality only with his own death. He can find in the threat of his own dissolution his only access to that "larger body," that true world from which his immediate society has so long deprived him. And it is exactly this that shows up all our deepest constraint. We have been deprived of truth not associated with our own effort. We have been deprived of the creation. Tommy Wilhelm is socially so impressionable and conformist that he is defenseless before his own merciless "interpersonal" examination of himself. What do I owe *you?* How do I look to *you?* How, according to *you,* shall I think of myself? This is the cruelty by which Tommy, poor *nebbish,* must live. And it is this unrelenting examination that makes Tommy's suffering vibrations in and out of the Hotel Gloriana in the West Seventies so ominous for the rest of us.

This use of environment is of course not new in realistic fiction; if anything, it is the very essence of fiction itself, a form which obviously depends on rendering the minute relationship between man and the world he creates. But what is distinctive about *Seize the Day* is that the story proceeds by sensations which are as individuated, warm, and vivid as they are in romantic poetry, but unfold into a dramatic action which is destructive of all hope in Tommy Wilhelm. Tommy Wilhelm coming down from his hotel room, hoping that his father will enter the elevator and so immediately give him the moral support he needs as much as money, finds all visible surfaces glittering in his eyes—and the promise of each sensation is *unconscious.* It is not the romantic egotism of nineteenth-century "genius" that puts the exciting world into play here; it is the constant promise offered to the average man that today, today of all days, he will yet make it: he will make the money that makes the day. The French writer Léon Bloy once wrote that "money is the blood of the poor." On the bustling, upsurging, massed West Side of New York, where the past poverty of so many parvenues is as evident as death disturbing the feast in a medieval allegory, money is the sure quicksilver in everybody's blood. "It was getting so that people were feeble-minded about everything except money: While if you didn't have it you were a dummy, a dummy! You had to excuse yourself from the face of the earth." Tommy impulsively left college because a shyster agent who would have been transparent to anyone else promised him a screen test. His estranged wife is after him for the money he owes, his mistress is a Catholic and will not be allowed to marry him. Tommy responds wildly to everything with leaps of hope or despair. We are tuned into Tommy, we are "with him," pulsation by pulsation, as if he were a rabbit whose exposed heart we hold in our hand.

Tommy starts his day, as he comes to breakfast, consciously posing the strength he no longer feels, still the actor he vainly tried to be. "He was smoking a cigar, and when a man is smoking a cigar, wearing a hat, he has an advantage." But though he "believed—he hoped—that he looked passably well: doing all right," his mood sinks with the elevator taking him down to breakfast as he goes past his father's floor without old Dr. Adler coming in.

> But there was no stop on the fourteenth, and the elevator sank and sank. Then the smooth door opened and the great dark red uneven carpet that covered the lobby billowed toward Wilhelm's feet. In the foreground the lobby was dark, sleepy. French drapes like sails kept out the sun, but three high, narrow windows were open, and in the blue air Wilhelm saw a pigeon about to light on the great chain that supported the marquee of the movie house directly underneath the lobby. For one moment he heard the wings beating strongly.

The force of definition in this writing is remarkable; the outer world is constantly a register of Tommy's ups and downs. The essence of Bellow's sense of fiction is to study the imposition of force on people who are too innocent, too hopeful, too eager to recognize their destiny until, as at the end of *Seize the Day,* they are engulfed by it. "Destiny" is an important word in Bellow's imaginative world; as important as money (no other American novelist with his intellectual perception has in recent years made such solid, wearing use of it as has Bellow); so is weakness or strength of the body, the instrument for living, the only power for resistance to so much force. (Tommy, in his middle forties, has a heavy and strong back, "if already a little stooped or thickened." Maurice Venice, the agent: "His breath was noisy and his voice difficult and rather husky because of the fat in his throat.") Bellow is always peculiarly attentive to such facts, and measuring the confusedly striving Wilhelm as an anthropologist might (he had some early training at this), he creates the style of definition, dry without being cold, which renders the environment as a series of pressures on this all-too-feeling but never-really-knowing hero.

So from the opening of *Seize the Day* we get the intensity of numbers in the West Seventies, the preponderance of old and sick people (here is your fate, Tommy Wilhelm), the anxious Jewish preoccupation with health—an allegory for survival. By contrast with Tommy's fatal immaturity, Rubin, who runs the cigar stand in the hotel lobby, is one of those who *know,* and so doesn't give out very much. He has poor eyes. "They may not have been actually weak but they were poor in expression, with lacy lids that furled down at the corners." Rubin is a judgment on Tommy because he can so easily take his measure. Everybody of a certain age, who has learned constraint, has this advantage over poor Tommy. The most depressing example to our hero is his father, old Dr. Adler, small, neat, professional, dry, whose cool autonomy is a horror to his son, for he cannot break through this privacy, and it humiliates as well as deprives him by the contrast it makes with his own foolish expectancies.

The most brilliant use of this knowingness as a human

characteristic is the mysteriously untrustworthy "Doctor" Tamkin, so ominously a charlatan and a crook, who becomes the very essence of the city environment by the way he manipulates Tommy Wilhelm's soul—and depleted bank account—as the all-explainer, the great brain and reassurer, the last possible guide through this metropolitan hell. Bellow is rather more of an "intellectual" than most good American novelists, and his protagonists, usually Jews, are typically implicated in the life of the intellect even when, like many intellectuals, they are incapable of thinking for themselves. Nevertheless, Bellow refuses to grant much value to intellectuals. His resistance is probably based on the fact that he has always lived among intellectuals, but wants his own creative difference to be recognized; he emphatically does not want to be confused with those whom Harold Rosenberg has called "the herd of independent minds." But deeper than this pride goes a profound distrust of all the fashionable literary, critical, psychological claims to knowledge, a conviction that the reality of life is to be found in personal experience, in works of literature as life-actions, not among the doctrinaires and ideologues, radical, Freudian, academic, who are usually deluded by their own pronouncements, and, like Tamkin, know they are well by ministering to the sick.

Still, no one is "like Tamkin" but Tamkin himself. If Tommy Wilhelm is the suffering rabbit, Tamkin is the magician who charms him out of the hat and puts him back in again. But who is to say *what* Tamkin is, where he begins, who he is, what he believes? His fathomlessness *is* Tamkin. He is the very personification of a kind of modern urban know-it-all, the quack analyst, the false guide to the many afflicted by their terrible uncertainty. Wherever it is that he lives with himself, whoever he may "really" be (and he may be the last to find out), Tamkin exists by explaining to lost souls like Tommy Wilhelm who *they* are and what their suffering is all about. What a marvelous touch this is. Tommy Wilhelm's unasked for "analysis" is conducted right on Broadway, over cafeteria pot roast and purple cabbage, at a stockbroker's Broadway branch office—by a faintly unclean, frighteningly dubious figure in a gray straw hat with a wide cocoa-colored band, who claims to have been everywhere, to have done everything, who pops up when you are least expecting him, is not to be found when you need him, and whose unending line of chatter, though he is an obvious faker, holds Tommy's attention as a bird is mesmerized by a snake.

Tamkin *knows.* Tamkin always knows. Where everything sickeningly turns under Tommy's feet, Tamkin presents himself as the source of light, the inspirer, the only solid underpinning in a world deprived of father, mother, wife, children, security, business, faith. This is indeed the role that many bogus analysts play to the suffering, deprived, and confused people in a world whose treachery confuses them after the bliss of earliest childhood. Forever afterward, the suffering man, who indeed suffers from the world because it daily robs him of his natural faith, will blame his faithlessness on "himself" rather than on the world that has robbed him of himself. He becomes not only the greatest possible sufferer but his own accuser. The victim makes himself guilty in the vain hope of securing some reprieve from the forces that indifferently block him.

What a world it is, indeed, in which Tamkin can alone give the illusion of faith and love and hope, in which Tamkin alone can seem to offer meaning, where everybody else around Tommy has turned savage in his pursuit of money. "Seize the day!" Tamkin's ridiculously affected yet singularly human poem says to our sufferer. No one speaks to his heart except the fake who in effect robs him. Yet who is to say, when the last of Tommy's money is gone speculating on lard in the commodities market, who is to say that Tamkin (now disappeared) has not been as much a victim of his own reckless self-confidence as Tommy is? Who can say what is truth and what is false in this foundationless world where at the end, as Tommy stumbles into a stranger's funeral, only death is real, and a man must mourn for himself more feelingly than anyone else ever will for him? At the end, Bellow's typically austere, witty, curt sense of the irony inherent in every human demonstration takes over.

> The great knot of ill and grief in his throat swelled upward and he gave in utterly and held his face and wept. He cried with all his heart.

> One woman said, "Is that perhaps the cousin from New Orleans they were expecting?"

> "It must be somebody real close to carry on so."

> "Oh my, oh my! To be mourned like that," said one man and looked at Wilhelm's heavy shaken shoulders, his clutched face and whitened fair hair, with wide, glinting, jealous eyes.

After *Seize the Day,* Bellow went on to write the full-length novels, particularly *Herzog,* that have given him his national reputation. But it is safe to say that none of his works is so widely and genuinely admired as this short novel. It has a quite remarkable intensity of effect without ever seeming to be forced. It is a particularly good example of what can be done with what Henry James called "that blessed form, the *novella.*" And not least, *Seize the Day* is probably the most successful rendering of the place, the time, the style of life, of Bellow's representative Jew. The protagonist is the city man who feels that the sky is constantly coming down on him. Before he dies, he will make it clear that his greatest need is not money nor love nor the "peace" he vainly seeks out of the city, but the reason of things. No one in history ever felt the loss of this so keenly as the modern man who lives in the most "developed" society of all time. (pp. 32-6)

> *Alfred Kazin, "Bellow's Purgatory," in* The New York Review of Books, *Vol. X, No. 6, March 28, 1968, pp. 32-6.*

John Jacob Clayton   (essay date 1968)

[*Clayton is an American novelist, educator, and critic. In the following excerpt from his book* Saul Bellow: In Defense of Man, *Clayton characterizes Tommy Wilhelm as a "moral masochist" who wilfully seeks out abuse to convince himself of his moral superiority.*]

Seize the Day is . . . an affirmation of human life; an affirmation of the possibility that the "salesman" need not go to his "death," need not live a life given to him by others and follow a masochistic strategy to preserve his childish self.

This affirmation is found most clearly in the poem which the charlatan-psychologist Dr. Tamkin presents to Tommy Wilhelm:

"Mechanism vs Functionalism: Ism vs Hism"

If thee thyself couldst only see
Thy greatness that is and yet to be,
Thou would feel joy-beauty-what ecstasy.
They are at thy feet, earth-moon-sea, the trinity.

Why-forth then dost thou tarry
And partake thee only of the crust
And skim the earth's surface narry
When all creations art thy just?

Seek ye then that which art not there
In thine own glory let thyself rest.
Witness. Thy power is not bare.
Thou art King. Thou art at thy best.

Look then right before thee.
Open thine eyes and see.
At the foot of Mt. Serenity
Is thy cradle to eternity.

When Tommy asks Tamkin "who this Thou is," Tamkin tells him, "Thou is you." He explains, "You were in my mind when I composed it. Of course the hero of the poem is sick humanity. If it would open its eyes it would be great." Tommy is, then, a representative man, an Everyman. To heal Tommy is to indicate the possibilities for healing the human race, to affirm the greatness of man. In none of Bellow's novels is it so clear that this greatness is dependent on a transformation of the individual. It is a transformation seen in terms of religious conversion: death and baptism and resurrection.

Tommy asks, "Yes, but how do I get into this?" He means, how does the poem refer to him; but, more broadly, the question means, how can he become the king that he is potentially, how can he reach the "greatness that is and yet to be"? The answer is given in the poem under the pompous, amateurish surface: reject the superficial of life and take its real prize, which is readily available if you can open your eyes. Opening them, you will become a child again and without striving you will reach "eternity." Seizing the present moment is equivalent to seizing the eternal.

The poem is a clumsy vehicle for ideas out of Blake (human divinity, eternity in the present), Reich (blindness of men due to character armor, as in *Listen Little Man*), and Gestalt therapists such as Goodman (living in the here-and-now). Bellow discounts the ideas by vulgarizing them. One of his continuing interests is in the reductions and debasements of great ideas. Through vulgarization, however, he is able to introduce healing ideas without sounding like a ventriloquist. For these *are* healing ideas. Bellow proposes that man can be great, that even Tommy, the common man who sees himself as more hippopotamus than man, can be great: he need only open his eyes.

Modern writers sin, says Bellow, if they pretend to know that the individual is defunct. "The subject of the novelist is not knowable in any such way. The mystery increases, it does not grow less as types of literature wear out. It is . . . Symbolism or Realism or Sensibility wearing out, and not the mystery of mankind." (pp. 28-9)

. . . . .

[*Seize the Day* is] about a moral masochist, Tommy Wilhelm. Tommy is his own most difficult obstacle, his own worst enemy. What he believes to be his troubles are not his real troubles. He allows Margaret to place burden upon burden on him, when he knows that "no court would have awarded her the amounts he paid." He chooses to live with a cold, carping father in a hotel for retired people. He chooses, out of pride, to leave the company where he had been employed, and does not look for other work.

Nor is it only present troubles that are self-imposed. Throughout his life Tommy has made bad decisions he knew in advance to be bad. "He had decided that it would be a bad mistake to go to Hollywood and then he went." He did not accidentally give Tamkin his last $700. "From the moment when he tasted the peculiar flavor of fatality in Dr. Tamkin, he could no longer keep back the money."

He constantly provokes his father into punishing him. Knowing his father's attitude toward his drug-taking, Tommy nevertheless (or rather, therefore) waits until they are together to swallow a phenaphen. He indulges in sloppy habits which disgust the old man. When he makes a scene in the restaurant, choking himself in demonstration of what Margaret does to him, he certainly knows that his father will snap, "Stop that—stop it!" He begs for pity, "almost bringing his hands together in a clasp," although he knows he can expect no pity. "Look out, Wilky, you're tiring my patience very much," his father says before he finally explodes. Tommy knows he is tiring his father's patience, and he wants to do so.

Yet Tommy only dimly suspects his self-destructive impulses. He, like Asa, sees himself as a victim: "It isn't my fault"—fate, the world, the hotel clerk are against him. He has bad luck at cards, takes a licking on the stock market. As Napoleon once told a young officer, "Bonheur est aussi une qualité." Tommy, however, believes that he is simply unfortunate. He is being murdered: "You must realize, you're killing me," he tells his wife. "Thou shalt not kill! Don't you remember that?" When his father gives him advice, he reflects on how much the old man is *not* giving him. When his father says, "Well, Wilky, here we are under the same roof again, after all these years," Tommy is suspicious: "Wasn't his father saying, 'Why are you here in a hotel with me and not at home in Brooklyn with your wife and two boys?'" The city itself is against him, slapping parking tickets on his car or frightening him with handbills that look like tickets.

But Tommy sees in the city what he is himself. Is the city grasping, money sucking, self-centered? So too is Tommy, who tries to drink or eat his way back to childhood security, who begs for love and pity. Tommy hates the city as he hates his own "pretender" soul.

Yet he has chosen the city. He remembers idyllically the suburbs around Boston. But no, "to be here in New York with his old father was more genuinely like his life." Indeed, he believes that to suffer is his fate, therefore his true occupation:

> He received a suggestion from some remote element in his thoughts that the business of life—the real business—to carry his peculiar burden, to feel shame and impotence, to taste these quelled tears—the only important business, the highest business was being done. Maybe the making of mistakes expressed the very purpose of his life and the essence of his being here.

What better summation could there be of the life of a moral masochist—or, in Reik's terminology, of a social masochist?

Still, it is important to note that Tommy's masochism does not warp *Seize the Day,* and that this is not a novel expressing the author's masochism but a novel about a masochist. There is, to be sure, a persecuted little man here, but as in *Dangling Man* and *The Victim,* it is a *self*-persecuted individual, created with the full awareness of the author. In other words, this is a far different thing from the authorial self-pity and masochism which Harvey Swados feels and attacks in Jewish writers.

Tommy needs to destroy himself and wants to see himself as a victim. There is social masochism, too, in the origin of his behavior and in its reinforcement.

According to Bernard Berliner, masochism does not result from the individual directing early sadism against the ego, but rather begins with another person and is from inception a pattern, literal or symbolic, directed toward a figure of both love and authority, a strong superego figure, generally a father. The masochist, acting out his childhood relationship, fulfills the expectations of the father. As Weiss says, "Wilhelm has the masochistic necessity to fail, to be destroyed at the hands of the punishing father, in order, under the terms of the moral masochistic commitment, to retain his love, and, in less obvious ways, to memorialize certain events in the past." It is for these motives that Tommy lives in New York, resides in his father's hotel, dresses and acts sloppily, behaves with cringing self-pity. I am reminded of Reik's discussion of the "provocative factor" found in both sexual and social (moral) masochism. Tommy acts the little boy; he provokes by childish behavior the punishment he needs to reproduce his childhood relationship with his father. Tommy uses Tamkin as a substitute father (*Tamkin* Tom-kin). Both are doctors, both give advice, and Tommy sees himself riding on the backs of both; thus to lose under the influence of Tamkin—to "take a licking" on the market—is to take a symbolic licking from his own father, a punishment which is a form of love. As Wilhelm Reich puts it, the masochist makes "demands for love in the form of provocation and spite."

This explanation does not cancel Freud's idea that masochistic behavior is self-punishment to remove guilt, generally oedipal. "You have lots of guilt in you," Tamkin tells Tommy. He judges himself by his father's criteria, from his father's perspective. "When he was drunk he reproached himself horribly as Wilky," his father's nickname for him: "'You fool, you clunk, you Wilky!'" And although in Hollywood he tried to break away from his father's judgment by changing his name (Wilhelm Adler to Tommy Wilhelm), he was unable to do so: "Wilky was his inescapable self." He "knows" his father is right, "knows" he should not have trusted Tamkin, or gone to Hollywood, or married Margaret, or left Margaret, or resigned from his job.

But as Reik and Berliner both show, the masochist gets positive rewards as well as guilt-reduction. Berliner says, "suffering has come to mean being worthy of love." "When I suffer—you aren't even sorry. That's because you have no affection for me, and you don't want any part of me." This is the baldest statement of Tommy's secret goal. And although Dr. Adler does not provide pity, or phenaphen, he does provide a duplication of the more or less secure father-child relationship. Tommy's worthiness of pity is in itself rewarding—whether or not he is actually pitied. It makes him feel, like Joseph, morally superior to his cold father. Thus, again like Joseph, Tommy refuses to dodge the draft during the war, becoming an ordinary GI rather than an officer. And, like Joseph and Augie, he feels superior to his father and Mr. Perls "because they adored money." But Tommy's suffering must seem to come from outside sources, and therefore he must keep "his troubles before him." If he did not, "he risked losing them altogether, and he knew by experience that this was worse." Worse not only because specific fear is milder than vague anxiety but also because his self-justifying construction might break down and, in confusion, his real motives would threaten to emerge.

Tommy luxuriates in his suffering. He sees himself as a sacrificial victim, remembers poem fragments like "Come then sorrow/Sweetest Sorrow! Like an own babe I nurse thee on my breast!" He does not know why he remembers these lines, but it is clear to the reader: his vision of himself as dead, his invitation of sorrow, his identification of sorrow with the state of infancy. Both doctors, his own father and Tamkin, tell him: "You make too much of your problems. . . . They ought not to be turned into a career" (his father); "Don't marry suffering. Some people do" (Tamkin).

Tommy has married suffering. Even more than Joseph, he moves toward death. He is in a hotel with old people waiting to die. He constantly feels pains in the chest, or choked, or suffocated, as he shows his father by strangling himself and telling him, "Dad, I just can't breathe. My chest is all up—I feel choked." He is being bled to death: "When I had it, I flowed money. They bled it away from me. I hemorrhaged money." Margaret is "trying to put an end to me." Tommy feels like the Brahma bull eaten by the piranha. "When I have the money they eat me alive, like those piranha fish. . . . when they ate up the Brahma bull in the river."

The bull in the river—Tommy also refers to himself as "wallowing hippopotamus"—connects the images of death by being devoured and death by water. Drowning is the most common image of death in *Seize the Day*. Tommy remembers from a college literature course the line, "Sunk though he be beneath the wat'ry floor" from *Lycidas,* about the drowning of Edward King. His father suggests a water cure, and in telling him to forget his trou-

bles, says, "Concentrate on real troubles—fatal sickness, accidents," a statement which seems an accidental invitation to die. Later, Tommy is afraid, "the waters of the earth are going to roll over me." When he discovered the loss of his investment, "his washed tears rose and rose and he looked like a man about to drown." It is as if he were going to drown in his own tears—a very precise symbolic statement. Choked, he visits his father by the pool in the steam room, and there he is, in a sense, told to die: "I'll see you dead Wilky . . . "; and at the stranger's funeral he symbolically does die by drowning: his eyes are blind and wet, there is heavy sea-like music which pours into him, he sinks "towards the consummation of his heart's ultimate need." Weiss exaggerates in believing that this scene represents Tommy's acceptance of the role of victim; but it is true that Tommy's self-pity and his drive toward self-destruction and even death are brought to climax here. (pp. 69-74)

Seize the Day does not end in Tommy's masochistic acceptance of his role as victim; it ends in hope for a new life. For if, on the one hand, Tommy is heading toward defeat, acceptance of suffering, perhaps literal death by suicide or heart attack, on the other hand, he is also committed to life. And if the final scene is a symbolic drowning, it is also a symbolic rebirth out of water.

Throughout the novel there are moments of serenity when striving has stopped. Just as Joseph lies at peace for a moment and sees "In the middle of the floor, like an accidental device of serenity, . . . a piece of red string"; just as Augie, lying for a moment with Thea, comes in touch with the axial lines in the same way, Tommy has found peace momentarily in the past. He has been in touch with his axial lines, has stopped striving and taken truth as a gift:

> When he was with the Rojax Corporation Wilhelm had kept a small apartment in Roxbury, two rooms in a large house with a small porch and garden, and on mornings of leisure, in late spring weather like this, he used to sit expanded in a wicker chair with the sunlight pouring through the weave, and sunlight through the slug-eaten holes of the young hollyhocks and as deeply as the grass allowed into small flowers.

It is as if the sunlight were pouring through Tommy, a simple living thing among other living things. Today again, remembering, in the whirring of the shining numbers on the commodities' board the birds of Roxbury:

> He breathed in the sugar of the pure morning.
>
> He heard the long phrases of the birds.
>
> No enemy wanted his life.
>
> Wilhelm thought, I will get out of here. I don't belong in New York anymore. And he sighed like a sleeper.

Always it is the sleeper in Bellow who is possessed of truth. Earlier he had said that to suffer in New York felt like "real life"; but if *"he doesn't belong in New York,"* the place of suffering, perhaps this means that he may be able to redeem himself from his impostor soul. These moments are few and brief, but in the materialistic atmosphere of the Hotel Gloriana and the commodities' market, they point the way toward Tommy's salvation. (One of the beauties in this novel is the picture of this gross man seeking salvation—a search distinct from that for self-justification—in the Hotel Gloriana and amid the whirring machines at the market.)

Just after his memory of Roxbury, Tommy thinks of how difficult it is in New York to communicate the simple need of a glass of water. "Every other man spoke a language entirely his own." Here is a favorite theme of Bellow's—the tower of Babel, or more generally, the lack of community. But this picture of alienation, Tommy thinks, finally does not matter:

> A queer look came over Wilhelm's face with its eyes turned up and his silent mouth with its high upper lip. He went several degrees further—when you are like this, dreaming that everybody is outcast, you realize that this must be one of the small matters. There is a larger body, and from this you cannot be separated. The glass of water fades out. You do not go from simple *a* and simple *b* to the great *x* and *y*, nor does it matter whether you agree about the glass but, far beneath such details, what Tamkin would call the real soul says plain and understandable things to everyone. There sons and fathers are themselves, and a glass of water is only an ornament; it makes a hoop of brightness on the cloth; it is an angel's mouth. There truth for everybody may be found, and confusion is only—only temporary, thought Wilhelm.

In tone and spirit this passage is like the conclusion of Isaac Singer's Yiddish story, "Gimpel the Fool," translated by Saul Bellow thus:

> Another *schnorrer* is waiting to inherit my bed of straw. When the time comes I will go joyfully. Whatever may be there, it will be real, without complications, without ridicule, without deception. God be praised: there even Gimpel cannot be deceived.

But the *there* is quite different. Gimpel refers to redemption in another world, Tommy to a redemption always at hand, found eternally in the here-and-now. If the false soul, the presentation self, is the individual, uncommunicating ego, the true soul is the common human soul which tells everyone the same message and which reveals the glory of the most common thing: a glass of water, Tommy Wilhelm.

And so the moment of truth is not isolating to the individual—quite the contrary. He feels himself part of a larger body. He feels love, as he did in the subway on his way to the Polo Grounds, when

> a general love for all these imperfect and lurid-looking people burst out in Wilhelm's breast. He loved them. One and all, he passionately loved them. They were his brothers and sisters. He was imperfect and disfigured himself, but what difference did that make if he was united with them by this blaze of love? And as he walked he began to say, "Oh my brothers—my brothers and sisters," blessing them all as well as himself.

In this moment of love Tommy, like Asa, is able to forgive himself. This is not the false love of the impostor soul but the true love which can rid Tommy of his burden. As Augie understands in his dream about the beggar-woman, instead of striving for individuality, one is to merge, to unite. At another time, acting with the impostor soul of his father, Tommy rejects an old fiddler begging for money—the figure comparable here to Augie's begging washerwoman—even though the "old bearded man with his bandaged beggar face and his tiny ragged feet and the old press clippings on his fiddle case to prove he had once been a concert violinist, pointed his bow at Wilhelm, saying 'You.' " Tommy refuses the identification, denies the omen. Or rather, seeing himself in the beggar who was once, as he himself was, a success, he rejects his common humanity with the beggar. And although he helps blind Mr. Rappaport to cross the street, he does it begrudgingly, out of duty, not love. The blaze of love passes; yet it is the center of the novel.

By the end of the novel Tommy is stripped bare. His lard and rye have no future; both his doctors have given him up. His unfinished telephone call to Margaret seems his final break in communication. She hangs up and he tries to rip the phone from the wall. He is cut apart from the world—without position, money, human contact.

But if he has lost his place in the world, he has also lost his artifices, his roles, his defenses. He is, like Lear, stripped bare. Perhaps now he will have to be reborn, have to love. Thus, if Tommy is symbolically the corpse in the funeral home, perhaps this death can be seen (as for Joseph in *Dangling Man*) as a release from the burden of selfhood, the death of the presentation self, the impostor soul. The real soul, according to Tamkin, tries constantly to kill the impostor soul, and unless it succeeds, "The pretender soul takes away the energy of the true soul and makes it feeble, like a parasite." When Tommy thinks, standing at the coffin, "If you want [my life] . . . then kill me. Take, take it, take it from me," is this resignation a moment in which by humility he is at least temporarily saved from his pretender soul? Is it Tommy's real or his pretender soul which is symbolically lying in the coffin? Since the defeats he suffers are at the expense of the pretender soul, it would seem to be this soul which is wounded. Although such defeats can be turned into victories by the masochist, it seems that this exhaustion and breakdown are not masochistic.

Bellow has learned a good deal from Reichian therapy; indeed, many of his friends, in particular the late Isaac Rosenfeld, have been Reichian devotees. Throughout the novel many of Tommy's physical symptoms are very much the kinds of symptoms dealt with by Reich in his discussions of "armoring"—in particular, the knot in Tommy's chest and his feeling of choking. "In certain patients," Reich reports, "we meet a syndrome stemming from the armoring of the chest which produces a particularly complicated system of difficulties. These patients complain, typically, of a 'knot' in the chest. . . . The lives of such patients are characterized by a general lack of initiative and by work disturbances based on the inability to use their hands freely." The condition cannot be changed "without the previous dissolution of the chest armor and without liberating the emotions of raving rage, of longing and genuine crying." Tommy's attempt to rip the phone from the wall is such rage, his weeping at the funeral, for Tommy such crying; thus, in Reichian terms, the end of the novel represents a healing release, a healing surrender of the armored self.

The moment before the coffin is very much like the moment of love in the subway—it is an expression of Tommy's true soul, his love for all men, and his acknowledgment of their common humanity. For if the corpse represents his father, himself, and (according to Klein) Dr. Tamkin, it is also simply a stranger, "another human creature."

> "It must be somebody real close to carry on so." . . .
>
> "The man's brother, maybe?"

Maybe the man's brother. And if so, insofar as this *is* so, the "consummation of his heart's ultimate need" is not death and the acceptance of his status as victim but, rather love, and if love, life for the true soul within Tommy.

This interpretation is supported by the passage immediately preceding the funeral, in which Tommy sees "the great, great crowd . . . on every face the refinement of one particular motive or essence—*I labor, I spend, I strive, I design, I love, I cling, I uphold, I give way, I envy, I long, I scorn, I die, I hide, I want.* Faster, much faster than any man could make the tally." It is like the municipal swimming pool in *Augie March,* like the sea of faces in the epigraph to *The Victim,* like the hunger of Eugene Henderson. It is out of this grasping crowd that the corpse appears to Tommy. Thus the corpse, "with his formal shirt and his tie and silk lapels and his powdered skin [which] looked so proper" is like Tommy's striving, inauthentic soul, his presentation self, and the man's corpse represents the death of this false soul and the possibility of new life, liberated from this soul.

The image of death-by-drowning offers hope. Tommy, who "dies" amid sea-like music, sinking "deeper than sorrow," has quoted, "Sunk though he be beneath the wat'ry floor." If in the death of Edward King, Milton expressed not only anxiety for his own life but also hope for the future ("Tomorrow to fresh woods and pastures new"), then by analogy the image of death-by-drowning hints at Tommy's rededication to life and to the living, his at least partial redemption from Selfhood. Further:

> Lycidas your sorrow is not dead,
> Sunk though he be beneath the wat'ry floor
> So sinks the day star in the ocean bed
> And yet anon repairs his drooping head. . . .
> So Lycidas sunk low but mounted high. . . .

and if Lycidas mounted high, perhaps so can Tommy Wilhelm.

This hope is sustained by the image of the fish under the water. . . . The fish is analogous to Tommy's true soul, "a mysterious being beneath the water, driven by hunger." Tommy is fishing *in* himself *for* himself. And if this fish

is an image of his soul, his soul seems safe: fish don't drown in water.

Finally, this is, as Klein notes, a moment of *Angst:* "At the point of death, he realizes existence, the 'true self,' the vitality which all men share, and which defines men." The confrontation of one's own death is always, in Bellow's novels, the beginning of new life within an admission of one's humanity.

It seems likely, then, that the "drowning" at the end is not an accession to masochistic failure, as Weiss believes, but a hint of new life for Tommy's true soul, an image of spiritual hope like that of the fisherman at the end of Eliot's *Waste Land.* If the final breakdown of Tommy's armoring signifies despair, more crucially it signifies hope. It is the wail of a baby at his birth. And if this ambiguous ending points toward possible redemption, it also affirms the beauty and dignity of Tommy Wilhelm and of all men. (pp. 128-34)

> *John Jacob Clayton, in his* Saul Bellow: In Defense of Man, *Indiana University Press, 1968, 273 p.*

Ralph Ciancio   (essay date 1969)

[*In the essay excerpted below, Ciancio examines religious and metaphysical issues in* Seize the Day.]

If the short novel *Seize the Day* is not the central story of our time, as one critic has commented, it is Saul Bellow's supreme achievement so far and, I think, a masterpiece of the first order. To be sure, it cannot lay claim to what is perhaps especially memorable about several of his full-length and more popular novels—the intellectual weight and lavish treatment of scene in *Herzog,* say; the rich variety of experience and linguistic range of *The Adventures of Augie March;* the comic and sweeping inventiveness of *Henderson the Rain King*—and its impact perhaps is not as immediately powerful. But its impact endures, and ultimately it is more satisfying because it derives from the achievement of perfect form. By this I do not mean to suggest that the book's content is more tractable because slighter in scope and less probing; that the difference between *Seize the Day* and Bellow's longer novels, in other words, can be reduced to a simple matter of purpose and the comparative freedom these dissimilar genres allow. Certainly its content is compressed, but one would hardly want to call it a thin or less complex story for that. To the contrary, its content, enlarged as well as intensified by metaphor, is far-reaching indeed: ostensibly an indictment of contemporary urban society, the story also encompasses religious and, ultimately, metaphysical issues. Nor, of course, do I mean to suggest that Bellow's longer novels are without discipline, the prime example to the contrary being *The Victim.* But as Leslie Fiedler has stated, the tight organization of *The Victim* represents only one tendency of Bellow's diverging styles; the tendency toward looseness and release, as in *Augie March,* is the other. Only in *Seize the Day* are both tendencies counterpoised, and to great effect, so as to produce a low-keyed but passionate "perilous rest," a tragic-comic tension and balance, Fiedler might have added, which is precisely the stylistic correlative to reality as Bellow's fiction explores it. In this respect alone, it is his most completely realized work.

In fact, *Seize the Day* coheres like a poem. " . . . I . . . think that the novel has imitated poetry far too much recently," Bellow has said [in Harvey Breit's *The Writer Observed*], "In its severity and style and devotion to exact form." He ought to know: by his statement Bellow meant to explain his adoption of the picaresque form in *Augie,* but by then he had already written *Seize the Day.* The aim of the analysis below, which hopefully will give to this remarkable work some measure of its due, is to explain its unity, how it holds together as a "poem" in conjunction with its meaning.

The story's controlling idea is propounded by Dr. Tamkin, a beguiling humbug sage posing as a psychologist and a friend in order to bilk Tommy Wilhelm, the protagonist, of his last seven hundred dollars.

> In here, the human bosom—mine, yours, everybody's—there isn't just one soul. There's a lot of souls. But there are two main ones, the real soul and a pretender soul.

Every man wants to live and to be loved, Tamkin argues, but because he lacks confidence in his real soul—what nature has made of him, the source of life—and the wisdom to comply with its strict demands, he finds nothing in himself to love and consequently seeks the approval of others as justification for self-approval; he turns his energies outward. In doing so, he activates the pretender soul, a false, theatrical self whose "interest . . . is the same as the social life, the society mechanism"—namely, vanity and the acquisition of financial power, the only value and criterion of success society honors—and the individual thus pursues money feverishly to prove his distinction. But he does so at the price of extinction, says Tamkin. To begin with, the pretender is sadistic; money-making is nothing but a disguised form of aggression:

> People come to the market to kill. They say, "I'm going to make a killing." It's not accidental. Only they haven't got the genuine courage to kill, and they erect a symbol of it. The money. They make a killing by a fantasy.

Misdirected by the pretender, the individual's love turns to hate, his passion for life to a passion for death; and when the real soul, victimized and maimed by its own energy, is laid to rest, the individual suffers a dehumanized, death-in-life existence. This is not all. After a time, enfeebled by efforts to overreach itself and scarred with guilt from having lived a falsehood, the real soul rebels and becomes masochistic:

> The true soul is the one that pays the price. It suffers and gets sick, and it realizes that the pretender can't be loved. Because it is a lie. The true soul loves the truth. And when the true soul feels like this, it wants to kill the pretender. The love has turned to hate. Then you become dangerous. A killer. You have to kill the deceiver.

The paradoxical corollary to this internecine and inward strife is twofold: every man is his own best lover and at once his own worst enemy, and all suicide is murder and all murder suicide.

Yet life is hardly meant to be so grave, as the affirmative and complementary side of Tamkin's philosophy stresses. The essence of it he writes out in a prescriptive poem, "Mechanism vs Functionalism [,] Ism vs Hism," the hero of which, the doctor says, is "sick humanity" in general and Wilhelm in particular. A ludicrous piece of doggerel, the poem nonetheless makes its humanistic point. Man is the center of all things; his eternity and rightful due, his cradle to joy and ecstasy rests with him. But it rests in the here-and-now and not in some future or transcendent state, "at the foot of Mt. Serenity" and not at the top; and it derives from his share in the brotherhood of man, in his common humanity rather than in his uncommonness as an individual. The poem thus urges man to put a halt to his strivings, to accept creation as it is given, the holiness of nature, "earth-moon-sea, the trinity," and his eminent place in its scheme; it urges man to know and to accept himself as he is, the limitations of his blessings as well as the blessings of his limitations; it urges man to seize the day and amen.

> Seek ye then that which art not there
> Is thine own glory let thyself rest.
> Witness. Thy power is not bare.
> Thou art King. Thou art at thy best.

Perhaps we should remark from the very start that Tamkin's ideas are the gauge of Bellow's primary interest, spiritual landscape, and in turn the gauge of his dramatic method, the fusion of the symbolic and the naturalistic, of metaphor and material image; to speak of one is to speak of the other. And whereas they perhaps seem conventional enough stated baldly and summarily, Tamkin's ideas cannot be separated either from his corny expression of them or from his motives as a confidence man: he obviously uses them as part of his pitch, he means to seize the day himself. Indeed, Tamkin's ambiguous character not only gives to his ideas vitality and depth but also is axial to both the structure of the story and to Wilhelm's fate; we shall have to ponder him at length. But the irony notwithstanding, and however commonplace, what is necessary to see first is that he in fact utters the truth, and a truth of considerable magnitude. What begins with the schizoid estrangement of the individual and his authentic self begets the estrangement of father and son, the individual and the contemporary urban world, the Jew and his spiritual heritage, the individual and humanity—issues which Bellow manages to encompass in the short breadth of his novel by focusing squarely on the plight of his protagonist and expanding centrifugally, as it were, the antagonism between the real and pretender souls according to Tamkin's diagnosis.

The perfect *schlemiel,* a failure at middle-age, Wilhelm enters the scene a desperate man on the day before *Yom Kippur.* Having lost his job with the Rojax Company; separated from his children and mercilessly hounded for alimony by Margaret, who refuses to give him a divorce; skeptical of his future with Olive, the woman from Roxbury he adores; and fearful that he will lose the money he has invested with Tamkin, he faces the total ruination of his life.

For all this he is largely to blame; he is the victim of his own blunders, a series of mistakes perpetrated even though he knew they would bring on disaster:

> This was typical of Wilhelm. After much thought and hesitation and debate he invariably took the course he had rejected innumerable times. Ten such decisions made up the history of his life. He had decided that it would be a bad mistake to go to Hollywood, and then he went. He had made up his mind not to marry his wife, but ran off and got married. He had resolved not to invest money with Tamkin, and then he had given him the check.

His feelings, the instinctual and the irrational, even the desire to fail, it is suggested, have governed Wilhelm's life. In everything, in fact, in all his habits as well as in all his endeavors, he is radically immature, emotionally a case of arrested development. Like the proverbial schoolboy, he stuffs his pockets with junk—packets of pills, strings of cellophane, pennies, and crushed cigarette butts—and affectionately humanizes his dog Scissors, his one-time companion; he whines with self-pity and looks to coca-cola bottles for security, sucking one after the other during the day; and he is indifferent to the neglect of his run-down and dirty car, not to mention the wall-to-wall slovenliness of his room. Further, for the same reason that the sight of children playing potsy and hopscotch eases his anxieties, we can assume that, before his improvident falling out with the boss, his moderate success with the Rojax Company derived from his feeling at home with its products—"Kiddies' furniture. Little chairs, rockers, tables, Jungle-Gyms, slides, swings, seesaws."

But if Wilhelm's feelings account for his failure, he at least *has* feelings, he at least evinces an eagerness for life, and in this sense his failure is also the measure of his human worth. If as willful and perverse as a child, he is also honest and direct as a child; if he allows people like Tamkin and Maurice Venice to dupe him, the reason is that he is trustful as well as naive. For everyone, in fact, he shows sympathy, compassion, love. When he hears that Venice was jailed for pandering, he grieves and wishes to express his sorrow in a letter; for the sake of his children, and even for the predaceous Margaret, he wants desperately to meet his alimony payments; and for reviling his father he suffers deep remorse. Being radically immature, in other words, Wilhelm is also radically innocent; indulgent with his own, "he would never willingly hurt any [other] man's feelings."

Or, as Tamkin would have it, Wilhelm's feelings are the inescapable source of his humanity as well as his inhuman adversary. Experience has made him aware that "he had been slow to mature, and he had lost ground, and so he hadn't been able to get rid of his energy, and he was convinced that his energy had done him the greatest harm," but he has yet to learn that it has done him the greatest harm not because it propels him against his will but because, although primordial and necessary, in itself it is not enough. His feelings need to be tempered by the acidity of hard facts and hard luck, the unpredictable in life and the consecrated if contingent clues to his identity as a human being—time, fallibility, death; they need, in short, to be-

come integral with and guided by reality. Reality, however, Wilhelm deliberately shuns. Implicit to his behavior is the romantic assumption that he is above or below, in one way or another beyond, the travails that assail the common lot of man. For example, sporadically, during the day, a glimmer of the truth comes forth from his real soul—

> he received a suggestion from some remote element in his thoughts that the business of life, the real business—to carry his peculiar burden, to feel shame and impotence, to taste these quelled tears—the only important business, the highest business was being done. Maybe the making of mistakes expressed the very purpose of his life and the essence of his being here—

but he lets the truth go, preferring instead to regard even his burdens and suffering as extraordinary. He must be different; he must prove his uniqueness; he must remain apart.

All "Ism," in other words, he has courted the pretender interest to his own detriment. Although still alive, although his real soul has not yet been crushed, he has allowed the pretender to scatter his energy outward and so far has defeated his own end. The salient example is his pseudonym, Tommy, which he adopted at the age of twenty while seeking fame and quick success in Hollywood, the land of make-believe—an attempt, he has come to see, to gain liberty from family ties, which is to say from his identity. And that he still hopes to redeem himself according to the ethos of cash-and-carry is shown in his investment with Tamkin, another bid for freedom initiated by "Tommy" and at the most precarious time of his life. This, too, Wilhelm faintly surmises, but it is a truth that neither his pride nor his guilt will permit him to believe in his heart. Again, he would rather believe that he is "a fool" and "a clunk" by nature, that the aspect of his personality he calls "Wilky" is his real soul, whereas "Wilky," to the contrary, denotes what "Tommy" has made of him, his own victim, and is another rationalization that blurs his true identity all the more. Rather, the name of his real soul is Velvel (evidence of this I shall present below), the name by which his grandfather called him; and until, amidst all this confusion, he begins to conceptualize the truth he is instinctively attuned to and to control the tropism of his feelings in accord with reality, his real soul will remain undiscovered in limbo and he a potential killer and suicide. For Wilhelm "is a visionary sort of animal. Who has to believe that he can know why he exists. Though he has never seriously tried to find out why." The events of the day, all of which take place within ten to twelve hours, are calculated to bring him unswervingly, shockingly to the answer.

But unfortunately Wilhelm has more to combat than just himself, and before the events of the day come to a close, his confusion is knotted over several times, which enlists our sympathies for him. Victimized from within, on the one hand, he is victimized from without, on the other hand, and ironically by the identical power, the externalization and metaphor of the same inhuman limits which bound his real soul and which he refuses to acknowledge in himself, the pretender interest. In other words, his external conflicts parallel the inner drama of his self-estrangement, amplifying his quest for identity and stifling further his growth as a human being.

Of a piece dramatically as well as metaphorically, these external conflicts unfold in dissolving view. But to take them in the order of their prominence, the first consists of his estrangement from his father, Dr. Adler, an affluent and retired diagnostician in whom the pretender has obviously usurped command. An eagle by name (the German and Yiddish meaning of "Adler") and description ("round-headed . . . with . . . feather-white, ferny hair"), he remains aloof from Wilhelm's anguish, stiff-backed and proud, unsullied, self-sufficient. A specialist in internal medicine, he knows nothing about the heart and its affections. He pockets rather than wears his hearing aid, having tuned out the human race. Even his clothes, the flamboyant shirts and vests he buys at a college haberdashery, betray at once his values—theatricality, hypocrisy, a concern for furbelows—and his obsession with death, the prospects of his dying in a year or two, the dread of which he suffers in silence, with style; a youthful facade, we see, to conceal his age and to arrest time, as if screaming colors might delay the entelechy of nature's juices. "And not only is death on his mind," Wilhelm notes, "but through money he forces me to think about it, too." This expresses succinctly the terms as well as the stakes of their bloody feud, life or death. On the one hand, Dr. Adler refuses to save his son from financial ruin because, by the perverse logic of his standards, Wilhelm is practically impoverished to begin with, not the kind of son a vainglorious father can boast of, not at all the right kind of Jew. On the other hand, Dr. Adler repudiates his son because Wilhelm threatens to drag him into the turmoil of life as he would drag Wilhelm into the grave.

This is the quirk of his obsession—it derives more basically from a fear of life than of death, and in fact he, even more than Wilhelm, cowers in the fact of reality. To Dr. Adler, life and death are synonymous; to him, the whole of life resides on the outskirts of time: in the future, with thoughts of his own death, and in the past, on the basis of which he condemns Wilhelm—on the basis of his son's dead mistakes. By thus objectifying death, he conveniently suspends the present, the here-and-now, the actual domain of human activity and the real stuff of life—struggle, defeat, suffering and, if struggle and defeat and suffering can be met with, joy. Joy Dr. Adler has no affinity with; the rest he wishes to suppress at all costs. In contrast, Wilhelm at least senses that "if he didn't keep his troubles before him he risked losing them altogether, and he knew from experience that this was worse." Dr. Adler has his legitimate complaints and miseries, to be sure, but he clings to them; they are death's miseries, moreover, not life's; abstract and cerebral, not concrete, not the flesh-and-blood miseries that accompany existential life. From such he has paid the price of immunity, he believes, by coming up the hard way, through aggressive entrepreneurism, and now is entitled to die in peace. Wilhelm is a blight in his eyes, then, because he lays his confusions and pains at his father's feet, begging him to flex his stiff carriage and pick them up. To accept the challenge is unthinkable: "You want to make yourself into my cross. But

I am not going to pick up a cross. I'll see you dead, Wilky, by Christ, before I let you do that to me." Seated on a table in the hotel's massage room as he lets fly his final renunciation, Dr. Adler appropriately "gathered over him a sheet," his shroud.

Wilhelm's second external conflict consists of his estrangement from the contemporary urban world, the collective soul of which Dr. Adler, pampered and "idolized by everyone," epitomizes. The setting is the Upper West Side of Manhattan—a world of shops and restaurants with gilded fronts and huge, baroque, mausoleum-like hotels whose clients—aged, decrepit, gaudily dressed businessmen—are waiting to die; a world of stockmarkets and electronic bookkeeping machines that cancel "you out automatically"; a world, as Wilhelm observes, that caters to the likes of the cruel and otiose Mr. Rappaport, a millionaire who has acquired his fortune in the chicken-killing industry and an obvious death-figure (he hardly has flesh enough to keep his trousers on) who clicks and clacks rather than talks when Wilhelm addresses him. And no wonder, still throbbing with life, Wilhelm is an alien to the city, an intruder, the violator, in fact, of its first taboo: he bewails his troubles before all, clamoring with anguish and operatic gestures in a society dedicated to spiritual suffering but, as if by tacit oath, to keeping its suffering buried. Mr. Perls' biological ailments, his clubfoot, for example, cannot be hidden, but about his flight from Germany and obscure tragedies not one illuminating word is mentioned; the business of the somnolent, droopy-eyed stockmarket manager, the overseer of daily catastrophe, is "to conceal his opinion"; and "the great weight of the unspoken" leaves Wilhelm and Reuben, a hotel clerk who suffers, like Wilhelm, marital and pecuniary problems, "little to talk about." Mum's the word, we see; no one dares articulate his genuine feelings lest he rattle society's bones. (pp. 49-57)

The third of Wilhelm's external conflicts consists of his struggle to regain his Jewish heritage and the spiritual values of his race. When Dr. Adler introduces him to friends and says, "I uphold tradition. He's for the new," of course the opposite is true. To be sure, Wilhelm does not go to synagogue, he cannot even translate into English the meaning of common Hebrew prayers. But in contrast to a society composed largely of assimilated Jews who pay homage to the bitch goddess and only lip service to the Hebraic God—the man Wilhelm pays to pray for his mother at the cemetery wants to be tipped for intoning *El molai rachamin;* and after the custom of theatrical performances people must purchase and reserve seats for *Yom Kippur,* the cost of atonement—Wilhelm "often prayed in his own manner" and "would occasionally perform certain devotions, according to his feelings." if not by the letter of the law, he lives by the spirit of the Law. Moreover, Wilhelm visits his mother's grave each year in keeping with Jewish custom, whereas Dr. Adler has forgotten even the year that she died; and when, outraged by the incident, Wilhelm learns that vandals have split in two the bench between her and his grandmother's grave and tells his father about it, Dr. Adler is unmoved and refuses to have it replaced. In one trenchant image, that of the broken bench, Bellow symbolizes simultaneously the loss of Wilhelm's consolations (another of his havens, like his children, is taken away from him); the power (money, needed to replace the bench) that alienates him from the succor of the past (the bench joins one generation to the next, his mother's grave to his grandmother's); and, more to the point here, Dr. Adler's denial of familial ties, traditional values, and the traits of his race—"sensitive feelings, a soft heart, a brooding nature, a tendency to be confused under pressure," traits which Mrs. Adler shared with her ancestors, and indeed with all mankind, and which Wilhelm has inherited from her. More profoundly than he suspects, then, Wilhelm is right when he declares to his father that Mrs. Adler's death marked "the beginning of the end," the end of their spiritual kinship as well as, potentially, the end of Jewish history.

The very fact that Dr. Adler fails in the least to comprehend his son's words confirms their acuteness. For like Wilhelm's distant and pretentious sister, who takes after her father and whose Philistine paintings convey meaning to neither Jews nor Gentiles (she has adopted Phillipa as a professional name!), and like society as a whole, which Wilhelm likens to the Tower of Babel, Dr. Adler has disavowed himself of a heritage nourished by the experience of humanity, in the permanence, universality, and continuity of which rests the *logos,* and hence he speaks an alien language. Wilhelm speaks from the heart, he from the glands—"voodoo," he says of Wilhelm's problems, and for therapy recommends steam. Consequently, he can be of no real help, for more urgently than money Wilhelm needs and seeks spiritual guidance, an authoritative, patriarchal word: "Father, listen! Listen" is his first and final plea. The cynical and solipsistic injunction he gets as advice—"Carry no one on your back!"—makes a mockery of Moses' farewell to the Jews:

> Remember the days of old;
> Consider the years of many generations,
> Ask your father and he will inform you.

With good reason, therefore, Wilhelm prays for deliverance, in Psalm-like cadences if in colloquial idiom—

> Oh, God, . . . Let me out of my trouble. Let me out of my thoughts, and let me do something better with myself. For all the time I have wasted I am very sorry. Let me out of this clutch and into a different life. For I am all balled up. Have mercy—

for he lives in a fallen world, "a kind of purgiatory [*sic*]," as Tamkin says, a world besieged by "plague."

Of these religious references "plague" is the most apt dramatically, as I shall explain in a moment. But first let me indicate that these and other religious references function only as one aspect of Jewish culture and are meant to crystallize the estrangement of the contemporary Jewish community not from orthodox Judaism or the Hebraic God but from the humanistic thrust of its spirtual past in secular terms, which in turn functions as the veil or projection of modern man's estrangement from humanity, from the Life Force—the last of Wilhelm's external conflicts against the suffocating grip of the pretender, to keep alive and to preserve his identity as a human being. It is in this secular and symbolic sense that plague of a biblical kind is given form in the novella. It is in this sense too, as part and parcel of his estrangement from his real soul, his father, the urban world and his Jewish consciousness, relating organically the furthest reach of Bellow's theme to the novella's controlling idea, that Wilhelm's total crisis comes down to a struggle against damnation.

All this Bellow manages through water imagery, which pervades the book from start to finish, in conjunction with variant expressions of one subsuming metaphor, the Waters of Life, the Stream of Humanity. According to its rationale, the Life Force originates in both an external and internal source, from Nature, the Fountainhead of the Human Spirit conceived of as God, and in man, whose real soul partakes of Nature. The holy life, therefore, the genuinely human life, consists of man living in organic unity with God and, as Tamkin observes, "rolls the waters of the earth." Now the urban world has fallen into damnation because it has sundered its attachment to God, the humanizing energy the Jewish religion has thrived on in the past, and at once denied the flow of its real soul, or *vice versa*. But more than this, as we have seen, the urban world has converted its human energy into inhuman energy; it has, according to Bellow's metaphor, drained its real soul from within and rechanneled the Life Force against its purpose, against God. Hence, as if by the wrathful God of Creation, it has brought upon itself a deluge, wholesale death by water reminiscent of the Flood, the symbolic form plague assumes in the story: The Ansonia Hotel looks "like the image of itself reflected in deep water, white and cumulous above, with cavernous distortions beneath"; people cross "the tide of Broadway traffic"; "in full tumult the great afternoon current raced toward Columbus Circle. . . . " The entire urban world, Bellow wants us to see, is inundated, a wasteland of plenitude, as it were.

Or, to sum up Wilhelm's total crisis as it is dramatized symbolically, against the pretender and damnation he struggles to keep himself from drowning: "The waters of the earth are going to roll over me." Instinctively he thus recoils from the "swirling green," "wall-locked and chlorinated" waters of the hotel pool in which the clean and immaculate Dr. Adler daily immerses himself; and from the "brackish tidal river smell . . . the smell of mop water" that rises high above the city from the Hudson River, whose currents separate him from New Jersey and from his children, who reside there. But his ordeal is more complicated than this. Although society has defiled the waters of life and makes it difficult for him to exist without sinking beneath them, they are nevertheless inherently holy, and this, as we have seen in another context, he has not yet acknowledged; he is right to say no to the pretender but yet must learn to say yes to the sacred fount of experience which alone can purify and make him a whole person, those brute realities he continues to oppose although floundering through life like a "hippopotamus" and soaking wet with them. In brief, his fear of drowning is inextricable from his fear of life: he uses "an electric razor so that he didn't have to touch water" and usually wears "his coat collar turned up as though he had . . . to go out in the rain." Thus resisting reality and a potential plague-carrier himself—he "smelled the salt odor of tears in his nose"—

he has become vulnerable to the pretender and ironically swells the very tide he would escape by frantically following its inclinations: on the day he invests his money on the stockmarket, a rainy, "weeping day," the water dribbles over his hat and transparent raincoat. And although he does not "wash his hands in the morning," significantly the commodity he invests in is lard, the rudimentary but essential ingredient of soap and hydrotherapy—hydrotherapy being what Dr. Adler grotesquely prescribes for Wilhelm's traumas, in particular the steam baths located at the very bottom of the Gloriana Hotel, below sea level, where an attendant passes out soap and where Dr. Adler damns him to death rather than listen to his miseries in their climactic encounter; a situation, if we wish to follow the tug of associations still further, that parallels what Wilhelm recollects of a movie in which the heroine Annie Laurie pleaded and "wrung" her hands before the Laird as he ordered the bagpipers "to drown her out." Once caught up in the cash nexus, in other words, Wilhelm's fate is set—"By and by, you'll get the drift," Tamkin assures him! He begins to vacillate like a "seaweed" in what Tamkin calls the "money-flow" of business transactions, the same deadly flow, we can assume, that has battened the fish-toothed Mr. Perls (his very name links wealth with the sea), who has a "drippy mustache," and made him successful. And finally, feeling the loss of his self-control, likened to "a ball in the surf washed beyond reach"; having taken barbituates throughout the day, with each Phanaphen capsule swallowing "a long gulp of water"; filled with "unshed tears" and looking "like a man about to drown" and recalling lines from "Lycidas"—finally Wilhelm sinks "beneath the wat'ry floor."

But not entirely. What begins in a paradox, the self-antagonism between the real and pretender souls, ends in a paradox. Wilhelm drowns insofar as, in the end, the pretender leads him to financial and social bankruptcy. But in the concluding scene, a scene, like "Lycidas," at once elegiac and redemptive, his resurrection is born of his defeat, he survives the waters, his real soul intact. (pp. 58-62)

> *Ralph Ciancio, "The Achievement of Saul Bellow's 'Seize the Day',"* in Literature and Theology, *edited by Thomas F. Staley and Lester F. Zimmerman, The University of Tulsa, 1969, pp. 49-80.*

M. Gilbert Porter (essay date 1974)

[*Porter is an American critic and educator who often writes on the fiction of Bellow and Ken Kesey. In the following excerpt, Porter examines "how the embodiment of theme in water imagery finds its larger objectification in individual scenes" that themselves "function like poetic images" in* Seize the Day.]

Critical opinion of *Seize the Day* reveals almost unanimous agreement that it is the most well made of all Bellow's novels. Plot, character, mood, and language are skillfully interwoven to produce the kind of "figure in the carpet" that Henry James prized so highly. Even more than *The Victim, Seize the Day* achieves a sustained intensity and a unity of effect that approaches the condition of poetry. Indeed, Keith Opdahl [in his *The Novels of Saul Bellow,* 1967] has seen the pattern of water imagery in the novel as its most dominant feature. His comments are both a description of imagery and a summary of plot:

> *Seize the Day* . . . depicts the death throes of a drowning man. Tommy Wilhelm faces complete submergence in failure. He begins his day plunging downward in a hotel elevator to a city sunk metaphorically beneath the sea. The New York streets carry a "tide of Broadway traffic" which is the "current" of the city. The baroque hotel he sees from the lobby window looks "like the image of itself reflected in deep water, white and cumulous above, with cavernous distortions underneath." Although Wilhelm struggles to keep "the waters of the earth" from rolling over him, he looks "like a man about to drown." He has foolishly quit his job and has no money to meet the demands of his wife, who seeks to punish him for leaving her. His relations with his elderly father, whom he has denied by changing his name, reach the breaking point; the physician denies his plea for help by calling him a slob. He finally loses the little money he has left on the commodities market, where he had speculated at the urging of a phony psychologist, Dr. Tamkin.
>
> The waters roll over him when he stumbles, defeated, into a funeral home. There, "where it was dark and cool," his troubles end. The quiet chapel has the wavering, dreamlike quality of an ocean grotto. Organ music "stirred and breathed from the pipes" and "men in formal clothes and black homburgs strode softly back and forth on the cork floor, up and down the center aisle." Wilhelm feels a "splash of heartsickness" as he stands before the corpse of a stranger. When he begins to cry, at first softly and then hysterically, his drowning is complete. "The heavy sea-like music came up to his ears," Bellow writes. "It poured into him where he had hidden himself in the center of a crowd by the great and happy oblivion of tears. He heard it and sank deeper than sorrow, through torn sobs and cries toward the consummation of his heart's ultimate need."

"Wilhelm's drowning," Opdahl explains further, "is first of all the climax of his day of failure. The water in which he drowns is both the world and his masochistic self which have murdered him." His death, however, is not purely negative, for in the death of the old self, there is the birth of a new self who will be, the novel implies, more capable of dealing with his own temperament and the world around him.

Clinton Trowbridge has also provided a sensitive reading of the water imagery in *Seize the Day.* Among many perceptive comments, he makes the following observation:

> The image of the drowning Wilhelm is the controlling one, but because of the book's ironic structure it is an image that functions in two ways. On a first reading, and on each rereading on the surface of our experience, it intensifies sympathy for Wilhelm's condition. Even when Wilhelm is being depicted least sympathetically, when he is most in the wrong, most a slob, we are continually made aware that we are witness-

ing the strugglings of a drowning man and we want to see him rescued. Thus our sympathy is continual in a way that it is not, for instance, with Dostoevski's underground man.

Both Opdahl and Trowbridge have provided provocative insights into the dominance of water imagery in the novel, but Trowbridge seems mainly interested in the affective functions of language and tone, and Opdahl seems content to provide an adumbrated description of the images, pointing to them but not examining in detail their cohesive function in the novel as a whole. Neither writer concerns himself with the skillful use Bellow makes of the scene as image in *Seize the Day.*

The purpose of the analysis offered here, then, is to show how the embodiment of theme in water imagery finds its larger objectification in individual scenes, for the individual scenes in this novel clearly function like poetic images, producing an integrated totality of impression that is very similar to the effect of a lyric poem. A novel is not a lyric poem, of course, and the methods of analysis that serve for poetry cannot without modification be applied to fiction, but with some allowance for the difference in genres, the formalist methods of analyzing poetic images can prove illuminating when applied to fiction. Such an analysis is especially productive in revealing Bellow's narrative strategy in *Seize the Day.*

That the scene in fiction frequently functions like the image in poetry has been established explicitly by W. J. Handy [in his *Kant and the Southern New Critics,* 1963]. . . .

How the fictional scene functions to "formulate the particularity, the texture of experience" in the life of Tommy Wilhelm and how these scenes approximate the poetic image provide the focus of this chapter.

Ezra Pound [in *Poetry,* March 1913] has defined the image in poetry as "that which presents an intellectual and emotional complex in an instant of time," and I. A. Richards has shown that a metaphorical image can be analyzed according to its tenor, the idea in or the subject matter of the implied comparison, and its vehicle, the particularity in which generality is embodied. The conception of the fictional scene developed in this chapter draws on both of these observations, for it is clear that at the center of *Seize the Day* is an extended metaphor which serves as the integrating principle of the narrative. The metaphor, as Opdahl and Trowbridge have shown, depicts human failure through the image of a drowning man. Tommy Wilhelm has made a mess of his life and now, gasping for breath and grabbing, panic-stricken, at straws (Tamkin), he sinks wearily beneath the pressures of his own making. The tenor of the total image that is the book is human failure. The vehicle in which this subject matter is embodied is the image of drowning, and each scene in the novel functions as a facet of the total image, the texture of the narrative presentation. The scenes render the particularity of the diverse pressures under which Wilhelm is submerged, and function thereby to extend the central metaphor.

Pound describes the poetic image as being presented in "an instant of time," that is, in a frozen moment. The ef-

fect is a kind of timelessness. In fiction, however, characters move through time; their experience occurs in successive moments. "Works of fiction," W. J. Handy has said in a recent essay [in *James Joyce: His Place in World Literature,* 1969], "express man's capacity to experience his experience, not in moments merely (as reflected in the lyric poem or the painting or the sculpture), but in time." The action of the novel necessarily involves the passage of time. Handy's emphasis on the scene as the basic presentational unit in fiction, however, suggests that within scene, time functions in a manner not dissimilar to Pound's concept of an "instant of time." What fiction achieves in the successful treatment of time and space within scene is what Joseph Frank [in *Sewanee Review* 53, 1945] has called "spatial form," the arrangement of action and setting in accentual levels of presentational unity. He illustrates his theory with an examination of the scene in [Flaubert's] *Madame Bovary* in which Rodolphe woos Emma with sentimental rhetoric, while below them on the street a country fair is in progress, the mobs being addressed by both local politicians and a livestock auctioneer. . . .

"Cutting back and forth between the various levels of action" in time-present enabled Flaubert, as Frank has demonstrated, to present movement within scene with a kind of simultaneity that approximates Pound's concept of an "intellectual and emotional complex in an instant of time."

Bellow performs a similar feat in *Seize the Day.* Tommy Wilhelm moves through time, from his pre-breakfast appearance outside his hotel room to his attendance at the funeral of a stranger in mid-afternoon; but the narration renders this successive movement in a series of eight stills, or scenes. Instead of cutting back and forth between levels of action in time-present, as Flaubert does, Bellow's omniscient narration most often cuts back and forth between time-present and time-past in the mind of Tommy Wilhelm. Setting and time-present form the frame which contains Wilhelm's reflections on time-past and its effect on his current situation. Since the integrating principle of time and place—and also of action—is the mind of Wilhelm, his mood is the primary device for establishing the limits of individual scene. Juxtaposing time-past and time-present within the context of setting and through the mind of the protagonist has the effect, if not of actually arresting time, of rendering it in slow motion, so that "spatial form" is achieved and the focus falls on the intrareferential relation among the parts that make up scene (language, action, character, mood, etc.) and, finally, that contribute cumulatively to the total image that is the book. Slow motion is appropriate to *Seize the Day* because it suggests the movements of a man under water.

Though it is usually easy for the critic to determine where one scene leaves off and the next begins, it is not always easy for him to explain his rationale for such division. Probably the difficulty lies in the eclectic nature of the scene in fiction. Like drama, the scene commonly involves action based on conflict. Other characters are therefore involved, and the action occurs in time and in a given place. The arrival or departure of a character or a shift in time or place is likely to entail a shift in scene—but not necessarily; for, like poetry, fiction can present attitudes or emotions in almost pure states, through dreams, say, or through omniscient narration, stream-of-consciousness, or a number of other techniques. Therefore, the mood of the protagonist or the central intelligence must be considered of major importance in determining the limits of scene. If a mood is sustained through several shifts in setting and characters, the scene must usually be judged continuous. The pace of a scene must also be considered, and narrative bridges (summaries, descriptive passages, etc.) must be accounted for. In practice these matters seem less complicated because the individual scene, like the whole work, creates a dominant impression and has an internal consistency of its own if it has been skillfully built. To discover this internal consistency, the critic must allow the scene to dictate from within the key to its analysis. The rationale behind the division of scenes in *Seize the Day* will, it is hoped, become clear in the discussions of each of its eight scenes.

Scene I begins with an archetypal descent. Wilhelm emerges from his hotel room on the twenty-third floor and goes down to the lobby. Water imagery begins immediately. "The elevator sank and sank" and the carpet in the lobby "billowed toward Wilhelm's feet": "French drapes like sails kept out the sun," and outside like an anchor chain is a "great chain that supported the marquee of the movie house directly underneath the lobby." The Ansonia Hotel across the street looks "like marble or like sea water, black as slate in the fog." Its image is reflected in the sun as though "in deep water." Wilhelm walks to the newsstand, which provides the setting for the first scene. In the glass cigar counter Wilhelm sees his reflection, but not clearly, because of "the darkness and deformations of the glass," a watery reflection. Three times in this scene he refers to himself as a "hippopotamus," an ungainly water creature. Wilhelm lights a cigar, buys a coke and a newspaper, and exchanges small talk with Rubin, the newsstand operator. He lingers at the newsstand to avoid entering the dining room to join his father, Dr. Adler, for breakfast because he fears that the day holds something ominous for him:

> Today he was afraid. He was aware that his routine was about to break up and he sensed that a huge trouble long presaged but till now formless was due. Before evening he'd know.

As Wilhelm fidgets at the newsstand, Rubin's casual remarks in time-present spark Wilhelm's reflections on time-past. Rubin remarks perfunctorily that Wilhelm is looking "pretty sharp today." Wilhelm reflects ruefully that once such an observation would have been accurate, but that now he has gone to seed. Other casual remarks by Rubin lead Wilhelm into three extended reflections, and each reveals some aspect of his past that has contributed to his present discomfort.

There is, first, his stock market investment with Dr. Tamkin, the glib, semiliterate pseudopsychologist. "With all this money around," Tamkin had told him enthusiastically, "you don't want to be a fool while everyone else is making." On the strength of this recommendation and in des-

peration, Wilhelm had entrusted the remainder of his savings to Tamkin. Though he sees himself as a porcine hippopotamus, Wilhelm perversely allowed his money to be invested in lard. Now he justifiably fears for his investment. But Tamkin is more to Wilhelm than a financial long-shot. Despite his obvious flaws, he is a surrogate father: "At least Tamkin sympathizes with me and tries to give me a hand, whereas Dad doesn't want to be disturbed."

The reflection on Tamkin leads by association into a reflection on Dr. Adler. Wilhelm's father is a retired physician, respected, wealthy, and gracefully aged. He wishes only to spend his autumn years in peace and security, which he feels he has earned. He is vain and healthy, the socially beloved object of flirtatious young women and fawning matrons. Having quit his job, left his wife, misplaced his money, and generally lost his way, Wilhelm remembers how he had confessed his troubles to his father in an implied supplication for aid and how his father had remained indifferent. . . .

The father is clearly a self-centered, uncompassionate old man, but Wilhelm is far from a blameless son. He has been, he knows, a great disappointment to his father: He was a college dropout, a bungling father, a misfit in the business world, and he has become an unhygienic slob. Unlovable though he knows he is, he yearns still to be loved. Two lines of poetry occur to him in connection with his reflections on his father: "Love that well which thou must leave ere long," from Shakespeare's Sonnet seventy-three, is the attitude that Wilhelm feels his father should take toward his declining son; and this line leads him to another even more elegiac in nature, Milton's "Sunk though he be beneath the wat'ry floor"—a line from "Lycidas" which carries out the water imagery and reflects Wilhelm's moribund personality. Then Wilhelm recalls another element in his personal history that might account in part for his father's attitude: When Wilhelm dropped out of college to go to Hollywood, he had changed his name from Wilhelm Adler to Tommy Wilhelm:

> He had cast off his father's name, and with it his father's opinion of him. It was, he knew it was, his bid for liberty, Adler being in his mind the title of the species, Tommy the freedom of the person.

Acknowledging this earlier rejection of the father leads Wilhelm to retrace the circumstances surrounding that event, and into his consciousness lumbers the figure of Maurice Venice, agent for Kaskaskia Films.

Water imagery continues in this reflection. Venice, whose name suggests water, has his office in the midst of the sides and roofs of buildings—"sheer walls, gray spaces, dry lagoons of tar and pebbles." Wilhelm remembers him as a relative of Martial Venice the producer and thus "the obscure failure of an aggressive and powerful clan." In describing for Wilhelm the condition of those nameless faces that make up movie audiences, Venice really describes his own condition: "Listen, everywhere there are people trying hard, miserable, in trouble, downcast, tired, trying and trying. They need a break, right? A break-through, a help, luck or sympathy." Venice knows what he is talking about, for he too is a drowning man; he speaks with difficulty in a "choked, fat-obstructed voice"; he is an objectification of failure whose warning Wilhelm fails to heed. To Venice, Wilhelm is the type who gets "stood up." He casts Wilhelm appraisingly as a loser, and the screen test Wilhelm makes shows Venice to be a prophet. Wilhelm goes on to California without Venice's backing, but his efforts to become an actor are futile. Wilhelm takes no pleasure in learning later that Venice has been arrested for pandering, and his true love, the bathing beauty Nita Christenberry, has been sentenced to three years for prostitution. There is a wry turn in the narrative here through allusion. The nebulous relative of "aggressive and powerful" Martial (Mars) whose last name is Venice (Venus) becomes a mock-Cupid at last in his touting of love, failing to retain the happiness he thought he had found in his water nymph. Wilhelm is too absorbed with the man's suffering to trouble himself with mythological overtones.

Having reviewed in his mind some of his major mistakes of the past, Wilhelm sums them up in a kind of self-flagellation. . . .

The pressures generated by this mental recital cause Wilhelm extreme depression and anxiety. The scene ends with his silent prayer for succor:

> "Oh God," Wilhelm prayed. "Let me out of my trouble. Let me out of my thoughts, and let me do something better with myself. For all the time I have wasted I am sorry. Let me out of this clutch and into a different life. For I am all balled up. Have mercy."

This is the drowning man's appeal for assistance from a divine source. Several times in this scene reference is made to Wilhelm's "panting laugh," a sound suggestive of both panic and frantic exertion to stay afloat. The anguished prayer which Wilhelm silently sends out at the end of the scene grows out of the cumulative effect of his reflections within time-present, his past mistakes, bad luck, and weakness in character culminating in his current condition. All of these are unified in a "single configuration of meaning" in the presentational form of the scene. The movement from his room to the newsstand, then, is really a single movement unified by the implied metaphor and the introspective, foreboding mood of the central character. This strategy sets the pattern for the scenes that follow.

Scene II is very brief. Wilhelm picks up his mail from the desk clerk, realizing as he does so—as much from the desk clerk's accusing attitude as from the day of the month—that his morning mail contains a bill for his rent, a bill that he cannot pay because all his money is tied up in his venture with Tamkin. Stimulated by the bill for his rent and his own shortness of funds, Wilhelm begins mentally to accuse his father of selfishness in knowing that his son is in trouble and refusing to offer him assistance. As if to corroborate his charge, Wilhelm then recalls the scene in which his father revealed to him that he had forgotten the date of his wife's—and Wilhelm's mother's—death. For a moment, the selfishness of the father is established and Wilhelm appears in a sympathetic light.

Almost immediately, however, the narrative strategy changes, and the focus of narration shifts. The omniscient narrator reveals Wilhelm as he appears in the eyes of his father: an overweight, jittery, whining, unkempt bungler. And then, from a still more detached view, Wilhelm's actions are described as he stands musing on his father's continued indifference:

> Unaware of anything odd in his doing it, for he did it all the time, Wilhelm pinched out the coal of his cigarette and dropped the butt in his pocket, where there were many more.

Suddenly the sympathetic light in which he has just appeared dims, for he shows himself no longer entitled to claim, as he has earlier, that "from his mother he had gotten sensitive feelings." Wilhelm's misery is too real to be negated by the revelation of such character traits, but the empathy which the reader regularly develops for Wilhelm is vitiated by this strategy. Such distancing through point of view—and it occurs repeatedly in the book—adds realistic dimension to Wilhelm's characterization and prevents his suffering from becoming maudlin.

Returning to the mail in his hand, Wilhelm finds a letter from his wife, protesting the recent postdated check he sent her and demanding that he pay the enclosed premiums on the boys' educational insurance policies. One of his most painful problems comes clearly into focus—money:

> They were his kids, and he took care of them and always would. He had planned to set up a trust fund. But that was on his former expectations. Now he had to rethink the future, because of the money problem. Meanwhile, here were the bills to be paid. When he saw the two sums punched out so neatly on the cards he cursed the company and its IBM equipment. His heart and head were congested with anger.

This scene accomplished at least two major things in documenting the pressures which are pushing Wilhelm under: It elaborates on the estrangement between Wilhelm and his father and between Wilhelm and his wife, and it insists on the immediacy of his financial problem. His mood throughout the scene is one of anger resulting from a sense of persecution. In accordance with the controlling metaphor of drowning, Wilhelm's head and heart at the end of the scene are congested, and in this condition he enters the dining room, putting an end to his long delay in meeting his father for breakfast.

Scene II takes place entirely in the dining room. The mood at breakfast is casual and, at times, almost lighthearted, at least on the surface. Water imagery pervades the scene, occasionally in mildly comic fashion. Wilhelm sees his father sitting in a sunny bay where water glasses cast light patterns on the tablecloth and the white enamel on the window frames is "streaming with wrinkles." Seated by Dr. Adler in this aquatic circumambience is, appropriately, Mr. Perls. Wilhelm immediately dislikes the fishy Mr. Perls: "Who is this damn frazzle-faced herring with his dyed hair and his fish teeth and this drippy mustache?" The faintly humorous suggestion here seems to be that one who sits down before Perls runs the risk of being classified as a swine. This is especially true of one who has invested his savings in lard and who frequently refers to himself as a hippopotamus. The initial humor in this suggestion is lost, however, in the truth of its application to Wilhelm and in his awareness of its truth. Narrative summary in this scene has revealed, for example, that Wilhelm is a careless, insensitive driver, that his car is filthy, that he does not wash his hands before meals, that he uses an electric razor to avoid touching water (the hydrophobia of a drowning man), and that he lives in his room with "worse filth than a savage." Furthermore, when the conversation turns to money, Wilhelm finds to his disgust that he is lying about his financial condition to please his father and to impress Mr. Perls, even though in his mind Wilhelm has just condemned both of them for their transparent greed. He feels dirtied by his pandering to their values, and his response is the usual one: He experiences congestion.

When the conversation turns to the dubious credentials of Dr. Tamkin, Wilhelm joins halfheartedly in the laughter while experiencing despair in his heart because the object of their ridicule is the man in whom Wilhelm has foolishly invested all his immediate financial hopes. His laugh is again his characteristic "panting laugh," an expression of panic and exhaustion. The combined weight of his misery provokes Wilhelm to see himself as a heavily laden leviathan: "The spirit, the peculiar burden of his existence lay upon him like an accretion, a load, a lump." The scene ends as Wilhelm thinks anxiously of the imminent opening of the stock market and of what the day's trading may portend for him.

Unlike the previous two scenes in which reflections were dominant, this scene conveys its meaning mainly through dialogue. The dominant impression left by the scene is the intensity of Wilhelm's self-disgust. When Mr. Perls excuses himself from the table, the mood changes and the subsequent scene begins.

Scene IV continues to rely heavily on dialogue in what amounts to a kind of verbal-emotional fencing match between Wilhelm and his father. Wilhelm is attempting to engage his father, to thrust through his defenses and turn up some form of deep feeling or genuine concern for the suffering of his son. Dr. Adler attempts to evade the emotionalism that Wilhelm is imposing on him, but finally strikes back at his son with feeling; the emotion he displays is anger, however, not sympathy, and it is provoked by selfishness, not paternal love. When Perls leaves their table, Wilhelm begins to gorge himself on the remaining food, causing Adler to reflect again on his son's obesity and slovenly ways. While Adler observes his son, Wilhelm is again feeling congested, partially from the vast amount of food he has just eaten but mainly from the pressure of suppressing his desire to discuss his problems with his father. The subject matter of each man's reflections reveals the distance between them: Wilhelm is concerned about his own emotional condition and his father's indifference to it; Adler is concerned about Wilhelm's physical condition and his son's indifference to it.

When they speak to each other these differences become more explicit. Adler recommends the "baths" to his son, then exclaims that the "Gloriana has one of the finest

pools in New York," but Wilhelm is repulsed by the "odor of the wall-locked and chlorinated water." Adler presses his point. "There's nothing better," he says, "than hydrotherapy when you come right down to it. Simple water has a calming effect and would do you more good than all the barbiturates and alcohol in the world." With unwitting irony here, Adler plays Hard-hearted Hannah to Wilhelm's drowning man. One does not prescribe hydrotherapy to a drowning man, unless, of course, one is totally indifferent to the conditions of others. It is clear from their exchange that selfish indifference is indeed Adler's condition. On the level of dramatic irony, however, Adler prescribes with more wisdom than he knows, for Wilhelm's final symbolic death by water—Adler's hydrotherapy—is necessary to restore him to psychic health.

That Wilhelm is a drowning man becomes clearer and clearer. Having overcome his feeble attempts to suppress the expression of his feelings to his father, Wilhelm explains what Margaret is doing to him, accompanying his description with an appropriate choking gesture:

> Well, Dad, she hates me. I feel that she's strangling me. I can't catch my breath. She just fixed herself on me to kill me. She can do it at long distance. One of these days I'll be struck down by suffocation or apoplexy because of her. I just can't catch my breath.

But Adler is unmoved; he accuses Wilhelm of victimizing himself by allowing his wife to dominate him and by expecting from the marriage a perfection which marriage is not capable of providing. The old man even accuses Wilhelm of contributing to his marital difficulties through extramarital affairs with both men and women. Wilhelm feels the pressure of this unjust accusation in conjunction with the pressure he feels from his wife's persecution. He struggles for breath, gets "choked up and congested" and thinks: "Trouble rusts out the system." "Wilhelm had a great knot of wrong tied tight within his chest, and tears approached his eyes but he didn't let them out." As he sinks beneath the wrongs piled upon him, Wilhelm cries out for assistance:

> He felt as though he were unable to recover something. Like a ball in the surf, washed beyond reach, his self-control was going out. "I expect *help!*" The words escaped him in a loud, wild, frantic cry and startled the old man, and two or three breakfasters within hearing glanced their way.

This cry for help (the hapless swimmer's plea for assistance) directed toward his earthly father parallels the silent prayer for aid which Wilhelm directed toward his heavenly father at the end of Scene I, but the intensity is greater here. In response, his father offers him again advice he cannot use: "I want nobody on my back. Get off! And I give you the same advice, Wilky. Carry nobody on your back." A drowning man, of course, is not likely to carry anyone on his back—though Wilhelm realizes later that Tamkin has been riding on his back, another pressure pushing him down. Adler's indifference to his son's need confirms the validity of the sense of persecution that emerges as Wilhelm's dominant feeling in this scene. The estrangement of son from father as a result of the father's self-centeredness is established dramatically here as a condition of long standing, a major contributing factor to Wilhelm's present problems.

Swearing silently at himself for breaking down in front of his father, Wilhelm moves into the lobby, where Scene V begins. Wilhelm's chest aches and he smells "the salt odor of tears in his nose." He thinks again of the line from "Lycidas"—to "sink beneath the watery floor"—and suddenly he encounters Tamkin, for whom references in earlier scenes have made dramatic preparation. With the appearance of Tamkin, Wilhelm feels himself "flowing into another channel." They exchange greetings and Wilhelm attempts, skeptically, to discover through cogitation if Tamkin is all he purports to be. Wilhelm remembers his own penchant for self-destructive choices and recalls how he thought five days ago, when closing the deal with Tamkin, that "when he tasted the peculiar flavor of fatality in Dr. Tamkin, he could no longer keep back the money." Tamkin had told him to invest some money in order to learn the stock market because "to know how it feels to be a seaweed you have to get in the water." Now, Wilhelm senses fearfully, he is in the water deeper than he had anticipated.

Much of this scene, which moves immediately from the lobby back to the dining room where Tamkin eats his breakfast, is taken up with Wilhelm's vacillating attitude toward Tamkin. Wilhelm's suspicions are aroused when Tamkin uses bad grammar, when he brags of his fantastic international financial deals, or when he reveals the details of his many "cases": the epileptic blonde, the eccentric nudist-dentist, the transvestite general. However, when Tamkin shows concern for human suffering, Wilhelm is drawn back to him. He believes that Tamkin reveals true insight into human aspiration when he declares: "Only the present is real—the here-and-now. Seize the day." Wilhelm responds from the heart when Tamkin describes the lonely person "howling from the window like a wolf when night comes." And Wilhelm thinks he finds a key to understanding his own problem in Tamkin's analysis of the two major souls in the man:

> "In here, the human bosom—mine, yours, everybody's—there isn't just one soul. There's a lot of souls. But there are two main ones, the real soul and a pretender soul. Now! Every man realizes that he has to love something or somebody. He feels that he must go outward. 'If thou canst not love, what art thou?' Are you with me?"

> "Yes, Doc, I think so," said Wilhelm listening—a little skeptically but nonetheless hard.

> " 'What art thou?' Nothing. . . . In the heart of hearts—Nothing! So of course you can't stand that and want to be Something, and you try. But instead of being this Something, the man puts it over on everybody instead. You can't be that strict to yourself. You love a *little*. Like you have a dog" (Scissors!) "or give some money to a charity drive. Now that isn't love, is it? What is it? Egotism, pure and simple. It's a way to love the pretender soul. Vanity. Only vanity, is what it is. And social control. The interest of the pretender soul is the same as the interest of the so-

cial life, the society mechanism. This is the main tragedy of human life. Oh, it is terrible! Terrible! You are not free. Your own betrayer is inside of you and sells you out. You have to obey him like a slave. He makes you work like a horse. And for what? For who?"

"Yes, for what?" The doctor's words caught Wilhelm's heart. "I couldn't agree more," he said. "When do we get free?"

"The purpose is to keep the whole thing going. The true soul is the one that pays the price. It suffers and gets sick, and it realizes that the pretender can't be loved. Because the pretender is a lie. The true soul loves the truth. And when the true soul feels like this, it wants to kill the pretender. The love has turned into hate. Then you become dangerous. A killer. You have to kill the deceiver."

Wilhelm sees in Tamkin's theory an explanation of his past action: In going to Hollywood, changing his name, marrying against his better judgment, and hastily investing in the stock market, Wilhelm realizes he was serving his "pretender soul," the agent of social control, and now he is enduring the bondage of his own creation. That this false self must be destroyed he is not yet ready to admit, nor is he comfortable with the knowledge that Tamkin has been "treating" him on the sly. "I don't like being treated without my knowledge," Wilhelm declares; "I'm of two minds"—that is, of two minds as well as two souls.

Tamkin too, it seems, is of two minds and souls, and he demonstrates his condition dramatically when he hands Wilhelm the stock market receipts along with one of his poems, evidence of his pretender soul on the one hand and, apparently, his true soul on the other. The poem is an anachronistic, ungrammatical, hypermetric piece of, in Wilhelm's words, "mishmash" and "claptrap." The bad quality of the poem throws Wilhelm in a panic again as he assesses the credentials of the man who represents his economic survival. "Kiss those seven hundred bucks goodby," he says, "and call it one more mistake in a long line of mistakes." Wilhelm feels "choked and strangled." In explicating his poem, Tamkin assures Wilhelm that in conflict between "*con*struct and *de*struct" money is "*de*struct" but nature is "creative": "It rolls the waters of the earth." The scene ends with Wilhelm's portentous vision of these waters as *de*structive: "The waters of the earth are going to roll over me."

With the introduction of Tamkin into the narrative, the pace of the novel increases. Movement from place to place is accelerated, and greater emphasis is placed on action and dialogue as more characters are admitted into each scene. In accordance with the metaphor developing in the novel, Wilhelm is being swept along faster by the currents that are carrying him to the sucking center of his personal maelstrom.

Scene VI begins with Wilhelm and Tamkin "crossing the tide of Broadway traffic" to enter the brokerage office. Here everything is strange to Wilhelm, and he is flooded with impressions of an impersonal, rapacious, money-mad world. Man's staples—wheat, rye, lard, eggs—are reduced in this place to flashing lights and whirring tumblers on a giant electric board. On his right and left sit secretive old men whose withered lives are devoted entirely to the pursuit of money, and all around him Wilhelm feels confusion:

> That sick Mr. Perls at breakfast had said that there was no easy way to tell the sane from the mad, and he was right about that in any big city and especially in New York—the end of the world, with its complexity and machinery, bricks and tubes, wires and stones, holes and heights. And was everybody crazy here? What sort of people did you see? Every other man spoke a language entirely his own, which he had figured out by private thinking; he had his own ideas and peculiar ways.

Wilhelm is clearly at sea here, bewildered and frightened, and his fear sparks two reflections. In the first he escapes in his mind to a farm he once owned in Roxbury—where the chickens and eggs were real—and for a moment he imagines the peace and quiet of a country day. In the second, he recalls an experience he had in an underground corridor beneath Times Square:

> In the dark tunnel, in the haste, heat, and darkness which disfigure and make freaks and fragments of nose and eyes and teeth, all of a sudden, unsought, a general love for all these imperfect and lurid-looking people burst out in Wilhelm's breast. He loved them. One and all, he passionately loved them. They were his brothers and his sisters. He was imperfect and disfigured himself, but what difference did that make if he was united with them by this blaze of love? And as he walked he began to say, "Oh, my brothers—my brothers and my sisters," blessing them all as well as himself.

Though the feeling he then had soon passed, Wilhelm concludes as he remembers his experience that "there is a larger body, and from this you cannot be separated." These two reflections provide Wilhelm with momentary respite from his immediate discomfort—and his transcendental vision prepares the way for the ambivalent final scene—but the insistence of the flashing lights and clicking wheels of the exchange board call him abruptly back to the feverish activity of the stock market.

Though the brokerage is strange to Wilhelm, it is familiar ground to Tamkin, who moves knowingly from place to place and from group to group in the room. His appearance and movements suggest to Wilhelm a bird of prey, perhaps a sea hawk: "A rare, peculiar bird he was, with those pointed shoulders, that bare head, his loose nails, almost claws, and those brown, soft, deadly, heavy eyes." Appealing to Tamkin to sell their rye in order to cover their losses in lard, Wilhelm finds himself chided by Tamkin for his faintheartedness. Tamkin recommends that Wilhelm try *"here-and-now* mental exercises" to compose himself:

> Nature only knows one thing, and that's the present. Present, present, eternal present, like a big, huge, giant wave—colossal, bright and beautiful, full of life and death, climbing into the

sky, standing in the seas. You must go along with the actual, the Here-and-Now, the glory—

As Tamkin drones on to the end of the scene, advocating through his water imagery focusing on the present, recognizing opportunity, seizing the day, Wilhelm recalls a chest condition he once had and how Margaret read to him the melancholy lines from Keats's *Endymion:*

> Come then, Sorrow!
>
> . . . . .
> I thought to leave thee,
> And deceive thee,
> But now of all the world I love thee best.

Margaret's voice from the past forms a counterpoint to Tamkin's voice in the present; both are appropriate to Wilhelm's condition. The combined effect of the two voices—Tamkin's water imagery and Margaret's elegiac tone—produce in Wilhelm a mood of resignation. His plight is too desperate, his resolve too weak, and the forces opposing him too strong for him to resist much longer. The waters are bearing him down. On this note of resignation to fate the scene ends.

Scene VII finds Wilhelm and Tamkin at lunch in a cafeteria with a gilded front. The scene is developed by statement and amplification. Taking his cue from Wilhelm's comments about how his estranged wife mistreats him, Tamkin provides the central statement in the scene:

> But Tamkin said, "Why do you let her make you suffer so? It defeats the original object in leaving her. Don't play her game. Now, Wilhelm, I'm trying to do you some good. I want to tell you, don't marry suffering. Some people do. They get married to it, and sleep and eat together, just as husband and wife. If they go with joy they think it's adultery."

"One hundred falsehoods," Wilhelm thinks, "but at last one truth. Howling like a wolf from the city window." Wilhelm knows, furthermore, that he is himself one of the compulsive sufferers that Tamkin has described:

> True, true! thought Wilhelm, profoundly moved by these revelations. How does he know these things? How can he be such a jerk, and even perhaps an operator, a swindler, and understand so well what gives? I believe what he says. It simplifies much—everything. People are dropping like flies. I am trying to stay alive and work too hard at it. That's what's turning my brains. This working hard defeats its own end. At what point should I start over? Let me go back a ways and try once more.

Tamkin makes the statement that stands at the center of this scene, and Wilhelm establishes its application through his reflections. The remainder of the scene provides dramatic corroboration of the fact that Wilhelm is "married to suffering," though it is his suffering that defines his humanity at last and enables him to break out of the imprisoning self.

As Tamkin and Wilhelm return to the brokerage, an old violinist singles out Wilhelm from the crowd, pointing his bow and exclaiming, "You!" in testimony to Wilhelm's status as a victim, a mark. On the sidewalk outside the brokerage, old Mr. Rappaport grabs Wilhelm's arm and insists that he be guided to the cigar store across the street. Begrudgingly, yet still passively, Wilhelm allows himself to be used. Rappaport delays Wilhelm, intensifies his anxiety over the status of his investment in lard, bores him with a story about Teddy Roosevelt, and causes him to be separated from Tamkin at a crucial moment. When Wilhelm finally escapes the old man and enters the brokerage, he discovers that both the lard and rye have dropped drastically. He is wiped out, and Tamkin has disappeared. The scene has demonstrated his bad judgment and passiveness and the resultant suffering. With "unshed tears" rising in his eyes, Wilhelm looks at the conclusion of the scene "like a man about to drown."

In Scene VIII, the final scene, Wilhelm does drown, but not without futilely thrashing about before he surrenders to his fate. The pace in this scene is very fast, and the water imagery is overwhelming. Wilhelm dashes to Tamkin's room at the hotel, but he is greeted there only by a maid, an empty room, and the "mop water smell" of the "brackish tidal river." Wilhelm then begins his final symbolic descent. Seeking his father, he goes down to the health club, past the swimming pool, into the misty massage room. He asks his father for assistance, describing his condition in desperate terms: "I just can't breathe. My chest is all up—I feel choked. I just simply can't catch my breath." But again his father is deaf to his cries for help. Wilhelm dashes to a phone booth and calls Margaret, asking her to give him some financial relief. The booth is oppressively close; he breaks into a sweat and warns Margaret that he is "suffocating." He yells at her—or to her—and she hangs up on him with the assertion, "I won't stand to be howled at"—and in her metaphor reverberates the cry in the night that Tamkin earlier attributed to the archetypal lonely person. Wilhelm now is painfully that person.

Rushing out into the street in a panic, Wilhelm encounters "the inexhaustible current of millions of every race and kind pouring out." Thinking he sees Tamkin nearby, Wilhelm gets caught in the crush of a crowd and finds himself in the "dark and cool" of a Jewish funeral home where "the stained glass was like mother-of-pearl." In the press of people Wilhelm is maneuvered alongside the casket and is suddenly totally engaged by the face of the strange corpse. He feels a "splash of heartsickness," and the tears he has held back so long quietly begin to fall:

> Standing a little apart, Wilhelm began to cry. He cried at first softly and from sentiment, but soon from deeper feeling. He sobbed loudly and his face grew distorted and hot, and the tears stung his skin. A man—another human creature, was what first went through his thoughts, but other and different things were torn from him. What'll I do? I'm stripped and kicked out. . . . "Oh, Father, Paul? My children. And Olive? My dear! Why, why, why—you must protect me against that devil who wants my life. If you want it, then kill me. Take, take it, take it from me."

> Soon he was past words, past reason, coherence. He could not stop. The source of all tears had suddenly sprung open within him, black, deep,

and hot, and they were pouring and convulsed his body, bending his stubborn head, bowing his shoulders, twisting his face, crippling the very hands with which he held the handkerchief. His efforts to collect himself were useless. The great knot of ill and grief in his throat swelled upward and he gave in utterly and held his face and wept. He cried with all his heart. . . .

> The flowers and lights fused ecstatically in Wilhelm's blind, wet eyes; the heavy sea-like music came up to his ears. It poured into him where he had hidden himself in the center of a crowd by the great and happy oblivion of tears. He heard it and sank deeper than sorrow, through torn sobs and cries toward the consummation of his heart's ultimate need.

This is Wilhelm's death by drowning, and every scene in the book has pointed toward this culminating moment. The salt water of his tears is the medium of his suffocation. Wilhelm cries for the failure that he has been, for the death-in-life that he has experienced. He cries for the pretender soul, now put to rest, whose misplaced values caused him to be married to suffering in all aspects of his existence. He cries for the time he has wasted and the mistakes he has made. His tears are tears of sorrow shed in personal grief.

He cries also, however, for mankind, for those millions—like himself—who have howled in anguish and loneliness like wolves from city windows at night. He cries for all men who must suffer and die; he cries for what Virgil called the *lacrimae rerum*, the tears in things.

An excerpt from *Seize the Day*

When it came to concealing his troubles, Tommy Wilhelm was not less capable than the next fellow. So at least he thought, and there was a certain amount of evidence to back him up. He had once been an actor—no, not quite, an extra—and he knew what acting should be. Also, he was smoking a cigar, and when a man is smoking a cigar, wearing a hat, he has an advantage; it is harder to find out how he feels. He came from the twenty-third floor down to the lobby on the mezzanine to collect his mail before breakfast, and he believed—he hoped—that he looked passably well: doing all right. It was a matter of sheer hope, because there was not much that he could add to his present effort. On the fourteenth floor he looked for his father to enter the elevator; they often met at this hour, on the way to breakfast. If he worried about his appearance it was mainly for his old father's sake. But there was no stop on the fourteenth, and the elevator sank and sank. Then the smooth door opened and the great dark-red uneven carpet that covered the lobby was dark, sleepy. French drapes like sails kept out the sun, but three high, narrow windows were open, and in the blue air Wilhelm saw a pigeon about to light on the great chain that supported the marquee of the movie house directly underneath the lobby. For one moment he heard the wings beating strongly.

Saul Bellow, in his Seize the Day, *Viking Press, 1956.*

Because he is able to transcend his personal grief, Wilhelm's tears are also tears of joy. In destroying the pretender soul, Wilhelm prepares the way for the coming of the true soul, who will not lead him to torture himself over an unworthy father, will not persuade him to go to Hollywood or marry unwisely or seek a quick fortune with a charlatan. In the termination of his marriage to suffering, Wilhelm's fragmentary glimpse in the underground corridor of a transcendental "larger body" comes to fruition in the tears of relief he sheds over his ability to find refuge "in the center of a crowd by the great and happy oblivion of tears." Where there has been alienation, there is now the possibility of communion. Wilhelm's drowning, then, is also a baptism, a rebirth. It is clearly a sea change, demonstrating that, as Saint John of the Cross stated, the way down is also the way up.

The unity of effect achieved in *Seize the Day* results from the skillful blending of all the elements of fiction in tightly constructed scenic units functioning very much like poetic images built around a controlling metaphor. Each scene extends the central image of Wilhelm's drowning by embodying a particular aspect of his life which has contributed to the pressure which finally overwhelms him in literal failure and symbolic death and rebirth. Unity is enhanced further by cross references between scenes. Wilhelm's appeal to his heavenly father in Scene I is paralleled by his two subsequent appeals (in Scenes IV and VIII) to his earthly father. Adler's advice to Wilhelm to "carry nobody on [his] back" in Scene IV is given ironic significance in Scene VIII when Wilhelm declares that Tamkin was "on [his] back." Tamkin's comparison of loneliness to a "howling wolf" (Scene V) is picked up in Wilhelm's reflection (Scene VII) on truth "howling like a wolf from the city window" and again in Margaret's assertion (Scene VIII) that she will not be howled at. The dramatic irony in Adler's prescription of hydrotherapy for Wilhelm (Scene IV), Wilhelm's gesture of self-strangulation (Scene IV), Tamkin's theory of the necessary death of the pretender soul (Scene V), and Wilhelm's vision of transcendental love in the underground corridor all coalesce in Wilhelm's symbolic drowning in Scene VIII. It is hydrotherapy, self-induced, which destroys the false self and opens Wilhelm's heart to true values and to communion with nature and man, ending his long alienation. "Spatial form" in a larger sense is achieved, then, both within and between scenes.

"The appeal the novel has," W. J. Handy has remarked, "must come in part from knowing that fiction is a symbolic formulation designed to give a more adequate account of the way human experience actually unfolds, not when it is merely known about or 'understood,' but when it is experienced in the course of human living." The combined effect of the scenes in *Seize the Day* presents the "full unabstracted bodiness" of Wilhelm's experience and—by extension—the human experience of everyone who has struggled, stumbled, fallen, and somehow picked himself up again. (pp. 102-26)

M. Gilbert Porter, in his Whence the Power?: The Artistry and Humanity of Saul Bellow, *University of Missouri Press, 1974, 209 p.*

Sanford Pinsker   (essay date Spring 1983)

[*Pinsker is an American scholar and poet who has written several books on contemporary American literature. His publications include the critical study* Between Two Worlds: The American Novel in the 1960's *(1978), and two books on the works of novelist Philip Roth. Pinsker has a particular interest in American humor and is known for his own witty critical style. In the following essay, Pinsker examines the significance of Andrew Marvell's poem "Eyes and Tears" in* Seize the Day.]

> He [Tommy] didn't like to think about his college days, but if there was one course that now made sense it was Literature I. The textbook was Lieder and Levott's *British Poetry and Prose,* a black heavy book with thin pages. . . .—from *Seize the Day*
>
> Thus let your streams o'erflow your springs,
> Till eyes and tears be the same things:
> And each the other's difference bears;
> Those weeping eyes, those seeing tears.
> —from Andrew Marvell's
> "Eyes and Tears"

Andrew Marvell's "Eyes and Tears" was not included in the anthology Tommy Wilhelm remembers from his undergraduate days in Literature I; nonetheless, the poem suggests a striking analogue of Tommy's situation. As a number of critics point out, *Seize the Day* is filled to the brim with water imagery. From the elevator that "sank and sank" in the opening paragraph (until it reaches the wine-dark sea of "dark red uneven carpet" in a lobby where "French drapes like sails kept out the sun") to the "waters of the earth" that are about to roll over Tommy at the end of Section III, liquefaction, rather than readiness, is all. Any addition, even a modest one, risks displacing the volume further, but Marvell's poem speaks more directly to Tommy's condition, and the critical debates about the novella's curious last paragraph, than the usual citations to the watery content of Milton's *Lycidas,* of Keats' *Endymion.*

Seize the Day is about drowning, both literally and figuratively, into the quotidian. But it is also about blindness and seeing, about evasion and insight. Indeed, there are nearly as many images of "blindness"—from a newsstand attendant with "poor eyes" to the elusive Tamkin Tommy is always "looking for"—as there are references to water. Tommy Wilhelm, the "fair-haired hippopotamus," the whining *schlemiel,* the sensitive flop, is bedazzled by the very dreams that are his destruction. Whether in Hollywood (where an aptly named Maurice Venice bathes him in promises) or on the floor of the commodities market (where his liquid assets evaporate), Tommy clumsily chases versions of the American Dream. Marvell's conceit fits him as snugly as Tamkin's "underwater suit":

> What in the world most fair appears,
> Yea, even laughter, turns to tears;
> And all the jewels which we prize,
> Melt in these pendants of the eyes.

In Tommy's case, the "jewels" include the sustaining love of a surrogate father and a quick killing in lard speculation—and both require a desperate faith in Tamkin; the "tears" are a recognition that an existential bottom has, at last, been reached and that liberation is, at last, possible.

Interestingly enough, what Marvel and Bellow share is a sense that eyes-and-tears are ineluctably related, that weeping is an inevitable result of truly seeing. As the conventions of "tear poetry" (developed along with the Counter-Reformation, and Richard Crashaw's *Saint Mary Magdalen or The Weeper* [1646]) would have it, weeping is a sign of strength, a superior activity, rather than an indicator of weakness. With that in mind, the last paragraph of *Seize the Day* takes on new and important meanings:

> The flowers and lights fused ecstatically in Wilhelm's blind, wet eyes; the heavy sea-like music came up to his ears. It poured into him where he had hidden himself in the center of a crowd by the great and happy oblivion of tears. He heard it and sank deeper than sorrow, through torn sobs and cries toward the consummation of his heart's ultimate need.

Which is perhaps to say, Tommy's Pretender Soul headed West for Hollywood; Tommy's True Soul, however, hankered, without quite knowing it, for a seminar in the Metaphysicals. (pp. 60-1)

> *Sanford Pinsker, "Bellow's 'Seize the Day'," in*
> The Explicator, *Vol. 41, No. 3, Spring, 1983, pp. 60-1.*

Patrick Costello   (essay date Spring 1987)

[*In the following essay, Costello examines Bellow's critique of three traditions in* Seize the Day—*the work ethic, the American Dream, and the Jewish tradition—and argues that much of the novella's ambiguity is dispelled through an understanding of the latter.*]

While many critics have acknowledged that Saul Bellow's *Seize the Day* is a masterpiece of contemporary fiction, the grounds for this judgment have been but slenderly put forth. There has been a great deal of useful and informative criticism of the story, but very little of it has addressed the source of its enduring power. In this essay I propose to locate that source and, in exploring it, to provide a frame of reference capable of dealing with a greater complexity and depth of experience than criticism has offered thus far. Yet the story's thickness of meaning and richness of suggestion, which afford the reader such variety of recognitions, demand that the measure of success for my essay be found in the reader's return to the story with a whetted appetite and increased capacity for the feast spead before him.

Let us begin by considering Dr. Adler's statement: "I uphold tradition. He's for the new." Dr. Adler is referring to his son's changing his name from Wilhelm Adler to Tommy Wilhelm, but the story as a whole poses much larger questions: which traditions are being upheld by whom; and what are the consequences? If "tradition" is taken in a rather loose sense, as any practice or way of life which is handed down from one generation to another, there are three traditions operating in the story: The American Dream, the Protestant (more accurately Secular) Work Ethic, and the Jewish tradition.

While much can be said about Bellow's handling of each of these traditions in the story, I will concentrate in this essay on Jewish tradition. It is here that the story is most subtle, profound, and humorous; and it is also where it makes its broadest, if not most obvious, appeal. In order to appreciate this appeal, however, we must first deal summarily with the other two traditions.

The Work Ethic and the American Dream are both shown to be incapable of answering Wilhelm's deepest needs. Both rest on the assumption that the acquisition and possession of money constitute success. They differ basically in the way or ways by which the money is acquired. The Work Ethic demands conscious, intelligent preparation and diligent, unremitting effort, while the American Dream is a "get rich quick" proposition, whose main ingredients are a good appearance and luck. A minor difference is that the successful pursuant of the Work Ethic is granted respect by the other members of society, while success in the American Dream is accorded fame.

Despite Wilhelm's reflection that his father considers himself the only "right kind of Jew," Dr. Adler is only peripherally associated with Jewishness. He is the embodiment of the Work Ethic. From humble beginnings, his father's selling dry goods in Williamsburg, Dr. Adler by his own efforts became "a diagnostician, one of the best in New York, and had a tremendous practice." He also has the respect and admiration of all the functionaries and casual acquaintances around him in the Hotel Gloriana. The adequacy of the Work Ethic is undercut from the beginning in the irony of his being a diagnostician, since he cannot diagnose what is wrong with his own family relationships. He does not remember the year of his wife's death, and he is no closer to his daughter, who also changed her given name, than he is to Wilhelm. His credo is dictated by the primacy of money: "And I want nobody on my back. Get off! And I give you the same advice, Wilky. Carry nobody on your back."

This is another aspect, perhaps the logical conclusion, of the high regard Americans have had for self-reliance at least from the time of Emerson. Dr. Adler repeatedly proclaims his self-reliance, his individualism; but he is finally alone, pathetically attempting to fend off his fear of death by clinging to his money. His position is reaffirmed in the story's final section in most violent language: "You want to make yourself into my cross. But I am not going to pick up a cross. I'd see you dead, Wilky, by Christ, before I let you do that to me." The last words Dr. Adler speaks to his son are: "Go away from me now. It's torture for me to look at you, you slob!" If the respect of functionaries and casual acquaintances masks this finally intolerable loneliness, so much the worse: Dr. Adler's "success" is illusory and encourages self-deception.

A supporting representative of the Work Ethic is Mr. Rappaport, whose fortune made in the chicken business suggests an ironic ambiguity. In Wilhelm's use of the term, "chicken" is a term of opprobrium meaning false and trivial. Rappaport's fortune may not be so fortunate for him after all. Rappaport is almost blind, an unpleasant old man who is a prisoner of the figures on the board of the Commodities Exchange, which he is unable to see. His hero is Teddy Roosevelt, T. R., the champion of rugged individualists. There is irony here too: Rappaport not only cannot read the figures which hold him captive but also is dependent on Wilhelm to be helped across the street to purchase his cigars. His physical blindness is an indication of his spiritual condition.

Rappaport can supply us with a transition to considering the American Dream, for the Commodities Market is the variation of "get rich quick" with which Wilhelm is involved on the day the story takes place. Since there must be a loser for every winner on each transaction in commodities, it is obvious that as a way of life it is at best untrustworthy. The untrustworthiness is humorously expressed by Dr. Tamkin, who is a monument of ambivalence. When he is talking Wilhelm into investing with him, he says: "They gamble, but I do it scientifically. This is not guesswork." When it comes to the crunch, however, Tamkin says: "But I have confidence: I'm sure I'll outguess them." The primacy of luck, "guessing," entails an absence of responsibility, no real investment of the self, which inevitably prevents full human significance or meaning. It is an operation of what Dr. Tamkin, in a phrase which powerfully affects Wilhelm, calls "the pretender soul."

Perhaps Hollywood is the most blatant variation of the American Dream. Maurice Venice, the failed talent scout, states it succinctly:

> You may plug along fifty years before you get anywhere. This way in one jump, the world knows who you are. You become a name like Roosevelt, Swanson. From east to west, out to China, into South America. This is no bunk. You become a lover to the whole world. The world wants it, needs it. . . . Listen, everywhere there are people trying hard; miserable, in trouble, downcast, tired, trying and trying. They need a break, right? A break through, a help, luck, or sympathy.

Venice himself tells Wilhelm that he has "found happiness" with 'Nita Christenberry, a "starlet"; yet several years after this conversation Wilhelm reads in a newspaper that Venice is given a fifteen-year prison term for using his studio connection to organize a ring of call girls. 'Nita Christenberry received a three-year sentence. Her case is sufficient to make the point. We do not need those biographies of other "starlets" which have flooded the book market since *Seize the Day* was written to realize that Hollywood, while appearing to offer freedom and the full life, is actually the locus of misery and the empty life. Bellow states it convincingly though off-handedly: Hollywood is empty and corrupt.

A final aspect of the American Dream which engages Wilhelm is baseball. While he thinks that baseball gives him an "advantage" over his wife in competition for the love of his sons, "When he went to fetch them to go to Ebbets Field, though, he was not himself. He put on a front but he felt as if he had swallowed a fistful of sand." In other words, he is not unaware that the commonplace attempt in our society to invest sports events with the myth-bearing significance of religious ritual in older cultures is futile. After all, baseball is not a revelation of total reality, nor can it supply, except in a very limited way, models of universally exemplary behavior.

A detail which radically undercuts baseball's myth-bearing potential is easily missed by the reader, unless that reader is a baseball historian or an old White Sox fan. In the story's third paragraph we are told that "the neighborhood's great landmark" was the Hotel Ansonia—the very place where members of the 1919 White Sox met with gamblers to fix the World Series. It can be seriously maintained that the fixing of the 1919 Series did more to undermine confidence in America as "the land of the free and the home of the brave" than anything prior to our involvement in Viet Nam. The fix certainly attests that where money is absolute, a certification for success for the American Dream, corruption is highly probable.

This brings us to the Jewish tradition; but before examining the tradition itself, we ought to take note of the narrator's tone revealed in the story's first paragraph. It is a kind of double negative: "Tommy Wilhelm was not less capable than . . . " This sets the tone for the whole story. The double negative will reappear in some of the narrator's most crucial comments about Wilhelm. While the double negative is not the tone of ecstatic faith, the tone of the prophets, it is an affirmative, admittedly the weakest in the language, but nevertheless affirmative. In our nihilistic age a real affirmation is no small accomplishment.

In the popular mind, what seems to be central to the Jewish tradition as a way of everyday life is the closeness and intensity of family relationships. That this is not the tradition Dr. Adler is upholding ought to be clear from very early in the story: "He behaved toward his son as he had formerly done toward his patients, and it was a great grief to Wilhelm; it was almost too much to bear. Couldn't he see—couldn't he feel? Had he lost his family sense?"

Wilhelm is distressed by this lack of relationship. His grief shows that he is more likely in tune with Jewish tradition than is his father. While the first section of the story mentions Wilhelm's difficulties and shows ground for his possible masochism, it also suggests the possibility of other values and standards: "Too much of the world's business done. Too much falsity." Here "world" is used in the Biblical sense of what opposes the reign of God. On one hand, the difficulties with his father at this point can be regarded as those expressed in hundreds of modern American stories. Dad was no pal; he was always at the office; he just doesn't understand. On the other hand, by the end of the first section, matters central to Jewish tradition are strongly though subtly suggested. Wilhelm admits changing his name was a mistake and a casting off of Dr. Adler. He considers the action itself a "sin" and wonders about "forgiveness." The section's final paragraph is a re-writing in contemporary gambler's idiom of the penitential Psalms, especially Psalm 51: "For all the time I have wasted I am very sorry. Let me out of this clutch and into a different life. For I am all balled up. Have mercy." The words are addressed to "God," and in his suffering we are told "Wilhelm prayed." This is not the usual expression of hundreds of stories of American adolescence.

It is a commonplace that the whole of Old Testament experience is summarized and re-expressed in the Psalms. Having been made aware of the presence and pressure of the Psalms by the language of Wilhelm's prayer, it is possible to see that his whole situation in considerable detail parallels Psalm 69. Wilhelm, like the Psalmist, fears that "the waters of the earth are going to roll over me." The Psalm places the oft-commented-upon fear of drowning in a traditional context which removes it from neurosis. Like Wilhelm, the Psalmist is insulted, ignominious, shamed and bereft of comforters.

The greatest difference between Wilhelm and the Psalmist is that the Father whom the Psalmist calls upon, unlike Dr. Adler, is one whose help is "constant," who is present in power to save, who "hears the poor." This last phrase throws a different light on the question of money in the story. It suggests that the absence of money is not damning as it seems to be in Dr. Adler's view of the world.

Is it fair to compare Dr. Adler with the God of Israel? The matter is integrally related to the question Wilhelm considers of what constitutes "the right kind of Jew." As we have already noted, in a religious world the conduct of God or the gods is always both universal and exemplary. As Martin Buber's work has shown of the Jewish experience recorded in the Bible, religion deals with the whole man in his entire being in all his relationships—a far cry from what religion is often reduced to in the twentieth century. In the Biblical experience, the Lord is the foundation of the Jewish father's authority and position in the family. If this is so, He is also the model of conduct.

From the secular point of view, Dr. Adler does not fare badly. He had warned Wilhelm against going to Hollywood, marrying Margaret, and giving his money to Tamkin. If only the son had listened to his dad's advice. Dr. Adler had also sent a check to Margaret every month while Wilhelm was in the service. Does not the reader side with Dr. Adler in demanding that a forty-four-year-old son stand on his own?

This may make secular sense, especially from the perspective of individualism (rugged or otherwise), but it is not the way of the Father with his child Israel. The whole of Scripture records the repeated disregarding of the Father, deserting Him, experiencing the pain of loss in idolatry, a calling for help and being reconciled. Psalm 106 lists eight rebellions or denials of the people against God, and the list is by no means exhaustive. God waits for his child Israel to turn again to Him. Then Israel will be comforted, renewed, set on high. Perhaps the most Jewish of all the parables of Jesus is the Prodigal Son—that terrifying, from a father's view, portrayal of unconditional acceptance.

The tension at the center of the complex of human difficulties in *Seize the Day* is this difference in the views of parent-child relationships. Is the fully satisfying model secular or religious? Wilhelm wonders who his father is and what it means to be a father and to be a son. He himself is both father and son. He knows that by walking out on

Margaret he is also walking out on his responsibilities as father. He admits his guilt and grieves, but he persists in his course of action. That the story emphasizes Wilhelm as son rather than father, however, says much about our primary relationships. At forty-four Wilhelm ought to be at the height of his powers, regarding power as something broadly social or political. But what if power is falsity? What if in our real primary relationship (our I in our I-Thou) we are always son or daughter? It is not for nothing that Scripture continually refers to the children of Israel.

Examination of the role of Jewish tradition in the story eventually will illuminate these central concerns, but the way is involved, complex, and allusive. In the second section of the story two specific details in the Jewish tradition are mentioned. In thinking about his sister's painting and painting in New York in general, Wilhelm reflects: "It was the Tower of Babel in paint." The lesson of this myth in Genesis is reenacted daily in our world. Arrogance, regarding oneself as a law unto oneself, inevitably leads to chaos, alienation, and isolation. The twentieth century may have specialized in these things, but we do not have a monopoly on them. Confusion of tongues and failure to communicate are undercurrents throughout the story.

Just before the mention of the Tower of Babel a wild joke comes up in Dr. Adler's conversation with Mr. Perls at breakfast. Dr. Adler says: "I have only this one son, one daughter. She was a medical technician before she got married—anesthetist. At one time she had an important position in Mount Sinai." The joke is in the resonance of references. The hospital is Dr. Adler's obvious reference, but the resonance is to the experience on Mount Sinai where a group of wandering peoples became a People, the Jews. If one were anesthetized there, he would have missed his identity, radically missed himself.

This is not a silly joke; indeed, it is full of significance. How many of us in present-day America (aptly figured by New York, the Big Apple) are anesthetized and so miss ourselves? Tamkin, in language reminiscent of Psalm 91, lists a number of the anesthetics: "Seven percent of this country is committing suicide by alcohol. Another three, maybe, narcotics. Another sixty just fading away into dust by boredom. Twenty more who have sold their souls to the Devil." Boredom (my brother, my double) and the devil (the old facilitator) are administering anesthetics more powerful and far more subtle than alcohol or chemicals. If we are anesthetized, how can we "seize the day" or our lives? Is Wilhelm one of the unanesthetized remnant? Is he "one of us"? Is he "the right kind of Jew"? Is he Tommy, Wilky, Velvel, or all three and more? Is he capable of seizing the day? Or is he a masochist or the loser that Maurice Venice pegged him as, the hopeless shlemiehl, the repulsive slob, a monument of self-pity? In a way he is all of these, but being the hopeless shlemiehl does not necessarily keep him from being either "one of us" or "the right kind of Jew."

There is a passage in the second section of the story which tells us a great deal about these matters and prepares us for an understanding of what the Jewish tradition is and what it demands. Before examining the passage, it is necessary to point out one or two things about the narrator and the tone he assumes in the passage.

The passage illustrates why this story requires an undramatized narrator, one who can both approve and disapprove of Wilhelm. (If we are honest, must not we do the same with ourselves?) The benefit of the undramatized narrator is the impression of distance from the subject, therefore of objectivity, therefore of credibility. Undue favoritism would destroy the effect of the following:

> In any moment of quiet, when sheer fatigue prevented him from struggling, he was apt to feel this mysterious weight, this growth or collection of nameless things which it was the business of his life to carry about. That must be what a man was for. . . . This Wilky, or Tommy Wilhelm, forty-four years old, father of two sons, at present living in the Hotel Gloriana, was assigned to be the carrier of a load which was his own self. There was no figure or estimate for the value of this load. But it is probably exaggerated by the subject, T. W. Who is a visionary sort of animal. Who has to believe that he can know why he exists. Though he has never seriously tried to find out why.

In the middle of the passage, following lines that have the flatness of a report on a police blotter or an insurance form, comes the first statement of purpose or meaning and what constitutes success in the Jewish tradition: "the carrier of a load which was his own self." Stated so flatly it is received flatly. We might notice it, but at this point we are not moved by it.

The word "business" also carries a meaning different from the world's business, speculating in lard or selling Rojax or diagnosing medical ailments. The usage here is tied to the living out of the Jewish tradition, but it requires further illumination and explanation.

After the flat tone of official forms the narrator switches to raillery in the matter of T. W. 's exaggerating the value. Then suddenly the narrator explodes a bomb or, better, a blaze of light. Maybe grammar is a tip-off. The final three sentences could be dependent clauses; in formal grammar they are. But for the narrator they are separate complete sentences. "A visionary sort of animal." A far grander and more satisfying descriptive definition than "economic," "political," "social" or even the older "rational." "Who has to believe he can know why he exists." Hope, dignity, meaning, the person. How much better than the pose of clever fellows with their silly school-boy competitiveness—"Nothing is meaningful. I know that, but you don't. Therefore, I'm better than you!" If they really believed that in the center of their being, they would either blow their brains out or keep their mouths shut and stop worrying about getting to R, let alone Z. "Though he has never seriously tried to find out why." Great blazing mounds of red-hot coals are heaped on our heads. O, Wilhelm, you are thoroughly representative, "one of us." Who has seriously tried? Martin Buber, Mother Teresa, and a handful of others?

Are the serious tryers the ten percent of Tamkin's remnant? The figure is the same one used by Dostoyevsky's Grand Inquisitor. Do ninety percent absolutely need the anesthesia of lies? The numbers are right off the computers and in the actuarial tables. Dare we dispute them? Better drop the cool and aloof "we." Which group am I in? That is the real, the important question.

Hold on a minute. Dr. Tamkin also says: "Now counting and number is always a sadistic activity. Like hitting. In the Bible, the Jews wouldn't allow you to count them. They knew it was sadistic." Wise advice. William Blake, Kierkegaard, and Buber have all been concerned with numbers as the adversary. Numbering is the spirit of abstraction, that which is antithetical to the person. Numbers and percentages always suggest that there are different kinds of people. What if there are not two kinds of people, just one? Although no one is normal, we are all ordinary.

The third section of the story focuses on Dr. Adler, the advice he gives to Wilhelm and his affirmation of the values of the Work Ethic. Along with the foolish advice to save his sympathy for victims of accidents and fatal illness, Dr. Adler gives Wilhelm some sound advice to go down to the baths. The significance of the water imagery of the bath extends beyond the old doctor's belief in the physical benefits of hydrotherapy. Much of the section dwells on Wilhelm's failure in money matters and how this disqualifies him in his father's eyes. Tears, building from the back of Wilhelm's throat in the first section of the story now "approached his eyes but he didn't let them out." The section concludes with Dr. Adler stating his credo: "Carry nobody on your back" and Wilhelm's miserable response: "Just keep your money . . . keep it and enjoy it yourself." This picture of alienation and isolation is the low point of the story.

At the opening of the fourth and middle section of the story, Wilhelm rushes from the dining room with the salt odor of tears in his nose, the most miserable of men. The narrator, returning to the double negative, tells us that things are not as bad as they seem with Wilhelm and in so doing states what constitutes success in the Jewish tradition:

> But at the same time, since there were depths in Wilhelm not unsuspected by himself, he received a suggestion from some remote element in his thoughts that the business of life, the real business—to carry his peculiar burden, to feel the shame and impotence, to taste these quelled tears—the only important business, the highest business was being done.

The passage hammers on the word "business," reinforcing, expanding, clarifying the meaning suggested in the previously quoted passage. It is important to note that these are not Wilhelm's thoughts about himself, which might be self-indulgent, flattering, or deluded. These are the narrator's thoughts and values. The materials between the dashes could certainly point toward masochism from a secular point of view. How are they regarded in the Jewish tradition?

Was the life of Moses without troubles? Did the prophet Hosea have an edifying home life? What about the "peculiar burden" Jesus carried? Right at the center of Jewish prophetic tradition stands a figure who characterizes all of the material between Bellow's narrator's dashes, the Suffering Servant in Isaiah. It is this figure of shame and impotence and no beauty who will restore Israel to the Lord and be a light to the nations (Is. 49:5-6). The secular mind may dismiss Isaiah (e.g., 53:3-5) as nonsense or wish-fulfillment or evidence of some aberrant psychological state; but there it stands. In light of the secularly inexplicable persistence of the Jews (How many Hittites, Assyrians or Babylonians are there in New York City? asks Walker Percy), it may be rash to dismiss Isaiah.

How different are Isaiah's values and terms of success from those of the American Dream or the Work Ethic? If Wilhelm embodies the Suffering Servant's condition, he might also embody, in his own limited way, the Servant's values and his success. Remember, we are in a bad time, perhaps a time capable only of the double negative. Wilhelm's weaknesses have been pretty thoroughly documented. It is perhaps necessary to rehearse some of his virtues.

What distinguishes him from many characters in modern fiction is that he acknowledges his responsibility for the difficulties he is in. It goes beyond admitting mistakes; he knows and admits that he is a sinner. He does not shift the blame onto the age, society, the government, capitalism, or chemistry. He admits that his life has been formed by his own choices.

Wilhelm, the sinner, is not reprobate, not a monster of evil. He desires the good, but he is unable to do it. Again, "one of us." He loves his sons but is no father to them. In walking out on Margaret, he also walked out on Tommy and Paul. Wilhelm has more than mere feelings: "Of course, of course I love him. My father. My mother—." His love remains largely inarticulate and ineffective, but it is real. Who of us can speak, so as to reveal fully the great longings that assail us, the same longings at ten and at fifty?

Wilhelm is scrupulously fair. He does not want any undue advantage over his sister. Though driven to the end of his rope, he can still become aware of the troubles of others, of Mr. Perls and Mr. Rappaport.

Like most of us, however, Wilhelm is caught in-between. He knows that the pursuit of money is finally a cynical choice: "Chicken! Unclean!"; yet he cannot by his own unaided force of will renounce it. The pursuit of money occupies the forefront of Wilhelm's mind throughout the story until the final scene in the funeral parlor. But all the while the depths of his mind and heart are concerned with relationships. It is in regard to these two different concerns, money and relationships, that we must look at the part Dr. Tamkin plays in Wilhelm's life. If one buys into the American Dream or the Work Ethic, with money as the measure of success, then Tamkin is simply a liar and a crook. If we subscribe to the Jewish tradition, where the highest business is the carrying of burdens, Tamkin may be what he says he is, a healer.

Through the first six sections of the story Wilhelm is ambivalent about Tamkin. His father and Mr. Perls warn him not to trust Tamkin. Much of what Tamkin tells him he regards as ridiculous lies; but every time he is about to render an adverse judgment on Tamkin, Wilhelm is struck by the truth of something Tamkin had said. Besides, he believes Tamkin cares for him.

If Tamkin is a financial counselor, then he should deal in facts that lead to profits. If he is a scientist, he should deal in facts that lead to demonstrable truth. But he says he is a psychologist (not necessarily a hard scientist) and a healer. What is truth to a healer?

One of the ways Tamkin fits into the Jewish tradition is in his approach to truth. The Greeks provide a contrast more in keeping with money or hard science. Euclid, Plato, and Aristotle all produce logical but abstract arguments. The Jewish approach is different: "In the land of Uz there was a blameless and upright man"; or "The kingdom of heaven is like . . . " The truth of Jewish tradition is personal or, in other words, the subject of a story. A teller of stories is a fabricator but not necessarily a liar.

What keeps Wilhelm from deciding that Tamkin is a healer or wise man or messenger of the Lord is that in addition to the merely fictitious (his stories are wild but no wilder than Job's) there is frequently something spurious, as in his inclusion of W. H. Sheldon in "the best of literature, science and philosophy." The effect is that Wilhelm must continue to think and decide for himself, however inadequate he feels. In short, he must continue to respond to the challenge to be free.

Tamkin and his words, both past and present, occupy Wilhelm throughout the fourth section of the story. As the narrator says: "What a rare, peculiar bird he was." In the world of nature, the cattle egret cleans parasites from the hippopotamus. If money is the most important business, then Tamkin is the parasite bleeding Wilhelm, an ironic reversal of nature's world; but, if money is not of utmost importance, perhaps the animal analogy is straightforward.

Many of Tamkin's words prepare for the awareness which must precede and accompany a radical change of heart. Loneliness and lack of direction that result in howling like a wolf from one's window are recognized by Wilhelm, as is the fear that comes from a lack of knowing. He agrees with Tamkin that "Maddest of all were the businessmen, the heartless, flaunting, boisterous business class who ruled the country with their hard manners and their bold lies and their absurd words that nobody could believe."

The most important of Tamkin's teachings is his identifying the real and the pretender soul—"That had awed him." This leads to the marvelous ambivalence of Tamkin's poem. As a poem Wilhelm knows it is a "mishmash." But the main idea as Tamkin explains it to Wilhelm is "*con*struct or *de*struct. There is no ground in between." This speaks to a number of ills afflicting our world of in-betweens.

In an embarrassed stumbling answer to Tamkin's question as to whether Wilhelm has followed the whole poem, Wilhelm says:

> "I'm trying to figure out who this Thou is."
> "Thou? Thou is you."

"Me! Why? This applies to me?"
"Why shouldn't it apply to you?"

For the poem as poem, the way a practitioner of New Criticism would address a poem, the dialogue is ludicrous, thoroughly nonsensical. In another sense, however, Tamkin might be telling Wilhelm it is possible for him to become a "Thou" in primary relationships, which according to Buber is the basis of all lived, meaningful life, a true seizing the day. Wilhelm, however, does not hear him this way. The section concludes with Wilhelm echoing the Psalmist: "The waters of the earth are going to roll over me." But what he is talking about is money.

The fifth section of the story takes place mostly in "the narrow crowded theater of the brokerage office." There are two passages of great importance for Wilhelm's awareness of himself and his situation. The first is a passage about New York City. It both details and diagnoses two of our greatest ills, alienation and isolation:

> Every other man spoke a language entirely his own, which he had figured out by private thinking; he had his own ideas and peculiar way. . . .
> You had to translate and translate, explain and explain, back and forth, and it was the punishment of hell itself not to understand or be understood, not to know the crazy from the sane, the wise from the fools, the young from the old or the sick from the well. The fathers were no fathers and the sons no sons. You had to talk with yourself in the daytime and reason with yourself at night. Who else was there to talk to in a city like New York?

Wilhelm is back to the Tower of Babel, arrogance, the confusion of tongues, and being alone. He has a very orthodox notion of hell. And with millions of people around, no one is present. How many times have we heard that story?

Another version of hell is not to be who I am, to miss myself completely. This is the death brought on by the pretender soul Tamkin spoke of: "The true soul is the one that pays the price. It suffers and gets sick, and it realizes the pretender can't be loved. Because the pretender is a lie. The true soul loves the truth." The cynical pursuit of money, fame, and reputation form the matrix of the pretender soul, the local habitation of the great lie.

The second passage is a kind of positive to the negative vision of hell. The experience occurs in a hellish place, an underground corridor where "all of a sudden, unsought, a general love for all these imperfect and lurid-looking people burst out in Wilhelm's breast." Wilhelm feels united with these people by "this blaze of love." He blesses himself and them as "my brothers and my sisters." However, "a few minutes later he didn't feel anything like a brother toward the man who sold him the tickets." The failure to sustain his love is intrinsically related to his confused relationship with his own father and his uncertainty about his Jewishness. Put simply, the question is, how can there be brothers and sisters without a common parent?

In section VI Wilhelm is cleaned out, which makes him either a total failure or puts him in a position to experience a saving conversion. Dr. Adler's advice to Wilhelm to take

the baths has resonance beyond the old man's intentions. In gambler's idiom "to take a bath" is to be cleaned out. Baptism, like crying, is an action which includes the three major associations of water: life, cleansing, and death. St. Paul writing about baptism stresses the necessity of the old man's dying before the new man can be reborn. Before one can be "cleaned up" one must first be "cleaned out"; no attachment to the old can remain. Being cleaned out of his money may be the necessary preparation for Wilhelm's turning his heart and seizing the day. Before disappearing, Tamkin includes him among "the small percentage of those who want to live." One indication of his preference for life is his ability, even when hardest pressed, to put off thinking only of himself and help others. He does not want to take Mr. Rappaport across Broadway to get cigars, but he does. The old man's talk of Teddy Roosevelt (T. R., unlike T. W., has "such snap, such class") is able, even in such a distressed moment, to draw a smile from Wilhelm.

Wilhelm's desire for life is also shown in his not condemning others. He accuses Margaret of committing a crime against him, but he does not condemn her. He expresses no wish for revenge. Even when Dr. Adler finally rejects him with violent language, "It's torture for me to look at you, you slob!" all Wilhelm answers is, "Okay, Dad. That'll be enough. That's about all we should say." He gives vent only to generalized thoughts of violence toward the nameless, faceless hoodlums who broke his mother's stone bench in the cemetery. He has no destructive or violent thoughts or fantasies about any particular person.

What he regards as Tamkin's lying to him produces no vindictiveness. Section VI concludes with a desire merely to get the two hundred dollars Tamkin owes him. The section opens in a key quite other than the revengeful:

> I was the man beneath; Tamkin was on my back,
> and I thought I was on his. He made me carry
> him, too, besides Margaret. Like this they ride
> on me with hoofs and claws. Tear me to pieces,
> stamp on me and break my bones.

He sees himself as a carrier of burdens. Like the prophets, he does not want the burden, but he carries it. The terms in which he acknowledges the burden, especially the last sentence quoted, are reminiscent of the language of Psalm 22.

Stripped, cleaned out, abandoned by all on whom he depended, Wilhelm is fully in the position of the Suffering Servant. His final choice for life occurs in the story's concluding passage, which is set in a funeral home. It is not surprising that the passage should be left relatively untouched by many commentators. Its significance is clear only in the light of Jewish religious tradition. The tears which Wilhelm finally sheds become a baptism, a conversion, the turning of his heart.

Nowhere is the undramatized narrator more important. We are told that Wilhelm "cried at first softly and from sentiment, but soon from deeper feeling." If Wilhelm had been telling his own story, we would always have to ask, how do you know it is deeper feeling? How do you know you are not exaggerating your worth again? Freed from this uncertainty by the undramatized narrator, we can be sure Wilhelm is approaching contact with the core of his being. In the story's final sentence we are told: "He heard it and sank deeper than sorrow, through torn sobs and cries toward the consummation of his heart's ultimate need." What is this ultimate need?

There is an apparent ambiguity which is, however, finally resolved. If one were an adherent of the American Dream or the Protestant Work Ethic, then, since Wilhelm is a failure according to those views, his need would be money. The story as a whole, however, has shown the spuriousness of these views of life; love of money is idolatry. Likewise, if one were cynical, a word frequently in Wilhelm's thoughts and always rejected, his need would be "not to be." Cynicism cannot be the narrator's or author's view. It is self-defeating. It is absurd for a real cynic to write a story. Sitting with one's hands folded is the only rational action for a cynic. But we have known for over a hundred years that one cannot do that even in the underground. The ultimate need, then, must be tied up with life.

What that link is is revealed in his seemingly confused final interior utterance—his last words in the story:

> What'll I do? I'm stripped and kicked out. . . .
> Oh, Father, what do I ask of you? What'll I do
> about the kids—Tommy, Paul? My children.
> And Olive? My dear! Why, why, why—you
> must protect me against that devil who wants
> my life. If you want it, then kill me. Take, take
> it, take it from me.

The whole passage is pregnant with the spirit of the Psalms. It would be a considerable and rewarding work to identify all the passages in all the individual Psalms off which this bounces. Not holocausts, but a crushed and humbled spirit is what the Lord desires. The "Father" is addressed; but to whom does Wilhelm appeal? The rules of standard grammar are no help; by rule it could be Dr. Adler. Maybe it is, but only in part. The "devil who wants my life" may at first be Margaret and Olive, his protectress. But the sentences which follow make no sense of that. Olive cannot be the antecedent of the pronoun "you." Why would Olive want his life? "You" refers back to "Father." Wilhelm is expressing his total abandonment, his willingness to be faithful "even unto death," so "Father" is also the one whose "F" is always capitalized.

The apparent confusion is appropriate. Wilhelm is not young Samuel on his cot nor Isaiah in the Temple nor a mystical poet. He is a Dodger fan and an out-of-work salesman, one who does not attend synogogue but who "often prayed in his own manner." Muddled as it is, the "you" is the primary Thou. (The terms in the ludicrous exchange over Tamkin's poem are reversed.)

The parallels in his final broken utterances with Jesus in the Garden of Gethsemane are inescapable. What must be remembered and stressed is Jesus' Jewishness. In the very beginning of the tradition, what is Abraham asked to do? Let go: abandon himself and more than himself to the Lord. And Moses and Israel at the Sea of Reeds with the chariots of Pharoah breathing down their necks? Let go: do nothing. Over and over again the same invitation: let go of your idols, those dead, empty things; abandon your-

self to me, the Living God. Indeed, "soon he was past words, past reason, coherence." Wilhelm is the acceptable sacrifice, total abandonment.

"The consummation of the heart's ultimate need" is communion with the Father. The effect of this communion is that now in truth all men can be addressed as brother and sister. There is a common parent. In a kind of humorous way the other people in the funeral parlor attest to Wilhelm acting as brother, not looking like a brother. A passage from Martin Buber helps to explain what is happening:

> But his is what he does now: he releases in himself a reserve over which only he himself has the power. . . . He will be able to tell no one, not even himself, what he has experienced. What does he now "know" of the other? No more knowing is needed. For where unreserve has ruled, even wordlessly, between men, the world of dialogue has happened sacramentally.

Wilhelm's dialogue is with the One who addresses him primarily, absolutely, and personally. He responds to the absolute Thou. He has become and is becoming a responsible person in the deepest and fullest sense of the word. Now he is literally able to respond to all men and to his whole world in its concrete everyday reality. He has managed to "seize the day." Buber helps to explain in conceptual terms what Bellow renders in concrete detail. Of course, Wilhelm's future will continue to be a series of failings. That is our everyday reality. But the primary word has been spoken. Responsibility has happened. Life, which is always a life of trust, is being realized.

Wilhelm is among that small percentage who choose to live, a choice which cannot escape dying to oneself. What is wonderful is that neither Prudential Insurance, General Motors, nor the Grand Inquisitor knows what the percentage is or who makes up its number. In fact, there is no percentage; only concrete particular persons choose to live, what Kierkegaard called the Single One. If Wilhelm can be one, so can I, so can any of us ordinary human beings who are "not less capable" than our fellows. This is the dazzling hope of this story and the deepest source of its appeal. A double negative is an affirmative. May His name be forever blessed. Not just by prostitutes and tax collectors, but even by an out-of-work salesman yet, by "one of us." (pp. 117-30)

> *Patrick Costello, "Tradition in 'Seize the Day',"* in *Essays in Literature, Vol. XIV, No. 1, Spring, 1987, pp. 117-31.*

FURTHER READING

Chavkin, Allan. " 'The Hollywood Thread' and the First Draft of Saul Bellow's *Seize the Day." Studies in the Novel* XIV, No. 1 (Spring 1982): 82-94.

Analyzes early versions of Bellow's novella, originally titled "One of Those Days," collected at the Humanities Research Center of the University of Texas in Austin.

Cronin, Gloria L. "Saul Bellow's Quarrel with Modernism in *Seize the Day*." *Encyclia* 57 (1980): 95-102.

> Discusses Bellow's departure from the Modernist tradition in *Seize the Day*.

Giannone, Richard. "Saul Bellow's Idea of Self: A Reading of *Seize the Day*." *Renascence* XXVII, No. 4 (Summer 1975): 193-205.

> Examines "the ways in which the self tries to establish a spiritual agreement with the outer world" in *Seize the Day*.

Glenday, Michael K. "Some Versions of Real: The Novellas of Saul Bellow." In *The Modern American Novella*, edited by A. Robert Lee, pp. 162-77. New York: St. Martin's Press, 1989.

> Focusing on Bellow's novellas *Seize the Day* and *What Kind of Day Did You Have?*, Glenday delineates what Bellow has called his "preoccupation with 'obvious and palpable' reality and the devices of 'distortion and blearing' which too often come between Americans and [the] fundamental recognition 'of what things are real'."

Guttmann, Allen. "Mr. Bellow's America." In his *The Jewish Writer in America: Assimilation and the Crisis of Identity*, pp. 198-201. New York: Oxford University Press, 1971.

> Characterizes *Seize the Day* as "a cautionary tale" in which Tommy Wilhelm's downfall is attributable to his inability to accept his fate as an ordinary man.

Harper, Howard M. "Saul Bellow—The Heart's Ultimate Need." In his *Desperate Faith: A Study of Bellow, Salinger, Mailer, Baldwin, and Updike*, pp. 7-64. Chapel Hill: University of North Carolina Press, 1967.

> Examines Tommy Wilhelm's "existential dilemma" in *Seize the Day*.

Jefchak, Andrew. "Family Struggles in *Seize the Day*." *Studies in Short Fiction* XI, No. 3 (Summer 1974): 297-302.

> Explores Tommy Wilhelm's frustrated relationship to his father.

Mathis, James C. "The Theme of *Seize the Day*." *Critique* VII, No. 3 (Spring-Summer 1965): 43-5.

> Ponders Bellow's untraditional treatment of the carpe diem theme.

Morahg, Gilead. "The Art of Dr. Tamkin: Matter and Manner in *Seize the Day*." *Modern Fiction Studies* 25, No. 1 (Spring 1979): 103-16.

> Explores Bellow's attempt to imaginatively communicate philosophical ideas through the "elusive and enigmatic" character of Dr. Tamkin.

Nelson, Gerald B. "Tommy Wilhelm." In his *Ten Versions of America*, pp. 127-45. New York: Alfred A. Knopf, 1972.

> Details Tommy Wilhelm's failure of identity in *Seize the Day*.

Raper, J. R. "Running Contrary Ways: Saul Bellow's *Seize the Day*." *Southern Humanities Review* 10, No. 2 (Spring 1976): 157-68.

> Examines the influence of the Jungian school of psychoanalysis on Bellow's novella.

Richmond, Lee J. "The Maladroit, the Medico, and the Magician: Saul Bellow's *Seize the Day*." *Twentieth Century Literature* 19, No. 1 (January 1973): 15-26.

> Rejects Daniel Weiss's treatment of Dr. Tamkin (see essay dated 1962 in entry above) as "cursory and misplaced" and emphasizes the importance of the character in *Seize the Day*.

Rodrigues, Eusebio. "Reichianism in *Seize the Day*." In *Critical Essays on Saul Bellow*, edited by Stanley Trachtenberg, pp. 89-100. Boston: G. K. Hall & Co., 1979.

> Explores the influence of Reichianism on *Seize the Day*.

Wilson, Jonathan. "*Seize the Day*." In his *On Bellow's Planet: Readings from the Dark Side*, pp. 96-111. London and Toronto: Associated University Presses, 1985.

> Highlights Bellow's ambivalent treatment of character in *Seize the Day*.

Additional coverage of Bellow's life and career is contained in the following sources published by Gale Research: *Contemporary Authors*, Vols. 5-8, rev. ed.; *Contemporary Authors New Revision Series*, Vol. 29; *Contemporary Authors Bibliographical Series*, Vol. 1; *Concise Dictionary of American Literary Biography*, 1941-1968; *Contemporary Literary Criticism*, Vols. 1, 2, 3, 6, 8, 10, 13, 15, 25, 33, 34, 63; *DISCovering Authors*; *Dictionary of Literary Biography*, Vols. 2, 28; *Dictionary of Literary Biography Documentary Series*, Vol. 3; *Dictionary of Literary Biography Yearbook: 1982*; *Major 20th-Century Writers*; and *World Literature Criticism*.

Bruno Bettelheim

1903-1990

Austrian-born American psychologist, psychoanalyst, educator, nonfiction writer, and essayist.

The following entry provides an overview of Bettelheim's career.

INTRODUCTION

A renowned child psychologist, Bettelheim is best known for his writings about emotionally disturbed children, the therapeutic value of fairy tales, and the experiences of Nazi concentration camp survivors. While many of his theories, which incorporate the work of Sigmund Freud, are considered outdated, critics concur that Bettelheim brought to the field of psychoanalysis an important humanistic element often missing from the clinical approach.

Born in Vienna, Bettelheim became interested in psychology after undergoing psychoanalysis as a teenager. He went on to study with Freud in Vienna, establishing himself in the late 1930s as an authority on childhood autism. In 1938 he was incarcerated in concentration camps at Dachau and Buchenwald, but was freed the following year due to international pressure for his release. Bettelheim moved to the United States, where he joined the faculty of the University of Chicago in 1944 and was appointed head of its Sonia Shankman Orthogenic School. Under Bettelheim's supervision the institution gained a reputation for helping the most severely autistic and emotionally challenged children. Many of Bettelheim's publications during this period chart the progress and setbacks he encountered with his students. In 1973 Bettelheim retired from the school, devoting his time to researching and writing. He died of self-inflicted suffocation in 1990.

"Individual and Mass Behavior in Extreme Situations," one of Bettelheim's earliest works written after his 1938 release from Nazi Germany, incorporates his own experiences of the concentration camps and describes how the Nazi leaders tried to rob Jewish prisoners of their identities and self-respect. Because the Nazi atrocities were generally unreported during the war, Bettelheim's descriptions were deemed unreliable and publishers were generally unwilling to print the article. When the piece was finally published in 1943, the essay garnered worldwide attention and became required reading for all United States military officers serving in Europe. Continuing with this subject in *The Informed Heart: Autonomy in a Mass Age* and the well-known "Surviving," an analysis of Lena Wertmüller's film *Seven Beauties,* Bettelheim outlined his survivor philosophy, asserting that an individual's psychological well-being and determination dictated his ability to endure the Holocaust and that most survivors felt guilty about surviving the experience. Although this theory was widely

accepted in the scientific community, Bettelheim was attacked for suggesting that the historical passivity of European Jews made them partially responsible for Nazi antagonism.

Bettelheim's views on child development and parenting, like his theories on survivors, are also drawn from personal experience and observation. His brief stay in an Israeli kibbutz in 1964, for example, resulted in a study of communal life entitled *The Children of the Dream,* and the majority of his writings—including *Love Is Not Enough: The Treatment of Emotionally Disturbed Children, The Empty Fortress: Infantile Autism and the Birth of the Self,* and *A Home for the Heart*—describe his work at the Orthogenic School. In these works Bettelheim details the attempts of his staff to treat individual patients by creating a nurturing environment and recognizing their basic needs through a process of empathetic identification. Although scholars faulted Bettelheim's conjecture, published in *The Empty Fortress,* that childhood autism is the result of either a parent's unspoken hostility for a child or a child's feelings of worthlessness, the Orthogenic School's high success rate is frequently cited as proof of the validity of Bettelheim's theories. Elsa First observed: "Bettelheim's myth of the embattled child served to inspire a powerful amount of goodness within the fortress of his school. His clinical intuitiveness and resourcefulness and the unfailing respect he showed toward his psychotic children were remarkable." Bettelheim's work at the institute, however, has proven to be a source of concern and consternation: after his death, former patients accused Bettelheim and his staff of brutality and abuse.

The Uses of Enchantment: The Meaning and Importance of Fairy Tales is often regarded as one of Bettelheim's more literary works. In this volume Bettelheim provides Freudian analyses of fairy tales, arguing that these stories act as therapeutic tools that help children—frequently subconsciously—to define and accept their desires and fears. While many critics have offered praise for *The Uses of Enchantment,* others have faulted Bettelheim for incomplete research of his subject, inaccurate documentation and citation of his sources, and failure to adapt Freud's theories to recent social and cultural changes. In addition to applying Freudian concepts in his work, Bettelheim also wrote biographical essays on Freud, many of which are collected in *Freud's Vienna, and Other Essays. Freud and Man's Soul* examines how the translation process has distorted Freud's theories.

Despite his many detractors and the controversy surrounding his life and work, Bettelheim remains an important figure in the field of pyschology and child development. Paul Roazen remarked: "Bruno Bettelheim stands as one of Freud's few genuine heirs in our time. Fearlessly independent and yet working within Freud's great discoveries, Bettelheim has sought to think through all of human psychology for himself."

PRINCIPAL WORKS

Dynamics of Prejudice: A Psychological and Sociological Study of Veterans [with Morris Janowitz] (nonfiction) 1950

Love Is Not Enough: The Treatment of Emotionally Disturbed Children (nonfiction) 1950

Symbolic Wounds: Puberty Rites and the Envious Male (nonfiction) 1954; revised edition, 1962

Truants from Life: The Rehabilitation of Emotionally Disturbed Children (nonfiction) 1955

The Informed Heart: Autonomy in a Mass Age (nonfiction) 1960

Dialogues with Mothers (nonfiction) 1962

Art: As the Measure of Man (nonfiction) 1964

The Empty Fortress: Infantile Autism and the Birth of the Self (nonfiction) 1967

The Children of the Dream (nonfiction) 1969; also published as *The Children of the Dream: Communal Childrearing and American Education,* 1970, and as *The Children of the Dream: Communal Childrearing and Its Implications for Society,* 1971

Obsolete Youth: Toward a Psychograph of Adolescent Rebellion (nonfiction) 1970

A Home for the Heart (nonfiction) 1974

The Uses of Enchantment: The Meaning and Importance of Fairy Tales (nonfiction) 1976

Surviving, and Other Essays (essays) 1979; also published as *Surviving the Holocaust,* 1986

Freud and Man's Soul (nonfiction) 1982

On Learning to Read: The Child's Fascination with Meaning [with Karen Zelan] (nonfiction) 1982

A Good Enough Parent: A Book on Childrearing (nonfiction) 1987

Freud's Vienna, and Other Essays (essays) 1989

Recollections and Reflections (essays) 1990

CRITICISM

Stanley Edgar Hyman (essay date 1956)

[*A longtime literary critic for the* New Yorker, *Hyman rose to a prominent position in American letters during the middle decades of the twentieth century. He is noted for his belief that much of modern literary criticism should depend on knowledge received from disciplines outside the field of literature; consequently, many of his best reviews and critical essays rely on his application of theories gleaned from such disciplines as cultural anthropology, psychology, and comparative religion. In the following essay, originally published in 1956, he discusses* Symbolic Wounds, *praising its revisionist approach to Freudian theory.*]

Such questions as what song the sirens sang, or what name Achilles assumed when he hid himself among women, Sir Thomas Browne assures us, though puzzling, are not beyond all conjecture. Now that Dr. Bruno Bettelheim, principal of the Orthogenic School at the University of Chicago, has published in **Symbolic Wounds** his theory that puberty rites and a great deal else are expressions of male envy of the female, we can make a new stab at conjecture. The song the sirens sang to each virile hero must have been "Come to Me, My Melancholy Baby," and the name Achilles assumed was of course "Thetis," the name of the mother with whom he was identifying.

This is bold stuff, despite Dr. Bettelheim's very moderate manner, and his book is of some significance as one of the latest attempts to revise Freudian theory drastically, in Freud's name. At a time when psychiatrists are becoming increasingly overbearing in areas of discussion they only dimly apprehend, such as literature, and seem to develop a splendid assurance in inverse proportion to the mousiness of what they bring forth, it is a pleasure to see at least one Freudian psychologist and psychiatrist making major challenges to theory, and large-scale forays into anthropology and culture, all with a tentativeness and humility akin to Freud's own. Even in the act of disagreeing with him, one must welcome the fashion in which Dr. Bettelheim puts his views: speculatively, offering alternatives, and hedging them with such disclaimers as "This is obviously a very complex question," "This interpretation of course may be correct only in individual cases," "I am still unable to explain," and so forth.

Symbolic Wounds is shaped around seven "hypotheses" about the meaning of puberty rites among nonliterate peoples. These are, in the author's words:

> 1. Initiation rites, including circumcision, should be viewed within the context of fertility rites, which play a primary role in primitive society.
>
> 2. Initiation rites of both boys and girls may serve to promote and symbolize full acceptance of the socially prescribed sexual role.
>
> 3. One of the purposes of male initiation rites may be to assert that men, too, can bear children.
>
> 4. Through the operation of subincision men may try to acquire sexual apparatus and functions equal to women's.
>
> 5. Circumcision may represent an effort to demonstrate sexual maturity or may be a mutilation instituted by women, or both.
>
> 6. The secrecy surrounding male initiation rites may serve to disguise the fact that the desired goal is not reached.
>
> 7. Female circumcision may be partly the result of men's ambivalence about female sex functions and partly a reaction to male circumcision.

The traditional Freudian explanation of initiation rites involving circumcision, subincision, scarification, the knocking-out or filing of teeth, or any ritual physical mutilation interprets them as symbolic castration of the young by their elders, an expression of Oedipal hostility. In place of this, Dr. Bettelheim argues a basic male motivation which he calls "vagina envy," equivalent to the Freudian "penis envy" in females. It is this "vagina envy," subsuming childbirth and nursing functions, which he believes inspires symbolic wounds and male puberty rites, and he strongly suggests that Freud was unable to recognize "vagina envy" because of the androcentric nature of his psychology. Dr. Bettelheim's interest in initiation rites originated in his clinical experience with disordered children at the Orthogenic School, when four of the pubescent children, two girls and two boys, invented a secret society with a monthly ritual in which the boys were to draw blood from their index fingers or some "secret place of their bodies" and mix it with the girls' menstrual blood. "At this point," Dr. Bettelheim says unhappily, "it became necessary to interfere," but he decided that the children's fantasy resembled primitive initiation rites he had read about, and apparently he went on to read widely in modern ethnography and ethnology. It is his claim that his theory of "vagina envy" and his other hypotheses fit such clinical experience as the four children, and the anthropological evidence he has read, better than traditional Freudian theory does.

Insofar as this is an ambitious revision of psychoanalysis, it displays several promising features. The first is Bettelheim's realistic weariness of what he calls the "deceptively pat biological model," the idea that such laws as Haeckel's "ontogeny recapitulates phylogeny" (the principle that the development of the individual repeats the evolution of the group) can be more than metaphors for psychology, if indeed they are more than that for modern biology. The second is Bettelheim's real cultural relativism, his insistence that "any event may be experienced, and its meaning understood, in vastly different ways in different societies," and that the same culture trait will produce varied results not only in different social configurations but on different personalities within the culture. The third, and most remarkable in a school principal who first encountered initiatory rites in the antisocial behavior of his disordered adolescent pupils, is a recognition of the high importance of rituals, the collective emotional experiences of nonliterate cultures, as neither institutionalized neurosis nor fantasy gratification (although they contain ingredients of both, surely), but as significant actions in the real world, filling vital social, psychological, and aesthetic needs that are less adequately filled in our own literate culture.

Psychoanalysis can stand serious modification in freeing it from the biological sciences and adjusting it to developments in other cultural sciences. Unfortunately, Dr. Bettelheim does not stop there. His major disagreement with Freudian psychology is in areas of philosophic depth and profundity where it is least in need of revision and has suffered from it most. If Freud's aim was laboriously to reclaim a little ego from the swamps of id, Bettelheim's policy is: ignore id, let us have only "ego psychology." Psychoanalysis, he says, is wrong to view "social institutions as mainly resulting from or expressive of man's destructive or irrational instinctual tendencies"; perhaps this was inevitable in those old fellows, fighting "entrenched denial and repression," but now with ego psychology we emphasize "positive human emotions and motivations."

For many of us, the answer to this was given by Freud himself in *The History of the Psychoanalytic Movement,* in response to the first of the "ego" psychologies, Alfred Adler's splintering in 1910. Freud writes, in Brill's translation:

> Psychoanalysis has a greater interest in showing that all ego strivings are mixed with libidinal components. Adler's theory emphasizes the counterpart to it; namely, that all libidinal feeling contains an admixture of egotism. This would have been a palpable gain if Adler had not made use of this assertion to deny, every time, the libidinal feelings in favor of the impelling ego components. His theory thus does exactly what all patients do, and what our conscious thinking always does; it rationalizes, as Jones would say, in order to conceal the unconscious motives.

Freud's conclusion is flatly that Adler's psychology "signifies an abandonment of analysis and a secession from it," and it would appear to this writer that Bettelheim's psychology signifies just about the same thing.

In his quest for "positive human emotions and motivations," Bettelheim consistently reinterprets the evidence in the cheeriest possible fashion. Thus sadistic impulses, such as the fantasies of some of his boy patients about tearing out female genitalia, represent only envy (sadism is not mentioned in *Symbolic Wounds*). Initiation rites are not imposed on the young by the old, but gratify constructive desires in the young (masochism is not mentioned either); if they are imposed they are imposed for the youngsters' own good. "What psychoanalysis has viewed so far as originating mainly in the id, the unconscious, and as the expression of unintegrated, destructive tendencies, may be much more the result or expression of ego tendencies that try, through ritual, to integrate chaotic instinctual desires and anxieties," Bettelheim writes. Instead of basely submitting to the father, the initiate bravely identifies with the mother; circumcision "clearly occurs because of the people's desire for it, not because of pressure from above"; "society may thus have been founded not on the association of homicidal brothers (postulated by Freud) but on a joint effort of men to master a common problem." Finally, Bettelheim asks rhetorically: "Under which frame of reference can human behavior best be understood, that of inner freedom and human autonomy, or that of coercion by blind instinctual forces or by the insensible powers of custom and tradition?" His answer, of course, is the former, since the latter does "injury to man's inherent dignity."

Unfortunately, such authorities on "man's inherent dignity" as the great tragic writers from Aeschylus to Joyce and the great stoic philosophers from Socrates to Freud himself seem consistently to have disagreed. What this is, as terms like "integrate," "joint effort," "inner freedom and human autonomy," and so forth make clear, is the same inspirational revision of Freud that Fromm, Horney, and the neo-Freudians have been purveying over the years. Water down libido, deny id, replace the Oedipus complex with something like Bettelheim's Christine complex, and heal and be healed by *caritas*. Bettelheim, whose earlier title *Love Is Not Enough* suggests that he should know better, trots out as usual "the child treated with love and tolerance," or finds "severe oral deprivation" traumatic for the newborn child "particularly when accompanied by cold and indifferent handling." "Important enterprises of human beings," he concludes, "and certainly those that have continued for centuries to give satisfaction, must serve positive rather than negative ends." Accentuate the positive is the slogan; love everybody or you will be left out of all the nice games. What Freud, to whose memory the book is dedicated, would have made of all this treacle can readily be imagined.

On examination, this "ego psychology" looks suspiciously like old-fashioned rationalism. A pyromaniac boy who set fires at the Orthogenic School out of urethral obsession was "rehabilitated" (ah, that word from the Bowery Missions) by "being permitted to set small, safe fires under supervision and to extinguish them by throwing jets of water from a hand fire pump." When he turned the stream of water through the window of his motherly counselor's room, that speeded up the rehabilitation. Bettelheim speaks of "the rather unusual custom of eating part of the female genitalia," or remarks cheerily, "Female pubic hair is a matter of great interest to modern children." His basic metaphor for primitive initiation is teaching or learning (where it is not integrating or adjusting). Other metaphors

are less overt: he believes that nonliterate peoples consciously add new rites to their ceremonies in an attempt to gain new effects (the primitive as stage manager), and impose taboos with similarly conscious ends in mind (the primitive as legislator). Myths are invented "after the rites of the cult with the intention of explaining them," and we may compare myth "with the experiences of a young and unsophisticated child."

Bettelheim devotes a great deal of attention to Jewish religion in his book, and here his Freudianism is rather more orthodox, since he recognizes that such Jewish customs as infant circumcision obviously do not fit his voluntaristic theories. *Symbolic Wounds* suggests somewhat more familiarity with Roellenbleck on traces of Magna Mater cult in the Old Testament and Zimmerman's theory of Jewish circumcision as permanent erection (to name two of his more abstruse citations) than it does with the Bible itself. Bettelheim speaks of "the original nature of Jahwe as a fire god, who appeared to Moses in the burning thornbush," and he is orthodox Freudian in seeing fire as a phallic expression, and Judaism as thus by extension a "phallic religion." All this seems unnecessarily labored. There appear to be traces of many primitive worships in the Old Testament, among them the sacrificial blood of the lamb and bread of life, later to flower in the New, but the characteristic god of the earliest J text is neither the priestly compilers' fire god of the altars who savors the smell of burned kidney fat (Exodus 29:13), nor the sky god of the E text who lives on mountain tops like Zeus and sends down storms and victories. It is a very primitive phallic deity, Buck Mulligan's "collector of prepuces," who makes male nakedness sacred (Genesis 9:23) and can show only his back parts to Moses (Exodus 33:23); who is appealed to by means of a genital oath (this has become a commonplace reading of Genesis 24:2 and 47:29) and in return confers fertility (Genesis 49:25); whose symbol of power is the rod that turns into a serpent (Exodus 4:3) and whose altar is a phallic herm on which oil is poured (Genesis 28:18) or a cairn of stones on which the sacred meal is eaten (Genesis 31:46). Judaism is an ancient religion containing such a variety of survivals that neither Bettelheim nor Freud can reduce it to any primitive monotheism, and its customs and taboos are magical, not practical, as Bettelheim recognizes when he insists that modern medical circumcision is the ancient sacrifice to the phallic deity "camouflaged as a hygienic or prophylactic manipulation." "I ignore medical rationalizations," he says grandly at one point.

The problem is, ultimately, the matter of motivation. Bettelheim quotes an Australian aboriginal's explanation for the *Kunapipi* ceremonies (a lengthy initiation rite involving circumcision and subincision) and adds "I cannot accept the obvious rationalization." When a Nandi in Africa explains tribal clitoridectomy with "We are Nandi. We don't want such a hanging down thing in our women," Bettelheim comments, "I believe that the custom originates in more positive desires." Rationalization is, of course, the name one vocabulary of motivations reserves for another. When an Australian informant justifies subincision of the young men with "It makes the old men strong," he is saying that it contributes to the psychic well-being of the tribe, which is precisely what Bettelheim is saying in another phrasing. Any monist interpretive system insists, "This is why they think they do it, but I will tell you why they *really* do it." In actual fact there are no motivations in the situation (except the neutral one that it is believed to be a good thing to do); they are put in by the interpreter, and you come out with whatever explanation your vocabulary smuggled in. Aristotle's fourth or Efficient Cause, God's inscrutable purpose, is here simply being argued against his third or Final Cause, man's motive, with various secular equivalents for the deity.

Bettelheim's conclusion, that initiation rites are "efforts at acquiring the functions of the other sex," begs this question: are they efforts in the minds of the initiates, the initiators, the tribe, the field worker, Bettelheim, Freud, History, or God? We would be better off, I think, accepting the fact that causation is relative to the vocabulary used and ultimately unknowable. Bettelheim recognizes that rites can "now satisfy needs different from those they served in the past"; he accepts Benedict's statement that rites continue stable while their associated symbolic meanings (myths) vary; and he admits "interpreting rituals on the basis of their possible symbolic meaning is hazardous." He has, however, a characteristically psychoanalytic distrust of Malinowskian social function, arguing that what Malinowski sees as means may in fact be the tribe's end and vice versa, and that functional explanations do not explain the individual's own wish. Of course they do not, which is why we need psychoanalytic explanations too, and both, along with other motivational systems, for a rich and meaningful interpretation. Our job is to learn how to translate from one vocabulary into another, to build bridges between systems, and insofar as Bettelheim limits his pluralism within one system and denies the validity of others, we must build his bridges for him.

Despite all these failings, *Symbolic Wounds* is a useful book. It points up the real need to revise Freud, not in the neo-Freudian direction of bowdlerizing or re-repressing his profound insights, but in putting them undiminished into a context of our later knowledge. Thus, as Kenneth Burke suggests in the section "The Temporizing of Essence" in *A Grammar of Motives,* we must translate what Freud called his "vision" of the Primal Horde from its characteristic nineteenth-century form as a theory of prehistoric "origin" back into its true form as a statement about the nature or "essence" of the Oedipal situation, generally recognizing all such statements of temporal priority as actually statement about logical priority. We must additionally replace the inherited "memory traces" (with which Freud anticipated Jung's racial unconscious) by cultural transmission, and adapt in general to new discoveries in sociology, anthropology, and mythology, which would include throwing out not only Freud's Moses the Egyptian (as Bettelheim does) but Moses the historical figure (as Bettelheim does not). *Symbolic Wounds* in addition points up the need for a serious reconsideration of the role and relationship of the sexes, transcending both Freud's androcentric view and the gynocentrism of Bettelheim's authorities: Mead, Bateson, Ashley Montagu. (They seem to be a new Cybele cult, convinced that all the boys want to be girls.) Here we would start from the post-

Malinowskian recognition of a universal Oedipus complex shaped differently in different cultures, and seek to balance in our own society the importance of the female-dominated childhood and the male-dominated adult world. Finally, *Symbolic Wounds* suggests the enormous importance of ritual. "Rudimentary forms of religious beliefs and rituals were probably the first inventions of the human mind," Bettelheim says, aware of ritual origins; "envy must be hidden and expressed only through ritual," he adds, alive to function. In the last paragraph of his book Bettelheim calls for "more civilized, less magic and more satisfying institutions" as our equivalents for primitive rites. These are, for some of us, the imaginative organizations of art, ritual structures more significant than factors of ritual origin and function, and they bring us whatever of psychic well-being our poor bedeviled tribe has. (pp. 121-29)

> *Stanley Edgar Hyman, "Jesting at Scars," in his* The Promised End: Essays and Reviews, 1942-1962, *The World Publishing Company, 1963, pp. 121-29.*

Paul Roazen   (review date 1 April 1969)

[*Roazen is an American critic and educator who has written several books about Sigmund Freud and psychoanalysis. In the following review, Roazen praises Bettelheim's insightful analysis of the psychological ramifications of kibbutz life in* The Children of the Dream.]

Freud's impact on his followers was overwhelming, and perhaps as a result many of his pupils have done little more than consolidate and preserve the master's findings. The relative absence of original thinking within psychoanalysis has become all the more distressing as psychoanalytic concepts have permeated the Western world. Freud himself was a great revolutionary who, for the sake of exploring new areas of man's relation to society, challenged all conventional ways of thinking and defied all established professional organizations. Yet as his own ideas influenced modern psychiatry, his formulations became part of a new conformism.

Bruno Bettelheim stands as one of Freud's few genuine heirs in our time. Fearlessly independent and yet working within Freud's great discoveries, Bettelheim has sought to think through all of human psychology for himself. Once again like Freud, Bettelheim has not been content to remain a closet philosopher but has sought to test his insights in a clinical context.

For alongside Bettelheim's prolific writing—*The Children of the Dream* is his eighth book—he has been an ardent clinician. His Orthogenic School at the University of Chicago is a brave enterprise devoted to the conviction that it is possible to help autistic children overcome the severest possible emotional conflicts. And the help Bettelheim's school offers is as unconventional as the very notion that these children can be rescued at all. The Orthogenic School tries to perform as an institution those parental functions which have misfired in the child's natural home.

Bettelheim's career and the evolution of his work have not

been without changes in course. He has himself movingly described in **The Informed Heart** how the experience of being an inmate in the Nazi camps at Dachau and Buchenwald shook him out of his earlier dogmatic psychological slumbers. If the environment of a concentration camp could have a radical effect on the personalities of its inmates, he reasoned, could not some positive lessons be gleaned from this for the creative use of institutions to promote human autonomy? The origins of the Orthogenic School lie in what Bettelheim had learned about the effects institutional life can have on human mental functioning.

Bettelheim has not been shy about speaking out on problems beyond the strictly therapeutic, and he is having a growing influence on social scientists throughout the world. Quite unlike many other post-Freudian thinkers, Bettelheim has never indulged in any soupy moralism. Drawing on his experiences with the children in his school he has become a severe critic of many middle-class American child-rearing practices. In fact he has never taken for granted the special virtues of middle-class life, and has made himself into a trenchant critic of the standards of contemporary culture.

The communal method of education developed on the Israeli kibbutz ("kibbutz" is a Hebrew word meaning "group"), although involving only a small fraction of Israel's total population, was almost bound to seem to Bettelheim a fascinating experiment in nature. To what extent is man the father of society, or society the father of man? Bettelheim's own experience with the institutional rearing of children had contradicted earlier claims that to rear children in groups must be damaging to their mental health. Moreover, the children of the kibbutz had been reared according to a variant of Freudian teaching. Like it or not, psychoanalysis has become a part of the modern world, and perhaps no one is more equipped to assess the effects of kibbutz society on personality formation than Bruno Bettelheim.

Not surprisingly his fascinating account of communal child rearing in Israel is appreciative of the best elements of kibbutz education, which takes place in a restricted society of high consensus functioning as an extended family. "Kibbutz children live from birth on (usually from the fourth day after delivery) with their age group, not at home with their families. That is, they are reared as a group, in separate children's houses, by members of the community assigned to the task."

Although kibbutz parents play a distant role in the upbringing of their children, by a conscious act of will the community is charged with assuming the over-all functions of direction and control in the life of its children. The kibbutz, and not the parents, provides the basic security for the child. Peer groups play a central role in the upbringing of children, while maternal substitutes by and large take over the mothering function.

Social philosophers over the centuries have speculated on the possibilities of human development in small societies, and Bettelheim has a keen eye for the gains (as well as the losses) of this unique Israeli subculture. In the kibbutzim he found an absence of drug addiction, juvenile delinquen-

cy and the kinds of cultural deprivations that have beset the young in our own society.

The kibbutzniks seem to have many fewer emotional disturbances than one would expect to find in a comparable group in the United States, although in a culture as different as the kibbutz it is difficult to say what would count as a sign of symptomatology. Freed from the anxieties bred by a competitive social order and the American premium on possessing things privately, the kibbutzniks have worked cooperatively in behalf of a joint community effort; their very consciences have been so formed by their society (instead of their parents) that to oppose the group would be to risk the greatest loss imaginable.

The ostensible purpose of the kibbutz movement had been to create a new way of life in a very ancient and hostile land. In fact, the dream of the first generation of kibbutzniks to found a new society has succeeded in contributing much to the uniqueness of modern Israel. Bettelheim puts this whole movement into the context of the revolt of Eastern European Jews against the constraints of ghetto life.

It took the deep devotion to a secular religion to undercut the faith of their fathers; instead of the unity of the ghetto, they evolved the solidarity of the kibbutz. Instead of the open show of familiar feeling, they substituted the calm detachment of comradeship. And in place of the values of intellectual achievement and the acquisition of property, they turned to physical labor and set themselves the task of transforming their physical environment. In the Promised Land former ghetto Jews could avoid overintellectualization by becoming farmers. Above all, the kibbutzniks rejected the powerful ghetto mother, and gratified their own fears of inadequacy as parents, by turning child-rearing into a specialized role.

Bettelheim ruthlessly pursues the psychological consequences of the special conditions of kibbutz life. These latter-day Puritans deliberately aimed to alter the relation between children and parents as typified in Freud's conception of the Oedipus complex. If they succeeded in removing some of the worst aspects of the hostility and ambivalence between child and parent, while protecting the child from fears of parental desertion and abandonment, the kibbutzim also managed to destroy the intimacy and deep attachments of traditional family life.

The author observed in the kibbutzniks an emotional flattening out and a fear of deep attachments, as they seemed to find it difficult to be fully intimate or autonomous as feeling human beings. To the degree to which they had given up to the community problems which in our society the individual must struggle over and internalize, the people of the kibbutzim lack a capacity for deep empathy with others. As critical as Bettelheim is of middle-class child-rearing, he is fully appreciative of some of the best aspects of our own culture, where in exchange for all the parents' dependent care, the child gives in return—ideally to be sure—through the full flowering of his personality.

No doubt other observers of kibbutz life will find much to quarrel with in Bettelheim's account. He freely admits that his report is very personal and impressionistic, based on an all too brief seven weeks field work, mainly in one kibbutz settlement. Others may well challenge the particular assets and liabilities of group rearing that Bettelheim found in Israel, but they should be grateful for his clarity, lucidity, and boldness in stating an argument. As long as we have workers like Bruno Bettelheim the Freudian tradition will remain very much alive. (pp. 3, 23)

> *Paul Roazen, in a review of "The Children of the Dream," in* The New York Times Book Review, *April 1, 1969, pp. 3, 23.*

Elizabeth Janeway   (review date 17 March 1974)

[*Janeway is an American critic, novelist, and lecturer. In the review below, she offers a favorable assessment of* A Home for the Heart.]

Bruno Bettelheim retired last year as director of the Orthogenic School, for disturbed children, at the University of Chicago. He had been there for 29 years and rebuilt the place, taking on children usually considered incurable, like the mute autistic ones, increasing the number of inmates from 30 to 50-odd, and adding adolescents and young people in their twenties. The school has achieved a salvage rate—"returned to full participation in life"—of better than 85 per cent, and done so, incidentally, on a budget quite comparable to those of more orthodox institutions.

Ex-patients are bankers, businessmen and barbers, teachers, professors, secretaries and construction foremen, nurses and airline pilots. Some have come back to work at the school. And of course Bettelheim has written about the work done here in volume after volume, which have reached a wider-than-professional audience: *Love Is Not Enough, Truants From Life* and *The Empty Fortress.*

The purpose of [*A Home for the Heart*] is to describe the heart of Bettelheim's method, which is the attempt to create a "total therapeutic milieu" as the setting and the means for curing the psychically damaged and crippled, in the hope that other institutions will be able to copy these techniques for their own use. At present, says Bettelheim, other institutions, even the best, fragment life both for patients and staff in a hurtful way. For the patients, a fragmented therapy results in a few hours a week of psychiatric work with specialists, plus some random occupational aid, against a background of merely custodial care. Institutions which fall below the best can tail off, as we all know, into the suburbs of hell.

In all of them, moreover, those who work most closely with the patients, like the nurses and orderlies, have little or nothing to say about the course of treatment, and those who prescribe treatment do so from afar, without personal involvement. This treatment is conceived as something done for, and to, the patient. His own efforts to control his life are hardly admitted and, in fact, control is taken from him even in areas where he is capable of operating well. Life in such an institution becomes even more confusing and unpredictable than in the outside world. The patient's madness, his inability to connect his inner self with functioning reality, is reinforced.

In Bettelheim's view, the patient's energy must be enlisted in his own cure. That means that those working with him must see him as a fellow human, worthy of respect. The traditional hierarchy of command, which distances doctors from patients, disvalues the patient in two sets of eyes, his own and that of the staff supposedly charged with curing him; this in turn devalues their work. In addition, this division between active-normal curers and passive-creature-to-be-cured deprives the therapist of what Bettelheim considers his most useful instrument, which is his own experience and his ability to see, in the experience of others, analogies with his own problems and emotions. He does not use this sense of likeness to teach, or to mold the patient in his own shape, but to understand what and where the patient is, how he is caught in his own human difficulties. The attitude developed thus in the therapist is not a sympathetic (and sentimental) urge to cure "the poor souls," it is the empathy which provides an understanding of how a human mind *like one's own* may be freed from confusion and terror.

Such work can only be done, says Bettelheim, in a structure that provides, so far as is humanly possible, a seamless web of concern for the patients and a continuing, concentrated process aimed always at the goal of bringing each individual back to a capacity for dealing with the world. In his description of the physical surroundings provided patients at the Orthogenic School, we see his theories worked out in everyday living. Those who come there arrive sunk in distrust and terror, uncertain of the meaning of the simplest word or gesture and ready to interpret them, therefore, as threats and maledictions.

Silent and barricaded within themselves as they may appear, they are not withdrawn from emotion, simply terrorized by it. Many are intensely sensitive to everything that can be read as concerning them and their state, at times uncannily so. Thus, since everything they see and hear may affect them, their ambience should support whatever shreds of self-esteem and active interest in others may be left them. The world speaks to them with great symbolic force, says Bettelheim; and if those who hope to heal the disabled know how to do it, they can enlist that force as an ally.

Eating and sleeping arrangements, bathrooms and toilets, degrees of possible privacy and room for one's own possessions, play-space whose use is not prescribed, food when it's wanted and plenty of it, attractive china and fittings which don't imply, "We can't give you anything nice because you'll destroy it" (which further implies, "You're unpredictably violent and we can't control it"), these all help to establish the patients' worth. Attractive living for patients also prevents any invidious comparisons with attractive staff quarters; all are treated alike. An accessible director; a staff which doesn't all go home at night; unlocked doors to the outside (though locked against incomers who might frighten or disturb); trips outside often and on demand; counselors who work intimately with the same patients so that personal affections can grow on a basis of realistic connections; regular and frequent staff meetings for all levels, with everyone expected to report on the progress of patients, not of "cases"; communication with service staff, so that janitors and cleaners and cooks and maids feel that they too have a hand in the healing process—all this and more is enlisted to weave a single fabric round the patients which supports them (though not their delusions) and is aimed at awakening in them that "justified self-esteem" which Bettelheim sees the proper goal of therapy.

This is spelled out in the modest definition he gives of mental health: "With some qualifications I suggest that nothing is more characteristic of mental well-being than a healthy self-respect, a regard for one's body and its functions, and a reasonably optimistic outlook on life." It is the patient's own positive feelings which can, in the end, work this cure, which, indeed, will be the cure; and so the efforts of the staff are much engaged in divining the flickers of such feeling and in responding positively themselves.

This is not easy work. For the staff too the "total therapeutic milieu" provides a much needed support. Letters from long-term staff members, some still at the school and some who have left, speak of their experience of this highly demanding vocation. Repeatedly they tell of finding themselves engaged in an integration of their experience into their own personalities, which is quite analogous to the patients' struggles to achieve a greater grip on their lives. It can be frightening indeed to see one's own half-resolved emotional binds reflected in a schizophrenic child. Perhaps only the conviction, conveyed by the school and its ethos, that such confrontations can supply the understanding through which a child can be reached and helped, will overcome fright and strengthen the self.

Yet the matter does not end there, for the very fact that counselors and therapists learn, grow and change reacts on the patients, telling them that they have actually affected someone important in their lives, in an important way. The result is positive, an increase in self-esteem; this, in turn, helps the staff to feel that their own struggles have been truly worthwhile. The therapeutic milieu, that is, sets up a magnetic field in which positive feed-back not only occurs but helps to sustain the milieu.

I have concentrated on the core of the book, but the general reader will find a great deal more here, for Bettelheim combines a capacity for lucid speech with a mind of rare strength and subtlety, as his readers well know. He is a natural parabolist, capable of seeing the universe in a grain of sand and passing the vision on. An example: In speaking of his own commitment to his work, he remarks that the enthusiasm he brought to it was more important to the staff he recruited and worked with, as a means of promoting their own commitment, than was his actual knowledge about psychiatric disturbances. Fair enough, but anyone not entirely self-absorbed might well see, if not say, that. But Bettelheim goes on to draw a further moral, citing the staff's awareness that his commitment, though it issued in rational courses of action, "had its mainspring in unconscious needs not to fail." And this, he concludes, was very useful indeed because it offered his fellow-workers a fine, immediate opportunity to observe that "specific 'irrational' pressures need not be repressed because they are all infantile, unhealthy, damaging, destructive, but that, to the contrary, they can be made to serve the most constructive endeavors."

Bettelheim has been called authoritarian and overbearing. For all I know he may be so in action, for the enthusiastically committed can certainly behave that way, when they imagine themselves to be merely vehement and engaged. But taking one's own subconscious and irrational urges as the subject for a parable is hardly the action of a didactic tyrant. And indeed the emphasis throughout Bettelheim's work, on the value of the individual and his autonomy, on the need to listen to those whom life has hurt instead of turning away in fright—and his own remarkable capacity for doing so—are answers in themselves to most of the charges made against him.

Like his early master, Freud, Bettelheim displays little interest in major, political, change. But do not be deceived. If he declares that the way to deal with reality is to integrate one's egostructure (excuse the jargon; to learn from the events of one's own life and modify one's behavior accordingly), he goes on to point out how the strengthened ego is then able to react upon reality—in short, to change the world. Those who get most from Bettelheim will be those who read him with eyes open and minds alert to the nuances and vistas of this thought. (pp. 27-8)

> *Elizabeth Janeway, "The Doctor Who Let the Patient Cure Himself," in* The New York Times Book Review, *March 17, 1974, pp. 27-8.*

[Bruno Bettelheim] has been a notable champion of freedom in an age when it has been fearfully assaulted by the forces of mass culture. With such works as *The Informed Heart* and *The Uses of Enchantment . . . ,* he has earned the gratitude of those who, to use the terminology of one of his earlier writings, are determined to develop their consciousness of freedom.

—*John R. Turner, in a review of* On Learning to Read, *in* The American Spectator, *September, 1982.*

Harold Bloom   (review date 15 July 1976)

[*Bloom is one of the most prominent contemporary American critics and literary theorists. In* The Anxiety of Influence *(1973), he formulated a controversial theory of literary creation called revisionism. Influenced strongly by Freudian theory, which states that "all men unconsciously wish to beget themselves, to be their own fathers," Bloom believes that all poets are subject to the influence of earlier poets and that, to develop their own voice, they attempt to overcome this influence through a process of misreading—a deliberate, personal revision of what has been said by another so that it conforms to their own vision. In the following review, Bloom provides a mixed appraisal of* The Uses of Enchantment.]

Freud's essay on "The Uncanny" (1919) can be said to have defined, for our century, what criticism once called the Sublime. An apprehension of a beyond or of the daemonic—a sense of transcendence—appears in literature or life, according to Freud, when we feel that something uncanny (*unheimlich*) is being represented, or conjured up, or at least intimated. Freud locates the source of the uncanny in our narcissistic and atavistic tendency to believe in "the omnipotence of thought," that is, in the power of our own or of others' minds over the natural world. The uncanny is thus a return to animistic conceptions of the universe, and is produced by the psychic defense Freud called repression, an unconsciously purposeful forgetting of drives that might menace our socially conditioned "ego-ideals," that is, the models we attempt to imitate.

It would have seemed likely for Freud to find his literary instances of the uncanny, or at least some of them, in fairy tales, since as much as any other fictions they seem to be connected with repressed desires and archaic forms of thought. But Freud specifically excluded fairy tales from the realm of the uncanny. "Who would be so bold," Freud asks, "as to call it an uncanny moment, for instance, when Snow-White opens her eyes once more?" Why not? Because, he goes on to say, in those stories everything is possible and so nothing is incredible, and therefore no conflicts in the reader's judgment are provoked. Freud concludes his essay, "The Uncanny," by an even more arbitrary judgment: "In fairy-stories feelings of fear— including uncanny sensations—are ruled out altogether."

Why Freud takes this attitude toward fairy tales is something of a mystery, at least to me, though two surmises immediately suggest themselves: there may be a hidden polemic here, against Jung and his excursions into daemonic romance, and there always is an ambivalence on Freud's part toward literary romance, so that the forms of what Northrop Frye, adapting Schiller, calls "naïve romance" are not tempting to Freud's interpretative skills. Essentially, Freud chose dreams and mistakes and neurotic symptoms in preference to stories, and his keen sense of texts did not betray him in such choosing; for even the simplest fairy tale tends to be a palimpsest, a textual jungle in which one interpretation has grown itself upon another, until by now the interpretations have become the story.

Where Freud would not venture, few orthodox Freudians have trespassed, though Karl Abraham and Otto Rank (in his earlier work) in different ways verged upon the area of the folk tale. Now Bruno Bettelheim, with a kind of wise innocence, has subjected fairy tales, in general and in particular, to very close, generally orthodox, and wholly reductive Freudian interpretations. [**The Uses of Enchantment**], written in apparent ignorance of the vast critical traditions of interpreting literary romance, is nevertheless a splendid achievement, brimming with useful ideas, with insights into how young children read and understand, and most of all overflowing with a realistic optimism and with an experienced and therapeutic good will. What Freud might have thought of it hardly can be conjectured, and many readers may find themselves somewhat baffled by its perpetual vigor in reductiveness, in discovering the same common denominators in what plainly are very varied stories. I myself am bothered by Bettelheim's need to see nearly all his stories as being equally coherent and consistent, but that is only a secondary reaction. Primarily, I am moved, charmed, and frequently persuaded by this humane effort to clarify the daemonic ground of romance and so to substitute the uses of enchantment for the uncanny actualities of the enchantment.

Bruno Bettelheim's major concern has been with autistic children, and inevitably his interpretative activity is directed against any child's tendency to defensive withdrawal, to submit to the temptations of an abnormal subjectivity or virtual solipsism. Throughout this book, Bettelheim argues for the child's legitimate needs, and against the parent's self-centeredness. The child's desperate isolation and loneliness, his inarticulate anxieties, are addressed directly by fairy tales, according to Bettelheim, and the parents' function is to mediate by telling the child the story, thus strengthening the therapeutic effect by the authority of their approval. But why should fairy tales, *in themselves,* be therapeutic? Bettelheim's answer depends upon the child being his own interpreter:

> The fairy tale is therapeutic because the patient finds his *own* solutions, through contemplating what the story seems to imply about him and his inner conflicts at this moment in his life.

Bettelheim proceeds on the basis of two complementary assumptions: that the child *will* interpret a story benignly, for his own good; and that the Freudian interpretations will yield an accurate account of the child's interpretations. The child, questing for help, and the analyst, attempting to find helpful patterns in the stories, thus read alike, though in different vocabularies. A layman, reading Bettelheim's interpretation of a fairy tale, will come into possession of a key to what the child finds. That both of his assumptions might be questioned does not occur to Bettelheim. Perhaps this is all to the good, since it leaves unimpaired his confidence as an interpreter; and a child analyst, like any analyst, would be destroyed without such confidence.

The first half of Bettelheim's book, in which he explains and justifies his approach to fairy tales, is almost wholly a success. Fairy tale is compared to fable and to myth, and preferred to either because of its realistic optimism. A gentle, persuasive reading of "The Three Little Pigs" becomes a masterly demonstration of the opposition between Pleasure Principle and Reality Principle, and Bettelheim develops a considerable defense of fantasy as a mode of overcoming the vestiges of infancy and bringing the young self to an early sense of autonomy.

Perhaps the best pages in this fine "Part One: A Pocketful of Magic" concern "The Goose Girl," a superb Grimm Brothers story, in which a princess is displaced by her wicked maid, whose crime of usurpation is augmented when she has the head of Falada, the faithful talking horse of the princess, chopped off. Reduced for a time to herding geese, the princess nevertheless ends happily, her true identity disclosed, while the unfaithful maid is stripped naked, placed inside a barrel with pointed nails, and dragged by horses up street and down until she is dead, a punishment she has unwittingly suggested as appropriate for someone with her guilt.

Bettelheim reads this as an Oedipal pattern, with the story warning the child against the desire to usurp the place of the parent of the same sex, just as the maid took the place of the princess. This displacement occurred after the princess lost a white handkerchief given to her by her mother, a handkerchief stained deliberately by three drops of the mother's blood. Noting that the Queen gave this handkerchief to her daughter as she was leaving home to be married, Bettelheim interprets the blood as symbolic of potential sexual maturity, and the loss of the handkerchief as indicating the princess was not ready for such maturity.

To have lost the handkerchief, Bettelheim writes, is a " 'Freudian' slip, by means of which she avoided what she did not wish to be reminded of: the impending loss of her maidenhood." It allowed her to revert to childhood as a goose girl. This regression brings about tragedy for poor Falada, whose head is nailed to a gateway. Each morning, the goose girl laments to the horse's head: "Falada, thou who hangest there," to which the head replies: "If this your mother knew, / Her heart would break in two." Bettelheim translates this as expressing the mother's helpless grief, and so as admonishing the goose girl to cease being passive, at least for her poor mother's sake. "All the bad things that happen are the girl's own fault because she fails to assert herself."

When the maid eventually is punished, Bettelheim urges us not to believe that children will be repelled by so ghastly an execution. Instead, they will say she chose it for herself, deserved it anyway, and fittingly is destroyed by horses in retribution for having killed the noble Falada. The Oedipal situation has been redressed, with the usurper serving as a scapegoat for the princess herself, who will believe no longer that her own mother was a usurper threatening the princess's true place, and whose story serves to warn other children against prolonging dependence with its attendant passivities. Here Bettelheim has been shrewd and observant, and his interpretation has a curious rightness.

"Part Two: In Fairy Land" is a descent, and I suspect that it will please fewer readers who have some care for romance and its interpretation. Bettelheim takes a series of the most famous tales—"Hansel and Gretel," "Little Red Riding Hood," "Jack and the Beanstalk," "Snow White," "Cinderella" among them—and tries to give rather straightforward Freudian readings that become less analyses of the texts, and rather more explanations of how and why young children *should* emerge with particular meanings to each story. Freud's belief that fairy tales lack a repressed element, a daemonic or uncanny aspect, is developed implicitly by Bettelheim's well-intentioned pleasure in uncovering only beneficent meanings, except in the instance of "Goldilocks and the Three Bears," which frustrates the analyst's best efforts, until he ends by condemning it as a story:

> Parents would like their daughters to remain eternally their little girls, and the child would like to believe that it is possible to evade the struggle of growing up. That is why the sponta-

neous reaction to "Goldilocks" is: "What a lovely story." But it is also why this story does not help the child to gain emotional maturity.

Why does "Goldilocks" fail Bettelheim? Because, as he says, it raises questions which it does not answer, "while the greatest merit of a fairy story is that it gives answers, fantastic though these may overtly be, even to questions of which we are unaware because they perturb us only in our unconscious." The more unresolved a text, the less therapeutic, thus threatens to become a Bettelheimian formula. But "Goldilocks" presents problems for Bettelheim precisely because "the three bears form a happy family, where things proceed in such unison that no sexual or oedipal problems exist for them." Unable to break into the happily balanced world of Father Bear, Mother Bear, and Baby Bear, Goldilocks achieves "no resolution of the identity problem . . . , no self-discovery, no becoming a new and independent person."

Bettelheim greatly prefers "Snow White" (which he recognizes as a precursor-text to "Goldilocks"), and his full, approving commentary upon "Snow White" ought therefore to be useful for assessing his interpretative method. I think that, as a reading, it fails, but the failure stems from the Freudian view of fairy tales as not belonging to the uncanny, to the sometimes Sublime world of romance.

Before giving the gist of Bettelheim on "Snow White," let me venture a brief sketch of a different reading, one that would assume a repressed or daemonic component in the story. [John] Ruskin, writing on "Fairy Stories" (1868), warned that their "fair deceit and innocent error . . . cannot be interpreted nor restrained by a wilful purpose," including surely a therapeutic one. Fairy stories, as Ruskin observed, cannot be "removed altogether from their sphere of religious faith," since in them: "the good spirit descends gradually from an angel into a fairy, and the demon shrinks into a playful grotesque of diminutive malevolence." For Ruskin what is repressed most strongly in fairy tales is a world of angels and demons, a world of energies that transcend familial conflicts, and that offer irrational solutions to the sorrows of "growing up." Those energies inform "Snow White" as a fiction, but are either unseen or evaded by Bettelheim.

What kind of a story is "Snow White," when an adult encounters it again in a good translation of the Grimms? It is about as uncanny as Coleridge's "Christabel," would be an accurate answer, and it is hardly a paradigm for the process of maturing beyond Oedipal conflicts, as Bettelheim wants it to be. Snow White's mother, like Christabel's, dies in childbirth. The relations between her wicked and disguised stepmother and Snow White, during the three attempts to murder the girl, are about as equivocal as the Sapphic encounters between Geraldine and Christabel. Trying to kill a girl by successively tight-lacing her, combing her hair with a poisoned comb, and sharing a partly poisoned apple with her—all these testify to a mutual sexual attraction between Snow White and her stepmother. The stepmother's desire to devour the liver and lungs of Snow White is demonic in itself, but takes on a particularly uncanny luster in the primal narcissism of a tale dominated by mirrors. When the tale ends, the wicked stepmother, dressed in her most beautiful clothes, has danced herself to death in red-hot slippers at the wedding feast of Snow White, a horror that is an expressive emblem of her frustrated desires.

Bettelheim seems on the verge of taking these hints as when, in one instance, he says: "That which is symbolized by the apple in 'Snow White' is something mother and daughter have in common which runs even deeper than their jealousy of each other—their mature sexual desires," to which I would add: "for each other," but that is to see a repressed element in a text where Bettelheim, faithful to Freud, cannot bear to see it. Where there is romance, I would argue, there *must* be repression, because enchantment is necessarily founded upon partial or misleading knowledge. Whatever the uses of enchantment may or may not be, the continuity of enchantment depends upon the ability of the enchanted reader or lover to sustain repression.

Bettelheim says of the stepmother's terrible end that: "Untrammeled sexual jealousy, which tries to ruin others, destroys itself," by which he means the stepmother's supposed jealousy of a love between Snow White and the father, but the father is nowhere involved in the story. All the text tells us is that the stepmother envies a beauty that is greater than her own, in the opinion of her mirror, which after all must represent her own repressed opinion. Rather desperately, Bettelheim tries to import the father into the text in the figure of the hunter assigned to kill Snow White. No moment in his book is lamer than Bettelheim's explanation for his naming the hunter as the royal father:

> At that time princes and princesses were as rare as they are today, and fairy tales simply abound with them. But when and where these stories originated, hunting was an aristocratic privilege, which supplies a good reason to see the hunter as an exalted figure like a father.

What can we do with this mode of interpretation, except to see it as confirming Ruskin's admonition against substituting the moral will for the spirit of the text?

Yet Bettelheim's moral will is so admirable that we are (and ought to be) uneasy at seeing him interpret so weakly. "Who is the interpreter and what power does he seek to gain over the text?" is the question that Nietzsche taught us to ask of every interpretation. Here the answer is: a benign healer of children is the interpreter, and his will-to-power is a will-to-health for young children who so badly require it. In the presence of motives so authentic and admirable as Bettelheim's, I feel a sense of shame in yet urging interpretations that would be closer, and better suited, to the daemonic text itself.

Bettelheim's polemic, as he keeps saying, is against a modern tradition in which parents have deprived their children of fairy tales, because they supposedly wished to protect the children from the pervasive violence of so many of the tales. I suspect that the true motive of many parents was founded rather upon a troubled apprehension, one that Freud, in his ambivalence toward romance, could not allow himself. "Snow White" is as Gnostic in its sexual and spiritual overtones as "Christabel" is; both are romances that set themselves *contra naturam*.

Bettelheim's [*The Uses of Enchantment*] is pragmatically right, but for the wrong reasons. Yes, fairy tales are good for young children, and for all the rest of us, but not because they are paradigms or parables that teach us how to adjust to an adult reality. They are good for us because their uncanny energies liberate our potential for the Sublime, for that little beyond ourselves that reason, nature, and society together cannot satisfy. As told by Bettelheim, a fairy tale may help a particular child, but the larger teaching of the tale, rather than the teller, is that the instinct for Sublime experience can never be satisfied, except perhaps by romance, human and literary. (pp. 10, 12)

> *Harold Bloom, "Driving Out Demons," in* The New York Review of Books, *Vol. XXIII, No. 12, July 15, 1976, pp. 10, 12.*

James W. Heisig (essay date 1977)

[*In the following excerpt, Heisig disputes many of Bettelheim's conclusions in* The Uses of Enchantment *but notes that Bettelheim "probably does more for the respectability of the fairy tale as an interpretative tool than has anyone before him."*]

[For those who know him] and are familiar with his work at the University of Chicago's Sonia Shankman Orthogenic School, Bettelheim's name has become synonymous with intelligent and devoted respect for the mysterious world of the child. In this latest book [*The Uses of Enchantment*] he carries on these same concerns by turning his attention to the function of the fairy tale in the development of the consciousness of the child. This is not the first time that Bettelheim has ventured beyond the psychologist's accustomed boundaries. Over twenty years ago he attempted a psychoanalytic study of puberty rites among preliterate cultures. The mixture of excitement and professional criticism which his theories aroused in that work has no doubt prepared him for similar reactions to the conclusions he arrives at in this full-length study of the fairy tale. Fortunately, it has not deterred him from setting forth his point of view boldly and without compromise—a fact which is all the more to be admired in a man in his seventies, a patriarch among child psychologists who refuses to rest comfortably on his considerable achievements.

Bettelheim is not the first, of course, to apply the principles of psychoanalysis to the fairy tale. Freud himself had suggested in his *Traumdeutung* (1900) that there is an unbroken line to be found between the origins and functions of dreams and of folklore in the psyche; and many since him, from a wide range of psychological persuasions, have carried the suggestion further. But the study of folklore in the past fifty years has become so specialized and so vastly documented a discipline and the distrust of psychological methods so widespread among orthodox ethnologists that it has become exceedingly risky to continue on with such investigations.

On the other hand, we cannot forget the inevitable popular

outrage still so easily incited by psychoanalytical ideas. Freud's interpretations of the polymorphous sexual perversity of the child is only beginning to settle into the modern mind, as Bettelheim himself, one of those who has done most to establish and refine the approach, must know only too well. Yet now we find him ordering such dear friends of imagination as Cinderella, Snow White, Rapunzel, Red Riding Hood, and Hansel and Gretel onto the analyst's couch—and the very idea sends a shudder down the spine in spite of ourselves. Surely this is the height of irreverence, the one sacrilege against memory for which psychoanalysis cannot be forgiven!

Indeed, left in the hands of a less sensitive observer of the human personality and a less skillful analyst, the worst might rightly be expected of such a project. Bettelheim's results however are impressive and generally hard to fault, given his stated intentions. Briefly put, the thesis he experiments with in the book is this: Using the psychoanalytic model of the psyche, fairy tales can be seen to communicate to the child an understanding of universal human problems in such a way as to encourage the development of his budding *ego,* give expression to *id* pressures, and suggest ways to relieve them in line with the requirements of the *superego.* The vagueness of the tales, he claims, is pedagogically suited to these tasks in that it engages the child's imagination to fill in the details and to invest his interests on whatever level he finds himself. The message of the tales, the argument goes on, is most critical at puberty, when the tangle of emotions which grip the child is most in need of sorting out and naming; and when the "separation anxiety" is keenest and most in need of some promise of deliverance. And in all of this, Bettelheim concludes, the fairy tale is much more reliable and therapeutic than attempts to educate parents in the arid complexities of child psychology could ever hope to be.

Working within that broad framework, Bettelheim brings to bear years of clinical experience, considerable research into the fairy tale, and a sharp eye for double entendre to uncover the mechanisms and meanings of enchantment in the child. In the end, he may not remove all the offensiveness of a rigorously Freudian perspective, but he probably does more for the respectability of the fairy tale as an interpretative tool than has anyone before him. His awareness of the limitations of his approach, together with occasional references to concrete cases of childhood disorder, ably protect the extreme subtlety which marks his reading of several of the stories from the usual charge of one-sided dogmatism.

In short, Bettelheim succeeds in opening the tales up, in leading us in and out between the lines where they can be made to deliver of their healing secrets. It is not surprising that he directs his strongest criticisms against attempts to detour the fairy tales from their natural functions in favor of other secondary ends and so to close off their power and meaning. Charles Perrault's seventeenth-century moralization of the tales is the object of Bettelheim's most telling complaints. Disney's famous animations (frequently biased in favor of Perrault's versions) are only mentioned twice as instances of apologic interference with the child's imaginative needs, although a general opposition to this treatment is unmistakable. All such closures remove the story from the genre of the folktale and relocate it amid the great bulk of so-called "children's literature" which he condemns as "empty-minded entertainment," shallow of substance and significance.

By the same token, Bettelheim argues that book versions of the fairy tales, even if accurate, can be counterproductive. Most obviously, the use of collections of these tales to teach reading skills or a love of written literature seriously threatens their effect on the child. Moreover, the use of illustrations bereaves the child of the imaginative freedom he should enjoy, and makes identification with the stories' heroes or heroines more difficult over a long period of time. Similarly, having the story read to one, or reading it oneself, tends to objectify it, to freeze its form and so to eliminate the essential contribution of the listener, who projects himself and significant others in his milieu into the tale. For Bettelheim, the ideal way to transmit the tales is in imitation of their folkloric means of communication: tell them orally and frequently; be faithful to the original without being slavish. Not only does such oral storytelling permit the greatest flexibility of response, but it sets up a valuable interpersonal event between the storyteller and the child. In addition, by separating the fairy tales from tacit interpretations—via the appendage of moral lessons, illustrations, or standardized wordings—their motifs may be taken over spontaneously by the child, Bettelheim suggests, to structure other forms of unconscious activity such as dreams, waking fantasies, and play.

Bettelheim's resistance to premature closure of the manifold of possible meanings contained in any given fairy tale is not simply a result of the same general interpretative principle which governs psychoanalysis' understanding of symptomatic languages. It has to do, he would insist, with the very genesis and structure of the tales themselves. He views the fairy tale as a corporate form of imagination which, so long as it meets the psychic needs of generation after generation of people who preserve it, will survive shifting patterns of reasoning and intellectual trends. Without denying this way of looking at the tales its validity, I think there are certain points in his argument where Bettelheim can be shown to have slipped into interpretative closures of his own which neither the fairy tales nor his own psychoanalytic perspective require. Accordingly, I turn now to a more critical examination of his project, focusing in the main on a number of general hermeneutical questions and adding a few specific remarks on selected tales by way of conclusion. Needless to say, these attempted disclosures will make best sense if read as marginal comments to the text itself and not as a complete substitute argument.

In the course of constructing his argument for the meaning and importance of fairy tales, Bettelheim draws upon a number of assumptions about the psyche of the child. Perhaps the first to strike us is his characterization of childhood modes of thought as essentially similar to those of primitive, preliterate peoples. As the child develops, he learns to replace them with more adult modes of thought which will enable him to live responsibly in our advanced civilization. Once one has understood the structure of this natural generation gap, Bettelheim would assert, it becomes clear that primitive forms of psychological insight—which is how he classifies the fairy tales—are more therapeutic for the child but unnecessary, even regressive, for the adult.

Standing behind this conclusion is the old notion that ontogeny recapitulates phylogeny, that is that the development of an individual organism telescopes and repeats the evolution of the entire species. Its promotion in modern times is associated with the evolutionary biologist, Ernst Haeckel (1834-1919). From there it was taken up for experimentation in theoretical anthropology by Claude Lévy-Bruhl, among others, and eventually found its way into psychology through Freud and Jung. The hypothesis itself fell speedily into disrepute, roughly in the same order, though it is one of those suggestive and stubborn ideas which seem to survive even the strongest contrary evidence and to reappear at the most unexpected times.

Bettelheim's subscription to this principle, implicit though it be here, seems to be unfortunate. First of all, the claim that primitive logics are inferior to and irrational in comparison with scientific views of the world is unnecessary to the claim (which Bettelheim makes, following Piaget) that children begin in a largely animistic world and only slowly learn the art of abstract thinking. Moreover, it has the disadvantage that it intimates a qualitative difference between adult and childhood thinking; and, consistent with that, a depreciation of the role of imagination in abstract thought. Bettelheim comes close to stating this explicitly in passages scattered throughout the book such as: "Every child believes in magic, and he stops doing so when he grows up (with the exception of those who have been too disappointed in reality to be able to trust in its rewards)."

Second, by grounding the comparison of thought-patterns in children and primitive peoples merely on their equidistance from our supposedly unquestionable commonsense world, the possibility of further insight from a study of the social functions of thought-patterns, including those found in the fairy tale, is prematurely closed off.

Third, these two closures combine to encourage further the original bias that fairy tales are really prescientific forms of psychology which are natural to the child's sphere but wholly unnatural to the adult's, which needs more rational means to integrate conscious and unconscious elements in the psyche. In this way, Bettelheim intends to support the usefulness of the fairy tale as a guide to the child's first halting steps in imagination. Yet it is hard to see how anything is gained in denying the tales any role at all in the mature imagination.

At this point the full and final implications of Bettelheim's attraction to the Haeckelian principle become clear. Personal maturity is measured, at least in great part, by one's ability to translate imaginative projections into the language of scientific psychology or some other rational interpretative frame. Enchantment is the necessary business of being a child. Becoming an adult, however, means extensive and deliberate disenchantment. What he calls the "illogic of the unconscious" continues to confront the "ratio-

nal order" of the "real world" throughout one's life. The difference between the integrated and the infantile personality is that the one can *understand* the objective truth about the real world, while the other can only *feel* it subjectively and so must revert to an unreal world. Each frame of reference has its own "truth," Bettelheim says, but there is no doubt that the truth of fantasy is more useful to the child's mind and harmful to the adult's.

There is a certain immediate appeal about such a point of view. For one thing, it seems to accord with our timeworn folk wisdom about raising children. For another, it supports our modern tendency to charge that wisdom more and more to the care of academic psychology, a tendency which Bettelheim seems to welcome readily enough. Parents are warned against trying to invent their own fairy tales to tell their children for fear of unwitting, but nonetheless dangerous, didactic interpretations. Only the rare individual—Goethe's mother is cited as an example—should extend creativity in storytelling beyond the addition of occasional details. What every parent can do, on the other hand, is grasp the psychological meaning of the fairy tales, and this gives him a decided superiority over the child, which must not be relinquished for the good of both sides. He may never be able to capture the many-leveled meanings of a single one of the tales or understand the varieties of influence involved in its retelling from infancy to adolescence. But "even if a parent should guess correctly why his child has become involved emotionally with a given tale, this is knowledge best kept to oneself." This because, Bettelheim argues, the child *wants* the meaning to be kept on a preconscious level. "Explaining to a child why a fairy tale is so captivating to him destroys the story's enchantment, which depends to a considerable degree on the child's not quite knowing why he is delighted by it. . . . He can gain much better solace from a fairy tale than he can from an effort to comfort him based on adult reasoning and viewpoints."

The advice is sound enough, even if the intellectual hubris it appears to cultivate may not be. I stress the point here not in order to take issue at this time with the social function of psychological theory, but because there are hints in Bettelheim's own treatment that he himself is aware of the enchantment which psychoanalysis has over him, not unlike that of the tale for the child in terms of its power and fictions.

To begin with, he sees that the basic charm of the fairy tale is due more to its literary form than to its psychological message. "The fairy tale could not have its psychological impact on the child were it not first and foremost a work of art." He then goes a step further to assert that no other form of literature and art is so "fully comprehensible to the child" as is the fairy tale, by which he means that it is capable of yielding new insights at each return. For this reason he concludes that the exploration of the psychological contribution of these stories to the child's development is more useful to parents than other forms of interpretation might be. The questions which are closed off by *petitio principii*, and which could as easily have been left open, are obvious. Surely educators of all kinds would be interested in seeing a balance between the psychological interpretations of the stories and some investigation of the literary-artistic form which Bettelheim sees as essential. Furthermore, by separating the enchantment of the fairy tale from the world of child psychology, the possibility of its range of relevant meanings to the adult becomes once more deserving of attention.

Likewise, Bettelheim takes pause on one occasion to talk about the limits of his interpretation in such a way as to suggest the inexhaustible intelligibility of the fairy tale. "Today adults use such concepts as id, ego, superego, and ego-ideal to separate our internal experiences and get a better grasp on what they are all about. . . . When we consider the emotional connotations these abstract terms of psychoanalysis have for most people using them, then we begin to see that these abstractions are not all that different from the personifications of the fairy tale." Except for one later remark about translating a story into "the pedestrian language of psychoanalysis," he does not return to the point. If we take the idea as given and add to it Bettelheim's acknowledgement that the fairy tales themselves are interpretations of inner human experiences—which is why they begin in concrete reality and pass into a magical, unreal world—then their "illogic" may be seen as a necessity and not simply as a pedagogic tool for the child who is unable to abstract. Just as the child "intuitively comprehends that although these stories are *unreal,* they are not *untrue,*" so too the adult may need to see that the same is true about his psychoanalytic stories. The familiarity with the workings of the mind which characterizes the mature personality may appear more true if we use psychoanalytic categories. But as Bettelheim notes: "Unfortunately, in doing so we have lost something which is inherent in the fairy tale: the realization that these externalizations are fictions, useful for sorting out and comprehending mental processes." With respect to the general argument of the book, therefore, the tales may yet be useful for adults, even if only to remind us of the inevitable gap between the things of our lives and the talk we use to appropriate them into the story of our life.

One final indication that Bettelheim's commitment to the view that the fairy tale belongs principally to the child is not absolute is his frequent allusion to different "levels" of meaning in the tales. Most often he uses the phrase merely to refer to the child's ability to project different psychic states into the stories. He makes brief note of the strata left in the tales by virtue of their long oral history, embracing cultural, religious, and mythical elements, but dismisses it at once from consideration as of little use for our understanding of the child. In this way his closure of the fairy tales in favor of child psychology is supported by his evidence; but it neglects to keep open his own intuition of the benefits of deeper research into their archaeology, whether for his own project or as a way to extend the meaning and importance of the tales into the adult world as well.

We may now consider certain aspects of Bettelheim's interpretation which fall within the general compass of his Freudian standpoint. First among these is his use of the theory of projection; that is, of the imaginative and largely unconscious transference of inner psychic states to artificial conditions which distort those states enough to provide a relaxation of anxiety. While such "externalization" is seen as necessary to relieve inner pressures—and at no time more necessary than during childhood—it is the very antithesis of maturation which requires the expansion of consciousness and the dissolution of projections. The benefit of fairy tales is that they prepare for mature consciousness in offering "figures onto which the child can externalize what goes on in his mind, in controllable ways. . . . Once this starts, the child will be less and less engulfed by unmanageable chaos." Bettelheim resists any attempt to specify which tales should be told at which time in the child's development, insisting that the way in which the tales teach by "indirection"—camouflaging feelings or displacing them onto secondary objects—can only be recognized but not organized for pedagogical purposes.

Although some theory of projection is essential for a psychological interpretation of the fairy tale, it is also likely to carry certain limiting biases with it. In Bettelheim's case, for instance, the concern with dissolving projections into their "real" components comes close to ignoring the need for criteria to determine what is real and what is not and overlooking the possibility that certain very real things of our life cannot but be spoken of in a language of apparent falsehoods, i.e. of projections. It is not necessary to get enmeshed in philosophical arguments about the mechanisms of perception to see these problems in Bettelheim's own method. On the one hand he allows the unavoidable projections of children and praises the fairy tales as helpful displacements of feelings too dangerous to be aimed at their direct referents. Adults do not need the tales for this, he says, but should remember enough of their own childhood not to deprive their children of them. On the other hand, he hints at possible uses of the stories as meditative devices for adults, only quickly to locate this function in a preliterate past where, according to his earlier assumption, men were more like the children of today in their modes of thought. "Like the patients of Hindu medicine men who were asked to contemplate a fairy tale to find a way out of the inner darkness which beclouded their minds, the child, too, should be given the opportunity to slowly make a fairy tale his own by bringing his own associations to and into it." The possibility of drawing a continuous line between the child's mind and the methods of the mystics, modern and ancient—Christian, Hindu, Islamic, Jewish, Buddhist, etc.—is not only sidestepped but directly closed off by Bettelheim's use of the projection theory.

In addition to infantilizing projection, he also tends to privatize it as simply a function of the individual psyche. That established patterns of projection are also used to transmit cultural values and views of the world cannot be dismissed out of hand simply because the individual is capable of casting his own fears and hopes into them. Bettelheim cites [Mircea] Eliade's interpretation of the tales as initiation rites by proxy, but only focuses on the person being initiated, overlooking the social context whereby a story relocates an individual in the heroic ideals of a common past.

Finally, some mention should be made of Bettelheim's

commitment to the universality and centrality of the Oedipus complex in childhood development. There is some indication that he recognizes how the application of Freud's idea to the subject matter of the fairy tales requires a common social structure based on a common definition of roles. "In the typical nuclear family setting, it is the father's duty to protect the child against the dangers of the outside world and also those that originate in the child's own asocial tendencies. The mother is to provide nurturing care and the general satisfaction of immediate bodily needs required for the child's survival." What we still want to know, or at least see questioned, is whether increasing control of once exclusively parental roles by service institutions might not make the tales so unreal a world as to be an ineffective source of projection for the contemporary child. Further, even if we were to accept with Bettelheim the universality of the Oedipus (or Electra) complex as the major psychic problem from age four until puberty, we might still want to distinguish those times at which it is peripheral or negligible to the child's world from those when it is central. This would mean a reevaluation of his discovery of oedipal symbolism as sufficient for understanding the tales he considers. For it is very difficult not to eye with considerable distrust the generalized hermeneutic principle Bettelheim devises to interpret number-symbolism in the fairy tale: one=superego or dominant parent; two=the two parents; three=the child in relation to his parents.

These closures brought about by the use of the projection theory point to four other assumptions which I do not believe the fairy tales share with Bettelheim's reading of them. Again, I state them here not to present a detailed alternative, but simply to suggest that the tales may be more open-ended than we often give them credit for.

In the first place, the use of a "growth model" to characterize the unfolding of childhood into adulthood is not to be found in the fairy tales which Bettelheim treats. In addition to using Freud's well known states, he refers favorably to [Erik] Erikson's epigenetic theory to describe the movement of the children through the tales. The difficulty with such models is that they require a notion of psychic betterment or progress according to some ideal, tacit or overt, of maturity. But the fairy tales seem to operate more simply, speaking only of some aspect or other of experience, some relationship, some insight which has yet to be appropriated by a particular character. The growth model, as Bettelheim uses it, stresses the ideal of a single ego which must gain mastery over the id, the superego and various ego-ideals, by "integrating" them, that is, by subduing them to its supremacy. "Complex as we all are—conflicted, ambivalent, full of contradictions—the human personality is indivisible." The fairy tales, in contrast, speak merely of individuals playing various roles, some of them surprisingly different, which give us an insight into their characters. There is no talk of a central unifying ego, and no assurance that the assumption need be made that each skin-bound individual can house only one personality. The goal of the character seems rather to be finding a place for each of the roles, as if the mature individual were more like a well-organized commune. The benefit of such a reading of the tales is not that it offers reliable criticism

of traditional psychological models, but only that it appears to reflect the actual world of the fairy tales whose enchantment over us we have set out to understand.

Second, Bettelheim is ambiguous about male-female differentiation in the fairy tales. He believes that both boys and girls can identify with characters of both sexes in the stories. His lengthy comparison of the stories of "Oedipus the King" and "Snow White" illustrates this well. Elsewhere he claims that the motif of heroine marrying hero at the tales' conclusions in fact indicates the integration of "male and female principles" found in each personality, the male representing the coming to terms with the outer world, the female with the inner world. Like the apportionment of parental roles in the nuclear family referred to earlier, the symbolism depends on cultural convention, which has proved highly volatile in industrialized societies. Bettelheim does not refer to this level of the problem, but skips over it to point to a mutual envy between the sexes seen on a biological level. The only real evidence he draws from the tales themselves is their frequent use of neuter names, as for instance in the heroines of the Grimms' collection: *Das Dornröschen, Das Schneewitchen, Das Aschenputtel,* etc. The idea of a counterbalance to a general male dominance in society by means of an exaggerated attention to female sexual mysteries, which seems a most promising one, is left untouched. In any case, Bettelheim's frequent reference to problems of female psychology reflects correctly the tales he is dealing with and needs an explanation not available within the limits of his chosen method.

A third problematic area has to do with the presence of morality in the fairy tales. While Bettelheim does not treat the stories as fables each with a specific moral—although he would surely have to admit that apologues and *Märchen* do occasionally overlap classifications—he does detect a certain moral world view which they all communicate. "A higher morality," he calls it, asserting that its unique trait is that good and evil are clearly polarized without ambivalence. This he finds helpful to the child who can thus identify without qualification with "good" characters in the stories and project his antipathies on "bad" characters. Where a fairy-tale character is involved in ethically questionable activity—stealing, murder, fornication, deception—the tales are treated by Bettelheim as "amoral." The argument is unconvincing and contrived. It is, after all, not to our interpretation of good and evil that the tales must conform, but rather the reverse. I believe it can easily be shown that good and evil are not so well polarized as Bettelheim supposes. There are numerous cases, and I would even venture to call them the rule in his selection of tales, where good and evil change appearances, where good comes out of evil and vice-versa, and where individual heroes and heroines are curious mixtures of good and evil. Here again, the meaning of the tales may frustrate our pedagogical interests, but in so doing may also lead us to a deeper level of meaning if we are only willing to follow.

In the fourth place, we may note that Bettelheim encourages the child's projection into the fairy tales because in this way the happy ending will promote the hope that adjustment to the real world will offer great rewards, and the fear that maladjustment will bring disgrace. It is not, for him, a matter of false wish-fulfillment as it is an appreciation of the need for wishes to be dramatized. "In the old days, when wishing still did some good . . . " opens the first story of the Grimms' collection. That "good" for Bettelheim is the promise of success which attends responsibility and perseverance. Wishing is then to be encouraged, but contextualized in reality. "Thus, a happy though ordinary existence is projected by fairy tales as the outcome of the trials and tribulations involved in the normal growing-up process." Once more, one wonders about this reading of the stories. The happy ending is not the universal element Bettelheim continually claims it to be. It is sometimes added abruptly, as a concluding device. And it is sometimes outright suspicious. The evident bias at work here is that the characters considered all do in fact mature and so are deserving of happiness. This in turn requires that we see happiness as the natural reward of virtue, a requirement which seems much closer to wishful thinking than to an acceptance of our real world. In the tales happiness is oftentimes given to the underserving, the naive, or simply the lucky-starred. Bettelheim's argument may well capture the child's simplistic expectations about endings to fairy tales. But that children's interpretative projections in what he calls "true fairy tales" are always correct and always therapeutic is something that needs more critical attention than Bettelheim gives it.

A psychological adaptation of the Haeckelian principle, the sharp separation of the worlds of fantasy and reality, and the full ramifications of his projection theory all circumscribe Bettelheim's analysis of the fairy tale as an aid to the child's natural process of development. The purpose of his method is to understand the effects of the tales and thereby to increase our insight into the mind of the child. If we begin, however, from the fairy tales themselves—even from those which he chooses for examination—and cast ourselves under their spell without any of these particular interests, a further level of meanings comes to light. Hints of this shadow-side to Bettelheim's treatment have come up in the course of our indication of those closures which seemed unnecessary to his overall project. It can now be portrayed more forthrightly, if in bold strokes, by way of introduction to some brief remarks on selected tales.

Bettelheim defines the generic difference of the fairy tale as the presence of magical or supernatural powers which come to the aid of the hero or heroine. I would argue that we need to go further and assert that these powers are not merely *dei ex machina* which highlight the heroism of the protagonists of the tales, but ought themselves to be seen as the prime movers of the plots which underlie these stories. Unbiased identification with the adventures of most all the human characters of the tales, it seems to me, produces less often a sense of heroic strength in adversity than one of victimization, at first in adversity and then often in victory as well. To enter the world of the fairy tale is to enter a world ruled by dark forces, unknown and uncontrollable, alternatively helpful and hostile, which have their own rules and are singularly disrespectful of our efforts to manipulate our own success. In general, they surround such realities as birth, death, suffering, separation, ambition, strife, misunderstanding, and sexuality. Where the main character of a story is a child, these dark forces tend to focus in particular on the despotic superiority of parents, the heartless rivalry of siblings, the accursed onslaught of puberty, or the like. Naming these things as dark forces reminds us that we have here to do with the most universal and deeply felt questions of our nature. It does little to tell us how to answer these questions, other than to promote a simple trust that as these forces interact with one another on the stage of our lives, our own well-being will somehow be served in the end.

Perhaps the best way to characterize the function of the fairy tale would be to adapt the term "superstitious" to that end. Superstition is a relational term. It refers to a mode of thought or behavior which stands above (super-stare) and against the current psychological, philosophical, religious, and cultural modes of thought, giving expression to perceptions and needs ignored by other forms of the corporate imagination. Superstitions are not primitive modes of thought (even though we may find in old superstitions of many forms insights later taken up systematically by modern science), but a contrapuntal tradition. The benefit of folkloric forms of superstition is that they have been purified of many particular details of time and space, losing almost all synchronic unity but gaining in diachronic consistency as a picture of the dark side of consciousness. In general they are fragmented and form no total world view, though they may have once belonged to one. This was Hegel's opinion for instance, when he referred to folk superstitions and tales as "the sad and indigent remains of an attempted independence" of the national imagination.

In contrast to Bettelheim's approach, such a view would not make the fairy tale strictly distinct in form and function from myth; nor would it focus on the heroic, self-salvific deeds of the protagonists as essential to a true tale. Most important, it would not require the restriction of the tales to children, which has been my most common complaint throughout the preceding analysis of Bettelheim's assumptions. This is not to say that many of the fairy tale characters are not easier for the child to identify with than for the adult and therefore of greater interest to the child psychologist, but only that the entire genre of the fairy tale need not be proscribed as pathological or immature for purposes of adult reflection.

Perhaps the most convincing argument for the dis-closure of Bettelheim's method is by way of attention to specific details in the stories themselves. We may begin with the tale of "Rapunzel."

In his cursory and incomplete analysis of the story, Bettelheim sees its central motif as a young girl's achievement of independence from a domineering mother by the use of her own body (the golden tresses). The image of the overly protective mother seems clear enough in the transformation from mother to ogre; but that Rapunzel's freedom is secured, in addition to being ardently desired, is not so clear. The maiden's long hair was hardly her salvation. It was the very source of her imprisonment and of her downfall. It was the point of contact between her and her mother and also between her and the young prince, who mounted it to impregnate her on the spot—apparently with her full consent, even though they hardly knew one another and even though she had never before even seen a man! Rapunzel is punished for her sin by being exiled to a desert, where she gives birth to twins. The prince is blinded by the old woman and only happens on his lover some years later while roaming about the woods eating wild berries after having been exiled from his kingdom. The "happy ending" which Bettelheim draws attention to was not part of the original story set down by Jacob Grimm, but was a later addition of brother Wilhelm. In any case, it is too abrupt to belong to the flow of events in the tale. Like the mother who longs ardently to have a child (a request which God grants) and then longs to keep it (a request which is ultimately refused), Rapunzel and her prince are themselves the unwitting victims of strong desires. In time, all three are punished, not for their desire—which is natural and pre-ethical—but for their blindness to its strength, for committing the original sin against human nature: the denial of consciousness. (Rapunzel, by the way, is named after the European bellflower, whose roots were known for their medicinal value as a cure to jaundice.) It is unlikely that a young child could appreciate much of this material in the tale, beyond some sense of the unfair restraint of the maiden in the tower of her parent's selfishness. Yet the message is there for the finding nonetheless.

In his treatment of "Sleeping Beauty," Bettelheim interprets the "curse" of the thirteenth wise woman fated to befall the young maiden in the fifteenth year of her age as symbolic of the arrival of puberty. Sexual awakening, and the isolation which accompanies it in the natural transition from childhood to adulthood, cannot be avoided, says the story, despite all the efforts made by parents to the contrary. Here Bettelheim comes close to abandoning his strict standpoint towards the "heroism" of the main character when he describes the central message with these words: "Don't worry and don't try to hurry things—when the time is ripe, the impossible problem will be solved, as if all by itself." But he avoids the temptation by insisting on the heroism of a "long, quiet concentration on oneself" as the meaning of the maiden's hundred-year sleep. The end result is a transformation of perception which Bettelheim attributes to Sleeping Beauty's personal strength of character, but which the story seems to attribute merely to the passage of time: her world falls asleep and then awakens, finding her richly rewarded for the period of dormancy. Where Bettelheim does renege on his principles is when he notes that the curse turns out to be a "blessing in disguise," thus denying the absolute polarization of good and evil.

The weakest aspect of the analysis, however, may be referring the young child's fascination with the story to preconscious sexuality, a sort of presentiment of pubertal problems just around the corner. It seems more likely that the puberty motif—a common and universal human experience of falling prey to the dark forces of human nature—is being used as an instance of a more encompassing mystery. Even the possibility that Sleeping Beauty can become a model for all turning points in life where transformation requires isolation does not capture the full meaning. The message needs a more mythical and cosmic frame of reference. Something like: death and life are parts of one and the same reality, in whose service they interact in the passage of time. Agriculturally, the image is that of the kiss of the warm spring sun enlivening the cold, sleeping winter earth. In the story's own context, the problem of life and death is introduced at the very outset. A king and a queen long for a child, as a way of insuring the continued life of the crown under their name after they die. And it ends with the statement that the maiden and her prince "live happily until their death." The curse of death by dark forces which marks the birth of the girl is changed into a promise of rebirth, just as the accursed thornbush forest (from which image she gets her original name, "Thorn Blossom") bursts into bloom sympathetically with the rebirth of the maiden. The overall feeling one is left with is that death is but a state of suspended animation. The tale does not argue the reality of life after death. It simply dramatizes the fundamental human desire for immortality. Hence, to read it purely in pubertal terms, or to assign it strictly to childhood problems, would seem a needless limitation on its meaning.

Bettelheim reserves his most extended analysis for the story of "Cinderella," and makes difficult reading of it by dealing simultaneously with a number of variants. This is perhaps the best example in the book of how he needs to overstep his own hermeneutic principle on the absolute polarization of good and evil. Far from seeing her as the wholly good and innocent object of others' derision which we typically see her as, Bettelheim shows how Cinderella is a pubescent young girl caught in the grip of a psychic condition which distorts her perception of her two sisters (sibling rivalry) and of her mother (who becomes like a stepmother and she herself like an unwanted orphan pining for the love of her "dead" mother). Oddly enough, he continues to maintain his position that it was her heroic deeds which saved her. In fact, she runs away from what she most wants (the prince at the ball), clings to a memory of past dependencies (weeping at the grave of her mother), and only yields to change when it is forced on her by magical forces (the birds who announce her presence to the prince). The evidence of the fairy tale itself is that it was dark forces which constellated the problem at home between her and the others in the family, dark forces which provided her with a temporary escape into fantasy, and dark forces which saved her. If anything, Cinderella was uncooperative and dangerously withdrawn, not traits we usually associate with heroism.

I find the most questionable part of Bettelheim's interpretation, however, in his reading of sexual significance into the slipping of Cinderella's foot into the golden slipper and the placing of the ring on her finger. There are sexual overtones to many images in the tales, to be sure. (Indeed, I could go further and point to the sexual symbolism in Cinderella's request for a hazel branch from her father, which she then plants on her mother's grave and ceremoniously waters with her tears until it blossoms into a magical tree fulfilling her every fantasy. The image of her desire that her father "be a man" in the home to save her from her unmerited ill fate, to give her everything she most desires with his magical hazel wand, is one of the most striking images in the Grimms' collection.) My criticism is rather that here, as elsewhere throughout his book, Bettelheim seems to confine sexual signification to *genital* signification, overlooking the more important functions of *phallic* signification. While there are instances in which an image can have both functions, the two should be kept distinct, since they point to distinct levels of meaning. As a genital symbol, the sexual image is a metonymic re-presentation disguised for purposes of good taste or even humor. The phallic symbol, however, is the metaphoric use of a sexual image to represent some deeper psychic reality.

Put in other words, the phallus represents desire—the impulse within which we can neither understand nor master in its entirety, but which is responsible for all human creativity. Desire is necessary (or "instinctual") and never satisfiable. It is premoral, chaotic, and far from always compatible with rational intentions; and for all these reasons, its repression is essential for effective social intercourse. To avoid such intellectual abstraction, the language of sexual metaphor is employed in the fairy tales, as in other mythical idioms. In this way, something is being said which is more than simply a statement about an emotional response to sexual factuality.

For his part, Bettelheim focuses rather on children's interest in genital symbols because of their preconscious sexual curiosity, and defends the use of symbolic representation over anatomical precision because it accords with the child's natural initial disgust with explicit talk of sexual realities and gradual discovery of their beauty. Nowhere is this more clear than in the tale of "The Frog King" of which Bettelheim remarks: "Preconsciously the child connects the tacky, clammy sensations which frogs (or toads) evoke in him with similar feelings he attaches to the sex organs. The frog's ability to blow itself out when excited arouses, again unconsciously, associations to the penis' erectability." The point is significant, but it may be more important to retrieve the function of the symbol as phallus—as representative of the inevitability and promise of a force which we neither like nor can control. The dark forces are not always pleasant and benevolent, but can be frightening and malicious in the extreme. We can only hope to understand them. (Here we might recall the image of the spirit Mercurius caught in the bottle, who is likened to "a frog jumping up and down.") In short, the genital symbol may be seen as an overtone nuancing a deeper symbolic function. Such possibilities escape Bettelheim's notice, once again, because of his method's limitations; but they are not therefore incompatible with his findings.

The recovery of silence necessary for the life of the fairy tale may seem to many . . . a thing of the past. To have plunged deeply into Bruno Bettelheim's *The Uses of Enchantment* can only rekindle the hope that this is not so. There one finds oneself, as it were, on the inside of a magic lantern of images at once so familiar and so unexpectedly unfamiliar. It is hard to resurface without at least a spark of that *amor fatae* which made childhood so enchanting. The fairy tale has not outlived its purpose so long as we need reassurance that there is more to life than our usual heavy words can tell. It is a well-known bit of psychoana-

lytic folk wisdom that an analysis terminates only when the patient realizes it could go on forever. We could just as well say of the fairy tales: you have invested enough time and imagination in wrestling with their meaning only when you finally come to tell the stories yourself, just as they are, without embarrassment, and to allow them to sleep quietly in your heart. (pp. 94-112)

> *James W. Heisig, "Bruno Bettelheim and the Fairy Tales," in* Children's Literature: Annual of The Modern Language Association Group on Children's Literature and The Children's Literature Association, *Vol. 6, 1977, pp. 93-114.*

William J. McGrath on the relationship between Bettelheim's writings and his theories:

Mr. Bettelheim builds a good case for personal engagement in all aspects of education and psychotherapy, and *Freud's Vienna and Other Essays* serves as an illuminating example of this philosophy. Rather than writing an autobiography, he has incorporated his experiences into his essays. Thus, he allows his life and work to speak directly to the reader on a personal level.

> *William J. McGrath, in his "City of Couches," in* The New York Times Book Review, *21 January 1990.*

Paul Robinson (review date 29 April 1979)

[*Robinson is an American critic, educator, and historian who has written extensively on social and intellectual history. In the review below, he provides a mixed assessment of* Surviving, and Other Essays.]

Born in Vienna in 1903, Bruno Bettelheim came to this country in 1939 and has enjoyed an illustrious career as a professor of psychology and psychiatry at the University of Chicago, founder of a psychiatric institute for children and the author of 11 books. [*Surviving, and Other Essays*], his 12th, is a collection of two dozen of his essays, written over nearly 40 years and treating matters as diverse as urban design, schizophrenia and the sexual revolution.

Several of the more recent essays offer a telling indictment of modern American culture, particularly its educational ideals and child-rearing practices. Bettelheim's position might be described as radical conservatism. In Freudian terms, he is an unembarrassed apologist for the superego. He makes the unstylish but (to me) persuasive point that education can never be painless. Like Freud in *Civilization and Its Discontents,* he argues that becoming a cultured human being means learning how to delay gratification, to restrain one's urges and to live one's life, at least in part, at the behest of imperatives that transcend the individual. And he is not afraid to state bluntly that fear plays a crucial role in this process: the child takes possession of its cultural heritage only through the vehicle of anxiety. On more than one occasion I was reminded of Christopher Lasch's recent book, *The Culture of Narcissism.*

Bettelheim's work has had two principal focuses: the psychology of children, an interest that culminated in 1976 in his widely acclaimed study of fairy tales, **The Uses of Enchantment;** and the psychology of what he calls "extreme situations," notably the concentration camps of Nazi Germany. The latter were the subject of his first professional paper in English, **"Individual and Mass Behavior in Extreme Situations"** (included in this collection and still a powerful essay). And he has returned to the subject more than 20 times since.

All of his work on the concentration camps emerges from his experience of being imprisoned in Dachau and Buchenwald for one year in 1938-39. He is the originator of a body of writing, now called simply "the literature of survival," to which many distinguished intellectuals have contributed. The common theme of this literature is the burden of guilt borne by survivors—their lifelong effort to understand why they were spared. They have an almost obsessive need to find purpose in life: Since they were granted a reprieve, their existence, they feel, must justify itself.

Among Bettelheim's many virtues are intellectual humility, analytic skill and unfailing clarity of expression. He is altogether compelling when he recounts his experiences as a camp inmate and survivor. He's not merely persuasive, but moving when he tells that he was able to retain his identity within the camps because, in his earlier life, he had cultivated the powers of observation and analysis: Once imprisoned, he began to watch and reflect upon his new circumstances, making them the object of critical examination. In his survival, one witnesses the triumph of civilization, of mind, of inner culture against almost impossible odds, and the prospect is exhilarating.

Over the years Bettelheim's thinking about the camps has undergone an interesting transformation. His early work, as noted, focuses on survivors. He maintained this perspective well into the 1960's, as can be seen from two of the best pieces in this collection, on Anne Frank and Hannah Arendt. But by the time of his 1976 essay for *The New Yorker,* **"Surviving"**—essentially an analysis of Lina Wertmüller's film *Seven Beauties* combined with a devastating critique of Terrence Des Pres's literary study *The Survivor*—he has done an about-face. The theme of survival now appears to him to have become a monster; and with (one suspects) a certain amount of bad conscience, he stresses repeatedly that surviving should not be allowed to seem the ultimate virtue. Bettelheim makes what is perhaps his finest point when he notes that the prisoners who did in fact survive were those who lived not for life's sake but for some ideal—cultural or religious—that transcended them. The argument is eminently sane, but it nonetheless sounds odd from the lips of the man who in 1960 criticized the Anne Frank family for not provisioning itself with knives and guns, as well as a back door.

Bettelheim is relatively unsuccessful when he attempts to translate his insights about surviving into a general critique of modern life. Here he falls into the parochialism of modernity, which holds that our age has been uniquely terrible and that its terribleness found perfect expression in the concentration camps of the Third Reich.

The proposition is historically naïve, and in overstating the case Bettelheim keeps us from a proper estimation of how our age differs from earlier ones and how the atrocities of the Third Reich differ from others. It is particularly misleading to suggest that the evils of the concentration camps were unprecedented: that is, it serves little intellectual or moral purpose, in my opinion, to insist that the victims of the camps occupy a status ontologically different from, say, the victims of Alexander the Great, Attila the Hun, The Albigensian Crusade, the Thirty Years' War, European imperialism or black slavery. The final example is especially pertinent because the historian Stanley Elkins, in his book *Slavery* (1959), developed an analysis of the American slave system based explicitly on Bettelheim's analysis of the concentration camps.

Three reasons might be advanced for placing the destruction of European Jewry in a distinct category. First, unlike previous horrors, it was "systematic," meaning that it was pursued with all the efficiency accessible to a modern technological society. Second, it had no apparent economic motive, indeed was economically counterproductive, and therefore, unlike an abuse such as slavery, seems "senseless," an adjective that Bettelheim himself often uses to characterize the holocaust. And finally, it meant not merely pain, humiliation and servitude, but death.

These are, obviously, important arguments, particularly taken together, but they do not categorically separate the holocaust from other historical acts of inhumanity. The first of the considerations carries the least moral weight, since it implies that an extermination effected through traditional rather than modern means would somehow be less horrible. I don't mean to dismiss this idea entirely, even though it has little logical force, because it does contain an undeniable emotional truth, the same truth that makes the destruction of Hiroshima and Nagasaki by atomic bombs seem somehow more awful than the destruction of Dresden by conventional weapons. Why this should be the case I'm not certain, but of its psychological reality I have no doubt.

The "senselessness" of the holocaust (as opposed to the "sense" of slavery) is, to a considerable extent, a matter of moral and social assumptions. We are inclined to believe that evil is less base when it has an apparent economic logic—in the instance of slavery, that of maintaining a particular form of agricultural production. But a confirmed racist would argue that the elimination of the Jews also had a purpose, though not an economic purpose: It represented an attempt to improve the "biological quality" of the German people. Bettelheim notes that the Nazis originally hoped to realize this objective through sterilization. Only after Stalingrad, when the war was lost and little time remained, did they turn to the radical measure of the death camps. I am by no means advocating moral relativism. On the contrary, we are fully justified in saying to the Nazis that their purposes were evil, that their "scientific" evidence was flimsy and that they must pay for their trespasses with their lives. What we cannot fairly say to them, however, is that they had no reason for what they did.

And lastly, death. Death has lain in store for many victims of persecution throughout history, though never before on the scale managed by Hitler and Stalin. But here, I think, one must ask: Is death the ultimate evil? Bettelheim pointedly argues that it is not, that worse things can happen to an individual or a people than extermination. Life, he insists, is a relative, not an absolute, value, and although he clearly rates it among the greatest goods, he notes that saving one's life while losing one's dignity is a hollow victory. With this in mind, we need to contemplate, as best we can, the relative evil of murdering Jews and—to remain with my example—of enslaving blacks. It is not a pleasant intellectual endeavor. But one can nevertheless make a plausible case that slavery was ultimately a greater evil because slavery, though it avoided death (save in extreme cases), meant an entire lifetime of unacknowledged and unrealized humanity. I would not myself subscribe to this opinion. It is, however, intellectually defensible.

The point I wish to stress is not that we should cease to distinguish between the horrors of the holocaust and those of slavery, but merely that we should resist the temptation to make the distinction categorical. By making it categorical we do not deepen our sense of shame about what we, as a species, have done to one another. Just the opposite: We impoverish that sense because we dismiss as relatively trivial all the sins that mankind has to answer for up to 1933. If one follows this line of reasoning to its logical conclusion, one would have to set aside as out of date the great historical portrayals of human wickedness left to us by, among others, Dante, Shakespeare and Milton, for the simple reason that there was no holocaust in the moral universe of any of these artists.

Bettelheim draws an inaccurate portrait of the state of the European soul before the 20th century. Until "the lamps went out" in 1914, Europe, he writes, was a civilization of uninflected optimism: first the optimism of Christianity (a remarkably crude psychological estimation), then the secular optimism of the culture of progress. Inevitably the historian must wonder what happened to Montaigne, Gibbon, Malthus, Schopenhauer, Kierkegaard and Dostoyevsky—to mention just some of our gloomier ancestors. Even members of the "party of humanity," such as John Stuart Mill, Alexis de Tocqueville and Jacob Burckhardt, were prey to frequent doubts. I don't question that the 20th century differs from earlier centuries, but it has had no monopoly on despair, and we will never understand its true character if we act as if it marked an unqualified departure from all that went before. The serious study of change requires attention to continuity as well.

These lapses are especially ironic in Bettelheim, because, like Hannah Arendt, he has been one of the most rigorous of modern Jewish intellectuals, maintaining a tradition that goes back to Freud, Marx and beyond. He strays from that tradition, and falls into habits of mind that he has criticized in others, only when he moves from psychological to social comment. His great strength is the analysis of individual behavior, and thus the book that one would most like to see him write—a book that lurks in the foot-

notes and prefatory remarks of the present collection—is his autobiography. Reticence, he says, has prevented him from doing so. If he can overcome that reticence, he should give us a masterpiece. (pp. 7, 63)

Paul Robinson, in a review of "Surviving and Other Essays," in The New York Times Book Review, *April 29, 1979, pp. 7, 63.*

Clara Claiborne Park   (review date 12 May 1979)

[*Park is an American educator who frequently writes and lectures about autism and mental illness. In the following review, she praises* Surviving, and Other Essays.]

When I accepted [*Surviving, and Other Essays*] for review, I had already worked out what I was going to say about it. I would begin with a frank admission of my combined qualifications and disqualifications, as a mother of an autistic child, for reviewing a book by a man who has done so much to persuade so many that the condition of children like my daughter is the result of their families' neglect, rejection, hostility and abuse. I would examine this thesis briefly and with impressive restraint, after which I would consider whatever else I might happen to find in the book with an objectivity and magnanimity which could not fail to elicit a reader's admiration. I would end with a generous appreciation of this old man in whom, as in the old Oedipus at Colonus, the capacity to curse and to love were so inextricably linked, recalling the words of Dmitri Karamazov: "Yes, man is broad, too broad indeed. I'd have him narrower."

But books often turn out to be different from the expected, especially when they are worth reading. In the event, Bettelheim is narrower than I thought him, not broader; his thought is to a rare degree all of a piece. Though he spent most of his mature life working with children, and *The Empty Fortress,* on autism, is his longest book, autism occupies only a few pages here, much muted, while the essays on the education of the young are peripheral to the book's central concerns. More than half the book—much more than half in interest and impact—is devoted to essays by means of which, over nearly forty years, he has thought his way through the experiences he underwent in 1938 and 1939 in Dachau and Buchenwald. Here is the center of his book, as of his life; if the bewildering behavior he saw later in the gravely damaged children called autistic seemed to him best explainable in terms of the withdrawal with which some prisoners responded to the systematic torture and brutalization of the camps, one can see why he needed it to be so.

> In times of trouble . . . the problem of life's purpose, or meaning, forces itself on our awareness. The greater the hardship we experience, the more pressing the question becomes for us. . . . It seems that if we could just grasp life's deeper significance, then we would also comprehend the true meaning of our agony—and incidentally that of others—and this would answer the burning question of why we have to bear it, why it was inflicted on us. If in the light of our understanding of life's design our suffering is needed to achieve its purpose, or is at least an essential

part of it, then as an integral element of life's great design our affliction becomes meaningful, and thus more bearable.

Surviving presents the record of a life constrained to a single focus; the necessity fully to experience that year in Dachau, to wring meaning out of it, and out of the even more terrible years experienced by others, the many dead and the few living, in the death camps liberated at last in 1945 by the Allied armies. There are interesting essays on other subjects—on the conflicts attendant on **"Growing Up Female"** in America in 1962 and to a lesser extent today; a reconsideration of Summerhill ("there is no socialization or learning without fear"); a very clever book review in the form of notes kept by the Dr. Spielvogel who undertook to psychoanalyze Portnoy. But the enduring force of the book lies in the essays on "the holocaust" (a term whose connotations Bettelheim emphatically rejects). These are impressive essays—much more impressive together than any one of them can be separately. It is compelling to follow their progression from the self-enforced, deliberately distanced objectivity of **"Individual and Mass Behavior in Extreme Situations"** (rejected everywhere until Gordon Allport published it in *The Journal of Abnormal and Social Psychology* in 1943), through considerations of Anne Frank, the Eichmann trial and various books by and about survivors, to the culminating essay, published in *The New Yorker* in 1976, which rightly gives the book its title. For this is much more than a collection of essays. Bettelheim has provided backward looks and introductory explanations that have done much to unify it formally, but this has been possible because of its single overwhelming subject: what it is, not merely to survive but to survive worthily. In the religious terms which Bettelheim cannot claim for himself, but which he never disparages, what is considered here is how to save one's soul alive.

In 1940, when Bettelheim began to write that first essay, the "final solution" was still in the future: it was not yet imaginable that a civilized country could apply the resources of advanced technology to systematically exterminate 11 million people, more than half of them Jews. "At that time, nothing was known in the United States about the camps, and my story was met with utter disbelief." So the language, today, shocks by its coolness:

> In this paper, an effort will be made to deal adequately with at least one aspect of the Gestapo's aforementioned aims: *the concentration camp as a means of producing changes in the prisoners which would make them more useful subjects* of the Nazi state. These changes were produced by exposing the prisoners to extreme situations particularly created for this purpose. These circumstances forced the prisoners to adapt themselves entirely and with the greatest speed. This adaptation produced interesting types of private, individual, and mass behavior.

The controlled academicism of **"Individual and Mass Behavior in Extreme Situations"** cannot have been easy for a survivor, but in 1943 it was still possible. It was more than possible, it was necessary, "to forestall the accusation that I distorted facts out of personal hatred," to make Americans listen to what even the American academic community shut its ears to. But objectivity was more than a strategic necessity; it was an inner imperative. "Trying to be objective became my intellectual defense against being overwhelmed." The experience had to be confronted, not because it could not be denied or left behind—others made that choice—but because only by confronting it, not once but over and over again, could meaning be found.

The full heroism of that early objectivity can be measured only after reading the later essays, most poignantly in certain details. A year after his release Bettelheim was analyzing with necessitated coolness how prisoners were humiliated by being forced "to develop types of behavior which are characteristic of infancy," in a paragraph on how the camp guards exploited their power over the places and times of the prisoners' defecation. It is only in 1976, in the essay written out of the anguish and outrage of his response to the widely praised *Seven Beauties,* Lina Wertmüller's travesty on survival, that he is ready to let us know, in its full immediacy, what that paragraph really meant. There are two characters in the film who retain their moral integrity. One is shot by the film's protagonist, Pasqualino, who is presented as the archetypal survivor, prevailing by the sheer amoral force of his vitality whatever the cost of his survival to others. The other commits suicide by jumping into the camp latrine into which other prisoners are defecating, shouting "Brothers, I go to jump into the shit!" Bettelheim is a real, not fictional, survivor, and it is with controlled fury that he notes how "asserting one's human dignity by . . . suffocating oneself in feces" is given, in the film, "a comic quality that is nearly as strong as its morbidity." It is here that Bettelheim tells us what he did not say in the cool paragraph on defecation that he wrote so long before: that he himself "witnessed in the camps prisoners dying in this way." They were not, however, committing suicide, which they could readily do in less sensational ways; they were pushed in by sadistic guards. For those who saw this happen, "the comic quality does not exist."

If Bettelheim is sometimes harsh and stubborn, we recognize that these too may be qualities of the survivor. He is, at any rate, as honest as he knows how to be.

—Clara Claiborne Park

The overwhelming necessity, for those who could save their souls alive, is to bear true witness to what they have known; it is what saves meaning out of the meaninglessness of despair. Objectivity was necessary, forty years ago, for bearing witness; controlled subjectivity is necessary today, when there is need to bear witness against those who would distort the concentration camp experience into a perverse hymn to a survivorship robbed of its meaning, won and enjoyed in the pure animality of the body and the repudiation of civilization and its irrelevant constraints.

Attractive Pasqualino is a guilt-free murderer, a two-time rapist, a betrayer; he is not to be accepted as the prototypical "little man" whose survival cheers us all. He is a monster, and it is monstrous to present him otherwise. Only in a world without morality can there be guilt-free survival of such experiences. Civilization nourishes guilt, and rightly. It is the capacity to feel guilt which more than any fear of disapproval is "a most powerful motivation for moral behavior."

So Bettelheim is drawn to confront the most painful feelings of all. Objectively, of course, no guilt attaches to survival. "The survivor as a thinking being knows very well that he is not guilty, as I, for one, know about myself." Yet the survivor's humanity, his existence "as a feeling being, requires that he feel guilty, and he does." He feels guilty for his luck in surviving. He feels guilty for having watched the destruction of others without intervening, for having heeded the counsels of that "better judgment" which preserved him at others' expense. Most of all he feels guilty "for having often felt glad that it was not oneself who perished, since one knew that one had no right to expect that one would be the person spared." But one was—and one cannot avoid the burden.

The psychoanalytic terms which spontaneously come to mind are in the end far less relevant than the religious. The words "working through," however appropriate they may superficially seem, can only trivialize the process by which Bettelheim has searched out meaning for himself and for us. For here near the end of his life he speaks, like so many other paradoxical Jewish atheists, with the voice of the Prophets. He writes not to explain and analyze the abomination that was, but to use it to recall us to the knowledge of what ought to be. There is no conflict, he tells us, between what he saw in the camps and the most deeply believed-in imperatives of nature and culture. The camps did not teach a morality of dog-eat-dog savagery, or that survival could be bought by the surrender of all about us that is not bestial. "Pasqualino's nihilistic vision of a battle of all against all for the survival of the strongest is a Fascist vision." Wertmüller's depraved female commandant tells Pasqualino, "You found the strength for an erection—that's why you'll survive and win in the end." But the actual survivor's experience is quite different: "the prisoners, to survive, had to help one another"; they "made common cause against the S.S. most of the time." "The greatest crime in the camps was stealing another prisoner's piece of bread; for this the other prisoners exacted the most severe punishment, as they had to if they wanted to live. But it hardly ever happened."

The most impressive pages of *Surviving* are those which present Bettelheim's masterly confrontation of Wertmüller's Johnny-come-lately romantic nihilism with the simple, terrible facts of 11 million people's daily existence in the years from 1936 to 1945. The most powerful prophecy is that which is grounded on truth. Fiction after fiction—falsehood after falsehood—fails the confrontation. Remembering Ilse Koch, Wertmüller makes the camp commandant a woman, so Pasqualino can escape by his willingness to exploit his sex. But Ilse Koch's power was through her husband; there could never have been a fe-

male commandant in Nazi Germany. No S.S. man would ever have handed Pasqualino a gun, to shoot his best friend or for any other reason; he would have known that the prisoner would shoot not his friend but the S.S. Treachery did not win survival in the camps; the guards as well as the prisoners despised it. The amoral *élan vital* attributed to Pasqualino would in fact have guaranteed not his survival but his early death, for the camp, in all its degradation, remained a human society.

It is finally to the humanity of society that Bettelheim has survived to bear witness. His experience has molded him, and as with all of us, that molding has been in some respects a deformation. He can be unjust here—in the essay **"Obsolete Youth"** there is no recognition of the generosity and idealism of the student activists of the 1960s, or of their part in bringing to an end another abomination, one the angry prophet has no words for, the Vietnam War. Events have rendered most of the essay obsolete, and there was little reason to reprint it. His theory of autism is also obsolete and also unjust, but it here assumes its true proportions as a minor corollary of his search for the meaning of his experience, still relevant only to those it injured. "Archaic," Bettelheim calls himself; perhaps it is the old Oedipus after all. If he is sometimes harsh and stubborn, we recognize that these too may be qualities of the survivor. He is, at any rate, as honest as he knows how to be. (pp. 544-46)

Clara Claiborne Park, "Survive and Remember," in The Nation, *New York, Vol. 228, No. 12, May 12, 1979, pp. 544-46.*

Jack Zipes (essay date 1979)

[*An American writer and educator, Zipes is the author of* The Trials and Tribulations of Little Red Riding Hood *(1983) and* Fairy Tales and the Art of Subversion: The Classical Genre for Children and the Process of Civilization *(1983). In the following excerpt, which is a significantly revised version of a review article that first appeared in 1977 in* Telos, *Zipes discusses the validity of Bettelheim's theories concerning fairy tales and their therapeutic value.*]

Bruno Bettelheim was impelled to write his book *The Uses of Enchantment* out of dissatisfaction 'with much of the literature intended to develop the child's mind and personality, because it fails to stimulate and nurture those resources he needs most in order to cope with his difficult inner problems'. Therefore, he explored the great potential of folk tales as literary models for children since 'more can be learned from them about the inner problems of human beings, and of the right solutions to their predicaments in any society, than from any other type of story within a child's comprehension'. This is, indeed, a grand statement on behalf of the folk tale's powers. However, despite his good intentions and moral concern in the welfare of children, Bettelheim's book disseminates false notions about the original intent of Freudian psychoanalytic theory and about the literary quality of folk tales and leaves the reader in a state of mystification. Not only is the manner in which Bettelheim would *impose* meaning onto child development through the therapeutic use of the folk tale authoritarian and unscientific, but his stance is symptomatic of numerous humanitarian educators who perpetuate the diseases they desire to cure.

This is not to dismiss Bettelheim's book in its totality. Since folk and fairy tales have played and continue to play a significant role in the socialization process, a thorough study of Bettelheim's position is crucial for grasping whether the tales can be used more effectively in helping children (and adults) come into their own. A critical examination of his theory may ultimately lead to a fresh look at contemporary psychoanalytic views on internalization and new insights about the production and usage of folk and fairy tales.

Bettelheim's major thesis is a simple one: 'the form and structure of fairy tales suggest images to the child by which he can structure his daydreams and with them give better direction to his life'. In other words, the folk tale liberates the child's subconscious so that he or she can work through conflicts and experiences which would otherwise be repressed and perhaps cause psychological disturbances. According to Bettelheim, folk tales present existential dilemmas in a clear-cut manner so that the child can easily grasp the underlying meanings of the conflicts. Most folk tales are an imaginative depiction of healthy human development and help children understand the motives behind their rebellion against parents and the fear of growing up. The conclusions of most folk tales portray the achievement of psychological independence, moral maturity and sexual confidence. Obviously, as Bettelheim admits, there are other approaches to folk tales. But, he maintains that it is primarily the psychological approach which uncovers the hidden meanings of the tales and their overwhelming importance for child development.

Given the immense volume of folk tales, Bettelheim limits his discussion to the better known tales. The book is divided into two parts. The first, fancifully entitled 'A Pocketful of Magic', focuses on a theoretical explication of his concepts, method and purpose. The second part, 'In Fairy Land', consists of 14 case studies of such different tales as 'Snow White', 'Sleeping Beauty', 'Hansel and Gretel', 'Jack and the Beanstalk', 'Little Red Riding Hood', 'Cinderella', etc. In the first part, Bettelheim asserts that adults should not explain the tales to children since that would destroy their 'magic'. However, adults should tell the tales because that shows approval of children's imaginative play. Children are allegedly drawn to folk tales because they symbolically depict the psychological problems which the children must work through *by themselves*. In doing this, a child supposedly attains a sense of his or her self. If we were to follow the logic of Bettelheim's argument, it is almost as though the folk tale could be considered a psychoanalyst in the manner in which it operates with a child. The tale by itself opens up unexplored realms of experience to children who learn to order their inner worlds by following the fantastic signposts of the tale and by identifying with the hero who becomes ruler of a kingdom, i.e. ruler of the self.

Characteristic of Bettelheim's orthodox Freudian approach is the arbitrary way in which he makes excessive claims for the therapeutic power of the folk tale and then diagnoses the power to fit his strait-jacket theory about neurosis and the family. For instance, he unabashedly asserts that 'unlike any other form of literature, they [folk tales] direct the child to discover his identity and calling'. Then he narrows the psychological meaning in a reductionist manner: 'the content of the chosen tale has nothing to do with the patient's external life but much to do with his inner problems, which seem incomprehensible and hence insolvable'. Such flat assertions, common throughout the book, rest on shaky grounds. Bettelheim provides no documentation to prove that the folk tale is better than any other imaginative or nonfiction literature for helping children develop their character. Moreover, Bettelheim has a one-dimensional way of examining the relation of literature to the psyche. To suggest that the external life is isolated from the inner life and that there is a literature which primarily addresses itself to the inner problems of a reader completely eliminates the dialectical relationship between essence and appearance. Existence is divorced from the imagination, and a static realm is erected which resembles the laboratory of an orthodox Freudian mind that is bent on conducting experiments with what *ought* to be happening in the child's inner realm.

The categorical imperative used by Bettelheim constantly prevents him from achieving his purpose of uncovering the significance of folk tales for child development. Folk tales are said to personify and illustrate inner conflicts, and Bettelheim wants to demonstrate to his adult readers how a child views folk tales and reality so that they can be more enlightened in their dealings with children. This stance is in actual contradiction to his previous argument that children must be allowed freedom to interpret the tales and that adults must not impose interpretation. It is the authority, Bettelheim, who *claims to know* how children subconsciously view the tales and who imposes this psychoanalytic mode of interpreting tales on adults. In turn they ought to use his approach if they care for children. This moral argumentation has nothing to do with a more scientific explanation of the tales and how they can be used to aid children in their development. Everything remains in Bettelheim's own realm of reified Freudian formulas which restrain the possibilities for a vital interaction between the tale and the child and between the adult and the child.

This can immediately be seen when he presents his theoretical explanation of how folk tales clarify the meaning of conflicts for children and how they provide for resolution. Like many cultural censors of morality, Bettelheim believes that only literature which is harmonious and orderly should be fed to the delicate souls of children who should be sheltered from harsh reality. Thus, the folk tale is perfect. In contrast to myths, fables and legends, folk tales are allegedly optimistic because they allow for hope and the solution of problems. In addition, they involve a conflict between the reality and pleasure principles and show how a certain amount of pleasure can be retained while the demands of reality are respected (as in the example of the oldest pig in 'The Three Little Pigs'). Indiscriminately using the discoveries of Piaget, who has demonstrated (among other things) that the child's thinking up till the ages of nine or ten is animistic, Bettelheim explains how the magic and fantastic images in the folk tale enable the child subjectively to come to terms with reality. The adventures in the folk tale allow for vicarious satisfaction of unfulfilled desires and subconscious drives and permit the child to sublimate those desires and drives at a time when conscious recognition would shatter or shake the child's character structure which is not yet secure. The folk tale provides freedom for the child's imagination in that it deals at first with a problematic real situation which is then imaginatively transformed. The narrative breaks down spatial and temporal limits and leads the child into the self, but it also leads him or her back into reality. Bettelheim argues against true-to-life stories for child development because they impinge upon the imagination of the child and act repressively as would the rational interference of an adult. In contrast, the folk tale transforms reality in such a way that the child can cope with it. Like the symbols of the id, ego and superego, which Freud created as operative constructs, the folk-tale symbols represent separate entities of the child's inner sanctum, and their representation in a folk tale (for a child) shows how order can be made out of chaos. In particular, the folk tale demonstrates how each element (ego, id, superego) must be given its due and integrated if character structure is to develop without disturbance.

Many folk tales like 'Brother and Sister' show how the animalistic (male/id) must be integrated with the spiritual component (female/ego, superego) to permit human qualities to blossom: 'Integration of the disparate aspects of our personality can be gained only after the asocial, destructive, and unjust have been done away with; and this cannot be achieved until we have reached full maturity, as symbolized by sister's giving birth to a child and developing mothering attitudes'. At the bottom of all the chaos and conflict which children experience are parents, leading Bettelheim to make the following claim: 'Maybe if more of our adolescents had been brought up on fairy tales, they would (unconsciously) remain aware of the fact that their conflict is not with the adult world, or society, but really only with their parents'. In other words, the ambivalent attachments to one's parents are the roots of all evil and must be worked out by the child (particularly the Oedipal conflicts) if a well-integrated personality is to be achieved. Symbolically folk tales are the most clear and distinct representations of children's anxieties and unconscious drives, and therefore they can stimulate children to explore their imaginations for resolutions to the conflicts with their parents. They are like guidebooks for achieving true identity and a true state of independence. Thus now we know what becoming a ruler over a kingdom means, and Bettelheim can conclude his first part by advising adults again to take an active part in the telling of the tale but not to interpret it for the child. The participation will (like the psychiatrist) bring the child and parent closer together by magically restoring order to the child's mind.

This theory is fallacious on two levels, the psychoanalytic and the literary. Not only does Bettelheim misinterpret some of Freud's key notions about psychoanalysis, but he also twists the meanings of the literature to suit his peculiar theory of child development. The intended 'humanitarian' goals of his study are undermined by his rigid Freudian abstractions which prop up irrational and arbitrary forms of social behaviour whose norms and values children are supposed to adapt. The patterns of the folk tales allegedly foster ideal normative behaviour which children are to internalize; yet, some of these literary patterns like the forms of social behaviour are repressive constructs which violate the imagination of both children and adults alike. Let me clarify both charges against Bettelheim, his betrayal of the radical essence of Freudianism and his corruption of the literary meaning of the folk tale.

The critical task of Freud's psychoanalytic theory was to demonstrate the manifold ways in which society made it impossible for the individual to achieve autonomy. His purpose was to expose the inner forces which hinder full development of the individual and cause psychic disturbances because of external pressures and conditions. His work in theory was to destroy illusions which society creates about the possibility of achieving autonomy and a happy life so that the individual could elaborate meaning out of the antagonistic relationship between self and society. As Russell Jacoby has demonstrated in his significant study *Social Amnesia: A Critique of Contemporary Psychology from Adler to Laing,* the basic radical thrust of Freudian theory has been forgotten and obfuscated. In particular, the orthodox Freudians have hampered the growth of Freudian theory by codifying the principles as absolute laws. Here it is important to make a distinction among orthodox Freudians as Jacoby does:

> Once the false opposition between orthodoxy and revisionism as that between obsolete dogma and contemporary insight is avoided, the notion of orthodoxy must be reformulated. To the point that the theories of Marx and Freud were critiques of bourgeois civilization, orthodoxy entailed loyalty to these critiques; more exactly, *dialectical* loyalty. Not repetition is called for but articulation and development of concepts; and within Marxism—and to a degree within psychoanalysis—precisely against an Official Orthodoxy only too happy to freeze concepts into formulas. . . . Freud and his students are clear enough as to what in psychoanalysis is to be preserved—not by thoughtless repetition but by reworking: the concepts of repression, sexuality, unconscious, Oedipal complex, infantile sexuality.

Unfortunately, Jacoby does not elaborate his critique of official orthodoxy. He spends most of his time defending the dialectical orthodox Freudians. Yet, as a result of his work, it becomes eminently clear that Bettelheim *does not* have a dialectical relationship to Freudianism but has contributed to the banalization of Freudian theory by blandly applying its tenets without rethinking and reworking them in the light of social and scientific changes. Moreover, he has also picked up one of the worst traits of the neo- and post-Freudians—their moralizing. Aside from Bettelheim's mechanical repetition of Freud's thought, his postulates read like 'Sunday sermons'. 'The positive is promoted to drive out the negative. One strives to be cheery because it is a cheerless world. Since reflection on the latter is taboo,' Bettelheim 'seeks to make palatable the unswallowable: the lie that the isolated and abandoned individual can "become", "love", "be". Hence, the "how to" nature' of his work. Bettelheim patches up his official orthodoxy with moral homilies about therapeutic self-help. He constantly asserts that the folk tale contains the answers to the good, happy life, implying that there is a social realm where individual autonomy can be reached. Yet, in *Civilization and Its Discontents,* Freud made clear just how repressive society was and how limited and varied the possibilities were to attain freedom and happiness.

> The liberty of the individual is not a benefit of culture. It was the greatest before any culture, though indeed it had little value at that time, because the individual was hardly in a position to defend it. Liberty has undergone restrictions through the evolution of civilization, and justice demands that these restrictions shall apply to all. . . . It is impossible to ignore the extent to which civilization is built on renunciation of instinctual gratifications, the degree to which the existence of civilization presupposes the non-gratification (suppression, repression or something else?) of powerful instinctual urgencies. This 'cultural privation' dominates the whole field of social relations between human beings; we know already that it is the cause of the antagonism against which all civilization has to fight.

What is significant in Freud's work is that he located the cause for psychosis and all mental sicknesses in the historical and materialistic development of social conditions. He may have misconstrued some theories which were based on inconclusive and partial data, but the basis of his research for studying the relationship of the human psyche to civilization was dialectical and provided the fundamentals for a social science that could be altered as the social conditions changed. Bettelheim not only fails to develop Freud's far-reaching findings for application to the massive changes in society and the human psyche, but he actually eliminates the dialectic from Freud's method. He holds the family primarily responsible for the conflicts a child experiences, thus not locating it as *one of the mediating agencies* through which civilization causes repression. Even worse, he employs Freudian terminology like a puritanical parson encouraging parents to have faith in the almighty power of the folk tale which will lead children through the valley of fear into the kingdom of grace. Gone is the dialectical antagonistic relationship between society and the individual. If anything, it is misplaced between child and family which shifts the real cause for repression and thus dilutes the dialectics. Bettelheim would have us believe that the child can voluntaristically work through internalized problems with the aid of a folk tale and become a well-adjusted, autonomous individual. Once familial conflicts are grasped and solved, happiness is just down the road. By assuming such a position, Bettelheim unwittingly becomes an apologist for a 'civilized' society noted for its abuse of children and its proclivity toward dehumanization. These negative tendencies of our contemporary society have been recorded not only by its critics but by its very own established news media which document the violation of human rights and violence of subjectivity every minute of every day.

Essentially Bettelheim's concern in children reflects a con-

servative Freudian notion of internalization and does not take into consideration the dire consequences which rational adjustment to the reality principle has for children. In contrast to Freud, for Bettelheim and other neo-Freudians,

> a theory of internalization is necessary which explains how the ego is formed through social interaction such that human beings come to comply with these laws rather than attempt to change them. Such a theory must recognize that internalization is a defense against unbearable reality, not a natural mode of constituting consciousness, necessitated by the opposition of the instincts. The idea of instincts has a role to play in the sense that the 'libido is the actual reality,' if we understand the libido as essentially object-seeking. Denial of this striving leads not only to illness but to compliance with authority, acceptance of helplessness. The way in which the striving for recognition is denied must be understood in the context of societal interaction rather than conceived as an eternal form of the ego. [Jessica Benhamin, 'The End of Internalization: Adorno's Social Psychology', *Telos* 32 (1977)]

Instead of recognizing the power of society to deny autonomy, Bettelheim encourages an internalization which furthers the split between mind and body. The fantasy of the child is to be given free rein only if it finally succumbs to instrumental reason. No wonder that his book is largely male-orientated and fails to make careful distinctions between the sexes, ages and class backgrounds of children. Nor does he bother to consider that the theories derived from Freud have to be made more historical and scientific to account for sex, age and class differences. It is no longer valid to postulate theories of the imagination, penis envy, and Oedipal conflicts without reworking them and perhaps even dismissing them in the light of changing social conditions and normative behaviour. Perhaps the greatest weakness of Bettelheim's book is his neglect of sociolinguistic studies and his own careless use of terminology which reflects just how faulty his theory of communication is. In one of the more important studies of this problem, *Class, Codes and Control,* Basil Bernstein has pointed out that

> as the child learns his speech or, in the terms used here, learns specific codes which regulate his verbal acts, he learns the requirements of his social structure. The experience of the child is transformed by the learning which is generated by his own apparently voluntary acts of speech. The social structure becomes the substratum of his experience essentially through the consequences of the linguistic process. From this point of view, every time the child speaks or listens the social structure of which he is a part is reinforced in him and his social identity is constrained. The social structure becomes the developing child's psychological reality by the shaping of his acts of speech. Underlying the general pattern of his speech are, it is held, critical sets of choices, preferences for some alternatives rather than others, which develop and are stabilized through time and which eventually come

to play an important role in the regulation of intellectual, social and affective orientations.

Bernstein discusses the ramifications of language for the psycho-social development of children, and he makes careful, empirically based distinctions between elaborated and restricted codes used generally by middle-class and working-class children respectively. Since 'the mode of a language structure reflects a particular form of the structuring of feeling and so the very means of interaction and response to the environment,' Bernstein investigates why working-class children respond differently and often negatively to the socialization process which has been developed to satisfy middle-class needs. In contrast, middle-class children adapt more readily and learn to use all sorts of codes to further their ends. The restricted code used by working-class children is not necessarily qualitatively poorer than the elaborated code of the middle-class child, but it is *different* and does reflect the more limited and authoritarian margins within which a working-class child is socialized. Thus, in a formal learning situation which is generally predicated on the elaborated code of the middle class, the 'I' of the working-class child is threatened. [Bernstein writes:] 'The attempt to substitute a different use of language and to change the order of communication creates critical problems for the working-class child as it is an attempt to change his basic system of perception, fundamentally the very means by which he has been socialized.'

In Bettelheim's discussion of folk tales and their use with children, there is no regard for the differences between children and their particular relationships to language which influences their receptivity to the linguistic and aesthetic codes and patterns of literature. In fact, differences are virtually levelled out as if the education process were a democratizing experience and as if there were no codes, either in public or private language or in the folk tales themselves. This brings us to Bettelheim's misuse of the folk tale as an art form.

Though aware of the historical origins of the folk tale, Bettelheim fails to take into account that the symbols and patterns of the tales reflect specific forms of social behaviour and activity which often can be traced back as far as the Ice and Megalithic Ages. As August Nitschke has documented in his book *Soziale Ordnungen im Spiegel der Märchen,* the contemporary psychological labels attached to the symbols and patterns of the tales are contradicted by the actual historical and archaeological findings. According to the data, the normative behaviour and labour processes of primitive peoples as depicted in the tales which they themselves cultivated cannot be explained by modern psychoanalytical theory. Properly speaking, any psychological approach to the folk tales would first have to investigate the socialization processes of primitive societies in a given historical era in order to provide an appropriate interpretation. Leaving aside the questionable methodology of the orthodox Freudians, who see penis envy and castration complexes everywhere in folk tales, and assuming that there is some validity to using folk tales therapeutically in educating children, one must still question the manner in which Bettelheim imposes meaning on the tales as well as his indiscriminate application of their meaning to

children of all ages, sexes, and class backgrounds. As Nitschke demonstrates, the creative purpose and major themes of the folk tales did not concern harmony, but the depiction of changing social structures and alternative forms of behaviour so that new developments and connections between humans and things could be better grasped by the people. Central to most tales is the concept of power. Where does it reside? Who wields it? Why? How can it be better wielded? Many of the tales bespeak a primitive or feudal ideology of 'might makes right'. Depending on the historical epoch the tales portray either the possibilities for social participation or the reasons for social conflict. The immanent meaning of the tales has little to do with providing suitable direction for a contemporary child's life. From a contemporary perspective, the tales are filled with incidents of inexplicable abuse, maltreatment of women, negative images of minority groups, questionable sacrifices, and the exaltation of power. Here I am only mentioning some of the more negative aspects of the tales which also contain positive features. . . . The point which I should like to make right now is that the psychological components and meanings can best be understood when first related to the contradictory developments of the historical period in which they originated.

To use the tales with children today as a means for therapeutic education demands first a historical understanding and secondly a careful delineation of the progressive and regressive ideological and psychological meanings of the tales. Here we are dealing with the entire question of reception. How does a child receive and perceive a given tale? It is necessary to ask whether a child actually knows what a king is. What does a king mean to a five-year-old, to an eight-year-old, to a girl or boy, to girls and boys of different races and class backgrounds? A prince who uses magical gifts which sometimes involve killing to become a king of a particular realm does not necessarily imply, as Bettelheim would have us believe, that the child (which child?) will psychologically comprehend this as a story about self-mastery. Could it not also serve to reinforce the aggressive instincts of a middle-class child to become more ego-centred, competitive and achievement-oriented? Could not the code be understood by a lower-class child so as to reinforce the arbitrary power of authoritarian figures and to accept a strict hierarchical world? What is obviously necessary in working with the impact of the tales on children is a method which takes into consideration the aesthetics of reception. Such a method would have to investigate the possibilities for comprehension by children in the light of the dialectical relationship of a specific audience to the tale at a given moment in history.

The ultimate weakness of Bettelheim's methodology can be seen in the second part of his book which contains his case studies of popular folk tales. Let us look at his exhaustive treatment of 'Cinderella' as an example of his approach. Bettelheim first discusses the various versions and cycles of the Cinderella story, in particular those of Basile and Perrault, and he diagnoses their major themes as those of sibling rivalry and the Oedipal complex. He then uses the basic plot of the Grimm version as the paradigmatic model for comprehending all the 'Cinderella' stories. Actually no matter what tale is touched by Bettelheim's orthodox Freudian wand, it is always transformed into a symbolic parable of self-realization and healthy sexuality. Here, as usual, Bettelheim is concerned with the hidden meanings which work wonders on children. 'Cinderella' teaches children about sibling rivalry and a young girl's endeavours to prove her worth. It is significant that Cinderella is given 'dirty' work to do since that reflects her own low self-esteem as well as the guilt she feels for desiring her father. Her thwarted Oedipal desires must be overcome if she is to prove her real worth and achieve complete sexuality. The hardships which Cinderella must endure are tests that involve the development of personality.

Using Erik Erikson's model of the human life cycle, Bettelheim talks about the 'phase-specific psychosocial crises' which an individual must go through in order to become the 'ideal human being'. In the case of Cinderella, she goes through five phases of the human life cycle to develop basic trust (the relationship with her original good mother), autonomy (acceptance of her role in the family), initiative (the planting of the twig), industry (her hard labours), and identity (her insistence that the prince see both her dirty and her beautiful side). Bettelheim is particularly penetrating on this last point.

> In the slipper ceremony, which signifies the betrothal of Cinderella and the prince, he selects her because in symbolic fashion she is the uncastrated woman who relieves him of his castration anxiety which would interfere with a happy marital relationship. She selects him because he appreciates her in her 'dirty' sexual aspects, lovingly accepts her vagina in the form of the slipper, and approves of her desire for a penis, symbolized by her tiny foot fitting within the slipper-vagina. . . . But as she slips her foot into the slipper, she asserts that she, too, will be active in their sexual relationship; she will do things, too. And she also gives the assurance that she is not and never was lacking in anything.

It is quite clear that the virginal Cinderella is the most suitable for Prince Charming because her step-sisters in their act of self-mutilation reveal through the blood (menstrual bleeding) that they are sexually too aggressive and cause the prince anxiety. In sum, 'Cinderella' as story 'guides the child from his greatest disappointments—oedipal disillusionment, castration anxiety, low opinion of others—toward developing his autonomy, becoming industrious, and gaining a positive identity of his own'. After reading Bettelheim's concluding remarks, one wonders why such books as Dale Carnegie's *How to Win Friends and Influence People* and *How to Succeed in Business* are necessary when we have folk tales.

In contrast to Bettelheim's moral primer about folk tales, Nitschke has demonstrated that Cinderella originated toward the end of the Ice Age. The norms of behaviour and social activity depicted in 'Cinderella' reveal that the tale revolves around a female who receives help and gifts from her dead mother, who continues living in the form of a tree, and from animals. Nitschke explains in some detail that the society which produced tales similar to 'Cinderella' was one of hunting and grazing in which the woman was accorded the place of honour. Death was not feared,

and women were sacrificed so that they could return to life in the form of a plant or animal to help their children develop. Life was seen in sequences and as eternal. Thus, a human being participated in his or her own time and, through transformation after death, there was a renewal of time. Most important is the function of the female. She was at the centre of this society and maintained it as nurturing element. 'Cinderella' does not reflect society undergoing great changes in production but a maintenance of the hunting and grazing society. However, when compared to tales of the early Ice Age, it does show how human beings have taken over centre stage from animals, and the growing importance attached to the woman. Love and mutual self-respect are accomplished through the intercession of the mother.

Nitschke's explanation of the historical origins and meaning of 'Cinderella' obviously cannot be grasped by children. But it does set the framework for a psychoanalytical approach which must first consider the people and their social behaviour if it wants to establish the psychological essence of a tale. The same thing holds true for the retelling of the tale today, but in a slightly different manner. And here the implications of the tale are remarkably different from what they were in the Ice Age. Instead of having a tale which does homage to women, we have a tale which is an insult to women. Here I want to concentrate on just one aspect of 'Cinderella' to question the relevance Bettelheim bestows upon it. In the American society today where women have been in the vanguard of the equal rights movement, where female sexuality has undergone great changes, where the central agency of socialization of boys and girls has shifted from the family to the mass media, schools and the bureaucratic state, a tale like 'Cinderella' cannot (neither explicitly nor implicitly) guide children to order their inner worlds and to lead fuller, happier sexual lives. Though it is difficult to speculate how an individual child might react to 'Cinderella', certainly the adult reader and interpreter must ask the following questions: Why is the stepmother shown to be wicked and not the father? Why is Cinderella essentially passive? (How Bettelheim twists the meaning to see 'Cinderella' as active is actually another one of his Freudian magic tricks.) Why do girls have to quarrel over a man? How do children react to a Cinderella who is industrious, dutiful, virginal and passive? Are all men handsome? Is marriage the end goal of life? Is it important to marry rich men? This small list of questions suggests that the ideological and psychological pattern and message of 'Cinderella' do nothing more than reinforce sexist values and a Puritan ethos that serves a society which fosters competition and achievement for survival. Admittedly this is a harsh indictment of 'Cinderella' as a tale. Certainly I do not want to make it responsible for the upkeep of the entire capitalist system. However, the critique of 'Cinderella' is meant to show how suspect Bettelheim's theory and methodology are. There is something ultimately pathetic and insidious about Bettelheim's approach to folk tales. It is pathetic because he apparently wants to make a sincere contribution in fighting the dehumanization of life. It is insidious because his banal theory covers up the processes and social mediations which contribute most to the dehumanization. Fundamentally, his instructions on how to use the folk tales can only lead to their abuse. Our task is to explore the possibilities for their positive utilization with children. (pp. 160-73)

Jack Zipes, "On the Use and Abuse of Folk and Fairy Tales with Children: Bruno Bettelheim's Moralistic Magic Wand," in his Breaking the Magic Spell: Radical Theories of Folk and Fairy Tales, *University of Texas Press, 1979, pp. 160-82.*

As a writer Bettelheim has always been pedestrian: he needs a theme on which he can spread himself, slowly and methodically deploying his special insights within a social or clinical setting.

—*Rosemary Dinnage, in her "No Surrender," in* The New York Review of Books, *19 April 1979.*

Howard Gardner   (review date 31 January 1982)

[*Gardner is an American educator and developmental psychologist whose works include* The Arts and Human Development *(1973) and* Artful Scribbles: The Significance of Children's Drawings *(1980). In the following review, he provides a mixed appraisal of* On Learning to Read.]

In past centuries, an entire Jewish community celebrated the day when a young boy began school. The child would first be shown an alphabet chart, onto which his father would toss a candy or coin while the teacher explained, "An angel threw this down so that you will want to study." Next would come a gift of cookies and cakes, each inscribed with a biblical passage. Finally, honey would be smeared all over the alphabet chart, and the child would be allowed to lick it off. After the ceremony at school, friends and family would go to a nearby river, and a blessing would be recited.

Nowadays, an American youngster is likely to be introduced to literacy by the cheerful refrain " 'Sesame Street' has been brought to you by the letter W." Further education is typically carried on through a primer, perhaps one of the Janet-and-Mark series, which have replaced the fabled Dick-and-Jane readers. The first day of school rarely involves the written word, let alone the pursuit of knowledge.

The renowned and highly outspoken child psychologist Bruno Bettelheim has surveyed the teaching of reading in the United States [in ***On Learning to Read***], and he does not like what he sees. With the same gusto he brought to his earlier criticism of the treatment of autistic children, the behavior of student radicals and, most recently, children's literature published in America, he now takes on the American reading establishment.

Bettelheim loathes the reading primers now in use, char-acterizing them as lifeless, patronizing, superficial and dishonest. In masterly fashion, he dissects these books and finds nothing of substance in them. He shrewdly points out their ambivalence about education; exalting fun above all else, the readers reveal a thinly veiled contempt for school and for work. The real value of learning to read and the rewards it can ultimately yield are hardly ever mentioned.

His particular bête noire is the emphasis on phonics, or the sounding out of words. For Bettelheim, the need to crack the code through graphemes—a skill deemed crucial by nearly all reading specialists—is a distinctly secondary concern, one which diverts the child from understanding that reading is the royal road to knowledge.

Enter the psychoanalytic perspective, leavened with a dose of John Dewey. Before we can hope to teach reading, Bettelheim suggests, we need to have a faithful picture of what children are like. These complex creatures, filled with fears, strong drives and powerful if usually unconscious motivation, are eager to unlock the secrets of the adult world and to meet new challenges. Easily seduced by the wonder and magic of words, which in fact exert a special power over the young mind, children can also be turned off by words.

Initially, children are pleasure-seeking creatures, but they have ample potential for learning discipline and skills: It is to these ends that school and education more generally should be directed. In Freud's terms, the child must move from being ruled by the pleasure principle to the reality principle; in Dewey's terms, from impulse to intelligence.

In order to investigate this process, Bettelheim, along with co-author Karen Zelan and several other researchers, visited eight schools over a four-year period. The team worked with approximately 30 teachers and 300 children to discover how reading is taught and how children's early reading efforts are handled. After familiarizing themselves with the children, the researchers focused particularly on the students' errors or misreadings.

Just as Freud saw "slips" as a pivotal cue to an individual's concerns, so do Bettelheim and his colleagues regard children's misreadings. In their view, understanding such misreadings is central to an understanding of the reading process, and extremely valuable in helping children to negotiate it. In the lengthiest (and to my mind the most eccentric) part of the book, the Bettelheim team reviews dozens of errors made by children and interprets these misreadings in terms of the children's personal agendas.

According to this analysis, children's reading errors are neither random accidents, nor simple manifestations of immaturity, nor symptoms of dyslexia. The mistakes don't signal inexperience, inattention or decoding problems; rather, they reveal the children's true feelings and thoughts—what is important to them, what they fear, what they desire. When seen as subjectively meaningful, the errors reflect a conflict between what is printed on the page and the child's own concerns: In fact, these mistakes are an act of self-expression by the child.

Consider a few of the examples on which Bettelheim

dwells. A child whose ability to read had been blocked for three years insisted on reading "Mom" for "Mother," Bettelheim writes, because the more formal word failed to connote his feelings for his own mother. The researchers suggest that one child who consistently read "saw" for "was" or "was" for "saw" did so not out of an inability to read the words but because he was struggling in his own life to separate past from present. A first grader read "can't" for "can" because he wanted to protest against a picture in his primer of a watchdog who was inexplicably asleep. And a little boy read "mane" for "name" because he wanted the cat in the story to be another more ferocious animal, such as a lion, that could protect him from a real dog that he feared.

In each case, Bettelheim takes the errors seriously, trying to figure out the psychodynamic processes that gave rise to the error and then, as appropriate, to share his perception with the child. Much as the analysis of dreams may help an adult cope with the anxieties of life, the interpretation of reading errors, Bettelheim believes, will produce a stronger ego in the child. In opposition to the mechanical focus on phonics, Bettelheim searches for the strong feelings that a given theme evokes in the child, as well as for the child's more general reactions to the challenges of reading. Repeatedly, Bettelheim expresses his frustration that American reading teachers have been remote from these psychological concerns. He believes that things need not be so.

The final part of **On Learning to Read** describes primers and reading programs that do engage students and yield higher levels of literacy. Bettelheim first pauses to praise traditional Hebrew and colonial-American methods of teaching reading as well as contemporary Japanese and Soviet methods, but reserves his greatest praise for the primer *Joyous Learning* from his native Austria. What strikes Bettelheim about the primers that he approves are the intellectual challenges that they pose and the seriousness with which education is treated. In the prototype, as Bettelheim describes it, one sees children and adults actually engaged in learning; individuals confronting and dealing with birth, death, rivalries—the stuff of reality (and also of fairy tales). As Bettelheim puts it, "These foreign primers treat the beginning reader with respect for his intelligence, for his interest in the more serious aspects of life, and with the recognition that from the earliest age on he will respond positively to writings of true literary merit." And Bettelheim reminds us of why children are taught to read: "Books are man's most important source of information and knowledge, and all later learning requires the ability to read."

In the end, Bettelheim's case hinges on the plausibility of the psychoanalytic approach to what has almost always been regarded by specialists as a perceptual and cognitive matter. And I find Bettelheim least convincing when he dons the garb of an experimental researcher in order to study children's errors.

In fact, the very idea of Bettelheim (who often sounds like an Old Testament prophet) as an empirical researcher is an odd one. In previous statements Bettelheim has been skeptical of "research teams," preferring to place his stock in intuition and clinical experience. Now Bettelheim adopts just enough of the paraphernalia and terminology of traditional empiricism to appear to have gone over to the "other side." But he seems uncomfortable writing as a behavioral scientist, and his own ambivalence about "data" (as opposed to "cases") seeps through.

Science cannot be done halfway; yet Bettelheim appears to rely on numbers while not really doing so. The reader is given little sense of how the researchers identified, collected and scored the children's errors. There is no discussion of the reliability of a given interpretation, and scant attention is paid to the numerous previous studies of children's reading mistakes that take different approaches. The major examples of the depth analysis of errors are unconvincing and at times seem almost ludicrous. I shudder to think of teachers practicing amateur psychoanalysis on their pupil's errors; in most cases, these mistakes will be the kinds of totally predictable reversals and substitutions that gradually disappear shortly after a child learns to read.

A clue to this odd business slips out in the introduction. Karen Zelan indicates that she was first drawn to this study through an examination of the errors made by autistic children. Has excessive involvement with pathology once again blinded clinicians to the obvious? As Freud's oft-repeated quip suggests, "Sometimes a cigar is only a cigar."

Nor am I sure that effective teaching of reading must take into account the child's unconscious or his major concerns. For instance, in traditional religious schooling, such as Koranic, Latin or Hebrew classes, reading is mastered by rote, with no attention to (or even comprehension of) the meaning of material. After the inaugural honey, there is only sweat. What keeps the children going is not the intrinsic interest of the often tedious material, but rather the belief that it is important to their society or to their religious creed—that it *matters* whether or not they learn to read.

Here, I think, we encounter Bettelheim's genuine and considerable achievement. He convincingly argues that the degree of our regard for reading reveals much—perhaps all too much—about what our society values and what it does not. We score poorly here. We approach reading with an amalgam of a sales pitch ("Sesame Street"), a denial of real seriousness and respect for work ("fun morality") and an unyielding faith in mechanics (if you master decoding, all will turn out O.K.). There is a virtual conspiracy of silence about why reading is important, how it makes and remakes one's world. Worse, children are trapped in a double bind. They are assured that school—and reading—is important, but the very primers that introduce them to these activities either do not mention education at all or carry the unmistakable message that learning is drudgery and any sensible person would rather—literally—go fishing.

But could it be otherwise? Can we change our primers, or must we first change our society? Can we re-create in modern America the world of Cotton Mather, of contemporary Japan or Bettelheim's beloved Vienna? Can a love for reading and learning replace our society's current passions? We have little reason for optimism. The reading atmosphere for which Bruno Bettelheim yearns presupposes a kind of commonality of experience (if not an ideology or a religion) that does not exist in our society. We *are* teaching what we as a society value; in fact, the primers themselves provide eloquent testimony to our success in promulgating our values. (pp. 11, 26)

> *Howard Gardner, in a review of "On Learning to Read," in* The New York Times Book Review, *January 31, 1982, pp. 11, 26.*

Bettelheim's achievement is that while his professional life *has* been concerned with the distresses of others, he has also been able to teach us through the writings— objective rather than passionate—that are based on his own distresses and endurance. Those experiences are the basis of his special understanding both of the growth and the destruction of what makes a person human.

—*Rosemary Dinnage, in her "No Surrender," in* The New York Review of Books, *19 April 1979.*

Anthony Storr   (review date 1982)

[*Storr is an English writer, lecturer, and psychotherapist. In the following review, he offers a mixed assessment of* Freud and Man's Soul.]

In [***Freud and Man's Soul***] Bruno Bettelheim's main contention is that Freud's message and attitude toward human nature have been misunderstood in the English-speaking world because of inadequate and inaccurate translation of his works. Since Bettelheim is a distinguished psychoanalyst and author, whose work with disturbed children is world-famous and whose description of life in Dachau and Buchenwald (***The Informed Heart***, 1960) has become a classic, his accusation must be taken seriously.

Bettelheim begins by pointing out that he himself comes from a background similar to that of Freud—"a middle-class, assimilated Jewish family in Vienna." Although Freud was born in 1856 and Bettelheim in 1903, he says that that there had been little cultural change in the years that intervened between Freud's student days and his own. Freud's psychoanalytic writings only began in the last decade of the nineteenth century, just before Bettelheim was born; thus he was able to study the "edifice of psychoanalysis" in the setting in which it was conceived, a study was facilitated by his being in analysis himself. After his liberation from the concentration camps, Bettelheim settled in the United States and was for many years a professor at the University of Chicago and director of the Orthogenic

School for disturbed children. He discovered that the staff of the school, though well read in psychoanalysis, was too detached, too "theoretical" in its approach to disturbed children. Whereas Bettelheim himself was not afraid of emotional closeness based on sympathetic understanding of, and identification with, disturbed children, his American staff remained distant and therefore unable to help their patients.

Bettelheim's claim is that this distant, detached attitude developed because Americans studied Freud only in translation. He believes that the effect of the English translation of Freud's ideas was to make them into an abstract intellectual system, something that might be applied to the understanding of others in a cerebral fashion, but that was not easily applicable to the study of one's own unconscious. Bettelheim maintains that Freud's writings were imbued with classical allusions that, though familiar to Viennese students who had been reared on Latin and Greek, lost much of their meaning when transferred to America, where classical studies were confined to the few. Words and concepts derived from classical myth—like Eros and Psyche and the legend of Oedipus—tend to become abstractions when denuded of the overtones and associations that have become part of the mental furniture of those who have been familiar with classical myth from early childhood.

These difficulties in comprehending Freud's real meaning have, so Bettelheim argues, been greatly increased by clumsy, insensitive translation and, even more, by the translators' tendency to substitute unfamiliar, technical, or medical words for Freud's use of terms that every German-speaking person would easily recognize.

Some of Bettelheim's examples are striking. He states that the German word *Mutterleib* can be translated only as "womb," a word that has quite different associations from the medical term "uterus" as used by the English translators. In Bettelheim's view, to translate *Das Ich und das Es* by their Latin equivalents the "ego" and the "id" is to misrepresent Freud's simplicity of language. *Ich* and *Es* are "among the first words used by every German child": "ego" and "id" are not to be found in the vocabularies of either German or English-speaking children. Bettelheim also criticizes the translators' use of "parapraxis" and "cathexis" to cover slips of the tongue and similar phenomena, and investment of an object with libido. These Greek terms, the first of which is an invention, do not, so Bettelheim asserts, reflect the original German, and present the reader with unfamiliar words that carry no emotional overtones.

Bettelheim states that

> The English translations cleave to an early stage of Freud's thought, in which he inclined toward science and medicine, and disregard the more mature Freud, whose orientation was humanistic. . . .

He believes that the translators wished "to perceive Freud strictly within the framework of medicine," and that this accounts for some of their misrepresentation of his language. He goes on to deplore the American decision to restrict the practice of psychoanalysis to physicians, which he believes reinforced the tendency, begun by the translators, to perceive psychoanalysis in scientific, rather than humanistic terms.

How far are Bettelheim's strictures justified? Many of his points concerning the translation are cogent, but in most instances Bettelheim himself has nothing better to offer. Although *The Interpretation of Dreams* may not be an exact equivalent for *Die Traumdeutung,* I am not convinced that Bettelheim's alternatives of *A Search for the Meaning of Dreams* or *An Inquiry into the Meaning of Dreams* are really more illuminating. "Free association" is, admittedly, an unsatisfactory translation of *Freier Einfall,* a point already made by Charles Rycroft in his *Critical Dictionary of Psychoanalysis,* but Bettelheim cannot suggest a succinct alternative. Although he pays lip service to the difficulties faced by the translators of Freud, he is less than generous to them. Moreover, his accusation of "medicalization" of Freud's thought cannot be laid at their door. James Strachey, the principal translator, was not a doctor, though he was analyzed by Freud and had a close acquaintance with his thought. Alan Tyson, one of his chief assistants, qualified as a doctor later in his career, but was not medically trained at the time of the translation. In fact *The Standard Edition* of Freud's writings was a labor of love, contributed to by many German scholars, and all the points raised by Bettelheim were in fact thrashed out in the greatest detail. The fact of the matter is that any translation is bound to evoke criticism, partly because many German words like *Seele* do not really have an English equivalent. Bettelheim is fair enough to mention that the whole of *The Standard Edition* was read and passed by Anna Freud, who was a passionate guardian of her father's reputation, and would certainly not have countenanced any distortion of his thought if she had believed that this was taking place.

Bettelheim's chief concern is to resuscitate Freud as a humanist with a deep perception of human nature and personal concern for human tragedy, and to play down his wish to be thought a scientist. This is an understandable aspiration. Psychoanalysis is not, and can never be, an exact science in the sense of chemistry or physics (although their exactness seems now to be in question). But Freud seems never to have lost his belief in science, which he unfavorably contrasts with religion in his late work *The Future of an Illusion.* Freud was a humane man, and contemporary accounts of his behavior as an analyst indicate that he sometimes showed quite human emotions to his patients, occasionally revealed personal matters like an accident to his son, and was even reported as thumping the table to hammer home a point. But Joan Rivière, who was analyzed by Freud and who became an analyst herself, chiefly recalls his interest in her as being "curiously impersonal."

Freud's desire to establish psychoanalysis as a science of the mind has had strangely contradictory results. If Freud had not been a detached investigator, who tried to regard his patients as objectively as possible, without becoming involved with their problems, we should never have understood the phenomena of transference as well as we do. For transference depends upon projection; and projections can only be understood or indeed fully evoked if the analyst remains somewhat of an enigma to the patient. But Freud's detachment also had an unfortunate result in that it gave birth to, and seemed to justify the behavior of, a breed of analysts who, one is glad to say, are fast disappearing.

These are the analysts whom Bettelheim is really attacking, and whose impersonality he found so therapeutically ineffective when he was in charge of the Orthogenic School. There is a revealing account of such an analyst in the person of "Aaron Green" in Janet Malcolm's recent, brilliant book, *The Impossible Profession.* In my review of the book [*The New Republic* (16 September 1981)] I wrote of Aaron Green:

> He calls psychoanalysis a science. He believes that Freud made certain fundamental discoveries concerning infantile sexuality and the Oedipus complex which ought to have been accepted and passed down in the way that discoveries in chemistry are handed on, and is amazed that this is still not the case. He considers psychoanalysis equivalent to a surgical operation; that is, it is both extremely intimate and yet entirely impersonal.

Bettelheim's advocacy of a more humanistic attitude in psychotherapy is entirely justified. Modern research into the efficacy of psychotherapy has demonstrated that genuine concern and warmth are important therapeutic factors. Moreover, for the therapist to show concern and warmth does not mean that he has to indulge in giving personal details about himself, the revelation of which might interfere with understanding the patient's transference projections.

But I don't really believe that mistranslation of Freud can have had quite the powerful effect in producing fundamentalist analysts like "Aaron Green" that Bettelheim attributes to it. Psychoanalysis is a body of knowledge and a technique of treatment that is passed down by training analysts to their trainees in the uniquely compelling situation of a training analysis. Bettelheim would allege that misunderstanding of Freud because of mistranslation was the cause of producing inhuman practitioners; but is there really any evidence that psychoanalysts brought up in Germany and Austria did not fall into the same trap? Bettelheim himself is, and has always been, a humane, concerned person, though sometimes feared as an authority. But not all his emigrant colleagues are like him, however much they have read Freud in the original German. Freud did not always practice what he preached; but the tradition of the detached, "scientific" analyst originated with him, and he certainly did not welcome the fact that his patients developed strong feelings toward him. In fact, he tried to protect himself from the emotional impact of his patients by lying them on a couch in such a position that they could not see his face or establish eye-to-eye contact with him. Bettelheim seems overconcerned with protecting Freud, whose influence, as today some of his most able followers are able to admit, was by no means always constructive. Insofar as England is concerned, most psychoanalysts there are quite warm and human in their approach to their patients, and Bettelheim is flogging a dead horse. In any case, Freud has now been dead for forty-three years, and disputes about what he actually meant or said are beginning to take on the aspect of medieval controversies about how many angels can be accommodated on the point of a pin. Bettelheim has written some marvelous books for which all of us are in his debt, but I would advise any reader who is unfamiliar with his work to begin with one of his other books, *The Informed Heart* or *The Uses of Enchantment*. (pp. 36-8)

> Anthony Storr, "Lost in Translation?" in The New Republic, *Vol. 188, No. 26, 1982, pp. 36-8.*

Robert Boyers   (essay date 1983)

[*Boyers is an American critic, editor, and educator whose works include* The Legacy of the German Refugee Intellectuals *(1972) and* Psychological Man: Approaches to an Emergent Social Type *(1974). In the following excerpt, he faults Bettelheim's strict adherence to humanistic philosophy and documented fact in his essay "Surviving," an analysis of Lena Wertmüller's film* Seven Beauties.]

In an essay on E. L. Doctorow's novel *Ragtime*, [contemporary historian John] Lukacs contrasts a nineteenth century genre, "the historical novel," with a twentieth century form, uneasily labelled "novelized history." Lukacs does not think his categories as flexible as I do, and he would no doubt resist my suggestion that "cinematized history" would serve the basic point of his distinction as well as "novelized history." My reader will, however, follow my advice, for the moment at least, and substitute the one term for the other in pursuing Lukacs' argument: "The new genre is the converse of the historical novel. In *War And Peace* or in *Gone With The Wind* history is the background. In the [novelized history, like *Ragtime,* or Solzhenitsyn's *Nineteen-Fourteen*] history is the foreground. In the classic historical novel the great events of history are painted on a large canvas in order to lend depth to the story, to give an added dimension to the main characters. In the [novelized history] the reverse: the main characters serve for the purpose of illuminating the history of certain events, of a certain time. In this historical novel the author's principal interest is *the novel*. In [novelized history] the author's principal interest is *history*—perhaps a new kind of history, but history nonetheless." Though recent popular works of novelized history may distort the historical record, at their best they do represent, in Lukacs' view, an advance in historical consciousness. [In his essay **"Surviving"**] Bettelheim does not think that cinematized history (my term, not his) can represent a fruitful advance in any kind of consciousness unless it registers historical events with documentary accuracy and rests upon a sound humanistic foundation. Though he does not make use of Lukacs' distinction, does not argue the necessary relation between fact and fiction, individual and collective, in the conception of a film like *Seven Beauties,* his paper everywhere cries out for just that sort of theoretical underpinning.

But let us look at Lukacs' distinction more closely. The novelized history is said to use characters and portray particular encounters "for the purpose of illuminating the history of certain events, of a certain time." Illumination—the truth of the historical record—is the goal. Works of art typically propose to illuminate the truth, of course, but it is not always easy to say what kind of truth is available to a given novel or film. When Lukacs writes that in the older genre—the historical novel—"the author's principal interest is *the novel*," he means to identify a certain kind of truth to which such works are principally suited. This is the truth of human feeling, a truth which is ratified by the accumulated experience of each reader or film-goer. Insofar as such works are persuasive, they appeal to our intuitive sense of things. If they present extraordinary persons involved in unusual exploits, they will develop their behavior and join events in such a way that our sense of the probable is tested no more than it may be without our turning from the spectacle in dismay. The truth to which we respond is, again, a truth of experience: we sense that, given a certain kind of extraordinary personage placed in very special circumstances, this is the way he would very likely behave; these are the likely consequences of initiating events; these are the sensations and thoughts an alert and intelligent observer ought to be permitted to have when confronted with such materials. This is the kind of truth we want and expect from most works of art.

Lukacs' notion of novelized history proposes to alter this expectation, to explain why it is we may be satisfied with another kind of truth when confronted with a book like *Ragtime*. It is the passion for historical truth which determines our response to these newer works, which have been created to answer to a demand earlier readers were not as likely to make as we: namely, the demand that no truth we are meant to accept be presented without the support of detailed context and place in time. Since all truth is presumed to be relative to particular circumstances and characterological disposition—itself a historical phenomenon which varies from one era to another—even a truth of feeling must be located in respect to time and general probability. Reader interest will tend to be less involved in the truth of human nature than in *a* truth of human nature in a given period. This is not to deny that general truths may emerge from the concentration on individual, specifically conditioned truths in their context, only that the terms of extrapolation will be differently weighted than they used to be. The issue is one of emphasis: as Lukacs writes, in the newer genre "the author's principal interest is *history*"—it is not the author's only interest, but his *principal* interest.

Bruno Bettelheim, in refusing to think through such distinctions, never really discovers what Wertmuller's *Seven Beauties* achieves. The issue here is not so much the success or failure of the film, but the expectations and responses it may be said to generate. Bettelheim assumes that Wertmuller's principal interest is history, that the film is an example of what we have called, following Lukacs, cinematized history. He assumes, moreover, that the film-goer cannot but be misled by the film, since what he is bound to find in it is a particular version of the historical truth which takes unforgiveable liberties with the actual historical record it presumes to enlarge upon. The actual record in this case is, of course, something with which Bruno Bettelheim is singularly familiar. As a concentration-camp survivor, as a scholarly authority in the field of holocaust studies, as author of several important works on terror and survivorship, he has at once a very large claim on our respect and attention. The problem is that his primary assumption is mistaken. No one believes while watching *Seven Beauties* that the historical record has been significantly clarified or enlarged. No one need feel that the actual experience of survivors has been betrayed, or demeaned. To argue the case as Bettelheim does is to mistake one kind of truth for another. There are more serious errors in Bettelheim's analysis, but the first one is crucial in directing the course of the others.

Bettelheim remembers the opening of the film—like the other parts—very well indeed, and what he makes of it may be said to stand for his response to the entire film:

> Before the film's story begins, we are shown a series of newsreels of Fascism: demonstrations, marches, Mussolini exhorting the masses, Mussolini shaking Hitler's hand; war, the bombing and destruction of cities, the killing and maiming of people. Though all this is presented as horrible, we are entertained by an amusing, mocking cabaret song accompanying the newsreel scenes. And Mussolini and Hitler are also presented partly as comic figures—an approach that is supported by the song, in which all the contradictions of life are accepted at the same time. The song says "Oh yeah" equally to "the ones who have never had a fatal accident" and to "the ones who have had one." And though most of the lyrics and the singing bitingly reject the world of Fascism we see on the screen, they are also funny, and this quality simultaneously adds to the rejection and takes the sting of true seriousness out of it.
>
> . . . The newsreels and the song accompanying them in *Seven Beauties* take us back to the period when we thought that we did not need to take Hitler and Mussolini seriously. But the war scenes show us at the same time what happened because we didn't take these men seriously. This is a contradiction that runs all through the film.

So, a combination of newsreel footage and "mocking cabaret song" frames Wertmuller's film and instructs us in Wertmuller's approach to her materials. She works, according to Bettelheim, on a principle of contradiction and alternation: the ludicrous and the obscene mingle freely in her imagination with the terrible, the good with the bad, the playful with the serious. The result, in Bettelheim's view, is confusion and irrelevance. If viewers cannot confidently tell an appropriate response from an intolerable impropriety, if they are asked to laugh when they should cover their eyes in shame and horror, they may decide that one thing is much like another, that truth is in vividness of presentation and the power to evoke feeling—not in the substance of the vision. When audiences are so manipulated, Bettelheim argues, they will come to feel that they may not trust their responses at all—including decent and once reliable responses to cruelty and torture. They will find ways to deny that they have such responses at all, or that

such responses are more legitimate, more worthy of their humanity, than others.

The opening of Wertmuller's film is no doubt full of incongruity and confusion, as Bettelheim rightly argues. What is its ostensible purpose and the effect it may be said to produce? As the frame for the film, rather than a part of the story, it may be said both to stand apart and to support or establish the central action. It stands apart in presenting what appears to be actual newsreel footage, while the central action is clearly fictional. No matter whether we take the story-line to reflect some accurate semblance of what actually took place in concentration camps. Insofar as the story is enacted; as it involves patently 'private' or 'exclusive' insights into very special characters; as it persistently juxtaposes the improbable and the probable with no trace of apology or regret—the audience knows that it watches the unfolding of a fiction. But what does it think as it labors to follow the opening sequence? Fact, or fiction? The distinction is not usually put so crudely when we speak of a film like *Seven Beauties,* but here there is no alternative. Bettelheim forces the issue in such a way that we cannot but go back to 'first' questions. If we take the newsreel footage to be authentic, which is to say, part of the documentary record—no matter how fragmentary—, must we therefore suppose that Wertmuller's intention was to prepare us for the unfolding of a cinematized history? The supposition might have been justified had the director not put in the accompanying cabaret song. As it is, the opening sequence undercuts any possible inference that Wertmuller is primarily interested in settling the historical record. If the song presents contradiction, if one interpretation of the holocaust experience vies with another—with no apparent means of reconciling them—the audience must see at once that it is not in for a definitive accounting. It is being asked to assimilate the frightening images on the screen to the shifting perspectives offered by the all-too-knowing lyrics mounted on the sound-track. Though the audience may try to manage this at first, it must recoil from the task with some unease after the opening minute or two of the film. Since there is no reliable way of adopting a single perspective on the imagery—not on the basis of the deliberately elusive cabaret lyrics, at any rate—the audience can do nothing but take in what is given, and wait for further 'instructions.' The unease we feel does not reflect the disappointed expectation that the definitive historical truth is about to be delivered. It reflects some feeling that we may have to work very hard to make sense of the film we are to see; also, that we shall be asked to focus not so much on what happened as on what the imagination is wont to make of the holocaust experience.

This is not an insignificant distinction, and the intelligence that registers the distinction in the opening minutes of the film will find its anticipations throughout unusually tense and uncertain. The film asks us to do several things at once: to compare and contrast what we know of the holocaust with the images projected on the screen—images which are patently fictional but which nonetheless refer unmistakably to real events we are not likely to forget; to think of the intrinsic dynamics of the imagination that contrives to move characters about and arrange events as peculiarly as it does in this film; to set up resistances to our own queasy impulses to reject what we are shown on the grounds that it violates a sombre decorum we take to be appropriate under the circumstances. In thinking about the way we perform these functions—here, as in our responses to many other works of art—we are required to differentiate between the way we ought to perform them, and the way we do perform them. Bettelheim thinks we ought to hold up the given images against the reality of the concentration camps and therefore to reject Wertmuller's images as specious and arbitrary—if *Seven Beauties* wanted to be taken as sheer fiction, it should not have suggested even for a moment that it was telling the historical truth. Also he thinks we ought not to be seriously interested in an imagination for which stacked corpses can as readily stimulate gallows-humor as evoke revulsion. Finally, Bettelheim feels that, far from resisting impulses to reject, we ought to dismiss *Seven Beauties* as a film which degrades and confuses—whatever the aesthetic discriminations we may feel tempted to introduce. Alas, we do not in general respond as we should. Wertmuller's images have a terrible authority which makes it difficult indeed to dismiss them as specious or arbitary. Even in the opening minutes of the film we are gripped by a central fact of human experience which is imposed upon us with ferocious authenticity: the fact that imagination can put to so many uses events which had seemed singular and astonishing almost to the point of numbing the senses which had long before engaged to deal with them. In witnessing *Seven Beauties,* though we may wish to turn away in horror or to cry out, we are persuaded by Wertmuller's invention to hang on, to watch for the trophies that persistent attention can win. Is it possible to laugh at stacked corpses and to do justice to the dead? The question here is almost beside the point. The film makes no pretense to do justice to the dead. Its business is another kind of remembering that has more to do with the dynamics of survival. Perhaps we ought always to think of the dead when we think of the Nazi period. Perhaps some of us are prone to think of little else, and may be blessed for so persisting. But it is a mistake to assume that everyone will be so disposed, or that *Seven Beauties* violates a mode of remembering to which it makes no claim, and to which it is obviously inadequate. If we resist impulses to reject what we are shown, we do so because those impulses are sometimes inflexible and unreliable, because they may inhibit the growth of our humanity as surely as Bettelheim thinks they will preserve and strenghten it.

But what exactly do we mean when we speak of this resistance? The film contains many sequences in which it is called into play. Not much resistance is required in the opening minutes because the presentation of materials there is so very tentative, the tension between image and cabaret song so deliberate that no 'statement' may be adduced, one way or another. If we are disposed to be sickened even by the newsreel footage and the 'improper' uses to which it is put we shall not be able to attend to the rest of the film in a satisfactory way, and there will be no more to consider. But resistance of the sort we have indicated *will* be required frequently afterwards. When the protagonist Pasqualino 'seduces' the monstrous female commandant in order to escape the fate to which others in the concentration camp are sentenced, we experience a revulsion so great that, for a moment, it threatens to swamp our more considered responses to the film. Pasqualino's behavior had been less than edifying in earlier sequences, but by this point, we feel, he has gone too far. The woman is as close to being a monster as we can imagine any human being to come. That Pasqualino should be willing to seduce her, to plead his love to one so fully terrible, in order to save his life, seems, at first, incredible. Why should she believe him? Why should he assume she'll find him appealing? How can a man who's been through so much seem to have learned so little, resorting to the tiresome deception by which men have so regularly sought to master women? Along with sheer physical revulsion at the prospect of a monstrous and unfeeling coupling, we experience a nausea that frequently accompanies an apprehension of the meaningless and incomprehensible. Though Wertmuller has had the effrontery to show us almost anything we can imagine—in *Seven Beauties* as in other films like *Swept Away* and *The Seduction Of Mimi*—we do not believe she will play out the seduction of the camp commandant. What point can possibly be made by pursuing an invention that so strains credulity and the limits of our tolerance?

Wertmuller allows us to resist impulses to reject the ghastly spectacle by detaching us from it and, strangely, by humanizing it. Resistance is an effect of discrimination, and discrimination is made possible by the complicating of an experience which had earlier seemed to offer nothing in the way of an enticing complexity. Revulsion is not so much overcome as, temporarily, held at bay, as the discriminative intelligence registers interesting distinctions between what we are given and what we'd expected. We resist the impulse to dismiss and to turn away because there is something for us in the spectacle, something we may not want to miss. This 'something' is signalled in the marks of Pasqualino's possession by his idea, his stratagem. He is so clearly given over to it, so fully convinced that he must act out his 'inspiration,' that we are almost persuaded he knows what he is doing. It is all thoroughly absurd, more than a little perverse, surely disgusting to think about too closely—but we are disposed progressively to feel that Pasqualino has to do what he has determined to do. We laugh at his overtures to the commandant, enjoy her amazement, anticipate that she may have him castrated and shot—didn't those big, 'sexless' German women go in for sexual butchery? we are apt to muse. Wertmuller detaches us from the spectacle by making us laugh at it and, simultaneously, by making us attend in a progressively disinterested way. We want to discover what it is about Pasqualino that drives him to the absurdity of his seduction-quest. We want to know why Wertmuller finds him so compelling, and how she manages almost to make him as interesting to us. But we know as well that, to the extent that we share this interest in Pasqualino, it is an interest not so much in his particular fate as in the peculiar, abstract depths of human invention. No one imagines that Pasqualino is Wertmuller's everyman, that anyone would be as likely as he to seduce the commandant. But no one will deny that he represents for us a certain kind of possibility to which present circumstances uniquely contribute. This is the possibility that human beings may well identify their humanity, their very sense of the self and of the values that sustain it, with the energy and cunning to remain alive and scamper, perpetually, beyond the outstretched hands of circumstance. If we are detached as we watch *Seven Beauties,* we experience nonetheless a very large interest in the issues raised, an interest we cannot satisfy by rooting for Pasqualino or against him; by passing secure judgments too quickly; or by giving in to the impulse to deny our laughter.

Bettelheim argues that detachment is fruitful only if we are detached from experiences that justify such a response. It is legitimate to conclude, early in the film, that Pasqualino is a relatively worthless person, and that we are therefore not required to feel concern for him. It is not legitimate to achieve detachment from the imagery of stacked corpses—whatever the way in which they are presented—, when to do so is inevitably to harden our responses to the murder of countless Jews. The operant principle here has to do with propriety, and it is not an idea anyone can take lightly. Over and over again, Bettelheim warns his reader that to confuse one mode of presentation with another is to forfeit the capacity to keep things in their rightful place. The comic and the horrible, persistently juxtaposed and intermixed, may make for a certain debased kind of aesthetic delight, but the "combination" will not yield to better purposes. Wertmuller's film, he argues, is a degrading experience because it induces us not to take anything seriously—not even something "that would ordinarily upset us greatly or move us deeply." Talk about detachment all you want, Bettelheim would seem to say. If the result is that the heart is hardened and the intelligence learns to yield too easily to the grotesque and fantastic, no good will come of what we call aesthetic discrimination and disinterestedness.

The problem is that, by failing to resist the impulse to condemn and recoil in sheer disgust, Bettelheim misses the film's invitation to participate in a crucial experience, wherein the dominant perspective is humanized with no corresponding refusal of judgment. This is an unfortunate feature of much self-consciously humanistic thinking. In insisting upon what it knows, it closes itself to all sorts of things it might otherwise have welcomed. To resist a "reflex" judgment is not, after all, to lose the capacity to judge, or to reflect, or to forfeit the right to judge at a later time. No doubt there is a sense in which we can take too much time making up our minds; a sense in which to wait, and split hairs, and search, perpetually, for nuance, is to lose any genuine prospect of moral intensity. But a film like *Seven Beauties,* after all, promises *something* in the way of a judgment. It is a work of art, of determinate length and scope and execution. The film, at least, may be judged, if nothing else, and there is bound to be some release of tension in this. We resist the impulse to judge and dismiss abruptly because we are secure in the knowledge that we shall have something on which to pass judgment later on. The film asks us to put up this necessary resistance by complicating our feelings and by humanizing our perceptions of what is going on. Bettelheim considers this sort of complication a disgrace. By making it difficult for us to know what we feel or, exactly, what we should be looking at, Wertmuller makes us doubt our right to judge. From such confusion, one thing looks much like another,

a crime might just as well have been an act of charity, and we are left in a muddle from which nothing in the film will extricate us.

Bettelheim's moral knowledge is based upon a number of truths to which every decent person is supposed to be as devoted as he. Because the film seems to go against the grain of these simple truths, Bettelheim feels, it is clearly a violation of the given and a disservice to the survivors of the holocaust, who know what to make of their experience. Examples:

> 1—Pasqualino: " . . . charmingly portrayed by Giancarlo Giannini as the prototypical 'little man,' who will be a Fascist under Fascism, a Communist under Communism, and a democrat in a democracy. But this portrait of the little man, which the film makes us believe in, is a lie. The world's little men do not rape or kill—not under Fascism or Communism or in a democracy. These little men do not think of or manage an erection and intercourse with an absolutely abhorrent woman, even if their lives are at stake. The little man is banal, but he is not evil."

> 2—The Commandant: "The closer she gets to being a woman, the more grotesque this mass of flesh becomes, but also the more human, and the greater depth she reveals, not least because of the way she is acted by Shirley Stoler. She is not only shown imprisoned in her body but shown to feel it and to suffer from it. Her being disgusted by Pasqualino and his lie of loving her—which she, knowing how repulsive she is, does not believe for a moment—is but a small reflection of her disgust with herself . . . When she says that Pasqualino, because he managed an erection, will survive and win in the end, while she is doomed, her dreams unattainable, she implies that, unlike Pasqualino, she is unable to have sex without the appropriate feelings. . . .

> . . . But this portrayal of a concentration-camp commander is no less a lie than the portrayal of Pasqualino as a sometimes charming but always utterly unimportant little man. If any one thing characterized the rulers of the concentration camps, it was their inability to reflect on themselves, to see themselves for what they were. Had they been able to recognize themselves as they really were—which the camp commander in this film is shown as being able to do—they could not have carried on for a moment. . . . Somebody with so much insight into herself could not behave toward the prisoners as we see her do."

In the first example, Bettelheim rejects the view of Pasqualino as capable of evil on the scale depicted in *Seven Beauties.* The little man as portrayed by Wertmuller "is a lie." How do we know? Bettelheim seems certain in his declarations on such matters, and assumes we will believe him. If Pasqualino were capable of evil on a grand scale, of indiscriminate killing and rape, he would not be a banal creature. This is the thrust of the argument. It is not, as such, a historical argument; nor is it an enlargement or application of a psychological thesis which has been experimentally validated. The argument is an argument from a body of shared knowledge which is often referred to as our fund of collective wisdom. "Little men do not rape or kill"—the conviction plainly expresses itself, with no hint of qualification or misgiving. Who, then, is responsible for the killing and raping? If not Pasqualino, presumably some other kind of social misfit will be held responsible. This misfit who commits evil deeds, according to Bettelheim, will not be banal. He will have some sense of what he is doing and what it means to do terrible things simply because one has been encouraged or empowered to do them. The evil man will not drift mindlessly into evil deeds, and will not think to defend himself by claiming he could not know how terrible his actions were. He will participate in brutality and terror because he stands to realize something from his participation, and he will know what he wants and how high the price may be. Pasqualino is incapacitated from this kind of participation by virtue of his mindless stumbling about from prospect to prospect with no resolute sense of what he really wants and may actually hope to achieve. He is banal because he is totally subject to the designs of others, and as such he is incapable of the resolve required to perform evil deeds which require a measure of fortitude, determination, even passion.

If I have properly represented Bettelheim's thought—and I do not see how I can have failed to represent it under the circumstances—I have also demonstrated that it is perfectly insupportable. It is a fact that many human beings in a number of European nations participated in brutal activities over a period of many years. That Hitler's programs were carried out by ordinary persons is not a fact anyone is in a position to dispute. It does not matter whether we call these ordinary persons banal or something else. We know what they did, and what they did was evil, if the word 'evil' has any ordinary meaning at all. To kill helpless people, to rape and pillage, is to do evil. Bettelheim argues that it is a slander upon ordinary men and women to show that they may be induced to support or to perform such evil actions. At one point he says he accepts Hannah Arendt's theory of Adolph Eichmann as the very embodiment of banality. But what can it mean to embrace the theory if one does not accept also what follows irrevocably from it? Namely, that banality is a condition to which human beings succumb; that certain cultures nurture in their citizens a complex of attitudes which incline them to deny responsibility for their deeds; and that such persons are to be judged by standards of civilized behavior whether or not they wish to assume responsibility for their actions. In this sense it is clear that banal persons are precisely those who, in our time, will perform evil deeds. Though they may pretend merely to be following orders, or to have acted out of confusion, they will be as capable of evil as though they had earnestly desired to murder Jews in order to steal their shoes or sleep with their daughters. For Bettelheim to deny the possibility of evil to banal little men is to deny that there have been responsible agents performing the many individual acts of brutality which together constitute the experience of the Nazi period.

Why does Bettelheim stake so much on this point? His concern is not really to assert that ordinary persons are fundamentally decent. He knows that any generalization of that kind is bound to seem dubious, at best. His more urgent contention is that Pasqualino, as the prototypical little man, can not have equated survival with the capacity to do terrible things. This is Bettelheim's central concern, to insist over and over again that survival in the Nazi period depended not upon the ability to kill or in other ways to dehumanize oneself, but to keep up one's sense of decency and honor. Though Terence Des Pres and other scholars of the holocaust have lately argued that survival often meant learning how to "live beyond the compulsions of culture," Bettelheim argues that persons like Pasqualino can not be said to represent the meaning of survivorship. Though some, like Pasqualino, may have reverted to sheer animalism, and may somehow have survived, most who came through the concentration camp experience did so because they were lucky, and because they knew better than to succumb entirely to the examples of monstrous debasement continually held up to them. The portrait of Pasqualino is a lie because it shows him to have survived by virtue of his capacity to do terrible things—things, moreover, such a person cannot have done in light of the banal characteristics attributed to him.

The argument sends us back, as it must, to Wertmuller's film, or at least to what we can recall of it. At once we are compelled to remember that Pasqualino seemed always a peculiar fellow, slippery and outrageous, something of a buffoon, at times a caricature of what we take to be a familiar Italian figure. It is the figure of the Italian male as the genial, simple-minded butt, hung up in the various ways played upon in a succession of popular films and novels. This is not *man,* but a certain kind of man, a certain kind of caricature of the Italian male animal. How do we know this? The opening sequences of the film had invited the viewer to wonder what might become the dominant perspective for an examination of the Nazi period. The peculiar tensions of the opening minutes—produced by a sound-track that seemed to know what it thought only to impress upon everyone the inherent uncertainty and contradiction of its knowledge—are extended to the entire film. The voice that glibly responds with an 'oh yeah' to everything it sees without being able to order its perceptions is the voice that controls the entire film. *Seven Beauties* is a vision of the past and of human possibility under the auspices of a cynicism whose manifest reason for being is the dominating presence of Pasqualino. Again, it is necessary to say, Pasqualino is not *man*—not for Wertmuller, not for the viewer of her film. He is a buffoon, a perennial victim who knows how to save his skin only by adopting the most transparent stratagems customarily available to the type. It never occurs to us to ask whether there is any actual human being who looks and behaves like the type because Pasqualino perfectly embodies what we have always taken the type to be.

Is it unreasonable that such a type should be said to have succeeded in saving his skin? Pasqualino may succeed, but nothing in the film suggests that anyone else would do as well in comparable circumstances. The strokes in Wertmuller's portrait are so broad, the caricature so playful and outrageously implausible, that no general conclusion may legitimately be drawn. We said earlier that the film asks us to focus "not so much on what happened as on what the imagination is wont to make of the holocaust experience." An imagination for which Pasqualino is a dominating presence is likely to be cynical in the extreme about the human truths revealed in the Nazi period. Who is to say, finally, what it takes to survive in a concentration camp? Surely Bettelheim understands that no program or strategy for survival was likely to be effective. Wertmuller's view is that while 'better men' perished, a man like Pasqualino might well have remained alive—not because he'd discovered a clever stratagem, but because he happened to be lucky. The film nowhere 'supports' Pasqualino or makes general claims for his shrewdness. On the contrary, he is ruthlessly exposed. We feel that he is detestable even as we want him to succeed in seducing the camp commander and saving his skin. When, finally, he shoots a fellow prisoner, he behaves only as we would expect him to under the circumstances. There is no use in denying that such a man might well do such a thing. Better men did worse things under pressure.

Bettelheim is surely mistaken in arguing that the film elaborates a morality of survivorship. There is nothing exemplary in Pasqualino's success, nothing anyone is encouraged to emulate. Wertmuller simply imposes upon us, with all the imaginative power at her command, an image we are not likely to forget. Though Pasqualino is not *man,* he is a figure of whom it is necessary to take stock when we think about our prospects and calculate the options. The imagination which cannot deal with Pasqualino, which cannot believe that he exists, does not know a very important part of the human condition. It may be that the type is overdrawn in Wertmuller's film; indeed, the elements of patent caricature and burlesque in the portrait encourage the view that Wertmuller deliberately exaggerated the features to provoke us and to indicate what were her major concerns. These have to do with the enlargement of imaginative potential, according to which it is possible to feel involved in Pasqualino's fate without capitulating to his view of the truth of things. Wertmuller's film succeeds precisely where Bettelheim thinks it fails: in its vivid distortions, in its strange conjunctions and grotesqueries, *Seven Beauties* compels a disinterested apprehension of issues. These are not primarily issues of historical fact but of imaginative resource: what, we consider, can the imagination do with the spectre of terror and banality acted out on a scale no one had previously imagined?

Bettelheim rejects not only the portrait of Pasqualino, but of the camp commander as well. The one is "no less a lie" than the other. Though the role is persuasively enacted by Shirley Stoler, though the viewer is led to "believe" in the character, she is a palpable untruth. This camp commander appears to know herself and to understand what makes other human beings behave as they do. In reality, camp commanders were nothing like this, Bettelheim argues. "Had they been able to recognize themselves as they really were. . . . they could not have carried on for a moment. . . . Somebody with so much insight into herself could not behave toward the prisoners as we see her do." This is one of those arguments it is difficult to win, whatever side you take. If you argue from experience, claiming that there are actual persons full of insight who nonetheless go right on doing terrible things, you will be told that such persons only *seem* to be in possession of the insights

they display. Just so, in the film, it is Wertmuller's dexterous manipulation of images that makes the camp commander *seem* plausible. The director's 'success' is a form of trickery, and we are duped because we do not know how to resist this kind of deception.

But Bettelheim's side of the argument is no easier to defend. It may be logical to suppose that someone capable of speaking seriously to herself about dehumanization would consequently wish to avoid dehumanizing others and so degrading herself. It is not therefore unlikely that this person will do what she despises and deliberately enact what others already take her to be. The logic of Bettelheim's argument is limited. It has very little to do with the peculiar logic of imagination, according to which truth and contradiction are often indistinguishable. Wertmuller might justly be attacked had she simply yielded to this peculiar logic, but she doesn't. She works at it, strenuously, and finds over and over again that her general suspicion of easy humanistic truths will not be dislodged. She remains cynical and resolutely disabused, largely because she is stuck with the figure of Pasqualino. If he is decidedly a part of *the thing itself,* what can his final antagonist be but a defiantly improbable and all too believable character? The working logic of *Seven Beauties* insists that the improbable is as potentially true to our experience of life as the probable. This has only marginally to do with the familiar notion of the absurd as a determinative factor in our experience. Wertmuller doesn't incline to make broad metaphysical statements. She is intent on following out a number of broad imaginative paths laid out by her involvement with certain kinds of human beings. These figures are, in her films, as likely to work in a factory as to be swept away on a desert island or to find themselves in a concentration camp. To think the portrait of the camp commander a lie is to reject the kind of imagination for which particular kinds of conflict and paradox are both interesting and important. There is nothing in *Seven Beauties* to prompt so determined a rejection.

But let us return, for a moment, to the question of historical truth. Suppose it was true that camp commanders were not persons of considerable depth, and that it was possible to prove this to anyone's satisfaction. Would Wertmuller's portrait be therefore less 'true,' less believable than it is? The circumstance as described here is so hypothetical that we are hard put to answer, but we must try. If Wertmuller's character ran counter to everything we know of camp commanders, we should naturally have greater difficulty in believing what we are shown. We should not readily be made to believe in a camp commander who did his best to save the lives of Jews and worked to make other Nazi camp officers cooperate in the effort to prevent destruction. No more can we believe in a camp commander who is nothing but a blundering fool, an idiot who is regularly taken advantage of by inmates and other officers. When we think of qualities of personal depth and insight, however, we are on more treacherous ground. Even if someone had proven beyond the shadow of a doubt that no camp commander possessed such qualities, we might well be induced to entertain further doubts. So vivid a portrait as Wertmuller draws would surely have a chance of shaking our faith in the efficacy of instruments used to test for personal qualities. We would, at least, suspend our disbelief in the possibility of an insightful camp commander. And this suspension of disbelief might well continue for the duration of the film—for so long as we continued to feel that issues raised and conflicts played out had something useful and entertaining to recommend them. Which is to say, the historical truth of the matter is only important to us when the context is such that we have been made to expect that kind of truth. Otherwise we are likely to be tolerant of 'violations' and to look for other truths the film may better get at.

Bettelheim assumes that *Seven Beauties* is an example of what we have called, following John Lukacs, cinematized history. It is nothing of the sort. It is a political film; it adumbrates political issues and asks political questions it does not feel required to answer. Like other works of this kind, it refuses to be held responsible for espousing correct positions. Its responsibility is to make us alert to problems it takes to be important, and to trace out the implications of various positions in a reasonably consistent way. It has room for considerable improbability and contradiction, provided only that primary expectations are not wantonly or cruelly violated. History is more than a background used to give depth to character, but it is not an end in itself. At most, history is that circumstance within which political conflicts work themselves out, and in which characters achieve usable designations. Without such 'history' as is furnished us in a film like *Seven Beauties,* we can distinguish victims from oppressors only by observing what

they do. We need to know as well what characters are supposed to be, what 'the record' has made of them. The early newsreel footage of the film indicates amply what we are to make of 'the record'; it can say ever so many different things depending on the predisposition we bring to it. Individual acts of brutality or cowardice are more difficult to get around. For Wertmuller, history is an uncertain domain within which we learn to fix particular acts and possibilities whose shape and meaning we both create and, in part, inherit. Politics, in a work for which history is more than background and less than determinate documentary fact, has to do with the problematic bringing to consciousness of social processes which for some persons always remain obscure and impenetrable. *Seven Beauties* is a political film in virtue of its persistent probing of the great social questions, in such a way that these questions come to seem unavoidable for each of us. Its use of history is instrumental to this end. (pp. 332-46)

Robert Boyers, "Politics & History: Pathways in European Film," in The Salmagundi Reader, *edited by Robert Boyers and Peggy Boyers, Indiana University Press, 1983, pp. 319-48.*

Piers Paul Read   (review date 12 September 1987)

[Read is an English novelist, editor, and nonfiction writer. In the review below, he provides a mixed assessment of A Good Enough Parent.*]*

Bruno Bettelheim, together with Erik H. Erikson, is rightly counted among the greatest child psychologists to have arisen since child psychology was invented. To the sceptical layman his greatest virtue is that his feet never leave the ground. On the whole he avoids jargon; the subconscious he refers to is one we can all accept; there are no grotesque presumptions of a Freudian, Jungian or Kleinian kind.

Like all professionals offering advice on the raising of children, he is faced with an immediate dilemma. If he is too forthright in laying down rules then he runs the risk of undermining the confidence of parents in their own instincts; yet if he fails to point out the common errors he has noticed in the course of his professional life, then children will continue to suffer from generation to generation.

[A Good Enough Parent] is a compromise. It is presented by the publishers as 'The Guide to Bringing Up Your Child'; but Dr Bettelheim himself is more cautious, saying that he only wants to

> encourage parents to do their own thinking about some aspects of child rearing in the hope that these examples will help them to find good solutions to whatever problems they may encounter in raising their child.

Nurturing is an art, not a science, but no one should aspire to genius. Being good enough is good enough: hence the title of the book.

Without trying to systematise Dr Bettelheim's thinking, since he never attempts to do this himself, it is possible to present some of his insights in an ordered form. His most important and fundamental point is that parents should

---

An excerpt from *A Good Enough Parent: A Book on Childrearing*

This book sums up my lifelong effort to discover and test what is involved and required for successful child-rearing—that is, the raising of a child who may not necessarily become a success in the eyes of the world, but who on reflection would be well pleased with the way he was raised, and who would decide that, by and large, he is satisfied with himself, despite the shortcomings to which all of us are prey. I believe that another indication of having been raised well is a person's ability to cope reasonably well with the endless vicissitudes, the many hardships, and the serious difficulties he is likely to encounter in life, and to do so mainly because he feels secure in himself. Although not always free of self-doubt—since only arrogant fools are entirely free of that—whatever happens in his external life, such a person who has been well raised possesses an inner life which is rich and rewarding, and with which he is hence satisfied. Last but certainly not least, to grow up in a family where good, intimate relationships between the parents and between them and their children are at all times maintained makes an individual capable of forming lasting, satisfying, intimate relationships to others, which give meaning to his and to their lives. He will also be able to find meaning and satisfaction in his work, finding it worth the efforts he puts into it, because he will not be satisfied with doing work that is devoid of intrinsic meaning.

Bruno Bettelheim, in his A Good Enough Parent: A Book on Childrearing, *Random House, Inc., 1987.*

---

beware of using their children for their own psychic purposes—projecting on to them their own values and ambitions, perhaps urging them to succeed where they failed in fields quite unsuited to the child's particular talents. They should also respect children's priorities: playing for them is quite as important as working for their parents. A child, he insists, must always be regarded as an autonomous personality, and the parents' 'most important task and obligation is to create in their child the inner conditions for his psychological and emotional well-being—and this not for the moment but for all his future'.

Parents should never underestimate the role they play in developing this sense of well-being. 'It is sad', writes Bettelheim, 'when parents fail to realise how terribly important they are to their children'; first in helping 'an infant to develop a healthy and positive attitude towards his body: to make him feel good about what it can do, and at the same time conveying to him how much they love and value it, so that the child will do the same'; and later in presenting a consistent system of values which they adhere to themselves.

He thinks it particularly important that parents should be honest and authentic with their children—even at an early age. A child can sense, for example, when 'you need your sleep' means 'we want you out of the way': it is better, says Bettelheim, to explain to the child that Mummy and Daddy want supper on their own. They should also practise what they preach: children will see through their parents' posturing, and sniff out their inconsistencies, becoming confused by contradictory signals from, say, the lecherous and greedy Christian or the Labour voter who sends his children to private schools (my examples, not his).

What makes things difficult for the parent is that the damage he does to his child's sense of security and self-esteem is invariably unconscious: thus Dr Bettelheim's message to parents is, in essence, 'know thyself', and get to know thyself by empathising with your own children, remembering how you felt at that stage in life. This leads to a somewhat indulgent attitude towards discipline. He is against punishment because

> any punishment, however justified in our eyes and even those of our child, interferes with our main goals, namely that our child should love us, accept our values, and want to live what we consider a moral life.

Instead of smacking a child, or even rebuking him, he would have us tell him that we are sure that if he had known he was in the wrong he would not have done it. This increases 'his self-respect and his love for us, and all this entails'.

Not only does this advice conjure up horribly cloying conversations between parents and their naughty children, it also seems to presume that there is no such thing as original sin—that children are never naughty, knowing that they are naughty, perhaps to test their parents' confidence in the rules they have made. Moreover since Bettelheim rarely makes clear the age of the child to which his advice pertains, it is difficult to judge upon the practicality of his advice. One might accept that 'during the period of adolescent turmoil, it is best when parents can *accept* their adolescent's odd, antagonistic or otherwise unpleasant behaviour *without approving it*'; but when one finds, for example, a six-year-old daughter in a towering rage, flogging her eight-year-old brother with a skipping rope, it seems absurd to consider, as Bettelheim suggests, 'the safeguards we are entitled to before we can be judged by society' (legal representation, trial by jury, etc). A quick smack seems the best solution.

One should bear in mind, perhaps, that while Dr Bettelheim was born and trained in Vienna, and was formed by European institutions (including Dachau and Buchenwald), his clinical experience has been largely in the United States. For this reason we can forgive him the odd horrible phrase like 'meaningful as part of a relationship' and the cautious, almost apologetic, way in which he urges parents to put their children's interests before their own. It is, after all, partly the spread of psychoanalytic concepts of individual fulfilment ('individuation') among analysis-orientated Americans, which has led to an egocentric attitude towards breeding. It would have been deemed evil, for example, in less enlightened times for educated women deliberately to conceive a child outside marriage. Now it is almost fashionable. In the same way divorce was abhorred because it destroyed what was necessary for the successful nurturing of the child. The importance of Dr Bettelheim's book is that it reteaches us many truths about raising a family which were common sense before. (pp. 33-4)

Piers Paul Read, "The Smack of Firm Government," in The Spectator, *Vol. 259, No. 8304, September 12, 1987, pp. 33-4.*

Ralph Tutt   (essay date 1989)

[*In the following excerpt, Tutt negatively assesses "Surviving" based on the arguments put forth in* The Uses of Enchantment.]

The 1982 film version of *Sophie's Choice* completed a cycle of mainstream novels, films, stage plays and TV dramas which in the sixties and seventies had increasingly appropriated the Holocaust for artistic purposes. No film in this cycle has commanded more attention and respect that Lina Wertmüller's *Seven Beauties* (1976), and no scholar has been more provocative in assessing its virtues—and defects—than Bruno Bettelheim. Although Wertmüller's stature as a filmmaker has diminished considerably in recent years, *Seven Beauties* remains a classic of the Holocaust genre. It is frequently revived at art houses, and Bettelheim's essay on the film, **"Surviving,"** first published in 1976, has become standard reading in the humanities curriculum, along with his book on fairy tales, **The Uses of Enchantment,** published the same year.

"It is every Italian director's dream to be loved in America," Wertmüller said on her first trip to this country in 1975. *Seven Beauties,* her fourth American release, was declared "a masterpiece" by the exacting—and frequently eccentric—John Simon, and lavishly praised by American critics generally. In reaction to its acclaim, Bettelheim filled fifty columns of *The New Yorker* with misgivings about its moral and political implications and objections to Wertmüller's perversion of fact in her treatment of concentration camp life. A survivor of Auschwitz and Buchenwald, Bettelheim was offended by the concentration camp setting for what *Time* had suitably called a "death-house-comedy." The success of *Seven Beauties* indicated to him the inability of the present generation to comprehend traumatic events suffered by their elders. For all the tribute Bettelheim pays Wertmüller's artistry, the skill with which she neutralizes horror with macabre comedy, he cannot accept the use of a concentration camp setting which falsifies and degrades experiences he and others survived during the War. He would remain silent on the subject of *Seven Beauties,* he tells us, were it not for the fact that the comedy of survival the film presents is a travesty of true survival. He rejects the idea that crude claims of the body alone can sustain the will to survive and holds himself, along with other concentration camp survivors, an embarrassing witness to the truth that without a sense of meaning in life there can be no survival. Accepting Hannah Arendt's thesis on the banality of evil in her book on the Eichmann trial [*Eichmann in Jerusalem: A Report on the Banality of Evil* (1963)], Bettelheim advises us to be on guard against that very banality: we must not allow it to desensitize us to the fact of evil and its consequences. In his view, Pasqualino, the protagonist of *Seven Beauties,* is banality personified.

"The trouble with Eichmann," Arendt wrote, "was precisely that so many were like him, and that the many were neither perverted nor sadistic, that they were and still are, terribly and terrifyingly normal." Pasqualino is banal in this sense, to be sure, but he is no Eichmann. Nowhere in *Seven Beauties* is he devoid of moral conscience. He is not a bureaucrat for whom genocide is all in a day's work. Throughout his criminal career, he is an honor-bound, conscience-stricken stumblebum who agonizes over his crimes and pays for them in descending circles of hell until, having learned the price of political apathy, he is equivocally reborn at the end of the film.

At the height of his beauty, groomed to kill with full moustache and slicked-back hair, Pasqualino Settebellezze as played by Giancarlo Giannini is a Chaplinesque Valentino blithely approaching an obstacle course which will take him from sunny Naples to a foggy chamber of horrors called Appleplatz. As he strolls the streets of Naples, all the young women moon over him, but the only one to whom he gives serious attention is an organ grinder waif named Carolina. Reduced to tears by her heckling audience, Carolina is consoled by Pasquilino. "If someone is disrespectful," he tells her, "you tell them you're engaged to me. Just repeat these words . . . I am engaged to Pasqualino Settebellezze."

At home in Naples, women lose their heads over him. At Appleplatz, he hits upon a plan to save himself by seducing Hilde, the beastly commandant, when he recalls advice his mother gave him as a child that, tucked away somewhere in every woman, no matter how wicked, there has got to be some sweetness, some goodness that will surface if a man finds the way of looking into her heart. The ultimate test of Pasqualino's "beauty" (moral and physical)

is sexual confrontation with the Beast of Appleplatz. As Bettelheim points out, Hilde is not without redeemable human qualities. To his credit as an esthetician, he does not complain of factual discrepancies between the fictional character, Hilde, and the Beast of Buchenwald, but he does overlook the obvious resemblance of Hilde to the male beast of the fairy tale, "Beauty and the Beast."

In *The Uses of Enchantment,* Bettelheim urges parents and teachers to assign fairy tales once again to the central role they held for centuries in the life of the child. He disapproves of the dominant cultural tendency to try and keep children safe from the dark side of human nature. Fairy tales, he insists, have traditionally met the child's need to know evil as well as good. They have helped children master a great many psychological problems in the process of growing up—"overcoming narcissistic disappointments, Oedipal dilemmas, sibling rivalries; becoming able to relinquish childhood dependencies; gaining a feeling of self-hood and of self-worth, and a sense of moral obligation."

Bettelheim's appreciation of the Dionysian energy of fairy tales for children is all the more generous for his assurance of their Appollonian after-effects. "Beauty and the Beast," as he summarizes it, is a "wonderfully healing story" about the transfer of Oedipal love from father to husband. Like "Bluebeard," it is one of the darker tales for children teaching the Freudian lesson that "only by struggling courageously against what seem like overwhelming odds can man succeed in wringing meaning out of his existence." *The Uses of Enchantment* is a book predicated on Freudian faith in the upheaval of the subconscious with Horatio Alger results. The meaning and importance of fairy tales for Bettelheim is that they communicate the harsher psychological realities of life while reassuring the child of moral victory in adulthood.

> This is exactly the message that fairy tales get across to the child in manifold form: that a struggle against severe difficulties in life is unavoidable, is an intrinsic part of human existence—but that if one does not shy away, but steadfastly meets the unexpected and often unjust hardships, one masters all the obstacles and at the end emerges victorious.

Bettelheim's appreciation of the meliorism of fairy tales for children is hard to fault; when he turns his attention to a fairy tale for adults like Wertmüller's *Seven Beauties,* however, his moralistic nature is perplexed. Surviving innocence is one thing; adult survival in the revolutionary world Wertmüller depicts in her films another. Child psychologist Bettelheim is so hopeful for the innocent that he can't embrace the quotidian of the fallen. (pp. 193-95)

According to Bettelheim, [Pasqualino] survives "without feeling, and without any purpose other than propagating himself. He does not feel guilty for Pedro's death, which he brought about; or for having said yes to Fascism; or for having killed Francesco and butchered Totonno." Guilt, says Bettelheim, is what separates the true survivor from those who applaud *Seven Beauties.*

If Wertmüller is guilty of perverting facts of concentration

> Bettelheim's appreciation of the meliorism
> of fairy tales for children is hard to fault;
> when he turns his attention to a fairy tale
> for adults like Wertmüller's *Seven
> Beauties,* however, his moralistic nature is
> perplexed. Surviving innocence is one
> thing; adult survival in the revolutionary
> world Wertmüller depicts in her films
> another. Child psychologist Bettelheim is
> so hopeful for the innocent that he can't
> embrace the quotidian of the fallen.
>
> —*Ralph Tutt*

camp life, Bettelheim is guilty of perverting the content of her film. His sense of reality and truth blind him to the reality and truth of Pasqualino who, in typical fairy-tale fashion, proceeds from callow youth in Naples to existential manhood at Appleplatz. In the final scene of the film, the liberated Pasqualino comes home to a brightly lit, garishly colored, liberated Naples overrun with GIs. His sisters, it is clear, have flourished in their [prostitution]. Carolina, innocent when he befriended her before the War, has fallen into the same profession, though she is still faithful to his memory. Pasqalino, gazing blankly into a mirror at the end, is not, as Bettelheim describes him, "nonchalant."

"Look how handsome you are!" his mother says. "Don't think about the past. . . . You're alive, Pasqualino . . . alive." "Yeah," he replies, "I'm alive." His voice and his eyes are those of a paranoid. Aware of tumultuous crowds high on victory in the alley outside his home, he expresses to Carolina in monotone the wish to marry and start having children at once. "We haven't got much time. I want lots of them, twenty-five, thirty . . . we have to become strong because we must defend ourselves. Do you hear them out there?"

If it is these lines that Bettelheim takes to indicate Pasqualino has embraced Fascism, he misses a major point of the film: the dangerous consequences of political apathy. In his traumatic state Pasqualino seems on the verge of political conversion. "In a few years we'll start killing each other for a glass of water . . . for a chunk of bread. . . . That's why there have to be a lot of us, in order to defend ourselves." It is Pedro's words that he echoes here; it would therefore seem to be Pedro's dream of a master race, not Hilde's, that he has in mind: "I believe in mankind. A new type of man must hurry up and appear . . . not the type of beast which has unbalanced the harmony of nature up to now, but a civilized man, a man who would be able to find peace and harmony within himself."

The presence of Carolina in the final scene suggests hope for Pasqualino and their children. Though she is no longer "pure," she is still innocent, and her eyes are radiant with love for him. Like Paola, the young girl on the beach at the end of Fellini's *La Dolce Vita,* she has within her the

power to redeem the humanity of a jaundiced older man. The Neapolitan Monster may yet be restored to Seven Beauties.

John Simon, Wertmüller's strongest booster in America, dismisses Bettelheim's essay on *Seven Beauties* as an "obtuse" and "notorious" attack. Whatever its notoriety, the essay is not obtuse; nor is it really an attack. Despite the length at which he discusses the film, the essay reveals more of Bettelheim than it does of *Seven Beauties;* if it is not exactly adulatory, neither is it a wholehearted indictment, and the length in itself is an indication of the film's hold on him. In his concern with its impact on those embarrassing witnesses to the truth—the actual survivors of Nazi concentration camps—and in his fear that its "raucous" humor may be intended for no purpose other than entertainment, Bettelheim suggests that audiences of the present generation have responded gleefully to that humor. He does not consider the possibility that those swept away by *Seven Beauties* may also be deeply disturbed by it, perhaps not so disturbed as the embarrassing witnesses, but disturbed nonetheless.

As a film analyst, child psychologist Bettelheim is at his best explaining the manner in which Wertmüller, by her swift alternation of mood, effectively plays on our emotions:

> We experience horror, then something grotesquely comic or funny, the scenes of brutality, then farcical humor again. With this technique, the horror becomes background for the comic scene, and the comic scene wipes out not the fact of the horror but its emotional impact, with the result that the horror adds, by contrast, to the effectiveness of the comic experience. Such quick manipulation of our emotions makes it impossible for us to go on taking seriously our emotional reactions to what we see on the screen, even though we do go on responding to it. . . .

His perception of Wertmüller's method is accurate enough, but his assumptions about its emotional effect questionable. Is the film a meaningless triumph of comedy over horror? Does the quick alternation of humor and horror necessarily diminish all serious sense of the action so that what we wind up watching is "a farce played in a charnel house?" What are we to make finally of his conclusion that Wertmüller's artistry is "dangerously seductive" because it does not induce us to commit ourselves seriously to events that would normally upset or move us?

Bettelheim esthetician is troubled and finally overcome by Bettelheim moralist. His purpose in writing the essay on *Seven Beauties* was to correct popular misconceptions about the Holocaust and sort out his own reflections on the relationship between life and art. He is finally unable—or unwilling—to accept a commonplace: between factual recording and artistic rendering of experience, there is a no-man's-land. Moreover, there are as many ways of looking at cold historical facts as there are of looking at a blackbird or at a jar on the top of a hill in Tennessee.

In *Seven Beauties* Wertmüller blends fact with fantasy as skillfully as she neutralizes horror with comedy. She cannot be faulted for misappropriation of a dreadful historic epoch, because she makes no claim to historical authenticity. Tornadoes, hurricanes, earthquakes, slave ships and shipwrecks, whips and lashes, mass murder and secret burial, starvation and cannibalism, moon landings, meltdown, and fallout—this is the stuff of history, both human and natural, past and possible—and all of us feed on it in our imaginings of the past as it impinges upon present fears about survival. The imagination never operates independently of facts. In the art of enchantment, facts of human evil are as valid—as those of natural cycles and catastrophe. In his attempt to reconcile the truth of life with that of art, Bettelheim misrepresents *Seven Beauties*. The film, he acknowledges, is a work of art. Because it is a work of art which resists his appeal for historical authenticity and an affirmative vision of survival, his argument fails. (pp. 199-201)

> Ralph Tutt, "Seven Beauties and the Beast: Bettelheim, Wertmüller, and the Uses of Enchantment," in Literature/Film Quarterly, Vol. 17, No. 3, 1989, pp. 193-201.

Alan Dundes   (essay date Winter 1991)

[*Dundes is an American instructor of English, anthropology, and folklore whose works include* Life Is Like a Chicken Coop Ladder: A Portrait of German Culture through Folklore *(1984), and* Parsing through Customs: Essays by a Freudian Folklorist *(1987). In the following essay, he praises* The Uses of Enchantment *as a book easily understood by popular audiences, but criticizes Bettelheim's research methods and scholarship.*]

The late Bruno Bettelheim (1903-1990) was one of a distinguished set of psychoanalysts going back to Freud himself who was not afraid to apply the insights gained from psychoanalytic practice to a wide variety of cultural materials. These individuals include Otto Rank, Ernest Jones, and Géza Róheim, among others. A common thread in their applied psychoanalytic writings is a fascination with folklore.

In 1911, Freud coauthored with mythologist Oppenheim a small but nonetheless insightful essay entitled *Dreams in Folklore* which was unfortunately not published until 1958. In this important paper, Freud and Oppenheim demonstrated that the symbolism of dreams which were told as part of traditional folktales corresponded exactly with so-called Freudian symbolism. Moreover, the exegeses of the dreams contained in the folktales were explicated by the folk who had no knowledge of Freudian theory. Since the tales were much older than Freud and his theories, the folk interpretations of dream symbols provided a valuable authentic confirmation of the validity of Freudian symbolism. This striking congruence of folklore data and Freudian theory has not received the attention it deserves from either folklorists or psychoanalysts.

Other landmarks in the psychoanalytic study of folklore include Otto Rank's pioneering *The Myth of the Birth of the Hero*, first published in 1909; Ernest Jones's provocative 1928 paper "Psycho-Analysis and Folklore," and Géza Róheim's 1952 *The Gates of the Dream*.

It is in this context that I wish to consider Bruno Bettel-

heim's remarkable foray into the world of fairy tales. In *The Uses of Enchantment: The Meaning and Importance of Fairy Tales,* first published in 1976, Bettelheim offers both an eloquent plea for the continued telling of fairy tales to children and a series of in-depth content analyses of a dozen or so of the best known Indo-European fairy tales. The basic position so ardently advocated by Bettelheim with respect to fairy tales is more obvious from the title of the German translation of the book: *Kinder brauchen Märchen,* that is, "Children need fairy tales." In Bettelheim's opinion, fairy tales were helpful to children "in helping them cope with the psychological problems of growing up and integrating their personalities." In a somewhat sentimental essay in which he confesses that "Hansel and Gretel" is his favorite fairy tale, Bettelheim relates its content to events in his own childhood.

For Bettelheim, fairy tales are absolutely essential for the mental health of children. Fairy tales function much like dreams, according to Bettelheim. "As we awake refreshed from our dreams, better able to meet the tasks of reality, so the fairy story ends with the hero returning, or being returned to the real world, much better able to master life." Just as dream deprivation research suggests that individuals prevented from dreaming during the night become emotionally disturbed, so Bettelheim argues, perhaps by analogy fairy tale deprivation will prevent children from working through the unconscious pressures in their lives. Bettelheim maintains that "fairy tales offer figures onto which the child can externalize what goes on in his mind" and that if the child is deprived of fairy tales, he may not be able to "invent stories on his own which help him to cope with life's problems." Bettelheim also points out aptly that "by denying access to stories which implicitly tell the child that others have the same fantasies, he is left to feel that he is the only one who imagines such things. This makes his fantasies really scary."

In Bettelheim's scheme of things, fairy tales provide a necessary forum for the playing out of interpersonal problems, for example, sibling rivalry or parent-child conflicts, but they supposedly do so without the child's being consciously aware of the fact. In his words, one should "let the fairy tale speak to his [the child's] unconscious, give body to his unconscious anxieties, and relieve them, without this ever coming to conscious awareness." In fact, Bettelheim insists that the parent and teacher should specifically refrain from telling children anything about the possible unconscious content of fairy tales. "Fairy tales can and do serve children well, can even make an unbearable life seem worth living, as long as the child doesn't know what they mean to him psychologically." Bettelheim is adamant on this point: "One must never 'explain' to the child the meanings of fairy tales." He further claims that explaining to a child why a fairy tale is so captivating to him destroys the story's enchantment.

Presumably then Bettelheim's essentially Freudian readings of such fairy tales as "Hansel and Gretel" (Arne-Thompson tale type 327A), "Little Red Riding Hood" (AT 333), "Jack and the Beanstalk" (AT 328), "Snow White" (AT 709), "Goldilocks and the Three Bears," "Sleeping Beauty" (AT 410), and "Cinderella" (AT

510A) are meant for parents and teachers. Bettelheim's goal appears to be to enlighten those parents and educators who unwisely seek to keep fairy tales away from children at precisely that point in children's lives when they most need them.

It is interesting that Bettelheim is dissatisfied with the story of the "Three Bears" in the light of his general overall approach—[in his review of *The Uses of Enchantment* appearing in *The New York Times Book Review* (23 May 1976), John] Updike characterizes Bettelheim's discussion of the tale as having a "rather grumpy tone." Bettelheim observes that the story lacks some of the important features of true fairy tales—no resolution of conflict, no happy ending. Goldilocks, according to Bettelheim, does not achieve any "higher selfhood" as heroes and heroines normally do in conventional folktales. The tale actually is not included in the Aarne-Thompson Indo-European folktale canon, perhaps because its initial orality is in some doubt. It is for the most part a tale that has flourished in literary rather than folk tradition. Bettelheim is quite right when he distinguishes the oral as opposed to the written transmission process. "When a story exists only in oral tradition," he notes, "it is largely the teller's unconscious that determines what story he relates, and what of it he remembers." Over the course of time, it is the many such oral repetitions of a story that hone its content to achieve what Bettelheim calls the tale's classic form which appeals to a consensus unconscious of many individuals.

Bettelheim is also to be praised for his strong opposition to illustrated children's book versions of fairy tales. He argues persuasively that the illustrations tend to be distracting rather than helpful and that they direct the child's imagination away from how he or she would experience the story. A child's imagination has no limits, but professional artists' illustrations tend to impose unnecessary and unwelcome restrictions on what a dragon or a princess looks like. Bettelheim's vocal opposition to artists' illustrations of fairy tales is entirely consonant with his overall view that fairy tales should not be explained to children. Printed illustrations are in effect an attempt to explain to the child how the characters or events of a fairy tale should be pictured. Bettelheim's criticisms of the literary rewriting of oral fairy tales were also just, especially his objections to the severe bowdlerizations of Charles Perrault.

Many of Bettelheim's readings of individual tales are exemplary. His ingenious identification of sibling rivalry in "Goldilocks and the Three Bears," his discussion of the underlying oedipal theme in "Cinderella," and his brilliant analysis of "Beauty and the Beast" as a successful resolution of the oedipal conflict whereby a girl's initial attachment to her father is transferred to an animal transformed into a husband, are all cases in point. However, the undeniable merits of Bettelheim's intellectual odyssey in the world of fairy tales are badly marred by several serious mistakes.

There are two major sins in *The Uses of Enchantment,* one of omission and one of commission. Let us consider the sin of omission first. If one wished to write a book devoted to the psychoanalytic study of folktales, one would in theory wish to consult two sets of sources. The first would be the folkloristic treatments of the tales under consideration and the second would be previous psychoanalytic exegeses of the same tales. From his footnotes, we can easily determine that Bettelheim did examine some relevant sources, but that he failed to read many others.

Bettelheim's lack of familiarity with conventional folkloristics leads him to make a number of erroneous statements. For example, he claims "in most cultures, there is no clear line separating myth from folk or fairy tale." The fact is that almost every society distinguishes between stories that are true and stories that are fictional. A myth is a sacred narrative explaining how the world and its human inhabitants came to be in their present form. It is set in the remote past. Folktales are fiction as signaled by an opening formula such as "Once upon a time" and they are set in no particular place or time. Bettelheim continues to blunder when he states that "German has retained the word *Sage* for myths, while fairy stories are called *Märchen.*" The second part of the statement is correct, but the first part confuses myth and legend. *Sage* in German definitely refers to legend, not myth. This error is surprising inasmuch as Bettelheim was a native speaker of German.

In other instances, Bettelheim is simply ignorant of relevant scholarship. For example, Bettelheim remarks that polarization dominates fairy tales. "A person is either good or bad, nothing in between. One brother is stupid, the other is clever. One sister is virtuous and industrious, the others are vile and lazy. One is beautiful, the others are ugly. One parent is all good, the other evil." Bettelheim is quite right, of course, but all this is what Danish folklorist Axel Olrik described under the rubric of the "Law of Contrast," one of what he termed epic laws which were characteristic of folk literature. Olrik carefully delineated these epic laws in the first decade of the 20th century in a classic essay which was translated into English in 1965 ["Epic Laws of Folk Narrative," in Alan Dundes's *The Study of Folklore* (1965)].

Similarly, Bettelheim wrestles with the possible significance of the number three in fairy tales. This corresponds to what Olrik called the "Law of Three." Bettelheim is well aware of the conventional Freudian interpretation of the number three as standing for the male genitals (penis plus two testicles), but he seems to prefer the non-Freudian reading of three as symbolizing two parents plus a child, thus explaining why the child can so readily identify with that number. However, the occurrence of tripartition as an all pervasive form of "three-determined" thought in Western culture generally—that is, outside of the immediate world of fairy tales—would tend to weaken his argument.

Since Bettelheim does not pretend to be a folklorist, one can understand why he might have missed several key folkloristic sources. What is less easy to forgive is his failure to read earlier psychoanalytic studies of the tales he selected for analysis. While Bettelheim does admit in a footnote that a few fairy tales had been previously discussed psychoanalytically, there is nary a mention of many of the most important pioneering studies, for example, Franz Ricklin's pathbreaking *Wishfulfillment and*

Symbolism in Fairy Tales, first published in German in 1908, or the many essays by Géza Róheim, perhaps the only psychoanalyst who began his career as a folklorist. Bettelheim's neglect of Róheim is especially egregious as Róheim wrote whole essays on many of the tales Bettelheim chose to analyze, for example, "Hansel and Gretel" and "Little Red Riding Hood." It is not that Bettelheim necessarily would have agreed with Róheim's interpretation of a particular tale, but only that it is a standard academic credo that one begins one's own research where previous investigators have ended theirs.

Bettelheim's discussion of the latent content of "Jack and the Beanstalk" (AT 328) is typical. First of all, he makes no reference whatever to previous psychoanalytic interpretations of the tale. Most of what Bettelheim has to say about the tale from a psychoanalytic perspective had already been noted by earlier analysts. On the other hand, his suggestion that the detail of the good cow, Milk White, suddenly stopping to give milk might represent a symbolic maternal expulsion from an infantile oral paradise (in which weaning abruptly begins) is brilliant. Far less persuasive is his strange contention that the hiding of Jack by the ogre's wife in her oven symbolizes oral regression. The oven from a Freudian perspective is a pretty standard womb symbol—cf. to have a "bun in the oven" is a folk metaphor for pregnancy. Jack's hiding in the ogre's wife's oven is either a return to the womb or an act of overt aggression against the threatening father-figure ogre by entering the mother-figure's genital area. Bettelheim also fails to discuss the cutting down of the beanstalk in terms of castration symbolism, and although he is cognizant of the masturbatory overtones of the tale, he does not comment on the possible symbolic implications of Jack's stealing the magical harp that *plays by itself* in this context. The upshot of all this is that Bettelheim's analysis is surely insightful, but his scholarship is sloppy. He certainly should have read what other psychoanalysts had to say about the same tale. Had he done so, his own analysis might have been much more comprehensive and complete.

In those instances where Bettelheim's interpretation of a fairy tale differs markedly from earlier ones, it is especially annoying for the sophisticated reader not to have the benefit of Bettelheim's criticism of the earlier analyses. For example, comparison reveals that Bettelheim and Róheim came to vastly different psychoanalytic readings of the same fairy tale. Bettelheim sees the tale of "Little Red Riding Hood" in oedipal terms. Little Red Riding Hood's "danger is her budding sexuality, for which she is not yet emotionally mature enough" and the tale "deals with the daughter's unconscious wish to be seduced by her father (the wolf)." Bettelheim specifically rejects any oral aggressive element in the tale stating baldly that Little Red Riding Hood "has outgrown her oral fixation" and that she "no longer has any destructive desires." This interpretation may be contrasted to Róheim's earlier one in which he argues that the tale is about infantile oral aggression. [Roheim writes in "Fairy Tale and Dream," *The Psychoanalytic Study of the Child* 8 (1953):] "Aggression is combined with regression and it follows that the idea of being swallowed, being eaten, is the talio aspect of this aggression. The cannibal child creates a cannibal mother." In

Róheim's defense, it is true that the oral versions of the tale found in Asia: China, Japan, and Korea, as well as in Europe (France and Italy), the heroine does eat the flesh of her grandmother, a detail obviously omitted from the sanitized versions of the tale to be found in Perrault and Grimm. In the majority of the oral French versions, the wolf having killed the grandmother puts her blood in a container and her flesh on a plate. When Little Red Riding Hood arrives at her grandmother's cottage, she complains of being hungry and thirsty. The wolf in disguise invites her to eat and drink what is in the cupboard. When she does so, the wolf, or in some versions a passing cat or bird, chastizes the girl by saying "You are eating the flesh of your grandmother and you are drinking the blood of your grandmother." From a Róheimian perspective, eating the flesh and blood of one's (grand)mother is clearly an act of oral aggression. In one explicit French text from Valencay, reported in 1893, a mysterious voice sings to Little Red Riding Hood: "Tu manges de ma titine" which might be rendered in English as "You are eating my breast" [Eugène Rolland, "Le Petit Chaperon Rouge," *Mélusine* 6 (1892-93)]. This kind of textual evidence would certainly tend to corroborate Róheim's reading of the tale and to give pause to anyone advocating Bettelheim's claim that Little Red Riding Hood no longer has any destructive desires.

There are other mistakes and omissions. It is bad enough that Bettelheim claims the story of Oedipus is a myth—Bettelheim calls it "that paradigmatic myth of psychoanalysis," a common enough error among psychoanalysts who are unaware of the fact that the story is a standard Indo-European folktale (AT 931)—but he goes on to exclaim "how different are the ways the fairy tale and this classic myth present oedipal relations and their consequences." The tale of Oedipus actually reflects a fair amount of wishful thinking insofar as a young male kills his father and marries his mother! Moreover, in the oral versions of the folktale (as opposed to the better-known literary adaptation by Sophocles), there are marvelous details which could provide grist for the psychoanalytic mill. For example, the hero often kills his father in the hero's mother's garden or orchard where the hero is standing watch at night. Killing an intruder *at night* who attempts to enter the mother's "garden" is an extraordinarily revealing element of the standard Oedipus folktale. In any event, Bettelheim in his own attempt to analyze the plot is totally oblivious of any of the huge mass of scholarship devoted to Oedipus including the superb paper by George Devereux, "Why Oedipus Killed Laius," that first appeared in the *International Journal of Psychoanalysis* in 1953, and the stunning psychoanalytic study of Greek mythology in general, *The Glory of Hera*, by Philip D. Slater in 1968.

There is little point in documenting Bettelheim's failure to consult relevant scholarship for each of the tales he considers. One further example can stand for all. Bettelheim references neither folklorist nor psychoanalyst in his discussion of "Snow White." He does mention [J. F. Grant Duff's "Schneewuttchen: Versuch einer psychoanalytischen Deutung," *Imago* 20 (1934)] elsewhere in a footnote but he evidently did not read the standard folkloristic studies by [Ernst Böklen, *Schneewittchenstudien* (1910), and Max Lüthi, *Schneewittchen. So leben sie noch hevle; Betrachtungan zum Volksmärchen* (1969)] or the psychological interpretations by [A. N. Foxe, "Terrorization of the Libido and Snow White" in *Psychoanalytic Review* 27 (1940), and A. S. Macquisten and R. W. Pickford, "Psychological Aspects of the Fantasy of Snow White and the Seven Dwarfs" in *Psychoanalytic Review* 29 (1942)].

Other outright errors could be mentioned. "Cupid and Psyche" is *not* a myth as Bettelheim claims, but a standard version of a widespread fairy tale, namely AT 425A, "The Monster (Animal) as Bridegroom." Perrault did *not* invent the glass slipper motif in "Cinderella", it is a traditional motif that has nothing whatever to do with an alleged homonymic relationship between "verre" [glass] and "vair" [fur], a spurious *explication de texte* which indeed only reaffirms the symbolism of the slipper as female genital.

Had Bettelheim read more of the relevant scholarship, he might have put it to good use. For example, he could have profited from a reading of Vladimir Propp's 1928 *Morphology of the Folktale* which has been available in English translation since 1958. Propp's 31-element syntagmatic structural scheme purportedly delineates the basic underlying sequential structure of all Russian (and perhaps Indo-European) fairy tales (Aarne-Thompson tale types 300-749). Bettelheim in the course of his analysis of "Brother and Sister" (AT 450) observes: "The story also suggests the two great upheavals in life: leaving the parental home, and creating one's own family." Propp's first element or function is: "One of the Members of a Family Absents Himself from Home" while the final, thirty-first function is: "The Hero is Married and Ascends the Throne." The point is that what Bettelheim noticed in one particular tale is to be found in *all* fairy tales. Moreover, the Proppian model would also lend credence to Bettelheim's oedipal remark made with respect to the tale of "Two Brothers" (AT 303) that "we must free ourselves of our oedipal attachments" and "we can do so most successfully by establishing an independent existence away from our parental home."

In his analysis of "Hansel and Gretel," Bettelheim might have benefited from the knowledge that in the original tale collected by the Grimm brothers, the character who sends the children to the woods is not the children's stepmother, but their actual mother. It was only in the fourth edition of the tales that the mother was changed by the Grimms to stepmother, precisely the kinds of meddling change deplored by Bettelheim, a change that tends to obscure the content of oral tales.

Thus far we have spoken only of Bettelheim's sin of omission, his failure to cite pertinent scholarship in folklore and psychoanalysis. But it is, unfortunately, Bettelheim's sin of commission that is more serious. Bettelheim did do some reading of sources in preparation for writing *The Uses of Enchantment* and it is his treatment of these sources that constitutes his second sin.

It is not surprising to find parallels between Bettelheim's book and earlier writings on the same subject. For example, Bettelheim attempted to distinguish between myth and folktale. "An even more significant difference between these two kinds of story is the ending, which in myths is nearly always tragic, while always happy in fairy tales." More than 35 years earlier, Róheim wrote, "A folktale is a narrative with a happy end, a myth is a tragedy" ["Myth and Folk-Tale," *American Imago* 2 (1941)]. Róheim is not cited at all by Bettelheim so this may be merely a matter of great minds thinking alike. The same holds for Bettelheim's remarks on projection or what I have elsewhere termed "projective inversion." In his discussion of "Snow White," Bettelheim remarks: "the wish to be rid of the parent arouses great guilt. . . . So in a reversal which eliminates the guilt feeling, this wish, too, is projected onto the parent. Thus in fairy tales there are parents who try to rid themselves of their child." This passage may be compared to a pioneering statement made by Otto Rank in his *The Myth of the Birth of the Hero* more than half a century before: "The fictitious romance is the excuse, as it were, for the hostile feelings which the child harbors against his father, and which in this fiction are projected against the father. . . . The child simply gets rid of the father in the neurotic romance, while in the myth the father endeavors to lose the child." I am not contending that Bettelheim consciously or unconsciously borrowed anything from Otto Rank, but only that Rank deserves credit for the insight seemingly articulated for the first time by Bettelheim.

One of the earlier books written on the psychoanalytic study of fairy tales was Julius E. Heuscher's *A Psychiatric Study of Fairy Tales: Their Origin, Meaning and Usefulness,* published in 1963. Although [James W. Heisig in his "Bruno Bettelheim and the Fairy Tales," *Children's Literature* 6 (1977)] wrongly chastizes Bettelheim for not mentioning this book, Bettelheim did refer to the book *en passant* in a footnote. A cursory comparison reveals that the order of the fairy tales discussed in both Heuscher's book and Bettelheim's book is similar. Heuscher discusses "Hansel and Gretel"; "Little Red Riding Hood"; "Snow White"; and "Briar Rose" ("The Sleeping Beauty") in succession. Bettelheim discusses "Hansel and Gretel"; "Little Red Riding Hood"; "Jack and the Beanstalk"; "Snow White"; "Goldilocks and the Three Bears"; and "The Sleeping Beauty." Except for the insertion of "Jack and the Beanstalk" and the tale of Goldilocks, the sequence of discussions is identical. Is this just coincidence?

One critic took Bettelheim to task for borrowing material from Heuscher's book without acknowledgment [Joan W. Blos, "The Emperor's Clothes," *Merrill-Palmer Quarterly* 24 (1978)]. One example unearthed by this author:

> Hansel and his sister Gretel appear successful at first. But the frustrations at home continue. The mother seems to be more shrewd in her plans for rejecting the children . . . [Heuscher]

> The children's successful return home does not solve anything. . . . The frustrations continue, and the mother becomes more shrewd in her plans for getting rid of the children. [Bettelheim]

It is sad to report that there are many examples of such

borrowing from Heuscher and others without any indication of sources. The following examples were not reported by previous critics.

In Heuscher's discussion of "Snow White," we find the following passage:

> Not wishing to deprive any one too much, she eats just a little from each of the seven plates and drinks just a drop from each glass (how different from Hansel and Gretel who, rather disrespectfully, start eating the gingerbread house).

In Bettelheim's discussion of the same title, we find the following passage:

> though very hungry, she eats just a little from each of the seven plates, and drinks just a drop from each of the seven glasses, so as to rob none of them too much. (How different from Hansel and Gretel, the orally fixated children, who disrespectfully and voraciously eat up the gingerbread house!)

It should be noted that it is not just a matter of occasional borrowings of random passages, but a wholesale borrowing of key ideas. For example, one of the important pieces of advice that Bettelheim gives throughout his book is not to explain fairy tales to children. With that in mind, let us consider the following passage from Heuscher:

> While one must never "explain" the fairy tales to the child, the narrator's understanding of their meaning is very important. It furthers the sensitivity for selecting those stories which are most appropriate in various phases of children's development and for stressing those themes which may be therapeutic for specific psychological difficulties.

Compare this passage with the following one from Bettelheim:

> One must never "explain" to the child the meanings of fairy tales. However, the narrator's understanding of the fairy tale's message to the child's preconscious mind is important. . . . It furthers the adult's sensitivity to selection of those stories which are most appropriate to the child's state of development, and to the specific psychological difficulties he is confronted with at the moment.

This is not coincidence. There can be no doubt about the genetic relationship existing between these two passages (and there are others). The parallels extend even to the placing of "explain" inside quotation marks. If an undergraduate were to turn in a research paper with this sort of borrowing without any attribution, he or she would almost certainly be accused of plagiarism, normally grounds for failing the class if not for actual dismissal from the college or university.

All this is not to say that Bettelheim's book is not infinitely superior to Heuscher's, which is a confusing mix of Freudian, Jungian, and anthroposophical theories. But that isn't the point. It is perfectly all right for one writer to borrow from an earlier one, but when one does so, one is expected to give proper credit to the earlier writer. Bettelheim's de-

scription of the symbolism of the glass slipper combined with an analysis of finger-ring symbolism in wedding ritual was singled out for comment by one reviewer who suggested that "Only a True Believer, washed in the blood of Freud, will buy this" [Anthony Arthur, "The Uses of Bettelheim's *The Uses of Enchantment,*" *Language Arts* 55 (1978)], but in fact the identical account appeared almost verbatim nearly ten years earlier than Bettelheim's book in a commentary to an essay in a psychoanalytic journal which Bettelheim briefly mentions. Again, Bettelheim failed to give credit to the earlier source from which he borrowed both the idea and the wording of it.

How then do we finally assess the contribution of Bettelheim's *The Uses of Enchantment*? There is little doubt that Bettelheim's book has brought Freudian readings of fairy tales to the attention of the general public. His readings on the whole are plausible if not always entirely persuasive. For the academy and that large segment of the public that tends to dismiss Freudian arguments out of hand, Bettelheim's book has had an important impact. Not only do fairy tales get a fair hearing, but the unique insights available through psychoanalytic reasoning are presented to the public in a most palatable form. To be sure, not everyone is pleased to see Cinderella, Snow White, Rapunzel, and Little Red Riding Hood reclining on the analyst's couch and there remain a host of conservative academics unalterably opposed to anything remotely psychoanalytic.

One of America's foremost fairy-tale scholars, Jack Zipes, enumerates a number of severe criticisms of Bettelheim's treatment of fairy tales. According to Zipes, Bettelheim is overly authoritarian—in claiming that he knows how children unconsciously understand the tales, he is overly moralistic, and he ignores social and class differences when he assumes that all children will understand a fairy tale in the same way.

There is no doubt that Bettelheim's book has made psychoanalytic readings of fairy tales accessible to a wide audience, taking the subject matter off the dusty library shelves lined with esoteric folklore and psychiatric periodicals and placing his genuine insights in the light of common knowledge. The vast majority of the readers of *The Uses of Enchantment* will not be aware of Bettelheim's sins of omission and commission. They will simply be informed, enlightened, and delighted. It is only the very few scholars familiar with the whole history of the psychoanalytic interpretation of fairy tales who will be disappointed or puzzled by Bettelheim's faults—which seem so unnecessary for a man of his stature and reputation. Whether it was a matter of laziness or outright intellectual dishonesty, Bettelheim's legitimate and worthwhile contribution in *The Uses of Enchantment* is permanently marred by his failure to observe conventional academic etiquette. (pp. 74-81)

Alan Dundes, "Bruno Bettelheim's Uses of Enchantment and Abuses of Scholarship," in Journal of American Folklore, *Vol. 104, No. 411, Winter, 1991, pp. 74-83.*

FURTHER READING

Biography

Angres, Ronald. "Who, Really, Was Bruno Bettelheim?" *Commentary* 90, No. 4 (October 1990): 26-30.

> Charges Bettelheim and his staff at the Orthogenic School with child abuse and neglect. Angres is a former patient of Bettelheim's.

Criticism

Bruner, Jerome. "Reading for Signs of Life." *The New York Review of Books* XXIX, No. 5 (1 April 1982): 19-20.

> Commends *On Learning to Read* as an attempt to reform the way reading is taught in America, but faults Bettelheim and Zelan for ignoring the "exquisite complexity involved in digging meaning out of what one reads."

Burgess, Anthony. "Last Words from an Optimistic Philosopher." *Observer* (25 March 1990): 67.

> Praises *Recollections and Reflections,* commenting: "In that a personality, an education, a career, and a set of hard convictions shine through, this book may be said to be autobiography."

Coles, Robert. "A Hero of Our Time." *The New Republic* 156, No. 9 (4 March 1967): 23-4.

> Favorably reviews *The Empty Fortress,* pointing out Bettelheim's "quiet heroism" in treating autistic and severely disturbed children.

Dinnage, Rosemary. "Reaching the Unreachable." *The Times Literary Supplement* (2 August 1974): 829.

> Positive review of *A Home for the Heart,* focusing on the keystones of treatment at the Orthogenic School, particularly the relationship between patient and caretaker.

Featherstone, Joseph. "Making a New Man." *The New Republic* 160, No. 21 (24 May 1969): 23-6.

> Provides a mixed review of *The Children of the Dream.*

First, Elsa. "Inside the Fortress." *The New York Review of Books* XXI, No. 9 (30 May 1974): 3-4.

> Discusses *A Home for the Heart,* concluding that "[in] spite of his often pontificating tone, there are many useful lessons to be learned from Bettelheim's retrospective look at his life's work."

Gorer, Geoffrey. "Freud among the Fairies." *The Times Literary Supplement* (1 October 1976): 1245.

> Mixed review of *The Uses of Enchantment,* concluding that "[apart] from an exhibition of paleo-Freudian pyrotechnics, Dr. Bettelheim's object in writing this book is to encourage agnostic but conscientious parents to tell their children fairy stories without feeling guilty."

Kendrick, Walter. "Thallic Symbols and Other Freudian Slippages." *The Village Voice Literary Supplement,* No. 14 (February 1983): 16-18.

> Compares Bettelheim's *Freud and Man's Soul* with Samuel Weber's *The Legend of Freud* and *The Collected Papers of Sigmund Freud,* edited and translated by Anna Freud, Ernest Jones, Joan Riviere, and Alix and James Strachey. Kendrick calls *Freud and Man's Soul* "a disingenuous attempt to deflect attention from the actual plight of American psychoanalysis, to discourage investigation into the intellectual barrenness, the crass self-serving, and the purblind provincialism that have brought the psychoanalytic establishment to its present dead-end state, and to shift all blame onto the shoulders of an imaginary cabal of people."

Kermode, Frank. "Freud Is Better in German." *The New York Times Book Review* (6 February 1983): 9, 25.

> Criticizes many of Bettelheim's contentions in *Freud and Man's Soul* concerning the Standard Edition translation of Freud.

Storr, Anthony. "Suffering of the Little Children." *The Spectator* (24 March 1990): 29-30.

> Favorable assessment of *Reflections and Recollections.*

Szajnberg, Nathan M., ed. *Educating the Emotions: Bruno Bettelheim and Psychoanalytic Development.* New York: Plenum, 1992, 222 p.

> In-depth examination of Bettelheim's contributions to psychoanalytic study.

Updike, John. Review of *The Uses of Enchantment,* by Bruno Bettelheim. *The New York Times Book Review* (23 May 1976): 1-2.

> Calls *The Uses of Enchantment* "a charming book about enchantment, a profound book about fairy tales."

Rita Mae Brown

1944-

American novelist, essayist, and poet. The following entry presents an overview of Brown's career.

For further information on her work, see *CLC*, Volumes 18 and 43.

INTRODUCTION

Brown is a novelist and essayist who writes conventionally structured novels about sometimes unconventional protagonists. Often ranked highly among feminist and lesbian writers, Brown herself rejects the classification of fiction by race, gender, or sexual orientation, stating that "I'm a writer and I'm a woman and I'm from the South and I'm alive, and that is that."

Brown was born in Pennsylvania and attended the University of Florida, New York University, and the New York School of Visual Arts. She became active in the feminist and lesbian rights movements in the late 1960s but left several feminist and gay rights groups, including the National Organization for Women (NOW) and Gay Liberation, when she found them intolerant or indifferent to the needs of lesbians. In 1971 she helped organize the Furies, a lesbian feminist separatist group in Washington, D.C. She later became one of the founding editors of *Quest,* a feminist research journal. Although she has been charged with abandoning her earlier radical stance since attaining literary success in the 1980s, Brown remains active in women's political issues. Brown chronicled her own and other lesbians' searches for a satisfactory outlet for their activism in her essay collection *A Plain Brown Rapper.*

Brown's first novel, *Rubyfruit Jungle,* sold widely in a first edition published by a small feminist publisher and has gone on to sell more than one million copies. A modern, female-centered picaresque, *Rubyfruit Jungle* has been compared to Mark Twain's *The Adventures of Huckleberry Finn* in the treatment of its protagonist, an intelligent, outspoken young woman who struggles and eventually triumphs in a social context that is often hostile to her identity as a woman and a lesbian. In subsequent novels Brown has written extensively about racial and sexual issues. *Southern Discomfort,* for example, concerns a wealthy white Southern socialite who falls in love with a black teenager, and *Sudden Death* is an acerbic account of professional dishonesty and sexual betrayal in the world of women's tennis. *High Hearts* is a thoroughly researched historical novel concerning a woman who fights in the Civil War to be near her husband. In her more recent work, Brown has shifted to different genres with *Starting from Scratch: A Different Kind of Writer's Manual* and the murder mysteries *Wish You Were Here* and its sequel *Rest in Pieces.*

PRINCIPAL WORKS

The Hand That Cradles the Rock   (poetry)   1971
Hrotsvitra: Six Medieval Latin Plays [translator] (drama)   1971
Rubyfruit Jungle   (novel)   1973
Songs to a Handsome Woman   (poetry)   1973
In Her Day   (novel)   1976
A Plain Brown Rapper   (essays)   1976
Six of One   (novel)   1978
Southern Discomfort   (novel)   1982
Sudden Death   (novel)   1983
High Hearts   (novel)   1986
The Poems of Rita Mae Brown   (poetry)   1987
Bingo   (novel)   1988
Starting from Scratch: A Different Kind of Writer's Manual   (nonfiction)   1988
Wish You Were Here   (novel)   1990
Rest in Pieces   (novel)   1991
Venus Envy   (novel)   1992

CRITICISM

Martha Chew   (essay date Fall 1983)

[*In the following essay, Chew surveys Brown's career through 1982.*]

Rita Mae Brown is known both for her political writing, which consists of the essays that came out of her activism as a lesbian feminist in the late sixties and early seventies and were collected in *A Plain Brown Rapper* (1976); and for her fiction, which to date consists of five novels, *Rubyfruit Jungle* (1973), *In Her Day* (1976), *Six of One* (1978), *Southern Discomfort* (1982), and *Sudden Death* (1983). Although the two bodies of work overlap chronologically, they come out of essentially different periods in Brown's life, and the novels have been increasingly directed toward a mainstream audience.

The movement of the novels away from the political focus of the essays is reflected in the way the two types of writing diverge in their publishing histories. Brown's essays originally appeared in lesbian and feminist publications; the collected edition, *A Plain Brown Rapper,* was published by Diana Press, a west coast lesbian-feminist press (which also published her second collection of poems, *Songs to a Handsome Woman* in 1973 and reissued in 1974 her first collection, *The Hand That Cradles the Rock*). Her first two novels, *Rubyfruit Jungle* and *In Her Day,* were published by Daughters, Inc., a Vermont feminist publishing house (co-founded by another Southern woman writer, North Carolina novelist June Arnold). When *Rubyfruit Jungle* became an underground best seller (selling 80,000 copies in hardcover), it was reissued by Bantam, a subsidiary of Harper and Row, and Harper and Row simultaneously contracted for her third novel, *Six of One.* Her next two novels, *Southern Discomfort* and *Sudden Death,* were published by Harper and Row and by Bantam, respectively.

Brown had evidently anticipated and planned these two publishing tracks with a clear sense of the different audiences that her political essays and her novels would eventually have. In 1976, a year before Bantam reissued *Rubyfruit Jungle,* she responded to a questionnaire on publishing policies sent to lesbian and feminist authors, "I see my political writing going to the feminist press while in time my fiction will go to establishment presses."

The widening gap between Brown's essays and her fiction is marked by the disappearance from the novels of the lesbian feminist political vision that is set forth with revolutionary fervor in the early writings. This apparent shift in her ideological stance is underlined by the change in her lifestyle from that of political activist and street-level organizer to that of Hollywood scriptwriter, celebrity novelist, and member of Charlottesville's polo-playing set. This change has, predictably, been noted with favor in some camps and disfavor in others. Jan Clausen, writing in *A Movement of Poets* about the relationship of poets to the

contemporary American feminist movement, notes that "it is a sobering experience . . . to read early 'underground heroine' Rita Mae Brown's musings on the joys of owning a Rolls Royce in a recent issue of *Savvy.*" The mainstream press, on the other hand, feels that Brown has "broken through" and that her success with standard publishers marks "the difference between being famous as a lesbian writer . . . and being a writer of greater substance and vision who is perhaps breaking new literary ground."

Brown, who points out that she gives ten percent of her after-tax earnings to women's political causes, talks about her feminist politics as having evolved, rather than changed. In her 1976 introduction to the essays in *A Plain Brown Rapper,* she explained that, although her vision of a feminist revolution remained "unchanged," she had come to see that revolution as "the slow, steady push of people over decades." And in a 1978 interview upon the publication of *Six of One,* after pointing out that fiction made her politics "more palatable," she added, "I still feel I'm part of the movement, but the form of my expression has changed."

Although the distance between the political viewpoint in Brown's essays and that in her fiction clearly signals more than a change in form, the essays and fiction are linked by Brown's concern with some of the same issues. We can begin to see that link, and to define the extent to which Brown's themes in her fiction reflect her early politics, if we look first at the account her essays provide of the development of her political thinking in the early sixties and late seventies.

> There is a growing movement of Lesbians dedicated to our freedom, to your freedom, to ending all man-made oppressions. You will be part of that surge forward and you will leave your fingerprints on the shape of things to come.
> **("The Shape of Things to Come,"** 1972)

Brown's political essays and speeches, which appeared from 1969 to 1975 in *The Ladder, Women: A Journal of Liberation, The Furies, Quest: A Journal of Feminist Liberation,* and other lesbian and feminist publications, chart the development of her vision of a feminist revolution. Looking back on that period in her 1976 introduction to her essays in *A Plain Brown Rapper,* Brown said, "In those days I ate, breathed and slept feminism. Nothing else mattered to me. We would bring about a revolution in this nation and we would do it now."

After making the Southern writer's archetypal journey to New York, she began to move from one political group to another. She helped found the New York University Homophile League, then left it because, as she explains in her 1972 essay, **"Take a Lesbian to Lunch,"** "the homosexual movement" was "male-dominated." She joined the National Organization for Women (and was appointed national administrative coordinator), then quit, reportedly blasting the leaders as "sexist, racist, reformist clubwomen" because of their reaction to the issue of lesbianism. She joined Redstockings (a New York radical feminist group that used consciousness-raising groups as a way of organizing women); found they reacted as negatively to her lesbianism as had NOW; joined and then left Gay Liberation.

She eventually became part of Radicalesbians, the New York collective that in 1970 issued the now-classic essay "The Woman-Identified Woman." In its definition of lesbianism as a political act, the Radicalesbians essay moves beyond "the traditional definition of women toward a concept of women defining themselves," as Brown explained in a later essay, **"Living with Other Women."**

What Brown has called the "burning intensity" of her commitment to a feminist revolution led her in 1971 to help organize the Furies, a Washington, D.C., collective of lesbian feminist separatists. The impact that the collective's newsletter, *The Furies,* had on *Feminary,* a Southern feminist publication, is described by M. Segrest in her article on writing by Southern lesbians in *Southern Exposure.* "The Furies collective was a religion to us in Chapel Hill between 1971 and 1974," Segrest quotes a former *Feminary* collective member as saying. After Brown was purged from the Furies, she went on to become one of the founding editors of *Quest,* a journal of feminist ideology and research.

Brown's movement from one group to another was typical of the experiences of other lesbian feminist activists at the time. In *Dreamers and Dealers,* Leah Fritz's account of the second wave of the women's movement, Fritz recalls that "Lesbians began to defect from one women's group after another, to move around in search of a place where they would feel at home, a place which would serve both the totality of their needs as women and their specific needs as lesbians." In documenting Brown's political odyssey during that period, the essays in *Plain Brown Rapper* are, as Brown says in the introduction, "as much a chronicle of the decade as of my own development."

The essays are also important, not just as history and personal biography, but as ideology. The collection—twenty previously published essays, plus an introduction, conclusion, and a new essay—is uneven. Often the essays fire movement rhetoric at the reader in a machine-gun style that makes one piece sound very like another. And some of Brown's prescriptions for bringing about the revolution are simplistic, just as some of her predictions seem amazingly naive—"Within five years we will have our party."

Yet many of the essays offer perceptive insights into class divisions and other artificial categories dividing human beings. Brown feels strongly that "Separation is what the ruling rich, white male wants: female vs. male; black vs. white; gay vs. straight; poor vs. rich." Her essays attack the tendency of society to put everyone into one category or another, and she points out the ways in which these categories are restricted by what she calls "the male culture's vulgar conceptual limitations." For example, her review essay **"The Last Picture Show"** offers a paradigm for analyzing films that depict only "the white, middle class heterosexual version of life." A later essay, **"I Am a Woman,"** offers an equally useful analysis, not just of the limitations of "the male concept of the female," but also of the limitations of a heterosexual view of women that ignores the fact that "even the most blatantly heterosexual woman has a relationship with her mother, her sisters, her girlfriends, aunts, grandmothers, office workers."

Perhaps the best writing in the collection has to do with class, which has always been an issue of great personal significance to Brown. She identifies herself as coming from a working class background: her mother was a bakery and mill worker, and her father was a butcher. Her interviews and essays repeatedly point to lack of class consciousness in the women's movement (along with lack of consciousness about lesbianism) as the source of her problems with the different groups that she joined and then left. In a 1978 interview she recalled the New York women's groups as hostile to "lower class" issues: "the early years of the movement were bitter years, especially for me because I was from poor origins and therefore 'lower class.' Let's face it, the Women's Movement is still a white middle-class movement: I was always bringing up the basic issues that faced the poor—food, shelter and clothing. But nobody wanted to hear that. . . . With NOW and the others it was bad enough that I was a lesbian and said so, but to call into question the very process by which we were organizing ourselves—in other words the unspoken assumptions of class privilege—well, you couldn't have asked to become a more unwanted person." Writing in the introduction to *A Plain Brown Rapper* about her experiences with the Furies, Brown says that, although the collective had tried to deal with class issues, "we ignored the psychology of class differences" and "in the end, it was this issue and the issue of identity which destroyed our collective."

In **"The Last Straw,"** perhaps her most important essay on class differences, Brown attacks two middle class assumptions: the idea that acquiring middle class income or status "removes the entire experience of our childhood and youth—working class life" and also the belief in "downward mobility" embraced by some middle class revolutionaries. She points out that "for those of us who grew up without material advantages downward mobility is infuriating—here are women rejecting what we never had and can't get!"

Brown's concern in her essays with class divisions is at times characterized by an ambivalence that foreshadows the movement of her novels away from her early political stance. For example, in **"The Last Straw"** her attack on "downward mobility" reveals an emotional defensiveness about capitalism, even though her official line in this and other essays is clearly a socialist one. Brown is not, of course, the first working class revolutionary to find her intellectual commitment to socialism in conflict with her need to protect herself by acquiring material possessions. In this defensiveness about capitalism in **"The Last Straw"** we can see the same conflicting feelings that turn up later in the ambivalence with which she portrays upper and middle class characters in her fiction.

On one level Brown's novels can be seen as a working and reworking of the interlocking problems of the oppressiveness of class and other artificial divisions of human beings and the isolation imposed by these divisions. As we might expect, in her essays Brown brings the expediency of the activist and the organizer to her analysis of society's readiness to put everyone in one category or another. Nonetheless, the essays reveal the intellectual basis of Brown's concern with the problems of class, race, and gender categories that her fiction explores in the lives of Southern women and in the context of the Southern environment in which Brown herself grew up.

> "I'm not saying it's easy but maybe that's just what we have to do, Adele, go back where we came from and fight this out."
> —Brown, *In Her Day*

Although Brown's political essays were an important influence on the Southern women putting out *Feminary* in Chapel Hill, it is her novels that identify her as a Southern writer for the majority of her reading public. On promotional tours for her novels Brown has repeatedly emphasized her Southern background and indicated that she wants to be identified as a Southern writer. For example, in a Boston interview she effusively expressed her pleasure in the enthusiastic reception to her appearances in the South: "I just love the South and I'm pleased to say it loves me right back. Everytime I speak there I'm just overwhelmed by love. I think Southerners are happy and proud when one of their own makes it." And she clearly wanted the *New York* interviewer to see her in the tradition of Southern writers when she called *Six of One* a Southern novel and described the South as a good environment for writers. "Actually I think the book is rather southern. The South allows itself eccentrics, and, of course, if you're going to be a writer it's fabulous to grow up with that, which I did in a way." In a recent interview in Philadelphia she was equally eager to identify herself as a Southern writer: "I pretty much dislike Yankees. They're no fun. They don't have a wild streak in them. They're too rational. Art is intensely emotive, and at least in the South you are allowed your emotions."

Each of Brown's first four novels can be seen as a different stage in her attempt to go back to her Southern roots, either in her choice of settings or in her focus on Southern characters. Most of the first half of *Rubyfruit Jungle* is set in Fort Lauderdale; *Six of One* is set in a Pennsylvania-Maryland town on the middle of the Mason-Dixon line; and *Southern Discomfort* is set in Montgomery, Alabama. *In Her Day* takes place in New York, but a central scene, and the only flashback, focuses on Carole's trip back home to Virginia to visit her family. (Brown's fifth novel, *Sudden Death,* which is about the world of women's professional tennis and depicts a love affair that has obvious parallels to Brown's relationship with tennis star Martina Navratilova, breaks the pattern of her increasing focus on the South in her fiction. Brown wrote the novel because of a promise to a dying friend, a sports writer, and she labels it an "interruption" in her writing plans: "I was all set to go on to my next novel about the War Between the States, and this came as an interruption." The biographical note at the end of *Sudden Death* is clearly intended to alert readers to Brown's intention to return to her focus on the South: "Rita Mae Brown is currently retracing Stonewall Jackson's steps during the War Between the States in preparation for her next novel.")

Brown's first four novels go back not only to the South but to specific events and places in Brown's own life. She was born in a small Pennsylvania town and moved at an early age to Fort Lauderdale. Her adoptive parents were working class. Her biological father was French—although Brown has said that she was "without knowledge of my ethnic origins"—and her biological mother at one time employed the woman who adopted her. After being expelled from the University of Florida for her lesbianism and civil rights activism, Brown put herself through New York University. In the late seventies she returned to the South to live, settling in Charlottesville, Virginia, which she says is "home" now: "It's the source of my power."

Different aspects of these experiences are reenacted by the various heroes of her four Southern novels. Molly in *Rubyfruit Jungle,* Carole in *In Her Day,* and Nickle in *Six of One* grow up poor in the South and leave. Brown's circuitous route from Pennsylvania to New York is specifically paralleled in Molly's move from Pennsylvania to Fort Lauderdale, her expulsion from the state university, and her flight to New York, where she puts herself through film school. Brown's move back to the South has parallels in two of the novels: at the end of *In Her Day,* Carole and her Southern friend Adele consider going back to the South to live; and in *Six of One,* Nickel returns to Pennsylvania after publishing a successful book, buys her grandmother's house, and prepares to settle down. Although *Southern Discomfort* does not for the most part have these literal autobiographical parallels, Catherine, like Brown, is adopted (as are Molly and Nickel in the two earlier novels) and, like Brown, has a non-Anglo biological father. (Catherine's father is black, and there is speculation that Molly's father and Nickel's father are black, although both are identified as French.) Catherine's biological mother employs her adoptive mother, just as Brown's biological mother once employed her adoptive mother.

Brown's novels are autobiographical not only in their portrayal of these experiences but, more importantly, in their exploration of the issue that concerned her both personally and politically during her activist years. All four of the Southern novels depict people who defy society's division of human beings into artificial categories and who struggle to come to terms with the isolation imposed by those categories, and they develop this theme in more depth and with more complexity than either the scope or the purpose of her political essays permitted. In exploring this theme in autobiographical novels about Southern women, Brown is using her fiction to do what Carole in *In Her Day* tells Adele (who is also a transplanted Southerner) that they must do about the oppression they face as lesbians, "go back where we came from and fight this out."

Brown treats the problem of class and other societal categories on two levels in the novels: a realistic, or literal, level, and a symbolic level. On the literal level, she shows women running head-on into the barriers imposed by class, race, and gender categories. Locked into some categories and locked out of others, her characters have varying degrees of success in breaking through the barriers and making contact with people in other categories.

On the symbolic level, Brown suggests a bridging of these divisions through the identification of the main character with two very different types of characters, an upper or middle class character (the "aristocratic" character) and a black character. The significance of the roles of these two types of characters as the doubles of the main character is underlined by the fact that in the first, second, and fourth novels the main character is adopted. (In the third novel, *In Her Day,* Brown offers a variation on the adoption motif in that Carole's parents are dead and she has adopted a friend to replace her dead biological sister.) Although the situation of the main characters as adopted children can be emblematic of the essential loneliness of the human condition, it also functions in a more specific way to underline the extent to which societal categories cut people off from one another. As Molly puts it in *Rubyfruit Jungle,* "I had never thought I had much in common with anybody. I had no mother, no father, no roots, no biological similarities called sisters and brothers."

This double-barrelled approach is evident in Brown's first novel, *Rubyfruit Jungle. Rubyfruit Jungle* became an underground best seller because of its reputation as a novel about "growing up gay in America" (as ads and reviews described it when it was reissued by Bantam in 1977), but Molly Bolt is, as her name suggests, in rebellion against the restrictions imposed on her by race and class as well as gender. When her family moves from Pennsylvania to Fort Lauderdale, her father tries to explain to her that racial segregation is more obvious in Florida: "Down South things are a little different than up in New York. Here the whites and the coloreds don't mix and you're not to mess with those people, although you are to be mannerly should you ever have to talk to one." Her mother puts it more bluntly: "If I ever see you mixing with the wrong kind, I'm gonna wring your neck, brat." Her family is poor—in her grandmother's words, "God knows with all of us working we can't make hardly enough to keep going"—but it is not until they move to Florida that Molly really becomes aware of class distinctions: "Back in the Hollow we were all the same. . . . Here it was a distinct line drawn between two camps and I was certain I didn't want to be on the side with the greasy boys that leered at me and talked filthy." Molly also comes up against the restrictions of gender roles. Early on her mother complains that "she don't act natural" because she "climbs trees" and "takes cars apart" instead of learning "the things she has to know to get a husband," and when Molly says she wants a "candy apple red Bonneville Triumph," her cousin Leroy echoes her mother's criticism: "you ain't natural. . . . It's time you started worrying about your hair and doing those things that girls are supposed to do."

Molly's reactions to the restrictions imposed on her by societal categories are in keeping with her strong sense of herself. Her reaction to racial segregation is to ignore it: "I ain't staying away from people because they look different." She tackles the problem of class like the survivor she is: "It took me all of seventh grade to figure out how I would take care of myself in this new situation, but I did figure it out." Her solution is to combine the traditional methods of "passing" (high grades, correct grammar, and a few good clothes) with humor: "I decided to become the funniest person in the whole school. If someone makes you laugh you have to like her." Although Molly opts for "passing" in high school, later on in New York she becomes more class conscious and insists on identifying her

working class background, so much so, in fact, that her friend Holly accuses her of "wearing your poverty like a badge of purity." She takes an even more defiant line when faced with gender roles. When her cousin Leroy labels her interest in motorcycles unfeminine, she retorts, "I'll buy an army tank if I want to and run over anyone who tells me I can't have it."

The success of Molly's defiance depends, of course, on her position in relation to the dominant culture. As white, she is a member of the dominant culture and can cross racial lines in a way that blacks cannot. As female, lesbian, and poor, she is in a more difficult position. She is able to gain the respect and liking of some people and survive the insults and attacks of others, but she can go only so far. Near the end of the novel, when she is by-passed for jobs in spite of her *summa cum laude* degree and her demonstrated talents and skills as a filmmaker, she says, "I kept hoping against hope that I'd be the bright exception, the talented token that smashed sex and class barriers." The novel's closing passage records her awareness of the power of barriers erected to maintain the power of the dominant culture: "Damn, I wished the world would let me be myself. But I knew better on all counts."

Molly's defiance of societal conventions concerning race, class, and sex is paralleled by the novel's symbolic identification of her with characters from different social worlds. Two of the women with whom she becomes romantically involved in New York, Holly, a beautiful black woman from a wealthy family, and Polina, an older white woman who is a medieval scholar, function as Molly's doubles, roles that are underlined by the similarity of the names of the three. Holly's role as Molly's black double is reinforced by Molly's childhood speculations about her own parents: "Since I don't know who my real folks are maybe they're colored." Her other double, Polina, a medieval scholar, represents aristocratic values to Molly; she needs Polina because of "the conversations, the theater, and her stories of Europe where she grew up." Although both relationships are short-lived, Holly's and Polina's roles as Molly's doubles identify her with women whose class and race are different from her own and, in doing so, foreshadow the more significant roles of the black and "aristocratic" characters in the later novels.

Brown's second novel, *In Her Day,* focuses on Carole Hanratty, a forty-four-year-old medieval art historian in New York. The break-up of her love affair with Ilse, a twenty-two-year-old lesbian feminist revolutionary from a Boston Brahmin family, is balanced against the stability of her friendship with Adele, her black friend. The novel has been described as "an embarrassing attempt to write a Lesbian-feminist novel of ideas," and, with the exception of a few reviews in lesbian feminist publications, it is generally agreed to be a failure, an assessment with which Brown herself agrees. Nonetheless, the novel develops the rebellion theme in *Rubyfruit Jungle* on both literal and symbolic levels. Although Carole is stately, reserved, and distrustful of Ilse's political enthusiasms, she has bucked the system in some of the same ways that Molly Bolt has. Carole's friendship with Adele in the fifties was, as Ilse reminds her, a form of "breaking the code," for "when you two became friends white and Black women weren't seen together." Like Molly, Carole has fought her way up from poverty: "I worked for everything I have. I didn't come from money. Honey, I grew up in the Depression in Richmond, Virginia. . . . We lived in the Fan. It was a slum pretty much, although we didn't call it that ourselves." As female and a lesbian she has rebelled against the restrictions of gender roles, first as a child ("I knew as a kid that boys got all the breaks but it made me mad—just made me fight that much harder"); then as a student at Vassar opting for a career at a time when "there wasn't a women's movement except in the direction of Yale;" and finally as a university professor in a department where "I would have been head . . . if I weren't a woman." Carole is, as Ilse somewhat patronizingly describes her, "a proto-feminist."

On the symbolic level of the novel, Adele functions as Carole's black double in a development of Holly's role in *Rubyfruit Jungle.* A beautiful black woman from a wealthy family, Adele is Carole's age and, like her, a Southerner. Her role as Carole's double is underlined by Carole's adoption of her as her sister. When Carole's biological sister is killed in an automobile accident, Adele comforts her, riding partway to Richmond with her on the train and meeting her returning train: "the hours, like a magic circle, closed around them and strengthened the bond of friendship already between them. As Carol boarded the train, finally, she turned to Adele and said, 'You're my sister now.' " Their identification is made even more explicit in the last scene, in which they talk about their need as Southerners to go back to their "roots" and the impossibility of their going unless they go together. "I love you more than anyone on earth," Carole tells Adele.

Ilse, Carole's "aristocratic" double, attended the same college, Vassar, that Carole had attended twenty years earlier, and she looks like "white America's dream of femininity," as Carole had at her age. Ilse's role as Carole's double is underlined by Carole's internalization of upper class values. Carole acknowledges that, like Molly Bolt, she had tried to overcome class barriers by "passing": "I spent close to a decade trying to pretend I was an aristocrat." Ilse remarks upon this ambivalence: "At first I thought she was some kind of aristocrat." As Adele puts it in explaining Carole's attraction to Ilse, "Carole has always been fascinated and repelled by people who had it easy." Although the relationship between them fails, they are, as Bernice Mennis notes in her review of the novel in *Conditions: One,* "two parts of a dialectic" and "by the end of the novel and of their relationship, each incorporates a small part of the other's vision." Ilse's role as Carole's "aristocratic" double builds on Polina's role in *Rubyfruit Jungle,* just as Adele's role builds on Holly's role, and the two characters prefigure the roles of the doubles in the novels that follow.

Brown's third novel, *Six of One,* portrays the women in two families in a small town in southern Pennsylvania between 1909 and 1980. The novel focuses on the lively feuding between two sisters, Juts and Louise, from their childhood (shown in flashbacks) to their old age (described by

the first-person narrator, Juts's adopted daughter, Nickel). Nickel had been a "bullheaded" child, "ready to get into trouble," and she had grown up to be an adult who "left the church, left the town, left [her mother] . . . writes books that disgrace the whole family," and sleeps with women. She and her mother, Juts, whose "hell-raising bent" she has inherited, are both reincarnations of Molly Bolt. Another hell-raiser in the novel is Celeste Chalfonte, the wealthy Southern white woman who employs Nickel's grandmother, Cora. (Cora was, Brown tells us, modeled on Brown's own grandmother and her "favorite character in the whole book.") Celeste defies convention by openly living with her female lover, but she cannot completely break through the class barrier. Her statement to her lover Ramelle reveals the power of the social structure in her life: "If I could choose a sister I would choose Cora. Our tragedy was to be born at opposite ends of the social spectrum. This [their employer-servant relationship] is the only way we can be part of one another's lives short of revolution."

The novel symbolically bridges this class division, however, through the identification of Nickel with Celeste, her "aristocratic" double. While a black double is absent in this novel, the speculation that Nickel's biological father may have been black identifies her to some extent with blacks, much as Molly's speculation about whether her parents were black functions in *Rubyfruit Jungle.* For example, when Cora decides to adopt Nickel, her sister warns her, "For all you know, the father could be black as spades," and one of the strike-breakers hired by the local munitions factory taunts Nickel, "I hear tell your father was a nigger."

Celeste and Nickel are repeatedly identified with one another throughout the novel, although the two never see each other. Nickel is born on Celeste's sixty-seventh birthday, and Celeste's unexpected death the night before ushers in the birth. Celeste's thoughts on the evening of her death suggest an identification with Nickel that has undertones of reincarnation: "Celeste found herself strangely excited about the baby. She hoped it would come forth tomorrow. . . . Celebrating earthly renewal with a new person might be fun." This identification of the two is continued by reminders of Nickel's resemblance to Celeste. For example, when Nickel says, "I hope I grow up to be like Celeste," her grandmother Cora replies, "I do, too." When Nickel's mother tells her, "Sometimes you remind me of Celeste Chalfonte with an engine on your back," Nickel replies that one of Celeste's Vassar friends "told me . . . that I reminded her a bit of Celeste." Celeste is further connected to Nickel through a bequest in her will that provides for Nickel to attend Celeste's alma mater, Vassar. The bequest links Nickel not only to Celeste but also to Celeste's social world.

The identification of Nickel with Celeste is underlined by the elaborate parallels between Celeste's two worlds. On the one hand there is her "aristocratic" world—her biological family, her lover, and her Vassar friends (who, significantly, were known as "the Furies" in college). On the other hand there is her working class family—her servant Cora, Cora's daughters Juts and Louise, and Cora's granddaughter, Nickel. When Celeste's lover becomes pregnant (by Celeste's brother), Celeste assumes the role of "a mother or mother number two" to Ramelle's child. Celeste is also a second mother to Cora's daughter Juts, a relationship suggested in part through the presence of Cora's daughters in Celeste's house when their mother is working there and in part through Celeste's love for Cora. (The bond between Celeste and Cora is put in physical, although not sexual, terms when Celeste, frightened and seeking comfort in Ramelle's absence, goes to Cora's house in the middle of the night and sleeps in the same bed with her.)

The parallels between Celeste's two "daughters," her daughter by her lover Ramelle, and her daughter by her servant Cora, are continued in the implied comparison of Cora's two "granddaughters," Ramelle's granddaughter and Cora's granddaughter Nickel. Significantly, the passage in which Ramelle and Cora compare their two granddaughters ends with Cora's summing up their similarity with the phrase from which the novel takes its title, "Six of one, half dozen of the other." Although attempts to break through class barriers are only partially successful on the literal level of the novel, on a symbolic level the two classes are brought together through the identification of Nickel with her "aristocratic" double, Celeste, an identification that is underlined by the complex paralleling of Celeste's two families.

Brown's recent novel, *Southern Discomfort,* takes place in Montgomery, Alabama, and is set in two periods ten years apart, 1918 and 1928. The first half of the novel focuses on the secret love affair between white society leader Hortensia Reedmuller Banastre (whose imposing demeanor recalls both Carole Hanratty in *In Her Day* and Celeste Chalfonte in *Six of One*) and Hercules Jinks, a black fifteen-year-old boxer. Their affair, which ends when Hercules is killed in a railway yard accident, leaves Hortensia pregnant with their daughter Catherine. Hortensia arranges for Catherine to be brought up by her black servant, and the second half of the novel focuses on Catherine's gradual discovery of her real heritage.

Hortensia rebels against race barriers in her love affair with Hercules, and against class barriers in her friendship with Blue Rhonda, a white prostitute. In a passage that recalls Celeste Chalfonte's envy of the "zest" and "immediacy" of Cora's family in *Six of One,* Lila, Hortensia's mother, acknowledges to herself that the hope for the upper class is to break out of their rigid mold: "Half of her longed to usher her daughter into the human race and the other half of her fought to preserve the stultifying social order over which she, Lila, presided."

In the end, the social order is preserved. In spite of Hortensia's love for Hercules, she is "not yet prepared to run away" with him, although she does not fully realize the significance of her reluctance until ten years later.

Brown suggests a possible transcending of class barriers in a key conversation in the second half of the novel between Hortensia and Blue Rhonda. Blue Rhonda makes a fumbling speech in which she calls societal categories "God's joke" because "God put beautiful spirits into these bodies, all kinds of bodies" and "we dumb humans are confused by the outside." She ends by saying, in a tone of finality, "We are one," a phrase picked up by Hortensia in their parting exchange:

> "How odd that we live so close to one another . . ."
>
> Rhonda finished her thought for her. "Same town, different worlds."
>
> Hortensia's smile caught the moonlight. "Ah, but we are one."

But this transcending of categories is clearly only momentary. For example, when Hortensia gets Blue Rhonda and two other prostitutes invitations to a society wedding, she sees their presence there as a joke, in spite of the debt she owes them and the bond forged by that debt in their private meetings.

Rebellion against gender roles is equally short-lived. After Blue Rhonda's death, she is revealed in the epilogue to the novel to be a man who has masqueraded as a woman. The letter she leaves behind for her friends echoes her reference to "God's joke" in her conversation with Hortensia, but her statement this time, "God played a joke on me and put me in a man's body," puts the emphasis on the power of societal categories, not their artificiality.

By virtue of her mixed heritage, Catherine defies both race and class barriers. Her feelings of isolation are movingly suggested in several scenes. When she realizes that she cannot join Hortensia's friends for drinks after a polo match, the ensuing dialogue between her and her mother reveals her sense of not fitting into any societal category:

> "It's because I'm piebald, isn't it?" Catherine flatly stated. . . .
>
> "What?" Hortensia inquired.
>
> "Piebald, pinto—half black and half white. I don't fit anywhere, do I?"

The reaction of one of Hortensia's otherwise obtuse friends links Catherine's isolation to the "discomfort" of the novel's title: "Sugar Guerrant felt her heart sink. For one flutter of an eyelash she had a sense of the child's displacement, and worse, an insight into what Southerners used to call 'our special problem.' "

Hortensia's acknowledgment of Catherine as her daughter does not really change Catherine's sense of not belonging, as the closing of the novel's last chapter suggests:

> "I don't feel like I belong to anybody but myself."
>
> Tears filled Hortensia's eyes. "You can belong to me if you want to."
>
> "I don't know," Catherine said thoughtfully.
>
> "As long as you like yourself, then if you do belong only to yourself perhaps you're ahead of the game."
>
> "I like myself." Catherine smiled, kissed Hortensia and then lay down and went right to sleep.

This last scene is inconclusive. The only time the novel suggests that these rigid divisions could be done away with permanently comes when Hortensia observes, "Still, if we wanted to, if we truly, truly wanted to, I think we could change the world." Although Hortensia believes in the possibility of change, she is nonetheless resigned to accepting the "stultifying social order" in much the same way that Celeste is when she says that, although she loves Cora like a sister, there is no way "short of revolution" that she and Cora can step out of their roles as employer and servant.

Although class and race lines ultimately prevail in *Southern Discomfort,* the symbolic bridging of these divisions in the novel is more complete than it is in Brown's earlier novels. The identification of the adopted character with a black character and/or a middle or upper class character (an "aristocratic" character) in the other works is brought to the forefront of the novel here in the casting of Catherine's father as her black double and her mother as her "aristocratic" double. Her father Hercules is a variation on Molly's black double, Holly, in *Rubyfruit Jungle,* and on Carole's black double, Adele, in *In Her Day.* (Hercules also recalls the biological fathers of both Molly in *Rubyfruit Jungle* and Nickel in *Six of One* in that both men are French but are suspected of being black.) Catherine's mother Hortensia is a development of the roles of the "aristocratic" doubles in the earlier novels, Polina in *Rubyfruit Jungle,* Ilse in *In Her Day,* and Celeste in *Six of One.*

The symbolic union of Catherine with both her "aristocratic" double and her black double is climactically brought about through Hortensia's murder of the younger of her two sons, Paris. Like Celeste Chalfonte in *Six of One* with her two families, Hortensia has children in two different worlds—Paris, her beautiful and immoral son by her white husband, and Catherine, her daughter by her black lover. Paris represents the shallow side of Hortensia that she must kill in order to accept the part of her that is Catherine. This process of becoming whole began earlier when Hortensia recognized the evil in Paris and when she saw Catherine's anguish at being rejected by the white children of Montgomery: "When Paris fully revealed his twisted self, and then recently when Catherine was unmasked at the Great Witch Hunt, she was pushed into herself." When Paris physically attacks Hortensia and Catherine, Hortensia kills him (in a more dramatic version of the killing or displacing of siblings than in Brown's earlier novels). The murder of Paris not only allows Hortensia to accept the part of herself that is Catherine but also brings Catherine into a fuller sense of herself. The act literally establishes Catherine in her rightful place as Hortensia's daughter and is followed by Hortensia's acknowledgment to Catherine that she is her mother. The murder also completes the union of Catherine with her black father, a process that began when Catherine had been given a picture of him and then was tutored by his mother. When the sheriff decides to report the murder as a suicide, he explains to Hortensia, "I owe Catherine's father one."

Catherine and Hortensia, like Brown's heroes in her three earlier novels, rebel against a system of values that infringes on their sense of themselves. In so doing, all these characters embody the definition of "the woman-identified woman" in the essay that Brown wrote with other members of the Radicalesbians: "She is the woman who, often beginning at an extremely early age, acts in accordance with her inner compulsion to be a more complete and freer human being than her society . . . cares to allow her. These needs and actions, over a period of years, bring her into painful conflict with people, situations, the accepted ways of thinking, feeling and behaving. . . ." While the Radicalesbians essay defines the "woman-identified woman" as one who rebels against "the limitations and oppression laid on her by the most basic role of her society—the female role" (**"Woman-Identified"**), Brown's heroes rebel against all roles that reflect society's "conceptual limitations." On the literal level, this rebellion has become progressively less open in Brown's novels, moving from Molly Bolt's free-swinging defiance of everyone who gets in her way in *Rubyfruit Jungle* to Hortensia's acceptance of the social order in *Southern Discomfort.* (Anne Gottlieb, in her review of *Southern Discomfort* in the *New York Times Book Review,* sees Brown as having become aware in this novel that no one can break "*all*" the rules" and that "every freedom must be understood within the bounds of a shared social structure that can, if stretched, yield painful renewal; if shattered, tragedy.") At the same time, the symbolic bridging of class and race divisions has intensified, reaching its height in *Southern Discomfort* in the biological identification of the adopted character with both a black character and an "aristocratic" one.

Jill Johnston, in writing about Brown's portrayal of herself in Molly in *Rubyfruit Jungle,* says, "What I admire most is her own early, or prepolitical, refusal to compromise her identity by permitting anybody to either closet or contain her." Molly Bolt is the most openly rebellious of Brown's heroes. But although the women characters in Brown's other novels do not rebel against societal categories in the same defiant way that Molly does, their rejection of the limitations that society attempts to place on them through class, race, and gender divisions is the essence of their being. It is in Brown's portrayal of the rebelliousness of her heroes that we can see how her concerns as a lesbian feminist underlie and inform her portrayal of Southern women and link her early political vision with her imaginative vision as a Southern novelist. (pp. 61-79)

Martha Chew, "Rita Mae Brown: Feminist Theorist and Southern Novelist," in The Southern Quarterly, *Vol. XXII, No. 1, Fall, 1983, pp. 61-80.*

James Mandrell (essay date Winter 1987)

[*In the following excerpt from his essay "Questions of Genre and Gender: Contemporary American Versions of the Feminine Picaresque," Mandrell discusses* Rubyfruit Jungle *as a modern picaresque.*]

Although at its appearance *Rubyfruit Jungle* was hailed as "a good and *true* account of growing up Un-American in America" by no less an authority than Gloria Steinem (who goes on to say, "for once, a *woman* has been honest and vulgar and political and funny enough to write about her *real life*"), the novel is nonetheless conventional in its literary form and discursive tendencies. Brown's novel is, for all intents and purposes, a *picaresque* novel, that is, an example of a narrative genre at least as old as the anonymous *Lazarillo de Tormes* (1554/1599) and Mateo Alemán's *Guzmán de Alfarache* (1599). As a genre, the picaresque novel possesses an extensive literary genealogy and even some modern offspring, including *El buscón* (c. 1604), *La pícara Justina* (1605), *Marcos de Obregón* (1618), *Simplicius Simplicissimus* (1668), *Gil Blas* (1715-35), and *Moll Flanders* (1722) as well as American novels in the Horatio Alger tradition. In large part, the appeal of this genre is to be found in its clear identification of the protagonist as an outsider, if not "rogue" or "delinquent." Whether or not the protagonist succeeds, as in the case of Defoe's Moll, or simply drifts off to conquer new lands, as does Quevedo's Pablos, these figures exist on the margins of society and attempt at least in economic terms to enter the social mainstream. On an ideological level, then, one must note the essentially conservative, if not reactionary, nature of the picaresque, since the genre tends to confirm the marginality of the protagonist; in fact, it is precisely in the act of confirming this marginality that the message of the picaresque novel is to be found. For example, in the case of the *Guzmán de Alfarache,* the *pícaro* is, according to Harry Sieber, "the product of poverty and of a social value system which prohibits him from being anything else." This means that the novel ought to be read as, in the words of Maurice Molho, "un violent réquisitoire 'anticapitaliste', le plus violent sans doute qu'ait produit l'Europe aristocratique des XVIᵉ et XVIIᵉ siècles contre l'argent, la banque et le négoce."

But is this conservative bias true of all of the classic Spanish picaresque novels? Probably. In a recent consideration of this aspect of the Spanish tradition of the picaresque, Anne J. Cruz takes as her point of departure the novels themselves as well as the historical, social, and cultural milieu of Spain. Cruz suggests that the picaresque as a genre had as its primary object the presentation of a "comic discourse—the misadventures of a buffoon written as a jest for the ruling classes." More insidious and pertinent yet is Cruz's analysis of the ways in which this comic discourse sustains the objective distance between fiction and reality even as it supports the political hegemony of the Spanish empire, since the army "finds" many of its new recruits in the population of beggars and *pícaros:*

> The picaresque's popularity domesticates its subversive nature, and the reading public's rejection of the harsh realities faced by an ever-increasing poor as it consumes more and more picaresque novels detailing these realities, discloses yet another example of collusion between literature and ideology. This discourse of poverty chronicles the social history of the marginalized substratum of pícaros all the while ridiculing their plight and colluding with the system by ultimately absorbing them into the Imperial war machine as an acceptable alternative to their destitution.

Thus, in the case of Spain, the picaresque genre must be

viewed as highly reactionary for the ways in which it treats the protagonists, evokes a special type of recognition from its readers, and elicits a response that reinforces the comic nature of its discourse while insisting on the *necessary* otherness of the *pícaros.* In our discussion, then, we should be particularly attuned to the ways in which adaptations and revisions of the picaresque novel "succeed" either in subverting *or* in recapitulating the ideological slant of their model, the necessary and enforced marginalization of the protagonist.

It might seem that **Rubyfruit Jungle,** [Sharon Isabell's] *Yesterday's Lessons,* and [Erica Jong's] *Fanny* are a far cry, historically at least, from the novels used in discussions of the classic tradition of the picaresque. In fact, when **Rubyfruit Jungle** is considered in the context of American society and even more acutely American *literary* culture, it is hard to conceive of anyone more marginal, more removed from access to power and authority, than a Southern lesbian from a poor, working-class family. With neither money nor the potential for upward mobility that would be offered by a husband, Molly Bolt is essentially condemned to her marginality. In this regard, the likely cohorts for such a figure would be black and, somewhat less probably, Jewish, as are the protagonists of [Ralph Ellison's] *The Invisible Man* (1952) and [Saul Bellow's] *The Adventures of Augie March* (1953), two earlier avatars of the *pícaro*. What is different here, however, apart from racial and ethnic identity, is the *gender,* not only of the protagonist but also of the author. On the one hand, Molly *could* form an unlikely literary and sisterly alliance with "la pícara Justina" and Moll Flanders. But on the other hand, these female protagonists of picaresque novels were written by men; and bypassing questions of the aims of representation, suffice it to say that these are, therefore, neither "true" nor "real life" accounts by a "woman."

Of course, autobiography (fictional or otherwise), along with its concomitant first-person narrative voice is a constitutive element of the picaresque novel, perhaps its single most important aspect. In the case of *Lazarillo de Tormes,* the narrating hero relates his *caso* to *vuestra merced* in an attempt to justify his life *and* to implicate his superior in his somewhat nefarious and illicit doings. So whether or not the Molly Bolt of *Rubyfruit Jungle* is, indeed, a surrogate for Brown is, at least initially, a moot point. The novel still conforms to the general outlines of its model and, in so doing, it partakes of what Paul de Man describes as the de-facement or disfiguring of autobiography. But the female protagonist's *and* author's double remove from the picaresque model renders the questions of genre and gender with which we began notably more complex.

Before proceeding too far in this discussion, it would be useful to situate **Rubyfruit Jungle** explicitly in terms of the picaresque. One of the classic descriptions is to be found in Frank Wadleigh Chandler's *Romances of Roguery:*

> The picaresque novel of the Spaniards presents a rogue relating his adventures. He is born of poor and dishonest parents, who are not often troubled with gracing their union by a ceremony, nor particularly pleased at his advent. He

comes up by hook or crook as he may. Either he enters the world with an innate love of the goods of others, or he is innocent and learns by hard raps that he must take care of himself or go to the wall. In either case the result is much the same; in order to live he must serve somebody, and the gains of service he finds himself obliged to augment with the gains of roguery. So he flits from one master to another, all of whom he outwits in his career, and describes to satirize in his narrative. Finally, having run through a variety of strange vicissitudes, measuring by his rule of roguery the variety of human estates, he brings his story to a close. Sometimes he has attained the modest satisfaction of his desires and is ready to relinquish overt fraud; sometimes he is farther than ever from the goal; and sometimes, asking with Ginés de Pasamonte in [the] *Quixote,* "How can my story be finished if my life itself be not finished?" he promises more when he shall have lived it.

This description clearly fits the picaresque novels of the Spanish tradition, and it also elucidates several aspects of Brown's novel. For example, in the opening chapter, the narrator announces:

> No one remembers her beginnings. Mothers and aunts tell us about infancy and early childhood, hoping we won't forget the past when they had total control over our lives and secretly praying that because of it, we'll include them in our future.
>
> I didn't know anything about my own beginnings until I was seven years old, living in Coffee Hollow, a rural dot outside of York, Pennsylvania.

Beginning, appropriately enough, with the question of origins as well as with the function of memory, and thereby the fact that this is an autobiography, the narrator's discussion of events from the past establishes the bias of the narrative voice and of the novel as a whole: the narrative is to be written from the perspective of a woman.

The important issue of beginnings is deferred, however, by the telling of the narrator's first memory, which significantly involves a loss of innocence and tangentially introduces her illegitimacy, which is to say, her *origins.* While watching a male friend urinate, the seven-year old Molly observes that her friend Broccoli has not been circumcised. This anatomical novelty eventually leads the two to form a business partnership in which Broccoli exhibits himself to other schoolchildren, and finally allows some of them to touch his member, for a price. He and Molly split the money fifty-fifty, Molly earning her share by rounding up prospective viewers. Of course, this enterprising realization and exploitation of sexual differences is brought to a conventionally abrupt end when one of the spectators reports the goings-on to a teacher, who in turn speaks to Molly's and to Broccoli's parents. The denouement of this opening chapter, however, reveals that Carrie Bolt is not Molly's *real mother:*

> "You shamed me in front of all of the neighbors, and I've got a good mind to throw you outa this house. You and your high and mighty ways, sail-
>
> ing in the house and out the house as you damn well please. You reading them books and puttin' on airs. You're a fine one to be snotty, Miss Ups, out there in the woods playing with his old dong. Well, I got news for you, you little shitass, you think you're so smart. You ain't so fine as you think you are, *and you ain't mine neither.* And I don't want you now that I know what you're about. *Wanna know who you are, smarty-pants? You're Ruby Drollinger's bastard, that's who you are.* Now let's see you put your nose in the air."
>
> "Who's Ruby Drollinger?"
>
> "Your real mother, that's who and she was a slut, you hear me, Miss Molly? A common, dirty slut who'd lay with a dog if it shook its ass right."
>
> "I don't care. It makes no difference where I came from. I'm here, ain't I?"
>
> "It makes all the difference in the world. Them that's born in wedlock are blessed by the Lord. Them that's born out of wedlock are cursed as bastards. So there."
>
> (my emphasis)

As in the traditional picaresque novel, origins are of special importance in this opening chapter of ***Rubyfruit Jungle.*** But here the protagonist's illegitimate beginnings are additionally inscribed in terms of sexual difference. The marginality of the outsider is compounded by the fact that the narrator is not just female but also illegitimate. The two axes upon which the novel depends are thus clearly delineated. First, and most significant for the question of genre, the novel assumes the guise of a picaresque novel. Second, sexual difference enters plainly into the economy of the somewhat ludicrous but nonetheless profit-oriented sideshow staged by Molly and Broccoli, since it is the phallus, that which is possessed by the male, that generates the income on which women are dependent.

The most subversive aspect of this novel is, however, neither its form nor its putative intent as read by Steinem but, rather, its rejection both of traditional male/female roles and even of non-traditional gender roles within the substrata of gay and lesbian culture. This occurs in several contexts of varying importance. Counter to any received notions of what it means to be a woman, Molly wants to be the doctor during the children's games of doctor-nurse; and she assumes tomboyish behavior, which ultimately leads to her father's declaration of what he views as the clearly unfeminine future of his daughter, prophesying that "Molly is going to college." Even more saliently, when Molly proposes marriage to her intimate childhood friend, Leota B. Bisland, she is shocked at the news that "Girls can't get married." Later she becomes council president, which in turn means, according to her mother and aunt, that she will not be prom queen. Finally she rejects marriage as an option for herself. This apparently complete repudiation of normative social value eventually leads her to New York and to her first real encounters with society's Other.

Yet even this "counter-culture" is typed, much to Molly's dismay and disappointment, in ways not unlike the world from which she fled. When her newfound friend Calvin, a gay black familiar with the ways of the big city (specifically, living on the street and cadging or scavenging means from local restaurants and trashcans), takes Molly to a lesbian bar, she is forced into the realization that lesbians play predetermined social roles *derived* from, *not independent* of, those of heterosexuals. Her first encounter is with "Mighty Mo," a "diesel dyke," who asks her to define herself:

> "Speaking of tits, sugar, are you butch or femme?"
>
> I looked at Calvin but there wasn't time for him to give me a clue for this one. "I beg your pardon?"
>
> "Now don't be coy with Mighty Mo, you Southern belle. They have butches and femmes down below the Mason-Dixon line, don't they? You're a looker baby and I'd like to get to know you, but if you're butch then it'd be like holding hands with your brother now wouldn't it?"
>
> "You're *[sic]* tough luck, Mo. Sorry." Sorry my ass. Thank God she'd spilled the beans.
>
> "You sure fooled me. I thought you were femme. What's this world coming to when you can't tell the butches from the femmes. Ha. Ha." She slapped me on the back fraternally and sauntered off.

This designation of roles, butch/femme, thoroughly perplexes Molly, even though Mo has "spilled the beans," and it elicits the following explanation from Calvin: "A lot of these chicks divide up into butch and femme, male-female. Some people don't, but this bar is heavy into roles. . . ." Disgusted by this version of the homosexual utopia, Molly asserts, "Goddammit. I'm not either one."

Although Calvin says that "some people don't" type themselves in terms of male or female roles and Molly rejects the notion of such typing, this binary view of social-sexual relations is not easy to overcome, even in a mono-sexual lesbian society. Relations with her lover Holly become strained when Molly refuses to accept financial support from a wealthy and influential female suitor. Not only does this refusal impoverish Molly, consequently consigning her to a ramshackle and uncomfortable apartment and a life of abject penury, it reflects ill on Holly, implying some criticism of the lover's reliance on an older, enamored sponsor. Because Molly sees something illicit in such support, like that which takes place in the heterosexual world where women are supported by men, Holly believes she is being censured, and the relationship between the two breaks up.

Molly's subsequent seduction of Polina Bellantoni (author of an academic tome entitled *The Creative Spirit of the Middle Ages*) is even more significant in this adumbration of the heterosexual assault on the gay/lesbian *weltanschauung*. The seduction involves several phases, including their initial meeting in the office where Molly works as an editorial assistant, the process of developing a friendship, and then Molly's announcement of her love for women. Although at first shocked and offended by Molly's

revelation, Polina overcomes her resistance and allows herself to be seduced. As a counterpoint to this seduction of the older female academic and as a means of learning more about the object of her affections, Molly contrives to meet and ultimately sleep with Polina's physically repulsive male lover, Paul Digita, an English professor and "a living study in human debris." The point of this mediated sexuality does not culminate with the seduction of Polina, as *ought* to be the case, nor with the anti-climactic ineptness of Paul's lovemaking, as *appears* to be the case. Rather, the mutually crippling and dependent relationship of the two heterosexuals is used to reveal the inherently liberating force of correct, i.e. non-role playing, homosexual contact. For Polina is only able to enjoy herself sexually while fantasizing that she is a man in the men's room of the Times Square subway station being picked up by another man; and Paul, likewise, is excited only when imagining himself as a woman in the ladies room at the Four Seasons where another woman admires his "voluptuous breasts." The role-playing that contaminated Molly's first experience in *organized* gay/lesbian society in New York during her run-in with Mighty Mo is here shown to be equally corrupting and disabling, to spawn sexually perverse and unfulfilled, morally unnatural individuals. The healthy a-social, a-gender individual at odds with the rest of society—a sick, smothering morass of guilt and repression—triumphs only in her realization of the benefits that accrue from her very marginality.

The outcome of this series of exploits is the seduction of Polina's lovely daughter, Alice. Fed up with Polina's increasingly perverse demands (the last straw is Polina's fantasy of being a "golden shower queen"), Molly discovers Alice, who "was there, all there with no hang-ups, no stories to tell, just herself." This is a somewhat ironic conclusion to the series of encounters, as Molly herself learns, at least in one sense. Alice is also susceptible to corruption, this time in the form of her mother's threat to cut off all financial support for Alice's upcoming college education if the affair with Molly is not brought to an end. Earlier, of course, Molly had stuck to her guns and had refused to be kept by another woman who would have been able to help fulfill her dream of a college education more quickly. That Alice gives in to her mother's pressure only serves to indicate how insidious is the collusion between conventionality and economic well-being, since, although in the guise of a mother-daughter relationship, Alice becomes a kept woman, the fetishized object of her mother's affection; in fact, both mother and daughter admit to a vague desire to sleep with one another.

Even more significant is the remark "no stories to tell." Clearly this refers to the fantasizing and fabulating tendencies/necessities of Polina/Paul, the crutches of their incomplete but outwardly normal sexual relationship. Yet, with this remark, the forthright field of reference notwithstanding, the narrative doubles back on itself, since it raises the question of whether or not *any* or even *every* type of narration and its narrator are not somehow suspect. In turn, to consider the nature of the role of the narrator and of the mode of the narration is to consider one other dimension of the picaresque novel, the representational aspects of the picaresque tradition and the impact that these have on individual novels.

In his book on the *Lazarillo de Tormes,* Harry Sieber shows how the form of "autobiography is not merely verbal self-creation but also self-conversion: Lázaro turns himself into a metaphor." This process of conversion to metaphor is traced by Sieber throughout the *Lazarillo* in treatments of the master/servant dialectic and its linguistic implications: what the narrator learns about language and the worldly ends to which it can be put. Essentially, Sieber's analysis takes what Chandler observes as the need to serve somebody in order to advance in the world and develops it in the context of increasing linguistic mastery made manifest through the diegetic presentation of the *pícaro's* adventures. The nature of the *pícaro* as servant translates into an inversion of the dialectic in which the servant becomes the eventual master of language and therefore of his master, and in which, as narrator, as speaker, he demonstrates a *narrative* authority.

Like Alice, Molly is there, all there with no hang-ups, just herself. But Molly *does* have a story to tell and she is telling it to us throughout **Rubyfruit Jungle.** She is both the narrator and the character whose development is chronicled over time and is, therefore, the very stuff of traditional, i.e. masculine, fiction. But this niggling detail is one never faced by Molly or by the novel, despite the radical exposure of relations between men and women. True, Molly assumes a role of power frequently assumed by a masculine voice, that of the narrator, a voice often masculine even when a woman has authored the text, and she has used her narrative authority to portray situations in which "normality" is obviously less preferable than "abnormality." But despite her rejection of traditional roles and the concomitant role-playing, Molly/Brown has implicitly condoned such activity by fulfilling an unproblematically normative role as the narrator. Because such powers of organization and fabulation are never called into question, issues related to storytelling are suppressed and the only indications of their insidious and detrimental nature surface in the explicit contrasts between Polina/Paul and Alice/Molly.

Nonetheless language is emphasized consistently throughout the novel and there are other, more straightforward instances in which it is scrutinized. We have already seen one occasion during which Molly learns a small lesson about language, specifically semantics, in the scene in the lesbian bar with Mighty Mo. But there are earlier examples of this type of inquiry. The child reporting Molly's and Broccoli's business to the teacher demonstrates the power of speech. The power of not speaking, of keeping secrets, is demonstrated when Molly and her cousin Leroy experiment sexually (more as a way of proving that Leroy is not "queer," despite some homosexual encounters, than for pleasure) and swear their secrecy. " 'You ain't saying anything, Molly, you promised.' 'I'm not breathing word one.' " And Molly learns the value of not speaking when she and a high school cohort catch two married teachers out together and are essentially bribed to obtain their silence.

Yet the real interest in the topic of language, in the power

of both speech and silence, begins somewhat earlier in the novel and centers on the learning of proper English. Moreover, it has to do with nothing less than how a type of linguistic competence ties into the economic and social hierarchy of the American system. When Molly begins junior high school after moving with her family to Florida, she begins to detect subtle differences among the students and to ascertain the nature of the distinction:

> That September I went to Naval Air Junior High School. . . . I kept to myself to see who was who in that place before I made any friends. There were a fair amount of rich kids at Naval Air. You could tell them by their clothes and by the way they talked. I knew enough from English lessons by this time to know they had good grammar. They held themselves away from the red-neck kids. I didn't mix with anybody. . . . Here it was a distinct line drawn between two camps and I was certain I didn't want to be on the side with the greasy boys that leered at me and talked filthy. But I had no money. It took me all of seventh grade to figure out how I would take care of myself in this new situation, but I did figure it out.

> For one thing I made good grades and they counted for a lot. You couldn't go to college without good grades. Even in junior high school, the rich kids talked about college. If I made those grades, I'd get a scholarship, then I'd go too. I also had to stop talking the way we talked at home. I could *think* bad grammar all I wanted, but I learned rapidly *not to speak it.(my emphasis)*

The American version of success is thus coded and couched in terms of language, and, more pertinently, in terms of the selection of certain types of discourse and the exclusion of others. Not only does Molly learn how to speak properly from this point on, but the language of the novel itself becomes more precise, more sophisticated, more *educated.* There is a process, therefore, by which the lessons learned by Molly translate directly into the narration of the novel, the ways in which the material itself is presented.

Yet these linguistic aspects of the picaresque (on the level of novelistic discourse) and Molly's ascension into the more ethereal realms of the Lacanian Symbolic order (in terms of plot) are most apparent not in the guise of narrative fiction, but rather when Molly's sense of purpose, always alluded to and at times openly discussed, becomes the focal point of the novel. All her other impulses have been set aside in deference to her single-minded ambition to get a college degree in filmmaking from New York University. When she is about to finish her studies, and her adviser inquires about her senior project, the problems inherent in being a woman in an otherwise all male preserve, come to a head:

> Professor Walgren, head of the department and dedicated misogynist, called me in his office for the routine consideration of a project.

> "Molly, what are you going to do for your senior project?"

"I thought I'd do a twenty-minute documentary of one woman's life." He seemed unimpressed. Porno-violence was in this year and all the men were busy shooting bizarre fuck scenes with cuts of pigs beating up people at the Chicago convention spliced between the sexual encounters. My project was not in that vein.

"You might have trouble getting the camera out for weekends. By the way, who will be in your crew?"

"No one. No one will consent to be my crew."

Prof. Walgren coughed behind his fashionable wire-rim glasses and said with a hint of malice, "Oh, I see, they won't take orders from a woman, eh?"

"I don't know. I hadn't noticed that they were too good at taking orders from each other."

"Well, good luck on your film. I'll be eager to see what you crank out."

All of the male violence against, and repression of, women detailed in the novel culminates in this interview. Effects seen only sporadically earlier, most explicitly when Holly decked a male customer who fondled her at a Playboy Club clone called The Flick, are here explicitly linked to the institutionalized nature of male dominance. The professor is not merely a misogynist but malicious to boot, the male students are into porno-violence, and Molly has neither the help nor the support of her fellow students or, worse yet, access to the equipment necessary to complete successfully the degree program. The marginality of her existence as a lesbian in a heterosexual world is now forcefully re-compounded by her gender. Because the odds are stacked against her, Molly sees no choice but to steal as much film as she can carry and to walk off with one of the cameras without signing it out. The equipment in hand, Molly catches a bus for Fort Lauderdale and a final confrontation with her mother, rather, her *adoptive* mother, Carrie, whom she films throughout a week-long visit. Molly then returns to New York with a cinematic biography of her stepmother as her final project.

The students' films are shown at an event known as Project Night. As the narrator tells it:

> Project night was a big event. All the other students had their "chicks" with them vying for who was best dressed in the downwardly-mobile category. They introduced their dates as "my chick" or "my old lady." I came by myself. It freaked them out that I didn't swish in with some bearded number sporting a tie-dyed tee shirt. And the projects began. The one that drew the most applause was a gang rape on an imaginary Martian landscape with half the cast dressed as Martians, the other half, as humans. All the men mumbled about what a profound racial statement it was. The "chicks" gasped.
>
> My film was the last on the list and by the time we got to it some of the audience had already left. There was Carrie speeding away in her rocking chair looking straight at the camera and being herself. . . . The last thing she said in the

film was, "I'm gonna turn this house into a big gingerbread cake with icing on the corners. Then when those goddamn bill collectors come after me I just tell 'em to break off a piece of the house and leave me alone. In time they eat the whole house," she chuckled, "then I'll be sittin' out in the sunshine that the good Lord made. I'll be out in the lilies of the field that's richer than all King Solomon's gold. That ain't a bad way to die when yer as old as I am." She laughed a strong, certain laugh and as that laugh died so did the light.
>
> No one clapped. No one made a sound. I began rewinding the film and they filed out by the projection table. I looked at these cohorts of mine through the last years and not one of them could look me in the face. They walked out of the room silently and the last one to go was Professor Walgren. He stopped at the door, turned to say something, thought better of it; his eyes on the floor, he slowly shut the door so that it didn't make a sound.
>
> I graduated *summa cum laude* and Phi Beta Kappa.

Despite the obstacles posed by the misogynistic institution of power at NYU, Molly succeeds in very specific and culturally correct ways. Not only did she succeed as a film student, she received the wider recognition and distinction of becoming a member of Phi Beta Kappa and of graduating at the head of her class. So some things do work out in the world. Yet, as if showing her disdain for the system that had seen fit to reward her (at least with titles), Molly neither participates in the commencement exercises nor in subsequent film department functions. She is more preoccupied with the pressing task of finding a job. But this, too, proves difficult, again, because she is a woman. "The guy who made the Martian rape went right into CBS as an assistant director for a children's program. CBS was full up, they told me." As confirmation of the institutionalization of misogyny and cripplingly violent sexual tendencies, a male filmmaker gets an important job in the production of children's programming, while the best Molly can come up with anywhere in the film world are jobs as a secretary at M-G-M, a copywriter for a PR office at Warner Brothers Seven Arts, or playing the role of a hermaphrodite in an underground film.

Molly remains in her present job as an editorial assistant. Her academic work and achievements have brought her no rewards beyond the useless proliferation of awards; and *Rubyfruit Jungle,* as if fulfilling the picaresque program to the letter, ends with these words of frustration:

> My bitterness was reflected in the news, full of stories about people my own age raging down the streets in protest. But somehow I knew my rage wasn't their rage and they'd have run me out of their movement for being a lesbian anyway. I read somewhere too that women's groups were starting but they'd trash me just the same. What the hell. I wished I could be that frog back in old Ep's old pond. I wished I could get up in the morning and look at the day the way I used to when I was a child. I wished I could walk down the streets and not hear those constant,

abrasive sounds from the mouths of the opposite sex. Damn, I wished the world would let me be myself. But I knew better on all counts. I wish I could make my films. That wish I can work for. One way or another I'll make those movies and I don't feel like having to fight until I'm fifty. But if it does take that long then watch out world because I'm going to be the hottest fifty-year-old this side of the Mississippi.

True to Chandler's observation that the *pícaro* "sometimes . . . promises more when he shall have lived it," Molly vows to make films, to continue her struggle and her story. This conclusion could be read, and probably was intended, as a strong assertion of a type of commitment; and, in fact, it does refocus several aspects of the novel we have discussed—but in a peculiar way. For it is important to recognize that the way Molly acquires her skills as a filmmaker is an allegory for the process of *Rubyfruit Jungle* itself. The narrator, who appropriates the cameras virtually denied her by her male colleagues and professors, co-opts the genre and means of expression that have been traditionally viewed as masculine and as presided over by men. The end result is the silencing of men, the "author's" (Molly Bolt/Rita Mae Brown) antagonists, and the recognition of an individual female voice. Molly and the complicitous author, Brown, stage a successful coup in that they demonstrate and represent respectively the vile and insidious nature of the world, supposedly turning what would be the tools of repression into a liberating force in society.

But we must ask in what sense Brown succeeds in overcoming either her version of traditional society or the conservative ideological determinants of the picaresque novel that she adapts for her own ends. Because Brown depicts both realistically and relentlessly the outcome of Molly's experiences, success is only a relative notion, not an absolute value, and the novel ends on a note of failure, with the isolation and alienation of the protagonist typical of the picaresque program. More significant, however, is the tenor of the isolation, the tone of Molly's final vow. Far from overcoming her male antagonists, Molly wins the battle only to lose the war. The silencing of her colleagues translates directly into the reinforcement of her marginality; she is utterly alien to the world around her. The novel ends, therefore, with the silencing of the narrator, with her inability to make films. Even those who ought to be sympathetic, who ought to understand her and her plight remain somehow apart from Molly, somehow an element of the status quo that rejects her and is rejected by her. In no way, then, does she or can she take part in the world around her. The world that she would reform, that she would expose, simply reaffirms and reinforces its judgment both with respect to Molly and to lesbians, to say nothing of women generally.

Furthermore, the story that Brown offers, in which she advocates an end to storytelling, *begins* by implicating those people presumably most sympathetic to her cause and who have the most to gain from any change in the general economy of repression of and discrimination against women: "*Mothers and aunts* tell us about infancy and early childhood, hoping we won't forget the past when

they had total control over our lives and secretly praying that because of it, we'll include them in our future." *Rubyfruit Jungle,* in tracing Molly Bolt's journey towards an independent life as an adult woman who loves women, begins as a recuperation of a past dominated by and ruled over by women, as if her childhood had been shaped solely by *matriarchal* forces of fabulation ("Mothers and aunts tell us"). In fact, the matriarchy suggested by the opening paragraph of the novel was shown to exist within the *patriarchal* strictures explicitly condemned, "Those constant, abrasive sounds from the mouths of the opposite sex," the social ideology inherent in the mere words of men. There is a twofold condemnation here, a rejection of both patriarchy and matriarchy, that necessitates a reconsideration of the touching reconciliation between Molly and her adoptive mother, and of the subsequent transcription of Carrie's life story, which characterizes *and embodies,* key moments of the narrative. Like Alice and Molly, "there was Carrie speeding away in her rocking chair looking straight at the camera and *being herself.*" The earlier suggestion that fabulation is somehow perverse, as in the cases of Polina and Paul, is here contradicted by both Carrie and Molly in the alternative stories they respectively relate and represent. Carrie imagines herself quite literally eaten out of house and home, "sittin' out in the sunshine that the good Lord made. . . . out in the lilies of the field that's richer than all King Solomon's gold." Likewise, but in minor key, at the end of the novel, Molly affirms her own poverty and alienation, this time not in the presumably triumphant terms of the Bible but, rather, in a dispirited lament. Indeed, one wonders whether or not Carrie is justified in her optimism as she sits "speeding away" in her chair without advancing one inch, whether or not there isn't more of a similarity between the stories of the two women than either would like to admit. The alternative story that Molly discovers in the life of her stepmother and offers to the world recuperates once again the alienation experienced by all women and, moreover, shows how Carrie acquiesces to the authority of that alienation. The supposedly serious exposé of the problems attending those whom society and its culture consider marginal ends by incriminating (perhaps not without reason), worse yet, by rejecting a large portion of its natural constituency, serving to corroborate the absolute otherness of *every* individual in society. [Mandrell adds in a footnote that Martha Chew, in her essay "Rita Mae Brown: Feminist Theorist and Southern Novelist,": "has a completely different reading of *Rubyfruit Jungle* and Brown's aims and role in these issues. Her reading of the novel primarily turns on the possibility of seeing both Molly's black lover Holly and her white academic lover Polina as doubles for the protagonist, as manifestations of a desire to identify with every aspect of culture and society. I think that this is too sympathetic a reading and that it fails to account for Molly's single-mindedness of purpose and for the ironic and oftentimes insensitive portrayal of the secondary characters. Similarities in names aside, these other characters represent, I believe, whatever is alien to Molly, that with which she cannot identify."] (pp. 150-63)

James Mandrell, "Questions of Genre and Gender: Contemporary American Versions of the Feminine Picaresque," in Novel: A Forum on Fiction, *Vol. 20, No. 2, Winter, 1987, pp. 149-70.*

John Blades (review date 14 February 1988)

[*In the following review, Blades commends the entertainment value of* Starting from Scratch.]

You'd better believe Rita Mae Brown when she calls her book **Starting From Scratch** a "different kind of writers' manual." As readers of **Rubyfruit Jungle** and her other novels already know, Brown is a different kind of writer—rowdy, irreverent and combative. Always a little eager to displease, she calls herself an "equal opportunity offender." Even so, there's almost nothing to offend anyone in **Starting From Scratch,** although embryonic novelists/screenwriters may feel cheated if they expect Brown to give them a quick fix on how to write marketable novels and/or screenplays.

"Writing can be taught," she insists. "It is not a mysterious process." But in the process of demystification, Brown occasionally neglects the practical advice in favor of philosophical digressions on such topics as the metaphysical properties of an open-faced sandwich, the "subconsciously homoerotic" tendencies of aggressively male writers and the "grammatical existentialism" of the passive voice. In her book, it's essential for a writer to be bisexual, to love cats passionately (she owns five, but concedes that two are enough for almost everyone else) and to know enough Latin to read Horace, Livy and Cicero. "If you don't know Latin, you don't know English."

Brown not only knows Latin and English, she also has an intimidating knowledge of Greek mythology, etymology and Western Civilization, among a multitude of other exalted subjects. She has evidently read and reread most of the Great Books, along with thousands of merely good and lousy ones, and compiled an annotated reading list that begins in 665 with "Caedmon's Hymn" and ends, 13 centuries and 30 pages later, with Anthony Burgess' *Earthly Powers.*

None of this is intended to suggest that Brown totally dispenses with the nuts, bolts, gears, springs and other structural components that make up a well-constructed, marketable manuscript. She devotes chapters to character development and plot, saying, "You need to know about people far more than you need to know about mechanical plot devices." She prescribes conditioning exercises, both literary ("Write a story about two gay waiters at the Last Supper") and physical ("Even if you don't want to hop in place while wearing pink tights and purple leg warmers, go to one good aerobics class."). She also includes consumer reports on dictionaries (recommending the 13-volume Oxford English Dictionary for those who can afford the $900, Webster's Third for those can't) and typewriters (her preference is the $945 IBM Correcting Selectric III).

When you get right down to the basics, however, **Starting From Scratch** is no more helpful (or no more harmful) than most how-to books for writers. What makes Brown's manual "different" from the others is its entertainment

value, which mostly comes from her natural exuberance, blunt charm and impudent humor. **Starting From Scratch** is at its most entertaining when Brown is speaking from experience, passing along autobiographical anecdotes about her voracious childhood reading habit, her struggles to earn a living from her novels (she still doesn't suffer from "Affluenza"), the hazards of promoting her books on the "literary vaudeville" circuit and her equally hazardous, but enriching, tours of duty as a movie and TV writer.

In whatever form it takes, writing makes her happy, Brown says, and her happiness is contagious, even when her wisdom is weirdly unconventional, her prose is graceless and her advice is utter nonsense. If for no other reason, Brown deserves our eternal gratitude for her warning to aspiring fiction writers about the unfortunate "rash of novels in the last decade (that) have been written in the present tense. It's a fad and it won't last. There are good reasons for writing in the past tense." On the other hand, there's no reason to be grateful for her defamatory remarks about book critics, whom she describes as people "who'd put a cyanide cap in an Easter Egg." Really, Ms. Brown, that description doesn't fit any critic I know.

> John Blades, "Wit, Wisdom, Nonsense from Rita Mae Brown," in Chicago Tribune—Books, *February 14, 1988, p. 3.*

Brown on categorizing authors:

Where do readers and publishers draw the line? What is homosexual, black or women's material and what is not? Who is a homosexual writer and who is not? Alice Walker's award-winning *The Color Purple* contains a lesbian episode. Are we to ponder Walker's sexuality, or is she just placed into the black category, which blots out any other considerations? What do we do with Noel Coward, Gertrude Stein, Henry James and Virginia Woolf? What about those risky poems Shakespeare wrote to his Dark Lady? Was the Dark Lady a man, as some scholars surmise, or was Shakespeare in love with an African? Does it matter?

Classifying fiction by the race, sex or sex preference of the author is a discreet form of censorship. Americans buy books by convicted rapists, murderers and Watergate conspirators because those books are placed on the bestseller shelf, right out in front where people can see them. Yet novels by people who are not safely white or resolutely heterosexual are on the back shelves, out of sight. It's the back of the bus all over again. Is this not a form of censorship?

Rita Mae Brown, Publisher's Weekly, *15 July 1983.*

Ed Quillen (review date March-April 1988)

[*In the following review, Quillen praises Brown's engaging prose and useful advice in* Starting from Scratch, *but faults her sometimes flawed logic.*]

In the latest round of books for writers, the most enjoyable to read, and yet the most disturbing, is Rita Mae Brown's **Starting from Scratch.** Her prose is engaging as she recounts her life, from growing up in a butcher's home where books were cherished through her struggle to write for a living in Manhattan.

Through her Tutorial Memoir, she dispenses useful advice—avoid the passive voice, learn Latin, cherish the richness of the English language, don't think you can snort and guzzle and still be a productive writer. Her story holds your interest and her guidance is generally good.

So why is Brown's book disturbing? For one thing, her use of "s/he" as a pronoun jars my traditional and male eyes. Good prose sounds good, and that is a construction you cannot read aloud. How do you pronounce it? "S slash he?" "Ssssheeee?" "She or he?" As someone who advises us to study English literature from *Beowulf* to Anthony Burgess, Brown owes us an explanation of the development of personal pronouns, as well as her reasoning for her pronominal choice. Instead, she just throws her assumptions at us, without an explanation. For another, she sometimes doesn't know what she's talking about. In a defense of the reality of auras, she assails Aristotle, and provides this as example of Aristotelian logic:

> A: *All birds sing.*
>
> B: *Madonna sings.*
>
> *Synthesis: Therefore, Madonna is a bird.*

Little wonder that Rita Mae Brown's Aristotle is so untrustworthy. But that's not an example of Aristotelian logic. It was Aristotle who gave us the tools to detect and categorize such flawed syllogisms. Despite those flaws, and several others, *Starting from Scratch* generally entertains while providing sound advice. You could do much worse. (p. 3)

> Ed Quillen, "Writers on Writing," in The Bloomsbury Review, *Vol. 8, No. 2, March-April, 1988, pp. 3, 10.*

Don G. Campbell (review date 27 November 1988)

[*In the following review, Campbell praises the humor in* Bingo.]

Tongue firmly in cheek, Rita Mae Brown has turned her fancy loose on the sleepy little town of Runnymeade—split, smack-dab down the middle, by the Mason-Dixon line—the feuding Hunsenmeir sisters and an adopted daughter of one of the sisters, Nickel Smith, and her mixed-up love life. In *Bingo* Brown has a field day with Julia Ellen Hunsenmeir Smith, 82 years old and a running kite flier of singular talents, and her sister, Louise, admitting to 80 and pushing 86, and the fight between them to nail the eligible new widower in town, Edgar Tutweiler Walters. Their sparring ring: the town's weekly Bingo game, held every Friday night in the St. Rose of Lima Catholic Church. Nickel (actually, Nicole), Julia's bisexual adopted daughter, has conflicts of her own to resolve: how to buy the Runnymeade Clarion, the newspaper for which she works, from the retiring publisher to keep the ownership local, and how to rationalize her torrid affair with her best friend's husband. Being half the town's admitted gay population (the other is Mr. Pierre, who oper-

ates the Curl 'n' Twirl) has its pressures. Underneath Runnymeade's placid, Southern exterior—where the statue of a Yankee general on a horse stands on the Pennsylvania side of the main street and faces Confederate soldiers and a Rebel cannon on the Maryland side—all hell is prepared to break loose when the Bingo game of the year, Bingo Blackout, reaches its climax.

While, at times, Brown's humor can get a tad arch, she's produced, on balance, a genuinely funny novel, and some of the one-line zappers between the two sprightly Hunsenmeir sisters are better than anything you'll hear at the Improv.

> Don G. Campbell, in a review of "Bingo," in Los Angeles Times Book Review, *November 27, 1988, p. 12.*

Daniel B. Levine (essay date Fall 1989)

[*In the following essay, Levine analyzes Brown's allusions to classical mythology in* Southern Discomfort.]

Rita Mae Brown is probably best known as a feminist/lesbian theorist, novelist, author of **Rubyfruit Jungle,** and former lover of tennis star Martina Navratilova. Less well-known is the fact that she majored in English and Classics at New York University before getting a doctorate in Political Science and becoming a popular author. Her senior thesis for the B.A. (1968) was on metaphor in Aristophanes' *Birds.* This paper shows that her interest in classical literature, especially Greek mythology, has strongly colored her best-selling novel **Southern Discomfort.**

The novel **Rubyfruit Jungle** brought Rita Mae Brown national attention as a writer, and may serve as a starting point for the present discussion. The story is thinly-disguised autobiography: protagonist Molly Bolt, like the author, was born in Pennsylvania in the mid-1940s, orphaned and adopted, raised in Florida, expelled from the University of Florida for political activism, and moved to New York for the completion of college and entrance into the world of activism. Molly Bolt, like Rita Mae Brown, studied Latin in high school and both Greek and Latin in college. The character's attitude towards this early classical influence is telling; she always found it immediate and relevant, although her attitude towards the Classics was not always mature. This is what Molly Bolt says of her high school Latin experience, which she shared with her friends Connie and Carolyn:

> All three of us took advanced Latin together, and in our junior year, we applied ourselves to the task of translating the *Aeneid.* Aeneas is a one-dimensional bore. We never could figure out how Virgil got it published, and the tedium of the main character encouraged us to enliven those sultry days in Latin class. The teacher, Miss Roebuck, only added to our energy. Miss Roebuck was from Georgia, and her Latin was Georgian Latin. It was always "all a ya chotaw est" rather than *alea jacta est.* We had heard the rumor from seniors who survived the *Aeneid* that Miss Roebuck would burst into tears when

we got to the part where Aeneas leaves Dido. Connie called her "Dildo," of course. So on that day Connie and I decided to cinch Latin for the rest of our high school career. We brought onions hidden in handkerchiefs. Miss Roebuck's voice started to quiver as Dido looked out her window at the departing Trojan. Then at Virgil's giving Dido her suicidal buildup, Miss Roebuck opened the waterworks. The class tried very hard not to look up from their texts and trots they were so embarrassed, but Connie and I started sniffling and showed tears on our cheeks. Carolyn looked at us in amazement and I flashed the onion at her. Her Presbyterian morality was offended, but she couldn't suppress a laugh. Soon the entire classroom was in hysterics which only highlighted our grief over the Carthaginian queen's plight. Miss Roebuck looked at us with infinite fondness and then in her stentorian voice, "Class, most of you are shamefully, shamefully insensitive. Great literature and great tragedy are beyond your grasp." She dismissed the class and called Connie and me aside. "You girls are true students of the classics." She patted us on the backs with tears in her eyes and ushered us out the classroom.

(Rubyfruit Jungle)

Molly Bolt grows in maturity in the course of *Rubyfruit Jungle,* and when she takes film and classics courses at N.Y.U., she describes her studies in a much different manner, probably reflecting Rita Mae Brown's own appreciation of what Classical Studies had done for her. Molly is at a dinner and surprises her hosts by reading out loud from Hrothsvitha's Latin play *Dulcitius.* When she is complimented, the following discussion ensues:

"Thank you. I studied [Latin] all through high school and I'm still at in in college. I'm reading Livy and Tacitus these days with a little Attic Greek thrown in for good measure." Polina clapped her hands and gave me a bear hug. "No wonder you've been so helpful to me! You're a classics scholar." . . .

"Well, I'm not really a classics scholar. I'm in film studies. I take Latin and Greek for the language credit, but I love them."

"I hope so. Greek is too difficult to take for laughs. If you're in film studies, why Latin and Greek?"

"Uh—this may sound funny to you, but Latin especially has helped my ability to discipline myself more than anything I've ever studied. It wouldn't matter what I would do, Latin would help me because it taught me how to think. And Greek, that adds a soaring quality, something that pushed my mind fast." . . .

Alice was sitting wide-eyed through all this. "Molly, is that true about the Latin or are you buttering the old lady up?" . . .

"No. I know it sounds weird but it was the best thing I ever studied. I take that back. Not the best thing, but the most useful."

(Rubyfruit Jungle)

In *Southern Discomfort* there is also a good deal of space devoted to Latin studies, and we gain insight into the author's early experience with the language when young Catherine (who probably represents the author) speaks of her first Latin lessons, saying that the endings on Latin words are like cuff links:

You know, little cuff links you pinch a sleeve with. If you didn't put those endings there, everything hangs open. The words wouldn't make any sense. . . . But, Aunt Tense, I don't understand how someone like Julius Ceasar, who was so smart, couldn't figure out how to talk like we do. We don't use endings and we make sense.

(Southern Discomfort)

Brown's comments outside of her novels corroborate her own love of classical language, myth, and history, especially in her recent book, *Starting from Scratch: A Different Kind of Writers' Manual.* In this work she insists that the study of Latin is absolutely essential to the modern English writer: "I'll be brutally frank: If you don't know Latin, you don't know English. If you want to write, you need this tool." In a chapter entitled "Myth and Symbol, as Opposed to Hit or Myth," Brown discusses the need to know the culture of the Greeks in order to understand western literature. She bemoans the lack of Latin in the modern secondary-school curriculum, calling its loss one of the reasons that Americans are so ignorant of Greek mythology. She cautions, "ignore mythology, and the force of writers before World War I will be lost upon you." She explains the importance of the Olympians, and divides them into "right brain" and "left brain" groupings, contrasting Apollo and Dionysus, Athena and Aphrodite, etc. In an interview (1983) with *Contemporary Authors* she says, "Those writers who have most influenced me are Aristophanes, Euripides, and Mark Twain. When I doubt, I return, always, to Athens, fifth century B.C. My next stop-off point is Rome, roughly 33 B.C." In the same interview, she says that she also enjoys reading "Horace, Terence, Eudora Welty, Alice Walker, Barbara Tuchman."

Ms. Brown wrote numerous political essays during her involvement in feminist and gay organizations between 1969 and 1975. These have been collected in the anthology *A Plain Brown Rapper,* which traces her activist odyssey. She founded the New York University Homophile League, and left it because the homosexual movement was too male-dominated. She joined the National Organization for Women and found it too anti-lesbian for her liking. She joined the radical feminists group Redstockings, but found them inimical to lesbianism also, so she left. She also joined—and left—Gay Liberation. Eventually she became part of the New York "Radicalesbians" collective, which defined lesbianism as a political act. In 1971 she organized a group of lesbian feminists who named themselves after the Greek spirits of vengeance, "The Furies." Brown's feminism and classicism again came together in the 1971 publication of her [translation of] *Hrothsvitha: Six Medieval Latin Plays.*

In the midst of this political turmoil, Ms. Brown met Alexis Smith, who encouraged her to become a serious writer instead of a pamphleteer. Subsequently, in 1973

Brown dedicated her first novel to Ms. Smith, who, she writes, gave her:

> a playful push in the direction of my typewriter. Of course, after you read the book, you may wish that she had pushed me in front of something moving faster than a typewriter.
>   *(Rubyfruit Jungle,* Dedication)

Other novels followed, including *In Her Day, Six of One, Southern Discomfort, Sudden Death,* and *High Hearts.* She also wrote screenplays for *Rubyfruit Jungle* and *Slumber Party Massacre,* and co-authored the award-winning television special *I Love Liberty* (ABC-TV, 1982). In the nine years between *Rubyfruit Jungle* and *Southern Discomfort,* the novelist grew in confidence and mischief. Ms. Brown begins *Southern Discomfort* with the following note, which sounds like something out of an Aristophanic parabasis:

> If you don't like my book, write your own. If you don't think you can write a novel, that ought to tell you something. If you think you can, do. No excuses. If you still don't like my novels, find a book you do like. Life is too short to be miserable. If you like my novels, I commend your good taste.

Southern Discomfort is a book about racism, among other things. The title refers to the shame and helplessness felt by Southerners about their racial caste system. Set in Montgomery, Alabama in 1918 and 1928, it is the story of Hortensia Reedmuller Banastre, a pillar of white society who does not love her husband and two sons, but has a passionate affair with a young black man and bears his child. The latter part of the book chronicles this child's difficulties in adjusting to a world where she is completely at home neither in white nor black society.

When the novel appeared in 1982, critics chose to concentrate on its political, racial, sexual, and "southern" themes; no one has remarked on its use of myth. However, its use is so pervasive that the novel could even be used as a textbook example of classical *Nachleben* in a college course on Greek Mythology.

There are three major focuses to the novel: Hortensia Banastre's aristocratic white family, the black family whose son Hercules becomes Hortensia's lover, and the prostitutes of Montgomery, Alabama's red light district. Each has its own association with Greek myth.

First, the Banastre family. Hortensia and her husband Carwyn have two sons—Edward and Paris—who are very much like the mythological Hector and his brother the bowman. Paris is beautiful, a seducer of women, and taunted by Edward for his lack of courage—in similar fashion to their Iliadic counterparts, especially in *Iliad* 3. At one point during a fight Paris hides under his mother's skirt while Edward taunts him:

> "Mama's boy, mama's boy," Edward chanted.
>
> [Hortensia] "Enough!"
>
> Edward shut up.

From underneath the skirt Paris called back, "I am not a mama's boy."
>   *(Southern Discomfort)*

Their father Carwyn does not love Paris as much as he loves Edward, just as Priam preferred Hector to all his other sons. Edward, like Hector, was always better than his younger brother, who was jealous of the older brother's successes. When Edward's team was victorious in the Halloween Great Witch Hunt, Paris says, "Just wait, Edward, I'll win." Brown continues: "Paris eyed his brother's shiny medal, tears in his eyes." Paris' life is dedicated to gaining the love of his mother Hortensia, and when he impregnates a local girl of good family, his mother says "I fear you'll bring our house down as did that Trojan." Paris counters: "He killed Achilles first, remember."

In the Greek myth, Hector does his best to save the state after Paris' fatal liaison with Helen brings the Achaean hosts to Troy. Likewise, in *Southern Discomfort,* older brother Edward nobly offers to marry the girl pregnant by his brother Paris, thus gaining the family a reprieve from the shame and ruin the profligate sibling has brought upon the house. Further parallel with the *Iliad* emerges in a scene when the boys receive their Christmas gifts. An epic Homeric battle of childish proportions erupts:

> Edward loved his set of lead soldiers and Paris had received a toy fire engine with pumps and hoses that worked. He lost no time in turning it on Edward's soldiers. . . .
>
> Later that day, a fight broke out between them. Paris threw half of Edward's soldiers in the fire. Livid, Edward struck his brother, a soldier in his hand. A deep four-inch gash sent Paris reeling, but it didn't prevent him from opening up his pocket knife and stabbing Edward's hand. The point of the blade ran clean through the fleshy part by the thumb.
>   *(Southern Discomfort)*

Paris eventually blackmails his mother into sleeping with him, and when he finds that this still does not bring her love, he attacks her illegitimate daughter and is killed by Hortensia herself. The young man's passion for Hortensia consumes the family, just as the Homeric Paris' passion for Helen destroyed Troy. Brown adds incest to the equation, enriching the mythological parallels by evoking the ruinous crime of Oedipus.

The novel's middle-class black family consists of Placide and Ada Jinks and their three children. Placide is a delivery man, and "looked like baby Atlas"; mother Ada is a strict Latin teacher. As a result of her influence, no doubt, their children are named Apollo, Athena, and Hercules. Apollo enters the army and is killed in the First World War. Athena is a bright girl who goes to college and then law school. Hercules, the youngest, is an excellent boxer and totally devoted to his sister. Their relationship closely parallels that of their mythological namesakes. Hercules was not as intelligent as his sister: "Hercules as yet showed no signs of an intellectual career." His labors are for her sake:

> The boy dreamed of sports. . . . Football, baseball, basketball, track and field—whatever the

sport, Hercules beat everybody at it. He's even taken up boxing, to the horror of Ada, who considered it truly low-rent. But there was money in pickup fights and Hercules, without a thought for himself, inevitably sent his earnings to Athena.

(Southern Discomfort)

People tease Athena because she does not have a proper beau, and although she eventually marries, she closely resembles the virgin goddess of wisdom. "Athena fascinated her brother with her knowledge." When Hercules suggests that his sister become a doctor, she responds, "I wouldn't mind being a doctor, but I think Apollo will become one." The Jinks children's names match the functions of their Greek mythological namesakes. As Hortensia Banastre says to Hercules when she knocks him over with her horse Bellerophon, "Hercules, you are aptly named."

Ada tutors Latin, and is passionate about education. The family dubbed her "Madam Cato": "Her *Delenda est Carthago* was 'Education is the hope of the Negro race.' " Her Christmas present from her husband was an illuminated manuscript, making that the best Christmas of her life. When her son tells her that he will fight on 15 March, she objects because the Ides of March is "the unluckiest day of the year!" Hercules responds: "Mother, you're the only person in the world still mourning Julius Caesar." When Hercules dies, his mother reacts "like a Roman matron of the Augustan age: no tears, hysteria or complaints."

The novel also makes use of the Apollo-Dionysus dichotomy. Hortensia is the first example of the struggle between the irrational and rational, changing from living a joyless life "from the neck up," to giving in to the wild passion she enjoyed with Hercules. More obviously, though, the prostitutes Blue Rhonda Latrec and Banana Mae Parker are part of the struggle between the Dionysian and Apollonine, very much in the vein of Euripides' Pentheus-Bacchae conflict. They are colorful, wild characters, constantly drinking and taking cocaine. They and the other whores of Water Street are outside of "proper" society (but supported by its pillars), and throughout the book suffer attacks from Reverend Linton Ray, who musters his religious flock to stamp out the evils of prostitution and alcohol:

> No drinking, no smoking, no dancing, no anything—this was Linton's creed. . . . Upright, self-righteous and joyless, Linton herded the one hundred or so souls under his protection. In his congregation the absence of feeling was declared a deliverance from temptation; emptiness was spiritual triumph.
>
> *(Southern Discomfort)*

This Pentheus constantly attacks the maenads on Water Street, who debate him on the "evil" of alcohol, and eventually attack their persecutor during one annual "Witch Hunt" at Halloween. Dressed up as ghosts, Blue Rhonda and Banana Mae knock the reverend unconscious and pour corn whiskey all over him and his Bible. Later, all the whores gather and disarm a mob of torch-bearing Christian zealots by dressing in choir robes (normally used to simulate Christian settings in fantasy sex-sessions) and singing pious hymns, reminiscent of Pentheus' mes-

senger who spied on the maenads and saw them worshipping Dionysus in a chaste and calm manner. Dionysus continually makes the argument to Pentheus in the *Bacchae* that his female followers are in reality pious. The whores, of course, are not, but only give the impression of piety to confound the reverend. In the Prologue, the prostitutes are further associated with maenads ("mad women") when Brown says:

> In this world, lying, fornicating and thieving are prerogatives of the sane. Small wonder that the two women, or any prostitutes, for that matter, were regarded as nuts.
>
> *(Southern Discomfort, Prologue)*

Later, Reverend Linton Ray runs for the legislature on a platform of Christian morality, trying to become like Pentheus: a moralist with state-sanctioned power to legislate morality. As one of the Water Street prostitutes puts it, "He'll make sinners into criminals."

Blue Rhonda Latrec is Linton's most persistent critic and tormentor. Even though she has a fatal disease, she goes to his church just to belittle the priggish preacher and flaunt her defiance of his religion. The parallel with Euripides' *Bacchae* is strengthened by the fact that in the book's epilogue Blue Rhonda dies and is revealed to be a man. Blue Rhonda's cross-dressing reminds us of the Pentheus-Dionysus struggle, when the king of Thebes remarks on the soft and feminine appearance of Dionysus in disguise, and of the transvestism of Pentheus himself when he dresses as a maenad.

Theban legend also surfaces in the parallel to be drawn between Blue Rhonda and the seer Tiresias. The myth that the latter was divinely changed into a woman and became a prostitute can help to explain the surprise ending of **Southern Discomfort,** when Blue Rhonda's letter to her friends states: "God played a joke on me and put me in a man's body, and not much of a man's body at that."

The Great Witch Hunt took place every Halloween in Montgomery, and it functions as a primitive religious background for the story. The white children divided into two teams that vied with each other to solve clues placed throughout town and to find the Great Witch, who would reward the winning team with medals:

> Legend had it that the Halloween game was as old as Montgomery, which was incorporated in 1819. A father made it up to soothe his tiny daughter's fear of ghosts about on that night. Whenever it started, no resident could remember being without it.
>
> *(Southern Discomfort)*

Parallel to this use of primitive ritual, Blue Rhonda thinks about dying, and "wondered if the origin of all religion was in the stark fear of death." The novel has a preoccupation with origins and creation, which reflects both Ms. Brown's wondering about her own biological parents and her love of things ancient.

For whatever reasons, Greek and Roman historical and mythological themes are second nature to Rita Mae Brown. Other classical references abound. When a judge dies in a whorehouse his corpse is rolled "in a rug like Cleopatra." There is an infelicitous reference to Thermopylae, where a character thinks that Athenians died there, as well as passing references to Aphrodite, the Titans, Olympus, Zeus, a character named Narcissa looking into a mirror, Persephone's rescue by Demeter from Hades, the Trojan Horse, Aeschylus, Sophocles, Euripides, and Aristophanes, Orestes chased by Harpies, Helen of Troy, Aeneas, Pandora, Adonis, the Delphic Oracle, Pericles and Augustus, Hector, Achilles, and Odysseus, Nike at Samothrace, Olympian laughter of the gods, Artemis, and Juno.

Greek myth lives for Brown and her characters, and provides another dimension to a story already rich in character and situation. The author's classical education has made a major contribution to her work; Rita Mae Brown practices in **Southern Discomfort** what she preaches in **Starting from Scratch,** using mythology's "cultural shorthand" to enrich her tale. Like Attic Greek for Molly Bolt, the all-pervasive mythological dimension of **Southern Discomfort** "adds a soaring quality, something that pushed my mind fast." (pp. 63-70)

> *Daniel B. Levine, "Uses of Classical Mythology in Rita Mae Brown's 'Southern Discomfort'," in* Classical and Modern Literature, *Vol. 10, No. 1, Fall, 1989, pp. 63-70.*

Mark Gerson   (review date December 1990)

[*In the following review, Gerson provides a positive assessment of* Wish You Were Here.]

Crozet, Virginia, isn't St. Mary Mead, and Mary "Harry" Haristeen isn't Jane Marple. But in **Wish You Were Here,** Rita Mae Brown uses village life much the same way Agatha Christie did: to illustrate that human emotions are no less complex in a rural backwater than they are in the big city. And they're kept just as well concealed. "It's a small-town illusion—thinking we know each other," Harry's best friend remarks shortly before the first of a series of seemingly senseless murders rocks this peaceful hamlet.

Using Harry, an eccentric cast of Southern characters, and a menagerie of household pets, Brown skilfully peels away Crozet's many layers of civilized veneer until we discover whodunit and why. In between, she manages to slip in a little local history, wry observations about social issues of the day—divorce, right-wing Christianity, the "cheapness and crass consumerism of American life"— and human nature in general.

The last of these suffers a bit of a beating at the paws of a Greek chorus of cats and dogs who play strong supporting roles in this mystery, often leading their unwitting masters to crucial clues. "Humans are crazy," Harry's dog concludes soon after the first victim is found ground up in a cement mixer. The animals' characters, in fact, are as clearly drawn as those of their masters. It could be cloying, but it's not (though the co-author credit for Sneaky Pie, Brown's cat, *is* a little silly).

All in all **Wish You Were Here** is funny, original, and clever, the perfect companion for a snowy December Sunday.

> *Mark Gerson, in a review of "Wish You Were Here," in* Quill and Quire, *Vol. 56, No. 12, December, 1990, p. 24.*

Marilyn Stasio   (review date 6 September 1992)

[*Stasio is an American novelist and critic. In the following review, she praises* Rest in Pieces.]

In Rita Mae Brown's **Rest In Pieces,** every house, barn, shop, rectory and civic building in the tiny Virginia hamlet of Crozet seems to have a resident cat. One sees in such details the fine paw of Sneaky Pie Brown, Ms. Brown's cat, who gets co-author credit for this cozy tale and who bears "an uncanny resemblance" to one of its heroines, the "wonderfully intelligent" Mrs. Murphy, a tiger cat who resides with the town postmistress, Mary Minor (Harry) Haristeen.

When she isn't lording it over the other animals on Harry's farm, Mrs. Murphy trains her formidable intellect on the appalling case of a corpse ("No fingerprints. No clothes. . . . No head") that turns up in bits and pieces all over town, just as a handsome stranger with a dark secret comes to Crozet and takes a friendly interest in Harry. The suspense isn't exactly killing, but it gets us jumpy enough to look over our shoulders in church.

Ms. Brown's earthy prose breathes warmth into wintry Crozet and pinches color into the cheeks of its nosy, garrulous residents. "How close it made everyone feel," Harry muses on their funny nicknames, "these little monikers, these tokens of intimacy." It is the shattering of this intimacy by acts of violence that Ms. Brown examines so thoughtfully, creating such an enchanting world of Crozet that we shudder to see any more of its citizens in their graves. Or caught with red hands.

> *Marilyn Stasio, in a review of "Rest in Pieces," in* The New York Times Book Review, *September 6, 1992, p. 17.*

R. C. Scott   (review date 27 June 1993)

[*In the following review, Scott characterizes* Venus Envy *as entertaining but overly didactic.*]

When a wealthy Virginia art gallery owner named Frazier Armstrong, convinced she's on her deathbed, confesses in writing to the Upper South's upper crust that she's a lesbian, the news goes down like warm Dr. Pepper on an August afternoon. The misdiagnosis of Frazier's condition, and her subsequent discovery that she'll live after all, boost the dramatic potential in Rita Mae Brown's clever recasting of this toothpaste-out-of-the-tube tale. Unfortunately, the combination of Frazier's epistolary style, flat and repetitive as a chain letter, and the title's pun is an early indication that **Venus Envy** will forsake character for the naive and irksome dogma of guilt-free and munificent sex. True to the polemical positions assigned them, Ms. Brown's characters behave predictably. What's more, they talk too much; in the din of righteous yammering, it's difficult to find a cogent observation about how anyone really feels. When relations here on earth stall, as they frequently do, Ms. Brown (best known as the author of the novel *Rubyfruit Jungle*) reverts to myth and parable, whisking Frazier off for a celestial romp with the gods, who are little help with problems of human frailty and disingenuousness. Though Ms. Brown delivers a sporadically entertaining story, Frazier seems less like a character than a device for extolling a credo; this kind of approach might be fine for the Op-Ed page, but it's seldom compelling as fiction.

R. C. Scott, in a review of "Venus Envy," in The New York Times Book Review, *June 27, 1993, p. 18.*

FURTHER READING

Ward, Carol Marie. *Rita Mae Brown.* New York: Twayne, 1993, 191 p.
    Biographical and critical survey.

Additional coverage of Brown's life and career is contained in the following sources published by Gale Research: *Contemporary Authors,* Vol. 45-48; *Contemporary Authors New Revision Series,* Vols. 2, 11, 35; *Contemporary Literary Criticism,* Vols. 18, 43; and *Major 20th-Century Writers.*

Roald Dahl

1916-1990

Welsh-born English short story writer, novelist, autobiographer, and children's writer.

The following entry presents an overview of Dahl's career. For further information on his life and work, see *CLC*, Volumes 1, 6, 18.

INTRODUCTION

Best known for his children's book *Charlie and the Chocolate Factory,* Dahl also published highly praised short stories for adults that feature dark humor, surprise endings, and subtle horror. While some critics comment that his characters lack depth, Dahl is considered a master of short story construction.

Dahl was born in Llandaff, South Wales, to Norwegian parents and spent his childhood summers visiting his grandparents in Oslo, Norway. After his father died when Dahl was four, his mother abided by her husband's wish that Dahl be sent to English schools. Dahl subsequently attended Llandaff Cathedral School, where he began a series of academic misadventures. After he and several other students were severely beaten by the headmaster for placing a dead mouse in a cruel storekeeper's candy jar, Dahl's mother moved him to St. Peter's Boarding School and later to Repton, a renowned private school. At Repton, instructors were unimpressed with Dahl's academic performance, one of them declaring in an end-of-term report: "Vocabulary negligible, sentences mal-constructed. He reminds me of a camel." Dahl would later describe his school years as "days of horrors" as well as the inspiration for much of his macabre fiction.

After graduating from Repton, Dahl took a position with the Shell Oil Company in Tanganyika (now Tanzania), Africa. In 1939 he joined a Royal Air Force training squadron in Nairobi, Kenya, serving as a fighter pilot in the Mediterranean. Dahl suffered severe head injuries in a plane crash near Alexandria, Egypt, an experience he recounted in his autobiography *Going Solo.* Upon recovering he was transferred to Washington, D.C. as an assistant air attaché. There Dahl began his writing career, publishing a short story in the *Saturday Evening Post* that would later appear in his first collection, *Over to You: Ten Stories of Flyers and Flying.* Dahl's next two collections, *Someone Like You* and *Kiss, Kiss,* contain his most celebrated short stories. In 1961, Dahl published his first work for children, *James and the Giant Peach,* and for the remainder of his career he continued writing stories for both children and adults. He died in 1990.

Critical commentary on Dahl's work has focused on his well-crafted and suspenseful short stories. Often com-

pared to the works of Guy de Maupassant, O. Henry, and Saki, Dahl's stories employ surprise endings and shrewd characters who are rarely what they seem to be. Of Dahl's work, Michael Wood has commented: "His stories are not only unfailingly clever, they are, many of them, *about* cleverness." In "Parson's Pleasure," for instance, an engaging con-man impersonates a parson to swindle priceless antiques from farmhouses for a fraction of their worth. When he tells a group of unwitting rustics that he only wants their original Chippendale commode for its legs, they assume they are doing him a favor by taking an ax to it. In "The Way up to Heaven" a woman leaves for a six-week vacation after arranging for her husband to become trapped in the elevator in their home. Murder and deceit are also central to "Lamb to the Slaughter," in which an angry wife kills her husband with a frozen leg of lamb, then serves the murder weapon to the detectives who are investigating her husband's death.

Dahl turned to less morbid, more comic themes for the novel *My Uncle Oswald.* The title character, Oswald Hendryks Cornelius, is a charming man of the world who enters a business venture with the alluring Jasmin Howcomely and A. R. Woresley, a chemist who has invented a method of quick-freezing sperm. Collecting the semen of geniuses and royalty and storing them in a sperm bank, they hope to attract a clientele of wealthy women desiring superior offspring. Seducing George Bernard Shaw, Marcel Proust, King Alfonso, and other notable figures of the time with Oswald's aphrodisiac, Powdered Sudanese Blister Beetle, Jasmin later runs off with Woresley and the sperm. Like Dahl's short stories, *My Uncle Oswald* features duplicitous characters and, as Mark I. West has observed, "deals with the major theme that runs through most of Dahl's adult fiction—the superficiality of civilization."

PRINCIPAL WORKS

The Gremlins (juvenilia) 1943
Over to You: Ten Stories of Flyers and Flying (short stories) 1946
Sometime Never: A Fable for Supermen (novel) 1948
Someone Like You (short stories) 1953
Kiss, Kiss (short stories) 1959
James and the Giant Peach (juvenilia) 1961
Charlie and the Chocolate Factory (juvenilia) 1964; revised edition 1973
The Magic Finger (juvenilia) 1966
Charlie and the Great Glass Elevator (juvenilia) 1972
Switch Bitch (short stories) 1974
Danny: The Champion of the World (juvenilia) 1975
The Wonderful World of Henry Sugar and Six More (short stories) 1977
The Best of Roald Dahl (short stories) 1978
My Uncle Oswald (novel) 1979
The Twits (juvenilia) 1980
The BFG (juvenilia) 1982
The Witches (juvenilia) 1983
Boy: Tales of Childhood (autobiography) 1984
Going Solo (autobiography) 1986
Two Fables (short stories) 1986
Matilda (juvenilia) 1988
Ah, Sweet Mystery of Life (short stories) 1989

CRITICISM

Nona Balakian   (review date 10 February 1946)

[*Balakian was a Turkish-born American critic and editor whose works include* Critical Encounters: Literary Views and Reviews, 1953-1977 *(1978), a critical study of literary journalism in America. In the following review, she praises* Over to You *for its craftsmanship and subtlety.*]

Roald Dahl, the RAF pilot who originated the gremlin story of some time ago, has a singular brand of talent, sin-

gular because he can communicate a feeling, a sensation, a state of mind that has often nothing to do with us as earthbound creatures. It is as if he had acquired new perspectives better suited to a life in which details lose their importance and the only reality is the release found in a moment's forgetfulness. A Norwegian, educated in England, Mr. Dahl saw the war in its worst stages of defeat and desperation as a fighter pilot in the deserts of Africa, in Greece and Syria. Yet he has not written the usual post-mortem adventure story but tried imaginatively to bring the flyer's separate world within the compass of our own.

With a feeling for essential truthfulness, he has singled out, in [*Over to You*] the inner experiences of some of the men who followed the Messerschmitts into the deserts of Egypt and Libya, into Greece and Palestine. What has impressed him most about them is not so much their heroism—for where is there heroism in doing what one must?—as their struggle to reconcile their dual existence as "great" pilots (who are supposed to know no fear) and human beings with very normal interests and hopes, which they cannot renounce, though they know "they shall not grow old."

Though they manage to sound casual and unimpressed, the most inveterate among them in the squadron is frightened when his turn comes up, haunted by a vision of his own dead body, lying disfigured on some lonely plain. But "like the sleeper who opens his eyes in the morning and forgets his dream," the fear strangely vanishes the moment he spots the enemy hiding in the sun. Then "the body of the Spitfire was the body of the pilot and there was no difference between the one and the other." When death finally comes in these stories the pilot is not sorry or afraid, but only relieved.

But the tone is not predominantly elegiac. The flier's sensitivity to death intensifies the moments for him, magnifies the worth of the simplest pleasures. One of the most vivid stories, **"Madame Rosette,"** tells of the wonderful adventures of three RAF fliers on a forty-eight hour leave in Cairo. After months of the "unnatural life" of the desert, sans water or women, they not only go to town in a big way, but end up with a good deed in the bargain, "rescuing" fourteen beautiful damsels of Mme. Rosette's famous establishment—who gratefully rush into their arms! Mr. Dahl has captured their spirit of mad abandon with marvelous subtle insight and genuine humor.

Sometimes amid the clouds, the war loses its reality, and the pilot begins to see everything in bright symbols, as in a dream. The planes of the enemy appear suddenly as "black crosses," with hands joined: "they made a circle and danced around my Gladiator . . . they were playing Oranges and Lemons. . . ." And as he falls, it seems "the blue of the sky and the black of the sea chased each other round and round. . . ." He sees his mother picking mushrooms in a field, and she asks, "Shall we go home?" And he wants to go, but he can't stop running. Actually, it is the pilot, the man of action, who always wins out; but in his visions, it is the human being with his intense desire for peace who triumphs.

Mr. Dahl occasionally overworks his endings in an effort

to make his point felt, but aside from this technical weakness, one senses the touch of the craftsman who weighs the effects of his words and his phrasing. He has, what is essential, an acute awareness of the narrow margin separating shadow and substance. He has not been afraid to venture into the realm of vision, where not only gremlins are born, but the very stuff of literature.

> *Nona Balakian, "Gremlins—and Mr. Dahl," in* The New York Times Book Review, *February 10, 1946, p. 6.*

James Kelly   (review date 8 November 1953)

[*In the following review, Kelly commends Dahl's suspenseful stories in* Someone Like You.]

At disconcertingly long intervals, the *compleat* short-story writer comes along who knows exactly how to blend and season four notable talents: an antic imagination, an eye for the anecdotal predicament with a twist at the end, a savage sense of humor suitable for stabbing or cutting, and an economical, precise writing style. No worshiper of Chekhov, he. You'll find him marching with solid plotters like Saki and O. Henry, Maupassant and Maugham. He doesn't really like people, but he is interested in them (to paraphrase the author of "Cakes and Ale"); the reader looking for sweetness, light and subtle characterization will have to try another address. Tension is his business; give him a surprise dénouement and he'll give you a story leading up to it. His name in this instance is Roald Dahl, here represented by **Someone Like You** (a collection of eighteen short stories, quite a few of which have appeared in *The New Yorker* and other magazines); and a more imperturbable young Englishman would be hard to find.

Mr. Dahl must bring off a tour de force every time out, since credibility seldom plays much part in the situations that interest him. His stories are like a fast game of badminton in which there's never a positive answer to the big question: Where's the bird? Honed dialogue, a masterful hand with nuance and an ability to keep the reader off balance through sheer astonishment are usually enough to see him through. Not always, though. For some observers (including this one) the spell will not extend to four or five of the stories where the humor is too ghoulish and the originality too intrusive. But it is safe to predict that anybody who responds to one entry will respond to all; Mr. Dahl is never, never dull.

For satirical burlesque, not many recent stories coming from either side of the Atlantic can compete with the outrageous **"Nunc Dimittis,"** an intricate tale of a man of culture and his resourceful revenge upon a young woman who had indiscreetly allowed her full-length portrait to be painted from the skin out. In a similar vein, **"The Great Automatic Grammatisator"** gravely explains what happens when an electronic genius named Adolph Knipe (who wants to be a man of letters) converts an electronic computing machine into a device for writing short stories and novels. The idea, of course, is to buy up all practicing writers and produce the world's creative output by Knipe's Grammatisator, which, Mr. Dahl estimates, must already be responsible for at least half the novels and sto-

ries published in the English language during the past year.

A short one—maybe the best one—called **"Taste"** captures the high drama and gourmet flavor of a dinner party where an expert wine-bibber backs his judgment of breed and vintage with a fraudulent bet and almost gets away with it. There's a story about a dubious host and hostess who put a microphone in the guest room and open up new horizons on cheating at bridge; another concerns a man who invents a sound machine which picks up cries of anguish from flowers and trees.

There's a wonderfully underplayed murder story in which the murderess gets off scotfree, thanks to a truly perfect crime. There's a pure horror story with muted sadism at its heart—and a last line guaranteed to raise most readers' hackles. There's one about a genteel commuter who mistakes his companion for a boyhood bully and falls into a "Stalky and Co." reverie. For many readers the final scarifying story about greyhound racing and the cheating men and willing dogs who share it will live as long as any in the book.

Someone Like You was made to be read—but tough-minded people who don't care which way the cat jumps will probably get the most fun out of it. Mr. Dahl could be a cult without half trying, and he deserves the warm welcome he'll get. No electronic machine will ever turn out *his* stuff.

> *James Kelly, "With Waves of Tension," in* The New York Times Book Review, *November 8, 1953, p. 5.*

Malcolm Bradbury   (review date 7 February 1960)

[*An English man of letters, Bradbury is best known as the author of such satiric novels as* Eating People Is Wrong *(1959) and* Stepping Westward *(1965). He has also, as a literary critic, written extensively on English and American literature. In the following review of* Kiss, Kiss, *he praises Dahl as a master of short story construction.*]

I don't want to suggest that Roald Dahl's latest collection, **Kiss Kiss,** has nothing more than good construction; it has. But construction, with Mr. Dahl (as with John Collier) is the premise from which he starts work; and on this score alone he gets straight A's in *my* creative writing class.

He builds his situations beautifully, and his punch-lines have so much punch that I was reeling for several days. In short, Mr. Dahl is a master of the beginning, the middle and the end; he enters completely into the crazy principality of the short story, accepts its local legislation and then, acting with irrefutable logic, does all the things that people say may not be done.

The odd thing about Mr. Dahl is that he is an Englishman who publishes almost exclusively in the United States; in his own land his work is scarcely known. This is an interesting commentary on the state of the short story in England—for, while in America the short story is a major, and a developing form, in England there are very few exciting practitioners of the genre; and of those few most, like Angus Wilson, Penelope Mortimer and Mr. Dahl, publish their work in this form mainly in the States. Why is this? One reason is that there are virtually no outlets in England—even non-paying ones—asking for the serious or even the well-crafted short story. England's loss is America's gain.

Read the two best stories first. One of them is **"The Champion of the World,"** which describes a poacher's dodge for doping pheasants with tranquilizers—a trick that is foolproof until the dénouement. The other is **"Parson's Pleasure,"** which tells how a London antique buyer, disguised as a dominie, plies his trade among the rustics, until he comes a cropper on a Chippendale commode. Both have great endings; both have enormous substance in the tale that is told. Slighter, but no less effective, are **"Royal Jelly,"** the story of a man who has begun to change his sickly daughter into a queen bee, and **"Edward the Conqueror,"** about a cat that takes over a household because the music-loving wife believes he is the reincarnation of Liszt.

Mr. Dahl shows us a curious England rather like the England in British Travel Association ads in The New Yorker. Deliberately, he makes it a bit more rural, a bit more quaint, a bit more lively than it really is, a foreigner's England, perhaps, but a wonderful world for his cunning adventurer-heroes to operate in. His characters are usually ignoble: he knows the dog beneath the skin, or works hard to find it. Exploitation and infidelity are normal doings in the *Kiss Kiss* set. But his touch is sure—read **"Mrs. Bixby and the Colonel's Coat"** (about the mink, the pawn ticket and the wife versus secretary), where the standard male magazine story becomes something immeasurably better because Mr. Dahl knows not only his market but his characters inside out.

His poorer stories (an allegory of Hitler's natal day, a horror-tale of a landlady who practices taxidermy on her lodgers) are weaknesses in idea—not in treatment. He is

also funny. No moralist, no profound seer—but a true craftsman.

Malcolm Bradbury, "Always a Dog Beneath the Skin," in The New York Times Book Review, *February 7, 1960, p. 5.*

Michael Wood   (essay date 20-27 December 1979)

[*Wood is an English critic and educator. In the following essay, he considers Dahl's ability to manipulate readers both an asset and a liability to the success of his stories.*]

"If your taste is for the macabre, the sick, the outrageous, the unexpected, the horrifying," the blurb says, "Roald Dahl will give you orgiastic delight." And if your taste is for something quieter, or if orgiastic delight is not exactly what you want after a long day at the boutique, then perhaps you'd better stick to Winnie the Pooh or the Marquis de Sade. As a matter of fact, the coy blurb does also say something about Dahl's writing.

He is certainly no slacker when it comes to the macabre, the sick, the outrageous and the rest. One story graphically describes a mother rabbit eating its baby. Another portrays a woman who has gambled away three fingers of one hand; another shows a long-suffering wife leaving her mate to die in a broken lift. Yet another introduces Franz Liszt, reincarnate in a strange and sensitive cat, which is burned by a jealous and conventional husband, who doesn't like the way things are going. In still another story, a man's severed but still living brain is delivered into the vengeful care of the wife he ceaselessly nagged in his earlier appearance. And there is one very brief story in which an anxious mother prays that her newborn boy may not die like her other three children. This piece is set in Austria, and the family's name is Hitler.

But macabre, sick and outrageous are the words of respectable people, and they suggest something well this side of pornography or unbridled horror. Dahl's stories propose only the faintest of flirtations with our disgust, and their virtues have very little to do with their more spectacular bits of nastiness. Dahl is at his best when he reveals the horrible thinness of much of our respectability; at his worst and most tiresome when he nudges us towards the contemplation of mere naughtiness.

My Uncle Oswald, published in October of this year, is billed as Dahl's first novel, but it is really only a long shaggy Dahl story about a rare beetle powder which turns men rabid with lust, and is used in a carefully planned scheme to collect specimens of semen from a roster of the world's most famous and brilliant men. There is an amusing scene with Alfonso of Spain, and some lumpish knockabout with Proust and Freud, but the whole thing is considerably less funny than an earlier, shorter work called **"Bitch,"** where a single sniff of a special perfume was enough to convert any man into a slobbering sex-fiend.

And even that story, well-timed and well-told as it is, is just a wringing out of an old joke, and conjures up a disturbing vision of nervously chortling readers, excited elbows digging into their neighbours' ribs, all of them dim and inhibited enough to be tickled by these sad, snickering approaches to the mysteries of Eros. Indeed, most of

---

Dahl on writing "The Way Up to Heaven":

I was once driving alone on a country road and an idea came for a story about someone getting stuck in an elevator between floors in an empty house. I had nothing to write with in the car. So I stopped and got out. The back of the car was covered with dust. With one finger I wrote in the dust the single word ELEVATOR. That was enough. . . .

The rich woman, the elevator, the maid . . . Possibly a murder rather than a chance death, when the elevator sticks between two floors in empty house . . . In love with the elevator repairer?

Roald Dahl in an interview with Christopher Sykes in The Times, *London, 30 November 1990.*

Dahl's recent work—this latest book and three out of the four stories in **Switch Bitch** (1974)—trades on the notion of sex as the great frightening secret, to be treated only with deliberate excesses of laughter. The exception—the fourth piece in **Switch Bitch**—concerns revenge, and points us back to Dahl's earlier and better work, that collected in **Over to You** (1945), **Someone Like You** (1953) and **Kiss Kiss** (1959).

There is another Roald Dahl, however. This one, who gives the impression of being the same fellow in other respects—born in Wales in 1916, went to Repton, was shot down in Libya during the war, is married to the actress, Patricia Neal, has four children, lives handsomely in Buckinghamshire—is an extremely successful author of children's books. A realm where the macabre, the sick and the outrageous are less in demand. Of course, a really tough egg might want to argue that there is plenty of orgiastic delight in *Little Red Riding Hood* if you're on the wolf's side, and certainly many fairy tales hand out executions in a way that would have pleased even Mme Defarge. But there are limits to the usefulness of this argument. Children have a larger tolerance than we sometimes think for images of violence and sudden death, but they do not usually cultivate their nightmares, and Dahl doesn't do it for them.

An outsize peach, in **James and the Giant Peach** (1961), flattens two awful aunts named Sponge and Spiker. In another book a near-miss with some nasties from outer space known as Vermicious Knids is celebrated in a breezy song with the lines:

> We even thought we heard the crunch.
> Of someone eating you for lunch.

But this is all part of the fun. Lewis Carroll—to say nothing of the Brothers Grimm—would have thought it child's play. There is an enormous crocodile, in Dahl's book of that name, published last year, who has a series of plans for putting children on his menu, but the story mainly concerns his witty, implausible and easily exposed attempts to imitate things like palm trees, seesaws, picnic benches, and wooden animals on a roundabout.

In fact, what is striking about Dahl's work, both for children and adults, is its carefully pitched appeal to its different audiences. In **Charlie and the Chocolate Factory** (1964), which is said to have sold nearly half a million copies, there is a chocolate waterfall and an edible landscape. There are tiny people, a magic lift, an assortment of ingenious gadgets, and a group of children so lamentably ill-behaved that even our own misbehaving children applaud their come-uppances.

In the sequel to that book, **Charlie and the Great Glass Elevator** (1973), there are more of the same things, and a trip to space, and a bit of time travel, and a lot more jokes—a President of the United States, for example, addicted to playing knock-knock. "Knock-knock." "Who's there?" "Warren who?" "Warren Peace by Leo Tolstoy." In most of Dahl's children's books there are splendid songs, one of which contains these lines:

> We may see a Creature with forty-nine heads
> Who lives in the desolate snow,

> And whenever he catches a cold (which he
>   dreads)
> He has forty-nine noses to blow . . .
> We may even get lost and be frozen by frost.
> We may die in an earthquake or tremor.
> Or nastier still, we may even be tossed
> On the horns of a furious Dilemma.

In Dahl's books for younger readers, like **The Magic Finger** (1966) and **Fantastic Mr Fox** (1970), the tone is simpler, more confidential, but quite uncondescending, and willing to count on children's alertness. "I am a girl and I am eight years old. Philip is also eight years old. William is three years older. He is ten. What? Oh, all right, then. He is eleven."

In his book for older children, **The Wonderful Story of Henry Sugar** (1977), Dahl's tone is different again, seems to assume an authentic capacity for indignation—which is more than Dahl will assume about his adult readers. "The beatings at Repton were more fierce and more frequent than anything I had yet experienced. And do not think for one moment that the future Archbishop of Canterbury [Geoffrey Fisher, then headmaster of the school] objected to these squalid exercises. He rolled up his sleeves and joined in with gusto."

Dahl tends to condescend to adults, because it seems that clever writers—the paradox invites further thought—can treat children as equals but can treat other adults only as victims. There is a hint of this attitude in the essay for older children I've just quoted from, where Dahl says that a sense of humour is "not essential when writing for grown-ups, but for children, it's vital." And there is more than a hint in Dahl's insistence, in interviews and in his introduction to the recent, star-spangled television series based on 22 of his stories, that the reader or viewer has to be hooked, snaggled in suspense, if he is not to close the book or change the channel.

Dahl is wrong, I think, about the imperative nature of this need for suspense—or rather, since a man who sells so well can't simply be wrong, I think he does his talent something less than justice when he subordinates it so entirely to the confection of the final twist. It has meant that his stories, increasingly, have become tall tales with punch lines, rather than bits of imagined life. His early work seems to belong to the tradition of Saki and Somerset Maugham; his later work to the tradition, if that's what it is, of the Two Ronnies.

Dahl's most obvious gift is also his most serious limitation. He has tact, timing, a clean, economic style, an abundance of ingenuity—none of them things to be sniffed at. But above all he knows how to manipulate his readers; and if no decent writer is without a touch of this talent, no really good writer, I suspect, ever lets it rule him. A writer who *only* manipulates his readers becomes a confidence man, a cousin to Thomas Mann's Felix Krull.

It is this quality in Dahl's stories which makes so many of them seem so wispy when they are done. You can't tell them to anyone, because you'll spoil the surprise; and you can't read them again yourself, because the surprise is all there was. This is not true of the better work of Maugham, or Saki, or Maupassant.

Fortunately, it's not true of the better work of Dahl, either. His stories are not only unfailingly clever, they are, many of them, *about* cleverness. Willy Wonka, Mr Fox and the enormous crocodile in the children's books correspond to dozens of characters in the stories for adults. "Secret plans and clever tricks," as the crocodile says, are the names of the game.

A wife kills her defecting husband with a frozen leg of lamb, then cooks it and invites the policemen in to eat the murder weapon. A man stakes two houses, against his host's daughter's hand in marriage, on his ability to tell the breed and vintage of a little-known claret—but he has sneaked a look at the label beforehand. A wife devises an elaborate plan to keep the mink coat her lover has given her; her husband manages to give it to a mistress the wife didn't even know he had.

A discontented young computer expert invents a machine that will write best-selling fiction without fail, and proceeds to buy out half the writers in England and America. All they wanted was the money and fame, after all; they were happy to sign contracts promising not to do any writing. The narrator, as the story ends, is still holding out: "This very moment, as I sit here listening to the howling of my nine starving children in the other room, I can feel my own hand creeping closer and closer to that golden contract that lies over on the other side of the desk. Give us strength. Oh Lord, to let our children starve."

This seems pretty close to home, and I don't want to belabour the point. Cleverness thwarted and rewarded in the stories plainly corresponds, on some level or other, to the writer's own ingenuity—getting away with it again, he may feel, but only just.

In these stories the ingenuity is everything, as much as we are going to get. In Dahl's best work the same subject acquires complication and depth, because it reflects a wider sense of what it means for cleverness to fail, and because cleverness in each case is related to an authentic expertise, an earned, painstaking knowledge which clearly echoes Dahl's own interests as well as his professional care in putting these stories together. I'm thinking especially of the pieces called **"Parson's pleasure"** and **"Nunc dimittis,"** and two stories about the amiable Claud Cubbage, poacher and greyhound fancier, called **"Claud's dog"** and **"The champion of the world."**

In the first of these, Mr Boggis, an antique dealer who likes to pose as a clergyman and pick up valuable items cheap in old farms and country houses, comes across a genuine Chippendale commode, complete with original bill of sale. It belongs to a pair of wily but ignorant rustics, and Mr Boggis nonchalantly pretends to want it only for its legs. The deal is settled, Mr Boggis showing excessive guile and offering only a laughable sum, scarcely able to contain his glee. But while he goes to fetch his car, the rustics obligingly chop off the commode's legs for him, and proceed to smash the whole thing up, on the assumption that parsons always have small cars and the complete commode wouldn't go in. Mr Boggis, who drives a large station wagon, had left it well away from the house because he

was working on exactly the same assumption and didn't wish to arouse suspicion.

In **"Nunc dimittis,"** a fussy bachelor and man about town makes a woman look ridiculous because she is supposed to have said uncomplimentary things about him, and he now regrets his act, because the woman has handsomely forgiven him, and has sent him some caviare, which she knows he cannot resist, as a token of her pardon. The only thing is, having had a few spoonfuls, he is beginning to feel a bit queasy. . . .

Claud, in the other two stories, has brilliant schemes for, respectively, cleaning up at a country dog track and beating the world record for pheasant poaching. The schemes, beautifully laid and patiently described, meet heartbreaking ends, similar to that of Mr Boggis's commode.

I don't think it's the apparent punishment of cleverness that matters in these stories—they are not more *moral* than the rest of Dahl's work. What matters is the pathos of failure, the sense of swindle seen from the inside. The triumph of trickery now seems downright dangerous, the walker could always fall from the high wire. Of course, Dahl himself is neither failing nor falling here, but at such moments, it seems to me, he is writing to us as he writes to children. We are on the same side of the fence for a while, crooks together; accomplices not stooges. We have been found worthy of the confidence man's confidence.

Dahl is unwilling to speculate about the meaning of his work. "I'm a fantasist," he told Michael Billington, in an interview. "I make up stories. That is my trade."

Perhaps we should leave it at that. Dahl makes things up, he constructs eccentricities, and this is what makes him so good at encouraging the child's resistance to adult seriousness. I would leave it at that, were it not for the persistence of the theme of deferred revenge in Dahl's stories. It is deviance's favourite mode.

A jilted boyfriend, now a successful doctor, met after many years in a strange, hostile town, amiably takes a woman to bed and drives her to despair and suicide by relentless medical innuendo. A cuckolded husband, finding his wife with her neck stuck in a modern statue, *almost* takes the opportunity of beheading her while ostensibly freeing her—and the almost is enough to bring colour to his cheeks and a smile to his eyes.

And then in the most haunting of all Dahl's stories, **"Galloping Foxley,"** we return to Repton, and a meticulous memory of the caning of a young boy by the older boy he was fagging for. The boy, grown up and commuting to the City as he has done for the last 36 years, now meets his tormentor on the train to Cannon Street. Foxley, he was called, Bruce Foxley. The victim ponders his revenge, and finally decides a simple reminder will be the subtle thing, accompanied perhaps by a few details for the benefit of the other occupants of the carriage. So the man quietly introduces himself. His name is Perkins, William Perkins, Repton, 1907. The bully lowers his newspaper and says, "I'm glad to meet you. Mine's Fortescue—Jocelyn Fortescue. Eton, 1916."

One could say a great deal about this delicate ending. We

shall see it, depending on our prejudices, as evoking an England so full of Foxleys and Fortescues that they cannot be distinguished, or as depicting an ancient rancour so strong that it deforms the most ordinary acts of perception. Or both. Michael Billington suggests that the caning at Repton, on which Dahl also swells in the children's piece I've quoted from, is the key to the cruelty of Dahl's stories.

That is too simple, no doubt, particularly since the caning is likely to be a focus for a whole lot of diffuse unhappiness, rather than a single, crucial memory; a representation, let's say, rather than a cause. But I do think it makes sense to see Dahl's writing as a kind of revenge on the world of which Repton was a picture for him. The vision is odd and tangential because the world is so deeply and finally in the wrong.

The stories are versions of the planned reminder on the train to Cannon Street, discreet mentions of the plentiful grounds for our shame. The trouble is that those of us whose taste is for the shameful (and the sick and the macabre) will lap them up. Foxley, if it had been Foxley, would have been perfectly unembarrassed by his exploits even supposing he remembered them.

So the thing is to make money from the world's Foxleys, lending them carefully crafted mirrors in which they recognise only the nastiness of others. That's entertainment; and in Dahl's best work it's more than that, but as an act of vengeance it bears a striking resemblance to the baffled schemes of Claud Cubbage and Mr Boggis. Or if we prefer a cheerier picture, it recalls the fantastic Mr Fox, in the story of that name, who is driven deeper and deeper into the earth by three ghastly farmers, and finally decides to tunnel round to the farmers' chicken houses and store rooms, thereby setting up himself and his friends with an extravagant supply of goodies.

What's more, he may never have to show his head above ground again. (pp. xiv-xvi)

> *Michael Wood, "The Confidence Man," in* New Society, *Vol. 50, No. 898-99, December 20-27, 1979, pp. xiv-xvi.*

L. J. Davis　(review date 20 April 1980)

[Davis is an American critic and educator. In the following review, he notes a lack of profundity in My Uncle Oswald *but praises the novel as a fairy tale for adults.]*

[In *My Uncle Oswald,* Dahl] has seen fit to undertake a children's book for grownups, a sort of *Charlie and the Chocolate Factory* featuring sex instead of fudge. In a way, it is an answer to the secret prayer of every literate parent who has ever succumbed to the literate parent's besetting vice: i.e., reading ahead in T. H. White's *Mistress Masham's Repose* rather than curling up with a good Mailer after the little ones are safely abed. Breathes there a mommy or a daddy with soul so dead who has not done just that?

Of course, there are rules to such an undertaking; we will not have our pleasures simple, and they must conform to certain hard and fast rules, largely of British inspiration. The fantasy should be exotic, but not so exotic that we can't imagine ourselves in the thick of it. Ideally, it should also begin with the discovery of a talisman possessing unusual powers. With this talisman, the ingenious hero will then set forth on a quest, from which he will emerge laden with riches and knowledge and, perhaps, an interesting wound. Along the way, he will encounter adventures, overcome adversity, behold wonders, confront perils and never be called upon to meet a dental appointment. He will acquire companions scarcely less qualified than himself, but they will be specialists with handy skills, whereas the hero is a generalist rather along the lines of Buckminster Fuller. In the more adult versions, he will also wench.

There is nothing very profound in any of this, but it's a lot of fun. It has been left to Roald Dahl, however, to introduce the element of gender—beyond, that is, the element of gender as represented by the hand of the princes, to which the rest of the princess is attached only by implication. Otherwise, the mixture conforms to type, but with certain inevitable modifications.

As his hero, he has chosen a youthful adaptation of Evelyn Waugh's detestable Basil Seal. He calls this creature Oswald Cornelius and obtains for him a quantity of Sudanese Blister Beetle powder, the world's most powerful aphrodisiac (the talisman). This event occurs in 1912, in Paris, in the highest diplomatic and social circles, and, needless to say, young Cornelius is not only in luck but, almost immediately, in the bucks. Reality intervenes in the form of World War I, but by 1919 our unscathed protagonist is back at the same old stand, assisted by a poverty-stricken Oxford don named A. R. Woresley and a luscious handful of jailbait named Yasmin Howcomely.

Woresley has invented a secret process for diluting and indefinitely storing fertile sperm. Howcomely is a sort of, er, mailbox. Once a hidden cryogenic vault is established in England under Woresley's supervision, Cornelius and his lissome companion sally forth into postwar Europe to obtain samples from the likes of King Alfonso of Spain, Jean Monnet, Albert Einstein and George Bernard Shaw (the quest), using a forged letter from George V as a foot in the door and Cornelius' magic powder as an icebreaker. The idea, noble in its simplicity, is to hold onto the stuff for a few years and then sell it for outrageous sums to royalty- and genius-crazed women whose husbands will, presumably, be none the wiser for having ostensibly sired an offspring with a Hapsburg lip. The reward . . . is riches beyond the dreams of avarice.

Frankly, I thought the seduction of Proust was in bad taste—Proust's. Shaw got what was coming to him, though, and Puccini was a dreamboat. As for the rest, the reader will doubtless have his own favorites. I suspect that Dahl's lighthearted little fairy tale will not exactly be all things to all men, if only because so many people take sex so much more seriously than they take, say, trees, nor does it have much to offer to the slap-and-tickle crowd. Alas, it is less than this, a delightful tale trimly told, all about sperm and greed and cunning and stuff like that.

> *L. J. Davis, "Oswald and the Sex Factory," in*

Book World—The Washington Post, *April 20, 1980, p. 7.*

Alan Warren   (essay date 1985)

[*In the following excerpt, Warren provides an overview of Dahl's fiction.*]

[It is] as a short story writer that Dahl is most renowned. His stories are not horrific in the usual sense. They have been likened to those of Saki, John Collier and James Thurber, and to the whimsically macabre cartoons of Charles Addams. The comparison is judicious. Praised for the "grinning skull" quality of the narration, and the technical excellence of their construction, his short stories have been well received by critics, though they disagree on whether Dahl is, at heart, a moralist. Although his evildoers are usually punished, the form that retribution takes is usually so outlandishly unexpected that opinions differ. Naomi Lewis of *New Statesman* believes " . . . these really are moral tales. Go wrong and you get some very peculiar desserts." Whether there is an unsuspected vein of profundity in Dahl's work, or whether Dahl is simply an entertainer (" . . . a master of horror—an intellectual Hitchcock of the writing world," says a reviewer for *Books and Bookmen*) who writes supremely well, one can hardly fault the originality of his plots, the economy of his storytelling, or his craftsmanship.

Dahl himself, in interviews, has stressed the importance of plot above all else, not only in his own work but in that of his contemporaries. "After having done my twenty-five years of short stories," he told Lisa Tuttle in a *Twilight Zone* interview, " . . . I think I probably ran out of plots, and that's the hardest thing in the world. If you write the sort of short stories I write, which are real short stories, with a beginning, a middle, and an end, instead of the modern trend, which is mood pieces . . . I found about thirty-five plots, and then I probably ran out of them. I don't know many now. I don't know *any*, I don't think. I couldn't sit down and write a short story now—it's very hard. And these people who are writing them now, they don't have any plots, they don't bloody well have them. Maupassant had them. Salinger had them. That's why they were so sparing. Salinger found eleven."

"Man from the South" is probably the quintessential Dahl story: civilized, unexpected, even savage, yet perfectly assured and balanced, the ending shocking yet entirely appropriate. As is usual with Dahl, there is a deceptively leisurely opening in which a young American meets and makes a strange bet with a wealthy South American: that his cigarette lighter will light ten times in a row. If the American wins the bet he wins a sleek new Cadillac; if he loses, the little man chops off the little finger of his left hand with a chopping knife.

Dahl frequently draws upon his own interests and background in his stories: **"Taste"** deals with a wine-tasting contest (Dahl is a connoisseur of fine wines); **"Galloping Foxley"** is set at Repton School, where Dahl was educated; **"Nunc Dimittis"** involves art and painting (Dahl is an enthusiastic collector of paintings); and **"The Visitor"** is set in the Sinai Desert just after World War II, a setting Dahl was familiar with at just that time.

This practice lends an air of verisimilitude to the unlikeliest of plots and characterizations. In **"Poison,"** Harry Pope, the protagonist, is lying in bed when he realizes a krait, a snake whose poison is almost invariably fatal, is lying asleep on his stomach, somewhere under the bedclothes. A native doctor is summoned. Dahl describes the proceedings with great accuracy and a fine eye for minute details:

> . . . one side of his mouth started twitching with rapid downward movements that continued for a while after he finished speaking. I took out my handkerchief and very gently I wiped the sweat off his face and neck, and I could feel the slight twitching of the muscle—the one he used for smiling—as my fingers passed over it with the handkerchief.

Dahl builds suspense to an almost unbearable pitch as the bedclothes are drawn back, the doctor having administered chloroform through a tube under the bedsheet to render the snake unconscious—only to find no snake in the bed; or anywhere else. Harry, enraged by the native doctor's dismissal of his claims, calls him a dirty little Hindu sewer rat. The "poison" is in Harry's head.

"Lamb to the Slaughter" is one of Dahl's most memorable tales, frequently anthologized and dramatized on *Alfred Hitchcock Presents,* as were several of Dahl's stories. As directed by Hitchcock himself, it remains probably the most famous of the half-hour segments. The plot concerns a policeman's wife who, upon learning her husband is leaving her, hits him over the head with an enormous leg of lamb, killing him, then serves the lamb up to the investigating policemen who sit around eating it while complaining they cannot lay their hands on the murder weapon. This is typical of Dahl in its mixing of humor and horror. The plot is just outrageous enough to be plausible, and his deadpan style sustains it to the last line. As always with Dahl, one is conscious of a master stylist at work, polishing every line, every phrase. This impression is not mistaken: Dahl estimates it took him six hundred hours over five months to complete his story, **"Mrs. Bixby and the Colonel's Coat."**

"Royal Jelly," another frequently anthologized piece, is one of Dahl's most famous stories. It concerns a beekeeper obsessed with royal jelly who begins feeding it to his baby daughter, unbeknownst to his wife. The baby begins to put on weight alarmingly while displaying other, unpleasant, characteristics. The wife is horrified, the beekeeper delighted. This is one of Dahl's more fantastic excursions, though, as always, he adds enough verisimilitude to anchor the story to reality. Dahl is often compared to the master fantasist John Collier, though this is more a matter of style than subject matter. Even in dealing with the most *outre* subject matter Dahl keeps both feet on the ground, or at least attempts to convince you he is doing so, whereas Collier leaves the real world far behind him whenever it suits his purpose. Collier's world is inhabited by lovesick young men who encounter devils, genii, and sentient department store mannequins. In Dahl's world the men are less likely to be in love and more likely to wind up betting their little fingers against shiny new Cadillacs.

Some of Dahl's other stories are less horrific and more like well-told jokes, elaborate leg-pulls by an amused, self-assured, sardonic and somewhat sadistic storyteller. **"Vengeance Is Mine, Inc."** concerns two entrepreneurs who set up a service that offers punching the nose, or blacking the eye, of a prominent vitriolic newspaper columnist. Their charges: five hundred dollars for the first, six hundred for the second, or one thousand dollars for both.

"Genesis and Catastrophe," also known as **"A Fine Son,"** is, as Dahl appends to the title, a true story, with a frightening historical significance. For once history has played into Dahl's hands, even supplying him with a surprising denouement of the kind he so obviously favors.

"The Landlady" was Dahl's attempt to write a ghost story. He explained later he wanted to make the title character a ghost, but couldn't bring it off, and settled on making her a murderess instead. It is not surprising that, given Dahl's strictness in regard to plot and narrative, he could not live up to his own standard in regard to ghost stories.

"William and Mary" is a bizarre tale of a man kept alive after death by a doctor who preserves his brain, minus the body, in a basin, only to have him fall prey to his wife, who now looks forward to dominating him.

"The Sound Machine" concerns a man obsessed with the idea of a tree as a living, thinking, feeling thing, who, with a pair of earphones, hears—or imagines he hears—roses shriek when a neighbor cuts them with a scissors.

"The Wonderful Story of Henry Sugar," the title story in Dahl's first collection of stories for all ages, is so sparely told it resembles an outline rather than a finished short story, much in the manner of one of Borges' fables. The plot concerns a wealthy man who learns the secrets of yoga, enabling him to see through cards, divining ranks and suits. He goes to casinos, taking care not to go to the same one more than once every twelve months, and of course breaks the bank time after time. In the end he decides to give his money to charity, though along the way Dahl employs another Borgesian device, declaring that his story is a true one and must end truly, but preferring another ending, the kind he would use if the story were fiction. He outlines this ending, in which Henry Sugar sees everything, including a small dark lump, a blood clot, inside the big vein leading into his own heart. He is thus left to die. Dahl, however, for once the munificent dispenser of fates, tells us that Henry instead went on with his philanthropic mission, finally dying happily. For Dahl, apparently, the good among us deserve a decent break now and then.

"The Boy Who Talked With Animals" is a fantastic fable about a boy's father who buys his son a giant turtle while they are on vacation in Jamaica, rather than allow the islanders to kill it. The boy winds up riding out to sea on the turtle's back. This story suffers somewhat from Dahl's attempt to make it suitable for his dual audience. It lacks

the nastiness of his better-known stories, and would probably have worked out better as a children's story.

"The Visitor" is very likely Dahl's masterpiece in the short story form. First published in *Playboy* in 1965 and later included in a somewhat longer form in his collection **Switch Bitch,** it was greeted with thunderous applause, many readers writing in to tell *Playboy* it was the finest piece of fiction they had ever published. The magazine's editors awarded it their prize for the best major work of fiction for the year. Surprisingly, it is not as well known as it deserves to be, probably because it does not fit into a convenient fictional niche. It is most certainly not a traditional horror tale. The genre it actually belongs to, more than any other, is that of the dirty joke. But with a difference: Dahl's story is a tour de force with a leisurely opening that soon slips into high gear and builds to a genuinely shattering climax. Echoing Poe's famous edict, every word contributes to the overall effect, seems unnecessary. In this, the narrator receives a large box containing elaborately bound books, twenty-eight in all, "identically and superbly bound in rich green morocco," containing the hand-written memoirs of the narrator's uncle Oswald. Nearly all of these are of a sexual nature. One—Dahl dubs it "The Sinai Desert episode"—seems safer to publish than any other, for fear of legal reprisals, and so the narrator reproduces it word for word from Oswald's diary.

"The Visitor" introduces Oswald Hendryks Cornelius, Dahl's supreme character creation, possibly created to confound those critics who have faulted Dahl in the past by deeming his characterizations flat or undeveloped. Uncle Oswald, as Dahl styles him, is a larger-than-life character: wealthy, extravagant, a connoisseur, collector of spiders, scorpions and walking sticks, and, as Dahl puts it, "without much doubt, the greatest fornicator of all time."

Uncle Oswald fits well into the scheme of Dahl's more recent fiction, for as the author notes, "For twenty-five years I was able to write stories that were untarnished by sexual undertones of any kind. But now, in my late middle age, they're riddled with sex and copulation. What, I wonder, is the reason for this?"

One reason is clearly the relaxing of laws in regard to the publication of sexual material. Dahl's later fiction could obviously not have been published early in his career. In **"Bitch,"** another episode from Uncle Oswald's diaries, Oswald stumbles upon a perfume with incredibly powerful aphrodisiac properties. As in so many of Dahl's stories, the fascination the author obviously has for the minutiae of exactly how this perfume works on the olfactory nerves is in itself fascinating.

Roald Dahl's position in the field of horror is difficult to judge, for he has always stood apart from other practitioners of the genre. One reason for this is the slimness of the volume of his published work. A contemporary of Dahl's, Robert Bloch, has for example published some five hundred stories over fifty years. Dahl, although he got a later start as a writer, has published perhaps one tenth as many. While it is arguably easier to produce first-rate work if you publish only two stories a year, as Dahl was doing in the late forties and early fifties, the consistent excellence of his work would not be possible otherwise. It is hardly fair to fault Dahl for remaining true to his ideal and never sacrificing quality for quantity. More horror writers, as well as "mainstream" short story writers, should follow his example. (pp. 121-26)

> *Alan Warren, "Roald Dahl: Nasty, Nasty," in* Discovering Modern Horror Fiction, *edited by Darrell Schweitzer, Starmont House, 1985, pp. 120-28.*

Gahan Wilson   (review date 12 October 1986)

[*Wilson is an American cartoonist, short story writer, and critic. In the following excerpt, he offers a mixed assessment of* Going Solo.]

Roald Dahl has written stories for adults and children, including the chilling **Switch Bitch, James and the Giant Peach** and **Boy,** the first volume of his autobiography. **Going Solo** is essentially a compendium of war stories taken from his experiences in the Royal Air Force. It is a kind of nonstop demonstration of expert raconteurship, and it's easy to imagine the comfortable, smoky pub about you or the feel of the huge leather chairs in the club as he goes on about the ops room at Elevsis airdrome or the time in Greece he ate black olives and drank retsina with a friend and fellow pilot who did not survive to become the Earl of Leicester while the two of them watched men burn to death in Argos Bay.

This steady tale spinning might, to tell the truth, be a little bit too much if it were unalloyed, but the author has wisely and cleverly inserted quotes from the actual adventurer, his younger self, in don't-you-worry letters he wrote to his worried mother. These, together with many photos taken with his trusty Zeiss Super Ikonta (eventually stolen by a peasant) and pages from his pilot's logbook (Mr. Dahl must be quite a pack rat), leaven things considerably.

The book actually starts with something even more nostalgic to the British heart than the horrors of World War II. It begins in 1938 with an account of the last days of the British Empire, before it was in any doubt whatsoever, as seen through the eyes of the 22-year-old Dahl, a brand-new employee of the Shell Company taking the steamer Mantola to Dar es Salaam, Tanganyika. He traveled with leathery professionals who had all gone mad, or at least been driven to extreme eccentricity by the rigors of building and maintaining the colonies. (One wonders what sort of mental cases the looming Third Reich Empire would have produced had it survived and thrived.). Mr. Dahl's telling of his fellow passengers' *Alice in Wonderland* doings is highly amusing, particularly his explanation of why his cabinmate, U. N. Savory ("I could hardly believe those initials when I first saw them on his trunk"), carefully sprinkled Epsom salts on the shoulders of his dinner jacket.

Mr. Dahl's account of colonial life itself manages to touch on almost all the reliable themes. There are a number of Africans, of whom the quaintest and most colorful is MISTER SHANKERBAI GANDERBAI OF BAGOMOYO, SELLER OF

DECORTICATORS (a decorticator converts sisal leaves into rope fibers, if you want to be one up at your next cocktail party). There is a first-rate lion story, together with an excellent bonus green mamba one, and there is an account of how sympathetic and understanding Mr. Dahl was toward his "boy," loaned him by the Shell Company as a personal servant, that ends with the horrible, pointless murder of a German national when Hitler's war breaks out at last.

Mr. Dahl joined the R.A.F. in Kenya, and aside from his basic flight training in a tiny, Gypsy-engined biplane with the delightful name of Tiger Moth, his personal war, in spite of the game face he puts on it, seems to have been an extended series of botches and bad decisions. His commanding officer sent him flying off over the Western Desert in the wrong direction to a near-fatal crash. At the end there was the dazzlingly bad strategy of the air defense of Greece—15 Hurricane fighters, of which Pilot Officer Dahl's was one, were expected to fend off and destroy at least 1,000 German fighters and bombers. The brave young British heroes failed, of course; most of them were killed; most of their beloved planes were burned to cinders ("It took somebody *thousands of hours* to build this!" a mechanic says, stroking a Hurricane lovingly with his greasy hand); and almost everyone concerned knew all along that the whole thing was a stupid waste.

Those evenings I listened to war stories from my British friends didn't go on so long as this celebration, and maybe it's better if you've had a few drinks. By the time I got done with the book, and it's not a long one, I really had had too much of brave young men being killed and of the wonderful machines that were used to kill them, and I was glad it was all over.

Except, of course, it isn't.

> *Gahan Wilson, "Young Man, Old Empire, Bad War," in* The New York Times Book Review, *October 12, 1986, p. 12.*

An excerpt from *Going Solo*

One morning I saw a medical orderly coming down this corridor carrying a very large tray with a white cloth over it. Walking in the opposite direction towards the orderly, was a middle-aged woman, probably somebody from the hospital clerical staff. When the orderly came level with the woman, he suddenly whipped away the cloth from the tray and pushed the tray towards the woman's face. On the tray there lay the entire quite naked amputated leg of a soldier. I saw the poor woman reel backwards. I saw the foul orderly roar with laughter and replace the cloth and walk on. I saw the woman stagger to the window-sill and lean forward with her head in her hands, then she pulled herself together and went on her way. I have never forgotten that little illustration of man's repulsive behaviour towards woman.

Roald Dahl, in his Going Solo, *Jonathan Cape, 1986.*

Frederic Raphael   (review date 4 October 1991)

[*Raphael is an American-born English critic. In the following review of* The Collected Short Stories of Roald Dahl, *he assesses Dahl's literary career.*]

Roald Dahl's name alone sold both books and television series. He aroused expectations which, with renowned professionalism, he regularly satisfied. Like Alfred Hitchcock, who might have relished his calculated *frissons,* he had the gift of consistent, not to say repetitious ingenuity. **"Parson's Pleasure"** and **"Royal Jelly"** may not be sublime, but they are small masterpieces, like the best of Conan Doyle's unHolmesian tales, or the worst of Edgar Allan Poe. Whatever his lack of high art, Dahl was a classic of a kind. . . .

Dahl addressed himself to the largest possible public. It may be that he craved critical applause, but he belonged to a tradition of self-reliant commercialism, in which the undeniable certificate of merit was top-dollar acceptance by best selling magazines. (Was it not Dorothy Parker who said that the sweetest phrase in the English language was "Cheque enclosed"?)

Fastidious critics tend to assume that only trash can result from writing for a mass market. However, commercialism can develop muscles which no grant-aided aesthete will ever be able to flex. The robustness of the American short story derives not least from the journalism in which Ring Lardner, Sinclair Lewis, John O'Hara, Scott Fitzgerald and Hemingway learned to box clever and, sometimes, a little dirty. Dahl was an Englishman, of Norwegian origins, but he mixed with American editors, in the years after the war, and the "universality" of his mean myths surely owes something to their demands for the unpretentious. In vocabulary and, as they used to say, level of intent, Dahl appears to be a low-flyer: he uses fancy words only to josh his readers. His only avowed purpose is to entertain; the anecdote is paramount. He seemed to have no trouble in devising stories with delicious twists, something which only fools and fine spirits imagine is a mere trick (it may be a trick, but it is not mere).

Dahl's trademark was his mercilessness. After **"William and Mary"**—you remember, the one about the man whose eye and brain live on after him in a dish which his embittered wife takes home—or **"The Champion of the World"** (who has not relished, or even poached, that ultimate poaching story about the pram full of narcotized pheasants?), or **"The Visitor"** (with its sour-creamy affinities with Karen Blixen's "The Immortal Story"), it is tempting to think that one has their creator's number: he is the definitive Mr Not-Nice Guy. The same charge, on a nobler plane, was sometimes levelled against Vladimir Nabokov, of whom there are certain echoes, in the unsentimental, but luxuriant, eroticism and in the lepidopteric minutiae. It might be argued that both men concealed their vulnerability, and their wounds, behind a carapace of heartlessness.

By leading off with the stories from *Kiss, Kiss* (1960), the compilers of *The Collected Short Stories* make sure that cruel expectations are promptly met: Dahl is here in the macabre vein which turned so regularly to gold. Yet by this prompt serving of old favourites, the line of his authorial progress is distorted. His published work began, significantly, with *Over to You* (1947), in which the stories derive less from *Esquire* or the *Saturday Evening Post* than from the H. E. Bates of "Flying Officer X", or the tales of "Gun-Buster" (whose pseudonym I have yet to hear blown). The latter's stories of the desert war, in particular, chilled and thrilled my schooldays. I remember an almost unpatriotic tale of surrendering Italians being run over by one of our tanks. Perhaps inadvertently, something horribly true bled through the hit-'em-for-six optimism.

Over to You announced Dahl's Royal Air Force provenance, and intimates how, and perhaps why, he came to turn bloody experience into well-done fodder. The stories written more or less immediately after the war are only superficially of a piece with the more characteristic later pieces. In these tales of RAF life, one is conscious of the unendurable being wilfully, desperately, recycled for a readership which is both solicited and despised. If Dahl's later avoidance of naivety smacked of Smart Alec, just as his want of sentiment looked like callousness, the flying stories sometimes resemble Richard Hillary with added sugar. **"They Shall Not Grow Old"**, for instance, tells of a young fighter ace who falls fatally in love with death: Fin's last words, as he plunges "like a dying eagle", leaving "a thin trail of black smoke", are "I'm a lucky bastard. A lucky, lucky bastard."

There was a kind of camp in Dahl's later outrageousness. The hate that dared not speak its name found it prudent to express itself in mordant piquancy. Inoffensive shamelessness became a winning gambit; no one else could have written **"Bitch"**—in which the hero is finally transformed into a walking, working phallus—without falling into tweeness or rising to pornography. The requirements of the marketplace served Dahl well; energy, rage, fancy, which might have taken monstrous wing—or been grounded entirely—were re-invested in toothsome ghoulishness.

In **"The Great Grammatizator"**, Dahl satirizes, with a rather unlight touch, the mechanical story-telling which word-processing has perhaps made imminent and which will allow editors to procure what they want by pressing the required button. His computer-operating "heroes" become filthy rich by buying up famous names and persuading them to abandon composition. Their husks are then filled with commercial corn until all individuality yields to market forces. A sour interpreter might claim that Dahl did his industrious best to impersonate just such a graceless machine, but a more sympathetic reading will detect repressed disgust (and shame perhaps) at mass culture's degradation of literature.

It may be that Dahl was not a nice man, but he seems to have been quite a nice young chap until the war introduced him, traumatically, to death. That it took him some time to come to terms with the realities behind *Over to You* is suggested by the fact that it was not until 1986, when he was seventy years old, that he published an excellent volume of autobiography entitled *Going Solo.* One cannot, of course, be sure how much of the manuscript already existed, in some form or other, nor to what degree the artful Dahl was dressing hind-sighted reminiscence in reconstituted youthfulness. Nevertheless, the metamorphosis of a nice young Shell executive in Tanganyika into a badly injured Battle of Greece veteran of twenty-five leaves one in no doubt as to the author's genuine sufferings. The ineptitude of authority, the absurdity of war, the arbitrariness of death had to be understated in order to be stated at all. Who but Dahl has pointed out that fighter pilots were often sent up without any instructions as to what to do in combat? War became a schoolboy story with death instead of half-holidays. The squeamish youth was callused into the hard case.

Dahl's misfortune was perhaps indistinguishable from his good luck: he survived (one of three out of sixteen pilots in his squadron), without much respect for those he obeyed or for whom he was said to be fighting. He remembered aces like David Coke, who died with aristocratic insouciance while cowards and time-servers went on to prosperous longevity. Living well and writing commercially were his best revenge, but the voice of Fin, hell-bent for infinity and immune to disillusionment, is audible behind all these artful, spun-out tales.

Frederic Raphael, "Stories from the Source of Heartlessness," in The Times Literary Supplement, *No. 4618, October 4, 1991, p. 28.*

FURTHER READING

Biography

Farrell, Barry. *Pat and Roald.* New York: Random House, 1969, 241 p.
    Overview of Dahl's life that focuses on his relationship with his former wife Patricia Neal after her near-fatal stroke in 1967.

Sykes, Christopher. "Unexpected to the Very End." *The Times,* London (30 November 1990): 18.
    Biographical sketch and interview with Dahl.

Criticism

Warren, Alan. *Roald Dahl.* Mercer Island, Wash.: Starmont, 1988, 105 p.
    Study of Dahl's fiction, including a chapter on television adaptations of his stories.

West, Mark I. *Roald Dahl.* New York: Twayne, 1992, 148 p.
    Biographical and critical study.

Additional coverage of Dahl's life and career is contained in the following sources published by Gale Research: *Children's Literature Review,* **Vols. 1, 7;** *Contemporary Authors,* **Vols. 1-4 (rev. ed.), 133 [obituary];** *Contemporary Authors New Revision Series,* **Vols. 6, 32, 37;** *Contemporary Literary Criticism,* **Vols. 1, 6, 18;** *Major Authors and Illustrators for Children and Young Adults; Major 20th-Century Writers;* **and** *Something about the Author,* **Vols. 1, 26, 65 [obituary], and 73.**

Owen Dodson

1914-1983

(Full name Owen Vincent Dodson) American dramatist, poet, novelist, librettist, short story writer, and nonfiction writer.

The following entry provides an overview of Dodson's career.

INTRODUCTION

Although critics have acknowledged Dodson to be an accomplished poet, dramatist, and novelist, his works have received little serious critical attention. As a drama professor at Howard University and as a major figure among black dramatists and poets, however, he acquired a devoted following that continues to recognize him as an important writer and a great man.

Born to Nathaniel Dodson, a free-lance journalist for black newspapers, and Sarah Elizabeth Goode Dodson, Owen Dodson grew up in poverty in Brooklyn, New York. His father, director of the National Negro Press Association, introduced young Dodson to such important black thinkers and artists as Booker T. Washington, W. E. B. Du Bois, and James Weldon Johnson. Receiving a scholarship in 1932, Dodson went to Bates College in Maine. There he soon became interested in classical English literature, informing his English professor that he could write a sonnet as fine as John Keats's "On First Looking into Chapman's Homer." The professor ordered Dodson to write a sonnet each week and submit it to him until he matched Keats or graduated, whichever came first. Dodson consequently was able to publish his work in the *New York Herald Tribune* and *Phylon* by the time of his graduation.

After receiving his B.A. in 1936, Dodson entered Yale Drama School on a fellowship. His first play, *Divine Comedy,* was produced there in 1938. In it he exposed "prophets" like Father Divine, an evangelist who claimed he was God. James V. Hatch wrote of Dodson's inspiration for *Divine Comedy:* "At ten, Owen met God, at least a man who called himself God. Owen and his brother Kenneth were taken out to Sayville, Long Island, and there they gazed upon Mother and Father Divine. Kenneth looked askance at Father Divine, who kept drawing milk from a spigot on the table that never ran dry; after everyone left the feast, Kenneth looked under the tablecloth and there was a little Negro boy with a large cask of milk and a pump." Dodson greatly enjoyed this childhood revelation, and the play he based on this early experience has been called the finest verse drama ever written by a black writer. Dodson's next play, *Garden of Time,* produced in 1939 at Yale, is a retelling of the Medea myth in terms of American race relations, with the conflict between black Medea

and white Jason shifting in the midst of the play from Greece to postbellum South Carolina. Upon graduation from Yale in 1939, Dodson taught drama and speech at several colleges and enlisted in the United States Navy, where he was charged with "raising the morale of the Negro seaman" through a series of plays about black war heroes. After being discharged from the service because of asthma, Dodson wrote and directed *New World A-Coming* in 1944. The play was a widely attended pageant designed to commemorate and gain recognition for the black American contribution to the war effort. The overwhelming success of the production guaranteed Dodson's appointment to the newly founded Committee for Mass Education in Race Relations at the American Film Center, where he worked with such artists as Richard Wright, Langston Hughes, and Arna Bontemps. Although he eventually became convinced of the committee's ineffectuality and resigned his appointment, Dodson continued to write plays and operas and to teach drama at Howard University and elsewhere. Among his students were such artists as Amiri Baraka, Roxie Roker, Earle Hyman, Debbie Allen, and Ossie Davis. Because of his experience as a teacher and dramatist he became known as the "Dean of Black Theater."

Although Dodson distinguished himself in the theater, Pulitzer Prize-winning poet Richard Eberhart once called him "the best Negro poet in the United States." Dodson's reputation as a poet was established in 1946 with the publication of his first volume of poetry, *Powerful Long Ladder*. Its epigraph expresses the work's theme: "It takes a powerful long ladder to climb to the sky / and catch the bird of freedom for the dark." After the publication of *Powerful Long Ladder,* however, Dodson temporarily stopped writing poetry and turned to a new genre, the novel. In 1951 he published his first and most acclaimed novel, *Boy at the Window*. This poetic and semi-autobiographical work is the story of Coin Foreman, a sensitive young boy who feels that his conversion to the Baptist church should have prevented his mother's death. Dodson later resumed writing poetry, producing, among other volumes, the work he considered his masterpiece: *The Confession Stone: Song Cycles*. This collection consists of monologues about Jesus spoken by New Testament figures. Despite his accomplishments as a poet, Dodson remained closely associated with the theater. Bernard L. Peterson, Jr. commented: "Although recognized as an outstanding poet whose work has been compared with that of Frost and Sandburg, it is perhaps as a drama director and playwright that Owen Dodson will be best remembered." Dodson died in 1983.

Though long recognized as exceptionally talented, Dodson never enjoyed much notoriety, evidently because he wrote in traditional rather than progressive forms and never maintained strong ties to black literary movements. Too young to have participated in the Harlem Renaissance and too traditional to be among the angry black militants of the 1960s, Dodson escaped categorization and, consequently, critical attention. His proficiency in many genres also makes his achievement difficult to gauge. Nevertheless, Dodson continues to be admired as a skilled writer and director, as well as a shaping force in African-American literature.

PRINCIPAL WORKS

Divine Comedy (drama) 1938
Garden of Time (drama) 1939
"Someday We're Gonna Tear Them Pillars Down" (poem) 1942; published in periodical *Harlem Quarterly*
Everybody Join Hands (drama) 1943; published in periodical *Theatre Arts*
"Black Mother Praying in the Summer of 1943" (poem) 1944; published in periodical *Common Ground*
Dorrie Miller (broadcast) 1944
"Jonathan's Song" (poem) 1944; published in periodical *New Currents*
"Martha Graham" (poem) 1944; published in periodical *Theatre Arts*
New World A-Coming (drama) 1944
"Pearl Primus" (poem) 1944; published in periodical *Theatre Arts*

Powerful Long Ladder (poetry) 1946
The Third Fourth of July [with Countee Cullen] (drama) 1946; published in periodical *Theatre Arts*
"Color USA" (nonfiction) 1947; published in periodical *Twice a Year*
Bayou Legend (drama) 1948
"College Troopers Abroad" (nonfiction) 1950; published in periodical *Negro Digest*
Boy at the Window (novel) 1951; also published as *When Trees Were Green,* 1967
Cages (poetry) 1953
"The Summer Fire" (short story) 1956; published in periodical *Paris Review*
The Confession Stone (poetry) 1968; also published as *The Confession Stone: Song Cycles* [revised and enlarged edition], 1970
"Playwrights in Dark Glasses" (nonfiction) 1968; published in periodical *Negro Digest*
Till Victory Is Won [with Mark Fax] (opera) 1974
Come Home Early, Child (novel) 1977
"Who Has Seen the Wind?" (nonfiction) 1977; published in periodical *Black American Literature Forum*
The Harlem Book of the Dead [with James Van Der Zee and Camille Billops] (poetry) 1978
Freedom, the Banner (drama) 1984; published in periodical *Callaloo*

CRITICISM

George Jean Nathan (essay date 1945)

[*Nathan has been called the most learned and influential drama critic the United States has yet produced. He is particularly known for his occasional stinging invective and verbal adroitness. In the following excerpt, he criticizes Dodson's* Garden of Time *for its complex scenario and its wordiness.*]

[Owen Dodson], quondam head of the drama department at Hampton Institute, has [in **Garden of Time**] undertaken something. "I believe," he stated in the public prints, "that the modern drama is too stingy. We don't use it for all it's worth. **Garden Of Time** is told in terms of the fable of the Golden Fleece instead of hard, realistic terms. It uses music and song and dance and poetry. It begins in ancient times in Colchis off the coast of Asia Minor and ends in a graveyard in Georgia, U. S. A., at the end of the nineteenth century. It's the story of one country, Greece, the ruling country of the world, going to a smaller country, Colchis, whose people are a dark people and trying to take its emblems. Jason, the Greek, captures the Golden Fleece, aided by Medea, priestess of Colchis, who has fallen in love with him. They flee to Greece, killing Medea's brother in their flight. Two children are born to them, but eventually Jason deserts Medea. 'You're dark,' he tells her, 'I can't stand you.' Actually he is spurred on by the chance of marriage with Creusa and its promise of new wealth and possessions."

Here, continued the author, "the play switches to the end of the last century, with Georgia substituted for Greece and Haiti for Colchis, and with the main characters going on and the Greek idea of vengeance and atonement being realized through Mama Leua, a Haitian voodooist, who is like the ancient goddess Hecate." Then, elaborating, "Jason and Medea could have gotten along together, but these passions that move them—ambition, lust, greed—destroy them. They realize what has been wrong when the play comes to its end but it's too late to turn back. The play foreshadows an end of all this, however, as the nineteenth century Medea says:

> The rats been eating at the
>   seeds of time,
> Eaten full the gullet
> But the end's coming."

Since Mr. Dodson's previous demonstrations of dramatic composition consisted chiefly in an unproduced play written while at college and in one or two shows executed for amateur performances while he was in the Navy, it is not to be wondered that his ambitious plan, which would come near to frightening even a dramatist like O'Neill, who seems rarely to be frightened by anything, has been too much for him. Like various other tyros, he has attempted to enlarge the scope of the "too stingy" drama without first mastering the stingy scope of such dramatists as, say, Ibsen, Strindberg, *et al*. His process of enlargement resolves itself mainly into fancy rhetorical flights which adorn his story like so many artificial beads; in the kind of experiment, however well-intentioned, which operates upon that story to its seriocomic undoing, like a small boy's improvement upon the telephone by attaching the dinner table bell to it; and in a garrulity which, while it undeniably enlarges the script, reduces to a minimum what active drama his theme may intrinsically possess. He might have profited by taking a cue from Charles Sebree's classical stage settings and by writing his play in equally simple terms.

The performance of a mixed company of Negroes and whites was as confused as the materials, only louder. (pp. 290-91)

> *George Jean Nathan, "The Year's Productions: 'Garden of Time',"* in The Theatre Book of the Year, 1944 & 1945, *1945, pp. 290-91.*

Richard Wright   (letter date 9 June 1946)

[*Wright established a reputation as a leading spokesman for black Americans with his first novel,* Native Son, *in 1940. In the following excerpt from a 1946 letter to Dodson, he urges his friend to continue portraying the realities of black American life.*]

One of the reasons that compel me to write you now is my memory of your description of what you saw on your Mississippi trip. What you told me is truly important, and since I've been here in Paris I've been wondering if you really realize just how important. The French people, like ours, are also ignorant of the Negro. The forces of commerce have done a damn good job in painting the Negro as something exotic, as a race of people with something queer in them that makes them write jazz music. I wonder if American Negroes really realize the vast harm that they are doing their cause by making themselves into something unreal, something that always sings, something that is always childish? While the great body of their life experiences are untouched and unexpressed? There is no reason why the Negro point of view cannot be put over in Europe, if the right people come over here. There are thousands of Frenchmen who know of our jazz, and no one here seems to realize the great tragedy of the Negro in America, or the meaning of his life. But few could really understand your poem about the Negro mother praying. . . . All of this is by way of saying that I do hope and wish that you continue to dig into the rich materials of Negro life and lift them up for all to see, and you ought to know while doing it that you'll be doing more than holding up Negro life for others to see, but you will be holding up human life in all of its forms for all to see. The more we dig into Negro life, the more we are digging into human life.

My work is already being translated over here, and the astonishment, bewilderment which greets it makes me know that they have never had an opportunity to look straight at Negro life. People just do not know what to say or think. It confounds them. They had been led to look at the Negro and laugh; well, they are learning to look at him and let their mouths fall open. So far, there is no opposition here to looking at the Negro honestly. They've just never had a chance to do so before now. So you must realize that it is your duty to keep plugging. (pp. 125-26)

> *Richard Wright, in a letter to Owen Dodson on June 9, 1946, in* New Letters, *Vol. 38, No. 2, Winter, 1971, pp. 125-27.*

John Holmes   (review date 29 September 1946)

[*In the following excerpt, Holmes criticizes Dodson for overemphasizing racial issues in* Powerful Long Ladder.]

With the friendliest intentions, I'll risk saying that Mr. Dodson makes too much of an issue of his race and color [in ***Powerful Long Ladder***]. It obtrudes, and that is bad art in any language. There is good poetry in his book, best when least self-conscious. There is awareness of the inevitable tragedy of life; there is rich, deep rhythm and feeling as in this **"Epitaph for a Negro Woman"**:

> How cool beneath this stone the soft moss lies
>   How smooth and long the silken threads have kept
> Without the taste of slender rain or stars,
>   How tranquilly the outer coats have slept.
> Alone with only wind, with only ice,
>   The moss is growing, clinging to the stone;
> And seeing only what the darkness shows,
>   *It thrives without the moon, it thrives alone.*

Or in this formal Shakespearean sonnet:

I loved the apple-sweetness of the air
   And pines that settled slanting on the hill,
Indians old and soft with needles there
   Where once we stood, and both so strangely
     still.
We must have surely known what other days
   Would come in other flaming autumn's flame
And even though we walk through different
    ways
   To different hills that hill remains the same,
Watch every splendor, envy all the sky. But rec-
   ognize the days we knew, and hear
The simple sounds we heard. As birds that fly
   Southward to warmth, we shall come back
   one year.
The little teeth of time will make no mark
   On any stone, on any leaf or bark.

Passages from longer works also indicate his power and promise. But he appears to be in some danger of falling into certain patterns somewhat expected of poets who are Negroes. Dodson uses language and rhythm in a way that I think is book-learned—slave songs, blues. It is clear from the bulk of his poetry that he can, if he will, outgrow this.

> *John Holmes, in a review of "Powerful Long Ladder," in* The New York Times Book Review, *September 29, 1946, p. 22.*

Alfred Kreymborg   (essay date 1 February 1947)

[*Kreymborg, a poet, editor, dramatist, and critic, was prominent among American writers in Paris in the 1930s and 1940s. According to biographical sources, Dodson was a great admirer of Kreymborg's poetry. In the following excerpt, Kreymborg praises* Powerful Long Ladder.]

A year ago, American poetry was enriched by the arrival of Gwendolyn Brooks and her thoroughly original poems, *A Street in Bronzeville.* In **Powerful Long Ladder,** our poetry is enriched once more by a compelling young man whose record in our social life is already impressive. Educated at Bates and Yale, [Owen Dodson] received a Rosenwald Fellowship, directed drama at various Negro institutions, headed a morale building program while in the Navy, won a Maxwell Anderson Verse Play Contest, and is now executive secretary for the Committee for Mass Education in Race Relations. From these factors it may be gathered that his principal medium of expression would be poetic drama. Even his lyrical poems have a dramatic tendency, notably a tragic sequence on estranged lovers, an old theme in poetry, but one now informed with fire, wisdom, and dignity.

The poems on Negro themes are composed of clear and supple images wedded to chanting cadences. Memorable lines reveal a whole race in a single strain. "Sorrow is the only faithful one." At times the tone is biblical, at others colloquial. In the title poem, a dramatic chant between a leader and a chorus of slaves, the vernacular is handled with realistic skill:

Ma father say: Freedom a story they tell that
   never happen.
When, O when, ma brothers, ma sisters, will the

well be drained of masquerading death?
When will the noosed rope strangle the nooser?
It take a powerful long ladder to climb to the sky
   an catch the bird of freedom for the dark.

Three choruses from a verse drama, **Divine Comedy,** are included, and they unfold "people in search of something to believe in when they are trapped in poverty, fear, and prejudice. They follow a false prophet for a time, but when he is killed, they turn to the strength in themselves for guidance and faith." Or, one might add, to prophets and leaders like Paul Robeson and Owen Dodson. There is only one poem in which this ardent poet assumes a satirical role. But that one suffices—a conversation on V:

They got pictures of V stamped on letter stamps;
Miss Eagle wear one in her lapel to her Red
   Cross suit;
Mr. Bigful, the bank president, got one in his
   lapel too;
Some of the people I do laundry with got big
   ones in they windows;
Hadley Brothers Department Store uptown got
   pictures of V on they store-bought dresses,
Even got a V ice-cream dish-girls selling them so
   fast had to run up a sign: NO MORE V
   SUNDAES;
And bless God, Lucy done gone up North and
   come back with one gleaming on her pocket-
   book.
Now let's get this straight; what do these V's
   mean?
V stands for Victory.
Now just what is this here Victory?
It what we get when we fight for it.
Ought to be Freedom. God do know that!

                    (pp. 32-3)

> *Alfred Kreymborg, "Exiles in Black and White," in* The Saturday Review of Literature, *Vol. XXX, No. 5, February 1, 1947, pp. 32-3.*

J. Saunders Redding   (review date 18 February 1951)

[*Redding is a distinguished American critic, historian, novelist, and autobiographer. His first book,* To Make a Poet Black *(1939), is a scholarly appraisal of black poetry; as one of the first studies of its type to be written by a black critic, this book is considered a landmark in criticism of black writers. In the following review, he deems Dodson's* Boy at the Window *a success.*]

The delineation of a sensitive boy's growing up is the business of **Boy at the Window.** As a poet's first novel, it is a real achievement. It is an achievement in the kind of writing that steers its tenuous way between the grossness of physical reality and the too nice refinement of emotional truth. "Clinographic" is the word Middleton Murry applied to this kind of writing in the works of Virginia Woolf. It is perceptive, but emotionally oblique and indirect without being obscure.

I have called **Boy at the Window** a delineation, a portrait. Rather, it is a series of portraits. It is as if Coin Foreman, the subject, were caught in various attitudes at the revealing heights of certain stages of his development. Limned carefully but in miniature around him are half a dozen other portraits—of his mother, father, brother, and of people in the house and on the street where Coin lives.

There is story only in the most tenuous narrative sense. It is not "And then . . . and then . . ." Yet this does not mean that there are no events, no happenings. It means only that the events, though arranged precisely in time, do not depend upon each other in such a way as to forge a chain of circumstances and bring about an inevitable result. It means further that Coin is more important than any happening.

The events are soon retold. Coin sees God; Coin gets religion (in the church where his father has been a deacon for twenty years); Coin's mother dies (after an illness that began with Coin's birth); Coin goes to live with a blind uncle in Washington. And that is all. And these events themselves are caught in a kind of static mobility, as in a picture, that does not exercise Mr. Dodson's narrative powers but does prove his sure talent in description.

Yet even this talent, it seems to me, is not the author's most noteworthy. His best talent shows itself in what he does with the between-events. It is a gift for total immersion in mood and for recapturing the feel of those deliciously painful and divine mysteries in the growing mind and the absorptive heart of a boy.

J. Saunders Redding, "The Pains of Growing Up," in The New York Times Book Review, *February 18, 1951, p. 4.*

Dodson on the quality of African-American theatre:

So many of our Negro playwrights are so saturated with the idea of Negro oppression, which of course they should be, that they have left out the lasting power, the universality, of their art: "They just keep trampin.' " They aren't trying to make heaven their home. They seem to prefer infernos to the blaze of light that can come in the future. Many of them have discipline . . . but they hardly have the daring or the flair to infuse high vision with our present angry condition.

Owen Dodson, quoted by Bernard L. Peterson, Jr., in his "The Legendary Owen Dodson of Howard University: His Contributions to the American Theatre," The Crisis, November 1979.

Owen Dodson with John O'Brien   (interview date 1971)

[*In the following excerpt from a 1971 interview conducted at Dodson's New York apartment, Dodson talks about his writing and gives his views of other black writers. The unpublished novel Dodson mentions in his first response was later published as* Come Home Early, Child *in 1977. According to the interviewer, "At the time (of the interview Dodson) was convalescing from a recent illness and tired after about the first hour of conversa-* tion. A year later he agreed to expand on some of his previous answers, which he did by mail."]

[O'Brien]: *I know that you wrote a sequel to your first novel* **Boy at the Window.** *Why wasn't it ever published?*

[Dodson]: I had proposed to do a series of novels, the first one of which was **Boy at the Window.** What I wanted to do was to follow the life of a little boy from his birth on. I started with **Boy at the Window.** Then I got a Guggenheim Fellowship and wrote the second novel which I now have in manuscript form. But I was told that the novel was not "black enough." Part of it won a prize in *Paris Review* and was put in *The Best Short Stories of* THE PARIS REVIEW. Of course, writers from all over the world were represented there, not just black writers. In **Soon One Morning** the first chapter of the novel, "Come Home Early Child," was published. So the second novel is here, but it ain't "black." It's about the growing up and fulfillment of a little boy, and that's why it has not been published. The book of poems which I have here and which I will read to you from later is not "black enough" either. They want Nikki Giovanni poems now. You know these poems. You can make them up in a minute. You can say: "Look, man, I am black / Don't you see how black I am? / I'm black as my fingernails / and I'm black to my toes / and if you smell me / I am black / And now I want you to give me a job / because I am black." That's the end of the poem. You can make them up by the minute. I myself have a sense of humor about the whole thing.

Then you have personally felt pressure to write certain kinds of novels and poems?

Any writer has got to write about what he sees and what he feels, his total observation. The black writer is no different from any other writer. White writers or Chinese writers walk along the same street and they observe what they observe. Then they put it down on paper. The black writer has no obligation to "blackness." He's got an obligation to what he sees and what he feels and what he knows. They sent me a letter from Bates College where I had received my undergraduate degree and asked me to join the Black Alumni Association of Bates. I wrote one sentence back: "Did I learn black Latin?" That was the end of that. Yale did the same thing. I didn't answer them at all. I think we have to begin to realize that people are people, they're not black or white or anything. They're themselves. People. And they have their own worth. That's the only thing that we can consider. If we try to do anything else, then we're lost.

Do you have positive feelings about the work being done by young contemporary black writers, writers like LeRoi Jones and Ed Bullins?

Well, I think that the strength and power of a work like Jones' *Dutchman* is tremendous. He had a drama there, he knew about conflict, knew about all the things that were important, that make drama work. So I have a great respect for what he has written in drama but not for what he has written in poetry. I had to lecture recently on Mr. Bullins and other black writers, mostly dramatists. I had a whole week at Lincoln University to prepare, so I read all of Bullins' things that I could get ahold of. Two weeks ago I read in the *New York Times* that Ed Bullins is one of the greatest dramatists in the world. And I said, "Bullshit!" That's what I said to myself, and that's what I meant. Here was a man who is presenting or thinks he is presenting a whole race and that race is doing nothing but cursing, fucking, and farting. And that's what he writes about. I don't see any spire of meaning, any richness of hope. I just came across a quotation which says that if you don't see any hope in the theater then flee from it. The people have fled from the New Lafayette Theater where Mr. Bullins is Playwright-in-residence. They have fled from it because there is nothing there. What he is doing is feeding garbage to people when that's what they've been brought up on. Garbage. And I know now that playwrights and writers like Richard Wright know that even in the degradation there is something golden in everybody's mind. There is gold even in those people, as you see them walking along Amsterdam, Broadway, and Lenox Avenue. They want to be something else. Richer in their spirits. But they don't know how to do it. The playwrights must say that it can be done. When people talk about praying at the table and all that, that's not important. God has given everybody an intelligence, a mind. That's what we work from. We don't work from God because God has given us what we need and we must use those gifts. You think of people like Richard Wright and Margaret Walker coming out of the depths of the South. They made themselves do it. I just wrote an article about Richard Wright and I tried to say something about this man. What education did he have? He didn't have any education at all. He educated himself. When he got to Brooklyn he wanted to know how to grow vegetables in his little yard, so he got all the books on it (laughing). I think it's ridiculous, but it's kind of wonderful too. Books about seeds and about growth and about how to make the earth fertile. And then he took up physics. And why would he do that? That man was after something. We can't excuse society but we can't excuse ourselves either. Never. We can't excuse ourselves for our behavior.

In your poetry and plays a recurrent theme is religion and history. You have an apocalyptic sense of both. Do you think this characterizes what your central concern is in your writing?

I have written three books of poetry. The first was—I would say—somewhat propaganda, but the third was filled with stories, diaries, and remembrances of Jesus. They are really framed in diaries by Mary, Martha, Joseph, Judas, Jesus, and even God. This, I believe, is my most dedicated work. But I have also been interested in history. A record company asked me to write some kind of history of black people from slavery to their entrance into the United States and now. I did this in *A Dream Awake*. It is illustrated and spoken by James Earl Jones, Josephine Premice, Josh White, Jr. and others who are dedicated to the mainstream of making the world a wide world, a blessed world, a step-in world where all races hold hands and bless God. I have written and fought somehow in my writing, but I know now that the courage and forthrightness of writers and poets will change something a little in our dilapidation. (pp. 56-9)

I know that you were acquainted with many of the writers from the Harlem Renaissance. Did any of them have a direct influence upon your work?

One writer is Langston Hughes. He presented the whole idea of Negro life. He said, "These are my people and I love them and I will live on 127*th* Street and I will grow flowers there." He wrote poems that had such thrust. Langston had a beautiful perception about people. In his will he wanted two things. He said, "Do nothing until you hear from me." And, of course, I've been writing and hearing from him. Second, he wanted a combo at his funeral. And he had a combo—ain't that nice? A combo. The combo was on a little stage. But when the combo came in, Langston had to get out because his coffin was too large for the combo. So they moved him out. Countee Cullen was another influence. He was black and lost because he made—or rather we did—his dedication to society. He wanted to be a lyric poet; that's what he wanted. He didn't want to write all these things about race, but he did. He was pushed into death. They say he died of some blood disease. No! That man was made to die, by himself and by us, because we did not recognize the universal quality of what he wanted to say. In one of his poems he wrote, "Wake up world, O world awake." That's what he wanted to write. He didn't want to write about rioting in old Baltimore. He wanted to write about the lyrical quality of life. (pp. 60-1)

Do you like talking about your novel **Boy at the Window?** *It has been about twenty years since it was first published.*

It's really difficult for me to remember specific things about the novel. Characters take over when you are writing a novel. They tell you what to do. It's very strange. It is no longer your writing. All you have to do is to sit down and begin to put things down on paper. If you want to know something about one of my characters, ask them. Of course, you will never find them. It's like when somebody asks me whether they can use such and such a poem. I say, "What poem?" They tell me the poem and I say, "Well, I didn't even remember it." It is especially difficult to talk about the protagonist, Coin, except to say that he has worked something out for himself when the novel ends. But I can't say where he will go or what he will do. Richard Wright in talking about Bigger Thomas could say a great deal, because Bigger Thomas is such a direct character and he has a direct ending. But Coin is just starting. (p. 61)

Owen Dodson and John O'Brien, in an interview in Interviews with Black Writers, *edited by John O'Brien, Liveright, 1973, pp. 55-61.*

C. James Trotman (essay date Spring/Summer 1986)

[*In the following essay, Trotman examines the major themes of* Powerful Long Ladder, *Dodson's first poetry collection.*]

Except for an occasional listing here and there, Owen Dodson's first collection of poems entitled ***Powerful Long Ladder*** (1946) has not received any serious written attention by the intellectual community and by literary scholars. This is a strange form of neglect because, until his death in June, 1983, Owen Dodson was known for his literary, cultural and academic accomplishments, ranging from his successful novel *Boy At The Window* to a multimedia presentation of his poetry done as recently as May 3, 1982, under the auspices of Joseph Papp and The Public Theatre in New York City. Before then, Dodson had been chairman and a member of the Drama Department at Howard University from 1947 until his retirement in 1970. Moreover, the neglect is regrettable because *Powerful Long Ladder* is an important book of American poetry and, in a particular manner, it adds substantively to collections of poetry, from Phillis Wheatley to Maya Angelou, expressing the development of American and Black American poetry in the United States.

Powerful Long Ladder is divided into five sections. Each varies in mood and texture, style and technique, but it does not exaggerate a reading of the collection to say that each section is calibrated to contribute to the book's major theme suggested by the title: to climb a ladder, which is to say that to go beyond the given, one must be willing to reach out over one's head and pull one's self up. The figure evokes images of struggle, sacrifice and searching—but to what end? In Dodson's poetry, the ends are practical though the routes are spiritual and psychological; and the passions for human understanding, freedom and love are goals to replace a world of experiences in which indifference, injustice and hate prevail.

We can do better, Dodson seems to suggest in these poems, and the reassurances are there for all who are interested in improving the quality of human life. Idealism is very much a part of the pitch one hears in this volume; however, it would be a mistake to think that this is poetry which shuns genuine feelings. The range is not only wide in its vision of human life, it also offers a broad scale in which the notes are sometimes somber, sometimes humorous, encouraging us to pause and reflect on the most cataclysmic personal struggles; and then sometimes we are, I think, seemingly urged to just sit back and allow a skillful writer to promenade with the rhymes and rhythms of his chosen craft.

Part one takes its title from the book, and we hear a lyrical voice which is resolute and determined to speak for those who won't or cannot speak because experience has paralyzed them, or they lack human recognition. Readers familiar with the poetry of Robert Frost and Langston Hughes will recall through Dodson the effective use of a controlling, sometimes omniscient voice in the lyric mode. In **"Lament,"** for example, the first poem, we see something of the demands Dodson presents to his readers. The poem begins with a directive to the dead: "Wake up, boy, and tell me how you died." Responding to the grief of death, the narrator's imperative dramatizes the futility of the situation. Its chief purpose is to remind us that while we cannot actually know death (or freedom or fear, or love, or other abstractions) we can nevertheless feel its power.

Not all of the poems in this first section carry their resolve in this way. **"Guitar,"** with its uses of the ballad, and **"Sorrow Is the Only Faithful One,"** with its studied contrast between nature and human nature, are two poems which emphasize a complex vision of human nature. Not very far into reading this volume does one proceed before becoming aware of the breadth of Dodson's vision. With Frostian detachment and Hughes' social sensitivity, Dodson makes **"The Signifying Darkness"** a journey into a private and public terror where the devastations of war and the ravages of cultural racism are like bomb craters on a map of humanity too blinded by its folly to see the ruins. The darkness that Dodson describes is at once existential in its suggestion of an indifferent universe; it is cultural atrophy; and it is the personal anguish, to use the poet's words, of human "condescension, greed and charity." The psychological invisibility being addressed in the poem is a theme in Afro-American writing that has received a great deal of attention from the outstanding contemporary example of *Invisible Man,* Ralph Ellison's modern masterpiece, where symbol and myth are two of the extraordinary techniques used in the novel. In Dodson's poem, the theme of psychological invisibility has mythic overtones. Pristine imagery opens the poem ("There was an evil darkness way before / The war rose clear, a darkness before that dawn"); and the poem closes on an image of human destruction as "The black, wet face / of a dark mother staring at . . . her boy." Beside its own qualities as a poem **"Signifying Darkness"** joins **"Black Mother Praying"** as one of several poems in which the poet is writing from a viewpoint that is both ethnocentric and universal.

In *Modern Poetry and the Tradition* (1939), Cleanth Brooks wrote that "a healthy tradition is capable of a continual modification." This is a helpful comment because several of Dodson's poems focus on familiar subjects. What are we to make of **"Epitaph for a Negro Woman"** and **"Black Mother Praying"** by Dodson when we have Paul Laurence Dunbar's "When Malindy Sings" and Langston Hughes' frequently anthologized and graceful "Mother to Son" and "The Negro Mother"? The Dodson poems also appear in this first section and it is clear that they owe their inspiration to other poems and people. An analysis of styles, language and metrical techniques would lead a reader to the conclusion that Dodson, like Hughes and Dunbar before him, knows how to control the elegy and to sustain his focus, but we would still be left without a response to the similarities existing between these poems. Others have also articulated a need to know about these similarities. Wellek and Warren, for example, remind us that literacy genres never remain fixed; with each new work a category shifts as our experiences with literature (and life) modify our conception of a literary kind. An analysis might yield a "winner" in some strange sense of literary competition, but it would not tell us about the poetry in the poems.

What these poems by Dodson bring is not worn imagery but renewed vigor and insight into poetry, the role of black women in the struggle for liberation and the role of women affirming their maternal and sexual contributions to human life. **"Epitaph for a Negro Woman"** is a dirge where even in death the only true companion is growing moss. **"Black Mother Praying"** returns the reader to the more familiar struggle of the individual seeking to find personal meaning in a society tearing itself apart; "And [where] Freedom is writ big and crossed out." The fullness of these women in Dodson's poetry is due to their stature. They are heroes. They are reminders in Afro-American life of the wealth of human potential frequently lost in the depersonalized, racist patterns of modern society. They are also symbols for a larger humanity, particularly women, because of the broad social canvas Dodson presents.

The centerpiece for the first section is **"Someday We're Gonna Tear Them Pillars Down."** It deserves our attention for several reasons. It is here that we find the book's title and, because it is verse drama, it is the first time we see Dodson employing this proscenium art. This form gives the poet more freedom to explore with greater metaphorical richness the personal need to be determined and stubborn about retaining the dignity of our lives. It isn't easy; transcendence never is, since nature and circumstance usually intrude. Dodson's poem takes us back to chattel slavery, a symbolic time when the human condition was at its lowest. Men who enslave men are themselves slaves, and Dodson personifies the voices of fear, doubt, cynicism and despair in order to suggest how much hope may have existed in spite of the dark midnight of that hour. As one might expect, the poem dramatizes its conflict by taking its readers through a series of images which thematically render the distortion that accompanied this spiritual holocaust. Fire does not warm, characters shiver in the heat of mid-day, and the simple expressions of song are "poisonous." Even the very air lacks comfort and support while freedom, the poem says, is "a story they tell that never happen."

Dodson was a careful writer and a careful observer of human behavior who reminds us of the longing to overcome barriers. When the longing becomes part of our selves, and our consciousness, it appears "like a miracle bird." The ideal and real clash in the poem when the voices of those requiring some form of assurance that everything will work out are juxtaposed to others expressing with equal determination that no such promise can be given. While a symbolic leader for the downtrodden does appear in the poem, the imagery carries the message: The ladder of the title is a symbol to be used for reaching out and up for the bird of freedom. Yet there is restraint. The leader admonishes his followers not to try and grab the bird but to allow it to serve as a source of inspiration for all to take on the risky business of attempting to be free.

The pillars, like the walls of Robert Frost's famous poem, "Mending Wall," are common symbols for human barriers, but Dodson, characteristically expansive in his thoughts, may have been thinking about aesthetics and craftsmanship as pillars to demolish also in order to reach a plane of artistic accomplishment. Dodson wrote about this concept in 1980, and with similar imagery, in an essay entitled **"Who Has Seen The Wind":**

> Beginning to master any art, especially playwriting, is an arduous, sometimes torturous task. A play is never fulfilled by one person: There are the producer, the director, the actors, designers, and, above all, the audience. But before these run interference, the writer must face the thick walls of craftsmanship, figuring how to blast

until they come tumbling down and he can enter the inner city of whatever life he chooses to portray. Some don't have to use the dynamite of experimentation; they walk into their city casually, almost carelessly, by themselves, tipping their hats to acquaintances, finding friends and family, sleeping with lovers, revealing the themes surrounding them astutely. But they are rare.

Dodson's interest in freedom for the individual would of course include examples. This is the intent surrounding the poem honoring Samuel Chapman Armstrong, who founded Hampton Institute, and the two white women, Miss Packard and Miss Giles, who founded Spelman College for (to use the historical term) Negro women in Georgia.

If a reader moves through the book in the order in which the poems are presented, as I have done, one is likely to feel growth with the next two sections, "Three Choruses from a Verse Drama: Divine Comedy" and "Poems for My Brother Kenneth." The spiritual themes of transcendence from human misery and sorrow certainly recall previously mentioned poems such as **"Someday We're Gonna Tear Them Pillars Down"** and **"Sorrow Is the Only Faithful One."** The familiarity, which is not to be confused with redundancy or stale imagery, is welcomed because it allows us to enjoy the poet working in concentration.

"Divine Comedy," with its allusion to Dante's world masterpiece in the title is, like its literary forebear, a study in faith. The sensibility that pervades Dodson's work is distinctively modern, yet the tone of the poem makes it more like its ancestor than the appropriation of a famous title. Here, as in Dante, the lyrical voice of the poet is submerged into the content of the dramatization by the poet's use of multiple personae. Some, in fact most, are allegorical figures representing groups (youth, a vacillating community, the chorus, a temple priest) whose presence is not felt by what they say to one another but what they say to us as readers. They cry out for "liberty, and peace and freedom," essential goals for experiencing human potential, which is exactly the vision they lack. In rendering these empty, despairing voices the poetry elevates their condition to the level at which the pain and confusion are not only felt but can be applied universally. For example, the despair is reflected in the barrenness of speech: no one has more than several lines, and the words in the lines are stark and linguistically stripped to the most elemental expressions:

> Chorus:
>   Where are the mirrors to show us normal
>   To pain
>   Love
>   Hate
>   Kindness?
>   To show we love our children?
>
> Crazy Woman:
>   We need a new star to live on.
>   The wind is fierce here.
>   I have rheumatism, arthritis, and cancer
>   in my left armpit.
>   The wind is fierce here and my heart . . .
>
> One:

Run before the wind slashes us together

Another:
>   Rip up the pavement and hide

Another:
>   Hide in the closets with automatic locks

Another:
>   Run into darkness for safety

Another:
>   Run to the attic

Another:
>   The cellar

Another:
>   Run!!!

Old Man:
>   If you run, the city hounds are faster,
>   The country hounds are more practiced.
>   Stand here and lean against each other.

Chorus:
>   Cancel us,
>   Let doomsday come down
>   Like the foot of God on us.

What moves us, however, in the verse dramatization is not the situation, because we have become conditioned to lonely voices in world and modern literatures. We are moved by the prospect of hope and the silent, powerful meditation that is called prayer.

Dodson is not proselytizing for a specific religious organization but for an awakening that is spiritual, inwardly directed and personal. The process is poetic, the symbols are recognizable (Christian, literary) and the journey is a sort of flight into feeling and moral enlightenment. This is what Dr. Johnson meant when he wrote: "The natural flights of the human mind are not from pleasure to pleasure, but from hope to hope." Dodson's poetry presents the same theme when a character at the end says to the masses:

>   I know, Lord, I know the deep well side of
>   life. . . .
>   The power and the glory.

"Poems for My Brother Kenneth," like *Divine Comedy*, is a separate section in the book, not a long one, but it stirs and touches. This section reminds one of Tennyson when he writes (from "In Memoriam"), "I sometimes hold it half a sin / To put in words the grief I feel / For words, like Nature half reveal / And half conceal the Soul within." This is the sensibility pervading this section: the struggle to find the strength to transform human pain. In addition to Tennyson, other poems and poets writing in English have brought dignity to the lyric-romantic tradition of poems about death. One hopes every school child would know Milton's "Lycidas," Donne's "Death Be Not Proud" and perhaps Gray's "Elegy in a Country Church-Yard." I mention these to acknowledge Dodson's participation in this tradition. For in spite of many social gains, the black writer remains the most oppressed figure in the publishing world because so many, many reviewers (readers of manuscripts, in particular) cannot conceive of the black writer dramatizing much that is not bare-knuckled racism. The poems for Kenneth contain some of Dodson's most beautiful writing in the collection and, like other good poems on the subject, they add something special to our vocabulary for struggling with grief and the inexorable human journey toward death. For example, in Section IV, the transformation of grief into a new enthusiasm is wrapped in child-like innocence, for memory and vividness make the poet assert that "There is a new language to learn / And I am learning like a truant child." But it is better to see the lines in their whole:

>   My chief citizen is dead
>   And my town at half-mast:
>   Even in speech
>   Even in walking,
>   Even in seeing
>   The busy streets where he stood
>   And the room where he was host to his friends
>   And his enemies, where we erased the night to
>   dawn
>   With conversation of what I had seen and he had
>   seen
>   And done and written during the space of time
>   we were apart.

With Dodson scorning the image of helpless mankind, we might expect that his spirit would not yield before the image of death in human life. This is in fact what we find in Section VIII where the poet's mind declares the figure of death a charlatan leaving itself in a world without a world. The small section is worth quoting:

>   Death, split-second guest, negative magician
>   When will you believe you are not final?

After the Kenneth poems comes "All This Review." If we can appropriate the language of music for describing this section, we can call it a melody of focused themes in which the orchestration of content and craft moves closest to realizing itself in a single voice. The themes of self-reliance and self-determination are here, but the most impressive characteristic is the lyricism itself.

In **"When I Am Dead"** and **"Countee Cullen,"** an encomium for the distinguished poet of the Harlem Renaissance, the lines sparkle with reversals and ironies. From the first and last stanzas:

>   Now begins the sleep, my friend:
>   Where the cold dirt blanket is, you will be warm,
>   Where seeds begin to root, you will flower.
>   and, . . .
>   Also in your brave and tender singing
>   We hear all mankind yearning
>   For a new year without hemlock in our glasses.

"Circle One" and **"Circle Two"** which follow are epigrams, with the trochaic foot carrying the metrical stress for these intellectual exercises. **"All This Review,"** the title piece, is a love song of lost innocence and unrequited love. Here one finds Dodson being conventional with the lyric tradition in poetry by seeking that correspondence between nature and human nature, taking imaginative flights that stimulate thought and action in order to relieve the burdens of an uneasy spirit and turning, as in **"The Verdict," "The Reunion," "I Break the Sky,"** and **"That**

Star," to the incidents of yearnings; or, as in the worlds from **"That Star,"** "Loves hours, only hours, never light."

"Counterpoint" is the concluding section of *Powerful Long Ladder.* It contains strong poems on established social and psychological themes; and we do not tire of them because the imagery is sharpened by exquisite phrasing. In **"Jonathan's Song,"** subtitled **"A Negro Saw the Jewish Pageant, 'We Will Never Die,' "** demonstrates Dodson's universal vision and his commitment to a spiritual view of humanity:

> I am part of this
> Memorial to suffering,
> Militant strength:
> I am a Jew.

Dodson's social consciousness, as Margaret Just Butcher has written, is also the subject of **"Conversation on V"** where race and war are Dodson's focus. But **"Iphigenia,"** because of its allusion through the title to the Greek myth of social innocence and ritualized sacrifice, has special significance. Its use of myth reminds one of Dodson's broad view of the materials capable of rendering authentically the truth of humanity; in **"The Watching"** Dodson turns to the Biblical saga of Samson to once again use material from the broadest elements of western culture to depict modern anguish and human fear.

The final four poems are compelling in their assertion of human potential and the risks involved; in fact they may be seen as lyrical refrains on the book's themes of hope and struggle, but they are presented with a vigor that derives from the craftsman's growing confidence in the truth of his vision and the agility with which he is saying it.

"Definition" has an ingenuous quality about its development. The first line establishes this tone: "Everyone says: fate is a bad number, . . . " Dodson's development in the poem leads to a challenge against that received perspective. In the third quatrain he writes: "Fate is ourselves awake and asleep." And to make the point more emphatic he turns to one of his favorite sources for the expression of human truth, Christianity and its rituals, by writing that:

> . . . Fate is the collection plate
> Of our sins and our loves—variety of coins,
> Stored away or stolen by fakirs
> Who blame the plus or minus of our condition
> On God or Devil or the sound of the sea.

There is a sense in which what **"Definition"** begins by way of reconstructing our perceptions of human possibilities continues in the remaining three poems. In **"The Precedent"** the poem moves from a description of nature desecrated by man to the poetic assertion of a new day which is, like the inexplicable in nature, itself "A precedent: spring will come / Like fire to the snow." In other words, there will be a rebirth, it is inexorable, and it will lead to a better day.

"Martha Graham" is about doing something to improve our common lot in the face of adversity. The imagery of the poem is full of signs and symbols for our technical capabilities for making war—indeed, there is some prescience here, a wisdom in the aftermath of WW II—that

rings all too familiar to the contemporary reader, and it is born out of the poet's search for a new vision.

> There is the world chasing the world
> In the dark, in the spaceless dark
> While the moon hides terrified
> At the mechanical cannon bark.

What are we to do? We are to "Dance them out of the speechless dark / Into the talking day." This, of course, is a symbol for human action, using the name of an artist most closely identified with modernizing the dance and revitalizing its forms to mirror the signs of our times.

"Open Letter" is an anthem. It is a paean and a plea for humanity to close ranks and to permit the time "when peace surrounds us like a credible universe."

As one might expect from a poet whose work engages reality and especially the dark side of experience, there are perspectives, sometimes even philosophies, and human truths to be found in this collection. Perhaps the largest among them is the necessary struggle of the human predicament to know that there is struggle and conflict, handicap and pain. It is sometimes brought on by war, racism, poverty, loneliness and misunderstanding; but it is painful. And that human pain, Dodson's poetry suggests, not only defines our common humanity but can lead to visions of independence and spiritual wealth, to sights and sounds of the impossible made possible by each of us. That statement on human potential is not going to be accepted by all, if that matters, but what is certain is the experience of responding to the verbal orchestration, the measured steps, that brought us to the point of making that decision for ourselves. (pp. 96-107)

> *C. James Trotman, "The Measured Steps of a Powerful Long Ladder: The Poetry of Owen Dodson," in* Obsidian II, *Vol. 1, Nos. 1 and 2, Spring-Summer, 1986, pp. 96-107.*

James V. Hatch (essay date Winter 1987)

[In the following essay, which has been revised and expanded since its original publication in 1984, Hatch, an expert on Dodson's life and works and a personal acquaintance, reminisces about an evening he spent with the writer.]

"You don't make decisions. You sweat into something that someone has made the decision for you. Life, most of the time, is a bitter hope that everything will be all right. There's a friend of mine who said, 'Hold me in your arms and tell me everything will be all right.' Marriage, all those things. You are not making a decision; you go into them and hope they'll be all right."

Owen never made a formal decision about dying. He provided no will, no lawyer, no witness. He just sweated into the bitter hope that it would turn out all right. His biography too: we drifted into it one evening, my curiosity and his caution loosened by two glasses of champagne.

A young playwright had invited me to a reading of his new play. The occasion, to be held near 8th Avenue, lay two or three blocks from Owen's New York City apartment at 350 West 51st Street, so I asked him to accompany me, thinking that the critique would benefit the playwright, and the outing might please Owen.

When I called at the Dodson flat, Owen's sister, Edith, opened the door. This four-foot-ten-inch warrior met nearly everyone at the door, and one might have as easily brushed past Ghengis Khan as ignore Edith on the qui vive. Tiny, tiny, she knew the secret: absolute self-assurance. She inspected each visitor for evidence of vodka running, for Owen depended upon runners. She waved me, a friend, to bend down and gave me a kiss on the lips. Her face revealed two Ediths: a sensual woman with clear, soft skin and full lips graced with a hint of moustache; a vigilant woman who balanced the budget of their retirement incomes, and protected her brother's reputation against young hustlers, against Owen himself. Edith, as a young girl, had been adorned with a marvelous set of buck teeth and seldom smiled in photographs until in later life she was able to afford the orthodontist. Owen had assumed she would have few boyfriends, and few she had. Following her divorce from a brief marriage at the age of thirty-nine, Edith became for Owen "the only faithful one," playing Wendy to his Peter Pan. Edith patted my arm and pointed me toward Owen, who sat wrapped in his velvet cape with his embroidered cap, his steel crutches gleaming against the red plush sofa. His moustache was neatly trimmed, and he touched his new spectacles, which made his eyes large and luminous.

"Chile, ain't these something? Don't they make me look like Dr. Eckleburg from what's his name's novel? I think they're kinda wonderful, don't you? Makes me seem wide-eyed with wonderment."

He refused my offer to hail a cab and committed himself to walk the three blocks. I did not know then how deeply he hated the embarrassment of begging for cabs, which speed past cripples. His neighborhood was not the best, and I sometimes worried that he was an easy mark for hoodlums. As he swung along, he spoke to a sullen man who supported himself against an iron grate of a window, and to a woman in a doorway who guarded her shopping bags. Unbeknownst to me, his subconscious was busy at work on "Life in the Streets," which would be performed at the New York Public Theater in about eight years. "How ya doin'?" Whether surprised by the greeting from an elegant gentleman, or by the sudden reminder that they still had the use of their legs, these street souls responded, "Evenin'." "Can't complain." "How you?"

When we arrived, we were confronted by two steep flights of wooden stairs, no elevator. I cursed. Why hadn't I asked before dragging him here? Owen handed me the crutches. "I'll pull myself up by the hand railing." And so we began our ascent, step by step by step, with me close behind, braced if he should fall. Before we reached the halfway, two young men appeared from the top to offer assistance. Owen refused them gently and, after a moment to catch his breath, climbed on. He remained strong in his arms and even his legs, but the metal ball-joints in his hips had never worked properly, and he shunned the physical therapist. When I would press him on this point, saying the exercises were necessary for his legs lest they degener-

ate, he would shake his head. "It doesn't matter . . . doesn't matter."

At the top, I introduced Owen to the playwright. I impressed the young man with his good fortune—he had in his audience an artist who had written or directed hundreds of shows, and who had led many talents to the discovery of their own genius. However, the attention of this writer, as it must be in nascent talent, was absorbed with his own work. We filed into the rows of steel chairs to witness the drama, a play that harbored a curious emotional power, somehow imprisoned in an improbable story of Vietnam veterans in a bar. (The author was not a vet.)

When the curtain came down, the writer invited us all to make comments so that he might be guided in his revisions. The actors spoke of their characters, the audience complained of confusion, and because I couldn't get a handle on the problem, I said something useless about the plot. Then Owen spoke: "This play is about love, the love of two men, one black and one white, who become as brothers in Vietnam. But once in America, they cannot find a way to express this love, physically or verbally, so they fight."

The mystery revealed! I was stunned. Owen had placed his finger upon the soul of the play. I looked to the writer to enjoy the revelation upon his face; there was none. He hadn't understood because the play had come from a place within him that he dared not yet know.

Later, as we crept along the dark street home, I extolled Owen's insights, and apologized that my playwright friend had not responded to them. "It's all right," he said. "If he continues to write, he'll find it himself." We had arrived at Owen's building, a nineteen-story white brick affair that housed nurses and interns from nearby St. Clare's Hospital, as well as retired people; these latter served by turns in the lobby in lieu of a doorman.

"Wanta come up for a drink?"

As we rode up in the elevator, my mind went back to 1958 to Professor Bill Reardon's playwriting workshop at the University of Iowa. There, Ted Shine, myself and other young talents attempted our first plays. Into our workshop one day, a guest, a black writer, a professor from Howard University, a poet without dark glasses, strode briskly in with Paul Engle of the Iowa Writers Workshop, trailed by an entourage of local dignitaries. That day, Owen spoke to us, chatting about people and things of the theater. He was, at first hearing, a shameless storyteller and a gossip. He would seize upon the famous and the near-great with gentle malice. He delighted in the naughtiness of people and the exposure of their vanities.

After the talk, Ted Shine introduced me to Owen, who had a way of paying each person a particular and unhurried attention, as though he searched for the wonderment in you. I sensed that Ted held this man in special reverence, but in my ignorance, racism, I assumed Ted's respect rested upon their both being black writers. It would be many years, and many knocks on heart and head, before I would meet Owen again.

The elevator reached the penthouse and its door slid open

into a hallway with Owen's apartment to the right, a funeral director's to the left. Immediately before us on the walls, framed posters: an Alvin Ailey dance performance, a huge kenti cloth textile exhibition, and others. In Owen's twelve years' residence there, none had been stolen or soiled with graffiti. Some guardian spirit hovered over the hall until the day he died, when, within hours, the posters were removed to protect them from theft.

When Owen let us into the apartment, the rooms were silent; Edith had gone to bed. "There's a bottle of champagne on the terrace, and glasses in the cabinet. Bring them to the living room. I want to read you a new poem."

I found the champagne, half a bottle that had been recorked with a tonic cap. I returned to find Owen in his place; I poured two glasses and settled into a deep chair. The room's distinction was not its floor-to-ceiling books, its square grand piano that had belonged to General Howard, nor even the paintings and prints—Cocteau, Kollwitz, Sebree—crowding the walls . . . not even the man-high candelabrum that he lent out to concerts, nor the wooden horse he planned to leave to the Brooklyn Children's Museum. These treasures were not possessions; rather, each seemed to have chosen for itself the distinction of being there.

Presently, he took from the coffee table two yellow legal sheets, scribbled over in a large hand. At the time he was composing poems for **The Harlem Book of the Dead** (1977), a collaboration with Camille Billops and James Van Der Zee. He took a long sip of champagne, put down the glass, and read slowly, twisting the paper to follow his inserts and rewrites.

> How many mothers with their grit
> With their bony and long dreams
> Have dared to splash with us out to sea?
> They weighed anchor while we,
> While we played marbles or dominoes;
> Hide-and-seek games
> With biology, spelling, geography;
> Then at twilight, crossed-legged the mothers
> Recited all the higher algebra of pride:
> Teaching of how to do, what not to do,
> With grace toward the chemistry of man.
> > Mothers hoping in the dark to God
> > Grunting spells into the decks,
> > Then mopping up with elbow grease
> > So we could walk safely
> > In any season's tantrum.
> > Mothers bargaining with
> >   ancient sins
> > To leave us be to learn
> >   and live and win;
> > Mothers milking nanny goats
> > To make us strong;
> > Telling the fortunes of bees
> > For honey to sweeten bile.
> In the suburbs of dreams
> They dug the earth with their
>   fingernails,
> Planted oaks to shelter us
>   with acorns for insurance.
> Nailed the Government to a cross
> For their stingy and when we
>   were desolate. . . .

He paused, as though remembering some private desolation. Then recollecting the champagne on the table, he took a sip.

> At night they played hymns
>   on their kazoos,
> Or whistled spirituals:
>   the haunted tunes.
> Sometimes whales accompanied them.
> They dived into the waters
> (where our ancestors might have died),
> Witnessed the intercourse
>   of mermaids
> As they scrubbed the ass
>   of the ship.
> And lo and behold a
>   new breed was born.
> How many mothers with their grit,
> With their bony and long dreams
> Have dared to splash with us
>   out to sea?

He stopped. I sat stunned. Mothers scrubbing the ass of the ship, "Nailed the Government to a cross . . . a new breed"—the resonance of growing up Black in America. It was an epiphany: for the first time I perceived what was Black in Black poetry. Owen's unique signature, his blend of classic and folk, his voice of erudition and innocence, his ambivalence between submission and defiance.

"When I die," he mused over his glass, "I would like to leave some memorable line . . . like Keats and Auden."

Until that moment, writing a biography had not crossed my mind, but as Owen read **"Allegory for Seafaring Black Mothers,"** the "bony and long dreams" had carried my imagination out to sea. Intrigued, I asked Owen about his family.

A baby born of a forty-year-old mother, as an old wives' tale has it, will be a bright, gifted, and peculiar child, in some ways, born already old. In the evening of November 28, 1914, Sarah Goode Dodson birthed her ninth and last, a Saturday's child. At the age of seven, Owen asked his father where he, Owen, had come from, and his father replied, "Dr. Owen Wallah rushed up the stairs of our apartment in Brooklyn with a little black bag, and he sat beside your mother and opened it and there you were." When relating this anecdote, Owen would look up out of the top of his eyes and add, "that was my first taste of sex; I was little and they all loved me."

For Owen's birth, the wood stove had surely been fired, warming the polished floors, floors noticeably bare of furniture. Neither Owen nor his sister Edith, when recalling their childhood, ever deigned to use the word "poor," and if one spoke of their childhood "poverty," at once they would recite the litany of cultural wealth they had been given; nonetheless, one may glimpse hungry days, and in the winter the family wore their coats in the house.

Perhaps the talisman of the doctor's good name insured Owen's survival. In this family, a boy and a girl, twins, had already died; before Owen would reach ten, two more would succumb, one to TB, the other to meningitis, familiar deaths for black children. Said Owen, "There was a great scent of death in the garden when I was born." The family took to the high ground; Owen's life became a struggle to hold that ground, not against poverty, but against racism and God.

The father, Nathaniel—elevator operator, college graduate, syndicated columnist, Sunday School superintendent at the Concord Baptist Church—wore his decorum clean and starched. His neighbors, privately, called him Reverend Dodson; children on the block tagged him "the preacher." On many days, the mother prepared oatcakes for breakfast, rice for lunch, and lima beans for dinner. No matter how parsimonious the servings, she always held back a spoonful so that Papa could have a second helping.

Seated at the head of the table, Papa would read from the Bible and then call out, "Momps, where are the napkins?" The mother would reply, "They're in the same place, Papa."

"Edith, fetch the napkins," and Owen's sister would go to the buffet and take nothing out of the top drawer and hand each person an air-shaped napkin. The children would giggle and clap hands.

Nathaniel referred to his two youngest sons as "his Chesterfields," not after the cigarette, but after Lord Chesterfield, the epitome of a gentleman. Although inconvenienced by impecuniosity, the boys wore freshly laundered sailor suits on Saturday and Sunday. An old acquaintance would later refer to the immaculate family as "those damnable Dodsons."

His father established the first syndicate for a Negro newspaper. He served Booker T. Washington and Dr. James Sheppard, who founded North Carolina College, as press agent. Owen told me, "Once Dr. Sheppard came to our house. I recall that day with glee. My father told us that he was bringing a great man to see us and wanted Kenneth and me both outside when they arrived. My mother had fixed the house up and we'd done the best we could. My father came up the street with Dr. Sheppard, and he introduced us, and he said, 'After you, Sir,' and when he opened the door, the knob came off in his hand; without hesitating, he handed the knob to me, saying, 'Son, tend to this.' I was eight, so I handed the knob to my brother who put it in his pocket. When we got to the dinner table, my father said in a loud voice that wasn't pompous, 'Momps, where are the napkins?' My mother said, very quietly, 'Papa, they didn't dry in time.'"

Before each meal, the father asked the Lord's blessing, in "megaphone tones, like he was praying before the whole Sunday school"; and after dinner mother or father read aloud. Often the Bible, sometimes poetry.

"In the beginning was the Word and the Word was God." The Dodsons' Baptist devotion to their Bible incarnated a reverence for literacy. Born to parents only five years out of slavery, Owen's father and mother made little distinction between their passion for Christ and their burning love for education. Their children, and Owen in particular, were ordained to a life sonorous in language and resonant with literature.

Owen courted glory. At ten, Owen met God, at least a man who called himself God. Owen and his brother Kenneth were taken out to Sayville, Long Island, and there they gazed upon Mother and Father Divine. Kenneth looked askance at Father Divine who kept drawing milk from a spigot on the table that never ran dry; after everyone left the feast, Kenneth looked under the tablecloth and there was a little Negro boy with a large cask of milk and a pump.

Owen delighted in that story (which became the inspiration for his verse play *Divine Comedy*), in lifting the tablecloth, in peeking behind the curtain, under the robe, behind the mask. Imagine, if you will, Owen kneeling before the Almighty, and kneeling in such a way that he can peek under the hem of the Lord's cassock, then turning to whisper, "Chile, do you know the Almighty uses cream on his ashy legs?" Much of Owen's narrative style derives from his delight in revealing the uneasy secrets of God and humankind.

However, for Owen, if God were not sacred, then Art—in great CAPITAL LETTERS—would be. To Beauty, to Art, to Theater, Owen would dedicate his life. Among the saints in his pantheon stood Eleanor Duse and Alla Nazimova.

"I must have been about thirteen or fourteen when I saw Nazimova in *A Month in the Country*. She taught me what spontaneous acting was. I learned from Ethel Barrymore, who played in *L'Aiglon*, a lesson I'll never forget: on stage, you never do anything you don't have to do. At the Majestic Theater in Brooklyn we saw her as Lady Teasdale; she was a little bit tipsy; they were taking their curtain calls in the manner of the period. Miss Barrymore came forward to the footlights and made a curtsy, and fell on her face, then the curtain came down."

White artists were not his only models. "My father took us to our first play, *Porgy*, given by the Theater Guild. Rose McClendon was the first black actress I had seen, and she made a great impression on me."

Not all Owen's early art experiences came from Broadway. He told me, "On Sundays, my brother and I would go to church together. The one we loved the most was Reverend Harten's Holy Trinity Church in downtown Brooklyn. He was spectacular: he dressed in a morning coat. Ritual! No informality. Black rimmed spectacles that clipped on his nose with a string attached. Twice a year he gave his famous sermon, *Dry Bones in the Valley*. On either side of the pulpit there was a long pole that went up to the ceiling, maybe holding the ceiling up. Anyway, Reverend Harten used to shinny up the pole as an athlete might, and he would preach from the top and point to the sinners in the congregation and call them by name. It was terrifying; then he would shinny down again and say, 'Now all you sinners are in hell.' At the end of each service, he would say, 'The Dodson boys are outside and they have the *Amsterdam News* and the *Pittsburgh Courier* and I want every one of those papers sold.' We would always leave the church with pocket full of money, maybe two dollars and fifty cents. Papers were only five cents; some of the old sisters would hug us to their bosoms and give us an extra nickel."

1932, Bates College, Maine, Owen received a scholarship.

Five foot six inches tall, weighing 135 pounds, this handsome, clear-skinned poet fell in love with the classics. In his first class in literature, a small balding professor, Robert Berkelman, extolled the beauty of Keats' sonnet, "On First Looking into Chapman's Homer." Young Dodson allowed that the sonnet was ok, but he could write one as good himself.

The little ball of saliva that rolled perpetually on Berkelman's lower lip glistened; then he spoke: "Mr. Dodson, you will write a sonnet every week and bring it to me each Monday," he paused, "until you write one as fine as Keats, or until you graduate, whichever comes first." And so, at this forge, Owen labored.

He mailed his first poems to James Weldon Johnson. In his letter Owen wrote, "I shall be very grateful if you will read those here enclosed and give me your opinion. Have I ability and an inherent sense of beauty and life and their expression in poetry that is better than mediocre? Or have I merely the usual adolescent outburst of morning glory expression that will fade by noonday?" Johnson returned the poems with marginal notes and, at the bottom of his letter, added: "I am enclosing your manuscripts; however, I note that you sent no return postage."

Owen's early poems reveal a talent wreathed in melancholy. Not many years after graduation, he wrote in *Powerful Long Ladder* (1946):

> There was a great scent of death
> In the garden when I was born.
> Sorrow is the only faithful one.

Indeed, Sorrow became his life companion. When Owen was twelve, his mother suffered a stroke, paralyzing her speech. Owen, who had suffered baptism gladly to bargain with God for his mother's life, felt betrayed when she died, and worse, he felt guilty for his failure. As Owen wrote in **Come Home Early, Child,** "He had his enemies, and the chief one was God." Within a year of his mother's death, his father died. But the blow that scarred Owen, the blow for which he never forgave God, was the death of his friend, his idol, his brother Kenneth.

"Kenneth always recited better than I. He had an irrepressible humor and he was smarter than any of us. He could fix things. I was awkward, couldn't dance; I was afraid to mingle. Once I awoke in the night and found myself wet. I was terrified. And I told Kenneth 'I don't know what's happened to me; I haven't done anything with anyone; I haven't even kissed anybody. You think I have syphilis or gonorrhea?' He said, 'Owen, you've had a wet dream'; he knew all those things.

"When Kenneth lay ill with pneumonia, I slept in my twin bed while he lay under his oxygen tent. We had a nurse. It was a sad time. At 1:30 in the morning, the nurse woke me up, but happened to poke her finger in my eye. The sadness of the time and the great pain in my eye complemented each other. She said, 'I think you better come and see your brother . . . he's going.' I remember opening the oxygen tent, and the last thing Kenneth said was 'I love you.'

"That day, I locked myself in the closet and wouldn't come out until my sisters, Lillian and Edith, dragged me out. A terrible time. Kenneth never leaves me; even now, I hear his voice. The first Christmas after he died, I made a wreath and went out to Evergreen Cemetery in Brooklyn. I wrote a poem, 'Here is holly, for you, brother, here is mistletoe . . . but woven in these blanket wreaths is sorrow, pared and wild.' It had been snowing and we had erected no tombstone; I couldn't find his grave, so I just left the wreath in the snow.

"I've tried to erase Kenneth from my mind by writing poems to get him out of my system, but every year the same mourning is there, the same anguish. I want Kenneth to leave. I just don't want to hear his voice anymore." Thus it came about that the accommodation between God and Owen suffered on God's side from an indifferent malice, and on Owen's side from deep resentment that the Creator had snatched everyone whom Owen loved. In a stunning poem entitled **"Summing Up by the Defendant,"** Owen addressed his adversary as the Judge, as the Examiner:

> Tell me my marks, Examiner, I've waited an
>   inch-worm time,
> seeing you raised, I think you are Eternal God
>   who bathed
> in the seven oceans at once like a leprous Moby
>   Dick,
> rattling up the waters, sizzling the air, eating the
> weather, teasing Ahab, forgetting your sperm of
>   men,
>   regretting Michael.
> Tell me my grades in conduct, arithmetic, ar-
>   thritis, human
>   love.
> I must be graded: A B or F and itch a torment
>   or eat my
>   roses of love.
> Registrar, Judge, Examiner, Jehovah of my knit-
>   ted world:
>   here I wish,
> Demand your furied mind to conference and
>   huddle. Let go
> The water, the firmament, the harpoons of
>   death, this
>   circled court.
> Clear my passport passage now or bite my leg in
>   two
> letting me stump away slimy on my ransom
>   blood.

Ten years after Owen wrote this poem, God gave Owen his marks in arthritis, crippling him to stump away, first on a cane, then a walker, and finally a wheelchair. But Owen would avenge himself.

The bitter year of his forced retirement from Howard University, Owen was but fifty-six years old. He sought work in other universities. Repeatedly, his applications were returned to him, stamped by an invisible hand: "Sorry, Professor Dodson. Our universities in these 1970s need your colleagues—Ralph Bunche, John Hope Franklin—to explain to us just what it is that is making black people behave in such a rebellious manner. We are also hiring the young militants Larry Neal, Amiri Baraka, Nikki Giovanni, so that our students may assimilate their idioms, their music. However, we have no need for a fifty-six-year-old black humanist to direct one more production of *Hamlet.*" (Owen had directed three.) Owen wrote,

> Now it is certain:
> The wedding is powerful as battle,
> Ahab screaming and the screaming whale
> and the destination among thorns.

Owen saw himself as Ahab, a desperate, lonely hero, wedded with "a leprous Moby Dick," at once the cruel God and a cruel America.

Until the week that he died of a heart attack, alone in his bedroom in Manhattan, Owen could, on occasion, be overheard holding conversations—out loud—with Kenneth and with Jesus. Owen often quoted a passage from *Blues for Mister Charlie:* "God can have his icy snow-white heaven. If he is somewhere on this fearful planet, if I ever see Him, I will spit in His face! In God's face!" Owen anointed himself the suffering Christ, the divine cripple with the deadly harpoon, "Ahab screaming and the screaming whale / and the destination among thorns."

But now, before we take another peek beneath the mask of Owen's art, we must glance briefly over his life, to note his victories. By the time of his death in 1983, he had published three volumes of poetry, anthologized in over sixty texts and translated into six languages. Twice he was invited to read his poems before the Library of Congress; Richard Eberhart, Pulitzer Prize poet, named Dodson "the best Negro poet in the United States." *Time* magazine called his poetry "peer to Frost and Carl Sandburg and other white American poets."

George Plimpton awarded Dodson's story, **"The Summer Fire,"** a *Paris Review* prize. Dodson's first novel, ***Boy at the Window,*** has been through three editions. Twenty-seven of his thirty-seven plays and operas have been produced—two at the Kennedy Center. In his career, Owen wrote, directed, or acted in over 300 productions. He was awarded two honorary doctorates of letters. President Johnson invited Dodson to the White House. He received Guggenheim, Rosenwald, and Rockefeller grants; his friends included W. H. Auden, Countee Cullen, Gordon Heath, Langston Hughes, Richard Wright, and Carl Van Vechten.

In his last years, he became the "Dean of Black Theater," who must speak at the fund-raiser, bless each art occasion. He had become an arthritic cripple. In this same critical period, he became addicted to alcohol; from lovers and family, he suffered deep psychic wounds. Sometimes he would say, "Chile, I'm a mess."

He suffered and there were no neighbors with whom he could lament the bloody plague that ate him up. Then his old foe, the Examiner, gave Owen a deadly mark: Owen's sister, Edith, his protector, his faithful idolator, his last close family tie, "the only faithful one"—died. To what source of ease could he turn when the heart-devouring suffering gave over?

By the year of his retirement, Owen had already hammered out the final razor edge of his response to God: he published ***The Confession Stone,*** a series of monologues spoken by Mary, Mary Magdalene, Joseph, Judas, Jesus and God. It is Jesus who addresses God:

> Father, I know you're lonely:
> talk to me, talk to me.
> We need not speak of Calvary
> or the lakes of Galilee:
> as my Father, talk to me.
> Notify my soul where
> You will be,
> send some message:
> answer me.
>
> I sign me, your son,
>   Jesus.

Then with typical Dodson audacity, Owen places a response into God's mouth.

> Dear, My Son
> my One, my constant One:
>   . . .
> Your Father has not deserted Thee
> to the gardens of Gethsemane.
> The stars are the tears We weep,
> the sun is Our Mercy,
> the moon is Our slumber.
> Sleep, Jesus, sleep.
> Mary is come with a bowl of wine.
> Sleep, Jesus, sleep.
> sleep, Jesus, sleep.
> Your father first, then God!

So God and Owen tried to work it out. The son would not speak of Calvary; the father would not deny the son. But not without laughter. One day Owen smiled and told me, "Jim, I have gotten more yardage out of Jesus and God than anyone you know."

Right up until his fatal heart attack, he was writing chapters for a new novel, calling on the telephone to read new poems to friends, friends who wearied of his midnight calls, friends who tired of his speech slurred with alcohol, friends who had heard him read the same poem the night before. One dear friend, late one night, lay her phone on the pillow beside her head. As Owen talked on and on, Vivian dozed, only to be awakened by Owen shouting, "Hello! Hello!"

"Yes, Owen," responded Vivian, "what do you want?"

"Chile," he said softly, "Who am I talking to?"

A month before Owen died, he wrote this letter to me: "They report that James Van Der Zee walked feebly to the platform of Howard University to receive his honorary degree awarded to him at last, then marched out and dropped dead. That is irony, all irony. Howard honored me on the 30th anniversary of the founding Phi Beta Kappa and wrote that if I wanted to bring a guest, it would cost me $25. I didn't go. Shit. The American Symphony Orchestra had a $50 shindig at Carnegie Hall and played 30 minutes of my libretto from 'Til Victory Is Won—didn't offer me a ticket and furthermore, didn't even list my name in the program. Shit. I am writing a song cycle for Edith, and spring will spring me back." And here at the end of the letter, his pen runs out of ink, but the point scratches on, etching the final dry words into the paper, "I will not break."

I will not break. Then one morning in June, the first day of summer, the Examiner slammed the book shut, flinging Owen's breakfast tray all over the quilt and rolling Owen's body onto the floor.

Did Owen curse God and die? I like to imagine that by using the Lord's own gift—the word aflame—Owen's soul blazed its way past the sword of that arthritic archangel Michael, and that, in heavenly concert, Owen now sits amid his dear friends, Edith, Countee, Wystan, Langston, Carl, and Kenneth. And when his turn comes round to praise the Almighty, Owen's smile collects impishly about his lips; he lurches to his feet and sings,

> The morning Duke Ellington praised the Lord
> The stars plus the moon shown out loud—
> Six little black Davids
> tapped danced unto:
> Gabriel trumpeted up arthritic Michael:
> Plus some Archangels who had slipped from
> grace
> Into Hell when God rode like a roaring
> General of peace into the universe.
> Trumpets: Who whee, who wheee—
> Duke's horns, all his brasses plus drums
> Did a dip pip pip-a-de doo.
> And so forth and what not; my testimony
> Is with Judges;
> "Don't judge me!
> "Yes, judge me—yes put me on the witness
> stand."
> Let the trumpet blow the candles out
> Then Naomi can kiss the cross in the dark.
> Do a dip-a-de do.
>
>   . . . . .
>
> The six black boys tapped dance up
>   the marble altar praising unto
>   God, our Lord and His Hosts.
> Whoo-whoo wee, whoo wee.
> Dip pip, pip-a-de doo
> dip-a-de-doo.
> Doo.

As the hosannas of the hallelujah chorus burst forth, rebounding like hail off the roof of the world, Owen's crutches dissolve into the clouds. God smiles, and with

His right hand, He blesses Owen; with His left, He pats a slash of cream on his ashy leg. (pp. 627-41)

James V. Hatch, "Owen Dodson: Excerpts from a Biography in Progress," in The Massachusetts Review, Vol. XXVIII, No. 4, Winter, 1987, pp. 627-41.

FURTHER READING

Bibliography

Hatch, James V.; Ward, Douglas A. M.; and Weixlmann, Joe. "The Rungs of a Powerful Long Ladder: An Owen Dodson Bibliography." *Black American Literature Forum* 14, No. 2 (Summer 1980): 60-8.
  Comprehensive bibliography of works by and about Dodson.

Criticism

Kramer, Aaron. "Remembering Owen Dodson." *Freedomways* 23, No. 4 (Fourth Quarter 1983): 258-69.
  Reminiscence of Dodson.

North, Jessica Nelson. "Somber and Real." *Poetry* LXIX, No. III (December 1946): 175-77.
  Positive review of *Powerful Long Ladder*.

Peterson, Bernard L., Jr. "The Legendary Owen Dodson of Howard University: His Contributions to the American Theatre." *The Crisis* 86, No. 9 (November 1979): 373-74, 376-78.
  Retrospective of Dodson's work in the theater.

Rosenthal, M. L. "Ideas Fused with Fire." *The New York Herald Tribune Weekly Book Review* 23, No. 30 (16 March 1947): 12.
  Review of *Powerful Long Ladder,* determining that Dodson has the power "to discover the best way to release a tremendous store of emotional and moral power."

Additional coverage of Dodson's life and career is contained in the following sources published by Gale Research: *Black Literature Criticism,* Vol. 1; *Black Writers; Contemporary Authors,* Vols. 65-68, 110 [obituary]; *Contemporary Authors New Revision Series,* Vol. 24; and *Dictionary of Literary Biography,* Vol. 76.

Jack Gelber

1932-

American playwright, director, novelist, and translator.

The following entry provides an overview of Gelber's career. For further discussion of Gelber's life and works, see *CLC,* Volumes 1, 6, and 14.

INTRODUCTION

An avant-garde dramatist primarily active during the 1960s and 1970s, Gelber is best known for supplanting the traditional realism of American theater by collapsing the usual boundary between audience and performer in his first play, *The Connection,* for which he won Obie and Vernon Rice awards in 1960. Often employing the structure of the play-within-a-play to allow characters to interact with the audience, Gelber's dramas are particularly noted for their improvisational nature, self-conscious theatricality, and unconventional staging.

Gelber was born in Chicago. He attended the University of Illinois and graduated with a degree in journalism in 1953. During the late 1950s he became associated with the Living Theatre, an experimental New York repertory company founded by Julian Beck and Judith Malina, who produced and directed *The Connection* in 1959. Following the play's critical success, Gelber received several major awards and honors through the mid-1970s, most notably garnering a total of four Guggenheim, Rockefeller, and National Endowment for the Arts fellowships. In 1964 he published an unsuccessful first novel, *On Ice,* in which a Greenwich Village hipster becomes a private eye. Gelber has also directed productions of various classic and contemporary plays, including his own, and won an Obie award in 1973 for his direction of *The Kid,* a play by the American avant-garde writer Robert Coover.

The Connection concerns four heroin addicts who wait in a run-down apartment for their "connection" to bring a supply of heroin. The drama uses a play-within-a-play structure to blur the distinction between reality and fiction; at the beginning of each performance, the "producer" and "writer" appear on stage to explain that the actors are "real" drug addicts who will be paid for their work with a fix, but then inform the audience that they won't be given real drugs. When the "junkies" overhear this and object, the "producer" explains that he was lying to the audience to reassure them. The following action similarly alternates between challenging theatrical illusion and affirming audience expectations, and the play ends inconclusively without expressing moral approval or disapproval for the addicts' situation. Initially panned by critics, *The Connection* eventually gained support from prominent reviewers, who praised the play's improvisational elements and mordant commentary on the similarities between the

drug addictions of the junkies and the unrealistic, morally superior outlooks of the audience. Gelber was later named the most promising playwright of 1960 by the New York Drama Critics Poll.

Gelber's next play, *The Apple,* is a self-reflexive work that also employs a play-within-a-play structure. Set in a coffeehouse, *The Apple* focuses on a group of actors from different social backgrounds and ethnicities who find their efforts to rehearse a play interrupted by a bigoted, drunken heckler. The first and third acts are presented from the point of view of the actors, while the second act is seen from the drunk's perspective. While some critics praised the originality and comedy of this work, most found *The Apple* obscure and generally less accomplished than *The Connection.* Gelber's later plays are also noted for their unconventional themes and techniques. *Square in the Eye* is a multimedia piece that uses film, slides, and audiotape to present, in nonchronological order, a tragicomic view of events surrounding the death of a high school art teacher's wife and his subsequent remarriage. *The Cuban Thing,* which presents Fidel Castro's 1959 revolution from the perspective of a middle-class Cuban family, suffered an extremely short run due to poor reviews and an incident in which anti-Castro activists bombed the theater shortly before opening night. Set in a dream research laboratory, *Sleep* focuses on two scientists, a man who is the subject of their studies, and the strange characters who occupy his dreams. *Jack Gelber's New Play: Rehearsal* returns to his play-within-a-play theme, presenting the story of a group of ex-convicts who develop and rehearse a drama about prison life only to see the production finally canceled.

While many critics believe that Gelber has failed to live up to the potential suggested by his first play, most nevertheless acknowledge the influence of *The Connection* on the development of contemporary experimental theater. As Catherine Itzin observed, "*The Connection* was a landmark in American theatre, more than any other single play at the time determining the direction of American alternative theatre in the 'sixties, doing effectively for American theatre what Osborne's *Look Back in Anger* did for British—putting a new kind of play with a new kind of subject in the public eye. Its parts may have been derivative, but as a whole it was, then, overwhelmingly innovative."

PRINCIPAL WORKS

The Connection (drama) 1959
*The Apple (drama) 1961
On Ice (novel) 1964
*Square in the Eye (drama) 1965
The Cuban Thing (drama) 1968
Sleep (drama) 1972
Barbary Shore [adaptor; from the novel by Norman Mailer] (drama) 1974
Farmyard [translator with Michael Roloff; from a play by Franz Xaver Kroetz] (drama) 1975
Jack Gelber's New Play: Rehearsal (drama) 1976

*These works were published as *The Apple & Square in the Eye: Two Plays* in 1974.

CRITICISM

Robert Brustein (review date 28 September 1959)

[*The artistic director of the American Repertory Theatre Company, Brustein is a well-known American drama critic who is highly respected for his devotion to excellence in all aspects of theater production and his belief in theater's "higher purpose." As the dean of Yale University's School of Drama from 1966 to 1979, Brustein introduced many innovative dramatic techniques, often considered controversial, which gave Yale a reputation as a leading American drama school. Brustein's criti-* cism, collected in such volumes as *The Theatre of Revolt (1964), The Culture Watch (1975), and* Critical Moments: Reflections on Theatre and Society, 1973-1979 *(1980), is highly regarded for placing drama within a social context. In the following production review, he offers a favorable appraisal of* The Connection. *A small portion of this essay, which was originally published in 1959, is excerpted in CLC, Vol. 1.*]

When you enter the Off Broadway theatre where **The Connection** is playing in repertory, you have a few moments before the action begins to formulate your expectations. The curtain is drawn, and on the stage some excessively seedy characters are arranged in various attitudes of weariness and gloom. The setting is a tawdry tenement, the furniture is dilapidated, the quarters cramped and dirty. Painted on the wall upstage is a crudely executed pyramid, a revivalist motto, and a huge disembodied eye; hanging from the flies is a single green light bulb. The play, you have been informed, is about drug addiction. The subject is unpromising, and Lower Depths naturalism, it appears, is to be the inevitable treatment. Yet, something is not in place here—the imaginary fourth wall has not been constructed. The actors are aware of the audience, and even somewhat distressed at its presence. It is making them nervous, disturbing their peace.

Soon, two actors, claiming to be the writer and the producer of the play, run down the aisle, and begin to speak to the spectators. Your expectations shift. Inductions, direct audience address, entrances through the house, these are the familiar, generally gratuitous techniques of experimental theatre (you may have seen them clumsily employed by the same company, just the evening before, in a pretentious and tiresome trifle by William Carlos Williams). Echoes of Brecht, Beckett, Pirandello, and O'Neill begin to resound, and your new expectations harden. The play is arty and derivative; the characters are dull; the dialogue is flat; the directorial pace is flagging; the acting is dreary. Nothing, in fact, is *happening*, and you wait for boredom to release you from the need to care.

It takes about ten minutes to realize that you are witnessing an extraordinary performance in which everything, including your initial response, has been planned with absolute precision. The acting and direction are so true that it would be some kind of violation to single out individuals for praise; and Jack Gelber's play, despite obvious literary derivations, soon emerges as highly original and unpredictable. Free from stylized Studio "reality," pumped-up [Elia] Kazan theatrics, and Broadway contrivance, **The Connection** even avoids that over-intellectualization of human behavior which informs the work of Beckett, Ionesco, and Genet. Gelber has managed to assimilate, and sometimes to parody, his borrowed techniques without a trace of literary self-consciousness; and by the use of live jazz (superbly played) as a rhythmic contrast to the cool junkie daze of the dialogue, he has introduced an effective theatrical device all his own. The most striking thing about this work is its Spartan honesty. The only false note of the evening is struck by your own conventional expectation, conditioned by years of phony drama and sociological indoctrination.

The play is structured like a work by Pirandello. A group of addicts, waiting throughout the first act for the arrival of their connection, are assumed to be "real" characters, improvising their parts in exchange for a free fix. The "playwright," the "producer," and a couple of cameramen (photographing them in action for an avant-garde movie) hope they will reveal themselves in melodramatic or sensational attitudes; but the junkies, although provided with strong, distinct characters, nervously follow the truth of their own lives, exposing themselves only piecemeal, through pointless stories and unfinished confessions. When Cowboy, their connection, finally arrives, accompanied by a bewildered Salvation sister, the junkies file into the bathroom one by one for their fix; a series of loaded ironies follows; the "playwright" is turned on himself and gets a real look at his subject; a fastidious hipster named Leach takes an overdose and almost dies; the action and the music turn phantasmagoric; the junkies scatter; and the play ends with two characters swaying over a phonograph, listening to the lonely, almost religious ritual of jazz.

Because the characters refuse to participate in false climaxes for the sake of dramatic excitement, the play goes nowhere, and—except for the conclusion that addicts find salvation in junk and jazz—it makes no strong point. But implicit in every moment is the understanding that human existence can no more be explained by social, psychological, moral or aesthetic theories than human life can be confined within the limits of a dramatic action. Thus, although Gelber borrows some of Pirandello's techniques, he is never guilty of Pirandello's operatic plot construction, for melodrama would merely be another distortion of reality. The characters of *The Connection* maintain their integrity in an atmosphere of frightening authenticity; and the naturalism of this anti-play functions as a sardonic comment on anything which would falsify for impure ends the truth of things as they are.

Quite clearly, then, the most severe indictment of the evening is reserved for the audience, and, by extension, for society at large. The spectator may think he attends the theatre for a few hours of harmless diversion, but if the dramatic characters are "real," then his presence is a violation of their privacy, motivated by a voyeuristic interest in freak shows. Similarly, the spectator may hold pat social attitudes toward addiction which he expects the play to confirm, but he soon finds himself under attack for seeking "connections" in tranquilizers, vitamin pills, alcohol, and success. By providing his downbeat characters with more dignity and self-awareness than the characters of most American drama, Gelber has managed to transcend the limitations of his subject. He has not only accurately stigmatized such bad drama as *A Hatful of Rain*, but opened out into a scathing criticism of the spectator's most cherished pieties.

Constantly tripping over the boundary between life and art, stripped of significant form, antagonistic to all theory or morality which does not accord with practice, *The Connection* is probably not a "good" play by any standard we now possess to judge such things; but it forms the basis for a brilliant theatrical occasion, and it lives in that pure,

bright, thin air of reality which few of our "good" playwrights have ever dared to breathe. The first hipster drama to be seen in New York, it offers promise that the language of "cool" might soon become a pulsing stage rhetoric similar to Odets' language of the blues. It may not be the healthiest sign for our culture that the only recent American play of honesty and imagination has issued from such alienated precincts. But when our commercial dramas genuflect before the cant, hypocrisy, and prosperity of our society, we must take our truth from whatever quarter it comes. (pp. 23-6)

> *Robert Brustein, "Junk and Jazz: 'The Connection'," in his* Seasons of Discontent: Dramatic Opinions, 1959-1965, *Simon & Schuster, 1965, pp. 23-6.*

Henry Hewes on *The Connection*:

For all of its wonders, there is no denying the fact that *The Connection* frequently strains its audience's indulgence with its refusal to use the artifices of theatre, its introspective unresolved improvisations, and its self-acknowledged failure to send us home with a riff. Furthermore, there is a basic non-dramatic lack of urgency to the action of the play, which translates itself to us in the form of unconcern and makes every speech pay its own way. But this is a choice made deliberately by the author, and it is probable that the sense of working against phoniness which is now the play's greatest virtue would not have existed had Mr. Gelber chosen to write his play in a more audience-satisfying way. Sure it lacks the impact of *Here Come the Clowns*, the dreamy glow of *The Time of Your Life*, and the extroverted desperation of *The Entertainer*. But it traverses the same area in its own distinctive way, and without the artistic pretension that curses *Waiting for Godot*, to which it also bears a resemblance. In its stubborn insistence upon being what it is, *The Connection* emerges as the most original piece of new American playwriting in a long long time, and the less fastidious of my readers are strongly urged to see it.

> *Henry Hewes, in his "Miracle on Fourteenth Street," in* Saturday Review, *26 September 1959.*

Nat Hentoff   **(essay date January-February 1960)**

[*Hentoff is an American journalist, novelist, and jazz critic. In the following essay, he examines the initial critical controversy over* The Connection.]

Both acts [of *The Connection*] are set in "Leach's pad," a large, bleakly impersonal room where several heroin addicts are waiting for Cowboy, their connection. A preliminary press release from The Living Theatre assured those who might have been told *A Hatful of Rain* was square that "The directors of The Living Theatre have shown the play to former drug addicts who state that it is the only accurate description of the junk scene that they have read."

Fortunately, however, *The Connection* turned out to be

more than a documentary on the endless aloneness and desperate apathy of junkies. The actors, to be sure, were disturbingly convincing and I would expect many in the audience at each performance needed to be reassured by the cast credits that the sullen, scratching, caged addicts on stage aren't all too real.

One of the shifting frameworks of **The Connection** is a play within a play, and in the "producer's" opening speech, the audience is told that these *are* addicts. He later discloses they'll be paid off for the night in heroin. The arrogantly ingenuous young "playwright," Jaybird, also confirms in his tense explanations to the audience and quarrels with the "producer" that living, so to speak, addicts are being used. Some of the "addicts" in turn look at the audience from time to time with contempt. ("Man, what do you think we do? Live in a freak show?") Throughout the play, Gelber has succeeded with remarkably effective control in making much of the audience believe it's looking into such private failure that it ought to have the good taste to stop staring or at the very least offer to pay for a round of fixes. In one of his less necessary maneuvers, a member of the cast circulates in the lobby at intermission and offers to trade picaresque in-group stories from his hip past in return for a contribution to his habit.

Jaybird maintains he has hired the addicts to implement his concept of "improvised theatre" but becomes increasingly querulous when they ignore his outline and go on instead with their obsessive preoccupation—when will Cowboy arrive with the heroin? The "producer" meanwhile brings two photographers on stage to make an avant-garde film of the play, and he anxiously tries to keep the addicts "working" so that he can get some return on his investment. After Cowboy's return with an old, lonely, Salvation Army sparrow whom he's used as a decoy to keep the Narcotics Squad off his back, the addicts turn on and finally tempt Jaybird into direct experience of his subject. He and one of the photographers get hooked hard. By the non-end of the anti-play, Jaybird is too sick to control the "action," having been locked inside himself like the other addicts.

The only ending is the putting out of the lights. The addicts will continue to gather at Leach's and grudgingly pay him off because he originally found the connection. Leach, who has almost died of an overdose, will probably always wonder why it took near-death for him to become high enough for once. And the Salvation Sister will remain terrified that faith is finding her wanting.

The morning after this morality-play-to-exterminate-morality-plays, it looked as if **The Connection,** if not the actors, had been busted. "Oh man, what junk," snapped Judith Christ in the *Herald Tribune.* Jim O'Connor of the *Journal-American* noted that "any connection with a dramatic production was accidental. . . . Worse it is studded with vile language not necessary to the action—if any. And I don't mean profanity; I mean four-letter words."

Louis Calta of the *Times,* as indignant as Mr. O'Connor but with a more limber vocabulary, called the play "a farrago of dirt, small-time philosophy, empty talk and extended runs of 'cool' music." (For long stretches in the

> Throughout *The Connection,* Gelber has succeeded with remarkably effective control in making much of the audience believe it's looking into such private failure that it ought to have the good taste to stop staring or at the very least offer to pay for a round of fixes.
>
> —*Nat Hentoff*

play, hotly improvised modern jazz is played by four musicians who *are* [even outside the play within the play] jazzmen, but who also act idiomatically.) During the rehearsals the actors watched the musicians for behavior clues, and the musicians observed the professionals for another kind of guideline. The result, due largely to Judith Malina, who directed, is an uncommonly consistent ensemble style that has the rhythms and other unpredictable appearances of improvisation.

To continue with the burial notices, Frances Herridge of *The New York Post* was a reluctant admirer of at least the acting "just in case it's acting." Bernard Krisher of the *World-Telegram* explained that the "playwright hasn't bothered to give us his point of view and has failed to edit this long drawn-out slice of life."

Minor encouragement came in the next few days from unlikely sources like the German-language *Aufbau,* and *Show Business,* a trade weekly whose circulation is concerned mainly with the casting notices it prints. *Variety,* however, was unimpressed. Gelber decided he'd failed once again, and wondered how soon the play would close.

On July 22, however, the first of the reviews appeared which were to save **The Connection.** Jerry Tallmer in *The Village Voice* pointed out Gelber, for one thing, has been the first playwright to use modern jazz "organically and dynamically . . . the music . . . puts a highly charged contrapuntal beat under and against all the misery and stasis and permanent total crisis." He also wrote that "the subject is still Illusion vs. Reality" and rightly insisted it was "high time that, everything else apart, reviewers everywhere finally started applauding Miss Malina and her colleague Mr. Beck for accomplishing in 1959 that which all the rest of the world just talks about—a repertory experimental theatre that is truly experimental and truly, actively, in repertory." Although he found "a certain amount of self-consciousness and over-obviousness throughout Mr. Gelber's work," he felt strongly that in staging **The Connection,** "the Living Theatre has once again excitingly justified the adjective of its title."

Henry Hewes in *The Saturday Review* agreed. Gelber, he wrote in a review headed, "Miracle on Fourteenth Street," "has tried to locate man's position in the universe not cleverly but well, with a method inspired by the one jazz musicians use, where the individual soloists take turns improvising on a more or less agreed-upon theme . . . we are conscious of a degree of non-wish-fulfilling truthfulness seldom found in the theatre." There is, Hewes conceded, "a basic non-dramatic lack of urgency to the action of the play, which translates itself to us in the form of unconcern and makes every speech pay its own way. But this is a choice made deliberately by the author, and it is probable that the sense of working against phoniness which is now the play's greatest virtue would not have existed had Mr. Gelber chosen to write his play in a more audience-satisfying way. . . . In its stubborn insistence upon being what it is, *The Connection* emerges as the most original piece of new American playwriting in a long long time."

The Connection proves to be nothing more than a farrago of dirt, small-time philosophy, empty talk and extended runs of "cool" music. There is a quality of sensationalism about the work that undoubtedly will offend the squares. On the other hand, the hipsters might dig its semi-serious, semi-facetious treatment of an unhappy social situation.

—Louis Calta, in his review of The Connection, in The New York Times, 16 July 1959.

On August 5, H. B. Lutz, who has helped finance experimental productions in the Village and occasionally writes with proselytizing urgency for *The Village Voice,* took a half-page ad in that weekly assaulting those of the critics who hadn't comprehended, he felt, the play's importance, and insisting it was a moral obligation to see it, if only to make up your own mind. Ten days later, Harold Clurman in *The Nation* thought the play was "a bit of naturalism not without point and not without talent" although "the play's form is unresolved, and some of the writing self-conscious as well as overlong." He concluded that "there is a sort of melancholy in the event, with touches of genuine pathos and even a wretched sort of lyricism."

Nathan Cohen, a columnist for the *Toronto Daily Star,* wrote as part of an enthusiastic recommendation on September 8 that "the cast is so persuasive in speech and movement, so authentic in texture and so lacking in counterfeit, that when they step forward after the show for their bows it comes as a jolt. . . . " The next most important review—in survival terms—after Tallmer's was Robert Brustein's in the September 28 *New Republic:*

> Free from stylized Studio 'reality,' pumped-up Kazan theatrics, and Broadway contrivance, *The Connection* even avoids that over-intellectualization of human behavior which informs the work of Beckett, Ionesco, and Genet. . . . The most striking thing about this work is its Spartan honesty; the only false note of the evening is struck by your own conventional expectation, conditioned by years of phony drama and sociological indoctrination . . . im-

plicit in every moment is the understanding that human existence can no more be explained by social, psychological, moral or aesthetic theories than human life can be confined within the limits of a dramatic action. Thus, although Gelber borrows some of Pirandello's techniques, he is never guilty of Pirandello's operatic plot construction, for melodrama would merely be another distortion of reality.

In *The Jazz Review,* however, Hortense Geist grumbled that "jazz and junk go together like ham and eggs in the world of Jack Gelber" and further that since the jazzmen on stage were called by their real names, "why are these musicians in the convention of the proscenium in the context of a play using their real names? Actors? Themselves? What? . . . This distortion smacks of the gimmick and it serves to distill Mr. Gelber's slight stage reality." The play, she wrote,

> may be "true to life," but it is not true to theatre. There is no illusion, no space in which the audience may co-create, and without the quickening of a spectator's thinking-feeling, there is no art. . . . Mr. Gelber would do well to listen to a good blues singer reveal great depth of misery, within the limits of a modest and infinitely fluid form and still make one remember the beauty and endurance of the human spirit.

The "thinking-feeling" of spectator Donald Malcolm of *The New Yorker,* however, had been quickened intensely. Malcolm had originally intended not to cover the play, but presumably at Kenneth Tynan's suggestion, he finally arrived, and his October 10 review insured *The Connection's* present existence. Describing it as "the first really interesting new play to appear off Broadway in a good long time," Malcolm was impressed at the "bitter, black vein of humor in their speech, a mordant criticism of the life, outlook, and interfering behavior of all 'squares' that gives to the play a terrible bite. . . . The lines I culled from the production, which look flat, lifeless, and scarcely comprehensible in my notebook, were vibrant with implication on the stage." Malcolm hastily added: "Most of the implications, to be sure, are stark nonsense." Nonetheless, "it has shape, pace, and point. It is an excellent piece of work."

Malcolm thought Mr. Gelber the "most accomplished spokesman" of the Beat. Brustein found the play to be "the first hipster drama to be seen in New York . . . the only honest and balanced work ever created by a Beat Generation writer." Gelber finds these references uncomfortable since he doesn't acknowledge belonging to any group, nor does his work reflect the raging romanticism, however various its guises, of the Beat. "It's funny," Gelber observed recently, "the people who liked the play called me and the play by the names I least like."

As for what *The Connection means,* Gelber isn't entirely sure himself. "Some of my feelings about how it can be interpreted are pretty hazy, but one thing it certainly says is that only knowing doesn't do anybody any good. Solly, the intellectual junky, knew why he was there and was able to make a bridge between himself and the other addicts better than the rest, but he was still there. Each one of them is by himself. None of them—with very few exceptions—is willing to back each other up. In the basic meaning of the word, they're 'apolitical.' They know no one else is going to take care of them. They'll take care of each other only against the outside world." And not even then. Leach's overdose led to a nearly unanimous flight. A corpse brings questions.

Part of Gelber's anti-playwriting (in the sense, for example, that [William Inge's] *Dark at the Top of the Stairs* is a play) is that the dialogue does not necessarily come out of a continuing action or a logically motivated or prepared situation. The people in *The Connection* speak, as Gelber puts it, "out of silence." Also, for the most part, the only feeling, the only recognition they can allow themselves to give others is the rancid nastiness that makes most of the dialogue in the play sound even more hopelessly hostile than a marriage that's gone on much too long.

The controversy about *The Connection* continues. People still walk out, some of them literally sick. The stronger dissidents are dissatisfied, among other reasons, because the play has no "solution." Gelber admits that while he's convinced "knowing isn't enough," he doesn't know what will make the junkies—and the rest of us—change. What he has done in *The Connection* is to present a situation that is. ("That's the way it is; that's the way it really is," one of the actors occasionally intones by way of ritual—gratuitously, it seems to me—from the back of the house.)

Gelber's point is that there is no easy (or even complicated) dramatic or sociological conclusion for the despair that rides not only the junkies among us. And he makes this point in terms of the theatre, not as a documentary. A documentary could hardly reach into audiences the way *The Connection* has. Many do indeed leave in disgust or stick it out and then leave in anger or frustration, but unless they succeed in pushing *The Connection* out of their minds entirely, I expect that vague but ominous and thoroughly unwelcome anxieties become inexorably associated with whatever memories they have of the play.

"You can't solve a social problem," says Gelber, "by merely having a scientific—or a humane—attitude toward it. Exposés are very square." To solve a serious social problem, obviously, the society itself must be operated on. To solve—not soothe—a serious personal problem, you have to go so far inside that, for nearly all of us, one way or another of passing or copping out is infinitely preferable. In *The Connection,* there is neither Kazan the circus barker nor Arthur Miller the righteous. This is the way it is. I don't mean the versimilitude of the junky subuniverse. I don't know how exactly accurate Gelber is in his field work, but that doesn't matter. Gelber is writing about more than junkies.

Certainly there are deficiencies in *The Connection.* There is the "self-consciousness" Tallmer describes, and the play could have been edited down by at least a fifth of its length. What *The Connection* does do, however, is provide a beginning for Gelber. The next Gelber play or the next three may or may not be an "improvement" but they should be worth seeing and arguing about if only because Gelber is doing what, as Harold Clurman recently pointed out in the *Partisan Review,* Brecht criticized the German classi-

cal stage for not doing. "There is little chance," said Brecht, "of hearing any genuine human voice, and one gets the impression that life must be exactly like a theater instead of the theater being just like life."

"Who else," says Solly of his colleagues in *The Connection,* "can make so much of passing out?" With a kindness that is rare in Gelber's first play, Solly did not then look at the audience. (pp. 170-77)

> *Nat Hentoff, "Who Else Can Make So Much Out of Passing Out?: The Surprising Survival of an Anti-play," in* Evergreen Review, *Vol. 4, No. 11, January-February, 1960, pp. 170-77.*

Kenneth Tynan   (essay date 1960)

[*Tynan was a highly esteemed English drama and film critic who achieved widespread fame as the creator of* Oh! Calcutta! *(1969), a play that became one of the most notorious successes of the 1960s due to its counterculture message and onstage nudity. In the following essay, which was originally published as the preface to the 1960 edition of* The Connection, *he discusses the play's early critical reputation, subject matter, and message, commending Gelber's work as "the most exciting new American play that off-Broadway has produced since the war."*]

In Moscow—or so they told me when I was there five years ago—you do not say to a friend: "Let's go to the Art Theatre and see [Anton Chekhov's] *The Three Sisters.*" Instead, you say: "Let's drop in at the Art Theatre and see how those sisters are getting on." I realized why as soon as I saw the celebrated Nemirovich-Danchenko production of Chekhov's play. The stage exuded a sense of life, pre-existent and continuing; it was not like going to the theatre, it was like paying a call on old acquaintances. I seemed to have met these people long before the curtain rose, and after it fell I found myself wondering what would become of them. I feel much the same, *mutatis mutandis,* about *The Connection.*

I first saw Jack Gelber's play in August, 1959. It had opened at the Living Theatre on Sixth Avenue about five weeks earlier, when it had received a fairly thorough bludgeoning from the daily press. A small cult of devotees, however, had formed around it, and it was on the recommendation of one of them that I went. Since then the cult has snowballed. As I write, six months later, it has developed into an obsession for some of its members, and there are few prominent Broadway figures who would admit, with anything like pride, that they had not seen the play. It has pervaded the consciousness of many people who had hitherto thought themselves immune to experimental theatre. It has become, in short, a cultural must. A few weekly reviewers gave it lavish praise; otherwise, it has had to depend for its success entirely on its own merits, supported by that most potent and unpredictable of critics, word of mouth.

The Connection is a difficult play to write about. Its atmosphere somewhat recalls Gorky's *Lower Depths;* its theme is akin to that of *Waiting for Godot;* and it tackles the same social problem as *A Hatful of Rain.* But to say what a work of art is *like* is often a tacit confession of inability to say what it *is.* Starkly yet unsensationally, compassionately yet unsentimentally, Mr. Gelber's play deals with a subject that the theatre (or the cinema, or television) hardly ever approaches except as a pretext for pathetic melodrama. The people with whom it is concerned are beyond the reach of drama, as we commonly define the word. They are heroin addicts, from which it follows that they are almost totally passive as human beings; their lives are spent in expectation of the next "fix," the next moment of glorious, transient reconciliation with the world and with themselves. They see themselves neither as victims nor as heroes, but merely as absentees from the daytime universe; their relationship to society is not one of enmity, but one of truancy. While they wait for their dope-purveyor—or "connection"—to arrive, they idly debate their condition. "That taste," one of them muses, "that little taste. If you don't find it there you look some place else. And you're running, man. Running . . . I used to think that the people who walk the streets, the people who work every day, the people who worry so much about the next dollar, the next new coat, the next vitamin, the chlorophyll addicts, the aspirin addicts, those people are hooked worse than me . . . " "They are," says a fellow junkie. "Man, they sure are. You happen to have a vice that is illegal." Later, the long-awaited connection turns up, and offers a sour comment on the official attitude toward narcotics: "Everything that's illegal is illegal because it makes more money for more people that way."

The Connection seems to me the most exciting new American play that off-Broadway has produced since the war. It explores a frightening territory with clear, unprejudiced eyes, and a gift of words that makes its vision ours.

—Kenneth Tynan

The play is not a defence of dope. Nor does it attack the wage-earning, clock-punching, home-making technique of survival; as one of the characters says, ". . . what's wrong with day jobs? Or being square? Man, I haven't anything against them. There are lousy hipsters and lousy squares." Leach, the snarling, snickering, putatively epicene hipster in whose apartment the play unfolds, has built up such a tolerance to drugs that he can no longer get high; and one of the most shattering moments of the stage production is that in which, tightening a belt around his arm to bring up the necessary vein, he gives himself an overdose that very nearly kills him. There is no softening of the agony. But equally, there is no shirking of the issues. The junkie seeks euphoria. The average citizen seeks happiness. How do these goals essentially differ? If the aim of life is pleasure, why is it more desirable to achieve it by injecting dollars into the bank account than by injecting dope into the bloodstream? If, on the other hand, the aim is spiritual en-

lightenment, how can we be sure that the insights provided by heroin (or mescalin, so eloquently hymned by Aldous Huxley) are less reliable than those supplied by religious mysticism? *The Connection* offers no answers; it simply states the problem, and implies the questions.

Theatrical characters—even inactive ones—must talk; and junkies, as a class, are contemplative rather than talkative. To overcome this handicap, Mr. Gelber employs the device of a play within a play. A nervous producer explains to us that he has hired a writer to bring together a group of addicts for the express purpose of improvising dialogue along lines that the author has previously laid down. The results are filmed, before our eyes, by a two-man camera crew. There are thus, acting as a collective bridge between us and the junkies, four intruders from the world of getting and spending. Some of them, by the end of the evening, have surrendered their credentials as squares and allowed themselves to be drawn into the hipsters' orbit. In the interim, we have learned a new language—the dry, wild, disenchanted *argot* of the confirmed and impenitent junkie. We have laughed at a kind of gallows-humour that eschews self-pity; we have listened to a plethora of reminiscences, wry in tone and phrased with the most perceptive frankness; and we have heard—if we attended the Sixth Avenue presentation—some exemplary jazz, blown by the quartet of musicians who are among the guests at Leach's pad. Some of the characters are Negro, others Caucasian. The colour of their skin is of negligible importance. *The Connection* is probably the first American play of which this could be said. In a preliminary note, the author stresses that, although he envisaged some of the characters as white and others as coloured, "there need not be any rigidity in casting." This constitutes a minor, but vital, revolution.

I could pick one or two holes in *The Connection.* For instance, it is sometimes guilty of repeating its effects; and with something approaching ferocity, it forbids us to admire any of its characters. But most of these minor flaws are inherent in the subject-matter—a way of life composed of recurrent lows and highs, all of which occur inside the nervous system and are seldom expressed in normal emotional relationships. Where Mr. Gelber overwhelmingly succeeds is in filling the stage with the kind of truth that goes beyond verisimilitude and achieves, at times, the robust, amoral candour of folk-poetry. As one of the squares keeps iterating: "That's the way it is. That's the way it really is."

The Connection seems to me the most exciting new American play that off-Broadway has produced since the war. It explores a frightening territory with clear, unprejudiced eyes, and a gift of words that makes its vision ours. (pp. 7-11)

> *Kenneth Tynan, in an introduction to* The Connection *by Jack Gelber, Grove Press, 1960, pp. 7-11.*

Jerry Tallmer   (essay date May-June 1962)

[*In the following essay, Tallmer comments on Gelber's*

efforts to reshape the form of contemporary drama and presents a favorable review of The Apple.]

As is usual with the unusual, *The Apple* has been greeted by most of its first critics as a willful enigma—and, of course, a nasty little mess. The first criticisms of *The Connection* were much on the same order; but as we know, *The Connection* has gone on to become world-famous, which *The Apple,* so far, has not. Both plays are the brain-work of a young American named Jack Gelber who casually hoards the ambition of shattering the entire known form of the drama from its beginnings until now. To be more specific, he has set out to blast the window-wall of the proscenium (or the encapsulating glass sphere of theater-in-the-round) to such smithereens as to render ridiculous any attempts at a repair job by the writers who come after him. Several things must immediately be said:

1. The idea is hardly unprecedented. Many playwrights now living or dead, most prominently [Luigi] Pirandello—Gelber's direct mentor—have wanted to do the same. Nobody has yet made it. The walls have splintered but not fallen.

2. Gelber probably won't make it either. Nevertheless there are those who think that his dynamite is fresher and stronger than any they have seen thus applied in their lifetimes. They think he will knock a few holes in the glass, at any rate, and that some new measure of the fluids of contact and communication must inevitably pour through—in both directions.

3. The idea may or may not really be a very good one. Art is long, it is in fact longer than long, it is not a horizontal line or an upslope or a downslope; it is a circle, or a whole collection of circles. What fades today can reappear again (if anything does) in 2000 years, and with full validity. Likewise the future is the past (see 1., above) and so forth. You come in where you come in and do what you think you have to.

To which the current corollary is that you can't concern yourself with the necessities of 2000 years from now in any event. Today the entire problem for every serious artist is to reverse the machine, keep humanity in business, break the glass, open the floodgates, get down to the basics, and let the individual once again burst free—somehow, if possible, which today doesn't seem very possible, before time runs out for every individual. Incontrovertibly, Mr. Gelber's fundamental interest is the individual: himself, his actors, Actor A, Actor B, the members of his audience, Member A, Member B . . . ; he is interested, to cut it more finely, in the return of the individual to individuality. Or to life. And that again is hardly an unprecedented idea, however much it may now, in certain quarters, and to a dread extent in every quarter, be out of fashion.

4. Mr. Gelber is young (almost exactly 30), brash, headstrong—a high-flying Aryan-looking Jewish Chicago laughing-boy—and he makes a lot of mistakes. That he has a deeply perceptive and thoughtful side is equally apparent. But the headstrong side (and the naive side) often gets the best of him. *The Connection* is cluttered, for all its novelty and power and truth, with a number of trite and embarrassing devices (much of the manipulation of

the play-within-a-play; the ingenuousness of Jaybird, stage "author" of that play-within-a-play; the suprabanality of the repeated cry of "That's the way it is, man, that's the way it really is!" from the "photographer" at the rear of the house) and its meandering sermon in the last minutes about narcotics and politics, while also true enough, is less than helpful to all that has preceded it. As with *The Connection,* so with *The Apple.* Mr. Walter Kerr, an intelligent and hostile critic—that is to say, his hostility toward what he classifies as avant-garde is always on sweet, sharp trajectory for the jugular—saw an obvious if tiny gift all wrapped up for him at *The Apple,* and seized it. In the *Herald Tribune,* the morning after: "I am beginning to detect a certain poverty of inspiration in the avant-garde business of bringing noisy intruders up out of the audience; after all, I have seen Ethel Merman do it." Next sentence, wrong as could be: "It is difficult to detect the possibilities of formal growth in a style that is deliberately without intelligible discipline." The truth being that as a thought-out drama *The Apple* is elaborately well-organized, tightly knit, if anything too symmetrical in the way the first and third acts balance around the nightmare passages of the middle, and that as writing it is a wonder-piece of short hard declarative sentences. Sentences, when they want to be, of the spoken language, which counts still more.

> Your humility is disgusting. Have a drink. I don't mean any harm. I talk too much. But, god-damn it, do you have to bring up this New York bull. Next thing I know you'll ask me: "And what do you do?" You people never lose control.

Notice the no question mark after *New York bull,* and the far-ranging explicitness of *You people never lose control* (where the speaker, like Mr. Kerr, is assaulting "intellectuals"). As for the sentence (Mr. Kerr's sentence) about Ethel Merman; it is one of those which is right for all the wrong reasons. For I too have seen her do it—as an amusement. Mr. Gelber's purposes are otherwise. Unfortunately he has had to come as something like 250th to this particular invention, which is indeed in such overuse these days as to have trickled even into as empty a vessel as (for an example off the top of the head) *J. B.* That does not make him a bad (or impoverished) playwright, but it does make him a young and vulnerable playwright. Without doubt he is well aware of it. One of the nice things about Jack Gelber is that he is alive.

The Apple is a remarkable conglomeration of the foregoing points 1, 2, 3, and 4. Perhaps it is time to try to describe the play.

There are seven characters. In the script they are given the working names of Ace, Jabez, Anna, Ajax, Mr. Stark, Iris, and Tom, but the title page of the script declares: "In production all the actors should use their own names." This means that in the opening weeks of its world première last December, . . . the actors spoke to one another throughout (not a new idea, except I think in scope) as James or James Earl (Jones), John (A. Coe), Marion (Jim), Julian (Beck), Mr. (Henry) Proach, Marilyn (Chris), and Fred (Miller). Since the opening there have, to present date, been two changes of personnel in one of the roles; until I go again, however, it will be impossible for me to "see" these seven people as any but James or James Earl, John, Marion, Julian, Mr. Proach, Marilyn, and Fred—in short, as themselves—and such was absolutely the intention of the author. The result is that in whatever remains for me to do here I shall employ these "real" names even though the bearer of one of them (James Earl Jones) at this moment is the male lead in a very different off-Broadway play and has twice been substituted for at the Living Theatre. For *The Apple* is what it is when you experience it, which is more than can be said for most other dramas in any theater.

James is ticketed in the cast list in the script as "A Negro," and James Earl Jones the actor is a young Negro of great stage presence, virile beauty, and sky-rocketing talent. The character's other main points of reference within *The Apple* are as some sort of waiter (the play takes place "in a restaurant or coffee shop"), an m. c., and a spelunker of life and death with his own built-in divining rod. John is listed as "A Con Man," but he is also a demi-intellectual demi-Bohemian, a gabber, a woman-baiter, a cynical romantic, and—not too successfully in performance—a Jew. Two others in the drama make reference to the last, one of them constantly and sneeringly. Marion is listed as "An Oriental-American," and Marion Jim, who plays her, is exactly that. Near the beginning and at intervals later throughout the work it is mentioned that this particular evening is in her charge, she's the "bosslady" of it—in other words, tonight's version of the play has to conduct itself and conclude as she desires. (It does neither.) She is deeply involved in a love-hate relationship with Julian, who is merely listed in the script as "A Nihilist," perhaps the understatement of the year. Julian is a true snob, true aesthete, skeptic, showman, with strong overtones of unashamed homosexuality, a wicked talent for infighting, and somewhere in the offing a psychological cushion of financial security. Mr. Proach is listed as "A Spastic," and is played that way, to the nines, with corkscrewing limbs and wildly lolling head and a gaggle of gurgling groans, by actor Henry Proach, who is finally revealed as not in fact a spastic; obviously Proach the actor has to externalize more than any of his fellows to assume the attributes of Proach the spastic, which is doubtless why I had to check, before writing, as to whether in the production he is called by his own name (as he is) or by the script name of Mr. Stark. There are two further roles. Marilyn is listed as "A Hustler," a description she only tangentially lives up to until, in the next-to-last instant of the drama, she smiles her blonde smile out toward the spectators, throws her arms wide in invitation, and proclaims to James Earl and to John: "Why don't you two guys get out of here. I'd like to take on this entire audience by myself." John *kvetches* and cogitates her out of it—the con man, remember?—and they go off together, evidently to bed.

Finally there is Fred, who must have a paragraph to himself. Fred is the noisy intruder from up out of the audience. And some intruder is he. It is his mission in life (or rather, in unlife) to murder everyone else in the house on either side of the footlights. Fred is a sheer unadulterated great American bastard, a bigot, a noisemaker, a man of violence, a drunk, a rotating son of a bitch. (In case you don't

know what that is, that's a son of a bitch no matter which way you look at him.) It is not in order to juice up this text—nor of course to issue free ammunition to the Freds of drama criticism (of whom Mr. Kerr is not one)—that I continue for a moment in the vernacular as just above. The following catalogue of some of Fred's turns of speech, taken in chronological order from the script, is inserted merely to shed some light on his native view of all others with him on stage and in the theater, or for that matter in Greenwich Village, where the theater is located, or New York City, or the world; it is also intended to shed some light on Mr. Gelber's qualifications as an explorer (or, if you like, if you are Mr. Kerr or others, but not myself, the Gelber bent for tedious juvenile sensationalism): "Hey! Who is that, Joe Louis?" (meaning the Negro, of course); "Kill 'em! Kill 'em all"; "bunch of goddamned intellectuals"; "jewboy"; "Kill the jews, niggers, obliterate the slants, let's see, who else is here, oh yes, that spastic must go"; "Get away from me you goddamn ballet dancer"; "heebie"; "You're probably all vegetarians" (clue to the Gelber method and private humor: Julian Beck and his wife Judith Malina, the director of *The Apple,* are in truth vegetarians); "Give a woman a job and she grows balls. Hey! Come here! Is it true what they say about Chinese girls?" (to which Marion replies: "Julian! We can't go on like this. I'm not Chinese. I'm Siamese-American"); "Faggot! Faggot!"; "Jesus Christ! What do you people do? I mean for a living?"; "Where I come from they don't let animals like you" (the spastic) "run around loose. That jew boy is all right though. . . . Hey, Steppin' Fetchit, bring something to drink!" "You little cunt!"; "You can't fool me. . . ." (jumping into audience near the end of the play and threatening the nearest onlookers with an object wielded like a club) "I'm going places but you're not sending me anywhere. . . . You know what I think! Wait a minute don't anybody move. (*A long pause.*) Don't worry about me. Worry about yourselves."

This last, which in the flesh is, in the exceptional performance by Fred Miller, extremely menacing, is also rather clearly the core of the apple, the pith of its message. For, oh yes, the main lines of the message of *The Apple* are as simple as all get out. Go back to what was said about getting down to the basics. Picasso was once hard to understand, but is not so hard any more; the most complicated novel in the history of literature, *Finnegans Wake,* deals essentially with standard root matters of parenthood, childhood, brotherhood, vigor, decline, life and deaths; so do the pulsing intricacies of Dylan Thomas. The individual, the basics. But there are many different basics, and Mr. Gelber's prime concern, as it happens—he might be startled to look up and find himself in such close company with the likes of E. M. Forster, Virginia Woolf, Henry James—is the vigor or decline of the human imagination, the human awareness. Some might call it the spirit, or even the soul. Or openness—merely that. With many people his age everywhere today, he is struggling in a closed society to keep something open. There is yet another word, one which has been so debased by its friends and enemies over the past fifty years that the typewriter, in its contempt, almost refuses to accept it. Tolerance. You don't hit me I don't hit you. There springs to mind a recent phone call from a woman, a smart career woman (magazine editor) who had just seen *The Connection* for the first time. "You'll laugh;" she said, "if I tell you the big thing I got from it, that I felt washing over me all the while I was there." I said I wouldn't laugh. "Togetherness," she said, and the laugh was hr own. "I was up there in that room with them and we were together." Years earlier I had once asked Warren Finnerty, the brilliant Leach of the original Living Theatre production, what he felt the whole play meant. He paraphrased one of the final lines: *If it wasn't junk it would be something else.* That was it. Corny old Oscar Wilde had said the same thing from his own pad in Reading Gaol. And *The Apple* says to us, from the lips of its drunken anti-social lunatic: *Don't worry about me. Worry about yourselves.*

But there is somewhat more to it than that. The point about Fred who comes up from the audience is that he is dead. The point about James the Negro is that he wishes to open the gates of life to those in the audience who have never left their seats. His means are those of theater. He has it all worked out:

> Okay! Okay! Let's everyone take a seat and do something right for a change. . . . Let's all take a deep breath. (*Takes a deep breath*) And let's start off alive. . . . I don't want a dead crew right from the jump. . . . When you breathe your muscles move and when your body is moving you get to feel good and warm all over. You keep moving, baby, because that's being alive. Alive. Don't look now but they can arrest you for that. Okay! Okay! We're together. . . . Don't despair. Smile, This is no joking matter. We are going to eat up the set, the audience, and nibble a little on ourselves. Don't get too smart now—a little knowledge is small potatoes. . . .

and after the entry of all the other characters and the ingress (or upgress) of Fred, the drunk:

> We're rolling. We're getting there. The theatre is an enormous eye. The audience is the eyeball. The light from the outside comes through the eyeball and focuses on the stage. I got the whole thing worked out. The cornea, the vitreous humor, the retina, the center of the blind spot—I got it all worked out. But why get technical. . . .

Early as it is in the play, Fred has already died for the first time. That is, in his drunken stupor he has let his head fall forward onto a tabletop where he sleeps. Marilyn: "He looks dead to me." James (the actors have the right to vote on anyone's participation including Fred's): "I vote no. I can't make any J. Louis scene. Later." Ten minutes later the drunk, who from the beginning has claimed a bad heart, finds himself forced into a fistfight with the spastic. John intervenes with a blow. Fred staggers into the audience and falls dead. Some of the actors are inclined to cut and run, as some of the addicts in *The Connection* are inclined to cut and run when Leach passes out from his overdose. Wiser heads prevail. James kicks the corpse. Julian goes out "to eat and put on some makeup" in preparation for the arrival of the police. Everybody not dead departs. The dead man slowly gets up. His lips move, but the voice is that of James, the Negro for whom he has so much contempt.

> Look at him showing you his credentials. Ha ha. As if he still had to prove that he had that thing called identity. You need more than that piece of paper. . . . Look at the person next to you. . . . Do you think death can be caught like the common cold? Take your mind off it. . . . Ooo-oh, look at the man saying: "I'm not dead. Can't you hear me? . . . "

Fred is now in silent frenzy, on his feet before the audience.

> " . . . Can't you see I'm alive? Are you deaf and blind? I'm not dead." Well it's his illusion. He doesn't know he's dead yet. We will see who is and who ain't dead.

First act curtain. It's pretty scary.

The second act, my least preferred act, is the nightmare of the dead Fred, a series of grotesque "blackouts" with the per-permanent members of the company, so to speak, baiting Fred from behind animal and insect masks.

> FRED. What is this?
>
> JAMES. You are dead.
>
> FRED. I am not.
>
> JAMES. You'll realize that you are dead in three or four days. The quicker you accept it the better off you will be.

Fred has hallucinations: the various "blackouts." He pulls out a gun and shoots Marion—for always and forever he has murder in his heart. He witnesses a scene, a sarcasm against marriage, between John and Marilyn—the two of them at the breakfast table with Mr. Proach the spastic as their dog. Neither wants to walk him. Fred kicks the dog. He starts to choke Marilyn. John (to Proach the spastic-as-dog): "I'll take you out now, boy. That should shut you up." Julian comes up in an insect mask and grabs the madman, then screams: "I'll release you if you kiss me." Quick exit by Fred. Julian (to the others and to the audience): "Come along to a pastoral life. Come along. Be careful of the one next to you. He has murder in his heart." And so on, through a number of similar scenes, until Fred suddenly reappears in S. S. uniform (his true colors), tries to arrest everyone, shoots John. The Jew does not fall. The cast closes in on Fred and Fred tries to shoot them all, crying: "Change the scene! Please God, change this scene! Hurry, hurry up!" Blackout. John and the spastic become a couple of jungle surgeons doing some terrible operation on a mannequin. Fred: "I can't stand the sight of copulating couples." Enter Julian and Marion wheeled in, locked in an embrace, in a baby carriage. James: "Doctor! Doctor! Two of my villagers are stuck together!" Fred: "I can't bear this any longer. I want to go back to living" (*collapses*). Second act curtain.

In the third act, which begins with everyone sitting around deciding that Fred isn't really dead since they can't find the body, we bit by bit learn that the actors are more truly approaching their own, "real" personalities. John, who has been straining all night to remember where he may have seen Fred before, now suddenly recalls him as an old-time silent-movie actor. Fred enters, and the internal evidence of his lines reveals that he is that actor; but Fred at this point is yet worse deranged than earlier, and trending toward violence. Marion expresses dissatisfaction with the way things are turning out: "I don't want a mood piece! I'm tired of satires on the race issue. And I'm tired of satires on satires." Julian begins to needle her, as is his frequent custom. A vicious little sexual-racial slugfest (verbal) ensues; Fred is not the only monster.

> JULIAN. Help! Help! I'm trapped in a Chinese restaurant!
>
> MARION. That's not very funny.
>
> JULIAN. Oh, baby, I didn't want to hurt your feelings. I'm a thoughtless rotten creature. My tongue doesn't belong to me. . . .
>
> MARION. I know all about your tongue.
>
> JULIAN. That's unfair! You sweet, lovely Oriental bitch!
>
> MARION. I know about your hands, too!
>
> JULIAN. Where is your Oriental calmness?
>
> MARION. You sonofabitch! You can afford to bait me. You haven't anything to lose. You can always fall back on your rich father.
>
> JULIAN. That's your fantasy! I can no more go back to my father than you to a hand laundry. Oh, my tongue again! Forgive it!
>
> MARION. You are more of an Oriental than I am. . . .
>
> MARILYN (*a peacemaker*). Tune in tomorrow. Will Anna, daughter of the rich and famous egg-roll manufacturer, keep her dignity masquerading as a coolie hipster. . . . Will Julian, son of rich father type 37-B, marry her and. . . . I like marriage as an end. It tells us that we have witnessed a comedy.

But we haven't, not in any customary sense. One may rest assured it is passages like the foregoing that have raised more Philistine hackles against *The Apple* than any quantum of dirty words per se, or any callousness toward the spastic, of which there is considerable, or any details like the two villagers stuck together in the baby carriage. For this is the tolerance of the dynamiter, the only true path to tolerance, self-awareness, social unselfconsciousness. It is the technique used by another dynamiter named Lenny Bruce, as cordially detested by the Philistines.

We are near the end. John the con man reverts more and more into the self that is the actor, worrying about the problems of having to chain smoke on stage. ("Is that fair? I ask you.") Marion discusses the perversions of a friend of her ex-husband's. ("Did you ever see him again?" "Sure, many times.") Fred assumes the role of a mad dentist who condemns the madhouse all around him. He starts dancing with the mannequin, propositions it, starts ripping it apart, plunges for its genitals, makes an awful discovery: "Oh, I'm dreadfully sorry. You are a man.

You're trying to mix me up!" He heads towards Marion with that good old murder back in his eyes, but at this Mr. Proach the spastic suddenly decides that enough is too much. The stage direction says it best; "Mr. Proach, no longer acting the spastic, intervenes."

> PROACH. Somebody call an ambulance. This is ridiculous.
>
> FRED. A miracle! I've performed a miracle! I made it happen! I am cause. I'm Christ.
>
> PROACH. Sssshhh! It's all right. I'm going to let you go. And you are going to take it easy. James, watch him. (*James sits Fred down. Proach begins to exit.*)
>
> FRED. Don't leave! You're my disciple.
>
> MARION (*to Proach*). . . . Who the hell are you?
>
> PROACH. An actor. Henry Proach, Hickory 4-4286. . . .
>
> MARILYN. But why did you want to play a spastic?
>
> PROACH. You've never wanted to play a spastic? It was an incredible opportunity.

Fred says: "Get out, creep, get out," and turns to place his rage upon the last available humankind—those sitting out front. He leaps down among them, shouting: "You can't fool me!" and then the savage words, and the warning, that I have said I believe contain the entirety of the play. He returns to the stage and the other actors ask him how did he ever get to the Living Theatre. Fred: "I knew you were here. You're in the papers. It wasn't what I expected." He turns on the company and in a last blind burst of complete lucidity tells each of them exactly what their faults are. Henry Proach leads him quietly away. Marilyn volunteers to take on the entire audience, which rather helps to clear the air. She goes off with John. James remains, solus. He says: "It don't always work itself out this way. . . . I mean we don't have a mad man every night. Some of us will be back tomorrow. Some of us won't. . . . A little of the old faces and a few of the new. It could be you up here. There's only one ingredient necessary. You got to want. I don't care if you want a meal or you come to steal. It'll work itself out. One way or the other. . . . Now don't come back without wanting something. Hear me? Okay. Okay."

The window has cracked a little and the fluids rush through. With Miss Malina's brilliant help, brilliant digging beneath the surface, brilliant realization of the work, the fluids rush through. You got to want. To want to feel, to be with, to understand. To live. (pp. 95-106)

> *Jerry Tallmer, "Applejack," in* Evergreen Review, *Vol. 6, No. 24, May-June, 1962, pp. 95-106.*

Bernard F. Dukore (essay date Fall 1962)

[*Dukore is an American educator, critic, and editor who has written extensively on American and world theater.*

In the following essay, he locates Gelber within the context of the Living Theater and assesses the critical response to The Connection *and* The Apple.]

New York's flourishing citadel of theatrical bohemia, the organization which produced Jack Gelber's two plays, *The Connection* and *The Apple,* is an ostentatiously avant-garde group called The Living Theatre. Its sponsors include such prodromal figures as John Cage, Jean Cocteau, Willem de Kooning, and William Carlos Williams. Jackson MacLow and Alan Hovhaness have composed music for them. Paul Goodman and Kenneth Rexroth have written plays which they have staged. The Living Theatre embodies those anarchistic concepts of art which most people think of when they hear the name "Greenwich Village."

The organization was incorporated in 1947 by designer-director-actor Julian Beck and director-actress Judith Malina (Mrs. Beck), but it was not until four years later that the group gave its first production. This was, appropriately enough, Gertrude Stein's *Dr. Faustus Lights the Lights,* and the performance took place in Greenwich Village's Cherry Lane Theatre. The other productions given during that first season included Picasso's *Desire* and T. S. Eliot's *Sweeney Agonistes.* The season was climaxed that summer by the Living Theatre's version of Jarry's *Ubu the King.* It was a considerably updated version (among those whom King Ubu threw into his pit, as I remember, were "Norman Thomas and Dylan Thomas and John Charles Thomas"; I think Harry Truman and Margaret O'Brien were also named), and an immensely exciting one. The whiff of Jarry reached the nostrils of some self-appointed moral defenders, and Comstockery prevailed as the New York City Fire Department, by a curious coincidence, found reason to close the theatre after a few previews and three regular performances.

The Living Theatre organization moved to a loft on 100th St. and Broadway, which is very far off the beaten track even for Off-Broadway. This location, in the heart of *West Side Story* country, was their home for the next few years. Their first post-*Ubu* production, presented in March, 1954, was W. H. Auden's *The Age of Anxiety,* with a twelve-tone score by Jackson MacLow and a cast which included the late James Agee as The Announcer. Other productions at the loft included Strindberg's *The Spook Sonata,* Cocteau's *Orpheus,* Pirandello's *Tonight We Improvise,* and—surprisingly—Racine's *Phèdre.* But again the theatre was closed, this time by the New York City Building Department. (pp. 146-47)

The Connection—the first play of a twenty-seven-year-old Illinoisan named Jack Gelber—opened on July 15, 1959, and was ripped to shreds by the newspaper reviewers. Judith Crist, second-string reviewer of the *Herald Tribune,* emulated the usual attitude and technique of Walter Kerr, the first-line reviewer, in what can be taken as the majority opinion of the daily journals: "*The Connection* has been touted as a tragi-comedy dealing with jazz and junk. The jazz is undistinguished, but oh man! what junk!" [*New York Herald Tribune,* July 16, 1959].

With this type of reception, one would not have expected the play to last a week. But *The Connection* is still running. Word-of-mouth and the repertory system (the suc-cessful *Many Loves* supported the initially unsuccessful *Connection*) kept the play alive until the reviews from the weekly press appeared—some during that summer, some in the fall—and the play caught on. Just as the dailies' reviews were almost unanimously pans, the weeklies' were almost unanimously raves. Whereas the play was "a farrago of dirt, small-time philosophy, empty talk, and extended runs of 'cool' music" to the man from the *New York Times* [Louis Calta, July 16, 1959], it was "the most original piece of new American playwriting in a long, long time" to the man from the *Saturday Review* [Henry Hewes, September 26, 1959]. Jerry Tallmer of *The Village Voice,* Robert Brustein of *The New Republic,* and Donald Malcolm of *The New Yorker* were among those critics who supported the play and who helped make it a success.

In *The Connection,* a producer and a playwright inform us that we are going to see an improvised performance by real dope addicts, whose payment for the evening will be a fix. The scene is "Leach's pad"—the apartment of one of the junkies. The language of the play is the language of its characters, with a great deal of color and extensive use of four-letter words. In the course of the evening, Cowboy, the junkies' "connection" (the one who supplies them—connects them—with heroin) arrives and "turns them on." Photographers take pictures of the dope addicts. Musician-junkies play jazz. The playwright and one of the photographers get a fix. One of the characters almost dies from an overdose of heroin. That is the "story" of *The Connection.* But although *The Connection* has little in common with the *pièce bien faite,* it is not structureless. The playwright explains the play's structure during the first few minutes of the first act when he informs the audience:

> I am interested in an improvised theatre. It isn't a new idea. It just isn't being done. Remember: for one night this scene swings. But as a life it's a damn bore. When all the changes have been played, we'll all be back where we started. We end in a vacuum. I am not a moralist.

The structure of *The Connection* is not linear, but circular. It is like a jazz composition: variations and improvised "rides" on a stated theme.

The printed script is merely a bare indication of the performance, for Gelber leaves room for what in this context may be called the actor's musicianship. When the producer tells the audience, "we are not actually using real heroin. You don't think we'd use the real stuff? After all, narcotics are illegal."—there is no response indicated on the printed page. But in the Living Theatre production, the junkies who happened to overhear this were highly indignant until the producer reassured them that he was lying for the audience's benefit. Here are the stage directions for the play's opening:

> *The players arrange themselves on stage a few minutes before the play begins. Solly is looking out of a window with binoculars. Behind him is a room full of homemade furniture. In center stage Sam is stretched out sleeping on a bed. Downstage left Leach and Ernie are slumped over a table. The 1st and 4th Musicians are at extreme right dozing at a piano.*

This is merely an outline. As one enters the theatre, one finds the curtain already drawn. The setting is a dilapidated New York tenement apartment. People wander about the stage with a curious combination of listlessness and nervousness. They appear to have barely enough energy to move about, and occasionally they do not seem to think that it is worth the effort to do so. They become aware, every so often, of the audience's presence, and they look at us—or, rather, they stare vacantly at us—in attitudes that combine contempt and lack of concern. We feel uncomfortable; we are annoyed that the actors do not do something; we want them to begin, and are impatient for them to get on with it. (Actually, we realize later, they have already begun.) At any rate, all of this is improvised as introductory melodies on the jazz theme of this jazz play.

The Connection is about dope addiction, but its subject is not limited to dope addiction. As one of the characters says:

> the people who walk the streets, the people who
> work every day,
> the people who worry about the next dollar, the
> next new coat,
> the chlorophyll addicts, the aspirin addicts, the
> vitamin addicts,
> Those people are hooked worse than me. Worse
> than me. Hooked.

We all need that connection, Gelber is telling us, that fix which enables us to go on living: "A fix of hope. A fix to forget. A fix to remember, to be sad, to be happy, to be, to be." The difference is that what these people need is illegal. But we all pay the price, whatever that price might be (say, a nine-to-five job) for our connection. Gelber emphasizes that there are no essential differences between these addicts and the people in our hustle-for-a-buck world. As Cowboy says:

> what's wrong with day jobs? Or being square?
> Man, I haven't anything against them. There are
> lousy hipsters and lousy squares. Personally I
> couldn't make the daily work scene. I like my
> work hours as they are. But it doesn't make me
> any better. No, man, no.

And the fact that our connection is more respectable, the corollary goes, does not make us any better. No, man, no.

But there is a basic difference between **The Connection** and, say, [Nelson Algren's] *The Man with the Golden Arm* or *A Hatful of Rain.* Most literature about dope addiction either takes the form of sin-and-redemption (taking dope and then kicking the habit—in effect, *The Drunkard* with pot instead of booze), or else society is condemned because it is not sympathetic, because it does not understand the problems of the addicts. **The Connection** fits neither of these categories. The evil is not society's failure to be sympathetic, but society's failure to realize that it too takes a form of dope. Its condescension toward the junkies is nauseating hypocrisy. Moreover, Gelber's junkies are society in microcosm, from Solly the intellectual to Ernie the "dope-addict psychopath." But it is the play's audience which not only represents but actually *is* respectable society, and it is that audience which is brought into the play

as its chief villain and chief addict. We are made painfully aware of *our* needs, *our* connections, and "the dues" which *we* pay. The play begins, as described above, by making us feel uneasy; it ends by making us feel guilty. As Robert Brustein succinctly puts it:

> the most severe indictment of the evening is reserved for the audience, and, by extension, for society at large. The spectator may think he attends the theatre for a few hours of harmless diversion, but if the dramatic characters are "real," then his presence is a breach of their privacy, motivated by a voyeuristic interest in freak shows. ["Junkies and Jazz," *The New Republic,* September 28, 1959]

We are not allowed to forget this even during the intermission. The producer tells us just before the end of the first act that these addicts "will be turned on a scientifically accurate amount of heroin in the next act. And that is their payment for the performance . . . " As we exit into the lobby—some of us reaching for cigarettes—we realize that we have paid for their fix, and for the pleasure of watching them receive it. The presence of the addicts is further kept in our minds when one of them panhandles from us in the lobby.

The form of the play is highly unusual. **The Connection** uses virtually every device of the theatricalist, anti-illusionistic theatre: there are entrances onto the stage from the house, and the reverse; actors comment on their roles and on the play; there is direct address to the audience, and interruption by behind-the-scenes personnel (lighting technician, writer, producer); and so on. However, these devices are used not to destroy illusion, but to enhance it. When Pirandello and Wilder use them, they do so to remind us of the artificiality of the process of theatre; when Gelber uses them, he does so to persuade us that we are witnessing reality. He sets up not actors who are going to perform a play, but junkies who are going to improvise a play. Thus, whenever the "illusion" is broken, we are returned to the more basic illusion: that these people are not actors playing junkies, but real junkies pretending to be actors, and not actors playing a producer, a playwright, photographers, etc., but a real producer, playwright, photographers, etc. Thus, the illusion-breaking devices become—in this context—illusion-making devices. Every time the "play" (actually, play-within-a-play) emerges as an artificiality, the play itself (the total performance) is made to seem real rather than the artificiality it actually is. The two levels (play and play-within-a-play) merge into one level of reality and illusion. We are finally presented with a successful slice-of-life achieved not by eschewing theatricalism, but by blending it with naturalism.

Between the initial performances of Gelber's first play and his second, more than two years elapsed. To be precise, the first performance of *The Apple* was given by The Living Theatre on December 7, 1961. During these two years, Gelber had received international acclaim. The New York daily press could not dismiss him as cavalierly as it had previously done. Nevertheless, **The Apple** does not have the clarity of **The Connection,** and this created an additional difficulty for them. In a [December 8, 1961, *New York Post*] review entitled "An Evening of Vast Perversity," Richard Watts, Jr. called the play a "baffling conundrum," but concluded that he was not bored. In some afterthoughts a few Sundays later, he explained:

> it didn't bore me for a minute, although my interest in it did arise more from Judith Malina's production than from an admiration for Mr. Gelber's writing. . . . [Its] obscurity, perverseness and suggestion of a bad little boy showing off turn it into an almost studiously esoteric stunt. [*New York Post,* December 24, 1961].

Taubman of the *Times* straddled the fence, refusing to commit himself, and Walter Kerr gave the following lucid commentary: "I do not admire *The Apple* . . . But . . . I did not hate *The Apple*" [*New York Herald Tribune,* December 8, 1961]. In *The Village Voice,* on the other hand, Jerry Tallmer intoned a veritable *Howl* about Gelber and his new play:

> fathers and teachers you are going to have to face up to it sooner or later; he is farther out on the space frontier than anyone writing in our time for the American theatre, and . . . what he does out there, with all its apprentice gaucheries, is going to get deeper and more itchingly under the skin than any comparable work this side of the School of Paris. Which today is rewriting the drama and lifting it to a plateau to be equated at some future date with the Elizabethans.

The Apple is a wildly extravagant play, with the vivid (and occasionally obscene) language and theatricality of *The Connection,* but without the naturalism of the earlier work. The scene is a coffee shop. In the Living Theatre production, the entire auditorium is a coffee house. The leader of the troupe, a Negro named Ace—but though Gelber names his characters, he advises the actors to use their own names in performance—interrupts the serving of coffee to the audience and starts the play rolling. Anna, an Oriental-American, brings in a bowl of apples. They are joined by a Jewish painter named Jabez, a homosexual named Ajax, a whore named Iris, and a spastic named Mr. Stark. They are also joined by Tom, a drunken heckler who climbs onto the stage from the audience, offers them a drink, and viciously insults them, calling Ace "Mister Bones," Jabez "Jewboy," and asking Anna, "Is it true what they say about Chinese girls?" Soon, Tom and Mr. Stark do battle, and Tom is killed. Following this, the entire company—including Tom—do a series of improvisation-like scenes set, among other locations, in a dentist's office, a breakfast nook, and a jungle in which actors don insect and animal masks and frighten the vicious bigot. Tom is revealed to have been an extra in silent movies, and the spastic to be an actor who has always wanted to play a spastic. Everyone leaves, and tomorrow night the same activities—or activities more or less the same—will recommence.

The title, as several reviewers have pointed out, is jazz musicians' slang for New York City. New York is the melting pot of the world, and as in *The Connection,* mankind is represented in *The Apple:* whore and queer; artist and worker; Jew and Gentile; Negro, Oriental, and Caucasian. Also like *The Connection, The Apple* is a series of jazz improvisations built around a theme, with extended rides.

But here the variations are more intricate, and the initial melody is more difficult to locate. *The Connection* is direct and works upon the senses in its use of naturalism; in *The Apple,* on the other hand, the author plans "a life behind the senses."

But although the title derives from jazz jargon, it also alludes to an older source: the Bible. We are back in the Garden of Eden, complete with the original insects and animals (symbolized by the masks) of the dawn of humanity. "Start from the beginning," says Jabez. "Do the Adam and Eve bullshit." And the stage is darkened, except for a table. As the light extends from the table to include a dentist's office, a record of the Grand Canyon Suite is played. Here is the beginning: the eternal dark, the gradual light, and the creation of the earth. The sexy Iris stimulates Jabez in a parody of the book of Genesis:

> IRIS. I'm your apple, baby.
>
> JABEZ. And I'm your snake doctor.
> (*Embraces* IRIS)
> Cover that native's eyes!

Compare the book of Genesis:

> she took of the fruit thereof, and did eat; and she gave also unto her husband with her, and he did eat. And the eyes of them both were opened, and they knew that they were naked; and they sewed fig-leaves together, and made themselves girdles.

The play begins with Ace setting the scene, creating the world of the play, and this is God creating with his breath the world and its people:

> Show about to begin. . . . Let's all take a deep breath. . . . we are not all here. Up here or down there, in here or out there we are not all here. . . . Breath creates. Yes sir and madam, I'll say it again: breath creates.

Ace soon gives orders for the lights to come up or to go down (day and night). In Genesis we find:

> And God said: "Let there be lights in the firmament of the heaven to divide the day from the night; and let them be for signs, and for seasons, and for days and years; and let them be for lights in the firmament of the heaven to give light upon the earth."

In *The Apple,* we find what may be considered a hipster treatment of that passage, as Ace, offstage, speaks through a microphone:

> We're rolling. We're getting there. The theatre is an enormous eye. The audience is the eyeball. The light from the outside comes through the eyeball and focuses on the stage. I got the whole thing worked out. The cornea, the vitreous humor, the retina, the center of the blind spot . . .

Anna compares the theatre with the universe. "It's like the solar system," she says. "Stars revolving around a sun." Then, as she moves about the stage:

> Can we have a play where our configuration is like the structure of a nucleus. . . . You know

(ACE *enters.*) Celestial and indifferent to one another.

The play presents the nucleus: the creation of the world, of Adam and Eve. Note, too, that as Ace (God) enters, we hear the adjective "Celestial."

The Oriental Anna is the Snake. She brings the apple onstage and gives it to Iris (Eve). Ajax is Christ. One of the characters says of him, "I'll bet he's only taken this job to prove to his rich father that he can make it on his own." Here is the Gelberesque version of the message of Jesus:

> Give up your homes which are not much anyway as you very well know. Give up your children and your nagging spouses. Come with me beyond the marked trails to a life of simplicity. I will teach you to take care of yourself.

Tom is, as Ajax characterizes him, "a false prophet." He is the evil in man, a Lucifer, a fallen angel, a man with—literally and figuratively—"a bad heart," at one point wearing an S.S. uniform and at another snarling his venomous credo: "Kill, kill, kill. Kill the Jews, niggers, obliterate the slants . . . " He battles, as he ultimately must, with Mr. Stark, the spastic, who is his opposite: the goodness in man. In fact, Mr. Stark (the only character known by a family name: the family of man) is brought onto the stage (the earth) by Ajax (Jesus) to be his replacement there. The goodness in man is usually inarticulate, and when it emerges it does so in spasms. But it does emerge. Nevertheless, even though Mr. Stark may kill Tom, Tom stubbornly refuses to die. The evil in man is not eliminated quite so easily.

Still, the play is not pessimistic. God's aim in creating the universe is: "Two people meeting on the street. Every gesture, every sound is singing. What a brotherhood! I'll work for that kind of universe." Although this has not been achieved, it may yet be. God is dynamic, not static. As Ace says, "change is my nature." At the play's end, Mr. Stark takes Tom to a hospital.

With the Bible in mind, scenes and passages acquire a richer texture and a more meaningful context. They also acquire a greater shock value, as, for example, when Ace says, "Call me a snake charmer or a paramour, it all comes out the same." You can call the omnipotent God who created the snake a snake charmer or snake controller; you can also call him a paramour, for Jesus is his son and the mother is wed to another.

The important point, however, is not that *The Apple* is obscure but that it is *purposely* so. Gelber deliberately tries to throw us off the track. He even has Ace tell the audience: "It's a good thing I'm doing the talking because if Ajax were here he'd break in and tell you that this apple is a golden Chinese apple and stands for knowledge." Intellectual comprehension is not his aim. If it were, he could have achieved it easily enough: he did so in his first play. His aim is—or seems to be—to involve the audience emotionally, to make us experience "a life behind the senses." "We relive it every night," Anna tells us. The oldest myths of mankind are as new as the youngest child. Gelber takes us back to creation and to original sin, and presents the mythic patterns in highly modern, almost sur-

realist terms, conducting an imagistic assault on our nerves. Like the playwrights whose works have come to be called (accurately or not) "the theatre of the absurd," Gelber supplements the literary means of the theatre with all of the stimulating and occasionally explosive nonliterary means available to him. Through these shrieks, movements, objects, rhythms, and thrusts into the very heart of the audience (as when the villain rushes into the auditorium ready to assassinate Lincoln), Gelber uses images and symbols in a manner which includes but goes beyond traditional means. We are placed in the position of the characters, and we are subjected to a direct assault on our nervous systems so that we will apprehend the scenic moment directly and become involved in it, rather than merely receive an intellectual understanding of it. When lights flash on and off, when hideous masks leer at us, and when voices rasp at us, we are placed in the position of the frightened character on-stage who is trying to reach sanctuary from this apparent chaos. When ludicrous farce alternates with sinister terror, we experience directly the whirl of confusion and the sparks of understanding experienced by the characters in the play itself. Gelber's fourth wall is at the rear of the auditorium. The audience is at center stage.

The Connection uses virtually every device of the theatricalist, anti-illusionistic theatre. However, these devices are used not to destroy illusion, but to enhance it. When Pirandello and Wilder use them, they do so to remind us of the artificiality of the process of theatre; when Gelber uses them, he does so to persuade us that we are witnessing reality.

—*Bernard F. Dukore*

A comparison with the films of Michelangelo Antonioni might be helpful. Antonioni attempts to achieve similar responses, but in a realistic context. Thus, in *La Notte,* there is a scene in a hospital in which a character lies dying. During the hushed conversation, a helicopter flies by, outside the window. The flight heavenwards is symbolic in the conventional literary manner. But—more important—we the audience are annoyed by the loud, harsh sound of the mechanical monster; we feel, we directly apprehend, an intrusion into the natural by a monstrous artificial society. In realistic terms, this is very close to Gelber's attempts to achieve "a life behind the senses" in *The Apple.*

It would be unwise to predict what the future holds for Jack Gelber, or vice versa. He may go farther along the lines of *The Apple.* He may return to anchor his work to a more recognizable reality, as in *The Connection.* He may do neither, and he may do both. "I have no theory of the theater to proclaim," an anonymous interviewer for *Newsweek* [December 18, 1961] quotes him as saying; and for this reason, he has refused to write articles and essays. Gelber stands at the beginning of his career. Fortunately for him, he has a congenial and enterprising theatre company to write for; and fortunately for the theatre company, it has Gelber's plays to perform.

When the Living Theatre brought **The Connection** to Paris's annual international theatre festival in 1961—where it won awards—Joseph Barry, Paris political analyst of the *New York Post,* took time out from his examination of the Algerian problem to write about this play:

> **The Connection** is the watershed of our culture; one's reaction to it means one falls this side or that of what's going on in the minds of the artists and poets. They are not ahead of their times. They are the only ones of it. The rest of us are living on the exhausted interest of accumulated culture. [*New York Post,* July 11, 1961]

This is true, I believe, of both of Jack Gelber's plays, and of the experimental theatre movement of which he is a vital part. (pp. 147-56)

> *Bernard F. Dukore, "Jack Gelber," in* Drama Survey, *Vol. 2, No. 2, Fall, 1962, pp. 146-57.*

John Simon   (review date Spring 1965)

[*A Yugoslavian-born American film and drama critic, Simon has been both praised as a judicious reviewer and censured as a petty faultfinder. He believes that criticism should be subjective, and as Andrew Sinclair has observed: "He is as absolute and arrogant in his judgements as any dictator of culture, a rigidity that is his great strength and weakness." In the following excerpt, he characterizes* On Ice *as a complete failure.*]

[*On Ice*] is about Manny Fells, a young Mid-Westerner ensconced in a roach-ridden loft just south of Greenwich Village, who under false pretenses gets a job with a shady and incompetent investigating firm. He is sent out as undercover agent to a suburban discount center where something is rotten in the camera department. He gets thoroughly embroiled with both outfits, and falls victim to undeserved envy and unwanted love. His private life is equally untidy: driftings through the Village, assorted dope parties, occasional Pyrrhic sexual victories, and a final entanglement with Louise, whom he doesn't really want and who is, besides, a sheep in wolf's clothing: under a swinging-chick exterior hides a solid little homemaker's heart. At novel's end, Manny has a clean apartment, a respectable job, and is tobogganing towards matrimony.

Despite incidental felicities, the novel fails on all counts. Consider the hero. On a morning after, he describes himself: "One hung-over male, Caucasian, third-generation American Jew, fledgling double agent, childless but with a stiff cock, standing his full length, holding his head which is much too heavy for his neck." After which, he enters the kitchen and, going Peter Orlovsky's immortal line, "There comes a time in life when everybody must take a piss in the sink," one better, pisses in his host's sink. For Manny is a hipster or, to put it more elegantly (since Mr. Gelber is fond of sudden elegancies: in the middle of

tough monosyllabic talk, there bob up words like "estivating," "griseous," "festinated"), a *picaro:* "Since when haven't the idiots run the world?" he asks, giving it a condign finger. But he is also, as we can see from that emblematic self-description, a shnook: authority can make him jump; a minor theft, weep. He is, moreover, a bit of a philosopher-poet, and an uptown party inspires in him the following rumination:

> The music said to the people: you are at a party. You may not like one another elsewhere but here you may like each other. Your miserable jobs are nothing if they can't buy your pleasure. Do not be ashamed about the money. Dance. You hear; you obey. Those wishing to investigate this remarkable phenomenon will do so at some future time. Listen you schmucks, we offer rapture.

> The people say to the music: don't say anything about our miserable life. These days generalizations are suspect. Sing but don't swing, for swinging is all inclusive and all we want to hear is the melody. Of course we're moving, we don't call it dancing, in nervous reaction to you. Rapture is too expensive; give us exhilaration.

Now, these three aspects of the hero refuse to jell: just when he should be hip, he goes square; when he is putting the world on, his prose puts us off by going lyrical-analytical, and the joke—if it is a joke—boomerangs. Of course, Gelber wants Manny to be inconsistent ("in the same breath he was a yokel and a hustler"), but he cannot carry it off: the sheer fun in the character is seldom acute enough, and the seriousness—for some seriousness is intended—never fully materializes. Nor are the contradictions in the lesser characters made believable, let alone resolved. Most of these characters, indeed, remain fixated somewhere between shadows and comic strips.

The basic technique of the novel is that of the cinema documentary: a roving camera wanders from supposedly symptomatic, nay symbolic, person to person along highways and subways, public and private places, sometimes stopping for a scrap of conversation allegedly charged with the pathos and absurdity of it all, sometimes merely itemizing endlessly. After all these dialectical catalogues and cataleptic dialogues, one cannot escape the sensation one gets from bad documentaries—that the camera is not searching for illumination, merely for a topic.

To bind all this flotsam together, Gelber resorts to leitmotivs such as references to movies or dedicated dwelling on sexual or scatological details, however humble. Not only is every masturbation, urination, defecation, windbreaking of the hero conscientiously recorded, but even erections that never transcended "early stages," and aborted micturitions ("he revised his opinion concerning his urge to piss"), are scrupulously set down. People and situations are repeatedly apprehended in terms of movies: one character is "a cross between Bogart and Von Stroheim," another looks "like Elisha Cook, Jr."; Manny will give "a fair rereading of Spencer Tracy playing Tom Edison" or wonder "what would Humphrey Bogart have done?" When as many as three such references appear on one page, the device usurps both our time and our patience.

Gelber's style is occasionally deft. He is good at one-line descriptions. A Village female neurotic is "the very picture of a mentally disturbed Israeli worker"; a shopkeeper asked to change a twenty-dollar bill becomes "a parody of a Jewish Philippine guerrilla fighter." Sometimes the comic successes have longer breath: "New York was turning Nelson into a vicious parasite where he had been just an ordinary one before." Manny muses: "Ten days ago there was nothing. Now a girl in my very own home and a fink job to boot. Still nothing, but nothing with added misery." But rarely does this humor extend beyond a paragraph, and then only with lapses along the way.

Mostly, however, the style is nondescript while trying to be clever, and sometimes it is downright uncouth: people "browse some shelves" or "gyrate their heads"; something "sags in dull symbols" and someone makes "a gesture of amelioration." One girl is "the prettiest of the two girls," another restrains amorous advances by pointing out she hasn't brought her diaphragm: " 'And,' Louise laid the final brick, the cunctation, 'I hate those awful rubbers, don't you?' " Not half so awful as brick cunctations.

Last and worst, the structure of the novel is lopsided. We are to be shown how Manny gets gradually sucked into respectability, how hypochondria and pusillanimity propel him out of hipsterism into bourgeois security. But the hipster phase, with only slight irruptions of the transitional, occupies three hundred and nine pages, whereas the *embourgeoisement* is accomplished in less than two. This, to me, is a major strategic blunder. The best one can say for **On Ice** is that it exhibits a certain pervasive good-naturedness, but even that is scarcely more than a chirrup in the cacophony of petty chaos. (pp. 295-97)

> John Simon, "Where Love Has Gone," in Partisan Review, *Vol. XXXII, No. 2, Spring, 1965, pp. 294-99.*

Robert Mazzocco   (review date 1 July 1965)

[*In the following production review, Mazzocco faults the characters, staging, and message of* Square in the Eye *as clichéd and uninteresting.*]

The themes of Jack Gelber's third play concern death and marriage. Significantly, in **Square in the Eye,** they go together like Scylla and Charybdis. We have characters who cannot act, and action without character. No one's in touch: neither with each other nor themselves. Within a rackety *mis-en-scène,* an arena of fallen idols, we hear of the death of domesticity and of the daily death of belief. Social identity is a mess, religious identity a scream. I'm laughing but don't ask me why, announces someone. No doubt it is Gelber's intention to allegorize America as a schizoid society, a sort of split-level consciousness. Certainly his style serves. On the one hand, pop art epic theater with vaudeville fantasy; on the other, old school psycho-drama. Further, at the Theatre de Lys the whole production is staged like a house afire, and the play is a false alarm.

Ed Stone, its aging hero, is a school teacher and a failed painter. His students are more or less juvenile delinquents,

his intimates are squalid and slick. A ballsy, panicky little guy, a quasi-bohemian malcontent, Ed has the manners of a stand-up comic: acrid gaze across the footlights, cigarette in mouth. He comes on heartless as a cigar store Indian, but he's really full of mush. He's also full of echoes. Ah the battle of the sexes, there's nothing like it! he twitters. Ah the old questions, there's nothing like them! (Beckett in *Endgame.*) Like Camus's Meursault [in *The Stranger*], Ed cannot make the appropriate response. With his wife, there's nothing but contretemps. He loves Sandy, but love's a drag. When Sandy dies, he trades jokes, not because he wants to, but because what's left? Unlike Meursault, when alone, he cries.

At the hospital, Sandy performs a sociological parody. *St. Joan of the Stockyards,* perhaps. She is for Civil Rights, Nuclear Disarmament, Marchers for Peace. And over the loudspeaker, the crowd cheers. (The winking that goes on in **Square in the Eye** could put a burlesque routine to shame.) At the funeral, one kid says: Ugh, Sandy, she wasn't even a good cook! The woman who wasn't a good cook has undergone the martyrdom of middle-class parents whose dream is Miami Beach. There's a Mama Dumpling (Oy, Sandy, how can you shame us, living in such a dump!), and a Papa Bear. He calls Ed a no-goodnik, he mawkishly remembers an immigrant past, he flutters greenbacks over his daughter's bed. Jewish self-hatred runs riot throughout, but it's merely authorial indulgence, or caricatured self-love.

Gelber is callous and he is coy. He's always unabashedly flirting. He wants to subvert like Mephisto (pronounced Brecht) and tickle like Puck (pronounced Murray Schisgal). To a degree, he succeeds. A whiff of sulphur hangs in the air, and Gelber the gagster is as persistent as a census taker. When the doctor garbles Sandy's medical report, a Chopin *étude* tinkles in the background. When the undertaker extols walnut caskets, Saint-Saens fiddles in the distance. As Ed remarries, with Sandy hardly in her grave, Cole Porter's "Just One of Those Things" grinds on the hi-fi. Do we need dialogue? I had to do it, Ed tells us. "I couldn't make it alone."

The actor who plays the doctor turns into the undertaker who turns into the rabbi who turns into the ballroom owner who becomes an off-the-street scavenger arriving to collect Sandy's clothes which Ed sells to pay his bills. The actor signifies the *reductio ad absurdum* of public rot, just as Ed and Sandy symbolize inner collapse. Gelber's pendulum really swings. The rabbi, for instance, solemnly blabbers in Hebrew; then, in English, he has a mock-Auschwitz harangue. The sheer effrontery jolts. And it is "funny." Still, what's the point? What, above all, is the point of Sandy's death? Why are the time sequences upside down? In the first act she's dead, in the second she's dying. Apparently, a random universe muddied with mendacity deserves an arbitrary chronology—not to mention other clichés.

It seems to me Gelber is a message-writer, an honorable calling; only his messages are always fragments from the latest *Kulturkampf.* "Be a secret hipster, slowly insinuating your own values into the hearts of millions." So goes the singing telegram of **On Ice.** In **The Apple,** the Negro says: You gotta want. Don't let your instincts dry up. Even with *The Connection,* Gelber's one authentic achievement, we have modish non sequitur relativism. Everyone's an addict. And the few who shoot-up on "horse" are no worse (actually, they're probably wiser, than the many who drug themselves with Beautiful Homes and Gardens. These messages may or may not be relevant. The point is that Gelber's characters simply (in both senses) embody bits and pieces of whatever message is on the boards.

Superficially, Ed and Sandy are dime-store bright; *au fond,* they are incredibly dim. Neither villains nor heroes nor "just folks," they are the indeterminate non-types, those collagist figurines of contemporary art—dramatic or otherwise. Haphazardly frustrated, perpetually baffled, these people sigh the roof down or balloon themselves up with inconsolable laughter. Sandy "desires" a life of dedication, of significance. Ed "wants" to relate. Each stifles the other. Why? We never know or else we know only too well.

In the old days, people would say: Ah, it's human nature, human cussedness. Now we say: It's only human not to know what being human means. Don't leave me, Ed, whispers Sandy in the elegiac finale. But the hero must leave. After all, she's going to die. And Ed must assume another mask, another marriage, only he will *try* not to assume the mask, *try* not to foul up the marriage. One must face up to sham, counsels Gelber, and the facing-up will set you free. To be sure, in the fading moments, one of Gelber's innumerable pinpricks of poignancy actually draws blood. Ironically, in parting, Ed and Sandy come alive. But the irony is accidental.

Gelber has provided an "evening's entertainment" for the downtown crowd. . . . Gelber's play is essentially Beatnik TV. (pp. 16-18)

> Robert Mazzocco, *"I'm Laughing but Don't Ask Me Why,"* in The New York Review of Books, *Vol. IV, No. 11, July 1, 1965, pp. 16-18.*

C. W. E. Bigsby   (essay date 1968)

[*Bigsby is a Scottish educator, critic, and editor who has written extensively on American literature and drama. In the following excerpt, he interprets the meaning of* The Connection *and discusses the play's significance in the development of contemporary American theatre.*]

The Connection is ostensibly a play about drug addiction. It invites the audience to believe that they are seeing a number of 'junkies' hired to take part in an improvisational drama. Jaybird, the supposed author of the play, appears on stage with the producer to explain his ideas but it soon becomes apparent that the junkies are not prepared to collaborate fully and they refuse to follow the guide lines which he has laid down. While the play is in progress two photographers wander around the set apparently in order to take a motion picture of what happens. Gradually they are drawn into the web of the addicts and by the end one of them has taken dope, in common with the supposed

playwright. The action of the play is concerned with this small group of people who await the arrival of the 'connection' with some heroin. Although this contact does eventually arrive there is no sense that the play has reached a climax for this is presented as merely another and accepted stage in the usual routine. One of the addicts takes an overdose of the drug and comes near to death but to be revived by two of the others. The play ends on an inconclusive note.

While the play ostensibly invites comparison with Michael Gazzo's *A Hatful of Rain* (1955) in fact such a comparison would be misleading for *The Connection* is in no sense a social play. Clearly George Wellwarth is incorrect in identifying it as a defence of drug addiction, in his book *The Theatre of Protest and Paradox.* Gelber is neither lamenting the plight of the dissolute junkie nor is he calling for reform. For him the addict, in the grip of an apparently remorseless need, is an image of the human situation and his play is an analogue of the condition of man in a universe which he identifies as empty, repetitive and cold. Indeed this is emphasised by Solly, the most lucid of the junkies and the one whose perception identifies him most closely with the author. He guesses that the author had chosen this 'petty and miserable microcosm' because of its 'self-annihilating aspects'.

Gelber is indeed unnecessarily concerned with establishing that the conclusions of the play have a relevence outside of the immediately destructive world of the drug addict. For if the junkie needs his fix so, Gelber insists, does a society which sublimates its need for hope and meaning in a frenzy of meaningless activity, ' . . . the people who walk the streets, the people who work every day, the people who worry so much about the next dollar, the next new coat, the chlorophyll addicts, the aspirin addicts, the vitamin addicts'. The meaningless repetition of a nine to five existence is seen by Gelber as an equivalent of the empty repetition of a junkie's life which is lived from one fix to the next. There is none of the hipster's contempt for the 'square' to be found in the play for Gelber's point is that there is basically no difference between them. They are both 'hungry for a little hope', and thus both make the absurdity of their situation more absurd by their response to it. If the junkie is 'hung up' on heroin then one of the addicts identifies the basic obsessions of society as money and sex.

Gelber's particular strength lies in his ability to establish the ironies of his terms. Indeed it is the ambiguity which surrounds his use of the word 'connection' which holds the clue to his central meaning. On the surface a connection, in the argot of the addicts, is the middle man between the junkie and the supplier. In a more general sense, however, it refers to the relationships between things—the relationships which create a semblance of order out of disorder. So that if the addict waits for his connection to bring him his heroin, on a more fundamental level man waits for that which will create some sense of meaning out of an apparently arbitrary life. Kenneth Tynan is clearly right in suggesting [in his preface to *The Connection*] that there are lines of force relating *The Connection* with *Waiting for Godot* for both plays are at first sight concerned with the same issues and both appear to have similar frightening implications. In fact a comparison will demonstrate how closely Gelber's play follows what is in many ways its European forbear.

Waiting for Godot is also an analogue of the human situation. Its basic premise is that man's life is spent waiting for something to bring meaning to the boring tedium of a repetitious existence. As Vladimir says, '. . . one thing alone is clear. We are waiting for Godot to come . . . Or for night to fall.' This is equally true of Gelber's play. The addicts are waiting for the connection to arrive or, like Leach who takes an overdose, for the darkness which will finally make that connection irrelevant. For Beckett's characters the choice is between distraction and suicide. Estragon and Vladimir, when they are not hiding behind their protective chatter, contemplate the feasibility of hanging themselves. So too the nature of the addicts' distraction is such that it presents both an escape and a flirtation with extinction. Although Cowboy, the connection, does eventually arrive it is clear that he fills a similar role to that of the young boy in Beckett's play. The addicts will go on waiting again and tomorrow will be the same as today and so on until increasing physical decay stamps out simultaneously both the individual and the hope or anticipation which was that individual's will to live and the source of his self-torture. The connection, in the fuller sense recognised by Solly, however, is no more identifiable with a particular person or philosophy than is Godot. As Solly says, 'We are waiting. We have waited before. The connection is coming. He is always coming. But so is education, for example. The man who will whisper the truth in your ear. Or the one who will shout it out among the people.'

The parallels between the two plays are not limited to their basic premise, however, for the similarity of their approach naturally leads to a similarity of detail. The drug addicts of **The Connection** relapse whenever possible into a sleep which protects them from the reality of their situation. This, however, tends to exacerbate the essential loneliness of those who remain awake. Leach, in whose apartment the action is presumed to take place, wakes up a fellow addict so that he can listen to the meaningless chatter which serves as his protection—an action which recalls not only *Waiting for Godot* but also *Endgame* (1957). When Solly objects that 'I haven't slept since the night I met you' we are reminded of the parallel situation in *Waiting for Godot* when Estragon, who wakes Vladimir because he feels lonely, is castigated by his partner. 'I was asleep! Why will you never let me sleep?' Looking for proof of existence the junkies seek it in the fix, 'A fix to remember, to be sad, to be happy, to be, to be' while Vladimir and Estragon similarly grasp at distraction as a proof of their existence, 'We always find something . . . to give us the impression that we exist'.

Nevertheless **The Connection** is not merely a transposition of *Waiting for Godot* to an American locale for there is a sense in which Gelber is aware of the possibility of transcending Beckett's deterministic absurdity. For Beckett the absurdity of the human situation makes man himself absurd *per se*. His attempts to seize dignity and to compre-

hend—those marks of the *gens humanus*—serve only to add self-ridicule to absurdity. Gelber, on the other hand, while recognising the validity of the absurdist's vision, granting, that is, that man is alone in an empty universe and that he is born 'astride of a grave', suggests that there are two possible responses to this fact. The response which serves to make man absurd is the debilitating need for distraction which, in avoiding a confrontation with reality avoids also that positive alternative which he goes on to outline. Gelber's characters are aware of the non-existence of established absolutes. They refuse to believe in 'the big connection', the man behind the connection, thus, in a wider sense the man behind the creation of order, the god. 'I have never seen the man because there is no man.' In the absence of such an absolute, however, they transfer the paraphernalia of religion to the drug addiction which becomes its substitute. When Sam has had his fix he returns to the room and announces, 'I've seen the light! Brethren, I used to be a sinner! A sinner . . . I am redeemed! From my eternal suffering I am redeemed!'

The sense of a possible alternative to the absurdity of this reaction is embodied in the person of Solly. It is an alternative, however, which Gelber presents only tentatively and which he refuses to trace to its logical conclusion. Solly derives from his sense of the human condition what amounts to an existentialist implication—an implication, moreover, which makes freedom and subjective meaning valid concepts. 'The man is you' he says, 'You are the man. You are your own connection. It starts and stops here.' It is Solly also who dismisses Jaybird who, as the author of the play, is ostensibly his creator, with what amounts to a declaration of freedom, 'Go ahead . . . it's our stage now.' In spite of this realisation, however, Solly fails to project his 'enlightenment' into concrete action. Although it is repeatedly suggested that he is not 'one of the people' and that he is 'out of it' he is sensible of a counter-force which he identifies as the 'tyranny of the majority'. To break away from the illusions accepted by those around him is to invite isolation and possible persecution. This dilemma is in fact reminiscent of Sartre's *The Flies* (1943) in which the apparent systematised order to which men subjugate themselves crumbles before the realisation of freedom. For freedom to be real, however, it has to be accepted and acted out. The irony which both Gelber and Sartre emphasize is that men would rather have apparent order with subjugation than the chaos of total freedom. In Sartre's play Orestes pictures the reality of his situation, 'I knew myself alone, utterly alone . . . I was like a man who's lost his shadow. And there was nothing left in heaven, no Right or Wrong, nor anyone to give me orders', but as Zeus points out, 'Your vaunted freedom isolates you from the fold; it means exile.' It is this fear of 'exile' which keeps Solly amongst the passive addicts—which prevents him from acting on the realisation that 'life begins on the far side of despair'. To 'kick' the habit is to embrace the gift of freedom and as Zeus insists 'Your gift to them will be a sad one; of loneliness and shame. You will tear from their eyes the veils I had laid on them, and they will see their lives as they are'. This, of course, is the 'momentous enlightenment' of the drama of confrontation and if Gelber's play does not progress from this enlightenment to the positive affirmation of *After the Fall* it does acknowledge a vision of the human situation which is more austere than that recognised by the earlier Miller. For it is through *The Connection* that the theatre of the absurd makes its most direct impact on the American theatre. Indeed it is the synthesis of the absurdist's vision and the humanist's faith which gives the drama of confrontation its particular quality of positive validity. Where the affirmative mood of *Death of a Salesman* had been largely unconvincing and unearned, the affirmation of the drama of confrontation is leavened by the cynicism of the absurd. In the words of Lorraine Hansberry's *The Sign in Sidney Brustein's Window* (1964), which also falls into this category, this is an affirmation 'seasoned, more cynical, tougher, harder to fool'. Where Albee's plays, like *After the Fall,* are concerned with redemption, *The Connection* is a play about the possibility of redemption.

While Gelber accepts the validity of the absurdist's vision of the human situation, however, he rejects that response which both Camus and Beckett advance as the only genuine reaction to an empty universe—a response embodied here in the persons of two photographers apparently hired to film the play. In *Act Without Words I* Beckett had shown man learning to distrust the senses which led him to participate in the world. At the end of the short mime the man had ended up, as does the boy in *Endgame,* motionless and unresponsive. This is in essence the state of the two photographers at the start of the action. When one of them is addressed by an actor he replies that he is not supposed to speak. They merely observe life without participating in it. In fact in a stage direction Gelber explains that in the course of the play they are to exchange their clothing and their personalities. Clearly then he sees this quietism as an absurd denial of existence while the comments which they interject into the action—'That's the way it is. That's the way it really is'—serve to stress the uselessness of an enlightenment which is not converted into a positive dialectic.

The drug addicts of *The Connection* are then only an image. As Jaybird suggests he could have chosen other examples. It is apparent that Gelber sees the modern neurosis over the bomb as an ironical method of inventing purpose, for worry, like waiting, presupposes a meaningful object for concern. Waiting and worry themselves become the fix to which not only the addicts surrender. 'So you wait and worry. A fix of hope. A fix . . . to be, to be.' *The Connection* rejects the popular image of the junkie as the outsider who must be rescued and brought back into society. This had been the import of *A Hatful of Rain* whose final curtain falls on the stirring sight of a wife telephoning the police who will bring with them the doctors to cure her husband's anti-social sickness. This, Jaybird confesses, is the solution which he had in mind at the start of the play. In fact in his drug-induced state he still insists on stating what has now moved beyond cliché to irony, 'I thought perhaps the doctors would take over. That's the message for tonight from me.' It is apparent by this time, however, that the junkie is not an outsider, that his sickness is shared by society and that the doctors themselves are offering the same destructive oblivion as the drug pushers. As Cowboy says, ' . . . the doctors would be the big connection' for it is they who 'mildly electrocute thou-

sands of people every year' and carry out prefrontal lobotomies. The drug addicts and the success addicts are finally indistinguishable from each other for as Cowboy insists, 'We all pay our dues whatever we do'. Both the junkies and society at large are hooked to an indefinable need which leads Leach to take an overdose of drugs and those outside to 'jump into the street against the lights'. This headlong flight towards destruction seems to Gelber the inevitable result of an addiction to distraction. The self-annihilating aspect of the addict group is emphasised by the sterility of their society. Leach, the greedy and repulsive host, is described as an incipient homosexual who, while enjoying the excitement of procuring women, usually by bribing them with drugs, can derive no satisfaction from them. So too Cowboy confesses that he has left love behind. In so far as this group of junkies can now be accepted as a valid microcosm it presents a horrifying picture of man's fear to confront reality and the resulting impotence and meaningless death. This connection between illusion and impotence is one which Edward Albee was to accept as valid in *Who's Afraid of Virginia Woolf?*

The Connection is, I believe, the first American play to confront the essential paradox of drama and the first play effectively to adopt from the European theatre the concept that form and content are indivisible. The central paradox of drama lies in the fact that the act of presentation is also an act of limitation. Unlike a novel, which is interpreted directly by the individual, a play is interpreted not so much by the audience as by the actor and the director. Thus in presenting the play as apparent improvisation Gelber is stating the dramatist's dilemma. He clearly does not imagine, as George Wellwarth seems to think he does, that he can resolve this dilemma. Nevertheless *The Connection* is not merely a petulant complaint against his craft any more than had been Pirandello's *Six Characters in Search of an Author* which Gelber's play resembles in some respects. In it Gelber is drawing attention to a form which is both an image in itself and a challenge to the theatrical norms of the American theatre.

In each of the two acts the stage directions indicate that there is approximately thirty minutes jazz—pure jazz, improvised, as in theory is the play of which it is a part. It is this very improvisational form which carries the key to Gelber's sympathies. For jazz itself is also an image. Its improvisational form is an image of an authentic response to the human condition. More than any other form of music it is dependent for its existence on the ability of individuals to create their own meaning and harmony and to establish their own relationships with their fellow musicians. So that it is apparent that neither the introduction of jazz nor indeed the ostensible improvisational nature of the play are the result of Gelber's perverse naïvete, as Wellwarth suggests, but that rather they re-inforce the freedom of action which is the basis of Solly's enlightenment. It is for the individual to accept his freedom and not to accept dictation from a majority 'hooked' on the need for distraction. For Gelber meaning derives from relationships deliberately created by individuals having a sense of their community with others.

The significance of the jazz image is emphasised not only

by the acknowledgement in the play's first minute of 'the authenticity of that improvised art' but by the presence of what amounts to a prophet for this authenticity—Harry McNulty. Harry appears twice in the play. He enters at the beginning and goes through a fixed ritual of plugging in a portable phonograph, playing a Charlie Parker record, unplugging the machine at the end and then going out again—the whole performed without dialogue. The music silences the self-pitying complaints of the junkies and temporarily unites them. Whatever understanding might result from this is aborted, however, by the interruption of Jaybird who insists that they follow the guidelines of his standardised plot. McNulty's second appearance occurs at the end of the play when Jaybird is forced to concede the freedom of his characters, 'It's all yours now'. This serves to herald Harry's entry. The ritual is repeated and the play ends with the sound of jazz penetrating the darkness of the stage.

The conventional response of desperate commitment to religion, characterised by the Salvation Sister brought back to the apartment by Cowboy, and the compulsive anaesthesia and isolation of the addict, both defer to the man who arrives with a phonograph record of improvised jazz. The Salvation Sister, obsessed by thoughts of death, turns naturally to Solly for insight into this superior salvation which she sees as a challenge to her own faith. Solly asks, 'What makes you think I would know him?'. The Sister replies, 'Oh, he loves jazz music. I thought perhaps . . . never mind, I'm probably wrong anyway. The Lord willing, that is.' She finds her religion neither proof against her loneliness nor able to grant any meaning to an existence dominated by the fact of physical disintegration. She begs to be allowed to stay but is forced out still muttering to herself the reassurance which we now see to be hollow, 'You are not alone. You are not alone. You are not alone.' Similarly Jaybird, in trying drugs for the first time, discovers that far from revealing meaning to him or destroying his loneliness it serves to erect walls between himself and others. Thus a retreat into illusion is revealed as ineffectual while the play concludes on Jaybird's admission of the freedom of his characters and the sounds of improvised jazz from Harry McNulty's phonograph.

Gelber's play is in fact an attack on the established American concept of drama. The play which Jaybird had planned would have been indistinguishable from the social and psychological theatre of Broadway—would in fact have been another version of Gazzo's comfortably reassuring play. When he intervenes, as the characters are apparently getting out of control, he does so to impose the rigidities of conventional drama, 'I had characters, with biographies for each of them. I thought that was clear'. The questions which he fires at the junkies serve only to emphasise his formularised concepts, 'Solly, where is your philosophy . . . Where are your confessions? Your capsule comments?', 'Leach, where is the plot?' Leach's reply sums up Gelber's dissatisfaction with standardised drama, 'I flushed it down the toilet'. When the junkies invite Jaybird to stay on the stage and really 'find out about things' they are indicating a schism between the contrivances of the theatre and reality which is precisely that which had motivated Pirandello. If *The Connection* is concerned

with repudiating the false logic of a desperate humanity trapped by its own rationalism it is also dedicated to destroying the self-justifying nature of the theatre. When Jaybird says, 'I believe it all fits together . . . We wouldn't all be on stage if it didn't' he is expressing both a deterministic vision of existence and an equally restrictive concept of drama. It is left to Solly, with the same dual relevance, to reply, 'It doesn't have to fit'. Perhaps the best comment on the significance of this declaration is to be found in the words of Oedipus in Cocteau's *The Infernal Machine* (1926), 'What we want . . . is not to fit, to breakaway. That's the sign of masterpieces and heroes.'

The horror of the group of junkies lies in their ignorance, with the exception of Solly, of the passive state into which they have betrayed themselves—of the breach which they have allowed to open up between themselves and reality. Granting the emptiness of their universe they invent an abstraction to which they can do obeisance and which will reveal a new order on a plane removed from the suffering of positive existence. Gelber is at pains to insist that the same can be said of the audience not just in the sense that it represents the macrocosm to the junkies' microcosm but in the attitude with which it approaches the theatre. Theatre, the conventional and reassuring stereotype of modern American theatre, acts as just such a drug. Under the guise of seeking truth the audience retreats behind its assurance of theatrical illusion, aware that the convention of American drama is one of reconciliation and resolution. *The Connection* is an assault on the audience not in the almost physical sense that [Kenneth Brown's] *The Brig* was to be but in the sense of jolting it with the apparent spontaneity of parts of its dialogue, the constant interruptions for a seemingly irrelevant jazz and the refusal to follow the normal lines of dramatic progression. The pseudo-improvisational nature of the play does not break down theatrical illusion but it does tend to diminish the effect of that illusion. Tennessee Williams, in *Camino Real,* had directed his characters up and down the theatre aisles but this had had the appearance of an arbitrary theatricality whose very flamboyance was a denial of its significance. In *The Connection* Gelber succeeds, where he was later to fail with *The Apple* (1961), in establishing a direct involvement on the part of the audience which is not dependent merely on the physical traffic between stage and auditorium.

The 'shock value' of the play lies, not in the fact of its stage presentation of addicts, which had been done before, but in Gelber's blunt refusal to adopt any of the simplicities of structure and theme which had been the mark of the bulk of American drama up to this time. The eccentricities of his play function, like the famous first word of Jarry's *Ubu Roi* in 1896, to jolt the audience out of its insulated self-satisfaction.

In Europe Strindberg and Maeterlinck had experimented with a 'non-linear' drama at the turn of the century while the absurdists, writing fifty years later, felt free where necessary to reject totally the logic of time and causality. While Williams had tended towards a similar non-linear form in *Camino Real* he had subverted his effect by imposing the structure of a dream. So that (with the exception of the surrealistic drama of the thirties) it is with *The Connection* that American drama turns away from what Marvin Rosenberg has called the standard 'linear pattern'. With *The Connection* Gelber firmly rejects Miller's contention that a play must 'end with a climax'. Like *Waiting for Godot* his play ends on a low note with the suggestion that the full stop could have been placed anywhere along the line for the action is a demonstration of a continuing state of consciousness. The only actions of any significance are the arrival of Cowboy, which occurs half-way through the play, and the overdose of drugs taken by Leach towards the end. Cowboy's arrival, however, takes place in the interval so that there is no element of suspense while Leach's overdose does not act as the climax to the play which simply comes to an end with the prospect that the action will be repeated over and over again. As Eric Bentley has said, however, ' . . . a new form always seems formless to the conservative mind'. The apparent formlessness of Gelber's play is illusory for it is in fact a strictly organised unit in which no element is extraneous to the whole. For *The Connection,* like *The Brig,* is an expression of a state of consciousness which therefore has no climax in the sense which Jaybird imagines essential to a play.

Jack Gelber's experimentation is not mere aestheticism for as Pirandello proved and Ionesco has insisted, ' . . . it is only when we have pulled apart the conventional characters in our plays, only when we have broken down a false theatrical idiom, that we can . . . try to put it together again—its essential purity restored'. Here, then, was evidence that at last an American dramatist was prepared to search out the fundamentals of his craft and was prepared to learn the advantage of a drama in which form and content were not strangers unhappily forced into the same bed. *The Connection* further serves as proof that philosophically based drama is not necessarily precocious for Gelber's 'philosophy' arises not from abstract speculation but from an acute awareness of the dilemma which is the human situation. As Ionesco says, 'In so far as an artist has a personal apprehension of reality, he is a true philosopher . . . The quality of a work of art directly depends on how "alive" philosophy is, on the fact that it springs from life and not from abstract thought.' Gelber's play was proof too that an American audience could become attuned to the nuances of a drama which rejects the turgid conventionalities of Broadway and those playwrights for whom drama was all too frequently a compromise with a society demanding reassurance and resolution.

Gelber's insistence on the need for confrontation is made with a full awareness of the frightening implications of the absurdist's vision. Influenced alike by Sartre and Beckett, two forces essentially antithetical, he is acutely aware of the essential dilemma which confronts modern man. While anxious to avoid facile resolution it is clear that for all Solly's failure to act Gelber sees his perception of the need for confrontation as a genuine one. While his failure to embrace reality frustrates the affirmation and redemptive love, which emerge as essential aspects of the drama of confrontation, it is clear that *The Connection* is the first American play to admit to the full horror of the absurdist vision while denying the validity both of illusion and qui-

etism. Solly's comprehension of the human situation is thus clearly greater than either Willy Loman's or Biff's while he differs from Quentin not in depth of perception but in the extent of his courage. *The Connection* thus defines for the first time the nature of that reality which Albee, Brown and the later Miller urge on their protagonists.

Gelber himself has produced nothing of any note since *The Connection* and his attempts to repeat his effects have necessarily resulted in failure. He has tended to slip back into a self-indulgent formalism which if successful in breaking down a false theatrical idiom has done little to put it together again with or without its purity restored. Nevertheless this does not detract from the value of *The Connection* for not only did this play a significant part in the development of the drama of confrontation but it also introduced a self-conscious note to American theatre which led eventually to the exciting experiment of Kenneth Brown's *The Brig.* (pp. 50-61)

> *C. W. E. Bigsby, "The Living Theatre," in his* Confrontation and Commitment: A Study of Contemporary American Drama, 1959-66, *University of Missouri Press, 1968, pp. 50-70.*

Gerald Weales (essay date 1969)

[*An American drama critic, Weales is the author of numerous books on drama as well as a theater critic for such journals as* Commonweal *and* The Georgia Review. *His books include, among others,* Tennessee Williams *(1965),* The Jumping-Off Place: American Drama in the 1960's *(1969), and* Canned Goods as Caviar: American Film Comedy in the 1930's *(1985). In the following excerpt, he examines Gelber's first three plays, emphasizing what he views as the highly conventional aspects of Gelber's work.*]

When *The Apple,* Jack Gelber's second play, opened in New York, he was quoted [in a December 18, 1961 *Newsweek* interview as saying]: "I don't believe I have the kind of talent that can produce a straight play in the nineteenth-century sense, which is what they are doing today." The remark had minimal relevance in a season in which few such straight plays were produced and even less were successful. If we accept the end of his sentence as the excessive statement of a man with a crying need to separate himself from a semifictional "they" and if we take the rest of the quotation as true after a fashion (like the strippers in *Gypsy,* he has to have a gimmick), his idea of his work is still false in a very basic way. All three of his plays—*The Connection* (1959), *The Apple* (1961) and *Square in the Eye* (1965)—make desperate attempts to shatter theatrical illusion, to force the actors and the audience into one another's arms, but behind his manipulation of devices a very conventional playwright is at work.

Gelber's sense of character, dramatic situation, emotional effects is stereotypical, even sentimental. Perhaps this quality can be seen more clearly in his nondramatic work where there are no audible jazz combos or visible movie screens (the jazz and movie references are there, of course) to obstruct the view of his soft-centered world. Take, for instance, **"Neal vs. Jimmy the Fag,"** a story that appeared in *Evergreen Review* (December, 1964), a confrontation tale in which an aging ex-con, with only his need to offer, tries and fails to take a young woman away from the titular faggot. "This is your last chance," comes Neal's final cry and then, "He could not control the shame he felt for his own pitifulness and did not wait for an answer, slamming the door." If it were a play instead of a short story, that would be a *schmaltz* curtain, all the more obvious because the whisper of low life—the criminal-homosexual subculture—is still as hokily romantic as it was at the turn of the century. To be fair to Gelber, although he clings to a semi-Bohemian milieu, he goes out of his way—particularly in **The Connection** and in his novel **On Ice** (1964)—to insist that there is no qualitative difference between the square and the hip worlds. "There are lousy hipsters and lousy squares," says Cowboy in **The Connection.** Even if this disavowal is taken as genuine, if Gelber's addicts (**The Connection**), actors (**The Apple**), and painters (**Square in the Eye**) are stripped of any implicit romanticism, Gelber cannot pull away the vestigial threads of ordinary stage psychology that—behind the bead curtains of avant-garde theatrics—can be seen clinging to them.

In his favorable review of **The Connection** (in *Seasons of Discontent*), Robert Brustein wrote, "The only false note of the evening is struck by your own conventional expectation, conditioned by years of phony drama and sociological indoctrination." Although Gelber is plainly suspicious of easy explanations of human behavior and overly neat formulations of human action, perhaps because he believes in the "random universe" that besets Manny Fells, the hero of **On Ice,** the note that Brustein heard at **The Connection** never sounded false to me. The conventional expectations—of character, plot and theme—are fulfilled. Not conventionally, of course, because Gelber's use of the play-within-a-play device and his on-again-off-again parodic stance let him back away from the characters and situations he is dealing with. **The Connection** tells how a producer brings together a group of addicts and has them improvise a scenario prepared by a sympathetic playwright and how—reality being stronger than art—the action on stage destroys any attempt to control it. This is obviously a workable dramatic metaphor for a statement about the inadvisability of putting labels on life, but there is a producer (Julian Beck) and a playwright (Gelber) beyond the fictional ones, and this fact—which not even the panhandling actor-addict in the lobby can hide—adds a probably unintentional ambiguity to the statement.

Jaybird, the fictional playwright, has presumably assigned characters to each of the main performers. In the first act, while they wait for the heroin to arrive, each of them is expected to do a revelatory turn, spelled by the jazz combo. At the beginning of the play, when the introductions are made, labels are distributed lightly, as the producer, joking ponderously, calls Ernie "our dope-addict psychopath" and Sam "our expert in folk lore." Presumably Gelber is playing with popular psychology when he plants references to Ernie's cruel father and Leach's orphanage upbringing, as though they were causes for a situation which he thinks cannot be explained in those terms. Yet, his and Jaybird's characters overlap. When Jaybird

loses control of his play, when presumably it passes into the addicts' hands, Ernie is still the psychopath, Solly still the intellectual, Sam still the uneducated wiseman, Leach still the female male, at once mothering and accusing. In the same way, Gelber both has his plot and dismisses it. Much of the activity in the play seems almost random—beginnings that are going nowhere, exchanges that are only isolated bits. This desultory quality is so strong that, at first glance, Roger Shattuck's description of the play as "the long ineptly timed *coitus interruptus*" (in his poem "New Years Afternoon 1961") seems as apt as it is clever. In fact, there are two conventional plots—one for each act—and both of them build to climax. The first has to do with the waiting, which is not an enclosed action, as it is in *Waiting for Godot.* Here the settlers (the addicts), trapped in the fort (Leach's room), wait for the arrival of the cavalry (the connection) so that they can be saved from the Indians (turned on). In naming his connection Cowboy, Gelber pays mock tribute to the plot he is using, and he lets Solly explain it to the audience. "So we wait for the trustworthy Cowboy to gallop in upon a white horse," he says, and then, for those who do not get the joke, he adds, "Gallant white powder."

In the second act, the fort having been saved (Sister Salvation arrives with Cowboy), there is a turning-on celebration, during which the second plot goes into operation. When Brustein says that Gelber is "never guilty of Pirandello's operatic plot construction," and Nat Hentoff (*Evergeen Review,* January, 1960) talks about "the non-end of the anti-play" *The Connection.* I have the feeling that I must have seen some other **The Connection.** Leach's overdose and the business about who will desert and who will try to help him is the purest melodrama, and it works in those terms even though Gelber uses Jaybird to belittle the convention. Through much of the play, Jaybird worries about his plot and his characters. "This part was to be blood and guts drama," he says near the end of the play, after he has turned on too, and a few speeches later, "I wrote a play with four heroes. . . . You are all heroes. I mean in the theatrical sense. Cowboy, can't you act like a hero?" It is at this point that Leach begins to go for the overdose, and within a few minutes the stage is deserted by all but the four heroes (Leach and the three men who stick by him—Cowboy, Solly, and Sam) and the playwright who will speak the nonheroic benediction over them: "No doctors, no heroes, no martyrs, no Christs." As a comment on addiction, the line may be valid. As a description of the drama, it is like a denial of operetta to the tune of "The Blue Danube."

Aside from what the play is trying to say about the distance between life and sociological, psychological, artistic descriptions of it, it has a conventional social point to make. As Zero Mostel's old night club act had it in more innocent days, "We're all a bunch of aspirin eatin' wrecks." Gelber uses his collection of addicts to remind the audience that we are all in search of some connection by which we may be, in Sam's words, "redeemed. From my eternal suffering I am redeemed! Like a pawn ticket." The analogy between the two worlds is made verbally in speeches by Cowboy (the one about lousy hipsters and lousy squares), by Sam (who describes working, worrying people as "hooked worse than me"), and by Solly ("You are your own connection"). It is made dramatically in the scene in which Solly joins Sister Salvation in an evangelistic exchange, music under, and sentimentally in the discovery that Sister Salvation is also on dope. It is illustrated when the line between the two plays disappears, when Jaybird and one of the photographers, who is supposed to be filming the play, take heroin. The juxtaposition of "eternal suffering" and "pawn ticket" in Sam's speech indicates what is implicit throughout the play—that whatever connection is made, the salvation is temporary. Only the need is permanent. Gelber, then, uses Leach's microcosmic pad to make a statement that is almost as formulistic as the sociology and psychology that the play ostensibly denies.

In *The Apple* a group of actors are supposed to be improvising a play. They are interrupted by a drunk who, like Sam in *The Connection,* annoys the audience in the lobby. He is aggressive, disruptive. It is never quite clear whether the actors' treatment of him as an outsider is part of the improvisation or part of the acting situation. If it is the latter—and I suspect that it is—the play is apparently making some kind of comment about the uses of theater. The play is full of real apples (bitten, passed around, the cores used as missiles) and verbal ones (Iris: "I'm whatever you want me to be . . . I'm your apple, baby"). In his speech at the end of the play, Ace explains that Ajax, who is somewhat grander in his concepts, would tell the audience "that this apple is a golden Chinese apple and stands for knowledge," a description that recalls the desire of Jabez to "Start from the beginning. Do the Adam and Eve bullshit." Ace settles for pointing out that "a lot of people wanted this apple" and ends by urging the audience to come back but not "without wanting something." Commenting on another actor and on the interrupting drunk, Ace says, "Stark would turn into an apple for you. And the madman would throw the apple at you." The assumption—at least, my assumption—is that this sentence and the whole knockabout evening is saying that the theater both gives an audience what it wants and confronts it with its desires.

In trying to fasten a specific label to *apple,* I may be imposing my own sense of order on a play that wants none of it. "Art is precision," says Jabez early in the play. "Control, control every gesture, every word." Ace says, "Relax. There isn't any grand design." What the audience gets from the play are the suggestion of conventional relations among the actors, a series of supposedly improvised sketches, a great deal of free-floating aggression, and many apparently random comments on death and art as well as on apples and wants. Except that the idiom is American and that there is a complete absence of delight for its own sake, the play suggests the kind of surrealist-dadaist theatrical games that were played in France at about the time of the First World War. Since the parts of the play, which are perhaps not supposed to make a whole, are not very interesting and since there is such an air of earnestness in its fun, I assume that Gelber wants the play to make a statement. If the audience (a random collection of shifting desires) dictates the performance, as one might assume from my definition of *apple* and from Ace's long theater-eye metaphor in which "The light from the outside comes through the eyeball [the audience] and focuses on the stage," then the statement may be no more than Jabez's answer to Ace, "No design is grand design." My own answer would have to be to Iris: not my apple, baby.

With *Square in the Eye,* we are back on familiar Gelber ground. This is a fairly obvious story disguised by machinery (movies and slides sharing stage with live actors), by antirealistic staging (entrances and exits through the audience, monologues in the style of the stand-up comedian), and by structural games (the story told out of sequence). In Act I the protagonist (if that is a possible word to use in talking about a Gelber play) appears to be Ed Stone, a would-be-artist schoolteacher who blames his wife, his family, the politics of the art world for his lack of success. At the end of the act, freed by the death of the wife, he is marrying a rich girl: "So I don't paint. Big deal. Or I do. That's my choice now."

In Act II, as we move back in time, the focus shifts from Ed to Sandy, the dying wife. In the long sequence in the hospital room she confronts all her failures—as daughter, as wife, as mother, as friend, as lover, as art critic, as crusader. The family and friends who body out these failures are obvious clichés—from the comic you-should-eat-something Jewish mother to the young daughter who does the Electra bit—but in expressionistic plays, too often, "That's the way it really is." Sandy's sense of loss, her unfulfilled desire for something more than she has had, is presumably to be taken seriously, which means sentimentally, and there is no way of avoiding the syrup of the ending. As Ed goes out through the audience, his and Sandy's voices can be heard on tape, ending with her declaration of love and "Don't go—Don't Ed."

Presumably this ending is supposed to be put in perspective by the first act. There is a long sequence in Act I in which, without a break, the scene shifts from the hospital corridor where Sandy's parents and Ed learn of her death, to the funeral parlor, to the funeral itself. This scene is played for satirical effect, the main device being the single actor who plays the doctor, the funeral director, and the rabbi, whose indifference in each case is presumably masked but actually emphasized by the jargon of his trade. In retrospect, in the light of the second-act hospital scene, this satiric material is probably supposed to take on another quality, to suggest that it is a social reflection of a failure of contact which is much more basic, which finally condemns Sandy to die alone. Unfortunately, in that last scene Gelber goes for easy ironies that misuse the material of the first act. For instance, Sandy predicts, "It'll be just your luck to marry some vapid rich doll and her docility will be the death of Ed Stone, the painter." If Gelber is prepared to work for that level of perception, there is little point in going in search of more subtle effects. One might as well take straight the tears in the last moments. In any case, it is difficult to escape the feeling that Sandy and Ed, their family and friends, are escapees from the William Inge world of the fifties, trying to pretend that they are at home in the setting Gelber has given them.

At one point in *On Ice,* Gelber begins to bring Manny Fells and a girl together; their approach is tentative, circumlocutory. "Louise interposed a complicated story, painting mechanistic sketches of the dramatis personae and elaborating the relationships based on incredibly subtle banalities." That line, when I read it, broke loose from the novel and took on a critical life of its own. Gelber, as playwright, refuses to use Louise's method, but—even in his best work, **The Connection**—he is working from the same base. (pp. 55-62)

> *Gerald Weales, "Front Runners, Some Fading," in his* The Jumping-Off Place: American Drama in the 1960's, *Macmillan, 1969, pp. 54-62.*

FURTHER READING

Biography

"Young Playwright." *New Yorker* XXXVI, No. 21 (9 July 1960): 24-5.

> Early biographical profile.

Criticism

Eskin, Stanley G. "Theatricality in the Avant-Garde Drama: A Reconsideration of a Theme in the Light of *The Balcony* and *The Connection.*" *Modern Drama* VII, No. 3 (September 1964): 213-22.

> Comparative discussion of the theme of self-conscious theatricality in Jean Genêt's *The Balcony* and Gelber's *The Connection.*

Jeffrey, David K. "Genêt and Gelber: Studies in Addiction." *Modern Drama* XI, No. 2 (September 1968): 151-56.

> Examines the play-within-a-play structure in Jean Genêt's *The Balcony* and Gelber's *The Connection* to comment on humanity's addiction to "inauthentic," or illusory, views of reality.

Mee, Charles L., Jr. "The Becks' Living Theatre." *Tulane Drama Review* 7, No. 2 (Winter 1962): 194-205.

> Ambivalent appraisal of the history of Judith Malina and Julian Beck's Living Theatre repertory company. The critic includes discussion of the group's productions of Gelber's *The Connection* and *The Apple.*

Interview

Kellman, Barnet. "The American Playwright in the Seventies: Some Problems & Perspectives." *Theatre Quarterly* VIII, No. 29 (Spring 1978): 45-50, 52-8.

> Transcript of a roundtable discussion with Gelber, Corinne Jacker, Leslie Lee, Janet Neipris, John Ford Noonan, Lanford Wilson, and Michael Weller on various issues facing American playwrights.

Additional coverage of Gelber's life and career is contained in the following sources published by Gale Research: *Contemporary Authors*, Vols. 1-4, rev. ed.; *Contemporary Authors New Revision Series*, Vol. 2; *Contemporary Literary Criticism*, Vols. 1, 6, 14; and *Dictionary of Literary Biography*, Vol. 7.

Nicolás Guillén

1902-1989

(Full name Nicolás Cristobal Guillén y Batista) Cuban poet, journalist, and editor.

The following entry presents criticism of Guillén's works from 1972 to 1990. For further information on Guillén's career, see *CLC*, Volume 48.

INTRODUCTION

Guillén has been recognized as one of Cuba's finest poets and as an important figure in contemporary West Indian literature. Named National Poet of Cuba by Fidel Castro in 1961, Guillén chronicled the turbulent social and political history of his native land. He is also credited as one of the first poets to affirm and celebrate the black Cuban experience. Robert Márquez characterized Guillén's work as "a poetry which is explicit, deceptively simple in style, militant in its assumptions, one which reaches out to the Third World and looks forward to liberation, then peace."

Guillén, a mulatto from the Cuban provincial middle class, was born in Camagüey to Argelia and Nicolás Guillén. His father, a journalist and Liberal senator, was assassinated in a political skirmish in 1917. According to Vera M. Kutzinski, after his father's death "the young Guillén became increasingly interested in poetry and journalism." He graduated from high school in 1920 and then attended the University of Havana, where he planned to study law. Guillén left school after a year, however, and founded the literary magazine *Lis* while also writing for various Cuban newspapers and magazines. In 1937 Guillén joined the Communist Party, campaigning for various political offices throughout the 1940s. He became president of the Cuban National Union of Writers and Artists in 1961, a position he held for twenty-five years. His honors include the Lenin Peace Prize from the Soviet Union in 1954 and the Cuban Order of José Martí in 1981. Guillén died after a long illness in 1989.

The majority of Guillén's poems are informed by his African and Spanish heritage, often combining the colloquialisms and rhythms of Havana's black districts with the formal structure and language of traditional Spanish verse to address the injustices of imperialism, capitalism, and racism. Guillén's first acclaimed volume of poetry, *Motivos de son,* introduced to a literary audience the *son,* a sensual Afro-Cuban dance rhythm. In this collection Guillén utilizes the rhythmic patterns of the *son* to evoke the energetic flavor of black life in and around Havana. Although some readers accused him of displaying negative images of black Cubans, Guillén was praised for originality and for blending Afro-Cuban idioms and traditional verse. Guillén expanded his focus in his next volume, *Sóngoro cosongo: Poemas mulatos,* to include poems depicting the

lives of all Cubans, with emphasis on the importance of mulatto culture in Cuban history.

Following the demise of the corrupt government headed by Gerardo Machado in 1933 and the increasing industrial and political presence of the United States in Cuba, Guillén began to write poetry with overtly political implications. In *West Indies, Ltd.,* a collection of somber poems imbued with anxiety and frustration, he decried the social and economic conditions of the Caribbean poor. Guillén attacked imperialism through his recurring description of the region as a vast, profitable factory exploited by foreign nations. The poet's commitment to social change grew when he traveled to Spain in 1937 to cover the Spanish Civil War for *Mediodia* magazine and subsequently participated in the anti-fascist Second International Congress of Writers for the Defense of Culture. That year he joined the Cuban Communist Party and produced an extended narrative poem chronicling the Spanish Civil War, entitled, *España: Poema en cuatro angustias y una esperanza.* In 1937 Guillén also published *Cantos para soldados y sones para turistas,* a volume of poetry denouncing the escalating military presence in Cuban society. He employed biting satire in poems that contrast the darkness and squalor of Cuba's ghettos with the garish atmosphere of downtown tourist establishments.

Guillén spent much of the 1940s and 1950s in exile in Europe and South America during the height of the Fulgencio Batista y Zaldívar regime. His works of this period reflect his opposition to Batista's repressive policies and denounce racial segregation in the United States. The poems in *La paloma de vuelo popular: Elegías* favor revolution, praising the activities of such political figures as Castro and Che Guevara. Guillén returned to Cuba following Batista's expulsion in 1959, and in 1964 he published *Tengo*. In this volume, Guillén celebrates the triumph of the Cuban revolution and the abolition of racial and economic discrimination.

Many commentators have distinguished between Guillén's early *poesía negra,* or Afro-Cuban-influenced poems, and the political poems he produced after converting to communism. There is little agreement among critics, however. As Richard Jackson noted, "Some critics have focused on Guillén as an exponent of Afro-Cuban poetry while others have viewed him as a poet having little to do with Africa. Some perceive a black aesthetic in his poetry; others say he is the most Spanish of Cuban poets. Some see him as a poet who stopped writing black poetry; others declare that he never wrote black poetry at all." Despite controversy concerning Guillén's treatment of racial themes and his status as a political poet, many scholars have found coherence in his oeuvre. Kutzinski argues: "Perhaps the best way to describe Guillén's poetic ventures is as processes of unraveling the intricate hieroglyphics of Cuban (and Caribbean) culture: his poetic texts are engaged in the forging of a literary tradition from the many disparate elements that constitute the cultural landscape of that region, and he is well aware that such a tradition can be established only on the basis of a perpetual reconciliation between black and white cultures."

PRINCIPAL WORKS

Motivos de son   (poetry)   1930
Sóngoro cosongo: Poemas mulatos   (poetry)   1931
West Indies, Ltd.   (poetry)   1934
Cantos para soldados y sones para turistas   (poetry) 1937
España: Poema en cuatro angustias y una esperanza   (poetry)   1937
Cuba Libre: Poems by Nicolás Guillén   (poetry)   1948
Elegía a Jacques Roumain en el cielo de Haití   (poetry) 1948
Versos negros   (poetry)   1950
Elegía a Jesús Menéndez   (poetry)   1951
Elegía cubana   (poetry)   1952
La paloma de vuelo popular: Elegías   (poetry)   1958
Buenos días, Fidel   (poetry)   1959
Prosa de prisa; crónicas   (prose)   1962
Poemas de amor   (poetry)   1964
Tengo   (poetry)   1964
   [*Tengo,* 1974]

Ché Comandante   (poetry)   1967
El gran zoo   (poetry)   1967
   [*¡Patria o muerte! The Great Zoo and Other Poems by Nicolás Guillén,* 1972]
Cuatro canciones para el Ché   (poetry)   1969
El diario que a diario   (poetry)   1972
Man-Making Words: Selected Poems of Nicolás Guillén (poetry)   1972
La rueda dentada   (poetry)   1972
El corazón con que vivo   (poetry)   1975
Poemas manuables   (poetry)   1975
Prosa de prisa: 1929-1972   (prose)   1975-76
Cerebro y corazón   (poetry)   1977
Por el mar de las Antillas anda un barco de papel   (poetry)   1977
Música de camara   (poetry)   1979
Páginas vueltas: Memorias   (poetry)   1982
Sol de domingo   (poetry)   1982

CRITICISM

Robert Márquez and David Arthur McMurray   (essay date 1972)

[*In the following introduction to their translation of* Man-making Words: Selected Poems of Nicolás Guillén, *Márquez and McMurray consider Guillén's role in* "the struggle between progress and reaction which continues to shape contemporary history."]

Just two years younger than the century, Nicolás Guillén came of age at a time when the peoples of the world were beginning consciously to move apart, to define their positions *vis-à-vis* the struggle between progress and reaction which continues to shape contemporary history. Today, as his seventieth birthday draws near, he is the dynamic National Poet of a country which has won and is consolidating an exemplary victory in that struggle.

By design, and with a great deal more consistency than many of his contemporaries, Guillén has spoken to, been formed by, the concrete human issues of both his immediate community and the larger world. But to conclude, merely for this reason, that his work as an intellectual has been political is to overlook what really distinguishes it. [In a footnote, the critic adds: Apart from his achievements as a poet, Guillén has always taken time to participate in important conferences and cultural gatherings in various parts of the world. These have included: the Congress of the League of Revolutionary Writers and Artists (LEAR), Mexico, 1937; the Second International Congress of Writers for the Defense of Culture, Valencia-Barcelona, 1938; the Association of Anti-Fascist Intellectuals, Madrid, 1938; the Cultural and Scientific Congress for Peace, New York, 1949; and the Continental Congress of Culture, Santiago de Chile, 1953. In 1937 he became a Communist and five years later in his home town, Camagüey, represented the Party as an unsuccessful candidate for Mayor. In 1953 he was honored in Moscow by the Stalin Prize. A contributor to Cuban journals since very early in his career, Guillén became through the years a first-class critical journalist. A selection of his articles (1938-1961) has been published as: *Prosa de prisa: crónicas* (Santa Clara: Universidad Central de Las Villas, 1962), and reprinted the following year in Buenos Aires by Editorial Hernández.] There should be no necessity at this advanced stage in the history of criticism to repeat that the responses—Combray as well as Macchu Picchu, Clarissa Dalloway along with Bigger Thomas—of an artist are always political; and even if Guillén had followed the poetic example of his Spanish namesake, Jorge, observations on the politics of his *oeuvre* would be no less germane.

Neither would it be particularly useful to characterize what Guillén has accomplished as *engagé* or militant. While these facile clichés can be applied to his poetry or, now and again, to the work of a few other modern artists, they are equally accurate with respect to the Lord's Prayer and the Monroe Doctrine. Militancy, as history so painfully demonstrates, has never been an exclusive province of those who share Guillén's world-view.

Concerning that world-view, it would be most exact to begin by calling the man a leftist. That is, in both intention and execution, his work is implacably antibourgeois or, what amounts in today's world to the same thing, anticapitalist. Even beyond this—and herein lies perhaps its greatest distinction—the poetry of Nicolás Guillén is revolutionary. But the revolution here is no simple matter of language, style, or form: that distracting swarm of "isms" which identifies the bulk of twentieth-century writing, and which may well emerge in the final analysis as historical curiosity, has not touched Guillén. In contrast to the majority of modern antibourgeois poets, he is direct, accessible, and, in the finest sense of the word, popular. Moreover, he has managed to apprehend and address himself to what one recent essay calls "the collective need for poetry in certain historical periods (the German occupation of France, for example) and in certain social situations (at rallies and demonstrations) when the group wants both to manifest and to structure its unity, its demands and its enthusiasm." [Michel Beaujour, "Flight out of Time: Poetic Language and the Revolution," in *Literature and Revolution*.]

April 20, 1930, marks Guillén's first response to that need, the debut of his revolutionary verse. On that day, *Ideales de una Raza,* the Sunday literary page of an otherwise conservative Havana newspaper, *Diario de la Marina,* published his **Motivos de Son** [*Son Motifs*]. "As soon as these poems had entered the cultural life of our island," writes critic-biographer Angel Augier, "we had the joyful sensation of discovering the essence of our own lyricism. . . . The *son,* a passionate dance born out of the Negro-white encounter under Caribbean skies in which the words and music of the people culminate in song, is the basic substance of the elemental poetry which Guillén intuitively felt as the expression of the Cuban spirit. . . . He specifically chose the *son* as the mixed artistic creation of the two races that make up the Cuban population for the *son,* in form and content, runs the full gamut of every aspect of

our national character." ["The Cuban Poetry of Nicolás Guillén," *Phylon,* XII (1951), 32. This is probably the most helpful article in English on the poet and his development up to the late forties. For a more scholarly account of the sources and evolution of the *son,* see: Alejo Carpentier, *La música en Cuba* (México, D.F.: Fondo de Cultura Económica [Colección Tierra Firme-19], 1946); and Fernando Ortíz, *La africanía de la música folklórica de Cuba* (La Habana: Publicaciones del Ministerio de Educación, Dirección de Cultura, 1950).]

While it has always been plain to the point of commonplace that Cuba is a lively protean synthesis, so to speak, of the white Spanish thesis and the black African antithesis, no one before Guillén had advanced such a bold affirmation of the latter. Among the few Negroes who had managed in the nineteenth century to achieve some standing in Cuban letters—Juan Francisco Manzano and Gabriel de la Concepción Valdes (Plácido), for example—the tendency was to assimilate the Spanish colonial culture, to "bleach out" any strains of a darker sensibility. The twentieth century, of course, brought a deepening self-consciousness among Blacks and that much-commented white cultivation of things African and Afro-American, both of which flowered—in genuine as well as pretended manifestations—during the post-World-War-One decade in Harlem and Paris. On a popular level, Cuba's association with this flowering is through the Afro-Caribbean movement which sprang up in Hispanic poetry around the mid-twenties. But the inaugurators of the movement (Luis Palés Matos, a Puerto Rican, and the Cubans, José Zacarias Tallet and Ramón Guirao) were white. Their achievement lay principally in the manipulation of exotic-sounding onomatopoeia and so-called primitive rhythm—a figure they commonly depicted is the stereotypical Black of mystery, sensuality, and dance. They were selective observers (even exploiters) of, rather than participants in, the world their verse purported to evoke.

In radical contrast to this local-color approach, Guillén's eight "*son*-poems" offered a provocative inside picture. It is the black inhabitant of Havana's slums who speaks here; what is more, he uses the argot and nonstandard pronunciation peculiar to his milieu, and sketches phenomena of his own daily existence. The result is a new and shocking authenticity. But gradually, through repeated confrontations with the text, it becomes clear that, just behind these entertaining and often happy-go-lucky slices of ghetto life, the people of **Motivos de son** (1) do not have enough to eat, (2) are often ashamed of identifiably Negroid features or coloring, and (3) commonly live in exploitative sexual promiscuity. One poem tells of a *chulo,* or small-time pimp, who is compensated for his nickname, "Nigger-lips," by a good white suit, two-tone shoes, and the fact that he lives well without ever working. In another a woman is told to cheer up and try to pawn her electric iron because the power is shut off for nonpayment and the cupboard as well as her man's pockets are empty. And in one more a woman announces that, since her man steps out in fine clothes and new shoes while she sits at home eating rice and biscuits, she will defy the censure of neighbors and leave him for someone else.

Social criticism implicit in these poems, then, finds its object in the unpleasant reality they evoke, not in the individuals who are forced to live it. As regards these latter, Guillén's affection is unmistakable; so is his admiration for the spirited and inventive manner in which they confront second- and third-class citizenship. On questions of color gradation among nonwhites, the first four lines of **"My Little Woman"** reveal the poet's attitude as one of healthy racial affirmation. Similarly positive is the piece in which a man responds to the derisory remarks of a light-brown woman. The individual in question is far from offended at having his flat nose likened to the knot of a necktie, and he assures the author of the comparison that with a fine black woman at home he need have nothing to do with the likes of her. Finally, Guillén also included an entertaining little piece in which a local fellow, Bito Manué (Victor Manuel), is teased good-naturedly for attempting a flirtation with an apparently-willing American tourist, when the best he can manage in English is counting to three with a horrible accent. Given both the island's national reality and the poet's concern for authenticity within the limitations of *Motivos de son,* at least this sort of passing reference to the United States is almost inevitable; undeniably, that country has been the greatest single "outside" influence on the unfolding of the above-mentioned Cuban synthesis. Soon enough Guillén will take more careful note of the United States influence and incorporate a progressive critique of it into his poetry. For the time being, however, imperialism is merely linguistic; there is no real exploitation, only embarrassment.

In both intention and execution, Guillén's work is implacably antibourgeois or, what amounts in today's world to the same thing, anticapitalist.

—*Robert Márquez and David Arthur McMurray*

The immature, highly personal, and *modernista*-inspired verse in which Guillén had dabbled without much distinction during the twenties has become clearly now a thing of the past. That single newspaper page of *Diario de la Marina* at once marks his real self-discovery as a poet and anticipates so much of what he will become. Carefully and surely, he moved from the urban black themes of *Motivos de son* to a more general, national concern in *Sóngoro Cosongo* (1931), then beyond to the broader Caribbean vision which shapes *West Indies Ltd.* (1934). In *Cantos para soldados y sones para turistas* (1937) [*Songs for Soldiers and Sones for Tourists*] he is continental in scope; some months later, with *España: poema en cuatro angustias y una esperanza* (1937) [*Spain: A Poem in Four Anguishes and a Hope*], his perspective has become international. After a decade of silence, *El son entero* (1947) [*The Entire Son*] appeared. Here the poet is revealed in his full thematic, formal, and ideological maturity; he is able to speak concretely to Cuba and the rest of Latin America, while conceding nothing with regard to universality. *La paloma de vuelo popular—Elegías* (1958) [*The Dove of Popular Flight—Elegies*], most of which was composed in exile, contains some of Guillén's most vigorous poems of praise and condemnation; in them he is more explicit than ever before as to his concept of complete social justice and the means of realizing it in today's world. And finally, *Tengo* (1964) [*I Have*], *El gran zoo* (1967) [*The Great Zoo*], and the as yet uncollected *La rueda dentada* [*The Serrated Wheel*] comprehend a hearty poetic endorsement of Cuba's new reality, a determined absorption in the day-to-day tasks and long-range goals of the Revolution.

All along this poetic itinerary Guillén has demonstrated an uncommon versatility. Beyond the *son,* his formal mastery extends to the *décima,* the *letrilla,* and the *romance,* as well as the sonnet, the ballad, and free verse. His ability to blend and juxtapose these forms effectively is evinced in the richly suggestive *Elegies.* If in such poems as **"Governor," "Little Rock,"** and **"Short Grotesque Litany on the Death of Senator McCarthy"** Guillén is caustic or malicious, others like **"Bars," "Paul Eluard,"** and **"Sunday Reading"** indicate his capacity for human affection. While **"The Flowers Grow High"** and, indeed, a great portion of the poet's work is intensely public, such pieces as **"Exile"** and **"Little Ballad of Plovdiv"** find him more quietly personal. **"Sputnik 57"** is a reaction to the scientific present; **"My Last Name"** explores an unrecorded past. If there is mordant condemnation in **"Wu-Sang-Kuei"** and **"Whatever Time is Past was Worse,"** there is spirited praise in **"Five Chinese Songs"** and **"Thus Sings a Mockingbird in El Turquino."** The coldness and severity of **"Mau-Maus"** or **"Execution"** is balanced by the vibrance and warm sensuality of **"Ovenstone," "Ana María"** or **"Words in the Tropics."** And while **"Soviet Union"** is specific and partisan, the spirit of **"Sell Me?"** is more general and nonsectarian. All this is not simply to assure the reader there is "something for everyone" in the work of Nicolás Guillén, but rather to underscore the richness of its texture. For while he maintains a consistent mass appeal, the poet has managed to avoid confusing simplicity with simplemindedness, the genuinely popular with what is merely ordinary.

On a level of theme and ideology it is useful to recall the racial affirmation, social criticism, and awareness of the United States which marked *Motivos de son.* These three features will continue to identify Guillén's poetry, and observations on their diverse presence in it are instructive with regard to his maturing world-view. Curiously enough, even prior to the publication of *Motivos de son,* the three appear as features of a single poem, **"Small Ode to a Black Cuban Boxer."** Collected later in *Sóngoro cosongo,* "they were lines of racial exaltation and disjointed rhythm, in which there was as yet nothing of the musical quality which would characterize subsequent production: 'the Negro reigns while boulevards applaud! / Let the envy of the whites / know proud, authentic Black!' As you can see, the poet asked little. Soon he would ask more." [Nicolás Guillén, from a talk given to the Lyceum Lawn and Tennis Club in Havana, 1945. The poem was first published on December 29, 1929, in *Ideales de una Raza.*]

What Guillén asks here—beyond his expression of admiration for the skills and triumphs of a particular boxer—is that black people in general take into account, even take advantage of, the "Negro craze" which had begun to make itself felt on the island. Around the same time he published an interview with Langston Hughes who was traveling in Cuba and another with the black Cuban songwriter, Rosendo Ruiz. In the former he praises Hughes' *Weary Blues* and *Fine Clothes to the Jew,* and commends his self-conscious blackness as the new stimulating ingredient in American verse. In the latter he chides Cubans for their indiscriminate acceptance of whatever happens to reach them from Paris or New York, and counsels a reacquaintance with and new respect for their own, and necessarily mulatto, expressions of popular culture. The poem in question also makes it plain that, whatever else he might be, this man with "fists of dynamite / and stylish patent leather shoes" is an easily-exploitable commodity; semiliterate even in his own language, he is trained to perform like "a brand new rubber monkey" for those bored and thrill-seeking crowds up there in "the North." Besides athletes and entertainers, the island has always exported sugar; and this better-known Cuban commodity also whets the appetite of what the poet refers to as "Broadway." Insatiable as the fan at ringside, the exploiter "stretches out its snout, its moist enormous tongue, / to lick and glut upon / our canefields vital blood!"

But for the present, Guillén's social criticism and awareness of the United States amount to little more than just that. While he is resentful of certain phenomena on general moral grounds and unassailable in his nationalism, he is not yet involved with thoroughgoing analysis and concrete solutions. As a response to the lionization of his boxer and imperialist incursions in his country, the poet's Marxism is still only incipient.

Not for almost thirty years, until the *Elegies,* will there appear anything quite so total as "Small Ode to a Black Cuban Boxer." Apart from these six extraordinary pieces, the poems as they are selected in the volume in hand exhibit in varying proportions the three features designated as central to Guillén's vision. Racial affirmation is at its most vivid in "Sports," "Words in The Tropics," and "Arrival," while in "Ballad of the Two Grandfathers" and "A *son* for Antillian Children" the poet also takes note of the white European ingredient in his particular admixture. In "I Came on a Slaveship" he is prideful of both who he has been and who he is today. Guillén's response to the presence of the United States in his part of the world varies according to the circumstances in question. He speaks with harsh censure in "Song for Puerto Rico," revolutionary confidence in "Far Off," militant resolve in "The Flowers Grow High," and triumphant celebration in "Thus Sings a Mockingbird in El Turquino." Social criticism, of course, is one of the more persistent elements of the poet's work. Particularly effective in this area are "Carioca Song," "Mau-Mau," and "Little Rock," while the readiness to temper his criticism with hope and encouragement is plain in "Brazil-Copacabana," "Neighborhood House," and "A Black Man Sings in New York City."

The *Elegies,* conceived and perfected over a period of ten years, were published (together with *La paloma de vuelo popular*) in Buenos Aires only weeks before Fulgencio Batista fled Cuba and "the decisive bearded ones from the Sierra" entered the city of Havana. While some audiences are likely to find these poems almost "heavy," too concentrated, and wanting in polemical subtlety, a close reading of them as well as some sensitivity toward their contexts will be essential to a full appreciation of who and what the poet is. "Elegy for Camagüey" is primarily an engaging, nostalgic tribute to the people and events of yesterday, of the poet's youth. But when he calls: "People of daily needs / . . . limpid, quotidian, unheroic / souls: bedrock of history: / know I speak and dream of you," he is identifying specifically with the common people of his home town and, by implication, with common people everywhere.

In "Elegy for Emmett Till" Guillén speaks with rage and indignation to an unpardonable act of savagery. A poignant juxtaposition of the victim's youth and vulnerability with the hellish brutality of the locale is accompanied by the plain allegation that this "ancient river, brother to the Black" has borne witness to a good many more incidents of the same nature.

Without question "My Last Name" will stand as one of the poet's most quietly moving and sensitively conducted pieces. It is a pilgrimage beyond the "notary's ink" from which "I know there will come distant cousins," an excavation of "my subterranean galleries / with great moist rocks / . . . where I feel the pure rush / of ancient waters." (pp. ix-xvii)

> *Robert Márquez and David Arthur McMurray, in an introduction to* Man-making Words: Selected Poems of Nicolás Guillén, *translated by Robert Márquez and David Arthur McMurray, University of Massachusetts Press, 1972, pp. ix-xviii.*

Lorna V. Williams   (essay date 1979)

[*Williams is an American educator, critic, and short story writer. In the following essay, she examines Guillén's poetry in relation to the concept of "an ideal African past, which predates contact with the 'corrupting' influences of Euro-American civilization."*]

For most blacks living in the Americas, Africa is the continent from which one's ancestors came, but it is hardly the place where one seeks poetic inspiration in the present. Time and space remain frozen in that mythical primeval moment, when one's ancestors were forced to embark on the slave ships traveling to the New World. Since few residents of the Americas have a first-hand knowledge of the land of their forefathers, popular fantasies of Africa form a standard part of the collective memory of black peoples in the New World. The presence that once was Africa has been displaced by Europe, as the languages spoken in the Americas so eloquently attest. And yet, centuries of miscegenation have failed to eliminate all trace of Africa from the socio-cultural repertoire of blacks in the New World. Or rather, the awareness that one is no longer as one's ancestors were has often led blacks to assert their continuity with an ideal African past, which predates contact with the "corrupting" influences of Euro-American civilization.

In this respect, the poetry of the Afro-Cuban, Nicolás Guillén, is instructive. In the opening lines of the **"Son número 6"** (**"Son number 6"**), Guillén declares himself to be Yoruba. However, by the middle of the second stanza, it becomes evident that the persona is no longer the representative of a particular ethnic group, but rather the spokesman for what M. G. Smith would term a generalized African culture [in "The African Heritage in the Caribbean," *Caribbean Studies: A Symposium*].

> Yoruba soy,
> cantando voy,
> llorando estoy,
> y cuando no soy yoruba,
> soy congo, mandinga, carabalí.
>
> I am Yoruba
> singing along,
> weeping,
> and when I am not Yoruba,
> I am Kongo, Mandinka, Calabar.

The poem thereafter becomes a celebration of that cultural convergence, which has often been regarded as a characteristic of black societies in the New World. If on the existential plane, ethnic identity becomes interchangeable, in rhetorical terms, the primacy of Yoruba culture is upheld through the force of repetition, thereby reflecting the cultural reality of Cuba.

Frequent references to Shango, and mention of his wife, Oshun, whose protection is invoked even for Stalin, also serve to highlight the predominance of the Yoruba influence in Cuba. Since it is generally acknowledged that the religious domain has remained the most faithful reflection of the African presence in the New World, it is possible to regard the red beads worn by the black woman who dances through the pages of **Sóngoro cosongo** as a sign that she is a worshipper of Shango, and to note that one of his sacrificial foods, *quimbombó* (okra stew), has become part of the national diet, which the nostalgic tourist dreams of in Paris. As the **"Balada del güije"** (**"Ballad of the River Spirit"**) makes clear, being a worshipper of Shango, or even wearing his insignia, does not offer unlimited protection against death or misfortune. It would appear that in this case, the necklace has lost its mystical power, and should have been specially treated by the priest so as to endow it with the miraculous power of the god that would have saved the child's life.

It should be noted that the cause of death is not found in the malfunctioning of the child's body, or even in an accident. Instead, intentionality is attributed to the river, which is peopled with beings that devour black children and other passers-by. In granting the river a spiritual dimension, Guillén reveals his characters to be living in an anthropomorphic universe, as did the members of traditional African societies. Since meaning is perceived in the objects of the natural world, which are often the dwelling place of a divinity, man is obliged to propitiate them to maintain harmony in the universe. In this case, words are used as incantation, as the mother hopes to dispel misfortune by repeating:

> ¡Neque, que se vaya el ñeque!
> ¡Güije, que se vaya el güije!
>
> Curse, may the curse go away!
> River-spirit, may the river-spirit go away!

Here the word, which ordinarily is believed to have the capacity to ward off disaster, by virtue of its symbolical role as a means of transmitting divine power, has ceased to be effective, as it too seems to have lost its mystical force.

That the word may possess this mystical power is amply demonstrated by *Sensemayá*, the "chant for killing a snake." In this instance, the word is charged with sufficient spiritual force as to produce the desired effect. Undoubtedly, the results of the chant are dependent on the manner in which it is uttered. In Guillén's hands, verbal expression attains the condition of music, as the author exploits the percussive possibilities in the name of one of the Kongo peoples to set the basic rhythm of the poem:

> ¡Mayombe—bombe—mayombé!
> ¡Mayombe—bombe—mayombé!
> ¡Mayombe—bombe—mayombé!

While the octosyllabic meter of the choral repetitions serves as the frame of reference for the entire performance, the call-and-response structure of the poem makes polymeter possible, for verses of contrasting meters are used to mark the states of the snake's progress. A syncopated rhythm is also achieved through the manipulation of a limited vocabulary, which depends for its effectiveness on the recurrence of set phrases with contrasting patterns of accentuation. This becomes most pronounced in the final stanza, where the heterophonic mode of the choral response marks the death of Sensemayá:

> ¡Mayombe—bomebe—mayombé!
> *Sensemayá, la culebra . . .*
> ¡Mayombe—bombe—mayombé!
> *Sensemayá, no se mueve . . .*
> ¡Mayombe—bombe—mayombé!
> *Sensemayá, la culebra . . .*
> ¡Mayombe—bombe—mayombé!
> *Sensemayá, see murió.*
>
> Mayombe—bombe—mayombe!
> *Sensemayá, the serpent . . .*
> Mayombe—bombe—mayombé!
> *Sensemayá, is not moving . . .*
> Mayombe—bombe—mayombé!
> *Sensemayá, the serpent . . .*
> Mayombe—bombe—mayombé!
> *Sensemayá, it is dead.*

The oral quality of the poem reveals its grounding in an African conception of the role of the human voice, which in musical composition is the primary instrument around which all others converge.

However, as Ruth Finnegan indicates [in her *Oral Literature in Africa*], in verbal compositions which are sung, sound often takes precedence over sense, as the rhythmic requirements of the music make the use of nonsense words and onomatopoeia necessary. Guillén's preference for the *jitanjáfora* in his early poetry is therefore in keeping with this widespread tendency of the African lyric. At the same time, it should be pointed out that whereas the lyric is only one of the many genres in African literature, and that while one of its characteristic features results from the subordination of meaning to melody, for many New World writers of Guillén's generation, the lyrical divorce between sound and sense comes to symbolize the nature of African man.

As G. R. Coulthard has observed [in his *Race and Colour in Caribbean Literature*], the Spenglerian atmosphere prevailing in Europe in the decade after the First World War was conducive to the adoption of such a stance, since many people who were disillusioned with European intellectual endeavor as manifested in its death-dealing technology, were searching for an Adamic world in which being was no longer inhibited by thought. Since Africa had always been perceived to lie on the periphery of Europe, which was the center from which all visions of culture were projected, it readily came to occupy that ideal space as a continent in which man lives in a state of nature, unencumbered by the processes of rational thought. To Caribbean writers who generally took their cue from Europe, and for whom Africa was equally out of focus, despite the fact that they were surrounded by living reminders of the African connection, the celebration of African spontaneity became a means of asserting their American vitality and originality in the face of the evident "decline" of Europe. In O. R. Dathorne's terms [in *The Black Mind: A History of African Literature*], ignorance and desire caused this literary vision of Africa to acquire the characteristics of a landscape of the mind, since it was required to be everything that Europe was not.

Many prevailing attitudes toward Africa are present in Guillén's early work. For example, the causes of the migration to the Americas are not sought in the internal structure of particular African societies, which would explain how many slaves arrived in the New World as a result of political expediency, socioeconomic necessity, or even human ruthlessness and greed, as recent scholarly research has since demonstrated. Instead, as the **"Balada de los dos abuelos"** ("Ballad of the Two Grandfathers") indicates, the African is portrayed as an innocent victim of superior European cunning, easily tempted by a few worthless beads into the holds of the slave ship. The pilgrimage to the Americas begins at an unlocalized point in space, where man has not yet imposed his imprint on the landscape. The hot, humid jungles teeming with monkeys and alligators therefore appear as a metonymic sign for a continent, whose most distinguishing feature is its primitiveness:

> Africa de selvas húmedas
> y de gordos gongos sordos . . .
> —¡Me muero!
> (Dice mi abuelo negro.)
> Aguaprieta de caimanes,
> verdes mañanas de cocos . . .
> —¡Me canso!
> (Dice mi abuelo blanco.)
> Oh velas de amargo viento,
> galeón ardiendo en oro . . .
> —¡Me muero!
> (Dice mi abuelo negro.)

> ¡Oh costas de cuello virgen
> engañadas de abalorios . . . !
> —¡Me canso!
> (Dice mi abuelo blanco.)
> ¡Oh puro sol repujado,
> preso en el aro del trópico;
> oh luna redonda y limpia
> sobre el sueño de los monos!

> Africa of the humid jungles
> and big, muffled drums . . .
> —I am dying!
> (Says my black grandfather.)
> Water blackish with alligators,
> mornings green with coconuts . . .
> —I am tired!
> (Says my white grandfather.)
> Oh ships sailing in a bitter wind,
> galleon on fire for gold . . .
> —I am dying!
> (Says my black grandfather.)
> Oh coasts of virgin necks
> deceived with glass beads . . . !
> —I am tired!
> (Says my white grandfather.)
> Oh pure, embossed sun,
> imprisoned in the hoop of the tropics;
> Oh moon, round and limpid
> above the sleep of monkeys!

Here man and nature share the same unspoiled condition, as conveyed by the references to "virgin necks," "pure sun," and "limpid moon." Equally significant is the fact that the European grandfather is characterized by his eyes, the principal organ of perception, while the African grandfather is presented as an earthy, muscular creature:

> Pie desnudo, torso pétreo
> los de mi negro;
> pupilas de vidrio antártico
> las de mi blanco.

> Bare foot, stony torso
> those of my black one;
> pupils of antarctic glass
> those of my white one.

Implicit in the vision of elemental strength embodied by the prototypical African ancestor is the idea of mindless energy, totally committed to a life of sensuality. In this connection, **"Madrigal"** comes readily to mind. To a certain extent, the poem can be regarded as merely a *machista* portrayal of the black woman:

> Tu vientre sabe más que tu cabeza
> y tanto como tus muslos.
> Esa
> es la fuerte gracia negra
> de tu cuerpo desnudo.

> Signo de selva el tuyo,
> con tus collares rojos,
> tus brazaletes de oro curvo,
> y ese caimán oscuro
> nadando en el Zambeze de tus ojos.

> Your belly knows more than your head
> and as much as your thighs.
> That
> is the strong black charm

of your naked body.

Yours is the mark of the jungle,
with your red necklaces,
your bracelets of curved gold,
and that dark alligator
swimming in the Zambezi of your eyes.

However, her metaphorical attributes reveal that her sensuality is an atavistic quality, transmitted to her by her African forebears.

The aconceptual propensity of the African explains his willingness to indulge in singing and dancing, preferably to the pulsating rhythms of the drum. Add alcoholic stupor, and we have the major ingredients of the then popular image of African man:

¡Yambambó, yambambé!
Repica el congo solongo,
repica el negro bien negro;
congo solongo del Songo
baila yambó sobre un pie.

Mamatomba,
serembe cuserembá.

El negro canta y se ajuma,
el negro se ajuma y canta,
el negro canta y se va.

Acuememe serembó,
        aé,
    yambó,
        aé.

Tamba, tamba, tamba, tamba,
tamba del negro que tumba;
tumba del negro, caramba,
caramba, que el negro tumba:
¡yamba, yambó, yambambé!

Yambambó, yambambé!
The Kongo solongo is ringing,
the black man, the real black man, is ringing;
the Kongo solongo from the Songo
is dancing the yambó on one foot.

Mamatomba,
serembe cuserembá.
The black man sings and gets drunk,
the black man gets drunk and sings,
the black man sings and goes away.

Acuememe serembó,
        aé,
    yambó,
        aé,

Bam, bam, bam, bam,
bam of the black man who tumbles;
drum of the black man, wow,
wow, oh the black man is tumbling:
yamba, yambó, yambambé!

"Canto negro" (**"Black Song"**) is no doubt one of the poems which Lloyd King has in mind when he states that Afro-Cubanism simply perpetuates the stereotypical image of the black man as primitive [in his "Mr. Black in Cuba," *African Studies Association of the West Indies Bulletin,* Vol. 5, 1972]. Indeed, the very form of the poem is

the expression of its referential dimension, for it defies translation because its semantic content is at such a minimum. It therefore establishes that the pleasure-seeking creature, which is its subject, has a limited capacity to articulate meaningful sounds.

And yet, perhaps the isolated fragments of intelligible sound—"congo," "Songo," "yambó"—correspond to what Edward Brathwaite would perceive as a genuine desire to reestablish the link with Africa [in his "The African Presence in Caribbean Literature" in *Slavery, Colonialism, and Racism*], particularly since, according to Fernando Ortiz [in his *Hampa afro-cubana: Los negros brujos*], there was still a significant number of the population who had been born in Africa living in Cuba at the time when Guillén came of age. However, as George Lamming has indicated, for the Caribbean writer who lives in a culture where the dominant values are European oriented, the attempt at reconnection is a problematic enterprise, because Africa is so carefully screened from his consciously lived experience. The result is often a feeling of ambivalence. Guillén's poem, ironically entitled **"Mujer nueva"** (**"New Woman"**), serves as an example of this ambivalent attitude, for in his enumeration of the positive qualities of this new African woman, he reduces her to an animal-like status by referring to her *anca fuerte* (strong haunch).

Undoubtedly, as Lamming has asserted, the dilemma of the Afro-Caribbean writer stems from the fact that while he recognizes Africa's contribution to the shaping of his own being, for him, Africa as historical and geographical entity has ceased to have tangible existence. Consequently, as in Guillén's poem, **"La canción del bongo"** (**"Song of the bongo"**), the name, "Bondó," comes to represent absolute negativity:

siempre falta algún abuelo
cuando no sobra algún Don
y hay títulos de Castilla
con parientes en Bondó:

some grandfather *is always missing,*
when some Sir is not left over
and there are titles from Castile
with relatives in Bondó: [critic's italics]

Since the negation of Africa also implies the negation of part of his being, the Caribbean writer often attempts to fill the void with "human significance" [according to George Lamming in *The Pleasures of Exile*]. But this attempt can only be partially successful, for in his engagement with that continent, the writer soon recognizes that he has lost the key to deciphering its true meaning. Names, places, people, kinship systems, political affiliation, nationality—in fact, all the relationships that serve to anchor the self in a society—have now passed into a state of otherness. Hence the sense of loss, so admirably expressed in Guillén's **"El apellido"** (**"The Family Name"**). The crossing of the Atlantic had led to a severing of the links with those who stayed behind: which explains the vaporous nature of the imagery, each time an effort is made to recall the point of origin:

¿Ya conocéis mi sangre navegable,
mi geografía llena de oscuros montes,
de hondos y amargos valles

que no están en los mapas?
¿Acaso visitasteis mis abismos,
mis galerías subterráneas
con grandes piedras húmedas,
islas sobresaliendo en negras charcas
y donde un puro chorro
siento de antiguas aguas
caer desde mi alto corazón
con fresco y hondo estrépito
en un lugar lleno de ardientes árboles,
monos equilibristas,
loros legisladores y culebras?

Do you already know my navigable blood,
my geography full of dark mountains,
of deep and bitter valleys
that are not on the maps?
Did you by chance visit by abysses,
my underground galleries
with big, damp stones,
islands jutting out from black pools
and where I feel a pure stream
of ancient waters
fall from my high heart
with a fresh and deep crash
into a place full of burning trees,
acrobatic monkeys,
legislating parrots and snakes?

No doubt because the new environment does not offer
enough scope for self-actualization, there is a stubborn insistence on inscribing oneself in the original frame of reference:

¿Seré Yelofe?
¿Nicolás Yelofe, acaso?
¿O Nicolás Bakongo?
¿Tal vez Guillén Banguila?
¿O Kumbá?
¿Quizá Guillén Kumbá?
¿O Kongué?
¿Pudiera ser Guillén Kongué?

Am I Yelofe?
Nicolás Yelofe perhaps?
Or Nicolás Bakongo?
Perchance Guillén Banguila?
Or Kumbá?
Maybe Guillén Kumbá?
Or Kongué?
Could I be Guillén Kongué?

However, the series of rhetorical questions point to the bewildering nature of such an undertaking. While the family
names selected are indeed authentic, they represent
groups widely separated on the continent, and so pose the
problem of belonging, or rather no longer belonging, even
more acutely.

The anguished search for roots has been created by a
breakdown in the system of communication:

¿No tengo pues
un abuelo mandinga, congo, dahomeyano?
¿Cómo se llama? ¡Oh, sí, decídmelo!
¿Andrés? ¿Franciso? ¿Amable?
¿Cómo decís Andrés en congo?
¿Cómo habéis dicho siempre
Francisco en dahomeyano?
En mandinga ¿cómo se dice Amable?

Don't I then have
a Mandinka, Congolese, Dahomean grandfa-
ther?
What is his name? On, yes, tell it to me!
Andrés? Francisco? Amable?
How do you say Andrés in Congolese?
How have you always said
Francisco in Dahomean?
In Mandinka, how do you say Amable?

By no longer speaking the language of his ancestors, the
persona is unable to share in those experiences which give
families their cohesion, and thereby signal his right to participate as a full-fledged member. Hence, he can only refer
now to *lejanos primos* (distant cousins).

Despite their remoteness, he still admits to a relationship
with them. However, the years of separation have resulted
in an alteration of both modes of perception. Consequently, acts which are performed in the new environment in
keeping with what is assumed to be the spirit of the old,
often take on a new significance, or undergo a shift in
focus. This is noticeable in the sphere of the dance. The
rumba, for example, was originally a neo-African secular
festival dance which had several movements, and, as with
dance forms in Africa, was dramatic in orientation. However, by the time Guillén came to write his poem,
"Rumba," the dramatic focus of the dance was still retained, but the emphasis was now solely on the erotic element, to the exclusion of other sequences such as the
yambú, which mimed old age:

Pimienta de la cadera,
grupa flexible y dorado:
rumbera buena,
rumbera mala.

Pepper of the hip,
flexible and golden rump
good (female) rumba dancer,
bad (female) rumba dancer.

The above comments by the narrator are African in flavor,
in that they reveal that the audience is not simply a passive
spectator of the performance by the dancing couple. Nevertheless, a new mode of consciousness has intervened,
which results in the simplification of the rhythm of the
music; as well as the reduction of the various movements
of the dance to the single movement of the *guagancó,* an
attraction/repulsion dance of courtship.

A similar transformation can be observed in **"Ebano real"**
("Royal Ebony"), which Olabiyi Yai has aptly defined as
a praise poem [in his seminar paper entitled "Influence
Yoruba dans la poésie Cubaine"]. Indeed, the poem is
structured on the principle of parallelism and repetition,
which Ruth Finnegan has observed to be marked features
of praise poetry [in her *Oral Literature*]. As is customary
in poems of this genre, the first stanza extols the virtues
of the tree:

Te vi al pasar, una tarde,
ébano, y te saludé:
duro entre todos los troncos,
duro entre todos los troncos,
tu corazón recordé.
Arará, cuévano,

arará sabulú.

On passing by one afternoon, I saw you,
ebony, and I greeted you:
hard among all trunks,
hard among all trunks,
I remembered your heart.
Arará, cuévano,
arará sabulú.

But in the rest of the poem, a disproportionate number of
stanzas are devoted to the pursuit of a reward by the pane-
gyrist:

> —Ebano real, yo quiero un barco,
> ébano real, de tu negra madera . . .
> Ahora no puede ser,
> espérate, amigo, espérate,
> espérate a que me muera.

> —Royal ebony, I want a boat,
> royal ebony, from your black wood . . .
> It can't be now,
> wait, my friend, wait,
> wait until I am dying.

While there are instances in African literature when the
panegyric will include the direct request for a reward from
the patron, particularly in the more democratic societies,
where the poet has to survive by his own initiative and enterprise rather than through royal patronage, nevertheless, the emphasis there is still on validating and affirming
the status of the patron, and not, as in Guillén's poem, on
boldly highlighting the profit motive.

In emphasizing the profit motive, perhaps Guillén wishes
to convey an idea of the exploitative nature of relationships in the Caribbean. Needless to say, the Americas are
not the only area where exploitation occurs, since Africa
too has proven vulnerable in that regard. Not only were
parts of the continent ravaged in the past to supply workers for the mines and plantations of the New World, but
even in the twentieth century, Europe has continued to
impose its imperial will on the African continent.

That this is invariably a violent situation is clearly seen
from the title of Guillén's poem, **"Soldados en Abisinia"**
("Soldiers in Abyssinia"). In Mussolini's case, the desire
to restore the empire of the Caesars leads to the incorporation of Ethiopia into the Italian sphere of influence. But
in Guillén's opinion, this gesture will ultimately be unsuccessful because it is founded upon an abstraction:

> El dedo, hijo de César,
> penetra el continente:
> no hablan las aguas de papel,
> ni los desiertos de papel,
> ni las ciudades de papel.
> El mapa, frío, de papel,
> y el dedo, hijo de César,
> con la uña sangrienta, ya clavada
> sobre una Abisinia de papel.

> His finger, child of Caesar,
> pierces the continent:
> the paper waters do not speak,
> nor do the paper deserts,
> nor do the paper cities.
> The cold paper map,

and his finger, child of Caesar,
with its bloody nail, already stuck
on a paper Abyssinia.

In his drive for self-aggrandizement, Mussolini evidently
does not take into consideration the possibility of local resistance to this threat to Ethiopian national sovereignty.
There is therefore a contrast between the passivity of the
"paper Abyssinia" envisaged by Mussolini and the dynamism displayed by a country determined to resist colonial
penetration:

> Abisinia se encrespa,
> se enarca,
> grita,
> rabia,
> protesta.

> Abyssinia gets angry,
> becomes confused,
> shouts,
> rages,
> protests.

By attributing the actions to the country as a whole rather
than to individuals, Guillén implies that this is a mass
movement for liberation.

Nevertheless, the defensive actions taken by the Ethiopians are clearly ineffectual, even if energetic. But instead of
underscoring the Ethiopian defeat, Guillén emphasizes
the high cost of victory to Italy in human lives:

> Entonces, los soldados
> (que no hicieron su viaje sobre un mapa)
> los soldados,
> lejos de Mussolini,
> solos;
> los soldados
> se abrasarán en el desierto,
> y mucho más pequeños, desde luego,
> los soldados
> irán secándose después lentamente al sol,
> los soldados
> devueltos
> en el excremento de los buitres.

> Then, the soldiers
> (who did not travel on a map)
> the soldiers,
> far from Mussolini,
> alone;
> the soldiers
> will be burnt up in the desert,
> and much smaller, of course,
> the soldiers
> afterwards will go on withering slowly in the
>   sun,
> the soldiers
> returned
> in the excrement of the vultures.

Moreover, for Guillén the Italian-Ethiopian War is not
simply a confrontation between colonizer and colonized.
It also represents a class conflict within the ranks of the
colonizers:

> Mussolini, bañado,
> fresco,
> limpio,

vertiginoso.
Mussolini, contento.
Y serio.

¡Ah, pero los soldados
irán cayendo y tropezando!
Los soldados
no harán su viaje sobre un mapa,
sino sobre el suelo de África,
bajo el sol de África.
Alla no encontrarán ciudades de papel;
las ciudades serán algo más que puntos que ha-
    blen
con verdes vocecitas topográficas:
hormigueros de balas,
toses de ametralladoras,
cañaverales de lanzas.

Mussolini, bathed,
fresh,
clean,
dizzy.
Mussolini, happy.
And serious.

Ah, but the soldiers
will go on falling and stumbling!
The soldiers
will not travel on a map,
but on the soil of Africa,
under the sun of Africa.
There they will not find paper cities;
the cities will be something more than dots that
    speak
with little green topographical voices:
swarms of bullets,
coughs of machine-guns,
canefields of lances.

By contrasting the cool calculations of Mussolini, who is isolated from the main theater of events, with the harsh realities encountered by his soldiers, Guillén suggests that the Italian soldiers who go to their deaths in Ethiopia are the unwitting executors of a policy which is contrary to their own interests. The implication is that like the Ethiopians, these soldiers are equally victims of a misguided imperialist decision.

If **"Soldados en Abisinia"** hints at the similarity of conditions among the ranks of the oppressed, and therefore offers the prospect of their potential solidarity, irrespective of race, culture or national origin, **"Mau-Mau"** is exclusively concerned with advocating self-determination for the African victims of colonial oppression. Guillén reveals the Mau Mau to be engaged in an unequal combat against the British settlers, who, supported by their government, use their military and technological superiority, as well as their control of the print media, to overwhelm the Kikuyu fighters physically and psychologically. Dual interpretations of the same event reflect the existence of a compartmentalized colonial world, "inhabited by two different species," already described by Fanon [in *The Wretched of the Earth*]:

Envenenada tinta
habla de los mau-maus;
negros de diente y uña,
de antropofagia y totem.

Gruñe la tinta, cuenta,
dice que los mau-maus
mataron a un inglés . . .
(Aquí en secreto: era
el mismo inglés de kepis
profanador, de rifle
civilizado y remington,
que en el pulmón de África
con golpe seco y firme
clavó su daga-imperio,
de hierro abecedario,
de sífilis, de pólvora,
de money, business, yes.)

Poisoned ink
speaks of the Mau Mau
blacks of tooth and nail,
of anthropophagy and totem.
The ink grunts, relates,
says that the Mau Mau
killed an Englishman . . .
(Confidentially speaking: it was
the same Englishman with the violating
shako, with civilized
rifle and Remington,
who in the lung of Africa
with a dry, firm stroke
stuck his dagger-empire,
of alphabet iron,
of syphilis gunpowder,
of money, business, yes.)

The fundamental conflict of interests lends to seemingly absurd gestures on the part of the Mau Mau:

Tinta de largas letras
cuenta que los mau-maus
arrasan como un río
salvaje las cosechas,
envenenan las aguas,
queman las tierras próvidas,
matan toros y ciervos.
(Aquí en secreto: eran
dueños de diez mil chozas,
del árbol, de la lluvia,
del sol, de la montaña,
dueños de la semilla,
del surco, de la nube,
del viento, de la paz . . .)

Algo sencillo y simple
¡oh inglés de duro kepis!
simple y sencillo: dueños.

Long-typed ink
tells that the Mau Mau
wreck the harvests
like a savage river,
poison the waters,
burn the productive lands,
kill bulls and deer.
(Confidentially speaking: they were
owners of ten thousand huts,
of the tree, of the rain,
of the sun, of the mountain,
owners of the seed,
of the furrow, of the cloud,
of the wind, of peace . . .)

Something plain and simple

Oh Englishman with the hard shako!
simple and plain: owners.

But the apparently illogical "strategy of immediacy" [Frantz Fanon, *The Wretched of the Earth*] that they adopt is in fact a dramatization of their need for a more just sociopolitical order.

Through their disruption of the agricultural economy, they are manifesting their refusal to participate in a system that ascribes to them a permanently inferior status. In attempting to negate the conditions of existence defined for them by the British other, the Mau Mau have taken the first step in what René Depestre would define as a process of "dezombification" [in *Casa de las Américas,* Vol. 58, January-February, 1970], as they strive to recover the land and liberty alienated from them by the British.

It is significant that Guillén refers to the group by the name, "Mau Mau," which, according to Kenneth Grundy [in *Guerilla Struggle in Africa*], was never used by its members to designate themselves, but rather was a term "more generally employed by Europeans, their governments, and their press." By a technique of ironic reversal, already studied by Antonio Ollíz Boyd in another context [in *Blacks in Hispanic Literature*], Guillén gives this originally derogatory term a more positive valorization by revealing the British to be capable of far greater savagery than the Kikuyu whom they denounce:

Letras de larga tinta
cuentan que los mau-maus
casas de sueño y trópico
británicas tomaron
y a fuego, sangre, muerte,
bajo el asalto bárbaro
cien ingleses cayeron. . . .
(Aquí en secreto: eran
los mismos cien ingleses
a quienes Londres dijo:
—Matad, comed mau-maus;
barred, incendiad Kenya;
que ni un solo kikuyus
viva, y que sus mujeres
por siempre de ceniza
servida vean su mesa
y seco vean su vientre.)

Abundant-inked type
relate that the Mau Mau
took British tropical
dream houses
and by fire, blood, death,
under the barbarous assault
one hundred Englishmen fell . . .
(Confidentially speaking: they were
the same one hundred Englishmen
to whom London said:
—Kill, eat Mau Mau;
sweep away, burn Kenya;
let not a single Kikuyu
live, and let their women
see their tables
forever served with ashes
and their wombs barren.)

What the British perceive as a "constitutional depravity" [Franz Fanon, *The Wretched of the Earth*] in the nature of the Mau Mau is thereby revealed to be a political response to a situation which denies the Kikuyu the right to be.

If Guillén's ethnic background, as well as the sociocultural composition of contemporary Cuba, serve to maintain his interest in the problems of twentieth-century Africa, there is no doubt that for him, the historical process is irreversible. While he acknowledges the continuity of the past in the present, he projects a vision of Africa that is not entirely situated in the mythical dimension but is also subject to the forces of contingency. Hence the multiplicity of African images evident in his work. The manifestation of the African presence displayed by the **"Balada del güije"** (**"Ballad of the River-Spirit"**) coexists with a lament for its absence in **"El apellido"** (**"The Family Name"**), while the stereotypical portrait of the primitive African appears side by side with its polar opposite in **"Mau-Maus,"** and the timeless, landless perception of the **"Balada de los dos abuelos"** (**"Ballad of the Two Grandfathers"**) exists alongside of the particularistic, historical version of **"Soldados en Abisinia"** (**"Soldiers in Abyssinia"**). Racial heritage, as well as common human experiences and ideals, make it possible for the poet to capture the African continent in a variety of attitudes. But cognizant of the effects of time and history, Guillén's interpretation is grounded in a recognition of his own difference. Hence there is no attempt

Photo of Guillén and Langston Hughes taken by Carl Van Vechten.

at a facile identification. The essential perspective on Africa remains that of "a Yoruba from Cuba." (pp. 124-43)

> *Lorna V. Williams, "The African Presence in the Poetry of Nicolás Guillén," in Africa and the Caribbean: The Legacies of a Link, edited by Margaret E. Crahan and Franklin W. Knight, The Johns Hopkins University Press, 1979, pp. 124-45.*

Ian I. Smart   (essay date 1982)

[*In the following essay, Smart discusses the presence of an idealized black female persona called the* mujer nueva *in Guillén's poetry.*]

One of the direct results of Nicolás Guillén's turning fully to his African roots as a source of poetic inspiration was the creation of the **"Mujer nueva."** This is the title of a poem published in **Sóngoro cosongo** in 1931; but more than a title, it stands as an apt description of the new poetic persona that began to grace Guillén's poetry. The *mujer nueva,* in contrast to the female poetic personae that preceded and some of those that followed her, is black. Now the fact that Guillén characterized his new interest in and assertion of African cultural values as a process of *mulatez* is of particular concern for today's readers. For certainly, *mestizaje,* its socio-political counterpart, has become suspect to many contemporary black scholars. And today, more than forty years after Guillén first made it his artistic rallying call, *mulatez* itself seems no longer to be an ingenious response to the centuries of neglect and scorn for the African component of Cuba's culture. The article will study the figure of the *mujer nueva* in the context of Guillén's total work, and with particular reference to the question of *mulatez* as a formula for fully expressing the African cultural heritage in a truly Cuban poetry.

Born in 1902, Guillén wrote his first verses as early as 1917 in clever imitation of both Latin American and European models—for example, Rubén Darío, Campoamor, Bécquer, and the poets of the Vanguard era. However, in April 1930, Guillén began to write an entirely new kind of poetry which for the first time showed appropriate recognition of and respect for African models, notably those Africans born in Cuba who had created a rich oral literature. An important form of this oral literature, the *son,* is in fact the central inspiration of the first of the new poems—**"Los motivos de son."** In October of the following year, the *Motivos* as well as other poems in the new style were published by the author in **Sóngoro cosongo,** which also bore the extremely provocative subtitle, *Poemas mulatos.* The prolog to the original edition contains these words of explanation and challenge: "Diré finalmente, que esos son unos versos mulatos. Participan acaso de los mismos elementos que entran en la composición étnica de Cuba, donde todos somos un poco níspero." He continues in the next paragraph: "Opino, por lo tanto, que una poesía criolla entre nosotros no lo será de modo cabal con olvido del negro. . . . Por lo pronto el espíritu de Cuba es mestizo. . . . " In an article published in 1937 [**"Cuba: pueblo y poesía"** in *Ultra,* No. 8, Feb., 1937], the poet gave a further explanation of what he meant by *versos*

mulatos. "No hay una poesía negra en Cuba, como no hay una poesía blanca. Hay, simplemente, una formidable contribucíon del hombre negro a la poesía nacional, liberada al fin, dueña de sí misma, y en la que no sea fácil discriminar las esencias que la integran."

Mulatez, then, is a fitting label for the artistic process to which Guillén's poetry was subjected in the 1930's, for it clearly consists of the injection of African cultural values into the exclusively European oriented Cuban literature. In the course of this article, *mulatez* will be seen through the creation of an African inspired set of metaphors to describe the female poetic persona. They are an example of *mulatez* because they result from the wedding of European form and language to an African world-view. The *son* poems are the best examples of the process, since they represent the purest form of what Guillén has called the *estilo mulato,* for they are a blend of the European with African forms as well as content. However, the image of the new woman, developed in poems like **"Mujer nueva," "Madrigal,"** and others to be studied here, represents the culmination of the process of *mulatez* in one of its applications, namely, to the female poetic persona. Guillén, in the 1930's, emphatically prescribed *mulatez* not only for his poetry but for all truly Cuban poetry. It is through this process that the poet found his true voice and rose to the level of model for other poets rather than being simply a clever imitator.

The first of the three free-verse stanzas of the poem **"Mujer nueva,"** from **Sóngoro cosongo,** reads as follows:

> Con el círculo ecuatorial
> ceñido a la cintura como a un pequeño mundo,
> la negra, mujer nueva,
> avanza en su ligera bata de serpiente.

The black woman is aptly called nueva, for prior to the process of *mulatez* she is conspicuously absent. The poet's earliest female personae came directly from the pages of his exclusively non-African oriented models, the Modernists, the post-Modernists, and the Vanguard poets. Thus in **"Mariposa,"** he speaks of: " . . . la linda rosa de tu cara," or more unequivocally in **"Madrigal trirrimo"**—written in the same year, 1921—he describes the persona as having "cabellera de oro." In **"Ven al jardín,"** a poem of this same period, the racial identity of the female persona is clearly revealed in the line: "tu mano de azucena entre las mías," while in **"Laca,"** another poem of the period, we see his amorous admiration centered on an Asiatic beauty: "Eres todo china, japonesa toda. . . . " These images then, even the last mentioned, are a clear consequence of the dominant influence exercised by the Modernists and others on the young poet.

Not only is the black woman presented as new, but she is also a cosmic figure closely tied to nature. This latter aspect is consistent with a cosmovision that was believed to be peculiarly African. In fact, the Afro-Antilleans and the Negritude poetry of the period abounds in images which personify nature and natural phenomena, giving a deep sense of the black man's closeness to nature. In Rosa Valdés-Cruz's estimation [in *La poesía negroide en América*], for example, the feature of humanizing nature accounts for Palés Matos' originality. Léopold Sédar Senghor, one of the original three Negritude poets, says quite clearly [in *Liberté 1: Négritude et humanisme*] that in African aesthetics " . . . toute la Nature est animée d'une présence humaine." The most stirring poetic expression of this approach is to be found in these lines of Aimé Césaire, another of the original Negritude poets, where he speaks of black people as:

> véritablement les fils aînés du monde
> poreux à tous les souffles du monde
>
> . . . . .
>
> chair de la chair du monde palpitant du mouvement même du monde!
>
>   (*Cahier d'un retour au pays natal*)

Guillén develops this idea in parallel fashion in the second stanza of **"Mujer nueva."** The woman/nature image is as clearly expressed as is the idea of her newness:

> Coronada de palmas,
> como una diosa recién llegada,
> ella trae la palabra inédita,
> el anca fuerte,
> la voz, el diente, la mañana y el salto.

In the significant opening poem, **"Llegada,"** of the same book (*Sóngoro cosongo*) the theme of the newly arrived black people is manifestly central. The poem is also written in free verse with neither rhyme not metric regularity, and its initial stanza strikes the same chords as those struck in the lines above:

> ¡Aquí estamos!
> La *palabra* nos viene húmeda *de los bosques*
> *y un sol* enérgico nos amanece *entre las venas.*
> El puño es *fuerte*
> y tiene el remo. [My italics]

The evident similarities are certainly not accidental. These new people like the new woman are strong beings, bringing a new word that is life inducing like the damp forests. They are a people infused with and almost transformed into nature. The poet is thus drawing from a consistent and profound vision in his elaboration of the series of metaphors describing the new black woman. In a **"Madrigal,"** he apostrophizes in similar terms:

> Signo de selva el tuyo,
>
> . . . . .
>
> y ese caimán oscuro
> nadando en el Zambeze de tus ojos.

There are disquieting echoes of the stereotyped, picturesque and ultimately unflattering depictions of Africa, popular with the white poets of the Afro-Antillean school. Such is the Africa painted, for example, in the following lines of Palés Matos:

> ¡Oh, mi fino, mi melado Duque de la Mermelada!
> ¿Dónde están tus *caimanes* en el lejano aduar del Pongo,
> y la sombra azul y redonda de tus baobabs africanos
> y tus quince mujeres olorosas a *selva* y a fango?
> [My italics]
>
>   ("Elegia del Duque de la Mermelada")

However, it can be said that at least Palés Matos and the others were of a single mind in their attempts, with varying degrees of success, to imbue their verses with an African spirit and flavor. And furthermore, their insights are corroborated by a long list of eminent scholars of African cultures and civilizations, whose findings point to a widely based and, in fact, characteristic tendency to personalize natural phenomenon and even attributes of God. Guillén, then, makes the black woman the representative of these personifications. She is the universe—"un pequeño mundo"—whose eyes are a river, and whose waist is the equator. She is a "diosa," the personification of a divine attribute.

Some of the most successful imagery created by the poet along these lines is to be found in another **"Madrigal"** which proclaims the black woman's singular beauty. The images in this poem are spontaneously appealing, but the careful reader will find that they are simply the translation into poetic language of the complex woman/nature associations. These associations are predicated on ontological principles that have been shown to be African. The poem is again in free verse, and reads as follows:

> De tus manos gotean
> las uñas, en un manojo de diez uvas moradas.
> Piel,
> carne de tronco quemado,
> que cuando naufraga en el espejo, ahúma
> las algas tímidas del fondo.

G. R. Coulthard indicates that the note of frank sensuality is struck in the descriptions of "coloured" women by Caribbean poets precisely through the use of fruit imagery [*Race and Colour in Caribbean Literature*]. Guillén here goes beyond the baseness of simply equating the woman to some succulent fruit, ripe for the plucking and eating. The "uvas moradas" are not to be eaten but to be admired. His image is thus touched with an unparalleled delicacy, and, indeed, like all the images of the poem, it is strikingly novel. The black woman is a mysterious presence like dark grapes, like a burned tree trunk, whose powerful smokey blackness penetrates to the depth of the mirror which is the sea and the world at the same time, and leaves its indelible stamp there.

The water related metaphor recalls these following stanzas from **"Rumba,"** yet another poem of the same book:

> En el agua de tu bata
> todos mis ansias navegan:
>
> . . . . .
>
> Anhelo el de naufragar
> en ese mar tibio y hondo:
> ¡fondo
> del mar!

Janheinz Jahn, who wrote extensively on the subject of African cultures and literatures, suggests that the *rumba* has its origin in another dance called the *yuka,* which is itself "obviously the secular equivalent of the dances of Oshún when she meets Shango" [*Munte: The New African Culture*]. Now Oshún is the divinity or orisha who "rules over rivers and over all fresh waters," and is in Yorubaland represented as a river, according to Jahn. Such religious tenets were, up until the very recent past at least, commonplace among the hundreds of thousands of Africans who still comprise a fair share of Cuba's population. These tenets must have provided the basis for Guillén's novel images. The poet seems to have taken the justifiable license of extending Oshún's dominion to include the sea.

The image of the "carne de tronco quemado" has resonances that are also of particular significance for Cuba's African population. Jahn and others point out the special place that trees have in African ontological systems. Speaking specifically of the Bantu, Jahn says that for them trees are " . . . the road travelled by the dead, the loas, to living men; they are the repository of the deified." Guillén converts this aspect of the philosophical system of many of his African ancestors and compatriots into successful poetry in works like, **"Ebano real,"** and **"Acana,"** poems from *El son entero* (1943). The *caña,* for obvious socio-economic, historical and geographical reasons, is the tree that most attracts the poet's creative imagination. His extremely beautiful poem, **"Caña"**—also from *Sóngoro cosongo*—is among the most important of the anti-imperialist works. In addition, the *caña* became an apt symbol of feminine beauty and grace, as is evidenced in this opening couplet of another **"Madrigal,"** this time from *West Indies Ltd* (1934): "Sencilla y vertical, / como una caña en el cañaveral".

The composite image is enriched by the new element contained in these lines which constitute the last stanza of **"Mujer nueva"**:

> Chorro de sangre joven
> bajo un pedazo de piel fresca,
> y el pie incansable
> para la pista profunda del tambor.

The *tambor,* of course, could not be left out. However, the image that is most important, in view of its repeated presence in Guillén's poetic universe, is "el pie incansable." Physical strength characterizes the new black woman, as it does the new people of **"Llegada."** "El puño . . . fuerte" of this latter poem was already seen. A similar image, " . . . el anca fuerte," appears in the second stanza of **"Mujer nueva."** In a **"Madrigal"** the poet speaks of " . . . la fuerte gracia negra / de tu cuerpo desnudo." More than mere brute strength, which would be appropriate in a horse or ox, the black men's strength has a quality of endurance and resistance to bodily hardship. Thus in **"Llegada"** the poet hails: "Nuestro pie, / duro y ancho." Like the black men, the black woman is as hard as nails. At the same time she is endowed with the flexible grace of the cane plant. So the **"Madrigal"** which began with the couplet quoted above ends with this telling image: " . . . tus muslos de metal."

Sensuality clearly has some role to play in the shaping of the image of the new black woman. Without any deeper underlying significance, the sensuous depiction of the black woman would richly deserve all the censure it has received from discerning critics, the most prominent of whom is G. R. Coulthard. Their view is that the white poets of the Afro-Antillean school—Palés Matos again being the best example—have converted the black woman into a mindless, hip-swaying, erotic animal. Some of Guillén's images display signs of this approach. In **"Mujer nueva"** he speaks of the black woman's *anca,* and in

"Rumba," it becomes a *grupa.* These terms, so dear to the Afro-Antillean poetic school, are more frequently used of animals than of persons. However, what distinguishes Guillén's treatment of the black woman is the overall, consistent, and real black consciousness from which it springs.

The corpus of metaphors examined in the preceding pages attests to the existence of precisely such a consciousness, and gives evidence of the direct and profound influence of the poet's African cultural roots. The image of the new black woman that these metaphors constitute is undeniably, then, a consequence of the process of *mulatez.*

There were some hints of these metaphors in the poet's works prior to 1930. The poem **"Aguafuerte,"** for example, from the collection *Cérebro y corazón,* compiled by the poet in 1922 but withheld from publication at that time, is a sonnet in which the woman's beauty is cleverly compared to that of nature. It begins: "Unió la noche al resplandor del día / para formar tus ojos." **"Granate,"** a sonnet from this collection, begins: "Ya en tu carne hay ardores meridionales," while in **"Sol de lluvia,"** a poem of the Vanguard period—it was published in 1927—the following startling image is used: "el sol está borracho / tendido en medio de la calle." The whole poem of three four-line stanzas is based on the image of a very human sun whose behavior is like that of a public drunk. The bold almost blasphemous tone of the image rather recalls Lautréamount's *Chants de Maldoror* and the school of those late nineteenth-century *poètes maudits.* It is very far removed from the dignity of the religious-oriented personifications of the African models.

"Agua del recuerdo," shows the female poetic persona as "una mulata de oro." The very same image reappears in **"El negro mar,"** another poem from *El son entero* (1943). This raises the question of the philosophical significance, if any, that Guillén attaches to the biological difference between the *mulata* and the *negra.* In the socio-economic realm, the distinction between the two is very important, and it provides the basic inspiration of the poem **"Mulata,"** one of the original *son* poems. The last stanza of this four-stanza *son* expresses an unmistakable sentiment:

> Si tú supiera, mulata,
> la veddá;
> ¡que yo con mi negra tengo,
> y no te quiero pa na!

This rather flat-footed formulation, in the so-called "black dialect" that Guillén used for the first and last time in *Motivos de son,* is a rare occurrence in his poetry. In fact it is extremely difficult to find any similar stated preference for the *mulata* over the *negra* or vice versa, even after a most careful reading of his works. The issue appears to be of no consequence, and there is good reason for this. A position of assertive African consciousness that adopts the name *mulatez* would certainly be an untenable absurdity if it posited any fundamental distinction between black and mulatto.

Whereas with the discovery of *mulatez,* the black woman (*mulata* or *negra*) exclusively occupies the poet's attention, this is not so in his published works subsequent to *La paloma de vuelo popular* (Buenos Aires: Losada, 1958). The poet clearly links his earlier works, in which the white female persona predominates to the complete exclusion of the black, to his imperfect understanding of what constitutes truly Cuban art. The reinstating of the white female persona might be construed as a renunciation of the principles of *mulatez*. In a fairly recent article the poet gives an explanation of the relationship between his work and his involvement in Cuba's political life. This explanation, which must be related to the poet's reason for returning to the apparently shelved motif, can be accurately represented by the following: "Repito que yo creo que mi adhesión permanente a lo largo de cerca de cuarenta años a la revolución, y por tanto a sus medios expresivos, dejó un poco en la penumbra de mi espíritu ciertas zonas creadoras . . . , lo cual hace que salga a flote lo que había estado sumergido." If Guillén's love poetry bears out the accuracy of this analysis, the same can also be said of the poetry of a more experimental nature within the European poetic tradition. Preoccupied with the revolution, of which *mulatez* is an integral part, the poet put aside his amorous verses. In 1964, quite consistent with his autoanalysis outlined above, he published a collection entitled *Poemas de amor* which contained all his previously unpublished love poems. It is in these poems, and others either not published or not composed prior to the full flowering of the Cuban revolution in 1959, that the white female persona reappears.

Although the very title of the poem **"Alta niña de caña y amapola"** (written in Moscow in 1957) brings back echoes of the new black woman, the female persona it presents does not seem to be racially black, for she has green eyes: " . . . la verde, la metálica / naturaleza de sus ojos." In addition, the poet's final salutation is couched in language that bespeaks the influence of *mulatez*:

> Oh tú, bienesperada,
> suave administradora
> del fuego y de la danza,
> alta niña de caña y amapola.

She is a vibrant and strong dancer. The rhythm of her dance is close to the rhythm of nature, for she is one with nature, a "niña de caña."

"Ana María," from *Poemas de amor,* was written in Bucharest in 1962. Again, the geographical location of its composition as well as certain other clues leave the impression that the persona is nonblack. The clue here is the reference to the "trenza que te cae / sobre el pecho, ..." Ana María is strong in exactly the same way that the *mujer nueva* is, having "un cuerpo metálico." The last lines suggest that her metalic body is somehow infused with a storm that stretches like a slow smooth suspended serpent, not unlike the flexible cane plant:

> Es cuando te recorren
> las nubes pensativas
> y en tu cuerpo metálico
> la tempestad se estira,
> como una lenta y suave
> serpiente suspendida.

In itself the metaphor is a meaningful image of a potential-

ly tempestuous woman, pensive to the point of brooding, with the flexible grace, strength, and perhaps venom of a serpent. Now this article has outlined a series of images which are associated with the figure of the *mujer nueva,* and which seem to be at the core of Guillén's poetic imagination in that they have been shown to be related to the most significant aspect of his work. In the light of this analysis, the stanza quoted above has to be considered a part of the broader and more fundamental *mujer nueva* cycle.

Even in this later phase there are poems that continue to be full expressions of the image of the new black woman as was elaborated in the period between *Motivos de son* and *La paloma de vuelo popular.* Such a poem is **"Julieta,"** the initial work of *Poemas de amor.* The woman portrayed has flesh that is "amasada con yodo, / con canela, con bronce y con agua del mar." She is then a *mulata* whose flesh is the flesh of the waters of the sea.

The image of the new black woman thus survives intact all the political and other vicissitudes that affected Guillén's art. When the poet apparently began again to preoccupy himself with the nonblack female poetic persona that once exclusively peopled his universe, he did so while remaining true to the essential vision of the *mujer nueva.* What results is not the substitution of the black *mujer nueva* by a return to the white female persona, but rather an attempt on the part of the poet to "universalize" the image of the new black woman. The set of metaphors that this article has shown to compose the complex image of the new black woman is the most frequently and consistently used. In fact it is difficult, if not impossible, to find any other set of metaphors used in a demonstrably systematic way by the poet to describe the female persona. This set of metaphors, then, is the most impressive and thus artistically the most successful. The fact that they are African inspired substantiates Guillén's assertion that the only true Cuban art—and for this very reason, the best—is that which incorporates African cultural elements.

Critics, notably Walterio Carbonell, have suggested that the *mulatez* period is the ultimate plateau in Guillén's artistic development precisely because *mulatez* is an inadequate formula. They sustain the point of view that the perfect blending of African and European aesthetic principles—a blend that Guillén definitely envisages and attempts to achieve—can only be attained when the two meet and merge as equals. Furthermore, they contend that, granted the centuries of neglect, the full and proper assertion of the African cultural heritage could not be achieved in a decade. Certainly in the socio-economic and political realm, *mestizaje* or *mulatez,* in Cuba as in the rest of Latin America, has always meant the subjugation of the African to the European principle, at best, and very frequently the total annihilation of the African principle. It would follow then that the formula devised by Guillén in the 1930's was a satisfactory means of drawing attention to the problem of cultural racism, but not an adequate solution. The incompleteness of the formula would also seem of necessity to predicate a corresponding incompleteness in the artistic expression that it gives birth to. (pp. 379-87)

Judgments always imply a risk, but for those who dare to judge, the evidence has been presented. However, it is perhaps more satisfying to enjoy and appreciate the beautiful and significantly black song that Guillén has created and sung, without making any quixotic attempt to measure it against an ideal "Black Poetry." It is certainly less problematic to do so, and perhaps infinitely wiser. (p. 388)

> Ian I. Smart, " 'Mulatez' and the Image of the Black 'mujer nueva' in Guillén's Poetry," in Kentucky Romance Quarterly, *Vol. 29, No. 4, 1982, pp. 379-90.*

Roberto González Echevarría (essay date Spring 1987)

[*González Echevarría is a Cuban-born American educator and critic. In the following essay, he argues for the literary merit of Guillén's poetry apart from its political significance.*]

The most advanced criticism on Nicolás Guillén has shown that he is not one poet but many. The monolithic Guillén, chiseled and shaped by official critics and bureaucrats into a monument called The National Poet of Cuba, simply will not do any longer. We are in a phase in which Guillén's work, having all of its moral and political battles behind it, must test itself in the broader arena of modern poetry. Who but the most recalcitrant ideologues would deny that Guillén made manifest the dignity of Afro-Antillean culture through his poetry, or that he eloquently denounced the many injustices to which blacks were and still are subjected? Who but, again, the most recalcitrant and dull-minded ideologues would want to persist in heaping praise on his works for reasons that, though in some ways valid, are not related to their poetic worth? One often hears the name of Guillén alongside those of the major Spanish-American poets of this century (César Vallejo, Pablo Neruda, Octavio Paz, José Lezama Lima), but one is always left with the impression that his inclusion obeys more a desire to do justice to the marginal to whom he gave a voice than to the conviction that his works are of the highest order. Is Guillén merely an Afro-Cuban poet or simply a poet? Does Guillén need the rhetorical pedestal erected by the State, or can he stand on his own two feet as poet? I would not be writing this essay if I did not believe the latter. Guillén is a major writer as Afro-Antillean poet—Afro-Antilleanism being not merely a thematic with sociopolitical relevance but also part of a general poetic revision at the core of modern poetry written in the Spanish language. Guillén's deserved prominence is due to his contribution to this revisionary process, which is as vast as the redefinition of poetry carried out by the English and German Romantics, and which distinguishes the history of Hispanic poetry from that of other Western traditions.

A central feature of that revision is a return to the Baroque, that is to say, to the work of the major poets of the language, Góngora, Quevedo, and Calderón, and to the Baroque aesthetics formulated by Baltasar Gracián. The inversion of the concept of representation from mimesis to expression envisioned by the Romantics was already implicit in the Spanish Baroque. As the Spanish and Spanish-American Romantics were a mere echo of their European counterparts, the great Hispanic poets of the avant-garde had to search for their poetic foundation not in the Romantics, as their English and German counterparts did, but in the Baroque. While it is a commonplace of Spanish literary history to say that the Generation of '27 in Spain looked to Góngora for inspiration, the fact is that the revision which brought about Góngora's rediscovery began in Spanish America with the *modernistas*—José Martí and Rubén Darío in particular—and continued in the writings of the Mexican Alfonso Reyes during the teens. It also has not been made sufficiently clear that both the Spanish-American and the Spanish writers looked to the Baroque poets because there were no Spanish language romantics worthy of rediscovery or rejection: no Goethe, no Coleridge, no Wordsworth, no Schiller, no Leopardi, only Espronceda, Bécquer, and in Spanish America Heredia, Echeverría, all minor poets, no matter how much we strain to find traces of originality in their works. The great Spanish-language poetic tradition that begins with the *modernistas* and makes yet another start in the twenties with the Generation of '27 has as foundation a rewriting of the Baroques. Guillén was no exception, though the way in which he rewrote them was certainly exceptional. To delve into the poetics of Afro-Antilleanism, one has to understand the Baroque poets. I will try to make my point by examining *Motivos de son* (1930), the book that established Guillén's reputation.

. . . . .

Why the Baroque? From outside the cultures of the Spanish-speaking world it is difficult to fathom why a movement that is so apparently European should be of any concern to modern Spanish-American writers. Even to those within the Spanish-speaking world who look at it from the perspective of the history of European literature, the Baroque seems to be something left behind a long time ago. And yet a host of modern Spanish-American writers have made of the Baroque a banner for their new art, calling it the Neo-Baroque. These artists, chief among them Severo Sarduy, are inspired in this endeavor by forerunners belonging to Guillén's generation, for whom the Baroque was a central source of concern: Alejo Carpentier and José Lezama Lima. Others, like Octavio Paz and Carlos Fuentes, have implicitly and explicitly paid homage to the Spanish and Spanish-American Baroque of the seventeenth and eighteenth centuries in works such as *Blanco* and *Terra Nostra.*

As a deviation from the classicist aesthetics of the Renaissance, the Baroque was the first literary movement to bear an original Spanish seal. It is precisely for this reason that the Spanish Baroque was considered anathema by Neo-Classicists in and out of Spain and Spanish-America. It was thought to be a species of Spanish malady, a penchant for excess, for ornamentation, that broke away from mainstream European aesthetics. In English, Gongorism has a negative connotation. The collegiate *Webster's* defines it as "the literary style of Góngora y Argote, Spanish poet (d. 1627), characterized by affected metaphor and the use of strained conceits." The unabridged *Webster's* displays an even more negative tone:

> *Gongorism . . .* a Spanish literary style esp. associated with the poet Góngora and his imitators characterized by a studied obscurity of meaning and expression and by extensive use of metaphorical imagery, exaggerated conceits, paradoxes, neologisms, and other ornate devices— compare EUPHUISM. 2a: an excessively involved ornate and artificial style of writing. . . .

Affectation, artificiality, obscurity of meaning—these are the symptoms of the disease which can only be cured by a good dosage of communicable meaning, essential features, clarity, transparency, in short, the classical ideal of symmetry. No one was more critical of Gongora than his own contemporaries, who lampooned him mercilessly while calling for a return to Renaissance aesthetics. Yet Góngora's influence was enormous, particularly in the New World, where he was not only imitated but annotated, and where a widespread fancy for his poetry generated what can now be seen as the first Spanish-American literary movement.

The Spanish poets of the Generation of '27 (so called because of the anniversary of Góngora's death), were the first to attempt a self-conscious revision of Baroque literature. Góngora, Dámaso Alonso claimed, was a poet of light not darkness; his complex language conveyed meaning as it created a world of pure beauty. To some, Góngora's world was not too far from that of Mallarmé, who had himself found a forerunner in the Spanish poet. The Spanish-American revision of Góngora and of the Baroque in general goes even further than the one proposed and practiced by the poets of '27. This reading does not attempt to make the Cordobesan into a poet of light, but to celebrate the difficulty of his language, his hermeticism, his eccentricity, his difference. It is here that Guillén fits in, though in many ways the Cuban belongs also to the Generation of '27. Yes, Góngora is obscure, but only because his poetics worked at the margins of the Western tradition, at the point where the tradition subverts itself by nurturing forces that negate its mainstream ideology. Góngora is, in fact, ornamental, artificial, obscure, because for him beauty is not found (paradoxically) in the tenets of the Greco-Latin tradition that he supposedly attempted to emulate. Góngora's poetry is inclusive rather than exclusive, willing to create and incorporate the new, literally in the form of neologisms. He is anxious to overturn the tyranny of syntax, making the hyperbaton the most prominent feature of his poetry. It is for this reason, and not by some quirk, that Góngora was the first to write poems imitating the speech of blacks, or better yet, *in* the speech of blacks. The sounds of African words, which were bizarre to the Spanish ear, were akin to those of the highly Latinate and Greek neologisms for which Góngora had such a penchant, and to the apparent breaks in syntactical flow. Although Latinate syntax was perhaps normal to the Latin ear (but when, and what Latin?), Góngora's version in Spanish is close to linguistic noise. The Greco-Latin tradition that Góngora supposedly idealized seems to me like an entelechy created by his commentators and critics. Góngora's style is not always "high"; nor does he

attempt to purge reality of base or heterogeneous elements. Reality did not enter into his formula either to be accepted or rejected; its representation did. And here Góngora, like Cervantes and Velázquez, liked to juxtapose received forms of representation—"high" and "low"— critically. Everything can be a part of beauty, even that which is not altogether comprehensible, and, worse yet, even that which appears to be ugly, grotesque, or monstrous.

This inclusiveness of Góngora's, whether he knew it or not, is seen as a break with tradition by Spanish-American artists and commentators, perhaps because they felt that it could contain their world. As I said before, Góngora was assiduously read, imitated, and annotated in the New World. The new American sensibility found in the Baroque an avenue for the different, the strange, that is to say, the American. Studies have shown that it was in Baroque churches that native artisans were able to include, in the cornucopia of figures, their own mythological beings, as well as elements of American nature, such as fruit that were exotic to the Europeans. The Baroque allowed for a break with the Greco-Latin tradition by allowing the fringes, the frills, as it were, to proliferate, upsetting the balance of symmetry, displacing the centrality of Renaissance aesthetics, and occupying an important position. Through its capaciousness and proliferation the Baroque inscribed the American. The speech of blacks in Góngora's poetry is like the presence of Inca or Aztec deities on church friezes.

Since it was in the Baroque that a creole sensibility began to assert itself, it was in the Baroque that the avant-garde sought the origins of its own poetic language. Hence, as we shall see, Guillén's "deviations" find their origin in the inclusiveness and assumed marginality of the Baroque.

This aesthetics of difference is another way of saying that the Baroque incorporates the Other; it plays at being Other. In the Renaissance the Other is analyzed, speculated about, described. According to Montaigne, the natives of the New World should have been left alone to worship their own gods and be different. The Baroque assumes the strangeness of the Other as an awareness of the strangeness of Being. Being is being as monster, at once one and the other, the same and different; Segismundo in the tower in Calderón's *Life Is a Dream* is half man, half animal. This is what is at stake in Baroque art: an awareness of otherness within oneself, of newness. In this way, the Baroque is a phenomenon parallel to Descartes's meditation on the self as thinking subject that questions all received knowledge. The feeling of being in the Baroque is more concrete than Descartes's *cogito;* it is more tangible. It is a sense of one's own rarity, of oddity, of distortion. Hence the plurality of New World culture, its being-in-the-making as something not quite achieved, of something heterogeneous and incomplete, is expressed in the Baroque.

Chief among those who discovered this foundational character of the Baroque was Alejo Carpentier. In his 1974 novella *Concierto barroco* [Baroque Concert] Carpentier suggests ways in which the Baroque is related to the aesthetics of Afro-Cubanism to which I am much indebted and which, I believe, clarify the perspective from which I read Guillén's poems in this essay. In *Concierto barroco* Carpentier creates two characters who chart the course of Baroque aesthetics in the New World: a rich *indiano* (a Spaniard born in the New World) who returns to the Old World from Mexico, and Filomeno, his black servant. Filomeno claims to be a descendant of Salvador Galomón, the black protagonist of *Espejo de paciencia* [Mirror of Patience], a Cuban Baroque epic written in 1608 by Silvestre de Balboa y Troya de Quesada. Filomeno's literary genealogy makes of Carpentier's novella a metafictional statement on literary history that is like a manifesto of Afro-Antillean Baroque aesthetics. Filomeno brings to the Old World his fiercely independent set of values as well as his shockingly visible physical difference: his color, which makes him an object of curiosity and desire. But the *indiano* also feels different in Europe. Home for him is already the New World, with its hybrid cornucopia of colors and forms.

Significantly, the only time when both master and servant feel at home is during a gigantic jam session organized at the Ospedale della Pietá. In this cacophonous celebration, mixing music from various parts of the world, Filomeno injects his own chant to kill a snake, with the refrain *"Cala-basón, / Son-són,"* that the others (which include Händel and Scarlatti) mispronounce as *"Kabbala-sum-sum."* Upon being deformed by the Europeans, "Calaba son" ["I am Carabali," "I am from Calabar"] reveals perhaps a common, plural origin in the Kabbala, a source of occult, encoded knowledge that, like the elements of black aesthetics, differs from the Western tradition. The "son," like Guillén's, is a celebration of the plurality of difference, with an emphasis on the physical joy and liberation of the ritualistic dance. Later in the novella Carpentier drives home his point by having Filomeno leave his master to attend a concert by Louis Armstrong in Paris; the time of the novel leaps from the eighteenth century to the 1920s, from the end of the Baroque to the years of Afro-Antilleanism and the Harlem Renaissance, thereby showing their common historical lineage. Carpentier's *Concierto barroco* is in many ways one of the most perceptive pieces of criticism on Guillén's poetry and a clarification of its vast genealogy and progeny.

. . . . .

It would be easy to document Guillén's indebtedness to the Spanish Golden Age poets, particularly the Baroques, by employing the conventions of philological criticism. Like the Spanish poets of the Generation of '27, the Cuban makes no secret of his admiration for those poets who are the classics of the language. Such admiration is not only explicit, but is inscribed in his verse. For instance, how can one fail to hear in the **"Que siga el son"** section of *West Indies, Ltd.* (1934) a clear echo of Quevedo's and Góngora's *letrillas*? When Guillén says:

> —Coroneles de terracota,
> políticos de quita y pon;
> café con pan y mantequilla.
> ¡Qué siga el son!

> Clay colonels,
> disposable politicos;

give me bread with butter on,
let the *son* go on!

one can hear Góngora's sardonic:

> Hablen otros del gobierno,
> del mundo y sus monarquías,
> mientras gobiernen mis días
> mantequillas v pan tierno;
> y en las mañanas de invierno,
> naranjada y aguardiente,
> ¡Y ríase la gente!

> Let others worry about
> the world and its monarchies,
> while my days are ruled
> by butter and fresh bread;
> and on winter morns,
> orange juice and a stiff drink.
> And let them laugh at me!

Quevedian echoes are heard in the "Sátiras políticas" and in the sonnet **"El abuelo"** [The Grandfather] in *West Indies, Ltd.,* whose theme is the Baroque *desengaño* so dear to Góngora and other poets of his time: here the blond hair's kink reveals the presence of a black ancestor. I wonder if anyone has noticed that the grandfather is a maroon—not only is he fleeing in the distant memory, but fleeing appears to be his mode of being: "La dulce sombra del abuelo que huye" [The sweet shadow of the fleeing grandfather]. That *sombra,* that shadow, is also a Baroque conceit that means both black and furtive, difficult to grasp. The truth hidden beneath the lady's white skin, the secret protected by her blond hair, is revealed in the curls. These are all Baroque figures, including the curls, but particularly the fact that the truth is concealed, encrypted in a proliferation of visual, yet false, signs. The Rubensian pinkness of the lady is a simulacrum, the niveous landscape of her skin is rushing headlong toward a darkness that is her true origin. Black is truth, white falseness; a reversal, an inversion of the traditional European meaning of these signs manifests their instability, their dependence on an economy of social exchange that devalues the real. Beauty, even the sonnet's, is dependent on an untruth, or at least on an interplay of superficial signs bearing both truth and the contrived beauty that conceals it. Light and shadow, black and white, inversions, conceits, chains of tropes—these are all contained in the one hundred and fifty-four syllables of the sonnet. Being is an elaborate simulation in a social space, changing one's appearance, one's body to conform, to pass. This Baroque sonnet is not the only one to be found in Guillén's works. He continues to produce sonnets in this style throughout his career, a display of virtuosity that is, in itself, an homage to the Baroque poets. Poems like **"El abuelo"** and **"Que siga el son"** are not isolated instances of an intermittent Baroqueness in Guillén, but part and parcel of the poetics of his Afro-Antillean works.

It almost sounds like a joke in very poor taste to say that *Motivos de son* is a book permeated by questions of color. But it is, and for reasons that are very much at the core of its Baroque aesthetics. In *Motivos de son* Guillén performed a kind of cultural catharsis, a public purge that showed Cuban society its black component, a component that was everywhere *visible* but generally repressed. This involved dealing with the surface of social relations, by which I mean the theatrical manifestations of the social, or the social as a form of play acting; life as theater. *Motivos de son* is a theatrical book because of the sharply differing poetic voices that perform in the poems, the thematic presence of color and costume in the speaking characters, and its links to Cuban theatrical tradition. Let us take these in order.

"Negro bembón" [Fat Lips] is addressed to someone who is ashamed of his big lips. The poem begins with a question, establishing immediately its dialogic nature; hence its inherent theatricality. In **"Mulata"** someone with a flat nose berates a woman for calling attention to his African features, while hers are not exactly European either; she sees others but not herself. Not seeing oneself is a mark of nonbeing outside of the critical gaze of the other. The male speaker tells the woman that he prefers black women anyway, not mulattas, and does not like her at all. There is a vocative in the first line that establishes at once that the poem is spoken and addressed to someone in a dialogue. In **"Si tú supiera . . . "** [If You Only Knew . . .] a jilted lover tells his tormentor that he knows that she will eventually leave the man for whom she left him. This poem, to which I shall return later, also begins with a vocative ["Ay, negra"] and is clearly part of a dramatic exchange with a woman. In **"Sigue"** [Pass On By] we find the same device. In **"Hay que tené boluntá"** [Got to Have

Will Power] and **"Búcate plata"** [Git Dough] there are commands that establish the dramatic convention. In the former the speaker is a male addressing a woman, in the latter it is the woman who is enjoining the man. **"Mi chiquita"** [My Honey] ends with a dramatized dialogue in which the male speaker acts out what his lover is supposed to say. In **"Tú no sabe inglé"** [You Speak No English] the speaker admonishes "Bito Manué," who again is addressed directly, in a vocative, and mocks him for pretending to know English.

The mini-dramas in these poems involve strained social relations among blacks. Love is thwarted by lack of money, lack of industry, shame of African features, false pretenses, ambition, lust for social status. All of the characters are black, and all judge each other and themselves according to rumor, hearsay, and the reactions that their most visible features will elicit. In other words, they live tortured by the anticipation of what other people will think or say about them. In **"Negro bembón"** the character with fat lips feels shame when someone calls him "bembón." The speaker in **"Mulata"** has heard that a woman says that his nose is flat and fat like the knot of a tie. In **"Sigue"** the speaker asks someone not to tell his lover that he or she has seen him. Hearsay is the social pressure to conform, visibility is that which one avoids at all costs or wishes to cover with clothes, jewels, and other status symbols. In **"Búcate plata"** the woman tells her

Langston Hughes, Mihail Kolstov, Ernest Hemingway, and Guillén, 1937.

lover that she has to get money to eat and will not put up with his spending it all on fancy clothes, shoes, and a watch. In **"Hay que tené boluntá"** the male speaker tells his lover to pawn her electric iron so that he can get his suit out of hock. The most dramatic instance of this fear of visibility and hearsay is to be found in **"Sigue"** where the speaker asks his friend not to tell the woman who jilted him that he or she has seen him, "no le diga que me bite" [don't tell her that you saw me]. In **"Si tú supiera,"** the poem that became the title poem of *Sóngoro cosongo,* the speaker tells his former lover that he saw her go by but did not want her to see him, and he predicts that she will leave her present lover as soon as he, too, runs out of money. Shame, fear of being seen, leads to the refrain in which the speaker asks people to come see how well the woman dances ("bengan a be" [all come'n see]). Being is the result of feeling odd and left out and of having to enter into an exchange of false signs in order to exist. One exists in the perception of others, one's own being generates shame or inability to actually see oneself, as in the case of the woman who mocks her man's African features while being oblivious to her own. Similarly, Segismundo, the monstrous wild man of Calderón's *Life Is a Dream* (1636), threatens to kill Rosaura "porque no sepas que sé / que sabes flaquezas mías" [so that you won't know that I know that you are aware of my weakness]. Outraged husbands in Calderón's honor dramas kill at the slightest hint that their honor has been tarnished.

The essence of Baroque poetry is that there is no interiority; everything is visible or audible, even if its meaning is not readily understood. In romantic poetry one always feels that there is a residue of meaning not conveyed by the language. What is not understood is not there; in Baroque poetry language is everything. In the Baroque, language is a social code; all emotions are codified and subject to social exchange. Baroque poetry in colonial times displayed the visible aspects of social and political power. Baroque art was a public art, an art of the city, of the festivals of the city, in which all wore or said that which established their social status. Emotion is objectified through the code in Baroque art. Sor Juana's great poem, **"Primero sueño"** [First Dream], is an outward projection of her inner life; Baroque buildings and monuments were the official manifestation of such outwardness. Life in the Baroque was public, taking the form of festival or theater.

Guillén uses this essential feature of Baroque art to present his drama of life among city blacks in *Motivos de son.* The sadness of these motifs is distanced, objectified like a gesture by the correlative humor in these mini-dramas. Are we to laugh? For whom is the humor intended? Obviously for Cubans, and for Cuban blacks in particular, who will recognize in the comical pathos their own insecurities and intracultural violence. Social life, which is the only life, is made up of these violent, comical encounters, in which all wear masks that both express and repress the pain. The consummate artistry of these poems lies in their teetering on the verge of bathos, from which they are saved by the humor. This humor is the result of yet another Baroque conceit, which we could call the literariness of the figures.

Afro-Antilleanism not only created a new literature but discovered the literature which was already there and showed that its essential feature was that it centered on blacks. The work of anthropologist Fernando Ortiz on the underworld of blacks in the Cuban cities, the musical theater of Alejo Carpentier, the poetry of Guillén and others, found that there was a wealth of literature dealing with blacks that harked back to the origins of Cuban literature of the 1830's. Afro-Antilleanism discovered the origins of Cuban literature and established that Cuban literature began as it faced the issue of the African presence on the island. Hence what it discovered was that any Cuban literature that seeks to be new returns obsessively to that issue. Breaking with tradition meant complying with that tradition. And that tradition had bequeathed a rich gallery of characters and situations to the novel as well as to the theater. Guillén integrates these theatrical and novelistic traditions with poetry. The characters who "speak" in Guillén's poetry are those who had already appeared in *Cecilia Valdés* and other antislavery novels, and who had spoken and were speaking in the Cuban theater. One can trace these characters, drawn from the underworld of the cities, from Cirilo Villaverde to Severo Sarduy, and they can be found in all kinds of artistic forms of expression, like the nineteenth-century cigarette labels recently collected by Antonio Núñez Jiménez in a handsome volume. But it was Guillén who created them for the twentieth century by not eluding their literariness or the lacerating self-analysis implicit in their stereotypical humor. Guillén's figures in *Motivos de son* are not only theatrical but metatheatrical; they had already been codified by Cuban literature, particularly by the theater. Hence, as they speak there is a double distancing, a layering that fixes the figures. The pimp, the mulatta, the dandy, the pretentious *catedrático* are stereotypes, which heightens their artificiality, their dependence on given codes in which black Cuban culture has been objectified. In so doing, the poems of *Motivos de son* are clearly denouncing the process by which black culture identifies itself, showing that it exists through the projection of the prejudices of the other, the dominant white majority. Here lies the double edge of the humor, the pain caught in the rictus of a false smile that half conceals the violence implicit in the social exchange. Baroque masks are always conceived by someone else and generally cover an absence of being, or being as an anguished lack of self-recognition, except as play-acting.

The best-known poem in *Motivos de son,* **"Si tú supiera,"** which became known later as **"Sóngoro cosongo"** and as the title poem of Guillén's next book, displays all of the features discussed above and brings them to an uneasy synthesis:

> ¡Ay, negra
> si tú supiera!
> Anoche te vi pasá
> y no quise que me biera.
> A é tu le hará como a mí,
> que cuando no tube plata
> te corrite de bachata,
> sin acoddadte de mí.
> Sóngoro cosongo,
> songo be;
> sóngoro cosongo

de mamey;
Sóngoro, la negra
baila bien;
sóngoro de uno
sóngoro de tre.
Aé,
bengan a be;
aé,
bamo pa be;
bengan, sóngoro cosongo,
sóngoro cosongo de mamey!

Hey, babe,
if you only knew!
Last night I saw you pass by,
and I didn't let you see me.
You'll do to him what you did to me,
when I ran out of money
you took off with another honey
and forgot all about me.
Sóngoro cosongo,
songo, see;
sóngoro cosongo
like mamey;
sóngoro, the black babe
dances well.
Sóngoro one,
sóngoro three.
Ae,
all come'n see;
ae,
all come'n see;
Come, sóngoro cosongo,
sóngoro cosongo like mamey.

The first part of the poem contains the typical mini-drama that I have been examining. The speaker is a jilted lover who is ashamed to be seen, but sees the woman pass by (in these poems people are always passing by, never still, affixed in one place). His prediction, appropriately, is that she will move on once her new love runs out of money. She forgot him, and he became invisible in the night, while she goes out to flash her gaiety and new-found wealth. In addition, all is set in a subjunctive world (*supiera*), unlikely to take place because it is unlikely that she will know. Though technically we have a dialogue, it is only an imagined one; she is not going to hear him. She cannot see him, and he cannot speak to her. Visibility and sound are foreclosed. The poem projects an entelechy, a play of shadows that does not and is not likely to exist. A play of colors and shadows, of imagined reality, this first part of **"Sóngoro cosongo"** is made up of Baroque conceits. But this is only the first part of the poem.

It is a revealing fact that Guillén's poetry, no matter what the real color of the critic, has been the object of exclusively "white" readings. I hate to use this terminology, but it may be necessary to awaken all of us out of a massive process of repression. It is only in the pioneering work by José Piedra and Vera Kutzinski that we begin to find a criticism that does not deal with what sounds to lay ears like music (or noise) as if it had no meaning. Even Ángel Augier refers to **"Sóngoro cosongo"** as the "sonorous refrain" that Guillén took from one of his poems for the title of his book. Mirta Aguirre, in her beautiful and powerful essay on the book, which contains the best prosodic analysis of

this particular poem, prefers to consider the phonemes in the refrain as "purely sonorous facts." But why empty this second part of the poem of meaning? **"Sóngoro cosongo"** is a poem in two parts, written in different languages. It is a diglossic poem. The first part is written in Spanish, the second in . . . what? Let us analyze in some detail the "sonorous refrain."

If we take some liberties with the syllabic arrangement of "sóngoro cosongo," we come up with at least three possible words: "son," "songo," and "congo." This simple exercise at once reveals that the poem alludes to or employs elements of the Congo or Bakongo culture, one of the three main African cultures in Cuba. We can thus quickly discard any idea that we are dealing with nonsense, or with purely sonorous effects. Congo culture is of undisputed importance in Cuba and its presence *at the end* of the poem, after the Spanish part, should be taken as at least suggestive, if not exceedingly meaningful. One should at the very least admit that there is a balance. But let us proceed.

The relevance of "son" need not be underlined. Song, ritual chant, the "son" became the central musical form of Afro-Cuban, or simply Cuban, culture. So "son," which alludes, of course, to the title of the book, means "this is a chant, a ritual song" that I am singing here; it is not merely words or much less pure musical sound. It is a defiant song that I sing on the face of the emptying of being that I have described in the first, Spanish part of the poem. The other two words are equally compelling.

It is at best hazardous for a lay critic like me to venture into the depths of Bantu philology, but there is no other way to understand **"Sóngoro cosongo."** What I offer here is tentative and amateurish, worthy perhaps only because of the *amateur* motivation. In the case of African languages in the New World, with no written records and the distance from the source, philological interpretation can either be totally loose or extremely cautious. It is easy to make anything mean anything. In the case of "songo" I have found similar sounding words that may or may not be derived from a real root. In any case, in his *Diccionario provincial casi razonado de vozes cubanas* (1836) Esteban Pichardo records the word *Songa:* "Feminine noun, used in familiar speech. Irony, jest, feigned threat or disdain; known for the gestures, style and way of expressing it. For example, 'He told me with *songa* . . . .' Could it be a corruption of *sorna*?" I think that one can easily discard Pichardo's last suggestion. It is possible to see the first part of **"Sóngoro cosongo"** as feigned disdained, a lover's insincere reproach, and move on from there to link *songa* to the origins of *choteo*. This is possible, but it could not be the whole story. There may be feigned disdain and threat in the poem, but there is certainly little humor. Without rejecting the previous interpretation, I find more promising a term included by Lydia Cabrera in her recent *Vocabulario congo (el bantú que se habla en Cuba)* (1984): "*Kusanga,* what is mine, what belongs to me." Here we have the advantage of the prefix. "Kusanga" sounds a great deal like "cosongo," and it could very well be the word in the back of Guillén's mind when he composed the refrain. "What is mine" is also an affirmation of being that can be related to "son": "I am singing my song." An alternative meaning of "songo" would be to show, demonstrate, convince. Leon Dereau's *Lexique. Kikôngo-Français—Français-Kikôngo* (1957) reads: "Songa-songele: to show, to indicate, to reveal, to demonstrate, to prove." And W. Holman Bentley's *Dictionary and Grammar of the Kongo Language* (1887) records "Songa, *v.t.*, to show, to point out, convince, prove, demonstrate, direct, describe, display, exhibit, expose, introduce (of friends), instruct, show how." "Cosongo," then, perhaps means to display or demonstrate what is Congo.

Congo means to be present: "I am here." Hence, I am here, present, singing my song, the song that enacts by being, that which is mine and which gives me substance. All of this, we see now, is opposed to the emptying of being of the first part, where the speaker was not visible and could not communicate with the woman. "Sóngoro cosongo" would then have a structure similar to "Mulata," where, at the end, the speaker affirms that he prefers black women. From the "hearsay" at the start, concerning his African features, we move to the celebration of those features in the black woman. In "Sóngoro cosongo" we go from the pain at his ruined love affair with the woman who only wants money to a refrain that is a recall of who he is, a memory made present through the words that will counter her forgetfulness. Through this gesture the poem is reaching back to the original *Son*, the mythical "Son de la Ma Teodora," modelled on African and *taíno* rituals (*areítos*) whose function is to awaken a collective memory.

Why is it that no one has dared interpret the second part of "Sóngoro cosongo"? I believe that it is partly because we are not meant to. The poem encrypts its meaning in an incomprehensible code that masks its ending, that leaves us babbling sounds not to be understood by the noninitiate. In this the poem enacts the Baroque feints and moves of the first part and also, of course, makes of encrypting its main trope, one so efficient that we tend not even to want to understand, intoxicated as we are with the music. Like the sonnet "El abuelo," "Sóngoro consongo" conceals, as in a secret yet public code, a truth—it is a complex hermeneutical process to get at it because of this visible concealment. There is nothing simple about Guillén's poetry; readers make it simple as an act of self-defense, or as an ideological imposition equating popular forms with simplicity (this is patently absurd in Cuba and other parts of the Caribbean where popular poetry is composed in Baroque *espinelas*).

From *Motivos de son* to *Sóngoro cosongo* and *West Indies, Ltd.* there occurs a noticeable evolution in Guillén's poetry. The underworld of urban Cuban blacks gives way to a broader setting, the whole Caribbean, and language begins to be invested with what can only be termed a religious sense, much like in the second part of "Sóngoro cosongo." Poems can now take on a ritualistic form, as in "Sensemayá"; can describe a ritual, as in "Velorio de Papá Montero" [Papa Montero's Wake]; or can present an encrypted meaning of religious significance, as in "Balada del Güije" [Ballad of the Güije]. Together with these poems, of course, there are those like "West Indies, Ltd." or "Balada de los dos abuelos" [Ballad of the Two

Grandfathers] that make broad historical statements or political appeals. The joint presence of these two kinds of poems in the books Guillén writes in the thirties can be explained in historical terms, but also opens up issues that hark back to the Baroque aesthetics within which he began his career in *Motivos de son.* This double presence, however, also brings forth the most profound contradiction of Afro-Antilleanism.

The historical explanation is clear, though a historical dimension was probably not apparent when the poems were first published. By invoking the underground discourse of Afro-Antillean religion, Guillén is making a statement about the current sociopolitical situation of Caribbean blacks and at the same time claiming that the subversiveness inherent in Afro-Antillean religion is at the core of all Caribbean struggles for independence. In short, the cohesiveness of Afro-Antillean culture, which made it resilient enough to survive the brutality of slavery, was due to the tenacious survival of religious beliefs and rituals. Today, as Lydia Cabrera has explained [in *Vocabulario*], African languages in Cuba have an essentially religious function. Hence, to sing a religious chant, such as "Sensemayá," then, has a political dimension, for it strengthens the bond uniting the oppressed and hardening their resolve to struggle, just as it joined blacks to fight against slavery in the nineteenth century. Yet to compose a sacred chant, or to invoke a ritual, in a poem written essentially in Spanish is to desacralize African signs, to divest them of their transcendental charge. The constant transfer from the African to the European code no doubt wears away the authority of the former, but at the expense of revealing, of making profane the latter. There is a double unveiling: the authority of the European code is shown to rely on convention or imposition, not to be invested with any inherent superiority; but, by relinquishing its secrecy, the African code gives up its sacredness, that which would presumably make its claim to superiority. On the historical level, of course, the answer is simple: this glossolalia of sacred signs—"Santa Bárbara on one side / Changó on the other"—aims to create a new, syncretic language endowed by the sacrifices in recent American history with its own aura of sacredness. But Guillén's best poems of the 1930s—e.g., "Balada del Güije" and "Sensemayá"—are those in which the force of the African component is preserved through a kind of encrypting in language. (pp. 302-15)

Roberto González Echevarría, "Guillén as Baroque: Meaning in 'Motivos de Son'," in Callaloo, *Vol. 10, No. 2, Spring, 1987, pp. 302-17.*

Ian Isidore Smart   (essay date 1990)

[*In the following excerpt from his critical study* Nicolás Guillén: Popular Poet of the Caribbean, *Smart examines the synthesis of European and African cultural influences, or* mulatez, *in Guillén's poetry.*]

Mulatez is a cultural concept of direct artistic relevance, which involves an awakening to the full importance of the African cultural heritage. This new awareness engenders conflict in every cultural sphere, be it social, political, economic, or psychological—the inevitable conflict between Eurocentered and Afrocentered realities. In Guillén's view, the conflict of thesis and antithesis must be faced and resolved through the harmonious blending or synthesis of the opposing elements. In a real sense, there is conflict at the heart of Guillén's creativity; it is the very fount of that creativity. Without the tensions generated by the clash between Europe and Africa, Guillén's best and most characteristic work would have no emotional core.

The concept of *mulatez* finds direct expression in several of Guillén's poems. The most significant is, perhaps, the **"Balada de los dos abuelos."** This work, from the collection *West Indies, Ltd,* is written predominantly in octosyllabic lines, combined with five- and three-syllable lines. There appears to be no regular rhyme scheme, but an assonance in *e-o* imposes itself throughout the entire poem. Significantly, this is the assonance in the words *abuelo, negro* and *veo* (I see), the last word of the first line. By the same token, the assonance *a-o*, as in *blanco* (white), is also frequently employed. The stanzas are irregular in length. The poet is clearly not making any great effort to stay within the well-worked traditions of Hispanic verse. However, this poem is not a *son;* it is close to the innovative, somewhat rebellious, spirit of contemporary Hispanic poetry and, in this regard, looks more to the *abuelo blanco* than to the *abuelo negro.*

The *abuelos* are introduced as *sombras* (shadows) and then presented in a series of paired images that symbolize and characterize them. In the second strophe, "lanza con punta de hueso" (lance with a bone tip) and "tambor" (drum), associated with the *abuelo negro,* are paired with "Gorguera en el cuello ancho" (Ruff on a wide collar) and the "gris armadura" (gray armor), associated with the *abuelo blanco.* Then in the third stanza, "Africa de selvas húmedas" (Africa with its damp jungles) is contrasted with the "galeón ardiendo en oro" (galley ablaze with gold). Of the two *abuelos,* one is dying and the other is tired. One is associated with the sun and the other with the moon.

In the fourth stanza, the historical and geographical context of their confrontation is clarified further. The opening lines evoke images of ships, black people, sugarcane, the whip, and the slaveholder. Then the horrors of slavery are suggestively presented:

> Piedra de llanto y de sangre,
> venas y ojos entreabiertos,
> y madrugadas vacías,
> y atardeceres de ingenio,
> y una gran voz, fuerte voz
> despedazando el silencio.

> A stone of tears and blood,
> veins and eyes wide open,
> and early morning emptiness,
> and dusks at the sugar mill,
> and a great voice, a loud voice
> ripping the silence to shreds.

These images are based on the implied, in fact preconscious, complicity of the reader, who thereby enters into the creative process with the poet. This aspect of Guillén's creative technique is, of course, consistent with the major trends in nineteenth-century and contemporary Western art.

In the penultimate stanza, the *sombras* metamorphose into more material existence. They become individuals with names, Don Federico and Taita Facundo—the "Don" that immediately precedes the given name is the traditional Hispanic formula for showing respect, and "Taita" has the same force as "Uncle," in "Uncle Remus" or "Uncle Tom" for example. The last line of this penultimate stanza manifests the powerful force of poetic volition and effects the synthesis, the harmonious blending of Europe and Africa, in the stark "Yo los junto" (I join them). The counterpoint carried on throughout the poem thus attains its intellectual peak.

The rhythm of the final stanza intensifies, mostly through the repetition of the line "los dos del mismo tamaño" (the two of the same stature). The new urgency of the rhythm gives the impression of an erotic coupling that is resolved in the climactic two-syllable line "Cantan" (they sing) with which the poem concludes, peaking affectively. A most appropriate final stanza for this ballad, it reads:

> —Federico!
> ¡Facundo! Los dos se abrazan.
> Los dos suspiran. Los dos
> las fuertes cabezas alzan;
> los dos del mismo tamaño,
> bajo las estrellas altas;
> los dos del mismo tamaño,
> ansia negra y ansia blanca,
> los dos del mismo tamaño,
> gritan, sueñan, lloran, cantan.
> Sueñan, lloran, cantan.
> Lloran, cantan.
> ¡Cantan!

> —Federico!
> Facundo! The two embrace.
> The two sigh. The two
> raise their strong heads;
> the two of the same stature,
> under the far-off stars;
> the two of the same stature
> black and white, both longing,
> the two of the same stature,
> they shout, they dream, they cry, they sing.
> They dream, they cry, they sing.
> They cry, they sing.
> They sing!

The rhythmic pattern is, of course, the familiar one of the *son* poems, the most effective rhythm of the poet's repertoire and the artistic element that accounts for much of the beauty of this poem. The poem represents the realization of *mulatez,* speaking through technique as well as theme to the fundamental relationship, the partnership, between Europe and Africa, the two *abuelos.* The harmonious aesthetic union in both form and content effectively symbolizes the cultural union that is *mulatez.*

Many other poems directly address the concept of *mulatez.* In fact, the image of the shadowy *abuelo* is used in the poem **"El abuelo"** of the same book, *West Indies, Ltd.* It is an alexandrine sonnet with a twist, entirely worthy of the Caribbean master bard who was also the consummate smartman. The first line presents:

> Esta mujer angélica de ojos septentrionales,
> que vive atenta al ritmo de su sangre europea,
> ignora que en lo hondo de ese ritmo golpea
> un negro el parche duro de roncos atabales.

> This angelic woman with her northern eyes,
> who lives attentive only to the rhythm of her European blood,
> in ignorance of the fact that deep within this rhythm a black
> beats the coarse skins of raucous drums.

The shadowy element is essential to the thrust of the sonnet, for the punch line in the final tercet reads:

> que ya verás, inquieta, junto a la fresca orilla
> la dulce sombra oscura del abuelo que huye,
> el que rizó por siempre tu cabeza amarilla.

> One day you will see, to your chagrin, close to the cool bank
> the sweet dark shadow of the fleeing grandfather,
> the one who put that permanent curl in your yellow hair.

The blonde female so proud of her European heritage is reminded by the poet, in his inimitably picaroon style, of the ubiquity of *mulatez.* These lines recall those of an earlier poem, **"La canción del bongo"** (The song of the bongo) from **Sóngoro cosongo:**

> siempre falta algún abuelo,
> cuando no sobra algún Don

> There's always either a grandfather missing,
> or some noble title slipped in.

Both poems depend for their effectiveness on the readers' understanding of, if not familiarity with, the whole question of race relations in Cuba—and, indeed, in the Americas in general. They could be written only by a poet honest enough to include into his poetic universe elements from both the thesis and the antithesis which create the synthesis that is Cuban culture.

The poem **"Dos niños"** (Two children), again from **West Indies, Ltd,** also explicitly addresses the question of the relationship between the sons of Europe and Africa in Cuba. In **"Poema con niños"** (A poem with children) from **El son entero,** the poet presents in dramatic form a conflict among four children, one Jewish, one European, one Chinese, and one African. The mother of the Euro-Cuban child resolves the conflict by invoking the principle of *mulatez.* **"Son número 6"** (*Son* number 6), also from **El son entero,** begins with a resounding proclamation of the persona's African heritage:

> Yoruba soy, lloro en yoruba
> . . . . .
> Yoruba soy, soy lucumí,
> mandinga, congo, carabalí.

> I am Yoruba, I weep in Yoruba
> . . . . .
> I am Yoruba, I am *lucumí* [a Yoruba speaker]
> Mandingo, Congo, *carabalí* [Ibo].

However, the theme of the racial blend that constitutes the Cuban ethos is also presented and, in fact, becomes paramount. The abiding image of the work is contained in the following lines from the central *son* portion of the poem:

> Estamos juntos desde muy lejos,
> jóvenes, viejos,
> negros y blancos, todo mezclado;

> We have been together for quite a long time,
> young, old,
> blacks and whites, all mixed together.

The Martinican critic Alfred Melon has been particularly struck with how often these, or remarkably similar, images turn up in Guillén's poetry (he uses the term *obsession* in his analysis) [in *Recopilación de textos sobre Nicolás Guillén,* edited by Nancy Morejón]: "The constant juxtaposition in fraternal solidarity of blacks and whites, rather, their constant mixing, is perhaps Nicolás Guillén's greatest obsession, and it is not mere sentimentality for it bespeaks a constructive efficacy and force." Since the mulatto is biologically at the crossroads where Europe and Africa meet, his physical duality has frequently been accompanied by sociological and psychological dysfunction. His identity is frequently assailed in the most fundamental fashion by external pressures and, indeed, intense internal pressures too. [In a footnote, the critic adds: Carl N. Degler, *Neither Black nor White: Slavery and Race Relations in Brazil and the United States,* confirms my assertion. Although he is speaking principally of the Brazilian situation, it is clear that the Cuban situation could not have been very different. The situation in Trinidad and Tobago, my native country, has been similar in many ways to that described in Degler's book. It seems quite reasonable to assume that analogous patterns would have developed in countries as similar as Cuba, Trinidad, and Brazil, along with many others that have had similar historical experiences in the matter of race relations. Degler asserts poignantly, with more than adequate demonstration, "The lot of the mulatto in Brazil can be anxiety-producing. Not white, yet often wanting to be so, the mulatto nevertheless can be classed as a black at any time a room clerk or maitre d'hotel chooses to treat him as such. This, too, is the negative side of the mulatto escape hatch." There is evidence that at least some of this turmoil was experienced by Guillén, and it is borne out in his remark about being a "mulato bastante claro 'y de pelo.' "] Neither black nor white, the mulatto's metaphysical alienation is likely to give him a clearer insight into the primordial contradiction of the human condition. Guillén seems to have developed the potential of this difficult position. He avoided the pathological pitfalls of his own biological and sociological *mulatez,* and, by elaborating on its positive aspects and incorporating these into his active artistic and psychological life, he converted a potential nightmare into poetic inspiration. The artist often builds beauty out of his own psychoses and neuroses; however, in this case, the aesthetic profit appears to have been made only after the destructive *mulatez* was transformed into a positive force.

Melon, being a Marxist critic, is naturally partial to the idea of synthesis and sees Guillén as "el poeta de la síntesis" (the poet of synthesis), a view he defends with masterful arguments [in his "El poeta de la síntesis" in *Recopila-ción*]. He asserts, for example, that the poet's "synthesiz-ing vocation" was already evident in his earliest works, and he cites the following lines from **"La balada azul":**

> Frente al mar, viendo las olas
> la quieta orilla besar,
> los dos muy juntos, muy juntos
>
> Facing the sea, seeing the waves
> kiss the still shore,
> the two of us together, close together.

Of course, the image of "los dos muy juntos" is natural in a love poem. However, Melon attaches special significance to it. He points out that it is repeated later in the same poem:

> al pie de la fuente clara
> juntos, muy juntos los dos.
>
> At the foot of the clear fountain
> together, the two of us close together.

He cites this as yet another example of "the obsession with pairs, the reiteration of the expressions *de dos en dos, los dos juntos, muy juntos,*" in Guillén's poetic work.

Samples of these recurring images of pairing and together-ness can be seen in the poems I analyzed previously in this chapter. Melon cites many other examples, especially in the poem **"No sé por qué piensas tú"** (I don't know why you think), from the collection **Cantos para soldados y sones para turistas,** which was first published in Mexico in 1937. Perhaps the most aesthetic example of Guillén's obsession with duality, this poem is a clever and moving play on "tú" (you) and "yo" (I). All the lines, except three, end with "tú" or "yo." The three exceptions act as the strong link, like two strong hands firmly clasped, uniting "tú" and "yo." Two exceptions come from the line "si somos la misma cosa" (if we are the same thing), which is repeated to heighten its intensity, and the third excep-tion is the only line in which the pivotal "juntos" is articu-lated, "juntos en la misma calle" (together in the same street).

Much of the effectiveness of the poem, and this is often the case with Guillén, comes from its simplicity. It begins:

> No sé por qué piensas tú,
> soldado, que te odio yo,
> si somos la misma cosa
> yo,
> tú.
>
> I don't know why you think
> soldier, that I hate you
> if we are the same thing
> I,
> you.

Written in 1937, the year Guillén joined the Communist party, the poem evokes deep emotions of revolutionary solidarity between the divided, and conquered, oppressed groups. It represents what Frantz Fanon called the Radi-calization phase, when the native artist or intellectual par-ticipates in the real revolutionary struggle. Guillén tries to persuade the soldier, who is one of the Cuban people, to open his eyes, become aware of, and desist from his com-plicity in the brutal oppression of his brothers, a complici-ty that is a necessary, and indeed sufficient, condition for the colonial process. In the stanza quoted above, three oc-tosyllabic lines are joined to the two one-syllable lines, "yo" and "tú," to take the strophe beyond the limits of the traditional, and very popular, romance form. The special structure is intimately bound to the content, with that im-pressive matching of form and content that always attends good art.

Building through the rhythmic interplay of "tú" and "yo," the final stanza comes to a climax:

> Ya nos veremos yo y tú
> juntos en la misma calle,
> hombro con hombro, tú y yo,
> sin odios ni yo ni tú,
> pero sabiendo tú y yo,
> a dónde vamos yo y tú . . .
> ¡No sé por qué piensas tú,
> soldado, que te odio yo!
>
> One day we'll meet, I and you,
> together on the same street,
> shoulder to shoulder, you and I,
> with no hatred either in me or in you,
> but knowing, you and I,
> where we're going, I and you . . .
> I don't know why you should think,
> soldier, that I hate you!

The obsession with pairing reaches its highest pitch of in-tensity in this last strophe, since not only are "tú" and "yo" matched by being the final words of the lines and hence the basis of the rhyme, but also, in most of the lines, they are actually joined as well: "tú y yo." The only line that does not enter into this pattern is the one that con-tains the very significant image "juntos." In fact, the sense of "juntos" is reaffirmed by the "misma" (same) that qual-ifies "calle," and so a double idea of unity is employed to bond "tú y yo."

. . . . .

Duality is at the core of reality. Guillén himself posited *mulatez,* an expression of duality and the creative dialogue between Africa and Europe, as the core of his art. . . . [It] is precisely this *mulatez* that links Guillén's art so closely to the Caribbean sensibility and culture, for this same du-ality is at the core of West Indianness or Caribbeanness. Every Caribbean artistic expression examined in these chapters—from the Cuban *son* to the kaiso from Trinidad and Tobago or the Colombian *vallenato*—results from some synthesis of African and European elements. For ex-ample, the particular process that produced the carnival in Trinidad and Tobago (with its accompanying kaiso) was seen to be a rich, complex synthesis uniting various European elements—Spanish, French, and English, in particular—with African culture, which was itself the end product of the synthesizing processes of New World slav-ery.

Anyone interested in forging, or merely exploring, a com-mon Caribbean sensibility, in order to remedy the perni-cious fragmentation imposed by the colonial experience, must, then, take the carnival kaiso from Trinidad and To-bago into very careful consideration. However, the *mu-*

latez at the core of Guillén's poetry is, in fact, synthesis enough—it provides an area of cultural communality within the fragmented Caribbean. It is interesting that, although this region is populated overwhelmingly by African-ancestored peoples, the fragmentation is found mostly in the European element, the most important element of diversity being the various European languages spoken in the area. The original African ethnic groups and their corresponding cultures quickly lost their functional specificities under the barbaric treatment meted out by the Europeans. However, the Africans' experience with the process of cultural synthesis will bear fruit in the Caribbean, through *mulatez,* as has already happened in Guillén's poetry. Thus, the creative dialogue, which generated this poetry by overcoming the stony silence imposed by Europe's cultural hegemony, must in time grow to fill the entire region with its rich cadences, to banish forever the hostile, self-serving, limitingly egocentric silences that once prevailed. (pp. 164-72)

> *Ian Isidore Smart, in his* Nicolás Guillén: Popular Poet of the Caribbean, *University of Missouri Press, 1990, 187 p.*

FURTHER READING

Benítez-Rojo, Antonio. "Nicolás Guillén and Sugar." *Callaloo* 10, No. 2 (Spring 1987): 329-51.

Analyzes Guillén's social poetry addressing the economic, political, and cultural problems associated with Cuba's sugar industry.

Coulthard, G. R. *Race and Colour in Caribbean Literature.* London: Oxford University Press, 1962, 152 p.

Explores various treatments of the theme of race in Caribbean literature and includes discussion of Guillén's poetry.

Ellis, Keith. *Cuba's Nicolás Guillén: Poetry and Ideology.* Toronto: University of Toronto Press, 1983, 251 p.

Examines Guillén's major works in the context of Cuban history and politics.

Infante, G. Cabrera. "Nicolás Guillén: Poet and Partisan." *Review: Latin American Literature and Arts,* No. 42 (January-June 1990): 31-3.

Presents a conversational retrospective on Guillén's life and career and evaluates his status as a poet.

Pérez-Firmat, Gustavo. "Nicolás Guillén between the 'Son' and the Sonnet." *Callaloo* 10, No. 2 (Spring 1987): 318-28.

Discusses Guillén's use of the sonnet form in his poetry.

Prescott, Laurence E. "A Conversation with Nicolás Guillén." *Callaloo* 10, No. 2 (Spring 1987): 352-54.

Guillén shares his views on politics and literature in Cuba.

Spicer, Eliose Y. "The Blues and the Son: Reflections of Black Self-Assertion in the Poetry of Langston Hughes and Nicolás Guillén." *The Langston Hughes Review* III, No. 1 (Spring 1984): 1-12.

Evaluates several early poems from *Motivos de son,* comparing Guillén's treatment of the *son* in his poetry with Langston Hughes's poetic use of the blues musical form.

Williams, Lorna V. *Self and Society in the Poetry of Nicolás Guillén.* Baltimore: Johns Hopkins University Press, 1982, 177 p.

Discusses Guillén's perspective on the Afro-Cuban experience of colonialism.

Additional coverage of Guillén's life and career is contained in the following sources published by Gale Research: *Black Literature Criticism,* Vol. 2; *Black Writers; Contemporary Authors,* Vols. 116, 125, 129 [obituary]; *Contemporary Literary Criticism,* Vol. 48; and *Hispanic Writers.*

E. D. Hirsch, Jr.

1928-

(Full name Eric Donald Hirsch, Jr.) American critical theorist and essayist.

The following entry provides an overview of Hirsch's career through 1988.

INTRODUCTION

A prominent contemporary critical theorist, Hirsch is known primarily for his concepts of typology and authorial intent—theories related to the interpretation of literary texts—and for *Cultural Literacy,* his best-selling critique of the American educational system. While Hirsch has received ample academic attention for his innovations in literary criticism, it was the publication of *Cultural Literacy* that gained him national recognition and significant notoriety.

Hirsch was born in Memphis, Tennessee, in 1928. He graduated from Cornell University in 1950 and completed the doctoral program at Yale University in 1957. His doctoral dissertation was later expanded and published as *Wordsworth and Schelling: A Typological Study of Romanticism.* Much of Hirsch's early career was devoted to the refinement of critical theories of interpretation, specifically typology and authorial intent. According to Hirsch's theory of typology, an author's writing is informed by the types, or distinctive patterns, that characterize that author's life, social and cultural background, worldview, and mode of literary expression. As Hirsch states in *Wordsworth and Schelling:* "A type may function as a guiding idea, which permits the student to examine minutely an individual mind in all its complexities without losing sight of the whole." In *Innocence and Experience: An Introduction to Blake,* Hirsch employed typology in a biographically grounded study of William Blake's verse collection *Songs of Innocence and of Experience: Shewing the Two Contrary States of the Human Soul* (1794). Hirsch subsequently asserted that an author's intent is the only meaning that can be justifiably attributed to a text, and that this meaning is both discernible and unchanging. He merged the ideas of typology and authorial intent, or intentionality, in his works *Validity in Interpretation* and *The Aims of Interpretation.* He writes in *Validity in Interpretation* that "our chances of making a correct preliminary guess about the nature of someone's verbal meaning are enormously increased by the limitations imposed upon that meaning through cultural norms and conventions." Both concepts relate to the development of a hermeneutic code that, according to Hirsch, allows the reader to pinpoint with precision and accuracy a text's meaning as intended by the author.

In *Cultural Literacy* Hirsch applies his critical theories to

contemporary culture in the United States, arguing that most Americans can neither fully communicate nor actively participate in society because of their cultural illiteracy—their ignorance of "the basic information needed to thrive in the modern world." Observing the relationship between Hirsch's critical theories in his early works and his educational theory in *Cultural Literacy,* Christopher Hitchens has stated: "Just as a reader, no matter how keen his analytic faculties, cannot divine the meaning of a text without understanding the author's intention and the work's place in a broader literary context, so students cannot hope to make sense of material they are given in a classroom without a shared pool of basic knowledge." In *Cultural Literacy* Hirsch stresses the necessity of a basic core curriculum for American schoolchildren and accentuates his idea with a list of names, dates, concepts, places, and phrases which are, according to the subtitle, "What Literate Americans Know." In the pursuit of national cultural literacy, Hirsch has established the Cultural Literacy Foundation in Charlottesville, Virginia, and has since published, with Joseph F. Kett and James Trefil, *The Dictionary of Cultural Literacy,* which defines the 5,000 terms listed in *Cultural Literacy.*

Critical reaction to Hirsch's work—both his earlier academic texts and his more recent social criticism—has often been harsh and unrelenting, with commentators citing a lack of skill and precision in the explanations of his philosophical arguments. Literary theorist Frank Lentricchia has considered Hirsch's suppositions in *Validity in Interpretation* and *The Aims of Interpretation* "theoretically questionable at best," and found that Hirsch misunderstood the writings of several German philosophers—whose work has been influential in the development of literary critical theory—"about as badly as it is possible to misunderstand them." The concepts presented by Hirsch in *Cultural Literacy,* particularly his list of terms, have also received an overwhelming amount of negative criticism, with many reviewers attacking the list as age-, gender-, and class-specific, racially and ethnically exclusionary, or random, vague, and subjective. Commenting on the ineffectiveness of Hirsch's list, Neil Postman stated that "its arbitrariness only demonstrates the futility of trying to do what he wants us to do." Some commentators object that Hirsch unjustly promotes memorization over comprehension and reasoning, while others such as Stanley Aronowitz and Henry A. Giroux have charged that the work is political in essence; they cite the traditional, fundamentalist nature of Hirsch's doctrine and the high degree of acceptance the concept of cultural literacy receives from conservative politicians and educators. A number of scholars have found potential in Hirsch's work for popular acceptance and the initiation of substantial social transformation. As William E. Cain has stated: "Hirsch's theory is in many respects bluntly authoritarian, and many beleaguered scholars and teachers will welcome it for its promise of a return to rigid authority and discipline." A proponent of *Cultural Literacy,* former U. S. Secretary of Education William Bennett has additionally contended that "this important book could, and should, change what goes on in our nation's classrooms."

PRINCIPAL WORKS

Wordsworth and Schelling: A Typological Study of Romanticism (criticism) 1960
Innocence and Experience: An Introduction to Blake (criticism) 1964
Validity in Interpretation (essays) 1967
The Aims of Interpretation (essays) 1976
The Philosophy of Composition (treatise) 1977
Cultural Literacy: What Literate Americans Know (nonfiction) 1987
The Dictionary of Cultural Literacy [with Joseph F. Kett and James Trefil] (dictionary) 1988

CRITICISM

Edward W. Said   (review date Fall 1967)

[*Said is a Palestinian-born educator and author. In the excerpt below, he discusses the critical theory presented by Hirsch in* Validity in Interpretation.]

E. D. Hirsch divides criticism into two moments, of which the first is intuitive and deeply sympathetic, the second reflexive and logical. Presumably, criticism as art and criticism as science. He focuses [*Validity in Interpretation*] exclusively on the second moment, although he seems unwilling to note how the first moment always influences the second. Nevertheless, his demand for a logical method for weighing evidence about verbal statements, and a means to secure validity, is a fair one. What it involves is that the critic turn himself on the work he criticizes, asking himself questions that will either legitimize his statements about the work, or, hopefully, correct them; in either case, he makes himself aware of what he is doing. Works of literature, Hirsch argues, have a meaning that is neither arbitrary nor changeable, and it is to his great credit that he recognizes the vast difficulties of construing the meaning not only of a work but of meaning itself. Consequently his book argues painstakingly (and rather drily) for a very modest "hermeneutic," in which intention (in Husserl's sense of the word) or meaning, as opposed to significance, is common to every use of language. Even nonsense has meaning, albeit nonsensical meaning. In literature, the broadest category of intention is genre: each literary utterance belongs to a "type" that performs a definable task, so that we can understand *Paradise Lost* because it is an epic which will always fulfill specific social and historical expectations. Hirsch proposes little that is more definite than this, for he is prudently hamstrung by a couple of limitations: 1), "there are no general rules which are at once general and practical," and 2), there are "no rules for generating insights." The rest of the time he spends in useful groundwork: making distinctions between meaning and significance, attacking relativism, generalizing about verbal meaning and probability.

Hirsch's most interesting observation is that in criticism "to understand is to understand as necessary." I doubt that his modesty will let him associate this remark made about the end of a critic's logical job of work with Heidegger writing about Hölderlin. For his essays on the poet are, Heidegger says, his method of showing how Hölderlin is a "necessity of thought," a series of actions that are necessary for the mind to perform. Hirsch might characteristically demand validation for such a project, yet when we read [the critics] Poulet or Blackmur validation is simply in the necessary beauty of their understanding of literature, which to them is the crux of thought. Criticism is notorious for its imperialism, carried out in the name of understanding: method swallowing work, argument dividing to conquer and variety colonized into periods and "ages." By contrast, Poulet's wish is to *prolong* literature in his criticism, Blackmur's to reveal literature taking, in Henry James's phrase, from "the enormous lap of the actual." Criticism is therefore a way of living up to and living with literature. Inner conversion rather than public quarrel.

We may say that such criticism flies too close to art, yet both are the more interesting for it, I think, and doubtless criticism is less concerned with accuracy as a result. Fiction makes its own canon of accuracy, however, to which Hirsch is too impervious, for even in criticism there are two cultures. (pp. 627-28)

Edward W. Said, "Sense and Sensibility," in Partisan Review, *Vol. XXXIV, No. 4, Fall, 1967, pp. 627-33.*

Paul Ricoeur   (review date 25 February 1977)

[*A French philosopher, educator and critical theorist, Ricoeur strove to blend structural and hermeneutical thought into a critical approach that successfully explains the processes of interpretation and the significance of speech. In the following review, he judges* The Aims of Interpretation *flawed but praiseworthy.*]

In 1967, E. D. Hirsch published *Validity in Interpretation.* Now, nearly ten years later, in *The Aims of Interpretation,* he proposes "to amplify important subjects that were dealt with only briefly in the earlier book". In speaking of amplification, the author denies having introduced any "substantive revisions of the earlier argument". I would say, for my part, that *The Aims of Interpretation* actually takes a middle course between amplification and revision.

On two points the earlier work left the reader in some confusion. The first concerned the relationship between the internal meaning of a work of art, what Professor Hirsch called the "verbal meaning", and the intention of the author, or "authorial meaning". He defended with equal vigour the idea that meaning must be determinate, is self-identical, in order to be sharable and the object of a valid interpretation, and the idea that the ultimate norm of validation of all interpretation was "authorial meaning". His purpose was to reinforce the autonomy of the meaning in order to prevent its usurpation by the reader, but he thereby risked falling into what W. K. Wimsatt called "intentional fallacy".

The second ambiguity in *Validity in Interpretation* was this: if in principle Professor Hirsch distinguished between the meaning of the work and its significance for the reader and critic, he did not succeed in elucidating this distinction, for this problem was finally overshadowed by the problem of validating our "guesses" about the possible ways of constructing the meaning of a text. The great originality of *The Aims of Interpretation* is to have made the distinction between "meaning" and "significance" the main line of his argument. The second ambiguity is thus resolved, but perhaps at the cost of an untenable separation. As for the first ambiguity, we shall see later on to what extent the re-orientation of all hermeneutics as a function of the couplet meaning significance removes that.

Criticism must therefore be concerned with the major distinction between meaning and significance. In my opinion Professor Hirsch is better when he argues and polemicizes in order to introduce his distinction than when he gets down to resolving the difficulties which result from it.

Broadly speaking, the distinction is one between "content" and "context": the term "meaning" refers to the verbal meaning within the text; the word "significance"designates the relevance of the text beyond itself, as a function of the interests, values and norms which preside over its evaluation. This demarcation extends beyond the confines of literature; it alone ensures in a general way the identity of the same objects of experience in time. Within the framework of literature, the autonomy of meaning in relation to significance achieves its full prominence once one recognizes that the private processes of verbal understanding follow the same rules as the public processes of validation.

Consequently, there are not two things: to understand and to validate. To understand is already to construe for oneself a scheme, a genre, a type which yield expectations, and are in their turn susceptible or not of being confirmed. In thus conceiving understanding to be a "validating, self-correcting process", Professor Hirsch transfers on to his theory of meaning all the weight of his earlier theory of validation. His purpose in so doing is to provide himself with weapons against all forms of relativism, thus giving his work a deliberately polemical tone. Among the relativists he naturally puts those literary critics who deny that meaning can be separated from significance, but he also includes all those who, following Heidegger, insist on the circular character of understanding; to these he adds, for good measure, French theorists like Barthes, Foucault and Derrida, who become, in his terms, "theologians of dogmatic relativism" and "cognitive atheists". I must confess that to me this process of amalgamation seems very debatable. In this work no more than in the earlier one has Professor Hirsch perceived the difference between a hermeneutic philosophy and a relativistic literary criticism which would impose the perspective of the reader as the criterion of meaning. To this mistake he now adds a second by enrolling under the same relativist banner the new wave of French theorists and the hermeneutists stemming from Heidegger.

If one forgets temporarily the universalizing pretentions of this work, its critique of some of the relativist arguments seems very persuasive. This is the case first of all with the "paradoxes of perspectivism": the author establishes in a very convincing fashion that the visual metaphor of perspective suggests exactly the opposite of what relativism sees in it; I can understand that the same object is seen by another spectator from a different angle than mine because I can depart from my own perspective, coordinate it with others, and recognize the identical object which relates my perspective to other people's. Professor Hirsch quite rightly concludes that all acts of interpretation necessarily include two perspectives, that of the author and that of the interpreter. (However, he refuses to see that H. G. Gadamer's notion of the "fusion of horizons" proceeds from a precisely similar reflection on double perspective.)

The same clear-sightedness shines out in the chapter on "Stylistics and Synonymity". The author at first picks his way between two extreme positions. If two different sentences are taken as synonyms, this is not to say that they are substitutable in every context, which would be to reduce them to an empty tautology; but neither is it to say that they do not have any meaning in common, which would be to ignore the independence of the stylistic level with respect to that of the structural analysis of content. Professor Hirsch reckons to escape these two pitfalls by distinguishing the proposition which is the kernel identical to both synonyms from the synonymous phrases themselves. One might think that the indeterminacy of the form with respect to the content furnishes an argument rather in favour of relativism. No, answers Professor Hirsch, for in freeing meaning from the tutelage of form, meaning recovers its identity at the level of the proposition. Thus synonymity becomes an argument in favour of the fundamentally determinable character of meaning. But Professor Hirsch does not tell us how one could transpose to the interpretation of a text the distinction between the identical proposition, underlying several synonymous sentences, and the sentences themselves.

Be that as it may, these two more technical studies are remarkably good. But Professor Hirsch's thesis finally stands or falls on whether it is possible clearly to separate meaning from significance, i.e., the descriptive from the normative aspects of interpretation. In a certain sense, the thesis becomes more radical the more it is clarified. Thus, the author now confesses that he gave too narrow a definition of the meaning of a text when he identified it with the "author's original meaning"; this is the second ambiguity of which I spoke earlier. How far is it resolved in the present book? The logic of the separation of meaning from significance would require that the author's intention be a case of "meaning for another", and therefore belong on the side of significance. However, Professor Hirsch does not wish to draw this conclusion: he concedes that the intention of the author is not the only *possible* norm of interpretation, but maintains that it is, in the strong sense of the word, the only *practical* norm. All verbal significance must be constructed; but there is no construction without choice, and no choice without a norm. It is at this point that the original authorial meaning asserts its claim: the most fundamental moral imperative of discourse is to respect the intention of the author.

I understand this answer. But it raises an even more fundamental problem which calls into question the distinction between meaning and significance. I have just said that meaning must be constructed—it is not given in the written signs; further, it is the minimal presupposition of a theory of validation that the meaning be first guessed before being validated. We must therefore admit that the identity of meaning with itself is not given in any intuition of essence, but yielded only by the test of validation. Now, it is precisely in the work of construction that choices occur, and with choice, aims, values, and norms. In other words, questions of choice are an integral part of the construction of meaning. We no longer have to deal with only the two aspects of interpretation—meaning and significance—but with the "three dimensions of hermeneutics" (which is the the title of the fifth essay in this book). The third dimension is the ethical choice itself which, on the one hand, intervenes in the field of description, since there must be a norm in order to realize the meaning of a text,

but on the other already belongs to the problematics of evaluation (which is why the fifth essay is meant to be a chapter of transition between the two parts of the book).

Part Two, which is devoted to evaluation, confirms the reader's suspicions that the demarcation between meaning and significance cannot be maintained without equivocation. Professor Hirsch is not prepared to say that Northrop Frye rather than René Wellek, is right in their quarrel over the possibility of separating value and meaning. On the one hand, the "separatists" are partially correct, in so far as description and evaluation constitute two distinct poles of interpretation. The argument of Professor Hirsch's work is solidly entrenched on this thesis, which is less clear-cut than that of demarcation. It is perfectly legitimate to ask of criticism that it situate its disagreements about the value of a work in relation to the meaning on which it tries to agree.

It is entirely legitimate even to give free rein to conflicts of evaluation as long as one strives elsewhere for a common description of the text. But in the concrete work of interpretation the two tasks never cease to become confused, and this means that the "anti-separatists" too are partially correct. This impossibility is foreseeable in as much as our knowledge of the meaning is in no way authorized by any intuitive insight into it. Because meaning has to be constructed, value and meaning are necessarily joined. In fact, Professor Hirsch's recourse to the "Analytics of the Beautiful" in Kant's third *Critique* can only reinforce the thesis of the indissoluble liaison between fact and value, because it is a subjective judgment of values which, in the Kantian theory of "common sense", is taken as communicable, sharable, and in this sense universal. One can understand why Professor Hirsch should insist in his final essay that, once conceded, this "interference" must not weaken the basic distinction between meaning and significance. That is the thesis which has to remain as the chief thrust of the book if the enemy to be overcome is relativism and if the latest form of this relativism is found among the French theorists, who are accused of reducing all textual commentary to a mere fiction. It is Professor Hirsch's combative spirit which leads him to subordinate the unstable realm of value to the stable realm of meaning. But has he not himself undermined the stability of this realm by showing that all textual meaning has to be constructed, that all construction requires choice, and that all choice involves ethical values?

Paul Ricoeur, "Construing and Constructing,"
in The Times Literary Supplement, *No. 3911,*
February 25, 1977, p. 216.

William E. Cain   (essay date November 1977)

[*In the following essay, Cain examines the critical theory presented by Hirsch in* Validity in Interpretation *and* The Aims of Interpretation, *which he contrasts with the deconstructionist critical approach espoused by French philosopher Jacques Derrida.*]

In both *Validity in Interpretation* and *The Aims of Interpretation,* E. D. Hirsch insists on the need for authority, order, and discipline in literary studies; and he directly challenges "relativist" attitudes towards textual interpretation that have been fostered by the New Criticism and, more recently, by Structuralist and Post-Structuralist theory. "Relativism" defines a state of affairs where, in Hirsch's view, subjectivity thrives without constraints, thereby ruling out the possibility for a common and determinate object of knowledge. When subjectivity is allowed free reign in scholarship and teaching, every person can legitimately claim authority for his or her own interpretation—there is no central authority, no firm and consistent set of principles to rely upon to arbitrate disagreements about what a text truly means. We require, Hirsch argues, an authoritative center around which to organize our profession, and to which we can relate in a disciplined manner our judgments about valid and invalid interpretations.

For Hirsch, this principle of authority should be based upon the distinction between "meaning" and "significance":

> *Meaning* is that which is represented by a text; it is what the author meant by his use of a particular sign sequence; it is what the signs represent. *Significance,* on the other hand, names a relationship between that meaning and a person, or a conception, or a situation, or indeed anything imaginable. (*Validity*)

A work's "significance" may change from one generation to the next, but its "meaning" (the "verbal meaning" willed by the author) does not. Though we often speak of changes in "meaning," we are in fact referring to changes in "significance"—how a particular "meaning" is (re)criticized during different historical periods. When Hirsch says "interpretation," he is speaking of our attempt to understand the author's "meaning"; and when he discusses the function of "criticism," he is referring to efforts to locate the "significance" attached to that "meaning." Because we possess this category of "meaning," which is changeless, determinate, and reproducible, we are able to judge textual interpretation (and its practice in the classroom) as a "discipline" rather than a "playground."

In *Aims,* his recent collection of essays, Hirsch maintains that his theoretical stance has changed little since *Validity* was published in 1967. His major themes in this new book are outlined in its opening chapter: the "futility" of "relativism," the "possibility of humanistic knowledge," and the importance of protecting the "stable determinacy of meaning"—the "object of knowledge" described in detail in *Validity.* The relativists, who deny our moral duty to advocate objective standards for interpretation, and who ignore the pressures of "ordinary experience" on teachers of literature, are treated with contempt. Literary study now suffers from a Post-Structuralist threat to its stability that is far more serious than that posed by the New Criticism. The proponents of "anti-rationalism, faddism, and extreme relativism," inspired by Heidegger, Derrida, and their "disciples," mount a frontal assault on the concept of centralized authority in interpretation, and therefore threaten to undermine the very basis for rule and discipline in the profession. These writers are the "cognitive atheists," who refuse to adhere to any common authority and shared principles; they degrade knowledge and value,

and disguise their self-indulgent "works of fiction" as "serious criticism." According to Hirsch, Derrida and his associates endanger literary and cultural order by calling into question the existence of and need for authority. Their theories subvert the goal of objective knowledge that should structure our interpretations, and encourage an interpretive solipsism that undercuts our belief in research and teaching as a shared, communal enterprise.

In *Aims,* as in *Validity,* Hirsch adheres to "principles" with which to combat the decadent "subjectivism" promoted by the Derridean group. His positions are forcefully (often aggressively) argued, and his stand on behalf of "validity" in our profession is admirable in its clarity and rigor. Yet it is interesting to note both in *Validity* and in *Aims* the potential radicalism of many of the "principles" which Hirsch deploys to counter "relativistic" dogma. He is, I believe, regularly misrepresented as a naive advocate of the "intentional fallacy" or as a supporter of crudely-defined generic categories. But many of his beliefs would prove difficult for "conservative" critics (both intentionalist and neo-Aristotelian) to accept; in fact Hirsch belongs in the "conservative" camp less for his theoretical insights than for his persistent retreat from their implications. Often he makes surprisingly radical statements—some which even resemble Derrida's and the relativists'—only to pull back to establish a line of defense against them. He sticks to his distinction between "meaning" and "significance," along with its promise of an authoritative object of knowledge, even when it seems not to be well served by the specific points of his theory.

In *Aims* some venerable dichotomies lose their prestige. Hirsch favors, for example, a "general" rather than a "local" hermeneutics, which means that he does not recommend the study of a "poetic" language divorced from other "ordinary" uses of language. For Hirsch, there is no distinction between "poetic" and (merely) prosaic or everyday properties of language: "General hermeneutics lays claim to principles that hold true all of the time in textual interpretation." Later references to "literature" and generic classification are equally straightforward:

> No literary theorist from Coleridge to the present has succeeded in formulating a viable distinction between the nature of ordinary written speech and the nature of literary written speech.
>
> Literature has no independent essence, aesthetic or otherwise. It is an arbitrary classification of linguistic works which do not exhibit common distinctive traits, and which cannot be defined as an Aristotelian species.
>
> . . . A true class requires a set of distinguishing features which are inclusive within the class and exclusive outside it; it requires a *differentia specifica.* That, according to Aristotle, is the key to definition and to essence. But, in fact, nobody has ever so defined literature or any important genre within it.

Although Hirsch challenges our usual understanding of the terms "literature" and "genre," he still preserves them in his theoretical system. He does not wish to grant privileged status to "literature" but neither does he want to deny, as he explains in the Afterword to *Aims,* the value of literary study and the knowledge to be acquired from it:

> Many modern defenders of literature rightly claim for literature a kind of truth not usually found in other modes of discourse—vivid truths about human nature and emotion, about the forms of human desire and resistance to human desire. Literature instructs still by being true.

Hirsch testifies eloquently here to the value of the knowledge to be attained through literature. But his position is nevertheless a curious one. Many of his local observations about "literature" and "genre" seem to conflict with his larger goal of defending the special place of literary studies, for he calls into question the terms that we usually judge to be (however mistakenly) privileged and unique. It is likely that many people, who, along with Hirsch, uphold the need for firm authority and discipline, will be made uncomfortable by his concessions to the other (relativist) side, which similarly criticizes the privileging of terms.

We also should not make the mistake of too quickly including Hirsch among those critics who find meaning to rest exclusively in the text, rather than in our codes and conventions of reading. He argues *against* theorists who claim that the text somehow projects messages, which are then (passively) understood by the reader. As Hirsch explains: "Meaning has existence only in consciousness. Apart from the categories through which it is construed, meaning can have no existence at all." But Hirsch's stand on the ongoing reader-text debate—where does the responsibility lie for generating meaning?—is again an intriguing one. While he refuses to explicitly locate meaning in the text, he also refuses to allow textual interpretation "from a perspective different from the original author's"—as though there *is* a particular meaning to be extracted from the text, which may be verified by referring both to the text and to other kinds of "relevant knowledge" (the biography of the author, historical information about the period, etc.). This argument finally inclines towards locating the meaning "in the text"—the author's intention, which the interpreter must understand, is represented by the sequence of verbal signs. But Hirsch's text-centered position is less the product of his statements about "meaning" (which can exist "only in consciousness") than of his desire for one special category of "meaning" to serve as an authoritative norm. Several passages in *Validity* help to clarify this point. While Hirsch does not deny that there may initially be disparate interpretations of "meaning," he does argue for strict controls. If the meaning proposed by the interpreter is not "verified in some way," then it "will simply be the interpreter's own meaning, exhibiting the connotations and emphases which he himself imposes." The interpreter should not "exhibit" (i.e., flaunt, display) "his own subjective acts," but should instead be ruled by the single authorial intention represented by the text. Otherwise we will be confronted by complete subjectivity in interpretation: "As soon as the reader's outlook is permitted to determine what a text means, we have not simply a changing meaning but quite possibly as many meanings as readers." From one point

of view the "text" (like "literature") is emptied of its usual weight, since it does not produce meaning itself. But the authority of the text remains in place, whatever Hirsch's concessions to the reader's "consciousness," for the text can represent *only* the "meaning" intended by the author.

When Hirsch discusses "form" and "content" in his chapter in *Aims* on stylistics and synonymity, he performs a similar move. He stresses that "synonymity" does exist— that an "absolutely identical meaning" can be expressed "through different linguistic forms." Undoubtedly many critics and teachers would like to share this belief in the availability of different "forms" to express the same content. But it is questionable whether they would endorse other statements in this chapter. Hirsch goes on to assert, for example, that "meaning" and "form" stand in an essentially indeterminate relationship. In fact, he points out, "the relation of form to meaning is so very flexible, even to the point of indeterminacy, that a word, or even a whole written text, is not necessarily synonymous with itself." This theoretical admission, however, allows room for the claims of the relativist critics who argue that, because understanding is an historical phenomenon, no two meanings can ever be spoken of as truly identical. While Hirsch declares the possibility of synonymity, he concedes that a word or text may not even be synonymous with itself; and once this concession is made, he leaves himself open to inviting the interpretive "chaos" he aims to oppose—the same "anarchic" state of affairs that his theory intends to protect us against. Perhaps Hirsch's repeated statements in favor of authority, order, and an "object of knowledge" partly arise from the apparent resemblance between some of his positions and those which he so vigorously attacks.

The ground for Hirsch's theory is his distinction between "meaning" and "significance." It is this "firm principle" which he uses both to refute Derrida's relativist claims and to avert the interpretive anarchy that some of his own insights might appear to generate. He can subscribe to what I have termed "radical" positions (despite his clear uneasiness about them) because he believes that his argument is firmly grounded in an authoritative center—in a principle of order that will prevent "radicalism" from undermining unity and objectivity in literary studies. But the origins of Hirsch's crucial tenet are again surprising. In *Validity* he emphasizes that "there is nothing in the nature of the text itself which requires the reader to set up the author's meaning as his normative ideal." In other words, there is no a priori necessity for treating "meaning" as the author's meaning. But in Hirsch's view only "authorial meaning" can exist as a compelling standard for interpretation: "On purely practical grounds, therefore, it is preferable to agree that the meaning of a text is the author's meaning." This definition of "meaning" is not in any sense forced upon us by the text, but is to be preferred for its practical advantages: it will act as a defensible norm to regulate the activities of scholars and teachers. Because we require a standard to govern our interpretive practice, we select (as preferable to disorder) a normative definition of authorial meaning.

But while Hirsch's category of "meaning" may supply the profession with a standard, its usage may not prove reassuring. At one point in *Validity* he presents a "hypothetical instance":

> We have posited that Shakespeare did not mean that Hamlet wished to sleep with his mother. We confront an interpretation which states that Hamlet did wish to sleep with his mother. If we assert, as I have done, that only a re-cognitive interpretation is a valid interpretation, then we must, on the basis of our assumed premise about the play, say that the Freudian interpretation is invalid. It does not correspond to the author's meaning; it is an implication that cannot be subsumed under the type of meaning that Shakespeare (under our arbitrary supposition) willed. It is irrelevant that the play permits such an interpretation. The variability of possible interpretations is the very fact that requires a theory of interpretation and validity.

If the critic or teacher hopes for a defense against relativism and a return to authority, he receives it here (as Henry James would say) "full in the face." The attempt to erect and justify an arbitrary authority—one which is "posited" and "assumed"—could not be more nakedly presented.

Hirsch differentiates "meaning" and "significance" to ward off the state of affairs signalled by his terms "chaos" and "anarchy." But it is important to recognize that this constitutes a desire rather than a firm proof. If there is only indeterminate meaning, then there is no norm for deciding among interpretations; but since we must have a norm if we ever hope to achieve objective knowledge, then we must assert that "meaning" is the determinate meaning intended by the author. Hirsch offers a variety of arguments for authorial meaning, yet it is too often forgotten that his choice of a "firm principle" is merely posited, not naturally grounded. His arguments for authority are the result of a need he perceives in the profession, and his proposal of the distinction between "meaning" and "significance" is chosen because it is (he feels) defensible, not because it is an a priori truth that no one could deny. Hirsch assumes that there will be "chaos" without a standard that all of us agree to honor; he does not consider the alternative that there might exist other kinds of standards, however uncodified, which already operate to forestall anarchy in interpretation. It is not as though we now write and teach without any kinds of constraints; and perhaps it is the case that our academic and other forms of behavior are "orderly" even though they are not impelled by a fully-articulated charter of rules. Hirsch believes that we cannot speak of a structured and orderly discipline unless we observe an authoritative standard. But the elusiveness of a single standard should not be taken to imply that in scholarship and teaching "anything goes." We are more conscious of all sorts of standards, rules, and proprieties, and less prone to anarchy, than Hirsch's arguments usually suggest. Simply because there is no *single* standard, privileged above all others, does not mean that there are *no* standards at all. This is an important point, and we will return to it when we discuss Derrida.

The authority which Hirsch claims for his category of "authorial meaning" may in fact be far less stable than he believes. When considering the problem of "implications," for example, he explains:

> If, for example, I announce, "I have a headache," there is no difficulty in construing what I "say," but there may be great difficulty in construing implications like "I desire sympathy," or "I have a right not to engage in distasteful work." (*Validity*)

But to claim that the verbal meaning of "I have a headache" is explicit assumes that it always comes attached to an identifiable (and irrefutable) context, and that this context will immediately be the same for both speaker and hearer. The meaning intended by the author of this statement, however, depends upon (for instance) whether he suffers from migraines or has had engine trouble with a new automobile; and the hearer or reader cannot always know in advance the appropriate context for understanding this authorial meaning. The author's intention is problematical for interpreters precisely because there *is* "difficulty" in construing what Hirsch "says" in these types of examples.

Other problems with Hirsch's distinction between "meaning" and "significance" become clear in *Aims,* where he qualifies somewhat the definitions presented in *Validity.* "Meaning" is now "simply meaning-for-an-interpreter," and "significance" is "meaning-as-related-to-something-else." This new emphasis on the interpreter greatly enlarges the category of "meaning" and, as Susan Suleiman has noted in a fine essay ["Interpreting Ironies," *Diacritics* (1976)], undermines the authority that Hirsch wants to claim for it. "Meaning," he argues, "now comprises constructions where authorial will is partly or totally disregarded." But by reducing the normative power of authorial intention, Hirsch has seriously weakened the forcefulness of the term "meaning" (whatever its other shortcomings) in his system. He still hopes to conceive of "meaning" as (more or less) centered in the text—the interpreter finds meaning in a text because he is confident that it is truly "there"; but of course it is "there" only because, as Hirsch often reminds us, it has been constructed by the interpreter. This description no longer provides for the "firm principle" of authorial will and intention: "No normative limitations are imported into the definition." There is, in other words, no single, reproducible, and determinate authorial intention "represented" by the text to confine the interpreter; and the boundaries to his responses to the text therefore are taken away. While Hirsch still speaks of "meaning" as a "principle" of authority, which guides and stabilizes our interpretations, he has eliminated its impact through his own revisions.

Perhaps the most admirable feature of Hirsch's work, which helps to account for his tough-minded theoretical stance, is his concern for the state of the profession. There is perhaps no other theorist today who speaks as passionately for responsibility in both scholarship and teaching; and certainly no other member of the profession so forcefully calls upon academics to address themselves to the dismaying trends in recent criticism, to the decline in writing skills among students, and to the pressures on teachers of the humanities to justify their performance in an era of decreasing budgets and enrollments. What disturbs Hirsch about the Derridean relativists is their impracticality and even hypocrisy. "Nobody could live" according to such theories in "his ordinary intercourse with the world," and no one would choose to do so even if it were possible. Derrida's thought is "faddish" and "decadent" to Hirsch not only because of its theoretical blindness to the need for authority and to the demands of the academy, but also because its proponents are not (and could not be) committed to living out the tenets of their own doctrine. For Hirsch, "empirical truth is the ultimate arbiter of theories in the practical disciplines" (*Aims*); and he emphasizes throughout his work the importance of attending to the "usefulness" of our theories, to "common sense," "practical questions," "concrete goals," and the "practical side of our present situation." There is a bottom-line:

> Poetry and fiction are worth studying, and if we don't keep them alive in humanistic education, nobody else will. That is the only justification we need.

The New Criticism committed a "philosophical error" in asserting the "centrality" and "autonomy" of literary studies; but, Hirsch adds, its success was due in large measure to its ability to define the roles and methods of those engaged in teaching "poetry and fiction." Now that the errors and excesses of New Critical practice have been exposed, we require a new theory. We need once again to define our identities as scholars and teachers, and to form our professional duties around a "center." But to find our self-definitions in the writings of Derrida would, Hirsch argues, deny our communal responsibility as teachers of others, preclude a common object of knowledge, and bring about "anarchy" in interpretation.

Perhaps the most admirable feature of Hirsch's work, which helps to account for his tough-minded theoretical stance, is his concern for the state of academia.

—William E. Cain

Hirsch maintains that literary theories and emphases in interpretation reflect "ethical choices." We must decide what should be the "goals of interpretation" and the priorities of the humanistic disciplines, and in making these decisions "we have to enter the realm of ethics." The source of Hirsch's strength both in *Validity* and in *Aims* is this ethical commitment, and his awareness that interpretation is never innocent of ethical motives and goals. Whatever our theoretical allegiances, we must at the very least be conscious of their ethical grounds, and measure them carefully against the ethical stances of those who argue from other points of view. For Hirsch the issue is clear: those who choose to ignore authorial intention are guilty of a vicious type of intellectual domination:

> To treat an author's words merely as grist for

one's mill is ethically analogous to using another man merely for one's own purposes.

When we engage a text "solipsistically," we in effect manipulate and abuse the intentions of another person. But while Hirsch's ethical point is forthright and persuasive, it is difficult to apply it fully to his own theory: his category of "meaning," as described in *Aims,* is no longer restricted to "an author's words," and his position therefore is no longer strictly centered in an authority that would ratify his ethical judgment.

Though Hirsch's reminders about the relationship between ethics and interpretation are valuable, he does not seem to me to recognize clearly the problems of authority and ideology that these imply. In *Validity,* for example, he recommends that interpretive debates proceed under an "advocacy system." Each critic "advocates" his or her interpretation of a certain text, and then participates in "adjudication" that will determine which is most probably correct. But of course it cannot be guaranteed that each advocate will voluntarily surrender his or her own claim; each person may remain firmly convinced (despite the attempt at adjudication) that his or her interpretation is the most accurate one. Hirsch's answer to this problem is to nominate a judge: " . . . Unless advocates sometimes serve as judges, none of this activity will actually contribute to knowledge." Hirsch makes no provision, however, for the selection of judges, and, while authority is often at issue in *Validity,* he fails to deal with it at its crucial points. There must be an authority to prevent the "chaotic democracy of readings" that could arise even under an advocacy system. But how this judge will be selected, and how an intellectual tyranny will be avoided in which certain interpretations are summarily over-ruled, are nowhere mentioned. Hirsch's theory is in many respects bluntly authoritarian, and many beleaguered scholars and teachers will welcome it for its promise of a return to rigid authority and discipline. But the ideology of this interpretive choice may be as alarming in its implications as that which it professes to guard against.

In several chapters of *Aims,* Hirsch deals provocatively with the issues of authority and evaluation, but again his answers are unsatisfactory. He observes that "preferential criteria" in evaluative criticism are necessarily problematical for us, since we lack "institutionalized authority" or a "genuinely widespread cultural consensus." Since, he elsewhere writes, "there is no papacy in intellectual affairs" in the modern world, we must judge literary value according to "principle, not authority." But when Hirsch advocates "principle," he is not offering a substitute for "authority" but instead proposing a new one. And when his "principles" lead in *Aims* to a return to the Arnoldian definition of "literature," their potential for authoritarian judgments becomes striking:

> Under that older conception, literature comprises everything worthy to be read, preferably the best thoughts expressed in the best manner, but above all the best thoughts.

But the criteria for "worthy to be read" and "best thoughts" have never been obvious: does the approved canon arise naturally (as Hirsch appears to imply), or is it decided upon by those with the authority to establish and enforce it? Later, when alluding to the Victorian critic Dowden, Hirsch presents a particular evaluation of "worth":

> . . . In the spirit of Dowden it is tempting to add that in English literature of the nineteenth-century, Charles Darwin is a greater and more interesting name than Walter Pater.

Darwin's name may associate nicely with the advocacy system set out in *Validity* ("the survival of the fittest"), but its ideological force is less than heartening. The dangers of authoritarianism exposed by the naming of Darwin, and by his placement (again as though it were self-evident) in the roster of "greater" and "more interesting," must be firmly resisted. The "principles" which inform these judgments are not simply alternatives to authority, but in fact promote an authority of the most ruthless kind: it is the survival of those who are *declared* to be the fittest.

In both *Validity* and *Aims,* Hirsch confronts major theoretical and professional issues. His effort to preserve authority and order in scholarship and teaching is admirable in its rigor, and his positions are often compelling and forcefully argued. But it is their persuasiveness, their skillfully presented appeal to the need for authority, which demands that they receive careful scrutiny. Before we accept Hirsch's proposals, we should consider the practice of what he preaches.

But it would be unfair to Hirsch to criticize his theoretical statements without also taking a brief account of Derrida—the most influential member of the "cognitive atheists" whom Hirsch roundly condemns in his books. Derrida's texts are varied, allusive (as well as elusive), obscure, and difficult to summarize—I will be forced to be extremely selective in my references to his work. And I also want to make clear that, while I do not endorse Derrida's position in all respects, I do believe it is necessary to try to remedy some common misunderstandings about his theories. My interest here will lie in several points: Derrida's "deconstructive" theory of literary criticism and its attack on the concepts of "origin" and "center"; his particular insights about the nature of authority, and why these have proven so disturbing to Hirsch; and finally, his recognition of the constraints on his "deconstructive" machinery, and his insistence that authority, discipline, and responsibility are crucial to his approach.

In "Positions" [*Diacritics* (1972)], Derrida describes "deconstruction" as the forced inversion of our usual textual hierarchies and systems. It "brings down the superior position while reconstructing its sublimating or idealizing genealogy, and the irruptive emergence of a new 'concept,' a concept which no longer allows itself, never allowed itself to be understood in the previous regime." Derrida strives to reverse the scale of authority in textual interpretation; he probes a particular text, hunting out the strand or element that serves as the authority for a certain reading or meaning, and then exposes it as yet another product of linguistic conventions—as, in other words, a feature of the text whose authority should not be privileged over others which are themselves constituted by language. The repressed reading, the group of other textual elements that

the former authority has subjugated, is then revealed, its structural contours brought to light.

"Deconstruction" denies the existence of a text governed by a center or an original core that organizes and authorizes a single system of meaning. When we deconstruct a text, we show that there is no privileged center for its interplay of meanings; rather, there is *only* a multiple and interwoven "play" of meanings, which is not bound to observe the strictures imposed by a claimant to centralized authority. In Derrida's terms, there is no single "referent" or "transcendental signified which would regulate all of [the text's] movements." We cannot identify a fixed goal or endpoint for our interpretations, and hence cannot justifiably speak of a truly privileged authority that verifies some interpretations, and rules others out of court. Interpretation never ends because it has nowhere to go:

> . . . The turbulence of a certain lack breaks down the limit of the text, exempts it from exhaustive and enclosing formalization or at least prohibits a saturating taxonomy of its themes, of its signifieds, of its intended meaning.

Once we acknowledge the lack or absence of a center around which the text is constructed, we shatter the notion of a text whose meanings will eventually be contained (enclosed) by our interpretations. The de-centered text excludes the the possibility of a final stage to our interpretations—there can *never* be a complete listing of patterns and themes or a single statement of authorial intention.

The conflict between Hirsch and Derrida should be clear from this brief summary and set of quotations. Derrida denies the availability of the key articles in Hirsch's theory: the notion of a fixed and determinate center; the belief in a final, authoritative meaning (in Derrida's words, an "exhaustive" or "enclosing" interpretation); and the possibility that a distinct interpretive goal can be established and reached by combining and sifting among the "meanings" advocated by different interpreters. No doubt Hirsch is also disturbed by the disruptive thrust of Derrida's highly politicized vocabulary—the overthrow of entrenched authority, the reversal of hierarchies, and the illumination of the subjugated "concepts" in the text. Hirsch fears the rebellious eruption of subjectivity, and the consequent emergence of each man as a claimant (without any constraints) to his own authority in interpretation. He can foresee only disorder and "chaos" in a world without centralized authority—without, that is, a "center" towards which all interpreters and interpretations owe their loyalty. Hirsch does in fact cross with Derrida in his perception in both *Validity* and *Aims* that his arguments for a "center" are not in any sense required or privileged by the nature of the text itself. But Hirsch maintains that the standard of "authorial meaning," even though it is our own creation, is *preferable* to the existence of a chaotic world which has no obvious standards, norms, and authorities—a world that he describes as unstructured, undisciplined, and fragmented by the irreconcilable demands of each interpreter upholding his or her private cause.

But, as we have seen, "constraints" do not disappear simply because they are left uncodified; nor does authority fail to exert its influence after its "center" is called into question. The analysis that Derrida devotes to systems and hierarchies, and to reversing their usual priorities, is confined (as he himself recognizes) by the reign of language. For Derrida, analysis never terminates, interpretation never ends, because "the hierarchy of the dual opposition always reconstitutes itself." What deconstruction works to tear asunder is immediately joined back together again, and the reversal of authority, brought about by the activity of the deconstructive critic, is itself reversed. Its identity is never precisely correspondent with what it was before, but its previous authority is "always" restored and again exposed for still another deconstruction. Our deconstructive procedures, undertaken through language, are therefore inescapably "trapped in a sort of circle":

> This circle is unique. It describes the form of the relationship between the history of metaphysics and the destruction of the history of metaphysics. *There is no sense* in doing without the concepts of metaphysics in order to attack metaphysics. We have no language—no syntax and no lexicon—which is alien to this history; we cannot utter a single destructive proposition which has not already slipped into the form, the logic, and the implicit postulations of precisely what it seeks to contest. [Jacques Derrida in "Structure, Sign, and Play in the Discourse of the Human Sciences," in *The Structuralist Controversy*, edited by Richard Macksey and Eugenio Donato, 1970]

Far from being able successfully to subvert authority, Derrida realizes that he can never break free from its hold; his intention to "destroy" and "deconstruct" is invariably challenged by the terms in which it is expressed. He is bound to observe the authority of a centered system even when his deconstruction reveals its linguistic base and, at that moment, tries to overthrow it. It is not the case for Derrida, contrary to Hirsch's view of him, that authority can be made somehow to disappear completely. Its origins can be examined and its priorities reversed, but its force "always reconstitutes itself." Although Derrida wants to analyze the foundations for authority, he perceives that his method must be limited to the same tools that support authority:

> It is a question of putting expressly and systematically the problem of the status of a discourse which borrows from a heritage the resources necessary for the deconstruction of that heritage itself.

The deconstructive critic's situation—he must always testify to authority in his act of opposing it—demands responsibility and discipline. These do not fade away under Derrida's method, but instead become all the more compelling, since we no longer have automatic recourse to a single authority that orders our interpretations for us. But again this should not be taken to mean that we are not conscious of, and obliged to observe, the presence of authorities—we are never free to ignore them and do so only at great risk. When we interpret a text and enter our interpretation into public and professional contexts, we are intensely aware of standards and authorities—and this holds true no matter how successfully we have exposed their suspect claims to special privilege over us. There are al-

ways authorities at work that govern our behavior, whatever our illusions or pretensions about living independently of them. Derrida specifically calls for "rigor" and "responsibility" in interpretation; he does not (and could not) advocate a state of affairs where these would not be required to serve as authoritative standards. His terms insist that efforts to dislodge concepts of authority and responsibility will always end in re-instituting them somewhere else.

Perhaps Derrida's most striking insight is that we cannot "get along" without "the center," no matter how persuasively we demonstrate its suspect claims for privilege. "The center," Derrida states, is "absolutely indispensable." We cannot rid ourselves of the notion of an authoritative center, or deny the existence of other kinds of authorities that hold sway over us in different contexts; and we should not delude ourselves that we can enjoy complete freedom from responsibility—both to ourselves and to others—in interpretation. But while authority cannot finally be overthrown, it is nevertheless always subject to our attempts to criticize it, and to reverse the conservative systems and hierarchies that it promotes: "It is a question of knowing where it comes from and how it functions." For Hirsch, on the other hand, once authority is (as in his *Hamlet* example) "posited" and "assumed," then it must remain unquestioned. The danger inherent in his position is that, in his effort to provide a "center" for the profession, he will establish an authority which does not merely limit interpretations but tyrannizes over them. (pp. 333-45)

William E. Cain, "Authority, 'Cognitive Atheism', and the Aims of Interpretation: The Literary Theory of E. D. Hirsch," in College English, *Vol. 39, No. 3, November, 1977, pp. 333-45.*

John M. Ellis   (review date Fall 1979)

[*Ellis is an English educator and critic who has published several studies of German literature. In the review below, he criticizes Hirsch's critical theory in* The Aims of Interpretation *as "not backed up by any real care or skill in the analysis of his key concepts or in the development of his argument."*]

[*The Aims of Interpretation*] is essentially a collection of essays previously published between 1968 and 1975. Hirsch explains that those essays, when first written, were "always conceived as parts of a coherent book." The dust cover presents the volume in like manner as a "major work" which extends Hirsch's "previous work in the theory of interpretation (hermeneutics), and breaks new ground in the theory of evaluation. The unifying theme of the book is Hirsch's convincing defense of the possibility of genuine knowledge in textual interpretation." The truth is, I think, that the volume does in fact have the character of a collection of occasional essays rather than of a systematically conceived major treatise. The individual essays do not form part of a chain of argument, but instead revolve around a small number of central tenets in Hirsch's view of criticism, continually returning to them in different contexts. The most important of these tenets are: an author's intention can be determined, and it should be central to interpretation; perfect synonymy is possible, so that meaning is not determined by linguistic form; meaning varies with perspective; "aesthetic" criticism is too narrow, and the canon of works of literature must be broader than that which aesthetic criteria would generate; and genuine objective knowledge is possible in criticism. At first sight, some of these might appear to be inconsistent with others (e.g., the last with the assertion that meaning varies with perspective). Hirsch manages to stitch them all together into what constitutes for him a unity (and the main drift of his thinking in literary theory) in the following way: the meaning of a piece of language is not determined by its linguistic form, but varies with each interpreter's perspective, and so the only stable objective knowledge we can have of it is that of its author's perspective, i.e., his intent. And since this account of meaning transcends purely formal (and therefore also aesthetic) factors, aesthetic criteria are insufficient and the canon of literary works ought not to be defined in terms of such criteria.

Hirsch's book has some virtues. He writes without the dogmatic ideological insistence, the flat assertive one-sidedness that characterizes so much literary theory; by contrast, he appears cool and low key, and relatively undogmatic. He appears to have read widely without brandishing his knowledge irrelevantly, and he pursues the central issues of linguistic form and the interpretation of meaning into a number of relevant other fields; he refers on occasion to philosophers of language such as Austin, Strawson, Searle, Grice, and Black; to logicians like Quine and Carnap; to the recent continental philosophers Husserl and Heidegger, as well as to classics like Kant and Aristotle; to linguists of the transformational kind like Chomsky, Katz, and Fodor, as well as to C. Bazell (who is rather more closely allied with J. R. Firth's work); to stylistics; to Piaget and developmental psychology; to both continental and Anglo-American literary theory; and more. He proceeds in what seems to be a consciously careful and sober analytic manner.

Nonetheless, I find this book ultimately disappointing, and I have serious doubts as to whether its argumentation can stand up to any kind of close logical scrutiny. Hirsch's analytic tone looks promising on the surface, but it is not backed up by any real care or skill in the analysis of his key concepts and in the development of his argument.

A good example of the book's shortcomings can be seen in its treatment of the concept of meaning. Early in his book Hirsch makes an issue of distinguishing the concepts *meaning* and *significance,* and that looks like a promising move—the word *meaning* has many distinguishable uses in English, and no serious theorist can avoid making some distinctions early in the game. But the way in which the distinction is drawn is immediately discouraging; meaning "refers to the whole verbal meaning of a text." This is not only vague but also uses the word *meaning* to explain itself. And throughout the book this and other concepts are frequently used without sufficient care to distinguish their various possible senses; as a result, Hirsch's argument flounders badly. When a key word is used in two or three

different senses, but as if the same notion were being developed, any argument simply falls to pieces. Here is an example:

> For instance, when on one occasion I speak the word "tangerine," I may be thinking of its flavor; on another of its texture and shape; on another of its color. Yet even though I may be attending to those different aspects of a tangerine (or to none of them), I can still be referring to the very same thing: a self-identical object or meaning. Moreover, this asymmetry is reversible. On both of two occasions I may be attending to the flavor of a tangerine, and yet I may mean something rather different when I use the word on these two occasions. In one of the cases the flavor could be my exclusive meaning; in the other my coincidental thinking about flavor could be irrelevant to my meaning.

This is a dreadful conceptual muddle. At least three different senses of meaning, some of them in any case very dubious, are being confused and conflated: the meaning of a word as its place in the language; meaning as the object referred to in a given context; and even meaning as an additional *unexpressed* thought about that object in the speaker's mind! When Hirsch says that he may mean something rather different by the word *tangerine* on two different occasions he is overlooking the much more important fact that in this passage he is using the word *meaning* in radically different ways. This kind of conceptual confusion renders many of Hirsch's key assertions literally meaningless. Take, for example, his statement that "my meaning exists and is construed only from my perspective"; given the amorphous use of the word *meaning* in Hirsch's text, this statement can hardly be interpreted at all.

**I find *The Aims of Interpretation*
ultimately disappointing, and I have
serious doubts as to whether its
argumentation can stand up to any kind of
close logical scrutiny. Hirsch's analytic
tone looks promising on the surface, but it
is not backed up by any real care or skill
in the analysis of his key concepts and in
the development of his argument.**

—John M. Ellis

My strongest impression of Hirsch's book is that it aspires to the elegance and logical finesse of philosophers like Austin and Grice, and cultivates a surface which is like theirs, but that the substance of his argumentation never really reaches into the world of such figures; the careful distinctions they make when talking about concepts such as meaning, and their consequent success in focusing and developing fundamental issues, are absent from his book. I find instead an attempt at precision (much use of technical terminology, much attempting to define words and issues) which too often achieves very little. For example, Hirsch announces at one point in his text yet another definition of meaning "as that which a text is taken to represent," but he does not elucidate the key word *represent* at all, nor does he explain to us why this definition must now replace his previous formulations. On the same page, he uses the logical term "any and all" quite irrelevantly and unnecessarily, as if it were a borrowed piece of jargon. What seems more revelatory of the substance and character of Hirsch's concerns and thought are those assertions which appear as a sudden break in the style of his book. On page 143, for example, he suddenly accuses those he disagrees with of being "specialists in elite verbal artifacts," and of trying to "seal off a work of art for contemplation"—crude and question-begging formulations which preclude any analysis of the issues involved.

Hirsch's display of references to relevant other fields, when looked at more closely, has the character of a spotty, superficial, and haphazard eclecticism rather than of a solidly grasped body of knowledge consistently and relevantly applied. Thus he seems to know very little about stylistics, even though he discusses it for 24 pages. During that time he does not refer to a single example or a single scholar in the field. Surely only a lack of any significant acquaintance with stylistics can lead to his saying that it is a "fundamental postulate" and a "basic assumption" of the entire field "that a difference in linguistic form compels a difference in meaning." There arises again the question of what this statement means in the general context of Hirsch's muddled use of the word *meaning,* and his failure to explain how he is taking style to relate to meaning. But in any case, the field of stylistics is evidently far too varied and chaotic for its practitioners to share any one view of the relation of style to meaning; transformationalist students of style, for example, would probably reject any sense of Hirsch's postulate, however it were interpreted. Anyone who has any acquaintance with stylistics knows that the field is characterized precisely by a complete lack of agreement on fundamental theoretical assumptions.

For the most part, Hirsch's book seems to me to do little to justify or analyze the positions he takes up; his text revolves around his articles of faith but ultimately achieves no more than the restating of them. Take, for example, the arguments he musters for his view that texts are indeterminate if taken only in themselves: "Stated bluntly, the nature of interpretation is to construe from a sign-system (for short, 'text') something more than its physical presence. That is, the nature of a text is to mean whatever we construe it to mean." Hirsch's "that is" tries to make these two sentences seem logically connected, but there is a huge gulf between them. The fact that a text means nothing merely as marks on a paper, but must be construed in relation to the rules of the linguistic system (Hirsch has that wrong too—the *text* is not the system), is a very long way from saying that it means whatever we construe it to mean. A similar gulf is casually bridged when Hirsch says that "if an ancient text has been interpreted as a Christian allegory, that is unanswerable proof that it can be so interpreted." This is extraordinary logic and avoids the obvious difference between the two senses of *can* which are in-

volved. Almost everyone has taken part at some time in a conversation such as this: "Can I fish for salmon with cheese for bait?" "You *can,* but you won't catch any." The mocking reply willfully takes up the *wrong* sense of can ("am I physically able to") instead of the sense which the context demands: "does it make any sense to" or "can anything useful be achieved by. . . ." The mere fact that I am able to say anything the English language allows me to say (two and two is five?) is unanswerable proof only of the fact that I am physically able to talk any kind of nonsense I want to. These elementary logical mistakes so permeate Hirsch's discussion of author's intention in relation to textual meaning that I am unable to see that he adds anything of substance to that debate.

Similarly, his discussion of synonymy does not really join the scholarly debate in a profitable way. To prove that *bachelor* and *unmarried man* can mean the same thing, Hirsch constructs a hypothetical piece of English in which the two terms are used frequently in strict alternation; that is, the text makes them interchangeable. But all that this odd example proves is that the inherent difference in the terms is so obvious that the context Hirsch invents has to give very firm signals to the reader that he must *ignore* any differences between them, since they are clearly used *as if* there were none. The context says, in effect: look only at similarity of function between the two, and disregard anything outside their overlap of meaning. This example makes it clear, in any case, that Hirsch misconceives where the problem of synonymy lies. It does not lie in the fact that any one of a number of different linguistic forms can *in a given context* achieve the purpose which is the main concern of that context (i.e., in that very limited sense, "mean the same thing"); it obviously can, and this was surely never in dispute. The problem is rather: are there two distinct linguistic forms which share the same range of functions to the point that there is no context in which they do not achieve something at least slightly different? Again, I am struck by Hirsch's not quite grasping the issues which predominate in those fields that he is trying to bring to bear on literary theory.

Hirsch does on occasion make a few shrewd remarks, but taken as a whole, his book cannot be judged as the major work announced by its dust cover. My own conclusion can only be that it does not penetrate any of the logical secrets of the problems which it raises, that it therefore offers only some articles of faith, in themselves not very remarkable, that it breaks no new ground in literary theory, and that it does not bring to bear on the problems of literary theory any solidly grasped insights from other fields. (pp. 417-20)

John M. Ellis, in a review of "The Aims of Interpretation," in Comparative Literature, *Vol. 31, No. 4, Fall, 1979, pp. 417-20.*

Robert Scholes   (essay date Fall 1986)

[*Scholes is an American author and educator specializing in the study of literary and critical theory. His works, which evince an interest in a wide range of literary aspects, include* The Nature of Narrative *(1966),* Structuralism in Literature *(1974), and* Elements of Literature Three: Fiction, Poetry, Drama *(1982). In the excerpt below, he attacks as ideologically grounded the definitions of "culture" and "literacy" presented by Hirsch in his 1983 essay "Cultural Literacy."*]

[The] current attempt to impose a canon on all humanistic study in this country presents itself in rhetoric designed to conceal its ideological bases. This attempt is most powerfully embodied in recent writings of E. D. Hirsch (Kenan Professor of English at the University of Virginia) and William J. Bennett (who published his views when he was chairman of the National Endowment for the Humanities and is now U. S. Secretary of Education). It has the support of the present administration of this country and of powerful foundations. It is anything but trivial. I am opposed to the establishment of a canon in humanistic studies because I believe such a move to be fundamentally undemocratic: a usurpation of curricular power by the federal government. I also believe, and hope to show why in the following discussion, that the establishment of a canon such as that proposed by William Bennett would entail severe restrictions upon the way that the canonical texts should be approached: restrictions of a quasi-religious sort designed to stifle any genuinely critical attitude toward the canonized texts. It is with these concerns in mind that I undertake a critical examination of the proposals of Bennett and Hirsch.

For both Hirsch and Bennett American education is presently in a state of crisis which they explain as a decline. Exactly what it is a decline *from* is somewhat less clear, but the rhetoric of their discourse is structured around the topics of present crisis and the myth of an earlier golden age. Their theme is *"O tempora, O mores,"* as Rome's greatest rhetorician put it, complaining about the decline of everything a few decades before the Augustan age. Their use of the notion of crisis is certainly understandable and thus perhaps forgiveable though hardly believable. In this country, at this time, we act only upon crises, just as we eat only olives that are large—or larger. We live, most certainly, in an age of inflation, of bloated rhetoric, or, to use our own word for it, of hype. None of us can escape this: not the Secretary of Education, nor you, nor I.

The myth of decline, however, is far less inevitable, which makes the choice of it by Bennett and Hirsch more interesting. They, of course, regard it as a fact not a myth, which will make it a key in the debate I am proposing. I see the myth of decline as a standard element in conservative ideology, just as the myth of progress is fundamental to liberal ideology. If we are to get beyond the repetitive confrontations of Tweedledum and Tweedledee on this matter, we shall have to get beyond both of these myths to the extent that we can. This means that on the present occasion we must subject the myth of decline to critical scrutiny. For Bennett this decline presents itself in terms of legal and economic metaphors. The "rightful heirs," as he calls them, have been deprived of "their heritage." The title of his report on the humanities in education is "To Reclaim a Legacy." A Victorian plot from the fertile brain of Dickens or Wilkie Collins underlies this version of the myth. Who is the guilty party? Who has deprived the rightful heirs of their heritage? You and I are the guilty

parties, brothers and sisters, but most guilty are those who should have led us:

> The decline in learning in the humanities was caused in part by a failure of nerve and faith on the part of many college faculties and administrators, and persists because of a vacuum in educational leadership. A recent study of college presidents found that only 2 percent are active in their institutions' academic affairs. ("To Reclaim a Legacy," *Chronicle of Higher Education,* 28 November 1984)

The logic of this is at best elusive. One implication seems to be that the bosses went fishing and the employees, without supervision, sat around goofing off. Is it, in fact, self evident that greater involvement by college presidents would improve education in the humanities? It would depend, I should think, upon who they were and what they did. Over the past few decades the office of college president, like that of university president, has become politicized, bureaucratized, and economized. Presidents mostly raise funds and negotiate with various constituencies that have funding power. This is a full-time job, necessitated by the socio-economic position of these schools in this historical situation. Mr. Bennett ought to know this. In fact, there is usually another officer whose job it is to take a lead in academic affairs, though this leadership normally involves some negotiation with faculty, other administrators, and trustees. Mr. Bennett must know this, too. Then why is he counting the number of presidents who double as deans of academic affairs? Why does he suggest this figure is so significant? Partly for rhetorical effect, no doubt, but also because he is bemused by a vision of the powerful leader, plentifully equipped with "nerve" and "faith," who can as he puts it, "reclaim a legacy," restore a lost heritage, "reverse the decline." (pp. 102-04)

Bennett's concern for teaching is in fact almost entirely ideological. Such matters as the size of classes . . . are not important to Bennett. Hirsch, on the other hand, has for some time taken a serious interest in pedagogical technique, which he uses as a point of departure for his curricular argument:

> For the past twelve years I have been pursuing technical research in the teaching of reading and writing. I now wish to emerge from my closet to declare that technical research is not going to remedy the decline in our literacy that is documented in the decline of verbal SAT scores. We already know enough about methodology to do a good job of teaching reading and writing.
> **("Cultural Literacy")**

Twelve years in that particular closet is a long time, and I am glad that Hirsch has come out of it, but I must confess to some scepticism as to whether anyone who has spent the last twelve years *in there* will be a reliable guide through our cultural perplexities. Hirsch seems to be saying that twelve years of technical research have persuaded him that technical research is inconsequential. Having thoroughly discredited his own recent enterprise, he then proposes to enlist us in his next one. This is, to say the least, a curious rhetorical strategy. The logic of his argument is equally curious.

Hirsch argues that steady but modest declines in SAT scores are symptoms of a national decline in what he calls "literacy." That is, lower scores are *caused by* a decline in students' ability to read, write, and understand the English language. He argues further that the decline in SAT scores has *"accompanied"* a decline in our use of common, nationwide materials in the subject most closely connected with literacy, 'English'. The decline in scores, Hirsch argues, has been caused by the decline in use of a common national curriculum. In moving from "accompanied" to "caused" Hirsch has introduced a new logical fallacy into argumentation. Even more fallacious than *post hoc, ergo propter hoc,* we now have *simul cum hoc, propter hoc.* This fallacy, however, is not the most serious weakness in Hirsch's argument. The real problems lie in the relationship between the test scores and what those scores are supposed to represent, that is, in the notion of literacy itself.

Hirsch claims that "the decline in our literacy and the decline in *the commonly shared knowledge that we acquire in school* are causally related facts" (my italics). His way of demonstrating the truth of this proposition is essentially to redefine literacy as a matter of culturally shared knowledge. For instance, he cites an elaborate experiment in which American and Indian students read and were tested upon two syntactically comparable texts, each of which described a wedding: one in India and one in the U. S. The test demonstrated conclusively that students read the description of the familiar wedding better than they read the other text. The test showed, in other words, that reading is not a pure skill but depends upon cultural information. But the cultural information used by the students in this test was not based upon their school curricula in English, nor, indeed, upon any school subjects. We learn about such customs as weddings from a cultural web of textuality in which school plays only a minor part. Surely, the ability to understand a description of a modern wedding does not depend upon having read such works as *Romeo and Juliet* or *The Taming of the Shrew,* which offer us a glimpse of cultural systems that are doubly (or trebly) removed from our own, being Elizabethan English versions of Renaissance Italian codes of behavior.

Part of the problem in arguments like Hirsch's is that they use words like "culture" in two quite different and even opposed senses. In the anthropological sense, "culture" means the textual web that young people enter as they are born and raised in any particular time and place. But "culture" also means "high culture," the "classics," or monuments of the past that have a quasi-religious or "canonical" status within a given society. Performing a verbal shell game with the two meanings of "culture," Hirsch argues that something called "cultural literacy" can be improved by having a common, classical curriculum taught throughout these United States.

A common curriculum would certainly make life easier for the compilers of the SAT. It might even produce higher scores, because everyone would now be teaching to the test. But this efficiently closed system would be effectively cut off from our actual culture, and would tell us nothing about literacy in *that* culture. If "cultural literacy" is our goal, we shall first have to decide what we mean

> **Hirsch's arguments for "cultural literacy" are deeply political and in the service of the same ideology that motivates the proposals of William J. Bennett for a curricular core that would restore its lost legacy to liberal education.**
>
> —*Robert Scholes*

by culture as well as what we mean by literacy. The end result of Hirsch's proposals, if they were enacted, might be more efficient testing of less significant behavior. Higher test scores would not in this case indicate a higher degree of literacy but only a more efficient test. All of which suggests that Hirsch may not have come far enough out of his educationist closet, since his proposals seem likely to benefit the makers of tests more than the students, the teachers, or the citizens of this country.

The arguments for "cultural literacy" are presented in the name of improved education, but education is never far from politics. Hirsch claims, for instance, that his proposal for a national curriculum established by a National Board of Education is free of political considerations and based merely upon his professional "expertise." He admits that politics would enter into the selection of the canon itself, but claims that the *need* for a canon has been established by arguments that are not in themselves political. I do not believe him. His arguments are deeply political and in the service of the same ideology that motivates the proposals of William J. Bennett for a curricular core that would restore its lost legacy to liberal education. (pp. 110-13)

[We] must consider one more dimension of Hirsch's case. If by "literacy" we were to mean mastery of a wide vocabulary and a broad range of syntactic structures, there is absolutely no reason why we should believe that a common national curriculum would lead students to achieve this result better than an eclectic set of curricula established locally to suit local conditions. There is no way to argue for a unified national curriculum except upon political grounds. If we wish to say, for instance, that a certain cultural competence is desirable for every person in order to exercise effectively their rights and responsibilities as *citizens*—that seems to me an entirely valid and proper argument. But, as [T. S.] Eliot pointed out, we need to discuss such possibilities within the framework of some consensus "about the kind of society we want." At its deepest level, beneath the absurd notion of making a great educational effort in order to raise the national median score on the SAT, lies the idea that a common curriculum—*any* common curriculum—would have a unifying effect upon a society that suffers from an excess of "pluralism," and this unifying effect, an achieved cultural consensus, would in itself be a good thing for the country socially and politically. This is sound conservative doctrine and I acknowledge its appeal, but I am keenly aware of the difficulties attendant upon enacting it. Hirsch says, essentially, let us decide to do it and then worry about exactly what we will do and how we will do it. I say, no, let us consider the problems first and then decide what action to take. The problems are posed vigorously by the proposals of William Bennett.

Bennett in fact cites Hirsch with approval and sees his own proposals as developing Hirsch's notion of "cultural literacy," but his argument is somewhat different. He sees Western Civilization as a consistent and coherent enterprise, a great tradition that has achieved what he calls a "lasting vision." We should, he asserts, "want all students to know a common culture rooted in civilization's lasting vision, its highest shared ideals and aspirations, and its heritage." It is hard not to respond to such rhetoric, and doubly hard to criticize it without appearing to join the ranks of the bad teachers, whom Bennett characterizes (in the words of David Riesman) as sophisticated cynics who are "witty, abrasive, and sometimes engrossing" but "really lifeless." Yet criticize it I must, for I believe Bennett is wrong in his assumptions and his proposals for American education.

He is wrong, first of all, in speaking of Western Civilization as a joint stock-company, in which we are all "shareholders." He is especially wrong in speaking of something he calls "civilization's lasting vision." I agree that we have a cultural heritage, and I agree further that it is satisfying and even useful to know as much as possible about it, but I see no evidence whatsoever to suggest that there is any such entity as "civilization" or that our cultural history embodies or expresses any single, durable vision. Bennett sees Western Civilization as a single coherent object, constructed of masterpieces built by geniuses. He sees teaching as the presentation of these masterpieces to students "with insight and appreciation." The students are to read these masterpieces "because an important part of education is learning to read, and the highest purpose of reading is to be in the company of great souls." Other masterpieces in other media are important for the same reason: "Great souls do not express themselves by the written word only: they also paint, sculpt, build, and compose." One wonders if they make movies? Probably not.

This justification for studying the humanities strikes me as deeply, disastrously wrong: designed to promote false emotions and to make actual engagement with important texts almost impossible. The trouble with establishing a canon—the great, insuperable problem—is that it removes the chosen texts from history and from human actualities, placing them forever behind a veil of pieties. This soulful rhetoric is guaranteed to drain the life out of the texts studied, because it permits only worship and forbids all criticism. These may indeed be texts that every young American should be studying in 1990; I am quite prepared to accept that as a possibility; but not for Mr. Bennett's reasons and, above all, not for study in the way that his reasons would compel. (pp. 113-14)

What I am opposing is the learning of a set of pious cliches about a set of sacred texts. What I advocate in its place . . . can be summarized as the critical study of texts in their full historical context. At the heart of my belief— separating me by a great distance from Hirsch and Ben-

nett—is the conviction that *no text* is so trivial as to be outside the bounds of humanistic study. The meanest graffito, if fully understood in its context, can be a treasure of human expressiveness. The purpose of humanistic study is to learn what it has meant to be human in other times and places, what it means now, and to speculate about what it ought to mean and what it might mean in the human future. The best texts for this purpose should be determined locally, by local conditions, limited and facilitated by local wisdom. Above all, they should not be imposed and regulated by a central power. (p. 116)

> *Robert Scholes, "Aiming a Canon at the Curriculum," in* Salmagundi, *Vol. 72, Fall, 1986, pp. 101-17.*

E. D. Hirsch, Jr. (essay date Fall 1986)

[*In the following essay, Hirsch responds to Scholes's 1986 essay, [above] by elucidating his position in the debate over a national literary canon and insisting that national literacy has undergone a dramatic decline.*]

The title of this reply to Robert Scholes echoes a title in a recent number of the *English Journal:* " 'Cultural Literacy' Does Not Mean 'Core Curriculum' ". That piece was also written by me, and it was also a reply to a college English teacher who had warned that the concept of cultural literacy might lead to the imposing of a canon of works on English teachers. Now, after I finish typing this answer to Scholes, I shall have to compose a reply to still another English teacher who writes in the *ADE Bulletin:* "Is Cultural Literacy A Worm in the Bud?" Like Scholes and the author of the *English Journal* article, this writer also assumes that I agree with William Bennett, the Secretary of Education, in desiring a central canon of texts.

Scholes says that there are *some* superficial differences between what Bennett is saying and what Hirsch is saying, but that Hirsch is deluding himself if he thinks these subtle distinctions make any practical difference. I'm sorry Scholes didn't overhear a conversation between Bennett and me in late 1984 at a conference where we ran into each other. I had recently sent Bennett a typescript of the essay entitled " **'Cultural Literacy' Does Not Mean 'Core Curriculum' ".**

> Bennett: "I got your essay, and I read it."
> Hirsch: "Well?"

Bennett (with hand on the door, preparing to make this his exit line): "You're right. 'Cultural Literacy' doesn't mean 'Core Curriculum'. But, on the other hand, 'Cultural Literacy' doesn't *not* mean 'Core Curriculum' either." (Exit)

There must have been a stylistic fault in **"Cultural Literacy,"** the essay cited by Scholes, because both he and Bennett inferred from it that my ideas imply a "canon" or a "common national curriculum." But I have now published eight essays on the subject of cultural literacy which make it emphatically clear that this is not the case. Bennett now grasps that point, and he doesn't cite my work any more. If Scholes decides to read further in this material, he will find that Hirsch is useful for *opposing* the idea of a national canon or common national curriculum.

Although it's true that literacy depends on common background knowledge, it's not true that common background knowledge requires a "common national curriculum" or "canon". *The common background knowledge required for literacy does not depend upon specific texts.* English teachers like Robert Scholes are used to thinking of education as being based upon texts. Their complaints about cultural literacy are always complaints about "canons" or lists of "works." But that model is far too limited; it doesn't fit the concept of cultural literacy. Except for a few short pieces like the "Gettysburg Address," Martin Luther King's speech "I have a Dream," the "Pledge of Allegiance," "The Star-Spangled Banner," there are no specific texts in the contents of cultural literacy. *To be culturally literate, one does not need to know any specific literary texts,* though one does need to know a few facts about some of them. Except for a few short texts which most literate people can recognize explicitly, *the contents of cultural literacy are not text-bound.* Thus my present choice of a title: "cultural literacy" does not mean "canon." I hope Robert Scholes will be pleased to discover this.

I also hope he will be pleased to find that I agree with his rousing conclusion:

> At the heart of my belief—separating me a great distance from Hirsch and Bennett—is the conviction that *no text* is so trivial as to be outside the bounds of humanistic study. The meanest graffitto, if fully understood in its context, can be a treasure of human expressiveness. . . . The best texts for this purpose should be determined locally, by local conditions, limited and facilitated by local wisdom. Above all, they should not be imposed and regulated by a central power.

There is not a single one of these platitudes that I don't subscribe to wholeheartedly, except for the claim that they separate Scholes a great distance from Hirsch. Scholes, like Bennett before him, has not grasped the simplicity of my ideas, or my lack of interest (as regards cultural literacy) in what goes on in college courses. When my ideas really do sink in, Scholes may have a very different sort of complaint: Hirsch not only isn't concerned with a canon of prescribed texts, he thinks it's acceptable to take one's entire knowledge of *Romeo and Juliet* from *Cliff Notes.* That is because cultural literacy is a canon of information, not of texts. If Scholes decides to read more widely in my writings on cultural literacy, he may not like what he sees, but he *will* find me quite useful for Bennett-bashing.

There is simply no disagreement among active reading researchers that true literacy requires widely shared background knowledge. Anyone who is interested in the subject of national literacy will probably have already read *Becoming a Nation of Readers: The Report of the Commission on Reading,* published jointly by The National Academy of Education, The National Institute of Education, and The Center for the Study of Reading in 1985. It should moderate Scholes's scepticism about the connection between literacy and cultural literacy to learn that the very essay of mine which he views with such distaste is endorsed by this report. Its authors include Richard Anderson, Director of the Center for Reading, and to my personal knowledge a Scholes-style libertarian, and two members of the National Academy of Education, Jeanne Chall of Harvard, and Robert Glaser of Pittsburgh, as well as several other distinguished researchers. These specialists did not detect in my essay an ideology hiding under a technical camouflage. Why not? Because they found that my technical claims converge with those of reading research (not to mention common sense.) In fact, *only* ideologues like Scholes and Bennett have inferred ideological consequences from my article.

Scholes's way of dealing with the technical claims of my work is to deny them, to deny that there has been a decline in literacy, to deny that literacy has really been defined adequately by me or anyone else, to deny a cogent relationship between SAT verbal scores and literacy. He's asserting there isn't really a problem, and that the pseudo-problem has been manufactured by the Right for ideological purposes. "The myth of decline as a standard element in conservative ideology." This line of argument is simply a mistake. Now that I have briefly disposed of the confusion between cultural literacy and a canon of texts, the most useful thing I can do in the rest of this short reply is to dispose of the idea that there is a "myth of a decline."

The most broadly based evidence about our national levels of literacy comes from the National Assessment of Educational Progress (NAEP). This nationwide measurement, mandated by Congress, shows that between 1970 and 1980 17-year-olds declined in their ability to understand written materials. Still more precise quantitative data have come from the Verbal scores of the Scholastic Aptitude Test (the Verbal SAT). According to John B. Carroll, a distinguished psychometrist, the Verbal SAT is essentially a test of "advanced vocabulary knowledge," which makes it a very sensitive instrument for measuring levels of literacy. It is well known that Verbal SAT scores have declined dramatically in the past fifteen years. Less well known is the fact that performance on the Verbal SAT has been slipping steadily *at the top.* Ever fewer numbers of our best and brightest students are making high scores on this test.

This fact has only recently been made public by the College Board. Before the full statistics were disclosed in 1984, anti-alarmists could argue that the fall in average verbal scores could be explained by the rise in the number of disadvantaged students taking the SAT's. That argument can no longer be made. It's now clear that not only our disadvantaged, but also our best educated and most talented young people are showing diminished verbal skills. To be precise, out of a constant pool of about a million test-takers each year, 56 per cent more students scored above 600 in 1972 than did so in 1984. More startling yet, the percentage difference was even greater for those scoring above 650—73 per cent.

The figures that are available from NAEP surveys, and the recently disclosed details of scores on the Verbal SAT are decisive evidence that literacy has been declining in this country just at a period when our need for effective literacy has been sharply rising. To these facts can be juxtaposed some evidence for another kind of educational decline, one that is related to the drop in literacy. During the period 1970-1985, the amount of shared knowledge which we have been able to take for granted in communicating with our fellow citizens has also been declining. More and more of the young people whom we meet don't know things we used to assume that they knew. The decline of literacy and the decline of shared knowledge are closely related, interdependent facts.

The evidence for the decline of shared knowledge is not just anecdotal. In 1977, NAEP issued a report which analyzed a large quantity of data showing that the civic knowledge of our children had dropped significantly between 1969 and 1976. The performance of 13-year-olds had declined eleven percentage points, from 53% to 42%, a relative drop of over twenty percent. That the decline has continued since 1976 was recently confirmed by a preliminary NAEP study conducted in late 1985. It was undertaken both because of concern about declining knowledge, and because of the growing evidence of a causal connection between the decline in shared information and the drop in literacy. The project, of which I am a member, is called "The Foundations of Literacy Project." It will measure some of the specific information about history and literature that American 17-year-olds possess. Although the report will not be published until 1987, the preliminary field-tests, conducted in 1985, have produced some disturbing results.

If these preliminary, nation-wide samplings hold up, as they usually do, then the results which we will be reading about in 1987 will show that two thirds of our 17-year-olds do not know that the Civil War occurred between 1850 and 1900. Three quarters do not know what "Reconstruction" means. Half do not know the meaning of "Brown Decision" and cannot identify either Stalin or Churchill. Three quarters are unfamiliar with the names of standard American and British authors. Moreover, our 17-year-olds have little sense of geography, or of the relative chronology of major events. The reports of youthful ignorance can no longer be considered merely anecdotal. The main causes of this decline are now clear, as is what we should do about it. But that is another subject.

I have wanted to provide these brief factual observations about the backgrounds to my emphasis on cultural literacy in the hope that these facts might make literary people, maybe Scholes himself, think twice before engaging in premature ideology on the subject of literacy. For someone who is alert to the ideological basis of ideas, Scholes seems, from my perspective, curiously blind to the connection of his own high liberal ideology with the class-bound interests of English teachers. So far, all attacks on cultural literacy have come from English or literature teachers. Cultural literacy looks at first glance (and wrongly) as if it were inimical to those interests, because from a vague distance it looks like an obligatory canon of works. But let me repeat the simple point that the needed information in cultural literacy can be conveyed in many different ways by many different texts.

The whole question of a literary canon is, in relation to literacy, a theological rather than a practical question. By all means let us engage in these interesting theological disputes. But meanwhile, in the realm of practice, there is no reason why all English teachers and all stripes of diversitarians should not cooperate in trying to raise the national level of literacy. I'm not in favor of a central ministry of culture any more than Scholes. But I'm also not in favor of reality-avoidance. No knowledgeable reading researcher disputes the fact that a higher level of national literacy will come only through a higher level of nationally shared information. What we need from ingenious and well-meaning people like Scholes are some good ideas for making that happen, particularly in the early grades of school-

---

An excerpt of the terms listed in *Cultural Literacy: What Every American Needs to Know*

anaerobic	Limbo
Anthony, Susan B.	Manifest Destiny
Appomattox	meiosis
basal metabolism	New Amsterdam
birthday suit	noble gas
capacitor	Ockham's razor
Congress of Vienna	Owens, Jesse
containment, policy of	parity price
Danton	pearl of great price
Dienbienphu	prevailing westerlies
Douglass, Frederick	Quisling
ethyl alcohol	reduction (chemistry)
fireside chat	Sarajevo
flying buttress	solstice
fourth estate, the	St. Paul's Cathedral
Gresham's law	Sun King, the
gung-ho	Talmud
Hector	thirty pieces of silver
hypotenuse	torque
Hz	vassal
Immaculate Conception	Vichy
justification by faith	xylem
Kelvin, Lord	yellow peril
Kitty Hawk	zero-sum

E. D. Hirsch, Jr., in his Cultural Literacy: What Every American Needs to Know, *Houghton Mifflin, 1987.*

ing where ingenuity and good will can make a difference. (pp. 118-24)

E. D. Hirsch, Jr., "Responses to Robert Scholes," in Salmagundi, Vol. 72, Fall, 1986, pp. 118-24.

Robert Stevens   (review date 26 April 1987)

[*Stevens is an American educator and a member of the National Council for the Humanities. In the review below, he praises Hirsch's* Cultural Literacy *for advancing innovative and potentially unpopular opinions.*]

[*Cultural Literacy*] is a delightful book. E. D. Hirsch says something new. He is probably wrong. He certainly is iconoclastic; but he should be read.

The Hirsch thesis is a variation on the current clamor about what is wrong with our schools and why our children cannot read and write. It is, however, an answer to a somewhat different concern. What worries Mr. Hirsch is an absence of what he calls cultural literacy. The author sees cultural literacy as the center of a spectrum that is bounded at one end by what he describes as our civil religion. Our civil religion, it turns out, is none other than the Declaration of Independence, the Gettysburg Address, even parts of the Bible. At the other end is the "vocabulary of our national discourse." As he says, this vocabulary is "hospitable to God and mammon, pornography and prudery, Catholicism and Zen."

What of this national culture, and how should it be imbibed? Mr. Hirsch and two of his colleagues at the University of Virginia—James Trefil, a physicist, and Joseph Kett, chairman of the history department—have set to work to devise a list of what literate Americans know or should know. The list, which appears as an appendix to this book, is inevitably, as the author says, heavily influenced by the English tradition. So one has to recognize 1066 as well as 1776, and know that World War II ran from 1939 to 1945. Then follows a list of 63 pages of what we should all know. We should all know Samuel Clemens, constitutional monarchy, Stonewall Jackson and Jack Sprat, manic-depressive and manifest destiny, Rhodes scholarships and saturated fatty acids. It is all good, clean fun.

As I said, Mr. Hirsch is an iconoclast. I admire that; it is a condition to which I aspire. It is therefore not surprising that I find myself agreeing with many of the observations in the book, and even more certainly with the analysis of the underlying causes.

Mr. Hirsch attributes all evidence of the ignorance of cultural history to the progressive movement in education. He is probably right. Beginning with the National Education Association's 1918 "Cardinal Principles of Secondary Education," this country went down the progressive path led, at least in popular mythology, by the pragmatist philosopher John Dewey. Process replaced substance, a concern with self-perception replaced rigor. Health and citizenship became more important than Greek and physics.

Efforts to halt the academic decline inaugurated by progressive education have been largely ineffective. We have

moments when we realize the seriousness of the problem—witness the panic after Sputnik 1 in 1957 and the later discovery that Americans are monolingual. These concerns have, however, paled into insignificance compared with the importance of football and fraternities. The situation does not seem to get any better. The recent Carnegie Report, "College: The Undergraduate Experience in America," is a mishmash of muddle-headed notions and platitudes—admittedly studded with occasional kernels of truth and wisdom—the effect of which, however, is to denigrate science and research (on the bizarre notion that most faculty members don't like doing it), and appears to conclude that the important thing is to make courses entertaining. Students who have had no structured education, who have been "educated" by the project method, so that they have little idea of the historical relationship between the Pilgrims and Jesus, must not be faced with the harsh reality that serious academic work may require intellectual effort.

Mr. Hirsch makes an extensive case for his claim that his vision of cultural literacy is in fact pluralistic, although national, in its demands. He also claims it is not elitist, arguing, historically, that national languages were not elitist. He does not prove that case. The concerns of the Chicano community in Southern California may not be the same as those of the Cuban community in Miami, let alone those of a predominantly WASP community in New England or the Midwest. All need some sense of national unity, which a shared understanding of certain basic information provides; that cannot be denied. Yet it seems highly unlikely that it could be provided in a way not in some sense geared to the values and assumptions of a rather narrow elite. That elite, in turn, would undoubtedly have its assumptions and values and notions shaped by its ethnic background and education.

If every primary or secondary school were to teach the 4,000-odd concepts that this book says educated Americans know, that process might bring back an element of rigor. It is, however, more likely to produce cram courses than anything else. That would not be all bad. Something would be learned, but it would not, I suspect, be the kind of cultural literacy that Mr. Hirsch has in mind.

Mr. Hirsch's argument is part of the wider debate about whether there is—or should be—a core to the liberal arts. Is there a core curriculum that every educated person should study? One's definition of education is inevitably related to one's beliefs about how many people should receive a liberal arts education. Core curriculums and a national cultural literacy may be inconsistent with diversity and democracy. We may yet have to settle for a survey course in English or, horrible thought, a rigorous course in American history replacing the babblings and ramblings of social studies.

Robert Stevens, "Ideas People Think With," in The New York Times Book Review, April 26, 1987, p. 36.

George Steiner   (review date 1 June 1987)

[*Steiner is a French-born American critic, poet, and fic-*

tion writer. A central concern of his critical thought is whether literature can survive the barbarism of the modern world. Although some commentators have found fault with his sometimes exuberant prose style, Steiner is generally regarded as a perceptive and extremely erudite critic. In the review below, he commends the observations made by Hirsch in Cultural Literacy *on the deficiencies of the American educational system, while questioning the premises of Hirsch's solution.*]

The indictment is by now widely known, but it remains appalling. Some fifty per cent of American teen-agers can identify neither Churchill nor Stalin. Two-thirds of American seventeen-year-olds do not know that the Civil War took place between 1850 and 1900. Geography is to almost three-quarters of high-school juniors and seniors a black hole: they can neither identify the less salient states on a map of the U.S.A. nor make even an informed guess as to whether Ireland is east or west of England. One qualified witness could not find a single high-school or college student in Los Angeles able to tell him the years in which either World War was fought. Only two could locate Chicago "even in the vaguest terms." A junior at U.C.L.A. opined that Toronto must be in Italy; a pre-law student confidently situated the nation's capital in the state of Washington. How, one student asked, can Latin be called a dead language when there is a country called Latin America?

But these are only pinpricks. The best evidence is that at least one-third of the adult citizens of the United States are illiterate; that is, they are unable to read at all or can decipher only rudimentary bits of written information. The instructions on most medicine bottles, let alone tax forms, driver's licenses, and insurance policies, are wholly beyond their grasp. Of the remaining two-thirds of our citizens, it is thought that at least one-half, while technically literate, scarcely read at all, or read only print of the simplest and most ephemeral kind. Even people at the top of the educational and social pyramid fall, on average, well below the standard of cultural recognition taken to be essential in Japan and Western Europe. The schooling in mathematics and language in the Soviet Union is sharply ahead of that in all but the most selective and privileged of American schools. Learning by heart—note the depth and power implied in that eroded idiom—is crucial to Russian, Japanese, and European education. It has all but vanished from American mores. Instead, there is throughout primary and secondary schooling a planned amnesia.

The consequences are manifold. It is to the lowest common denominator that the mass media and the marketplace make their pitch. A deafening emptiness pours out of the television screens, radios, and jukeboxes that spangle the land. The press, except for a rather restricted mandarin sector, knows that the world must be blazoned to skimming readers in words of one syllable. Dependent clauses introduce into life a hostile mystery. Vital information—vital in the sense that it must inform sane political debate and decision—remains blocked in the conduits of the specialists. In a context of illiteracy and semiliteracy, the Ciceronian-Jeffersonian program for a republic founded on the articulate discussion of demanding and evolving issues, for a free polis based on remembrance of

the historical past and on the dissemination of new knowledge breaks down. The problem is not only that the United States is being outstripped in both the volume and the quality of economic production by rival societies, or that it can no longer recruit into its military and administrative cadres men and women of even minimal intellectual calibre; it is that the axiom of mature perception and debate on which the great, proud experiment that is the United States is conceived may crumble into a morass of demagogy and apathy.

The alarm bells have been ringing since Sputnik. It is to the imperative task of remedy that E. D. Hirsch addresses himself. His *Cultural Literacy* is a brief, crystal-clear, and condignly urgent tract. Even within its brevity, it is repetitive. But this is a legitimate device of impatient virtue. The hour is late.

Professor Hirsch sets forth his postulate as follows:

> We Americans have long accepted literacy as a paramount aim of schooling, but only recently have some of us who have done research in the field begun to realize that literacy is far more than a skill and that it requires large amounts of specific information. That new insight is central to this book.

One is left mildly numbed by this solemn, almost Mosaic promulgation of a "new insight." Did it truly require recent research (one hears the deep, supportive breath of the relevant foundations and of national powwows) to discover that human beings cannot read intelligently—cannot make sense of a message—unless they have mastered a more or less extensive corpus of previous background knowledge? Is it a novel discovery that semantics—the structure and performative means of meaning—is almost invariably "contextual," that it depends on a measure of familiarity with the codes and objects of reference, with the preceding "textuality," from which it derives its own sense? The very notion of uninformed reading is one of those idiotic spooks conjured by hayseed populism and by psychologists in American departments of education. Never mind. Whether his insight is original or not, Hirsch is emphatically right.

Who are the villains of the piece? Again, Professor Hirsch's answer is unambiguous: Jean-Jacques Rousseau and John Dewey. It is they who preached a "content-neutral" schooling for children. It is they who held up the mirage of the development of a child's capacities by means of vaguely defined and roseate stages of personal exploration, of, as Dewey puts it, "personal acquaintance with a small number of typical situations with a view to mastering the way of dealing with the problems of experience, not the piling up of information." That we find here a drastic misreading of Rousseau—whose education toward solitude in *Emile* is one of the most complex and tragic analyses of human defeat ever argued—is immaterial. Hirsch is surely right in asserting, over and over, that the evacuation of concrete knowledge—names, dates, texts, the vocabulary and grammar of one's own language and others—from American education in the name of pastoral license and utopian play has been sheer catastrophe. It is, moreover, exponential: when almost nothing is known, nothing further can be learned.

Hirsch is surely right in asserting, over and over, that the evacuation of concrete knowledge—names, dates, texts, the vocabulary and grammar of one's own language and others—from American education in the name of pastoral license and utopian play has been sheer catastrophe.

—*George Steiner*

Hence the pressing need for a return to more traditional ideals and practices. Hirsch argues, "It isn't facts that deaden the minds of young children, who are storing facts in their minds every day with astonishing voracity. It is incoherence—our failure to ensure that a pattern of shared, vividly taught, and socially enabling knowledge will emerge from our instruction." The establishment of this pattern of minimal shared reference—of "common readership," to borrow Virginia Woolf's designation—constitutes the heart of Hirsch's manifesto. What ought every American child to be taught so that as an American adult he can exercise his talents, his political rights, his spiritual and emotional maturity within a coherent community of values and of recognitions? It is this delineation of an essential "cultural literacy" that is proving to be the most widely noticed and most controversial element in Professor Hirsch's case.

Actually, the proposals he makes are not easy to encapsulate. There is in them more than a dash of the Great Books program developed by Mortimer Adler and Robert Hutchins in those palmy days at Chicago. There are (though these precedents are passed over entirely in silence) echoes of the visionary plea in Paul Goodman's classic *Growing Up Absurd* and of the pioneering work on illiteracy in America by Jonathan Kozol. Hirsch's trump card comes from an impressive background of psychological and sociological research, and from a certain specificity. It is his dream (that Martin Luther King phrase sounds and resounds through the book) that the greatest possible number of American men and women be educated to the linguistic-contextual level required to read intelligently the news stories and editorial page of a serious, adult newspaper—say, the *Times*. The ingenuity and the advantage of so focussed a target are clear. If we take this particular standard of performance as canonic, we can fairly readily establish the vocabulary needed, the syntax that has to be internalized, and much of the "primary content"—historical, geographical, political, literary, and scientific—to which an American reader must have unforced access if he is to understand both his own national life and, to a certain degree, that of the planet at large. He must, even to make sense of the sports pages, be able to identify "Waterloo" if a home team is said to have suffered one;

he must be able to make out what is meant by a "Pyrrhic victory" if the hockey game has resulted in excessive injuries. To characterize either of these events as a "Donnybrook" would, on the other hand, represent an instance of editorial preciosity beyond what might be reasonably expected of the normal reader.

This example derives from a list supplied by Hirsch and two of his colleagues at the University of Virginia, Joseph Kett, a historian, and James Trefil, a physicist, of basic words, terms, names, and proverbial tags that all literate Americans must be capable of grasping and locating accurately if literacy is to be regained. The list is intrinsically fascinating. A wicked soul could construe from it a psychobiography of E. D. Hirsch and his two associates. On a more serious level, it represents a peculiarly graphic image of the American liberal imagination—of the national mythologies of common sense—at a certain point in our history. Having only this listing to hand, future historians, sociologists, or political theorists could go a long way toward formulating with some accuracy the ways in which the United States in the later nineteen-eighties looked upon the past, upon its own institutions, and upon the outside world. Here was a society that had to remember Orestes but not Electra; Dickens but not Thackeray; the massacre at My Lai but not that of St. Bartholomew's Day; George McGovern but not Adlai Stevenson. Lee Iacocca makes the roll, but not Louis Sullivan, the originator of the skyscraper; John Philip Sousa, yes, but not Charles Ives, the most inventive figure in American music; Emily Dickinson is of the pantheon, Ezra Pound not; the oratory of Webster is assured inclusion, but not that of Demosthenes. The ideological reflexes discernible in this catalogue are sometimes transparent: Verdi is home and dry, but Richard Wagner, the greatest aesthetic influence on modernity, goes unnamed. Auschwitz must (praise God) be part of basic literacy, but not the Gulag. Wittgenstein is, hauntingly enough, part of the cultural alphabet for Americans, but not Heidegger, the begetter of modern existentialism and of all deconstructive movements, and a presence who more and more towers over twentieth-century thought. Irregular verbs must be identified, but not irrational numbers; Spiro Agnew is assigned a place in the echo chambers of the literate; syphilis endures, but herpes is not yet listed.

One could play this game ad absurdum (a tag omitted, while "ad hominem" is present). Nor is it a trivial game, for it is precisely via this basic lexicon and primer of cognizance that Professor Hirsch lets one divine what he has in mind. It is only here that one can make out the material and psychological contours of that "middle ground of cultural knowledge" which must be mastered and universally shared if the republic is to accomplish its promised destiny. There is a deliberate politics—almost a metaphysics—in the principles of selection which array Betty Friedan next to Milton Friedman or put *Pilgrim's Progress* immediately above the Pill. What emerges is the profile of a well-schooled man or woman with not only a sound knowledge of American history and of the numerous popular and populist elements alive within that history but also a quite remarkable alertness to science: mesons, quarks, pulsars, nucleic acids are postulated as indispensable signals. Nothing less will insure "that new generations will continue to be enfranchised in our medium of national communication as securely as they are enfranchised at the polls."

The attacks on Professor Hirsch's entire conception of a central cultural literacy—of an indispensable core of shared learning—have, predictably, come from the spokesmen for ethnic and sex-polarized diversity. Those who regard Mohican history as being at least as important as the sort of history that compels a child to know something about Julius and Augustus Caesar do not acquiesce in Hirsch's assumption of Judeo-Christian or European and Anglo-Saxon centrality. Radical feminism lays claim to its own syllabus of long-neglected facts and allusions. (In turn, how betrayingly characteristic it is of an academic in arcadian Virginia to include in his primary baggage of awareness Joe Louis but not Rocky Marciano!) Any canonic content is, in short, a piece of more or less naked power politics. Given the stridency and the personal tenor of the current ethnic, feminist, and minority-group polemics in the United States, Professor Hirsch is both elusive and defensive in his plea. The core must, he agrees, be flexible. It must be open to the currents of diversity in the singular mixture of races, inheritance, and historical provenance that make up the American mosaic. Classical markers will fade away as new configurations arise from American political and social experience. Booker T. Washington and Paul Robeson *must* appear on today's vade mecum (unlisted), even if Toussaint-Louverture does not. Nevertheless, insists Hirsch, there are prime numbers, as it were, that cut across all claims of splintered singularity. A play by Neil Simon is, if fundamental civility and civilization are at stake, never a substitute for one by Shakespeare.

Other polemics are bound to come from the more pessimistic and conservative right. Is it really evident that certain levels of linguistic manipulation and abstract thought are accessible to all human beings, or even to the overwhelming majority? What level of coaching, of continued education, of directed reading is necessary if some two hundred million Americans are to be able to cope even on a modest plane—to have a nodding acquaintance—with the Fourth Gospel, with the art of Vermeer, with the concept of a quantum leap or that of genetic recombination (all of which figure in the cardinal catalogue)? Is E. D. Hirsch's whole program not going to water down to the level of a bland digest those very virtues and fascinations of culture, of textuality, which have always been the possession and the joy of the few? It would not, I imagine, be difficult for Professor Hirsch to counter that the sheer informational demands of modern American life call for a heightened ambition in regard to human capacities, and that there is no definite evidence—certainly not on biological grounds—that such capacity is denied to any given group, class, or ethnic component of our society. Such a reply *may* be erroneous, but hope and decency must underwrite it.

My own uneasiness is twofold. "To be culturally literate," proclaims Hirsch, "is to possess the basic information needed to thrive in the modern world." The postulate is unashamedly Benthamite. I am not certain that thriving in the modern world—in the palpably economic and socially integrated sense intended by Hirsch—is an unquestionable ideal. And I am fairly certain that it is essential for a genuine inward culture to be acutely critical of the information and the values offered it by the body politic. The "modern world" is, in fundamental respects, a fairly hellish place. We inhabit the century of Himmler and Pol Pot. The nuclear arsenal has long since spiralled into homicidal lunacy. We are laying waste what is left of the natural resources and the vestiges of the Edenic on our planet. In many of its fundamental motions of spirit and of policy, the era of the superpower and the terrorist is one not of progress, as Hirsch seems to imply unexaminedly, but of reversion to barbarism. "Animal kingdom" is immediately preceded by "angst" in the Hirsch lexicon. To "thrive" in these conditions and to do so via "information" are perfectly arguable predications, but they need to be argued.

The second point is more of a luxury. Here is an important tract on behalf of eloquence—that of Cicero, of Jefferson, of Lincoln, of Martin Luther King. There is not in it an eloquent, a memorable sentence. Here is a plea for literacy in a dynamic, even joyful, sense, a plea for eyes that will light not only at the name of Shakespeare but at that of Rabelais. There is not a phrase, not a passage in this book that sings, that makes the language come alive with its matchless magic. When Bacon composed his *Advancement of Learning,* when John Stuart Mill and Matthew Arnold discussed education and culture, they demonstrated by their very means of discussion just what was at stake. Perhaps it is now too late for that in the American circumstance. Perhaps it is, indeed, one of the merits of Professor Hirsch's discourse that it is as gray, as joyless, and as utilitarian as the realities and needs it addresses. (pp. 106-10)

> George Steiner, "Little-Read Schoolhouse," in
> The New Yorker, *Vol. LXIII, June 1, 1987,*
> *pp. 106-10.*

Stefan Kanfer   (review date 20 July 1987)

[*An American novelist and non-fiction writer, Kanfer has served on the staff of* Time *magazine for more than two decades. In the review below, he criticizes the educational theory presented by Hirsch in* Cultural Literacy *and questions the usefulness of the 5,000-term list entitled "What Literate Americans Know."*]

What is Brownian motion? Who said we should burn with a hard, gem-like flame? How do you translate the phrase comme il faut? Failure to answer questions like these signifies a catastrophic ignorance, according to E. D. Hirsch Jr., a professor of English at the University of Virginia and inventor of the latest intellectual parlor game.

Hirsch did not set out to produce an entertainment. But this summer, readers seem eager for masochistic diversions. Another finger-wagging polemic about American education, Allan Bloom's *The Closing of the American Mind,* has been on the New York *Times* best-seller list for eleven weeks. **Cultural Literacy** is equally cranky, and it has already made best-seller lists in New York City, Dallas, Denver, Seattle, San Francisco and Boston.

Hirsch establishes his dour tone early on by distinguishing between literacy (the ability to read one's own language) and cultural literacy (possession of specific information). Students may be able to read at a ninth-grade level, according to Hirsch, and still be ignorant of history and society. He quotes a Latin pupil astonished to find that she is learning a dead language. "What do they speak in Latin America?" she demands. A California journalist testifies, "I have not yet found one single student in Los Angeles, in either college or high school, who could tell me the years when World War II was fought." The Federal Government's Foundations of Literacy project recently tested 17-year-olds; samplings show that half cannot identify Stalin or Churchill.

Hirsch proposes to recover what has been lost: a set of common references. "The more computers we have," he maintains, "the more we need shared fairy tales, Greek myths, historical images, and so on." The reason for this seeming paradox is that "if we do not achieve a literate society, the technicians, with their arcane specialties, will not be able to communicate with us nor we with them. That would contradict the basic principles of democracy and must not be allowed to happen."

Stripped of its apocalyptic tone, what this amounts to is an advocacy of teaching names, dates and places by rote and providing a context later. Hirsch acknowledges that the method has been derided since Dickens satirized Pedant Thomas Gradgrind ("Facts, sir; nothing but Facts!") in *Hard Times*. But, he counters, "it isn't facts that deaden the minds of young children, who are storing facts in their minds every day with astonishing voracity. It is incoherence—our failure to ensure that a pattern of shared, vividly taught, and socially enabling knowledge will emerge from our instruction."

And exactly what knowledge will be vividly taught? *Cultural Literacy* is obviously meant to provoke serious debate. But when it leaves the theoretical and lands on the practical, it executes a pratfall. Hirsch and two academic colleagues offer a 64-page appendix of references that constitutes their version of vital information. They never do get around to telling the reader that Brownian motion is a random movement of microscopic particles suspended in liquids or gases, that Walter Pater said we should burn with a hard gemlike flame and that comme il faut means proper. They are too busy moving their curriculum between the trendy and the arbitrary. Why, for example is Sartre listed but not Camus? Why Norman Mailer but not Saul Bellow or John Updike? Leonardo but not Michelangelo? Venereal disease but not AIDS? Why Beverly Hills but not St. Louis? Cole Porter but not Leonard Bernstein? Muammar Gaddafi but not François Mitterand? Bogart but not Olivier or even Cagney? Such questions guarantee that the book will indeed spur discussions all summer long, but perhaps not the ones the author intended. (pp. 72-3)

Stefan Kanfer, "Appendixitis," in Time, *New York, Vol. 130, No. 3, July 20, 1987, pp. 72-3.*

Hugh Kenner   (review date 9 October 1987)

[*Kenner, a Canadian-born American educator, editor and author, is the foremost critic and chronicler of literary Modernism. In addition to his reputation as an important scholar, Kenner is also noted for his often eccentric judgments and a critical style that relies on surprising juxtapositions and wit. In the following excerpt, he finds merit in Hirsch's theory of cultural literacy.*]

[In addition to Allan Bloom's *The Closing of the American Mind*,] this year's other surprise best-seller, hovering around number three on the *New York Times* list, is *Cultural Literacy,* by E. D. Hirsch Jr. It is a very different book from Bloom's, but they share an important part of their thesis: American schools and colleges are failing to impart to their students our common culture. As a people, we are no longer reading from the same text.

This wouldn't be half the catastrophe Bloom and Hirsch say it is if the text itself were the point. But the question is not whether we know our Thucydides—who does, the day after the quiz?—but whether we and our fellow Americans have sufficient common cultural experience to enable us to communicate . . .

There is some reason to doubt that the message will get through. *Time,* our largest university, certainly missed it—was all but obliged to miss it given the implications.

Hirsch, with his straightforward claims—he supplies a 63-page list—about what every literate American should know, must have seemed an easy target to *Time* Senior Editor Stefan Kanfer, writing in the book-review section. (Ezra Bowen, in the Education section, later did a better job, though not good enough to repair the damage.) Here's Kanfer: "Who said we should burn with a hard, gemlike flame? How do you translate the phrase comme il faut? Failure to answer questions like these signifies a catastrophic ignorance, according to E. D. Hirsch Jr., . . . inventor of the latest intellectual parlor game."

That's simply, crassly wrong, as is Kanfer's claim that Hirsch advocates "teaching names, dates, and places by rote and providing a context later." It's tempting to say that Kanfer can't read and feels sure his consumers can't either. He bad-mouths, while he's at it, an "equally cranky" book—[Allan] Bloom's [*The Closing of the American Mind*]. So how come two cranks are outselling Bill Cosby and the Carters? Well, "This summer, readers seem eager for masochistic diversions." Ungratified sex, that's the surest explanation for anything. (Bloom can tell us how *that* came about.)

That the lo-cal *New York Times Book Review* also got it wrong goes without saying. Its browsers were offered a five-minute entertainment, a list of excerpts from Hirsch's notorious List, at which to go blank amid reassurances that it's all in fun, really, though there *is* this cranky professor who thinks one really should recognize such things, ho ho.

Back when I reviewed frequently for the *Times Book Review* I came to expect routine calls just before press time from sharp voices with revisions to propose. Their concern, so they said, was always for "the reader." There was so much that "the reader" might be unsure of. Afloat near the word "uncertainty," just the word "Heisenberg" was enigmatic; let's change that to "the physicist Werner Heisenberg, OK?"—even add that he formulated an "uncertainty principle," OK? And "I grow old, I grow old": shouldn't we say, "As T. S. Eliot's Prufrock put it," OK?

As it happens, I can date the inception of those calls; the first one came in mid-1982. About then, it seems, the *Times* people awoke to what Professor Hirsch has documented, that all writing beyond Dick-and-Jane is inherently allusive, and that much of the readership just isn't up to the challenge. They may even have realized that readers of the *Book Review* are not necessarily readers of books. They began to cajole the bylined authors into tolerating lots of explanatory asides. I used to ask why they didn't just write the stuff in-house, and got known, I fear, as a crusty writer to deal with.

I also proposed, more than once, that the *Times* underrated its "reader." In the light of Professor Hirsch's *Cultural Literacy* I'm no longer so sure. I now don't even suspect that addiction to the *Times* is what induces catatonia. For Hirsch tells us how it came about. With ample documentation he argues, explicitly and somewhat laboriously, that from about 1918, American education has been caught in a fatal drift toward teaching Reading in the abstract. You learn to *Read,* never mind by reading what. The idea could seem democratic, because people with diverse talents, facing diverse futures, will be employing the all-important skill on quite different things. Reduce it, then, to its essence, which is skill at decoding. Dick-and-Jane books aim at teaching exactly that skill. Unfortunately, they don't teach anything else. Hence the debacle.

"Decoding" means getting swiftly from the marks on the page to the sounds: "Oh, see Spot!" Unhappily, such skill however well mastered won't help with "I'm stuck in Siberia," where "Siberia" has an acculturated meaning we need to have somehow acquired.

We needn't know—this is important—Siberia's area, latitude, longitude, mean temperature, typical fauna: only that it's shorthand for "a place of punitive exile." The "meaning" of all spoken or written discourse is a weave of such elements by the hundred: not just "words" to see and say, but words and phrases that carry schemata with them. These shared schemata hold a culture together; it's important that we all have access to the same ones. That needn't mean swallowing encyclopedias; the schemata rely on the close-enough.

Fifty years back—and I'm not about to hunt up the reference—Ezra Pound, paraphrasing something or other, remarked, "I have forgotten which book," then looked up at his reader to utter a golden apophthegm: "Culture begins when one *has* 'forgotten which book.' "

Culture is a huge mosaic of *partial* knowledge, a fact invisible to Senior Editors who hang suspended in a web of "fact-checkers." The point of the List is not, as Kanfer had it, that we need to know "Who said we should burn with a hard, gemlike flame?" Since Hirsch doesn't tell us (Walter Pater), *Time* had to send out a researcher, and Kanfer grumps. No, the point is that one criterion of liter-

acy is ability to pick up from those words an allusion to the intense life. That means having met "hard, gemlike flame" before, and acquired some hint of what it connotes. Far from being "the latest intellectual parlor game," Hirsch's 63-page listing documents, suggestively, the common—and vanishing—shorthand of American writing. (pp. 37-8, 40)

Hugh Kenner, "The Department of Factual Verification," in National Review, New York, Vol. XXXIX, October 9, 1987, pp. 37-8, 40-1.

Barbara Herrnstein Smith (essay date Winter 1990)

[*Smith is an American educator and critic who is prominent in the field of composition studies. In the essay below, she claims that Hirsch's* Cultural Literacy *"does a very good job of obscuring the nation's very real educational problems."*]

It should be a matter of some concern, I think, that the current movement for educational reform duplicates so many of the perennial (indeed classic) themes of apocalyptic cultural criticism: most obviously, of course, the recurrent images of a civilization in decline (the young corrupted, the masses stupefied, barbarians at the gates of the *polis*), but also the nostalgic invocations of an allegedly once "whole" but now "fragmented" community (lost shared values, lost shared knowledge, lost shared attitudes, and so forth), where historical as well as contemporary diversities are, in one stroke, both forgotten and wishfully obliterated.

The force of this general concern will be apparent in my remarks, but I mean to focus specifically on E. D. Hirsch's book, *Cultural Literacy,* and I don't mean to mince words. I believe that the immediate objective it proposes— that is, the acquisition, by every American child, of the alleged "common," "traditional," information, attitudes, and values shared by all literate Americans or, as Hirsch also refers to it, "*the* national culture"—is meaningless as stated and if not meaningless then, given what it evidently means to Hirsch, undesirable; that such an objective, if it were desirable, could not be achieved by the pedagogic methods it proposes; and that, if it were actually adopted on a national scale (as is clearly Hirsch's serious and now institutionalized intention), the pursuit of that objective by those methods—that is, the attempt to equip every child in the country with a putatively finite, determinate, measurable store of basic "American knowledge" in the form of standard definitions or "sets of associations" attached to disarticulated terms and phrases—would not only *not* alleviate the conditions it is supposedly designed to cure (among them, widespread illiteracy and a cycle of economic deprivation, social marginalization, and political ineffectuality), but would postpone even longer adequate analyses of, and appropriate responses to, those and other problems of the nation's schools.

I will amplify these points by examining several key passages in *Cultural Literacy,* beginning with the one, early in the book, in which Hirsch introduces the notion of a "national culture" and sets up his argument for a uniform national school curriculum based on his now-famous List.

The failure of our schools, Hirsch tells us, can be attributed to the educational theories of Rousseau, Dewey, and "their present-day disciples." In contrast to these, he writes, his own "anthropological" theory of education

> deems it neither wrong nor unnatural to teach young children adult information before they fully understand it. The anthropological view stresses the universal fact that a human group must have effective communications to function effectively, that effective communications require shared culture, and that shared culture requires transmission of specific information to children.

Each link in this argument bears scrutiny, as does also the nature of the logical/rhetorical syntax by which they are joined.

To begin with, the term "human group" is vague and, as Hirsch uses it here, slippery. The statement containing the phrase—that is, "a human group must have effective communications to function effectively"—makes sense when we think of a relatively small group of mutually interacting people, such as a family, a company of coworkers, or, given the quasi-anthropological auspices, a tribal community. A *nation,* however, and particularly what Hirsch refers to repeatedly as "a modern industrial nation," is not a "human group" in that sense; and, although his subsequent allusions to "our national community" manage to evoke, under the sign of scientific precision, a questionable (and, as will be seen, otherwise disturbing) nationalist communitarianism, the phrase is clearly question-begging here and the concept has no anthropological or other scientific credentials whatsoever.

The existence of an American "national culture" is by no means self-evident. Every citizen of this nation belongs to numerous communities (regional, ethnic, religious, occupational, etc.) and shares different sets of beliefs, interests, assumptions, attitudes, and practices—and, in that sense, cultures—with the other members of each of those communities. There is, however, no single, comprehensive macroculture in which all or even most of the citizens of this nation actually participate, no numerically preponderant majority culture in relation to which any or all of the others are "minority" cultures, and no culture that, in Hirsch's term, "transcends" any or all other cultures. Nor do these multiplicities describe a condition of cultural "fragmentation" except by implicit contrast to some presumed prior condition of cultural unity and uniformity—a condition that could obtain only among the members of a relatively isolated, demographically homogeneous and stable community, and has never obtained in this nation at any time in its history.

The invocation of *transcendence* noted above is justified in the book by an illegitimate analogy between language and culture: indeed, doubly illegitimate, for not only are cultures not like languages in the way Hirsch implies (that is, sets of discrete items of "information" analogous to "vocabulary" lists), but languages themselves are not the way he describes them and requires them to be for the analogies in question. Just as every national language, Hirsch writes, "*transcends* any particular dialect, region,

or social class," so also does the "national culture." There is, however, no "national language," either in the United States or anywhere else, that all or most of the inhabitants of a nation speak *over and above* various regional and other (ethnic, class, etc.) dialects. There are only *particular* regional and other dialects, some—or one—of which may be privileged over and above all others in the state educational system and/or by various cultural agencies. An analogy from language to culture, then, would support a view of the latter quite different from that urged by Hirsch. Indeed, as his critics observe, what he refers to as "*the* national culture," and exemplifies by his List, is nothing but a *particular* (egregiously classbound and otherwise parochial) set of items of "knowledge" that Hirsch himself privileges and that he *wants* the state educational system to make "standard." (His recurrent reply to this observation is to dismiss it as "ideological," in presumed contrast to his own beliefs and proposals.)

Hirsch puts the culture/language analogy to other, remarkable uses. "[F]ixing the vocabulary of a national culture," he writes, "is analogous to fixing a standard grammar, spelling, and pronunciation"; and, he claims, Americans "need to learn not just the associations of such words as *to run* but also the associations of such terms as *Teddy Roosevelt, DNA,* and *Hamlet.*" Indeed, he assures us, if children can all learn the associations of common words such as *to run,* there is no reason why they cannot all learn the associations of *Teddy Roosevelt, DNA,* and *Hamlet.* To speak of the "vocabulary" of a culture, however, is to presuppose the altogether Hirsch-generated culture/language analogy and thus, as usual, to beg the question. (It is because Hirsch characteristically presupposes the key points of his arguments—either as self-evident or as already proved by his mere statement of them—that question-begging formulations are so recurrent in *Cultural Literacy.*) Moreover, the dubiousness—and, in fact, absurdity—of the analogy becomes increasingly apparent from the very use he makes of it. Can we really speak of "*the* associations" of *Teddy Roosevelt, DNA,* and *Hamlet* or, to choose some other items from Hirsch's List, of *Woodie Guthrie* or *Harlem*? Are there "standard associations" and, as he also claims, "traditional values" already in existence for such items, and are they really shared by all literate Americans? Or, if they are not already in existence (Hirsch is equivocal on the point), could associations and values for such items be "fixed" or "standardized" so that they really would be *independent,* as he implies, of the specific personal histories of whoever was doing the sharing and associating and valuing? And, if we really managed to teach children from Houston, Boston, Alaska, and Nebraska to memorize and recite standard associations and values for *Teddy Roosevelt, Woodie Guthrie, Hamlet, Harlem, DNA,* and five thousand other terms, do we really suppose that the "human group" constituted by the citizens of this country would have acquired a "shared culture," and would only then "have effective communications," and would only thereby and thereupon "function effectively"? What *are* we talking about?

Hirsch's claim that "effective communications require shared culture" is, in fact, false. For, given any sense of the term "culture" relevant to the passage under discussion—that is, either (a) as anthropologists would define it, the system of beliefs, skills, routine practices, and communal institutions shared by the members of some society as such, or (b) as Hirsch implies, familiarity with a list of academic set-phrases and vintage items of middle-class cultural lore—then it is a "universal fact" that people can communicate *without* a "shared culture" and that they do it all the time. Japanese suppliers, for example (a group whose presence hovers over the pages of **Cultural Literacy**), communicate with European and African buyers without sharing the latter's cultures in the anthropological sense; and, just to speak of other Americans, I communicate quite effectively with my eighty-five-year-old ex-mother-in-law from Altoona, Pennsylvania, my twenty-five-year-old hairdresser from Hillsborough, North Carolina, my five-year-old grandson from Brooklyn, New York, and my *cat,* without sharing much, if anything, of what Hirsch calls "the shared national culture" with any of them. The reason I can do so is that all the activities that Hirsch classifies as "communication" and sees as *duplicative transmissions* that presuppose *sameness*— "common" knowledge, "shared" culture, "standardized" associations—are, in fact, always *ad hoc,* context-specific, pragmatically adjusted negotiations of (and through) *difference.* We never have sameness; we cannot produce sameness; we do not need sameness.

From the conjunction of the two questionable statements considered above, Hirsch would have us conclude that "[o]nly by accumulating shared symbols, and the shared information that the symbols represent, can we learn to communicate effectively with one another in our national community"—from their conjunction, that is, by way of a crucial link in the argument: namely, the observation that "[l]iteracy, an essential aim of education in the modern world, is no autonomous, empty skill but *depends upon literate culture.*" The link is crucial because it joins the two terms, *literacy* and *culture,* the recurrent, varied, and thoroughly ambiguous operations of each of which underwrite the remarkable notion of "cultural literacy" and, with it, the rhetorical force of Hirsch's entire program for educational reform.

Literacy, Hirsch tells us, is no empty, autonomous skill. To be sure. But does it follow that it depends on "literate culture"? Indeed, what does this latter, rather barbaric phrase mean? It seems to be equivalent to the condition of "cultural literacy," or what he characterizes, for the citizens of this nation, as that which "all literate [but *not illiterate*] Americans know"—as represented by his List. But it is not clear, then, whether "literate culture" is the information possessed by people who *are able to read adequately* or, alternatively—and, of course, quite differently—the knowledge had by people who are "literate" in the sense of *well-educated* and thus also, as we say and as Hirsch's own uses of the term certainly suggest, "cultured."

In the first case, the statement in question (that literacy depends on literate culture) is, as formulated, vacuous, self-contradictory, or a Catch-22 clause: that is, it is the same as saying that, in order to read, you must know what is known (only) by people who are able to read. In the second case, it is empirically wrong, and—in relation to the

ambitious claims made for it—importantly wrong. For one's ability to read adequately (including one's ability to understand what one reads) certainly does not depend on one's having already read many worthy books, or having a B.A. degree, or being familiar with high culture. And, more significantly for the specific pedagogic reforms Hirsch proposes, it certainly does not depend on one's ability to identify or recite standard definitions for all (or even a large number) of the items on Hirsch's List—or, which may or may not be the same thing, having one's head furnished with the particular assortment of bric-a-brac that furnishes the heads of people like the Kenan Professor of English at the University of Virginia and his various friends, relatives, and associates.

The verbal slippage noted above—that is, between "literate" in the sense of being able to read adequately and "literate" in the sense of being well-read, well-educated, and, in that sense, "cultured"—is crucial to the shimmering ambiguity of the term and concept "cultural literacy" and, one suspects, responsible for a good bit of the popularity of the book (which seems to offer easy access to the socially desirable states thus named). It also permits Hirsch to deal handily with a number of significant objections:

> There are many things to be said against making a list, and in the past two years I have heard them. Ideological objections to codifying and imposing the culture of the power structure have been among them. These are objections to the whole concept of spreading cultural literacy and are consequently objections to spreading literacy itself, not to making lists.

Period. End of reply. Hirsch's answer to these objections consists, in other words, of labeling them (as usual) "ideological," putting the rabble-rousing words "power structure" in the mouths of those who raise them, and deftly identifying the questioning of his List and its use in the schools with not wanting people to be literate. The deftness of this identification depends, of course, on the verbal slippage just noted.

We may turn, however, to the more general operation of the idea of "literacy" in Hirsch's book. As everyone who has dealt with the question knows, the term names something notoriously difficult to determine or measure, even taken in its common, pedagogic sense of adequate reading competence. For not only are there many different levels of reading competence, but also many different varieties, and "adequacy" itself is, of course, a variable concept, changing its specific value in relation to different criteria, including specific purposes. It is also well known that the ease with which someone reads a text plus the extent to which she or he understands it—a legal contract, a newspaper editorial, a historical novel, printed directions for installing and operating an appliance, etc.—will always depend on a number of variable conditions, including the extent of (a) the reader's interest in that *particular* text, (b) his or her prior experience with its *particular* subject matter and domain, and (c) his or her skill in handling its *particular* verbal idiom. Contrary, however, to Hirsch's unshakable belief and central contention, none of these conditions can be equated with or reduced to the reader's mastery of *general* "background information," nor could the interests, experiences, and skills in question be derived from someone's knowledge of some list of things—any list, no matter who compiled it or how long it was.

As it happens, Hirsch cites a number of studies bearing on these points, but he interprets them bizarrely. Since appeals to the laboratory lend authority to many of his claims, it will be useful, for this and other reasons, to look at one such characteristic appeal. Citing a particular study of the conditions that enhance reading facility, Hirsch maintains that its results demonstrate the "*national* character of the knowledge needed in reading and writing." The experiment apparently consisted of a comparison of the rates of speed with which people from India and the United States could read texts that described either "an Indian wedding" or "an American wedding." As Hirsch reports it, what the data indicated (hardly surprisingly) was that the Indians read the descriptions of the Indian wedding faster, and the Americans read the description of the American wedding faster. But, of course, the same contrasts would have been obtained if the study had compared the ease with which auto mechanics and pastry chefs could read texts that described either how to take apart a carburetor or how to bake a strudel, since what mattered was not the different nationalities of the readers as such but, rather, the different extents of their prior familiarity with the particular practices described in those texts—a difference that would, with other texts, fall along occupational lines, age lines, class lines, or regional lines rather than, as was the case here, along national lines. In other words, whatever else the study demonstrated, it did not support Hirsch's views either of the general conditions required for reading facility or of the specifically "national character" of the knowledge presupposed by literacy.

The idea that "background information" is in some sense "*national*" is attended by a set of claims that are crucial to Hirsch's general argument, dubious in every detail, and worth examining very closely:

> Although nationalism may be regrettable in some of its worldwide political effects, a mastery of national culture is essential to a mastery of the standard language in every modern nation. This point is important because educators often stress the importance of a multicultural education. Such study is indeed valuable in itself; it inculcates tolerance and provides a perspective on *our own* traditions and values. But however laudable it is it should not be the primary focus of national education. It should not be allowed to supplant or interfere with *our* schools' responsibility to insure *our* children's mastery of American literate culture.

It is not clear what Hirsch understands and implies here by "multicultural education," and the vagueness is not without consequences. For many educators in this country, it would mean schooling that recognizes either the internal multiplicity of American culture and/or the significance for Americans of the cultures of other groups and nations. The indeterminate reference here permits Hirsch to ignore the former as such and, at the same time, to conflate it with the latter: in other words, he can imply (and may, of course, himself believe) that (certain) internal

American cultures are *foreign* or, in any case, not "our own." The question is, which traditions and values *are* "our own," or, to put it the other way around, which traditions and values, shared by members of various communities in America and/or elsewhere in the world, are *not* "our own," and who exactly are "we"? Hirsch's answer to each part of this question, though never explicit, is a subtextual drumbeat throughout the passage and the book.

Because the reference of "multicultural education" is vague, we also do not know what specific curricular practices Hirsch's imperatives are meant to discourage. The study of African-American fiction and the history of jazz by Philadelphia schoolchildren, for example? The study of Chinese and Mayan art in some California high school where Asian-American and Hispanic-American students are a majority? The study of French literature, architecture, and cooking in an elite New England prep school? Never mind the details; we are given to understand that, whatever we suspect it is (probably not a course in French civilization at the Concord Academy for Girls), we don't want too much of it. The passage concludes as follows:

> To teach the ways of *one's own* community has always been and still remains the essence of the education of *our* children, who enter neither a narrow tribal culture nor a transcendent world culture but a national literate culture. For profound historical reasons, this is the way of the modern world. It will not change soon, and it will certainly not be changed by educational policy alone.

What this deeply allusive and determinedly grim statement is meant to suggest, I take it, is that, however much pluralistic- or international-minded educators might wish to ignore the stark realities of life, modern (American) children have no use for local, ethnic cultures (at least not for *certain* of them—dare we guess which?), and, furthermore, should not be encouraged to identify, as their own community, any social unit either smaller, larger, or other than the *nation*. What is indicated here as ironclad fact, however ("This is the way of the modern world"), is, of course, thoroughly ideological and, for "profound historical reasons" plus many other—sociological, geopolitical, etc.—reasons, profoundly questionable.

American children "need to know" a great many things, and no doubt many more than the schools are now teaching most of them. It would be all to the good—in many different ways and for various reasons (including, but not only, their chances of prospering economically)—for them to know things about the history, government, demography, and geography of their own nation, their own state, and their own local region, *and* various other regions of the world that quite properly engage their attention. It would also be all to the good for them to know things about the ecologically, economically, and politically global, international world that they "enter" just as surely as they enter the United States of America when they are born somewhere within its borders. And, of course, it would be good for children everywhere to know things such as mathematics, biology, ecology, and computers that are not about—and the knowledge of which is not confined to or especially distinctive of—any particular society or culture, American or otherwise; for, contrary to Hirsch's odd notions regarding its "national character," most knowledge in "the modern world" (background, foreground, and middle ground) does not have any citizenship papers attached to it at all.

Cultural Literacy (book, list, term, and concept) does a very good job of obscuring the nation's very real educational problems and assuring the American public that those problems are caused primarily by befuddled education professors and school administrators following what scientists have shown to be the incorrect principles of progressive education.

—Barbara Herrnstein Smith

Given that there is more that American children "need to know" than they can be taught during their school years, the schools must, of course, establish educational priorities. Given also, however, that the social backgrounds and individual competencies of American schoolchildren vary in numerous ways related to the unique social/regional/demographic history of this very large, very populous, and exceptionally diverse nation, the *specific* priorities of their education (and sequence of their studies) are most responsively and effectively determined on a local—region by region, school by school, classroom by classroom—level, not a national level. This is not to say that those priorities are being determined now as well as they should be. But there is no reason to think that attempting to determine them uniformly at a national level would be more responsive and effective, and, moreover, no reason, aside from Hirsch's personal illusion of the essentialness, basicness, and proper standardness of some particular bag of things that he (along with what he is pleased to call "all literate Americans") happens to know, why the alphabetically listed contents of that bag should be given absolute priority in this regard.

What literate Americans know. What every American needs to know. So Hirsch claims for his List, and so Americans in the hundreds of thousands may now be inclined to believe. The force of the claim is equivocal, however, and hedged throughout the book. Hirsch states, for example, that the appendix to *Cultural Literacy* is not meant to be "prescriptive" but is only "a *descriptive* list of the information actually possessed by literate Americans," forgetting the book's subtitle and his recurrent imperatives concerning the centrality of the List to the educational reforms he is proposing. The continuous eliding of the prescriptive/descriptive distinction is significant because it permits Hirsch to evade the responsibilities of each kind of claim by moving to the other when criticisms are pressed. Thus, if the List's claims to descriptive adequacy

and accuracy are questioned (is it really what literate Americans—*all* of them?—"actually" know?), Hirsch can claim to be offering only provisional recommendations and "guideposts"; conversely, when objections are raised to the manifestly patrician, self-privileging norms promoted by the List, Hirsch can claim that it has nothing to do with what *he* knows or thinks should be known, but simply describes the way things are among "literate Americans."

The method by which the List was generated is, in any case, exceedingly mysterious. According to Hirsch, it is not "a complete catalogue of American knowledge," but "is intended to illustrate the character and range of the knowledge literate Americans tend to share" and to "establish guideposts that can be of practical use to teachers, students, and all others who need to know our literate culture" (which is, of course, according to Hirsch, "every American"). But, one might ask (granting the double absurdity of a specifically "*American* knowledge" and a possible catalog of *any* actual human knowledge), what sorts of persons *are* the "literate Americans" whose knowledge is illustrated or represented by the List? How, for example, could one distinguish them from Americans who merely know how to read? And how does Hirsch himself know what "the literate reader" knows?

The answers to these questions cannot be determined from any explicit statements of procedure in the book. Indeed, the accounts of the List given by way of introduction and explanation could hardly be briefer or vaguer. Hirsch notes that "different literate Americans have slightly [*sic*] different conceptions of our shared knowledge," but assures his readers that "more than one hundred consultants reported agreement on over 90 percent of the items listed." Wonderful: more than one hundred, over 90 percent. But agreement on *what*? Was each "consultant" asked to compile an individual list and then all the lists compared for overlap? Or, quite differently, were the consultants asked, for each item on an already compiled list, to say whether they were themselves familiar with it? Or, again, and again quite differently, were the consultants asked, for each item, whether they agreed that every "literate American" (however defined for them—if at all) *knew* it—or, and also quite differently, whether they thought every literate American *should* know it? Nor does Hirsch indicate how the consultants themselves were chosen. At random from the Charlottesville telephone directory? From among his classiest friends, best students, and most congenial colleagues at the University of Virginia? Were they, by any chance, selected to be representative of various regions of the nation, and a range of ages, occupations, and degrees of formal education? Were they chosen, in fact, by any consistent and appropriate sampling principle?

The questions raised here are important because, depending on the specific procedures and selection criteria used, very different lists would have been produced. Moreover, without consistent and appropriate procedures and criteria, the claims of representativeness (not to mention implications of unbiased, statistical authority) made for Hirsch's List—copies of which are now being delivered by the truckful to teachers and children across the nation—

might seem, relative to the standards of responsible social science research, dubious. But never mind all that: like the old Ivory Soap ads, *99 and 44/100 percent pure—it floats!*

Toward the end of the book, Hirsch acknowledges the objection from "some educators" that there might be some "difficulties" putting the idea of cultural literacy into practice since information is not remembered "unless it is embedded in interesting material" and, as he phrases the objection, knowledge of that sort is acquired only through "years of communication with other literate people." His reply is that "the predicted difficulties . . . simply do not apply to young children" because the latter are "fascinated by straightforward information and absorb it without strain": young children, Hirsch remarks, really *like* "to pick up adult information long before they can make sense of it" and, besides, "even untraditional schools have not found a way to avoid rote learning," as in the alphabet and multiplication tables.

But Hirsch's reply evades the point of such objections and misses their decisive implications for the value of his educational program. If "cultural literacy," as he defines it, cannot be formally taught, then it makes no difference how early you start teaching it; if it cannot be acquired by memorizing lists and dictionaries, then it makes no difference that children memorize alphabets and multiplication tables. Moreover, if children learn List-items such as *coup d'état, The Charge of the Light Brigade,* and *consumer price index* only as "adult information" that they cannot "make sense of," and their lives, then and subsequently, give them no other way to use that information or otherwise make sense of it, then it will not operate as knowledge at all. It will not, that is, function for those children in the way one presumably wants it to function (in relation to reading or otherwise), namely as a part of their intellectual resources—to say nothing of their creative or critical thinking, the first of which (and, indeed, creativity of any kind) Hirsch never mentions in the book, and the second of which elicits only his patient condescension as among the sadly misguided goals of progressive education.

Indeed, the acquisition of information of that sort in those ways (that is, children's memorization and recitation-on-cue of discrete pieces of information that they did not understand and never had any need or extra-academic occasion to use) would be no different in kind and effect from that bare "word recognition" and mere "knowledge of phonics" that Hirsch always contrasts to genuine literacy and excoriates as only a facsimile of competence. It appears, then, that this "educational reform" would not, as it promises, eliminate illiteracy and make all merely technically literate Americans truly, functionally literate, but would only create a new classification of functional illiteracy—"functional *cultural* illiteracy"—on which we can blame all our national problems and by which we can explain why the jobless can't get jobs, the powerless don't vote, and the poor don't have enough money.

It is no wonder that Hirsch's book is acclaimed by numerous government officials and by the neoconservative wing of the nation's intellectual/educational establishment. For *Cultural Literacy* (book, list, term, and concept) does a very good job of obscuring the nation's very real educa-

tional problems and assuring the American public, many of whom are naturally happy to hear it, that those problems (along with other social and economic ills, both real and imaginary, from poverty and unemployment to "cultural fragmentation" and the "competitive edge" of the Japanese) are caused primarily by befuddled education professors and school administrators following what scientists have shown to be the incorrect principles of progressive education—and, consequently, can be solved by school reforms that require no funding, entail no social or political changes, create no uncomfortable feelings for anyone except teachers and school administrators, and do not touch the structure of a single American institution, including its school system.

Cultural Literacy promises practically everything, costs practically nothing, and is produced, packaged, and promoted in a form quite familiar to Americans, whose shared national culture consists as much of media hype and 4th of July speeches as it does of anything on Hirsch's List from *auf wiedersehen* to *vestal virgins*. "[O]nly a few hundred pages of information," says Hirsch, "stand between" literacy and illiteracy, "between dependence and autonomy"—only a few hundred pages between us and the fulfillment of our dreams. And not only our individual dreams but the American Dream. For, as he tells us in the concluding words of the book, the stakes here are high:

> breaking the cycle of illiteracy for deprived children; raising the living standard of families who have been illiterate; making our country more competitive in international markets; achieving greater social justice; enabling all citizens to participate in the political process; bringing us that much closer to the Ciceronian ideal of universal public discourse—in short, achieving the fundamental goals of the Founders at the birth of the republic.

Wild applause; fireworks; music—*America the Beautiful;* all together, now: *Calvin Coolidge, Gunga Din, Peter Pan, spontaneous combustion.* Hurrah for America and the national culture! Hurrah!

The project of cult-lit will, I am certain, fail. It will fail because, even if children all over the country began to study cultural literacy lists, it would make little if any dent in the conditions that actually produce and perpetuate illiteracy, poverty, social inequities, and political ineffectiveness (not to mention the prosperity of the Japanese in industry and business, and the communication gap between Puerto Rican teenagers and Bridgeport bank executives or between middle-class grandparents and their postmodern grandchildren). As I have been suggesting, however, the very pursuit of Hirsch's project would itself have substantial consequences and, it seems, is already having them, not the least of which is the continued deferral of responsible analysis of the nation's enormous—but quite complex and *various*—educational problems (in some places, deteriorated facilities and insufficient, obsolete materials; in other places, large numbers of children from poor, illiterate, non-English speaking, and otherwise educationally disadvantaged families; in most places, underpaid, undervalued, overburdened teachers; and, throughout the system, but for different reasons and to different extents, unresponsive and ineffective teaching), and the deferral also of the identification and mobilization of the substantial and *varied* resources that would be needed to begin to address those problems adequately.

It is for this reason that I think members of the educational community should not dismiss Hirsch's book as silly, well-meaning, and harmless but, rather, should examine it closely, devote some energy to the exposure of its oversimplifications and incoherences, and remain alert to its echo and endorsement by state officials and agencies. For, we must remember, the fact that the arguments for a proposal are vague and muddled, that its recommendations are patently absurd, and that the possibility of its success is rejected by all of the most eminent people in the field does not mean that it won't become national policy. After all, just think of Star Wars. (pp. 69-84)

> *Barbara Herrnstein Smith, "Cult-Lit: Hirsch, Literacy, and the 'National Culture',"* in South Atlantic Quarterly, *Vol. 89, No. 1, Winter, 1990, pp. 69-88.*

FURTHER READING

Aronowitz, Stanley, and Giroux, Henry A. "Schooling, Culture, and Literacy in the Age of Broken Dreams: A Review of Bloom and Hirsch." *Harvard Educational Review* 58, No. 2 (May 1988): 172-94.

Discusses the premise of *Cultural Literacy,* finding that "Hirsch's argument is more than a popular and politically innocent treatise on educational reform, but rather serves at best as a veiled apology for a highly dogmatic and reactionary view of literacy and schooling." The critics also observe an ideological similarity between *Cultural Literacy* and Allan Bloom's *The Closing of the American Mind.*

Booth, Wayne C. "Cultural Literacy and Liberal Learning: An Open Letter to E. D. Hirsch, Jr." *Change* 20, No. 4 (July-August 1988): 11-21.

Objects that Hirsch's goal in *Cultural Literacy,* "despite its deep-felt democratic claims, too often sounds not like the education of free men and women, but rather the training of functionaries."

Colomb, Gregory B. "Cultural Literacy and the Theory of Meaning: Or, What Educational Theorists Need to Know about How We Read." *New Literary History: A Journal of Theory and Interpretation* 20, No. 2 (Winter 1989): 411-50.

Debates the validity of Hirsch's educational theory as presented in *Cultural Literacy,* concluding: "To have a theory of reading is to have a theory of meaning, and Professor Hirsch has the wrong theory of meaning."

Danneberg, Lutz, and Müller, Hans-Harald. "On Justifying the Choice of Interpretive Theories." *The Journal of Aesthetics and Art Criticism* XLIII, No. 1 (Fall 1984): 7-16.

Applauds Hirsch's *Validity in Interpretation* and The

Aims of Interpretation for providing "a forceful critique of the arguments conventionally put forward in support of interpretive theories" as well as "a new set of standards for justifying the theories."

Hitchens, Christopher. "Why We Don't Know What We Don't Know: Just Ask E. D. Hirsch." *New York Times Magazine* (13 May 1990): 32, 59-60, 62.

Provides a brief summary of Hirsch's career and an overview of the controversy surrounding *Cultural Literacy.*

Lentricchia, Frank. "E. D. Hirsch: The Hermeneutics of Innocence." In his *After the New Criticism,* pp. 256-80. Chicago: The University of Chicago Press, 1980.

Argues against Hirsch's critical theory of authorial intent presented in *Value in Interpretation* and *The Aims of Interpretation,* finding Hirsch's assertions "theoretically questionable at best."

Madison, G. B. "A Critique of Hirsch's *Validity.*" In his *The Hermeneutics of Postmodernity: Figures and Themes,* pp. 3-24. Bloomington: Indiana University Press, 1988.

Asserts that "the main value of Hirsch's book can be found in its deficiencies, for it is precisely these which can force us to recognize the urgent need for a theory of human understanding capable of overcoming them."

Postman, Neil. "Learning by Story." *The Atlantic* 264, No. 6 (December 1989): 119-24.

Declares of the 5,000-term appendix to *Cultural Literacy:* "Hirsch's list is the disease for which it claims to be the cure—that is to say, its arbitrariness only demonstrates the futility of trying to do what he wants us to do." Postman states that individuals need a framework in which to synthesize and evaluate facts such as those offered in Hirsch's list.

Ray, William. "E. D. Hirsch: Individual Meaning as Shared Meaning." In his *Literary Meaning: From Phenomenology to Deconstruction,* pp. 90-103. Oxford: Basil Blackwell, 1984.

Analyzes the critical theory presented by Hirsch in *Validity in Interpretation* and *The Aims of Interpretation,* concluding that "Hirsch's fragmentation of meaning can be understood as a response to the threat that a non-simple notion of meaning might pose for the objectivist project."

Scholes, Robert. "Three Views of Education: Nostalgia, History, and Voodoo." *College English* 50, No. 3 (March 1988): 323-32.

Criticizes Hirsch "because the sweetly reasonable facade of his book is just that—a facade" and finds *Cultural Literacy* to be "a bizarre and dangerous book."

Tuttleton, James W. "Literacy at the Barricades." *Commentary* 84, No. 1 (July 1987): 45-8.

Applauds Hirsch's challenge of the educational system and agrees that literate Americans share a pool of facts and informational items—but not necessarily values or ideals. Tuttleton considers Hirsch's views on the nature of cultural literacy to be "solidly buttressed by the conclusions of serious research in cognitive psychology, anthropology and sociology.''

Additional coverage of Hirsch's life and career is contained in the following sources published by Gale Research: _Contemporary Authors,_ Vols. 25-28, rev. ed.; _Contemporary Authors New Revision Series,_ Vol. 27; _Dictionary of Literary Biography,_ Vol. 67; and _Major 20th-Century Writers._

Brave New World
Aldous Huxley

The following entry presents criticism on Huxley's novel *Brave New World* (1932). For information on Huxley's complete career, see *CLC*, Volumes 1, 3, 4, 5, 8, 11, and 18. For criticism focusing on Huxley's utopian and dystopian fiction, see *CLC*, Volume 35.

INTRODUCTION

Often considered an archetypal dystopian novel, *Brave New World* combines Huxley's comprehensive scientific knowledge with satire of contemporary society to project a future totalitarian state based on values and trends of the modern world. Examining the fate of the individual in a technologically advanced society, Huxley criticizes the results of unchecked scientific achievement, intensive social conditioning, and single-minded pursuit of pleasure, which together could turn humans "into a kind of uniformity." Regarding the aim of establishing a utopian society, Huxley stated: "Anyone who believes that there is some magical shortcut out of man's chronologically tragic situation is inviting either violent catastrophe through an ideological crusade or else a slower but equally sure disaster through the creation of a brave new world."

Huxley was born into a family renowned for its scientific and intellectual achievements. Among his noted relatives were his grandfather Thomas Henry Huxley, an eminent biologist during the advent of Darwinism; his father Leonard, a respected editor and essayist; his brother Julian, also a prominent biologist; and his half brother Andrew, who received the Nobel Prize in 1963 for his work in physiology. As a young man Huxley extensively studied the fields of medicine and the arts and sciences, and utilized his experience in these areas in such works as *Ape and Essence, Island,* and "Young Archimedes." This scientific background is also evident in his descriptions of the technologically advanced society of *Brave New World.*

Brave New World depicts life in the year 632 A.F. (after Ford, or occasionally Freud). Free from war, disease, and suffering, the society described by Huxley enjoys an abundance of physical pleasures and material luxuries. In order to maintain this state, human beings are mass-produced in test tubes and genetically engineered with standardized traits. As children they are socially conditioned through subliminal programming and drugs; as adults they fulfill prescribed roles in one of five social classes and enjoy carefree, promiscuous lives. Although in rare instances individuals become aware of intellectual and spiritual dissatisfaction, the most significant conflict arises when an uncon-

ditioned outsider—a young man named John, or "the Savage"—is introduced from the wilderness into this allegedly advanced society. Capable of independent thought and able to express diverse emotions, John recognizes the limitations placed upon the individual in this standardized world and rebels against mass conformity. However, he eventually succumbs to the temptations of the "brave new world" and, wracked with guilt, commits suicide.

Brave New World is generally regarded as a classic examination of modern values, and critical attention to the novel has often focused on the nature of Huxley's satire. Commentators have noted the cynicism with which Huxley depicts the authoritarian state in *Brave New World*, as evidenced by his parodies of contemporary figures, institutions, and theories. Critics perceive Huxley's dystopia to be a mockery of the scientific and social progress generally sought by government and industry in the early twentieth century. As Jerry W. Carlson has stated: "In *Brave New World*, Huxley explores the . . . problem of how modern mass society could destroy the values of individualism by accepting a false belief in perfection by standardization."

PRINCIPAL WORKS

The Burning Wheel   (poetry)   1916
The Defeat of Youth and Other Poems   (poetry)   1918
Leda and Other Poems   (poetry)   1920
Limbo   (short stories and drama)   1920
Crome Yellow   (novel)   1921
Antic Hay   (novel)   1923
On the Margin   (essays)   1923
Those Barren Leaves   (novel)   1925
Jesting Pilate: An Intellectual Holiday   (travel journal)
    1926
Point Counter Point   (novel)   1928
Brave New World   (novel)   1932
Eyeless in Gaza   (novel)   1936
The Gioconda Smile   (short stories)   1938
After Many a Summer Dies the Swan   (novel)   1939
Time Must Have a Stop   (novel)   1944
The Perennial Philosophy   (essay)   1945
Ape and Essence   (novel)   1948
*Gioconda Smile   (drama)   1948
The Doors of Perception   (essay)   1954
Heaven and Hell   (nonfiction)   1956
Brave New World Revisited   (essay)   1958
Collected Essays   (essays)   1959
Island   (novel)   1962
Literature and Science   (essay)   1963
The Collected Poetry of Aldous Huxley   (poetry)   1971

*Adapted from the short story of the same name; also published as
Mortal Coils.

CRITICISM

Margaret Cheney Dawson   (review date 7 February 1932)

[*In the review below, Dawson declares* Brave New World *a "lugubrious and heavy-handed piece of propaganda."*]

Mr. Huxley has the jitters. Looking back over his career one can see that he has always had them, in varying degrees, that the flesh and the intellect have exasperated him in almost equal proportions, that love and lust and art and science and religion and philosophy have been so much pepper to his nostrils. Time was when these and other phases of the human experiment appeared to him ridiculous and he exposed them, brutally to be sure, but with charming malice and suave literary grace. As the years went and novels came, the dry wine of his wit began to sour and his satire to toughen into something closely resembling didacticism. To the astonishment of those who had counted as much on his thoroughgoing erudition as his brilliance for stimulation, the second phase of his development failed to produce any outstandingly powerful or original results. The fine edge of his bitterness was worn down to querulous argument. And now, with what can only be called a straight case of jitters, he abandons his genius for mere ingenuity and rushes headlong into the great pamphleteering movement.

Brave New World is intended to be the Utopia to end Utopias, the burlesque of grandiose modern schemes for futurity. It is described by the publishers as "witty and wickedly satirical," but unless the substitution of Ford for God ("Ford's in his Flivver, all's well with the world") and the introduction of such scintillating nursery rhymes as "Streptocock-Gee to Banbury T, to see a fine bathroom and W. C." can be relied on to stop the show, it must stand on its merits as a lugubrious and heavy-handed piece of propaganda.

The world which is here revealed to shock us has taken for its motto "Community, Identity, Stability." In it babies are hatched out of bottles (decanted, rather) and the word "mother" has become a nasty joke. Due to a process known as Bokanovskification, whereby one normal egg can be made to yield as many as ninety-six embryos, this world is largely peopled by huge groups of twins or should one call them centruplets? This is true, however, only in the lower classes, which result from purposeful stunting of the embryo by doses of alcohol and regulated oxygen shortage. These people, classified as Gammas and Epsilons and Semi-morons, and made to wear, respectively, green, khaki and black uniforms, are predestined to perform all unpleasant work. As their brains have been conditioned and their subconscious desires shaped by suggestions whispered while they slept, they are perfectly happy in the environment to which the World Directors have seen fit to call them. The Alphas and Betas, on the other hand, who were allowed as eggs to develop without benefit of Bokanovsky and whose hypnopaedia (sleep teaching) has inspired them with a sense of superiority, are perfectly suited to the fields of higher intellectual endeavor. Thus everybody is happy, since everybody has been conditioned to like the life which he will be forced, for society's sake, to lead. When any little maladjustments occur, there is always *soma,* the equivalent of the clumsy old time drugs, but without any of the unpleasant after effects.

The description of the fertilizing room, the decanting room, the predestinating room, etc., have a horrible fascination. Every detail is conceived and depicted with the utmost ingenuity, and if Mr. Huxley had confined himself to such vivid grotesqueries, he might have given us a first rate case of the horrors. It is when he runs into plot development that the illusion fails. By way of supplying adverse comment on the system, he brings on the scene a "savage," i.e. the child of a "civilized" woman who had been abandoned with her viviparous shame in a New Mexican Indian reservation. This boy, John, had grown up in a very confused state, his mother extolling the wonders of civilization on the one hand, while his Indian playmates and an old copy of Shakespeare taught him an utterly different set of values on the other. He learned to prize heroism, to honor self-discipline, to believe in chastity. In the new world to which an enterprising Alpha Plus transported him, these virtues were useless, in fact, incomprehensible. But John could not relinquish his belief in them nor resist trying to convert the placid herds to his own credo of divine discontent. Trouble ensued, and at last John the Savage was arrested and brought face to face with his Fordship Mustapha Mond, Resident World Controller for Western Europe. There follows a dialogue that contains the meat of the matter, during which John pleads for the "right to be unhappy" and protests against "getting rid of everything unpleasant instead of learning to put up with it." Both arguments the Controller meets with commendable placidity, while showing John out the door. The unhappy savage retires to seclusion and eventually to suicide. And then at the very end, after all the sound and fury, Mr. Huxley relents for a moment and gives us a few plangent phrases in which lie the only echo of his former work, the only whisper of better things to come.

> Margaret Cheney Dawson, "Huxley Turns Propagandist," in New York Herald Tribune Books, February 7, 1932, p. 5.

Henry Hazlitt   (review date 17 February 1932)

[*Hazlitt is an American journalist and editor who has written extensively on government and economics. In the review below, he favorably assesses the satiric elements of* Brave New World *and identifies their twentieth-century social and political contexts.*]

On the flyleaf of [**Brave New World**] is a quotation from Nicolas Berdiaeff: "Les utopies apparaissent comme bien plus réalisables qu'on ne le croyait autrefois. Et nous nous trouvons actuellement devant une question bien autrement angoissante: Comment éviter leur réalisation définitive?" Mr. Huxley has portrayed here a Utopia that obviously he would wish to avoid. It is set ostensibly in the far future, the year of Our Ford, 632. One has not read very far, however, before one perceives that this is not really Mr. Huxley's idea of what the future will be like, but a projection of some contemporary ideals. So far as progress in invention is concerned, there is very little in this Utopia, outside of the biological sphere at least, that does not seem realizable within the next twenty years—though people do go to the "feelies." Economically, the ideals that prevail are those usually associated with Henry Ford—mass production and particularly mass consumption. Everyone spends freely, and games and other pleasures that do not require the use of elaborate and expensive apparatus are frowned upon. The social organization is communistic—there is a World State managed by ten World Controllers, who head an almost Catholic hierarchy; everyone is assigned his job, is educated to identify his interests with those of everyone else, and is suspected if he is ever found alone. The official religion is Fordianity: people under stress of emotion say "Ford forbid!" or "Ford's in his flivver; all's well with the world," and make the sign of the T. "My Life and Work" has replaced the Bible, and all old books are forbidden to circulate because they suggest the past and history is bunk. Moreover, reading wastes time that should be given to consumption.

The sexual *mores* stem from the ideals associated with the names of Freud and Bertrand Russell. There is complete promiscuity; every woman carries a set of contraceptives with her; the children are taught erotic games in the kindergarten; marriage and the home have disappeared; any approach to monogamy is considered hardly decent; children are brought to birth in bottles in laboratories, and mother and father have become merely obscene words. Sentimentality and a curious bottle-fixation seem to have survived, however, for the people sing such popular songs as:

> Bottle of mine, it's you I've always wanted!
> Bottle of mine, why was I ever decanted?
> > Skies are blue inside of you,
> > The weather's always fine;
> For
> There ain't no Bottle in all the world
> Like that dear little Bottle of mine.

Curiously enough, there is no democracy, but, on the contrary, a rigid caste system. Each caste is set off from the others not only by the work it does, but by the color of its clothes and even by physical constitution. The Alphas represent the highest intellectual class, from which all the directors are recruited; they are selected from the finest chromosomes, and developed in their bottles under optimum chemical conditions. The classes graduate down through Betas, Gammas, Deltas, and finally Epsilons, who do the most menial work, and are even purposely stunted in growth by a shortage of oxygen in their incubator bottles. The purpose of the caste system is social stability. There could obviously be no social stability if everyone were an Alpha. The lower castes are prevented from being dissatisfied by having brains geared down to the work they have to do. In addition to these hereditary and prenatal precautions, conditioning along the lines discovered by Freud, Pavlov, and Watson begins at birth. The secret of happiness and virtue, as one director points out, is liking what you've *got* to do; therefore all conditioning aims at making people like their unescapable social destiny. Children are conditioned to hate flowers by giving them regularly an electric shock when they touch them. In their sleep certain maxims, like "Everybody belongs to everybody else," are repeated to them over and over again, so that the adult mind accepts them as axioms. Finally, these people are also protected from whatever physical and emotional pain there may be left in the world by regular doses of *soma,* a drug somewhat similar in its qualities to morphine, with none of the latter's bad after-effects.

What is wrong with this Utopia? Mr. Huxley attempts to tell us by the device of introducing a "savage," brought up under other ideals on an Indian reservation, and having read that author unknown to the Model T Utopia, Shakespeare. In the admittedly violent and often irrational reactions of the "savage" we have the indictment of this civilization. Not only is there no place in it for love, for romance, for fidelity, for parental affection; there is no suffering in it, and hence absolutely no need of nobility and heroism. In such a society the tragedies of Shakespeare become not merely irrelevant, but literally meaningless. This Model T civilization is distinguished by supreme stability, comfort, and happiness, but these things can be purchased only at a price, and the price is a high one. Not merely art and religion are brought to a standstill, but science itself, lest it make discoveries that would be socially disturbing.

Even one of the ten World Controllers is led to suspect the truth, though of course forbidding the publication, of a theory holding that the purpose of life is not the maintenance of well-being, but "some intensification and refining of consciousness, some enlargement of knowledge."

Brave New World is successful as a novel and as a satire; but one need not accept all its apparent implications. A little suffering, a little irrationality, a little division and chaos, are perhaps necessary ingredients of an ideal state, but there has probably never been a time when the world has not had an oversupply of them. Only when we have reduced them enormously will Mr. Huxley's central problem become a real problem. Meanwhile reformers can continue to strain every muscle in the quiet assurance of their own futility. They may, for example, form their Leagues of Nations, draw up their Kellogg Pacts and Nine-Power Treaties, and hold their disarmament conferences, in the calm confidence that a Japan will still brutally attack a China. (pp. 204, 206)

> Henry Hazlitt, "What's Wrong with Utopia?" in The Nation, *New York, Vol. CXXXIV, No. 3476, February 17, 1932, pp. 204, 206.*

Hermann Hesse   (review date May 1933)

[*Recipient of the 1946 Nobel Prize in literature, Hesse is considered one of the most important German novelists of the twentieth century. Lyrical in style, his novels focus on protagonists who search for self-knowledge and insight into the relationship between physical and spiritual realms. In the following review originally published in 1933, Hesse praises* Brave New World *while objecting to the unrealistic quality of utopian literature.*]

Huxley's utopian novel [**Brave New World**] has all the pleasant characteristics of his earlier books, the good ideas, the nice humour, the ironic cleverness. Its effectiveness is only diminished by the utopian element itself, through the unreality of its human beings and situations. With perspicuity and irony a completely mechanized world is depicted, in which the human beings themselves have long since ceased to be human but are only 'standardized' machines. Only two of them are not wholly machines, one superior and one inferior; they still have remnants of humanity, of soul, of personality, of dream and passion. In addition there is a savage, a complete human being who, with logical consistency, quickly succumbs in the standardized civilized world: the last human being. There survive the two half-human beings and one of them may well be the symbol of Huxley's own tragic fate: the figure of the clever, gifted, successful, brilliant man of letters who, to be sure, has been too far engulfed by civilization in order to be a poet, as his ambition desired, but who knows well enough about the magic and miracle of poetry, perhaps has plumbed the depths of what it means to be a poet more thoroughly than any real poet ever could, for he sees with perfect clarity that poetry rises from other roots than technology, that like religion and genuine learning it thrives on sacrifices and passions, which are impossible on the asphalt of a standardized superficial world with its cheap department-store happiness.

This book does not reach the level of tragedy. We remain on the level of a slightly melancholy irony, but one loves Huxley for the sake of this figure, one loves his deep love for Shakespeare and his gently ironic gesture of resignation. (pp. 221-22)

> Hermann Hesse, in an extract, translated by G. Wallis Field, in Aldous Huxley: The Critical Heritage, *edited by Donald Watt, Routledge & Kegan Paul Ltd., 1975, pp. 221-22.*

Philo M. Buck, Jr.   (essay date 1942)

[*In the excerpt below, Buck examines the vision of scientifically standardized human life presented by Huxley in* Brave New World.]

Is contemporary science, engaged successfully upon the ordering and perfecting of the practical business of life, liable so to standardize it and fit it to the environment as to endanger man's amateur standing, and thus disqualify him ultimately in the game of life? It is an interesting question, whether or not science in its exceeding care to reduce human life, as it does with all nature, to a formula, has not forgotten some essential aspects of life that are beyond and above any scope of science.

Aldous Huxley is well equipped to raise and perhaps to answer this question. He has the sensitiveness and imagination of the artist whose domain is not the commonplace but the unique. For, as he himself once said in criticism of the proletarian literature, 'Life's so ordinary that literature has to deal with the exceptional—Drama begins where there's freedom of choice. Even proletarian books will deal with exceptional proletarians.' There is more than a grain of truth in the generalization, hotly though some may debate it. He is a close observer of the life about him—this anyone can discover from even the most cursory reading of his essays and novels. He is an intellectualist interested in what he observes, as is the scientist, that he may understand. 'My thinking is predominantly extraverted; but I have a great dislike of practical activity. I am interested in the outside world, but only intellectually.' True, one can hardly fancy him in a band of martyrs, but there is still a deal of deep feeling in his intellectual observation. Then he has the rare gift of pointed satire, and satire without the indignation to prompt it is less than a blank cartridge. 'Fecit indignatio versus,' and indignation is a moral virtue.

But above all he knows science and the aim of true scientists. The grandson of Thomas Henry Huxley, he belongs to a family famous in its devotion to science. More than any other, he knows the difference between the true scientist who is concerned only with pure and humble intellectual understanding, and those who with inordinate pride would extend its boundaries. When in his **Ends and Means** he writes, 'We are living now, not in the delicious intoxication induced by the early success of science, but in a rather grisly morning after, when it has become apparent that what triumphant science has done hitherto is to improve the means for achieving unimportant or actually deteriorated ends,' he is thinking not of Newton or Einstein, but of the appliers of scientific discovery to human comfort and leisure. He can afford to be the critic of science when he understands that true scientists differ by a horizon from those, like the political scientists and economists, who try to translate its findings into objects of comfort and into social and political systems. It is these blunderers who cause him again to write bitterly: 'The scientific picture of the world is what it is because men of science combine this incompetence with certain special competence.' Blunderers and incompetent because they overlook the portion of human life that is the domain of art and ethics.

The essays and novels, which are Huxley's most significant work, are a timely criticism of precisely this oversight of the contemporary mind. He is a creative artist, but like Swift it is his critical insight into the sins of the age—sins against human nature—that prompts his art and gives it substance. He is thinker and observer first, and his fiction a means of enforcing his moral. Perhaps of all contemporary creative writers he most resembles the prophet of old who to enforce his teaching turned to well-known parables and tales. In this he again resembles the honest, intrepid battler, his grandfather, who in his day also was a prophet with a mission. Thomas Henry Huxley wrote and lectured, when he might have devoted himself to research in biology, that he might set the world right about the nature and need of science. His mission was successful, and the domain of science was expanded until now it threatens to become absolute. The grandson, in his turn, neglecting pure art, turns to prophecy and satire that again he may set the world right about science and rescue from its misuse the forgotten domain of human nature.

Nowhere has he done this more potently than in the satire *Brave New World,* which is the *Gulliver's Travels* of the twentieth century. To be sure it is exaggerated, so is Gulliver. To be sure it overlooks much, so does Gulliver, and above all it is cynical, at times bitterly brutal and offensive, and so also is Gulliver. There can be no omelet without the breaking of eggs. But the breaking of painted eggs is the motive of satire. It is not meant to amuse or entertain, but to shock. The *Brave New World* is shocking and is meant to be, as Jeremiah was shocking when he described the finery and the emptiness of the daughters of Zion.

In his earliest novels, as in *Crome Yellow,* he had visibly portrayed the autumnal shade of contemporary life, life from which, as from autumn foliage, all vigor has departed, melancholy and monotonous and ready for death. It has its false gaiety and its substitute for vitality and spontaneous growth. But the aimlessness and emptiness of contemporary life is a theme that many have essayed and more have felt; for with the advance in the comfort and luxuries of life has come a brilliance of color and a swiftness of movement and an abandonment to sensuous caprice that was impossible in the days before science gave us comfortable houses and the means of rapid locomotion and the leisure for sensuous living. All this can easily be mistaken for a richer living, as the colors of autumn might be read as a debauch of life instead of the omen of death. All this many novelists and essayists have pointed out, until it takes no great imagination to repeat the foreboding. *Brave New World* on the contrary is a prophecy on a new, or at least a different theme: the seeds of death are already planted for us in the triumphs of science. When science turns its eyes to the conquest of the whole of the human world—and this conquest already is almost achieved—it will be a conquest which will mean also the death of science.

Brave New World is a satire, again as Thomas More's *Utopia* is a satire, in the form of a novel, a description of our lives as they will be in the none too distant future, if the present obsessions persist for standardization according to the sciences—eugenics and psychology, as well as economics and mechanics. Thus, though it purports to be a look into the future, it is much more an assessment of the present. For example, the little song in which the scientifically processed inhabitants of the world find a substitute for the emotion of art:

> Hug me till you drug me, honey;
> Kiss me till I'm in a coma:
> Hug me, honey, snugly bunny,
> Love's as good as soma.

Any night on the radio, or from the dance orchestra, drug like this is poured out by crooners. It is not a caricature of the theme song—it is Hollywood. And people like it.

The *Brave New World* is not a fantastic Utopian *jeu d'esprit.*

—Philo M. Buck, Jr.

It is the emotional substitute for art, as 'soma' in the *Brave New World* is the artificial substitute for the exhilaration of experience. Soma is cheaper, for it comes in medicinal pellets, and it is safer, for it leaves no aftereffects of misadventure or danger. Again we think of substitutes that the safety of modern life offers for the thrill of real danger. Then, that there be nothing lacking in the way of emotional outlet in this brave new world, with perfect safety for all, there are the 'Feelies.' The movies today have one thing lacking, the response of the audience to their emotional thrill is not quite perfect. It requires some imaginative labor to respond to the emotions of the hero and the heroine. So the New World invented the 'Feelies' where the full play of all emotions is remotely distilled into the nerves of each member of the audience, merely by his putting his arms on the chairs in the theatre. But is not that day of the brave new world not much more than just around the corner, if Hollywood and the technicians have their way?

'Soma' and 'Feelies' compensate for the instinctive striving for unique self-expression. They are spillways, safe and practicable, for the personal dissatisfaction with his environment that each individual will some time feel, the craving for God, for danger, for excellence, even for sin when sin is unique and personal. But already with these fortunate inhabitants of the brave new world, dissatisfaction and sin were impossible. This new deal began after a great world war that had for the last time made disorder prevail, and discomfort. So the director of the new world, the super-dictator, declared things must be altered once and for all, and human nature changed. All the old incitements to extravagance and uniqueness and personal freedom were abolished by the psychologist, biologist, and efficiency engineer. The age of Ford was made to prevail.

> You can't make tragedies without social instability. The world's stable now. People are happy; they get what they want, and they never want what they can't get. They're well off; they're safe; they're never ill; they're not afraid of death; they're blissfully ignorant of passion and old age; they're plagued with no mothers or fathers; they've got no wives, or children, or lovers to feel strongly about; they're so conditioned that they practically can't help behaving as they ought to behave.

This is a dawn that can be made to last forever. But no poet's imagination can ever give it hail or sing its praise, for there will be no poets.

Yes, people are here conditioned for the role they are to play in life before they are born, no, before they are decanted, for they are conceived in a test tube and decanted from a flask in which are all the ingredients, the hormones and fluids, that will make them what they are to be. Strict census is kept of all classes of society and babies are planned ahead, like crops, to meet a foreseen shortage. There is the 'alpha' class, the administrators-in-chief and the intellectuals, the 'betas' below them, though yet a class of dignity. Below are the varied lower ranks, the 'gammas,' the 'deltas,' and last and lowest the 'epsilons.' Each class is exactly designed for its position and function; there are no errors or misfits. An 'epsilon' can no more dream of being an 'alpha' than a mosquito can compose elegies on the unhappy fate which kept him from being an elephant. So much virtue is there in science. 'Abandon all hope ye that enter.' This motto with its ominous warning might equally be inscribed above the arch of this scientific paradise. And it carries a more sinister warning than Dante's, for Dante's damned had had at least one chance in life where hope might have been of avail. In this paradise of the physiological-psychological-biologist, the faculty of hope is not abandoned; it has been atrophied even before it is decanted.

Nor is this quite so fantastic a forecast of what may be as one might imagine. The reign of the biologist-psychologist is already upon us, and none of even its more extravagant pictures is very far around the corner. Modern science has already available many of the techniques, and the others are predictable. I recall an article in a well-known magazine on the next century in science, by Julian Huxley, the author's half-brother. It is not a mere coincidence that what the biologist predicts the writer of fiction makes into the plot of his satirical novel. For science can, if it is given the rule, reduce life to its greatest comfort and maximum efficiency. If our two gods are to be the efficiency engineer and the expert in eugenics and the ductless glands, here is a picture of the universe into which we can expect to be translated. And reference is obvious to experiments in standardization that are being talked about and even made

in various parts of the world, and efforts to promote happiness through technology.

Is the job worth the while? Is there something supremely precious that evaporates in the laboratory of the decanter and the shop of the mechanical contriver? Is this 'civilization wrapped in cellophane,' and made safe for everyone's taking, worth the sacrifice? The answer to this question is the theme of the philosophical satire. What is lost when comfort is valued above experience, stability above experiment, and happiness above art? When people are 'immune from life,' is life worth living? Is the expense of biological and psychological insurance against failure too great for humanity to pay? Can humanity pay too much even for perfect safety and cellophane?

Huxley answers these questions in the course of the novel in the experiences of an unsuccessfully decanted hero, 'who had too much alcohol in his blood-surrogate,' and of a savage who had been preserved in a reservation for the unblessed and who had never been exposed to the regimen of science. Here are two interesting people. The first is a young man who should be a perfect 'alpha,' qualified for the conditioning of others, and whose life of work for which he is geared, and the emotional outlets of sex, 'soma' and 'feelies,' should leave nothing in life to be desired. But there is gnawing at his imagination a need for an unexpressed something, a dissatisfaction with perfection and desire for desire. 'God manifests himself as an absence, for he isn't compatible with machinery.' Nor is art. 'You're making flivvers out of the absolute minimum of steel—your works of art are practically nothing but pure sensations.' It was this absence that troubled him, this something that could not be stilled by the tickle of sensation and safe sensuality. It was a world without Romance.

The savage was never more than a savage, but he had been born of the illegitimate union of a stray 'beta' and an 'alpha' official. These savages were people of the old regime, living not according to science but to nature, kept behind fences lest they contaminate the blessed, and yet not exterminated because their blind state could serve as a perpetual moral. He is discovered for what he is, a mongrel in breeding, an aristocrat in blood; and he is brought to the light, for his responses are unexpected and illuminating. He becomes the latest novelty. But in his native haunts he has discovered and learned to read Shakespeare—a highly objectionable and forbidden book. It is his reactions, unblessed and unconditioned, that are the theme of the novel. Poetry he has, rude and untrained, and love of the unattainable. He supplies the gloss and detailed commentary to the unexpressed dissatisfaction of the hero. He is the Nihilist, as great art and poetry is always the nihilist to complacency and comfort.

'I don't want comfort, I want God, I want poetry. I want real danger, I want freedom, I want sin.' 'He ate civilization and it killed him.' Is modern civilization more and more becoming a poison to the best in human nature? In sensitive souls all over Europe, as in Huxley, there is the active fear that science can displace or destroy poetry.

Poetry is one way out of inescapable situations. These are the causes of passion, passion that can express itself and find its discharge in the laughter of comedy or tears of tragedy. But once bring perfect comfort, perfect standardization and stability—and this can be done through science—and the very source of passion is dried up, the fear of failure gives place to the fatness of complacency, and life becomes a mere routine as automatic as the composite life of the beehive or ant hill, where all individual initiative has been lost. The *Brave New World* is not a fantastic Utopian *jeu d'esprit*. (pp. 173-81)

> Philo M. Buck, Jr., "Sight to the Blind: Aldous Huxley," in his Directions in Contemporary Literature, *Oxford University Press, Inc., 1942, pp. 169-91.*

Aldous Huxley   (essay date 1946)

[*In the following essay, which originally appeared as the foreword to the 1946 edition of* Brave New World, *Huxley discusses the relevance of his novel in the technologically advanced post-World War II era.*]

Chronic remorse, as all the moralists are agreed, is a most undesirable sentiment. If you have behaved badly, repent, make what amends you can and address yourself to the task of behaving better next time. On no account brood over your wrongdoing. Rolling in the muck is not the best way of getting clean.

Art also has its morality, and many of the rules of this morality are the same as, or at least analogous to the rules of ordinary ethics. Remorse, for example, is as undesirable in relation to our bad art as it is in relation to our bad behaviour. The badness should be hunted out, acknowledged and, if possible, avoided in the future. To pore over the literary shortcomings of twenty years ago, to attempt to patch a faulty work into the perfection it missed at its first execution, to spend one's middle age in trying to mend the artistic sins committed and bequeathed by that different person who was oneself in youth—all this is surely vain and futile. And that is why this new *Brave New World* is the same as the old one. Its defects as a work of art are considerable; but in order to correct them I should have to rewrite the book—and in the process of rewriting, as an older, other person, I should probably get rid not only of some of the faults of the story, but also of such merits as it originally possessed. And so, resisting the temptation to wallow in artistic remorse, I prefer to leave both well and ill alone and to think about something else.

In the meantime, however, it seems worth while at least to mention the most serious defect in the story, which is this. The Savage is offered only two alternatives, an insane life in Utopia, or the life of a primitive in an Indian village, a life more human in some respects, but in others hardly less queer and abnormal. At the time the book was written this idea, that human beings are given free will in order to choose between insanity on the one hand and lunacy on the other, was one that I found amusing and regarded as quite possibly true. For the sake, however, of dramatic effect, the Savage is often permitted to speak more rationally than his upbringing among the practitioners of a religion that is half fertility cult and half *Penitente* ferocity would actually warrant. Even his acquaintance with Shakespeare

would not in reality justify such utterances. And at the close, of course, he is made to retreat from sanity; his native *Penitente*-ism reasserts its authority and he ends in maniacal self-torture and despairing suicide. "And so they died miserably ever after"—much to the reassurance of the amused, Pyrrhonic aesthete who was the author of the fable.

Today I feel no wish to demonstrate that sanity is impossible. On the contrary, though I remain no less sadly certain than in the past that sanity is a rather rare phenomenon, I am convinced that it can be achieved and would like to see more of it. For having said so in several recent books and, above all, for having compiled an anthology of what the sane have said about sanity and the means whereby it can be achieved, I have been told by an eminent academic critic that I am a sad symptom of the failure of an intellectual class in time of crisis. The implication being, I suppose, that the professor and his colleagues are hilarious symptoms of success. The benefactors of humanity deserve due honour and commemoration. Let us build a Pantheon for professors. It should be located among the ruins of one of the gutted cities of Europe or Japan, and over the entrance to the ossuary I would inscribe, in letters six or seven feet high, the simple words: SACRED TO THE MEMORY OF THE WORLD'S EDUCATORS. SI MONUMENTUM REQUIRIS CIRCUMSPICE.

But to return to the future . . . If I were now to rewrite the book, I would offer the Savage a third alternative. Between the utopian and the primitive horns of his dilemma would lie the possibility of sanity—a possibility already actualized, to some extent, in a community of exiles and refugees from the Brave New World, living within the borders of the Reservation. In this community economics would be decentralist and Henry-Georgian, politics Kropotkinesque and co-operative. Science and technology would be used as though, like the Sabbath, they had been made for man, not (as at present and still more so in the Brave New World) as though man were to be adapted and enslaved to them. Religion would be the conscious and intelligent pursuit of man's Final End, the unitive knowledge of the immanent Tao or Logos, the transcendent Godhead or Brahman. And the prevailing philosophy of life would be a kind of Higher Utilitarianism, in which the Greatest Happiness principle would be secondary to the Final End principle—the first question to be asked and answered in every contingency of life being: "How will this thought or action contribute to, or interfere with, the achievement, by me and the greatest possible number of other individuals, of man's Final End?"

Brought up among the primitives, the Savage (in this hypothetical new version of the book) would not be transported to Utopia until he had had an opportunity of learning something at first hand about the nature of a society composed of freely cooperating individuals devoted to the pursuit of sanity. Thus altered, *Brave New World* would possess an artistic and (if it is permissible to use so large a word in connection with a work of fiction) a philosophical completeness, which in its present form it evidently lacks.

But *Brave New World* is a book about the future and,

whatever its artistic or philosophical qualities, a book about the future can interest us only if its prophecies look as though they might conceivably come true. From our present vantage point, fifteen years further down the inclined plane of modern history, how plausible do its prognostications seem? What has happened in the painful interval to confirm or invalidate the forecasts of 1931?

The theme of *Brave New World* is not the advancement of science as such; it is the advancement of science as it affects human individuals.

—*Aldous Huxley*

One vast and obvious failure of foresight is immediately apparent. **Brave New World** contains no reference to nuclear fission. That it does not is actually rather odd; for the possibilities of atomic energy had been a popular topic of conversation for years before the book was written. My old friend, Robert Nichols, had even written a successful play about the subject, and I recall that I myself had casually mentioned it in a novel published in the late twenties. So it seems, as I say, very odd that the rockets and helicopters of the seventh century of Our Ford should not have been powered by disintegrating nuclei. The oversight may not be excusable; but at least it can be easily explained. The theme of **Brave New World** is not the advancement of science as such; it is the advancement of science as it affects human individuals. The triumphs of physics, chemistry and engineering are tacitly taken for granted. The only scientific advances to be specifically described are those involving the application to human beings of the results of future research in biology, physiology and psychology. It is only by means of the sciences of life that the quality of life can be radically changed. The sciences of matter can be applied in such a way that they will destroy life or make the living of it impossibly complex and uncomfortable; but, unless used as instruments by the biologists and psychologists, they can do nothing to modify the natural forms and expressions of life itself. The release of atomic energy marks a great revolution in human history, but not (unless we blow ourselves to bits and so put an end to history) the final and most searching revolution.

This really revolutionary revolution is to be achieved, not in the external world, but in the souls and flesh of human beings. Living as he did in a revolutionary period, the Marquis de Sade very naturally made use of this theory of revolutions in order to rationalize his peculiar brand of insanity. Robespierre had achieved the most superficial kind of revolution, the political. Going a little deeper, Babeuf had attempted the economic revolution. Sade regarded himself as the apostle of the truly revolutionary revolution, beyond mere politics and economics—the revolution in individual men, women and children, whose bodies were henceforward to become the common sexual property of all and whose minds were to be purged of all the natural decencies, all the laboriously acquired inhibitions of traditional civilization. Between sadism and the really revolutionary revolution there is, of course, no necessary or inevitable connection. Sade was a lunatic and the more or less conscious goal of his revolution was universal chaos and destruction. The people who govern the Brave New World may not be sane (in what may be called the absolute sense of that world); but they are not madmen, and their aim is not anarchy but social stability. It is in order to achieve stability that they carry out, by scientific means, the ultimate, personal, really revolutionary revolution.

But meanwhile we are in the first phase of what is perhaps the penultimate revolution. Its next phase may be atomic warfare, in which case we do not have to bother with prophecies about the future. But it is conceivable that we may have enough sense, if not to stop fighting altogether, at least to behave as rationally as did our eighteenth-century ancestors. The unimaginable horrors of the Thirty Years War actually taught men a lesson, and for more than a hundred years the politicians and generals of Europe consciously resisted the temptation to use their military resources to the limits of destructiveness or (in the majority of conflicts) to go on fighting until the enemy was totally annihilated. They were aggressors, of course, greedy for profit and glory; but they were also conservatives, determined at all costs to keep their world intact, as a going concern. For the last thirty years there have been no conservatives; there have been only nationalistic radicals of the right and nationalistic radicals of the left. The last conservative statesman was the fifth Marquess of Lansdowne; and when he wrote a letter to the *Times,* suggesting that the First World War should be concluded with a compromise, as most of the wars of the eighteenth century had been, the editor of that once conservative journal refused to print it. The nationalistic radicals had their way, with the consequences that we all know—Bolshevism, Fascism, inflation, depression, Hitler, the Second World War, the ruin of Europe and all but universal famine.

Assuming, then, that we are capable of learning as much from Hiroshima as our forefathers learned from Magdeburg, we may look forward to a period, not indeed of peace, but of limited and only partially ruinous warfare. During that period it may be assumed that nuclear energy will be harnessed to industrial uses. The result, pretty obviously, will be a series of economic and social changes unprecedented in rapidity and completeness. All the existing patterns of human life will be disrupted and new patterns will have to be improvised to conform with the nonhuman fact of atomic power. Procrustes in modern dress, the nuclear scientist will prepare the bed on which mankind must lie; and if mankind doesn't fit—well, that will be just too bad for mankind. There will have to be some stretching and a bit of amputation—the same sort of stretchings and amputations as have been going on ever since applied science really got into its stride, only this time they will be a good deal more drastic than in the past. These far from painless operations will be directed by highly centralized totalitarian governments. Inevitably so; for the immediate future is likely to resemble the immediate past, and in the immediate past rapid technological changes, taking place in a mass-producing economy and among a population predominantly propertyless, have always tended to produce economic and social confusion. To deal with confusion, power has been centralized and government control increased. It is probable that all the world's governments will be more or less completely totalitarian even before the harnessing of atomic energy; that they will be totalitarian during and after the harnessing seems almost certain. Only a large-scale popular movement toward decentralization and self-help can arrest the present tendency toward statism. At present there is no sign that such a movement will take place.

There is, of course, no reason why the new totalitarianisms should resemble the old. Government by clubs and firing squads, by artificial famine, mass imprisonment and mass deportation, is not merely inhumane (nobody cares much about that nowadays); it is demonstrably inefficient—and in an age of advanced technology, inefficiency is the sin against the Holy Ghost. A really efficient totalitarian state would be one in which the all-powerful executive of political bosses and their army of managers control a population of slaves who do not have to be coerced, because they love their servitude. To make them love it is the task assigned, in present-day totalitarian states, to ministries of propaganda, newspaper editors and schoolteachers. But their methods are still crude and unscientific. The old Jesuits' boast that, if they were given the schooling of the child, they could answer for the man's religious opinions, was a product of wishful thinking. And the modern pedagogue is probably rather less efficient at conditioning his pupils' reflexes than were the reverend fathers who educated Voltaire. The greatest triumphs of propaganda have been accomplished, not by doing something, but by refraining from doing. Great is truth, but still greater, from a practical point of view, is silence about truth. By simply not mentioning certain subjects, by lowering what Mr. Churchill calls an "iron curtain" between the masses and such facts or arguments as the local political bosses regard as undesirable, totalitarian propagandists have influenced opinion much more effectively than they could have done by the most eloquent denunciations, the most compelling of logical rebuttals. But silence is not enough. If persecution, liquidation and the other symptoms of social friction are to be avoided, the positive sides of propaganda must be made as effective as the negative. The most important Manhattan Projects of the future will be vast government-sponsored enquiries into what the politicians and the participating scientists will call "the problem of happiness"—in other words, the problem of making people love their servitude. Without economic security, the love of servitude cannot possibly come into existence; for the sake of brevity, I assume that the all-powerful executive and its managers will succeed in solving the problem of permanent security. But security tends very quickly to be taken for granted. Its achievement is merely a superficial, external revolution. The love of servitude cannot be established except as the result of a deep, personal revolution in human minds and bodies. To bring about that revolution we require, among others, the following discoveries and inventions. First, a greatly improved technique of suggestion—through infant conditioning and, later, with the aid of drugs, such as scopolamine. Second, a fully developed

science of human differences, enabling government managers to assign any given individual to his or her proper place in the social and economic hierarchy. (Round pegs in square holes tend to have dangerous thoughts about the social system and to infect others with their discontents.) Third (since reality, however utopian, is something from which people feel the need of taking pretty frequent holidays), a substitute for alcohol and the other narcotics, something at once less harmful and more pleasure-giving than gin or heroin. And fourth (but this would be a long-term project, which it would take generations of totalitarian control to bring to a successful conclusion) a foolproof system of eugenics, designed to standardize the human product and so to facilitate the task of the managers. In *Brave New World* this standardization of the human product has been pushed to fantastic, though not perhaps impossible, extremes. Technically and ideologically we are still a long way from bottled babies and Bokanovsky groups of semi-morons. But by A.F. 600, who knows what may not be happening? Meanwhile the other characteristic features of that happier and more stable world—the equivalents of soma and hypnopaedia and the scientific caste system—are probably not more than three or four generations away. Nor does the sexual promiscuity of *Brave New World* seem so very distant. There are already certain American cities in which the number of divorces is equal to the number of marriages. In a few years, no doubt, marriage licenses will be sold like dog licenses, good for a period of twelve months, with no law against changing dogs or keeping more than one animal at a time. As political and economic freedom diminishes, sexual freedom tends compensatingly to increase. And the dictator (unless he needs cannon fodder and families with which to colonize empty or conquered territories) will do well to encourage that freedom. In conjunction with the freedom to daydream under the influence of dope and movies and the radio, it will help to reconcile his subjects to the servitude which is their fate.

All things considered it looks as though Utopia were far closer to us than anyone, only fifteen years ago, could have imagined. Then, I projected it six hundred years into the future. Today it seems quite possible that the horror may be upon us within a single century. That is, if we refrain from blowing ourselves to smithereens in the interval. Indeed, unless we choose to decentralize and to use applied science, not as the end to which human beings are to be made the means, but as the means to producing a race of free individuals, we have only two alternatives to choose from: either a number of national, militarized totalitarianisms, having as their root the terror of the atomic bomb and as their consequence the destruction of civilization (or, if the warfare is limited, the perpetuation of militarism); or else one supra-national totalitarianism, called into existence by the social chaos resulting from rapid technological progress in general and the atomic revolution in particular, and developing, under the need for efficiency and stability, into the welfare-tyranny of Utopia. You pays your money and you takes your choice. (pp. vii-xx)

Aldous Huxley, in a foreword to his Brave

New World, *Harper & Row, Publishers, 1946, pp. vii-xx.*

Theodor W. Adorno   (essay date 1951)

[*A German-born philosopher, literary and cultural critic, musicologist, and sociologist, Adorno greatly influenced the intellectual foundations of revolutionary thought in postwar Europe. He is closely associated with the Frankfurt Institute for Social Research, a center for Marxist studies, and aided development of the Institute's "Critical Theory." Critical Theory—an approach to the analysis and criticism of philosophies and ideologies—is intended to allow movement toward an objective and creative view of society untainted by false theories and inherited assumptions. In* Minima Moralia *(1951) and* Dialektik der Aufklärung *(1947;* Dialectic of Enlightenment, *1972), Adorno stated that the arrogant denial of our oneness with nature is the original sin of our society. Below, in an essay originally published in 1942 and revised in 1951, he claims that in* Brave New World *Huxley implicitly advocates conceptions of society and human nature that are dogmatic and stagnant.*]

Those who came to the new world [from Europe] in the nineteenth century were lured by the unlimited possibilities it offered. They emigrated to make their fortunes or at least find enough to make ends meet, something they could not achieve in the overpopulated European countries. The interests of self-preservation were stronger than those of preserving the self, and the rapid economic growth of the United States took place under the aegis of the same principle that drove the emigrant across the ocean. The newcomer strove for successful adjustment; critical attitudes on his part might have compromised the prospects and the claim to legitimacy of his own efforts. Neither their backgrounds nor their position in the social process enabled the new arrivals to avoid being overpowered by the turbulent struggle for the maintenance of life. Any utopian hopes they might have attached to their resettlement took on a different character in the new context of the saga of struggling upwards, the horizon of a still uncharted existence, the prospect of advancing from dishwasher to millionaire. The skepticism of a visitor like De Tocqueville, who a century ago already perceived the element of unfreedom in unrestrained equality, remained the exception; opposition to what in the jargon of German cultural conservatism was called 'Americanism' was to be found in Americans like Poe, Emerson, and Thoreau rather than in the new arrivals. A hundred years later it was no longer individual intellectuals who emigrated but the European intelligentsia as a whole, by no means only the Jews. They sought not to live better but to survive; opportunities were no longer unlimited, and thus the necessity for adjustment which prevailed in the sphere of economic competition extended implacably to them. In place of the wilderness which the pioneer intended to open up spiritually as well as materially and through which he was to accomplish his spiritual regeneration, there has arisen a civilization which absorbs all of life in its system, without allowing the unregimented mind even those loopholes which European laxness left open into the epoch of the great business concerns. It is made unmistakably clear to the intellectual from abroad that he will have to eradicate himself as an autonomous being if he hopes to achieve anything or be accepted as an employee of the super-trust into which life has condensed. The refractory individual who does not capitulate and completely toe the line is abandoned to the shocks which the world of things, concentrated into gigantic blocks, administers to whatever does not make itself into a thing. Impotent in the machinery of the universally developed commodity relation, which has become the supreme standard, the intellectual reacts to the shock with panic.

Huxley's *Brave New World* is a manifestation of this panic, or rather, its rationalization. The novel, a fantasy of the future with a rudimentary plot, endeavours to comprehend the shocks through the principle of the disenchanted world, to heighten this principle to absurdity, and to derive the idea of human dignity from the comprehension of inhumanity. The point of departure seems to be the perception of the universal similarity of everything mass-produced, things as well as human beings. Schopenhauer's metaphor of nature as a manufactured article is taken literally. Teeming herds of twins are prepared in test tubes: a nightmare of endless doubles like that which the most recent phase of capitalism has spawned into everyday life, from regulated smiles, the grace instilled by charm schools, to the standardized consciousness of millions which revolves in the grooves cut by the communications industry. The here and now of spontaneous experience, long corroded, is stripped of its power; men are no longer merely purchasers of the concerns' mass-produced consumption goods but rather appear themselves to be the de-individualized products of the corporations' absolute power. To the panicked eye, observations that resist assimilation petrify into allegories of catastrophe; it sees through the illusion of the harmlessness of everyday life. For it, the model's commercial smile becomes what it is, the contorted grin of the victim. The more than thirty years since the book's appearance have provided more than sufficient verification: small horrors such as the aptitude tests for elevator boys which detect the least intelligent, and visions of terror such as the rational utilization of corpses. If, in accordance with a thesis of Freud's *Group Psychology and Ego Analysis,* panic is the condition in which powerful collective identifications disintegrate and the released instinctual energy is transformed into raw anxiety, then the person seized by panic is capable of innervating the dark basis of the collective identification—the false consciousness of individuals who, without transparent solidarity and blindly subjected to images of power, believe themselves one with the whole whose ubiquity stifles them.

Huxley is free from the foolhardy sobriety which emerges from even the worst situations with a temporizing 'It's not all that bad'. He makes no concessions to the childish belief that the alleged excesses of technical civilization will be ironed out automatically through irresistible progress, and he scorns the consolation upon which exiles so readily seize: the notion that the frightening aspects of American civilization are ephemeral relics of its primitiveness or potent safeguards of its youth. We are not permitted to doubt that American civilization has not only not lagged behind that of Europe but has indeed forged ahead of it, while the Old World diligently emulates the New. Just as the world-state of *Brave New World* knows only artificially maintained differences between the golf courses and experimental stations of Mombasa, London, and the North Pole, Americanism, the butt of parody, has taken over the world. And that world supposedly resembles the utopia whose realization, as the epigraph from Berdyaev indicates, is foreseeable in the light of technology. But, by extension, it becomes hell; Huxley projects observations of the present state of civilization along the lines of its own teleology to the point where its monstrous nature becomes immediately evident. The emphasis is placed not so much on objective technological and institutional elements as on what becomes of human beings when they no longer know need. The economic and political sphere as such recedes in importance. It is stipulated only that there is a thoroughly rationalized class system on a planetary scale and totally planned state capitalism, that total domination goes along with total collectivization, and that a money economy and the profit motive persist.

'Community, Identity, and Stability' replaces the motto of the French Revolution. Community defines a collectivity in which each individual is unconditionally subordinated to the functioning of the whole (the question of the point of this whole is no longer permitted or even possible in the New World). Identity means the elimination of individual differences, standardization even down to biological constitution; stability, the end of all social dynamics. The artfully balanced situation is an extrapolation from certain indications of a reduction in the economic 'play of forces' in late capitalism—the perversion of the millennium. The panacea that guarantees social stasis is 'conditioning'. The expression is a product of biology and behaviouristic psychology, in which it signifies the evocation of particular reflexes or modes of behaviour through arbitrary transformations in the environment, through control of the conditions; and it has made its way into colloquial American English as the designation for any kind of scientific control over the conditions of life, as in 'air-conditioning'. In *Brave New World* conditioning means the complete preformation of human beings through social intervention, from artificial breeding and technological direction of the conscious and unconscious mind in the earliest stages of life to 'death conditioning', a training that purges children of the horror of death by parading the dying before their eyes while they are being fed candy, which they then forever after associate with death. The ultimate effect of conditioning, which is in fact adjustment come into its own, is a degree of introjection and integration of social pressure and coercion far beyond that of the Protestant ethic; men resign themselves to loving what they have to do, without even being aware that they are resigned. Thus, their happiness is firmly established subjectively and order is maintained. Conceptions of a merely external influence of society upon individuals, through agencies like psychology or the family, are recognized to be obsolete. What today has already happened to the family is inflicted upon it once again in *Brave New World,* from above. As children of society in the literal sense, men no longer exist in dialectical opposition to society but rather are identical with it in their substance. Compliant exponents of the collective totality in which all antitheses have been absorbed, they are 'socially conditioned' in a non-metaphorical sense, not merely adjusted secondarily to the dominant system through 'development'.

The system of class relationships is made eternal and biological: directors of breeding assign each person to a caste designated by a Greek letter while he is still an embryo. Through an ingenious method of cell division, the common people are recruited from identical twins, whose physical and intellectual growth is stunted through an artificial addition of alcohol to the blood. That is, the reproduction of stupidity, which previously took place unconsciously under the dictates of material necessity, must be taken in hand by triumphant mass civilization now that scarcity could be eliminated. The rational fixation of irrational class relations indicates their superfluity. Today class lines have already lost their 'natural' character, an illusion created during the undirected history of mankind, so that classes can be perpetuated only through arbitrary selection and co-option, only through administrative differentiations in the distribution of the social product. By depriving lower-caste embryos and infants of oxygen in the Hatching and Conditioning Centres of *Brave New World,* the directors create an artificial slum atmosphere. In the midst of unlimited possibility they organize degradation and regression. Such regression, however, devised and automatically induced by the totalitarian system, is truly total. Huxley, who knows his way around, points out the signs of mutilation in the upper class as well: 'Even alphas have been conditioned.' Even the minds of those who credit themselves with being individuals are caught up in standardization by virtue of their identification with the 'in-group'. They automatically produce the judgments to which they have been conditioned, rather like the member of the present upper middle class who babbles that the real problem is not material circumstances but a religious regeneration or who insists that he cannot understand modern art. Non-comprehension becomes a virtue. Two lovers from the upper caste fly over the Channel in stormy weather, and the man wishes to delay the flight so as to escape from the crowds and be alone with his beloved for a longer time, closer to her and more himself. In response to her reluctance, he asks whether she understands his wish. ' "I don't understand anything," she said with decision, determined to preserve her incomprehension intact.' Huxley's observation does more than just point up the *rancune* that the statement of the most modest truth provokes in persons who can no longer allow such statements lest their equilibrium be disturbed. It diagnoses a powerful new taboo. The more the existing society, through its overwhelming power and hermetic structure, becomes its own ideological justification in the minds of the disillusioned, the more it brands as sinners all those whose thoughts blaspheme against the notion that what is, is right—just because it exists. They live in airplanes but heed the command, tacit like all genuine taboos, 'Thou shalt not fly'. The gods of the earth punish those who raise themselves above the earth. Avowedly anti-mythological, the pact with the existing order restores mythic power. Huxley demonstrates this is the speech of his characters. The idiocy of mandatory small talk, conversation as chatter, is discretely pursued to the extreme. The phenomenon has long since ceased to be a mere consequence of conventions intended to prevent conversation from becoming narrow shop talk or unabashed presumption. Rather, the degeneration of talk is due to objective tendencies. The virtual transformation of the world into commodities, the predetermination by the machinery of society of everything that is thought or done, renders speaking illusory; under the curse of perpetual sameness it disintegrates into a series of analytic judgments. The ladies of *Brave New World*—and in this case extrapolation is hardly required—converse only as consumers. In principle, their conversation concerns nothing but what is in any case to be found in the catalogues of the ubiquitous industries, information about available commodities. Objectively superfluous, it is the empty shell of dialogue, the intention of which was once to find out what was hitherto unknown. Stripped of this idea, dialogue is ripe for extinction. People completely collectivized and incessantly communicating might as well abandon all communication at once and acknowledge themselves to be the mute monads they have been surreptitiously since the beginnings of bourgeois society. They are swallowed up in archaic childlike dependency.

They are cut off both from the mind, which Huxley rather flatly equates with the products of traditional culture, exemplified by Shakespeare, and from nature as landscape, an image of creation unviolated by society. The opposition of mind and nature was the theme of bourgeois philosophy at its peak. In *Brave New World* they unite against a civilization which lays hands on everything and tolerates nothing which is not made in its own image. The union of mind and nature, conceived by idealist speculation as the supreme reconciliation, now becomes the absolute opposition to absolute reification. Mind, the spontaneous and autonomous synthesis achieved by consciousness, is possible only to the extent to which it is confronted by a sphere outside its grasp, something not categorically predetermined—'nature'. And nature is possible only to the extent to which mind knows itself as the opposite of reification, which it transcends instead of enthroning it as nature. Both are vanishing: Huxley is well acquainted with the latest-model average citizen who contemplates a bay as a tourist attraction while seated in his car listening to radio commercials. Not unrelated is hatred of things past. The mind itself seems a thing of the past, a ridiculous addition to the glorified facts, to the given, whatever it may be, and what is no longer around becomes bric-à-brac and rubbish. 'History is bunk,' an expression attributed to Ford, relegates to the junkpile everything not in line with the most recent methods of industrial production, including, ultimately, all continuity of life. Such reduction cripples men. Their inability to perceive or think anything unlike themselves, the inescapable self-sufficiency of their lives, the law of pure subjective functionalism—all result in pure desubjectivization. Purged of all myths, the scientifically manufactured subject-objects of the anti-*Weltgeist* are infantile. In line with mass culture, the half-involuntary, half-organized regressions of today finally turn into compulsory ordinances governing leisure time, the 'proper standard of infantile decorum', Hell's laughter at the Christian dictum, 'If you do not become as little children. . . .' The blame rests with the substitution of means for all ends. The cult of the instrument, cut off from

every objective aim (in *Brave New World,* the implicit religion of today—the auto—becomes literal with Ford for Lord and the sign of the Model T for that of the cross), and the fetishistic love of gadgetry, both unmistakable lunatic traits ingrained in precisely those people who pride themselves on being practical and realistic, are elevated to the norm of life. But that substitution is also in force in areas of the *Brave New World* where freedom seems to have won out. Huxley has recognized the contradiction that in a society where sexual taboos have lost their intrinsic force and have either retreated before the permissibility of the prohibited or come to be enforced by external compulsion, pleasure itself degenerates to the misery of 'fun' and to an occasion for the narcissistic satisfaction of having 'had' this or that person. Through the institutionalization of promiscuity, sex becomes a matter of indifference, and even escape from society is relocated within its borders. Physiological release is desirable, as part of hygiene; accompanying feelings are dispensed with as a waste of energy without social utility. On no account is one to be moved. The original bourgeois *ataraxia* now extends to all reactions. In infecting eros it turns directly against what was once the highest good, subjective eudaemonia, for the sake of which purgation of the passions was originally demanded. In attacking ecstacy it strikes at all human relations, at every attempt to go beyond a monadological existence. Huxley recognizes the complementary relationship of collectivization and atomization.

His portrayal of organized orgiastics, however, has an undertone which casts doubt upon his satirical thesis. In its proclamation of the bourgeois nature of what claims to be unbourgeois, the thesis itself becomes ensnared in bourgeois habits. Huxley waxes indignant at the sobriety of his characters but is inwardly an enemy of intoxication, and not only that from narcotics, which he earlier condemned, thus endorsing the prevailing attitude. Like that of many emancipated Englishmen, his consciousness is preformed by the very Puritanism he abjures. He fails to distinguish between the liberation of sexuality and its debasement. In his earlier novels libertinism already appears, as it were, as a localized thrill without an aura—not unlike the way men in so-called 'masculine' cultures habitually speak of women and love with a gesture in which pride at having won the sovereignty that enables them to discuss such matters is inevitably mixed with contempt. In Huxley everything occurs on a more sublimated level than in the Lawrence of the four-letter words, but everything is also more thoroughly repressed. His anger at false happiness sacrifices the idea of true happiness as well. Long before he acknowledged Buddhist sympathies, his irony displayed, especially in the self-denunciation of the intellectual, something of the sectarianism of the raging penitent, a quality to which his writing is usually immune. The flight from the world leads to the nudist colony, which destroys sexuality by overexposure. Despite the pains Huxley takes to depict the pre-mass-civilization world of the Savage (who is brought to the Brave New World as a relic of humanity), as being distorted, repellent, and insane in its own way, reactionary elements find their way into his portrayal. Freud is included among the anathematized figures of modernity, and at one point he is equated with Ford. He is made a mere efficiency expert of the inner life.

With all too genial scorn he is credited with having been the first to discover 'the appalling dangers of family life'. But this is in fact what he did, and historical justice is on his side. The critique of the family as the agent of oppression, a theme familiar to the English opposition since Samuel Butler, emerged just at the time when the family had lost its economic basis and, with it, its last legitimate right to determine human development, becoming a neutralized monstrosity of the sort Huxley so incisively exposes in the sphere of official religion. Huxley ascribes to the world of the future the encouragement of infantile sexuality, in complete misunderstanding, incidentally, of Freud, who all too orthodoxly adhered to instinctual renunciation as a pedagogical aim. But Huxley himself sides with those who are less concerned with the dehumanization of the industrial age than with the decline of its morals. Whether happiness is dependent upon the existence of prohibitions to be broken is an endless dialectical question, but the novel's mentality distorts the question into an affirmative answer, into an excuse for the perpetuation of obsolete taboos—as if the happiness produced by the transgression of taboos could ever legitimate the taboo, which exists not for the sake of happiness but for its frustration. It is true that the regularly occurring communal orgies of the novel and the prescribed short-term change of partners are logical consequences of the jaded official sexual routine that turns pleasure to fun and denies it by granting it. But precisely in the impossibility of looking pleasure in the eye, of making use of reflection in abandoning one's whole self to pleasure, the ancient prohibition for which Huxley prematurely mourns continues in force. Were its power to be broken, were pleasure to be freed of the institutional reins which bind it even in the 'orgy-porgy', Brave New World and its fatal rigidity would dissolve. Its highest moral principle, supposedly, is that everyone belongs to everyone, an absolute interchangeability that extinguishes man as an individual being, liquidates as mythology his claim to exist for his own sake, and defines him as existing merely for the sake of others and thus, in Huxley's mind, as worthless. In the foreword he wrote after the war for the American edition, Huxley claimed, as the ancestor of this principle, de Sade's statement that the rights of man include the absolute sexual disposition of all over all. In this, Huxley sees the foolishness of consequent reasoning consummated. But he fails to see that the heretical maximum is incompatible with his world-state of the future. All dictators have proscribed libertinage, and Himmler's much cited SS-studs were its piously patriotic opposite. Domination may be defined as the disposition of one over others but not as the complete disposition of all over all, which cannot be reconciled with a totalitarian order. This is even more true of work relations than of sexual anarchy. A man who existed only for the sake of others, an absolute ξωον Πολιτιχον, would, to be sure, have lost his individual self, but he would also have escaped the cycle of self-preservation which maintains the Brave New World as well as the old one. Pure fungibility would destroy the core of domination and promise freedom. The weakness of Huxley's entire conception is that it makes all its concepts relentlessly dynamic but nevertheless arms them against the tendency to turn into their own opposites.

> In *Brave New World* conditioning means the complete preformation of human beings through social intervention, from artificial breeding and technological direction of the conscious and unconscious mind in the earliest stages of life to "death conditioning," a training that purges children of the horror of death. . . .
>
> —*Theodor W. Adorno*

The *scène à faire* of the novel is the erotic collision of the two 'worlds': the attempt of the heroine, Lenina, a well-groomed and polished American career woman, to seduce the Savage, who loves her, in a way consonant with the mores of the conscientiously promiscuous. Her opponent belongs to the type of shy, aesthetic youth, tied to his mother and inhibited, who prefers to enjoy his feeling through contemplation rather than expression and who finds satisfaction in the lyrical transfiguration of the beloved. This type, incidentally, is bred at Oxford and Cambridge no less than are Epsilons in test tubes, and it belongs to the sentimental standby of the modern English novel. The conflict arises from the fact that John feels the pretty girl's matter-of-fact abandonment to be a debasement of his sublime passion for her and runs away. The effectiveness of the scene works against its thesis. Lenina's artificial charm and cellophane shamelessness produce by no means the unerotic effect Huxley intended, but rather a highly seductive one, to which even the infuriated cultural savage succumbs at the end of the novel. Were Lenina the imago of Brave New World, it would lose its horror. Each of her gestures, it is true, is socially preformed, part of a conventional ritual. But because she is at one with convention down to her very core, the tension between the conventional and the natural dissolves, and with it the violence in which the injustice of convention consists; psychologically, poor conventionality is always the mark of unsuccessful identification. The concept of convention does not survive its opposite. Through total social mediation, from the outside, as it were, a new immediacy, a new humanity, would arise. American civilization shows no lack of tendencies in this direction. But Huxley construes humanity and reification as rigid opposites, in accordance with the tradition of the novel, which has as its object the conflict of human beings with rigidified conditions. Huxley cannot understand the humane promise of civilization because he forgets that humanity includes reification as well as its opposite, not merely as the condition from which liberation is possible but also positively, as the form in which, however brittle and inadequate it may be, subjective impulses are realized, but only by being objectified. All the categories examined by the novel, family, parents, the individual and his property, are already products of reification. Huxley curses the future with it, without realizing that the past whose blessing he invokes is of the same nature. Thus he unwittingly becomes the spokesman of that nostalgia whose affinity to mass culture his physiognomic eye so acutely perceives in the test-tube song: 'Bottle of mine, it's you I've always wanted! Bottle of mine, why was I ever decanted? . . . There ain't no Bottle in all the world Like that dear little Bottle of mine.'

The Savage's outburst against his beloved, then, is not so much the protest of pure human nature against the cold impudence of fashion, as was perhaps intended; rather, poetic justice turns it into the aggression of the neurotic who, as the Freud whom Huxley treats rather shabbily could easily have told him, is motivated in his frantic purity by repressed homosexuality. He shouts abuse at the girl like the hypocrite who trembles with rage at things he has to forbid himself. By putting him in the wrong, Huxley distances himself from social criticism. Its actual advocate in the novel is Bernard Marx, an Alpha-Plus who rebels against his own conditioning, a skeptically compassionate caricature of a Jew. Huxley is well aware that Jews are persecuted because they are not completely assimilated and that precisely for this reason their consciousness occasionally reaches beyond the social system. He does not question the authenticity of Bernard's critical insight. But the insight itself is attributed to a sort of organic inferiority, the inevitable inferiority complex. At the same time, following the time-honoured model, Huxley charges the radical Jewish intellectual with vulgar snobbism and, ultimately, with reprehensible moral cowardice. Ever since Ibsen's invention of Gregers Werle and Stockmann, actually since Hegel's philosophy of history, bourgeois cultural politics, claiming to survey and speak for the whole, has sought to unmask anyone who seeks to change things as both the genuine child and the perverse product of the whole which he opposes, and has insisted that the truth is always on the side of the whole, be it against him or present in him. As novelist, Huxley proclaims his solidarity with this tradition; as prophet of civilization, he detests the totality. It is true that Gregers Werle destroys those he seeks to save, and no one is free from the vanity of Bernard Marx who, in raising himself above the general stupidity, thereby imagines himself untainted by it. But the view which evaluates phenomena externally, in a detached, free, superior way, deeming itself above the limitations of negation and the arbitration of the dialectic, is for this very reason neither one of truth nor one of justice. A just reflection should not delight in the inadequacy of things which are better in order to compromise them before things which are worse, but should draw from inadequacy additional strength for indignation. The forces of negativity are underestimated in order to render them impotent. But it befits this position that what is set up as positive and absolute against the dialectic is no less powerless. When, in his crucial conversation with the World Controller Mond, the Savage declares, 'What you need is something with tears for a change,' his deliberately insolent exaltation of suffering is not merely a characteristic of the obdurate individualist. It evokes Christian metaphysics, which promises future salvation solely by virtue of suffering. But, despite all appearances to the contrary, the novel is informed by an enlightened consciousness in which Christian metaphysics no longer dares to assert itself. Hence the cult of suffering becomes an absurd end in itself. It is a mannerism of an aestheticism whose ties to the pow-

ers of darkness cannot be unknown to Huxley; Nietzsche's 'Live dangerously', which the Savage proclaims to the resigned, hedonistic World Controller, was a perfect slogan for the totalitarian Mussolini, himself a World Controller of a similar sort.

In a discussion of a biological paper which the World Controller has suppressed, the all too positive core of the novel becomes clearly visible. It is 'the sort of idea that might easily de-condition the more unsettled minds among the higher castes—make them lose their faith in happiness as the Sovereign God and take to believing instead, that the goal was somewhere beyond, somewhere outside the present human sphere; that the purpose of life was not the maintenance of well-being, but some intensification and refinement of consciousness, some enlargement of knowledge'. However pallid and diluted or cleverly prudent the formulation of the ideal may be, it still does not escape contradiction. 'Intensification and refinement of consciousness' or 'enlargement of knowledge' flatly hypostatize the mind in opposition to praxis and the fulfilment of material needs. For mind by its very nature presupposes the life-process of society and especially the division of labour, and all mental and spiritual contents are intentionally related to concrete existence for their 'fulfilment'. Consequently, setting the mind in an unconditional and atemporal opposition to material needs amounts to perpetuating ideologically this form of the division of labour and of society. Nothing intellectual was ever conceived, not even the most escapist dream, whose objective content did not include the transformation of material reality. No emotion, no part of the inner life ever existed that did not ultimately intend something external or degenerate into untruth, mere appearance, without this intention, however sublimated. Even the selfless passion of Romeo and Juliet, which Huxley considers something like a 'value', does not exist autarchically, for its own sake, but becomes spiritual and more than mere histrionics of the soul only in pointing beyond the mind towards physical union. Huxley unwittingly reveals this in portraying their longing, the whole meaning of which is union. 'It was the nightingale and not the lark' is inseparable from the symbolism of sex. To glorify the aubade for the sake of its transcendent quality without hearing in the transcendence itself its inability to rest, its desire to be gratified, would be as meaningless as the physiologically delimited sexuality of **Brave New World,** which destroys any magic which cannot be conserved as an end in itself. The disgrace of the present is not the preponderance of so-called material culture over the spiritual—in this complaint Huxley would find unwelcome allies, the Arch-Community-Songsters of all neutralized denominations and world views. What must be attacked is the socially dictated separation of consciousness from the social realization its essence requires. Precisely the *chorismos* of the spiritual and the material which Huxley's *philosophia perennis* establishes, the substitution of an indeterminable, abstract 'goal somewhere beyond' for 'faith in happiness', strengthens the reified situation Huxley cannot tolerate: the neutralization of a culture cut off from the material process of production. 'If a distinction between material and ideal needs is drawn,' as Max Horkheimer once put it, there is no doubt that the fulfilment of material needs must be given priority, for this fulfilment also involves . . . social change. It includes, as it were, the just society, which provides all human beings with the best possible living conditions. This is identical with the final elimination of the evil of domination. To emphasize the isolated, ideal demand, however, leads to real nonsense. The right to nostalgia, to transcendental knowledge, to a dangerous life cannot be validated. The struggle against mass culture can consist only in pointing out its connection with the persistence of social injustice. It is ridiculous to reproach chewing gum for diminishing the propensity for metaphysics, but it could probably be shown that Wrigley's profits and his Chicago palace have their roots in the social function of reconciling people to bad conditions and thus diverting them from criticism. It is not that chewing gum undermines metaphysics but that it *is* metaphysics—this is what must be made clear. We criticize mass culture not because it gives men too much or makes their life too secure—that we may leave to Lutheran theology—but rather because it contributes to a condition in which men get too little and what they get is bad, a condition in which whole strata inside and out live in frightful poverty, in which men come to terms with injustice, in which the world is kept in a condition where one must expect on the one hand gigantic catastrophes and on the other clever elites conspiring to bring about a dubious peace.

As a counterweight to the sphere of the satisfaction of needs, Huxley posits another, suspiciously similar to the one the bourgeoisie generally designates as that of the 'higher things'. He proceeds from an invariant, as it were biological concept of need. But in its concrete form every human need is historically mediated. The static quality which needs appear to have assumed today, their fixation upon the reproduction of the eternally unchanging, merely reflects the character of production, which becomes stationary when existing property relations persist despite the elimination of the market and competition. When this static situation comes to an end needs will look completely different. If production is redirected towards the unconditional and unlimited satisfaction of needs, including precisely those produced by the hitherto prevailing system, needs themselves will be decisively altered. The indistinguishability of true and false needs is an essential part of the present phase. In it the reproduction of life and its suppression form a unity which is intelligible as the law of the whole but not in its individual manifestations. One day it will be readily apparent that men do not need the trash provided them by the culture industry or the miserable high-quality goods proffered by the more substantial industries. The thought, for instance, that in addition to food and lodging the cinema is necessary for the reproduction of labour power is 'true' only in a world which prepares men for the reproduction of their labour power and constrains their needs in harmony with the interests of supply and social control. The idea that an emancipated society would crave the poor histrionics of Lametta or the poor soups of Devory is absurd. The better the soups, the more pleasant the renunciation of Lametta. Once scarcity

has disappeared, the relationship of need to satisfaction will change. Today the compulsion to produce for needs mediated and petrified by the market is one of the chief means of keeping everyone on the job. Nothing may be thought, written, done, or made that transcends a condition which maintains its power largely through the needs of its victims. It is inconceivable that the compulsion to satisfy needs would remain a fetter in a changed society. The present form of society has in large measure denied satisfaction to the needs inherent in it and has thus been able to keep production in its control by pointing to these very needs. The system is as practical as it is irrational. An order which does away with the irrationality in which commodity production is entangled but also satisfies needs will equally do away with the practical spirit, which is reflected even in the non-utilitarianism of bourgeois *l'art pour l'art*. It would abolish not merely the traditional antagonism between production and consumption but also its most recent unification in state capitalism, and it would converge with the idea that, in the words of Karl Kraus, 'God created man not as consumer or producer but as man'. For something to be useless would no longer be shameful. Adjustment would lose its meaning. For the first time, productivity would have an effect on need in a genuine and not a distorted sense. It would not allay unsatisfied needs with useless things; rather, satisfaction would engender the ability to relate to the world without subordination to the principle of universal utility.

> **Despite many ingenuities of execution, *Brave New World* fails because of a basic weakness—an empty schematism. Because the transformation of men is not subject to calculation and evades the anticipating imagination, it is replaced by a caricature of the men of today, in the ancient and much abused manner of satire.**
>
> **—*Theodor W. Adorno***

In his critique of false needs Huxley preserves the idea of the objectivity of happiness. The mechanical repetition of the phrase, 'Everybody's happy now,' becomes the most extreme accusation. When men are products of an order based on denial and deception, and that order implants imaginary needs in them, then the happiness which is defined by the satisfaction of such needs is truly bad. It is a mere appendage of the social machinery. In a totally integrated world which does not tolerate sorrow, the command from Romans (xii.15), 'Weep with the weeping,' is more valid than ever, but 'Be joyous with the joyful' has become a gory mockery—the job the order permits the ordered feeds on the perpetuation of misery. Hence the mere rejection of false happiness has a subversive effect. Lenina's reaction when the Savage finds an idiotic film obnoxious, 'Why did he go out of his way to spoil things?' is a typical manifestation of a dense network of deception.'One shouldn't spoil it for the others' has always been one of the stock maxims of those who spoil it for the others. But at the same time the description of Lenina's irritation provides the basis for a criticism of Huxley's own attitude. He believes that by demonstrating the worthlessness of subjective happiness according to the criteria of traditional culture he has shown that happiness as such is worthless. Its place is to be taken by an ontology distilled from traditional religion and philosophy, according to which happiness and the objective good are irreconcilable. A society which wants nothing but happiness, according to Huxley, moves inexorably into insanity, into mechanized bestiality. But Lenina's overzealous defensiveness betrays insecurity, the suspicion that her kind of happiness is distorted by contradictions, that it is not happiness even by its own definition. No pharisaical recollection of Shakespeare is necessary to become aware of the fatuousness of the feelies and of the 'objective despair' of the audience which participates in it. That the essence of the film lies in merely duplicating and reinforcing what already exists, that it is glaringly superfluous and senseless even in a leisure restricted to infantility, that its duplicative realism is incompatible with its claim to be an aesthetic image—all this can be seen in the film itself, without recourse to dogmatically cited *vérités éternelles*. The holes in the vicious circles which Huxley draws with so much care are due not to inadequacies in his imaginative construction but to the conception of a happiness subjectively consummate but objectively absurd. If his critique of subjective happiness is valid, then his idea of a hypostatized objective happiness removed from the claims of humanity must be ideological. The source of untruth is the separation of subjective and objective, which has been reified to a rigid alternative. Mustapha Mond, the *raisonneur* and devil's advocate of the book, who embodies the most articulate self-consciousness of *Brave New World,* formulates the alternative. To the Savage's protest that man is degraded by total civilization he replies, 'Degrade him from what position? As a happy, hard-working, goods-consuming citizen he's perfect. Of course, if you choose some other standard than ours, then perhaps you might say he was degraded. But you've got to stick to one set of postulates.' In this image of the two sets of postulates, exhibited like finished products between which one must choose, relativism is apparent. The question of truth dissolves into an 'if-then' relation. Similarly, isolated by Huxley, the values of death and interiority fall prey to pragmatization. The Savage reports that he once stood on a cliff with outstretched arms in burning heat in order to feel what it was like to be crucified. Asked for an explanation, he gives the curious answer: 'Because I felt I ought to. If Jesus could stand it, and then, if one has done something wrong . . . Besides, I was unhappy, that was another reason.' If the Savage can find no other justification for his religious adventure, the choice of suffering, than the fact that he has suffered, he can hardly contradict his interviewer, who argues that it is more reasonable to take *Soma,* the euphoria-producing cure-all drug, to dissolve one's depressions. Irrationally hypostatized, the world of ideas is demoted to the level of mere existence. In this form, it continually demands justification according to merely empirical norms and is prescribed for the sake of precisely that happiness which it is supposed to negate.

The crude alternative of objective meaning and subjective happiness, conceived as mutually exclusive, is the philosophical basis for the reactionary character of the novel. The choice is between the barbarism of happiness and culture as the objectively higher condition that entails unhappiness. 'The progressive domination of nature and society,' Herbert Marcuse argues, 'does away with all transcendence, physical as well as psychical. Culture, the all-embracing title for one side of the opposition, subsists upon lack of fulfilment, longing, faith, pain, hope, in short, on that which does not exist but leaves its mark in reality. That means, however, that culture exists on the basis of unhappiness.' The kernel of the controversy is the hard and fast disjunction that one cannot be had without the other, technology without death conditioning, progress without manipulated infantile regression. However, the honesty of the thought expressed in the disjunction is to be distinguished from the moral constraint of ideology. Today, only conformism could acquiesce in considering objective insanity to be a mere accident of historical development, for retrogression is essential to the consistent development of domination. Theory is not free to choose good-naturedly that which suits it in the course of history and to omit the rest. Attempts to come up with a *Weltanschauung* which takes a 'positive attitude' to technology but advocates that it ought to be given meaning provide shallow comfort and serve merely to reinforce an affirmative work morale which is itself highly questionable. Nevertheless, the pressure that ***Brave New World*** exerts on everyone and everything is conceptually incompatible with the deathlike stasis that makes it a nightmare. It is no accident that all the major figures in the novel, even Lenina, show signs of subjective derangement. The alternative is false. The perfectly self-contained state which Huxley depicts with such grim satisfaction transcends itself not by virtue of an ineffective melange of desirable and reprehensible elements brought in from the outside, but by virtue of its objective nature. Huxley is aware that historical tendencies realize themselves behind men's backs. For him the essential tendency is the self-estrangement and perfected externalization of the subject, which makes itself into a mere means in the absence of any end whatsoever. But he makes a fetish of the fetishism of commodities. In his eyes the character of commodities becomes ontic and self-subsistent, and he capitulates to this apparition instead of seeing through it as a mere form of consciousness, false consciousness which would dissolve with the elimination of it economic basis. Huxley does not admit that the phantasmagoric inhumanity of ***Brave New World*** is actually a relation between human beings, a relation of social labour which is not aware of its own nature—that the totally reified man is one who has been blinded to himself. Instead, he pursues in succession various unanalysed surface phenomena, such as 'the conflict between men and machine'. Huxley indicts technology for something which does not, as he believes (and in this he follows the tradition of romantic philistinism), lie in its essential nature, which is the abolition of labour. It is rather a result of the involvement of technology in the social relations of production; this insight, moreover, is implicit throughout the novel. Even the incompatibility of art and mass production today does not originate in technology as such but rather in the need of these irrationally persisting social relations to maintain the claim to individuation (in Benjamin's words, an 'aura') which is only honoured in the breach. Even the process for which Huxley censures technology, the displacement of ends by means to the point where the latter becomes completely independent of the former, does not necessarily eliminate ends. Precisely in art, where consciousness makes use of unconscious channels, blind play with means can posit and unfold ends. The relation of means and ends, of humanity and technology, cannot be regulated through ontological priorities. Huxley's alternative amounts to the proposition that mankind should not extricate itself from the calamity. Humanity is placed before the choice between regression to a mythology questionable even to Huxley and progress towards total unfreedom of consciousness. No room is left for a concept of mankind that would resist absorption into the collective coercion of the system and reduction to the status of contingent individuals. The very construction which simultaneously denounces the totalitarian world-state and glorifies retrospectively the individualism that brought it about becomes itself totalitarian. In that it leaves no escape open, this conception itself implies the thing that horrifies Huxley, the liquidation of everything that is not assimilated. The practical consequence of the bourgeois 'Nothing to be done', which resounds as the novel's echo, is precisely the perfidious 'You must adjust' of the totalitarian Brave New World. The monolithic trend and the linear concept of progress, as handled in the novel, derive from the restricted form in which the productive forces developed in 'prehistory'. The inevitable character of the negative utopia arises from projecting the limitations imposed by the relations of production (the enthronement of the productive apparatus for the sake of profit) as properties of the human and technical productive forces *per se*. In prophesying the entropy of history, Huxley succumbs to an illusion which is necessarily propagated by the society against which he so zealously protests.

Huxley criticizes the positivistic spirit. But because his criticism confines itself to shocks, while remaining immersed in the immediacy of experience and merely registering social illusions as facts, Huxley himself becomes a positivist. Despite his critical tone, he is in basic agreement with descriptively oriented cultural criticism, which, in lamenting the inexorable decline of culture, provides a pretext for the strengthening of domination. In the name of culture, civilization marches into barbarism. Instead of antagonisms, Huxley envisages something like an intrinsically non-self-contradictory total subject of technological reason, and correspondingly, a simplistic total development. Such conceptions belong to the currently fashionable ideas of 'universal history' and 'style of life' which are part of the cultural façade. Although he gives an incisive physiognomy of total unification, he fails to decipher its symptoms as expressions of an antagonistic essence, the pressure of domination, in which the tendency to totalization is inherent. Huxley expresses scorn for the phrase, 'Everybody's happy nowadays'. But the essence of his conception of history, which is better revealed by its form than by the events which make up its content, is profound-

ly harmonious. His notion of uninterrupted progress is distinguished from the liberalist idea only in emphasis, not through objective insight. Like a Benthamite liberal, Huxley foresees a development to the greatest happiness of the greatest number, but it discomfits him. He condemns the Brave New World with the same common sense whose prevalence there he mocks. Hence, throughout the novel there emerge unanalysed elements of that worn-out *Weltanschauung* which Huxley deplores. The worthlessness of the ephemeral and the catastrophic nature of history are contrasted to that which never changes—the *philosophia perennis,* the eternal sunshine of the heavenly realm of ideas. Accordingly, exteriority and interiority move into a primitive antithesis: men are the mere objects of all evil, from artificial insemination to galloping senility, while the category of the individual stands forth with unquestioned dignity. Unreflective individualism asserts itself as though the horror which transfixes the novel were not itself the monstrous offspring of individualist society. The spontaneity of the individual human being is eliminated from the historical process while the concept of the individual is detached from history and incorporated into the *philosophia perennis.* Individuation, which is essentially social, reverts to the immutability of nature. Its implication in the network of guilt was discerned by bourgeois philosophy at its zenith, but this insight has been replaced by the empirical levelling of the indvidual through psychologism. In the wake of a tradition whose predominance provokes resistance more readily than it invites respect, the individual is immeasurably exalted as an idea while each individual person is convicted of moral bankruptcy by the epigones of disillusioned romanticism. The socially valid recognition of the nullity of the individual turns into an accusation levelled against the overburdened private individual. Huxley's book, like his entire work, blames the hypostatized individual for his fungibility and his existence as a 'character mask' of society rather than as a real self. These facts are attributed to the individual's inauthenticity, hypocrisy, and narrow egoism, in short, to all those traits which are the stock-in-trade of a subtle, descriptive ego psychology. For Huxley, in the authentic bourgeois spirit, the individual is both everything—because once upon a time he was the basis of a system of property rights—and nothing, because, as a mere property owner, he is absolutely replaceable. This is the price which the ideology of individualism must pay for its own untruth. The novel's *fabula docet* is more nihilistic than is acceptable to the humanity which it proclaims.

Here, however, Huxley does not do justice to the very facts on which he puts his positivistic emphasis. **Brave New World** shares with all fully worked-out utopias the character of vanity. Things have developed differently and will continue to do so. It is not the accuracy of imagination which fails. Rather the very attempt to see into the distant future in order to puzzle out the concrete form of the non-existent is beset with the impotence of presumption. The antithetical component of the dialectic cannot be conjured away syllogistically, for example by means of the general concept of enlightenment. Such an approach eliminates the very material which provides the moving force of the dialectic—those elements that are external to the subject and are not already 'spiritual' and transparent. No matter how well equipped technologically and materially, no matter how correct from a scientific point of view the fully drawn utopia may be, the very undertaking is a regression to a philosophy of identity, to idealism. Hence the ironic 'accuracy' for which Huxley's extrapolations strive does his utopia no service. For however surely the unselfconscious concept of total enlightenment may move towards its opposite, irrationality, it is nevertheless impossible to deduce from the concept itself whether this will occur and if so, whether it will stop there. The looming political catastrophe can hardly fail to modify the escape route of technical civilization. *Ape and Essence* is a somewhat hasty attempt to correct a mistake which derives not from insufficient knowledge of atomic physics but from a linear conception of history, a mistake which thus cannot be corrected by the elaboration of additional material. Where the plausibility of *Brave New World*'s prognoses was oversimplified, those of Huxley's second book dealing with the future bear the stigma of improbability (as, for instance, the devil cult). These characteristics can scarcely be defended in the midst of a novel which is realistic in style by allusions to philosophical allegory. But the ideological bias of the conception revenges itself in this inevitability of error. There is an unwitting resemblance to the member of the upper middle class who solemnly insists that it is not in his own interest but in that of all mankind that he advocates the continuance of a profit economy. Men are not yet ready for socialism, the argument runs; if they no longer had to work, they wouldn't know what to do with their time. Such platitudes are not only compromised by the usage to which they are put; they are also completely devoid of truth, since they both reify 'men' in general and hypostatize the observer as a disinterested judge. But this coldness is deeply embedded in Huxley's conceptual framework. Full of fictitious concern for the calamity that a realized utopia could inflict on mankind, he refuses to take note of the real and far more urgent calamity that prevents the utopia from being realized. It is idle to bemoan what will become of men when hunger and distress have disappeared from the world. For although Huxley can find nothing more to criticize in this civilization than the boredom of a never-never land which is in principle unattainable anyway, it is by virtue of the logic of this civilization that the world is subject to hunger and distress. All his indignation at the calamitous state of things notwithstanding, the basis of Huxley's attitude is a conception of a history which takes its time. Time is made responsible for that which men must accomplish. The relation to time is parasitical. The novel shifts guilt for the present to the generations of the future. This reflects the ominous 'It shall not be otherwise' which is the end-product of the basic Protestant amalgamation of introspection and repression. Because mankind, tainted with original sin, is not capable of anything better in this world, the bettering of the world is made a sin. But the novel does not draw its life from the blood of the unborn. Despite many ingenuities of execution, it fails because of a basic weakness—an empty schematism. Because the transformation of men is not subject to calculation and evades the anticipating imagination, it is replaced by a caricature of the men of today, in the ancient and much abused manner of satire. The fiction of the future bows before the omnipotence of

the present; that which does not yet exist is made comic through its resemblance to that which already is, like the gods in Offenbach operettas. The image of the most remote is replaced by a vision of that which is closest to hand, seen through inverted binoculars. The formal trick of reporting future events as though they had already happened endows their content with a repulsive complicity. The grotesqueness that the present assumes when confronted with its own projection into the future provokes the same laughs as naturalistic representations with enlarged heads. The pathetic notion of the 'eternally human' resigns itself to the less humane one of the normal man of yesterday, today, and tomorrow. It is not for its contemplative aspect as such, which it shares with all philosophy and representation, that the novel is to be criticized, but for its failure to contemplate a praxis which could explode the infamous continuum. Man's choice is not between individualism and a totalitarian world-state. If the great historical perspective is to be anything more than the *Fata Morgana* of the eye which surveys only to control, it must open on to the question of whether society will come to determine itself or bring about terrestrial catastrophe. (pp. 97-117)

Theodor W. Adorno, "Aldous Huxley and Utopia," in his Prisms, *1967. Reprint by The MIT Press, 1981, pp. 95-118.*

William M. Jones (essay date Summer 1961)

[*In the essay below, Jones studies the tragic aspects of* Brave New World, *tracing Huxley's allusions to Shakespeare's* Othello.]

The first half of Aldous Huxley's *Brave New World* is devoted almost entirely to the presentation of a society in which the only major freedom is a sexual one, a society built entirely on "Community, Identity, Stability." Communal security has replaced all individual freedom. Ford-Freud has replaced God, and all the crosses have become T's. As Huxley is presenting this society to his reader, however, he is also preparing his plot structure. Eventually Lenina Crowne and Bernard Marx take a vacation to a New Mexico reservation together. There another society is presented, a primitive tribal one similar to that of the Brave New World in its emphasis on physical sensation and community. Their religious ceremony, in which a member of the tribe is beaten, is, in its basic urge, similar to the Solidarity Service of the Brave New World. And both societies demand total conformity.

Within this world is one person who does not belong to either. John Savage, as the son of an exile from the Brave New World, is not accepted by the primitive community. But, as the only one who has read Shakespeare, he is not suited to the Brave New World either. The Savage's knowledge of Shakespeare, which differentiates him from the other characters, makes him useful to Huxley as the plot-mover in the second half of the book.

When Lenina and Bernard return from their visit to the New Mexico reservation, they bring with them John Savage and his mother. The second half of the book then utilizes the device of introducing a stranger into a new society. This stranger, however, is not, as most outsiders are, an exact equivalent of our own society; he is part savage, part Brave New World, and part Shakespeare. As a Shakespearean he plays his part as deceived lover, and as Shakespearean he judges the society. From his first glimpse of Lenina, when he blushes and quotes Miranda, "How beauteous mankind is!" to his last condemnation of her, "Fry, lechery, fry!" he is guided by Shakespearean attitudes and quotations.

Underneath the attitudes and quotations is also a Shakespearean construction. Huxley prepares the reader for this construction by giving a detailed account of the "feelie" that Lenina and John see on their first date: in a helicopter accident a big Negro receives a concussion that destroys his conditioning. He develops an exclusive passion for a blonde, she resists, he kidnaps her, keeps her alone in a helicopter, she is rescued by three young men, the Negro is sent to an Adult Reconditioning Center, and the film ends happily with the blonde becoming the mistress of all her rescuers.

Later, when Lenina attempts to kiss John, he recalls this "feelie" with horror. And almost at the conclusion of the book, he questions the World Controller about the movie: " 'Why don't you let them see *Othello* instead?' " The obvious similarities between the movie and *Othello* suggest this play rather than some other. As a matter of fact, through his whole conversation with the Controller, the play the Savage refers to most often is *Othello*. " 'Goats and monkeys!' " the Savage says, quoting Othello to show his contempt for the feelie-viewers. And the World Controller says that " ' . . . our world is not the same as Othello's world. You can't make flivvers without steel— and you can't make tragedies without social instability.' "

But the irony of the situation is that Huxley has made the "feelie" plot show us the Brave New World's version of *Othello,* and he has built his own plot on the outline of *Othello* as well. We are given in the second half of the book two variations on a theme by Shakespeare. Huxley's whole development denies the statement made by the Controller: " ' . . . if it were really like *Othello* nobody could understand it, however new it might be. And if it were new, it couldn't possibly be like *Othello.*' "

Shakespeare's *Othello* presents an outsider who marries a beautiful girl and carries her off against the wishes of her father. A villain, Iago, poisons the mind of the outsider against his wife, suggesting that all Venetian women are promiscuous and unfaithful. The outsider, in a fit of rage, murders his wife. The Brave New World's Othello is an outsider, the Negro, who carries off a girl against the wishes of society. Society, however, is able to recondition the outsider so that all is well. Huxley's Othello character is an outsider who loves a girl, but whose mind is poisoned against her, not by an individual villain, but by the entire society which has produced her. From our own point of view, the entire society that produced Lenina is the Iago. That society's stability has made true affection impossible, and in so doing has contributed to the tragedy which its Controller felt was impossible.

Huxley's structure, however, makes Shakespeare himself, whose whole ethic differed from that of the Brave New World, serve as Iago. Shakespeare kept John Savage from a satisfactory relationship with the girl he loved, just as Iago kept Othello from Desdemona. Othello was duped by lying Iago, who corrupted his mind against the purity of Desdemona. In a society such as Shakespeare's, where purity and virtuous living were respected by all, the disturbing influence would be an Iago. In the Brave New World, where the Desdemona character Lenina is praised for her promiscuity and where the characteristics of Shakespeare's Desdemona would be frowned upon, the Iago character becomes a disturbing influence of another sort. It is Shakespeare who causes the Savage to fail in his adjustment to the new world. In both *Othello* and **Brave New World,** the Othello character has the same basic attitudes. He is a just and honest man duped. In an honest society, the villain, therefore, would be evil; in a perverted one the villain would be, in our eyes, good.

John Savage, the Othello character, is the pivotal one. He parallels Othello, whereas all else in the novel is the reverse of the play. The Desdemona of the Brave New World is unchaste, as her perverted society demands, and the Iago of the Brave New World is not a villain, but the man an upright society regards as one of its leading representatives: Shakespeare. In a perverted society, the good of one society becomes, naturally, the evil of the other.

Only by recognizing, either consciously or unconsciously, this Othello pattern, can the reader accept the conclusion of the novel. After two chapters devoted to a discussion of art, science, and religion, two main characters are sent to an island for the hopelessly unconditionable, and John Savage is left to solitude within the new society. Why Huxley did not end the book happily by permitting the Savage to accompany the two can be answered only in terms of *Othello.* Huxley has been building to a tragedy with a new Othello, one incapable of becoming one-eyed in a one-eyed society, one who refuses to play insane to seem sane in an insane society. The Savage's tragedy, like Othello's, is that of a man deceived by himself as well as by a villain. At the moment when Lenina comes forward in true affection, "two tears rolled down her cheeks," the Savage's own lack of control causes him to rush upon her and kill her.

Huxley has prepared us for the depth of tragedy here by once more setting up an Othello parallel. Earlier the Savage has protested against the new world's happiness: " 'But the tears are necessary. Don't you remember what Othello said? "If after every tempest came such calms, may the winds blow till they have wakened death." ' " Lenina's tears show her return to sanity at the moment the Savage, like Othello, gives way to momentary madness. Without the *Othello* parallels the conclusion might seem vaguely pessimistic, but with the echo of *Othello* behind it this conclusion takes on the positive power of deep tragedy: the Othello character destroying at the moment of potential fulfillment. After this temporary loss of control comes the terrible enlightenment that precedes the suicide. Both Othello and the Savage have been forced to murder and suicide by a villain, one a soulless Iago, one an honest Shakespeare.

At the end of the story Huxley's reader feels the same

sense of tragic loss that the reader of *Othello* feels. Here were men of promise duped by disturbing influences. In the enlightened society of the new world Shakespeare brought John Savage to destruction by revealing truth to him; in *Othello* Iago brought the destruction by revealing lies. Huxley has wisely chosen the Shakespearean play that would best fit his Brave New World and has built upon it while his characters are protesting against it. (pp. 275-78)

> William M. Jones, "The Iago of 'Brave New World'," *in* The Western Humanities Review, *Vol. XV, No. 3, Summer, 1961, pp. 275-78.*

Ira Grushow   (essay date October 1962)

[*Grushow is an American critic and educator. In the following essay, he studies allusions to Shakespeare's* The Tempest *in* Brave New World.]

In ***Brave New World*** Aldous Huxley enforces in us disgust toward the future society largely through constant reference to our own society. We find the World State intolerable largely because we see in it perversions of our most cherished ideals and institutions. Their proverbs ("The more stitches the less riches") are refutations of our own ("A stitch in time saves nine") and their Solidarity Service is a travesty of Christian ritual.

Parody and allusion extend to our literary heritage as well. In a brilliant *tour de force* at the beginning of Chapter Five, Huxley translates Gray's *Elegy in a Country Churchyard* into the terms of Fordian society. The sound of curfew becomes the announcement over the loud speakers of the closing for the day of the Stoke Poges Club House, the lowing herd is the cattle of the Internal and External Secretion Trust, and the beetle's droning flight is the incessant buzzing of helicopters. The meditation on death in the *Elegy* is frighteningly paralleled by the dialogue between Henry Foster and Lenina Crowne on the physicochemical equality of all men and on the contribution to society after death of even the lowest of Epsilons in the form of phosphorus pentoxide, recoverable from their cremated bodies. Our shock at realizing the violation of one of the most famous and beloved poems of our language assures us once more that we want no part of the Brave New World.

Allusions to Shakespeare are the most frequent in the book. The Savage speaks, we realize, very largely in quotations from Shakespeare, one of the principal sources of his education. The contrast between his poetically inspired ideas and Lenina's hypnopaedically instilled maxims serves to point up linguistically the great gulf which separates their two worlds. John is not simply a well-read savage, however: Shakespeare's morality has invaded his consciousness. It is not by accident that the book of plays opens to Hamlet's denunciation of his mother. John identifies himself with the young prince, and he sees in Linda's liaison with Popé a re-enactment of the incestuous union of Gertrude and Claudius. Later in ***Brave New World*** in his frenzied attacks upon lechery John identifies himself with Othello and Lear.

These references are for the most part casual; they are more ornamental than functional; they display the author's ingenuity, but they cannot be said to constitute a pattern of sustained allusion. One play of Shakespeare's, however, *The Tempest,* bears a more intimate relationship to ***Brave New World*** than the others. Huxley has taken his title, of course, from Miranda's exclamation upon meeting the party of the King of Naples, the first men other than her father Prospero and her betrothed Ferdinand whom she has ever seen:

> O wonder!
> How many goodly creatures are there here!
> How beauteous mankind is! O brave new world,
> That has such people in't!

John Savage repeats these words several times in the course of the novel, first when he learns that Bernard Marx intends to take him back with him to civilization. As in Shakespeare (Alonso, Sebastian, and Antonio are, after all, plotters, usurpers, and would-be assassins) the words "O brave new world!" are ironic. John, no less than Miranda, is in for a few surprises when he gets to civilization. His education has not prepared him for the world outside the reservation, just as Miranda's education, one feels strangely apprehensive, may not be wholly adequate for a princess of Naples. Huxley's book may be said to begin where Shakespeare's play leaves off. Just as W. H. Auden, in *The Sea and the Mirror*, has explored the thoughts and feelings of the characters of *The Tempest* on their boat trip from the enchanted island back to Naples, so Huxley treats of the reaction of John Savage, a type of Miranda, to the world of "civilized" men and women.

The irony of John's exclamation, "O brave new world," pervades the whole relationship of Huxley's novel to Shakespeare's play, and even after the reader has accepted the fact of reference to *The Tempest,* he may not readily see the identifications that Huxley makes. It is not immediately apparent, for example, that Bernard Marx represents Caliban, the deformed monster and unwilling slave of Prospero, described by his master as "a devil, a born devil, on whose nature / Nurture can never stick; on whom my pains, / Humanely taken, are all lost, quite lost." But the resemblance is unmistakable. Like Caliban's, Marx's questionable birth, or decanting, is against him, his physical deformity breeds discontent and rebellion, and his education or conditioning has failed to produce its desired results. "You taught me language," Caliban upbraids his master, "and my profit on't / Is, I know how to curse; the red plague rid you, / For learning me your language!" So might Bernard Marx rail against the hypnopaedic instruction he has been subjected to. Again, like Caliban, Marx takes part in an unsuccessful insurrection, and, terrified of his master's wrath, he abjectly begs for mercy when the plot is discovered.

If Marx is Caliban, then who is the Savage? We have already established that one of his functions in the novel is to play the role that Miranda might have in a sequel to *The Tempest.* He is the innocent suddenly brought into an evil world. But as Lenina's virtuous lover he identifies himself with Ferdinand as well. Like Ferdinand's, John's sorrow for the loss of a parent is gradually displaced by a love which is not filial. Like Ferdinand, John believes in taking a bride, not for the asking, but by winning her through the accomplishment of some arduous task. He quotes Ferdinand to the effect that "some kinds of baseness / Are nobly undergone." And again like Ferdinand, John is committed to strict chastity before marriage. At one point the Savage quotes Prospero's injunction to Ferdinand:

> If thou dost break her virgin knot before
> All sanctimonious ceremonies may
> With full and holy rite be minister'd
> No sweet aspersion shall the heavens let fall
> To make this contract grow. . . .

John also quotes Ferdinand's assurance that

> The most opportune place, the strong'st suggestion
> Our worser genius can, shall never melt
> Mine honour into lust. . . .

It is, of course, one of the bitterest morsels of Huxley's irony that John can only speak for himself. If he represents Ferdinand, then Lenina must be Miranda. The measure of the difference between Shakespeare's fresh, innocent, intelligent virgin and Huxley's jaded, experienced, automated Alpha is the full measure of the difference between Shakespeare's vision of an ideal world and Huxley's. The confused exchange of dialogue between John and Lenina in the scene where she tries to seduce him once more enforces linguistically the incompatibility of their two worlds.

If Lenina represents an unreluctant Miranda, then her father is Prospero. But a properly decanted female Alpha of A. F. 632 has no parent of either sex. As the law regards certain persons not progenitors as acting *in loco parentis,* however, so may we consider the Controller, Mustapha Mond, as a father-surrogate to Lenina and, indeed, to all under his care. Through his planning and coordination their generation has been brought about, and through his direction and supervision their conditioning has been effected. Moreover, like Prospero in the play, the Controller is the guiding figure in Huxley's novel: he knows what is going on at all times and he determines the fate of all those under his dominion. His wrath is fearful: just as Caliban cringes before Prospero, so does Marx before Mustapha Mond. But here again there is a gross distortion of character. Mond is a Prospero who has elected to stay in Milan, a Prospero who for the sake of security and worldly power has renounced his scientific studies. Given a choice (as in a sense Shakespeare's Prospero was) of getting on in the world or of continuing his quest for truth, Mond does not choose as Prospero does. And as in Shakespeare so in Huxley an island, remote from all commerce with the rest of the world, is the only escape open to the nonconforming thinker.

Some of the lesser themes of *The Tempest* also find their way into **Brave New World**. The society of A. F. 632 is not merely one of the future—it has idealistic pretensions, it is a utopia. It bears a number of resemblances to the ideal commonwealth described in *The Tempest*. In Act II Scene I Gonzalo, to beguile the sorrows of his king, diverts the company, by telling the others what he would do, had he "the plantation of this isle":

> *Gonz.* I' the commonwealth I would by contraries
> Execute all things; for no kind of traffic
> Would I admit; no name of magistrate;
> Letters should not be known; riches, poverty,
> And use of service, none; contract, succession,
> Bourn, bound of land, tilth, vineyard, none;
> No use of metal, corn, or wine, or oil;
> No occupation; all men idle, all;
> And women too, but innocent and pure;
> No sovereignty,—
>
> *Seb.*   Yet he would be king on't.
>
> *Ant.* The latter end of his commonwealth forgets the beginning.
>
> *Gonz.* All things in common nature should produce
> Without sweat or endeavour: treason, felony,
> Sword, pike, knife, gun, or need of any engine,
> Would I not have; but nature should bring forth,
> Of its own kind, all foison, all abundance,
> To feed my innocent people.
>
> *Seb.* No marrying 'mong his subjects?
>
> *Ant.* None, man; all idle; whores and knaves.

The World State realizes many of the provisions of Gonzalo's fanciful account, especially in its freedom from the economic and political trammels of common life. It is true that the abolition of labor is not a feature of the World State, although the technology is so far advanced that it is almost a possibility. However, as Mustapha Mond explains, the masses require a certain amount of work or else they would find their increased leisure unendurable. The World State is also not without sovereignty, but since the subjects have been predestined and conditioned for their roles in the state, physical restraint is unnecessary. The final exchange between Sebastian and Antonio is particularly revealing, for while in Shakespeare it is set forth as a reductio ad absurdum to shatter Gonzalo's idle dream, in Huxley sexual promiscuity becomes one of the basic assumptions of Fordian civilization.

Caliban's plot, already mentioned, finds its parallel, too, in **Brave New World.** As in *The Tempest* there are three conspirators who attempt to overthrow the established order. In the play it is the wine saved from the shipwreck which gives Caliban, Stephano, and Trinculo the false courage to rebel. In the novel it is soma which obliterates thought and action; administered to Bernard, Helmholtz, and John it soon dispels all their antisocial inclinations.

It should by now be apparent that in **Brave New World** Huxley has hardly written a *version* of The Tempest for a future or even a modern audience. For one thing, the basic identifications are constantly shifting. At times John Savage is Ferdinand and at others he is Miranda, for the novel is in part both an ironic repetition and an ironic continuation of Shakespeare's play. What is more important than demanding exact correspondences between the characters and incidents of play and novel is the recognition that *The Tempest* stands behind *Brave New World* for contrast. In effect Huxley rings constant variations upon the characters and themes of *The Tempest*.

To some this may appear as nothing more than a demonstration of Huxley's virtuosity, the charade of a litterateur, and it must be admitted that one may read *Brave New World* intelligently without being overwhelmed by its pattern of allusions to *The Tempest*. Yet the power of Shakespeare's play is such that it informs with additional meaning any literary work that comes near it. What distinguishes *The Tempest* (and indeed the other romances) from Shakespeare's earlier comedies is the fact that it is openended. At the conclusion of the play evil is overcome and good seems to win the day. But in *The Tempest* there is the uneasy apprehension that, although evil is subdued, it has not been vanquished, and the certain realization that, although good is temporarily in the ascendancy, it has purchased this victory at a tremendous cost.

This is the problem posed by *The Tempest*. Prospero clearly triumphs—on the island. But when he returns to his dukedom, can he ever fully trust Antonio? Or can Alonso sit securely on his throne in Naples while his brother Sebastian is around? Virtue has no difficulty in surviving in isolation. On the island Prospero can thwart the murderer and the rebel. On the island. But when he leaves the island he leaves his power and magic behind.

This, it seems to me, is also the problem Huxley poses in *Brave New World,* and one which we may overlook by simply accepting John as a noble Savage. Certainly he is the most admirable character in the book, the one with whom we can most closely identify. He suffers humiliations, but not defeat on the reservation. The great challenge comes when he enters civilization. Stronger in his convictions than most of us, he is nevertheless vanquished in the World State. Is his code of morality any less obsolete (never mind how admirable it is) in our own world than it is in the Brave New World? This becomes the central question of the novel: Is this life of the spirit, of poetry, of pure science and of pure knowledge, of chastity, of human relations, of the sanctification of carnal pleasures—is this life, to which we are all so ostensibly devoted, viable in the common, everyday world? (pp. 42-5)

Ira Grushow, " 'Brave New World' and 'The Tempest'," in College English, *Vol. 24, No. 1, October, 1962, pp. 42-5.*

Stephen Greenblatt   (essay date 1965)

[Greenblatt is an American educator and critic. In the excerpt below, he considers Huxley's pessimism as evidenced in Brave New World.*]*

Although all of his fiction has strong ironic elements, Al-

dous Huxley did not write satire exclusively, and [after *Antic Hay*] his next truly satirical novel is not, I believe, *Those Barren Leaves* (1925) or the long, semi-autobiographical *Point Counter Point* (1928), but *Brave New World* (1932), published almost ten years after *Antic Hay.* Huxley has stated that a utopian novel by H. G. Wells was the motivation for *Brave New World*; but it is obvious that the dangers of scientific materialism, blind faith in progress, and hedonism had long been troubling him, and his concern finally found full expression in this fine novel. In *Brave New World* Huxley has managed to sustain a structural simplicity and dynamism he sorely lacked in earlier works. He has also divested himself of the aura of the Jazz Age that has rather dated the novels of the 1920s, while retaining all of his standard devices of irony and satire—the contrapuntal themes, the dizzy piling up of arguments and incidents, the witty caricatures. More important, working in a definite framework—the utopian novel—he is able to integrate fully his great talent for fantasy which he exhibited in **"The History of Crome Manor"** and his brilliant and bitter social criticism.

Point Counter Point is prefaced with lines by Greville which express the basic problem of all of Huxley's characters:

> O, wearisome conditions of humanity!
> Born under one law, to another bound,
> Vainly begot and yet forbidden vanity:
> Created sick, commanded to be sound.
> What meaneth Nature by these diverse laws—
> Passion and reason, self-division's cause?

In *Brave New World* this self-division is allegorized and forced to its ultimate conclusions. The realms of reason and passion are totally apart in Huxley's utopia, passion having been vanquished and exiled to a few remote, forbidding corners of the world. It is important to note that passion, for Huxley, is not necessarily or even probably gratification and pleasure, physical or otherwise. Rather, it is a sort of primal, *natural* emotion, which man experiences when he achieves profound union with nature. It is also important to see that *Brave New World,* like Orwell's *1984,* is primarily concerned not with what will happen in the future but what is happening to mankind now. A futuristic detail like the hatching of babies from bottles, for example, is less an interesting scientific speculation than an ironic comment on the dissociation of sexuality and childbirth and on the ultimate artificiality of the inhabitants of our brave new world. (pp. 95-6)

Brave New World is a remarkable novel and, in many respects, the culmination of Huxley's art.

—Stephen Greenblatt

The basic goal of this [Brave New World] is the happiness of all, even if this happiness is purchased at the cost of imagination, discovery, free will, poetry, and pure science. The Trinity of the world state is "Community, Identity, Stability," and to achieve these ends, life is totally planned, *ab ovo*. Citizens of this "last word in organized good times and of secular revolutions," [as termed in Sisirukmar Ghose's *Aldous Huxley*,] are hatched from bottles and predetermined as members of a strictly defined caste—alpha, beta, gamma, delta, or epsilon. Women undergo an "Operation . . . voluntarily for the good of Society, not to mention the fact that it carries a bonus amounting to six months' salary," and the remarkable "Bokanovsky's Process" successfully produces "scores of standard men and women from the same ovary and with gametes of the same male." By means of mass suggestion during sleep and other devious psychological techniques, the children are completely reconciled to their own caste and are given a strong aversion for beauty, art, and solitude. In their place are endless rounds of promiscuity and meaningless games, as well as "liquid air, television, vibrovacuum massage, radio, boiling caffeine solution, hot contraceptives, and eight different kinds of scent . . . in every bedroom." The creatures of this world are doomed to be happy. No other kind of life is possible or imaginable. And if any vexations arise—like the mention of the obscene word "mother" or the arousal of a passion—there are always the pregnancy substitutes, the V.P.S. ("Violent Passion Surrogate—the complete physiological equivalent of fear and rage. All the tonic effects of murdering Desdemona and being murdered by Othello without any of the inconveniences"), and of course, that most delightful of all wonder drugs, soma ("All the advantages of Christianity and alcohol; none of their defects."). Such is the state of the world in the year 623 After-Ford ("Our Ford—or Our Freud, as, for some inscrutable reason, he chose to call himself whenever he spoke of psychological matters" is the deity of the Rational State). Man, in using his reason to create the ultimate life of pleasure, has ceased to be man.

Into this realm of unceasing and sterile happiness comes the Savage, the natural-born son of Linda, an ex-beta-minus who was abandoned on an Indian Reservation by the man who was "having" her for the week end, and discovered by Bernard Marx, one of the rare deviants from the Fordian norm (rumored cause—"alcohol in his blood surrogate"). The Savage has many unheard-of qualities and strange habits—he quotes Shakespeare, actually *loves* his mother, is a romantic, and believes in God. Living on the reservation, he is also disease-ridden, unhappy, filthy, and masochistic. Brought to London by Bernard, the Indian is a sensation among the fun-loving and curious citizens, but unfortunately the Savage's reaction to the Brave New World is not as favorable. He refuses to take soma, is not impressed by the titillating entertainments, and retches violently at the sight of the great numbers of mindless and identical creatures. Disgusted and desperate, the Savage flees to a lonely lighthouse and seeks solitude and self-punishment, but he is hounded unmercifully—yet without malice—by curiosity seekers and "feelie" makers and is finally driven to suicide.

In the last scene of the novel, the Savage's lifeless body hangs in the lighthouse and, turning slowly, sightlessly

gazes on a world in which creativity, love, and God have been crushed by the weight of human happiness:

> Slowly, very slowly, like two unhurried compass needles, the feet turned towards the right; north, north-east, east, southeast, south, south-south-west; then paused, and, after a few seconds, turned as unhurriedly back towards the left. South-south-west, south, southeast, east.

In **Brave New World** the few true human beings who have managed to resist Progress are deviants from the majority of society. Bernard Marx, Helmholtz Watson, and the Savage are all oddities in a world where the average man can't stand to be alone, blushes at the word "mother," and goes through life reciting the slogans which are, in fact, his total being. It is clearly not possible to be human and part of the system at the same time, for the essence of man is seen by Huxley as creativity, free will, recovery of natural passion, and these are heresies which the Brave New World has suppressed. The only member of the establishment who has remained human is Mustapha Mond, the world-controller, who, with a thorough knowledge of society both before and after Ford, freely chooses to side with the state and helps mold it with a brilliant but perverse creativity.

Bernard Marx is an unusual characterization in Huxley, for he is not a typed and static figure. Gradually, Huxley induces a shift in the reader's attitude toward Marx, from a thorough sympathy at the beginning of the novel to a scornful disdain at the close. Marx appeals to the reader at first because he does not fit into the Brave New World, but Bernard himself would very much like to be part of his society—to have the most pneumatic women, to be admired by the other alphas and feared by the lower castes. Unfortunately, a mistake during his hatching has made him smaller than average, neurotic, and maladjusted. Marx's intellectualism, his professed scorn for the values of his society are motivated not by an insight into the meaning of truth and beauty but by a hasty reaction formation to his alienation from the Brave New World. He loses the reader's sympathy when he uses the Savage as a device to gain attention. From this moment on, he diminishes from heroic to comic proportions and is finally revealed as a coward, begging to be allowed to stay in London rather than be sent to an island of misfits.

Helmholtz Watson, Bernard's friend, is a much more sympathetic character but remains a minor figure. If developed further, Watson could have been the successful alternative to the irreconcilable Savage and Mustapha Mond, as the person who finds meaning in creativity and poetry. But Watson is apparently introduced into the novel only to point out the decline of art into "emotional engineering" and the impossibility of free expression in the Brave New World.

Lenina Crowne, a pneumatic alpha whom the Savage at first adores as a goddess and a symbol of ultimate beauty, is generally a comic figure but with some tragic overtones. The reader senses that the ability to experience passion lies dormant within Lenina, but she has been trained to experience only mechanical, "rational" responses and does not have the imagination to transcend them. To the Savage's poetic ardors she can only respond with the words of a popular song, "Hug me till you drug me, honey."

Brave New World is a remarkable novel and, in many respects, the culmination of Huxley's art. The gruesome utopian vision, presented in marvelous detail and with awesome imaginativeness, holds the reader in horrified fascination. Huxley has escaped from his self-conscious pedantry, his uncertainty, his lapses in style, and writes with boldness and assurance. *Crome Yellow* and *Antic Hay* had been seriously marred by a lack of dramatic tension, but *Brave New World* manages to achieve such tension through the direct confrontation of equally powerful, conflicting philosophies. Unlike the earlier novels, there is a very real debate in *Brave New World,* and, interestingly enough, the outcome of the debate as presented within the novel is a grim stalemate.

Near the end of the novel, the Savage and the World-Controller, Mustapha Mond, have a crucial argument. Mond was a brilliant theoretical physicist with a knowledge of the Bible, literature, and philosophy; but given a choice to be sent to an island where he could continue his research or to be taken on to the Controllers' Council, he chose the latter and abandons the research. On the assumption that the happiness and stability of man are the only ultimate ends, all troubling qualities which upset men such as truth, beauty, love, knowledge, pure science *are* dangers and must be suppressed. "God isn't compatible with machinery and scientific medicine and universal happiness," Mond argues. The poetic Savage, who mortifies his flesh and worships a stern and terrible God, does not view this happiness and contentment as man's end. "What you need," he says to the World-Controller, "is something with tears for a change. Nothing costs enough here." Mustapha Mond astutely observes that the Savage is "claiming the right to be unhappy." When the Savage agrees defiantly, Mond goes on:

> "Not to mention the right to grow old and ugly and impotent; the right to have syphilis and cancer; the right to be lousy; the right to live in constant apprehension of what may happen tomorrow; the right to catch typhoid; the right to be tortured by unspeakable pains of every kind."

> There was a long silence.

> "I claim them all," said the Savage at last.

> Mustapha Mond shrugged his shoulders, "You're welcome," he said.

Who has won the argument? Both men on their own terms, and neither; for Huxley and the reader, caught in between the conflicting claims of "passion and reason, self-division's cause," are locked in an irresolvable conflict, an unbreakable stasis. Huxley is able to offer no solution, no reconciliation, no alternative. D. H. Lawrence's notion of Noble Savagery, which Huxley had flirted with, and even the fusion with nature he had claimed as man's ideal, must be rejected in the terms of *Brave New World.* Caught in the basic conflict of the novel, they are torn apart and discredited. Half of the creed resides with the closeness to nature and the savagery of the Indian reservation but inextricably is mingled there with disease, guilt,

masochism, the hostile God. The other half is found in the sexual release and rejection of abstractions of the Brave New World, but is likewise sullied by the total dehumanization and absence of communication of its inhabitants. *Brave New World* is the darkest point and final stage of Huxley's pessimism. He is torn by irreconcilable views of man, and, admittedly, offers the reader the unenviable choice between "insanity on the one hand and lunacy on the other."

With *Brave New World,* Huxley ends the first and most productive period of his life. It is obvious, at the close of this novel, that the spiritual crisis in Huxley had reached its greatest intensity and could go no further. Sadly enough, the author could find no earthly solution. Rejecting this world entirely in bitterness and disgust, Huxley adopted the philosophy of nonattachment, a mystical belief of Buddhist origins, which leads man away from the ugliness of bodily existence and immerses him in eternal, changeless verities. Huxley did not cease writing satirical novels, but even the best of his later satires, *After Many a Summer Dies the Swan,* is marred by the spirit of a man who hates life and is sinning against it. The subtle irony, the surprise of a beautiful passage, the delicate portrayal of character have disappeared and are replaced by a ruthless and brutal hatred.

Huxley's dilemma was a conflict between a skeptical, sophisticated mind and essentially Victorian morals. His scientific outlook, the First World War, the disillusionment of the '20s—these destroyed intellectually the validity of all but relative moral standards, but emotionally, he was in desperate need of absolutes. It was as if the spirits of his two famous ancestors, T. H. Huxley and Matthew Arnold, were locked in a mortal embrace in Huxley's soul. Huxley's tragedy is that of a man caught between two worlds, each with its own particular demands, truths, and horrors. Who can blame him for abandoning the struggle? (pp. 96-101)

Stephen Greenblatt, "Aldous Huxley," in his Three Modern Satirists: Waugh, Orwell, and Huxley, *Yale University Press, 1965, pp. 75-101.*

R. T. Oerton   (essay date 1967)

[*In the essay below, Oerton examines contemporary society's development toward the future as predicted in* Brave New World.]

Before long we shall have the means to translate Aldous Huxley's fictional *Brave New World* into solid fact; and it seems that we intend to do it.

No one who reads the newspapers, however casually, can have failed to notice that science has now put within our grasp the most important and revolutionary of those instruments of social engineering which Huxley foresaw, and that many others which he did not visualise are also being made available to us.

In *Brave New World,* human beings (if this phrase may be used for the moment without begging any of the questions which may later arise) were not born of women but cultured in bottles from unfertilised eggs obtained by surgical operation and subsequently fertilised by immersion "in a warm bouillon containing free-swimming spermatazoa." On 22 July 1966, the *New Statesman* reported that "at the physiology laboratory in Cambridge, Dr. Robert Edwards has been working with immature egg cells obtained from the ovaries of women who had undergone some necessary gynaecological operation. He has been able to culture these human eggs in a jar, and bring them to a stage of development at which they are capable of being fertilised by spermatazoa. In some cases he has achieved what he will only claim as 'apparent fertilisation' . . . There is no theoretical reason why such embryos should not be artificially sustained until they are 'full term' babies—alive and kicking." Waiting only to be (if we may borrow Huxley's word) decanted.

In *Brave New World,* some of the fertilised ova were subjected to "Bokanovsky's Process" to which the eggs responded by budding to produce "identical twins—but not in piddling twos and threes as in the old viviparous days, when an egg would sometimes accidentally divide; actually by dozens, by scores at a time." On 13 November 1966, *The Observer* told us that "it may soon be possible to propagate people in much the same way as we now propagate roses—by taking the equivalent of cuttings. According to . . . Professor Joshua Lederberg . . . it would offer the 'possibility of making dozens or hundreds of genetically identical individuals like multiplied identical twins'. Biologists are agreed that such techniques are likely to come; the main uncertainty is when? Professor Lederberg suggests . . . in 'a few years rather than decades'."

No one would doubt that *Brave New World* was a brilliant book, and few who read it can have failed to react with revulsion to the civilisation which it foresaw.

—*R. T. Oerton*

In *Brave New World,* the role and status of human beings was unalterably determined not just from their birth but before their birth. A worker in the Central London Hatchery and Conditioning Centre explained: "We predestine and condition. We decant our babies as socialised human beings, as Alphas or Epsilons, as future sewage workers or future . . . Directors of Hatcheries." On 30 October 1966, the *Sunday Times* led its Colour Supplement with a report on "The Super Babies"—babies whose South African mothers had been subjected in pregnancy to special treatment and who had as a result been born with quite exceptional intelligence and capacities. Even the treatment employed bore a close resemblance to Huxley's prediction, because it involved increasing the availability of oxygen to the brain of the foetus, and in *Brave New World* the foetuses destined to be lower-caste human beings were deprived of oxygen: "The lower the caste . . . the shorter the oxygen. The first organ affected was the brain", because there was "nothing like oxygen-shortage for keeping an embryo below par." There is of course an obvious difference, in that the technique used in South Africa is designed to increase intelligence not to stunt it; but it does demonstrate nonetheless that the method of stunting which Huxley suggested is not only valid but (in principle at least) available. Indirectly, indeed, the results he predicted are already being achieved, because those children whose mothers do *not* receive this treatment are in fact condemned automatically to a status inferior to that enjoyed by those whose mothers do.

The social engineering in *Brave New World* did not stop at the baby's birth, but continued long afterwards with the aid of conditioning techniques. In the "Neo-Pavlovian Conditioning Rooms" babies destined to be lower-caste manual workers who "you couldn't have . . . wasting the Community's time over books" were made to hate books from childhood. This was done by giving them books to play with and terrifying them when they did so by loud noises and electric shocks. In the Winter 1962/63 issue of *Twentieth Century,* Professor H. J. Eysenck described an experiment performed by J. B. Watson in which a little boy was given a "conditioned fear response" to white rats, of which he had previously been fond, by very similar methods: an iron bar was banged by a hammer "producing a tremendous noise" whenever he reached for the rats. The Pavlovian principles which underlay this experiment have since been developed and form the basis of the treatment technique known as aversion therapy. The newspapers recently carried reports of a case in which this had been used to make a man reject his mistress in favour of his wife, and on 24 November 1966 *New Society* noted that it was being used in the treatment of criminal offenders.

Another conditioning technique employed in *Brave New World,* known as "sleep teaching, or hypnopaedia" involved the giving of moral instruction to children by recorded messages softly and repeatedly played over while they were asleep. In his book, *Uses and Abuses of Psychology,* Professor Eysenck described another experiment in which a group of children were induced to stop biting their nails by "a large electric gramophone which was put on rather softly after the children had gone to sleep and which repeated endlessly 'I will not bite my finger nails. Finger nail biting is a dirty habit . . . '" Of this experiment, Professor Eysenck remarks: "Thus does reality catch up with the wild extravagant fantasies of Huxley's *Brave New World*!"

And so indeed it does. In fact reality has now in some ways outstripped Huxley's fantasies. In the forseeable future we may be able to implant "memories" by injection, to freeze the dying and preserve them in indefinite frigidity until a cure is found for the disease of which they were about to die, to determine the sex of our children before their birth, and to preserve sperm in cold storage so that a man may father children long after his death. Spare-part surgery, too, has made great strides of late and posed several problems. A surgeon has succeeded in removing a monkey's brain from its head and preserving it in living isolation. In this state it could remain indefinitely and although the surgeon said he thought it was probably not conscious, a writer who made the not implausible assumption that it was would have to hand and ready-made the plot of a horror story too horrible to write.

No one would doubt that **Brave New World** was a brilliant book, and few who read it can have failed to react with revulsion to the civilisation which it foresaw. But one thing which it did not do was to provide them with a good *reason* for rejecting this civilisation. Some may think that revulsion is itself a reason good enough for anyone. Revulsion, however, is a feeling which tends to abate as we become familiar with the object which inspired it, and the initial wave of disgust which **Brave New World** aroused has very nearly spent itself. Things which once seemed terrible seem much less terrible when we read about them every week in our newspapers. They evidently seem less terrible still to the scientists who work with them, and no scientist today seems inclined to stop, or even to pause, as his journey takes him through one discovery after another. The atomic bomb was built, and then the hydrogen bomb: why not the Central London Hatchery and Conditioning Centre?

It is in any case beside the point to say that we do not *like* the Brave New World; for if the Brave New World should ever come to pass we may rest assured that we should be *built* to like it. And if any last vestige of rebellion should remain in us, it would be treated as a flaw of personality to be eradicated at once by the conditioning process. "And that," as the Director of the Central London Hatchery and Conditioning Centre put it, " . . . is the secret of happiness and virtue—liking what you've *got* to do. All conditioning aims at that: making people like their inescapable social destiny."

And after all why not? Humanity today is a sprawling and uncontrolled mass, breeding at will, often hungry, sometimes starving, frequently at war within itself and hardly notable for its happiness or its contentment. If all these evils could be effectively abolished by methods of social engineering like those described in **Brave New World,** why should we not seek eagerly to employ them? There is of course one obvious reason why not—namely, that their efficacy is doubtful. Present knowledge indicates, for instance, that a child cannot be deprived entirely of parents or parent-figures, as were the children in the Brave New World, without suffering lasting pathological damage to his personality. Again, present knowledge does not enable us to confirm the effectiveness of Pavlovian conditioning in making such deep and permanent changes in behaviour as those which Huxley envisaged. But these objections are rather superficial ones since they could be overcome, in theory at any rate, by future scientific development and by increasing scientific knowledge and expertise. So if we are to find a good reason for rejecting the Brave New World we must look a little deeper.

What exactly is it about **Brave New World** which gives it so strong an atmosphere of nightmare? Above all else, surely, it is the fact that the human race has come to a dead end. The horror comes not only, perhaps not even primarily, from the way things *are* in the Brave New World, but from the certain knowledge that they can never be any different. The reader knows not only that humanity has achieved this state, but that this state is all humanity will ever achieve. For change depends upon individual discontent and individual rebellion and the very possibility of these things is excluded for ever by system which has grown up. The nightmare comes from the oppressive sense of minds closed, of feelings castrated, of self-perpetuating blindness. For a mess of happiness and contentment man has bartered his birthright of freedom and lives now like a laboratory rat in a cage from which there is no possibility of escape. His imprisonment is perpetual and complete because he does not know he is imprisoned. He has become his own jailer and the bars of the cage are built into his mind.

If this diagnosis is correct and these really are the aspects of **Brave New World** which we find most oppressive, it still remains to ask why we should do so. The answer to this question may well be found to lie at the very core of man's nature. We had our origin long ago in the slime at the waterside where, for the first time on this planet, something came to exist in whose substance lay the power to increase, to develop and to strive. Nowadays we call it life. And then a process began which stretched through time and which created time, a process of groping search down blind alleys and along the high road, through an infinity of deaths and an infinity of births, out of the extinction of old species and into the creation of new. Nowadays we call it evolution.

And yet although we call the thing life and the process evolution, we do not feel we understand the process or the thing. We question our existence and wonder why we struggle, but no one yet has found an answer which satisfies us all. Perhaps we can hardly expect one, because in truth we *are* the thing and we *are* the process, and perhaps if we are true to our nature we must submerge ourselves and submit unquestioningly to what we cannot question. This, quite simply, is the way it is. For man is essentially a product of evolution, and not only its product but its instrument.

If we bear this in mind and bear in mind, too, the fact that evolution itself is essentially a process of continual change, we may begin to see why Aldous Huxley's Brave New World would be quite literally a dead end for the human race. The need to preserve the possibility of change (which is in truth no more and no less than the need to preserve the possibility of future evolution) is very close to the heart of mankind; and so indeed it should be—so it is bound to be—since man with all his imperfections is still the crowning achievement of the evolutionary process. There was a time when change could mean no more in this context than physical change, but this time is long past and at the present stage of our development our need is to preserve the possibility of ideological evolution, of changes in ideas, changes in values, changes in our way of looking at the world, changes in our conception of man's nature and man's role. In our hearts we know this. We cling to democracy, and what is democracy but an instrument for preserving the possibility of changes such as these? We demand freedom, and what else is freedom but the right to differ and to change?

The real objection to the kinds of social engineering which the Brave New World has adopted—and which we ourselves may soon adopt—is that under the guise of evolutionary progress they ushered in the death of evolution and, with it, the death of the human race. For it is hard to see how the creatures which inhabited this World could be described as human beings. In truth, it seems to us, the human race had died and been replaced by a carefully controlled laboratory culture which had altogether ceased to play its part in the story of man's adventure on this planet. And so the story was finally at an end. (pp. 48-50)

> *R. T. Oerton, "The End of the Beginning," in* The Twentieth Century, *Vol. 175, First quarter, 1967, pp. 48-50.*

George Woodcock   (essay date 1972)

[*Woodcock is a Canadian educator, editor, and critic best known for his biographies of George Orwell and Thomas Merton. He also founded Canada's most important literary journal,* Canadian Literature, *and has written extensively on the literature of Canada. In the following excerpt, Woodcock identifies elements that distinguish* Brave New World *within the genre of utopian literature.*]

If any vision runs more persistently than others through Huxley's works, from **Crome Yellow** in 1921 down to **Island** in 1962, it is that of Utopia, the world where a kind of perfection has been attained, change has come to a stop in a temporal parody of eternity. As a young man he saw Utopia as Hell on earth; as an old man he saw it as the earthly paradise. The difference between the two sides of the vision derives from a change in Huxley's views of human potentialities. For the greater part of his life he believed that only a tiny minority was capable of the highest thought or—in later years—of spiritual enlightenment, yet, apart from the brief period when he wrote **Proper Studies,** he distrusted the idea of a world which the élite planned for mankind as a whole. In his final years he believed that he had discovered the way, through mystical discipline and the intelligent use of drugs, to give every man an equal chance of an enlightened existence, and so a Utopia based on a balance of the physical and spiritual, the temporal and eternal, seemed possible to him; such was the vision he gave concrete form in **Island.**

Huxley's preoccupations with Utopias belong to a wider movement, for many writers in the earlier twentieth century were turning away from the facilely benign Utopias of the Renaissance and the nineteenth century. Some followed the example of Samuel Butler in *Erewhon* by creating negative Utopias, pictures of a future which, by reason of some flaw in human capabilities, has turned out to be the opposite of the ideal worlds that early socialists and early writers of science romance conceived. Even the most distinguished of the science romancers, H. G. Wells, balanced his positive Utopia *Men Like Gods* with the terrifyingly negative vision of *When the Sleeper Wakes.* Years before Huxley wrote **Brave New World,** E. M. Forster ('The Machine Stops') and Karel Čapek (*R.U.R.*) already portrayed in varying ways the withering of man's spiritual life and even of his physical capacities when he becomes too reliant on a machine-oriented world, and in 1924 there had appeared the first of the three great anti-Utopias of the twentieth century, Evgeny Zamiatin's *We.*

While *We* had a profound influence on the third of the key anti-Utopian novels, *1984,* its influence on **Brave New World** is obviously—if it exists—less profound and direct, despite the many striking resemblances between the two novels.

Both Huxley and Zamiatin see Utopia as a possible, even a probable outcome of twentieth-century technological developments, especially of the refinement of techniques in psychological suggestion. Both assume that in the process of creating Utopia man's outlook on life will be radically altered, since the stability necessary to maintain society unchanged will mean the elimination of the idea of freedom and the knowledge of the past, and the reduction of culture to a pattern of mechanical enjoyments. Both envisage the economic structure of Utopia as collectivist, and see its political structure as hierarchical, a pyramid topped by a tiny group of guardians who rule through effective police systems and conditioning techniques. They foresee the destruction of the very ideas of individuality and privacy, of passionate personal relationships, of any association outside the state. Both make happiness the goal of their Utopias, and equate it with non-freedom. Both use a passionless sexual promiscuity, based on the theory that each belongs to all, to break down any true intimacy between persons. The individual becomes an atom in the body of the state and nothing more. Even the rebellions in the two novels are alike, for in each case the hero—D.503 in *We* and Bernard Marx in **Brave New World**—is physically and mentally an atavistic throwback, and both heroes are tempted to rebellion by contact with men who have escaped the conditioning hand of the state: the hairy people who live outside the protective green wall of the Utopian city in *We,* the primitives of the New Mexican reservation in **Brave New World.** Needless to say, both rebellions fail; the unitary world utopian state continues on its course.

Striking as the resemblances may be, it is hard to prove that Huxley was influenced by Zamiatin at the time he wrote **Brave New World.** Unlike Orwell, he never admitted such an influence. And though, given Huxley's omnivorous reading habits, it seems unlikely that he failed to read *We* during the seven years between its publication and that of **Brave New World,** this appears to have affected only secondary details of his book. The essential outline of **Brave New World** was sketched already in **Crome Yellow,** and while it is true that *We* was written in 1920, and was secretly circulated as a forbidden text in Soviet Russia, it is improbable that Huxley saw a copy of it or even learnt of its existence before he conceived the character of Mr. Scogan and filled his mind with Utopian ideas.

The concept of Utopia, implicitly rejected in **Crome Yellow,** haunted Huxley as he watched the advance of the applied sciences and particularly of physiology and psychology. Utopia, he realized, was not entirely an impossible abstraction. Perhaps it cannot be made with men as they are. But science can change—if not men themselves—at least their attitudes and reactions, and then Utopia becomes feasible as a society in which men cease to be individuals and become merely the components of a social collectivity.

Utopia, of course, is a matter of imposing a pattern, of subordinating human life to a discipline of abstraction analogous to geometry. 'A mind impregnated with music', said Huxley in *Beyond the Mexique Bay,* 'will always tend to impose a pattern on the temporal flux.' But it seemed evident to him that any human attempt to impose an ideal order on Nature or on men would be perverted by man's limitations. So, for all his love of order in geometry and architecture and music, he distrusted it in political or social planning.

Brave New World marks a fundamental change in Huxley's use of the novel; it is no longer fiction intended to describe and satirize. The satirical element remains, but the primary function is now to exhort. Like Orwell's *1984,* *Brave New World* was deliberately devised as a cautionary tale. The earlier novels may have been didactic in part, as *Point Counter Point* clearly was whenever Rampion held the field; *Brave New World* is the first that will be didactic in total intent. This function of the novel, quite apart from any entertainment value it may have as a piece of futurist fantasy, is clearly stated in the description which Huxley gave his father in August 1931: he saw it as

> a comic, or at least satirical, novel about the Future, showing the appallingness (at any rate by our standards) of Utopia and adumbrating the effects on thought and feeling of such quite possible biological inventions as the production of children in bottles (with consequent abolition of the family and all the Freudian 'complexes' for which family relationships are responsible), the prolongation of youth, the devising of some harmless but effective substitute for alcohol, cocaine, opium etc:—and also the effects of such sociological reforms on Pavlovian conditions of all children from birth and before birth, universal peace, security and stability.

(pp. 173-76)

[From] now to the end of his life Huxley was to remain concerned with the fundamental social issues of peace and freedom and the preservation of the environment; even after his conversion to mystical religion he did not retreat out of social responsibility, as many self-styled mystics have done, but remained—even if he did not long continue as a political activist—intensely concerned with the plight of man in his temporal existence.

Music at Night, the volume of essays which in 1931 followed the vitalist manifesto of *Do What You Will,* can be read with particular profit as a kind of notebook for *Brave New World.* It discusses a whole series of possibilities which Huxley sees as latent in the European-American world of the late 1920s, and which will form part of the fabric of *Brave New World*: the cult of perpetual youth, the problem of leisure, the perils of Fordism to the human psyche, the possible development of eugenics as a means of shaping the man of the future, the implications of the attempt to make man primarily a consumer, and the perils to freedom of a dogmatic egalitarianism. A reading of the relevant essays shows that, though *Brave New World* is

projected on to the screen of the future, it is derived almost entirely from tendencies which Huxley observed with alarm and distrust in the world around him.

Music at Night is less definite in its expression than *Brave New World,* for Huxley often presents his possibilities neutrally, with the suggestion that men in the future may use them either for good or for ill. This is the case in his discussion of the ideal drug, which in his essay, **'Wanted, a New Pleasure',** he presents as a possible benefit to mankind. He suggests endowing a band of research workers to find 'the ideal intoxicant.'

> If we could sniff or swallow something that would, for five or six hours each day, abolish our solitude as individuals, atone us with our fellows in a glowing exaltation of affection and make life in all its aspects seem not only worth living, but divinely beautiful and significant, and if this heavenly, world-transfiguring drug were of such a kind that we could wake up next morning with a clear head and an undamaged constitution— then, it seems to me, all our problems (and not merely the one small problem of discovering a novel pleasure) would be wholly solved and earth become paradise.

This ideal drug will be used both negatively and positively in Huxley's novels; in *Brave New World* it provides a conditioning technique and its effect is therefore negative and life-constricting, but in *Island* (written in 1962 after Huxley had experimented with LSD) it is used in a positive Utopia as part of a technique of mental liberation.

Music at Night includes several essays which develop a theory of literature that reflects Huxley's changing practice. In **'Tragedy and the Whole Truth'** he draws the opposition between two types of literature: that which, like Shakespearian tragedy, acts quickly and intensely on our feelings by isolating the dramatic elements in life, and the Wholly Truthful literature, represented by writers like Proust and Dostoevsky and Lawrence, which is 'chemically impure' and mild in its catharsis because it is based on 'the pattern of acceptance and resignation', on taking life as it is. Huxley grants that we need both kinds of literature, but it is clear that he is most attracted to Whole Truthism. In **'Art and the Obvious'** he points out how high art has retreated completely from certain areas of life because popular art has vulgarized them. But these aspects of life do exist.

> And since they exist, they should be faced, fought with, and reduced to artistic order. By pretending that certain things are not there, which in fact *are* there, much of the most accomplished modern art is condemning itself to incompleteness, to sterility, to premature decrepitude and death.

Vulgarity in literature lies not in the content, as Huxley points out in the essay which ends *Music at Night,* but in a pretentiousness unrelated to real life. He illustrates this with a brilliant comparison between Dostoevsky and Dickens, between the death of the child Ilusha in *The Brothers Karamazov* and the death of Little Nell. Why is the first moving and the second not? It is, Huxley suggests, because Dickens isolates in a cloud of emotion the suffering and the innocence of Nell, while Dostoevsky evokes vividly the factual details of everything that happens around Ilusha's deathbed, and so relates it constantly to 'the actual realities of human life'.

These discussions of literary form are as closely related to *Brave New World* as are the speculations regarding scientific and social developments, for they draw one's attention to one of the principal reasons why this is still the most widely read of Huxley's books. It is a fantasy of the future and a satire on the present. And in both roles it carries conviction because of the expert and convincing handling of detail to create a plausible world. It is England six hundred years ahead, and Huxley has been wise enough not to change it beyond recognition. It is the country we know and a different world, and this paradox sustains our attention.

As we have seen, *Brave New World* projects happiness as the principal goal of Utopia and equates it with non-freedom. The society of the future is a parody of Plato's republic, with a small group of World Controllers ruling five castes of subjects, divided not merely socially but biologically, since they have been conditioned to their future tasks in the bottles where they were bred. To preserve happiness, the World Controllers throw away everything that might provoke either thought or passion.

> The world's stable now [says Mustapha Mond, Controller for England]. People are happy; they get what they want, and they never want what they can't get. They're well off; they're safe; they're never ill; they're not afraid of death; they're blissfully ignorant of passion and old age; they're plagued with no mothers or fathers; they've got no wives, or children, or lovers to feel strongly about; they're so conditioned that they practically can't help behaving as they ought to behave.

The most striking difference between *Brave New World* and *1984,* with which it has so often been compared, is the absence of violence and overt repression.

> In the end [says Mond] the Controllers realized that force was no good. The slower but infinitely surer methods of ectogenesis, neo-Pavlovian conditions, and hypnopaedia. . . . '

Men are so conditioned from the time the spermatozoon enters the egg in the Hatchery that there is little likelihood of their breaking into rebellion; if they do become discontented there are always drugs to waft them into the heavens of restorative illusion. Thus the Controllers are able to govern with a softly firm hand; the police use whiffs of anaesthetic instead of truncheons, and those over-brilliant individuals who do not fit the established pattern are allowed to indulge their heretical notions in the intellectual quarantine of exile.

The daily lives of the conditioned inhabitants of the brave new world are passed in a carefully regulated pattern of production and consumption. Since it was found that too much leisure created restlessness, scientists are discouraged from devising labour-saving inventions, and the working day is followed by gregarious pleasures so organized that elaborate machinery is required and maximum

consumption is encouraged. Complete freedom of sexual behaviour, plus the availability of soma, provide releases from all ordinary frustrations. The abolition of viviparous birth has made families and all other permanent attachments unnecessary; individuals have become merely cells, each occupying his special position in the carefully differentiated fabric of society.

All this would not make a novel of its own; Utopian fiction that merely describes a futuristic society is notoriously tedious. Huxley brings his to life by showing the perils of any attempt at a perfect society. The higher castes of the community, the Alphas and the Betas, cannot be as closely conditioned as the worker castes, because their tasks involve intelligence and the occasional need to use judgement; and even the best conditioning is not foolproof. So we get sports like the stunted Bernard Marx who has a heretical longing for solitude, like the pneumatic Lenina Crowne who is inclined to remain a little too constant in her attachments, like Helmholtz Watson who secretly writes forbidden poems about the self instead of slogans for the state.

Bernard is already suspected of disaffection and threatened with exile to Iceland, but the crisis in the life of all these three misfits in Utopia is provoked . . . by a journey into unfamiliarity. Bernard takes Lenina on a trip to the reservation for primitive people in New Mexico. For Lenina the first sight of dirt and disease is traumatic, but Bernard is rewarded by the discovery of a woman from Utopia who was lost years ago and has since lived and brought up her child among the Indians. The young man—John—is not only a savage; he has also, accidentally, acquired a copy of Shakespeare which, with the mixed heathen and Christian cults of the Indians, has enriched his language and shaped his outlook. In our sense he is far more 'cultured', if not more 'civilized', than the utopians.

Bernard brings the savage back to London, where he creates a sensation by his baroque behaviour and Elizabethan speech. On Bernard and Helmholtz he has the effect of crystallizing their sense of difference from the society to which they have been bred. Lenina, who is merely a Beta Plus and therefore not so inclined to intellectual rebellion, lapses into an old-fashioned infatuation for the savage, who meanwhile has conceived a romantic attachment to her. There is an extraordinarily comic scene of crossed purposes, in which the savage declares his love in resounding Shakespearian terms, whereupon Lenina, reacting in the only way she knows, unzips her garments and advances upon him in all her pneumatic nakedness, and the savage, shouting Elizabethan curses, drives her from him.

The rebellion, slight as it is, fails. The three young men, Bernard, Helmholtz and the savage, after creating a minor riot by interrupting a distribution of soma, are brought before Mustapha Mond. There is a Peacockian interlude in which each of the four characteristically reacts to the situation, and then Bernard and Helmholtz are exiled to join those who have shown themselves unreliable in the past (the real intellectual élite of the brave new world). The savage is forbidden to join them, because Mond wants to continue the experiment of subjecting him to 'civilization'.

Since he cannot go anywhere else, the savage tries to establish a hermitage in the Surrey countryside of Huxley's youth, but Utopia's equivalents of newshounds discover him, and the fervent pleasure-seekers of the brave new world, hearing that he is flogging himself like a New Mexican penitent, descend on him in their helicopters. Lenina is among them. There is a great orgy in which the savage first whips and then possesses her. The next day, revolted by Utopia and his surrender to its seductions, he hangs himself.

In thematic terms, *Brave New World* opposes the scientific-industrialist ideal of Mustapha Mond (and, by derivation, of Henry Ford) to the primitivist vitalism of Lawrence, the acceptance of life with all its joys and miseries, as it exists. A decade later Huxley criticized himself for having failed to add a third possibility, that of the decentralized, libertarian society, where industry is minimized and man is liberated to pursue the life of time by the illumination of eternity. Yet it is difficult to see how the novel could have been changed to include this third possibility. The anti-individualist tendencies latent in our society have to be opposed by the poetic primitivism of the savage, who alone, since he is the only character conscious of the nature of tragedy, can embody the tragic possibilities of man's future.

One is tempted to consider *Brave New World,* because it is a Utopian fantasy, as an exceptional work that stands outside the general pattern of Aldous Huxley's fiction. In reality, its function is to close the sequence of the earlier novels. The central characters belong clearly in the Huxleian succession. Bernard is a latter-day Gumbril who has to inflate himself perpetually in order to feel equal to others, and who can only fulfil himself in exceptional circumstances. Helmholtz is a Calamy, an expert amorist who has lost his taste for sensual delights and longs for something more elevated and intelligent. The savage is a more acceptable vehicle for the Lawrencian viewpoint than the excessively didactic Rampion. And Mustapha Mond, with his orotund delivery, is a Scogan or a Cardan who has at last made good. As for the world of the novel, it is the Bohemia of *Antic Hay* and *Point Counter Point,* carried to its logical end, its pleasures sanctified and its personal irresponsibilities institutionalized so that the freedom of the libertine is revealed as the most insidious of slaveries. There can be no doubt of the continuity between *Brave New World* and the earlier novels. It is the direction of the journey that has changed. (pp. 176-81)

> *George Woodcock, in his* Dawn and the Darkest Hour: A Study of Aldous Huxley, *The Viking Press, 1972, 299 p.*

John Colmer   (essay date 1978)

[*Colmer is an English-born Australian educator and critic whose writings include book-length studies of S. T. Coleridge, E. M. Forster, and Patrick White. Colmer has stated that his central preoccupation as a critic is the relationship between literature and politics. In the excerpt below, he studies Huxley's social criticism in* Brave New World.]

Thirty-seven years separate [H. G. Wells's] *The Time Machine* (1895) and Aldous Huxley's *Brave New World* (1932). Wells's story was written to appeal to the products of the Education Act of 1870, the readers of the new popular penny newspapers; it was also conceived before the great advances in the biological sciences and in psychology. Thus the popular oversimplified treatment of science and the patronising tone arise in part from the nature of Wells's public. Huxley, on the other hand, addresses an altogether different class of reader. He expects a high level of education and sophistication; consequently, he feels free to employ a wide variety of narrative techniques and literary allusions. He counterpoints speeches and scenes for ironic effect in a highly sophisticated manner—a technique already tried in *Point Counter Point* (1928)—and he introduces scattered quotations from Shakespeare, the meaning of which depends on knowledge of their original context, in order to establish human norms in the abnormal world of the future. His theme is man's use of biology and psychology to achieve an ordered world. Inevitably it takes the form of a vision of the future. But, whereas Wells placed the action of *The Time Machine* in the year AD 802,701, Huxley places it in the foreseeable future AF 632, that is, 632 years after the birth of 'our Ford', Henry Ford, the founder, in some sense, of modern industrial society. The closeness makes the fantasy world more frightening, easier to apply to our own world (obviously there are some disadvantages in choosing too close a date, as Orwell did in *Nineteen Eighty-Four*). There is a further major difference between Wells and Huxley. Huxley's theme is not man's control over the physical world, but the much more radical and challenging one of man's control over human nature itself by the use of science. Wells lived in a world that worshipped mechanical inventions, Huxley in a world of biological discovery, psychological conditioning, and authoritarian ideologies. Thus, the major hypothesis of *Brave New World* is that a time may soon come when men will create a society in which the production of human beings will be scientifically planned, so that by artificial and selective breeding each man will fit in perfectly to his destined environment. With all the tensions between man and his environment removed, the result should be perfect harmony and happiness. It should be COMMUNITY, IDENTITY, STABILITY, the World State's motto, the words on the shield outside the CENTRAL LONDON HATCHERY AND CONDITIONING CENTRE. But is the outcome desirable? *Brave New World* suggests that it is not. It is one of the many anti-utopias that seek to demonstrate that certain kinds of order would destroy our essential humanity. Here is the paradox on which all utopias hinge. We long for a perfect world, but the worlds we dream of turn out to be enemies of our individual perfection.

Huxley's title, *Brave New World,* is ironic. And there is already an implicit irony in its original context in Shakespeare's *The Tempest,* for when Miranda cries out in rapturous happiness

> O wonder
> How many goodly creatures are there here;
> How beauteous mankind is! O brave new world
> That has such people in it

the faces she gazes at are the faces of the conspirators, the villains of the play.

Huxley expects his readers to be familiar with general scientific principles. But he constructs his work so that all the essential scientific information is released indirectly in the early chapters. Where Wells introduced the stupid Philby to ask questions about the Time Machine, Huxley employs a conducted tour of the Hatchery and Conditioning Centre and a modified, ironic lecture technique. It is not necessary that the writer of Utopian fiction should give us a comprehensive description of every aspect of life in his fantasy world. What is essential is that he himself should have imagined it so intensely that it possesses inner coherence and therefore obeys the laws of its own being. Huxley succeeds triumphantly in creating a coherent, absolutely convincing world, a world in which we feel free to move around because we know the essential laws of its nature.

First, the reader enters the wintry, antiseptic atmosphere of the Fertilising Room at the Central London Hatchery, and listens to the Director explaining the process to a newly arrived troop of students.

> 'I shall begin at the beginning,' said the D.H.C., and the more zealous students recorded his intention in their notebooks: *Begin at the beginning.* 'These,' he waved his hand, 'are the incubators.' And opening an insulated door he showed them racks upon racks of numbered test-tubes. 'The week's supply of ova. Kept,' he explained, 'at blood heat; whereas the male gametes,' and here he opened another door, 'they have to be kept at thirty-five instead of thirty-seven. Full blood heat sterilizes'.

The Director then goes on to explain the fertilising process: how if any egg remained unfertilised it was again immersed in free-swimming spermatozoa, and if necessary again; how the fertilised ova went back to the incubators, where the Alphas and Betas remained until definitely bottled, while the Gammas, Deltas, and Epsilons were brought out again after only thirty-six hours to undergo the Bokanovsky process.

> 'Bokanovsky's Process,' repeated the Director, and the students underlined the words in their little note-books. One egg, one embryo, one adult—normality. But a bokanovskified egg will bud, will proliferate, will divide. From eight to ninety-six buds, and every bud will grow into a perfectly formed embryo, and every embryo into a full-sized adult. Making ninety-six human beings grow where only one grew before. Progress. . . . But one of the students was fool enough to ask where the advantage lay. 'My good boy!' The Director wheeled sharply round on him. 'Can't you *see*? Can't you *see*?' He raised a hand; his expression was solemn. 'Bokanovsky's Process is one of the major instruments of social stability!'
>
> *Major instruments of social stability.*
>
> Standard men and women; in uniform batches. The whole of a small factory staffed with the products of a single bokanovskified egg.

Next, in **Brave New World,** the reader enters the NEOPAVLOVIAN CONDITIONING CENTRE. The secret there is hypnopaedia, the process of teaching, indoctrinating, and conditioning responses while people are asleep. The lesson that is in progress when the Director arrives with his class is 'Elementary Class Consciousness'. He asks the nurse to turn up the voice that is murmuring into the eighty identical cots so that his students may hear.

> 'Alpha children wear grey. They work much harder than we do, because they are so frightfully clever. I'm really awfully glad I'm a Beta, because I don't work so hard. And then we are much better than the Gammas and Deltas. Gammas are stupid. They all wear green, and Delta children wear khaki. Oh no, I *don't* want to play with Delta children. And Epsilons are still worse. They're too stupid to be able. . . .

As the Director explains to his listeners, hypnopaedia is 'the greatest moralizing and socializing force of all time'.

Huxley, by carrying twentieth-century trends to their logical conclusion and by clever parodies of modern social rituals, makes us feel the pressing relevance of *Brave New World.*

—*John Colmer*

Once the preliminary explanations have been dramatised in this fashion in the opening two chapters, Huxley bounces his readers straight into his world of the future and we begin to discover in detail what the people are like, how they act, what they believe in, and how they enjoy themselves. Although it is certainly a fantasy world it is remarkably self-consistent. We soon come to learn how everything works and therefore to suspend all disbelief. But the ominous thing is that it constantly reminds us of the worst features of our own society. Sex has become separated from love, procreation, and marriage, and has become pointless. Literature has degenerated into mere emotional engineering, in other words, advertising and propaganda. Religion has become meaningless mumbo jumbo, emotional rituals for achieving group solidarity. Soma has replaced alcohol as the source of joyful oblivion but, unlike alcohol, it is non-addictive and produces no hangovers. Sport has become completely mechanised, its main purpose being to maximise consumption. Huxley, by carrying twentieth-century trends to their logical conclusion and by clever parodies of modern social rituals, makes us feel the pressing relevance of **Brave New World.**

A typical example is the description of the Solidarity Service. Here Huxley parodies some of the rituals of the Christian church and introduces incongruous elements (erotic dancing and nursery rhymes) to suggest that religion is either a sublimation of sex or a return to childishness.

> Round they went, a circular procession of dancers, each with hands on the hips of the dancer preceding, round and round, shouting in unison,

stamping to the rhythm of the music with their feet, beating it, beating it out with hands on the buttocks in front; twelve pairs of hands beating as one; as one, twelve buttocks slabbily resounding. Twelve as one, twelve as one. 'I hear him, I hear him coming.' The music quickened; faster beat the feet, faster, faster fell the rhythmic hands. And all at once a great synthetic bass boomed out the words which announced the approaching atonement and final consummation of solidarity, the coming of the Twelve-in-One, the incarnation of the Greater Being. 'Orgy-porgy,' it sang, while the tom-toms continued to beat their feverish tattoo:

Orgy-porgy, Ford and fun,
Kiss the girls and make them One.
Boys at one with girls at peace;
Orgy-porgy gives release.

'Orgy-porgy', the dancers caught up the liturgical refrain, 'Orgy-porgy, Ford and Fun, kiss the girls. . . . ' And as they sang, the lights began slowly to fade—to fade and at the same time to grow warmer, richer, redder, until at last they were dancing in the crimson twilight of an Embryo Store.

By such parodies Huxley could have allowed the world he creates in this novel to make its own implicit criticism of itself. But utopian fiction and satire are two closely connected literary forms. And most satirists have felt the need to create some kind of formal detached critical perspective. If everyone were happy in *Brave New World* because bred and conditioned to be happy, how could anyone be critical of this world? That was the technical problem Huxley faced as a writer. He solves it by a couple of ingenious cheats. He imagines that there are some 'misfits' who haven't quite turned out as they should have. Something went wrong with Bernard Marx's blood surrogate and Helmholtz Watson has discovered that poetry offers a truth higher than emotional engineering. As a result these two are more critical of the system than anyone else and provide the necessary critical viewpoint. The second cheat is that Huxley imagines that within the world state, but quite uninfluenced by it, is a Savage Reservation where people live the old primitive life involving love, childbirth, dirt and ignorance. This invention produces two critical perspectives: one arises from the ironic juxtaposition of two such contrasted worlds, and the other develops when John the Savage leaves the Savage Reservation and visits the Brave New World, when the reader begins to see the scientifically ordered society through John's innocent incredulous eyes. The Savage becomes a norm of sanity, not so much because he has been brought up in a non-test-tube, non-psychologically conditioned environment, but because his one book has been Shakespeare's plays. And that is really cheat number three. But it works reasonably well, especially for the reader who can recognise his quotations from Shakespeare's bitterest and most tragic plays, *Troilus and Cressida, Othello* and *King Lear*. John soon becomes sick of civilisation and hangs himself. And that's what many readers feel like doing at the end of this grimly pessimistic anti-Utopia.

Why? Because neither of the alternatives that Huxley offers us is acceptable. No one, except the inhabitants of totalitarian countries or the underprivileged in the undeveloped countries of Asia and Africa, would be prepared to buy happiness and social solidarity at the price of losing all individuality. And no one would be prepared to return to the filth and ignorance of a pre-scientific primitive life. If these are the only choices then John's suicide seems the only answer. This bleak pessimism, this clever paradox, was very typical of Huxley's views when *Brave New World* was first published in 1932.

But when he wrote a Preface for the book in 1946 he said that he now thought that he had been wrong to offer only an absurd choice between two impossible worlds. The Preface holds out a hope to mankind. It talks about the peaceful use of nuclear energy and contains pious platitudes about the need for de-centralisation and the use of science to extend, not to limit, man's freedom. There is little of the old satiric rage and indignation. And it was really that that made Huxley a powerful critic of society.

What in the end does Huxley's criticism in *Brave New World* amount to? First and foremost, it warns us that in our present society man is ceasing to exist as an end in himself. This is the danger that was foreseen by Coleridge and the nineteenth-century critics of society. They saw that industry, which holds out the promise of infinite wealth, in fact tends to reduce man to a cog in a machine; that science, which promises to explain the universe, explains little and becomes applied science, concerned with means not ends; that the utilitarian philosophy, based on the principle of the greatest happiness for the greatest number, turns into Gradgrind's worship of fact and the destruction of those very qualities that constitute our full humanity; that economic planning which should improve the quality of life tends to reduce man to a mere statistical unit.

This whole conflict between the individual as an end in himself and as insignificant part of a social plan is finally dramatised in the confrontation between the Controller of the World State, Mustapha Mond, and John the Savage, a confrontation reminiscent of Dostoevsky's Fable of the Grand Inquisitor and Christ. John rejects Mond's world:

> 'But I don't want comfort. I want God, I want poetry, I want real danger, I want freedom, I want goodness. I want sin.'
>
> 'In fact,' said Mustapha Mond, 'you're claiming the right to be unhappy.'
>
> 'All right then,' said the Savage defiantly, 'I'm claiming the right to be unhappy.'

In addition to making this one great major criticism of the tendency of our planned industrial societies to dehumanise and create totalitarian order, *Brave New World* also criticises the misapplication of scientific discovery, the misuse of religion and mass emotion, and the reduction of literature to state propaganda.

One of its chief weaknesses, as even its author came to see, was that it had too little to say about the nature of power; about the psychology of power and the means now available for securing and retaining power. In this respect, Orwell's *Nineteen Eighty-Four* is a much more impressive book. . . . However, we need to remember that by the time Orwell wrote his anti-utopia, after the Second World War, he had had the advantage of studying the European dictators and their propaganda machines. Yet even if *Brave New World* had been written much later than 1932, one suspects that it would still not have had much to say about the cult of power. Although Huxley failed to foresee many of the instruments of slavery that Orwell incorporated into *Nineteen Eighty-Four,* his satire in *Brave New World* is remarkably comprehensive. Despite its pessimistic message, it is a high spirited work, continuously entertaining, deeply serious and with enough emotional complexity to make it a successful piece of fiction as well as a powerful criticism of society. (pp. 168-74)

> *John Colmer, "Utopian Fantasy," in his* Coleridge to Catch-22: Images of Society, *St. Martin's Press, 1978, pp. 162-76.*

Jerome Meckier   (essay date Spring 1979)

[*Meckier, an American educator, is the author of* Aldous Huxley: Satire and Structure *(1969). In the essay below, he studies Huxley's 1929 preface to J. H. Burns's* A Vision of Education *as a nonfictional synopsis of many of the ideas subsequently dramatized in* Brave New World.]

Few students of utopianism recognize the name J. H. Burns. He authored *A Vision of Education, Being an Imaginary Verbatim Report of the First Interplanetary Conference.* Published in London by Williams and Norgate four years before one of the century's most famous dystopias, this imaginary convocation deserves remembering for the "Preface" Aldous Huxley contributed. Ignoring Burns and his book, Huxley took the occasion to describe an impending future bleaker than anything the Interplanetary Conference anticipates. The description is worth reprinting in future editions of Huxley's collected prose. It amounts to a synopsis of the themes of breeding and education in *Brave New World.* In an unlikely place, one finds clues to the genesis of Huxley's most popular novel.

The clues alter current conceptions about the novel's origin and composition. According to Grover Smith's generally useful "Chronology," Huxley wrote *Brave New World* between May and August of 1931. Mrs. Bedford states that Huxley's "bad utopia" was not begun until April of that year. "In the three years after *Point Counter Point,*" Mrs. Bedford recalls [in *Aldous Huxley: A Biography*], "Aldous did not attempt any major work." Admittedly, the "Preface" does not offer definite proof to the contrary. But the advanced state of development Huxley's ideas on breeding and education had attained by the 1929 introduction to Burns's volume suggests that the actual writing may have begun much earlier. Planning for the novel certainly did.

Huxley's letters first mention *Brave New World* unexpectedly in the penultimate paragraph for May 18, 1931, to Mrs. Kethevan Roberts:

> I am writing a novel about the future—on the horror of the Wellsian Utopia and a revolt against it. Very difficult. I have hardly enough imagination to deal with such a subject. But it is none the less interesting work.

The self-deprecating remark about insufficient inventiveness need not be taken too seriously. But the letter fosters the impression that Huxley had not given much prior thought to his task. It also initiates the legend that *Brave New World* was simply a parody of Wells that got out of hand. On the contrary, Huxley's dystopia puts into fictional form the outcome of trends that disturbed him for several years before the accepted date when composition commenced. The "Preface" to Burns's book contains definite allusions to Wells, but it is Huxley's Swiftian prose and its immodest proposals that make this document interesting work.

The "Preface" quickly dismisses the possibility of a genuinely benevolent system of genetics and education. "The dreams of Helvetius and the modern Behaviorists," Huxley reports, are not likely to be realized. It is improbable, he continues, that "every child" can be "turned, according to taste and social necessity, into a Newton, a Shakespeare, a Napoleon, a Mozart, a St. Francis, a Samuel Smiles." Huxley does not expect the scientific production of exceptional individuals, which is often given as the justification for beginning genetic experiments. The trend, Huxley believes, is in the opposite direction, not toward improvement of the race. While utopians, notoriously wishful thinkers, talk about eugenics and salutary systems of education, the approaching dystopia will be founded on a scheme of dysgenics. This is the "really revolutionary revolution . . . not in the external world, but in the souls and flesh of human beings" later referred to with distaste in the "Foreword" to *Brave New World.* The Swiftian satirist of the "Preface" predicts this "really revolutionary revolution." He suggests that scientists will soon realize that education methods are "antinatural" whenever they "consider the welfare of the individual before that of the species as a whole." The goals in future will be mediocrity and sameness, not excellence and individuation. To be natural, therefore, does not require talking lessons from the lilies of the field. Instead, as will be seen, it means emulating the wisdom of communities established by termites.

Huxley's reference to the "dreams of Helvetius" is extremely important. It reveals the eighteenth-century philosopher as one of the unjustly forgotten founding fathers of the brave new world. The idealistic "modern Behaviorists" Huxley mentions in the same sentence bear little resemblance to the Pavlovian mechanists responsible for education in Our Ford's London, but Claude Adrien Helvétius (1715–1771) leaves his imprint on Huxley's dystopia in several crucial places. Denying free will, the French philosopher built a utopian educational system on a purely sensationalist basis. Man, Helvétius contended, responds mechanically to outside stimuli. The cornerstone of Helvétius' philosophy is the assertion that *education is everything.* The brave new world seconds this notion. All minds, Helvétius argued, are equal and void at birth. Subsequent differences in intellectual achievement must therefore be attributed to external environment. Any man, Helvétius believed, could be made into a genius, for intellectually superior individuals are made, not born.

Helvétius' unfounded idealism is parodied in Huxley's "Preface." Parodists frequently disembowel generalities with carefully chosen specific illustrations. Thus the idea of mass-producing geniuses becomes ridiculous if it means cranking out a Newton or Napoleon upon demand. The definition of genius being relative, the eugenic impulse might even lead to the not-so-laughable proliferation of Samuel Smiles. Helvétius' idealism is also refuted by the brave new world. Mond and his cohorts have no desire to produce geniuses. Their one attempt, the infamous "Cyprus Experiment," proved that a society of Alphas, a community of geniuses, will always be a disaster. As Mond explains to Helmholtz Watson and John Savage, the island of Cyprus was "recolonized with a specially prepared batch of twenty-two thousand Alphas." Left to manage their own affairs, these products of superior breeding were by nature inadequately diversified. "All the people detailed for a spell of low-grade work," recalls Mond, "were perpetually intriguing for high-grade jobs, and all the people with high-grade jobs were counter-intriguing at all costs to stay where they were." Disagreements led to civil war and the destruction of nineteen out of twenty-two thousand. As a consequence, the brave new world decides that its "optimum population" should be "modelled on the iceberg—eight-ninths below the water line, one-ninth above." Geneticists and behaviorists of the future, Huxley fears, will work with this model in mind.

The "Cyprus Experiment" gives Huxley the opportunity to parody Helvétius and H. G. Wells simultaneously. He reveals that Helvétius' utopian theories of education find more recent support in Wells's excessively rosy view of the benefits derivable from applied science. In **"A Note on Eugenics,"** Huxley negates the possibility that "eugenic states" can permit all of their superior individuals "to make full use of their powers. . . . no society provides openings for more than a limited number of superior people." "But if . . . every individual is capable of playing the superior part," Huxley wonders, who

> will consent to do the dirty work and obey? The inhabitants of one of Mr. Wells's numerous Utopias solve the problem by ruling and being ruled, doing high-brow and low-brow work in turns. While Jones plays the piano, Smith spreads the manure. At the end of the shift, they change places; Jones trudges out to the dung-heap and Smith practices the A minor Etude of Chopin. An admirable state of affairs if it could be arranged . . .

Future societies, Huxley forecasts, will have to be dysgenic at least in part. They will condition some men to be Alphas and play Chopin, others to be Deltas or Epsilons and spread manure. This is an unpleasant but realistic prospect. It is central to the strategy employed throughout **Brave New World.** A modern satirical novelist of ideas, Huxley sets up difficult choices for the reader. One cannot take any of the options with much enthusiasm. The reader must choose between Mond, who stands for happiness and comfort, and the Savage, who insists on truth and beauty. Similarly, one can hope for Helvétius' society of geniuses,

which is absurd; Wells's solution of voluntary job rotation, which seems scarcely more credible; or a future in which the state predetermines the amount of intelligence each person will need for his assigned occupation, which is nightmare. This third choice, Huxley makes clear, springs from suggestions made by Helvétius and Wells that must be altered for the worse if they are to work. When he discredits the commune mentality prevalent in such Wellsian utopias as *In the Days of the Comet* (1906), Huxley again makes use of a telling example to explode a general principle. Job rotation loses its allure when translated into Chopin and manure. By parodying Wells and Helvétius at the same time, Huxley discloses hitherto unsuspected affinities in their thoughts and inclinations.

Although Helvétius' program for creating genius comes to grief on the island of Cyprus in A.F. 473, the Controllers have adopted almost every other aspect of the French philosopher's system, including his definition of man. They subscribe almost entirely to his theory of education. As he did, they regard the human being as a pleasure-pain calculating machine: man learns to seek pleasure and avoid pain. Good must therefore be redefined as whatever is pleasurable; evil brings pain. This is the rationale behind the Neo-Pavlovian Conditioning Rooms Mr. Foster, the D.H.C., and his students inspect in Chapter Two of **Brave New World.** The state creates good by attaching pleasure to certain objects and actions. It designates evil by connecting them with pain. Alarm bells and electric shocks persuade the babies of the brave new world to shy away from books and flowers, two inexpensive delights a community dedicated to consumerism need no longer provide. The only criterion for morality in Ford's London is whether or not an act or item promotes the general happiness. Mond's ideal of social stability owes its origin, at least in part, to Helvétius' *De l'esprit* (1757). Society, this controversial book argued, can insure the greatest happiness of the largest number by establishing a system of rewards and punishments that coerce men to act in accord with the public welfare. Despite a predilection for creating geniuses, Helvétius was fundamentally mechanistic and utilitarian. The boast that his philosophy of education enables society to rear superior specimens cannot conceal the reductive, behavioristic tendencies in Helvétius' thought. When Huxley expresses his fear that the future will ignore the individual in favor of the species, he responds negatively to developments clearly implied in the system Helvétius proposed as utopia.

According to the French philosopher, earthly happiness, not eventual salvation, constitutes the object of existence. Mustapha Mond, it is evident, agrees. Helvétius eulogized the passions, especially the sex urge. Instead of stifling man's passions, Helvétius contended, society must develop and use them. The sex urge in particular was one any utopia should exert itself to satisfy abundantly. Otherwise, happiness and tranquility are unlikely. Man's sexual drive, Helvétius went on to explain, was a manifestation of his self-love. The key to social harmony was the encouragement in men of enlightened self-love. The men with the strongest passions, he concluded, had more to work with and were therefore potentially capable of greater self-love. They were most likely to grow into geniuses. They would also prove easiest to condition. Helvétius' philosophy clearly anticipates Pavlov, Ford, Freud, and Bentham. His concern with genius foreshadows Wells's conception of utopia as a Eugenic State. As do Ford and Pavlov, Helvétius sees man as a machine. This machine is driven, as Freud maintained, by a strong sex urge, a willing pursuit of the Pleasure Principle. Nevertheless, it is feasible to bring happiness to the greatest number—"everybody's happy now"—if man is taught some form of the enlightened self-interest utilitarians were subsequently to celebrate. Above all, as the hypnopaedic maxim quoted by Lenina enjoins, the individual must feel nothing that will make the community reel.

The "Preface" to Burns's book reveals the important role Helvétius played in Huxley's earliest conceptions of imminent dystopia. Unfamiliar with this introduction, critics have been unable to assign Helvétius his proper part. *Brave New World* should acknowledge Our Helvétius as respectfully as it hails Our Ford. The completed novel, however, never cites him. Huxley left this seminal but now unread eighteenth-century philosopher out of *Brave New World* in favor of more recent thinkers who appeared to be, wittingly or not, his intellectual heirs. The decision to omit Helvétius by name is one that only a writer aspiring to become a popular novelist could make. Few persons in Huxley's original audience would have heard of the French philosopher. Besides, he was unfairly persecuted for his views. Thousands would be better acquainted with Ford, Freud, J. B. Watson, Wells, and Pavlov. Their ideas were current and, to many, unreservedly attractive. Huxley chose topicality. *Brave New World* attacks and parodies the philosophies of prominent writers, industrialists, and scientists by showing how dreadful a future constructed in accord with their combined theories would be. Proving that their theories interconnect was no sophomoric feat. Huxley's anti-utopia is probably the most topical of his satirical novels of ideas. This, of course, is not a bad trait for a dystopia.

Excluding Helvétius' name and concealing the tip-offs it would have provided had some adverse consequences. Thanks to the "Preface," one can reestablish Helvétius' formative impact. His recovery via the "Preface" palliates his nominal expulsion from the novel. Had he been included, Huxley could have driven home more vigorously his disclosure that the brave new world was no more *new* than it was *brave*. The scientific elimination of motherhood, for example, is costlier but no more effective than the reorganization of the family in primitive Samoan and Trobriand societies alluded to early in *Brave New World*. Huxley constantly delights in showing how primitive brave new worlders really are. Far from being highly original, Huxley could also have argued, the brave new world was merely Helvétius revamped. This charge would have made Mond's utopia a greater threat. Disaster could hardly be in the remote future if Huxley presented it as the logical fulfillment of eighteenth-century ideas applied with better effect by their twentieth-century adherents. Helvétius had hoped to be recognized as a benefactor to humanity. Instead, he was scorned, ridiculed, and censored. In the future, Huxley fears, he will have his revenge. His ideas are being sanctioned by the passage of time.

As Wells does, Helvétius could speculate about the creation of geniuses. But he could not discuss the scientific means because he lacked the technology. Science has now furnished it. Huxley wishes that science had been employed to support profounder conceptions of man's nature and Final End. It would appear that science can make the delusions of the past into modern realities. Behaviorists in A.F. 632 can easily test the twofold contention that education is everything and environment all-important. They can take both points well beyond Helvétius' feeble imaginings. Scientists can convert the entire island of Cyprus into a behaviorist's laboratory. When the experiment fails, it merely necessitates an ignobler view of man. Mond and the other Controllers continue to adopt other features of Helvétius' program but jettison the one trace of aspiring idealism it contained. The brave new world can mass-produce genius, but it decides that stability is not served by such a step. Consequently, it probably manufactures fewer extraordinary individuals than the life process would were it left alone.

Helvétius could not manipulate the environment to the extent that Mond's behaviorists can. They elaborate his belief that education is paramount by instituting the biological conditioning of bottle babies. The prenatal environment can be controlled by geneticists familiar with Pavlov's discoveries. As the brave new world perceives, Helvétius was talking about conditioning, not education. The eighteenth-century Frenchman was one of the earliest behaviorists. Huxley later blames the brave new world partially on educators who failed to oppose the substitution of conditioning for genuine instruction. Conditioning, it turns out, can be extended into the womb. Prior to birth and at the exact moment of decanting, environment and conditioning in the brave new world have already been at work. Breeding is made an aspect of education and vice versa. The idea that men are made into what they are, not born, is given a literal turn Helvétius could never have expected. In *Brave New World*, thinkers are held accountable for the perversions their ideas invite.

Incorporation of Helvétius' name into the completed novel would have emphasized Huxley's suspicion that no radically new solutions to the human condition will be found. This belief is at the core of his anti-utopian satire. Perfectabilitarians and their earthly paradises, he insinuates, are seldom as new as they seem or half as attractive. Since the brave new world is Helvétius reheated, Huxley could have used the revelation that Mond and his allies were looking backward as a justification for his own search through the past, for an antidote. Huxley permits Helmholtz Watson to reactivate a tradition. As he develops introspective tendencies, Watson begins to make contact with the timeless Vedantic truths Huxley subsequently celebrates in *The Perennial Philosophy*.

In this way, *Brave New World* pointedly repudiates Helvétius. Despite an enviable sexual prowess and unlimited opportunities, Watson, an Alpha-plus, proves hardest to condition. If education was an absolute and strong passions an asset, as Helvétius claimed, Watson should prove easiest. He should never rebel. But Helmholtz develops into a true genius, a Huxley-Heard superman. He senses within himself a surplus of internal energy, an "extra power" that Heard identified as a reservoir of unused evolutionary force. Looking inward, Helmholtz begins to exploit this untapped reservoir to expand his mental awareness. He responds to an internal stimulant, and it proves to be spiritual rather than sexual. His religious drive, Huxley theorizes, is stronger than his sex urge. Had he specifically positioned Helvétius among the founders of the brave new world, Huxley could have cemented more firmly the alliance of Ford, Freud, Bentham, Pavlov, and Wells. Conspirators against individuality and human development, these thinkers derive from common intellectual currents, such as the one personified by Helvétius.

Huxley criticizes Burns for omitting from his deliberations the real impending future. The inventor of imaginary reports, Huxley claims, should have summoned a speaker from still another planet, where the good of the species takes precedence over the welfare of the individual child. This unheard-from planet is the sort of place London was soon to become when Huxley projected present trends into the future and wrote *Brave New World.* On this planet, says Huxley in his "Preface," a child's powers

> would be allowed to develop only so far as was compatible with the advantage of the race. Any signs of outstanding individuality would be ruthlessly suppressed, or at any rate canalized in racially useful channels. Every art of compulsion and suggestion would be used to enforce the ethics of total self-abnegation. The systematic breeding of useful individuals and the systematic suppression of the useless would form a natural complement to this system of more than Spartan education. Special sub-species would be bred (and, having been bred, specially educated) for the purpose, for example, of working in hot climates, at high altitudes, in the dark, under great atmospheric pressure; while other varieties would be produced by selection to perform specialized intellectual functions.

All major twentieth-century writers of dystopia, Huxley included, foretell the demise of "individuality." This appears to be the worst prospect the future holds. By stressing "the advantage of the race" and the canalizing of energy into "racially useful channels," Huxley anticipates several actual dystopias, such as the Third Reich. "Total self-abnegation" describes Russian Communism if the state is substituted for the race. Huxley differs from Orwell and Zamyatin, however, in his use of the word "outstanding." He makes no impassioned plea for ordinary humanity. Apparently, they constitute no great loss. The "Preface" reveals that Huxley primarily fears what the future state will do to the extraordinary person, not to the common man. It is the defeat of the exceptional individual that will hurt the common man the most. Beginning in *Brave New World* with Helmholtz Watson, who shows mystical promise, Huxley entrusts the genuine future to special individuals capable of expanding the human mind and taking the evolution of the race one step further. Pioneers of Watson's caliber are more advantageous to the race than the uniform men and women modern utopian systems seem to require. Huxley foresees the complete subordination of the gifted individual to the group, whereas a truly utopian order would cultivate the exceptional person, not suppress him. Oppressive, group-oriented utopias stem the evolutionary tide and doom the race they purport to assist. One of the cruelest ironies behind Huxley's complaint against a system like that of the brave new world is that its presuppositions—"Community, Identity, Stability"—compel it to quash the unusual individuals who hold the real key to a brighter, saner future, individuals, one might add, such as Huxley himself.

The 1929 "Preface" implies the kind of revolt Helmholtz Watson must attempt if he is to forestall the horrors of oncoming dystopia. Watson develops into an anti-utilitarian. Instead of the greatest happiness ("the advantage of the race"), he pursues a vision of personal well-being. Once highly useful, he begins to withdraw from societal activities, to become quite useless. In place of group solidarity, he elects solitude and writes a poem on this forbidden subject. Completion of this somewhat mediocre effort signals his eventual salvation. Under the circumstances, it is a remarkable achievement. Having rescued the creative urge, Watson can proceed to the religious drive that Huxley locates behind it. For the canalizing of energy into racially useful channels, Watson substitutes a traditional form of sublimation: cutting back on sexual and professional activity, he transforms the energy conserved and activates a latent spiritual drive, his dormant religious sense. Instead of self-abnegation, he practices meditative introspection. Helmholtz experiences the preliminary stages of an expansion of the mind, a broader, mystical awareness, that Huxley and Gerald Heard posited as the next step in man's evolutionary growth. In a society dedicated to arrested development and scientifically controlled infantility, Helmholtz will try to realize Bernard Marx's ambition "to be an adult all the time," "not just a cell in the social body." On men such as Watson, the improvement of the race depends. His is the only "deep, personal revolution" Huxley can countenance.

Burns's book gave Huxley text and pretext. His "Preface" outlines most of the educational program for *Brave New World.* Conceivably, Huxley's impatience with Burns provided a stimulus. Having formulated general educational principles upon which the brave new world will rest, Huxley had only to summon "enough imagination" to invent specific illustrations. Some of these he may already have had in mind in 1929, for the general principles reveal the kinds of things he must invent. "Every art of compulsion and suggestion," for example, leads to such devices as hypnopaedia, Neo-Pavlovian Conditioning Rooms, and farcical Solidarity Services. It also helps to coin the maxim, "when the individual feels, the community reels." A Central London Hatchery and Conditioning Centre and the genetic distribution of the population into the ideal number of Alphas, Betas, Gammas, Deltas, and Epsilons are implicit in the need for "systematic breeding."

With its reference to the coming system "of more than Spartan education," the "Preface" dispels the notion of the brave new world as a pleasure palace. It discloses the starkness and simplicity of Huxley's basic design. This is a society committed to arrested development on a universal scale. The brave new world is an enormous nursery.

Everyone is "allowed to mature only so far as [is] compatible" with the needs of society. Such a guiding principle is fundamentally anti-evolutionary. Individuals who have the temerity to grow—Bernard Marx walking in the Lake District, Watson sensing unused energies within himself, and the doomed biologist who suggests in a paper that life be lived in accord with some higher purpose—"some intensification and refining of consciousness"—are not exactly "ruthlessly suppressed," but they are effectively exiled. Some men still have presentiments of a society dedicated to human fulfillment. But Ford's religion of consumerism, Freud's definition of the Pleasure Principle as an all-powerful determinant, and the use of Pavlov's findings to condition people into contentment unite to perpetuate the utilitarian obsession with the chimera known as the Greatest Happiness Principle.

In *Brave New World* one finds precisely the subspecies Huxley's "Preface" to Burns predicts. They are peculiar divisions within the larger categories that make up the novel's caste system. By 1929, Huxley not only had some of the larger conceptions worked out but had gotten round to a number of specifics. The "Preface" actually lists some examples of dysgenic experimentation that are used soon afterward in Huxley's dystopia. Huxley could not have felt unequal to the task of contriving illustrative instances if these had been occurring to him since 1929. The "Preface" may even be summarizing episodes he had already written down, for the material it shares with the novel appears exclusively in Chapter One.

Special subspecies must be bred, the "Preface" forecasts, for undesirable occupations, such as "working in hot climates." Mr. Foster explains in *Brave New World* how this is accomplished. A group of bottle babies undergoes "Heat conditioning." After Metre 170 on Rack 9 of the procreation assembly line, these bottles perform the remainder of their journey to the decanting room "in a kind of tunnel." Hot tunnels alternate with cool ones, but the cool enclosures are "wedded to discomfort in the form of hard X-rays." Accustomed to subterranean conditions, these embryos will have a horror of cold. Their fear predestines them "to emigrate to the tropics, to be miners and acetate silk spinners and steel workers." Foster also points out Rack 10, where "rows of next generation's chemical workers" are being trained to tolerate "lead, caustic soda, tar, chlorine."

A special subspecies is also being created to enjoy working "at high altitudes, in the dark, under great atmospheric pressure." On Rack 3 the containers of embryonic rocket-plane engineers are kept in "constant rotation." This improves their sense of balance. "We slacken off the circulation when they're right way up," Foster explains, "so that they're half starved . . . They learn to associate topsy-turveydom with well-being; in fact, they're only truly happy when they're standing on their heads." Consequently, they will relish the "ticklish job" of "doing repairs on the outside of a rocket in mid air." By 1929 Huxley had already conceived the idea of social predestination, on which the stability of the brave new world is contingent. One of the sharpest points Huxley raises against Burns and hones still further in *Brave New World* is that

education in the future is likely not to be education at all. Instead, as Helvétius surmised, it will be "conditioning," a process of "making people like their inescapable social destiny."

Specially bred subspecies and the idea of community welfare taking precedence over individual development combine to form what Huxley calls a "termite-ideal." The satirical utopian in Huxley joins forces with the zoologist of fiction. The perfect society of the future, Huxley points out, already exists in termite communities of the present. Sounding more and more like the Swiftian economist of "A Modest Proposal," Huxley suggests in his "Preface" that we try not to find this "termite-ideal" revolting because its arrival appears inevitable. Although we believe in freedom and individual rights, Huxley's argument proceeds, such beliefs are "functions of the prevailing economic conditions." In future, our beliefs will be increasingly harder to afford. "As terrestrial conditions become more difficult," Huxley summarizes in a tone now definitely and accurately prophetic, "the welfare of the species, not of the individual, will become the single aim of all political action, all religious idealism, all educational theory and practice." Individuals, Huxley concludes, will be advised to model themselves on the termite. If they decline, it will probably be done for them.

As the Savage leaves the Park Lane Hospital for the Dying, where Linda has just expired, he passes through a queue of 162 Deltas awaiting their *soma* ration. John beholds around him a "nightmare of swarming indistinguishable sameness." The "maggoty" children he has just seen being death-conditioned in the Galloping Senility ward "swarmed defilingly over the mystery of Linda's death." They were "like maggots." The Deltas are "Maggots again, but larger, full grown, they now crawled across his grief and his repentance." John's experience confirms the aerial epiphany the unmindful Lenina and Henry Foster should have had when they flew over a monorail station: the approaches to it are "black with the ant-like pullulation of lower-caste activity." Similarly, the leaf-green Gamma girls and black Semi-Morons they see when shifts change at the Television Corporation at Brentwood resemble "aphides and ants." The brave new world is the termite-ideal in full swing. It would appear that this satirical ideal came first, and then Huxley had the inspiration to amplify its unpleasantness by contrasting it with Shakespeare's notion [in *The Tempest*] of a utopian diversity, a "brave new world" staffed by "many goodly creatures."

By 1929 the resolve to parody Wells had formed in Huxley's mind. Burns's interplanetary conference provided a rehearsal. The specialized subspecies mentioned in the "Preface" and discussed in the preceding paragraphs of this essay are a fact of life in the Selenite community that Cavor discovers beneath the lunar surface in Wells's *The First Men in the Moon* (1901). "The Natural History of the Selenites," Chapter Twenty-Three, discloses that the moon is "a kind of super-anthill." As Cavor transmits back to earth important messages about his discovery, one can designate him the speaker from yet another planet whom the negligent Burns omits.

Dwelling in a series of subterranean galleries, a remarkable community of utilitarian ants contrive the perfect society. Every Selenite, observes Cavor, "is exquisitely adapted to the social need it meets." The Selenites have already begun to implement the future Huxley's "Preface" foresees. Training, education, and surgery fit each ant for the place it is to occupy. No Selenite possesses organs unconnected with his social role. A prospective mathematician, for example, is tutored so that "the mathematical faculties of his brain grow," the rest of him maturing only so far as is necessary to sustain his essential part (limbs shrivel, heart and digestive organs shrink). To perform the "specialized intellectual functions" that Huxley mentions in his "Preface," some Selenites become distended brains, human computers in whom knowledge is stored. The closest equivalent in *Brave New World* are the Alpha-Plus Intellectuals Mr. Foster mentions.

Cavor witnesses young Selenites "confined in jars from which only the fore limbs protruded." Bred for machine-minding, these vital limbs receive normal nourishment, while the rest of the body is practically starved. "Fine work," Cavor reports, "is done by fined-down workers amazingly dwarfed and neat." Chapter Twenty-Three of Wells is clearly the inspiration for the subspecies Huxley's "Preface" envisions being specially bred and educated. It is Helvétius put to worst possible use: instead of turning out another Shakespeare or Mozart, Selenites produce deformed workers who can be drugged and stored until they are required; the brave new world creates rocket repairmen, only content when upside down, and workmen for the tropics, who equate happiness with heat.

As is Wells, Cavor appears to be of two minds about the Selenite utopia. His indecision opens the door for Huxley's parody. Lunar educational methods affect Cavor "disagreeably" with a sense of "lost possibilities." Yet he terms their community a "wonderful social order," "an altogether strange and wonderful world—a world with which our own must now prepare to reckon sooner or later." Cavor even suggests that it is "a far more humane proceeding" to stunt individuals prior to birth than to follow the "earthly method of leaving children to grow into human beings, and then making machines of them." As he scores a blow against industrial England, Cavor expresses Wells's ambiguous feelings. The Selenite system, though definitely inhuman, is remarkably efficient, perhaps even kinder in the long run than Britain's.

Huxley's attitude toward special species is different from Wells's. The examples of experimental breeding in the "Preface" and subsequently in *Brave New World* are absurdly comic, unmistakably outrageous. Those in Wells's utopia, although grotesque, remain disturbingly practical despite the inhumaneness involved. Selenites whose physiologies and personalities are subordinate to their functions guarantee a stability and efficiency beyond Mond's fondest hopes. Cavor's anthill becomes Huxley's termitary. Huxley's parodies draw all the logical attractiveness out of Wells and accentuate the perils for humanity his ambiguous thinking contains. Huxley exposes the irrationality of utilitarian reason taken to its logical extremes. The earthly method of making machines out of full-grown human beings, which Cavor deplores, may even have suggested to

Huxley an attack on the techniques for increasing production devised by Henry Ford. Implicit in the notion of society as a "super-anthill" is the metaphor of society as a factory, which becomes Huxley's satiric image for modern life in *Brave New World.* Never mentioned in the "Preface," Ford could later be installed as one of the archvillains in Huxley's dystopia because his industrial methods and the kind of workers ideally suited to capitalize on them enhance the credibility of the Selenite blueprint for utopia. Recalling the visit he made to America in 1926, Huxley could eventually couple Ford and Wells as men apparently bent on the same perverse errand. When Cavor exclaims that the Selenite community is "an altogether strange and wonderful world," he certainly sounds like Shakespeare's Miranda and Huxley's John Savage. The Selenite machine-minder with the hypertrophied arm, "a perfect unit in a world machine," the young Beta-Minus mechanic . . . busy with screw-driver and spanner on the blood-surrogate pump of a passing bottle," and the assembly-line worker in a Ford factory could all have come out of a common bottle.

To construct a satirical novel of ideas, many thought currents must be made to converge. There is more to a novel of ideas than placing amusing theories in the mouths of its characters. The dreams of Helvétius, the deficiencies of J. H. Burns's views on the future of education, the ambiguities of the scientific enthusiasms in H. G. Wells, and the similarities between a Ford plant and a lunar anthill— here are merely four factors that contributed to a complex process. In the case of *Brave New World,* this process began at least four years prior to the novel's completion.

Huxley's "Preface" to Burns delineates the trends in education that humanitarians should unite against. The long passage from the "Preface" quoted earlier then proceeds to parody instances of these trends already dramatized with some admiration in Wells's *The First Men in the Moon.* Parodying Wells became one way of expressing opposition to tendencies Huxley felt must not prevail. One can therefore suggest that Wells was not solely or primarily responsible for the inception of *Brave New World.* Helvétius' claim is at least as good. The idea of manufacturing individuals to meet precise social needs occurred to Helvétius long before Wells invented the Selenites. Freud's concern with the libido, Bentham's felicific calculus, indeed the utilitarian concept of ethical hedonism, would not have seemed very original to Helvétius. In Huxley's mind, as reflected in the Swiftian "Preface," Wells is used to corroborate certain possibilities that the satirical novelist dislikes. This makes Wells a logical, perhaps an obligatory, target, but not the earliest of inspirations.

Burns's book was negligible because it possessed no awareness of approaching disasters. As the "Preface" undercuts the text it introduces, Huxley taunts modern educators with impending realities they seem unable to prevent. The harmlessness of Burns augmented the threat imposed by Ford, Pavlov, and Wells. Huxley's utopianism began, it is safe to say, with his contempt for the unqualified theoretical and practical visionaries of his day. Neither Wells nor Ford impressed Huxley as philosophers intelligent enough to determine the future. Neither had any sense of what man was made for. This could be seen, Huxley felt, in the way the Selenite community and the Ford factory, two separately conceived manifestations of the coming age, made no satisfactory provision for the "outstanding individual," such as the mind-expanding mystic, who might be the salvation of the race.

Huxley's "Preface" is brief but extraordinary. It gives a concise statement of his views on education and records his anxieties for the future of this vital process. The Swiftian satirist suggests that man's Final End, enrichment and expansion of consciousness, may soon be at odds with "the purpose of the Genius of the Species," or the common good. "Thanks largely to our present wastefulness and extravagance," Huxley laments, the inhuman laws of nature are reasserting themselves. These laws may soon compel "insect-like self-sacrifice to the Genius of the Species." Ironically, the system employed by Mond and the brave new world is *natural:* it is in accord with nature, where the individual ant's or termite's claims are never permitted to overrule the needs of the group. No ant is more important than the anthill. Group needs will soon be met, Huxley prophesied, by mass production, mass culture, mass education. Hence the immodest proposal of a termite-ideal. "Go to the termite, thou individualist"—this, says Huxley, "will be the advice of the wise men" in the future, wizards such as Mustapha Mond and the Grand Lunar; "and to the termite the individualists will duly go."

Comparing modern schools of the 1920s with "child-taming establishments" such as Dotheboys Hall, Huxley concedes that children of his generation are certainly no worse off than the adult products of old-fashioned educational methods. But they soon will be. "Our world," his "Preface" begins, "is a world of humanitarians and individualists." It is rapidly coming to an end. "Luckily," Huxley's "Preface" concludes, his generation can still educate its children to believe in liberty and individual rights. Perhaps they will be among the last to do so. The so-called "Genius of the Species" seems to be unsympathetic toward individual genius. If forced to conform to the mediocre majority, exceptional beings like Helmholtz Watson, a salutary psychological mutation, will be prevented from taking humanity forward. The "Preface" betrays an uncertainty about evolution not as evident in the subsequent novel. In *Brave New World,* the termite-ideal appears to have triumphed, but Watson can discover the Atman within himself and begin to mature spiritually in spite of unfavorable circumstances. Thus, man's evolution toward his Final End, namely a participatory awareness of the Divine Ground, cannot be stopped. Exceptional individuals *are* made, not born (Helvétius was right); but they are self-made, not turned out by society. They will continue to appear. The "Preface" is not so sure about continuing evolution. Heard's influence is not yet at work. Comparing the harbinger "Preface" with the completed *Brave New World* furnishes the earliest indication of the tremendous change Heard was to work on Huxley's thought. By the time he finishes his dystopia, Huxley believes that the "Genius of the Species" need not be ascertained zoologically by analogies with the insect kingdom. Unlike Mond and the Controllers, he prefers to position

that Genius within the soul of the exceptional man and encourages this individual to find Vedanta's version of the Life Force by spirited introspection. The sardonic critic might interject that the Huxley-Heard fascination with genius is dreamier than Helvétius. But the "Preface" cannot manage anything of the kind; it is actually less optimistic than the novel. In 1929 Huxley expects the worst. Four years later, when he looks ahead to A.F. 632, the worst has already happened; but some men refuse artificial contentment; one of them seems strong enough to continue toward the best.

Brave New World does not merely signal the start of a new era, an era of enlightened individuals versus the termite-ideal. It also marks the end of the old one, the period of unchallenged individualism and comfortable humanitarianism. Burns's *Vision,* despite its forward-looking title, belongs to the old era; *Brave New World* anticipates and tries to see beyond the new. (pp. 1-17)

> *Jerome Meckier, "A Neglected Huxley 'Preface': His Earliest Synopsis of 'Brave New World'," in* Twentieth Century Literature, *Vol. 25, No. 1, Spring, 1979, pp. 1-20.*

Edward Lobb   (essay date Summer 1984)

[*In the essay below, Lobb—who considers* Brave New World *to be a meditation on the political and metaphysical dimensions of freedom—examines how plots within the novel undermine the ostensible happiness offered by the utopian state depicted.*]

Aldous Huxley's *Brave New World* (1932) is usually and rightly called a novel, but it is a novel of a problematic type. Satirical in technique, it is torn between the exaggeration peculiar to satire and the realism which is characteristic of the novel. Moreover, as a work in the tradition of utopian and dystopian literature, Huxley's fable walks a line between the overt discussion of ideas, which is normal in the utopian tradition, and the novel's tendency towards more dramatized conflict.

A highly conscious artist and an omnivorous reader, Huxley was well aware of the difficulties involved in writing a work of this type. There were few precedents for the juxtaposition of the novel form, the satiric mode, and the utopian debate (*Erewhon* is one possible example), so Huxley was in territory which was not only dangerous but largely uncharted. It is a measure of his success that *Brave New World* not only overcomes its potentially centrifugal tendencies, but actually uses its various traditions to work out, in subtle fashion, themes which are more directly stated elsewhere in the novel. *Brave New World* is thus—against the odds, and contrary to the opinions of several critics—a work in which form and content are artfully combined.

The themes are stated most overtly in the long dialogue between the World Controller and the Savage which forms the climax of the novel as a utopian debate. Despite the clarity of that dialogue, there has been much confusion about what the themes of *Brave New World* are, and it has been aggravated, unwittingly, by Huxley himself. In 1946,

Huxley wrote a "Foreword" for a new edition of *Brave New World.* He admitted the novel's defects as a work of art and acknowledged the distance between his present self and "the amused, Pyrrhonic aesthete who was the author of the fable," but had decided that the book could not be rewritten: ". . . in the process of rewriting, as an older, other person, I should probably get rid not only of some of the faults of the story, but also of such merits as it originally possessed." Whatever its faults, Huxley insisted, the novel should be read for what it was. "The theme of *Brave New World* is not the advancement of science as such; it is the advancement of science as it affects human individuals. . . . The only scientific advances to be specifically described are those involving the application to human beings of the results of future research in biology, physiology and psychology."

Huxley made this point, one year after Hiroshima, to explain the absence from the novel of phenomena such as atomic energy, which was a theoretical possibility even in 1932. His specifying of "the theme," however, has led to unfortunately narrow interpretations of *Brave New World.* It is generally treated now as a scientific dystopia, a cautionary reply to H. G. Wells's vision of infinite social progress under the aegis of a benevolent caste of scientist-samurai. Although this level of meaning does exist, it is almost entirely overt and requires little comment. The Huxley who adapted the "conversation-novel" of Peacock to the twentieth century knew how to make his points clearly and wittily.

But Huxley was an artist as well as an intellectual; despite his obvious concern with contemporary issues, his novels are never (as Shaw's plays sometimes are) merely vehicles of debate. Thus, while *Brave New World* deals with the effects of science on human beings, its larger theme is the political and metaphysical dimensions of freedom. Critics generally treat the limitation of freedom in the novel in scientific terms, simply because the means of scientific control are so thoroughly and entertainingly described. Nevertheless, to paraphrase Huxley's own foreword, we could say that he is not interested in the limitation of freedom as such, but in the effect of this limitation on human beings. If conditioning and ceaseless propaganda effectively deprive us of freedom, what significance can human actions have? The question is almost absurdly large, but Huxley never shrank from large questions, and his treatment of this one is brilliantly "literary": it explores the issues through the use and parody of literary forms and particular works, and reflects in its own form the problems of free action in the world it depicts.

The best means of approach to Huxley's use of literary forms is Northrop Frye's outline of the four *mythoi* or generic plots. In using this, I am not assuming the correctness of Frye's system as a whole, but employing a system of classification which seems uncontroversial in itself and peculiarly well suited to discussion of *Brave New World.* Frye sees all literature as a large circle which is divided in half horizontally: "The top half of the natural cycle is the world of romance and the analogy of innocence; the lower half is the world of 'realism' and the analogy of experience. There are thus four main types of mythical

movement: within romance, within experience, down, and up. The downward movement is the tragic movement, the wheel of fortune falling from innocence toward hamartia and from hamartia to catastrophe. The upward movement is the comic movement, from threatening complications to a happy ending and a general assumption of post-dated innocence in which everyone lives happily ever after" [Northrop Frye, *Anatomy of Criticism: Four Essays,* 1957]. It is important to note that only two of the *mythoi* involve change. Within the world of "romance," of the ideal, change is unnecessary; within the world of "irony," it is impossible. These two realms, modeled on heaven and hell, are immutable. Normal human life, which occupies the middle ground, can move in either direction and issue in comedy or tragedy.

Huxley involves all four *mythoi* in portraying the world of A. F. 632, which presents itself as "romance." It is, in its own terms, idyllic—a realm of static, perfected social forms. In the reader's terms, on the other hand, the World State is a parody of romance; it is changeless but infernal, the nightmare world of what Frye calls irony. This antithesis not only emphasizes the contrast between what the World State claims to be and what it is, but also reinforces the theme of freedom, for the protagonist of ironic narrative (*The Trial,* for example) is defined by his lack of freedom. "If inferior in power or intelligence to ourselves, so that we have the sense of looking down on a scene of bondage, frustration, or absurdity, the hero belongs to the *ironic* mode. This is still true when the reader feels that he is or might be in the same situation, as the situation is being judged by the norms of a greater freedom" (Frye). The inhabitants of the World State and the Savage who serves as the novel's protagonist display different sorts of bondage.

But Huxley is not content to present us with a romantic fiction and an ironic reality. Much of the latter part of *Brave New World* involves burlesques of the other two *mythoi,* those of tragedy and comedy. It is easy to see why. Comedy and tragedy are both social in focus: one deals with the reconciliation of individual desire and social good, the other with their sundering and conflict, and both take for granted the freedom to make choices. It is fitting, therefore, that a novel about freedom and society should show us the fate of tragedy and comedy in a world which denies individual freedom.

Let us begin with tragedy. The Savage, also known as John Savage, comes to the heart of the World State from the New Mexico Reservation, and is appalled by everything he sees. His "pity and fear" suggest that he is witnessing a tragedy, and despite his ignorance of critical terminology (he argues from Shakespeare, not Aristotle) he suggests that the narcotized efficiency of A. F. 632 is tragic in implication:

> "Do you remember that bit in *King Lear?*" said the Savage at last. " 'The gods are just and of our pleasant vices make instruments to plague us; the dark and vicious place where thee he got cost him his eyes,' and Edmund answers—you remember, he's wounded, he's dying—'Thou hast spoken right; 'tis true. The wheel has come full circle; I am here.' What about that now? Doesn't

there seem to be a God managing things, punishing, rewarding?"

"Well, does there?" questioned the Controller in his turn. " . . . 'The wheel has come full circle; I am here.' But where would Edmund be nowadays? Sitting in a pneumatic chair, with his arm round a girl's waist, sucking away at his sex-hormone chewing-gum and looking at the feelies. The gods are just. No doubt. But their code of law is dictated, in the last resort, by the people who organize society; Providence takes its cue from men."

"Are you sure?" asked the Savage. "Are you quite sure that the Edmund in that pneumatic chair hasn't been just as heavily punished as the Edmund who's wounded and bleeding to death? The gods are just. Haven't they used his pleasant vices as an instrument to degrade him?"

This is a good point, but a bad definition of tragedy. Without conflict and isolation there can be no tragedy, and the World Controller makes this point in questioning the idea of "degradation." A properly organized society simply precludes tragedy; nobility and heroism are useless gestures or "symptoms of political inefficiency." The words of Shakespeare and other old writers are banned in the World State, presumably because, like nature, they encourage contemplation rather than consumption. But, as the World Controller points out, they are virtually incomprehensible anyway.

If the postulates of the World State make tragedy impossible for its inhabitants, there remains the possibility that the encounter of the Savage and the State has tragic potential. The plot of **Brave New World** in fact includes most of the elements of classical and Shakespearean tragedy: conflict, isolation, the reestablishment of order at the cost of the protagonist's life. There is a doomed romance (that of the Savage and Lenina Crowne) and, as I shall show later, a whole host of allusions to situations in Shakespeare's plays, as well as the direct quotations which make up a large part of the Savage's speech.

But the Savage's tragic potential is subverted, for reasons which he himself has unwittingly made clear. When Edmund says "The wheel has come full circle; I am here," he makes his tragedy comprehensible: his end is plausibly related to his own actions and to a cosmology. But the Savage can make no such connections, nor can we. His actions are innocent, unrelated to his fate, and the forces which drive him to madness and suicide are arbitrary, not inevitable. His "enlightenment" is of a wholly negative and destructive kind. What undoes the Savage is not his introduction to alien values, which he could reject or assimilate in altered forms, but the vision of a society without real values of any kind. Huxley's undercutting of the tragic vision is not meant to deny the values of Shakespeare's world, but to increase our horror at their irrelevance in the "scientific" world order of the future.

The supplanting of the tragic by the ironic—of the intelligible by the absurd—is underlined by the discussion of *Othello* in Chapter XVI. The World Controller attempts to explain why literature in general and tragedy in particular are dead letters: " 'Because our world is not the same as Othello's world. You can't make flivvers without steel—and you can't make tragedies without social instability. The world's stable now. People are happy; they get what they want, and they never want what they can't get. . . . ' The Savage was silent for a little. 'All the same,' he insisted obstinately, '*Othello*'s good, *Othello*'s better than those feelies.' 'Of course it is,' the Controller agreed. 'But that's the price we have to pay for stability. You've got to choose between happiness and high art. We've sacrificed the high art.' " But the novel has in fact provided its own version of *Othello* five chapters earlier in the "feely" film *Three Weeks in a Helicopter*. It is the story of "a gigantic Negro and a golden-haired young brachycephalic Beta-Plus female" whose affair goes awry when the man has a helicopter accident and falls on his head:

> The concussion knocked all the Negro's conditioning into a cocked hat. He developed for the Beta blonde an exclusive and maniacal passion. She protested. He persisted. There were struggles, pursuits, an assault on a rival, finally a sensational kidnapping. The Beta blonde was ravished away into the sky and kept there, hovering, for three weeks in a wildly anti-social *tête-à-tête* with the black madman. Finally, after a whole series of adventures and much aerial acrobacy three handsome young Alphas succeeded in rescuing her. The Negro was packed off to an Adult Re-Conditioning Centre and the film ended happily and decorously, with the Beta blonde becoming the mistress of all her three rescuers.

Still earlier, Bernard Marx has stopped his helicopter over the English Channel at night and attempted, unsuccessfully, to interest Lenina Crowne in the beauties of nature. Lenina and the Beta-Plus blonde are thoroughly modern, unromantic, and hedonistic; Bernard and "the black madman" are absurd figures whose anachronistic values mock Othello's (and the Savage's) tragic earnestness.

Another tragedy of passion, *Romeo and Juliet,* is travestied in the relationship of the Savage and Lenina Crowne. They are truly the representatives of different worlds, but their affair, if they were to have one, would be a matter of no importance to either family, since there are no families. The Savage's Elizabethan courting is laughably out of place, and creates, as George Woodcock has noted [in his *Dawn and the Darkest Hour: A Study of Aldous Huxley,* 1972], "an extraordinarily comic scene of crossed purposes, in which the Savage declares his love in resounding Shakespearean terms, whereupon Lenina, reacting in the only way she knows, unzips her garment and advances upon him in all her pneumatic nakedness, and the Savage, shouting Elizabethan curses, drives her from him."

If the potential for tragedy is systematically reduced to farce, the possibility of true comedy is similarly undercut, for comedy no less than tragedy issues in enlightenment. A familiar pattern in Shakespearean comedy is that of the journey from city or court to a strange and freer world, often associated with dream and magic, and a journey back which results in the reconciliation of reason and imagination, law and love, etc. The most obvious example is *A Midsummer Night's Dream*, but *As You Like It, The*

Winter's Tale, and *The Tempest* take the same form. In **Brave New World** these journeys are entirely fruitless. Bernard and Lenina travel to the New Mexico Reservation as tourists, but Lenina is disgusted by everything she sees, and Bernard, despite his attraction to some of the features of Indian life, remains one of Huxley's contemptible intellectuals, incapable of changing his dishonest life in any real way. The opposite journey, that of the Savage to the heart of the World State, results in "enlightenment" of only the bitterest sort, as we have seen.

The Shakespearean comedy which Huxley alludes to more often than any other, directly and indirectly, is *The Tempest.* It is quoted at least ten times, usually in contexts which make use only of a line's immediate meaning. The Savage's echoing of Miranda's words, which give the novel its title, are typical of Huxley's occasionally heavy-handed irony:

> How many goodly creatures are there here!
> How beauteous mankind is! O brave new world
> That has such people in't!

But *The Tempest* has a more complex function in **Brave New World.** As a play, it shows us a genuine near-utopia—one which works by education, not conditioning—and thereby underlines the inadequacies of the World State. Huxley also develops a series of parallels between **Brave New World** and *The Tempest* which emphasizes the difference between comic growth in Shakespeare and the immobility of the characters in Huxley's novel.

In *The Tempest,* we learn that Prospero's Island was once the home of Sycorax, a witch. Abandoned on the island by sailors, she gave birth to Caliban, the "natural man" haunted by dreams of beauty. In **Brave New World,** the Savage's mother is Linda, a Beta-Minus from the World State who was left behind on the New Mexico Reservation during a storm—a tempest. On the reservation she gave birth to John, the "natural man" of Huxley's fable, who is troubled by dreams of beauty inspired in large part by Shakespeare himself. Caliban is governed by appetite, superstition, and credulity; after drinking Stephano's liquor, he offers to worship Stephano as a god. The Savage keeps his appetites strictly under control, but his syncretistic religion is superstitious and barbarous, little better than a nature-cult which demands ritual punishment and sacrificial victims. These parallels underline the fact that the Savage, like Caliban, is incapable of change, and cannot therefore undergo the redemptive trials of a Ferdinand. He can only rail at the rulers of a world he does not understand, and attempt to overturn them. In *The Tempest,* Caliban, Stephano, and Trinculo plot against Prospero; in **Brave New World,** the Savage throws boxes of *soma* tablets out the window. Neither rebellion constitutes the slightest threat to the established order.

We balk, of course, at the implied identification of the Savage with the brute Caliban. For all his limited understanding, the Savage is concerned with moral values and strikes most readers as the most sympathetic character in the novel—in part, of course, because of the "noble savage" tradition which Huxley also invokes. But in either capacity, as brutish victim or noble savage, he is a static figure incapable of comic or tragic growth, and this is part of

Huxley's ironic design. There is no point of contact between the Savage and the society he is at odds with, and therefore no point from which comic reconciliation or tragic conflict might begin. As a result, the Savage's encounter with the World State is not a tragedy but a farce of mutual incomprehension. The *dynamis* of drama has been replaced by the stasis of irony, the frozen world of Frye's winter *mythos.*

A similar conflation of roles can be seen in the portrayal of Mustapha Mond, the World Controller. In the system of ironic allusions to *The Tempest,* the World Controller is Prospero, but he is a Prospero who is not interested in effecting a "sea-change" in anyone's life. His sole object is to keep things exactly as they are; he has broken his wand—his free-ranging intelligence—in the interest of the higher social good. As he explains to Helmholtz Watson, " 'Happiness has got to be paid for. You're paying for it, Mr. Watson—paying because you happen to be too much interested in beauty. I was too much interested in truth; I paid too.' 'But *you* didn't go to an island,' said the Savage, breaking a long silence. The Controller smiled. 'That's how I paid. By choosing to serve happiness. Other people's—not mine.' " In *The Tempest,* Antonio took advantage of Prospero's absorption in his studies to usurp his position as Duke of Milan, an implied warning to intellectuals of the danger of ivory-tower attitudes. In **Brave New World,** the *trahison des clercs* is complete: not only does Mond reject the modern equivalent of Prospero's island (one of the few places where free intellectual inquiry is still allowed), but chooses instead to serve the new order and perfect its "happiness."

If Mond is a demonic travesty of Prospero, he is almost a mirror-image of that earlier World-Controller, the Grand Inquisitor in *The Brothers Karamazov,* who promises to relieve men of the burden of freedom. At the conclusion of **Brave New World Revisited** (1958), Huxley cited the essence of Dostoevsky's parable: " 'in the end,' says the Grand Inquisitor . . . 'in the end they will lay their freedom at our feet and say to us, "make us your slaves, but feed us." ' " And when Alyosha Karamazov asks his brother, the teller of the story, if the Grand Inquisitor is speaking ironically, Ivan answers " 'Not a bit of it! He claims it as a merit for himself and his Church that they have vanquished freedom and done so to make men happy.' " The meaning of this in the novel is clear. Change and growth are possible only with freedom, which can result in comedy or tragedy. A society which is "perfect," and which denies the need for growth and change, is frozen in the logic of its own assumptions and doomed to the stasis of incomprehension and irony. It is therefore our responsibility, paradoxically, to avoid utopia. The epigraph to **Brave New World,** a passage from Berdayev, sums up the problem: "La vie marche vers les utopies. Et peut-être un siècle nouveau commence-t-il, un siècle ou les intellectuels et la classe cultivée rêveront aux moyens d'éviter les utopies et de retourner à une société non utopique, moins 'parfaite' et plus libre."

To summarize: Huxley's theme, the meaning of freedom, is developed not only through the final debate between the Savage and Mustapha Mond, but also through the structure of **Brave New World,** which is not a moving picture but a series of frozen tableaux. The "stability" of the World State is ironically reflected in the immobility of the novel and the failure of its plot to resolve itself meaningfully. Its deliberate burlesque of the more active plots of tragedy and comedy further emphasizes the lack of freedom and the death of tragedy, the death of meaning itself, which results from it.

For all the seriousness of its theme, however, **Brave New World** remains a remarkably lighthearted book. Huxley's talents as wit and farceur are everywhere in evidence, for he was less concerned with the prophetic aspects of his fable than with its depiction of mental attitudes. The masters of the World State are enthusiasts in the old sense—zealots possessed by a single idea. As such they are the legitimate descendants of the projectors in *Gulliver's Travels* and part of a particular tradition of intellectual satire to which Huxley contributed throughout his writing career. **Brave New World** is best read as Menippean satire, in which evil and folly are seen not as social or moral problems but as diseases of the intellect, "as a kind of maddened pedantry which the *philosophus gloriosus* at once symbolizes and defines" [Frye]. It is satire of this kind, in fact, which ties together the various literary elements (prose narrative, utopian debate, parody, burlesque, etc.) which make up Huxley's novel, and which suggests the possibility of a generic approach to it. It is therefore peculiarly fitting that the last act of Huxley's novel should allude to the most satirical of Shakespeare's tragedies, *Timon of Athens.*

Disgusted by the amorality of London, the Savage retreats to an old "air-lighthouse" near Puttenham in Surrey, much as Timon withdraws from Athens after cursing its inhabitants. The "air-lighthouse" itself seems a deliberate recollection of Timon's hermitage,

> His everlasting mansion
> Upon the beachèd verge of the salt flood,
> Who once a day with his embossèd froth
> The turbulent surge shall cover

Just before this, his last speech, Timon has promised to help the Athenians avoid the wrath of Alcibiades. The senators are encouraged, but Timon's solution is brutally cynical:

> Tell my friends,
> Tell Athens, in the sequence of degree
> From high to low throughout, that whoso please
> To stop affliction, let him take his haste,
> Come hither ere my tree hath felt the axe—
> And hang himself!

The Savage has read his Shakespeare well, and has earlier thought of a line from *Timon.* He hangs himself in the lighthouse—an abandoned beacon—and the discovery of his death concludes **Brave New World,** not with a sounding curtain speech but with scientific detachment: "Slowly, very slowly, like two unhurried compass needles, the feet turned towards the right; north, north-east, east, south-east, south-south-west; then paused, and, after a few seconds, turned as unhurriedly back towards the left. South-south-west, south, south-east, east. . . ." Even in death, the Savage is pursued by ironies: the inability of his

compass-needle feet to find true north is the final "amused, Pyrrhonic" comment of Aldous Huxley on the fortunes of his unenlightened hero. (pp. 94-101)

> *Edward Lobb, "The Subversion of Drama in Huxley's 'Brave New World',"* in The International Fiction Review, *Vol. 11, No. 2, Summer, 1984, pp. 94-101.*

Peter Edgerly Firchow   (essay date 1984)

[*An American educator and critic, Firchow is the author of* Aldous Huxley: Satirist and Novelist *(1972) and* The End of Utopia: A Study of Aldous Huxley's "Brave New World." *In the following excerpt from the latter work, he examines narrative technique, literary allusions, and characterization in* Brave New World, *which he considers a modernist novel.*]

If there are plenty of good scientific and technological reasons—ectogenesis, cloning, serial mass production, TV—why **Brave New World** could not have been written before it was, there are also some very good literary reasons. For **Brave New World** is, literarily speaking, a very modern book; modern not only because it deals frankly with a typically "modern" subject like sex, but modern in the very ways it conceives of and presents its subject and characters.

There are in **Brave New World** no long introductory descriptions of landscape or environment in the Victorian or Edwardian manner; there is, initially, no attempt to give more than a very rudimentary outline of the physical and psychological traits of the characters. There is no elaborate explanation of how we came to be where we are, nor even at first an explanation at all why we are where we are: six-hundred-odd years in the future. The starting assumption is simply that it is quite normal to be in a big factory in the middle of London. Only gradually and indirectly does that assumption also become startling, as it becomes clear to us what the products of this factory are and what kind of a world we have entered.

This technique of indirection is one that Virginia Woolf ascribes, in *Mr. Bennett and Mrs. Brown* (1924), to the moderns. For her—and by extension for the modern novelist—the way to get at the heart of a character and a situation is not to add up every item of information we can gather about them; the whole is not to be found in the summing up of all of the parts. That way lies dullness—and Arnold Bennett. The better way is to try to get at the whole by being, as it were, paradoxically content with the part. To get at the essence of Mrs. Brown—Woolf's hypothetical example—we need to be told nothing directly of her history and background; we merely need to overhear her conversation in a railway compartment for an hour or so. Out of the apparently random odds and ends of this conversation, we can, by an act of the imagination, reconstruct her life and penetrate her soul.

What happens when a modern novelist resolves to transfer a Mrs. Brown or any other person into a work of fiction is that, inevitably, the author himself more or less disappears; the reader is left alone, seemingly at least, with the character(s). The modern novel therefore involves a shift of responsibility for character and situation away from the author and toward the reader, who must reach his conclusions about both "unaided." This is clearly what happens in Virginia Woolf's own novels, or in the novels of other modern writers like Waugh, Bowen, Isherwood—and Huxley.

This is not to say that Huxley or Isherwood or anyone else read Woolf and then decided to write a new kind of novel. Woolf is merely, as she knew full well herself, making explicit theoretically a conclusion that she had noted in practice for some years, in Joyce and others. Huxley himself had employed this new and modern manner from the very outset of his career in stories like **"The Farcical History of Richard Greenow"** (1918) and novels like *Crome Yellow* (1921).

The first three chapters of *Brave New World,* especially, are masterfully composed in the indirect manner. Very little is heard; almost everything is overheard. To this manner Huxley also adds a refinement of his own devising, a technique perhaps best called "counterpoint," since Huxley had used it most fully before in *Point Counter Point* (1929), though there are intimations of it as early as *Those Barren Leaves* (1925). This technique involves a simultaneous juxtaposition of different elements of the narrative, much as musical counterpoint means sounding different notes simultaneously with a *cantus firmus.* The result in music is—or should be—a complex harmony; in Huxley's fiction the result is, usually, a complex dissonance, a subtle and often brilliant cacophony of ironies. The third chapter of *Brave New World* is set up entirely in this kind of counterpoint, gathering together the various narrative strains of the first two chapters and juxtaposing them without any editorial comment, slowly at first and then with gathering momentum, climaxing in a crescendo that fuses snatches of Mond's lecture, Lenina's conversation with Fanny, Henry Foster's with Benito Hoover, Bernard Marx's resentful thoughts, and bits of hypnopaedic wisdom.

The result is astonishing and far more effective in drawing us into the noisy and frantically joyless atmosphere of the new world state than pages of descriptive writing would have been. It is one of the most remarkable pieces of writing in the modern British novel.

Brave New World is modern, too, in another literary respect. It is shot through with literary allusions. Most of these allusions—such as the title and much of the conversation of the Savage—are to Shakespeare, but there are also more or less direct or indirect allusions to Shaw, Wells, T. S. Eliot, D. H. Lawrence, Voltaire, Rousseau, Thomas Gray, and Dante. The point of these allusions is not, I think, to show how clever and sophisticated and knowledgeable a writer Aldous Huxley is; the point is, rather, as in the poetry of T. S. Eliot—or Huxley's own poetry, for that matter—to reveal ironically the inadequacies of the present (or the present as contained in the future) by comparing it with the past. This is primarily how the literary allusions function in *The Waste Land* or in "Whispers of Immortality"—from which Huxley derives Lenina's peculiarly pneumatic sexuality—and that is also how they function primarily in *Brave New World.* The

juxtaposition of Cleopatra with a bored modern woman who has nothing to do or of Spenser's and Goldsmith's lovers with the dreary amorous adventures of a modern secretary serves the same purpose as the juxtaposition of the love of Othello and Desdemona with that of the hero and heroine of the "feely" "Three Weeks in a Helicopter," or even the love of Romeo and Juliet with that of Lenina and the Savage. The effect in both cases is that of a literary double exposure, which provides a simultaneous view of two quite distinct and yet horribly similar realities. The tension between the two—that which pulls them violently apart and at the same time pushes them violently together—produces a powerful irony, which is just what Eliot and Huxley want to produce. By means of this irony it then becomes possible for Huxley, or the "narrator" of his novel, to guide the reader's response without seeming to do so, without requiring any overt interference on his part. By merely hinting, for example, at the analogy between the Fordian state and Prospero's island, Huxley manages to convey ironically a disapproval of that state without ever having to voice it himself. And he can safely leave it to the reader to make the rest of the ironic identification; Mond is Prospero; Lenina is Miranda; the Savage is Ferdinand; Bernard Marx is Caliban. Or, if one prefers, Mond is a kind of Prospero and Alonso combined; the Savage, as befits his name, is Caliban, and his mother, Linda, is Sycorax; Lenina is a perverse Miranda and Bernard a strange Ferdinand. Or, to give another twist to it, the Director of Hatcheries and Conditioning is a kind of Alonso who abandoned Linda and John to the desert; they in turn are, respectively, Prospero and Miranda, with their sexes reversed; the Indians and especially Popé are a kind of collective Caliban; Lenina, the aggressive lover, is a female Ferdinand, and Bernard a sort of rescuing Ariel. The same kind of ironic game can be played with *Romeo and Juliet* and *Othello.* In this way the ironies multiply until they become mind-boggling.

This is not to say that there is no direct narrative guidance in Huxley's novel. The reader is explicitly told, for example, that mental excess has produced in Helmholtz Watson's character the same results as a physical defect has in Bernard Marx. Or Bernard's psyche is analyzed for us in terms of an inferiority complex that finds its chief victims in his friends rather than his enemies. These are all acts of narrative interference and by no means isolated ones, but even so they are kept in the background and are, generally speaking, confined to attempts to make the psychological functioning of the characters more comprehensible.

Brave New World is a novel that is very carefully planned and put together. As Donald Watt has recently shown in his study [in *Journal of English and Germanic Philology* 77 (July 1978)] of Huxley's revisions in the typescript of *Brave New World,* a number of the best stylistic effects and one of the best scenes—the soma distribution riot— were afterthoughts, inserted by Huxley after he had finished the rest of the novel. This is not unusual for Huxley, who always revised his work thoroughly and in the process often came up with some of his best ideas. Just when Huxley started work on the novel is, however, not clear, though it is certain that the novel was finished, except for a few final touches, by the end of August 1931. *Brave New World* is first mentioned, though not by name, in Huxley's correspondence on May 18, 1931, and about a week later he wrote to his brother, Julian, that "all I've been writing during the last month won't do and I must re-write in quite another way." This clearly means that Huxley must have started the novel no later than the end of April or the beginning of May 1931. There is, however, some evidence to suggest that he may have been planning and perhaps even writing *Brave New World* as early as the latter part of 1930. For in an essay published in January 1931, entitled **"Boundaries of Utopia,"** Huxley describes a future world that in general—and in some striking details—anticipates the new world state. "Served by mechanical domestics," Huxley writes in this essay,

> exploiting the incessant labour of mechanical slaves, the three-hundred-a-year men of the future state will enjoy an almost indefinite leisure. A system of transport, rapid, frequent and cheap [taxicopters and passenger rockets], will enable him to move about the globe more freely than the emigrant *rentier* of the present age. . . . The theatres in which the egalitarians will enjoy the talkies, tasties, smellies, and feelies, the Corner Houses where they will eat their synthetic poached eggs on toast-substitute and drink their substitutes of coffee, will be prodigiously much vaster and more splendid than anything we know today.

Huxley concludes the essay by asserting that continuous progress is possible only on condition that the size of the population be limited and genetically improved.

The focus on leisure, rapid transport, amusements, synthetic substitutes, and genetic improvements in humans all suggest close links with *Brave New World,* so close indeed that it is difficult to believe that the novel was not already germinating in Huxley's mind and perhaps even on his typewriter. If this is true, then Huxley spent the better part of a year—nine or ten months—writing and rewriting *Brave New World.* If it is not true, then Huxley must have planned and written the novel in the astonishingly short time of a little less than four months. In either case, it is a remarkable achievement in a remarkably short time, though it should be remembered that utopian and anti-utopian ideas had been floating through Huxley's mind and popping up occasionally in his fiction since as early as 1921. However short a time the actual writing may have taken, there were clearly years of general preparation and preliminary thought that went into the novel.

One of the chief problems Huxley had with *Brave New World,* according to Donald Watt, was with the characters. On the evidence of the revisions, Watt concludes that Huxley seems first to have thought of making Bernard Marx the rebellious hero of the novel but then changed his mind and deliberately played him down into a kind of anti-hero. After rejecting the possibility of a heroic Bernard, Huxley next seems to have turned to the Savage as an alternative. According to Watt, there are in the typescript several indications, later revised or omitted, of the Savage's putting up or at least planning to put up violent resistance to the new world state, perhaps even of leading

a kind of revolution against it. But in the process of rewriting the novel, Huxley also abandoned this idea in favor of having no hero at all, or of having only the vague adumbration of a hero in Helmholtz Watson.

Watt's analysis of the revisions in *Brave New World* is very helpful and interesting; he shows convincingly, I think, that Huxley was unable to make up his mind until very late in the composition of the novel just what direction he wanted the story and the leading male characters to take. From this uncertainty, however, I do not think it necessary to leap to the further conclusion that Huxley had difficulty in creating these characters themselves. Huxley's supposedly inadequate ability to create living characters, the result of his not being a "congenital novelist," is a question that often arises in discussions of his fiction, and in connection with longer and more traditionally novelistic novels like *Point Counter Point* or *Eyeless in Gaza* (1936) appropriately so. But *Brave New World* is anything but a traditional novel in this sense. It is not a novel of character but a relatively short satirical tale, a "fable," much like Voltaire's *Candide.* One hardly demands fully developed and "round" characters of *Candide,* nor should one of *Brave New World.*

This is all the more the case because the very nature of the new world state precludes the existence of fully developed characters. Juliets and Anna Kareninas, or Hamlets and Prince Vronskys, are by definition impossibilities in the new world state. To ask for them is to ask for a different world, the very world whose absence Huxley's novel so savagely laments. Character, after all, is shaped by suffering, and the new world state has abolished suffering in favor of a continuous, soma-stupefied, infantile "happiness." In such an environment it is difficult to have characters who grow and develop and are "alive."

Despite all this, it is surprising and noteworthy how vivid and even varied Huxley's characters are. With all their uniformly standardized conditioning, Alphas and Betas turn out to be by no means alike: the ambitious "go-getter" Henry Foster is different from his easy-going friend Benito Hoover; the unconventional and more "pneumatic" Lenina Crowne from the moralistic and rather less pneumatic Fanny Crowne; the resentful and ugly Bernard Marx from the handsome and intelligent Helmholtz Watson. Huxley, in fact, seems to work consistently and consciously in terms of contrastive/complementary pairs to suggest various possibilities of response to similar situations. So, too, Helmholtz and the Savage are another pair, as are the Savage and Mond, Mond and the DHC, Bernard and Henry Foster. The most fully developed instance of this pairing or doubling technique is the trip that Bernard and Lenina make to the Indian reservation, a trip that duplicates the one made some years earlier by the DHC and a "particularly pneumatic" Beta-Minus named Linda. Like the DHC, Bernard also leaves Lenina, another pneumatic Beta, (briefly) behind while returning to civilization, and during this interval she, too, is lusted after by a savage, much as Popé and the other Indians lust after Linda. Even the novel as a whole reveals a similar sort of doubling structure, with the new world state on the one hand and the Indian reservation on the other.

Within limits, the characters, even some of the minor and superficial characters like Henry Foster, are capable of revealing other and deeper facets of their personality. Returning with Lenina from the Stoke Poges Obstacle Golf Course, Henry Foster's helicopter suddenly shoots upward on a column of hot air rising from the Slough Crematorium. Lenina is delighted at this brief switchback, but "Henry's tone was almost, for a moment, melancholy. 'Do you know what that switchback was?' he said. 'It was some human being finally and definitely disappearing. Going up in a squirt of hot gas. It would be curious to know who it was—a man or a woman, an Alpha or an Epsilon. . . . '" Henry quickly jolts himself out of this atypical mood and reverts to his normally obnoxious cheerfulness, but for an instant at least there was a glimpse of a real human being.

Much more than Henry, Bernard Marx and Helmholtz Watson are capable of complexity of response. The latter especially and partly through his contact with the Savage grows increasingly aware of himself as a separate human entity and of his dissatisfaction with the kind of life he had led hitherto. As an Emotional Engineer and contriver of slogans, Helmholtz has been very successful, as he also has been in the capacities of lover and sportsman; but he despises this success and seeks for a satisfaction for which he has no name and which he can only dimly conceive. He comes closest to expressing it in the poem that eventually leads to his exile, the poem in which an ideal and absent woman becomes more real to him—in the manner of Mallarmé's flower that is absent from all bouquets—than any woman he has ever actually met.

In the end Helmholtz agrees to being sent into frigid exile in the Falkland Islands. The reason he chooses such a place rather than possible alternatives like Samoa or the Marquesas is because there he will not only have solitude but also a harsh climate in which to suffer and to gain new and very different experiences. His aim, however, is not, as some critics have suggested, to seek mystic experience; he simply wants to learn how to write better poetry. "I should like a thoroughly bad climate," he tells Mustapha Mond. "I believe one would write better if the climate were bad. If there were a lot of wind and storms for example. . . . " This hardly represents a search for mysticism and God; in this novel only the Savage, and he in only a very qualified way, can be described as seeking after such ends. Helmholtz merely wants more and better words. In the context of Huxley's work, he harks back to a character like Denis Stone in *Crome Yellow,* not forward to the pacifist Anthony Beavis in *Eyeless in Gaza* or in the inner-directed Propter in *After Many a Summer* (1939).

The same is true of Bernard Marx. Despite the apparent fact that Huxley once had more exalted intentions for him, Bernard belongs very much to the familiar Huxleyan category of the anti-hero, best exemplified perhaps by Theodore Gumbril, Jr., the so-called Complete Man of *Antic Hay* (1923). Like Gumbril, Bernard is able to envision and even seek after a love that is not merely sexual, but, like Gumbril again, his search is half-hearted. He is willing to

settle for less because it is so much easier than trying to strive for more. Bernard is weak and cowardly and vain, much more so than Gumbril, and this makes him an unsympathetic character in a way that Gumbril is not. Nevertheless Bernard is undoubtedly capable of seeing the better, even if in the end he follows the worse.

Bernard is certainly a more fully developed character than Helmholtz; he is, in fact, with the exception of the Savage, the character about whom we know most in the entire novel. Just why this should be so is a question worth asking, just as it is worth asking why Bernard is the first of the novel's three malcontents to be brought to our attention.

Bernard's importance resides, I think, in his incapacity. The stability of the new world state can be threatened, it is clear, from above and from below. In the case of Helmholtz the threat is from above, from a surfeit of capacity; in Bernard's case it is from below, from a lack of sufficient capacity. This is not simply to say that Bernard is more stupid than Helmholtz, which he probably is, but rather that because of his physical inferiority he has developed a compulsive need to assert his superiority. It is this incapacity which, paradoxically, seems to make Bernard the more dangerous threat, for it compels him to rise to a position of power in his society; he wants to be accepted by his society, but only on his own terms, terms that are not acceptable in the long run if stability is to be maintained. Helmholtz, on the other hand, is a loner who really wants to have nothing to do with the society at all, and in this sense he represents much less of a threat. The Savage, on the other hand, though most violent and uncompromising in his hatred of and desire to destroy the new world state, is really no threat at all, for he originates from outside the society and is a kind of *lusus naturae.* There is never likely to be another Savage, but it is very probable that there will be or that there are more Bernards and Helmholtzes.

Both Bernard and Helmholtz are fairly complex characters. What is surprising, however, is that the same is true of Lenina Crowne. She seems at first to be nothing more than a pretty and addle-brained young woman without any emotional depth whatever. And at first it is true that this is all she is; but she changes in the course of the novel into something quite different. She changes because she falls in love.

The great irony of Lenina's falling in love is that she does not realize what it is that has happened to her; like Helmholtz she has no name for the new feeling and hence no way of conceiving or understanding what it is. She can only think of love in the physiological ways in which she has been conditioned to think of it; but her feeling is different.

So subtle is Huxley's portrayal of the change in Lenina that, as far as I know, no critic has ever commented on it. Yet Lenina is clearly predisposed from the very beginning to a love relationship that is not sanctioned by her society. As we learn from her conversation with Fanny, Lenina has been going with Henry Foster for four months without having had another man, and this in defiance of what she knows to be the properly promiscuous code of sexual behavior. When Fanny takes her up on this point of unconventionality, Lenina reacts almost truculently and replies that she "jolly well [does not] see why there should have been" anyone other than Henry. Her inability to see this error in her sexual ways is what predisposes her for the much greater and more intense feeling that she develops for the Savage.

The stages of her growing love for the Savage and her increasing mystification at what is happening within herself are handled with a brilliantly comic touch. There is the scene following Lenina's and the Savage's return from the feelies when the Savage sends her off in the taxicopter just as she is getting ready to seduce him. There is the touching moment when Lenina, who had once been terrified of pausing with Bernard to look at the sea and the moon over the Channel, now lingers "for a moment to look at the moon," before being summoned by an irritated and uncomprehending Arch-Songster. There is Lenina's increasing impatience with the obtuseness of Henry Foster and his blundering solicitousness. There are the fond murmurings to herself of the Savage's name. There is the conference with Fanny as to what she should do about the Savage's strange coldness toward her. There is her blunt rejection of Fanny's advice to seek consolation with one of the millions of other men. There is the wonderful scene in which she seeks out the Savage alone in his apartment, discovers to her amazement that he loves her, sheds her clothing, and receives, to her even greater amazement, insults, blows, and a threat to kill. There is the final terrible scene at the lighthouse when Lenina steps out of the helicopter, looks at the Savage with "an uncertain, imploring, almost abject smile," and then "pressed both hands to her left side [i.e., to her heart], and on that peach-bright, doll-beautiful face of hers appeared a strangely incongruous expression of yearning distress. Her blue eyes seemed to grow larger, brighter; and suddenly two tears rolled down her cheeks." Again the Savage attacks her, this time with his whip, maddened by desire, by remorse, and by the horde of obscenely curious sightseers. In the end, however, desire triumphs and the Savage and Lenina consummate their love in an orgy-porgian climax. When the Savage awakens to the memory of what has happened, he knows he cannot live with such defilement. For him the end is swift and tragic. For Lenina, however, there is no end; her tragedy—and for all the comedy and irony in which her love for the Savage is immersed, the word *tragedy* is not entirely inappropriate—her tragedy is that she has felt an emotion that she can never express or communicate or realize again.

The characters of *Brave New World,* it is safe to conclude, are not merely made of cardboard and *papier-mâché.* That they are nonetheless not full and complete human beings is quite true; but for all the technology and conditioning and impulses toward uniformity, there is still something profoundly human about them. As Lenina's development in the novel indicates, it is possible, as it were, to scratch the plasticized "doll-like" surface of a citizen—at least of an Alpha or Beta citizen—of the new world state and draw actual blood. In this sense and to this degree, Huxley's vision of the perfectly planned future is not without hope; for all the genetic engineering and conditioning,

basic humanity remains much the same as it always was. Its imperfections and its needs, even under such greatly altered conditions, inevitably reappear. And it is for this reason, I think, that Huxley's vision is so extraordinarily powerful and compelling; because in the people he portrays we can still somehow recognize ourselves. (pp. 13-24)

> *Peter Edgerly Firchow, in his* The End of Utopia: A Study of Aldous Huxley's "Brave New World," *Bucknell University Press, 1984, 154 p.*

FURTHER READING

Baker, Robert S. *Brave New World: History, Science, and Dystopia.* Boston: Twayne Publishers, 1990, 156 p.
    Examines several aspects of *Brave New World,* including Huxley's treatment of time, love, technology, ideology, and historical progress.

Calder, Jenni. *Huxley and Orwell: "Brave New World" and "1984."* London: Edward Arnold, 1976, 61 p.
    Compares the dystopias of Huxley and George Orwell, emphasizing their viewpoints on politics and technological progress. Calder concludes that "both books were written out of the same impulse to protect the individual and to protect history."

Hankins, June Chase. "Making Use of the Literacy Debate: Literacy, Citizenship, and *Brave New World.*" *The CEA Critic* 53, No. 1 (Fall 1990): 40-51.
    Applies Huxley's vision of the future in *Brave New World* to the contemporary literacy debate. Hankins finds that "*Brave New World* can be read as a vision of what happens when a culture abandons the written word as its dominant medium of public discourse and adopts the electronic media instead."

Hébert, R. Louis. "Huxley's *Brave New World,* Chapter V." *The Explicator* XXIX, No. 9 (May 1971): item 71.
    Considers the opening paragraphs of the fifth chapter of *Brave New World* to be "a skillfully structured parody of the first four quatrains of Thomas Gray's 'Elegy Written in a Country Churchyard.' "

Huxley, Aldous. "Brave New World." *Life* 25, No. 12 (20 September 1948): 63-4, 66-8, 70.
    Examines the contemporary human condition apropos the "myth of Progress" dramatized in *Brave New World.* Huxley states: "Anyone who believes that there is some magical shortcut out of man's chronologically tragic situation is inviting either violent catastrophe through an ideological crusade or else a slower but equally sure disaster through the creation of a brave new world."

Kessler, Martin. "Power and the Perfect State: A Study in Disillusionment as Reflected in Orwell's *Nineteen Eighty-Four* and Huxley's *Brave New World.*" *Political Science Quarterly* LXXII, No. 4 (December 1957): 565-77.
    Contrasts the world of "conspicuous production" depicted in George Orwell's *Nineteen Eighty-Four* with the

society founded on "conspicuous consumption" in Huxley's *Brave New World,* yet concludes that both novels plead for the rights of the individual.

Leeper, Geoffrey. "The Happy Utopias of Aldous Huxley and H. G. Wells." *Meanjin Quarterly* XXIV, No. 1 (March 1965): 120-24.

Discusses the influence of Wells's fiction on Huxley's utopian novels, and examines the change from Huxley's "horrible utopia" of *Brave New World* to his "happy utopia" of *Island.*

Le Roy, Gaylord C. "A.F. 632 to 1984." *College English* 12, No. 3 (December 1950): 135-38.

Contrasts the authorial intents of Huxley's *Brave New World* and George Orwell's *Nineteen Eighty-Four.* Le Roy considers the former novel "the better written of the two."

Macey, Samuel L. "The Role of Clocks and Time in Dystopias: Zamyatin's *We* and Huxley's *Brave New World.*" In *Explorations: Essays in Comparative Literature,* edited by Makoto Ueda, pp. 24-43. Lanham, Md.: University Press of America, 1986.

Explores "the dangers inherent in a technological society dominated by the clock" as seen in several examples of dystopian fiction, including *Brave New World.*

Matter, William. "On *Brave New World.*" In *No Place Else: Explorations in Utopian and Dystopian Fiction,* edited by Eric S. Rabkin, Martin H. Greenberg, and Joseph D. Olander, pp. 94-105. Carbondale: Southern Illinois University Press, 1983.

Provides an overview of *Brave New World,* particularly discussing Huxley's criticism of scientific progress and mechanization.

Meckier, Jerome. "Shakespeare and Aldous Huxley." *Shakespeare Quarterly* 22 (Spring 1971): 129-35.

Studies the role that Shakespeare's writings play in Huxley's fiction. Meckier finds that "*Brave New World* is constructed around an extended contrast of Shakespeare and H. G. Wells."

"Best of Bad Times." *Newsweek* LVI, No. 14 (3 October 1960): 80-1.

Huxley relates his opinions on human potential and the fate of humankind.

Snow, Malinda. "The Gray Parody in *Brave New World.*" *Papers on Language and Literature* 13, No. 1 (Winter 1977): 85-8.

Elucidates the parody of Thomas Gray's "Elegy Written in a Country Churchyard" that begins the fifth chapter of *Brave New World,* stating that it "serves the satire by reminding the reader of specific concepts he [or she] values and finds missing in the society Huxley describes."

Watt, Donald. "The Manuscript Revisions of *Brave New World.*" *Journal of English and Germanic Philology* LXXVII, No. 3 (July 1978): 367-82.

Examines Huxley's alterations to the manuscript of *Brave New World* and determines that "besides diversifying his characters and dramatizing the action, Huxley in his revisions was in the act of discovering what he really wanted to say in *Brave New World.*"

Wilson, Robert H. "*Brave New World* as Shakespeare Criticism." *Shakespeare Association Bulletin* XXI, No. 3 (July 1946): 99-107.

Questions the nature of Huxley's references to Shakespeare in *Brave New World,* stating that "Huxley may be taken to imply that we can best profit from [Shakespeare's] plays if we view them esthetically and not . . . as textbooks of thought and conduct."

Dorothy Livesay

1909-

(Full name Dorothy Kathleen Livesay) Canadian poet, critic, playwright, nonfiction writer, and short story writer.

The following entry contains criticism published from 1951 through 1991. For further coverage of Livesay's life and works see *CLC*, Volumes 4 and 15.

INTRODUCTION

A prolific author in several genres, Livesay is best known as a poet whose work combines personal introspection, social commentary, and political observation. D. V. Smith has written that Livesay "is a poet remarkable for her strong, pioneering personality. . . . She is probably a major poet of the English language of the twentieth century."

Born in Winnipeg, Manitoba, Livesay moved with her parents, both writers, to Toronto, Ontario, in 1920. She received her bachelor's degree at the University of Toronto in 1931 and later attended the Sorbonne in Paris. In the 1930s, spurred on by the Depression in Canada and threats of fascism in Europe, Livesay began what would become a lifelong involvement in social work and women's rights, eventually leading to her position with the United Nations Educational, Scientific, and Cultural Organization (UNESCO) as an English teacher in Northern Rhodesia (now Zambia) from 1960 to 1963. She has since continued publishing and has served as an associate professor of English and writer in residence at several Canadian colleges and universities.

Having written mostly pastoral poems and love lyrics early in her career, Livesay began writing political poetry while she worked at social service agencies. This led to the publication of *Day and Night,* a collection of poems that includes examples of both her earlier style and her less-structured, politically oriented work. The book was well received by critics for its artistic merits. Lee Briscoe Thompson has praised "the crystalline imagery, the refreshing intelligibility, the precise control of sound, and the purity of tone" in the collection. Livesay's experience observing African music and dance inspired her to experiment further with poetic structure, most notably in "Zambia," a socio-political documentary poem that employs metrically what Livesay refers to as "song and dance." Critics also commend Livesay's adept handling of the conflict between giving oneself to another in a relationship and remaining an individual—a problem, according to Livesay, more significant for women. The poems about her affair with a younger man in *The Unquiet Bed* explore this dichotomy, concluding that a woman should not lose her selfhood in romantic involvement. More recently Livesay has concentrated on writing prose, publishing the novella

The Husband and the autobiographical *Journey With My Selves: A Memoir, 1909-1963.*

PRINCIPAL WORKS

Green Pitcher (poetry) 1929
Signpost (poetry) 1932
Day and Night (poetry) 1944
Poems for People (poetry) 1947
Call My People Home (poetry) 1951
New Poems (poetry) 1955
Selected Poems of Dorothy Livesay (poetry) 1957
The Colour of God's Face (poetry) 1964
The Unquiet Bed (poetry) 1967
The Documentaries: Selected Longer Poems (poetry) 1968
Plainsongs (poetry) 1969
Collected Poems: The Two Seasons (poetry) 1972
A Winnipeg Childhood (short stories) 1973
Ice Age (poetry) 1975
Right Hand Left Hand (nonfiction) 1977

The Woman I Am   (poetry)   1978
The Raw Edges   (poetry)   1981
The Phases of Love   (poetry)   1983
Feeling the Worlds   (poetry)   1984
Beyond War: The Poetry   (poetry)   1985
Selected Poems: The Self-Completing Tree   (poetry)
   1986
Les ages de l'amour   (poetry)   1989
The Husband   (novella)   1990
Journey With My Selves: A Memoir, 1909-1963   (autobi-
   ography)   1991

CRITICISM

Northrop Frye   (essay date April 1951)

[*Frye was a Canadian critic who exerted a tremendous influence in the field of twentieth-century literary scholarship. In his seminal work* Anatomy of Criticism *(1957), Frye argues that judgments are not inherent in the critical process and asserts that literary criticism can be "scientific" in its methods and its results without borrowing concepts from other fields of study. In the following excerpt from an essay originally published in April 1951, Frye evaluates Livesay's poetry.*]

Dorothy Livesay is a poet who has remained within a single convention, though with modulations. . . . Miss Livesay is an imagist who started off, in *Green Pitcher* (1929), in the Amy Lowell idiom:

> I remember long veils of green rain
> Feathered like the shawl of my grandmother—
> Green from the half-green of the spring trees
> Waving in the valley.

The virtues of this idiom are not those of sharp observation and precise rhythm that the imagists thought they were producing: its virtues are those of gentle reverie and a relaxed circling movement. With *Day and Night* (1944) a social passion begins to fuse the diction, tighten the rhythm, and concentrate the imagery. . . . From **"Prelude for Spring"** on, the original imagist texture gradually returns, and is fully re-established by the end of the book. . . . (pp. 84-5)

Imagism tends to descriptive or landscape poetry, on which the moods of the poet are projected, either directly or by contrast. The basis of Miss Livesay's imagery is the association between winter and the human death-impulse and between spring and the human capacity for life. Cutting across this is the irony of the fact that spring tends to obliterate the memory of winter, whereas human beings enjoying love and peace retain an uneasy sense of the horrors of hatred and war. That man cannot and should not forget his dark past as easily as nature I take to be the theme of **"London Revisited,"** and it is expressed more explicitly in **"Of Mourners."** . . . (p. 85)

The dangers of imagism are facility and slackness, and one

reads through [the retrospective *Selected Poems 1926-1956*] with mixed feelings. But it is one of the few rewards of writing poetry that the poet takes his ranking from his best work. Miss Livesay's most distinctive quality, I think, is her power of observing how other people observe, especially children. Too often her own observation goes out of focus, making the love poems elusive and the descriptive ones prolix, but in the gentle humour of **"The Traveller,"** in **"The Child Looks Out,"** in **"On Seeing,"** in the nursery-rhyme rhythm of **"Abracadabra,"** and in many other places, we can see what Professor Pacey means [in the book's introduction] by "a voice we delight to hear." (p. 86)

> *Northop Frye, "Letters in Canada," in his* The Bush Garden: Essays on the Canadian Imagination, *House of Anansi Press, 1971, pp. 1-127.*

Jean Gibbs   (essay date Spring 1970)

[*In the following essay, Gibbs considers Livesay's poetry in the tradition of Transcendentalist writing, especially as represented by the works of Henry David Thoreau.*]

To entertain seriously the idea that the poet of the celebration of sex in *The Unquiet Bed* and *Plainsongs* could have a poetic vision shaped considerably by a Thoreauvian trancendentalism—at times mystical and consistently asexual—may at first glance appear to be fatuous. For Thoreau wholeness of being came through an acute sensual awareness of the physical world, so that he in a sense became the tree, the flower, the pond that he saw, smelled, touched and in which he immersed himself. His metaphysic, then, consists essentially of this awareness of his fusion with the natural elements, eternal in their cyclical patterns. Whitman, D. H. Lawrence, Dylan Thomas all possess a metaphysic equally grounded in a return to the elements, but with a significant difference. They see sexuality as the most elemental force in the natural cycle of birth, growth and decay. The act of sex, therefore, unites man with the cosmos. Their celebration of life is more full-bodied than Thoreau's, which appears at times, in spite of its sensuality, unattractively sterile in comparison. For this very reason, however, the transcendent or mystical side of Thoreau's vision is more obvious to readers whose literary consciousness is still often restricted by Puritanism where asceticism and spirituality are equated. The fusion of sex and spiritual awareness that D. H. Lawrence preaches, on the other hand, requires a return to the primitive consciousness where such dissociation of sensibility does not exist. It is necessary to make these distinctions between the metaphysics of Thoreau and Lawrence in a study of Dorothy Livesay's poetry because on the surface her poetry appears to be a celebration of life much in the manner of D. H. Lawrence whose influence she acknowledges. But a closer examination of her work reveals an unexpected, and what I would call Thoreauvian, twist in her way of seeing things which works in opposition to the more obvious Laurentian view of life. What is significant in this distinction is that it sets up opposing forces that find expression in various guises in Miss Livesay's poetry and that create a basic tension which acts as the unifying principle in her work.

I do not mean to say that Dorothy Livesay has a highly developed system of belief in the way that the metaphysic of Thoreau or Lawrence is both complex and profound. She herself is ready to acknowledge her relatively simplistic approach to the questions of existence. This is how she summarizes her basic beliefs in a recent article:

> Recently I read in a *New Republic* review of my admired critic, Herbert Read, that although he had achieved the modern techniques sufficiently to be a great poet, he admitted failure because he lacked the necessary modern concomitant, "a sense of the tragic." Perhaps that sums me up also? We are optimists, Blakeian believers in the New Jerusalem. We cannot see man's role as tragic but rather as divine comedy. We are alone—so what? We are not always lonely. Laughter heals, the dance captures, the song echoes forth from tree-top to tree-top. I won't stop believing this until every tree in Canada is chopped down! I thumb my nose at those who say that nature and with it, human nature, is becoming "obsolete."

Although it is understandable that in an article of limited length Miss Livesay must necessarily deal in general observations, I feel, nevertheless, that she is doing her poetry somewhat of a disservice by statements like these that play down this basic conflict which enriches and expands her vision considerably.

In any poet whose mode of expression is chiefly lyrical, as Dorothy Livesay's is, the search for fundamental truth takes the form of an exploration of the self. So to arrive at a full vision of life is to achieve complete self-awareness, a sense of the self as a perfect entity—what Yeats calls unity of being, a state where all antinomies are held in a perfectly resolved balance. Miss Livesay, a minor poet in relation to Yeats to be sure, nevertheless possesses a vision that moves in this direction, for her poetic quest is a search for a means of bringing her conflicting responses to life into some kind of reconciliation. Her poetry seldom, if ever, becomes mere rhetoric—with the exception of some of her socialistic poems—for "the quarrel with oneself" is always present in her work, even in her latest most exuberant love poetry.

The basic conflict in the poetry of Dorothy Livesay centres around the problem of communication. (That she sees the question of communication as central to her poetry is evident in a statement such as this: "Behind it all [is] a belief in love, in communication on all levels".) What comes into opposition is the individual's desire for a sense of selfhood and his innate need to see himself as part of some larger order of things if life is to have any significance. An enlarged vision means moving outside the self to communicate with other people or, more transcendently, with nature itself. Thoreau chose this latter means of communication while D. H. Lawrence attempted to enlarge his vision through a physical and spiritual union with others—to return to the broad distinctions I made earlier. Thoreau was singularly self-contained. Most often he regarded any close human relationship forced on him as an encroach-

ment on his self-integrity, as dissipation of his energies and senses that he wished to expend only in reaching a more spiritualized state of awareness. A chronological study of Miss Livesay's poetry will reveal, I think, a rather Thoreauvian sense of self-sufficiency and wish to avoid human entanglements specifically sexual and a transcendental sense of unity with nature predominating in her earlier poetry, and giving way to a more Laurentian attitude to life in her later work. This approach may appear on the surface to be based simply on the freer and more explicitly sexual expression of her later poetry. A closer look at individual poems will reveal that this is not the sole basis of such an approach, and at the same time will point to further complexities in this central issue of communication. Hardly less significant is the question of man's response to nature which acts as a corollary to the central problem of the poetry. The predominance of natural imagery is perhaps indication enough of the important role nature plays in Miss Livesay's poetic vision.

Although the very early poetry of *Selected Poems* often expresses the typical adolescent sense of isolation and loneliness, the poet's empathy with her natural world appears in poem after poem. The beautifully neat poem, **"Such Silences,"** in addition to expressing her close relationship with nature, suggests that the poet finds her self-contained world in this kind of communion where human intrusions would destroy the calm self-awareness that comes from contact with the silences of the little wood:

> Some silence that is with beauty swept
> With beauty swept all clean:
> Some silence that is by summer kept,
> By summer kept all green. . . .
>
> Give me such silence in a little wood
> Where grass and quiet sun
> Shall make no sound where I have run
> Nor where my feet have stood.

Such a poem as **"Autumn"** captures the sense of transcendental awe that would readily find a prose counterpart in Thoreau:

> To recapture
> The light, light air
> Floating through trees
> As a river through rushes:
>
> To walk on feet made aerial,
> Meeting the grey atmosphere
> With one's own colourless wraith:
>
> To feel again the wind
> Drawing down leaves
> To their last surrender:
>
> To see even children walking apart,
> Unreal,
> Smelling the day
> In brief snatches of wonder!

It is an almost epiphanic moment where fusion with nature is so nearly perfect that the children are unreal and the poet, herself, a "colourless wraith".

The poet cannot, however, for very long remain in this isolated world. Human contacts cannot be avoided. But they appear as threats to the sense of selfhood that comes to the poet through her empathy with nature—they hurt. Her self-sufficiency is destroyed:

> Lest I be hurt
> I put this armour on:
> Faith in the trees
> And in the living wind.
>
> Lest I be hurt
> I walk above the sky—
> Taller than Sagittarius
> I grow.
>
> Lest I be hurt. . . .
> But O, what shields, what swords
> Can save me, if you too proclaim
> My faith, you too invade my skies?

The final stanza suggests the possibility that such a world can be shared with some one else, in fact ought to be shared with some one: the strength of the other's faith from which the poet has no real protection implies that a force larger than themselves has brought about their meeting. Unlike Thoreau, Miss Livesay can seldom shut out other human beings from her poetic world, as often as she may express the wish to do so.

Once her world is invaded, fragmentation of her selfhood sets in. Her allegiances are divided: the perfect fusion of the poet with both nature and that other person is rare. Someone in the triangular relationship is always on the outside—in this instance the poet herself:

> What was it, after all,
> The night, or the night-scented phlox?
> Your mind, or the garden where
> Always the wind stalks?
>
> What was it, what brief cloak
> Of magic fell about
> Lending you such a radiance—
> Leaving me out?
>
> What was it, why was I
> Shivering like a tree,
> Blind in a golden garden
> Where only you could see?

Here the poet is blind and suffers from alienation. In this next poem, it is the other person's blindness that preserves the poet's integrity:

> You did not see me dancing.
> No!
> I did not dance for eyes to see.
> Only a fluttering breath of me
> Flashed with the sunlight on the wall,
> Sank—and grew tall,
> Taller than my own ecstasy.
>
> You did not see me dancing,
> Even then!
> Your blindness saves my self's integrity.

Although the natural imagery is not immediately apparent, we remember this Miss Livesay generally sees the dance as an expression of the universal rhythms. And a closer look at the poem reveals a transcendental experience most certainly, if only a momentary one. The poet's

dance is the sun's dance—"only a fluttering breath of me / Flashed with the sunlight on the wall." For a brief ecstatic moment her spirit becomes one with the sun. This is the kind of integrity she wishes to preserve and may, only if the other person is sufficiently blind to remain alienated. Once he gains the insights to share in her vision, there is a real fear that this diffusion of her senses and emotions, now shared, may destroy her oneness with nature. What Thoreau would call her "sphericity" is threatened.

This almost totally Thoreauvian way of looking at things characterizes Miss Livesay's earliest poetry. Very soon the Laurentian and sexually centred principle exerts itself, and from that point on in the poetry these two poles of vision are in almost constant opposition. Whichever direction the poetic quest takes toward communication and completion of the self the alternate is present either by direct statement or by implication.

With this change in emphasis comes a change in the poet's world of nature. It now often takes on sexual characteristics. The poet's communion with nature becomes the working out of the male-female principle. The poem which most clearly marks this transition is **"Prelude for Spring"**. On one level, the poem may be seen as a Laurentian immersion in nature, the kind of sexual union with the landscape that Lawrence's women often undergo, Lou Carrington in *St. Mawr*, for example—here to a lesser degree, although the mystical element is unmistakable. The framing of the poem by the statement "These dreams abound" readies the mind for this "other" view of the landscape so familiar in waking moments, and whose normality breaks into the poem at one point:

> Somehow, the road rolls back in mist
> Here is the meadow where we kissed
> And here the horses, galloping
> We rode upon in spring. . . .

But for the remainder of the poem we are in another realm from objective reality, as the dream setting suggests. It is the same silent, enclosed world that the poet finds in the "little wood" of the earlier poem, **"Such Silences"**. It may be a silent world, but it is far from quiescent. A very vital force is in evidence:

> He comes. Insistent, sure
> Proud prowler, the pursuer comes
> Noiseless, no wind-stir
> No leaf-turn over;
> Together quiet creeps on twig,
> Hush hovers in his hands.

That he is described in terms of silence—"noiseless", "quiet", "hush"—clearly marks the pursuer as this same Thoreauvian spirit of nature (later in the poem he is depicted as a bird) of the earlier poetry. Here, however, he appears as a threat to the poet's integrity rather than an extension of herself. The poem begins as a flight from his relentless pursuit, and what the pursued hopes to escape is an intrusion on her self-sufficiency:

> Then on, on
> Furrow, fawn
> Through wall and wood
> So fast no daring could
> Tear off the hood

Unmask the soul pursued.

But soon the soul, the fawn, succumbs to the enchantments of the natural world around him. Immersed in its loveliness, he loses all fear (the pursuer is by his side) and experiences a kind of epiphany when everything is bathed in light. The sensuous richness of the imagery and the heightened lyricism of the language emphasize this moment of ecstasis:

> O green wet, sun lit
> Soaked earth's glitter!
> Down mouth, to munch
> Up hoof, to canter
>
> Through willow lanes
> A gold-shaft shower,
> Embracing elms
> That lack leaf-lustre
>
> And copse' cool bed
> All lavendered
> With scentless, sweet
> Hepatica—
> Till side by side
> In field's brown furrow
> Swathe sunlight over
> Every shadow!

The pursuer and the pursued become one. But the soul discovers that it must lose itself even more completely to achieve that final mystical union with nature, the eternal force "soaring unspent":

> But still
> On heart's high hill
> And summit of
> A day's delight
> Still will he swoop
> From heaven's height
> Soaring unspent,
> Still will he stoop to brush
> Wing tip on hair,
> Fan mind with fear.

With this threat to the sense of selfhood, the move outside the self becomes a terrifying and shattering revelation:

> And now the chill
> Raw sun
> Goes greener still—
> The sky
> Cracks like an icicle:
>
> Frozen, foot-locked
> Heart choked and chafed
> Wing-battered and unsafe,
> Grovel to ground!
> A cry lashed the sky—

This final subjugation in its imagery of force and mastery strongly suggests the climactic union of physical love. This is strengthened by the pattern of pursuit, meeting and withdrawal that shapes the poem. It is not difficult, then, to see the pursuer and the pursued as male and female forces and the mystical union with nature as clearly Laurentian.

It is possible to see **"Prelude for Spring"** and the two poems that follow it, **"Annunciation"** and **"Nativity"** as a trilogy. In this case, **"Prelude for Spring"** becomes clearly the physical conquest by the man. In **"Annunciation"**, he again appears in terms of bird imagery and as a threatening force:

> Steel bird prey intent
> Flight imminent
> I see your stride (no walk)
> Cleaving the air,
> Cloud treading, your hair
> Sickle bent.

The central concern of the poem has to do with the woman's acquiescence and compliance after the initial act of conquest. She is engulfed in the dark (Laurentian) life force, taken out of herself, and attuned to the universal rhythms:

> Night's soft armour welds me into thought
> Pliant and all engaging; warm dark,
> No scintillations to distract
> Nor any restless ray, moon-shot.
> I am still of all but breathing—
> No throbbing eye, no pulse; and a hushed heart.
>   . . . . .
> Only the heaven sent
> Pulse of the universe
> Beats through the buried heart
> Its steady course.

Now fusion with the elements lies in sexual union. This letting go of the self to be subjugated to the man's will is not easy, as it is not in the later poem **"The Taming"** (*The Unquiet Bed*). But it is the only way to communication with a larger order of things, to becoming one with the natural cycle—the reiterated drift—and nature itself is the teacher:

> Look, it takes long to grow a listener
> To bend his bough, let fall his leaf to earth;
> Upward and on his own words speeding
> Leaps the self to light.
>
> But wind is teacher. Rain is kind,
> Down-sailing, soaking deep
> And summer ruddying to sear
> Reiterates the drift:

Then, all of life falls into place. Death is seen as an essential part of the natural process:

> Be earthward bound; and here
> In the strata of flown flowers
> And skeleton of leaf, set self down
> Hurry ear to ground.
> Not burials; not dust and ashes' crumbs
> But world's own cry resounding!

And **"Nativity"**, the third poem of the trilogy falls readily into place. It is a poem about the birth of the poet's son. The woman, having lost herself in the life force, now participates in the act of creation itself.

What emerges in this rather detailed consideration of the trilogy is a poetic vision in which the self-contained Thoreauvian world struggles with the Laurentian world and finally succumbs to it. That they are in conflict implies, however, that the loss of the poet's sense of "sphericity" and her subjection to the life force are not readily accepted, although the experience of **"Nativity"** in the end is undoubtedly joyful. **"Prelude for Spring"** and **"Annunciation"** are pivotal poems in Miss Livesay's total body of work in the sense that they are the poetic enactment of this major conflict in her vision. Their intensity comes through in the heightened lyricism of the language and the richness of the multi-levelled imagery. The imagery suggests not only the sensual and emotional range of physical love, but moves beyond this level to an area of meaning approaching the mystical where the self is moved outside the body to an awareness of elemental life. These are among Miss Livesay's best love poems, I feel, because she does not linger unduly over concrete physical details, as she quite often does in her later love poetry, but rather deals with the intensity of passion.

From this moment of equilibrium where antinomies are resolved in the act of love, the poet returns to the problem of her divided self. In **"At Sechelt"** she is torn between the pull of the sea and the need for a lover to share in this transcendent experience. In Section I of the poem the poet experiences a sense of oneness with the sea, the primal source of life. It is "our mind's ocean":

> Sea is our season; neither dark nor day,
> Autumn nor spring, but this inconstancy
> That yet is continent: this self-contained
> Organic motion, our mind's ocean
> Limitless as thought's range, yet restrained
> To narrow beaches, promontories
> Accepting her in silence; the land's ear
> Forming a concave shell along the sands
> To hear the sea's shuffle as she leaps in gear

Although the ocean is self-contained (as the poet wishes to be), it yet must depend on the land to give it definition. The image implies, in other words, that the interaction of opposites is necessary for a state of completion—land and sea, convex and concave, male and female. So in Section II, the poet looks for the lover to complete herself. He must, however, never interfere in her communion with nature and share in it only at her request: he must be the "lover who could share the song / Yet bow to the denial; laugh, or be mute". Even if such a lover is found, she accepts him reluctantly:

> Calling, and yet reluctant to forego
> For otherness, the earth's warm silences
> Or the loquacious solace of the sea.

Immersion in nature holds greater attractions because by it her integrity is not threatened. A lover means sharing or "otherness", and this endangers her sense of selfhood. The conflict, then, remains unsolved.

Selected Poems ends with a further poetic enactment of the union of woman and man and nature through art—an extension of the vision of **"Prelude for Spring"** and **"Annunciation"**. The first section of the poem moves through a series of paradoxical antitheses which suggest the perfect fusion of mass and space, form and the formless, of a Henry Moore sculpture—each is contained in the other and contains the other. The work of art is intrinsically perfect, and this is the kind of wholeness the poet looks for in love where each is the complement of the other. From such a union would come self-awareness:

> When I have found
> Passivity in fire
> And fire in stone
> Female and male
> I'll rise alone
> Self-extending and self-known.

Even this kind of union, however, is not wholly satisfactory for the poet, because she sees herself as a part of a larger order of things. She does not belong to the static, self-enclosed world of art, but shares in the vital forces of nature. The tree, more than the sculpture, speaks to her and its message is that she will find true self-knowledge only when she views herself in the context of the cycle of life:

> The message of the tree is this:
> Aloneness is the only bliss
>
> Self-adoration is not in it
> (Narcissus tried, but could not win it)
>
> Rather to extend the root
> Tombwards, be at home with death
>
> But in the upper branches know
> A green eternity of ice and snow

Narcissistic preoccupation with the immediate self is not enough. Communication must extend outside the self to a larger existence.

The third section of the poem, in its imagery, is again the unmistakeably Laurentian and mystical immersion in nature. The woman finds her essential self through the man, but moves beyond him. The act of love is a baptism of fire into the deepest human experience, a sense of oneness with the universe:

> The fire in the farthest hills
> Is where I'd burn myself to bone:
> Clad in the armour of the sun
> I'd stand anew, alone.
>
> Take off this flesh, this hasty dress
> Prepare my half-self for myself:
> One unit, as a tree or stone
> Woman in man, and man in womb.

Poetically, at least, Miss Livesay has achieved a perfect reconciliation in the conflict of man and woman with nature.

The poetry of *The Unquiet Bed* as a whole reflects this oneness with nature. As the opening poem, **"Without Benefit of Tape"**, makes clear, real life is the simple existence of people close to the land in the outposts, on the backwoods farms, in the North, in Zambia. The land, the senses, sex are recurrent themes for praise and jubilation. The elemental life triumphs unquestionably, and there is far less room for the metaphysical doubts about the self, that we find in the earlier poetry of *Selected Poems*. The poet is the complete woman who finds a full life in her family and her art in **"Postscript"**, and whose ties with the land are reaffirmed in **"Roots"**. In the uncle of this poem, the Laurentian man makes a brief reappearance:

> Only outdoors
> tending his seedlings
> in the black earth, May-awakened,
> only setting out tomato plants

and Grannie's geraniums
(generations of fire)
only as he looks up suddenly
beyond, out into sky
his blue eyes
terrify.

His mysterious detachment from others and his closeness to the dark soil terrify only momentarily, however, for the poet has achieved a nearly perfect understanding of the order of nature and her place in it, and this man's close union with the soil is no longer a mystery. **"Sunfast"** expresses the kind of sensuous immersion in nature that Thoreau might enjoy, although of a slightly more rollicking variety:

I lurch
        into the sun
fasten on green
        leaves dripping
                in golden butter
I break
        fast
        munch morning
I am one
with rolling animal life
        legs in air
green blades scissoring
        the sun

In **"Empress"** the poet is a banquet for the hornets, "bussed huzzahed!" In **"Eve"** she holds all the power of nature in her hand, the fatal apple that started the whole process of birth, growth and decay. There are moments, although they are few, when this state of equilibrium is for the time destroyed. In **"Ballad of Me"** nature has done the poet an injustice—she is misbegotten—and her life appears to be an aborted effort to dance to the world's tune:

What happened was:
the world, chuckling sideways
tossed me off
left me wildly
treading air
to catch up.

In the love poetry of *The Unquiet Bed*, although an affirmation of life is made through sex, doubts about the self's integrity intrude. **"The Touching"** clearly portrays sexual union as the means to fusion with the elements with the lyrical and wrenched intensity of Lawrence:

Each time you come
        to touch caress
me
        I'm born again
                deaf dumb
each time
        I whirl
                part of some mystery
I tear through the womb's room
                give birth
and yet   alone
                deep in the dark
                earth
I am the one   wrestling
the element re-born.

And **"The Notations of Love"** records the same transcendence through passion, contained in the natural imagery:

You left me nothing, yet
Softly I melted down
into the earthy green
grass grew between my thighs

and when a flower shot
out of my unclenched teeth
you left me nothing but
a tongue to say it with.

In **"Taming,"** on the other hand, there is the sense that the woman is not ready to subjugate her will to the man's. The measure of the words "be woman" demands too great an invasion of the self if the last vestiges of privacy are destroyed:

Be woman. I did not know
the measure of the words
until that night
when you denied me darkness
even the right
to turn in my own light.

The poet of **"Four Songs"** finds that love may be a disintegrating force in one's sense of oneself—it may be as destructive as Dido's passion for Aeneas:

It is the fire you love
not me not both
burning my body
it envelops you
attracts the moth
and the murderer too

Dido knew
this fire
and chose
that funeral

And the man in the first song works from "design," not as the woman, from compulsion by a larger force. In **"And Give Us Our Trespasses,"** again passion moves the woman outside herself as the natural imagery suggests:

Yet charged
your beauty charged me

quivering water
        under the smite
        of sunlight

But she is plagued by a feeling of inadequacy, and their trespasses on each other do not bring perfect communication—"Forgive us our distances."

Thus, although in the poetry of *The Unquiet Bed* the poet appears to have achieved a reconciliation of her conflicting attitudes to life—the Thoreauvian and Laurentian viewpoints complement one another—there are indications of struggle and conflict. What is most threatened is the self's integrity. The man is less than perfect and union with him leads to a less than perfect transcendent awareness.

Plainsongs presents the same alternation between doubt and affirmation in the poet's attitude to love. **"Another Journey"** records the kind of complete mystical release into another world that we find in **"Prelude for Spring"** where an ascending climb through a natural setting again becomes the metaphor for the climatic experience of physical love. By implication—because of the poet's choice of natural metaphor—such an experience leads to fusion with the elements:

> I am aware
> of cedars breathing
>   turning the trees
>   move with me
>   UP the mountain

The woman has moved beyond the man to an awareness of her place in the permanence of nature and she is self-contained:

> Now you have released me
> from your grip
> now I can slip alone
> into the forest
>
> rest
> upon stone

More often, however, the woman's dependence on the man appears as a prison of sorts: in **"Birdwatching"** she is a caged bird; in **"Dream"** she is imprisoned by blindness; in **"Auguries"** all nature has turned against her (I am alone in´a garden / with trees yelling); in **"The Journey East"** she is chained to a wire bed; and in **"Sorcery"** she pleads for the man to "magic me / out of insanity." Disintegration of the self, rather than wholeness of being, seems to be the end result.

With the final poems of **Plainsongs** comes a plea for the return of the self-sufficient woman of the early poetry of **Selected Poems.** In **"Operation"** love is a sickness which "split[s] the mind's peace." The essential operation is the one which will restore a sense of integrity through a transcendent awareness of one's place in the natural order of things, as the image of "animal sun" coupled with the metaphor for fusion with the elements (the torn and scattered poet) suggests:

> I decide to complete the operation
> tear myself into four quarters
> scatter the pieces
> into uncoiling
> animal sun—
> another kingdom

Only when the poet is restored to her singularity, can she hope to attain the full measure of herself by transcending self:

> I did not know how shrunk
> I had become
> for now the *he* the *you* are one
> and gone
> and I must measure me
>
> O let me grow and push
> upright!
> even aware of height
> and the cry
> to reach a dazzled strangeness
> sun-pierced sky

"De-Evolution" states the case even more plainly. A return to the asexual world of Thoreau may perhaps be the only way to retain one's sphericity:

> Bi-sexual, we
> the human kind
> cannot procreate
> alone
>
> but flower, plant
> without a meeting
> greets only the light
> and is made quick
> Shall animal man
> searching the universe
> return/ radiant
> self-creating?
>
> the thing
> in itself?

Ultimately, then, communication with a larger existence resides in communication with the self. (pp. 24-38)

> *Jean Gibbs, "Dorothy Livesay and the Transcendentalist Tradition," in* The Humanities Association Bulletin, *Vol. XXI, No. 2, Spring, 1970, pp. 24-39.*

Peter Stevens   (essay date Winter 1971)

[*In the following excerpt, Stevens addresses the differences between Livesay's early and late love poems.*]

In her social poetry of the 1930's Dorothy Livesay is concerned principally with human fellowship and the poems call for freedom from capitalist tyranny. There is no mention of the problem of freedom for each individual: the question of the roles played in society by man and woman is not raised. . . .

Her later poems, however, show a greater interest in woman's individuality, her need for freedom, her right to exist in her own way. Woman as herself is very much a part of her love poems. . . . The love poems in **The Unquiet Bed** are preceded by a section of personal poems in which the poet concentrates on various aspects of herself as woman. (p. 26)

[Most of the poems in the second section] are directly concerned in an unpretentious way with the problem of woman's position in modern society. Dorothy Livesay still insists that woman is involved in the natural cycle of growth. In **"Sunfast"** she sees herself as part of the whole life force symbolized by the sun. She takes in the sun like food; the sun refreshes and re-orders the world just as human beings try to establish patterns. . . .

The feeding on nature, the immersion in it as well as the recognition of one's place in it, is expressed in several poems in the second section of **The Unquiet Bed,** for instance, **"Process"**. **"Pear Tree"** has the same notion at its centre. (p. 27)

The question of individuality in relation to the male-female principle Dorothy Livesay herself finds so prevalent in her poetry crops up humorously in the poem **"Flower Music"**, particularly in the section titled

"Peony." . . . [The] sense of opposition and contradiction between male and female, expressed somewhat obliquely in the poem, is very much a part of Dorothy Livesay's view of human love, and it turns up in the next section of *The Unquiet Bed* which is devoted exclusively to love poems.

But these love poems were not the first that Dorothy Livesay wrote. There are quite a number of love poems in *Signpost,* and it is interesting to look at them now to see how her views on the role of woman have changed. The love poems in *Signpost* are attempts to express the changing moods and emotions of a love affair. They are personal poems but they are also objectified to make more universal statements about love. . . . I think that Dorothy Livesay is much surer of herself as a woman in the later poems so that she can afford to be more open, direct and honest, make the poems in fact much more personal. The early poems still have some romanticism clinging to them, although some of the poems are admirable statements of the wayward passions, misgivings, deceits and contradictions of love. And certainly they are the first attempts in Canadian poetry to express a modern approach to love, even though they are not always successful. (pp. 27-8)

[In these early poems Dorothy Livesay], in talking of the immense external reality in terms of an outer darkness, often used the image of enclosed space within which she kept the darkness at bay. But even in erecting a shell around one, one senses that it is futile. In the same way, love seems to be an enormous force in the love poems in *Signpost* and defences against it are fragile, particularly as love demands frankness and searches out the private sanctities of personality. Even if one of the partners takes refuge in nature, as the poet suggests in **"Sun,"** recognizing the naturalness of love, then the other partner can uncover the whole, can see everything open to his eye as he looks at nature. (p. 29)

The notion . . . of distance, a notion that crops up time and again in Dorothy Livesay's poetry, a distance between people, . . . is part of the poet's concept of love. She seems to be suggesting that union through love is only momentary and that it includes struggle for dominance. The release from individuality through complete union seems to be too open a position, may bring about such a thorough nakedness of soul as to threaten the very basis of the personality. (p. 30)

The [early love] poems are attempts to express the varying moods occuring during the course of a love affair with images pointing to psychological states and conflicts. Not all the poems dealing with love in this volume are successful. Some retain a kind of adolescent vagueness of romantic feeling, some strive for ambivalence of meaning which results only in obscurity or, conversely, oversimplification. . . . [But on the whole, these poems] convince as personal statements; they are believable as notations on personal experience. At the same time, however, they reach a certain objectivity because of the tone of directness amounting in most cases to a starkness. The images are not often over-developed; the poems themselves are generally short and to the point, as if the poet—and this is somewhat surprising considering both the age of the poet when she wrote these poems and the general poetic atmosphere in Canada when these poems were published—as if, then, the poet is determined to get to the root of her emotions in order to express them as openly and frankly as possible without making them too private in their connotation. (pp. 31-2)

Honesty and candour are essential components of the poems she wrote about her later experience of love in *The Unquiet Bed,* and *Plainsongs.* These poems, stemming as they do from her maturity as both poet and woman, taking into consideration her wholehearted concern about the position of woman in society and therefore the integrity of woman in a love relationship, are obviously for the most part more compelling statements than those in *Signpost.*

The poet prepares us for the section devoted to the love poems in *The Unquiet Bed* by closing the previous section, which as we saw earlier concentrated on the individual liberty of woman in personal life, with two poems ["**Eve**" and "**Second Coming**"] about the re-awakening of love within woman. And again she expresses this in an intensely personal manner. (pp. 32-3)

["**Second Coming**"] prefigures perhaps the insistence on physicality in the love poems which follow. But the titles of both these poems with their general religious implications also suggest that physical manifestations of love, however momentary, may include some spiritual meaning and revelation, and in some of the love poems the spirituality does arise from the physical presences of the lovers themselves, so that the ideas of separation, darkness, silence and distance in these poems take on weightier values because of the context in which they have been placed.

An insistent demand runs through the love poems, a demand that comes from her essential individuality but also a demand that comes from the masculine opposite partner. "Be woman", is the opening line of "**The Taming**" and in this poem being a woman means being submissive in sexual union but paradoxically that basic femininity has its own strength which will take away some of the mastery of the male. In a way "**The Taming**" is a poem that emphasizes the give-and-take of love in the strictest sense. . . . [The] sexual experience makes her face her essential self, her womanhood with both its submissive qualities and its strength. Through the physical experience comes a release from physicality. Woman is not to be considered merely as a physical piece of property. Love must give her freedom to remain herself even within the gestures of submission. . . . She wants the freedom to be part of a unity, a loss of one kind of freedom in order to release a true individuality. (pp. 33-4)

In spite of the ecstasies and freedom of love, in spite of the joy she experiences in rediscovering love at this point in her life . . . the poet acknowledges the terrors, failures, and paradoxes of love. She sees its creative joys but also its abysses, gaps, and silences. (p. 34)

Images of dream and sleep figure a great deal in the love poems in *The Unquiet Bed.* The poet sees the experience of love as something other-worldly and dream-like ("**A Book of Charms**"), something beyond words as in a dream

("**The Dream**"), but at times sleep and dream represent loneliness and distance, as in "**The Vigil**".

Some poems in *The Unquiet Bed* and *Plainsongs* attempt to describe the momentary blisses and fearful transient qualities of human love. "**Old Song**", in *The Unquiet Bed*, expresses in controlled and resigned tone the passing of love, the impermanence of a human relationship even though it may achieve harmony and union. . . . In a later poem in *Plainsongs*, "**Con Sequences**", Dorothy Livesay uses images drawn from nature to suggest the distances between lovers and also the growth and violent surge of love. (pp. 35-6)

Throughout the love poetry in *The Unquiet Bed* and *Plainsongs* Dorothy Livesay emphasizes the physical aspects of human love, so it is not surprising that the poem "**The Operation**" (*Plainsongs*), connects her experience of love and her recovery from it, together with a general reassessment of her situation of her life as she found it at that time.

"**The Operation**" opens with a sense of crisis. The poet has reached a crucial point in her life, this crisis made all the more emphatic in her mind because it happened after her tremendous experience of love. . . . (p. 41)

Just as she has to rely on herself to effect a complete physical cure after the operation, so she must assess her chances in the aftermath of love, which she now sees as "a sickness" which the lovers attempted to cure in many ways: by separation or even by physical indulgence. . . .

The last section of the poem returns to a key image in Dorothy Livesay's poetry—a doorway—used generally as an entrance to new experience, as a release, a revelation or emergence into some new world. Here, as she stands in a doorway, she takes stock of herself. . . . (p. 42)

The sequence of the love poems in *The Unquiet Bed* and *Plainsongs* are the most candid revelations of the experience of love as seen by a woman in Canadian poetry. Some poems fall short of their aims because the poet seems more concerned with poetic theories about form and lining. Sometimes the structure of lining seems arbitrary, although in most cases the use of broken short lining together with rhyme, half-rhyme and assonance mirrors the changing and breathless quality of the experiences themselves, as well as rendering some sense of the spirituality of the experience, for the best poems in the sequence seem enclosed in suspension, caught in an ecstatic calm. At other times the poet mars a poem by making the reader too conscious of an image, so that it becomes for him a conceit, a rhetorical device that militates against the tone of honesty and directness in most of the poems. There is occasional overemphasis and repetition, even (though rarely) and indulgence in romanticism and sentimentality. But these are only minor blemishes on an otherwise distinguished set of poems. They are examples of the very best in Dorothy Livesay's later work in which she is not afraid to be intensely personal and frank because she is able to express her feelings immediately and yet objectively so that she herself is subjected to the appraising and critical apparatus she uses in her own poetry. (p. 43)

Peter Stevens, "Dorothy Livesay: 'The Love Poetry'," in Canadian Literature, *No. 47, Winter, 1971, pp. 26-43.*

Joyce Whitney   (essay date 1979)

[*In the following essay, Whitney examines themes relating to death and transfiguration in Livesay's later love poems.*]

Poetry is a distillation of life, not the photograph of *a* life, and nowhere is this truth more evident than in the mature love poems of Dorothy Livesay. Some forty years separate these poems from *Green Pitcher* and the young love lyrics which Livesay herself calls "**The Garden of Love**" in her *Collected Poems: The Two Seasons.* In the years between, what Livesay learns about the human heart, about being a woman, about existence itself is thought about, "simmered," and finally appears as poetry; it is, therefore, worthwhile tracing the spiritual evolution which leads from the music of first love to the stillness of fulfilment.

Perhaps the most interesting characteristic of Livesay's work is the imagery of death, which finds its way into poems most expressly concerned with life; especially telling is the shift in its meaning over the years, and it is this aspect of her work I should like to consider here.

The early poems are filled with delight in the world in which young Dorothy finds herself: "How lovely now / Are little things: / Young maple leaves— / A jet crow's wings." The reverse side of this joy is a marked hesitation before life which sometimes descends to despair. Indeed, these early poems show a wish to escape from the prison of the body which reminds one of Yeats' distaste for the condition of the human being on this planet: "my heart . . . sick with desire and fastened to a dying animal" ("Sailing to Byzantium"). Listen to Livesay's "**Autumn**," when she longs to "recapture the light, light air," "to walk on feet made aerial," not to be a part of life at all, but rather "one's own colourless wraith"; briefly, the young Livesay yearns to return to whatever silent bodiless realm she inhabited before life. The feeling of actually being a wraith comes into "**Impuissance**," where she observes a young harvester—what could be more a part of life than bringing in the hay?—and her impulse to communicate with the boy is defeated by her feeling that she is, once again, a wraith:

> I longed to cry out
> "Stay, stay, I am here."
> But the words would not come:
> My feet were held fast.

Under this image of the invisible ghost is the other image of life as a force which imprisons her in a shape which is alien and unfriendly. Again, in "**The Forsaken**," the poet is "shaken, suddenly, discovering myself " in stones which are "grey with the kiss of the wind and the sweep of the water," but which can only react passively to passion by being worn smooth. The girl recognizes, and so do we, the traditional male-female relationship: the male integrated into the sweep and flow of life, as free to act as wind and water, the female restricted to being acted upon, a lifeless object. Young Livesay has every reason to feel shaken.

Sometimes it is the young poet who rejects life in a deliberate veering away, as in **"The Shrouding,"** where, although spring is on the way "still snow clings," a neat description of the girl's indecision; the poet herself clings to the sleep of winter (death) where she will be "safe":

> Let me lie safe on lonely northern ground
> Safe in the snow;
> Wrap me in silence, let me not ever know
> Where the sun burns, nor whither flies the crow.

Here we find the fear of life (life symbolized by the sun) stemming from the instinctive knowledge that life inevitably brings suffering; "the sun burns"; so, reasons the poet,

> Must we awake from this long quietness of sleep,
> Must we arise and find
> Beauty in wakening?

Here, in three lines, are all the weariness and disappointment which await the person who holds out her arms to the colours and sounds of the world, and the vulnerability of the sensitive spirit. Those colours and sounds are ephemeral, and in another poem, the "Widow-woman" knows the "defeat of the sun," and sees the only touch of colour in the poem, the goldenrod, fade; death is welcome for "the starkness of the earth"—and the human heart— "cries for some covering," the end of life is "the wind's *gift* of snow," and its numbing power puts us beyond the reach of pain. A more explicit refusal of life occurs in **"Explanation,"** where pain is a fanged animal, reminiscent of Blake's tyger, crouching ready to spring; notice that the "pain" has not yet been inflicted, life has not yet been tried, yet already death (darkness) seems preferable. Here again the warm colours of life—the sun, goldenrod, the "sombre eyes gleaming"—are rejected. **"A Dream"** shows young Dorothy walking through her life, "the sombre woods," and refusing passion, implied by "the dark scarlet of the painted trees"; she disappears, but "great flocks of heavy birds soon filled the sky": the archetypal dream of escaping frustration (imprisonment in the body) through flight into "the pale sky." Once again, colour is cast aside.

This hesitancy before life is remarkable in a woman who, alone among contemporary Canadian poets, has always felt completely at home in nature; she is kinswoman to the birds who perch on so many of her poems, and she is as much at home in water as Undine. **"The Gulls"** recalls an ecstatic moment when for once Dorothy was a joyful part of a harmonious whole,

> My body no longer mine, but something loos-
>   ened, free,
> Yet bound forever to the rock,
> Possessed forever by the wind.

One feels that she is bound by understanding, and not against her will, and for a brief moment the life of the spirit and the life of the body are at peace. There are no other persons in this landscape; perhaps what drives Dorothy to dream of flight and death is that puzzling part of life, human relationships. **"The Gulls"** remains an exception among Livesay's early published work which, generally, reveals a fear of life and a regret that the condition attached to being here is a very long term of imprisonment in a human form. This regret is never completely resolved

but recurs as late as **"Ballad of Me"** from *The Unquiet Bed:*

> Misbegotten
> born clumsy
> bursting feet first
> then topsy turvy
> the fear of
> joy of
> falling.

The poet is mature enough to look back and laugh ruefully, but only after many years and much living.

The title, **"The Garden of Love,"** which Livesay gives to her poems of young love in *Collected Poems: The Two Seasons* is deliciously ironic, for few flowers bloom there; it contains no signpost saying "Thou shalt not," and Blake's priests are nowhere in sight, yet life remains stubbornly outside that garden. Here, the imagery shifts so that birds and winds symbolize physical and spiritual life while the garden of love is a sterile box. First love is, apparently, a fragile thing, so while "doves dive up and down across our window," the young woman feels it "preferable to imagine" rather than lean out to see all Paris spread below. Clouds send the poet's thoughts back to snow drifting from hemlocks; snow here is a lovely moment in life and no longer stands for the sleep of death. There is no yearning for flight here; love is a peaceful interlude from the constant motion of life, and the speaker is content that it should be so.

"Let not our love grow mildewed, out of use," begs Livesay in another lyric, and she follows with an image of the sepulchre when love grown stale becomes "a closet room walled from the sun." In the sad little poem which begins "I am merry; / till I lie alone encased within the dark," the word "encased" shoves us back into the claustrophobic coffin; "strange womb," remarks Livesay, and we agree, for no life will be brought forth from it; the poem goes on to describe love as a sickness that enfeebles the sufferer. In the last line, the equation is stated: love is, simply, pain. More than once in this sequence of poems, love is darkness, a usual image of death.

> Love has come back now like a cloud
> And made the world a sober place—
>   . . . . .
> Love has come back like a cloud
> And darkened all except your face.

And again:

> Dark ways we led each other, though we sought
> Only to catch the sun—

The last poem of the group combined most movingly images of life and growth:

> I have struggled toward the light
> And borne the wind in my branches—
> Grown upwards with the wind.

with images of death:

> But I think I have not learned
> Not yet
> Not after this terrible, beautiful loving
> The way of love when it goes—

The way to pierce myself
To run cleanly on the sword.

The poet has experienced life and found it good—no longer a passive stone, she has "grown upwards with the wind"; she knows that the next thing to be learned is to experience death and find it good, too; here, it is the small death which is the end of love, but already Livesay's mind is reaching out beyond this one moment to the years ahead; the use of the present perfect points movingly to the certainty that death will be there.

The years which lie between the young love lyrics and the love poems written when Livesay was in her fifties were spent living a typical woman's life. After her studies at the Sorbonne, Livesay returned to Canada, which was badly hit by the depression. Perhaps a Diplôme d'Etudes Supérieures was no help in getting a job, but she had brought back something else: images of class warfare fought out in the streets of Paris. Coupled with her experiences as a social worker, these memories led to her interest in the Communist party, and to her deliberately putting aside for the time being all thought of writing poetry concerned with just one human heart. Humanity, oppressed and without hope, blotted out all thought of self. From this period come the "public" poems; these are like posters, catching the attention by their bright primary colours and their unsubtle messages, and they remain one-dimensional occasional pieces. While there is little to explore beneath the surface, we do find that snow, previously the symbol of pleasant death, then of the movement of life itself, now appears as the living death of the working classes. "Snow will be shaken off, / Stripped from the trees by struggling fists and arms—" (**"In Green Solariums"**). One feels that Livesay wrote these poster poems out of a sense of devotion to the cause she had so wholeheartedly embraced, and that she is not at ease handling this material. In those moments where, almost in spite of herself, she treats an individual's inner life, the voice is true, the verse three-dimensional. Take the symphonic poem **"The Outrider"**: the decisive moment for the narrator comes when he decides to banish his morbid fear of life (here, the crow); the challenge of life accepted with joy leads him to quit the farm and he finds himself working on the assembly line in an abattoir. After the strength and elation of the stanza where man faces crow and wins, the reader is left with a feeling of disappointment at being tossed back into the trade union movement—the death-in-life of the poor again.

Marriage and a family turn Livesay's thoughts back to explorations of the human heart: poems about relationships, woman-man, mother-child, and everywhere in the background the puzzle of life and death. We can notice, however, an evolution in imagery which reveals a change of attitude towards death. If we compare two poems, one early, **"The Invincible,"** the other later, **"On Looking into Henry Moore,"** the change is striking. The first poem is permeated with images of death and violence: the "dark garden" and the elms who deeper and deeper

delve their arms
Into the helpless earth
And suck the young wines
Of spring.

This is life thriving on the death of innocents; the word "helpless" turns aggression into murder. If we next listen to the second part of **"On Looking into Henry Moore,"** all violence is gone, and there is a hint that the life-death cycle can be a peaceful one:

Rather, to extend the root
Tombwards, be at home with death

But in the upper branches know
A green eternity of fire and snow.

This train of thought leads Livesay to the felicitous **"Pear Tree,"** where light and dark are more perfectly balanced.

Lucky this pear tree . . .
can grow and glow in whiteness
sunlightness

. . . . .

Lucky this pear tree hears
if anything
small bird cries percolating
through downwhite foam

. . . . .

Lucky this pear tree seeped in sun . . .
taps with her roots
the worms' kingdom.

Life is there, and death; the pear tree, being part of both, is happy. That Livesay had long been growing towards this serene viewpoint is apparent if one reads **"Fantasia,"** a poem from *Day and Night* published in 1944; death is called "diving" and "imagination's underworld," as though the poet sees it as a mirror image of life, present wherever life is. She accepts, too, the fact that some may want to choose their moment for passing through that mirror:

Wise to have learned: how diving's done
How breathing air, cool wafted trees
Clouds massed above the man-made tower
How these
Can live no more in eye and ear:
And mind be dumb
To all save Undine and her comb . . .

Perhaps the most moving example of this evolution is found in the two versions of the poem on abortion which begins "Everyone expected guilt / Even I." The first version ends in a bleak, dry-eyed condemnation of a woman's life:

No. Not for her
no tears for her
whatever she has missed
she has gained also.

Later, this is changed to let transfiguration bloom out of death:

No. not for her
no tears
I held the moon in my belly
nine months' duration
then she burst forth
an outcry of poems.

From the moment Livesay can accept the life-death cycle as naturally as she has always accepted the circle of the seasons, she has only a small step to take to comprehend the act of love as a microcosmic death-life cycle, ever renewing, ever nourishing. This rhythm underlying the love poems gives them a quality of peacefulness which is rare in the *genre;* indeed, these poems could well be described in Wordsworth's phrase, "emotion recollected in tranquillity," for love has been purified of all dross: notions of force and submission, winning and losing, superiority and inferiority, and what is left is female and male uniting to form a whole. The act of love is described over and over again as a complete surrender of the self, comparable to the surrender made to death; from this comes a feeling of rebirth and transfiguration and a sense of inevitability. Livesay chooses traditional poetic forms for some of these poems, but more often she simply moulds each poem around its content.

Sometimes the ideas of death and transfiguration are specifically stated. **"The Touching"** reaches back before time, the creation of the world, death, giving birth, and being born are experienced all at the same time; the effect of this on the reader is of the universe created out of chaos. The poem, by its sequence of ideas (born again-whirl-mystery-drown-root-shell-fire) spirals down to the primeval in the last lines:

> each time you come
> I tear through the womb's room
>   give birth
> and yet   alone
>   deep in the dark
>   earth
> I am the one   wrestling
> the element re-born.

Another instance is **"The Woman"** where, after the lines

> O hurry hurry on
> and down
> break me again
> (until the bliss begins)

the second part of the poem goes on to the idea of birth and creation:

> When you make me come
> it is the breaking of a shell
> a shattering birth
> how many thousand children
> we have conceived!

The tenderest of the death-transfiguration poems is surely the first of the **"Notations"** group, which begins:

> You left me nothing, when
> you bared me to the light
> gently took off all my skin
> undressed me to the bone.

Out of the love sprang poetry:

> and when a flower shot
> out of my unclenched teeth
> you left me nothing but
> a tongue to say it with.

"The Operation" pulls the reader once more down into chaos:

> The second time I turned

swam with you into darkness
> was the foetus
> fed by blood
> and breath
> fighting to grow
> gasping for air
> world's door . . .

The effort of love-making (or birth or giving birth) is in the verbs: pull, gasp, demand, swim, fight, drown; from this effort comes a dreamy, healing peace which makes the poet whole:

> . . . healing me
> with gentle breath and tongue
> lulling me down
> tender   rocking   ease
> and a quick come.

Notice the rhythm of the heartbeat in "tender rocking ease." In other poems, death and rebirth are not stated but lie under the words. In the second of **"Four Songs,"** Livesay says,

> It is the fire you love
> not me . . .
> it envelops you
> attracts the moth
> and the murderer too
>
>   Dido knew
>   this fire
>   and chose
>   that funeral

In the third **"Song,"** she speaks of

> the body blunt
> needing the knife . . .
>
> your blow
> eased me so
> I lay   quiet
> longer.

Again, this moves towards creation or transfiguration. Livesay ends with the words:

> I drink the liquid flow
> of words   and taste
> song in the mouth.

In **"The Dream,"** Livesay takes her poetic vocabulary from mythology: an encounter with a unicorn; she "dissolved," sank to the ground, since when "strangeness blazes in my blood." This is, interestingly enough, the only one of this group in which she describes a body, her own, when she mentions "my small white breasts" "ponderous and round."

Whether stated or implied, the equilibrium between life and death on which the mature love poems are built makes them something other than mere descriptions of love-making; it removes sex from the realm of the exciting, the sensational, and the extraordinary, and places it in the quiet region where the great work of the universe goes on: the ebb and flow of the tides and the movement of the planets on their curved courses. It is a place of peace. For peace is the magic which these poems exercise upon the reader; all imbalance between partners and all precariousness are eliminated, and although one meets turbulent lines (e.g., **"The Operation"** quoted above) the underlying rhythm never falters.

Livesay's technique here reminds us just how far she has come since those early love lyrics which flow along horizontally with no heavy consonants to interrupt.

> we who still
> Were longing to be kind, to do no hurt.
> Two innocents expelled, outside the gate.
> (from **"Dark Ways We Led Each Other"**)

Now, take a mature poem on the same theme, the death of love, and you hear something quite different.

> Listen! when rain rattles the branches
>   our ghost shivers. (from **"The Operation"**)

This is not meant to flow; we must take time over the consonants of "rattles" and "branches," we must finish the "t" of "ghost" before passing to "shivers." The pauses—the blank spaces on the page—are just as important as the printed words; we are made conscious of a steady beat underlying the lines; there is all the time in the world.

What of the man in all this? Most of the poems are addressed to him, so he is not described, and there is no need to find a masculine equivalent of all those pointed breasts. As he is loved and valued as a whole person, we easily recognize him as such, and do not require a list of his component parts. He is a human being, not a sexual object, and his presence in these poems perfectly balances that of the woman. Man and woman come together as they are meant to, as equals, and the feeling of serenity which lingers with the reader of these poems stems from the harmonious equilibrium between each lover's delight in sexual pleasure and the unimportance of the separate self. This serenity is reinforced by the absence of colour, for the colours of passion are not set in contrast to one another, but are fused to make light; the visual movement is invariably from light to darkness as each poem descends to its climax, followed by a resurgence towards the light.

These mature love poems are the fruit of Livesay's long evolution towards understanding; they set a standard of taste and wisdom against which all love poetry yet to be written will be measured. (pp. 100-12)

> *Joyce Whitney, "Death and Transfiguration: The Mature Love Poems of Dorothy Livesay," in* Room of One's Own, *Vol. 5, Nos. 1-2, 1979, pp. 100-12.*

Dorothy Livesay with Alan Twigg (interview date 1981)

[In the following interview, Livesay discusses her own work and that of other Canadian writers.]

[*Twigg*]: *You've always been a great believer in proletarian literature or writing which is readily accessible to everybody. Do you think Canadian writers are adequately responding to their social obligations?*

[Livesay]: No, not at all. We have no writers like Sartre or Simone de Beauvoir who believe that the writer in any country must be committed to seek better things for humanity. If he doesn't speak out then he's committed to reaction.

Certainly there must be some writers whom you read nowadays and admire, whom you could recommend to other people?

I had high hopes for the grass roots poets in Canada like Milton Acorn, Al Purdy and Pat Lane. And Pat Lowther was certainly very much a committed poet before her murder. And Tom Wayman. It would seem to me that these poets and those that follow with them are speaking out, but there isn't anything like the commitment of the writers in the 30's. We were so stirred up by what was happening in Spain. The takeovers by Mussolini and Hitler created an anti-Franco situation in Canada which was very strong.

We have lots of capable wordslingers, but very few people are concerned with international matters.

It's pitiful what some of the young writers are doing. They are completely ignoring what's happening in this world, which is the threat of nuclear war. But it isn't so with the youngest group. I've been in contact with students in Ottawa and Manitoba who are nineteen and twenty and they seem very concerned.

In the 30's, when you were writing for New Frontier, *you were more consciously propagandist in your poems than compared to the work in your most recent collection,* Ice Age.

Well, in those days you didn't have any mass media. You didn't have people participating so much in the level of say, folk songs or jazz. Now the scene is changed. Beginning with the 60's, in Canada and perhaps around the world, the poet is now asked to come and speak to musical gatherings or pop weekends. There was never any of this in the 30's. Of course we tried to join in on picket lines and have mass chants that we read, but it was somewhat schematic, or unreal. What's very good today is that poets are now part of popular art. I don't spurn popular art. Many songsters are very good poets.

In your poem, **"Last Letter,"** *you write: "I am certain now, in love, women are more committed." Do you think that opinion will ever change?*

It's going to be very tough. Young men are having an awful time adjusting to the idea that a woman is a person, completely free to do what she pleases. I have confessions from young men who tell me their problems with their girlfriends. I sympathize with them, but we're absolutely flooded with television and magazines which work against change. The consumer market for women's products is appalling! Girls must have more and more dresses for more and more occasions to attract men. How are you ever going to break that down?

It seems there's a freedom now not to conform, but still the majority is conforming.

Up to a certain age, they do wear blue jeans. But a time comes when most of them change.

Speaking of ages, let's talk a little about your latest book of poetry. Is the title **Ice Age** *intended to have personal and political implications?*

And human. I had been reading, as we all have, of the possible changes in our world climate. The ice age is moving down again. This is a symbol of what's happening to humanity psychologically and spiritually. And of course personally, as one is approaching seventy, one begins to sense that this will be the end. All I have said will turn to ice.

Young men are having an awful time adjusting to the idea that a woman is a person, completely free to do what she pleases. We're absolutely flooded with television and magazines which work against change. The consumer market for women's products is appalling! Girls must have more and more dresses for more and more occasions to attract men. How are you ever going to break that down?

—Dorothy Livesay

Your style as a poet has not fluctuated a great deal since you began writing in the 30's. How consciously have you been concerned with manipulation of technique?

I used to be very conscious of punctuation. All my early poetry was very carefully punctuated. But I think my style changed when I came back from Africa in '63. That was the year the Black Mountain thing descended on Vancouver. Earle Birney brought Robert Creeley and Robert Duncan and that whole crowd. I heard them that summer and met Phyllis Webb and all the Tish people. But I got bored with the way they were all talking the same way. Lionel Kearns would use a metronome finger as he read. But I did come around to thinking that capitals at the beginning of a line were unnecessary. So I started arranging my lines as much as I could according to the breath. [George] Bowering helped me quite a bit on that. But I'm conservative. I don't want to make it look far out, like Bissett and these people.

Many poets nowadays write poetry which is meant to be read aloud. Do you keep that in mind when you write?

If I'm alone, I'll go over a poem aloud. I'll pace it out. I'll find that a particular stress or syllable doesn't work there at all.

You mentioned at an SFU Heritage seminar on poetry in the 30's that P. K. Page had never given a poetry reading until the 60's. Did you undergo a problem of adjustment becoming a poet as performer?

Well, I remember the Ford Foundation once invited Canadian poets to come from all over the country to Kingston to discuss the literary scene for a weekend. The government was concerned with setting up the Canada Council. This would be around '56. Between these long sessions

with publishers on the state of publishing, we organized little poetry circles. Layton and Dudek were there, people of that sort. I was asked to read. I read a recent poem that hadn't been published called **"Lament,"** about the death of my father, I was absolutely terrified. I believed in the poem before I read it, but while I was reading it didn't believe in it at all. It didn't make much of an impression. Now it's probably the most anthologized of my poems, that and **"Bartok."** But it was definitely not an easy time to read aloud.

Did you get much support from the CBC?

I don't know when I was first asked to read for the CBC. I had a long standing fight with Bob Weaver who was doing *Anthology.* He insisted that the poetry be read by an actress. I couldn't stand their women actresses. They read it all wrong. I didn't think my voice was that bad. Some of us had a ten year fight with Weaver to allow the poet to read it his own way. They swore an actor could do it better. Part of it was they had to pay the actor, to help them survive. Now it's pretty well the rule that a poet reads his own poems.

Most of the power of your poetry comes from your ability to make the personal reflect the universal. Do you ever consciously write poetry as a social function, starting with the universal deliberately?

My earlier documentaries were full of immediate passion, like **Day and Night.** It just sprang out of my experience. But **Call My People Home** was planned. I had to present what happened to those people. So I did a lot of research beforehand. The same is true of an Indian play I wrote for the CBC called **Momatkom.** This was in the 50's, long before *The Ecstasy of Rita Joe.* I was dealing with these radical conflicts way back. In '45 I was writing a poem about Louis Riel. I had to get a Guggenheim grant for that because there were no Canadian grants. Well, I missed getting the grant and couldn't finish the poem. It's now called **"The Prophet of the New World."** Now suddenly there's nothing but Louis Riel poems, plays and operas! [laughing]

Do you ever look back on things you wrote perhaps forty years ago and want to change them?

No, I've objected very much to W. H. Auden changing his poems about Spain. I think it's dreadful, sinful. Because that was the feeling at the moment and that's what made the poem. Earle Birney's done the same thing. He's revised and I think it's wicked.

Birney was a Trotskyite when you knew him aside from his poetry.

Yes. We were all against Hitler during the war. That's how I got to know Earle best. He brought Esther home from London and they had a son born about when my children were born. We met often on picnics and literary evenings. But I had known him even in his Trotskyite days. Earle at that time wasn't a poet at all, as far as I knew him. He was a Canadian interested in literature while he was becoming a Trotskyite. Harold Cassidy, who is the father of Michael Cassidy of the Ontario NDP, asked us to come together and talk politics.

Then Earle corresponded with me during the war from Europe. We were always quite close. I dedicated the poem **"West Coast"** to him. He represented the poem's central figure, the intellectual, who didn't know what to do. So he finally went down to the shipyards to see what that was all about. Then he enlisted. We've had terrible schisms since.

Generally do you have a low opinion of Canadian critics?

They're myopic. They have no vision.

Has reading the criticism of your work ever been a learning experience for you?

I don't think I had any serious critical work done on me in the earlier years. The whole group that centred around Frye ignored me completely. You won't find any of them even looking at my books.

Is the Canadian writing scene more fragmented than ever?

Well, I don't think we ever were fragmented because we were small enough to be a company, a community of writers. We all knew each other. Now it's just become more regional. You have communities in five regions but you don't have a unification for the country. That's significant for the future.

In a remark he made in the introduction of Emily Carr's first book, Ira Dilworth said she was absolutely rooted in her region, in the history of B.C. and Indian life. But because she was dedicated to that region she's an international genius. It's true of Hardy; it's true of Balzac. The more you really absorb a locale or community, the more international you become.

Do you think the Crossing Frontiers conference in Banff [1978] crossed any frontiers between American and Canadian?

It proved there was a difference. It gave us quite a lift, in fact. We thought, "We are real! We have an identity!" I felt that tremendously.

Even though the gathering was organized to throw some light on our similarities?

Yes, it was a great thing. Canadians identified with the western American experience, but they felt ours was different. The great thing is that Canadians are writing from their roots. A lot of young people are doing this in the West, on the Prairies, and in the Maritimes. The urban experience is common, I suppose, to all North America. So urban writers in Toronto and Montreal don't seem to have much to say that's new or real.

Are there poems of yours which you think will stand the test of time?

Some poems have meaning now and some poems have meaning for always. A poem like **"Bartok and the Geraniums"** might have meaning for always. It's a male/female poem, but it's also about art and nature. Then there are poems about women's plight. And perhaps a poem which predicts the androgynous future, **"On Looking Into Henry Moore."** I think he was androgynous. He saw the humanity of man and woman, the complete thing, which I've been striving to express. I also think in the Canadian scene that my documentaries will have importance. **Day and Night** and **Call My People Home** are being put into anthologies quite frequently.

Has your writing been affected by your earlier work as a journalist?

Yes, I think that helps. I hated newspaper work because you have to do such dirty things to people. My year of apprenticeship on *The Winnipeg Tribune* was painful. I had to compromise people to get my story. I hated that. Then I worked for *The Star.* I sent articles about France and then after the war I did a series on post-war rehabilitation in England. I was freer then, but as a younger reporter you simply had to get a story out of people. I hated that.

I don't think there's any particular route one should follow to become a writer. However, would you recommend a career in journalism as opposed to the university route?

Both things that I did, journalism and social work, have been significant. But I actually would have liked to have been an anthropologist. There are a number of anthropologists who are also poets and writers. That sort of area is far better than going into English. The last thing I'd tell people to do would be to go through as an English major. I took languages, French and Italian, and that was far

Page from Livesay's journal, 1928, describing a dinner with Bliss Carman and Charles G. D. Roberts.

more broadening. But then I'd read all the English literature at home in my teens. I tell every single promising poet, "Don't go through and be an English major. It kills your poetry." That's my great message. [laughing]

Yet you were in Vancouver teaching a course on woman writers. Which are your favorites?

I've always tremendously admired Virginia Woolf, Katherine Mansfield and Edith Sitwell. Recently, Doris Lessing, Rebecca West, Simone de Beauvoir. I don't know American writers very well at all. I've had to close myself off from that. I'm doing so much Canadian reading.

Canadian women writers have been neglected. All the best and first Canadian women fiction writers have come from the West. The Canadian novel had its roots in the West, certainly not in Montreal or Ontario. But when Mordecai Richler came to give a talk in Alberta, he hadn't read anything by Frederick Philip Grove. He didn't know he existed. It's that kind of incredible insularity that I've been fighting against. Emily Carr's style was utterly unusual and she had a brilliant mind. And the other B.C. writer, Ethel Wilson, also had a totally individual style. But all people think of back east is Marian Engel or Margaret Atwood. These weren't the first, and they're not the best. But I should mention that I have not read as much as I should have of French Canadian women writers. Gabrielle Roy is absolutely a top novelist. And Anne Hebert.

But it seems like the Canadian theatre scene, as a whole, is coming along well?

It's the healthiest. It's not looking at its navel. That's the worst thing about the poets in this country; they're writing from an ivory tower. Even the young ones. All that Tish group is ivory tower in my view.

Are there major projects on your mind that you're worried about not getting done?

Well, I've done a lot of work on the first woman poet in Canada, who was a Confederation poet, Isabella Valancy Crawford. She was an Irish child brought to Canada in 1855 or 1858. She was a remarkably visionary poet. I discovered and edited an entirely new manuscript that had never been seen. There are now about five people writing theses on her.

The other writing I would like to do is some work on popular women writers like Pauline Johnson, Mazo de la Roche and Nellie McClung, who were neglected and spurned by the critics. There needs to be a whole critical book looking at popular writers in Canada. Their work laid the basis for more mature work like Margaret Laurence's. I don't think a mature novel can arise in a country unless there's been a lot of popular writing as a base.

Certainly one of the signs of maturity in a country's literature is when all books do not have to aspire to be War and Peace.

Yes! What's wrong with the ballads of Robert Service? It's a genre. It's great fun. A lasting literature has to have a base from which to grow. She who went before Margaret Laurence was Nellie McClung.

And Dorothy Livesay. That must be a good feeling, to know you helped lay the foundation for what others are now writing.

Yes, it is. But I've never felt that the poetry belonged to me. I am the vessel through which it comes. My tentacles are out recording. What's coming through has been for everybody. (pp. 130-37)

> *Dorothy Livesay and Alan Twigg, in an interview in* For Openers: Conversations with 24 Canadian Writers *by Alan Twigg, Harbour Publishing, 1981, pp. 127-37.*

Jon Peirce (review date October 1983)

[*In the following review, Peirce favorably assesses* The Phases of Love.]

One might be tempted to come to Dorothy Livesay's latest book of love poems expecting to find a graphic, even lurid treatment of sex. After all, many of the poems are about sex. As Livesay has said in a recent *Quill & Quire* interview, the previously unpublished second section, "Fire and Frost," deals with her love affair with a younger man. Even now, she admits, she is a bit fretful about publishing those poems because of the other individual involved. Certainly the collection contains frank description enough. In the first stanza of **"Let your hand play first,"** for example, Livesay shows that she can be fully as explicit as that notable puritan-baiter, Irving Layton—and a good deal less self-conscious to boot:

> Let your hand play first
> fanning small fires
> over the arms, the breasts
> catching responses all along the spine
> until the whole body flowering
> 's enveloped in one flame
> that shudders wildly out
> to meet your thrust

But even here, in what is probably the most explicit poem in the whole collection, Livesay has her eye on more than just physical passion. In the very next stanza, she takes us from the realm of the physical to that of the metaphysical:

> Then burn, my fire
> burn with a flame so tall
> it can unshape the shaping clouds
> unearthly move the sphere

All this is much more in the spirit of John Donne than that of, let us say, Erica Jong. And the emphasis is consistent throughout the collection. Not content, as she suggests in **"The hard core of love,"** with mere "muscle, thrust / to an intensity / of lust," she seeks

> . . . more
> than skin, flesh, blood
> I seek the coursing
> heaving heart
> for my soul's food

Clearly those seeking mere titillation, those who would view the collection as simply a literate sort of peep-show, must inevitably be disappointed. *Phases* is by no means all passion, flame, and shuddering, not even in the second section. Livesay is a poet of considerable complexity and many moods; the introspective and the whimsical (to name just two of those moods) probably have as much of a place in love poetry as does the steamily passionate. And these emotions get their full play, particularly in the third section, "Voices of Women," in such poems as **"Friday's Child," "The Twins,"** and **"On Seeing The Day of the Dolphin".**

What I find most admirable about *Phases* is Livesay's persistent refusal to oversimplify, her recognition that while love is intense it is also quite mysterious. In the final poem of "Fire and Frost," **"The Step Beyond,"** Livesay provides us with perhaps the best evidence of just how rewarding her complex and demanding sort of truth-telling can be.

Here, though

> The doorway appeared
> luminous
> as if light were music
> and music light

the speaker is pushed backwards, falls into old patterns, takes up "my sewing in a confined room." But eventually she is able to reconcile these seemingly contradictory forces. In the end, it is her recognition that even though the doorway did appear luminous,

> . . . never was it meant
> I'd enter in:
> for entering, I knew
> would be loss of all
> my dross and dress
> and need
>
> I would find not you
> but you-ness
> and no necessity
> to seize   possess
>
> that enables her
>
> to discern the vision: blue green
> essence of bird flashing
> his colours weaving   a wild song

A totally consummated love, then, a total merging of souls, as desirable as it might seem, isn't possible—not for people who wish to retain any independent identity of their own, at least. And this conflict between the lover's desire for merger and union and the independent woman's need to hold fast to some part of herself is central to Livesay's love poetry. Early on, in **"Analysis,"** Livesay declares:

> I am ashamed to be so intimate with you,
> And yet so much more intimate
> With my own thoughts:
> Telling you all,
> And finding
> That it was only half.

The same theme is dealt with more subtly and at greater length in such poems as **"The Search for Wholes"** and **"This Page My Book."** In the latter, we also sense a related conflict between the lover's desire to experience passion

to the fullest and the artist's desire to record that passion as fully and faithfully as possible.

While poems like **"This Page My Book"** are among my personal favourites because they manage to combine a sensuous description of the pleasures of love with an appreciation of the problems facing the woman who would be both a lover and independent human being, I also think section III, "Voices of Women," will be of special interest to many readers. Here, Livesay starts to move away from the specifically romantic love of "Fire and Frost" and starts talking about love as a universal healing force. The poems of this section, dealing with love for family, friends, teachers and the earth and its creatures generally, should be read with particular care by anyone who thinks of Livesay purely as a personal poet; they prove that love, to Livesay, means a great deal more than the private passion between a man and a woman, important though that undoubtedly is.

Again in *Phases,* as in her earlier love poems, Livesay earns our admiration by her insistence on describing love in all its complexity—hesitancies, reticences, conflicts, silences and all. And again, though space permits only the briefest mention of technical matters, the collection demonstrates that her craftsmanship remains as superb as ever. Lines like "Bliss me with your mouth," from **"Dawnings,"** and "magic magic me / out of insanity / from scarecrow into girl again," from **"Sorcery,"** achieve their remarkable intensity and originality from the transformation of a noun into a verb. Described thus baldly, the technique seems straightforward enough—but how many other poets would have had the imagination or guts to attempt it?

There are two problems with the collection, though one is perhaps unavoidable. Because Livesay didn't write much love poetry during the 1930's and early 1940's, and those few love poems she did write during that period have already been published, there is a big gap between the pieces in section I ("Adolescence") and those in II ("Fire and Frost")—a gap which makes the collection as a whole seem just a bit cryptic. There needs to be some kind of bridge. While Livesay obviously couldn't have included poems that simply aren't there to include, even a brief prose explanation might have helped the reader over the hurdle.

What's more, though the book is beautifully printed—a veritable visual delight—it might have been made easier to read. There is no real table of contents, only a listing of the sections, and this, combined with the lack of titles for many poems, often makes it hard to figure out where one poem ends and the next begins.

These minor quibbles notwithstanding, *Phases of Love* is clearly a book to buy and treasure, to read and reread, and to pass on to friends, lovers, and children. It will, I suspect, be many years before a Canadian poet produces an equally sensitive and incisive anatomy of love—unless, perchance, Livesay should herself be working on another volume. (pp. 28-9)

Jon Peirce, "Warts, Reticences and All," in

Canadian Forum, *Vol. 63, No. 732, October, 1983, pp. 28-9.*

Alex Kizuk   (essay date 1983)

[*In the following excerpt, Kizuk argues that many interpretations of Livesay's work are inherently flawed because most theoretical approaches are "male-oriented."*]

After reading Dorothy Livesay's poetry for many years, and trying to write about it, I began to feel that the methods of interpretation in which I had been trained were not adequate to the task. My instincts as a reader told me that my interpretations were only partially accountable. I began to think that my interpretations were oriented toward motives and justifications of the poetry as a communicative act which were not in the poetry itself, but existed outside of it—and originated in my habits of reading, habits that have been conditioned by the ideological investment of our culture in reading. I began to see that my reading was a form of power that our culture put into my hands like a stock-holder's year-end dividends. I began to believe that my interpretations failed to ring true because of the sexual one-sidedness of this ideological investment, and that such poetry as Livesay's bore witness to its own motives and justifications as a communicative act. It seemed clear that the methods of interpretation in which I have been trained were methods bonded to my culture, and that this bonding resulted in forms of male-oriented criticism which could not, in every case, impose its meanings and patterns with absolute certainty. (p. 47)

[Writing] by women by and large continues to be approached and understood through those elements that touch upon how men understand one another. In the case of Livesay's poetry, what little critical attention it has received has been male-oriented. There was a brief flurry of interest after Livesay's publication of *The Unquiet Bed* in the late sixties. This was a time when the voices of radicalism were re-appearing in Canada, after the wound-healing somnolence of the fifties. Filled with rebelliousness, young people like myself gravitated toward Livesay's book because of its sexual frankness. In 1971, Peter Stevens praised these lyrics as the "most candid" of articulations of sex coming from a female perspective. In another article of the same year, Stevens described the unity of Livesay's oeuvre, in such a way as to situate Livesay's poetry in the dominant and traditional opposition of Canadian literary criticism: that opposition between the silence and isolation of indifferent nature, and the voice of human creativity, which seeks to find a cultural vision in this silence and isolation. But Stevens went on to other work, and criticism of Livesay returned to the complimentary, if not patronizing, sort of treatment that Desmond Pacey gave us in 1957. Stevens and Pacey recognized in Livesay's poetic world what they expected to see, which nevertheless signalled her acceptance by the Canadian literary establishment. In his review of *The Unquiet Bed,* Pacey tells us that Livesay's sexual frankness has an "almost frightening vitality," which, he goes on to say, would be monotonous were it not for the poet's modesty, morality, and compassionate empathy. Stevens, concerned with a vision of Ca-

nadian identity, and Pacey, concerned with what, one supposes, he expected a woman writer should be striving after, were not reading the same book as the young, who were full of protest, living on communes in the bush, and outrageously dirty.

By 1974, the integration or unity of Livesay's oeuvre was being abstracted from her recurring images of house and home. One article describes what is feminine about Livesay's poetry as a unity, or "individuation," of images of the woman writer as a wife and mother. At about the same time, in the United States, the poet Adrienne Rich was writing vitriolic articles demanding the expansion of the severely repressed female self. She developed these into a unique and specifically feminine discourse on wife-right, mother-right, daughter-right, sister-right, and so forth. Stevens had recognized in *The Unquiet Bed* the assertion of a woman's "right to exist in her own way," but Livesay's oeuvre came to be thought of as a series of phases through which a woman passes under a man's roof: resistance, acceptance, eventual adjustment to the "traditional role of keeper of the hearth." Livesay's "right to exist in her own way" became obscured by an interpretation that imposed traditional sexual stereotyping and role-models on a period in Livesay's career the poet herself describes, in her article **"Song and Dance"**, as a period of defeatism, mystical experience and existential despair.

The male-oriented criticism that has dealt with Livesay's oeuvre has apparently imposed a dominant and traditional theme of Canadian identity on Livesay's ways of categorizing reality, and an equally dominant and traditional stereotype of woman as wife and mother on her ways of understanding herself. But Livesay's poetry demands that the male-oriented critic change his or her ways of understanding himself or herself, and his or her world, by coming to terms with the poet's own local, private and elemental experience of herself as herself. The female-oriented text makes a demand for changed perception, which, if honored, would change criticism in such a way that it could include this female-oriented way of seeing and knowing. This is not only a matter of sexual chauvinism but also of the limits of perception. Livesay's poetry encourages the reader to discover the "palimpsest" under the lacunae of his or her reading experience; this requires the stripping away of certain cultural models, and certain ways of knowing what a woman is.

Livesay's poetry attempts to teach its reader how to read it: how to effect a personal alteration in one's reading experience so that the experience of a woman becomes accessible as a form of knowledge. Her method is a dialectic between male and female modes of perception. The subject of this dialectic is a woman's will or struggle to discover a language of her own; the object is to effect a change in the reader's habits of reading, which have been imprinted by the ideological investment of our culture. The motives and justifications of this dialectic as a communicative act lie in the poet's commitment to personal relationships and social conditions. Yet she often feels thwarted in her struggle to be heard on her own terms, to "assemble a world of poetry from a vast silence," as Stevens said. In the poem **"One Way Conversation"**, from the *Ice Age* volume of

1975, Livesay tells us that what a woman wants is to be "touched, caressed," and that what she "carries away / the next day / is pride of flesh / love of link with man." This is no chauvinistic sex-pride, but a pride in the sexual dialectic. Livesay knows that men will find it hard to accept "the womb's intrusion" into the "great illusion" of their order of words, and so she reassures her male-oriented reader that:

> You have a role
> valid as sunshine
> of speech as equal
> of man in parallel
> pain . . . joy . . .
> partner to woman
> You have a role gently caressing
> human to human

As reassuring as this poem is, we must remember that what Livesay is saying here is both political and ironic: a woman's language, even though it links man and woman, is put forward as having equal validity as the great illusion of man's "thundering gods". But despite this parity, the statement is made in a "one way" conversation. This irony betrays an awareness on the writer's part that her communication can break down in static on the receiver's end. As Livesay says in **"And Give Us Our Trespasses"** from *Unquiet Bed:*

> The telephone
>   hangs on the wall
> always available
>   for transmitting messages:
>
> Why is it
>   to lift the receiver
> is to push the weight
>   of a mountain?

The communication of a woman's experience of herself as a form of knowledge is as heavy as the stone of Sisyphus to Livesay because it can only be revealed in a *two*-way conversation: a sexual dialectic in which the male reader of such poems as these must freely participate. Livesay's poetry facilitates this participation by using language in such a way as to render the reading experience incomplete without some effort on the reader's part to perceive what, in the poem **"De-Evolution,"** she calls "the thing / in itself," revealed by the sexual dialectic.

The Unquiet Bed has a special importance to the criticism of Livesay's poetry for two main reasons: it marked a sizeable increase in Livesay's audience because it happened to touch upon concerns that were very much talked about at the time, and it addressed itself to Canadian literary criticism outright. What I would like to do at this point is to try to illustrate the idea that Livesay's language forces the reader to alter his or her reading experience by discussing a few poems from *The Unquiet Bed.*

In one of these poems, **"Without Benefit of Tape"**, Livesay tells us that "The real poems are being written in outports / on backwoods farms" they are shouted out "by men and women leaving railway lines," and "in a corner store / it booms upon the river's shore." These statements recall a poem Livesay had written for Alan Crawley in the early fifties. Crawley's magazine *Contemporary Verse: A*

Canadian Quarterly had initiated a trend in the little magazines of creative writing in this country, which effected a "decentralization of Canadian letters". Crawley's regionalization of Canadian taste in poetry was aided by the editorial services of Livesay and three other women writers: Anne Marriott, Doris Ferne and Floris Clarke McLaren. Livesay received friendly support in her writing from Crawley, and it is as her critic and friend that she praises him in **"Nocturne"**, written just before Crawley ended his editorship in 1953. Here, the blind Crawley moves across Livesay's experience of herself as the shadow of an eclipse over a country of the mind. She is thankful that working with Crawley gave her self-knowledge as a writer:

> Only now the shout
> of knowledge hurls, amazing:
> O bind me with ropes of darkness,
> blind me with your long night.

But in this praise there seems to be a note of anxiety in the violent imagery of binding and blinding. If the image were only of blindness, it would be empathetic with Crawley's blindness. That it is also an image of bondage perhaps suggests some unhappiness with her dependence on the knowledge Crawley helped to develop.

In **"Ballad of Me"**, Livesay adds a personal and familial aspect to the local and regional side of her experience of herself as a writer. Here she speaks of an abortionist in language that suggests not the clinic of a doctor but the arena of critical discourse: "the abortionist / who added one more line / to his flat perspective." The personal side of her experience is again treated in the documentary **"Roots"**. This poem has a strange ambiguity to its closing lines, which can suggest both castration and an affirmation of origins:

> I walk beside you where I grew
> amongst the flowers
> and retain
> in the scent of the sweet-pea
> my mother's scissors, snipping
> in the musk of nasturtium
> my father's thumbs, pressing
>
>   heart planted then
>   and never transplanted.

The suggestion is, if one disregards the apposition of "snipping" and "pressing", and reads them as verbs rather than adjectives, that the poet has her origins in this violent expression of the sexual dialectic.

In the poem **"The Touching"**, Livesay's first heart, which is to say the father, is complemented by her lover's penis, which becomes a "second heart", and completes the woman's experience of herself during coitus. This wholeness is made possible only in so far as the "second heart", has been completely incorporated into the woman's experience of herself. When Livesay says that she drowns in the lover's identity, becoming "root / shell / fire", she expresses a moment of reconciliation between the male root and fire, and the female shell. Fire and the sun are almost always images of masculinity and domination in Livesay's work. These lines from the 1971 poem **"Disasters of the Sun"** will illustrate this orientation:

> Sun, you are no goodfather
> but tyrannical king:
> I have lived sixty years
> under your fiery blades
> all I want now
> is to grope for those blunt
> moon scissors

There is no complete submission of the woman to the man in **"The Touching"**. The unity is transient, and "deep in the dark / earth" the woman remains alone. Her incorporation of the man's fire in this most personal expression of the sexual dialectic allows her to become "the element re-born".

Images of water, earth and growing things such as plants and children are always associated with Livesay's experience of herself as a woman. However, these elemental images are also associated with the practice and production of poetic language. In the poem **"Pear Tree"** we find an image of children "chugging on chains / of sound / practicing language." In the poem **"For Abe Klein: Poet"** Livesay reads her body, the elemental ground of this feminine way of seeing things, like a language: "I read where my roots go / assess the green / count leaves' ascension / into heaven's blaze." In the poem **"A Book of Charms"** the lover untangles the woman from "petals and from sleep", and then reads her like a book. In **"Four Songs"** the reader should be aware of the sexual dialectic when Livesay says she drinks "no fiery stuff," but rather the "liquid flow / of words and taste / song in the mouth." This poetic language has something to teach us, and Livesay says in the poem **"Old Song"**: "What you will learn / is this / you cannot hold / what vanishes." Here we find that what is essential to Livesay's poetic language is temporary, transient, as the woman's incorporation of male fire was transient in **"The Touching"**. What is essential, fleeting and yet always "the element re-born" is also the subject of the title poem of *The Unquiet Bed:* "The woman I am / is not what you see." The woman in and for herself has an existence other than that which the lover can perceive. Moreover, in the poem **"Poet and Critic"**, we find that this essential woman is precisely what, to Livesay, gives language its meaning: "Words are so much more / than the thing seen, touched", she says in this poem. What Livesay brings to her poetic language is herself, or rather her experience of herself, which she seals "on the poem's mouth" with the pressure of a kiss. What is disturbing, what is a challenge to male-oriented criticism, is that the reader is held to be incapable of perceiving the essential woman unless he allows himself to be incorporated into her experience of herself as a woman.

In the poem **"Sunfast"**, the woman's will to know herself is expressed in a kind of sacramental conjunction of metaphors of light and the vegetable kingdom. In the opening part of the poem Livesay's awareness of herself moves outward in an empathetic communion with the sun:

> I lurch
> into the sun
> fasten on green

> leaves dripping
> in golden butter

> I break
> fast
> munch morning

Since the sun is a key term in Livesay's poetic language, this expresses a communion not between a woman and a natural object, but rather a communion between the poet and the language she uses to communicate herself. In the second part of the poem, the "you" to whom Livesay is speaking, the reader, is told to speak *his* language into the sun's mouth:

> If you want to tell me anything
> shout it out loud
> into the sun's mouth

> he grins and combs
> our underworld
> with his golden teeth

Recalling that Livesay spoke of her poetry as having a mouth in **"Poet and Critic"**, and that she has incorporated the sun by munching morning-sunlight, dripping like butter on green leaves, as she incorporated the lover of **"The Touching"** by making love with him, we can see that the reader is here expected to direct his commentary towards Livesay's poetic language. The poem invites communication between itself and the reader. It also assumes that we will have something to tell the poet. As the sun grins at this assumed communication, so does Livesay, since she and the sun are one. This is to say that what is essential about the woman's experience of herself as herself is the same thing as what is essential about her language. In the essay **"Song and Dance"**, Livesay says that what is essential about her poetry is song and dance—or to put it another way, euphony and rhythm. She says there that she avoids academic poets and academic critics because "They miss the essence." And in the poem **"Old Song"** we saw that what this language teaches us is that which is transient and fleeting.

And so, in the third and final section of **"Sunfast"**, the transient and fleeting sounds and aspects of the morning are put forward:

> Lawnmower's purr
> caressing grass
> in my next-door-neighbour's
> garden
> probes me
> as if I stroked
> cat's fur
> played with
> green claws

> I am one
> with rolling animal life
> legs in air
> green blades scissoring
> the sun.

If Livesay is here at one with her poetic language, the language generated out of her experience of herself, nothing the reader might have to say about it, shouted into the sun's mouth, can be displeasing to her. Even the irritating sounds of the lawnmower are pleasing. The oneness that she feels with the objects of her language, stated in the opening lines, is restated in the third part of the poem in a oneness with her physical sensations. As the lawnmower caresses grass, so its sound caresses the woman, and this sensation becomes similar to stroking a cat's fur. The lawnmower caresses instead of mows because Livesay has fashioned an identity between her pleasure and the grass, just as she made an identity between her munching and the sun's golden teeth combing "our underworld". With the phrase "green claws" we discover that the woman may not really be all that sure that what the reader has to say will be included in her pleasure. Even the claws of cats can draw blood.

As the sun is an image of masculinity and domination throughout Livesay's oeuvre, and since it is fastened to the lawnmower through Livesay's moment of pleasure and affirmation, the lawnmower can be seen to be an image of domination over the grass. The "green claws" become "green blades scissoring / the sun." In this chain of identities, in which Livesay is, like the children in **"Pear Tree"**, "practicing language", there is a sudden reversal and insurrection of the poem's subject, in which she is suddenly at one with the grass. There is a certain violence in the image that closes the poem; this recalls the mother's and moon's scissors of **"Roots"** and **"Disasters of the Sun"**. The "green blades" would unman the male sun.

In these poems the sexual dialectic alternates between a truth-oriented communion and a reality-oriented struggle, and this alternation operates within what Elaine Showalter calls the "object/field" of her experience of herself as herself. Livesay's commitment to fathers, husbands, friends and lovers motivates her to seek the origin of self in union and communion. The self claims its own truth, right to individuality, and power to create a language of its truth and right. Her commitment to perceive and to know herself in and for herself justifies her struggle with the ideological imprint of our culture upon the experience of union. Thus, though she wants to be "caressed, touched", every caress is for her an occasion for a creative struggle in which this caress is rendered into a poetic discourse that is essentially her own. The resulting poems tell us that even pleasure and desire are modulated by history and culture, and they show us one woman's attempt to come to terms with this modulation by developing a language of her own. (pp. 50-7)

Peter Stevens, who has written most cogently on Livesay, believes that the real unity in her oeuvre must be sought in her imagery of silence and isolation, and in the way that Livesay articulates her response to silence. This is quite true. However, what I want to say is that literary criticism in this country, from the point of view of the woman writer, belongs to that part of our culture that is indifferent to private, local, regional or transient forms of knowledge. I want to suggest that the silence out of which Livesay's dialectic emerges is, in a sense, *our* silence. Literary criticism does have access to a number of different ways with which it can study, as Foucault says, the means by which discourse marks the other in itself. Foucault's notion of reversal denies that discourse can continue indefinitely to

rarefy itself out of silence into order. It denies that any male-oriented discourse, for example, can expect to proceed without reversals, insurrections, rival claims to truth arising from within it. My point is this: that such writing as Livesay's—Isabella Valancy Crawford's, Atwood's, Susanna Moodie's—can be understood as feminine less in its ordering of genre, convention, form, beliefs, ideas or images, than in the ways in which these features of the work organize the experience of a woman into a kind of language.

It is interesting that the theoretical and methodological developments I have been discussing all seemed to come to a head in the period during which Livesay wrote *The Unquiet Bed.* My own feeling is that this book is a development simultaneous with the works of Foucault, Dumézil and R. D. Laing, and that Livesay has participated in a spurt of cultural growth. To criticize *The Unquiet Bed,* as I have suggested, one must allow for a certain degree of modulation in the way in which we habitually perceive the body of a text. I have been forced into attempting some such modulation of my own methods of reading poetry out of frustration with Dorothy Livesay's work; however, this study has shown that avenues exist which can lead toward a female-oriented criticism. In conjunction with more traditional routes, such ways of seeing and knowing may produce a critic who, as Livesay says in **"Green Solariums"**,

> . . . can take me, and be glad of that—
> But will not let himself be lost for love.
> There's bigger things than love to be worked out;
> There's darkness, madness to be fought against:
> The men who will not see the only way,
> The men who choose religion or some crank
> Philosophy wherein to lose themselves—
> These must be battled with before we'll find
> The going easy.

(pp. 60-1)

Alex Kizuk, "Some Theoretical Considerations on Reading Dorothy Livesay's Poetry: 'Green Blades Scissoring/The Sun'," in The Journal of Literary Theory, Vol. 4, 1983, pp. 47-63.

Beverley Mitchell   (review date Spring 1989)

[*In the following review, Mitchell asserts that the sexually explicit nature of the poems in* The Self-Completing Tree *detracts from their artistic value.*]

Just recently I read somewhere that there should be a ten-year moratorium on poetry—and after reading Dorothy Livesay's latest and "most definitive" collection (as the cover blurb claims), I am almost inclined to agree. You see, I like Dorothy Livesay, I admire much of her work, and I really looked forward to reading this book. She had chosen the poems herself from published and unpublished works which span some sixty years, and she had said, "This is the selection of poems that I would like to be remembered by." What an incentive to reading—a poet's choice of her own works arranged thematically. I was even taken in by the unrestrained hyperbole of the jacket blurb:

Half verdant, half in flames, the divided tree symbolizes the androgynous wholeness of the self. This is the theme of much of Dorothy Livesay's writing and the central metaphor for her most definitive collection of poetry, *The Self-Completing Tree.*

Perhaps a divided tree does symbolize the androgynous wholeness of the self—whatever that means—but there is precious little of androgynous wholeness in this collection. Moreover, the tree, which apparently serves both as a metaphor for the poet and as the title for this collection, is not divided; it is "self-completing," as these lines indicate: "Happy the self-completing tree / that brews, in secret, / its own seasons. . . ." Sadly, the poems reveal that Livesay is neither self-completing nor one who brews in secret—and I wish she had taken a lesson from that tree she writes of and kept a few things to herself.

"Winter Solstice," published in 1986, is a case in point. If anything, it shows that the poet who wrote these lines from **"Green Rain"** in 1930 has not lost her touch:

> I remember long veils of green rain
> Feathered like the shawl of my grandmother—
> Green from the half-green of the spring trees
> Waving in the valley.

Some fifty-six years later, Livesay's ability to make you feel as if the top of your head is coming off is as powerful as ever. *How* does she manage the perfect blend of sound and sight as in, for example, the following stanzas from **"Winter Solstice"**?

> Early morning: skirts of fog sweep in   hang
>   over rumpled sea
> till clouds explode   loosening their white dancers
> from window's view nothing is there: only whiteness
> only swirling snow
> Inside: beside the fire we nod and drowse. An hour?
> No, two. Then there is light:
> a hidden sun pierces the curtain
> fog vanishes   snow lies prone
> spreadeagled over the garden grass
>
> Below the cliff a darkening sea emerges
> rippling   sinuous   slow
>
> We wait. We listen half expecting
> not ready for the song
> that bubbles round the lighthouse rock.
> Sea lions are here!   talking again
> no male bark
> but female chuckle   soft
> yet strong with joy
> bells within shells
>
> We window watch: entranced
> he steams up   close
> and now he has her pinned
> rocking her till the curling waves
> seal them in   locked in a triangle
> heads together clipped
> their movements underwater based
> And are there others   farther out
> repeating these same calls?

> We stand   amazed

Now, these lines are worth remembering Livesay by—they reveal her ability to capture all the mysterious beauty of the West Coast and to evoke the innocence of the natural world which is so close to our own. But the poem doesn't stop here. In its entirety, the last stanza reads:

> And are there others   farther out
> repeating these same calls?
> We stand   amazed
> rocked in our own embrace
> then fling ourselves upon the couch
> and beat that rhythm in our heaving cries

And so the top of your head crashes back into place, and you don't know whether to laugh hysterically or weep—because a beautiful poem has been trivialized, made bathetic, and just plain ruined. (The seals at least had the delicacy to make "their movements underwater based"—which is more than can be said for the poet.)

It is the inclusion of so many poems that show an almost obsessive concern with sex in its limited (and limiting) physical aspects that I dislike most about this collection. I don't want people to remember the sensitive, intelligent poet I know as "The Old Bawd"—but the poems in "The Unquiet Bed: Fire and Frost," which were "fired by an intense love affair with a younger man," invite this judgement. My objection to these poems is twofold. First, the intimate physical details of a sexual encounter are interesting only to the participants—and then only so when the hormones are raging, not when recollected in tranquillity; second, expressed in their crudest terms, these details make for incredibly *awful* poetry.

For example, what is poetic about the following stanza from **"Sorcery"**?

> My breasts are withered gourds
> my skin all over   stiffens
> shrinks—the pubic hair
> bristles to an itch

Try flashing that image on the inward eye which is the bliss of solitude and see where it gets you! Why would Livesay want to be remembered by these lines—or by the following ones from **"The Woman"**? "When you make me come / it is the breaking of a shell / a shattering birth." Oh, come now! This is *not* poetry, this is *not* about love, and this is *not* worth remembering the poet by. (One wonders how the partners of these passionate encounters feel today, knowing that anyone can read about them—violated? degraded? used?) The reader is placed in the embarrassing position of voyeur, and wishes that either Livesay or her editors had exercised some discretion and left many of these poems private.

Of course there are many other poems in this collection, and most of them reflect the sensitivity and control that make Livesay one of Canada's most respected poets. As the following lines from **"Song from the Multitude"** indicate, she can write about love with dignity and restraint when she chooses:

> Not until the mad impossible day
> Arrives, when you and I return again

> To the wide heaven and farstretched earth,
> And know ourselves through knowing quiet-
>   ness.
> Not until then, dear love, will there be joy
> To cover us with gold, a sun-like web.

The most exultant of Livesay's poems, **"Serenade for Strings,"** is included, as is **"Windows,"** with its sober triumph of

> a woman gone through drought
> now full whole
> blessedly
> complete

Despite these poems and others like them, which reveal Livesay at her poetic best, the collection is disappointing. Nearly three-quarters of the selections consist of poems published in the last twenty years—and because those not previously published appear to have been written during this time, some forty years of poetry gets short shrift. Moreover, the thematic arrangement is weak. The reader expects to find some development in the themes, both in the ideas expressed and in the poetic techniques used—but the preponderance of recent works, the overlapping of themes, and the apparently random order in which the poems are presented preclude this. Consequently, this collection does not satisfactorily represent "the cyclical nature" of Livesay's art as the jacket blurb claims, but rather a limited and somewhat muddled view that seems contrived.

How sorry I am to come to these negative conclusions. My particular affection for Livesay and genuine respect for her poetry began years ago when she replaced the guest speaker at a convention. Harried and out of breath, she seemed so frail and vulnerable—and she had a run in her stocking. Then she began to read. The power, beauty, and sheer music of her words held us absolutely enthralled—and poetry became somehow real for me that night. I will always remember this experience with gratitude, and love her for the run in her stocking. But I wish her selection of poems for this collection had been different. (pp. 73-7)

> *Beverley Mitchell, "The Self-Defeating Tree,"*
> in Essays on Canadian Writing, *No. 37,*
> *Spring, 1989, pp. 73-7.*

Kristjana Gunnars   (review date September 1991)

[Gunnars is a Canadian poet and novelist. In the following review, she praises Livesay's autobiographical Journey With My Selves: A Memoir, 1909-1963.*]*

Dorothy Livesay goes over five decades of her life in *Journey With My Selves,* and tells the story in outline, without embellishment, in a wonderfully mellow voice. It is the voice of someone who has come to terms with life and gained wisdom in her experience. Reading this gentle account of an interesting life is a surprising experience; surprising in that the prose is so matter-of-fact and even ordinary one almost forgets that what is being told is quite extraordinary. The voice lulls the reader into submission and then quietly tells an "unquiet" tale.

Much of the territory covered in Livesay's memoir of her life from 1909 to 1963 has been dealt with in greater detail elsewhere. Some of the turmoil skimmed over lightly in this book can be found in other titles, in particular the short-story collection *A Winnipeg Childhood* (1973), where Livesay half-fictionalizes her early life. Then there is *Right Hand, Left Hand* (1977), a quasi-documentary book that blends poetry and memoir, where Livesay gives an account of her experiences in the turbulent, highly politicized 1930s, and her fascination with agit-prop writing.

But these books, as well as Livesay's many poetry collections, are more "point-works," to borrow a Norwegian term, wherein certain details are elaborated on at the expense of an overview of the whole. *Journey With My Selves* is really the first chance Livesay's readers have had to see the landscape of her life and career from a distance, as if flying over it. The pace of her telling is very comfortable and entirely free of the corrosive elements that mar so many other memoirs: bitterness, cynicism, regret, guilt, unresolved emotions, and so forth. This book is the account of a woman who gives the impression of being satisfied with her life, fulfilled in her career, and happy in her later years.

We do not, of course, get the whole story. Livesay herself admits in her chapter on "love":

> As I reread these passages I ask: is that the
> whole truth? And I am bound to say, no! . . .
> The truth: all the truth! "Tell all the truth but
> tell it slant," said Emily Dickinson. My father
> was more uncompromising: "If you can't tell the
> truth, shut up." It must be said, sadly, that the
> truth is cutting. It injures.

There is a tacit assumption here that the truth cannot be told. Everything is interpretation. Since Livesay does not want to venture into fiction—an assumption made possible by her choice of straightforward expository prose, delivered without the poetic nuances we know she is capable of—she sometimes attempts the work of being her own biographer, resorting to documents to show how she was feeling at a certain time. Livesay knows the value of a document; you cannot argue with a personal letter, for example, that was as true as a story could be at the time it was penned. So the reader is pacified into an unarticulated contractual agreement with the author that the truth, as truths go, is unnecessary. *Journey With My Selves* is, in other words, as satisfying to read as it must have been to write.

There are elements of the book that will prove interesting, and possibly new, to even the most knowledgeable Livesay scholars. Those who know her books and are acquainted with her papers (now in the Elizabeth Dafoe Library of the University of Manitoba) may still find unexpected information in her newest book. Some things that are already well known, such as her parents' relationship with each other and her own relationship with her husband, are treated summarily but with understanding. One interesting feature, not dealt with so much elsewhere, is Livesay's understanding of adolescent lesbianism. Her final comment is " . . . I never lost the knowledge that ecstasy was possible in the communion created by the union of two bodies. I came to realize that for some human beings these bodies could be of the same sex." The memoir is also interesting for what appears to be Livesay's final comment on her relationship with Raymond Knister and his death. A great to-do was made of Livesay's comments in *Books in Canada* (April, 1987) about Knister ("uproar," as she calls it), but here she calls in a referee, Leon Edel, and allows him the final word. Knister's death, Edel asserts, "was probably an accident" rather than a suicide.

One of the distinctive features of Dorothy Livesay's career is that she has been an important part of the Canadian literary scene for six decades. She has changed with the times and always been ready to take on the most advanced, and sometimes provocative, ideas of each decade. She delved into imagism early, before many Canadian poets. She took up left-wing ideologies and social agitation when most of the important North American and European intellectuals were doing so. She was in the forefront of the women's movement before many Canadian women knew what time of day it was. She spoke freely about human sexuality before the veil of prudery in Canada had been lifted. And now she is showing us what a woman of 80 can do: live a full life, express herself freely, and go on performing, reading, and writing as energetically as ever. *Journey With My Selves* offers a brief, gentle glimpse into how and why this remarkable woman has done so much.

> *Kristjana Gunnars, "An Unquiet Tale," in* Books in Canada, *Vol. XX, No. 6, September, 1991, p. 40.*

Additional coverage of Livesay's life and career is available in the following sources published by Gale Research: *Authors in the News,* **Vol. 2;** *Contemporary Authors,* **Vol. 25-28, rev. ed.;** *Contemporary Authors Autobiography Series,* **Vol. 8;** *Contemporary Authors New Revision Series,* **Vol. 36;** *Contemporary Literary Criticism,* **Vols. 4, 15;** *Dictionary of Literary Biography,* **Vol. 68; and** *Major 20th-Century Writers.*

Ayn Rand

1905-1982

(Born Alice Rosenbaum) Russian-born American novelist, nonfiction writer, playwright, scriptwriter, and editor.

The following entry provides criticism on Rand's fiction, plays, and philosophy. For further information on her life and works, see *CLC,* Volumes 3, 30, and 44.

INTRODUCTION

Rand is chiefly remembered for her controversial novels *The Fountainhead* and *Atlas Shrugged,* which promote her philosophy of objectivism. This extreme form of individualism has been defined by Rand as "the concept of man as a heroic being, with his own happiness as the moral purpose of his life, with productive achievement as his noblest activity and reason his only absolute."

Alice Rosenbaum left the Soviet Union in 1926 and came to the United States, where she changed her name to Ayn Rand. Before she left her native country, Rand was determined to become a writer. Having watched her prosperous middle-class family reduced to near starvation in the aftermath of the 1917 Communist revolution, Rand developed strong anticollectivist sentiments that would stay with her all her life. After moving to Hollywood, she worked as a film extra, and later as a junior scriptwriter. In 1929 Rand married actor Frank O'Connor in order to remain legally in America. Rand's first published work was the play *Night of January 16th,* but she became disgusted with the way various producers treated her work. She subsequently concentrated on writing novels, in which she began to formulate her controversial philosophy. While scorned by many critics, Rand's novels found a sizable audience, particularly among college students. Over time she developed a considerable cult following that flourished through the 1960s. After the publication of *Atlas Shrugged* in 1957, Rand devoted her time to lecturing about her philosophy and defending it in several collections of essays, including *The Virtue of Selfishness* and *Introduction to Objectivist Epistemology.* She also edited the *Objectivist Newsletter,* later renamed *The Ayn Rand Letter.* Rand died of lung cancer in 1982.

Each of Rand's four novels celebrates the primacy of the individual versus collective society. *We the Living* is a polemic against totalitarianism and its disregard of the individual. *Anthem,* a science fiction novella, concerns a future primitive society in which the word "I" is forbidden. In this work, Rand suggests that the individualism essential for building a complex technological civilization has been smothered by collectivism.

In the novels *The Fountainhead* and *Atlas Shrugged,* Rand dramatizes her philosophy of objectivism in lengthy works designed to glorify characters who fulfill her ideals. How-

ard Roark of *The Fountainhead* is an architectural genius who refuses to bend to bureaucratic pressure. John Galt, Rand's spokesperson in *Atlas Shrugged,* leads a strike of the most productive and creative members of society in an effort to collapse the prevailing collectivist social system to prepare the way for a new society based on Rand's ideals. In the closing sentence of a long oration, Galt presents the credo of objectivists: "I swear—by my life and my love of it—that I will never live for the sake of another man, nor ask another man to live for mine."

Critical and reader response to Rand's work has been sharply divided, with much of the disagreement focused on her philosophy. Inherent in her concept of the ego as the moving force behind all creative human endeavors is an unwavering advocacy of self-centeredness and its concomitant opposition to the altruism so important to Christian ethics. While some critics have praised Rand for writing novels of ideas, calling her a thoughtful spokesperson for laissez-faire capitalism, many others have found her work too simplistic and didactic. Since her death, interest in Rand's personal life and work has spawned several biographies and critical analyses of her fiction and philosophy.

PRINCIPAL WORKS

Night of January 16th (drama) 1936
We the Living (novel) 1936
Anthem (novel) 1938
The Fountainhead (novel) 1943
The Fountainhead (screenplay) 1949
Atlas Shrugged (novel) 1957
For the New Intellectual: The Philosophy of Ayn Rand (philosophy) 1961
The Virtue of Selfishness (essays) 1964
Capitalism: The Unknown Ideal (essays) 1966
Introduction to Objectivist Epistemology (philosophy) 1967
The Romantic Manifesto: A Philosophy of Literature (philosophy) 1969
Philosophy: Who Needs It (philosophy) 1971
The New Left: The Anti-Industrial Revolution (essay) 1982
The Ayn Rand Lexicon: Objectivism from A to Z (philosophy) 1984
The Early Ayn Rand: A Selection from Her Unpublished Fiction (short stories) 1984

*First produced as *Woman on Trial,* 1934.

CRITICISM

Daniel Aaron (essay date Fall 1947)

[*An American critic and educator, Aaron has written extensively on American literature and history. In the essay below, he dismisses as "vulgar" both Rand's philosophy and her writing style in* The Fountainhead.]

The Fountainhead, published in 1943, has already sold something like 350,000 copies and has been on the "best seller" list for three or four years. This, in itself, is no excuse for its extended treatment here. It has simply enjoyed the success shared by other bad novels which are 754 pages long and boast of heroines with long legs and high breasts. But there are other facts about the popularity of Ayn Rand's novel which give it a sociological if not a literary significance and make it the kind of novel, to quote an advertisement, "that becomes an active force shaping the lives of its readers."

Unlike its popular counterparts, this novel was not launched with the noise and lights we have now come to expect whenever a new and sultry hussy is about to set forth on her erotic adventures. Apparently the book achieved its reputation through genuine reader response. Ayn Rand writes in an open letter to "every reader who had the intelligence to understand *The Fountainhead,* the integrity to like it and the courage to speak about it," that twelve publishers rejected the manuscript on the grounds that it was "too intellectual" and "too unconventional." But Ayn Rand's readers proselytized for her, spreading her message over the land, and even though Bobbs-Merrill has not stinted in advertising the novel, it belongs very definitely to the category of books that people thrust into their friends' hands with the air of evangelists dispensing religious tracts.

When we realize that the protagonist of *The Fountainhead* is not Forever Amber but a man, an architect, and a philosopher, its success becomes all the more remarkable. It is true that Miss Rand makes real concessions to the slicks. The hero, Howard Roark, has magnificent muscles and orange hair and rapes the heroine, Dominique Francon, with considerable aplomb. But he is also given to philosophizing about the fit and the unfit, functional architecture, and "integrity." In fact many of the characters in *The Fountainhead* are great talkers, and despite the violence and lust and sadism and masochism glowing fitfully through hundreds of murky pages, *The Fountainhead,* compared to *The Manatee* or *The Turquoise,* is an intellectual book. It is built around an idea. It carries a message.

If we follow the main lines of the story and ignore the seductive byways, the plot is roughly this. Howard Roark (for Roark read "the male principle," "the creative urge," Individualism, Thoreau, Frank Lloyd Wright, Carlyle, William Graham Sumner, Alexis Carrel, Tom Girdler, Priapus) is fired out of the Stanton Institute of Technology because his ideas about architecture don't happen to jibe with the administration's. Like most solipsists Roark is a little hard to deal with, but the reader knows from the beginning that no misfortune can make a dent on his flinty personality. He cuts through the obstacles of authority, institutions, society, convention as easily as Superman, to whom he bears an esoteric relationship, and sustained by Nature and by a high-powered unabashed ego, he ultimately achieves an unsought-for success. Indeed Roark is so omnipotent, his unblushing indifference to the most formidable barriers is so colossal, that Miss Rand must work very hard to set up counterforces which will even temporarily stall her juggernaut.

Roark has to face the swinishness of the masses, the tastelessness of the vulgar, but the most dangerous heresy he strives to extirpate is something Ayn Rand calls "collectivism," a protean word respectively identified with "the common good," altruism, planning, democracy, humanitarianism, Russia, Germany, housing projects, social workers, and mass imbecility. The collectivists hate men who make $40 a week or over, independent artists, Nature, functional architecture. Their spokesman in *The Fountainhead* and Roark's only respectable antagonist is Ellsworth Toohey, a diabolical newspaper columnist and art critic who conspires to paralyze society by preaching the vicious doctrine of self-abnegation and by deliberately enshrining mediocrity. Toohey pulls down genius, exalts the "second-handers" (Miss Rand's term for timid, second-rate group-men), and almost perverts America with his gospel of sentimental altruism.

It looks at first as if Roark is going to be sucked into this humanitarian bog. Like Frank Lloyd Wright, whose ideas Miss Rand misconstrues and perverts, Roark serves his apprenticeship with some one meant to suggest Louis Sullivan and then begins his slow ascent to notoriety. Somewhere between page one and page 754 his spiritual and physical complement, Dominique, marries several times—first to a second-hander architect and then to a Hearstian publisher—while Roark builds buildings that aren't appreciated. Toward the end of the novel he finds out that the plans for his housing project have been tampered with by the second-handers, that they have added features of their own to the clean symmetry of his original designs. His response is as simple as his architectural principles. He blows up the uncompleted constructions.

At the trial Roark explains to the jury that his action was necessary and inevitable. And it is at this point that Roark makes the statement which Miss Rand tells us is the key to *The Fountainhead:* "I wished to come here and say that I am a man who does not exist for others. It had to be said. The world is perishing from an orgy of self-sacrificing." The true creator, he argues before a remarkably receptive jury, serves no one. He lives for himself. He simply responds to self-generative primal forces. A man can be either a parasitical borrower or an independent creator. "All that which proceeds from man's independent ego is good. All that which proceeds from man's dependence upon men is evil." It is the creator, Roark continues, who denies, opposes, persecutes, and exploits. "The only good which men can do to one another and the only statement of their proper relationship is—Hands off!" America, "the noblest country in the history of men," was erected on that principle, not "on selfless service, sacrifice, renunciation, or any precept of altruism. It was based on a man's right to the pursuit of happiness . . . a private, personal, selfish motive. Look at the results." The jury hardly bothers to deliberate. Not guilty, the foreman says.

Lest the point of the book be missed by her fans, Miss Rand explains in her letter that she is offering "a new code of ethics," a "morality of individualism." What it amounts to is a kind of watered-down existentialism: don't live through other people. The Great Heresy may be seen in the squashy submissiveness of Dominique's first husband, Peter Keating, and in the power-loving spirit of her second, the arrogant publisher, Gail Wynand. The equilibrium is maintained in the unsullied egoism of Roark who neither seeks to repress his ego for the sake of the herd, nor to live through the herd by ruling it.

So much for the philosophy of *The Fountainhead.* One can only guess whether Miss Rand's reflections helped to sell her book or whether her insights were submerged by the glamour of Dominique's boudoir and the long descriptions of "frozen music" that read like the program notes of Olin Downes. Part of its appeal must lie in its charm for young readers obsessed by thoughts of their own identities; they can respond, perhaps, to its vision of power and sex, to its particular brand of romantic anarchism, shot through with an equally spurious idealism, which inspire dormitory bull-sessions and stimulate adolescent reveries.

And yet this dreary and vulgar equivalent of Carlyle or Nietzsche is symptomatic of certain postwar attitudes that have become more sharply outlined in the last few years. It is indiscriminately anticollectivist, antidemocratic, anti-humanitarian. Howard Roark's challenge to the bureaucrats and the system-makers—"I don't work with collectives. I don't consult. I don't co-operate. I don't collaborate"—becomes in this novel more than a cry against authoritarianism; it is a glorification of the solitary Titans, a polemic against the collaborating, co-operating masses. This is the book that thousands of readers, many of them of the more literate variety, have found inspiring. It is significant, if not portentous, that a woman like Ayn Rand can write a best seller in which the word "collectivism" is distorted beyond all recognition and "democracy" becomes another name for vulgarity, stupidity and viciousness. (pp. 442-45)

Daniel Aaron, "Remarks on a Best Seller," in Partisan Review, *Vol. XIV, No. 4, Fall, 1947, pp. 442-45.*

Whittaker Chambers   (essay date 28 December 1957)

[*An American memoirist, journalist, and critic, Chambers is best known for his involvement in the 1948 trial that led to State Department official Alger Hiss's conviction for passing government documents to Soviet agents. Once a member of the Communist Party, Chambers later became an editor and columnist for the staunchly conservative journal* National Review, *an evolution he chronicled in his autobiography* Witness *(1952). In the following essay, which was originally published in 1957, Chambers finds it difficult to take seriously the plot and philosophy of* Atlas Shrugged, *and maintains that the work is more a tract than it is a novel.*]

Several years ago, Miss Ayn Rand wrote *The Fountainhead.* Despite a generally poor press, it is said to have sold some four hundred thousand copies. Thus, it became a wonder of the book trade of a kind that publishers dream about after taxes. So *Atlas Shrugged* had a first printing of one hundred thousand copies. It appears to be slowly climbing the best-seller lists.

The news about this book seems to me to be that any ordinarily sensible head could possibly take it seriously, and that, apparently, a good many do. Somebody has called it: "Excruciatingly awful." I find it a remarkably silly book. It is certainly a bumptious one. Its story is preposterous. It reports the final stages of a final conflict (locale: chiefly the United States, some indefinite years hence) between the harried ranks of free enterprise and the "looters." These are proponents of proscriptive taxes, government ownership, Labor, etc. etc. The mischief here is that the author, dodging into fiction, nevertheless counts on your reading it as political reality. "This," she is saying in effect, "is how things really are. These are the real issues, the real sides. Only your blindness keeps you from seeing it, which, happily, I have come to rescue you from."

Since a great many of us dislike much that Miss Rand dislikes, quite as heartily as she does, many incline to take her at her word. It is the more persuasive, in some quarters, because the author deals wholly in the blackest blacks and the whitest whites. In this fiction everything, everybody, is either all good or all bad, without any of those intermediate shades which, in life, complicate reality and perplex the eye that seeks to probe it truly. This kind of simplifying pattern, of course, gives charm to most primitive story-telling. And, in fact, the somewhat ferro-concrete fairy tale the author pours here is, basically, the old one known as: The War between the Children of Light and the Children of Darkness. In modern dress, it is a class war. Both sides to it are caricatures.

The Children of Light are largely operatic caricatures. In so far as any of them suggests anything known to the business community, they resemble the occasional curmudgeon millionaire, tales about whose outrageously crude and shrewd eccentricities sometimes provide the lighter moments in Board rooms. Otherwise, the Children of Light are geniuses. One of them is named (the only smile you see will be your own): Francisco Domingo Carlos Andres Sebastian d'Antonio. This electrifying youth is the world's biggest copper tycoon. Another, no less electrifying, is named: Ragnar Danesjöld. He becomes a twentieth-century pirate. All Miss Rand's chief heroes are also breathtakingly beautiful. So is her heroine (she is rather fetchingly vice-president in charge of management of a transcontinental railroad). So much radiant energy might seem to serve an eugenic purpose. For, in this story as in Mark Twain's, "all the knights marry the princess"—though without benefit of clergy. Yet from the impromptu and surprisingly gymnastic matings of the heroine and three of the heroes, no children—it suddenly strikes you—ever result. The possibility is never entertained. And, indeed, the strenuously sterile world of *Atlas Shrugged* is scarcely a place for children. You speculate that, in life, children probably irk the author and may make her uneasy. How could it be otherwise when she admiringly names a banker character (by what seems to me a humorless master-stroke): Midas Mulligan? You may fool some adults, you can't fool little boys and girls with such stuff—not for long. They may not know just what is out of line, but they stir uneasily.

The Children of Darkness are caricatures, too; and they are really oozy. But at least they are caricatures of something identifiable. Their archetypes are Left Liberals, New Dealers, Welfare Statists, One Worlders, or, at any rate, such ogreish semblances of these as may stalk the nightmares of those who think little about people as people, but tend to think a great deal in labels and effigies. (And neither Right nor Left, be it noted in passing, has a monopoly of such dreamers, though the horrors in their nightmares wear radically different masks and labels.)

In *Atlas Shrugged,* all this debased inhuman riffraff is lumped as "looters." This is a fairly inspired epithet. It enables the author to skewer on one invective word everything and everybody that she fears and hates. This spares her the plaguy business of performing one service that her fiction might have performed, namely: that of examining in human depth how so feeble a lot came to exist at all, let alone be powerful enough to be worth hating and fearing. Instead, she bundles them into one undifferentiated damnation.

"Looters" loot because they believe in Robin Hood, and have got a lot of other people believing in him, too. Robin Hood is the author's image of absolute evil—robbing the strong (and hence good) to give to the weak (and hence no good). All "looters" are base, envious, twisted, malignant minds, motivated wholly by greed for power, combined with the lust of the weak to tear down the strong, out of a deep-seated hatred of life and secret longing for destruction and death. There happens to be a tiny (repeat: tiny) seed of truth in this. The full clinical diagnosis can be read in the pages of Friedrich Nietzsche. (Here I must break in with an aside. Miss Rand acknowledges a grudging debt to one, and only one, earlier philosopher: Aristotle. I submit that she is indebted, and much more heavily, to Nietzsche. Just as her operatic businessmen are, in fact, Nietzschean supermen, so her ulcerous Leftists are Nietzsche's "last men," both deformed in a way to sicken the fastidious recluse of Sils Maria. And much else comes, consciously or not, from the same source.) Happily, in *Atlas Shrugged* (though not in life), all the Children of Darkness are utterly incompetent.

So the Children of Light win handily by declaring a general strike of brains, of which they have a monopoly, letting the world go, literally, to smash. In the end, they troop out of their Rocky Mountain hideaway to repossess the ruins. It is then, in the book's last line, that a character traces in the air, "over the desolate earth," the Sign of the Dollar, in lieu of the Sign of the Cross, and in token that a suitably prostrate mankind is at last ready, for its sins, to be redeemed from the related evils of religion and social reform (the "mysticism of mind" and the "mysticism of muscle").

That Dollar Sign is not merely provocative, though we sense a sophomoric intent to raise the pious hair on susceptible heads. More importantly, it is meant to seal the fact that mankind is ready to submit abjectly to an elite of technocrats, and their accessories, in a New Order, enlightened and instructed by Miss Rand's ideas that the good life is one which "has resolved personal worth into exchange value," "has left no other nexus between man and man than naked self-interest, than callous 'cash-payment.'" The author is explicit, in fact deafening, about these prerequisites. Lest you should be in any doubt after 1168 pages, she assures you with a final stamp of the foot in a postscript: "And I mean it." But the words quoted above are those of Karl Marx. He, too, admired "naked self-interest" (in its time and place), and for much the same reasons as Miss Rand: because, he believed, it cleared away the cobwebs of religion and led to prodigies of industrial and cognate accomplishment.

The overlap is not as incongruous as it looks. *Atlas Shrugged* can be called a novel only by devaluing the term. It is a massive tract for the times. Its story merely serves Miss Rand to get the customers inside the tent, and as a soapbox for delivering her Message. The Message is the thing. It is, in sum, a forthright philosophic materialism. Upperclassmen might incline to sniff and say that the author has, with vast effort, contrived a simple materialist system, one, intellectually, at about the stage of the oxcart, though without mastering the principle of the wheel. Like any consistent materialism, this one begins by rejecting God, religion, original sin, etc. etc. (This book's aggressive atheism and rather unbuttoned "higher morality," which chiefly outrage some readers, are, in fact, secondary ripples, and result inevitably from its underpinning premises.) Thus, Randian Man, like Marxian Man, is made the center of a godless world.

At that point, in any materialism, the main possibilities open up to Man. 1) His tragic fate becomes, without God, more tragic and much lonelier. In general, the tragedy deepens according to the degree of pessimism or stoicism with which he conducts his "hopeless encounter between human questioning and the silent universe." Or, 2) Man's fate ceases to be tragic at all. Tragedy is bypassed by the pursuit of happiness. Tragedy is henceforth pointless. Henceforth man's fate, without God, is up to him, and to him alone. His happiness, in strict materialist terms, lies with his own workaday hands and ingenious brain. His happiness becomes, in Miss Rand's words, "the moral purpose of his life." Here occurs a little rub whose effects are just as observable in a free enterprise system, which is in practice materialist (whatever else it claims or supposes itself to be), as they would be under an atheist Socialism, if one were ever to deliver that material abundance that all promise. The rub is that the pursuit of happiness, as an end in itself, tends automatically, and widely, to be replaced by the pursuit of pleasure with a consequent general softening of the fibers of will, intelligence, spirit. No doubt, Miss Rand has brooded upon that little rub. Hence, in part, I presume, her insistence on "man as a heroic being" "with productive achievement as his noblest activity." For, if Man's "heroism" (some will prefer to say: "human dignity") no longer derives from God, or is not a function of that godless integrity which was a root of Nietzsche's anguish, then Man becomes merely the most consuming of animals, with glut as the condition of his happiness and its replenishment his foremost activity. So Randian Man, at least in his ruling caste, has to be held "heroic" in order not to be beastly. And this, of course, suits the author's economics and the politics that must arise from them.

For politics, of course, arise, though the author of **Atlas Shrugged** stares stonily past them, as if this book were not what, in fact, it is, essentially—a political book. And here begins mischief. Systems of philosophic materialism, so long as they merely circle outside this world's atmosphere, matter little to most of us. The trouble is that they keep coming down to earth. It is when a system of materialist ideas presumes to give positive answers to real problems of our real life that mischief starts. In an age like ours, in which a highly complex technological society is everywhere in a high state of instability, such answers, however philosophic, translate quickly into political realities. And in the degree to which problems of complexity and instability are most bewildering to masses of men, a temptation sets in to let some species of Big Brother solve and supervise them.

One Big Brother is, of course, a socializing elite (as we know, several cut-rate brands are on the shelves). Miss Rand, as the enemy of any socializing force, calls in a Big Brother of her own contriving to do battle with the other. In the name of free enterprise, therefore, she plumps for a technocratic elite (I find no more inclusive word than technocratic to bracket the industrial-financial-

engineering caste she seems to have in mind). When she calls "productive achievement" man's "noblest activity," she means, almost exclusively, technological achievement, supervised by such a managerial political bureau. She might object that she means much, much more; and we can freely entertain her objections. But, in sum, that is just what she means. For that is what, in reality, it works out to. And in reality, too, by contrast with fiction, this can only head into a dictatorship, however benign, living and acting beyond good and evil, a law unto itself (as Miss Rand believes it should be), and feeling any restraint on itself as, in practice, criminal, and, in morals, vicious—as Miss Rand clearly feels it to be. Of course, Miss Rand nowhere calls for a dictatorship. I take her to be calling for an aristocracy of talents. We cannot labor here why, in the modern world, the pre-conditions for aristocracy, an organic growth, no longer exist, so that impulse toward aristocracy always emerges now in the form of dictatorship.

Nor has the author, apparently, brooded on the degree to which, in a wicked world, a materialism of the Right and a materialism of the Left, first surprisingly resemble, then, in action, tend to blend each with each, because, while differing at the top in avowed purpose, and possibly in conflict there, at bottom they are much the same thing. The embarrassing similarities between Hitler's National Socialism and Stalin's brand of Communism are familiar. For the world, as seen in materialist view from the Right, scarcely differs from the same world seen in materialist view from the Left. The question becomes chiefly: who is to run that world in whose interests, or perhaps, at best, who can run it more efficiently?

Something of this implication is fixed in the book's dictatorial tone, which is much its most striking feature. Out of a lifetime of reading, I can recall no other book in which a tone of overriding arrogance was so implacably sustained. Its shrillness is without reprieve. Its dogmatism is without appeal. In addition, the mind, which finds this tone natural to it, shares other characteristics of its type. 1) It consistently mistakes raw force for strength, and the rawer the force, the more reverent the posture of the mind before it. 2) It supposes itself to be the bringer of a final revelation. Therefore, resistance to the Message cannot be tolerated because disagreement can never be merely honest, prudent or just humanly fallible. Dissent from revelation so final (because, the author would say, so reasonable) can only be willfully wicked. There are ways of dealing with such wickedness, and, in fact, right reason itself enjoins them. From almost any page of **Atlas Shrugged**, a voice can be heard, from painful necessity, commanding: "To a gas chamber—go!" The same inflexibly self-righteous stance results, too (in the total absence of any saving humor), in odd extravagances of inflection and gesture—that Dollar Sign, for example. At first, we try to tell ourselves that these are just lapses, that this mind has, somehow, mislaid the discriminating knack that most of us pray will warn us in time of the difference between what is effective and firm, and what is wildly grotesque and excessive. Soon we suspect something worse. We suspect that this mind finds, precisely in extravagance, some exalting merit; feels a surging release of power and passion precisely in smashing up the house. A tornado might feel this way, or Carrie Nation.

We struggle to be just. For we cannot help feel at least a sympathetic pain before the sheer labor, discipline and patient craftsmanship that went to making this mountain of words. But the words keep shouting us down. In the end that tone dominates. But it should be its own antidote, warning us that anything it shouts is best taken with the usual reservations with which we might sip a patent medicine. Some may like the flavor. In any case, the brew is probably without lasting ill effects. But it is not a cure for anything. Nor would we, ordinarily, place much confidence in the diagnosis of a doctor who supposes that the Hippocratic Oath is a kind of curse. (pp. 313-18)

> *Whittaker Chambers, "Big Sister Is Watching You," in his* Ghosts on the Roof: Selected Journalism of Whittaker Chambers, 1931-1959, *edited by Terry Teachout, Regnery Gateway, 1989, pp. 313-18.*

Nora Ephron   (essay date 5 May 1968)

[*Ephron is an American essayist, film director, and screenwriter. In addition to the films* Sleepless in Seattle *(1993), which she wrote and directed, and* When Harry Met Sally *(1989), for which she wrote the screenplay, Ephron is known for her novel* Heartburn, *which chronicles her divorce from reporter Carl Bernstein. In the following excerpt, Ephron reflects on how she enjoyed but "missed the point" of* The Fountainhead *in her youth.*]

Twenty-five years ago, Howard Roark laughed. Standing naked at the edge of a cliff, his face gaunt, his hair the color of bright orange rind, his body a composition of straight, clean lines and angles, each curve breaking into smooth, clean planes, Howard Roark laughed. It was probably a soundless laugh; most of Ayn Rand's heroes laugh soundlessly, particularly while making love. It was probably a laugh with head thrown back; most of Ayn Rand's heroes do things with their heads thrown back, particularly while dealing with the rest of mankind. It was probably a laugh that had a strange kind of simplicity; most of Ayn Rand's heroes act with a strange kind of simplicity, particularly when what they are doing is of a complex nature.

Whatever else it was, Howard Roark's laugh began a book that has become one of the most astonishing phenomena in publishing history. *The Fountainhead* by Ayn Rand was published on May 8, 1943, by the Bobbs-Merrill Company, at the then-staggering price of $3. Its author, a Russian émigré with a Dutch-boy haircut, had written the 754-page book over a period of seven years, six months of which were spent hanging around an architect's office learning the lingo of the profession Howard Roark was to romantically exemplify. The book was turned down by 12 publishers; the editor-in-chief of Bobbs finally bought it over the objections of his publisher.

In the years since, *The Fountainhead* has sold over 2.5-million copies in hard and soft cover. Bobbs-Merrill, which is about to issue its 32nd printing, a 25th-anniversary deluxe edition that will sell for $8, calls it "the book that just won't stop selling." Along with Miss Rand's other blockbuster, *Atlas Shrugged* (1957), it forms the theoretical basis for the Rand philosophy known as Objectivism. New American Library considers the two books the prize possessions of its paperback backlist. "Once or twice a year, we reissue these books," said Ed Kuhn, former editor-in-chief of N.A.L. who recently became publisher of the World Publishing Company. "And I'm not talking about a printing of 10,000. These books are reprinted in runs of 50,000 and 100,000 copies. What this means is that every year, 100,000 new people read *The Fountainhead*—a new generation of readers every five years. Other than with Fitzgerald and Hemingway—and I couldn't even say Faulkner and Sinclair Lewis—this just doesn't happen."

The Fountainhead is the story of Howard Roark, modern architect, and his fight for integrity, individualism and ego-fulfillment against the altruistic parasites who believe in Gothic architecture, and more important, against the near-heroes who do not believe the fight can be won. It is also the story of Roark's thoroughly peculiar love affair with one Dominique Francon (whose body is also a clean composition of straight, clean lines and angles, notwithstanding the fact that conventional curves might have been better). Miss Francon is first attracted to Roark while he is working splitting rocks in a granite quarry on her property; she is raped by him on page 219 of the new deluxe edition and page 209 in the paperback. When she discovers, somewhat later, that he is the only architect whose work she admires, she sets out to protect him from disappointment by making certain no one ever gives him a job. She marries two men just to tick him off. "Dominique is myself in a bad mood," Miss Rand has said.

The book ends in a blaze of ego when Roark blows up a housing project he has designed after details of it have been altered; he is ultimately acquitted; and he marries Dominique. They live happily ever after, one supposes, in a steel and glass house.

When *The Fountainhead* was published, almost every critic who reviewed it missed the point—that the welfare of society must always be subordinate to individual self-interest. Rather than dealing with this theme of ego, most of the reviewers treated it as a Big Book, and treated it badly. The reviewer for *The New York Times* called it "a whale of a book about architecture" and thought it overwritten and melodramatic. Wrote the critic for *Architectural Forum*, "The architecture profession, may the Lord protect it, has at last been made a background for a novel. According to its publishers, *The Fountainhead* will do for architects what *Arrowsmith* did for doctors. Though we do not recall precisely what *Arrowsmith* did for doctors, it seems likely that *The Fountainhead* may do a lot less for the architects."

Like most of my contemporaries, I first read *The Fountainhead* when I was 18 years old. I loved it. I too missed the point. I thought it was a book about a strong-willed architect—Frank Lloyd Wright, my friends told me—and his love-life. It was the first book I had ever read on modern architecture, and I found it fascinating. I deliberately skipped over all the passages about egotism and altruism.

And I spent the next year hoping I would meet a gaunt, orange-haired architect who would rape me. Or failing that, an architect who would rape me. Or failing that, an architect. I am certain that *The Fountainhead* did a great deal more for architects than *Architectural Forum* ever dreamed: there were thousands of fat, pudgy non-architects who could not get dates during college because of the influence *The Fountainhead* had on girls like me.

In any case, about a year after I read the book, I sat in on a freshman orientation seminar which discussed the book (among other novels it was suspected incoming Wellesley girls had read) and was shocked to discover:

That Howard Roark probably shouldn't have blown up that housing project.

That altruism was not bad in moderation.

That the book I had loved was virtually a polemic.

That its author was opposed to the welfare state.

I also learned, though not in the seminar, that architects were, for the most part, nothing like Howard Roark.

I recently reread *The Fountainhead,* and while I still have a great affection for it and recommend it to anyone taking a plane trip, I am forced to conclude that it is better read when one is young enough to miss the point. Otherwise, one cannot help thinking it is a very silly book. (*Atlas Shrugged,* the saga of a group of Roark-like heroes who go on strike, move to a small Atlantis somewhere in Colorado, and allow the world to go to pot in their absence, is not a silly book. It is a ridiculous book. It is also quite obviously a book by an author whose previous work readers have missed the point of. It is impossible to miss the point of *Atlas Shrugged.* Nevertheless, it is a book that cannot be put down, and therefore probably should not be picked up in the first place.) (p. 8)

Nora Ephron, "A Strange Kind of Simplicity," in The New York Times Book Review, *May 5, 1968, pp. 8, 42-3.*

Paul Deane   (essay date 1970)

[*In the following essay, Deane praises the psychological realism of the characters in Rand's novels.*]

The philosophy of Ayn Rand, Objectivism, has been subject to intensive analysis and discussion. Interest in her theories has led critics to overlook largely her work as novelist. While it may fairly be said that her plots, except for *We the Living,* are amorphous and loose, that there is endless repetition in *Atlas Shrugged,* and that characters are generally two-dimensional vehicles for ideas, in *The Fountainhead* she has been almost totally successful in creating thoroughly realized characters whose motivations are psychologically valid. It is always dangerous to talk of "influences" on writers; it may be wiser to talk about "parallels." Howbeit, there are close resemblances between personality types described by Karen Horney in *The Neurotic Personality of Our Time* (1937) and by Ayn Rand in *The Fountainhead* (1943). Whether or not one can point to a definite knowledge of Horney and a deliber-

ate use of her conclusions, it is clear that both psychologist and novelist-philosopher have been impressed by the same personality characteristics in American society.

Horney feels that when judgement is passed on individual "neurotics," in a real sense it is being passed on society at the same time. As *The Fountainhead* makes abundantly clear, a person may deviate from social norms without being neurotic—Howard Roark is a case on point; others, such as Peter Keating, Catherine Halsey, Gail Wynand, and Ellsworth Toohey, who have severe neuroses, may be accepted as fulfilling social values exactly. A neurotic is usually characterized by rigidity of behavior, by lack of flexibility: he has a limited number of options available in adjusting to a given situation. But rigidity may also not be "neurotic" unless it departs from the "normal" cultural pattern (i.e., rigid suspicion of everything new is a quality of small, isolated, peasant cultures; to be suspicious in these circumstances is "normal").

Karen Horney recognizes two major trends in neurosis in our time; both of them figure prominently in *The Fountainhead.* First is the excessive dependence on the approval or affection of others. Wishing to be liked is neurotic only when it is indiscriminate and out of proportion. Peter Keating, for instance, needs constant reassuring that his work is good, that he is valuable—from everyone. Feelings of inferiority seem to be among the chief evils of our day: Keating's neurosis is based on inferiority.

Though openly successful, Keating is actually a bundle of anxieties. These he attempts to obscure by amassing money, dressing in the prescribed way, following the proper opinions (those of Ellsworth Toohey). He has difficulties making decisions for himself and he hesitates to express selfish wishes. In important areas, such as marriage to Catherine Halsey, he lets himself drift. Without a clear conception of what he wants to do in his work, he ends by doing nothing. Envying everyone more secure and self-confident than himself, Keating becomes a parasite incapable of self direction. Dominique Francon marries him (he does not decide), Howard Roark gives him ideas for his work, Ellsworth Toohey directs his values.

Keating's need for approbation faces an additional cultural hurdle. Our society is based upon competition. This competition implies that each individual has to fight with others, and in any fight, inevitably someone loses. The result is a generally widespread hostility and tension, generated by fear of the potential hostility of others; fear of retaliation for one's own hostility; fear of failure, with resulting economic insecurity, loss of prestige; and fear of success, which, out of envy, may produce the hostility of others. Peter realizes that if he pursues his own desires and achieves success, others may retaliate and he will lose their approval. He sees that he must be modest, inconspicuous, and conventional; he must negate his potentialities; he must be "normal" in a society that paradoxically extols both competitive success and Christian self-sacrifice.

The quest for affection is one reassurance against fear mentioned by Karen Horney. The search for power, prestige, and possession (both of things and of people) is another. The wish to dominate, acquire, and be admired is as normal as the desire for approval. The feeling of power in a normal person may be a recognition of his superior strength (physical or mental). The striving for power may be connected with some cause: religion, patriotism, or work. The neurotic craving for power is born of anxiety, hatred, and feelings of inferiority. Thus "the normal striving for power is born of strength, the neurotic of weakness."

Comparative texts are sometimes revealing. From *The Fountainhead*:

> Ellsworth Monkton Toohey was seven years old when he turned the hose upon Johnny Stokes. . . Johnny Stokes was a bright kid with dimples and golden curls: people always turned to look at Johnny Stokes. Nobody had ever turned to look at Ellsworth Toohey.

From *The Neurotic Personality of Our Time:*

> The quest for power is . . . a protection against helplessness and against insignificance . . . The neurotic that falls in this group develops a stringent need to impress others, to be admired and respected . . . Usually they have gone through a series of humiliating experiences in childhood . . . Sometimes the ambition is not centered on a definite goal, but spreads over all a person's activities. He has to be the best in every field he comes in touch with.

From *The Fountainhead* descriptions of Gail Wynand:

> One day he walked up to the pressroom boss and stated that they should start a new service—deliver the paper to the reader's door . . . he explained how and why it would increase circulation. "Yeah?" said the boss. "I know it will work," said Wynand. "Well, you don't run things around here," said the boss. "You're a fool," said Wynand. He lost the job. One day he explained to the grocer what a good idea it would be to put milk up in bottles . . . "You shut your trap and go wait on Mrs. Sullivan there," said the grocer, "don't you tell me nothing I don't know about my business. You don't run things around here."

The name of Gail Wynand's boat is *I Do*. *The Neurotic Personality of Our Time* describes Wynand's character:

> Neurotic striving for power serves as a protection against the danger of feeling or being insignificant. The neurotic develops a rigid and irrational ideal of strength which makes him believe he should be able to master any situation. [*I Do*] . . . He classifies people as either "strong" or "weak," admiring the former and despising the latter . . . He has more or less contempt for all persons who agree with him or give in to his wishes.

In her chapter "The Meaning of Neurotic Suffering," Horney draws a solid portrait of Dominique Francon, the most interesting and unbearable character in *The Fountainhead*. Dominique's deliberate incurring of suffering accompanies "the realization of a growing discrepancy between potentialities and factual achievements"; Her suffering is "prompted by anxiety" and has "direct defense value against imminent dangers." Even stronger is Horney's suggestion that "having to realize a definite weakness or shortcoming of his own is unbearable for one who has such high-flown notions of his own uniqueness . . . abandoning oneself to excessive suffering may serve as an opiate against pain."

Dominique is in love with Howard Roark; she applauds his ideas. Yet she consistently tries to ruin him and thwart his projects. Through marriages to Peter Keating and Gail Wynand, she puts herself out of Roark's reach. Early in the novel she buys a beautiful statue, which she finds especially satisfying, but she flings it down an elevator shaft to smash it. These are all neurotic signs, but the reasons for them are more interesting than masochistic motives: they are explained by Horney. Dominique is afraid to believe that Howard Roark is as self-contained and dedicated as he seems, because such a person makes terrible demands on others; if she can find a flaw in him, she need not make an effort to be a complete individual. She also wants to take Roark out of a position where he can be hurt: i.e., if he is broken, if his ideals are gone and his work no longer his most important—and vulnerable—aspect, then the world cannot hurt him. By various experiences with men, she strives to humiliate herself in order to experience some of the pain she believes Roark is feeling. Sex for her is a degrading experience, a subduing one because carried on with inferior men.

Horney continues: "The obtaining of satisfaction by submersion in misery is an expression of the general principle of finding satisfaction by losing the self in something greater, by dissolving the individuality, by getting rid of the self with its doubts, conflicts, pains, limitations, and isolation." Roark will not have Dominique until she learns *not* to submerge herself, until she learns not to submit herself to something greater. He does not wish her to be Mrs. Howard Roark as much as he wants her to be Dominique first. *The Fountainhead* is a long account of the education of Dominique Francon.

As a foil for Dominique is Catherine Halsey, a tragic, beautifully drawn figure. She is what our society regards as the perfect social worker: a figure of utter altruism, of complete submersion in the lives of others. When she is first encountered in the novel, she is a delightful, open girl. After Peter Keating throws her over for Dominique, Catherine dedicates her life to serving others; in so doing, she impoverishes her whole personality, and becomes a bitter, prematurely old woman who worries about the bowels of her friends. Society, however, would applaud her dedication, failing to see that until she has a self of her own, she cannot possibly be of any value to others.

Howard Roark does not strictly speaking belong in a discussion of Ayn Rand's neurotic personalities, because he is not neurotic; he is, however, the touchstone for all the other characters in the novel and as such points up their particular neuroses. Roark needs no approval, acclaim, or admiration: whether he is liked is immaterial to him. He knows his work is good; no one needs to confirm the fact for him. He feels all the emotions except inferiority. While in social terms he is openly a failure, his inner calm and confidence belie the idea. Roark creates his own taste and follows none. In terms of fundamental values and ideals, his important decisions have already been made; he knows exactly what he wants to do, and for 754 pages of novel, expresses only his own selfish point of view. The potential hostility, retaliation of others do not affect him, nor does the prospect of success. And unlike a more typical romantic hero, he does not give up all for the woman he loves: his work and his integrity are more important.

The Fountainhead, chiefly through its characters, points up a number of paradoxes in our time and culture. There is first the paradox of the drive for competition and success on the one hand *vs.* the constant demand for brotherly love and humility on the other. On one side, the individual is spurred on to greater and greater heights of success, which means he must be assertive and aggressive, while on the other he is deeply imbued by the principle and ideal of unselfishness. A second paradox is that one's desires and needs are constantly kept stimulated, while the possibilities of fulfillment are slim or impossible. Through advertising, television, and films, the demand for conspicuous consumption keeps the desires pitched high. But for most the ability to realize this level is not commensurate with the wish, and there is a constant discrepancy between desire and achievement. The third paradox is that a gap exists between the alleged freedom of the individual and his actual limitations. One cannot choose his parents or his early environment, which limits his potential for meeting certain kinds of people. For the majority of people the possibilities are limited but not insurmountable. For the neurotic the conflicts are intensified, and as mentioned in regard to Keating, Toohey, and Wynand, a satisfactory solution is impossible.

The whole force of these paradoxes is to show that society as a whole is neurotic, in that its constitution encourages the neuroses found in *The Fountainhead.* If all society is faced with these paradoxes, and all the conflicts implied in them are essentially impossible to solve, then the Howard Roarks, the really well balanced and secure individuals, will be the ones considered neurotic by the society around them. Thus we end with a fourth paradox. (pp. 125-29)

> *Paul Deane, "Ayn Rand's Neurotic Personalities of Our Times," in* Revue des langues vivantes, *Vol. XXXVI, No. 2, 1970, pp. 125-29.*

Barbara Grizzuti Harrison (essay date September 1978)

[*Harrison is an American journalist noted for combining objectivity with personal experience in her nonfiction works. She has written several books, including* Unlearning the Lie: Sexism in School *(1969), and* Visions of Glory: A History and a Memory of Jehovah's Witnesses *(1978). In the following excerpt, Harrison argues that Rand's philosophy, as outlined in* The Fountainhead, *is destructive and dangerous, especially to the many women who admire Rand's fictional heroines.*]

The literary establishment has never really taken Ayn Rand seriously. She couldn't care less. She has the imperturbable arrogance of one who knows she has The Truth.

"There are very few guide-posts to find," she says. "*The Fountainhead* is one of them." Those who reject the ideas set forth in *The Fountainhead* "are of no concern of mine; it is not me or *The Fountainhead* that they will betray; it is their own souls."

She is not adorable. But she can't be shrugged off. Although it requires inordinate patience and devotion to turgid prose to read Rand's books—and although her sex scenes reek with sadomasochism—the lady speaks (as they say) to a lot of women; it's interesting to consider why.

The 1949 movie version of *The Fountainhead*—Rand adapted it for the screen—does little to explain the success or the appeal of the novel. A posturing Patricia Neal kept doing these jerky things—like throwing her favorite sculpture down an air shaft because it was too beautiful to exist in a world of commies and mystics and parasites and crowds of insipid people who resembled "soft shivering aspic"; and she kept getting married a lot to men she didn't love, while resolutely refusing to marry the man she *did* love—because the thought of his perfection in an imperfect world drove her bonkers. ("Dominique," says Rand, "is myself in a bad mood.")

Gary Cooper, Neal's hero-lover, an architect rebuked and scorned for his excellence in a world of "second-handers," had to make a lot of speeches about man's spirit and skyscrapers and the virtues of selfishness, looking all the while as if he profoundly wished for a six-gun and a horse—which would have enlivened the proceedings considerably, inasmuch as Cooper looked about as comfortable at a drawing board as Frank Lloyd Wright would have looked on Trigger. The movie was not even fun-bad enough to be resurrected as camp.

The book, on the other hand, *is* fun-bad, though no less pretentious. *The Fountainhead* is a ripe and fanciful mixture of politics and sex. In case anybody can possibly have forgotten, Rand's architectural genius hero Howard Roark is thwarted (up to page 757) by liberals and mystics from building New York in his own image. Rand's novels end happily (which is to say, in *her* image); on page 758, the victorious Roark (a man with cruel eyes and hair "the exact color of ripe orange rind") is united atop New York with Rand's Dominique Francon (a woman with "an exquisitely vicious mouth," long legs, and emerald bracelets too heavy for her fragile wrists). The lovers deny themselves the right to marry until all of New York capitulates to Roark's architecture and his ego. In the closing scene, a windblown Dominique ascends in an open elevator to Roark, who is standing atop one of his buildings, blotting out the ocean and the sky. Heady stuff.

Rand describes herself as a Romantic Realist. Romantic? Yes—if one's ideas of romance derive from gothic novels and forties movies ("Nothing but your body, that mouth of yours, and the way your eyes would look at me if . . . "). A Realist? She says that her purpose is the "presentation of an ideal man." Well, if you're going to create heroes, you must, in conscience, give them real worlds to conquer. Rand, instead, sets up straw figures for her heroes and her heroines to knock down: her villains have names like Wesley Mouch and Ellsworth Toohey—and execrable physiques to match.

Rand's knowledge of the real world approximates that of one who has been hermetically sealed in the Chrysler Building since birth. (Anybody who can write a sentence like *Plato was the transmission belt by which Oriental mysticism infiltrated into Western culture* does not, to put it kindly, live anywhere but in her own head.) On the evidence of her novels, Rand appears to believe that the very poor have a terrific time because they can buy radios on the installment plan and do not mind "the feel and smell of one another's flesh on public beaches and public dance floors." And in *Atlas Shrugged,* she implies that American economic intervention in the "pestholes of Asia" and in the underdeveloped countries of Latin America is motivated by demented, savagely liberal altruists who wish wrongheadedly to lend a hand to the undeserving poor. (Now *you* didn't know that's what United Fruit was doing in the banana republics, did you?) Unreal.

Well, about those heroes of hers. I happen to think that women who devoured *The Fountainhead* and *Atlas Shrugged* were attracted, not to them, but to Rand's *heroines;* but we might as well get the gents out of the way first.

In Ayn Rand's tidy, black-and-white universe, all reasonable, rational men are also inordinately good-looking—and fast on the draw. In *The Fountainhead,* Roark and Dominique *don't* waste any time talking before their first sexual encounter—which consists, as it happens, of Roark's raping Dominique. Roark's physical presence hits Dominique "like a slap in the face." She sees him working in a stone quarry, "his long fingers continuing the straight lines of the tendons that spread in a fan from his wrist to his knuckles," and she's a goner, longing to be "broken . . . weak with pleasure," all before she knows whether or not he has passed third-grade math. (Rand's assembly-line heroes all have pitiless eyes and scornful mouths; they discourse on the joys of oil derricks and power plants and the Industrial Revolution while they're unzipping their flies.)

There are three heroes in *Atlas Shrugged,* all in love with the same woman, and all remarkable examples of male bonding. Neither of the losers in the sweepstakes for Dagny Taggart's affections minds at all, when, after a lumbering Pilgrim's Progress, she chooses the most heroic of the heroes in the valley of heroes. (They're like the Seven Dwarfs in their devotion to one another and to her.) One of the heroes distinguishes himself by destroying his own nationalized copper mine, in order to prove that the world cannot exist without unfettered capitalists to make things work.

In spite of their bizarre activities, justified by the Objectivist premise that it is moral to put one's own profit and achievement first, all Rand's heroes are given to the utterance of bromides, which they deliver as if they were unfurling defiant banners: "If one doesn't respect oneself, one can have neither love nor respect for others." Rand may lay claim to eminence and singularity, but platitudes like that are just as likely to crop up in assertiveness-training manuals or pop-psychology books—and just as

likely to be accepted as gospel by needy people with low self-esteem.

One thing can be said about Rand's heroes: they don't take any crap. I suppose it's possible that women who cohabit with wishy-washy, effete, ineffectual men—men who wield worldly power, but who have little authentic authority—have been drawn to Rand's juggernaut heroes because they are able to take the reins so firmly and make the world work for them, and for their women.

Maybe. But I'm inclined to believe that the women who love Rand's books are seduced by an age-old formula: they identify themselves, in fantasy, with a strong, dominant woman who is subdued by an even stronger, more dominant male; with the independent woman who must, to preserve her integrity, capitulate to a more powerful man. Rand gave women romantic heroines who managed to combine hothouse femininity with stern military precision of thought and action.

Rand told women what their experience had unhappily prepared them to believe—that man was the life-force and woman could respond to nothing else, that man had the "will" of life, and prime power. Then she added a thrilling kicker: she placed these men at the feet of her heroines. " 'Kiss my hand, Roark.' He would kneel and kiss her ankles . . . she felt herself owned more than ever, by a man who could . . . still remain controlled and controlling—as she wanted him to remain." Rand gave women haughty, indomitable, fierce heroines—who sang in their chains and found ecstasy in surrender.

There is—provided one lobotomizes the political-feminist part of one's brain—a certain amount of delicious, randy fun to be found in this stuff. Rand knows how to push the atavistic dream-machine buttons. Her "delicately austere" heroines move serenely and aristocratically through crowds of overblown, overdressed women, standouts and knockouts in their chaste severe costumes (which are usually your basic black with lots of diamonds and shoulder bones showing, or dresses "the color of ice" melded to bodies that have never heard of cellulite). And nobody ever *telephones* anybody in her novels. The heroes make Superman-dramatic unannounced visits to the always immaculate penthouse apartments of their waiting perfumed heroines. They come bearing crude bracelets made of some new revolutionary steel they've just invented.

There are some yummy visual set pieces in *The Fountainhead.* Dominique dines in solitary splendor: "a shallow crystal bowl stood in a pool of light in the center of a long table, with a single water lily spreading white petals about a heart yellow like a drop of candle fire." She bathes in a sunken bathtub, "the hyacinth odor of her bath salts, the aquamarine tiles polished, shining under her feet, the huge towels spread out like snowdrifts to swallow her body. . . ." Ah, shades of Cecil B.—Rand's apprenticeship in Hollywood served her well.

She said it before Gloria Vanderbilt did: you can't be too skinny or too rich.

Executive women were hardly popular in the fiction of the forties and fifties. Rand—who says, somewhat obscurely, that men are "metaphysically the dominant sex"—created imperious women who melted at superheroes' touch. She never made the mistake of scaring traditional women off with shoulder-padded Joan Crawford types. She gave us women who were capable of running the world—but who rejoiced in being "a luxury object" for "the amusement" of a powerful man; Dagny Taggart can make transcontinental trains run on time, but she is never happier than when she is sewing buttons on the stained and sweaty work clothes of her man. Rand gave us women who were ruthless with those they perceived to be their inferiors, but who blissfully received "dark satisfaction in pain" from the men they adored.

From there, of course, it's a skip and a jump to sadomasochism.

The question of whether women's oppression has so damaged us that we enjoy wallowing in masochistic fantasies is a vexing one (and I don't propose to try to resolve it). But if women want S-M dream trips, they have only to read Ayn Rand.

On Dominique's second meeting with Roark, she, on horseback, slashes him across the face with a branch . . . because she hates herself for longing to be "defiled" by him. Next thing you know, there he is in her hyacinth-scented bedroom, "austere in cruelty, ascetic in passion." And he rapes her. And she loves it, purple bruises (which go well with emeralds) and all.

> He did it as an act of scorn. Not as love, but as defilement. And this made her lie still and submit. One gesture of tenderness from him—and she would have remained cold, untouched by the thing done to her body. But the act of a master taking shameful, contemptuous possession of her was the kind of rapture she had wanted.

After that first fine careless rapture, D. discovers that Roark is not just a common laborer but an architect whose buildings are so beautiful they give her multiple orgasms. Precisely because his buildings are so beautiful, she decides to destroy him. She cannot bear the thought of his buildings, in a world of neoclassical architecture and tenements, being desecrated by such plebeian artifacts as "family photographs . . . dirty socks . . . and grapefruit rinds." (And I thought the rich *lived* on grapefruit.)

"I hate you, Roark," Dominique says, ". . . for what you are, for wanting you, for having to want you. . . . I want to be owned, not by a lover, but by an adversary who will destroy my victory over him, not with honorable blows, but with the touch of his body on mine." After this extraordinary speech, Roark says—and under the circumstances, it's hard to think what else he could say—"Take your clothes off." Sex is all "clenched teeth and hatred" from there on in, till Roark and Dominique blow up a public-housing project in a final act of cathartic violence that paves the way for them to marry and raise little skyscrapers in their gladiatorial image.

Rand says that she appeals to "rational egoists." I think, on the contrary, that she appeals both to narcissism and to self-hatred, traits which are apparently mutually exclusive but which in fact often coexist in one fragmented personality: scratch a narcissist, and you often find, beneath the veneer of braggadocio, a frightened self-loather.

One way to bolster weak egos is to tell people that they're better than all those other poor slobs they see around them. It isn't rational—but it can be ego-enhancing for people with terminally poor self-images.

In Rand's books, the sick and the unemployed are the victims of their own incompetence—all poor slobs. When children appear in her novels, they are sniveling, squalling, soggy, ugly brats, given to writing dirty words on sidewalks and grotesquely in need of orthodontics. Villains are likely to be "mama's boys." "Breeders" (mothers) are overprotective, corseted, squashy women with fat ankles and bullying personalities. Rand's idea of polar opposites is "a starving genius" and "a pregnant slut."

I hate to think that women hold themselves in such low esteem that they'll buy this . . . ; I'm bound to conclude, however, that for many women, traditional wife/mother roles are so unrewarding that they'll lap up fantasies of a pure, clean, competent, radiant life that most definitely does not include damp babies and runny noses. (In a 1964 *Playboy* interview with Alvin Toffler, Rand allowed as how it was okay for a woman to have as her vocation the raising of a family provided it was done with "science" and without "emotional indulgence.")

I guess by now it's obvious that I'm straining hard to find a charitable explanation for Rand's continuing appeal to women. Basically, I think the appeal to women who have spent so much energy—with so little return—on gaining the approval of others, and the appeal to women who have led sacrificial lives, is Rand's clarion call to selfishness. If you've spent a lifetime being "nice"—and not being rewarded for being nice—it must feel very good when someone comes along and makes a virtue of selfishness. It certainly short-circuits political analysis; it also puts women right back, masochistically, into thinking that *they* are the cause of their own oppression, and hooks them with the less-than-novel idea that all oppressed people can pull themselves up by their own bootstraps.

Rand allows women to have their sacrificial cake and eat it too: she would, she says, step in front of a bullet aimed at her husband, not because she is altruistic (heaven forbid!), but because he is an objective value she cannot live without. That's what's known as being *selfishly* sacrificial. (Rand's husband, to whom she's been married for 48 years, is Frank O'Connor, an artist whose work has decorated her book jackets.)

I've been writing as if only women buy and read and follow Ayn Rand. That's unfair and untrue. Men love Rand too. They are people who enjoy a measure of economic comfort but suffer from the pervasive fear that "welfare looters" and Third World "bums" will take it all away from them. Rand panders to the fears of the middle class; she does so with phony equations: give housing to the unemployed, she says, and people who work to earn a modest living will go homeless. Government bureaucrats are inept, she says (and she's not going to find many who will contradict her); so the answer is not to regulate industry at all.

And since so many Americans are indeed overtaxed and underrewarded, Rand's false and pernicious equations—which refuse to name our real enemies—exert an enormous appeal. She flourishes in a climate of despair.

I think of her man who once worked in the White House; and I am afraid of Ayn Rand. (pp. 26-30, 34)

> *Barbara Grizzuti Harrison, "Psyching Out Ayn Rand," in* Ms., *Vol. VII, No. 2, September, 1978, pp. 24-30, 34.*

Judith Wilt   (essay date November 1978)

[*In the following essay, Wilt discusses* Atlas Shrugged *as a feminist work.*]

I *could* wish that the cancer-causing cigarette were not the ultimate symbol of glowing mind controlling matter in the book, I could wish that the rails which reflect the self-assertion of the heroine were not envisioned running to the hands of a man invisible beyond the horizon—most of all I wish the author had resisted the temptation to have her hero trace the Sign of the Dollar over the devastated earth before his Second Coming. But yes, I agree with Mimi Gladstein, there is a feminist element in Ayn Rand's *Atlas Shrugged,* and it's on my ideal Women's Studies reading list too.

It made a deep impression on me at nineteen and now I can see at least two feminist reasons why. First, the book's opening sections on Dagny Taggart's childhood and adolescence depict with great power the most shattering discovery the awakening womanmind makes—this world is not the one the vigorous confident girlchild expected to find and to help run when she "grows up." And second, the book's middle and final sections depict with still greater power, nay satisfaction, the destruction of that false usurpers' world.

Rand's extended invocation of catastrophe feels astonishingly like the 1970's: "On the morning of September 2 a copper wire broke in California, between two telephone poles. . . . On the evening of September 7, a copper wire broke in Montana, stopping the motor of a loading crane. . . . On the afternoon of September 11, a copper wire broke in Minnesota, stopping the belts of a grain elevator. . . . On the night of October 15, a copper wire broke in New York City, extinguishing the lights . . . " In fact, *Atlas Shrugged* partakes of the general post-nuclear apocalypticism of the 1950's. But there is also a special quality of *feminine* rage discernible not only in the analysis of the Originating Sin behind the usurping world—"altruism," selflessness, the worship of "the other" and his need before one's own—but in the nature of the destruction.

According to her vision of the great age of progress (the nineteenth century, that is—not, I admit, perfectly recognizable to the historian in Rand's form), humanity civilized, indeed organicized, material nature by infusing it with its own purposeful creativity—metal plus mind equals the living copper wire, the bridges and motors and lights which are, so to speak, the mystical body of the human mind, the "material shapes of desire" as Rand

phrases it. When mind goes astray or is withdrawn, the enterprise collapses upon itself, and the plot of *Atlas Shrugged* is predicated upon the desire of the best minds in the world to "go on strike," to destroy the old shapes of desire because they have been appropriated, usurped. Thus in the novel destruction of what is outside the self becomes the measure of greatness, purposefulness, authenticity, even more than construction or preservation of what is inside the self. The heroine's adolescent lover, Francisco D'Anconia, devotes his life to "destroying D'Anconia Copper in plain sight of the world." The hero, John Galt, who organizes the strike and convinces the suppliers of oil, then coal, then steel to withdraw just as the national economy, swinging wildly about in its search for a savior, needs them most, is the hated "Destroyer" to Dagny before she actually meets him. Even after she meets him and knows him, complicatedly, as the full shape of her desire, that desire remains destructive to the measure of its authenticity. Before entering his Atlantis she understands that she would have destroyed the Destroyer if she could—but not until she had made love to him; after she leaves it to go back and try to halt the world's self-destruction, she goes to see him in his hideout in New York despite the risk that she will lead his enemies to him. He describes, to her horror, the trap she has probably enclosed them both in, and urges

> "It's our time and our life, not theirs. Don't struggle not to be happy. You are."
>
> "At the risk of destroying you?" she whispered.
>
> "You won't. But—yes, even that. . . . Was it indifference that broke you and brought you here?"
>
> "I—." And then the violence of the truth made her pull his mouth down to hers, then throw the words at his face: "I didn't care whether either one of us lived afterwards, just to see you this once!"

This subterranean commitment to a cleansing violence, an ethic of destruction, is evident in Rand's vision of both work and sex, is indeed what makes the two functions of the same desire. What attracts Rand, and Dagny, to the industrial barons of the nineteenth century, is unmistakably the sense of their successful smashing of opposition. What brings Dagny back to her job after one early frustration is the disastrous train wreck which destroyed the Taggart tunnel through the Rockies—she cannot accept that destruction and wants to mitigate it. The test of her ethical adulthood at the end of the novel is her willing desertion of the railroad she runs just as the Taggart bridge across the Mississippi, the last link to the West, is destroyed. Leaving, she sanctions this and all following destruction. Dagny first comes to John Galt by crashing her plane into his private mountain retreat; when they return to the city he follows her, running, into the dark tunnel of the terminal, and they share a love scene not easily distinguishable from mutual rape: "she felt her teeth sinking into the flesh of his arm, she felt the sweep of his elbow knocking her head aside and his mouth seizing her lips with a pressure more viciously painful than hers."

At the root of all this eager violence is an equivocal passion for the display of *will* in a world where will seems to Rand's heroine to have either utterly rotted away or else become so devious in its operations as to be unrecognizable, a world "feminized" in the worst sense of the word. "Oh, don't ask me—do it!" she prays at seventeen when Francisco, too, "seizes" her, and she receives his violence thankfully as an anodyne for the disappointment of the formal debut party months before, where "there wasn't a man there I couldn't squash ten of." What she doesn't realize then, what Francisco and Galt are about to learn, is that the power to create *or* to squash that comes from will is not in fact equal to the power to expropriate or squash that comes from will-lessness, not only because there is more of the latter than the former in the world, but more because the people of will have accepted the chains of certain moral systems which short circuit or diffuse their desires.

Dagny suffers from the quantity of will-lessness opposed to her will. Gaining the position she requires, Operating Vice President of the Taggart railroad, was "like advancing through a succession of empty rooms," deathly exhausting but productive of no violence, cleansing or otherwise. Her disgust and near despair are in this respect interestingly like that of an ambitious *man*. Indeed, at the wedding of her wealthy brother and the energetic little shopgirl he marries, the bride challenges the sister-in-law she has heard of as a cold and unfeminine executive: "I'm the woman in this family now," and Dagny replies, "That's quite all right, I'm the man." At the same party Francisco, the self-proclaimed womanizer who is actually one of the Destroyers, answers Hank Rearden's contemptuous "Found any conquests?" with "Yes—what I think is going to be my best and greatest." Rearden is himself the conquest Francisco is after; Dagny's first lover wants her second lover not for explicitly sexual purposes, of course, but for the Cause. And yet, in several senses Rearden is the female to Francisco and Dagny in the novel:

> "I'm saying that I didn't know what it meant, to like a man, I didn't know how much I'd missed it—until I met him."
>
> "Good God, Hank, you've fallen for him!"
>
> "Yes, I think I have."

This is more than the love of one man for another, though it is certainly that too, and eloquently described by Rand, and welcome. It is the love of one being whose desire has been short-circuited, "hooked to torment instead of reward" as Rand describes it, for another whose desire is direct and confident of its ends. And it is this kind of frustration, desire short-circuited, will "contravened," as Lawrence would say, that makes Rearden a kind of female icon. It is the archetypal female plight that Rand explores in his story, displacing it cleverly from her heroine, whom she values too much to subject to it, to her middle-rank hero, whom she loves and pities.

Rearden's existence at book's opening is a schizophrenic shuttling between an unendurable dead family and marriage, and a profoundly satisfying work life whose very satisfaction is a guilty torment because all his love is concentrated there among the machines, mill schedules, and

metals which are, inexplicably and "shamefully" to the usurpers of altruism, alive and lovable to him. He makes the classic "female" adjustment: he accepts the world's definition of his work-life, love, and productivity as guilt and his withdrawal of pure love from his family as shame. He hates and tries to eliminate the sexual desire which is at the heart of the corrupt world of marriage and family and relies on sheer strength, doubled and redoubled, to support both sides of his existence and the conflicts between them. "Well, then, go on with your hands tied, he thought, go on in chains. Go on. It must not stop you." When he finds himself desiring Dagny Taggart, the mind and spirit his working soul most admires, it is a catastrophe to his split self—"the lowest of my desires—as my answer to the highest I've met. . . . it's depravity, and I accept it as such." Dagny does not challenge his definition, knowing that their living experience as lovers will teach him the truth, but it is Francisco who actually tells him the truth. In this novel it is still true that women, even the heroine, mainly exist and demonstrate, while men develop and articulate. "Only the man who extols the purity of a love devoid of desire, is capable of the depravity of a desire without love," Francisco argues; only "the man who is convinced of his own worthlessness will be drawn to a woman he despises." Led by Francisco and Dagny, Rearden emerges from the schizophrenia, reconnects the circuits of his sexual and productive desire to his sense of self-worth, and achieves in the end, like Dagny, that act of abandonment-destruction which, again, is Rand's rite of passage from the usurpers' world to the "real" one. Only it is not just the mills which, like Dagny's railroad, must be destroyed: it is also Rearden's family—mate, mother, brother—which, deprived of his coerced strength, must be let slide into poverty and degradation and madness before the new beginning is possible.

Finally, interestingly, Rearden's reward for making his passage does not include a mate, as Dagny's does. Discovering that Francisco, whom he loves, was Dagny's first lover, Rearden "seized" the woman (again) and consummated an act of love that included, through the woman's body, "the act of victory over his rival and of his surrender to him," just as Dagny too "felt Francisco's presence through Rearden's mind." When Dagny chooses John Galt, the purest shape of her desire and the full expression of her sense of self-worth, Rearden is left, as Francisco was before him, with only his maturity, his recaptured sense of being. Solitary, but not alone, for all three men and the woman are "in love—with the same thing, no matter what its forms." And in Rand's world, which is above all Aristotle's and Euclid's world, "A is A," as the title of her last section proclaims, all movement arises from the unmoved mover of legitimate self-love, and four people who are equal to the same first principle are equal to each other, as long as they live.

Essentially, Rand's novel portrays the victory of Aristotelian and Euclidean thought over Platonic and Planckian relativism. For them, as for John Galt, "reality" stays put and yields its truths to human observation. Only the villains celebrate, only the psychotic accept, the message of much twentieth-century physics and psychology, that matter is not solid nor perfectly predictable and that the mind is at some level simply "a collection of switches without shape." In this respect, in addition to being, as Mimi Gladstein argues, both a science fiction romance and a feminist model, **Atlas Shrugged** is genuinely a "novel of ideas," and it belongs, all 1100 pages of it, on that reading list too. (pp. 333-36)

> *Judith Wilt, "On 'Atlas Shrugged'," in* College English, *Vol. 40, No. 3, November, 1978, pp. 333-37.*

Mimi Reisel Gladstein　(essay date 1984)

[*In the following excerpt, Gladstein discusses Rand's major themes and use of symbolism in her fiction.*]

Although Ayn Rand became known as a philosopher whose ideas influenced people as diverse as politicians and tennis superstars, she was initially a writer of fiction. It was through her fiction that her ideas were first disseminated and it is still through her works of fiction that the majority of readers are introduced to her essential concepts. Though many literate individuals would recognize such titles as **The Romantic Manifesto** or **The Virtue of Selfishness,** by far the greater number of readers are familiar with Rand's novels: **Anthem, The Fountainhead,** or **Atlas Shrugged.** The latter titles are all still in print in hardcover as well as in paperback. The nonfiction works, while still immensely popular, do not compare in sales to the fiction.

Rand's fiction is her foremost achievement. It has made her a world-class author. It is the medium through which her message is most widely and most palatably broadcast. Even those who oppose her politically and philosophically acknowledge the impact of her fiction.

Though she has not published much in comparison to other writers of similar popularity, what she has written continues to sell remarkably well. Her popularity transcends the generations. The sales figures continue to be a publishing phenomenon.

Rand published four novels and one play and one short story. For the purposes of this study, the play will be discussed with the works of fiction. The basic elements of fiction such as plot, character, and theme pertain to both genres.

Rand's major literary works follow similar plot patterns. In each, an exceptionally able and individualistic protagonist battles the forces of collectivism and mediocrity which are threatening or have destroyed a nation or the world. Though Rand personally became more pessimistic about the prospects for individualism in the real world (in 1975 she ceased publishing her newsletter with the announcement that the state of culture was so low, and so many of the dire events that she had predicted had occurred, that to continue to write about and warn of them would be redundant), in her fictional worlds the plot structures become, chronologically, more optimistic. Of course, she quit writing fiction in 1957, nearly a generation before she stopped publishing her newsletter.

Her initial works hold out little hope. In her first published work, **Night of January 16th,** the outcome for the protagonist is dubious. There is a new jury for each performance and Karen Andre's fate hangs on the "sense of life" of a different dozen jurors nightly. Whether or not she is convicted, her main value in life, Bjorn Faulkner, is dead. **We the Living,** begun earlier but published later, has a very depressing ending. Of the three major characters, two die and the third is on his way to sure self-destruction. It is not until **Anthem** that the worthwhile people begin winning. At the end of that novelette, though the world is still in a benighted state, the young Edenic couple have escaped and are ready to establish a refuge for others of their ilk, thereby holding forth hope for the future. **The Fountainhead** paints a roseate picture. Not only does Howard Roark prosper, but Dominique, who had been convinced that the world would destroy anyone with his integrity, has changed her mind and has become his wife. The most optimistic ending is reserved for **Atlas Shrugged.** Although Roark succeeds in **The Fountainhead,** the Ellsworth Tooheys of the world are still solidly in place. In **Atlas Shrugged,** however, the strike of the "men of the mind" vanquishes the looters, leeches, and "second-handers," leaving the world firmly in the hands of the creative and the productive. (pp. 21-2)

Of Rand's five protagonists, three are women and two are men. However, the great preponderance of her other characters, major and minor, is male. Her main female characters share certain characteristics: they have slender physiques, defiant stances, and inner calm. The major male characters have distinctive coloring and bearing: John Galt's hair is chestnut-brown and his eyes are deep grey in a face that reflects no pain, fear, or guilt; Francisco d'Anconia has black hair, blue eyes, and lots of style; Howard Roark's hair is a startling orange and his eyes are grey; Andrei Taganov's face carries a battle scar and projects the look of a caged tiger. Grey eyes predominate as do supple and hard physiques. Rand's heroes are all tall, straight, and strong. As with their feminine counterparts, defiance is a keystone of their characters. Fear is never part of their demeanor. Dominance is reinforced with whip imagery: Bjorn Faulkner treats Karen as if she were an animal he was trying to break; Leo Kovalensky is described as being born to carry a whip.

Rand also uses a technique, traditional in comedy and allegory, by which characters' names are indicators of their personalities. Such names as Wesley Mouch, Ellsworth Monkton Toohey, Homer Slottern, and Balph Eubank carry strong suggestions of their wearers' offensive natures. There are, to be sure, many villains with neutral names such as Robert Stadler or James Taggart. However, even if the character has a handsome physical appearance and a neutral name, the reader is never left in doubt about Rand's attitude toward him or her. Ambiguous characters are extremely rare in Rand's writing. The author/narrator, who is most definitely subjective, communicates quite clearly whether a character is to be viewed positively or negatively. Rand's usual method of character introduction is a brief biographical sketch in which the individual's virtues or vices are clearly delineated. Though Pavel Syerov is described as nice-looking, if a bit of a dandy, the reader is quickly informed that while he represents himself as a revolutionary hero, in fact, "Pavlusha" stayed home with a cold during the initial forays of the revolution. Lillian Rearden, whose classic beauty fools Hank into thinking she is someone to strive for, turns empty eyes and a superficial gaiety on those who encounter her. Although she claims to love her husband, she does not value what he does or appreciate his abilities.

Instant recognition of the like-minded is an ability shared by Rand's heroes and villains alike. Though Kira has never seen Leo before, she is willing to let him believe she is a prostitute rather than let him go out of her life. Equality 7-2521 and Liberty 5-3000 need only eye contact to establish a bond strong enough to make them defy their collectivist society. After minimal conversation, she is sure enough of him to follow him into the Uncharted Forest. In two of Rand's stories, the first meeting of hero and heroine is accompanied by a rape-like encounter, which, rather than distancing the couple, cements the relationship. Howard Roark's rape of Dominique establishes an unspoken bond as neither speaks during the entire episode. Bjorn Faulkner rapes Karen Andre when she comes for a job interview and she remains his business partner and mistress for the rest of his life. John Galt's first sexual experience with Dagny is a ritualized rape in the tunnels of Taggart Transcontinental. For Rand these romanticized rapes are symbolic of the head-on clash of two strong personalities. The rapist is conquered just as his victim is. A readership with a raised consciousness about the nature of rape might find this symbolism unpalatable.

When Rand's characters love, they love without reservation. Since for Rand the emotion of love is a response to values, then the object of one's love is a representation of all that one holds dear; therefore, just as a Rand character does battle for that which he or she values, so a Rand character will do anything for the loved one. This is demonstrated in each of Rand's works of fiction. In *The Night of January 16th* Karen Andre is willing to do anything for Bjorn Faulkner. She defies the law, engages in criminal acts, and even allows Bjorn to marry Nancy Whitfield since that is what Bjorn thinks is necessary to buttress his failing financial empire. She allows herself to be tried for his murder because she thinks that she is helping him engineer a fake suicide. "Guts" Regan is also willing to help Andre and Faulkner stage the fake suicide. His reason is that he loves Karen; he loves her so much that he would help her run off with the man she loves after she has turned down his advances. As he explains to the district attorney, even a lowlife gangster such as he can be moved to nobility when "something passes us to which one kneels."

Leo's health is so important to Kira that she becomes Andrei's mistress so that she will have the money to send Leo to a sanatorium in the Crimea. Prior to that she has risked her life attempting to escape with Leo, although she doesn't even know his name. Kira, who never lies, lies to both Andrei and Leo in order to save Leo's life and pride. She pretends that she loves Andrei and she lies to Leo about where she gets money.

Roark, who is fiercely independent, openly acknowledges to Dominique how much she controls him. When she at-

tempts to play power games with him, he shows her immediately that she owns him—"all . . . that can be owned." His love for her is so great that he will not ask her to be his wife because he knows that she cannot be whole until she comes to him with a healthy ego. He stands by when she marries first Peter Keating and then Gail Wynand, enduring the pain while she goes through her perverse penance.

Gail Wynand explains to Dominique that "love is exception-making." He has broken every person of supposed integrity that he can find in order to prove his power, but he doesn't want to break her, although he tells her that she is in love with integrity and in his eyes is a person who has it, a "person who matches inside and out."

John Galt puts his life in danger in order to be with Dagny. Eventually his association with her results in his capture and torture. Before the government agents arrive he tells her that he does not regret her action. Dagny exclaims, "I didn't care whether either one of us lived afterwards, just to see you this once!" The life-worshipping Galt tells Dagny that he will kill himself rather than allow her to be tortured.

Rand's vision of the world was set when she was very young. She had a very clear sense of the kind of individual she admired and the kind of person she wanted to be. Once she had set her goals, she worked toward them with unswerving determination and integrity. She did not compromise her values. She was determined to do it her way. As she strove to understand why people were beset by the problems they were beset by, she developed a set of principles by which she judged individuals and events. Though there are reasons to believe that she was not unswervingly consistent in her application of her own principles, she claimed that she was. The first sentence of the Afterword to *Atlas Shrugged* reads, "My personal life . . . is a postscript to my novels; it consists of the sentence: '*And I mean it!*'"

A detailed working out of all of Rand's major themes would occupy an entire book; after she stopped writing fiction, Rand published seven works of nonfiction in which she did just that. This [essay] will focus *only* on the literary works and on some of the implications of Rand's predominant message that can be inferred from the actions and words of Rand's fictional spokespersons.

The major theme of Rand's fiction is the primacy of the individual. The unique and precious individual human life is the standard by which good is judged. That which sustains and enriches life is good; that which negates and impoverishes the individual's pursuit of happiness is evil. All of the secondary themes in Rand's fiction develop as the logical consequence of her major theme. If the individual human life is the standard by which good is judged, then it follows that political, economic and ethical systems and institutions which encourage and protect individual freedom and happiness are the proper systems to develop and sustain. While her major theme is explicitly developed in all of her novels, it is not until *Atlas Shrugged* that she works out all of the political, economic, and metaphysical implications of that theme.

Rand repeatedly articulated her respect for America's Founding Fathers and the premises upon which this country was based. If there is a phrase in the Constitution which synthesizes Rand's philosophy, it is the statement that each individual is endowed with certain inalienable rights: the rights to life, liberty and the pursuit of happiness. As Rand worked out her interpretation of what those rights entailed she saw three areas of conflict in which those rights were held in the balance.

THE THREE ANTIPODES

Individualism versus Collectivism
Egoism versus Altruism
Reason versus Mysticism

In Rand's philosophy all of these areas are interconnected. Reason is the tool by which the individual discerns that which is life-sustaining and ego-nourishing. Collectivism, altruism, and mysticism all work against individual freedom, a healthy ego, and rationality.

In all of Rand's works, the individual human is the most important being in the universe. Not God, nor country, nor cause, precedes the individual in Rand's hierarchy of values. In her first novel, *We the Living,* she pointedly illustrates how putting one's state or political cause above the self is detrimental to human happiness and ultimately creates a destructive and poorly functioning state.

The value that Rand places on the individual is clearly seen in Kira's affection for Andrei. Though she hates Communists, she sees Andrei's worth as an individual and worries about him, expressing fear for his safety when he fights rebellious farmers.

Whitfield, the villainous banker who kills Bjorn Faulkner, states his credo on the witness stand, "I believe in one's duty above all; Bjorn Faulkner believed in nothing but his own pleasure." One of Rand's favorite techniques is this kind of dramatic irony whereby the speaker, in trying to explain what is wrong with a character by his standards, is explaining what is right with that character by Rand's standards.

The Fountainhead is Rand's fullest explication of the primacy of the individual. One of her stated purposes in writing it was to develop a defense of egoism, which Rand has also called selfishness and rational self-interest. Howard Roark explains the virtue of selfishness in his defense at the Cortlandt trial. In his explanation of how independent creators have benefited humankind he says, "The creators were not selfless. It is the whole secret to their power—that it was self-sufficient, self-motivated, self-generated." He goes on to explain that only by living for oneself can one accomplish those things which are the crown of human achievement. The mind, in which great creations are conceived, is an individual thing. "There is no such thing as a collective brain."

The much-quoted rule of living of Mulligan's Valley—the utopia of *Atlas Shrugged*—is another of the specific articulations of Rand's belief in the primacy of the individual. Carved in granite on the door to the structure which holds the motor, product of one mind, that could power the world is the oath: "I swear by my life and my love of it

that I will never live for the sake of another man, nor ask another man to live for mine."

Parallel to Rand's development of the dichotomy of the individual versus the collective is her working out of the analogous situation of the productive versus the parasitical. In Rand's fictional world, the elite are the able, the doers. The ability to create, to produce, to do is a primary virtue. For Rand, you are what you do.

This is not as evident in her early works as it was to become in the novels that were the hallmarks of her philosophy. Bjorn Faulkner has a great financial empire, but it is not clear that this is as much a result of his productive capabilities as it is of his financial manipulations and wheeler-dealering. His callous appropriation of his stockholders' funds for his own purposes is more appropriate to those that Rand was later to describe as "looters" than the kind of scrupulous achiever she depicts in Howard Roark. Karen Andre is an excellent secretary; she can take any shorthand assignment Faulkner throws at her. She also becomes an expert at forging his signature. However, her productive capabilities are not on a par with later Rand heroines.

In *We the Living* the only person of actual achievement is Andrei. He is a hero whose bravery has been demonstrated in battle. At the Battle of Melitopol, he risks his life to convince the White Army soldiers in the trenches that the red flag should be their flag. His recognition of like quality in another is demonstrated when he first helps and then allows Captain Karsavin, one of the ablest of the White Army leaders, to commit suicide rather than risk capture. Though Kira and Leo have the raw materials for later achievement, neither of them is allowed to develop those natural resources. Kira has grand aspirations; she wants to be an engineer and build bridges and buildings. To that end she is a good student at the Technological Institute. Though the reader is convinced that she could be an able engineer, Kira is prevented from becoming one. She is expelled from the Institute because she is the daughter of a former factory owner. Her talents are buried in a deadening job as an excursion guide. Leo Kovalensky's only demonstrated talents are in the attraction of women. Though Kira believes in him and though he does begin study in the University, his promise is also stultified by the reverse discrimination practised against children of those who were once in power. Leo's only accomplishments are a bitter bravado and black marketeering.

In *We the Living* Rand had not yet fully developed her concept of the parasitical. The negative characters are more specifically opportunistic than parasitical. Of course, the opportunists are not productive and therefore as they do not contribute materially, they are in a very real sense feeding off the contributions of others. Not only are the Communists not productive, but their system does not promote productivity. What counts is not ability, but party membership or congeniality. Pavel Syerov trades upon his supposed friendship with Andrei Taganov, who is a real hero. He also benefits from the dangerous activities of speculators. They take the chances and he is paid off. Victor Dunaev has some real abilities, but he uses them to further his political aims, not to accomplish anything concrete.

It is not until *Anthem* that the Rand hero whose abilities are society-shaking in a positive sense is introduced. Equality 7-2521 is a creator and inventor in the tradition of Galileo, Edison, and Einstein. In a world where all technological advancement has been lost, he rediscovers electricity. Through hands-on experimentation, he is able to move beyond the shackles of his limited education. Not only does he invent, but he defies. When his society is not ready to accept what he offers, he escapes through uncharted forests to form a new colony of his own where he and others who wish to throw off the chains of collectivism can develop individually.

In *Anthem* there is really only one person of exceptional ability. There is a suggestion that International 4-8818 may be an artist with a real comic talent. And Liberty 5-3000 is brave and loyal. But the only one whose productive capabilities are fully displayed is Equality 7-2521. The villains in the story are not so much parasitical as inert and anti-progress. They do not want to benefit from Equality 7-2521's invention, nor do they want anyone else to.

The theme of the productive versus the parasitical is developed more fully in *The Fountainhead.* The term Rand uses to describe the parasitical in this work is "second-handers." One of the main plot lines of the novel traces the careers of the two architecture students the reader is introduced to in the first few chapters: Peter Keating and Howard Roark. Though Keating possesses a modicum of talent, rather than developing his gift, he guides his life by pursuing what other people think is important. He never learns his craft, and when important commissions are called for he must put his name on other people's work. When he achieves everything he thinks he should want, he does not understand the hollowness of it. He will never be satisfied because he has never gone after what he wants.

Howard Roark, on the other hand, knows exactly what he wants and is not the least bit interested in what other people think of it. In architectural terms, Roark's work is original. He does not follow an already established school or style. His designs proceed organically from the site and each building has an intrinsic integrity. As Roark explains to Austen Heller, "Your house is made by its own needs." The architecture produced by second-handers is derivative. John Erik Snyte's firm stocks one architect for each of a number of derivative styles: Classic, Gothic, Renaissance, and even Miscellaneous. Roark is hired because he fits the slot of "Modernistic."

What Roark respects is productivity. What he calls it is competence. He tells Gail Wynand that there is no substitute for it. Not all the love, personality, charity, good feeling in the world will hold up a poorly designed building.

Ability is the touchstone by which all of Roark's friends and Rand's characters are measured. The field does not matter. The social class does not matter. One of Roark's dearest friends is Mike, an electrician he meets on his first construction job. Mike, whose real name is Sean Xavier Donnigan, is passionate about his work and the people he respects are passionate about theirs; "He worshiped expertness. . . ." Once he is convinced about Roark's quality as an architect, he arranges to work on every one of Roark's commissions.

All of Roark's other friends, the ones who support him through the trial, are persons of exceptional accomplishment. Steve Mallory, who sculpts the statue of tribute to the human spirit, explains it. When Howard Roark wants to hear what he *thinks* and not who his family or friends are or about his childhood, he is overjoyed. He exclaims, "You want to know what I do and why I do it, you want to know what I think?" For Mallory, that means Roark really wants to know what counts about him. They become fast friends. Though Steve has been tried for attempted murder, what counts about him for Roark is his talent as a sculptor.

First-handers don't need others' approval. They know when what they have done is good. Peter Keating needs Ellsworth Toohey to tell him that he is a great architect. Second-handers need committees, and unions, and groups to reinforce themselves.

There is room in Rand's world for people who are not creative giants, but only if they are appreciative of those who create, who produce. In Rand's depiction of contemporary society this proper relationship has been overturned. Those who are unable to do have made the producers their slaves. In the characterization of employers as evil, the employee has forgotten that without the employer there would be no work.

The "second-handers" of *The Fountainhead* are the "moochers" and "looters" of *Atlas Shrugged.* While the "second-handers" are not productive and litter the cultural world with mediocre works, there is still room in the world of Howard Roark for genuine geniuses to function. In the world of *Atlas Shrugged* the "moochers" and "looters" not only hamper the producers' abilities to function, they pass laws and directives which confiscate both the means and the ends of their efforts.

One of John Galt's rationales for the "strike of the mind" is that if the weak have harnessed the strong to their service (as they claim the strong have exploited the weak in the past), then the strong should use the same means that the weak have used—a strike. When the productive withdraw their talents and abilities, the "looter" economy crumbles. When there is no host to feed on, a parasite cannot exist. This is the lesson that Rand teaches in *Atlas Shrugged.* In one of Francisco's speeches to Rearden he explains that Rearden is helping those who torment and hobble him because he still tries to produce even with all of the "looters" restrictions. Francisco suggests that the only way to defeat looters is by not giving them anything to loot.

Certain motifs recur in Rand's fiction. The flamboyant or extravagant gesture is one. Bjorn Faulkner gives Karen Andre a dress of platinum mesh; "Guts" Regan sends her one pound of orchids; Hank Rearden buys Dagny an exorbitantly priced pear-shaped ruby to wear for his eyes alone; Dominique purchases a priceless sculpture of Helios from a museum and then destroys it because she considers it too beautiful for a world of second-handers. For

Rand's characters, these gestures indicate freedom from monetary and mundane restraints.

Music also plays an important role in Rand's works. It symbolizes the creative and inspirational capacities of humanity. **We the Living** and **Atlas Shrugged** have the strongest musical components. For Kira, "The Song of Broken Glass," a tune from an operetta, encapsulates a sense of the gaiety and joy possible in life. Its promising notes echo in her brain as she dies. Richard Halley's unpublished Fifth Concerto initiates Dagny's search for the great minds that have vanished. Its triumphant strains reverberate in her head through much of the book. As Ayn Rand's body lay in state, light operetta music played as the crowds paid her their last respects.

Trials act as significant plot junctures in the majority of Rand's works of fiction. The most important trial in terms of plot structure is Howard Roark's arraignment for blowing up the Cortlandt Housing Project. His acquittal is evidence that justice can prevail and that the individualist does not have to be destroyed. Hank Rearden's trial for defying an unfair government edict also results in his winning. In Rearden's case, he contests the court's jurisdiction over him. In both of these trials, the accused act as their own defense attorneys and in both their summation speeches are important statements of Rand's philosophy of personal rights. Since the juries agree with the accused in each case, one could infer that Rand has faith that an average dozen citizens will respond to reason and appreciate greatness. **Night of January 16th** is a courtroom drama. The trial is the plot of this play. There are also trials in **Anthem** and **We the Living.** But whereas the trials in **The Fountainhead** and **Atlas Shrugged** demonstrate the value of the jury system, the trials in the former works are travesties of justice. When Equality 7-2521 will not tell where he has been, he is sent to the Palace of Corrective Detention without a trial. There, on the instruction of two Judges, he is lashed repeatedly. Later, his actions and invention are condemned by the ignorance of The World Council of Scholars. When Kira and Leo go to the People's Court to protest the fact that one of their rooms is taken from them, they are judged not on the merits of their case, but upon their ancestry.

Cities, especially those with a skyscraper skyline, are the preferred setting for Rand's stories. Skyscrapers serve as a positive symbol. They represent the potential for human conquest over nature. Rand is not ecology-minded. She is enamored of technology and the urban landscape. Kira's chosen profession is engineering. She keeps a picture of an American skyscraper over her bed. Howard Roark's most important commission is the Wynand Building, which will tower over Hell's Kitchen in New York. When Dagny walks on the streets of New York, she is filled with reverence by the sight of the skyline. Rand is the antithesis of a primitivist. Her characters are not refreshed by interaction with nature. For them, nature is there to be harnessed. (pp. 22-30)

Mimi Reisel Gladstein, in her The Ayn Rand Companion, *Greenwood Press, 1984, 130 p.*

James T. Baker (essay date 1987)

[*Baker is an American educator and critic who, in addition to his critical study on Rand, has written biographies of Thomas Merton, Eric Hoffer, and Jimmy Carter. In the following excerpt, Baker analyzes Rand's play,* Night of January 16th, *and short stories.*]

Most people familiar with Ayn Rand know her primarily as the author of **Night of January 16th, The Fountainhead,** and/or **Atlas Shrugged.** They may be vaguely aware of her strong social and political opinions, but few remember her as a philosopher, and fewer still know her philosophic essays. Her fame, for better or worse, rests on her fiction.

This is no real cause for regret, for while her philosophy has its strengths and her fiction its weaknesses, the fiction is far and away her more lasting achievement. She wrote at least one stage play and two novels that deserve to be counted among the landmarks of twentieth-century American literature. Though they are all imperfect, primarily because they are so conspicuously and unremittingly ideological, they have met the psychological and aesthetic needs of multitudes of readers, perhaps owing to the very energy of their ideological biases. They may never be included among the "American Classics," but they have passed one major test of classicism: they will live on.

Although Alissa Rosenbaum decided to be a writer when she was nine years old and wrote a number of short stories and made outlines for novels and plays before leaving Russia, Rand was forced upon her arrival in the States in 1926, at age twenty-one, to start over—with a new language in a new land with a new culture. Yet she did not become a "Russian émigré" writer; nor did she abandon, despite frustrations, her dream of being famous. She started right in, perhaps haltingly, to write fiction in English, and she kept at it until she was successful.

Rand's executor, Leonard Peikoff, has collected in **The Early Ayn Rand** her unpublished first work, from the period between her arrival in this country to the time she was writing **Penthouse Legend** and **We the Living** six years later. These stories provide an interesting window through which to view her development. They show how quickly she mastered a new tongue. They show how rapidly her fluid images and principles crystallized into characters and action. They show her becoming an "American" writer, yet remaining essentially a unique individual in her adopted country.

The first of these stories, written in 1926, is called **"The Husband I Bought."** The English is remarkably good for someone so recently "off the boat," and it dispels some of the mystery of how Rand so quickly landed a job in Hollywood. The story's protagonist, Irene Wilmer, is an early Kira Argounova of **We the Living.** Her husband, Henry Stafford, is an early version of Leo from the same novel, or perhaps even an early Howard Roark of **The Fountainhead.** The story was written while Rand was doing scenarios for silent pictures; she signed it Allen Raynor, perhaps still uncertain of her identity.

Henry Stafford loses his wealth and Irene marries him, pays off his debts, and restores him to polite society, thus "buying" herself a husband. But she loves—actually worships—the man so much that when he falls in love with another woman, she pretends to have an affair with another man so that Henry will think she has been unfaithful and grant her a divorce. In the end he marries the other woman and lives happily ever after while Irene lives her life alone, satisfied that she has done the right thing, kneeling before his photograph in tribute to this ideal man.

There are hints here of the later Ayn Rand. Already we see the strong, intelligent woman worshipping a man who brings out the best in her. Already there is the strong element of masochism. Already there is the individualism that never looks back, never feels remorse. Leonard Peikoff suggests that Rand's attitude toward romantic love may have been formed as much by losing an early love to Siberian exile as by reading nineteenth-century fiction; and if so we may be dealing with a writer whose romantic tendencies will always be dependent on a twist of irony.

Yet in Rand's second story another, contradictory tendency is already raising its head, one that will eventually lead in a more positive direction—Rand's love for the happy ending, the kind that grace (some say disgrace) her mature novels. **"Good Copy,"** written in 1927, was completed while Rand worked for DeMille; and it is much like the synopses she was writing at the time: pure romantic fantasy, with daring heroes, loving heroines, slapdash action, and happy endings. There is virtually no philosophic content. Its English is better than that of **"The Husband I Bought."**

A reporter named Laury McGee is stuck in a small-time job with a small newspaper without prospects when he comes up with a great idea: he will kidnap a pretty young heiress named Jinx Winford, hold her hostage while he scoops all the competition with inside information on the abduction, and make himself famous. Naturally things go wrong. While he is making hay with his stories, a real kidnapper takes Jinx from him, threatens her life, and forces McGee to go to the police with the whole story. The quick-witted Jinx, however, escapes the bad guy and tells the world that the first kidnapping was a ruse to cover her elopement with the man she loves, McGee. They live happily ever after.

For Rand in those days happy endings came easily, for life was good. But soon there came rejection and with it a return to the dark Russian psyche of earlier times. She would long, while writing the wrenching *We the Living, The Fountainhead,* and *Atlas Shrugged,* to do stories with lighthearted themes. She even had a name, Faustin Donnegal, for the slaphappy Irish boy who would star in her farces. But she seemed never to free herself from the pessimism of the late 1920s and early 1930s; and despite what she called victorious, "happy" endings, her later fiction was called comic opera only by uncharitable critics.

The early years saw a great deal of experimentation. Rand read and liked the stories of O. Henry and tried to match his light manner and surprise endings. A story called **"Escort,"** written in 1929, the year she married, is a good example. It was signed O. O. Lyons for Oscar and Oswald, a pair of stuffed lions O'Connor had given her. In the story the young husband Larry Dean keeps from his wife, Sue, the fact that he pays the rent by working as a professional escort, showing rich ladies around town while Sue stays home each night. Sue is so lonely that she uses her meager savings to hire an escort for one night of dancing. Both feel guilty about what they are doing and will doubtless feel more guilty shortly after the story ends; for Sue calls the service where Larry works, and Larry is told to pick up a "Mrs. Dean" at his own address.

There is little here of the later, darker Ayn Rand, except perhaps the thrill of trying to buy a man. There is a great deal here of the Ayn Rand who kept a stiff upper lip when she could find only menial jobs and was married to an actor out of work who might be earning his keep in ways she did not know.

So far Rand's stories, despite strong hints of Russian pessimism, were more or less upbeat, with strong women who knew what they wanted and got it. A fourth story, **"Her Second Career,"** also written in 1929 but after Rand had started working for R.K.O.'s wardrobe department, features a woman who loses control of her life. Also signed O. O. Lyons, this is the story of one Claire Nash, a starlet in a Hollywood that is superficial, trite, and vain. Claire is so sure that her success is due to talent—as perhaps Rand believed about her own early success at DeMille—that she makes a bet she can fake a European holiday, take a new name, and make it big a second time on merit alone.

She soon discovers the hopeless plight of an unknown extra, working for greedy, mindless, dictatorial directors (with German accents), herded around back lots with other human livestock, growing ever more aware of life's injustices. At last she books herself home from her fictitious vacation and prepares to meet her public on the day the plane she is supposed to be flying arrives in Los Angeles. The plane crashes and she is presumed dead. Her advisers tell her that a grieving public would hate her if they learned of her deception. She must indeed assume a new identity and start all over. The story ends with her playing a bit part in a film that features a girl she once discouraged from continuing a career in films. Critics are cool to the "amateur" who had once been a star.

About all that can be said for **"Her Second Career"** is that it shows Rand in that "bad mood" she would retain most of the rest of her writing career. She was in fact entering a new phase in her American life, one in which she would find more rejection than acceptance, and she was not amused. She felt unappreciated, used, angry. Yet out of her anger she would create three heroines, Joan Volkontez of **"Red Pawn,"** Kira Argounova of *We the Living,* and Karen Andre of *Penthouse Legend,* the best female characters of all her fiction, all three courageous, all three lovers of strong men, all three assaulted but unconquered by injustice. Adversity was for Rand the mother of invention.

She was writing *Penthouse Legend* and *We the Living* when in 1932 she sold the story **"Red Pawn"** to Universal Studios. Although it was never produced, it enabled her to leave R.K.O. wardrobe. The synopsis demonstrates Rand's flair for the dramatic. It also demonstrates her antisocialist bias, which in the 1930s worked against the story's production and retarded the success of *We the Living.* The setting of **"Red Pawn"** was unfamiliar to Hollywood producers, its characters improbable, its ideology unacceptable. Its energy and plot sold it.

"Red Pawn" is the story of a strong young woman—in early versions a Russian countess, in later ones an American married to a Russian activist—who sets out to free her husband from prison by any means necessary. Frances Volkontez assumes a new identity, calling herself Joan, and volunteers to be mistress to a prison island's commandant, Comrade Kareyev. This will be a familiar theme in Rand's later fiction, what some call her *Tosca* theme, that of a woman who gives herself sexually to one man to save another.

Joan becomes Kareyev's mistress and arranges an escape—for a moment—for her dying husband. In the process she learns to love Kareyev, who is a good man serving an evil system, and he helps them escape. When they are caught she is told that her husband, "the convict," must return to the island to be executed, while she and the commandant are to go on to trial for conspiracy. She identifies the commandant as the convict, the commandant does not dispute her, and she takes her husband away to trial, knowing he will at least die on the mainland, as the commandant returns to the island to be executed. The commandant goes to his death with his head held high for the first time in years.

As in *We the Living,* Rand's true souls in **"Red Pawn"** do not survive the cruel Soviet system; but again they end their lives with dignity. With these two stories Rand seems to have found her message. *Penthouse Legend* still leaves a woman's fate in the hands of an unpredictable jury, and **The Fountainhead** and **Atlas Shrugged** shift the focus of attention to male characters as well as to North America; but by 1932 Rand had committed herself to the tale of the individual against the collectivist state, in **The Fountainhead** a state run by men without taste, in **Atlas Shrugged** a state run by men without reason.

Frustration with **"Red Pawn,"** a script that sold but was not produced, led to further frustration with **Penthouse Legend,** a script that sold and was produced. Rand claimed that she had merely set out to write a courtroom drama about a woman on trial for pushing her wealthy boss-lover from a Manhattan penthouse, a play in which each night's jury would be chosen from the audience. Once she began writing, however, she decided to do this and much more; yet the woman on trial for killing her lover and the "gimmick" of selecting the jury from the audience were to be what most people enjoyed and remembered about the play. Even those who found the story simplistic, the characters cardboard, and the dialogue childish admitted and still admit that the play, with its female lead and its "gimmick," is worth an evening.

The story was inspired by public reaction to the suicide of Swedish "match king" Ivar Kreugar on 12 March 1932, followed almost immediately by the collapse of his financial empire. He had lent money to several European governments in exchange for match monopolies, the governments had reneged on their payments, and his company had gone bankrupt. Rand noted the "spree of gloating malice" at his death and the failure of his corporation, how he was one day called a genius and the next denounced as a criminal, and she concluded that it was not his dishonesty but his ambition and success that mediocre people despised. The play would be her vehicle for telling what she considered the truth about the life of such a man and the public's judgment of him.

She called the play **Penthouse Legend** and would prefer that title the rest of her life. It opened in Hollywood in the fall of 1934 under the direction of veteran character actor E. E. Clive, with the title **Woman on Trial,** Clive's choice. While the production was too "naturalistic" for Rand, she gloried in its success; and after a year battling New York producer A. H. Woods, what Rand called its "mangled corpse" opened on Broadway in September 1935. It was directed by John Hayden and appeared under Woods's title, **Night of January 16th.** Despite its success, Rand took no pleasure in it.

Reviews gave most of the credit for success to producer Woods and to leading lady Doris Nolan. *News-Week* did not even mention Rand, referring instead to Woods's more than three hundred previous productions and to the fact that eighty of them over a thirty-year period had run longer than a year. The article commended him for discovering Miss Nolan but did not note the discovery of Ayn Rand. *Commonweal* did call the play "well constructed, well enough written, admirably directed . . . and excellently acted," particularly by Doris Nolan; but it referred to the author, only once, as "Mr. Rand."

Time got Rand's name and sex right but spent most of its space on Woods's previous successes, particularly his similar 1927 hit *The Trial of Mary Dugan.* **Night of January 16th,** it did admit, went *Mary Dugan* one trick better by selecting its jury from the audience. But *Theatre Arts* dismissed the play as no more than a parlor game: "It is fun in a parlor with some bright wits about. It seems pretty foolish in a theatre." No one caught Rand's deeper meanings, the clash of philosophies, the praise of heroic behavior, the ultimate victory of individualism; but this did not surprise her at all. No one foresaw great things for the author, and this undoubtedly surprised, angered, and frustrated her. The play ran for six months, not a Woods record but a successful run; and Karen Andre was found not guilty of the murder sixty percent of the time. This too was frustrating for Rand because she often said it should have been obvious to everyone that the woman was innocent.

The rest of the play's history, until 1968 when Rand's official edition was published, was "pure hell." In 1936 she sued Woods for paying another writer to make changes in the script. An unauthorized "amateur" version, which mangled the script even more than Woods had done, became popular with little theater groups around the country and an embarrassment to the author. A film version was, according to Rand, "cheap, trashy," and a further source of embarrassment. The whole experience taught her never to trust anyone with her work again. From this time she would guard her manuscripts, defending them against editing as though they were Holy Writ.

In 1960 the Nathaniel Branden Institute decided to do a public reading of the play, and Rand returned to her original manuscripts to provide the players with an authentic script. In 1968 that script was published by New American Library as the definitive text; the only bow to popular taste Rand made was to retain the title **Night of January 16th.** Otherwise it was all hers again, completely and forever, and she welcomed it home like a long lost child. At last she could be proud of it, and in a long preface she explained what the play was originally intended to say and do. A Manhattan revival, with her blessing, was held at the McAlpin Rooftop Theater beginning 22 February 1973, this time under the title **Penthouse Legend.** It had only a brief run, with few favorable reviews, and Rand put it to rest.

What surprises many readers of the play—and despite the magic of the lighted stage even some who see it performed—is its inaccurate portrayal of an American courtroom trial. One has to wonder if Rand had ever really spent time in court. At several points in the action the judge could and should declare a mistrial. Toward the end of act 3 there certainly should be a recess until two bodies are identified. The case against Karen Andre, which probably should never have come to trial, has been lost long before the jury is asked to decide her fate. In short, it is one of the most contrived courtroom dramas in the history of the theater. But of course the play was never intended to portray real life, certainly not the life of a courtroom, and audiences across the years have found the revelations of shady business deals and illicit love affairs so much fun that they have forgiven the play's shortcomings.

In act 1 the prosecution argues that on the night of January 16th, just before the Faulkner financial empire fell, Bjorn Faulkner's secretary-mistress pushed him from the Faulkner Building's penthouse to his death on a Manhattan street below. The doctor who examined the body is unable to say if the man were dead before he fell or had been previously wounded or even how long he had been dead when he was examined. The night watchman explains that Faulkner and Andre lived in the penthouse together until his marriage the previous October and that Andre then lived there alone. At 10:30 P.M. the night of January 16th, Faulkner, Andre, and two men entered the building, one of the men drunk, and went upstairs. Later the drunk man, now somewhat sobered, came down and left on foot, followed by a car; and later still the second man left. After an hour there were screams, Andre appeared in the lobby with her dress torn, and when the night watchman followed her outside he found the body on the street.

A private investigator hired by Faulkner's wife to watch him verifies that Faulkner, Andre, and the two unidentified men entered the building, the two men later left, and then he swears he saw Andre push Faulkner off the balcony. The defense is able to weaken this testimony by making the private eye admit he had tossed a few drinks while he waited in another building. A police investigator tells of finding Faulkner's "suicide note" in the penthouse and of taking Andre's immediate testimony that Faulkner had made his intentions known to her, struggled with her as she tried to stop him, and jumped to his death. The house-keeper makes no effort to hide her contempt for Andre, describing how Faulkner wasted money on her and how she saw her kissing another man the day Faulkner married Nancy Lee Whitfield. The man she was kissing, by the way, was one of those who came up to the penthouse January 16th.

Faulkner's wife, Nancy Lee, daughter of financier John Graham Whitfield, describes how she met her husband the previous August, married him in October, and loved him very much, as he did her. She admits that when she met him he had overextended himself financially and was on the verge of bankruptcy and that her father had bailed him out; but she contends that he married her for love and that he gladly dismissed Karen Andre after he proposed to her. She says that she hired a private investigator to watch Faulkner because a gangster named "Guts" Regan had threatened his life, not because she ever suspected his fidelity. The act ends with insults hurled between Nancy Lee and Karen Andre.

Act 2 brings to the stand financier Whitfield, Nancy Lee's father. He admits lending his new son-in-law $25 million and argues that Faulkner could have survived his crisis had he not died. He also admits irreconcilable differences between himself and Faulkner over money and social responsibility, what Rand would call in the 1968 preface to the published edition their "sense of life." As Whitfield puts it: "I believe in one's duty above all; Bjorn believed in nothing beyond his own pleasure." Rand would say that the play's primary purpose was to make a clear distinction between these two types of men.

At this point the prosecution rests, without making much of a case, and the defense begins. A handwriting expert explains that it is possible but not probable that Karen Andre forged the suicide note. Faulkner's male secretary, Siegurd Jungquist, demonstrates canine loyalty by testifying that a man like Faulkner never intended to do wrong, that Whitfield constantly taunted him about his business troubles, that he was driven to suicide. A note is given to the defense attorney asking that Andre not be put on the stand until the writer arrives at court, and Andre insists on taking the stand immediately.

There she describes her relationship with Faulkner, how he made love to her the first day she came to his Stockholm office looking for work, how she became his mistress, how he loved her until he died. She says he married Nancy Lee only because her father would not otherwise extend a $10 million loan, which he could not pay on time. He did promise to dismiss Karen, but all along he planned to return to her. When Whitfield reneged on the extension, she and Faulkner forged Whitfield's signature to $25 million worth of stock securities, but it was not enough. She is about to testify that Faulkner preferred death to poverty and that he committed suicide when "Guts" Regan enters the courtroom and blurts out that Faulkner is dead. This is apparently a surprise to Andre, who suddenly faints.

Act 3 begins with the conclusion of Andre's testimony. She now admits that she and Faulkner faked the suicide. Faulkner sent Whitfield's millions to South America, "Guts" found a corpse the same size as Faulkner, they brought it to the penthouse "drunk," and Faulkner changed clothes with it and left. Regan was to fly him to Buenes Aires, and Andre to meet him there. "Bjorn never thought of things as right or wrong," she says. "To him, it was only: you can or you can't. He always could." So could Andre, who threw a corpse over the balcony.

Regan picks up the story. He arrived at the airstrip to find the getaway plane gone. He did find a limousine hidden in the trees nearby. In the morning a man returned to it, disheveled, and gave him a check for $5,000 to keep quiet. Submitted as evidence, the check was dated January 17th and signed "John Graham Whitfield." Regan says he went looking for Faulkner in Argentina, returned to the states to look for the plane, and only yesterday found it in New Jersey. A charred skeleton in the burned shell, which he says was Faulkner, had been shot twice before the plane was torched. "Guts" admits to the prosecutor that he loves Karen Andre, that it was he who was kissing her at Faulkner's wedding, and that he would do anything, including lie or kill, to save her.

John Graham Whitfield testifies that Regan's story is a complete fabrication and explains that he hired Regan and paid him $5,000 to guard his daughter the day after Faulkner was killed. He knew nothing about the money sent to Argentina. Jungquist blurts out that he told Whitfield about the money, unaware that he was sentencing his patron to death; but the prosecution says that it is one man's word against another, and the defense rests.

The jury is taken away, where a simple majority is needed to convict or acquit. They may either decide that a jilted Karen Andre, in a fit of jealousy, forged a suicide note and pushed her lover (who was drunk or drugged) to his death. Not likely, given what the jury has seen and heard. Or they may decide that Faulkner and Andre concocted an elaborate hoax, that a dead man's body was thrown from the balcony, that Faulkner is either still alive or dead at the hands of Whitfield or Regan. Rand thought it obvious that Andre was innocent—innocent of murder, certainly not of perjury. Yet her juries, perhaps enjoying punishing this bad girl, found Andre guilty forty percent of the time. Fortunately Rand provided two endings: if not guilty, Andre thanks the jury and is released without a word said about her perjury; if guilty, she announces there will be no appeal, that the verdict has saved her the effort to commit suicide. Nothing is said about arresting Whitfield or Regan, and no one suggests performing autopsies to discover just who is and who is not dead.

The real question for Rand was not who was dead and who was guilty but who in the cast had the superior "sense of life." When she published the script in 1968, she defined "sense of life" as a person's "emotional, subconsciously integrated appraisal of man's relationship to existence." Her play contrasted that of Bjorn Faulkner (and Karen Andre) with that of John Graham Whitfield (and Nancy Lee). The events and characters were not to be taken literally; they were intended merely to dramatize "certain fundamental psychological characteristics, deliberately isolated and emphasized in order to convey a single abstraction: the character's attitude toward life." The play, she said, should be considered "romantic symbolism."

Bjorn Faulkner and Karen Andre represented passionate self-assertiveness, self-confidence, ambition, audacity, and independence from social norms. John Graham Whitfield and Nancy Lee represented conventionality, servility, envy, hatred, and lust for power over other people. Rand knew from the start that audiences would mistake her message, think the play a murder mystery, enjoy "the gimmick," and go home unenlightened; but she wrote it, offered it, and suffered embarrassment in order to build a foundation for a career that would attract an audience to understand.

She always felt she had to defend what people called the play's immorality. Bjorn Faulkner, she explained in the 1968 preface, is not an ideal man. She was not ready in 1933 to portray the ideal man. Howard Roark was five years away from birth. Bjorn Faulkner is already dead when the play begins and is seen only through the eyes of those who loved and hated him. This is Karen Andre's story, and it portrays "a woman's feeling for her ideal man." It is Karen Andre and not Bjorn Faulkner who is on trial; and we are told to judge her only by the standards of loyalty. She cannot be immoral—or guilty—even if the life she lives is immoral, even if she is guilty. Because Faulkner was a man of supreme self-confidence, because he won and held the love of a woman like Karen Andre, it is irrelevant whether or not he is a crook.

Night of January 16th was a popular success and brought Rand the fame she so desperately desired. Yet it does not bear close scrutiny, and it does not really convey the "senses of life" Rand thought it did. In the final analysis, despite its significance for her career, it is held together by an enormously attractive woman and a gimmick. It is great entertainment, but it is not philosophy. Rand would gladly have sacrificed the first for the second, and in her later fiction she would consciously do just that.

While *Night of January 16th* entertained without indoctrinating, *We the Living* indoctrinated without entertaining. Novels "with a message," whatever the message, often fail to achieve the level of great fiction. Rand believed that this novel was long rejected by publishers and ill-treated by critics because it told the truth about the Soviet system, when in fact it was rejected and criticized because it was preachy. Those who bought and continue to buy it liked, and still like, Rand's sermon.

We the Living was written between 1931 and 1933 and published in 1936. Thus it is a contemporary of **"Red Pawn"** and *Night of January 16th.* Its central figure, Kira (for Cyrus) Argounova, is a woman, as are the central figures Joan in **"Red Pawn"** and Karen Andre in *Night of January 16th.* But in this novel Rand at last attempts to create a male hero, not one seen through a woman's eyes, not one already dead, and not one but two. Leo Kovalensky and Andrei Tagonov are not yet Howard Roark and John Galt, but they are vital first steps in that direction. It may come as a shock to those who think of Rand as an anticommunist to learn that the most admirable men in **"Red Pawn"** and *We the Living* are both communists.

In her preface to the 1958 edition, Rand wrote that *We the Living* is "as near an autobiography as I will ever write." Not literally, she hastened to add, but intellectually. Kira is a student of engineering while Rand studied history; Kira wants to build, Rand wanted to write; and Kira dies trying to escape Russia, while Rand escaped and lived a full life. But Rand, like Kira, knew from childhood that she hated the communist system, from the moment it told her that man exists for the state. And so to a large extent, though we can never know how faithfully she portrayed her university friends and experiences, this story is Rand's pilgrimage.

It will be the last time she sets a story in Russia, unless we surmise that Russia is the backdrop for the nebulous and futuristic *Anthem.* The "great" novels, *The Fountainhead* and *Atlas Shrugged,* are both set in America. *We the Living* is the only one of her novels with an atmosphere akin to that of Boris Pasternak's *Doctor Zhivago.* Yet Rand always said that this is not really a story about Russia or even about the Soviet system as such. To her it was a story about man against the state, its theme universal, its philosophy timeless. To her it happened in any state at any time where and when men and women are enslaved and made to serve the common good.

The 1958 paperback edition, which most people read today, contains revisions. Rand explained that she changed certain language to make it sound more American, less stilted, easier for the casual reader to follow. Her English, she admitted, was in 1933 still a bit uncertain. Yet as she reread it twenty-five years later she found her original philosophy of life unchanged, and she was pleased at how well she had been able to express it. While she improved her English, she was unable to improve her philosophy. It was essentially unchanged through the course of her adult life.

The story of *We the Living* begins in 1922 as the Argounova family—Kira, her parents, her older sister—return to Petrograd from four years in the Crimea. Her father, once a textile manufacturer, has lost his business during the revolution and is a broken man. The escape to the south has proven futile. Kira, who has never had a boyfriend but who dreams of a Viking she once read about in a novel, wants to be an architect. Above her bed, like an icon, hangs a picture of a New York skyscraper. She does not believe in God, but she believes in man.

As soon as she enters the Technological Institute she meets a young communist leader named Andrei Taganov and spends her spare daylight hours with him, while she spends nights with a mysterious young resister named Leo Kovalensky. Andrei cautions her to keep quiet about her opposition to the Party. He sees in communism hope for the downtrodden, for people like his father who died in a czarist camp in Siberia. Kira argues with him that the state should exist for the people, not the people for the state, and that she will never be reconciled to the idea of sacrificing the individual for "the common good." The other man, Leo, tells her not to hope for things to get better. His father was a great captain in the czar's fleet who was blinded during the war and then executed by the communists as a subversive. When she tells him her dream of building skyscrapers, he asks her why she bothers. When she replies that she wants to be admired, he warns her that

it is a curse "to be able to look higher than you're allowed to reach."

Thus in the opening chapters Kira becomes involved with two men, one intellectually, the other both intellectually and physically, whose backgrounds and philosophies differ not only from each other but also from her own. She has a stronger commitment than Leo, though it is to a different faith, and a stronger resolve than Andrei, though it is to a different cause. As in earlier works, Rand's woman, though she pretends to worship maleness, is superior to Rand's men. One wonders what inner conflict she was trying to resolve as she created women superior to men, while forcing them to bow to male dominance.

While Kira keeps her relationships with Andrei platonic, she makes an ill-fated attempt to flee Russia with Leo and gives up her virginity to him in midflight. After they are caught and then released because an official fondly remembers Leo's father, Kira goes to live with him in his father's old apartment. Leo has the body of a Greek god and the soul of a Greek hero. Although he hates the Soviet regime, he works for the government, translating foreign novels that demonstrate the evils of capitalism. When this work is done, he is forced to do manual labor and becomes ill. Kira is expelled from the Technological Institute for bourgeois attitudes. Leo must go away, to the Crimea, if he is to live; and to save him Kira pretends to love Andrei to secure money from him to send Leo to a sanatorium in Yalta.

Once again, as in **"Red Pawn,"** Rand makes a woman give herself to one man in order to save another, again to a communist to save a lover. This seems to be the only type of self-sacrifice she ever approved. Perhaps to a greater degree than in **"Red Pawn,"** this communist turns out to be a more admirable person than the man the woman saved. The entire second half of *We the Living,* in fact, deals with the corruption of Leo and the heroism of Andrei. Despite her desire to condemn the system that Leo despises and for which Andrei works so faithfully, despite pages and pages of commentary and dialogue aimed at making her anti-Soviet point, she permits Andrei's dedication to the revolution to ennoble him, while she permits Leo's efforts to make money by subverting the system to pull him ever deeper into disrepute. One has to wonder if Ayn Rand, the self-described "radical for capitalism," was fully aware of what this novel and **"Red Pawn"** were saying. In her own defense she would probably have pointed out how depraved she made all the other communists in the story. She might particularly have singled out the case of Kira's cousin Victor, a man totally without scruples who sees in the Party a path to power over other men and its subsequent comforts.

Leo returns from the Crimea physically well but still spiritually tortured. Although Kira has been sleeping with Andrei and working as a guide in the Museum of the Revolution by his grace, she moves back in with Leo. Before long Leo is prospering in a job of his own, working a store stocked by a smuggler who happens to be the lover of a woman he met in the south. The communist system is being reborn in rewards given to good party members, certain chosen professions valuable to the party are being given priorities, and young people are denouncing relatives, not for corruption but for deviation from party dogma. Rand paints a touching picture—possibly autobiographical—of a pair of young lovers separated forever when the boy is sent to Siberia for dissident behavior. In this atmosphere Leo's cynical exploitations are rewarded, while Andrei's faith in the new regime is shaken. Oddly enough, Kira is more attracted to Leo in his "fallen" state than she was earlier and even proposes marriage to him while refusing to escape the country with the more admirable and honest Andrei.

Throughout this ordeal Leo and Andrei do not know that they share Kira's affection. Andrei sets out to expose corruption without knowing he is closing in on Leo. He is warned by Party members that to continue his crusade will injure the cause; but he is too honest to sweep matters under the rug. In his investigations he discovers that Kira is living with Leo and that she only pretended to love him (Andrei), used him, to help another man. Kira shows no remorse for what she has done, and Andrei does not condemn her. Instead, nobler still, he promises to save Leo from the net he has cast.

At a Party gathering Andrei delivers a speech that will end his career. "Every man worth calling a man lives for himself," he says. "The one who doesn't—doesn't live at all. You cannot change it. You cannot change it because that's the way man is born, alone, complete, an end in himself. No laws, no party, no G.P.U. will ever kill that thing in man which knows how to say 'I'." This of course sounds more like Howard Roark than the Andrei earlier in the novel; but it is supposed to show the change that Kira and his recent experience have had on him.

He blackmails a Party official to secure Leo's release, assures Leo that he and Kira are only friends, and takes his own life. While misguided before he met Kira, Andrei was all his life a noble person, dedicated to noble causes, far superior to men who sought power or creature comforts. His spirit emerges victorious, even in death. In later novels he is represented by Howard Roark and John Galt.

Again the heroine Kira is boldly honest. She admits to Leo that she has been Andrei's mistress, whereupon he announces that he has decided to go away with another woman. Kira moves back to her parents' house, applies for a passport to leave Russia, and is turned down. It then becomes a matter of living her life out under a system she despises or risking it once more in an attempt to escape. While trying to cross the far northern frontier wearing white clothing in the snow, she is shot by a border guard who takes her for a rabbit. She dies thinking of the things that might have but will not be. (pp. 29-44)

> *James T. Baker, in his* Ayn Rand, *Twayne Publishers, 1987, 168 p.*

Joseph Sobran   (essay date 27 January 1989)

[*In the following excerpt, Sobran praises* We the Living *for its convincing depiction of life in a totalitarian state and for characters who are more believable than those in* The Fountainhead *and* Atlas Shrugged.]

Ayn Rand's first novel, *We the Living,* was published in 1936. It holds up well after fifty years, thanks to a gripping plot and a property in which it's almost unique: social realism about the Soviet Union.

It was also filmed, in 1942, but without Miss Rand's consent or knowledge. The Fascist government of Italy sponsored a production that ironically violated her property rights, thereby indicating a certain deafness to her message.

Nevertheless, when Miss Rand saw the film after the war, she was pleased. It's generally faithful to her book, and the casting is superior to that of the Hollywood version of *The Fountainhead,* which starred Gary Cooper and was made with her close cooperation.

The postwar settlement gave her the rights to the movie of *We the Living,* and her estate has now released it for general circulation. In Italy it was shown in two parts (and was a hit); here, it has been edited to a single three-hour film, with English subtitles.

The plot is simple. In the early Twenties, in Petrograd, a girl named Kira falls in love with a young man named Leo, son of an executed aristocrat. Because of his "class origins," Leo is denied medical care when he contracts tuberculosis. In order to save him, Kira becomes the mistress of a powerful but essentially decent Communist Party official, Andrei. When Leo recovers, Kira has to prevent her two lovers from finding out about each other.

Inevitably, they do find out. Andrei searches Leo's apartment in connection with a black-market investigation, and there discovers Kira's dresses. Leo is arrested and faces the death penalty. But with Leo apparently lost, Kira furiously tells Andrei the whole truth: she was only his whore, and she did it all for Leo. She defies him to do his worst. But Andrei is shattered at the realization of what he has done, and of what Communism is. He contrives to save Leo's life, then shoots himself. Leo, however, cynically spurns Kira and chooses instead the life of a prosperous gigolo. Here the film ends; in the book, Kira is killed while trying to flee to the free world.

The dénouement reveals Andrei as the nobler of the two men: unlike Leo, he prefers death to dishonor. He serves Communism only as long as he can believe in it. Except in his love for Kira, he serves it incorruptibly. Leo, on the other hand, is willing to compromise himself. When Andrei sees the truth, he sacrifices himself for Kira as she has sacrificed herself for Leo. But Leo is as incapable of such love as he is of understanding what Kira has done for him, and she never tries to explain her actions to him: rather mysteriously, she simply allows him to think the worst about her and to sink further into cynicism. Is she sparing him the torment of full knowledge? Or is it futile to try to keep his love, and pointless to justify herself? Or is this perhaps simply one of those old-fashioned stories in which characters don't discuss their own motives too much?

Be that as it may, Kira loves Leo, not the more deserving Andrei. When it comes to winning maidens' affections, the smart money is still on reckless virility rather than moral rectitude, and reckless virility happens to be Leo's long suit. He tells off Soviet officials (including Andrei) with a courage that frightens Kira for him, even as it makes her admire him all the more. Andrei has his own courage, as his final Sydney Carton gesture shows, but as a GPU officer he's hardly in a position to display it: in executing his duties he simply appears ruthless.

The book's power lies in its depiction of the grim, grimy terror that prevailed even in the supposed golden age of Lenin. Everyone is reduced to a debasing dependence on the state, less because of the fear of arbitrary arrest than because of the total absence of property rights and economic freedom. You can be suddenly deprived of anything—job, possessions, living quarters—that is coveted by some Party hack. The characters are driven to toadying, corruption, prostitution, and treachery by the system that promised them "liberation."

We the Living makes the issue of property rights vivid and vital as no other fiction does, as far as I know. It also shows the formation of a malign status system in a society in which everything is up for grabs, where connections are everything and talent is next to nothing. Miss Rand does for Lenin's Soviet Union something like what *Bonfire of the Vanities* does for New York—again ironically, because she'd have had only scorn for Tom Wolfe's notion that status information is the stuff of the novel. (p. 52)

Miss Rand's characters, on the page, often seem to be played by mediocre thespians who can't resist making their lines pat and their gestures extravagant. This tendency got worse in her two big novels, *The Fountainhead* and *Atlas Shrugged,* where every speech seems to hammer home Objectivist doctrine. The doctrine was still embryonic, fortunately, in *We the Living,* and in the movie the characters seem to speak for themselves rather than on Miss Rand's behalf.

What's more, they develop. Life changes them. Howard Roark and John Galt are demigods, self-created, without ancestors or blood ties. They can no more have children than parents. When they fall in love, it's the instantaneous mutual recognition of a breed apart. (Roark rapes Dominique Francon, having quickly read her mind. Luckily, his reading is accurate.) Love neither follows nor is followed by growing intimacy: being perfect and autonomous, the Randian hero may desire, but never need, another. Randian desire is never merely randy. But this is the man of Miss Rand's later immaturity. Kira has needs, and parents. And she has what John Galt lacks: life.

But even Kira's parents are ineffectual. They have no wisdom to impart. She has no debt to them. From early childhood she has rejected their religion, and they've long since given up taking her to church; it doesn't even seem to matter to them. Their speeches expose them as small, deluded people.

When Miss Rand includes parents in her picture at all, she shows them as they look to unhappy adolescents: kind but potentially tyrannical, and—above all—uncomprehending. Kira's parents understand nothing: neither the nature of the Soviet state (they think it will pass quickly) nor her own desire to be independent (they disapprove of her living with Leo out of wedlock).

Miss Rand's appeal has always been to young people, people of Kira's age, for whom "society" is just parents writ large, and in whom the desire to *be* parents is still unborn. Individualism and collectivism are the only options; no network of affection and obligation has reality.

Born Jewish in Leningrad when it was still St. Petersburg, Miss Rand was able to escape to America thanks to her relations in Chicago, whose name, by the way, was Portnoy. This pivotal fact made no impression on her outlook. She never wrote about her Jewishness (her original name was Rosenbaum) and seems to have attached no significance to it. All her heroes and heroines are Nordic, verging on Viking.

But just as some Christians could only see Communism as "Jewish Bolshevism," Miss Rand seems to have thought of Communism as the logical extension of Christianity, for which her euphemisms were "mysticism" and "altruism." An atheist herself, she made no connection between Communism and atheism and never expressed sympathy for Communism's Christian victims. "Religion," she wrote in her private notebook in 1934, "is the first enemy of the ability to think. . . . *Faith is the worst curse of mankind.*" She audaciously opposed the dollar sign to the Cross, exalting "the virtue of selfishness."

Like Christian socialists, though from the other side, she confused the counsel "Give all you have to the poor" with the somewhat distinct command "Give all your neighbor has to the poor." But renunciation and expropriation are, after all, two different things.

And the villains of *We the Living* are selfish people, whereas Kira engages our sympathy because she loves another so much that she commits a monstrously unselfish act. True, the concept of selfishness underwent a drastic high redefinition in Miss Rand's hands, but it's still stretching a point to call Kira *more* selfish, in any sense, than the grubby little Party worms she has to contend with. She may have more genuine self-respect, but we didn't need Ayn Rand to point this out to us.

In her biography *The Passion of Ayn Rand,* Barbara Branden, who was well situated to know, recounts how Miss Rand's own selfishness destroyed two marriages. Nor did she gracefully release her lover—Mrs. Branden's husband—when his fancies took a different turn: she insisted that he owed her everything, and she would destroy him for rejecting her. ("I don't even care what it does to *me!*" she roared, throwing rational self-interest to the winds.) She could be amazingly bullying toward her young disciples, demanding of them humiliating self-abasement. Even her eccentric aesthetic tastes became Objectivist credenda: Rachmaninoff was superior to Beethoven, Mickey Spillane to Shakespeare. And while obeying the strange swerves of her party line, her followers would parrot her denunciations of "second-handers"—people whose opinions were merely derivative (unlike those of us rational beings). After her break with Nathaniel Branden, you couldn't even sign up for the Objectivist lectures without a written promise that you would never buy any of his books.

Such was the fate of the man she had once called a "genius," a "hero," and "my intellectual heir." He's in California now, still making a living.

Even so, I think Ayn Rand is a much better novelist than, say, Mickey Spillane. And she does force you to think straight: not a contemptible virtue, in this world. She wrote *We the Living* before she had set up shop as the Oracle of Reason, while she was still human. Read it, if you haven't already. (p. 53)

Joseph Sobran, "Mussolini Shrugged," in National Review, *New York, Vol. XLI, No. 1, January 27, 1989, pp. 52-3.*

Nathaniel Branden   (essay date 1989)

[*A Canadian-born American psychologist and author, Branden was a close friend and professional colleague of Rand's for nearly two decades. During their association Branden was instrumental in the popularization of the objectivist philosophy described in Rand's novels. He founded the Nathaniel Branden Institute and under its patronage presented a series of lectures on Rand's philosophy. Although Branden and Rand parted ways in 1968, Branden still credits Rand with broadening his intellectual outlook. In the following excerpt, Branden assesses the impact that* The Fountainhead *had on him as an adolescent and young adult.*]

"Howard Roark laughed." That was how it began.

There are extraordinary experiences in life that remain permanently engraved in memory; experiences that represent turning points; moments, hours, or days after which nothing is ever the same again.

The writing had the most marvelous purposefulness and clarity. I had the sense that every word was chosen with excruciating care; the book seemed absolutely devoid of the accidental. This was stylization of a kind I had never seen before, and it was maintained consistently down to the smallest detail. The author's ability to provide an experience of visual reality was instantly evident, and it was visual reality of the highest level of luminosity and precision. Years later the analogy that would occur to me was that it was like stepping into a painting by Vermeer.

The author's constructions, images, rhythms, all took hold of me in some profound way. The style reflected a manner of processing experience, a way of being conscious, which I had never encountered before and yet that seemed intimately familiar.

Six years later, at one of my early meetings with Ayn, I told her, "My excitement wasn't just at the stylization of the writing—your particular way of seeing and re-creating reality, which runs through everything—it was like being in a *stylized universe.*" She clapped her hands in appreciation of this image and later referred to it many times.

The first chapter of the novel establishes the basic character and context of Howard Roark, a young man passionately committed to becoming an architect, who has just been expelled from school for designing buildings that represent a total break with tradition. Unmoved by the expulsion, he knows he will not be stopped. His direction comes not from the opinions or values of others but from his own inner vision and convictions.

The novel covers nearly two decades in Howard Roark's life. The plot-theme of *The Fountainhead* is the battle of a great innovator, an architect of genius, against a society geared and committed to tradition and mediocrity. In terms of its abstract theme, the novel is a dramatization of the morality of individualism.

Every work of art is an act of psychological self-disclosure. An artist declares to the world: "This is what I think is important; important for me to project and for others to perceive." By the same token, an intense response to a work of art is also psychological self-disclosure. More often than not, the roots of our responses lie deep in our subconscious, but our values, philosophy, and sense of life are necessarily engaged when we encounter a work of art and fall in love.

I was aware that Ayn Rand had reached me in some unique way, and that in the cardinal values of the novel—independence, integrity, love of one's work, and a sacred sense of mission about one's life—I had found a world more interesting, more energizing, more challenging, and in a way more real, than the world around me. I experienced it as more relevant to my growth and development than anything I was hearing from my elders. To me, at fourteen, the vision offered by *The Fountainhead* was a great and inspiring gift. (pp. 14-15)

Between the ages of fourteen and eighteen, I read and reread *The Fountainhead* almost continuously, with the dedication and passion of a student of the Talmud. It was the most important companion of my adolescence. When I opened its pages, I was transported into a world where the issues I cared about really *mattered.*

There were particular scenes I returned to again and again, like favorite pieces of music. One such scene occurs at the conclusion of Part I. At a time when he is struggling and destitute, Roark receives an enormously important commission, one that could virtually make his career, on one condition: that he agree to modify the unconventional design of his building. Roark explains why it is as important for a building as it is for a man, to have integrity, why it cannot borrow pieces of its soul. They concede that he may be right, but in practical life one can't always be so consistent. They give him an ultimatum: " 'Yes or no, Mr. Roark?' " After a long, agonizing moment, Roark says, " 'No.' " Appalled, one member of the board of directors cries, " 'You need the commission. Do you have to be so fanatical and selfless about it?' " Pressing his architectural drawing to his body, Roark answers, " 'That was the most selfish thing you've ever seen a man do.' "

In first reading this, I knew immediately what Roark meant. Maintaining the integrity of his own convictions, values, and commitments above fame, worldly success, or money was not an act of self-sacrifice but a supreme expression of selfishness in the noblest possible meaning of that word. If he had perceived his action as self-sacrificial, it would have lost all moral grandeur.

Everything I had ever heard about the virtue of self-sacrifice and selflessness became preposterous and irrelevant. It missed the point of what life—and greatness—demanded. Not to sacrifice the self but to remain true to it at all costs—that was the heroic vision *The Fountainhead* offered.

"That was the most selfish thing you've ever seen a man do." I pondered those words as one might meditate on some esoteric saying containing a treasure of secrets. If self meant consciousness, thought, judgment, creativity—how could it be evil? How could people think self-surrender was noble? I asked these questions of everyone—from people on the block to visitors in our home to almost anyone who professed to take ideas seriously. I was not satisfied by the answers I received which ranged from "Everyone knows it's evil to be selfish," to "Wait until you grow up."

To keep faith with the best within yourself was clearly *selfish* and clearly a *virtue*. I knew what a break from the beliefs of the people around me this way of seeing things represented and I welcomed that.

Another scene of great personal meaning to me was "the boy on the bicycle scene" at the beginning of Part IV. A young man, newly graduated from college, is wheeling his bicycle through a forest, thinking about his future. He wants to love and admire others, but he is most happy when he is alone. This saddens him because he longs for the sight of human joy and achievement as fuel and inspiration. He comes to a clearing and stands overlooking a valley; he sees a series of breathtaking structures, a magnificent symphony in stone. Lost in contemplation of this answer to his longing, he finally notices a man sitting alone on a rock, looking at the same sight. Who built this? the boy wants to know. " 'I did,' " the man says. " 'What's your name?' " the boy asks, and the man answers, " 'Howard Roark.' " The boy thanks Roark and walks away. "Roark looked after him. He had never seen that boy before and he would never see him again. He did not know that he had given someone the courage to face a lifetime."

There was one scene in *The Fountainhead* that I reread a hundred times. For one sentence only, this one scene was more important to me than any other in the book. Peter Keating, a parasitic yet successful fellow architect, asks Roark to design the government housing project, Cortlandt Homes, and let him, Keating, take the credit. Years earlier, Keating graduated from architectural school with honors on the day Roark was expelled. Later, when they were both in practice—Roark struggling desperately, Keating rising to the top of his profession—Keating went to Roark again and again for help with his work. Keating is the "second-hander," the man without independent values or judgment, the man who lives through and by others. Roark, the innovator, the egoist, the man who lives for his own sake and by his own mind, has fought a battle of eighteen years against the society around him. Now his architectural ideas are beginning to win; clients are coming to him in increasing numbers. Keating, having ridden for years on a prestige he had not earned, is now slipping. Roark, inspired by the challenge of Cortlandt Homes, agrees to design the project for Keating on one condition: that it be built exactly as Roark designs it. In a rare, pathetic groping for honesty, Keating struggles to understand Roark's motive. " 'Everybody would say you're a fool. . . . Everybody would say I'm getting everything. . . . ' " Roark answers: " 'You'll get everything society can give a man. You'll keep all the money. You'll take any fame or honor anyone might want to grant. You'll accept such gratitude as the tenants might feel. And I—I'll take what nobody can give a man, except himself. I will have built Cortlandt.' "

To me, aged fourteen, fifteen, sixteen, seventeen, eighteen, those words, " 'I will have built Cortlandt,' " were like a hymn or a battle cry, celebrating an almost reverential feeling for the activity of creative work and the self-sufficiency of the creative process. This feeling has never changed.

Many years later, in an introduction to the twenty-fifth anniversary edition of *The Fountainhead,* Ayn said that her novel is a confirmation of the spirit of youth. My own experience quite supports this assessment. A confirmation of the spirit of youth—and a confirmation of the conviction that joy is possible to human beings, that doom and defeat are not our inevitable fate.

I cannot discuss the impact of *The Fountainhead* upon me without discussing the much-debated climax of the novel—Roark's blowing up of Cortlandt Homes. How many discussions—how many arguments!—among how many readers must that event have inspired! On my first reading of the novel, and at each successive rereading through my teenage years, I was inspired by the integration of the various characters and their conflicts at the climax, and by the story's final resolution.

Ellsworth Toohey, the architectural critic who secures the government commission, Cortlandt Homes, for Peter Keating, is Ayn Rand's first major literary portrait of evil. Toohey is a socialist who preaches self-surrender, self-sacrifice, and collectivism as a means to power over other human beings. Now, after years of plotting and scheming, he is at the height of his fame and influence; his goal at present is control of the Wynand newspaper chain for which he works as a columnist. His boss, and the target of his manipulations, is Gail Wynand.

Gail Wynand is projected as the great tragic figure of *The Fountainhead.* Having succumbed in his youth to the belief that virtue and integrity have no chance in human society, he concludes that one's only choice is to rule or be ruled—and chooses to rule. He pours his energy and genius into the creation of a vast newspaper syndicate that does not express his own values or convictions, but panders to the lowest values and tastes of the mob. With the exception of the *Banner,* his New York paper, Wynand finds only two passions in life: Dominique Francon, whom he marries—and Howard Roark, whom he first attempts to corrupt and later virtually worships. Roark is the embodiment of the impossible: a man of integrity. But the realization toward which Wynand is moving is that if Roark can be practical *and* successful on his own moral terms, then there is no justification for his, Wynand's, life.

Wynand does not know that Dominique and Roark are in love. Dominique had left Roark years earlier, before she met Wynand, because she could not bear to witness the destruction to which she felt certain he was doomed. Like Wynand, she believes that the good has no chance in human society, but she does not seek any values from a world she despises. She marries Wynand, her symbol for evil, in a deliberate act of self-destruction, seeking to kill her own ecstatic sense of life. Then she witnesses Keating's disintegration, she sees Roark winning his battle, she observes Wynand's helplessness before him, and she begins to grasp the impotence of evil.

The book dramatized for me, and no doubt for many young people seeking a rational view of life, the idea that the moral and the practical are not in conflict, provided one knows what is, in fact, moral. This was hardly what I was hearing from my peers and elders.

When the first building of Cortlandt Homes is completed, Roark discovers that it has been totally disfigured. The government officials have used Roark's structural and engineering plans, without which the project would have been impossible, but they have drastically altered the design, for petty and personal reasons. No legal recourse is available to Keating or Roark: the government bureau cannot be sued or forced to honor its contract.

Roark dynamites Cortlandt and waits at the scene of the explosion to be arrested. The storm of public indignation against him, led by Ellsworth Toohey, emphasizes Cortlandt's status as a housing project for the poor. Roark has no right to a motive.

Peter Keating, who has made a final, desperate effort to save his career by another act of parasitism, is brought to public disgrace and to the full realization of his own emptiness and mediocrity. From my teenage perspective, Keating's characterization illuminated the conventional mentality I found so inimical. He was the quintessential "good boy."

Gail Wynand attempts to use the *Banner,* for the first time in his life, for a cause in which he believes: his defense of Roark. His readers desert him—and Wynand learns that it is not he who has directed public opinion, but public opinion that has controlled and directed him. To save his newspaper, he finally joins the voices denouncing Roark, but recognizing the futility of his career, recognizing that his pursuit of power has delivered him to slavery, he finally closes the *Banner.* He sees that a man cannot sacrifice his values all his life and expect to escape the consequences. " 'You were a ruler of men,' " he tells himself. " 'You held a leash. A leash is only a rope with a noose at both ends.' "

A leash is only a rope with a noose at both ends—how I treasured that sentence with its masterly, elegant way of conveying the self-humiliating and self-defeating nature of the quest for power over other human beings. In my later teenage years, I would have many arguments with people who accused Ayn Rand of being a Nietzschean. By the time I knew who Nietzsche was, it seemed obvious that the character of Gail Wynand was intended to be an indictment of Nietzsche—a conviction that Ayn would subsequently confirm. "A true and consistent egoist," she would say, "would never seek power over other human be-

ings. He would be too independent for that. And power-seeking always means dependency." To me, this could not have been clearer.

The dynamiting of Cortlandt puts Dominique to the severest test possible: her highest value, Roark, is in far worse danger than he has ever faced before. But she is not afraid for him; she knows that he is right, that he has won—no matter what happens. She makes peace with her love for him, and joins him.

I found the character of Dominique the most troublesome in the book; I could not really make sense out of her psychology. She must be read very abstractly, symbolically. Once, Ayn rather bluntly acknowledged, "If you take Dominique literally, she's quite stupid. You have to see her more as the projection of a certain attitude, taken to an extreme—an idealist paralyzed by disgust." But what nonetheless attracted me was Dominique's passion and her spirituality, a priestess run amok, as it were, and certainly more interesting than the "normal" girls I met in Toronto.

Dominique's love for Roark focused another issue that influenced me profoundly: the supreme importance of admiration in romantic love, as contrasted with the mixture of affection and contempt that seemed to pass for love with so many people. This total dedication, I thought, is what I want to feel for a woman one day and what I want her to feel for me.

At his trial, Roark's statement to the jury is a summation of the novel's philosophy: that all progress and achievement come from the independent mind; that altruism, the doctrine that self-surrender in service to others is the highest ideal, is a device for controlling and ultimately enslaving productive men and women; that a human being is not a sacrificial animal, but has a right to exist for his or her own sake; that society depends on the work of the creators and has a right to that work only on the creator's terms. Roark is acquitted.

I listened to the boys on the block talk about girls and popular songs and baseball; I sat in class while teachers talked about geography and social studies; I listened at family dinners to my parents arguing with each other or lecturing my sisters or me—but what I was seeing and hearing were the events and characters of *The Fountainhead,* the ecstatic laughter of the book's sense of life.

This, of course, is precisely the inspirational power of Romantic art. Contrary to the claims of Naturalism, a young person does not require descriptions of the people next door but an escape from them to a wider view of life's possibilities.

The Fountainhead was for me an invaluable aid to psychological survival. Not many novels have that power. (pp. 18-23)

Nathaniel Branden, in his Judgment Day: My Years with Ayn Rand, *Houghton Mifflin Company, 1989, 436 p.*

George H. Smith   (essay date 1991)

[*In the following excerpt, Smith compares Rand's objectivism to other philosophies.*]

Ayn Rand was one of the most intriguing and dynamic figures in twentieth-century thought. She had enormous power to inspire or to frustrate, to engage one's sympathies or to enrage them. While primarily a novelist, Ayn Rand constructed a philosophic system, which, although sketchy at times, is integrated, coherent, and compelling.

Many modern libertarians came to their present views by reading Ayn Rand. Whether they now favor limited government or some form of anarchism, it was Rand who first fired their imaginations and impressed upon them the crucial role of principles in thought and action.

Possibly because of the fierce emotions, pro and con, that Rand evokes, there has appeared relatively little in the way of competent reflection on Ayn Rand as philosopher. Accounts of Objectivism written by Rand's admirers are frequently eulogistic and uncritical, whereas accounts written by her antagonists are often hostile and, what is worse, embarrassingly inaccurate.

Evaluations of Rand in the academic community vary widely. On one extreme, the head of a philosophy department at a major university once called Rand "the worst philosopher in the history of Western Civilization." On the other extreme, the late Hiram Hadyn, an accomplished scholar who disagreed with Rand, remarked that Rand had constructed the most impressive philosophic edifice since Thomas Aquinas in the thirteenth century.

How, then, are we to evaluate the work of Ayn Rand as philosopher? How are we to judge the work of this astonishing woman who wrote with such intellectual passion?

I shall not attempt to analyze or criticize Rand's theories; this complex task would require far more than a single essay. Nor shall I assess Rand's influence on the climate of opinion, for this requires a perspective that can come only with the passage of time.

Another approach to Rand's ideas, and the one I shall adopt here, is to examine Objectivism for points of similarity to other philosophies. As I shall demonstrate, many features of Objectivism can be found elsewhere. In epistemology and ethics, some of Rand's arguments are strikingly similar to the arguments of Aristotelians, especially to those modern followers of Thomas Aquinas known as Thomists. In political philosophy, Rand's approach to natural rights and limited government falls squarely in the tradition known as Classical Liberalism.

Although Rand is often represented as a philosophic maverick, she actually represents a throwback to philosophy in the classical sense. The true mavericks are found in logical positivism, ordinary language philosophy, existentialism, and other schools that (until recently, perhaps) dominated much of modern philosophy. Unlike many of her contemporaries, Rand addressed the same basic questions that have vexed philosophers for centuries: What is the nature of existence? How do we acquire knowledge? What

are concepts? What is ethics, and why do we need this discipline? What is the proper role of government?

Uncovering precedents and parallels to Rand's philosophy is not a popular enterprise among her more ardent disciples. For these true believers, it is not enough for Rand to be totally right; she must also be totally *original*. The problem here, of course, is what we mean when we call a philosopher "original."

Ayn Rand was not especially well-read in philosophy, and this fueled some of her originality. If previous philosophers anticipated some of her arguments or if some of her contemporaries made similar points, Rand seemed largely oblivious to those facts. Thus, in citing precedents and parallels, I don't wish to suggest that Rand borrowed from other philosophers without acknowledgment (although this does seem likely in a few instances). Rather, I believe that Rand originated most of her ideas; that is, she worked them out for herself, unaware that they had been previously worked out by others. She reinvented a number of wheels, so to speak. Whether this kind of originality is especially praiseworthy is an open question, but it at least demonstrates a remarkable ingenuity.

I do think that Rand was original in a more fundamental sense. A philosophy is (or should be) more than unconnected theories and arguments bundled together by a common name. A philosophy is an integrated and organized system of theories and arguments. Therefore, even if many elements of Objectivism can be found in other philosophers, this does not mean that Objectivism, considered as a philosophical system, is unoriginal.

In the final analysis, originality may or may not be admirable. A new method of torture may be original, but this does not recommend it. Conversely, to say that torture is wrong may be unoriginal but important nonetheless. It is always better to reaffirm old truths than to originate new falsehoods.

Another problem haunts Ayn Rand's philosophy. Rand was a sharp polemicist who gave no quarter to her adversaries. Many philosophers have retaliated by exiling her beyond the pale of respectable discussion. This is a mistake. Whether you like the woman or not, her brilliance and influence cannot be gainsaid. If Rand is to be excluded from serious consideration because of her polemicism, then why not exclude other polemical philosophers as well?

Nietzsche was an ardent polemicist, as was Marx, but both are taken seriously. The same is true of Arthur Shopenhauer, whose caustic attack on Hegel (the most respected philosopher of his day) was more vindictive than anything ever written by Rand. (pp. 193-95)

There is another reason why some philosophers snub Ayn Rand: she was not an academic. She addressed a popular audience, not other philosophers. Here again, Rand was a throwback to an earlier conception of philosophy. Rand sincerely believed that philosophy *matters,* that it influences not just other philosophers, but the general culture as well. Quoting Rand:

> The professional intellectual is the field agent of

the army whose commander-in-chief is the *philosopher*. The intellectual carries the application of philosophical principles to every field of human endeavor. He sets a society's course by transmitting ideas from the "ivory tower" of the philosopher to the university professor—to the writer—to the artist—to the newspaperman—to the politician—to the movie maker—to the night-club singer—to the man in the street.

Rand was at once a philosopher and a professional intellectual who wished to transmit ideas to a broad audience. Furthermore, she was a *market* intellectual. Like the Sophists of ancient Greece, she sold her ideas in the intellectual marketplace; and, like those unjustly maligned teachers, she has incurred the wrath of the establishment.

As a market intellectual, Rand addressed the nonacademic masses, using vigorous and lively prose. She believed in the ability of the average person to deal with basic philosophical issues. This should count in Rand's favor, but more often it is used against her. She is dismissed as a "popularizer"—rather like Plato's attack on the Sophists. Plato distrusted the average person's ability to discern philosophic truth, so he assailed the Sophists—itinerent teachers of wisdom—who sold their wares to all comers. Perhaps modern philosophers agree with Plato's assessment; if so, such elitism is their problem, not Rand's.

Lastly, some of the disdain for Rand has been caused by her more dogmatic and abrasive disciples. Ironically, some of these disciples, having praised Rand as the savior of western civilization, later turn against her with a vengeance—thereby exhibiting a kind of true-believer/heretic syndrome. As true believers, these persons praised Rand as the greatest philosopher in history; then, as heretics, they assail Objectivism as worthless and even harmful. Ayn Rand is transformed from the Pope to the Antichrist—two sides of the same dogmatist coin. The true believer turned heretic has accomplished nothing more than to reverse direction in a sea of ignorance.

William James once observed that a new philosophy often passes through three stages during its reception: First, it "is attacked as absurd; then it is admitted to be true, but obvious and insignificant; finally it is seen to be so important that its adversaries claim that they themselves discovered it." This, perhaps, is the fate of Objectivism.

Rand's view of philosophy is grand and delightfully old-fashioned. In the style of Aristotelian philosophers, who call philosophy "the queen of the sciences," Rand writes:

> Philosophy studies the fundamental nature of existence, of man, and of man's relationship to existence. As against the special sciences, which deal only with particular aspects, philosophy deals with those aspects of the universe which pertain to everything that exists. In the realm of cognition, the special sciences are the trees, but philosophy is the soil which makes the forest possible.

Similarly, Cardinal Mercier, a major figure in the revival of Thomism in the late nineteenth century, maintains that philosophy "does not profess to be a particularized science." Instead, philosophy "comes *after* the particular sci-

ences and ranks *above* them, dealing in an ultimate fashion with their respective objects, inquiring into their connexions and the relations of these connexions. . . ." Philosophy, Mercier concludes, "deserves above all to be called the *most general science*. . . ."

A key element in Rand's philosophy is what she calls the "primacy of existence." For Rand, any attempt to prove the existence of a world external to consciousness is absurd on its face. We cannot begin, as Descartes did, with the certainty of consciousness while doubting the existence of an external world. Why? Because consciousness presupposes the existence of something external to consciousness, something to be conscious *of*. In Rand's words:

> If nothing exists, there can be no consciousness: a consciousness with nothing to be conscious of is a contradiction in terms. A consciousness conscious of nothing but itself is a contradiction in terms: before it could identify itself as consciousness, it had to be conscious of something. If that which you claim to perceive does not exist, what you possess is not consciousness.

Rand's argument is sound, but it is scarcely new. On the contrary, it has a long and distinguished history. We find essentially the same argument, for example, in Thomas Aquinas:

> No one perceives that he understands except from this, that he understands *something*: because he must first know *something* before he knows that he knows; and the consequence is that the mind comes to actually know itself through that which it understands or senses.

Thomistic philosophers sometimes refer to this as the reflexive nature of consciousness. We first become aware of something external to consciousness, and then (and only then) we become aware of our awareness by reflecting on the process by which we became aware. The distinguished Catholic philosopher Jacques Maritain put it this way:

> One cannot think about a "thought thing" until after one has thought about a "thinkable thing"—a thing good for existing, i.e., at least a possible real. The first thing thought about is being independent of the mind. . . . We do not eat what has been eaten; we eat bread. To separate object from thing . . . is to violate the nature of the intellect.

Celestine N. Bittle, an author of Thomistic textbooks, has described the reflexive nature of consciousness in words that are almost identical to Rand's: "Consciousness has a content. In order to be conscious, we must be conscious of something." Bittle also agrees that consciousness, as Rand puts it, is an axiomatic concept—an irreducible primary that cannot "be reduced to other facts or broken into component parts." Consciousness, according to Bittle, is "an ultimate datum of experience" that "lies at the very root of all mental activity." Bittle, like Rand, argues that consciousness "*admits of no strict definition*" and can only be defined ostensively, i.e., "pointed out and described."

A venerable epistemological debate concerns the reliability of sense perception. Do our senses somehow deceive us or transmit inaccurate data about the external world? Rand defends the reliability of sense perception as follows:

> [T]he day when [man] grasps that his senses cannot deceive him, that physical objects cannot act without causes, that his organs of perception are physical and have no volition, no power to invent or to distort, that the evidence they give him is an absolute, but his mind must learn to understand it, his mind must discover the nature, the causes, the full context of his sensory material, his mind must identify the things that he perceives—that is the day of his birth as a thinker and scientist.

Many philosophers have argued this way, but, again, Rand's formulation most closely resembles the arguments of Thomists. Consider this passage from Peter Coffey's *Epistemology,* published in 1917:

> [T]he *senses themselves neither err nor deceive.* They do not err because they do not judge or interpret, but merely present, register, report a "something," a "datum," an "object" to the conscious perceiver. They do not *themselves* deceive because they always present or register or report that precisely which under the circumstances they must: they simply could not present a datum other or otherwise than they actually do; according to the organic condition in which they are, and according to the condition in which the external influence impresses them, so much the presented datum be, nor can it be otherwise: nor can the perceiver be deceived in judging that he has this datum consciously present to him.

Another problem addressed by Rand is causation. In opposition to David Hume, who denied any necessary connection between cause and effect, Rand links causality to the law of identity and locates necessity in the natures of the entities involved in the causal process. Quoting Rand:

> The law of causality is the law of identity applied to action. All actions are caused by entities. The nature of an action is caused and determined by the nature of the entities that act; a thing cannot act in contradiction to its nature.

This argument may be found in H. W. B. Joseph's book on logic, published in 1916:

> [T]o say that the same thing acting on the same thing under the same conditions may yet produce a different effect, is to say that a thing need not be what it is. But this is in flat conflict with the Law of Identity. A thing, to be at all, must be something, and can only be what it is. To assert a causal connection between *a* and *x* implies that *a* acts as it does because it is what it is; because, in fact, it is *a*. So long therefore as it is *a,* it must act thus; and to assert that it may act otherwise on a subsequent occasion is to assert that what is *a* is something else than the *a* which it is declared to be.

The philosopher Brand Blanshard, writing in 1939, also links causation to the law of identity: "To say that *a* produces *x* in virtue of being *a* and yet that, given *a, x* might not follow, is inconsistent with the laws of identity and contradiction."

Although Rand defends necessary causation, she also defends free will, or volition, in humans. Working from an agency theory of causation, where the human agent is said to be the cause of his actions, Rand locates free will in the choice to think or not to think. Man, says Rand, is "a being of volitional consciousness."

A few Thomistic philosophers have presented arguments similar to Rand's. For instance, Michael Maher, in a Thomistic work on psychology, refers to "the active power of selective attention" and to the "power of the mind to modify through selective attention." Maher elaborates:

> If I study by introspection any process of voluntary attention, such as that involved in recalling a forgotten incident, or in guessing a riddle, I observe that *I myself* deliberately *guide* the course of my thoughts. I am conscious that I do this by fostering the strength of some ideas, and starving others. . . . I determine not only what representations, but what *aspect of those representations* shall occupy my consciousness. In such cases I am conscious of exerting *free volition.* Further, throughout this process I apprehend myself as *causing* my mental activity—I am immediately conscious of my attention as the exercise of *free causal energy* put forth by me.

Arthur Koestler, himself a philosophic maverick, has offered a similar view of volition. Koestler discusses activities that can be performed automatically until something unexpected happens.

> At that moment a strategic choice has to be made, which is beyond the competence of automatized routine, and must be referred to "higher quarters." *This shift of control* of an ongoing activity from one level to a higher level of the hierarchy—from "mechanical" to "mindful" behaviour—seems to be of the essence of conscious decision-making and of the subjective experience of free will.

According to Rand, morality (or ethics)—"a code of values to guide man's choices and actions"—is necessary for human survival, well-being, and happiness. The "law of existence"—the need to achieve particular values in order to sustain and promote life—applies to all living beings, including man. Quoting Rand:

> They, who pose as scientists and claim that man is only an animal, do not grant him inclusion in the law of existence they have granted to the lowest of insects. They recognize that every living species has a way of survival demanded by its nature, they do not claim that a fish can live out of water or that a dog can live without its sense of smell—but man, they claim, the most complex of beings, man can survive in any way whatever, man has no identity, no nature, and there's no practical reason why he cannot live with his means of survival destroyed, with his mind throttled and placed at the disposal of any orders they might care to issue.

As this passage illustrates, Rand's theory of ethics is based on natural law, an approach that was exceedingly popular for many centuries (we find it in the ancient Stoics, for instance). As natural-law ethics fell into disfavor, Rand was one among a minority of philosophers (mainly Aristotelians) who attempted to resurrect this tradition—although, here as elsewhere, Rand labored under the misapprehension that she was giving birth to a new approach rather than breathing new life into an old one. In *Moral Values,* an introductory text published in 1918, Walter Everett expressed views very similar to Rand's:

> Moral law is just as real as human nature, within which it has its existence. Strange, indeed, if man alone of all living beings could realize his highest welfare in disregard of the principles of his own nature! And this nature, we must remember, is what it is—is always concrete and definite. Indeed the sceptic nowhere else assumes the absence of principles through obedience to which the highest form of life can be attained. He does not assume that a lily, which requires abundant moisture and rich soil, could grow on an arid rock, nor that a polar bear could flourish in a tropical jungle. No less certain than would be the failure of such attempts, must be the failure of man to realize, in disregard of the laws of his being, the values of which he is capable. The structure of man's nature, as conscious and spiritual, grounds laws just as real as those of his physical life, and just as truly objective.

An important feature of Rand's meta-ethics—one cited frequently by Objectivist writers—is her contention that the concept of "value" is conceptually dependent upon the concept of "life." "It is only the concept of 'Life'," she writes, "that makes the concept of 'Value' possible. It is only to a living entity that things can be good or evil." Similar statements have been made by other philosophers (although, in fairness to Rand, it should be mentioned that she develops this insight in more detail than most other philosophers).

According to Friedrich Nietzsche, "When we speak of values we do so under the inspiration and from the perspective of life. . . ." The modern theorist G. H. von Wright has argued in a similar vein: "The attributes, which go along with meaningful use of the phrase the good of 'x', may be called *biological* in a broad sense. . . . [T]hey are used as attributes of beings, of whom it is meaningful to say that they have a *life*." Richard Taylor stands in basic agreement: "[T]he things that nourish and give warmth and enhance life are deemed good, and those that frustrate and threaten are deemed bad."

It is in her ethics that Rand most closely follows in the footsteps of Aristotle. (Ironically, though she acknowledged the importance of Aristotle's epistemology, she badly misinterpreted his ethical theory and so failed to understand its significance.) Rather than deal with Aristotle directly, I shall call on Henry Veatch, whose book *Rational Man* provides an excellent summary of an Aristotelian ethics. The similarities between *Rational Man* and Rand's essay **"The Objectivist Ethics"** are more than superficial.

Rand and Veatch agree in their rejection of the modern dichotomy between facts and values. According to Rand, "the validation of value judgments is to be achieved by reference to the facts of reality." And, in a similar vein, Veatch contends that "values are simply facts of nature."

Rand and Veatch agree in other areas as well. Ethics, Veatch contends, "can be based on evidence and . . . is a matter of knowledge." Rand concurs: "Ethics is an *objective, metaphysical necessity of man's survival*" and falls within "the province of reason."

Both philosophers maintain that happiness is properly the purpose of ethics. Following Aristotle, who held that "whatever creates or increases happiness or some part of happiness, we ought to do," Veatch maintains that "moral rules are more in the nature of counsels of perfection or instructions as to what one ought or ought not to do in order to attain happiness." Or, as Rand puts it: "The task of ethics is to define man's proper code of values and thus to give him the means of achieving happiness."

Both writers view happiness objectively, within the total context of one's life, and not merely as momentary satisfaction or pleasure. "Happiness," Rand contends, "is possible only to a rational man." Similarly, Veatch argues that any so-called happiness that comes from something other than "living intelligently" has "somehow become perverted and corrupted."

In other words, both Rand and Veatch see happiness as a concomitant of the good life, which consists of pursuing rational goals in a rational manner. Writes Veatch: "[M]an's true good, his natural end or goal, and his living intelligently, may, in turn, be equated with happiness." Rand stands in basic agreement: "The maintenance of life and the pursuit of happiness are not two separate issues. To hold one's own life as one's ultimate value, and one's own happiness as one's highest purpose are two aspects of the same achievement."

Although Veatch does not call himself an egoist, he makes it clear that "learning how to live," which is what ethics teaches us, "is no more than [learning] what is in one's best interests." As for the view that the goal of ethics is self-sacrifice, Veatch writes:

> [A]ny such identification of ethics with altruism is radically at variance with the sort of ethics of the rational man that we have been trying to defend in this book. In Aristotle's eyes ethics does not begin with thinking of others, it begins with oneself. The reason is that every human being faces the task of learning how to live, how to be a human being, just as he has to learn how to walk or to talk.

Although the terminology differs, this passage is clearly in accord with the following statement by Rand:

> A being who does not know automatically what is true or false, cannot know automatically what is right or wrong, what is good for him or evil. Yet he needs that knowledge in order to live. . . . And *this* . . . is why man needs a code of ethics.

The least original part of Rand's philosophy is her political theory. Indeed, she says little that was not said many times over by Classical Liberals—advocates of natural rights, free markets, and limited government—during the eighteenth and nineteenth centuries. Here, more than else-where, many parallel quotations could be placed alongside passages from Rand. I shall confine myself, however, to a few representative passages.

Let's begin with Rand's defense of natural rights:

> *Rights* are conditions of existence required by man's nature for his proper survival. If man is to live on earth, it is *right* for him to use his mind, it is *right* to act on his own free judgment, it is *right* to work for his values and to keep the product of his work. If life on earth is his purpose, he has a *right* to live as a rational being: nature forbids him the irrational.

Compare this to the argument of Herbert Spencer, one of the greatest Liberals of the last century:

> Those who hold that life is valuable, hold, by implication, that men ought not to be prevented from carrying on life-sustaining activities. In other words, if it is said to "right" that they should carry them on, then, by permutation, we get the assertion that they "have a right" to carry them on. Clearly the conception of "natural rights" originates in recognition of the truth that if life is justifiable, there must be a justification for the performance of acts essential to its preservation; and, therefore, a justification for those liberties and claims which make such acts possible.

Rand condemns the initiation of force or the threat of force in human relationships:

> The precondition of a civilized society is the barring of physical force from social relationships—thus establishing the principle that if men wish to deal with one another, they may do so only by means of *reason:* by discussion, persuasion and voluntary, uncoerced agreement.

Auberon Herbert, like Herbert Spencer and many other nineteenth-century Liberals, made exactly the same point:

> Nobody has the moral right to seek his own advantage by force. That is the one unalterable, inviolable condition of a true society. Whether we are many, or whether we are few, we must learn only to use the weapons of reason, discussion, and persuasion.

Rand points out that the prohibition of force applies only to the *initiation* of force; individuals may use force in self-defense:

> The necessary consequence of man's right to life is his right to self-defense. In a civilized society, force may be used only in retaliation and only against those who initiate its use. All the reasons which make the initiation of physical force an evil, make the retaliatory use of physical force a moral imperative.

Again, Auberon Herbert sounds like an early version of Rand:

> [A]s long as men . . . are willing to make use of [force] for their own ends, or to make use of fraud, which is only force in disguise, wearing a

mask, and evading our consent, just as force with violence openly disregards it—so long we must use force to restrain force. That is the one and only one rightful employment of force . . . force in the defense of the plain simple rights of property, public or private, in a word, of all the rights of self-ownership—force used defensively against force used aggressively.

For Rand, the proper function of government is to protect individual rights:

> The only proper purpose of a government is to protect man's rights, which means: to protect him from physical violence. A proper government is only a policeman, acting as an agent of man's self-defense, and, as such, may resort to force *only* against those who *start* the use of force.

This is a concise statement of the role of government as defended by Classical Liberals. Wilhelm von Humboldt, writing in 1791, argued that "any State interference in private affairs, where there is no reference to violence done to individual rights, should be absolutely condemned." Humboldt continues:

> [I]n order to provide for the security of its citizens, the state must prohibit or restrict such actions, relating directly to the agents only, as imply in their consequences the infringement of others' rights, or encroach on their freedom or property without their consent or against their will. . . . Beyond this every limitation of personal freedom lies outside the limits of state action.

With Ayn Rand no longer on the scene, it is interesting to speculate on the future of Objectivism. Two distinct trends have already emerged. We have the official school of Objectivism headed by philosopher Leonard Peikoff, a talented thinker and writer—and Rand's self-proclaimed "intellectual heir" (a peculiar label at best). Peikoff has decreed Objectivism to be a "closed system" and has rooted out heretics, thereby assuming the role of a Randian Grand Inquisitor. Such tactics will accomplish nothing more than to plunge Objectivism into a deep intellectual coma. A philosophy will not attract young philosophers with first-rate minds if they must agree with everything Rand has written. Inquisitive, original thinkers are unwilling to confine themselves to exegesis, even if the text to be interpreted is a good one.

Fortunately, the fate of Objectivism does not depend solely on the official Randians. Some capable neo-Randians have emerged during the past two decades; and these philosophers, while willing to credit Rand where credit is due, are also willing to criticize Rand where criticism is due. Most importantly, the neo-Randians are philosophers, not expositors; they wish to expand the frontiers of Objectivism, not build walls around it.

Prominent among the neo-Randians are Tibor Machan, who has argued extensively for a Randian approach to rights in *Human Rights and Human Liberties, Individuals and Their Rights,* and other books; and David Kelly, who has ably defended Rand's epistemology in *The Evidence of the Senses: A Realist Theory of Perception.* Important work has also been undertaken by Douglas Den Uyl, Douglas Rasmussen, Eric Mack, Jack Wheeler, and others. (A sample of their work may be found in the anthology *The Philosophic Thought of Ayn Rand.*)

If Objectivism is to have a future beyond the works of Ayn Rand, the hope lies with the neo-Randians rather than with the official school. Randian clones can mimic her writing style, regurgitate her ideas, and denounce heretics—but that is all. They can never duplicate her genius. As Etienne Gilson has written:

> I wish I could make clear from the very beginning that in criticizing great men, as I shall do, I am very far from forgetting what made them truly great. No man can fall a victim to his own genius unless he has genius; but those who have none are fully justified in refusing to be victimized by the genius of others. . . . There is more than one excuse for being a Descartes, but there is no excuse whatever for being a Cartesian.

Paraphrasing Gilson: There is more than one excuse for being an Ayn Rand, but there is no excuse whatever for being a disciple of Ayn Rand. Her admirers should heed the words of Aristotle: I love Plato, but I love the truth more. (pp. 196-208)

> *George H. Smith, "Ayn Rand: Philosophy and Controversy," in his* Atheism, Ayn Rand, and Other Heresies, *Prometheus Books, 1991, pp. 193-211.*

Ronald E. Merrill   (essay date 1991)

[*In the following excerpt, Merrill praises* Atlas Shrugged *for its complex literary style and compelling characterizations.*]

With the publication of *Atlas Shrugged* in 1957 Rand reached the destination of her intellectual journey—the Taggart Terminal. She had purged the last vestiges of Nietzsche's errors from her thinking, and completely integrated her ideas into her own philosophical system, Objectivism. The great question of her life, the dilemma of the rational person in an irrational society, at last was solved to her satisfaction. The concept of the "sanction of the victim" provided her answer—and provided also the key plot device, the strike of the men of the mind, for her greatest novel.

Atlas Shrugged, from a purely stylistic or literary point of view, is inferior to *The Fountainhead.* But as an intellectual achievement, it is far superior. A complete, radically new philosophy is expounded, and with astonishing clarity. The practical implications of philosophical ideas are illustrated on every level, from metaphysics to epistemology to ethics to politics to economics to esthetics. The novel's plot is a miracle of organization. And with all this, the book is a thrilling page-turner.

. . . . .

Rand described her fiction style as 'Romantic Realism'. She regarded herself as a Romantic in that her fiction dealt with ideal people and their pursuit of important values; and a Realist in that the settings of her stories and the issues they dealt with were those of real life rather than fantasy. This description is quite appropriate to most of her work. However, *Atlas Shrugged* marks somewhat of a departure. Stylistically, it represents a considerable change from *We the Living* and *The Fountainhead.* Building on the techniques with which she had experimented in *Anthem,* Rand made *Atlas Shrugged* a more abstract, conceptual, and symbolic work than her earlier novels; it might best be described as a work of Romantic Surrealism. The cover painting by George Salter accurately conveys the mood and style of the novel.

Atlas Shrugged takes place in the United States, and cities such as New York and Philadelphia are recognizable. But Rand goes to considerable pains to create an ambiance that is far from realistic. The United States of the novel has no President, but a "Head of State"; no Congress, but a "National Legislature". Most of the world is Communist, but this word does not appear in the book at all; instead, Communist countries are referred to as "People's States". The story takes place in no particular time, and in 'realistic' terms is a tissue of anachronisms. The American economy seems, structurally, to be in the late nineteenth century, with large industrial concerns being sole proprietorships run by their founders. The general tone is however that of the 1930s, a depression with the streets full of panhandlers. The technological level, and the social customs, are those of the 1950s. And the political environment, especially the level of regulation and the total corruption, seems to anticipate the 1970s. We are simultaneously in a future in which most of the world has gone Communist, and the past in which England had the world's greatest navy.

With a subtle choice in literary technique Rand adds to the effective mystery of the story. In *The Fountainhead* Rand adopts the universal viewpoint; we see inside the head of almost every significant character and many very minor ones. (The only important exception is Henry Cameron.) In *Atlas Shrugged* Rand uses what might be called a 'half-universal' viewpoint. We are told the thoughts of nearly every significant character, hero or villain—except the strikers.

In further contrast to Rand's other works, *Atlas Shrugged* is permeated with symbols—from Atlantis to Wyatt's Torch, from Galt's motor, which draws on the power of the lightning, to Nat Taggart's statue. The symbolic theme of the stopping motor provides a powerful motif throughout the book. And of course there is the famous dollar sign.

. . . . .

One of the paradoxes in Rand's style is her combination of extremely serious philosophical themes and a sense of humor that occasionally verges on the literary equivalent of the practical joke. In *Atlas Shrugged* one of her puckish tricks involves the sly use of Jewish symbolism and myth. For instance, considerable emphasis is laid on Rearden's gift to Dagny of a ruby necklace. It is hard to escape the allusion to the famous biblical quotation:

> Who can find a virtuous woman? for her price
> is far above rubies. [Proverbs 31:10]

But more interesting is her use of a Talmudic doctrine to provide the basic device of the book: The doctrine of the 36 Just Men. The idea of the 36 Just Men derives from the story, in Genesis, of the destruction of Sodom and Gomorrah. Lot, who resided in the former city, was warned by God to leave, as the place was condemned to destruction because of the evil of its inhabitants. Lot attempted to avert the catastrophe, promising to find other good men in the place; when he failed, he and his family left and the cities were destroyed.

It is interesting to note that—contrary to the popular misconception—the great sin of the Sodomites was not sexual perversion but collectivism. According to the Talmudic account, Sodom's egalitarian government institutionalized envy, even forbidding private charity because some recipients might get more than others. The judicial system was perverted into an instrument for expropriating the wealthy and successful. The ultimate crime for which the Sodomites were destroyed was placing envy and equality above benevolence and justice.

From the biblical account of Sodom and Gomorrah, Jewish scholars evolved the idea that God would destroy the earth if ever it lacked some minimum number of good people. The exact number needed to avert His wrath was hotly debated, and finally settled, for numerological reasons, as 36.

In *Atlas Shrugged,* Rand (who was Jewish by background, though not religious) takes as her theme the destruction of civilization when its 'just men' are withdrawn. The analogy with the 36 Just Men is striking, particularly when one notes that exactly 36 strikers are specifically identified in Galt's Gulch. An incident near the end of the story convinces me that the symbolism is intentional.

As Dagny, Galt, and the other strikers are returning to the valley after rescuing Galt, they pass over New York City. (This in itself is suggestive of some special significance, since New York is nowhere near the great circle route between New Hampshire and Colorado.) As they fly over, the lights of New York go out. Dagny gasps, and Galt orders, "Don't look down!"

What?!

Can this be the same John Galt who said, "Nobody stays in this valley by faking reality in any manner whatsoever."? The incident is totally out of character. And that's Rand's little joke; Galt is saving Dagny from being turned into a pillar of salt.

. . . . .

The plot of *Atlas Shrugged* is marvelously constructed, an intricate machine that meshes smoothly with the novel's philosophical themes.

There are, it must be conceded, some notable flaws. For instance, during his affair with Dagny, why does Francisco not tell her about his college friends—Galt and Danneskjold? Obviously this would make hash of the mystery element of the plot, so Rand simply makes Francisco be-have out of character. Later she is forced to make Hugh Akston lie to Dagny for the same reason.

A more serious problem is Galt's refusal to let Rearden learn that Dagny is alive, after her crash in the valley. As Nathaniel Branden has pointed out, this gratuitous cruelty does not reflect well on Galt—nor on Dagny. Apparently Rand regarded this incident as essential to the plot; Rearden's loyalty to values, as demonstrated by his continued search for Dagny, is a major factor in her motive for leaving the valley. But surely the dilemma could have been dealt with otherwise.

These are minor problems. Overall, the plot of *Atlas Shrugged* is one of the greatest accomplishments of world literature. Not only is it a masterpiece of logic in itself, but it integrates perfectly the needs of the story with Rand's exposition of a series of philosophical principles. And, with an absolutely insolent arrogance, as if to show off, Rand neatly organizes this extraordinarily complex book into three tidy, cleanly structured sections of ten chapters each.

To analyze the plot of *Atlas Shrugged* thoroughly would require far too much space. But we may consider the main strands.

The primary sequence is the story of how Dagny and Rearden discover the secret of the strike and are led to join it. On the political level, this is integrated with the account of the final destruction of statist society. On the personal level, it is integrated with Dagny's romantic involvement with Francisco, Rearden, and finally Galt. These three strands are braided into the primary plot-line of the novel.

Half-a-dozen subplots are woven into the structure. One is Francisco D'Anconia's Monte-Cristo-like crusade of destruction. Two follow the fates of minor heroes, Eddie Willers and Cherryl Brooks. Three more describe the degradation and destruction of the villains James Taggart, Lillian Rearden, and Robert Stadler. Is this pleasing symmetry intentional? Quite possibly.

. . . . .

The unifying principle of *Atlas Shrugged* is the connection between philosophical ideas and their consequences. It is worth examining one passage in detail to study Rand's technique. The primary incident in the chapter, 'The Moratorium on Brains', is the catastrophe at the Taggart Tunnel in which an entire passenger train is annihilated. At least one critic has cited this passage as evidence that Rand took a malicious, sadistic pleasure in killing (fictional) people. What is really involved here?

Rand makes the tunnel accident play an important role in the novel's plot mechanics. It brings Dagny back from her self-imposed exile so that she can receive Quentin Daniels' letter. It interrupts Francisco's explanation of the strike at a crucial point, and sets up the confrontation between Francisco and Hank Rearden in Dagny's apartment. The disaster also necessitates the journey that will put her on a frozen train and propel her into her meeting with John Galt.

The sequence also plays an important part in a more subtle

aspect of the plot, by beginning the process of final preparation for Dagny to be confronted with the secret of the strike. The first step is Directive 10-289. Dagny's instinctive rejection of this irrational horror results in her resignation from Taggart Transcontinental. But this, to Rand, could not be a satisfactory resolution; Dagny must reach this stage of emotional revulsion, but she could not be Rand's heroine if she made her decision on the basis of emotion. What has been accomplished however is that Dagny (and the reader) have been presented with the solution to the novel's dilemma—the strike.

Dagny's resignation is followed by a month of meditation in the woods, in which for the first time her basic dilemma is made explicit. Then the pressure is turned up. Francisco appears to present her with the key concept of the sanction of the victim. It is at this point that the tunnel catastrophe intervenes. Francisco fails to recruit Dagny—because Dagny, having quit due to emotional revulsion, returns due to emotional revulsion.

It is important to understand that Dagny's emotional reaction to the disaster plays a critical role. She is not merely annoyed by a sublime piece of incompetence. She is not just outraged by the destruction of an important item of her railroad's property. She is horrified by the human destruction, the loss of life. Rand is building up here to a major, dual climax in the novel's plot: Dagny's discovery of the secret of the strike, and her meeting with John Galt. The tunnel catastrophe plays a key role in building the tension that will be (partially and temporarily) resolved in Galt's Gulch.

During this chapter Dagny is put under increasing emotional stress, until she nears the breaking point. Directive 10-289 drives her from her job in disgust—and separates her from Rearden (on whom it also puts pressure). Her month in the woods wrestling with an insoluble problem focusses her emotional state. Then there is the astounding revelation that Francisco is in fact faithful to her—a scene interrupted by the report of the tunnel catastrophe. The sequence continues with the confrontation between Rearden and Francisco, which raises the tension of Dagny's sexual relationship with Rearden to a maximum. We can begin to see how masterfully Rand pulls these two strands of the plot together in preparation for Dagny's encounter with Galt.

But the Taggart Tunnel catastrophe is not merely an incident in the plot; it also functions as a demonstration of an important principle: the relationship between political oppression and the breakdown of social responsibility—and the consequent destruction of social function. Rand in this chapter provides us with a vivid picture of the way even everyday activities disintegrate when the men of ability and rationality are driven underground. This is the function of the scene on the book's philosophical or intellectual level.

Rand begins preparation for this scene early and carefully ties it into the other events of the plot. Early in the story we learn of the bad condition of the Taggart track near Winston, Colorado. Accidents happen on this stretch of the road. The need to repair it is casually mentioned. But it is merely a nuisance, a potential problem.

With Dagny's resignation, Rand begins her demonstration. First, the repairs at Winston are cancelled; the rail instead is used on the Florida line, which is more frequently travelled by politicians. This decision is allowed to stand—because Dagny is gone. Then the spare diesel at the Taggart Tunnel is withdrawn, again to please a politician. Eddie Willers attempts to stop it, but with Dagny gone he is helpless.

The process by which the accident happens is, to anyone acquainted with industrial safety principles, entirely realistic. It is exactly the sort of sequence which creates real-life disasters such as the Bhopal and Chernobyl accidents.

The petty politician Kip Chalmers, inconvenienced by a derailment near Winston, insists on immediate continuation of his journey—through the tunnel—though no diesel engines are available. The men of intelligence and integrity, who could prevent the ensuing catastrophe, are gone because of Directive 10-289, just as Dagny is. The best of those who remain are, like Eddie, of insufficient rank to intervene successfully. One by one, the safeguards set by rational men are violated by political appointees, driven by their fear of political reprisals.

It would take only one man to prevent the tragedy—but that one man is not present any more. The Superintendent of the Division has been replaced by an incompetent. Higher management, with Dagny gone, evades all responsibility. The one man who fights the disaster, Bill Brent, lacks authority. The physical order is signed by a boy who lacks knowledge.

So the inexorable march to disaster continues. The dispatcher knows he is sending men to their deaths. But he no longer cares; his beloved brother committed suicide, his career ruined by Directive 10-289. It appears that disaster may be averted when the chosen engineer walks out rather than take a coal-burner into the Tunnel—but a replacement is found, an alcoholic who kept his job by political pull and union corruption. The conductor, who might have warned the passengers, has become embittered and cynical; he limits his action to saving himself. Even the switchman might have averted the wreck at the last minute. But in the new environment of the railroad, he fears for his family if he disobeys orders, even to save lives.

So the Comet proceeds into the tunnel. And with magnificent irony Kip Chalmers, having succeeded in scaring the Taggart employees into sending him to his death, proudly proclaims, "See? *Fear* is the only effective way to deal with people!"

. . . . .

By her own account, in **Atlas Shrugged** Rand finally succeeded in portraying her ideal man, John Galt. And indeed, she has met the challenge of showing completely moral persons in a way that she did not achieve in *The Fountainhead*. Dominique and Wynand are, as we have seen, contaminated by Nietzschean morality and the corresponding despair. Roark is morally perfect, but he is not a full ideal because he is naive. He is good without knowing fully why he is good. John Galt, however, has moral stature and philosophical knowledge.

Atlas Shrugged has a complex plot involving a number of major and minor heroic characters. Rand takes as her primary heroes the giants of intellect and productivity, particularly business entrepreneurs. The basic fabric of these characters derives from the hero of one of her favorite books, Merwin and Webster's *Calumet K.* Charlie Bannon, an engineer and construction supervisor, a natural leader and compulsive worker who solves problems with effortless ingenuity, is described as skeletally thin. Appropriately, Rand fleshes out this skeleton with full personalities to create her business heroes.

The modern reader may not realize how radical it was, in 1957, to make a businessman a hero. It should be kept in mind that Rand wrote this book in an environment in which 'entrepreneur' was almost a dirty word. It is interesting to note, however, that there was one other significant writer of the period who defended businessmen, and who may have influenced Rand: Cameron Hawley.

In Hawley's second novel, *Cash McCall* (1955), the theme is ethical conflicts in business, and the author comes down squarely for the position that commerce is an honorable activity. McCall is what would now be called a 'corporate raider', and Hawley skillfully depicts his economic value and productiveness.

Even more interesting for our discussion is the theme of Hawley's first novel, *Executive Suite* (1952). This is the story of a struggle for control of a major company after its CEO, Avery Bullard, suddenly dies. Here is the scene in which the hero, looking out over the company town, decides it is his responsibility to take over the leaderless corporation:

> They were his . . . all of them . . . the uncounted thousands, born and unborn. If he failed them there would be hunger under those roofs . . . there had been hunger before when the man at the top of the Tower had failed them. Then there would be no food . . . and the belongings of the dispossessed would stand in the streets . . . and a man in a black coat would come to take the children to the orphans' home . . .
>
> . . . Did the people under those roofs know what Avery Bullard had done for them? Did they realize that if it had not been for Avery Bullard there would be no Tredway Corporation . . . that the Pike Street plant would never have been built . . . that the Water Street factory would have rotted and rusted away like the steel mill and the tannery and the wagon works . . . that there would be no Tredway jobs, no Tredway paychecks?
>
> No, they did not know . . . or, if they did, they would not acknowledge their belief . . . or, if they believed, they were not willing to pay the price of gratitude. Had any man ever thanked Avery Bullard for what he had done? No. He had died in the loneliness of the unthanked.
>
> Don Walling accepted his fate. He would expect no thanks . . . he would live in loneliness . . .

but the Tredway Corporation would go on. There would be jobs and pay checks. There would be no hunger. The belongings of the dispossessed would not stand in the streets. No children would be sent to the orphans' home.

Though the motives of Hawley's character are hardly those of an Objectivist, the theme of the entrepreneurial businessman as an unappreciated hero who gives society far more than can ever be repaid clearly prefigures Rand's use of the same theme. There is no external evidence to support it, but she may well have been influenced by Hawley's heroes. (She would certainly, however, have been disgusted by *The Lincoln Lords* [1960], which idealizes a man who bears no small resemblance to Peter Keating.)

Into the gray-suited bodies of her business executive heroes Rand poured the souls of her childhood idols from the melodramas she devoured as a girl. There resulted those extraordinary characters who have inspired so many of her young readers—especially the central heroes of ***Atlas Shrugged,*** Dagny Taggart and the three men who become her lovers: Francisco D'Anconia, Hank Rearden, and John Galt.

. . . . .

In Dagny Taggart Rand creates her ideal woman. Her earlier female protagonists are mostly Nietzschean and, as such, tragic figures. Dominique Francon, it is true, renounces her allegiance to Nietzsche, but this decision does not come until nearly the end of ***The Fountainhead,*** so that we can only project what her life and personality will be like as an Objectivist. Gaia, the teenaged heroine of ***Anthem,*** is not a well-developed character. It is only with the appearance of Dagny that we can see how Rand visualizes the 'ideal' woman.

Dagny, like the other heroes of ***Atlas Shrugged,*** is an incarnation of the virtue of competence. In her mid-thirties she is the de facto CEO of the country's largest railroad. Intelligent, decisive, self-confident, she embodies the prime characteristic of the natural leader: she is the person who knows what to do.

As one might expect from Rand's literary technique, Dagny's characterization is rooted in a seeming paradox. On the one hand, she appears neuter, if not masculine, in her aggressiveness and career dedication. Lillian Rearden describes her as "an adding machine in tailored suits". When Cherryl Taggart claims her place as the woman of the Taggart family, Dagny responds, "That's quite all right. I'm the man."

On the other hand, Dagny is an intensely feminine woman. (She is, in fact, the kind of woman who wears a dress and stockings to explore an abandoned factory!) She is attracted to strong, dominant men, and desires to play an explicitly submissive role in her sexual relationships.

The key to the seeming contradiction is that Dagny has repressed her sexuality in the hostile society in which she exists. Dagny's air of coldness and unemotional, pseudo-masculine behavior are a consequence of her immersion in a society which contains nobody to whom she can respond naturally. This is hinted at in Rand's depiction of the Rearden anniversary party, at which Dagny is described as presenting a challenge which nobody can perceive. There is a vivid contrast between Dagny's unexpressed personality in the statist world and her temperament in Galt's Gulch, where she happily becomes—a housewife! That this was Rand's conscious intention is shown by her notes for *Atlas Shrugged:*

> Dagny, who is considered so hard, cold, heartless, and domineering, is actually the most emotional, passionate, tender, and gay-hearted person of all—but only Galt can bring it out. Her other aspect is what the world forces on her or deserves from her.

Rand herself was profoundly ambivalent on the issue of feminism. She was a strong advocate of careers for women, of course, and said (in her *Playboy* interview), "There is no particular work which is specifically feminine." She endorsed (with some political reservations) Betty Friedan's *The Feminine Mystique.* She was contemptuous of 'housewives' in general. On the abortion issue, Rand took a vigorously 'pro-choice' position.

Yet Rand could scarcely be classified as a feminist. Though most of her heroines lack interest in marriage and family life, there are exceptions. Gaia, in *Anthem,* shows no ambition beyond following her man, and is pregnant at the end of the novel. Rand sympathetically portrays the anonymous young woman who chooses motherhood as a 'profession' in Galt's Gulch, as well as Mrs. William Hastings, who appears to be a 'mere' housewife. Rand's notorious statement that a woman ought not to aspire to be President of the United States hardly sounds like feminism. And, in response to a question about her position (at her 1981 Ford Hall Forum appearance) she said, "I'm a male chauvinist."

Rand could hardly have meant by this—in a literal dictionary sense—that she exhibited "unreasoning devotion" to the male sex and contempt for the female sex. She did not say that men in general are superior to women. What, then, did she mean? Consider this:

> Hero-worship is a demanding virtue: a woman has to be worthy of it and of the hero she worships. Intellectually and morally, i.e., as a human being, she has to be his equal; then the object of her worship is specifically his masculinity, not any human virtue she might lack.

Later in the same essay, Rand says, "[the feminine woman's] worship is an abstract emotion for the metaphysical concept of masculinity as such". It appears that Rand would attach a special, exceptional value to 'masculinity' as 'the fact of being a man', and that she was a 'male chauvinist' in this sense. Rand is explicit that the feminine woman's desire to look up to man "does not mean dependence, obedience or anything implying inferiority".

When we examine Rand's fictional heroines, we find that they certainly exhibit this intense admiration for the masculinity of their lovers. But, despite Rand's stated opinions, her fiction suggests that she regarded men as being inherently superior to women. Gaia, for instance, is far from being an intellectual equal of her mate. For that matter, Dominique does not seem to be quite a match for Howard Roark in ability, nor Dagny for John Galt.

All Rand's heroines are explicitly submissive in a sexual sense. Indeed, it is hard to avoid the suggestion of a certain degree of masochism in the physically vigorous couplings of Dagny and Rearden, in Faulkner's burning Karen Andre with hot platinum, and of course in Dominique's first sexual encounter with Roark.

Rand herself married a man who was far from being a John Galt in intellectual stature. Frank O'Connor, protective, nurturing, and pliable, gave her the emotional support of a husband without the inconvenient demands. She could pursue her career as she wished, and he accommodated her. Like Dagny, she was the man in her family.

But she really didn't want to be a man. Her struggle over the decades compelled her to become mannish in many ways; a 'womanly' woman could never have waged the war Rand fought. Yet through it all she battled to remain a woman. The desire to reclaim and assert her femininity, contends Barbara Branden, impelled her into the affair with Nathaniel Branden.

One can find a psychological explanation for Rand's portrayal of the sexes in her personal conflict. As a woman she longed for a mate who could match or even surpass her ability, a hero who would fill her need for romance and passion, a man who would dominate her sexually. Yet hero-worship has its obligations as well as its privileges; a marriage with a real-life John Galt, even if she could have found one, would have imposed demands she could never have accepted. Nothing could be allowed to interfere with her intellectual growth or achievements. Devastating as this paradox was to her personal happiness, its tension contributed to her art, in which she portrayed a series of fascinating man-woman relationships.

From a more abstract point of view, Rand's vision of men and women reflects her uncritical acceptance of the twentieth-century cliché that human behavior has no genetic component. Accepting that humans are born *"tabula rasa"*—blank slates—she could not develop a theory of sexuality that accounted for the inherent differences between the sexes in a coherent manner. As we will see, this contradiction also had its effect on the Objectivist ethics.

Rand may not have understood what made the male sex an ideal for her, but she knew what she liked, and the heroes of *Atlas Shrugged* demonstrate her vision of man at his best.

. . . . .

Francisco Domingo Carlos Andres Sebastian D'Anconia is the favorite character of many readers of *Atlas Shrugged.* Like Dagny, he embodies a paradox: He is at once a man of extraordinary *joie de vivre,* gay, light-hearted, sophisticated; and a man of tragedy, frozen, unemotional, implacable.

The light side of Francisco embodies the sense of life that Rand aspired to, the unobstructed, effortless achievement of joy in a totally benevolent universe. As the young boy who can do anything, and do it superbly, who fears nothing and hates nobody, he presents an extraordinarily attractive figure.

The other side of the coin is the tortured but self-controlled man who allows no feeling or suffering to affect him, much less deflect him. His relentless pursuit of his terrible purpose invokes our awe and admiration.

We love Francisco precisely because of the union of these aspects of his personality. It was a stroke of artistic genius to create a character paradoxically embodying these disparate traits, and it is a tribute to Rand's literary skill that she could integrate them into a convincing personality.

. . . . .

Hank Rearden is older than the other major heroes of *Atlas Shrugged.* (He is 45 as the novel opens.) He also presents a different sort of inner conflict. Unlike Dagny, he feels a fundamental sense of guilt, which has been carefully nurtured over the years by his wife, the despicable Lillian. He has responded by emotional withdrawal.

It is critical to emphasize that Rand does not present Rearden's obsessive fixation with his business as an ideal. On the contrary, his struggle with emotional repression is a key thread of the plot.

We see Rearden, when he is first introduced, as a man who is interested in nothing but steel. He literally falls asleep when forced to deal with any other topic. The only hint that he is anything beyond a stereotypical workaholic is a jade vase in his office.

But this is not the real Rearden. As his affair with Dagny flowers, he expands as a person. Without losing his passionate commitment to his career, he begins to develop the full personality that he had so long repressed. He takes an interest in ideas, begins to express his love of beauty, becomes more relaxed and gay. As this process unfolds, his emotions open up. He finds himself able to love Dagny. He also responds more effectively to his coworkers; his relationship with his secretary, Gwen Ives, visibly expands and becomes more personal as his affair with Dagny progresses. And he is able to de-repress his resentment of, and contempt for, his worthless family.

Much of the novel is devoted to showing Rearden's gradual emotional blossoming, as he responds to Dagny and to Francisco D'Anconia. This is a vital factor in the plot; before he can join the strikers, he must not only deal with his unearned guilt, but he must establish new, interpersonal values so that his mills are not the be-all of his life—otherwise he could not abandon them.

. . . . .

To depict an ideal man in a work of literature is a difficult assignment for any author. Few have attempted it; none have attempted such an ambitious ideal as does Rand.

John Galt, by the nature of the novel's plot, carries a heavy burden to start with. As the leader of the strikers, and the core of the novel's mystery element, he does not even appear on stage (except in disguise) until the last third of the book. We see him for two chapters; then he again disappears until the book's climax. Galt receives so

little exposure to the reader that only Rand's superb technique can make him real at all.

Unfortunately, it is not quite sufficient to fully expand his character. John Galt, like Howard Roark, is too perfect to sustain a convincing internal conflict. Indeed, Galt was explicitly intended to represent man-become-god, and Rand deliberately avoided any details of characterization that might have made him seem more 'human' in the usual, self-deprecatory sense of the word. John Galt is Rand's ultimate answer to Nietzsche; he is an assertion that we need not evolve any 'superman', that man can become godlike himself if he so chooses.

But of course, the Randian paradox appears as always. John Galt, the ideal man, the pinnacle of the human species, is condemned to work underground, as a greasy laborer in the Taggart tunnels. This idea, that in a corrupt society the best men will be found at the bottom, plays a part in all of Rand's novels. Kira encounters Leo in a red-light district. In *The Fountainhead* Dominique discovers Howard Roark working, like a slave or a convict, in a quarry. The hero of *Anthem* is assigned as a street-sweeper and does his illicit scientific work in an abandoned subway tunnel—underground.

(An interesting inversion takes place in the strikers' valley. Galt, the lowly trackworker, becomes the revered leader of society. And Dagny, the wealthy executive, finds herself penniless and must find work as a maid.)

Galt was not merely Rand's ideal man; he was the projection of Rand herself. He verges on pure intellect; he is a philosopher and teacher; he is the leader of an intellectual movement; and he is, through most of his life, frustrated by the inability to find a partner worthy of him.

If John Galt sometimes seems more a symbol than a person, it reflects Rand's difficulty in visualizing her ideal man. When she tried, she ran up against the contradiction implicit in her *tabula rasa* model of humanity: to be an ideal man, John Galt would have to be inherently different from a woman. He would have to be distinctively male, not just a pure intellect happening to inhabit a male body. Just as Rand could not make herself fully female, so she could not make her ideal hero fully male. Her concept of humanity, for all its novel and perceptive insights, was incomplete. (pp. 59-74)

. . . . .

Rand also creates an incredible rogues' gallery of villains, and provides them with some beautifully appropriate names: Wesley Mouch, Tinky Holloway, and Cuffy Meigs are classics. Floyd Ferris has just the right ring for the handsome, slick, and vicious scientist-bureaucrat. Robert Stadler's name gives a hint of the statist views which make him a villain. Perhaps best suited of all is that undistinguished politician Mr. Thompson, an old-fashioned gangster very similar in style to the weapon suggested by his name.

Though Rand has been criticized for creating two-dimensional villains, the fact is that she devotes considerable effort to digging into the psychology of evil. Three villains are analyzed in considerable depth: James Taggart, Lillian Rearden, and Robert Stadler.

Jim Taggart is visualized by most readers as short, fat, and ugly; some critics have even attacked Rand for making all her villains physically unprepossessing. This is a tribute to her skill; the actual description of Jim Taggart in the book is as tall, slim, and aristocratic in appearance. It is the reader who unconsciously visualizes him as ugly, giving him a physical appearance to fit his character.

For ugly he is—psychologically. A man of mediocre talent, he inherits control of Taggart Transcontinental. At the opening of the story, he is 39 and a neurotic whose response to the problems of the railroad he nominally heads is, "Don't bother me, don't bother me, don't bother me." Gradually we watch his psychological disintegration, until he ends up as a catatonic. He is unable to face the fact that he is "a killer—for the sake of killing", and psychosis is ultimately his only escape.

Lillian Rearden is a marvelous portrayal. She is a fitting foil for Dagny: intelligent, capable of shrewd psychological insight, and completely dedicated to relentless pursuit of a single goal. Her campaign to destroy Hank Rearden is masterfully conceived and flawlessly executed. It is only his extraordinary inner strength, and some timely help from Dagny and Francisco, that saves him.

In the story of Dr. Robert Stadler, Rand achieves a Trollopian depiction of temptation and the consequences of surrender to it. When we first see Stadler, he is a great mind, a brilliant scientist, who has compromised with statism to get the money to continue his research. This initial sin inexorably presents him with a series of moral dilemmas, and each failure to turn back leads him deeper into the morass.

In his first crisis, the State Science Institute issues an attack on Rearden Metal. Though Stadler knows it is false, he dares not contradict it, for fear that the Institute's funding might be reduced. Later Floyd Ferris attacks science and reason explicitly, and even uses Stadler's name in doing so. This time Stadler protests—but not publicly. Ferris goes on to create Project X, using Stadler's discoveries to forge a weapon of terror. And now, under Directive 10-289, the consequences of rebellion are more serious; Stadler faces not mere embarrassment but the threat of starvation. Under compulsion, he publicly praises his tormentors and commends them for their perversion of the knowledge he had created. By the novel's end Stadler has surrendered utterly to corruption, and his last act in life is an undignified scuffle with a drunken criminal for possession of the murderous weapon he had once scorned.

Most of Rand's villains fill bit parts. The mystic Ivy Starnes, the whining Lee Hunsaker, the pretentious Gilbert Keith-Worthing, and many others are portrayed with a few deft strokes and used as needed. Each, however, is used to make a unique point.

Rand is careful, despite her 'black and white' moral code, to avoid any hint of moral determinism. One villain, the "Wet Nurse", demonstrates that it is possible to turn away from evil. Another, the labor racketeer Fred Kinnan,

shows a certain blunt honesty that makes him more sympathetic than his colleagues.

. . . . .

Perhaps the most neglected characters in discussion of *Atlas Shrugged* are what one might call the 'lesser heroes'—people who are morally good, but lack the immense ability of Dagny and the other strikers. Rand treats sympathetically such tiny roles as the police chief of Durrance (who helps Dagny locate the Starnes heirs) and Mrs. William Hastings. Another such character, the hobo Jeff Allen, supplies a key piece of information in the main mystery of the plot. Three of these characters, however, receive considerable attention: Tony (the "Wet Nurse"), Cherryl Brooks, and Eddie Willers.

Tony, the young, amoral bureaucrat who is sent to supervise Rearden's production under the "Fair Share Law", represents the human potential for moral redemption. At his first appearance, he is a total cynic. The very concept of morality has been educated out of him, so that he finds Rearden's integrity disturbing and incomprehensible. Gradually, in the productive environment of the Rearden mills, he develops a desire for an ideal to believe in. Tony begins to feel admiration and sympathy for Rearden. He offers assistance in bribing the bureaucracy to obtain higher quotas, which Rearden of course rejects. Later, when Rearden defies the State Science Institute's order for Rearden Metal, Tony is concerned for Rearden's safety and chides him for taking such a risk. His commitment to Rearden becomes progressively stronger: he cheers Rearden's triumph at his trial; he fails to report Rearden's violations of regulations, and later volunteers to actively conceal them; he asks Rearden to let him quit the bureaucracy and work for the mill, even if only in a menial job. In the end he has accepted Rearden's ideals and fights to defend them; Tony's murder is the final straw before Rearden joins the strike.

Cherryl Brooks is the most tragic character of *Atlas Shrugged.* She is a slum girl determined to rise. (Had the book been written ten years later, Rand might well have made Cherryl a Black.) She is not brilliant, not an intellectual, has no career ambitions. But she is fiercely honest, idealistic, and courageous. Finding herself married far 'above her station' to James Taggart, she applies her limited ability to the task she considers appropriate to her: becoming a high-society 'lady'. Zealously she studies etiquette, culture, and style to become the kind of wife Taggart, in her vision of him, deserves. And she succeeds; the slum girl from the five-and-dime transforms herself into a sophisticated member of the aristocracy of wealth. Again we see a classic Randian cliché-reversal. Taking off from Shaw's *Pygmalion*, Rand invents an Eliza Doolittle who transforms herself into a lady on her own initiative and by her own efforts—against the opposition of her 'benefactor', who wants her to remain a slum girl. But Cherryl's effort to become a worthy consort for her husband goes for nothing; Taggart is not a hero but a rotter; he has married her, not to ennoble her, but to destroy her.

The most important of the lesser heroes is Dagny's assistant, Eddie Willers, the very first character to whom we are introduced as the novel opens. It is easy to underestimate Eddie Willers. Standing beside Dagny Taggart or Hank Rearden he seems ordinary, not very competent, almost a bit wimpish. This, however, is due merely to the contrast with Rand's extraordinary heroes, as the moon seems dim in sunlight. Hank Rearden, who ought to know, says that Eddie has the makings of a good businessman. In fact, he is a highly able executive. Toward the end of the book, he bribes his way onto an Army plane and flies into a city torn apart by civil war. In the space of a few days, singlehanded, he negotiates immunity with three separate warring factions, reorganizes the Taggart terminal, revitalizes its personnel, and gets the trains running again. Some wimp!

All three of these lesser heroes come to bad ends. Tony is murdered when he defies his masters and attempts to warn Rearden of the plot against his mills. Cherryl commits suicide when she discovers the horrifying truth about her husband. Eddie strands himself in the desert, sobbing at the foot of a dead locomotive. Why is there no happy ending for these characters?

Mimi Gladstein suggests that Eddie's fate is punishment for his refusal to accompany Dagny to Galt's Gulch. Certainly it is a consequence of that decision, but it is wrong to see it as punishment for a moral failing.

In her treatment of the lesser heroes Rand expresses an important truth. The essence of statism is the destruction of all that is good in the human spirit. The ablest heroes frequently escape, to make new lives for themselves elsewhere. Such people as Rachmaninoff and Sikorsky and Rand escaped from the Bolsheviks. Such people as Einstein and Fermi and von Mises escaped from the Nazis. It was mostly the people of more ordinary intellect that perished at Vorkuta or Auschwitz. These were the people who attempted to fight, but lacked the ability to do so effectively—like Tony. Or they were the people who died of sheer despair, facing a horror beyond their conception—like Cherryl. Or, they were those who might have escaped, but could not bring themselves to give up their old life and start over again with no capital but their own minds—like Eddie. Rand had known such people; her own father died under the Soviet regime, unwilling to leave Russia and give up the hope that he might somehow get his business back. She pities them, does not condemn them. (pp. 74-8)

It should be evident to the reader that a great deal more could be said about **Atlas Shrugged.** This book is one of the most complex novels ever written, and its analysis poses hundreds of fascinating problems which will occupy scholars for decades.

I lack the space to properly cover the many concepts that Rand developed in this novel: 'sanction of the victim' and the impotence of evil; envy and the hatred of the good for being good; the 'individual surplus' of the great innovators; the intimate connection of philosophical premises and personal and social character; and many others.

Atlas Shrugged is not merely a novel to be read for entertainment, enjoyable though it is. Nor is it a treatise to be read for enlightenment, instructive though it is. The reader will benefit most who regards the book as a sort of magical box full of tightly folded intellectual *origami,* each of which should be carefully opened, contemplated, and cherished. (p. 85)

Ronald E. Merrill, in his The Ideas of Ayn Rand, *Open Court, 1991, 191 p.*

FURTHER READING

Biography

Branden, Barbara. *The Passion of Ayn Rand.* Garden City, N.Y.: Doubleday, 1986, 442 p.
Critical biography written by a former associate of Rand. Gives special attention to Rand's relationship with the author and with Nathaniel Branden.

Criticism

Cain, Edward. "Ayn Rand as Theorist." In his *They'd Rather Be Right: Youth and the Conservative Movement,* pp. 37-50. New York: Macmillan, 1963.
Explores the relationship of Rand's philosophy to conservatism and the reasons why her writings appeal to the young.

Den Uyl, Douglas J., and Rasmussen, Douglas B., eds. *The Philosophic Thought of Ayn Rand.* Urbana and Chicago: University of Illinois Press, 1984, 235 p.
Collection of essays on the philosophical aspects of Rand's works.

Evans, M. Stanton. "The Gospel According to Ayn Rand." *National Review* XIX, No. 39 (3 October 1967): 1059-63.
Analyzes Rand's views from a conservative perspective.

Fletcher, Max E. "Harriet Martineau and Ayn Rand: Economics in the Guise of Fiction." *American Journal of Economics and Sociology* 33, No. 4 (October 1974): 367-79.
Compares Rand's fiction and philosophy to that of Martineau, a nineteenth-century English writer who used her own fiction to defend capitalism.

Hunt, Robert. "Science Fiction for the Age of Inflation: Reading *Atlas Shrugged* in the 1980s." In *Coordinates: Placing Science Fiction and Fantasy,* edited by George E. Slusser, Eric S. Rabkin, and Robert Scholes, pp. 80-98. Carbondale and Edwardsville: Southern Illinois University Press, 1983.
Discusses *Atlas Shrugged* as science fiction especially suited to the political tensions of the early 1980s. Contains an afterword in which the author speculates about the impact of Rand's death and the enduring popularity of her work.

Letwin, William. "A Credo for the Ultras." *The Reporter* 27, No. 6 (11 October 1962): 56, 58, 61-2.
Finds Rand's fiction and philosophy unrealistic and potentially dangerous.

Machan, Tibor R. "Ayn Rand: A Contemporary Heretic?" *Occasional Review* (Winter 1976): 133-49.
Explores Rand's basic philosophical concepts and makes comparisons to other philosophies.

Malcolm, Donald. "The New Rand Atlas." *The New Yorker* XXXIII, No. 36 (26 October 1957): 194, 197-98.

Review of *Atlas Shrugged.*

O'Neill, William F. Review of *Introduction to Objectivist Epistemology,* by Ayn Rand. *Teaching Philosophy* 3, No. 4 (Fall 1980): 511-16.

Evaluates the potential value of *Introduction to Objectivist Philosophy* as a philosophy course text. O'Neill is the author of *With Charity Toward None,* an extended study of Rand's work.

Peikoff, Leonard. *Objectivism: The Philosophy of Ayn Rand.* New York: Dutton, 1991, 493 p.

Summary and application of the objectivist philosophy by Rand's chosen successor as the chief expositor of objectivism.

Rolo, Charles. "Come the Revolution." *The Atlantic Monthly* 200, No. 5 (November 1957): 249-50.

Review of *Atlas Shrugged.*

Rosenbloom, Joel. "The Ends and Means of Ayn Rand." *The New Republic* 144, No. 17 (24 April 1961): 28-9.

Review of *For the New Intellectual.*

Smith, George H. "Atheism and Objectivism" and "Objectivism as Religion." In his *Atheism, Ayn Rand, and Other Heresies,* pp. 181-92, 213-30. New York: Prometheus Books, 1991.

These essays respectively examine the objectivist argument for atheism and the religious aspects of objectivist thought.

Tracy, Honor. "Here We Go Gathering Nuts." *The New Republic* 155, No. 24 (10 December 1966): 27-8.

Review of *Capitalism: The Unknown Ideal.*

Additional coverage of Rand's life and career is contained in the following sources published by Gale Research: *Authors and Artists for Young Adults,* Vol. 10; *Contemporary Authors,* Vols. 13-16, rev. ed., Vol. 105 [obituary]; *Contemporary Authors New Revision Series,* Vol. 27; *Contemporary Literary Criticism,* Vols. 3, 30, 44; *DISCovering Authors; Major 20th-Century Writers;* and *World Literature Criticism.*

Yves Thériault

1915-1983

French-Canadian novelist, short story writer, and playwright.

INTRODUCTION

The author of over thirty novels and nearly a thousand short stories, Thériault is one of French-Canada's most prolific and widely acclaimed literary figures. He is best known for his novel *Agaguk,* which centers on an Inuit eskimo torn between traditional culture and the necessities of modern life. While Thériault's works incorporate a wide spectrum of characters ranging from Canada's indigenous peoples to orthodox Jews and Italian immigrants living in Montreal, they all address such themes as cultural assimilation, self-identity, and environmental degradation.

Thériault grew up in Montreal. He acquired an early appreciation for non-Western culture from his father, who, being half Montagnais Indian, taught Thériault the language and customs of the Montagnais people. After quitting school during the eighth grade, Thériault worked a number of odd jobs, including bartending and truck driving. Following an eighteen-month stay in a sanatorium where he was treated for tuberculosis, he lived for a short time with a group of trappers, an experience that gave him firsthand knowledge of the Canadian wilderness. From the early 1930s through the early 1960s, Thériault worked intermittently for several radio and television stations, writing his first radio play in 1940. The following year he began publishing short stories in a Montreal newspaper, and in 1945 he and his wife signed a contract to anonymously write six "ten-cent" detective and romance novels per week over a four-year period. In 1950 he published his first serious novel, *La fille laide,* followed by three more in 1951. With the success of *Agaguk* and later *Ashini*— a lyric novel that celebrates Montagnais culture and laments its decline—Thériault earned recognition as a spokesman for native peoples and served as director of Cultural Affairs in the Ministry of Indian Affairs from 1965 to 1967. Despite suffering partial paralysis from a stroke in 1970, Thériault recovered and continued to write until his death in 1983.

While Thériault's works are considered extremely diverse, critics note that the author's fundamental themes remain constant. The novels *Aaron* and *Amour au goût de mer,* for instance, respectively examine the problems faced by orthodox Jews and Italian immigrants in Montreal. Thériault also addresses the cultural denigration that occurs when native peoples are forced to conform to Western beliefs and mores in such novels as *Ashini, Le ru d'Ikoué,* and *Tayaout, fils d'Agaguk.* The protagonist of *Tayaout,* for example, attempts to save himself and his

people by reintroducing cultural symbols and reviving such traditional practices as stone carving. Although Tayaout initially succeeds in reinvigorating his people's culture, his efforts ultimately fail when members of his village agree to sell their work to a white trader and thus transform sculpting into a commercial activity devoid of cultural meaning.

The conflict between traditionalism and modernism is also a principal theme in *Agaguk* and *Agoak, l'héritage d'Agaguk* (*Agoak: The Legacy of Agaguk*). In both novels an Inuit and his wife flee to the remote wilderness, enduring tremendous suffering to preserve their personal and cultural integrity in the face of an encroaching white civilization. For Thériault, the violence and dangers of the wilderness add emotional and spiritual vitality to one's existence as evidenced by the intense love and compatibility that Agaguk and his wife, Iriook, share while traveling together across the tundra. As Allison Mitcham has written: "Yves Thériault explores such contemporary issues as the function of the wilderness in a twentieth century context, the necessity of solitude for self-knowledge, and the role of love and art in the regeneration and expansion of human perceptions. Above all, Thériault seems concerned that we stop short in our head-long pursuit of material goals and examine the position of contemporary man—before all opportunities for choice and for heroism vanish with the impending destruction of the wilderness."

PRINCIPAL WORKS

Contes pour un homme seul (short stories) 1944; enlarged edition, 1965
La fille laide (novel) 1950
Le marcheur (drama) 1950
Le dompteur d'ours (novel) 1951
Les vendeurs du temple (novel) 1951
La vengeance de la mer (novel) 1951
Aaron (novel) 1954
Agaguk (novel) 1958
    [*Agaguk*, 1963]
Ashini (novel) 1960
    [*Ashini*, 1972]
Amour au goût de mer (novel) 1961
Les commettants de Caridad (novel) 1961
Cul-de-sac (novel) 1961
    [*Kesten and Cul-de-sac*, 1973]
Séjour à Moscou (travel essay) 1961
Le vendeur d'étoiles, et autres contes (short stories) 1961
Le ru d'Ikoué (novel) 1963
Berangère ou la chair en feu (drama) 1965
Les temps du Carcajou (novel) 1965
N'Tsuk (novel) 1968
    [*N'Tsuk*, 1972]
Tayaout, fils d'Agaguk (novel) 1969
Agoak, l'héritage d'Agaguk (novel) 1975
    [*Agoak: The Legacy of Agaguk*, 1979]
Moi, Pierre Huneau (novel) 1976
Les aventures d'Ori d'Or (children's fiction) 1979
Cajetan et la taupe (children's fiction) 1979
La quête de l'ourse (novel) 1980
La femme Anna, et autres contes (short stories) 1981
Valère et le grand canot (short stories) 1981

CRITICISM

Gilbert Farthing (review date Autumn 1961)

[*In the following review, Farthing offers a mixed assessment of* Ashini.]

[In *Ashini*] Theriault harps again on an old grim theme, the casual destruction of traditional pride by civilized inability to feel back in time. The victims in this tragedy are the North American Indians, represented in the person of an unredeemed Montagnais.

Ashini tells his own story: how his family one by one were taken from him by the cruelty of nature or the cruelty of

the white men, alike devoid of personal malice yet devastatingly destructive; how he refused the degrading comforts of the reservation, though the presence of white men had driven the few remaining animals into the northern wilderness; of his vision of freedom for his people, his attempt to parley with the Great White Chief from Ottawa, his pathetic failure and his death.

The author shows the shortcomings of the civilized, even those fundamentally sympathetic to the Indians; and damns with faint praise that paternalism which condemns great hunters to the spiritless dragging out of a pensionary existence. Ashini is doomed because his point of view is so far removed that there can be no common meeting-place. The ultimate irony comes when, home at last in the happy hunting ground, he learns that his messages in blood were never forwarded to the Great White Chief. His ritual death has earned him a few lines on the official death certificate: Ashini, Montagnais, 63 years, committed suicide while temporarily mentally deranged.

Like all of Theriault's work, this novel is written in clear and straightforward French, and says what it has to say with disarming simplicity. It is less effective than either **Aaron** or **Agaguk,** partly because of a conscious exaggeration of the author's usual forthright style. The publisher's blurb claims that the result is poetic, but if so it is a clipped, bare poesy somewhere halfway between Hemingway and the Authorised Version. The style is not unpleasant, but it is affected and occasionally monotonous.

Judged as a novel, the book is inferior to the earlier works mentioned; at any rate if one agrees that a novel should tell a good story against an interesting background. There are fine moments in **Ashini,** but too many pages are taken up with the musings of the central character. Though it is not quite fair to say that none of the minor characters have life, they are certainly fewer and less alive than one might have expected from an author with Theriault's talents. The book, containing just 173 pages of large (and attractive) type, gives an impression of having been spread a little, so as to give it reasonable bulk. It might have been more satisfying if the author had written in the third person, leaving out some of the philosophy, and putting in more of the nature lore which added so much to the interest of **Agaguk.**

Theriault, however, has made a point of trying to avoid repetition in his technique. He had displayed a good deal of versatility between **Le Dompteur d'Ours** and **Agaguk,** and was doubtless eager to carry on the tradition. The attempt does not quite succeed in this case, yet it is to be hoped that the criticism offered will not discourage potential readers. (pp. 84-5)

Gilbert Farthing, "An Indian Tragedy," in Canadian Literature, *No. 10, Autumn, 1961, pp. 84-5.*

Herbert R. Percy (review date Winter 1963)

[*Percy is an English-born Canadian nonfiction writer, novelist, and critic. In the following review, he comments favorably on* Agaguk, *commending Thériault for conveying events from the Eskimo point of view.*]

This is the first appearance in English of [*Agaguk*], a novel that has won wide acclaim both here and in France since its publication in 1958. Despite passages of sometimes needlessly stark realism the book escaped the attention of certain petty censorious and censorship-loving minds to win the *Prix de la Province de Quebec* and the *Prix France-Canada,* and to run rapidly into several editions.

Agaguk, a young Eskimo, takes a bride from his tribe and goes to live alone with her on the inhospitable tundra to escape certain evil forces which he senses to be at work in his father the chief, and in the tribe. Returning to the village to trade his furs, Agaguk is so incensed at being cheated (inevitably) by the whisky-peddling white trader that he kills him and returns to his woman Iriook, saying nothing. From then on, although little is said, and the story concerns itself with the couple's continual battle for survival against the inimical wilderness, justice impends and suspense is accumulated with a subtlety that is reminiscent of [Fyodor Dostoyevsky's] *Crime and Punishment.*

Although horror abounds, to dwell upon it or to imply that it is the book's *raison d'etre* would be to belittle the author's very considerable achievement. Indeed, it would be no exaggeration to say that the story succeeds as literature in spite of, rather than because of, its sensational plot. The account of the day-to-day life of Agaguk and Iriook, which makes prodigious demands upon their fortitude, cunning, and faith, might well stand alone not only for the social record but as an adventure in reading.

Several things emerge from the story that are not explicit. One is the quality of the author's understanding of and feeling for his people. The simplicity and essential barbarism of the Eskimo, while occasionally stated and often demonstrated in action, are most effectively and credibly conveyed by some mysterious congruity of style, and it is of great credit to Miriam Chapin that this felicity has survived translation. It is by this compatibility of language, which obviously is born of Mr. Thériault's profound *rapport* with the Eskimo mind, that the reader is made to react as an Eskimo to the ineptitudes of the white man's justice, and to hope that Agaguk will escape legal, if not divine, retribution.

While some of the events are not easily credible, the people, the setting and the mood always are. One comes from the book with a sense of having lived through the long arctic months, of having been harrowed by the stark but ultimately ennobling experiences of Agaguk, and of being a better person for it. Surely a book could exact from its reader no higher tribute. (pp. 15-16)

> *Herbert R. Percy, in a review of "Agaguk," in* Canadian Author & Bookman, *Vol. 39, No. 2, Winter, 1963, pp. 15-16.*

Gerard Tougas   (essay date 1966)

[*In the following excerpt, Tougas comments on eroticism, naturism, and symbolism in Thériault's fiction, and argues that* Aaron *and* Agaguk *constitute his highest achievements.*]

There are two main sources of Yves Thériault's sensibility and thought: naturism and a sharp criticism of French-Canadian society. In this regard Yves Thériault is very representative of the first generation of novelists, often impatient when confronted with the impediments to modern sensuality set up by a religion which subdues the flesh and by a conservative society.

Thériault makes liberal use of the symbol to represent the liberation of instinct in his main characters. His ***Contes pour un homme seul*** (1944) heralds the entry into French-Canadian literature of a whole current of eroticism whose very numerous representatives in France and the United States include Jean Genêt and Henry Miller. If it is true that there is practically no real pornography in Thériault and that his most suggestive pages are indeed innocent if compared with the imaginings of Jean Genêt, everything seems to indicate that the ambient atmosphere of materialism will be responsible for finding more daring successors to Thériault.

His language, deliberately popular and tough, is the expression of a reality made up of carnal desires and murders, which are used as expressions of sexuality. In the ***Contes*** Thériault is trying to produce a style to match as closely as possible the primitive sensations he wants to evoke; but it betrays him too often.

La fille laide (1950) is more successful. A murder and a marriage, which satisfy the demands of primitive instincts, consecrate the union of Fabien and the ill-favoured girl. It is a picture of integral naturism.

Le dompteur d'ours (1951), Thériault's third work in his first manner, heralds the social criticism of the novels that follow. Hermann, the bear-tamer, the man with the muscular body, makes the village women dream when he decides to come and live there. We see the confusion that his presence, symbol of sexual delight and personal liberty, brings to the village people: Lubin, the adolescent, who comes to maturity in a single day; Geneviève Cabirand, who throws herself to no avail into the arms of this handsome male; Adèle, who grows vegetables and who succeeds where the village women fail because she asks nothing in return for her ready love. Finally the bear-tamer is outdone when the whole village assembles to see him in single combat with a bear. Liberty admits of no bondage.

All through ***Le dompteur d'ours*** one feels the condemnation of a society which torments man in his instincts. It is by this expedient that Thériault doubtless came to the point of bringing to trial a section of the clergy, too inclined, according to him, to wield its influence. Leaving the symbol for the time being, the author makes a direct attack on abuses of all kinds which, according to him, would corrupt the moral and political atmosphere of his native province. Instead of the hearty Rabelaisian jesting that Thériault would like to have produced in ***Les vendeurs du temple*** (1951), we have only a poorly fashioned and unconvincing work, inferior to the first attempt of the kind in Canada, Rodolphe Girard's *Marie Calumet.*

Brought back after this failure to the symbolist novel, Thériault writes his ***Aaron*** (1954) and succeeds finally in effecting the difficult junction of life and symbol. This time by means of a thin plot which brings on stage the Montreal

Jewish community, Thériault sets forth the sorry choices offered to any minority. In other words his criticism becomes more objective. For the first time also his use of the symbol loses the stiffness of the theorem, giving to the anguish of Jethro, a Jew of the old school, a feeling of deep tragedy, universal in the way it is developed. Between Jethro and his son-in-law there is the same chasm that widens between all the minorities in the world, those who remain faithful to the old beliefs and those who belong to tomorrow.

Still more than *Aaron* it is *Agaguk* (1958) which furnishes proof of the artist in Thériault. In this latter novel he succeeds, according to the old formula, in making something out of nothing. The plot consists of showing the effect produced on an Eskimo by the very relative sophistication of his wife. To keep the reader's curiosity alive Thériault varies his tempo with remarkable skill. The searching study of the male, charmed and uneasy at the unsuspected talents of his wife, stays in one's mind for a long time. There is one doubt, however: has the Eskimo mentality not been too easily adapted to our modern tastes? Does Agaguk not react a little like a white man when Iriook, his wife, leads him on along the path of sexuality?

In 1958, Thériault, the most prolific of French-Canadian novelists, was beginning to be established in the role, new in French Canada, of the master capable of weakening and falling below his own standards, but whose development, whatever it might be, could not fail to have an influence on the course of the novel. What demon took possession of this bear-tamer to prompt the disastrous words of advice which go by the names of: *Ashini* (1960), *Cul-de-sac* (1961), *Les commettants de Caridad* (1961), *Le vendeur d'étoiles* (1961), *Amour au goût de mer* (1961)?

Ashini is nothing but a caricature of *Agaguk*. The conventional portrayal of the White Man, destroyer of Indian tribes, furnishes the theme of this sermon in story form. *Cul-de-sac* reveals another side of this moralizer, a role that does not fit Thériault and makes the heroine, Fabienne, unbearable. *Le vendeur d'étoiles,* a dreary collection of stories the author ought to have left in the drawer where they gathered dust, is unworthy of the man who breathed so much life into the French-Canadian novel after the war. Finally, as if to prove that the sacred fire of the first years has not gone out completely, Thériault gives us *Les commettants de Caridad.* In a so-called Spain one witnesses the development of the irresistible male. All he needs to do is wink to have every woman his, unless, unleashed, she swallows him whole. In spite of the fact that Heron has to take on the appearance of a palm tree with his "two metres and more," it is of no importance; the Spanish women react to this man, even taller than Charles de Gaulle, as if he were the incarnation of all the seductiveness of a Casanova. "We are made to enjoy," is the conclusion of the widow Inez. Can it be that the novelist is desperately trying to evoke his vigorous past? Worse still, Thériault affects a contrived and archaic French which he simply does not have the scholarship to reproduce successfully. The false linguistic note underlines the mediocrity of this French-Canadian lesser *Decameron.*

Thériault will have left to the novel two strong works,

Aaron and *Agaguk,* symbolizing one of the great victories of his generation. The savage energy with which he has been trying to maintain his creative powers since 1958 is certainly to his credit; but it is doubtful that he will add much to his stature in the years ahead. (pp. 155-58)

Gerard Tougas, "The Contemporary Period," in his History of French-Canadian Literature, *translated by Alta Lind Cook, second edition, The Ryerson Press, 1966, pp. 144-250.*

An excerpt from *Agaguk*

"Leave me my baby."

Nailed to the ground, Agaguk was incapable of budging. Something kept him there, a power so complete that he did not wish to oppose it. Iriook held against herself the arms she had held out, begging him to lay the baby in them. Hate took the place of entreaty and pain on her face, a hate such as Agaguk had never imagined, in her expression, in the twist of her lips, in her whole face, burning and indescribable. A new need rose in the man's heart, to destroy this hate, for all at once it appeared to him that the future would be lived in silence, one day after the other. Never again would he know the former caresses, only this hate with which he would have to learn to live. He knew he was incapable of that. But why would she not understand?

"You must understand," he said. But in pronouncing the words he realized their uselessness. If he killed the baby, he would be killing Iriook with the same blow. At least he would be killing all that in the woman had been his joy, his pleasure. As the image of the years to come suddenly appeared intolerable, so his memory of former times revived. Iriook's smile, her tender gesture, her sensual wail in the night, what she had been to him, each step that she had taken beside him, the feeling of peace and security that he had with her beside him, their entire life together came back to him, pushing aside the ugly image of the future. None of this harmonized with Iriook's present implacable, unfeeling look.

"Go kill the baby," she said in a cold voice. "Go ahead. Do what you like. You are right, you are the master."

She turned away, fell on the ice bench and cried, "But go on. Since you want to, go on. I'm not hindering you. I will go away. I have no need of you, nor of Tayaout, nor of the baby."

It was true that she could go away, at night, silently. And even if he caught up with her the next morning, would he not have to kill her? But then? Dead or living, would she be as he saw her now? After a long while, Agaguk came slowly toward the woman. Hesitatingly, he held out the child to her.

"Take her," he said.

Yves Thériault, in his Agaguk, *translated by Miriam Chapin, McGraw-Hill Ryerson, 1963.*

Jack Warwick   (essay date 1968)

[*Warwick is an English-born Canadian educator and critic. In the following excerpt from his* The Long Journey: Literary Themes of French Canada, *he examines Thériault's treatment of vitality, nature, and personal freedom in* Le dompteur d'ours, Agaguk, *and* Cul-de-sac.]

Le Dompteur d'ours springs ultimately from a moral principle. It shows a group of people in a village, which is a simplified way of posing the problem of living in society. They have accepted a moral code, yet the spirit of emancipation is necessary. The lives of the different characters revealed in the course of the narrative have one thing in common. They are cramped by the pressures of habit or public opinion. Escape being offered in the form of the bear fighter, they all undergo a crisis. Hermann himself is eventually to disappear without actually fighting the bear they provide. Yet his effect is in each case real. The spirit of emanicipation, even of licence, has entered those who suffer from constraint. Dissatisfied women have dared to imagine running away with him, angry parents have reconsidered the problems of youth, youth has made its various gestures of independence. The episodes, jointly and individually, culminate in a new vigour for facing the human lot, a vigour derived from the will to escape brought by the pseudo-savage.

The same therapeutic association has been observed in English-Canadian novels. Hugh MacLennan's *The Watch that Ends the Night* deals mainly with Jerome Martell, a Montreal surgeon. Martell is the bringer of life, both personally and professionally. His only memories of childhood take him to a forest up a lonely river, and to the brutal vitality on which he was nurtured there. In *Sick Heart River,* John Buchan describes the therapeutic journey of a French-Canadian financier. His health can only be renewed by returning to the *pays d'en haut* [a region of Quebec] without plans or any other sop to his organized life in New York. In the Far North an enclave of vitality is discovered on a river which is half real and half dream. This is the simplest expression of the magic which the man of nature finds in the *pays d'en haut.*

Yves Thériault's Agaguk and Ashini together form the most interesting new development historically. They are respectively an Eskimo and a Montagnais Indian whose characters are drawn from the author's observations in Ungava. Like the early missionaries, Thériault has made his observations in the light of an existing tradition. The result is in some ways a renewal of the whole noble savage process. Yet in Agaguk there is also a definite *coureur de bois* coefficient. [Warwick describes the *coureurs de bois* as follows: "the *coureurs de bois* were partly assimilated to the life and character of the Indians. Affranchised from the excessive controls of the colonial church and government, yet not subjected to the social restrictions of their Indian hosts, they indeed seemed free, happy mortals. They were civilized men who had successfully returned to nature, it seemed. Their dependence on trade notwithstanding, the *coureurs de bois* were a kind of happy savage, and heirs to both the abhorrence and admiration that the savage inspired."] Agaguk is the man who has left the village and chosen to live in his own way outside its jurisdiction. Yves Thériault warns his reader that the society depicted is not of the Eskimos as they are, but as they used to be. This device both recalls the element of distance which has always been necessary to happy savage stories and creates a fictitious world in which the forces of *rayonnement* and personal liberty are dramatized together.

It would be an understatement to say that Agaguk is free, since the whole of the action involves the dual struggle for freedom, that of the village, and that of the individual. The action, too, shows him to be noble and good. It is not his fault that he sometimes goes wrong: each crime is the direct reaction to a swindling trader's frustrating Agaguk's worthy plans. Like Joseph-Charles Taché's Père Michel, he kills an unjust man and pays the full price in a long struggle with his conscience. The outcome of the struggle is the emancipation of his wife, and a break with the custom of infanticide.

The struggle itself is not a conscious one, since Agaguk and Iriook are ignorant of morals. All they have learned from the priest is to drink tea. Their own natural goodness is unconscious and unreasoned, which probably explains why it is so drastically upset by outside interference in the form of the whisky trader. Their conscious knowledge is of nature, mainly through the medium of hunting. The struggle is therefore set in Agaguk's contact with nature. He is hunted by a strange white wolf.

The boundary between internal and external nature is completely abolished as the struggle goes on. Agaguk has always been aware of the threat of wolves in the ordinary way, especially when he has accumulated too much meat. But the prize in this contest is the new man. Firstly, Agaguk becomes convinced that the real prey of the white wolf is his son, in whom are vested his vague hopes for the future and the better life he is building. Finally, he wins the struggle when his face has been mauled enough to destroy his original identity, the unregenerate man. This accident saves him from being arrested for murder, but at the same time completes his break with the corrupt village and certain Eskimo traditions. Not only is Agaguk a noble savage, he has also been reborn into a purer state. The struggle with the white wolf is greater, for him, than the break with custom, and a more decisive step in his regeneration. It represents the growth of conscience which must accompany his increased prosperity and ambition. Because Yves Thériault realizes that moral simplicity or neutrality is not enough, he shows a hero transformed by the responsibility of a man who wants to do the right things in a world full of wrong.

An essential of this state is vitality, which Agaguk has in the form of virility and hunting prowess, underlined by Thériault's insistence on sexual activity, in blunt, short sentences. It is the vitality of nature. When Agaguk exults in his wife's pregnancy, he thinks about teaching his son to hunt, and in his dream lesson the whole predatory chain of Ungava's wild life is reconstructed, with victorious man precariously successful in it.

> . . . Viens, viens avec moi jusqu'à ces herbes. Ici la piste du vison, regarde! Elle se confond avec celle du rat musqué. Bon, avance et regarde, là!

Du sang, du poil. Un rat musqué est mort, dévoré par le vison. Pour eux aussi, l'un comme l'autre, la rançon de la survie. Pour que le vison vive, le rat musqué est sacrifié.

. . . . .

Mais il n'y avait pas que les bêtes. Il y avait aussi les armes. Ceci est un fusil . . . Examine comment il est fait. Voici le canon par où surgit la balle d'acier. Ici l'âme de ce canon. Et la crosse. Voici comment il faut charger l'arme. Comment il faut l'épauler, tirer. Vois là-bas ce caribou qui fuit . . . Je presse ici, la balle jaillit, va frapper l'animal.

. . . . .

Il lui dirait tout cela à ce petit qu'il aurait. Chaque jour il lui enseignerait les mystères de leur propre survie accordée à celle des animaux de la toundra.

Vitality gives Agaguk the ability to make progress, which the village Eskimos lacked. The point is not that Yves Thériault has left a careless contradiction in his picture of Eskimos; judged as sociology, *Agaguk* would not go very far in spite of its trappings of language and custom. This apparent inconsistency is a novel way of endowing natural man with perfectibility instead of perfection. His wife, Iriook, represents the emancipation of Eskimo women. References to Eskimo women who are more submissive to tradition suggest a lack of any recognizable human dignity. Iriook's emancipation is distinctly expressed by her giving advice to Agaguk, by speaking up for him in front of the police and in general by participating constructively in their day to day life. It is also shown by untraditional sexual liberties, by insisting on saving the life of a female baby, and generally by being on the side of life in the most elementary ways. Iriook is not wholeheartedly supported by Agaguk, but she wins because in her maternity she holds the life-giving force. She completes Agaguk's break with the obnoxious sexual customs of the village. These, whatever their foundation in the Arctic past, have become corrupt, and support the tyranny of the aging chief and his sorcerer lieutenant. Agaguk wins, not because he is less guilty, but because he is less decadent. In fact, it is Agaguk's crime which leads to the collective fall of the village, and his own disfigurement. Under the influence of his wife, Agaguk is able to begin thinking of himself as a free moral agent, a better being than the one who impulsively killed a swindler. From this he is able to see his past act as a crime, and develops from his remorse the first awareness of conscience. For Thériault, aimless personal freedom and natural vitality are the first sources of moral dignity. He has given this idea a novel if at times highly spiced expression, and developed one more meaning from the myth of the *pays d'en haut.*

Agaguk and Iriook make this moral progress in defiance of sorcerer and chief. Their village represents societies where church and state conspire against individual freedom. They refuse to participate in its decadent customs and to share its fate. For French Canadians of the Duplessis era the use of national solidarity as a battle cry to mask corruption and stifle opposition was a live question. It is

no surprise that Yves Thériault should have gone to northern settings for their traditional anti-conformism, and to the happy savage for the equation of freedom with moral good. What is strikingly original is the way in which so many of the main *pays d'en haut* themes have been brought together: the noble savage, his special variant in the *coureur de bois* type, the mystic ordeal with nature (admittedly in this case not a journey) and *rayonnement,* including both cultural conflict and a saved savage. This must account for a great part of the force and consequent popularity of *Agaguk.* (pp. 120-24)

Cul-de-sac, as its title indicates, is mainly concerned with the problem of escape. Freedom is no longer good without complication, as it was in Yves Thériault's earlier novels. The positive good is to be found in love, and personal freedom is an essential prerequisite, capable of extending from good to evil. It is characterized by reference to a restrictive society, so that inevitably there is a certain amount of social protest. However, *Cul-de-sac* is not simply a satire; the inner struggle remains and destroys its hero even after the immediate restrictions of society have been removed. His choice is not between a good nature and a corrupt society.

Victor Debreux's picture of provincial society is none the less integral to his escape. The figure of his father, seconded by that of his employer, amounts to a stifling patriarchy. Its virtues are self-interest, respectability and polished hypocrisy; its vices are scandal, art and social heresy. Yves Thériault obviously felt under no obligation to develop these points at length in 1961, because this is already an accepted way of dealing with French-Canadian society in French-Canadian novels.

Debreux's empty existence is controlled by the collective "we" of family and friends, or by economic and similar circumstances. His employer and his father are both successful men, whose every action, word and gesture is calculated and controlled. Both work and pleasure are dictated to the young man, who follows like a sheep even to the extent of having a fiancée incorporated into his weekly habits without having felt any interest in her. His idea of freedom was that of his ambient culture:

La liberté, cela signifiait l'occasion de commettre le mal à l'insu de ses parents. Le devoir des parents étant de protéger leurs enfants contre le péché, et le péché de l'impureté étant . . . *quod erat.* . . . On n'en sortait pas.

Il ne devrait pas être nécessaire de le dire. Nous sommes les produits de cet âge et nous ne savons plus trop bien comment en sortir. Le danger, me disait un directeur de conscience, en première philo, c'est de se sentir pris au piège, de faire un effort terrible pour se dégager, et que cet effort, mal calculé, nous libère en effet, mais nous projette tête première dans l'abîme.

(Debreux has in fact literally fallen into an abyss at the time of recalling all this).

Sa conclusion était simple: par prudence, rester dans le piège. (Je lui avais demandé conseil sur la sensation d'étouffement que me procurait l'étude de Saint Thomas dans le manuel imposé.)

Debreux was the perfect passive creature desired by the authoritarians, and imprisoned in their plan for French-Canadian manhood.

By the device of having his hero recall his life story while awaiting death in a stark granite crevice, the author is able to transpose upon that society its culmination in a physical and figurative prison. His is a history of wandering that has led only from one kind of prison to another. The helpless victim is being eaten by a hawk while recalling how his days were consumed in a fruitless search. The story of Montreal society has been transposed into an Ungava setting, which gives it a new perspective. The northern countryside adds a meaning; it gives a spiritual dimension to what might otherwise be a purely social problem:

> J'ai aimé ce pays chaque fois que j'y suis venu.
>
> Je l'ai aimé parce qu'il savait je ne sais trop comment ni pourquoi me combler, m'emplir l'âme. Il me rassurait. Ici, mon vide était parfois moins vide, et ce qui en restait alors rendait des échos bizarrement tendres.

Debreux is an engineer, and he is a man caught in a trap of raw granite. It is in the symbolic suggestions of these two sides of the central character that the meaning of the novel is most evident. As an engineer he has been trained to submit everything to measurements. He frequently mentions mathematical tables with a metaphorical sense for measuring human values and he challenges the reader to work out the *cote morale* of his love affair as if challenging the worth of their measuring instruments. Another aspect of his profession is controlling the forces of nature in forms such as dams. As a trapped man he thinks of the futility of measurements or controls, and looks back on love and life as something to be wallowed in: instead of control he looks for spontaneity. Through love properly understood, he would have lived with nature and man; this is mainly what is meant by introducing a passage from Teilhard de Chardin.

Four ways of escape are present in the total narrative: drink, work, love, and death. Drink is a false escape which lands young Debreux in a dipsomaniac clinic, still under the supervision of his family. Finally it leads him into his fatal predicament in Ungava. Still, it is an initial escape. In the beginning Debreux feels grateful to an alcoholic stranger who made him see his own futility so clearly. Their meeting brings in the first reference to rebirth, introducing the theme of spiritual regeneration. The stranger's finger, with which he prods Debreux while telling him of his inner void, is like an umbilical cord. Debreux does escape to the extent of realizing that the word "pareil" is an accusation, not an approbation. This is his first chance to become himself. The second drinking crisis is regarded with more indulgence, because it is an escape from sudden grief. This is a feeble echo of its first potentiality. The last reference to drink (apart from the very end of the book) shows a complete debasement of this kind of freedom: he is free to be drunk because he is underpaid by his last employer.

A more effective escape is hard work. This is more toxic than drink, because it absorbs his lucidity, gives him peace with society, and so takes his mind off his real problem. This kind of activity could be called "escapism." [Blaise] Pascal's comments [in his *Pensées*] on how *divertissement* blinds us to the tragedy of man are recalled by the alcoholic's explanation of the human condition:

> —Lorsqu'on craint le vide, on se tient loin des bords. Mais loin des bords, c'est le désert. Et le désert est plat, le désert est sans fin, le désert est mort. La mort de nous, la mort du désert. Nous sommes donc une partie du désert tu vois? Par peur de l'abîme. Et la peur de l'abîme, c'est la peur du vide. Si l'on s'arrête un seul instant, si l'on se détache du quotidien pour regarder au-dedans de soi, on trouve le vide. Un vide qui donne le vertige. . . .

Debreux had always suffered from lack of purpose, because as a perfect conformist he had surrendered his will to authority. Work gives an illusion of purpose.

Love is not escapism. It brings a true feeling of responsibility. It was a real release to Debreux and he compares it with grace, because it freed him from his fear of the void and gave him purpose which made him free to act in professional and personal life. A sketchy anecdote demonstrates (with too much evidence of the author's intention) how it released his intellectual energies into constructive channels. Love is identified with healthy vitality. It changes construction into creation, and management into the service of man.

This portion of the novel, abruptly ended by the senseless death of the loved one for the purpose of dramatic effect, is rather insubstantial. The message of love is plain enough, and the qualification that this does not mean fleshless charitable intentions leaves no doubt as to the author's meaning. Yet it lacks conviction, because the characters and actions do not speak for themselves as much as in the rest of the novel. Love is supposed to be full and invigorating, and then completely destroyed by a motoring accident. True, Debreux mentions his attempt to live up to the level of Fabienne after her death. His failure is explained by the weakness which he has always had. He has always been the prisoner of narrowness and mediocrity, and his escape seems to be dashed by fate. It is only in the journey to Ungava that he acquires any lasting freedom to choose his own end.

Failure has led Debreux into the face of certain death, trapped in a hole. The novel opens with a physical and figurative fall. A long mixture of seeking and avoiding has ended with the hero facing his real situation. Before his bare, broken bone he is able to contemplate his impotence beside nature:

> Reculeur de granit! J'ai dirigé des chantiers où l'on a bougé des montagnes. . . . Et ce jourd'hui de mort, ce temps de la haine de l'homme envers lui-même, alors qu'il sait jauger brusquement la véritable étendue de sa faiblesse, je ne savais même plus reculer deux parois de granit bleu qui m'enserraient et me retenaient stupidement.
>
> Plus de calculs, plus d'invention, plus d'audace.

Pour une fois l'homme, l'homme originel, aux
prises avec le granit. . . .

Démuni, réduit à mon identité originelle, j'étais
impuissant contre la nature.

There is nothing left but to welcome his tormentor, the
giver of death. He begs the hawk which has been eating
him alive to bring deliverance.

This thorough discovery, this acceptance of ultimate
truth, is one of the main ends of the journey. It has a considerable paradoxical value. In vast space, Debreux has
found a narrow prison; in his enemy he has found his
friend; in evasion he has found truth; in his absolute dejec-
tion there is a certain exaltation. At this point he is hoisted
out of his crevice by a helicopter. This is not only to add
a picture of physical elevation. The sequel which his rescue provides takes him to a Quebec hospital, and there is
the whole feeling of coming down from the *pays d'en haut*
to ordinary men and ordinary problems. Debreux has to
become an ordinary living man again. He is given a mocking last chance of regeneration through the hospital priest
who tells him that he is in any case dying of liver cancer.
He can drink and die quickly, or abstain and live a little
longer. He will be released from the hospital and, apparently for the first time in his life, obliged to make a choice
in real freedom. Reversing Pascal's famous hypothesis
that a man condemned to death could not waste time playing cards in prison, Debreux plays a game of argument
with the almoner, avoiding the question until the last minute. Yet in the taxi that takes him from his hospital, he
makes his choice with the rapid lucidity that once made
him a great engineer. The memory of Fabienne tells him
of purpose in life, but he is filled with repugnance at the
thought of giving his dead father the satisfaction of an edifying death. The reader realizes that the story has come
full circle: he is the young man in the bar, and Debreux
is the alcoholic stranger showing him the emptiness of our
existence. Despite his own negative end (in effect the refusal of grace, since that is what Fabienne means to him) Debreux's impending death may have the value of making
others assume their freedom more readily than he did. (pp.
135-40)

> *Jack Warwick, "Regeneration" and "Revolt,"
> in his* The Long Journey: Literary Themes of
> French Canada, *University of Toronto Press,
> 1968, pp. 101-28, 129-59.*

Ben-Zion Shek (essay date 1977)

*[Shek is an Israeli-born Canadian educator and critic.
In the following excerpt, he comments on Thériault's
characterizations and use of social realism in* Aaron.*]*

In Yves Thériault's book, **Aaron,** we get an original and
striking portrayal of a social type heretofore absent from
the French-Canadian novel: the self-employed craftsman—in this case, a tailor. Moishe Cashin, who emigrated
to Montreal from his native Russia, via the United States,
took a certain pride in conserving "l'héritage d'habileté
transmis de père en fils depuis tant de générations."
Moishe wishes his grandson Aaron to continue the family
tradition of tailoring. He also wants to protect his sole re-

maining blood relative from what he considers to be the
impure influences of modern society, which tend to weak-
en the rigid tenets of orthodox Judaism.

Although Moishe is attached to his trade, he has nonetheless suffered because of it, and worked under difficult conditions:

> . . . Moishe avait été comme son père avant lui
> un être obscur et silencieux qui cousait patiem-
> ment les tissus chez les tailleurs, courbé sur une
> table à l'arrière d'une boutique, sorte de machine
> humaine qui accomplissait une besogne aride,
> sans joie, y mettant son meilleur mais sans
> songer qu'il eût pu souhaiter mieux.

After the death of his son David (Aaron's father), Moishe
took up his trade again. He preferred working at home in
order to be able to look after Aaron, and thus picked up
bundles of cloth at factories. Near a window in one of the
rooms of his tiny flat he set up a work-table. There he
sewed linings, collars, pockets: "À tant la pièce, les gages
étaient minces parce que Moishe dont les yeux s'étaient
usés avec l'âge travaillait lentement." After Aaron fell
asleep, the old man would be back at his work-bench, toil-
ing by the light of a table-lamp until late at night.

The economic themes, in [**Aaron**], deal with the difficult
Depression years . . . and the toll they took in human suffering.

The effect on individuals and groups of the economic crisis
constitutes the main social theme in [**Aaron**]. (pp. 159-60)

Yves Thériault has written several novels centred on aboriginal peoples and ethnic minorities. In **Aaron,** he generally succeeded in overcoming a near insurmountable obstacle, that of describing in depth a milieu totally strange
to him. Thériault has admitted that the Eskimo setting of
Agaguk was accidental. In the case of **Aaron,** it is difficult
to imagine the story of Moishe and his family, in their
wanderings half-way around the world, and in their life of
privation in a crowded section of Montreal, as being other
than that of orthodox Jewish immigrants. Thériault
mounts a strong attack against anti-Semitism in his novel,
and does not hesitate to attach to Christians in general and
to Catholics in particular, some of the blame for animosity
towards Jews, which has found its way into fictional literature.

And yet, after all this is said, one tends to agree with those
critics [such as Pierre de Grandpre, in *Dix ans de vie lit-
téraire au Canada français,* (1966)], who also see in **Aaron**
a possible allegory of French-Canadian life. The conflict
between the new and the old, between Aaron and Moishe,
between a religion forged centuries ago and life in a modern metropolis, can also be interpreted as the very struggle
which has shaken French Canada's religious and secular
life to its foundations in recent years. This seems implicit
in such passages as the following:

> Inconscient de l'être, mais puisant en de seules
> écritures les chemins à suivre, Moishe avait ou-
> blié qu'un homme dépasse sa tradition. . . .
> Moishe, lui qui avait été nourri à ces mamelles
> ensuite offertes à l'enfant, n'avait pas songé qu'il
> y avait un monde sur cette terre, et une vie qui

se vivait, et une évolution qui suivait son cours,
non selon un rythme constant et régulier, mais
par à-coups.

(pp. 163-64)

Aaron can be studied on different levels. It has already
been suggested that it could be analyzed as an allegory in
which French-Canadian life is transposed and placed in
a setting that at first glance seems far removed from it. The
novel could be viewed, also, from the angle of the symbols
which permeate it—the Biblical names of the characters
and their historic and fictional relationships; the ironic
role of the mountain as compared with the sacred incident
in which Moses received the Law on a similar site; the
many quotations from the Scriptures and the element of
eternity they bestow on the work, etc. Of primary interest
here is the socially realistic level of the novel, in its portrayal of a poor immigrant worker living in a drab dead-
end street in the centre of Montreal, and the social drama
that ensues between himself and his grandson.

Yves Thériault has succeeded in *Aaron* in creating a setting that becomes real from the very first page by the pro-
fusion of impressions that appeal to all our senses. On that
initial page, too, he has placed the two main characters,
subtly suggesting the different approach that each will
have before the reality that surrounds them:

> Impassible à la fenêtre Moishe regardait sans
> voir, écoutait sans entendre. Sur le lit, l'enfant
> à qui il interdisait d'aller hurler avec les autres
> restait les yeux grands ouverts, écoutant le pouls
> de cette vie nerveuse qui battait jusqu' à lui . . .

In a rhythmic way, the author brings us back, throughout
the novel, to the noisy, dirty, crowded street where the
Cashins live. Similarly, Moishe the worker reappears
often, with his bundle of cloth going to or from the factory, or bent over his work-bench late at night. Not only
does the author focus on two characters; he also concentrates his setting in a small, sharply-defined area of Montreal which, until recently, was heavily populated by poor
Jewish immigrant families: "Dans le quadrilatère formé
par les rues Saint-Laurent, Mont-Royal, Saint-Denis et
Sherbrooke . . . ." This quadrilateral is situated south-
east of Mount Royal. The synagogue, Malak the butcher's
store, the library frequented by Aaron (the Jewish Public
Library) are all nearby. Viedna's apartment is a little to
the west, and just south of Mount Royal.

The characterization of Moishe is the outstanding
achievement of [*Aaron*]. We see both his external actions
and, very often, his innermost thoughts as he contemplates life around him and especially the evolution of his
grandson's thinking and actions. We often hear him talking, reciting holy texts, calling to Aaron in broken English, conversing with his friend Malak, with a sigh. His
voice has many registers. His gestures are eloquent,
whether he is carrying his bundle, praying or slapping
Aaron for impertinence. Moishe is a character in constant
development, and at the end of the novel his deeply-rooted
faith in the Almighty, and in what he considers to be his
people's mission on earth, is rudely shaken, and he begins
to doubt. With striking images the author depicts the last

days of a man who was able to survive persecution and
deep sorrow, but not betrayal by his grandson Aaron.

The other characters, including Aaron, are overshadowed
by the old man, and often leave something to be desired.

The author generally succeeds in *Aaron* in depicting the
various scenes from the point of view of one of the characters—almost always Moishe. Sometimes, however, he is
the omniscient author who predicts an event, or chastises
the character for being limited in his outlook. His zeal in
combatting prejudice against Jews, which was seen in
Chapter One to have been encouraged by clerical and lay
right-wing nationalists, leads him to direct author comment on that subject at several points in the story.
Thériault tends to exaggerate, for dramatic purposes, the
role of material wealth for Aaron and, for the same reason,
he makes Moishe insist, somewhat unnaturally, that the
young man follow the traditional family career of independent tailoring, in spite of Aaron's academic success and
great thirst for knowledge. Nonetheless, *Aaron* is an original and moving work, not the least of the merits of which
is the believable and striking depiction of a heretofore ignored social and occupational milieu and a poignant gen-
erational conflict, made more tense by the elimination of
Aaron's father and mother. (pp. 166-68)

> *Ben-Zion Shek, "Theme and Variations I," in
> his* Social Realism in the French-Canadian
> Novel, *Harvest House, 1977, pp. 157-69.*

George Woodcock   (review date May 1979)

[*Woodcock is a Canadian educator, editor, and critic
best known for his biographies of Thomas Merton and
George Orwell. He founded the journal* Canadian Literature *and has written extensively on the literature of
Canada. In the following excerpt, he favorably reviews*
Agoak, l'heritage d'Agaguk, *noting the thematic similarities and reversals between this work and Thériault's
earlier novels,* Agaguk *and* Tayaout, fils d'Agaguk.]

It is more than 20 years since Yves Thériault published the
novel he is best known by, *Agaguk,* in which he narrated
the powerful story of an Inuit hunter's emergence out of
the darkness of a primitive and harsh life among the ice
and tundra. *Agaguk* became and has remained a best seller
beyond the dreams of most Canadian writers; up to now
it has sold more than 250,000 copies and in sheer financial
terms it has certainly been Thériault's most successful
novel.

It may also have been his most successful in terms of fictional art, for though Thériault has been a consistently
productive novelist, he has written nothing since that
caught the imagination quite so powerfully. His later
books took him back to the Quebec marginal farmlands
of his earlier novels, into the slums of Montreal, and—in
novels such as *Ashini* (perhaps the second most important
of his works)—into the boreal forest of the northern Indians. Almost always, whether his protagonists were native
Canadians, or habitants, or Italian immigrants, he was
concerned with the way in which men lived under extreme

conditions, and at times the powerful merged into the grotesque, the drama shifted over into melodrama.

Thériault never lost his interest in the native peoples of the Canadian North. In 1969 he returned to the Inuit way of life with a sequel to his earlier masterpiece, *Tayaout, fils d'Agaguk,* in which the old hunter is corrupted by the commercialism that emerged during the popularization of Eskimo art in the 1960s, and is eventually killed by his son Tayaout, who is appalled when his father sells images in which are secreted the most sacred traditions of the Inuit. Tayaout himself, the upholder of the primitive past, is killed by a great white bear.

The same inescapable conflict between the primitive past and the civilized present dominates Thériault's . . . novel, *Agoak,* in which he returns after another decade to the world of the Inuit. During the time that has elapsed since *Tayaout,* there has been a further shift in the relationship of the Inuit to the modern world. Agoak, grandson of Agaguk and son of a full-time stone carver, enters the commercial world of the North and as the novel begins seems poised on the verge of a successful career as a computer expert.

The links with the earlier novels are tenuous, for though Agaguk and his wife Iriook and their travails in the wilderness are recalled in *Agoak,* the drama of Agaguk and Tayaout is not mentioned, and Agoak's stone-carving father is evidently another son of the old hunter; he has departed so successfully from the ancestral life that Agoak, when the novel begins, has almost no knowledge of the hunting techniques that were essential to the survival of his forefathers.

In *Agoak* the civilizing process that is central to *Agoak* goes into reverse as circumstances force Agoak back into the wilderness and relentlessly primitivize him.

In the earlier part of the novel, Agoak is portrayed as an Inuit eager to adopt the skills of white men and to succeed in a way that will make him indistinguishable from them. In Frobisher he masters the white men's ways of organization, and dreams of going south to Montreal to make a career in the centre of Canadian financial power. The more traditional Inuit regard him as a traitor, and even his wife Judith, passionate as their sexual relations may be, fears leaving the North lest she lose her Inuit identity.

But they do achieve a kind of emotional compromise, and a happy future seems assured. Then two visiting Americans break into Agoak's house and rape Judith. Agoak catches them in the act, kills and mutilates them, and then, rather than risk life imprisonment, steals sleighs and teams of dogs and, with Judith, sets off across the ice with Ellesmere Island as his final destination.

As they travel, the primal Inuit emerges in Agoak; the self-preservative instincts of his people reassert themselves, and he becomes the adept hunter he never was before, surviving and for months successfully evading the police. As the hidden knowledge emerges, so does the harshness of behaviour that went with the old life, and Agoak becomes brutally dominant towards Judith, who begins to lose her traditional inclinations and to think even

prison preferable to the enslavement she now feels herself experiencing. She tries to escape, but in a sense of monumental terror Agoak kills not only two Mountie pursuers but also a whole family of nomad Inuit whose ammunition he needs. The final assertion of primitive domination is a bitterly ironical reversal of one of the key scenes of *Agaguk.* In the earlier novel a crucial point in the civilizing of Agaguk occurs when Iriook prevents him, rifle in hand, from murdering in the traditional manner the girl child she has born him. Judith is too defeated, when her child comes, to defend it, and at this point, as he crushes his daughter's head with a rifle butt, we know Agoak has been wholly recaptured by the primal past.

Agoak builds up in a steady crescendo. The early chapters in Frobisher are rather prosy, and the long discussions between Agoak and Judith about their future are improbably self-conscious. But once we are in the world of ice and danger, where Thériault portrays the life of the hunter with unsentimental ferocity, the novel gains steadily in strength, and in its final chapters, if not in its beginning, *Agoak* is a darkly powerful book, bitterly pessimistic in its view of the regressive potentialities of human nature. (pp. 15-16)

> *George Woodcock, "Short Day's Journey into Night," in* Books in Canada, *Vol. 8, No. 5, May, 1979, pp. 15-16.*

Lynn Kettler Penrod   (review date February 1983)

[*In the following excerpt, Penrod favorably reviews the short story collection* Valère et le grand canot.]

This collection of twenty-eight short stories [*Valère et le grand canot*] is the second volume in VLB's projected series of heretofore unpublished short fiction by Quebec's Yves Thériault. As in the first volume of the series, *La femme Anna et autres contes,* Thériault's versatile story-telling gifts are here once again abundantly displayed.

Typical of Thériault's writing, one of the pervasive images in almost all these stories of rural Quebec is that of the mysterious land itself: "On ressentait comme un trouble bizarre à vivre là. Une désunion de l'homme et de la nature: comme si l'homme, justement, ne savait trop comment prendre cette végétation revêche, ces couleurs sombres, l'espèce de deuil continuel à sa vue."

Yet despite the struggles involved for Thériault's characters as they attempt to adapt to a hostile environment and make everyday existence bearable, we see in these tales the genuine triumph of the human spirit as ordinary people cope, realistically and optimistically, with grief ("Le gué dans le torrent"), poverty ("Le choix"), physical illness and disability ("L'eau de Pâques"), attempted suicide ("La robe déchirée"), village superstition ("La forge," "Le disque de Caruso") and the difficulties of marriage ("L'arbre," "La tour").

Thériault's painstaking miniature portraits of small-town eccentrics ("L'insaisissable Breyon!," "Valère et le grand canot," "La fille Eva"), his ability to capture the colorful speech of rural Quebeckers ("Le disque de Caruso"), and, most of all, his marvelous sense of humor ("La robe de laine," "L'uranium") make the selections in this volume eminently readable.

> *Lynn Kettler Penrod, in a review of "Valère et le grand canot," in* The French Review, *Vol. LVI, No. 3, February, 1983, p. 517.*

Lynn Kettler Penrod   (review date March 1983)

[*In the following excerpt, Penrod favorably reviews the short story collection* La femme Anna, et autres contes.]

Although perhaps best known to readers of French-Canadian fiction as a novelist (*La Fille laide, Le Dompteur d'ours, Aaron, Agaguk*), Yves Thériault is also a prolific writer of short stories. Nevertheless, from among the nearly one thousand stories he has written, only about sixty have as yet appeared in book form. Accordingly, this work, *La Femme Anna et autres contes,* is the projected first volume in a series of Thériault short-story collections to be published by VLB. It contains twenty-seven stories and one radio play, the prize-winning "Aaron." The title story, "La Femme Anna," is a new version of the story by the same name that first appeared in Thériault's *Le Vendeur d'étoiles*; "La Baleine" is a revised version of "Ambroise, la baleine et Gabrielle," which was published originally in *L'Ile introuvable*. All stories selected for this collection were chosen by the author himself; and a thirty-page preface by Thériault's editor, Victor-Lévy Beaulieu, provides readers unfamiliar with Thériault's works and literary career with a lively introduction to this important Quebec writer.

With their deliberately popular and tough language and their powerful sensuality, Thériault's short stories evoke a sharply realistic impression of the world of rural French Canada, which is consistently described in loving detail: "l'été doux des orées, la quiétude des tièdes jours sans vent, les étranges moucharabies du soleil à travers les ramures, le chant long et lancinant des cigales, le bourdonnement zélé des guêpes à miel brun, les chants divers de mille oiseaux identifiant leur géographie, et dans les échappées d'azur, dans le haut du jour, le vol attentif des éperviers épiant la prochaine proie."

Thériault gives his readers tales of many kinds: stories of small-town rural Quebec morality ("La Fille noire", "La Femme Anna"), stories of the always difficult relationship between man and his environment ("Les Terres impossibles," "La Courageuse"), stories about the difficulties of human communication ("Le Secret de Justine," "Le Terroriste"), stories of human love at its most tender ("La Fleur qui disait amour") and at its most violent and destructive ("Elle est pour moi"), stories of the everyday struggles and problems of ordinary people ("Denis le boiteux," "Dimitri"), and stories that consistently remind the reader of the fund of French Canadian humor that makes a difficult existence bearable ("Le Cog pondeur," "La Montre de Pâcome").

We meet memorable fictional characters, from the loving and energetic Nicole of "Le Foin de Martial" and the twelve-year-old narrator of "Licorice" to the wily old Ambroise of "L'Intrus" and the wise father of "La Grange d'Emilien." We visit the farms and villages of the Gaspé peninsula and the Côte Nord, with brief stops in Montreal and Quebec City. From theft, murder, and jealous revenge to love, generosity, and cooperation, we travel through the world of Yves Thériault. Questions of money, greed, despair, hatred, and love preoccupy the characters of *La Femme Anna et autres contes.* Theirs is the world, in the words of Beaulieu, of "l'homme dur ou de silencieuse tendresse, la beauté de la campagne profonde et aussi sa violence toujours prête à se manifester, le lancinant besoin d'eau pour que d'elle naisse le mouvement de vie et de mort, ou la grasse plaisanterie venant presque toujours de questions d'argent, à gagner, à ne pas perdre ou à s'approprier par actes de fourberie, d'envie ou de désespérance." (pp. 674-75)

> *Lynn Kettler Penrod, in a review of "La femme Anna, et autres contes," in* The French Review, *Vol. LVI, No. 4, March, 1983, pp. 674-75.*

Yves Thériault with M. G. Hesse   (interview date 1983)

[*Hesse is a Canadian educator, critic, and translator. In the following interview, Thériault discusses his career, his literary influences, and his thoughts on writing.*]

[*Hesse*]: *Yves Thériault, you seem to have a tendency to think and identify yourself in terms of a* conteur, *a storyteller. That term doesn't seem to do justice to the creator of a work like* **Aaron** *or* **Les Commettants de Caridad.** *Just what do you mean by being a* conteur? *Does this suggest a special role in a given milieu or society?*

[Thériault]: I like to think that if I had lived a couple of thousand years ago, I would have been one of those guys who walked about with the tribes in the desert and told stories to allay fears, to perpetuate history. If I had lived my adult life fifty years ago, I would have been hired by a lumber camp at the time when they had those big camps. There was no TV, no radio at that time. I would have told stories.

I've recorded in Gaspé stories from one of those lumber camp story-tellers. I have about three hours. It's fantastic. I can see the way his mind was working. It was working as mine was. I could see how he structured his telling and I would have done what he did. So you see I'm not an intellectual writer. I don't want to be one. I am a story-teller!

This means also that communicating with your audience or public is very important to you.

Yes, three weeks ago I was invited to a small village. They want me to go to a party and tell stories. This will be the first time—I'm 67 years old—that I actually create a story verbally. I tell you frankly, it gives me the greatest joy because I dreamed of doing that.

What do you consider the essential elements of storytelling? What aspects can be learned or developed? Since you have taught creative writing, you have the advantage of your experience as a natural story-teller and writer and as a teacher.

One of them is purely mechanical. It's the *esprit de synthèse.* You must be able to take the elements of a story and bunch them together so tightly so that you can write a story in one page or in two pages. That is a faculty. That is not something you can learn. It is something that you can practise. Me, I have it naturally. This is my basic talent. Also, the ability to see what makes a person move, talk, think, exist is all part of being a story-teller.

Years and years ago I had workshops for writers. From my end of the table, I told the pupils how to write a story, how to create structures, how to assemble the elements that would make a story verbally.

But now in that village for the first time not only will they expect me to tell a story at a party, but they will pay me to do it. So it will be professional.

In other words, story-telling or writing satisfies also an inner necessity, so to speak, for you.

Yes, I have to tell my stories. I am a ham, a *cabotin.* I'm not taking anything of this back. That's what I am, because my business, my human endeavour is to tell stories. Now I am going to do that as long as I can. That is my motivation. There is no other.

What personality traits do you consider essential for a creative writer or artist?

The important part is observation, curiosity, and the ability to judge people rapidly; wrongly, it's possible, but it doesn't matter. Because if you look at a person walking in the street and I say, "She is a *megere,*" it doesn't matter whether she's really a shrew or not. It's just that there's one person with an aura that strikes me. She will never know. Nobody will ever know that it's her.

The important thing is that you want to know "why?". You want to know why a person walks like that; what's happening in his or her life; why he gestures like this; why he has this fear. These are the important things because this is what you can transfer.

I have to tell my stories. I am a ham, a *cabotin.* . . . That's what I am, because my business, my human endeavour is to tell stories. Now I am going to do that as long as I can. That is my motivation. There is no other.

—*Yves Thériault*

Do you remember incidents in your childhood that illustrate that curiosity? Or did someone make you aware of this gift?

No, no. I have a feeling I've always had it. I don't remember at what point I noticed it. As a child, as an adolescent, I was a bit apart from the others in a certain sense. I was a good, strong, little boy. I was not interested in sports un-less they brought me something. I've always been that way. In fact, I would have been a damn good grocer, or a butcher. I'm a *commerçant,* a businessman.

Well, I was an *enfant de choeur,* an altar boy. Because I could do six masses per morning, I was making more money when I was ten years old than all the other kids, even though the best had allowances. When the Dominican brother insisted that I should be an *enfant de choeur, le servant de messe,* I asked, "How much does it pay? How many can I do?" And he told me, "ten cents for a high mass in the morning and five cents for the low masses." I said, "How many can I do?" Our parish was of the Dominican fathers, and they had a whole convent full of fathers, and everyone of them said a mass every morning. So we had six altars in the church and one in the monastery. From 5:15 on in the morning was a rolling business of masses. So I was getting up at 4:30. I was serving the masses. I was the only boy who would do it. They loved me. I was making quite a lot of money for a ten-year-old. It's always been like that.

That's also how I got into sports. As soon as possible I became a pro, because I thought if I was going to play tennis and get tired at playing tennis, it might as well bring me a buck, or the hell with it. Boxing was the same. I got into that because of the money. I played lacrosse for a while for the same reason.

So all my life I've been intent on never doing anything unless it paid. Not being crass about it, because I've done quite a few things where there was no money involved, but generally speaking. That's why, when I was aware that I could write, immediately I turned around and said to myself OK, I write and you're using my stuff, so pay me. And that's it. I never was conscious of a time when I wasn't curious about things.

That curiosity probably created a few problems for you.

I was disliked by certain people because I was too inquisitive. You know an inquisitive boy of fifteen can be detestable. Personally, I would kick him in the pants right now. But I was like that. I couldn't help it.

The diversity of your writing is quite striking. How do you account for this? It suggests a varied background.

I have had a diverse life as far as trades or work go. It's logical that the total of my work is diverse. It touches everything and everywhere. I am not—*comment dirais-je? un écrivain en chambre.* The world is there and I've been there. You see, I travelled all over Europe; I travelled in the East, the Eastern Block; I was in Bulgaria, Czechoslovakia, Roumania; I was in Russia. I lived in France—I lived in Paris for a while. Incidentally, I don't like Paris. For the beautiful things yes, but not the people. My vision of the world is much more complete.

To what extent do you consider your writing autobiographical?

Not that much. Not directly. I dig into my memories, my souvenirs, my many backgrounds, if I can say that. I never consciously organize or create a character which could be me.

In fact in **Agaguk** I would feel that if I am in that book, it's in the character of Iriook rather than Agaguk. Agaguk is not me. Not at all. I'm not like that.

In **La Quête de l'ourse,** yes. The young Indian is me. If I were to admit to one character.

Ashini is not me. Ashini is the me I would probably have been if I had lived my life as an Indian.

You don't come from a so-called literary background or family. Are there particular persons or events that steered you in a literary direction—perhaps without your or their awareness at the time?

Yes, things happened in my life, I tell you, a lot. Luck and strange events.

There was a man in Westmount who had a magnificent library and one of my mother's cousins was working there as a maid. She called my mother and said, "Yves should go and see Monsieur McMann. He's throwing out a lot of books. He told me if I knew somebody who'd like them, they could have them." So my mother called M. McMann, who was a Francophone despite his name, and she said, "Those books, are they good books?" My mother was a very Catholic person. What she wanted to know was, are there any dirty books? He answered on the basis of quality and said, "They are very good books." So mother very confidently told me: "Go and get the books." So I went and got several cartons of books. So from the moment I read those books, I loved those books. Now I had the complete works of Balzac. The complete works of Zola. Pierre Louys—*Aphrodite, Chrysis.* His complete works, the *Chansons de Bilitis.* Things like that. There was all of Mauriac. I was thirteen. I had to look for words in the dictionary. Unfortunately all I had was a *Petit Larousse.* Some of the most beautiful words in those books I couldn't find in the *Larousse.* But I managed to find out later what they meant.

So at thirteen I had more knowledge about things than most boys at that time. I knew things they didn't. But it gave me something, something most peculiar. I had culture. I had read authors that other boys couldn't even dream to attain, because the libraries of their fathers were probably closed up or locked up.

How did you actually start writing?

If I put into my head that I want to go somewhere or do something—don't ever tell me don't do that. . . . I'm going to do it. That's the story of my life.

You know how I started writing? Because of a little girl, a beautiful little girl. She was a student at a college, I was intent on possessing her. That's normal. I was reading a book at a soda fountain and she came in for a coke. "Madeleine," I said, "you know, I think I could write like that." She said, "No. Come on. Only people with a doctorate in literature from a university can write." "Oh?" "Yes." Then I had some, what I call, ritualistic liturgical words. I went down and rented a typewriter. They gave me fifty sheets of paper and I took them back home in the streetcar. I learnt to work on the typewriter because I had never seen one before that close. When it was OK, I wrote

my first story. I sent it to a weekly paper called *Le Jour.* Jean-Charles Harvey's paper. I didn't put my address or anything on it. Just my name. I sent the story and about six weeks later that story came to that drugstore where the soda fountain was. They had fifteen copies for sale, every week on Thursday. So six weeks later, there's my story on the front page. So the girl came in every noon for a coke. I showed her the story and told her I had written it. Then she said, "But how do I know there isn't somebody else named Yves Thériault?" So I thought, you little bitch. I went home and wrote another story. And I sent it in. Six weeks later again the new story on the front page.

By the way, that second story is **"La Jeannette."** The first one was called **"La Marie."**

How old were you at the time?

I was twenty-two. I started late.

But what an achievement. The intensity of feeling in "La Jeannette" and its stylistic expression are impressive.

You'll find **"La Marie"**—a very short story—in **Les Contes pour un homme seul** that was published by Hurtubise HMH. The third one is called **"La Malnou"** and the fourth is **"Lorgneau le Grand."** All these first stories are in **Les Contes pour un homme seul.** You see, what finally master-minded my career was that I never had a single piece of writing refused. I don't know what it is. I had about six stories in *Le Jour.* They didn't even know who I was.

I didn't want to tell them because I felt somebody would come to my door and say, you have no right to write. I had no schooling, I had no diploma, nothing. I felt I was entering a forbidden world. But never in my whole life as a writer of whatever kind of text—radio script, novel, short stories—never have I had a piece refused, and somehow this was the confirmation that I was doing it right. Also, it was my own personal confirmation. I could continue writing with perfect faith in me.

Those first stories reveal also that on a thematic level, you are already concerned with questions of morality that seem to be running like a thread through many of your works.

Possibly because I come from a period when it was not easy to be free in Quebec. Free is one way of saying it. Society . . . the structures were very strong, very heavy, very tyrannical. I was brought up in a very religious, very Catholic family.

I got out of it when I was sixteen. That's when I started boxing, and it was a far cry from all the structures that were there for me before that time. Then I became a truck driver, a tractor operator, and eventually a radio announcer. In that first part of my life I was doing tough, rough jobs. When I entered radio, to me it was tantamount to entering an intellectual world. It was not, but to me it seemed that way at the time. It was between two radio jobs that I met this girl Madeleine who challenged me.

I ended up in radio, and from radio I went into an advertising agency, and then I became a writer. This is a cycle. It's almost a closing up of a cycle. But it was always a challenge, and it was always entering new doors, doors that I thought were closed, stratas that I felt I had no place in.

It took me until 1950 to write a novel. In the meantime, I had done a lot of short stories. I had done radio. I had done radio drama. I had my own show at the CBC every week, and I had done little dime novels. And I felt I could not, did not, have the *souffle nécessaire* to do a novel. I did a novel, **La Fille laide,** on the defensive, as far as I was concerned. I was afraid, in a panic.

My first wife sent it to a publisher. He kept it for about four months. We recovered the manuscript. He hadn't even read it, and it was sent to another publisher. There, you see, luck. Luck has always played a very rich part. I sent it to Beauchemin. M. Hurtubise, who was the director at Beauchemin, travelled from Montreal to Quebec on the train. He travelled with Paul Michaud, a guy who operated a book club in Quebec. He read the novel on the train and he said, "I'll take 2,000." Two thousand copies sold in advance before publication was unheard of. So the book came out and because of that advance sale, it came out with a nice fanfare of publicity; the critics were very good, and that was the start of my career. Pure luck! You know, that one man would be travelling with another on the train. It's been like that. The story of my life. It's just been chance.

Apart from chance and luck, as you call it, a lot of hard work must also have entered into the picture.

When I started writing, I had to learn more about this damn language. So I bought myself a lot of books. There was an author called Rene Georgin. He wrote all kinds of books about syntax. I had about ten or twelve of these books. Every night I read his books going to sleep.

I also read in the dictionary. The dictionary I didn't like because if you're sitting in bed with a big dictionary, you can read only ten or twelve pages. I liked words, preferred words. I had a pad, which I still have, for words. I wrote down words because I had to learn.

If you read **La Fille laide** and **Les Contes pour un homme seul,** you'll see the style is initially *patois.* I could not conjugate words. So notice how I used them. I trick around them. I use the present rather than another tense. It's fake. It's simply because I could not conjugate those verbs. I learnt because I bought the books and I have a good memory. That always served me very well. I have a visual memory, so learning like that was easy.

*Before publishing **Les Contes** and **La Fille laide,** you had a special kind of apprenticeship.*

Well, there again destiny was favourable to me. Right after the war there was a classified ad. I had nothing to do. I was looking for work. "Writer wanted." How many times do you see in the classified ads: "Writer wanted?" They ask for husbands, they want to sell a car. Anyway, "writer wanted." So I called. The next day this guy ended up at my place. He was a little drunk, an enormous man. He was looking for people to write dime novels. Mystery, love, and detective stories. Thirty-two pages long. They had the characters already delineated. All you had to do was write the story.

From 1942 to 1946 I didn't write much. I was a radio announcer. I had done some writing before 1946, but not much until this guy comes up with that proposition. I looked at my wife and she said, "Can we do it?"

"Sure."

"Will you?"

I said, "Yes. Anything, fifty cents is fifty cents. A page is a page."

So anyway, my first wife and I ended up after about three months by writing every single dime novel published in Quebec at that time. There were about twelve of them a week. We went completely crazy. We weren't even speaking to each other. We had it down pat to a system. Twelve pages an hour.

"What are you doing, Joe?" the guy says to the detective.

"I'm going to Quebec."

"Where?"

"Quebec."

"Why?"

"Well, I have some things to do there."

"Are you going alone?"

You could go on and on like that for whole pages, flowing. All this time we were paid fifty cents a page, typewritten. What it gave me is that easy flow of writing. It's like practising the piano, and we had to write fifteen hours a day. Finally each of those stories was forty typewritten pages. We were making about $250 a week. In 1946 that was a fortune. But we couldn't talk to each other. From 8 o'clock in the morning to 12 o'clock at night we were writing. Four years. But what practice!

Later, when you have to write anything, you have that facility, that ability to pick up words from your memory, to get them together. You don't have to look for words or to work very hard at creating a structure; you've had to create the damn structures as they came, and often in one day. So some writers ask, where did you learn to write that fast, that quickly? You do that for four years. At the end of four years, you've learned to get it together, which is the hardest part. For most writers, it is the writing. For me it never was a problem.

*Your work includes all major forms of writing, except poetry. Yet many passages in **Ashini** or **La Quête de l'ourse,** for example, may be regarded as poetic prose. This happens particularly when you describe nature and the characters' relationships with their environment.*

The closest I came to poetry is **Ashini.** It's poetry in prose. Poetry has not been my medium.

To what extent did the various media and prose forms influence your style, the choice of subject matter and characterization?

It did once influence the mechanics of writing. You see, most of my writing is spoken, rather than written. That's the influence. My very first writing after those stories in

Le Jour were radio scripts that I did for station CKCH where I was working. After the war Roger B. Duceppe gave me Studio G7. It was half an hour a week and it lasted for two and a half years. I had to write one show per week. Then if I say I earned my living by writing, I must be precise.

Books, no. Books would represent a rather low salary. Maybe $15,000 to $20,000. Radio, TV—that rounds the income to about $45,000, which is comfortable.

At the time I had to write a lot. Actually I had at that time only *La Fille laide, Contes pour un homme seul,* and *Le Dompteur d'ours. Les Vendeurs du temple* and *Cul-de-sac* came after that. *Agaguk* came before *Ashini.* My income was radio. But I had two growing kids. Books sold very slowly. If you sold 1,000 or 2,000 books you thought you had a good sale. Now it's much better because distribution has improved and because of those libraries spread out around the province. This encourages reading. But still there's inflation, new presses, a new economy, as compared to twenty or twenty-five years ago. I still would not be earning enough by just books. So I still do radio.

Writing for children has also been an important aspect of your career, especially in the sixties and again quite recently. Even before publishing, you had a children's programme of story-telling on radio.

I liked it. I still do. It's very much a question of business, if there were publishers of children's literature that would have decent distribution. That would be a good deal to work out because I like writing for kids. I wrote a book for Les Editions Paulines—*Cajetan et la taupe.* It's a book for little kids that's read by the parent. *Les Aventures d'Ori d'Or,* that's three stories in one little album. Ori comes from a planet called Or. So he is called Ori d'Or and he has magic, tremendous magic; he meets a boy on earth and they have adventures. You see, he can compress time. So the boy says to his mother: I'm going to *le dépanneur* to get a sucker. Actually he has gone to Africa with Ori, because in five minutes they can do something that takes five days. All this time his mother thinks he's just five minutes away. That's my last book for kids. Yes, I like writing for kids, because you see, you can tell a kid anything. You can say his father's Cadillac is transforming itself into a pumpkin and he agrees. For adults you have to explain the facts of life.

Now that you've established your reputation as a writer, your working pattern has quite changed.

Oh yes. You see, I don't write every day. Most of my writing is done under contract. Previously signed with an advance or payment before I write. I can do that now after thirty-seven years. So I do it. I have no fixed hours. I don't write better in the morning than at night. I write when I feel like it. Right now, I have to write a dramatic script for the CBC in Montreal. Sunday I'll probably write about two-thirds of the script and the last third Monday night.

Leaving the contract aside, what is the starting point for writing a given story or novel?

I have always proceeded with a question. What happens? Take *La Fille laide.* When a girl is considered ugly, how

will she be treated? Will there be a man to love her? That's the story of *La Fille laide;* that there is a man to love and a girl who's considered ugly. But she's not ugly actually. She's by comparison, I'll admit. It's a simple story. But it's a story that has tempted girls in Quebec and they are still buying the damn book. There are about four editions of it. Last year's sale was over 12,000 to 14,000. I know next year it's going to be the same thing. Who buys it? Little girls, fifteen to eighteen years old, the age when a girl thinks she is ugly. The title *La Fille laide* is catching. She wants to know. She thinks she is ugly. Very few girls of fifteen think they are beautiful. Ten books with that kind of sales. I'd be a rich old writer.

The first printing of *Agaguk* by Les Editions de l'Homme was in two volumes. Very few of them are left. They sold 100,000 copies of each. But it's in the hand of collectors. You can't find it anymore; even libraries don't have it. Two volumes because Les Editions de l'Homme had decided to publish literature. Jacques Hébert was going to publish books at $1, printed on newsprint, and when he came to *Agaguk,* he couldn't print it in one volume. He had to sell it for $2. At the time the books were cheap. Here in Quebec a sale of 325,000 is enormous. You see, the big success now is Yves Beauchemin's *Le Matou* with a sale of 50,000. Louis Caron's *Le Canard de bois* is 35,000. But they made a TV series for Radio Quebec so that pushed up the sales. Ryerson-McGraw-Hill sold *Agaguk* in English Canada with a total sale of about 3,000.

Agaguk is to be made into a film, I understand.

Yes, *Agaguk* is to be made into a film if all goes well. It should be finalized in September or October.

Then there are other film projects?

I'm doing some things for *Playboy. Oeuvre de chair,* you know, those erotic stories with recipes, are the inspiration for a *Playboy* First Choice program. It's a ten-minute erotic with a cooking recipe included, and it's going to be done here in Montreal by Claude Leger Productions. It's a complicated contract. The financing comes from Royal Trust.

Oeuvre de chair *has a rather unique origin, as you once said, tongue in cheek.*

OK, I come to Saint Peter and he says, "You're a writer." I say, "Yes." He says, "We have a few people in here who have written cookbooks. Very successful cookbooks. I have given them a very beautiful place in heaven. Now what did you say you were writing?" I say, "Novels." "Oh. We have no place in heaven for novel writers."

So I went home and wrote a cookbook—an erotic cookbook.

So your place in heaven is guaranteed.

Yes, at the right of God, at least. I'll do the cooking up there.

Cooking is hardly my dream of heaven.

Well, there are all kinds of heaven.

Well, I'll tell you the real story behind that book. I went to Alain Stanké. I said to him, "Alain, how can we make a buck . . . ? I want to be rich." So, *Oeuvre de chair* was started as a joke. I said to him, "the only books that sell are cookbooks. I'm going to write a cookbook." "Do you think I'm going to publish your cookbook? No, sir! Write me novels, not cookbooks." So it stayed there, but I talked with his literary director, André Bastien, and I told him, "Let's fool the guy. I've an idea—I'm going to write short stories and recipes." He said, "Yes, let's try it." Stanké never reads a manuscript. Never, but never. So I bring the manuscript to André Bastien and we called it *Oeuvre de chair* and it's published. When it's published, Stanké finds out it's a recipe book. He wouldn't pay for a single line of advertising saying that it was a cookbook. André didn't dare put it on the cover. Stanké wouldn't pay for it. So the public never knew that it was a cookbook, only those that bought it. Yet it sold quite a few thousand copies because by word of mouth. And then if I went to readings or something like that, well, then I talked about it. So it's not a very big sale—about 12,000, I think. It was enough to justify it.

For the majority of your titles you draw on the main character, which suggests that characterization is of primary importance in the inspiration of your works.

Yes.

At the same time there is, generally speaking, a very strong sense of place. How important do you consider the setting you create?

Eighty to ninety percent of a book, as far as I am concerned. It has to be a *cadre,* a setting where I feel at ease. It's a place I know intimately. Otherwise I won't touch it. Never have I written all that much about the cities. In *Aaron,* yes.

But *Aaron* represents a setting that is completely different from the real city setting. It's the Jewish quarter in Montreal. There again a question.

I was walking along Saint-Laurence. At that time Saint-Laurence was the main street of the ghetto. And I saw an old man with a long black coat and a fur hat. By his side was a boy of about thirteen. He was thin, emaciated. He had just a white shirt buttoned at the top, sleeves down to here and curly hair. I was walking behind them. So I crossed the street to see them better from afar, and I kept asking myself this question. That boy, in North America, what happens to him? The old man evidently was an orthodox Jew. Now I knew about Jews. I'll tell you later why. Evidently he was from Poland and that very strict, very structured Hassidic sect. I kept thinking about that boy and went home. If he stays with that structure, nothing can happen to him. So I finally wrote a radio script.

Now I wrote that script under a strange motivation. Olivier Mercier-Gouin—the son of the dramatist Yvette Mercier-Gouin, a friend of mine—had just been hired by CKAC as a producer-director. He was very young—about twenty years old. So he had asked me for a script and I gave him *Aaron.* The script was put on and it won the Beaver award. That was the first time that CKAC had won the Beaver award.

I took the script with me to Italy, where I was going a little later. And I had signed a contract with Paul Michaud in Quebec to write a novel. So, I said, what the hell, why don't I take that and make it into a novel? Which I did. The first version was published by Michaud. The second version was augmented by forty more pages and published by Grasset in Paris.

I was interested in the Jews for all kinds of reasons. First of all on the street where I lived when I was a kid, there were Italians and Irish and Jews and Germans and French and English. I spoke French and English.

My mother was a buyer in ready-made confection. She was buying from the trade in Montreal, which was entirely Jewish. She knew all the Jewish manufacturers. And a lot of them came to our home. So I was brought up not hating Jews, but knowing Jews.

A little later—I was about twelve years old—one of the Jewish boys I played with said, "I can't play. It's Saturday. I got to go to the synagogue." I said, "Ok, I'll go with you." So we went together. And I was fascinated by the music, the singing, the atmosphere. I was a Catholic. I was practising because my parents sent me to church. I was interested, but no more than that, you know. But that interested me, and I kept going to the synagogue. One day I told that friend of mine, "Hey, tomorrow morning is Sunday, why don't we do something?" He said, "I can't because I go to Hebrew classes." "Hey" I said, "when do you go there? I'm going to go there with you." And so I went there. They won't bother you, you know. They won't ask you who you are.

You've made it well known that you write your novels very quickly. Sometimes in a matter of weeks. But I wonder if you write your books in your mind first to allow you then to proceed so quickly?

To a point.

There is a book I would have liked to write this summer. The structure, the principal elements of the book, *le cadre géographique,* the setting, the principal character, the era and most of the information that I need to describe are in my mind.

It's going to happen somewhere around 1910, which is the end of the century or the beginning of the next century. Well, most of the information I have in my head because of my age, first of all. I was born in 1916. So, writing about 1910-1915, I have the information in my head. There was not much evolution between 1900 and 1920.

The character is in my head. It's been in my head for quite a while. I've seen that woman, I've seen her live, I've seen her think for five years. So when the writing begins, the writing is nothing. It's like putting bricks on a house. All the structure is there.

But I'll have to look through documentation because I want to use the language used in Quebec at that time. So I have about four principal dictionaries and documents that were published by the University of Trois-Rivières and by Boreal Publishers. So there's enough there.

I've listened very attentively to the way my grandmother and my grandfather and my father were speaking. My father died at 87. So he was of that era. So I can remember the words.

I wrote a well-documented book that was published by Hurtubise HMH called *Moi, Pierre Huneau.* That was a book where all the language is completely authentic. It purports to reproduce the language used on the Gaspé coast around 1925, with adjuncts to the language from the Beauce region and from the upper part of the St. Lawrence River, the Boucherville Islands.

Do you think that a kind of "readiness" is also necessary before you start the actual composition of a book? You emphasize that largely with regard to sculpture in **Tayaout.**

It's the soul of the stone in part, usually it's a beast. The animal is in the stone. The artist has to extract it. To a point that's true with words. I make jokes sometimes about reassembling the dictionary: it's all the talent a writer needs. It's quite true. In a sense he must reassemble the dictionary in another sequence. If you look at words like that, you're not going to be afraid of them. You master them. I like a lot to master words. To master words is to have language do what I want it to do. That's the fun of writing.

The book about that woman is also well documented as far as that's concerned. It happens in St. Côme, which is about fifteen miles from here, in a very different type of environment than this one here in Rawdon. The mountains are higher. The woods are thick. St. Côme lives from lumber—lumber and the paper mill. We call it in vulgar Quebec French *"la pitoune."* St. Côme was founded by a woodsman, and people have always been living from the wood and still do.

So you see, the book, the writing of it is the easy part. The hard part is the structure. To give it reality, to give it authenticity, that's the hard part.

Does **La Quête de l'ourse** *have a special place among your works, collectively speaking? You've indicated that it took you twenty years to write it.*

No, it didn't take twenty years to write. But it sounds like it. The way I said it. And I said it deliberately because I had been accused by a lot of people of writing too fast, and for once I could say a cryptic thing about *La Quête de l'ourse.* The real story behind *La Quête de l'ourse* is this: It was written in two or three months. That's a little longer than most books, because I was doing a lot of dramatic radio work at the time. I didn't have much free time, but I wrote the book. Then I gave it to a publisher and there was a falling out between the publisher and me, and eventually he closed his publishing house. And since he had paid quite a fat sum for Quebec as a royalty advance on the book, he didn't want to give it up to another publisher unless that publisher reimbursed him. And, you see, it was not published until I found another publisher that was willing to reimburse the original sum.

So Stanké bought the manuscript actually from Paul Michaud. And it was published with a twenty-year delay. I had written it twenty years ago. So I wasn't sure of that manuscript. I thought that it was an elongated manuscript with a lot of useless material because I wrote it at the time

at so much per page and I felt that I was stretching the manuscript. But no, it wasn't that stretched and I cut maybe twenty pages. The manuscript was well-structured. But *La Quête de l'ourse* surprised a lot of people. You see, your view of things evolves. You don't notice it. You don't feel it at the time. But when you read something that you've written that many years ago, you find how you have evolved. I wouldn't deny any of the material in that book. But I see that I was not looking at things the same way. Yet I was looking at things in a way that was quite acceptable. So the book finally was a success as far as Quebec publishing was concerned.

I had the greatest compliment about it. It came from Paul Provencher who died about a year ago. Paul had always been a woodsman. He was an engineer. He was the expert on the forest in all its aspects. Now he had a message given to me by a common acquaintance who was a trapper. And this guy came to me and told me, "Paul is very sick. He has just read your book and he said he would recommend it as a very good trapping manual. He said it's that authentic." I thought that was a great compliment. I didn't give a damn what critics would say about it. What is important is what Paul Provencher said about it. "It was a beautiful book" and he said, "the forest in it is almost a character by itself. It has such presence."

You've won most of Quebec's and Canada's most prestigious literary prizes and awards. How important is such public recognition to you?

Let's put it this way. Provencher is more important, because you see that's not impersonal. Recognition is more important when it's man-to-man recognition of a specific thing. Take the Molson award. I was given the Molson award for the bulk of my writing. That was impersonal.

But do readers discover you perhaps through such awards so that they become a stepping-stone to personal recognition?

No. It's too officialized. I never met anybody who discovered me through that. It's possible, but I've never met anyone that said, "Hey, you got the Molson prize, so I read your book." I'm quite cynical. The only interest the prizes have to me is the cheque. To be able to put into your *curriculum vitae*—Molson Prize, Governor General's Award. Yes, but so what? There are prizes that I didn't get, and that's all right, but I'm sorry I didn't get the cheque. It would have been useful. That's cynical, I know. But it's a fact.

It seems frank and realistic rather than cynical.

In France, if you win the Goncourt, you sell about half a million books because of that. In Canada, you win the Governor General's Award and you sell ten books or so. The recognition is not really public. Maybe that is why I am so cynical. If I knew that by winning the Prix David or the Prix Molson, my work would be spread out immediately and really appreciated, it would be different. But it's not the case.

Academic recognition—I won't say I'm totally indifferent. But it does not represent an end in itself. Whereas I know writers who dream of being recognized by all the universities. Hubert Aquin was one; he was recognized; he was one of them. I'm not. You see I don't dream of being recognized by the universities.

You see, when I say I'm going to that party and improvise and tell stories, that's more important to me than being invited to a university. Much more important. It's an achievement I dream of, whereas the other thing is routine. Part of the structure. It's fun. It would be fun to go and all that, but it's no more than that.

Nevertheless, your works—particularly **Agaguk** *and* **Ashini**—*are being studied in colleges and universities and you do make readings there.*

Logically enough the University of Ottawa—the French Department there invited me. But I was never invited even by Laval University. I tell you, I'm not a writer for the academics. They'll go for Marie-Claire Blais, Roch Carrier. You see, they all go for *Agaguk.* But the writer of *Agaguk* is forgotten.

Where I have an academic response is through the secondary schools, the equivalent of high school, the *polyvalentes.* There I have a response. But higher, they teach me, but they will not invite me. This spring [1983], I did a tour of fifteen universities in the Maritimes—Saint John, Halifax, Truro. It was an organized continuous tour of the French Departments. And I've just been to the University of Sherbrooke. I spent the afternoon there. Sherbrooke is extremely active in the summer. That was completely different from what I've done all my life. It was with the *Faculté de droit.* They were Anglophone students from all provinces. They are there for an immersion course in the Napoleonic Code, that is the Common Law in Quebec.

There's probably a reluctance to invite you if one considers the time and energy that must be spent on such occasions, especially if there's only a small audience.

I love it when it's a small group. If you'd ever see me work, you'd find I don't spend energy because I communicate in a very natural, easy way. The only thing that would spend energy would be the trip.

I've regained my energy, my strength almost miraculously—because I was paralyzed in 1970 from a massive stroke. I had to relearn everything: to talk, to walk, to pick up things. I spent a couple of months in panic because I did not know if my memory was affected. And a writer with no memory is not a writer. But other cells took over. I'm OK now. That was thirteen years ago. It was a rough time.

You don't think you are vulnerable. You think you'll never be sick in your life. You wake up one morning and you're paralyzed. Just like that, as if something fell on you.

Your stroke occurred shortly after you had completed **Le Dernier Havre.**

Le Dernier Havre was written in about a week in the two months preceding my illness. When the proofs came from the publisher to be proofread, my wife could not read them. She said there's a premonition there. Something was going to happen to me. So that was a bad time.

What helped you in your recovery?

I was so angry that I was paralyzed. I was so angry to a point that it saved me.

You are at a stage in your career when younger writers, like Claude Jasmin and Victor-Lévy Beaulieu, acknowledge your influence and their debt to you. Are you aware of writers that have influenced you or whom you admire particularly?

Influence is a great word, because it's not detectable in anything I write. Giono has been a writer that I admired. I read a lot because I found that when I read him, we had the same vision of things, of nature, of people. Not a similitude in vision, but we had the same approach. He saw things pretty much the way I saw things. What he did with them was different from what I did. That is the most important of the influences.

Saint-John Perse came very, very much later and was not an influence on me either. I admired him. I admired his command of language, the immense quantity of very exotic words. I liked that. That was a bit depraved and vicious to know so many strange words.

But the man who has been most influential for me was Mauriac. Mauriac was among the first writers I consorted with. What I admired in him was that he could in three or four lines, or a very short paragraph, create or recreate a world. I was trying to figure out how he did it. So I started dissecting pages and pages of Mauriac and found it was in the use of the precise meaning of a word that permitted him out of a verb and a couple of attributes to create a world. I wasn't capable of imitating Mauriac and I wasn't trying to do that. But I was capable of pastiching him, of using the same technique of checking my meanings. For a long time I did that. Now I have enough memory so that I can work with the vocabulary I have in my memory bank. But at that time I had to check my words, and I checked them. So I was told eventually by my readers and critics, or professors, how clear and concise my style is. And I attribute that to my frequentation with Monsieur Mauriac.

Yes, I think **L'Etreinte de Vénus,** *for example, is a book that could easily be used by students of French. The detective and mystery stories of that collection must have surprised many readers familiar with some of your other works.*

These are stories I wrote for *La Patrie du Dimanche,* way back in 1960. I was working for *La Patrie* as a reporter, and I was selling them a story every two weeks. It became a book because Québec-Amérique wanted to publish something of me and so they picked that up.

How does **Amour au goût de mer** *fit into your collective works?*

Roland Sasseville was working at Beauchemin's in 1961. I had just come back from Italy. He said, "Why don't you write something about Montreal and the Italians?" At the same time I had just discovered Saint-John Perse, the poet. So I invented a story. It's not a very good story. The first part of the book is OK. The second. . . .

No, I think **Amour au goût de mer** *deserves to be better known. It has some beautiful moments of emotional intensity. And the empathy for these immigrants is so well developed.*

Possibly. There again, you see, much, much of human relations is vastly improved when people can communicate in their own language. And when, as a stranger, you can communicate with them in their language it is oh, ten million times better than communicating with them through translators or guessing at some other person's communication.

When I went to Italy, of course, I lived in Florence. But then it didn't take very long to pick up the *lingua pura.* And I came to speak it almost fluently.

That facility of acquiring different languages must be linked with your awareness of language. In **Aaron** *and in* **La Quête de l'ourse** *you delve into the significance language has in people's lives and speak of the "soul" of a language. That must be very revealing to many of your readers, especially if they speak only one language.*

I hate to say this, but it's true. I have to have my character express himself in the language of publication, that is for the communication with the reader.

Now one thing is very seldom taught or even known by a lot of white people of Canada is that there are no Indian arts other than the art of speaking—*l'art oratoire.* So there are actually two Indian languages. The language of usage and the noble language. You see, Montagnais is divided into six dialects. It is also a sublanguage of the Cree. It's not a dialect proper, but the six dialects do not understand each other, or only with difficulty.

Even if your message doesn't reach Indians, it's important that it be heard by the white people.

The Algonquin language, the Cree being one of the languages of Algonquin, is a very rich language. If it were spoken by fifty million people, it would be a beautiful and rich language. So would Eskimo, although Eskimo is not pleasant to hear. It's a very harsh language, and there's a disagreeable "K" in Eskimo. But you have thirty-five words for snow. There is a richness. This is a wealth of expression to be able to delineate snow so well that to give all the minute details of what kind of snow. We look at snow, you see, it's white, just white stuff. They look at snow and they have thirty-five different white stuffs in their eyes, in their minds. So these languages are usually extremely interesting because of that.

Then in the Cree language and its various dialects, you proceed with roots, prefixes, infixes and suffixes. So if you are talking with somebody who knows his language, you can invent a word. You can create a word with a root. You can create an action, first by using the root and then by using the various infixes or suffixes that you need to make a new word. That's why I say a language like that, if spoken by a great number of people and with an economy to go with it, can be a very rich language. Which is not the case with French or English.

You don't create a word in French. You can, but you have to stop and think and probably use a Greek root or a Saxon root. But the creation is a long-term process. Whereas in Cree you can create the word instantaneously for the person to understand, to know what you are talking about. But it will be a word not in the sense that it would. . . . I'm trying to think of the English word to describe that. In French it is *locution.*

A phrase, an expression.

It's a complex thought, reunited in one word. I think you have something like that in German. It looks like one big word, but actually it's two or three things expressed through that word. Well, it's the same thing in Cree—which we don't have in French or English.

Is the complexity of language a mirror of a complexity of personality and thought?

Yes. Unfortunately if you know an Indian through one of the common-use languages, like French or English, you don't notice the complexity. You notice that after a while. If you know him very well, then you see what he expresses is probably a very primitive, very simple type of thought. Whereas inside his head in his own language, he could discourse for half an hour on a thought because, you see, he possesses a means of expression.

Your perception of the world of Indians and of the White Man is quite unique in Canadian fiction. And I think it furthers a better understanding of these two respective worlds, as you do in **Ashini, N'Tsuk** *or* **La Quête de l'ourse** *because you open so often your readers' eyes to the richness and complexity of the Indians' world.*

On the one hand, I'm a very contemporary white person. Within the next week or so I'll have a computer delivered with a word processor. Because I crave to write on that kind of a machine. That makes me, I think, a very contemporary, a very modern white person of Canada. But I partake of the two worlds.

I also learned about the forest. In a way I lived in it; not in the way of the ordinary hunter who goes on a weekend to shoot a bear or to shoot a moose. My forest experience was actually living from the forest. Not carrying food or anything like that. I'd trap.

Pessimism and the dark side of life show up very much in your writing.

The funny part is, I am a joyous man. I'm a guy who jokes all the time. I cannot take myself seriously and I can, with great difficulty, act seriously. I like to laugh. I like to have a good time. I'm not a pessimist. If I'd been a pessimist, I would have killed myself a long time ago. Economically at least. But when I write. . . .

There's only one book I've written which was treated as a funny book. And that's **Les Vendeurs du temple.** This, this was really a satire. Generally speaking, I don't like laughing subjects. I prefer drama, tragedy, the struggle of man. I didn't say that. Critics said that. The struggle of man against himself and against the elements. I don't know why.

I've kept dreaming of writing some sort of a last book that

would be a vast joke. I might still do it. Because I have a story in my head about a village. Something like **Les Vendeurs,** but contemporary because that dates back about thirty years. My idea is that of a man, the mayor, who has nine children, and he feels a bit sick. He doesn't know what the hell it is. And the doctor can't diagnose anything. So he ends up at the Mayo Clinic and he finds out that he's turning into a woman. So he comes back to his village. A good Catholic, French-Canadian with nine kids, turning into a woman. And the problem is—well, the problem is for the village. What is he? Is he a man, is he a woman? What do you call him? *Monsieur le maire,* ou *Madame la maire? La Mairesse?* And his kids, are they going to call him Poppa or Mamma? So it could be a very funny book, you know. Take a village of today with a population and the politics of today. It's not written yet. But someday I'll write it.

Les Vendeurs was also a satire in that respect. It's the moving of a cemetery. You know, you move a cemetery in a small village, anywhere in Germany or in Canada, in French-Canada or in English-Canada. You move a cemetery in a small village. What happens? You are really throwing something into the fan.

What writing projects have you planned for the future?

There's this book I wanted to write this summer. I don't know now. Then there's this book I want to write in English because I want to die a millionaire.

Isn't a living millionaire a better idea?

Oh, if I die a millionaire, mind you, I had the chance to live a millionaire. It's a book in English. It has all the elements. In a way it's about Indians, but only in a way. The story of a shaman. It's an adventure story. It's not written yet; it's in my head. I will write it. It won't take long.

At one point I'll go down to New York with my manuscript. You see, that *Playboy* First Choice thing is a door opener with publishers. I won't have to go down there and wait around to see somebody. I'll be the guy writing those things. And the book is not a religious book, it's not particularly authentic. It has all the necessary elements. It has enough violence, enough eroticism, enough magic. I'm methodical. I've always been methodical.

I don't like to be read by a very high-faluting, intellectual person. There are people who dissect my book *Agaguk* like a frog on a lab table. . . . Are you a psychiatric case or what? Through your writings they strive to bare your soul. I detest that.

—Yves Thériault

Since critics have often disappointed you, I'd like to know

what expectations you have of your readers, or who is your ideal reader?

All writers in the world are disappointed by critics. All the time. Critics have a tendency not to know what they are writing about or else of creating around a book or an author a sort of myth. I know what kind of a myth they created here around me. I find it funny, amusing. But I will not respect the critics for having formed that sort of myth.

My reader, my reader. I write on my typewriter and a lot of the sentences that I write I say in a whisper, over and over. In fact, people can hear me write like that. And I'm talking to someone, to a reader. It's usually interchangeable as to sex, not necessarily a man or a woman. My ideal reader is around thirty to thirty-five years old. He or she has read a lot. I will him to be capable of reading what I write. I expect him to be capable without having to refer to documentation, without going to the dictionary or explanations. I expect my reader to know the forest, for example, if I talk about the forest, to know what I'm talking about. The same thing with the St. Lawrence River or a foreign land. I'm not going to explain things. I want my reader to know, to reflect. So, I do not underestimate my reader and rarely overestimate him. It's an average person.

*If the reader "knows what you are talking about," as you put it, you can concentrate on the essentials. This, in turn, makes your works accessible on a universal level and accounts for the popularity of **Agaguk** in Japan and Portugal, for example.*

I don't like to be read by a very high-faluting, intellectual person. There are people who dissect my book like a frog on a lab table; I dislike that! There's a tendency for certain people to analyse more and more. Are you a psychiatric case or what? Through your writings they strive to bare your soul. I detest that.

You are certainly one of Canada's best known writers. But are there works which are perhaps especially dear to you or which you consider have been unjustly neglected?

Well, not for the subject, but for the way I handled it, I think. **Le Temps du carcajou** is a very good book. Bruno Juchereau is a character I love to have created.

Another book, I feel, that has been grossly neglected is **Les Commettants de Caridad.** Because it's the same story told three times. It's never *ennuyant* because the three tellings of the story are completely different in structure. But, you see, what bothered the critics was the fact that it is set in Spain. Most of them had not even gone to Spain, so they couldn't even say whether it was right or authentic or things like that. So the book was published at the wrong time. Nineteen sixty-one was the wrong time. I had just won the Governor General's Award with **Ashini,** and that book came out three or four months after that. That was the wrong time. But someday it may get a new start. (pp. 36-56)

Yves Thériault and M. G. Hesse, in an interview in The Canadian Fiction Magazine, *No. 47, 1983, pp. 32-57.*

Allison Mitcham   (essay date 1983)

[*In the following essay, Mitcham examines Thériault's interest in the Canadian wilderness and its relation to his vision of love, sexuality, and art.*]

In part, both Thériault's imaginative vision and his moral stand stem from his link with the romantics and his endorsement of primitivism. Like the American transcendentalists, [Ralph Waldo] Emerson and [Henry David] Thoreau, and of course like the European romantics before them, Thériault is convinced that man must look to nature for his most significant lessons in living. He shows many times in such novels as *Ashini, Le Ru d'Ikoué, Agaguk,* and *Tayaout, fils d'Agaguk* that the man who fails to respond to nature-as-teacher is doomed to emotional and spiritual sterility.

However, Thériault differs in several ways from both earlier and contemporary writers on this theme in other countries. His concern is specifically with twentieth century Canada and with the environmental difference which he finds distinguishes Canada from other industrial western nations—namely, the extensive reserves of virtually unspoiled wilderness which still remain. He explores this environmental peculiarity and calls attention to the moral responsibility which it creates for contemporary Canadians.

Before probing the most original aspects of Thériault's vision, it is also important to call attention to certain Thoreauvian attitudes to which Thériault clearly subscribes. Such famous Thoreauvian statements as: "In Wildness is the Preservation of the World," "Simplify, simplify, simplify," and "In civilization, as in a southern latitude man degenerates at length, and yields to the incursion of more northern tribes"—are also basic to Thériault's vision, although because he is a novelist his work is not reducible to mottos. Like Thoreau too, Thériault is obsessed with North America's first inhabitants, and the important secrets which he feels they have preserved and may reveal about life's basic essences. Thoreau's thesis and Thériault's too, for instance, is that we must not seek to 'civilize' the Indian. In his unspoiled state only indigenous man can keep the balance of nature because he does not want to use up more than he needs for survival.

The point at which Thériault parts company with Thoreau is over the Thoreauvian idea that the wilderness exists to revitalize a tired and decadent civilization. Thériault, writing well over a century after Thoreau, looks back over a much longer period of technological 'progress' and sees absolutely no merit in nineteenth or twentieth century civilization. Contemporary civilized man, for Thériault, is invariably degenerate man. Chiefly because of his greed and softness he is responsible for walling himself up in urban ghettos. (The 'cul-de-sac'—"une rue sans issue"—is one of Thériault's favorite urban images.) To such streets, he notes at the beginning of *Aaron,* no purifying fragrance of pine or spruce can ever penetrate.

Thériault in such novels as *Ashini, Agaguk,* and *Tayaout fils d'Agaguk* warns that the destructive march of civilization and technological progress into the pure northern wilderness is so far-advanced that only a miracle will save the wilderness. Thus his plea through his northern novels and his attempt to awaken our consciences before the destruction is complete. For skeptics who consider that Thériault is unnecessarily gloomy in his moral stand—in his depiction, for instance, of Ashini and Tayaout as would-be but ironically misunderstood saviours—one has only to pick up almost any newspaper or news magazine to find factual accounts of the disastrous consequences which he has been forecasting over the past decades. Thériault's insights in *Ashini* (1961) and in *Le Ru d'Ikoué* were in fact substantiated within a decade by *Time.* The caption of one 1972 article states:

> If all goes well according to Premier Robert Bourassa's preliminary plan, about 140,000 sq. mi. of Northern Quebec will be flooded or drained to marshall headwaters for the projected James Bay hydro development. To Bourassa's Liberal government, the mammoth project—which could cost as much as $10 billion and take up to ten years to build—holds the promise of 125,000 new jobs during the construction phase alone. But to the 5,000 Cree Indians who roam the wilderness as trappers and hunters, the coming of the bull-dozers will ultimately mean cultural annihilation.

Of course we all know what happened here: how the warnings in fact and fiction came to nothing.

From Thériault's perspective there can be no compromise with the forces of civilization. The individual who wishes to preserve his integrity and humanity must somehow escape to the most remote wilderness where the bulldozer and the company town will not follow him. If he weakens and returns to a softer life he is undone—as Agaguk is at last in the sequel to *Agaguk, Tayaout, fils d'Agaguk.* Thériault makes it clear then that because of the harshness and perils of the Canadian wilderness, the individual who goes there in pursuit of a dream must be fully committed because invariably within the dream he has to contend with the nightmare. The northern nightmare—visible or invisible—is inevitably white, like the 'agiortok', the white wolf, in *Agaguk* or the white bear in *Tayaout, fils d'Agaguk.* Always the demon of a white death lurks. Because of the continuous struggle against almost insuperable odds, the individual, if he does 'overcome', emerges from an epic battle Canadian style as a hero—the tested, tried and proved hero of epic proportions that Agaguk becomes at the end of the novel *Agaguk.*

It is above all, however, Thériault's conception of love and sexuality in connection with social evolution and with the wilderness obsession which distinguish his vision from that of other writers—particularly North American ones. In both the nineteenth and twentieth centuries a considerable number of writers have sought the ideal relationship between man and woman. D. H. Lawrence is of course particularly notable in this century for his pursuit of the truth about human sexual relationships, and his conclusion seems to be that fulfilment in the relationships between man and woman is rare, primarily because the human social environment is wrong. Lawrence underscores the fact that the ideal and equal relationship in which the man and the woman meet like "two eagles in mid air" [*Aaron's Rod*] in a "lovely state of free, proud singleness, which . . . submits to the yoke and leash of love but never forfeits its own proud singleness, even while it loves and yields" [*Women in Love*] rarely occurs because of the constricting pressures of modern society.

It is above all . . . Thériault's conception of love and sexuality in connection with social evolution and with the wilderness obsession which distinguish his vision from that of other writers—particularly North American ones.

—Allison Mitcham

In the nineteenth century such writers as Margaret Fuller (*Woman in the Nineteenth Century*—1855), George Gissing (*The Odd Women*—1893) and Nathaniel Hawthorne (*The Scarlet Letter*—1850) also concluded that the social climate was unsatisfactory to the ecstatic and lasting sort of sexual relationship of which they caught elusive glimpses. For all these writers there is the realization that until the role of woman changes, man too is a lesser creature both spiritually and intellectually. Thus a New Woman is seen as the salvation of Man. Margaret Fuller writes:

> that the idea of Man, however imperfectly brought out, has been far more so than that of woman; that she, the other half of the same thought, the other chamber of the heart of life, needs now to take her turn in the full pulsation, and that improvement in the daughters will best aid in the reformation of the sons of this age.

And one of Gissing's women states:

> There must be a new type of woman, active in every sphere of life: a new worker out in the world, a new ruler of the home. Of the old ideal virtues we can retain many, but we have to add to them those which have been thought appropriate only in men. Let a woman be gentle, but at the same time let her be strong; let her be pure of heart, but none the less wise and instructed . . . The mass of women have always been paltry creatures, and their paltriness has proved a curse to men. So, if you like to put it in this way, we are working for the advantage of men as well as for our own.

In the light of statements such as these it is ironic that the New Woman sought after and envisaged by Fuller, Gissing, Hawthorne, Lawrence and mid-twentieth writers as well, emerges in the contemporary northern Canadian wilderness as an untutored Eskimo woman—strong and gentle, pure of heart, yet deeply wise and able to hold her own in a man's world—and it is clearly because of her that Agaguk attains both peace and heroism.

Nevertheless, Thériault makes it apparent that the relationship of Iriook and Agaguk is only possible because of their wilderness environment. Other couples Thériault introduces us to appear at first equally blessed by compatibility—Pippo and his wife in *Amour au goût de mer* and Aaron and Viedna in *Aaron*. But Thériault shows that they are doomed—doomed ultimately by their urban environment. Fabien and Edith in *La fille laide* have a deeper relationship, chiefly because they live in the country, but they too cannot escape far enough from existing social patterns.

Civilized society with its frivolous and transitory fashions is no setting, Thériault indicates, for a deep and basic relationship. He is particularly critical of superficially alluring women, like Bernadette in *La fille laide,* who prove empty behind the mask of their beauty. Always warning against trite and superficial judgements, Thériault shows us that it is Edith, 'la fille laide', who possesses the essential femininity. Speaking for Thériault, Fabien persuades Edith of the basic truth of his statement that "Being beautiful is not the important thing; being womanly is."

Still it is Iriook who is the complete woman—although ironically Thériault implies that she would not even draw a second glance from a 'civilized' contemporary urban male. She is nonetheless the embodiment of a male dream. Responding completely to the sexual act, faithful, courageous, vital, a devoted mate and mother, she also possesses an intuitive feminine perception and wisdom which is often shown as a complement to and check on Agaguk's sometimes foolhardy bravery and his aggressively destructive male impulses. Together they fulfil and improve each other with primitive vitality.

Love is the basis of Iriook's and Agaguk's life together. Yet, chiefly because of the wilderness setting in which it flourishes, it is a violent as well as a tender emotion. Violence, in fact, must be considered crucial to Thériault's vision. Thériault at once makes it apparent that the wilderness provides not only a sanctuary for love, but also a series of trials to test its strength and endurance. The violence of these trials proves the courage of those who can endure and survive them. For this reason Thériault sees violence not only as a significant fact of life but even as a beneficial one.

Iriook's and Agaguk's love on the tundra begins as an exhausting but satisfying animal passion. The violence of their passion alerts all their senses, paradoxically bringing to life delicate and hitherto undiscovered subtleties and loyalties. Thus Thériault considers that a sexual experience of this sort is a form of rebirth. Agaguk, for instance, decides that the accepted Eskimo custom of lending one's wife to friends on special occasions will not work for him. It happens because Iriook has totally grasped his imagination that physically he cannot bear to take another woman or to lend Iriook. Iriook, he concludes in opposition to tribal customs, must be for him alone.

Such a development of an emotional-intellectual decision from a violent physical response happens many times to Agaguk in the course of the novel. Agaguk, for instance, although at the height of his masculine strength and assertiveness, learns on a number of occasions, as after the birth of their daughter, to allow Iriook's decision to stand. He does this with difficulty—against all traditional practices again—because he is forced to realize that he must let Iriook develop as a strong individual too or he will destroy the special nature of their relationship. However, for Agaguk such decisions are painfully achieved: his emotions, Thériault shows, are tested and finally purified in the fires of violence.

Thériault obviously believes that the violence of Iriook's and Agaguk's life lends the spice of their vitality and love. Because they live so near to death and destruction in its many forms and because they both face frightful perils daily—in the snows, on the ice, in lonely hunting expeditions, from the white wolf, from unfriendly tribesmen—they are, paradoxically always deeply conscious of the power of life. With their vitality always at white heat and their courage always being proved, their admiration and consequently their love for each other increases as they struggle to preserve themselves and each other in their formidable environment.

Finally, Thériault's vision extends to art. Art, like love, Thériault believes, flourishes in its most honest, most spiritual and consequently most intense form in the wilderness, remote from the fads and mercenary motives of civilized societies which often, he feels, prevent the fulfilment of its deepest meaning and purpose. Thériault is concerned with this thesis briefly in *Agaguk* and more specifically in *Tayaout, fils d'Agaguk.* Art inspires the individual with the capacity to dream and thence to conquer brutality and acquire self-knowledge.

Tayaout, Agaguk's son, seeks to save himself and his people by his rediscovery of the symbolic green stone which in former generations had held such significance for his people. Finding the stone and removing it to the Eskimo settlement is in itself an incredibly difficult undertaking. But the significance that Tayaout assigns to the stone is immense. Its proper use, he is convinced, could mean salvation for his people. Thus he sets himself and each individual of his tribe the task of interpreting dreams and memories in stone so as to bring out, Thériault says, the 'soul' in the stone. The Eskimos, inspired by Tayaout's sincerity and courage, succeed beyond their wildest hopes and begin through their achievement to acquire self-respect. But this is short-lived. During one of Tayaout's absences to replenish the stock of stone, the others agree to sell their work to a white trader who of course will remove it to the 'decadent' south. When sculpting becomes a commercial venture and the figures fall into the hands of those who cannot comprehend the creators, their culture or inspiration, Thériault, like his hero Tayaout washes his hands of the whole undertaking. Tayaout soon perishes, like Ashini, without completing his mission of saviour to his people, because the rest of the tribe lack his strength and moral fibre.

Thus, through his studies of sensitive and perceptive char-

acters engaged in the individualistic quests—quests which frequently take them into the northern Canadian wilderness—Yves Thériault explores such contemporary issues as the function of the wilderness in a twentieth century context, the necessity of solitude for self-knowledge, and the role of love and art in the regeneration and expansion of human perceptions. Above all, Thériault seems concerned that we stop short in our head-long pursuit of material goals and examine the position of contemporary man—before all opportunities for choice and for heroism vanish with the impending destruction of the wilderness. (pp. 85-91)

Allison Mitcham, "Yves Thériault: The Conscience of Contemporary Canada," in her The Northern Imagination: A Study of Northern Canadian Literature, *Penumbra Press, 1983, pp. 85-92.*

FURTHER READING

Bibliography

Kandiuk, Mary. "Thériault, Yves (1915-1983)." In her *French-Canadian Authors: A Bibliography of Their Works and of English-Language Criticism,* pp. 175-82. Metuchen, N. J.: The Scarecrow Press, 1990.

   Lists works by Thériault as well as criticism of his fiction.

Criticism

Shek, Ben-Z. "The Modern Novel: 1938-1959" and "The Sixties: The (Not So) Quiet Revolution." In his *French-Canadian and Québécois Novels,* pp. 24-44, pp. 45-85. Toronto: Oxford University Press, 1991.

   Brief discussion of *Aaron* and Thériault's treatment of the differences between Inuit and white culture in *Agaguk; Tayaout, fils d'Agaguk;* and *Agoak, l'héritage d'Agaguk.*

Smith, Donald. "Yves Thériault, Storyteller." In his *Voices of Deliverance: Interviews with Quebec and Acadian Writers,* translated by Larry Shouldice, pp. 57-81. Toronto: House of Anansi Press, 1986.

   Interview in which Thériault discusses his career and literary influences.

Urbas, Jeannette. "The Primitive Hero." In her *From Thirty Acres to Modern Times: The Story of French-Canadian Literature,* pp. 76-84. Toronto: McGraw-Hill Ryerson, 1976.

Examines the theme of the individual in conflict with society in *Agaguk* and *Ashini*.

Additional coverage of Thériault's life and career is contained in the following sources published by Gale Research: *Contemporary Authors,* **Vol. 102;** *Dictionary of Literary Biography,* **Vol. 88; and** *DISCovering Authors: Canadian Edition.*

☐ Contemporary Literary Criticism

Indexes

Literary Criticism Series
Cumulative Author Index
Cumulative Nationality Index
Title Index, Volume 79

How to Use This Index

The main references

list all author entries in the following Gale Literary Criticism series:

CLC = *Contemporary Literary Criticism*
CLR = *Children's Literature Review*
CMLC = *Classical and Medieval Literature Criticism*
DC = *Drama Criticism*
LC = *Literature Criticism from 1400 to 1800*
NCLC = *Nineteenth-Century Literature Criticism*
PC = *Poetry Criticism*
SSC = *Short Story Criticism*
TCLC = *Twentieth-Century Literary Criticism*

The cross-references

list all author entries in the following Gale biographical and literary sources:

AAYA = *Authors & Artists for Young Adults*
AITN = *Authors in the News*
BLC = *Black Literature Criticism*
BW = *Black Writers*
CA = *Contemporary Authors*
CAAS = *Contemporary Authors Autobiography Series*
CABS = *Contemporary Authors Bibliographical Series*
CANR = *Contemporary Authors New Revision Series*
CAP = *Contemporary Authors Permanent Series*
CDALB = *Concise Dictionary of American Literary Biography*
CDBLB = *Concise Dictionary of British Literary Biography*
DA = *DISCovering Authors*
DLB = *Dictionary of Literary Biography*
DLBD = *Dictionary of Literary Biography Documentary Series*
DLBY = *Dictionary of Literary Biography Yearbook*
HW = *Hispanic Writers*
MAICYA = *Major Authors and Illustrators for Children and Young Adults*
MTCW = *Major 20th-Century Writers*
SAAS = *Something about the Author Autobiography Series*
SATA = *Something about the Author*
WLC = *World Literature Criticism, 1500 to the Present*
YABC = *Yesterday's Authors of Books for Children*

Literary Criticism Series
Cumulative Author Index

A.
See Arnold, Matthew

A. E. . . . . TCLC 3, 10
See also Russell, George William
See also DLB 19

A. M.
See Megged, Aharon

Abasiyanik, Sait Faik   1906-1954
See Sait Faik
See also CA 123

Abbey, Edward   1927-1989 . . . . . . CLC 36, 59
See also CA 45-48; 128; CANR 2, 41

Abbott, Lee K(ittredge)   1947- . . . . . . CLC 48
See also CA 124; DLB 130

Abe, Kobo   1924-1993 . . . . CLC 8, 22, 53
See also CA 65-68; 140; CANR 24; MTCW

Abelard, Peter   c. 1079-c. 1142 . . . CMLC 11
See also DLB 115

Abell, Kjeld   1901-1961 . . . . CLC 15
See also CA 111

Abish, Walter   1931- . . . . CLC 22
See also CA 101; CANR 37; DLB 130

Abrahams, Peter (Henry)   1919- . . . . . CLC 4
See also BW; CA 57-60; CANR 26;
DLB 117; MTCW

Abrams, M(eyer) H(oward)   1912- . . . CLC 24
See also CA 57-60; CANR 13, 33; DLB 67

Abse, Dannie   1923- . . . . CLC 7, 29
See also CA 53-56; CAAS 1; CANR 4;
DLB 27

Achebe, (Albert) Chinua(lumogu)
1930- . . . . . CLC 1, 3, 5, 7, 11, 26, 51, 75
See also BLC 1; BW; CA 1-4R; CANR 6,
26; CLR 20; DA; DLB 117; MAICYA;
MTCW; SATA 38, 40; WLC

Acker, Kathy   1948- . . . . CLC 45
See also CA 117; 122

Ackroyd, Peter   1949- . . . . CLC 34, 52
See also CA 123; 127

Acorn, Milton   1923- . . . . CLC 15
See also CA 103; DLB 53

Adamov, Arthur   1908-1970 . . . . . . CLC 4, 25
See also CA 17-18; 25-28R; CAP 2; MTCW

Adams, Alice (Boyd)   1926- . . . CLC 6, 13, 46
See also CA 81-84; CANR 26; DLBY 86;
MTCW

Adams, Douglas (Noel)   1952- . . . CLC 27, 60
See also AAYA 4; BEST 89:3; CA 106;
CANR 34; DLBY 83

Adams, Francis   1862-1893 . . . . . . NCLC 33

Adams, Henry (Brooks)
1838-1918 . . . . TCLC 4
See also CA 104; 133; DA; DLB 12, 47

Adams, Richard (George)
1920- . . . . CLC 4, 5, 18
See also AITN 1, 2; CA 49-52; CANR 3,
35; CLR 20; MAICYA; MTCW;
SATA 7, 69

Adamson, Joy(-Friederike Victoria)
1910-1980 . . . . CLC 17
See also CA 69-72; 93-96; CANR 22;
MTCW; SATA 11, 22

Adcock, Fleur   1934- . . . . CLC 41
See also CA 25-28R; CANR 11, 34;
DLB 40

Addams, Charles (Samuel)
1912-1988 . . . . CLC 30
See also CA 61-64; 126; CANR 12

Addison, Joseph   1672-1719 . . . . LC 18
See also CDBLB 1660-1789; DLB 101

Adler, C(arole) S(chwerdtfeger)
1932- . . . . CLC 35
See also AAYA 4; CA 89-92; CANR 19,
40; MAICYA; SAAS 15; SATA 26, 63

Adler, Renata   1938- . . . . CLC 8, 31
See also CA 49-52; CANR 5, 22; MTCW

Ady, Endre   1877-1919 . . . . TCLC 11
See also CA 107

Aeschylus   525B.C.-456B.C. . . . . . . CMLC 11
See also DA

Afton, Effie
See Harper, Frances Ellen Watkins

Agapida, Fray Antonio
See Irving, Washington

Agee, James (Rufus)
1909-1955 . . . . TCLC 1, 19
See also AITN 1; CA 108;
CDALB 1941-1968; DLB 2, 26

A Gentlewoman in New England
See Bradstreet, Anne

A Gentlewoman in Those Parts
See Bradstreet, Anne

Aghill, Gordon
See Silverberg, Robert

Agnon, S(hmuel) Y(osef Halevi)
1888-1970 . . . . CLC 4, 8, 14
See also CA 17-18; 25-28R; CAP 2; MTCW

Aherne, Owen
See Cassill, R(onald) V(erlin)

Ai   1947- . . . . CLC 4, 14, 69
See also CA 85-88; CAAS 13; DLB 120

Aickman, Robert (Fordyce)
1914-1981 . . . . CLC 57
See also CA 5-8R; CANR 3

Aiken, Conrad (Potter)
1889-1973 . . . CLC 1, 3, 5, 10, 52; SSC 9
See also CA 5-8R; 45-48; CANR 4;
CDALB 1929-1941; DLB 9, 45, 102;
MTCW; SATA 3, 30

Aiken, Joan (Delano)   1924- . . . . CLC 35
See also AAYA 1; CA 9-12R; CANR 4, 23,
34; CLR 1, 19; MAICYA; MTCW;
SAAS 1; SATA 2, 30, 73

Ainsworth, William Harrison
1805-1882 . . . . NCLC 13
See also DLB 21; SATA 24

Aitmatov, Chingiz (Torekulovich)
1928- . . . . CLC 71
See also CA 103; CANR 38; MTCW;
SATA 56

Akers, Floyd
See Baum, L(yman) Frank

Akhmadulina, Bella Akhatovna
1937- . . . . CLC 53
See also CA 65-68

Akhmatova, Anna
1888-1966 . . . . CLC 11, 25, 64; PC 2
See also CA 19-20; 25-28R; CANR 35;
CAP 1; MTCW

Aksakov, Sergei Timofeyvich
1791-1859 . . . . NCLC 2

Aksenov, Vassily . . . . CLC 22
See also Aksyonov, Vassily (Pavlovich)

Aksyonov, Vassily (Pavlovich)
1932- . . . . CLC 37
See also Aksenov, Vassily
See also CA 53-56; CANR 12

Akutagawa Ryunosuke
1892-1927 . . . . TCLC 16
See also CA 117

Alain   1868-1951 . . . . TCLC 41

Alain-Fournier . . . . TCLC 6
See also Fournier, Henri Alban
See also DLB 65

Alarcon, Pedro Antonio de
1833-1891 . . . . NCLC 1

Alas (y Urena), Leopoldo (Enrique Garcia)
1852-1901 . . . . TCLC 29
See also CA 113; 131; HW

Albee, Edward (Franklin III)
1928- . . . CLC 1, 2, 3, 5, 9, 11, 13, 25, 53
See also AITN 1; CA 5-8R; CABS 3;
CANR 8; CDALB 1941-1968; DA;
DLB 7; MTCW; WLC

Alberti, Rafael   1902- . . . . CLC 7
See also CA 85-88; DLB 108

Alcala-Galiano, Juan Valera y
See Valera y Alcala-Galiano, Juan

Alcott, Amos Bronson   1799-1888 . . NCLC 1
See also DLB 1

Alcott, Louisa May   1832-1888 . . . . NCLC 6
See also CDALB 1865-1917; CLR 1; DA;
DLB 1, 42, 79; MAICYA; WLC;
YABC 1

Aldanov, M. A.
See Aldanov, Mark (Alexandrovich)

Antoninus, Brother
See Everson, William (Oliver)

Antonioni, Michelangelo 1912- ..... **CLC 20**
See also CA 73-76

Antschel, Paul 1920-1970. ...... **CLC 10, 19**
See also Celan, Paul
See also CA 85-88; CANR 33; MTCW

Anwar, Chairil 1922-1949 .... **TCLC 22**
See also CA 121

Apollinaire, Guillaume .. **TCLC 3, 8, 51; PC 7**
See also Kostrowitzki, Wilhelm Apollinaris
de

Appelfeld, Aharon 1932- ...... **CLC 23, 47**
See also CA 112; 133

Apple, Max (Isaac) 1941-. .... **CLC 9, 33**
See also CA 81-84; CANR 19; DLB 130

Appleman, Philip (Dean) 1926- ..... **CLC 51**
See also CA 13-16R; CANR 6, 29

Appleton, Lawrence
See Lovecraft, H(oward) P(hillips)

Apteryx
See Eliot, T(homas) S(tearns)

Apuleius, (Lucius Madaurensis)
125(?)-175(?) .... **CMLC 1**

Aquin, Hubert 1929-1977. .... **CLC 15**
See also CA 105; DLB 53

Aragon, Louis 1897-1982........ **CLC 3, 22**
See also CA 69-72; 108; CANR 28;
DLB 72; MTCW

Arany, Janos 1817-1882........ **NCLC 34**

Arbuthnot, John 1667-1735.......... **LC 1**
See also DLB 101

Archer, Herbert Winslow
See Mencken, H(enry) L(ouis)

Archer, Jeffrey (Howard) 1940- .... **CLC 28**
See also BEST 89:3; CA 77-80; CANR 22

Archer, Jules 1915- .... **CLC 12**
See also CA 9-12R; CANR 6; SAAS 5;
SATA 4

Archer, Lee
See Ellison, Harlan

Arden, John 1930- .... **CLC 6, 13, 15**
See also CA 13-16R; CAAS 4; CANR 31;
DLB 13; MTCW

Arenas, Reinaldo 1943-1990 .... **CLC 41**
See also CA 124; 128; 133; HW

Arendt, Hannah 1906-1975 ...... **CLC 66**
See also CA 17-20R; 61-64; CANR 26;
MTCW

Aretino, Pietro 1492-1556 .... **LC 12**

Arguedas, Jose Maria
1911-1969 .... **CLC 10, 18**
See also CA 89-92; DLB 113; HW

Argueta, Manlio 1936-........... **CLC 31**
See also CA 131; HW

Ariosto, Ludovico 1474-1533........ **LC 6**

Aristides
See Epstein, Joseph

Aristophanes
450B.C.-385B.C........ **CMLC 4; DC 2**
See also DA

Arlt, Roberto (Godofredo Christophersen)
1900-1942 .... **TCLC 29**
See also CA 123; 131; HW

Armah, Ayi Kwei 1939-......... **CLC 5, 33**
See also BLC 1; BW; CA 61-64; CANR 21;
DLB 117; MTCW

Armatrading, Joan 1950-.......... **CLC 17**
See also CA 114

Arnette, Robert
See Silverberg, Robert

Arnim, Achim von (Ludwig Joachim von
Arnim) 1781-1831 .... **NCLC 5**
See also DLB 90

Arnim, Bettina von 1785-1859.... **NCLC 38**
See also DLB 90

Arnold, Matthew
1822-1888 .... **NCLC 6, 29; PC 5**
See also CDBLB 1832-1890; DA; DLB 32,
57; WLC

Arnold, Thomas 1795-1842 ...... **NCLC 18**
See also DLB 55

Arnow, Harriette (Louisa) Simpson
1908-1986 .... **CLC 2, 7, 18**
See also CA 9-12R; 118; CANR 14; DLB 6;
MTCW; SATA 42, 47

Arp, Hans
See Arp, Jean

Arp, Jean 1887-1966............... **CLC 5**
See also CA 81-84; 25-28R

Arrabal
See Arrabal, Fernando

Arrabal, Fernando 1932-... **CLC 2, 9, 18, 58**
See also CA 9-12R; CANR 15

Arrick, Fran.................... CLC 30

Artaud, Antonin 1896-1948 ..... **TCLC 3, 36**
See also CA 104

Arthur, Ruth M(abel) 1905-1979.... **CLC 12**
See also CA 9-12R; 85-88; CANR 4;
SATA 7, 26

Artsybashev, Mikhail (Petrovich)
1878-1927 .... **TCLC 31**

Arundel, Honor (Morfydd)
1919-1973 .... **CLC 17**
See also CA 21-22; 41-44R; CAP 2;
SATA 4, 24

Asch, Sholem 1880-1957 .... **TCLC 3**
See also CA 105

Ash, Shalom
See Asch, Sholem

Ashbery, John (Lawrence)
1927- ...... **CLC 2, 3, 4, 6, 9, 13, 15, 25,**
41, 77
See also CA 5-8R; CANR 9, 37; DLB 5;
DLBY 81; MTCW

Ashdown, Clifford
See Freeman, R(ichard) Austin

Ashe, Gordon
See Creasey, John

Ashton-Warner, Sylvia (Constance)
1908-1984 .... **CLC 19**
See also CA 69-72; 112; CANR 29; MTCW

Asimov, Isaac
1920-1992 ...... **CLC 1, 3, 9, 19, 26, 76**
See also BEST 90:2; CA 1-4R; 137;
CANR 2, 19, 36; CLR 12; DLB 8;
DLBY 92; MAICYA; MTCW; SATA 1,
26, 74

Astley, Thea (Beatrice May)
1925- .... **CLC 41**
See also CA 65-68; CANR 11

Aston, James
See White, T(erence) H(anbury)

Asturias, Miguel Angel
1899-1974 .... **CLC 3, 8, 13**
See also CA 25-28; 49-52; CANR 32;
CAP 2; DLB 113; HW; MTCW

Atares, Carlos Saura
See Saura (Atares), Carlos

Atheling, William
See Pound, Ezra (Weston Loomis)

Atheling, William, Jr.
See Blish, James (Benjamin)

Atherton, Gertrude (Franklin Horn)
1857-1948 .... **TCLC 2**
See also CA 104; DLB 9, 78

Atherton, Lucius
See Masters, Edgar Lee

Atkins, Jack
See Harris, Mark

Atticus
See Fleming, Ian (Lancaster)

Atwood, Margaret (Eleanor)
1939- ..... **CLC 2, 3, 4, 8, 13, 15, 25, 44;**
SSC 2
See also BEST 89:2; CA 49-52; CANR 3,
24, 33; DA; DLB 53; MTCW; SATA 50;
WLC

Aubigny, Pierre d'
See Mencken, H(enry) L(ouis)

Aubin, Penelope 1685-1731(?)........ **LC 9**
See also DLB 39

Auchincloss, Louis (Stanton)
1917- .... **CLC 4, 6, 9, 18, 45**
See also CA 1-4R; CANR 6, 29; DLB 2;
DLBY 80; MTCW

Auden, W(ystan) H(ugh)
1907-1973 ...... **CLC 1, 2, 3, 4, 6, 9, 11,**
14, 43; PC 1
See also CA 9-12R; 45-48; CANR 5;
CDBLB 1914-1945; DA; DLB 10, 20;
MTCW; WLC

Audiberti, Jacques 1900-1965 ...... **CLC 38**
See also CA 25-28R

Auel, Jean M(arie) 1936-.......... **CLC 31**
See also AAYA 7; BEST 90:4; CA 103;
CANR 21

Auerbach, Erich 1892-1957 .... **TCLC 43**
See also CA 118

Augier, Emile 1820-1889 .... **NCLC 31**

August, John
See De Voto, Bernard (Augustine)

Augustine, St. 354-430.......... **CMLC 6**

Aurelius
See Bourne, Randolph S(illiman)

Austen, Jane
  1775-1817 . . . . **NCLC 1, 13, 19, 33**
  See also CDBLB 1789-1832; DA; DLB 116;
  WLC

Auster, Paul 1947- . . . . **CLC 47**
  See also CA 69-72; CANR 23

Austin, Frank
  See Faust, Frederick (Schiller)

Austin, Mary (Hunter)
  1868-1934 . . . . **TCLC 25**
  See also CA 109; DLB 9, 78

Autran Dourado, Waldomiro
  See Dourado, (Waldomiro Freitas) Autran

Averroes 1126-1198 . . . . **CMLC 7**
  See also DLB 115

Avison, Margaret 1918- . . . . **CLC 2, 4**
  See also CA 17-20R; DLB 53; MTCW

Axton, David
  See Koontz, Dean R(ay)

Ayckbourn, Alan
  1939- . . . . **CLC 5, 8, 18, 33, 74**
  See also CA 21-24R; CANR 31; DLB 13;
  MTCW

Aydy, Catherine
  See Tennant, Emma (Christina)

Ayme, Marcel (Andre) 1902-1967 . . . **CLC 11**
  See also CA 89-92; CLR 25; DLB 72

Ayrton, Michael 1921-1975 . . . . **CLC 7**
  See also CA 5-8R; 61-64; CANR 9, 21

Azorin . . . . **CLC 11**
  See also Martinez Ruiz, Jose

Azuela, Mariano 1873-1952 . . . . **TCLC 3**
  See also CA 104; 131; HW; MTCW

Baastad, Babbis Friis
  See Friis-Baastad, Babbis Ellinor

Bab
  See Gilbert, W(illiam) S(chwenck)

Babbis, Eleanor
  See Friis-Baastad, Babbis Ellinor

Babel, Isaak (Emmanuilovich)
  1894-1941(?) . . . . **CLC 73**
  See also CA 104; TCLC 2, 13

Babits, Mihaly 1883-1941 . . . . **TCLC 14**
  See also CA 114

Babur 1483-1530 . . . . **LC 18**

Bacchelli, Riccardo 1891-1985 . . . . . **CLC 19**
  See also CA 29-32R; 117

Bach, Richard (David) 1936- . . . . **CLC 14**
  See also AITN 1; BEST 89:2; CA 9-12R;
  CANR 18; MTCW; SATA 13

Bachman, Richard
  See King, Stephen (Edwin)

Bachmann, Ingeborg 1926-1973 . . . . . **CLC 69**
  See also CA 93-96; 45-48; DLB 85

Bacon, Francis 1561-1626 . . . . **LC 18**
  See also CDBLB Before 1660

Bacovia, George . . . . **TCLC 24**
  See also Vasiliu, Gheorghe

Badanes, Jerome 1937- . . . . **CLC 59**

Bagehot, Walter 1826-1877 . . . . . . **NCLC 10**
  See also DLB 55

Bagnold, Enid 1889-1981 . . . . **CLC 25**
  See also CA 5-8R; 103; CANR 5, 40;
  DLB 13; MAICYA; SATA 1, 25

Bagrjana, Elisaveta
  See Belcheva, Elisaveta

Bagryana, Elisaveta
  See Belcheva, Elisaveta

Bailey, Paul 1937- . . . . **CLC 45**
  See also CA 21-24R; CANR 16; DLB 14

Baillie, Joanna 1762-1851 . . . . **NCLC 2**
  See also DLB 93

Bainbridge, Beryl (Margaret)
  1933- . . . . **CLC 4, 5, 8, 10, 14, 18, 22, 62**
  See also CA 21-24R; CANR 24; DLB 14;
  MTCW

Baker, Elliott 1922- . . . . **CLC 8**
  See also CA 45-48; CANR 2

Baker, Nicholson 1957- . . . . **CLC 61**
  See also CA 135

Baker, Ray Stannard 1870-1946 . . . **TCLC 47**
  See also CA 118

Baker, Russell (Wayne) 1925- . . . . . . **CLC 31**
  See also BEST 89:4; CA 57-60; CANR 11,
  41; MTCW

Bakshi, Ralph 1938(?)- . . . . **CLC 26**
  See also CA 112; 138

Bakunin, Mikhail (Alexandrovich)
  1814-1876 . . . . **NCLC 25**

Baldwin, James (Arthur)
  1924-1987 . . . . . . **CLC 1, 2, 3, 4, 5, 8, 13,
           15, 17, 42, 50, 67; DC 1; SSC 10**
  See also AAYA 4; BLC 1; BW; CA 1-4R;
  124; CABS 1; CANR 3, 24;
  CDALB 1941-1968; DA; DLB 2, 7, 33;
  DLBY 87; MTCW; SATA 9, 54; WLC

Ballard, J(ames) G(raham)
  1930- . . . . **CLC 3, 6, 14, 36; SSC 1**
  See also AAYA 3; CA 5-8R; CANR 15, 39;
  DLB 14; MTCW

Balmont, Konstantin (Dmitriyevich)
  1867-1943 . . . . **TCLC 11**
  See also CA 109

Balzac, Honore de
  1799-1850 . . . . **NCLC 5, 35; SSC 5**
  See also DA; DLB 119; WLC

Bambara, Toni Cade 1939- . . . . **CLC 19**
  See also AAYA 5; BLC 1; BW; CA 29-32R;
  CANR 24; DA; DLB 38; MTCW

Bamdad, A.
  See Shamlu, Ahmad

Banat, D. R.
  See Bradbury, Ray (Douglas)

Bancroft, Laura
  See Baum, L(yman) Frank

Banim, John 1798-1842 . . . . **NCLC 13**
  See also DLB 116

Banim, Michael 1796-1874 . . . . . . **NCLC 13**

Banks, Iain
  See Banks, Iain M(enzies)

Banks, Iain M(enzies) 1954- . . . . **CLC 34**
  See also CA 123; 128

Banks, Lynne Reid . . . . **CLC 23**
  See also Reid Banks, Lynne
  See also AAYA 6

Banks, Russell 1940- . . . . **CLC 37, 72**
  See also CA 65-68; CAAS 15; CANR 19;
  DLB 130

Banville, John 1945- . . . . **CLC 46**
  See also CA 117; 128; DLB 14

Banville, Theodore (Faullain) de
  1832-1891 . . . . **NCLC 9**

Baraka, Amiri
  1934- . . . **CLC 1, 2, 3, 5, 10, 14, 33; PC 4**
  See also Jones, LeRoi
  See also BLC 1; BW; CA 21-24R; CABS 3;
  CANR 27, 38; CDALB 1941-1968; DA;
  DLB 5, 7, 16, 38; DLBD 8; MTCW

Barbellion, W. N. P. . . . . **TCLC 24**
  See also Cummings, Bruce F(rederick)

Barbera, Jack 1945- . . . . **CLC 44**
  See also CA 110

Barbey d'Aurevilly, Jules Amedee
  1808-1889 . . . . **NCLC 1**
  See also DLB 119

Barbusse, Henri 1873-1935 . . . . **TCLC 5**
  See also CA 105; DLB 65

Barclay, Bill
  See Moorcock, Michael (John)

Barclay, William Ewert
  See Moorcock, Michael (John)

Barea, Arturo 1897-1957 . . . . **TCLC 14**
  See also CA 111

Barfoot, Joan 1946- . . . . **CLC 18**
  See also CA 105

Baring, Maurice 1874-1945 . . . . **TCLC 8**
  See also CA 105; DLB 34

Barker, Clive 1952- . . . . **CLC 52**
  See also AAYA 10; BEST 90:3; CA 121;
  129; MTCW

Barker, George Granville
  1913-1991 . . . . **CLC 8, 48**
  See also CA 9-12R; 135; CANR 7, 38;
  DLB 20; MTCW

Barker, Harley Granville
  See Granville-Barker, Harley
  See also DLB 10

Barker, Howard 1946- . . . . **CLC 37**
  See also CA 102; DLB 13

Barker, Pat 1943- . . . . **CLC 32**
  See also CA 117; 122

Barlow, Joel 1754-1812 . . . . **NCLC 23**
  See also DLB 37

Barnard, Mary (Ethel) 1909- . . . . **CLC 48**
  See also CA 21-22; CAP 2

Barnes, Djuna
  1892-1982 . . . **CLC 3, 4, 8, 11, 29; SSC 3**
  See also CA 9-12R; 107; CANR 16; DLB 4,
  9, 45; MTCW

Barnes, Julian 1946- . . . . **CLC 42**
  See also CA 102; CANR 19

Barnes, Peter 1931- . . . . **CLC 5, 56**
  See also CA 65-68; CAAS 12; CANR 33,
  34; DLB 13; MTCW

Baroja (y Nessi), Pio 1872-1956 . . . . **TCLC 8**
  See also CA 104

Baron, David
  See Pinter, Harold

Baron Corvo
See Rolfe, Frederick (William Serafino
    Austin Lewis Mary)

Barondess, Sue K(aufman)
1926-1977 . . . . **CLC 8**
See also Kaufman, Sue
See also CA 1-4R; 69-72; CANR 1

Baron de Teive
See Pessoa, Fernando (Antonio Nogueira)

Barres, Maurice 1862-1923 . . . . . . **TCLC 47**
See also DLB 123

Barreto, Afonso Henrique de Lima
See Lima Barreto, Afonso Henrique de

Barrett, (Roger) Syd 1946- . . . . **CLC 35**
See also Pink Floyd

Barrett, William (Christopher)
1913-1992 . . . . **CLC 27**
See also CA 13-16R; 139; CANR 11

Barrie, J(ames) M(atthew)
1860-1937 . . . . **TCLC 2**
See also CA 104; 136; CDBLB 1890-1914;
    CLR 16; DLB 10; MAICYA; YABC 1

Barrington, Michael
See Moorcock, Michael (John)

Barrol, Grady
See Bograd, Larry

Barry, Mike
See Malzberg, Barry N(athaniel)

Barry, Philip 1896-1949 . . . . **TCLC 11**
See also CA 109; DLB 7

Bart, Andre Schwarz
See Schwarz-Bart, Andre

Barth, John (Simmons)
1930- . . . . . . **CLC 1, 2, 3, 5, 7, 9, 10, 14,
27, 51; SSC 10**
See also AITN 1, 2; CA 1-4R; CABS 1;
    CANR 5, 23; DLB 2; MTCW

Barthelme, Donald
1931-1989 . . . . . . **CLC 1, 2, 3, 5, 6, 8, 13,
23, 46, 59; SSC 2**
See also CA 21-24R; 129; CANR 20;
    DLB 2; DLBY 80, 89; MTCW; SATA 7,
    62

Barthelme, Frederick 1943- . . . . **CLC 36**
See also CA 114; 122; DLBY 85

Barthes, Roland (Gerard)
1915-1980 . . . . **CLC 24**
See also CA 130; 97-100; MTCW

Barzun, Jacques (Martin) 1907- . . . . **CLC 51**
See also CA 61-64; CANR 22

Bashevis, Isaac
See Singer, Isaac Bashevis

Bashkirtseff, Marie 1859-1884 . . . **NCLC 27**

Basho
See Matsuo Basho

Bass, Kingsley B., Jr.
See Bullins, Ed

Bass, Rick 1958- . . . . **CLC 79**
See also CA 126

Bassani, Giorgio 1916- . . . . **CLC 9**
See also CA 65-68; CANR 33; DLB 128;
    MTCW

Bastos, Augusto (Antonio) Roa
See Roa Bastos, Augusto (Antonio)

Bataille, Georges 1897-1962 . . . . **CLC 29**
See also CA 101; 89-92

Bates, H(erbert) E(rnest)
1905-1974 . . . . **CLC 46; SSC 10**
See also CA 93-96; 45-48; CANR 34;
    MTCW

Bauchart
See Camus, Albert

Baudelaire, Charles
1821-1867 . . . . **NCLC 6, 29; PC 1**
See also DA; WLC

Baudrillard, Jean 1929- . . . . **CLC 60**

Baum, L(yman) Frank 1856-1919 . . . **TCLC 7**
See also CA 108; 133; CLR 15; DLB 22;
    MAICYA; MTCW; SATA 18

Baum, Louis F.
See Baum, L(yman) Frank

Baumbach, Jonathan 1933- . . . . . . **CLC 6, 23**
See also CA 13-16R; CAAS 5; CANR 12;
    DLBY 80; MTCW

Bausch, Richard (Carl) 1945- . . . . . . **CLC 51**
See also CA 101; CAAS 14; DLB 130

Baxter, Charles 1947- . . . . **CLC 45, 78**
See also CA 57-60; CANR 40; DLB 130

Baxter, George Owen
See Faust, Frederick (Schiller)

Baxter, James K(eir) 1926-1972 . . . . **CLC 14**
See also CA 77-80

Baxter, John
See Hunt, E(verette) Howard, Jr.

Bayer, Sylvia
See Glassco, John

Beagle, Peter S(oyer) 1939- . . . . **CLC 7**
See also CA 9-12R; CANR 4; DLBY 80;
    SATA 60

Bean, Normal
See Burroughs, Edgar Rice

Beard, Charles A(ustin)
1874-1948 . . . . **TCLC 15**
See also CA 115; DLB 17; SATA 18

Beardsley, Aubrey 1872-1898 . . . . . **NCLC 6**

Beattie, Ann
1947- . . . . **CLC 8, 13, 18, 40, 63; SSC 11**
See also BEST 90:2; CA 81-84; DLBY 82;
    MTCW

Beattie, James 1735-1803 . . . . **NCLC 25**
See also DLB 109

Beauchamp, Kathleen Mansfield 1888-1923
See Mansfield, Katherine
See also CA 104; 134; DA

**Beauvoir, Simone (Lucie Ernestine Marie
Bertrand) de**
1908-1986 . . . . **CLC 1, 2, 4, 8, 14, 31, 44,
50, 71**
See also CA 9-12R; 118; CANR 28; DA;
    DLB 72; DLBY 86; MTCW; WLC

Becker, Jurek 1937- . . . . **CLC 7, 19**
See also CA 85-88; DLB 75

Becker, Walter 1950- . . . . **CLC 26**

Beckett, Samuel (Barclay)
1906-1989 . . . . . . **CLC 1, 2, 3, 4, 6, 9, 10,
11, 14, 18, 29, 57, 59**
See also CA 5-8R; 130; CANR 33;
    CDBLB 1945-1960; DA; DLB 13, 15;
    DLBY 90; MTCW; WLC

Beckford, William 1760-1844 . . . . **NCLC 16**
See also DLB 39

Beckman, Gunnel 1910- . . . . **CLC 26**
See also CA 33-36R; CANR 15; CLR 25;
    MAICYA; SAAS 9; SATA 6

Becque, Henri 1837-1899 . . . . **NCLC 3**

Beddoes, Thomas Lovell
1803-1849 . . . . **NCLC 3**
See also DLB 96

Bedford, Donald F.
See Fearing, Kenneth (Flexner)

Beecher, Catharine Esther
1800-1878 . . . . **NCLC 30**
See also DLB 1

Beecher, John 1904-1980 . . . . **CLC 6**
See also AITN 1; CA 5-8R; 105; CANR 8

Beer, Johann 1655-1700 . . . . **LC 5**

Beer, Patricia 1924- . . . . **CLC 58**
See also CA 61-64; CANR 13; DLB 40

Beerbohm, Henry Maximilian
1872-1956 . . . . **TCLC 1, 24**
See also CA 104; DLB 34, 100

Begiebing, Robert J(ohn) 1946- . . . . . **CLC 70**
See also CA 122; CANR 40

Behan, Brendan
1923-1964 . . . . **CLC 1, 8, 11, 15, 79**
See also CA 73-76; CANR 33;
    CDBLB 1945-1960; DLB 13; MTCW

Behn, Aphra 1640(?)-1689 . . . . **LC 1**
See also DA; DLB 39, 80, 131; WLC

Behrman, S(amuel) N(athaniel)
1893-1973 . . . . **CLC 40**
See also CA 13-16; 45-48; CAP 1; DLB 7,
    44

Belasco, David 1853-1931 . . . . **TCLC 3**
See also CA 104; DLB 7

Belcheva, Elisaveta 1893- . . . . **CLC 10**

Beldone, Phil "Cheech"
See Ellison, Harlan

Beleno
See Azuela, Mariano

Belinski, Vissarion Grigoryevich
1811-1848 . . . . **NCLC 5**

Belitt, Ben 1911- . . . . **CLC 22**
See also CA 13-16R; CAAS 4; CANR 7;
    DLB 5

Bell, James Madison 1826-1902 . . . **TCLC 43**
See also BLC 1; BW; CA 122; 124; DLB 50

Bell, Madison (Smartt) 1957- . . . . . . **CLC 41**
See also CA 111; CANR 28

Bell, Marvin (Hartley) 1937- . . . . . **CLC 8, 31**
See also CA 21-24R; CAAS 14; DLB 5;
    MTCW

Bell, W. L. D.
See Mencken, H(enry) L(ouis)

Bellamy, Atwood C.
See Mencken, H(enry) L(ouis)

Bellamy, Edward   1850-1898 . . . . . .   NCLC 4
See also DLB 12

Bellin, Edward J.
See Kuttner, Henry

Belloc, (Joseph) Hilaire (Pierre)
1870-1953 . . . .   TCLC 7, 18
See also CA 106; DLB 19, 100; YABC 1

Belloc, Joseph Peter Rene Hilaire
See Belloc, (Joseph) Hilaire (Pierre)

Belloc, Joseph Pierre Hilaire
See Belloc, (Joseph) Hilaire (Pierre)

Belloc, M. A.
See Lowndes, Marie Adelaide (Belloc)

Bellow, Saul
1915- . . . . . .   CLC 1, 2, 3, 6, 8, 10, 13, 15,
25, 33, 34, 63, 79
See also AITN 2; BEST 89:3; CA 5-8R;
CABS 1; CANR 29; CDALB 1941-1968;
DA; DLB 2, 28; DLBD 3; DLBY 82;
MTCW; WLC

Belser, Reimond Karel Maria de
1929- . . . .   CLC 14

Bely, Andrey . . . .   TCLC 7
See also Bugayev, Boris Nikolayevich

Benary, Margot
See Benary-Isbert, Margot

Benary-Isbert, Margot   1889-1979 . . .   CLC 12
See also CA 5-8R; 89-92; CANR 4;
CLR 12; MAICYA; SATA 2, 21

Benavente (y Martinez), Jacinto
1866-1954 . . . .   TCLC 3
See also CA 106; 131; HW; MTCW

Benchley, Peter (Bradford)
1940- . . . .   CLC 4, 8
See also AITN 2; CA 17-20R; CANR 12,
35; MTCW; SATA 3

Benchley, Robert (Charles)
1889-1945 . . . .   TCLC 1
See also CA 105; DLB 11

Benedikt, Michael   1935- . . . .   CLC 4, 14
See also CA 13-16R; CANR 7; DLB 5

Benet, Juan   1927- . . . .   CLC 28

Benet, Stephen Vincent
1898-1943 . . . .   TCLC 7; SSC 10
See also CA 104; DLB 4, 48, 102; YABC 1

Benet, William Rose   1886-1950 . . .   TCLC 28
See also CA 118; DLB 45

Benford, Gregory (Albert)   1941- . . . .   CLC 52
See also CA 69-72; CANR 12, 24;
DLBY 82

Bengtsson, Frans (Gunnar)
1894-1954 . . . .   TCLC 48

Benjamin, David
See Slavitt, David R(ytman)

Benjamin, Lois
See Gould, Lois

Benjamin, Walter   1892-1940 . . . . .   TCLC 39

Benn, Gottfried   1886-1956 . . . .   TCLC 3
See also CA 106; DLB 56

Bennett, Alan   1934- . . . .   CLC 45, 77
See also CA 103; CANR 35; MTCW

Bennett, (Enoch) Arnold
1867-1931 . . . .   TCLC 5, 20
See also CA 106; CDBLB 1890-1914;
DLB 10, 34, 98

Bennett, Elizabeth
See Mitchell, Margaret (Munnerlyn)

Bennett, George Harold   1930-
See Bennett, Hal
See also BW; CA 97-100

Bennett, Hal . . . .   CLC 5
See also Bennett, George Harold
See also DLB 33

Bennett, Jay   1912- . . . .   CLC 35
See also AAYA 10; CA 69-72; CANR 11;
SAAS 4; SATA 27, 41

Bennett, Louise (Simone)   1919- . . . . .   CLC 28
See also BLC 1; DLB 117

Benson, E(dward) F(rederic)
1867-1940 . . . .   TCLC 27
See also CA 114

Benson, Jackson J.   1930- . . . .   CLC 34
See also CA 25-28R; DLB 111

Benson, Sally   1900-1972 . . . .   CLC 17
See also CA 19-20; 37-40R; CAP 1;
SATA 1, 27, 35

Benson, Stella   1892-1933 . . . .   TCLC 17
See also CA 117; DLB 36

Bentham, Jeremy   1748-1832 . . . . .   NCLC 38
See also DLB 107

Bentley, E(dmund) C(lerihew)
1875-1956 . . . .   TCLC 12
See also CA 108; DLB 70

Bentley, Eric (Russell)   1916- . . . .   CLC 24
See also CA 5-8R; CANR 6

Beranger, Pierre Jean de
1780-1857 . . . .   NCLC 34

Berger, Colonel
See Malraux, (Georges-)Andre

Berger, John (Peter)   1926- . . . . . .   CLC 2, 19
See also CA 81-84; DLB 14

Berger, Melvin H.   1927- . . . .   CLC 12
See also CA 5-8R; CANR 4; SAAS 2;
SATA 5

Berger, Thomas (Louis)
1924- . . . .   CLC 3, 5, 8, 11, 18, 38
See also CA 1-4R; CANR 5, 28; DLB 2;
DLBY 80; MTCW

Bergman, (Ernst) Ingmar
1918- . . . .   CLC 16, 72
See also CA 81-84; CANR 33

Bergson, Henri   1859-1941 . . . .   TCLC 32

Bergstein, Eleanor   1938- . . . .   CLC 4
See also CA 53-56; CANR 5

Berkoff, Steven   1937- . . . .   CLC 56
See also CA 104

Bermant, Chaim (Icyk)   1929- . . . . . .   CLC 40
See also CA 57-60; CANR 6, 31

Bern, Victoria
See Fisher, M(ary) F(rances) K(ennedy)

Bernanos, (Paul Louis) Georges
1888-1948 . . . .   TCLC 3
See also CA 104; 130; DLB 72

Bernard, April   1956- . . . .   CLC 59
See also CA 131

Bernhard, Thomas
1931-1989 . . . .   CLC 3, 32, 61
See also CA 85-88; 127; CANR 32;
DLB 85, 124; MTCW

Berrigan, Daniel   1921- . . . .   CLC 4
See also CA 33-36R; CAAS 1; CANR 11;
DLB 5

Berrigan, Edmund Joseph Michael, Jr.
1934-1983
See Berrigan, Ted
See also CA 61-64; 110; CANR 14

Berrigan, Ted . . . .   CLC 37
See also Berrigan, Edmund Joseph Michael,
Jr.
See also DLB 5

Berry, Charles Edward Anderson   1931-
See Berry, Chuck
See also CA 115

Berry, Chuck . . . .   CLC 17
See also Berry, Charles Edward Anderson

Berry, Jonas
See Ashbery, John (Lawrence)

Berry, Wendell (Erdman)
1934- . . . .   CLC 4, 6, 8, 27, 46
See also AITN 1; CA 73-76; DLB 5, 6

Berryman, John
1914-1972 . . . . . .   CLC 1, 2, 3, 4, 6, 8, 10,
13, 25, 62
See also CA 13-16; 33-36R; CABS 2;
CANR 35; CAP 1; CDALB 1941-1968;
DLB 48; MTCW

Bertolucci, Bernardo   1940- . . . .   CLC 16
See also CA 106

Bertrand, Aloysius   1807-1841 . . . .   NCLC 31

Bertran de Born   c. 1140-1215 . . . . .   CMLC 5

Besant, Annie (Wood)   1847-1933 . . .   TCLC 9
See also CA 105

Bessie, Alvah   1904-1985 . . . .   CLC 23
See also CA 5-8R; 116; CANR 2; DLB 26

Bethlen, T. D.
See Silverberg, Robert

Beti, Mongo . . . .   CLC 27
See also Biyidi, Alexandre
See also BLC 1

Betjeman, John
1906-1984 . . . .   CLC 2, 6, 10, 34, 43
See also CA 9-12R; 112; CANR 33;
CDBLB 1945-1960; DLB 20; DLBY 84;
MTCW

Bettelheim, Bruno   1903-1990 . . . . . .   CLC 79
See also CA 81-84; 131; CANR 23; MTCW

Betti, Ugo   1892-1953 . . . .   TCLC 5
See also CA 104

Betts, Doris (Waugh)   1932- . . . .   CLC 3, 6, 28
See also CA 13-16R; CANR 9; DLBY 82

Bevan, Alistair
See Roberts, Keith (John Kingston)

Beynon, John
See Harris, John (Wyndham Parkes Lucas)
Beynon

Bialik, Chaim Nachman
1873-1934 . . . .   TCLC 25

Bickerstaff, Isaac
See Swift, Jonathan

Bidart, Frank 1939- .... **CLC 33**
See also CA 140

Bienek, Horst 1930- .... **CLC 7, 11**
See also CA 73-76; DLB 75

Bierce, Ambrose (Gwinett)
1842-1914(?) ..... **TCLC 1, 7, 44; SSC 9**
See also CA 104; 139; CDALB 1865-1917;
DA; DLB 11, 12, 23, 71, 74; WLC

Billings, Josh
See Shaw, Henry Wheeler

Billington, Rachel 1942- .... **CLC 43**
See also AITN 2; CA 33-36R

Binyon, T(imothy) J(ohn) 1936- .... **CLC 34**
See also CA 111; CANR 28

Bioy Casares, Adolfo 1914- .... **CLC 4, 8, 13**
See also CA 29-32R; CANR 19; DLB 113;
HW; MTCW

Bird, C.
See Ellison, Harlan

Bird, Cordwainer
See Ellison, Harlan

Bird, Robert Montgomery
1806-1854 .... **NCLC 1**

Birney, (Alfred) Earle
1904- .... **CLC 1, 4, 6, 11**
See also CA 1-4R; CANR 5, 20; DLB 88;
MTCW

Bishop, Elizabeth
1911-1979 ...... **CLC 1, 4, 9, 13, 15, 32;
PC 3**
See also CA 5-8R; 89-92; CABS 2;
CANR 26; CDALB 1968-1988; DA;
DLB 5; MTCW; SATA 24

Bishop, John 1935- .... **CLC 10**
See also CA 105

Bissett, Bill 1939- .... **CLC 18**
See also CA 69-72; CANR 15; DLB 53;
MTCW

Bitov, Andrei (Georgievich) 1937- ... **CLC 57**

Biyidi, Alexandre 1932-
See Beti, Mongo
See also BW; CA 114; 124; MTCW

Bjarme, Brynjolf
See Ibsen, Henrik (Johan)

Bjornson, Bjornstjerne (Martinius)
1832-1910 .... **TCLC 7, 37**
See also CA 104

Black, Robert
See Holdstock, Robert P.

Blackburn, Paul 1926-1971 ..... **CLC 9, 43**
See also CA 81-84; 33-36R; CANR 34;
DLB 16; DLBY 81

Black Elk 1863-1950 .... **TCLC 33**

Black Hobart
See Sanders, (James) Ed(ward)

Blacklin, Malcolm
See Chambers, Aidan

Blackmore, R(ichard) D(oddridge)
1825-1900 .... **TCLC 27**
See also CA 120; DLB 18

Blackmur, R(ichard) P(almer)
1904-1965 .... **CLC 2, 24**
See also CA 11-12; 25-28R; CAP 1; DLB 63

Black Tarantula, The
See Acker, Kathy

Blackwood, Algernon (Henry)
1869-1951 .... **TCLC 5**
See also CA 105

Blackwood, Caroline 1931- .... **CLC 6, 9**
See also CA 85-88; CANR 32; DLB 14;
MTCW

Blade, Alexander
See Hamilton, Edmond; Silverberg, Robert

Blaga, Lucian 1895-1961 .... **CLC 75**

Blair, Eric (Arthur) 1903-1950
See Orwell, George
See also CA 104; 132; DA; MTCW;
SATA 29

Blais, Marie-Claire
1939- .... **CLC 2, 4, 6, 13, 22**
See also CA 21-24R; CAAS 4; CANR 38;
DLB 53; MTCW

Blaise, Clark 1940- .... **CLC 29**
See also AITN 2; CA 53-56; CAAS 3;
CANR 5; DLB 53

Blake, Nicholas
See Day Lewis, C(ecil)
See also DLB 77

Blake, William 1757-1827 .... **NCLC 13**
See also CDBLB 1789-1832; DA; DLB 93;
MAICYA; SATA 30; WLC

Blasco Ibanez, Vicente
1867-1928 .... **TCLC 12**
See also CA 110; 131; HW; MTCW

Blatty, William Peter 1928- .... **CLC 2**
See also CA 5-8R; CANR 9

Bleeck, Oliver
See Thomas, Ross (Elmore)

Blessing, Lee 1949- .... **CLC 54**

Blish, James (Benjamin)
1921-1975 .... **CLC 14**
See also CA 1-4R; 57-60; CANR 3; DLB 8;
MTCW; SATA 66

Bliss, Reginald
See Wells, H(erbert) G(eorge)

Blixen, Karen (Christentze Dinesen)
1885-1962
See Dinesen, Isak
See also CA 25-28; CANR 22; CAP 2;
MTCW; SATA 44

Bloch, Robert (Albert) 1917- .... **CLC 33**
See also CA 5-8R; CANR 5; DLB 44;
SATA 12

Blok, Alexander (Alexandrovich)
1880-1921 .... **TCLC 5**
See also CA 104

Blom, Jan
See Breytenbach, Breyten

Bloom, Harold 1930- .... **CLC 24**
See also CA 13-16R; CANR 39; DLB 67

Bloomfield, Aurelius
See Bourne, Randolph S(illiman)

Blount, Roy (Alton), Jr. 1941- ..... **CLC 38**
See also CA 53-56; CANR 10, 28; MTCW

Bloy, Leon 1846-1917 .... **TCLC 22**
See also CA 121; DLB 123

Blume, Judy (Sussman) 1938- ... **CLC 12, 30**
See also AAYA 3; CA 29-32R; CANR 13,
37; CLR 2, 15; DLB 52; MAICYA;
MTCW; SATA 2, 31

Blunden, Edmund (Charles)
1896-1974 .... **CLC 2, 56**
See also CA 17-18; 45-48; CAP 2; DLB 20,
100; MTCW

Bly, Robert (Elwood)
1926- .... **CLC 1, 2, 5, 10, 15, 38**
See also CA 5-8R; CANR 41; DLB 5;
MTCW

Bobette
See Simenon, Georges (Jacques Christian)

Boccaccio, Giovanni 1313-1375
See also SSC 10

Bochco, Steven 1943- .... **CLC 35**
See also CA 124; 138

Bodenheim, Maxwell 1892-1954 ... **TCLC 44**
See also CA 110; DLB 9, 45

Bodker, Cecil 1927- .... **CLC 21**
See also CA 73-76; CANR 13; CLR 23;
MAICYA; SATA 14

Boell, Heinrich (Theodor) 1917-1985
See Boll, Heinrich (Theodor)
See also CA 21-24R; 116; CANR 24; DA;
DLB 69; DLBY 85; MTCW

Boerne, Alfred
See Doeblin, Alfred

Bogan, Louise 1897-1970 ..... **CLC 4, 39, 46**
See also CA 73-76; 25-28R; CANR 33;
DLB 45; MTCW

Bogarde, Dirk .... **CLC 19**
See also Van Den Bogarde, Derek Jules
Gaspard Ulric Niven
See also DLB 14

Bogosian, Eric 1953- .... **CLC 45**
See also CA 138

Bograd, Larry 1953- .... **CLC 35**
See also CA 93-96; SATA 33

Boiardo, Matteo Maria 1441-1494 .... **LC 6**

Boileau-Despreaux, Nicolas
1636-1711 .... **LC 3**

Boland, Eavan 1944- .... **CLC 40, 67**
See also DLB 40

Boll, Heinrich (Theodor)
1917-1985 .... **CLC 2, 3, 6, 9, 11, 15, 27,
39, 72**
See also Boell, Heinrich (Theodor)
See also DLB 69; DLBY 85; WLC

Bolt, Lee
See Faust, Frederick (Schiller)

Bolt, Robert (Oxton) 1924- .... **CLC 14**
See also CA 17-20R; CANR 35; DLB 13;
MTCW

Bomkauf
See Kaufman, Bob (Garnell)

Bonaventura .... **NCLC 35**
See also DLB 90

Bond, Edward 1934- .... **CLC 4, 6, 13, 23**
See also CA 25-28R; CANR 38; DLB 13;
MTCW

Bonham, Frank 1914-1989 .... **CLC 12**
See also AAYA 1; CA 9-12R; CANR 4, 36;
MAICYA; SAAS 3; SATA 1, 49, 62

Bonnefoy, Yves 1923-........ **CLC 9, 15, 58**
See also CA 85-88; CANR 33; MTCW

Bontemps, Arna(ud Wendell)
1902-1973 .... **CLC 1, 18**
See also BLC 1; BW; CA 1-4R; 41-44R;
CANR 4, 35; CLR 6; DLB 48, 51;
MAICYA; MTCW; SATA 2, 24, 44

Booth, Martin 1944-............. **CLC 13**
See also CA 93-96; CAAS 2

Booth, Philip 1925-............. **CLC 23**
See also CA 5-8R; CANR 5; DLBY 82

Booth, Wayne C(layson) 1921- ... **CLC 24**
See also CA 1-4R; CAAS 5; CANR 3;
DLB 67

Borchert, Wolfgang 1921-1947 ..... **TCLC 5**
See also CA 104; DLB 69, 124

Borel, Petrus 1809-1859........ **NCLC 41**

Borges, Jorge Luis
1899-1986 ... **CLC 1, 2, 3, 4, 6, 8, 9, 10,**
13, 19, 44, 48; SSC 4
See also CA 21-24R; CANR 19, 33; DA;
DLB 113; DLBY 86; HW; MTCW; WLC

Borowski, Tadeusz 1922-1951...... **TCLC 9**
See also CA 106

Borrow, George (Henry)
1803-1881 .... **NCLC 9**
See also DLB 21, 55

Bosman, Herman Charles
1905-1951 .... **TCLC 49**

Bosschere, Jean de 1878(?)-1953... **TCLC 19**
See also CA 115

Boswell, James 1740-1795.......... **LC 4**
See also CDBLB 1660-1789; DA; DLB 104;
WLC

Bottoms, David 1949-............. **CLC 53**
See also CA 105; CANR 22; DLB 120;
DLBY 83

Boucicault, Dion 1820-1890...... **NCLC 41**

Boucolon, Maryse 1937-
See Conde, Maryse
See also CA 110; CANR 30

Bourget, Paul (Charles Joseph)
1852-1935 .... **TCLC 12**
See also CA 107; DLB 123

Bourjaily, Vance (Nye) 1922- .... **CLC 8, 62**
See also CA 1-4R; CAAS 1; CANR 2;
DLB 2

Bourne, Randolph S(illiman)
1886-1918 .... **TCLC 16**
See also CA 117; DLB 63

Bova, Ben(jamin William) 1932-.... **CLC 45**
See also CA 5-8R; CANR 11; CLR 3;
DLBY 81; MAICYA; MTCW; SATA 6,
68

Bowen, Elizabeth (Dorothea Cole)
1899-1973 ...... **CLC 1, 3, 6, 11, 15, 22;**
SSC 3
See also CA 17-18; 41-44R; CANR 35;
CAP 2; CDBLB 1945-1960; DLB 15;
MTCW

Bowering, George 1935-........ **CLC 15, 47**
See also CA 21-24R; CAAS 16; CANR 10;
DLB 53

Bowering, Marilyn R(uthe) 1949-... **CLC 32**
See also CA 101

Bowers, Edgar 1924- .... **CLC 9**
See also CA 5-8R; CANR 24; DLB 5

Bowie, David .... **CLC 17**
See also Jones, David Robert

Bowles, Jane (Sydney)
1917-1973 .... **CLC 3, 68**
See also CA 19-20; 41-44R; CAP 2

Bowles, Paul (Frederick)
1910- .... **CLC 1, 2, 19, 53; SSC 3**
See also CA 1-4R; CAAS 1; CANR 1, 19;
DLB 5, 6; MTCW

Box, Edgar
See Vidal, Gore

Boyd, Nancy
See Millay, Edna St. Vincent

Boyd, William 1952-........ **CLC 28, 53, 70**
See also CA 114; 120

Boyle, Kay
1902-1992 ..... **CLC 1, 5, 19, 58; SSC 5**
See also CA 13-16R; 140; CAAS 1;
CANR 29; DLB 4, 9, 48, 86; MTCW

Boyle, Mark
See Kienzle, William X(avier)

Boyle, Patrick 1905-1982......... **CLC 19**
See also CA 127

Boyle, T. Coraghessan 1948-.... **CLC 36, 55**
See also BEST 90:4; CA 120; DLBY 86

Boz
See Dickens, Charles (John Huffam)

Brackenridge, Hugh Henry
1748-1816 .... **NCLC 7**
See also DLB 11, 37

Bradbury, Edward P.
See Moorcock, Michael (John)

Bradbury, Malcolm (Stanley)
1932- .... **CLC 32, 61**
See also CA 1-4R; CANR 1, 33; DLB 14;
MTCW

Bradbury, Ray (Douglas)
1920- .... **CLC 1, 3, 10, 15, 42**
See also AITN 1, 2; CA 1-4R; CANR 2, 30;
CDALB 1968-1988; DA; DLB 2, 8;
MTCW; SATA 11, 64; WLC

Bradford, Gamaliel 1863-1932..... **TCLC 36**
See also DLB 17

Bradley, David (Henry, Jr.) 1950- .. **CLC 23**
See also BLC 1; BW; CA 104; CANR 26;
DLB 33

Bradley, John Ed 1959-........... **CLC 55**

Bradley, Marion Zimmer 1930-..... **CLC 30**
See also AAYA 9; CA 57-60; CAAS 10;
CANR 7, 31; DLB 8; MTCW

Bradstreet, Anne 1612(?)-1672 .... **LC 4**
See also CDALB 1640-1865; DA; DLB 24

Bragg, Melvyn 1939- .... **CLC 10**
See also BEST 89:3; CA 57-60; CANR 10;
DLB 14

Braine, John (Gerard)
1922-1986 .... **CLC 1, 3, 41**
See also CA 1-4R; 120; CANR 1, 33;
CDBLB 1945-1960; DLB 15; DLBY 86;
MTCW

Brammer, William 1930(?)-1978 .... **CLC 31**
See also CA 77-80

Brancati, Vitaliano 1907-1954..... **TCLC 12**
See also CA 109

Brancato, Robin F(idler) 1936-..... **CLC 35**
See also AAYA 9; CA 69-72; CANR 11;
SAAS 9; SATA 23

Brand, Max
See Faust, Frederick (Schiller)

Brand, Millen 1906-1980.......... **CLC 7**
See also CA 21-24R; 97-100

Branden, Barbara .... **CLC 44**

Brandes, Georg (Morris Cohen)
1842-1927 .... **TCLC 10**
See also CA 105

Brandys, Kazimierz 1916-........ **CLC 62**

Branley, Franklyn M(ansfield)
1915- .... **CLC 21**
See also CA 33-36R; CANR 14, 39;
CLR 13; MAICYA; SAAS 16; SATA 4,
68

Brathwaite, Edward (Kamau)
1930- .... **CLC 11**
See also BW; CA 25-28R; CANR 11, 26;
DLB 125

Brautigan, Richard (Gary)
1935-1984 .... **CLC 1, 3, 5, 9, 12, 34, 42**
See also CA 53-56; 113; CANR 34; DLB 2,
5; DLBY 80, 84; MTCW; SATA 56

Braverman, Kate 1950- .... **CLC 67**
See also CA 89-92

Brecht, Bertolt
1898-1956 ..... **TCLC 1, 6, 13, 35; DC 3**
See also CA 104; 133; DA; DLB 56, 124;
MTCW; WLC

Brecht, Eugen Berthold Friedrich
See Brecht, Bertolt

Bremer, Fredrika 1801-1865 ..... **NCLC 11**

Brennan, Christopher John
1870-1932 .... **TCLC 17**
See also CA 117

Brennan, Maeve 1917-............. **CLC 5**
See also CA 81-84

Brentano, Clemens (Maria)
1778-1842 .... **NCLC 1**

Brent of Bin Bin
See Franklin, (Stella Maraia Sarah) Miles

Brenton, Howard 1942-........... **CLC 31**
See also CA 69-72; CANR 33; DLB 13;
MTCW

Breslin, James 1930-
See Breslin, Jimmy
See also CA 73-76; CANR 31; MTCW

Breslin, Jimmy .... **CLC 4, 43**
See also Breslin, James
See also AITN 1

Bresson, Robert 1907-............. **CLC 16**
See also CA 110

Breton, Andre 1896-1966... **CLC 2, 9, 15, 54**
See also CA 19-20; 25-28R; CANR 40;
CAP 2; DLB 65; MTCW

Breytenbach, Breyten 1939(?)- .. **CLC 23, 37**
See also CA 113; 129

Bridgers, Sue Ellen　1942-　.........　**CLC 26**
See also AAYA 8; CA 65-68; CANR 11,
36; CLR 18; DLB 52; MAICYA;
SAAS 1; SATA 22

Bridges, Robert (Seymour)
1844-1930　..................　**TCLC 1**
See also CA 104; CDBLB 1890-1914;
DLB 19, 98

Bridie, James....................　**TCLC 3**
See also Mavor, Osborne Henry
See also DLB 10

Brin, David　1950-...............　**CLC 34**
See also CA 102; CANR 24; SATA 65

Brink, Andre (Philippus)
1935-　...................　**CLC 18, 36**
See also CA 104; CANR 39; MTCW

Brinsmead, H(esba) F(ay)　1922-　....　**CLC 21**
See also CA 21-24R; CANR 10; MAICYA;
SAAS 5; SATA 18

Brittain, Vera (Mary)
1893(?)-1970　.................　**CLC 23**
See also CA 13-16; 25-28R; CAP 1; MTCW

Broch, Hermann　1886-1951......　**TCLC 20**
See also CA 117; DLB 85, 124

Brock, Rose
See Hansen, Joseph

Brodkey, Harold　1930-...........　**CLC 56**
See also CA 111; DLB 130

Brodsky, Iosif Alexandrovich　1940-
See Brodsky, Joseph
See also AITN 1; CA 41-44R; CANR 37;
MTCW

Brodsky, Joseph　.......　**CLC 4, 6, 13, 36, 50**
See also Brodsky, Iosif Alexandrovich

Brodsky, Michael Mark　1948-　.....　**CLC 19**
See also CA 102; CANR 18, 41

Bromell, Henry　1947-..............　**CLC 5**
See also CA 53-56; CANR 9

Bromfield, Louis (Brucker)
1896-1956　.................　**TCLC 11**
See also CA 107; DLB 4, 9, 86

Broner, E(sther) M(asserman)
1930-　.....................　**CLC 19**
See also CA 17-20R; CANR 8, 25; DLB 28

Bronk, William　1918-.............　**CLC 10**
See also CA 89-92; CANR 23

Bronstein, Lev Davidovich
See Trotsky, Leon

Bronte, Anne　1820-1849.........　**NCLC 4**
See also DLB 21

Bronte, Charlotte
1816-1855　.............　**NCLC 3, 8, 33**
See also CDBLB 1832-1890; DA; DLB 21;
WLC

Bronte, (Jane) Emily
1818-1848　.............　**NCLC 16, 35**
See also CDBLB 1832-1890; DA; DLB 21,
32; WLC

Brooke, Frances　1724-1789..........　**LC 6**
See also DLB 39, 99

Brooke, Henry　1703(?)-1783.........　**LC 1**
See also DLB 39

Brooke, Rupert (Chawner)
1887-1915　.................　**TCLC 2, 7**
See also CA 104; 132; CDBLB 1914-1945;
DA; DLB 19; MTCW; WLC

Brooke-Haven, P.
See Wodehouse, P(elham) G(renville)

Brooke-Rose, Christine　1926-......　**CLC 40**
See also CA 13-16R; DLB 14

Brookner, Anita　1928-......　**CLC 32, 34, 51**
See also CA 114; 120; CANR 37; DLBY 87;
MTCW

Brooks, Cleanth　1906-　...........　**CLC 24**
See also CA 17-20R; CANR 33, 35;
DLB 63; MTCW

Brooks, George
See Baum, L(yman) Frank

Brooks, Gwendolyn
1917-　......　**CLC 1, 2, 4, 5, 15, 49; PC 7**
See also AITN 1; BLC 1; BW; CA 1-4R;
CANR 1, 27; CDALB 1941-1968;
CLR 27; DA; DLB 5, 76; MTCW;
SATA 6; WLC

Brooks, Mel.....................　**CLC 12**
See also Kaminsky, Melvin
See also DLB 26

Brooks, Peter　1938-..............　**CLC 34**
See also CA 45-48; CANR 1

Brooks, Van Wyck　1886-1963......　**CLC 29**
See also CA 1-4R; CANR 6; DLB 45, 63,
103

Brophy, Brigid (Antonia)
1929-　.................　**CLC 6, 11, 29**
See also CA 5-8R; CAAS 4; CANR 25;
DLB 14; MTCW

Brosman, Catharine Savage　1934-....　**CLC 9**
See also CA 61-64; CANR 21

Brother Antoninus
See Everson, William (Oliver)

Broughton, T(homas) Alan　1936-　...　**CLC 19**
See also CA 45-48; CANR 2, 23

Broumas, Olga　1949-..........　**CLC 10, 73**
See also CA 85-88; CANR 20

Brown, Charles Brockden
1771-1810　.................　**NCLC 22**
See also CDALB 1640-1865; DLB 37, 59,
73

Brown, Christy　1932-1981........　**CLC 63**
See also CA 105; 104; DLB 14

Brown, Claude　1937-　.............　**CLC 30**
See also AAYA 7; BLC 1; BW; CA 73-76

Brown, Dee (Alexander)　1908-　..　**CLC 18, 47**
See also CA 13-16R; CAAS 6; CANR 11;
DLBY 80; MTCW; SATA 5

Brown, George
See Wertmueller, Lina

Brown, George Douglas
1869-1902　.................　**TCLC 28**

Brown, George Mackay　1921-....　**CLC 5, 48**
See also CA 21-24R; CAAS 6; CANR 12,
37; DLB 14, 27; MTCW; SATA 35

Brown, (William) Larry　1951-......　**CLC 73**
See also CA 130; 134

Brown, Moses
See Barrett, William (Christopher)

Brown, Rita Mae　1944-.....　**CLC 18, 43, 79**
See also CA 45-48; CANR 2, 11, 35;
MTCW

Brown, Roderick (Langmere) Haig-
See Haig-Brown, Roderick (Langmere)

Brown, Rosellen　1939-............　**CLC 32**
See also CA 77-80; CAAS 10; CANR 14

Brown, Sterling Allen
1901-1989　.............　**CLC 1, 23, 59**
See also BLC 1; BW; CA 85-88; 127;
CANR 26; DLB 48, 51, 63; MTCW

Brown, Will
See Ainsworth, William Harrison

Brown, William Wells
1813-1884　.............　**NCLC 2; DC 1**
See also BLC 1; DLB 3, 50

Browne, (Clyde) Jackson　1948(?)-...　**CLC 21**
See also CA 120

Browning, Elizabeth Barrett
1806-1861　.........　**NCLC 1, 16; PC 6**
See also CDBLB 1832-1890; DA; DLB 32;
WLC

Browning, Robert
1812-1889　.............　**NCLC 19; PC 2**
See also CDBLB 1832-1890; DA; DLB 32;
YABC 1

Browning, Tod　1882-1962　.........　**CLC 16**
See also CA 117

Bruccoli, Matthew J(oseph)　1931-　...　**CLC 34**
See also CA 9-12R; CANR 7; DLB 103

Bruce, Lenny.....................　**CLC 21**
See also Schneider, Leonard Alfred

Bruin, John
See Brutus, Dennis

Brulls, Christian
See Simenon, Georges (Jacques Christian)

Brunner, John (Kilian Houston)
1934-　..................　**CLC 8, 10**
See also CA 1-4R; CAAS 8; CANR 2, 37;
MTCW

Brutus, Dennis　1924-.............　**CLC 43**
See also BLC 1; BW; CA 49-52; CAAS 14;
CANR 2, 27; DLB 117

Bryan, C(ourtlandt) D(ixon) B(arnes)
1936-　.....................　**CLC 29**
See also CA 73-76; CANR 13

Bryan, Michael
See Moore, Brian

Bryant, William Cullen
1794-1878　.................　**NCLC 6**
See also CDALB 1640-1865; DA; DLB 3,
43, 59

Bryusov, Valery Yakovlevich
1873-1924　.................　**TCLC 10**
See also CA 107

Buchan, John　1875-1940........　**TCLC 41**
See also CA 108; DLB 34, 70; YABC 2

Buchanan, George　1506-1582　........　**LC 4**

Buchheim, Lothar-Guenther　1918-　...　**CLC 6**
See also CA 85-88

Buchner, (Karl) Georg
1813-1837　.................　**NCLC 26**

Buchwald, Art(hur) 1925-.......... CLC 33
See also AITN 1; CA 5-8R; CANR 21;
MTCW; SATA 10

Buck, Pearl S(ydenstricker)
1892-1973 .... CLC 7, 11, 18
See also AITN 1; CA 1-4R; 41-44R;
CANR 1, 34; DA; DLB 9, 102; MTCW;
SATA 1, 25

Buckler, Ernest 1908-1984......... CLC 13
See also CA 11-12; 114; CAP 1; DLB 68;
SATA 47

Buckley, Vincent (Thomas)
1925-1988 .... CLC 57
See also CA 101

Buckley, William F(rank), Jr.
1925- .... CLC 7, 18, 37
See also AITN 1; CA 1-4R; CANR 1, 24;
DLBY 80; MTCW

Buechner, (Carl) Frederick
1926- .... CLC 2, 4, 6, 9
See also CA 13-16R; CANR 11, 39;
DLBY 80; MTCW

Buell, John (Edward) 1927-........ CLC 10
See also CA 1-4R; DLB 53

Buero Vallejo, Antonio 1916-... CLC 15, 46
See also CA 106; CANR 24; HW; MTCW

Bufalino, Gesualdo 1920(?)-........ CLC 74

Bugayev, Boris Nikolayevich 1880-1934
See Bely, Andrey
See also CA 104

Bukowski, Charles 1920-.... CLC 2, 5, 9, 41
See also CA 17-20R; CANR 40; DLB 5,
130; MTCW

Bulgakov, Mikhail (Afanas'evich)
1891-1940 .... TCLC 2, 16
See also CA 105

Bullins, Ed 1935- .... CLC 1, 5, 7
See also BLC 1; BW; CA 49-52; CAAS 16;
CANR 24; DLB 7, 38; MTCW

Bulwer-Lytton, Edward (George Earle Lytton)
1803-1873 .... NCLC 1
See also DLB 21

Bunin, Ivan Alexeyevich
1870-1953 .... TCLC 6; SSC 5
See also CA 104

Bunting, Basil 1900-1985.... CLC 10, 39, 47
See also CA 53-56; 115; CANR 7; DLB 20

Bunuel, Luis 1900-1983 .... CLC 16
See also CA 101; 110; CANR 32; HW

Bunyan, John 1628-1688 .... LC 4
See also CDBLB 1660-1789; DA; DLB 39;
WLC

Burford, Eleanor
See Hibbert, Eleanor Alice Burford

Burgess, Anthony
1917- ...... CLC 1, 2, 4, 5, 8, 10, 13, 15,
22, 40, 62
See also Wilson, John (Anthony) Burgess
See also AITN 1; CDBLB 1960 to Present;
DLB 14

Burke, Edmund 1729(?)-1797........ LC 7
See also DA; DLB 104; WLC

Burke, Kenneth (Duva) 1897-.... CLC 2, 24
See also CA 5-8R; CANR 39; DLB 45, 63;
MTCW

Burke, Leda
See Garnett, David

Burke, Ralph
See Silverberg, Robert

Burney, Fanny 1752-1840 .... NCLC 12
See also DLB 39

Burns, Robert 1759-1796....... LC 3; PC 6
See also CDBLB 1789-1832; DA; DLB 109;
WLC

Burns, Tex
See L'Amour, Louis (Dearborn)

Burnshaw, Stanley 1906-..... CLC 3, 13, 44
See also CA 9-12R; DLB 48

Burr, Anne 1937- .... CLC 6
See also CA 25-28R

Burroughs, Edgar Rice
1875-1950 .... TCLC 2, 32
See also CA 104; 132; DLB 8; MTCW;
SATA 41

Burroughs, William S(eward)
1914- .... CLC 1, 2, 5, 15, 22, 42, 75
See also AITN 2; CA 9-12R; CANR 20;
DA; DLB 2, 8, 16; DLBY 81; MTCW;
WLC

Busch, Frederick 1941-... CLC 7, 10, 18, 47
See also CA 33-36R; CAAS 1; DLB 6

Bush, Ronald 1946- .... CLC 34
See also CA 136

Bustos, F(rancisco)
See Borges, Jorge Luis

Bustos Domecq, H(onorio)
See Bioy Casares, Adolfo; Borges, Jorge
Luis

Butler, Octavia E(stelle) 1947- ..... CLC 38
See also BW; CA 73-76; CANR 12, 24, 38;
DLB 33; MTCW

Butler, Samuel 1612-1680 .... LC 16
See also DLB 101, 126

Butler, Samuel 1835-1902 ...... TCLC 1, 33
See also CA 104; CDBLB 1890-1914; DA;
DLB 18, 57; WLC

Butler, Walter C.
See Faust, Frederick (Schiller)

Butor, Michel (Marie Francois)
1926- .... CLC 1, 3, 8, 11, 15
See also CA 9-12R; CANR 33; DLB 83;
MTCW

Buzo, Alexander (John) 1944-...... CLC 61
See also CA 97-100; CANR 17, 39

Buzzati, Dino 1906-1972 .... CLC 36
See also CA 33-36R

Byars, Betsy (Cromer) 1928-....... CLC 35
See also CA 33-36R; CANR 18, 36; CLR 1,
16; DLB 52; MAICYA; MTCW; SAAS 1;
SATA 4, 46

Byatt, A(ntonia) S(usan Drabble)
1936- .... CLC 19, 65
See also CA 13-16R; CANR 13, 33;
DLB 14; MTCW

Byrne, David 1952-............... CLC 26
See also CA 127

Byrne, John Keyes 1926-......... CLC 19
See also Leonard, Hugh
See also CA 102

Byron, George Gordon (Noel)
1788-1824 .... NCLC 2, 12
See also CDBLB 1789-1832; DA; DLB 96,
110; WLC

C.3.3.
See Wilde, Oscar (Fingal O'Flahertie Wills)

Caballero, Fernan 1796-1877..... NCLC 10

Cabell, James Branch 1879-1958 ... TCLC 6
See also CA 105; DLB 9, 78

Cable, George Washington
1844-1925 .... TCLC 4; SSC 4
See also CA 104; DLB 12, 74

Cabral de Melo Neto, Joao 1920-... CLC 76

Cabrera Infante, G(uillermo)
1929- .... CLC 5, 25, 45
See also CA 85-88; CANR 29; DLB 113;
HW; MTCW

Cade, Toni
See Bambara, Toni Cade

Cadmus
See Buchan, John

Caedmon fl. 658-680............. CMLC 7

Caeiro, Alberto
See Pessoa, Fernando (Antonio Nogueira)

Cage, John (Milton, Jr.) 1912-..... CLC 41
See also CA 13-16R; CANR 9

Cain, G.
See Cabrera Infante, G(uillermo)

Cain, Guillermo
See Cabrera Infante, G(uillermo)

Cain, James M(allahan)
1892-1977 .... CLC 3, 11, 28
See also AITN 1; CA 17-20R; 73-76;
CANR 8, 34; MTCW

Caine, Mark
See Raphael, Frederic (Michael)

Calderon de la Barca, Pedro
1600-1681 .... LC 23; DC 3

Caldwell, Erskine (Preston)
1903-1987 .... CLC 1, 8, 14, 50, 60
See also AITN 1; CA 1-4R; 121; CAAS 1;
CANR 2, 33; DLB 9, 86; MTCW

Caldwell, (Janet Miriam) Taylor (Holland)
1900-1985 .... CLC 2, 28, 39
See also CA 5-8R; 116; CANR 5

Calhoun, John Caldwell
1782-1850 .... NCLC 15
See also DLB 3

Calisher, Hortense 1911-.... CLC 2, 4, 8, 38
See also CA 1-4R; CANR 1, 22; DLB 2;
MTCW

Callaghan, Morley Edward
1903-1990 .... CLC 3, 14, 41, 65
See also CA 9-12R; 132; CANR 33;
DLB 68; MTCW

Calvino, Italo
1923-1985 ..... CLC 5, 8, 11, 22, 33, 39,
73; SSC 3
See also CA 85-88; 116; CANR 23; MTCW

Cameron, Carey 1952-............ CLC 59
See also CA 135

Cameron, Peter 1959-............ CLC 44
See also CA 125

Campana, Dino 1885-1932 . . . . **TCLC 20**
See also CA 117; DLB 114

Campbell, John W(ood, Jr.)
1910-1971 . . . . **CLC 32**
See also CA 21-22; 29-32R; CANR 34;
CAP 2; DLB 8; MTCW

Campbell, Joseph 1904-1987 . . . . **CLC 69**
See also AAYA 3; BEST 89:2; CA 1-4R;
124; CANR 3, 28; MTCW

Campbell, (John) Ramsey 1946- . . . . **CLC 42**
See also CA 57-60; CANR 7

Campbell, (Ignatius) Roy (Dunnachie)
1901-1957 . . . . **TCLC 5**
See also CA 104; DLB 20

Campbell, Thomas 1777-1844 . . . . **NCLC 19**
See also DLB 93

Campbell, Wilfred . . . . **TCLC 9**
See also Campbell, William

Campbell, William 1858(?)-1918
See Campbell, Wilfred
See also CA 106; DLB 92

Campos, Alvaro de
See Pessoa, Fernando (Antonio Nogueira)

Camus, Albert
1913-1960 . . . . **CLC 1, 2, 4, 9, 11, 14, 32,
                 63, 69; DC 2; SSC 9**
See also CA 89-92; DA; DLB 72; MTCW;
WLC

Canby, Vincent 1924- . . . . **CLC 13**
See also CA 81-84

Cancale
See Desnos, Robert

Canetti, Elias 1905- . . . . . . **CLC 3, 14, 25, 75**
See also CA 21-24R; CANR 23; DLB 85,
124; MTCW

Canin, Ethan 1960- . . . . **CLC 55**
See also CA 131; 135

Cannon, Curt
See Hunter, Evan

Cape, Judith
See Page, P(atricia) K(athleen)

Capek, Karel
1890-1938 . . . . **TCLC 6, 37; DC 1**
See also CA 104; 140; DA; WLC

Capote, Truman
1924-1984 . . . . . . **CLC 1, 3, 8, 13, 19, 34,
                    38, 58; SSC 2**
See also CA 5-8R; 113; CANR 18;
CDALB 1941-1968; DA; DLB 2;
DLBY 80, 84; MTCW; WLC

Capra, Frank 1897-1991 . . . . **CLC 16**
See also CA 61-64; 135

Caputo, Philip 1941- . . . . **CLC 32**
See also CA 73-76; CANR 40

Card, Orson Scott 1951- . . . . **CLC 44, 47, 50**
See also CA 102; CANR 27; MTCW

Cardenal (Martinez), Ernesto
1925- . . . . **CLC 31**
See also CA 49-52; CANR 2, 32; HW;
MTCW

Carducci, Giosue 1835-1907 . . . . . . **TCLC 32**

Carew, Thomas 1595(?)-1640 . . . . **LC 13**
See also DLB 126

Carey, Ernestine Gilbreth 1908- . . . . **CLC 17**
See also CA 5-8R; SATA 2

Carey, Peter 1943- . . . . **CLC 40, 55**
See also CA 123; 127; MTCW

Carleton, William 1794-1869 . . . . . **NCLC 3**

Carlisle, Henry (Coffin) 1926- . . . . . . **CLC 33**
See also CA 13-16R; CANR 15

Carlsen, Chris
See Holdstock, Robert P.

Carlson, Ron(ald F.) 1947- . . . . **CLC 54**
See also CA 105; CANR 27

Carlyle, Thomas 1795-1881 . . . . . . **NCLC 22**
See also CDBLB 1789-1832; DA; DLB 55

Carman, (William) Bliss
1861-1929 . . . . **TCLC 7**
See also CA 104; DLB 92

Carossa, Hans 1878-1956 . . . . **TCLC 48**
See also DLB 66

Carpenter, Don(ald Richard)
1931- . . . . **CLC 41**
See also CA 45-48; CANR 1

Carpentier (y Valmont), Alejo
1904-1980 . . . . **CLC 8, 11, 38**
See also CA 65-68; 97-100; CANR 11;
DLB 113; HW

Carr, Emily 1871-1945 . . . . **TCLC 32**
See also DLB 68

Carr, John Dickson 1906-1977 . . . . . . **CLC 3**
See also CA 49-52; 69-72; CANR 3, 33;
MTCW

Carr, Philippa
See Hibbert, Eleanor Alice Burford

Carr, Virginia Spencer 1929- . . . . . . **CLC 34**
See also CA 61-64; DLB 111

Carrier, Roch 1937- . . . . **CLC 13, 78**
See also CA 130; DLB 53

Carroll, James P. 1943(?)- . . . . **CLC 38**
See also CA 81-84

Carroll, Jim 1951- . . . . **CLC 35**
See also CA 45-48

Carroll, Lewis . . . . **NCLC 2**
See also Dodgson, Charles Lutwidge
See also CDBLB 1832-1890; CLR 2, 18;
DLB 18; WLC

Carroll, Paul Vincent 1900-1968 . . . . **CLC 10**
See also CA 9-12R; 25-28R; DLB 10

Carruth, Hayden 1921- . . . . **CLC 4, 7, 10, 18**
See also CA 9-12R; CANR 4, 38; DLB 5;
MTCW; SATA 47

Carson, Rachel Louise 1907-1964 . . . **CLC 71**
See also CA 77-80; CANR 35; MTCW;
SATA 23

Carter, Angela (Olive)
1940-1992 . . . . . . **CLC 5, 41, 76; SSC 13**
See also CA 53-56; 136; CANR 12, 36;
DLB 14; MTCW; SATA 66;
SATA-Obit 70

Carter, Nick
See Smith, Martin Cruz

Carver, Raymond
1938-1988 . . . **CLC 22, 36, 53, 55; SSC 8**
See also CA 33-36R; 126; CANR 17, 34;
DLB 130; DLBY 84, 88; MTCW

Cary, (Arthur) Joyce (Lunel)
1888-1957 . . . . **TCLC 1, 29**
See also CA 104; CDBLB 1914-1945;
DLB 15, 100

Casanova de Seingalt, Giovanni Jacopo
1725-1798 . . . . **LC 13**

Casares, Adolfo Bioy
See Bioy Casares, Adolfo

Casely-Hayford, J(oseph) E(phraim)
1866-1930 . . . . **TCLC 24**
See also BLC 1; CA 123

Casey, John (Dudley) 1939- . . . . **CLC 59**
See also BEST 90:2; CA 69-72; CANR 23

Casey, Michael 1947- . . . . **CLC 2**
See also CA 65-68; DLB 5

Casey, Patrick
See Thurman, Wallace (Henry)

Casey, Warren (Peter) 1935-1988 . . . **CLC 12**
See also CA 101; 127

Casona, Alejandro . . . . **CLC 49**
See also Alvarez, Alejandro Rodriguez

Cassavetes, John 1929-1989 . . . . **CLC 20**
See also CA 85-88; 127

Cassill, R(onald) V(erlin) 1919- . . . **CLC 4, 23**
See also CA 9-12R; CAAS 1; CANR 7;
DLB 6

Cassity, (Allen) Turner 1929- . . . . **CLC 6, 42**
See also CA 17-20R; CAAS 8; CANR 11;
DLB 105

Castaneda, Carlos 1931(?)- . . . . **CLC 12**
See also CA 25-28R; CANR 32; HW;
MTCW

Castedo, Elena 1937- . . . . **CLC 65**
See also CA 132

Castedo-Ellerman, Elena
See Castedo, Elena

Castellanos, Rosario 1925-1974 . . . . . **CLC 66**
See also CA 131; 53-56; DLB 113; HW

Castelvetro, Lodovico 1505-1571 . . . . . **LC 12**

Castiglione, Baldassare 1478-1529 . . . **LC 12**

Castle, Robert
See Hamilton, Edmond

Castro, Guillen de 1569-1631 . . . . **LC 19**

Castro, Rosalia de 1837-1885 . . . . . **NCLC 3**

Cather, Willa
See Cather, Willa Sibert

Cather, Willa Sibert
1873-1947 . . . . . . **TCLC 1, 11, 31; SSC 2**
See also CA 104; 128; CDALB 1865-1917;
DA; DLB 9, 54, 78; DLBD 1; MTCW;
SATA 30; WLC

Catton, (Charles) Bruce
1899-1978 . . . . **CLC 35**
See also AITN 1; CA 5-8R; 81-84;
CANR 7; DLB 17; SATA 2, 24

Cauldwell, Frank
See King, Francis (Henry)

Caunitz, William J. 1933- . . . . **CLC 34**
See also BEST 89:3; CA 125; 130

Causley, Charles (Stanley) 1917- . . . . . **CLC 7**
See also CA 9-12R; CANR 5, 35; CLR 30;
DLB 27; MTCW; SATA 3, 66

Caute, David 1936-.............. **CLC 29**
See also CA 1-4R; CAAS 4; CANR 1, 33;
DLB 14

Cavafy, C(onstantine) P(eter)...... **TCLC 2, 7**
See also Kavafis, Konstantinos Petrou

Cavallo, Evelyn
See Spark, Muriel (Sarah)

Cavanna, Betty .... **CLC 12**
See also Harrison, Elizabeth Cavanna
See also MAICYA; SAAS 4; SATA 1, 30

Caxton, William 1421(?)-1491(?)..... **LC 17**

Cayrol, Jean 1911-.............. **CLC 11**
See also CA 89-92; DLB 83

Cela, Camilo Jose 1916-...... **CLC 4, 13, 59**
See also BEST 90:2; CA 21-24R; CAAS 10;
CANR 21, 32; DLBY 89; HW; MTCW

Celan, Paul .... **CLC 53**
See also Antschel, Paul
See also DLB 69

Celine, Louis-Ferdinand
.... **CLC 1, 3, 4, 7, 9, 15, 47**
See also Destouches, Louis-Ferdinand
See also DLB 72

Cellini, Benvenuto 1500-1571 .... **LC 7**

Cendrars, Blaise
See Sauser-Hall, Frederic

Cernuda (y Bidon), Luis
1902-1963 .... **CLC 54**
See also CA 131; 89-92; HW

Cervantes (Saavedra), Miguel de
1547-1616 .... **LC 6, 23; SSC 12**
See also DA; WLC

Cesaire, Aime (Fernand) 1913-.. **CLC 19, 32**
See also BLC 1; BW; CA 65-68; CANR 24;
MTCW

Chabon, Michael 1965(?)- .... **CLC 55**
See also CA 139

Chabrol, Claude 1930-........... **CLC 16**
See also CA 110

Challans, Mary 1905-1983
See Renault, Mary
See also CA 81-84; 111; SATA 23, 36

Challis, George
See Faust, Frederick (Schiller)

Chambers, Aidan 1934-........... **CLC 35**
See also CA 25-28R; CANR 12, 31;
MAICYA; SAAS 12; SATA 1, 69

Chambers, James 1948-
See Cliff, Jimmy
See also CA 124

Chambers, Jessie
See Lawrence, D(avid) H(erbert Richards)

Chambers, Robert W. 1865-1933... **TCLC 41**

Chandler, Raymond (Thornton)
1888-1959 .... **TCLC 1, 7**
See also CA 104; 129; CDALB 1929-1941;
DLBD 6; MTCW

Chang, Jung 1952-.............. **CLC 71**

Channing, William Ellery
1780-1842 .... **NCLC 17**
See also DLB 1, 59

Chaplin, Charles Spencer
1889-1977 .... **CLC 16**
See also Chaplin, Charlie
See also CA 81-84; 73-76

Chaplin, Charlie
See Chaplin, Charles Spencer
See also DLB 44

Chapman, George 1559(?)-1634...... **LC 22**
See also DLB 62, 121

Chapman, Graham 1941-1989 ...... **CLC 21**
See also Monty Python
See also CA 116; 129; CANR 35

Chapman, John Jay 1862-1933 ..... **TCLC 7**
See also CA 104

Chapman, Walker
See Silverberg, Robert

Chappell, Fred (Davis) 1936-.... **CLC 40, 78**
See also CA 5-8R; CAAS 4; CANR 8, 33;
DLB 6, 105

Char, Rene(-Emile)
1907-1988 .... **CLC 9, 11, 14, 55**
See also CA 13-16R; 124; CANR 32;
MTCW

Charby, Jay
See Ellison, Harlan

Chardin, Pierre Teilhard de
See Teilhard de Chardin, (Marie Joseph)
Pierre

Charles I 1600-1649 .... **LC 13**

Charyn, Jerome 1937-........ **CLC 5, 8, 18**
See also CA 5-8R; CAAS 1; CANR 7;
DLBY 83; MTCW

Chase, Mary (Coyle) 1907-1981 ...... **DC 1**
See also CA 77-80; 105; SATA 17, 29

Chase, Mary Ellen 1887-1973....... **CLC 2**
See also CA 13-16; 41-44R; CAP 1;
SATA 10

Chase, Nicholas
See Hyde, Anthony

Chateaubriand, Francois Rene de
1768-1848 .... **NCLC 3**
See also DLB 119

Chatterje, Sarat Chandra 1876-1936(?)
See Chatterji, Saratchandra
See also CA 109

Chatterji, Bankim Chandra
1838-1894 .... **NCLC 19**

Chatterji, Saratchandra .... **TCLC 13**
See also Chatterje, Sarat Chandra

Chatterton, Thomas 1752-1770 .... **LC 3**
See also DLB 109

Chatwin, (Charles) Bruce
1940-1989 .... **CLC 28, 57, 59**
See also AAYA 4; BEST 90:1; CA 85-88;
127

Chaucer, Daniel
See Ford, Ford Madox

Chaucer, Geoffrey 1340(?)-1400 ..... **LC 17**
See also CDBLB Before 1660; DA

Chaviaras, Strates 1935-
See Haviaras, Stratis
See also CA 105

Chayefsky, Paddy .... **CLC 23**
See also Chayefsky, Sidney
See also DLB 7, 44; DLBY 81

Chayefsky, Sidney 1923-1981
See Chayefsky, Paddy
See also CA 9-12R; 104; CANR 18

Chedid, Andree 1920-............ **CLC 47**

Cheever, John
1912-1982 ...... **CLC 3, 7, 8, 11, 15, 25,
64; SSC 1**
See also CA 5-8R; 106; CABS 1; CANR 5,
27; CDALB 1941-1968; DA; DLB 2, 102;
DLBY 80, 82; MTCW; WLC

Cheever, Susan 1943-.......... **CLC 18, 48**
See also CA 103; CANR 27; DLBY 82

Chekhonte, Antosha
See Chekhov, Anton (Pavlovich)

Chekhov, Anton (Pavlovich)
1860-1904 ...... **TCLC 3, 10, 31; SSC 2**
See also CA 104; 124; DA; WLC

Chernyshevsky, Nikolay Gavrilovich
1828-1889 .... **NCLC 1**

Cherry, Carolyn Janice 1942-
See Cherryh, C. J.
See also CA 65-68; CANR 10

Cherryh, C. J. .... **CLC 35**
See also Cherry, Carolyn Janice
See also DLBY 80

Chesnutt, Charles W(addell)
1858-1932 .... **TCLC 5, 39; SSC 7**
See also BLC 1; BW; CA 106; 125; DLB 12,
50, 78; MTCW

Chester, Alfred 1929(?)-1971....... **CLC 49**
See also CA 33-36R; DLB 130

Chesterton, G(ilbert) K(eith)
1874-1936 .... **TCLC 1, 6; SSC 1**
See also CA 104; 132; CDBLB 1914-1945;
DLB 10, 19, 34, 70, 98; MTCW;
SATA 27

Chiang Pin-chin 1904-1986
See Ding Ling
See also CA 118

Ch'ien Chung-shu 1910-........... **CLC 22**
See also CA 130; MTCW

Child, L. Maria
See Child, Lydia Maria

Child, Lydia Maria 1802-1880 .... **NCLC 6**
See also DLB 1, 74; SATA 67

Child, Mrs.
See Child, Lydia Maria

Child, Philip 1898-1978 .... **CLC 19, 68**
See also CA 13-14; CAP 1; SATA 47

Childress, Alice 1920-.......... **CLC 12, 15**
See also AAYA 8; BLC 1; BW; CA 45-48;
CANR 3, 27; CLR 14; DLB 7, 38;
MAICYA; MTCW; SATA 7, 48

Chislett, (Margaret) Anne 1943-.... **CLC 34**

Chitty, Thomas Willes 1926-....... **CLC 11**
See also Hinde, Thomas
See also CA 5-8R

Chomette, Rene Lucien 1898-1981 .. **CLC 20**
See also Clair, Rene
See also CA 103

Chopin, Kate .... TCLC 5, 14; SSC 8
See also Chopin, Katherine
See also CDALB 1865-1917; DA; DLB 12, 78

Chopin, Katherine 1851-1904
See Chopin, Kate
See also CA 104; 122

Chretien de Troyes
c. 12th cent. - .... CMLC 10

Christie
See Ichikawa, Kon

Christie, Agatha (Mary Clarissa)
1890-1976 ...... CLC 1, 6, 8, 12, 39, 48
See also AAYA 9; AITN 1, 2; CA 17-20R;
61-64; CANR 10, 37; CDBLB 1914-1945;
DLB 13, 77; MTCW; SATA 36

Christie, (Ann) Philippa
See Pearce, Philippa
See also CA 5-8R; CANR 4

Christine de Pizan 1365(?)-1431(?) .... LC 9

Chubb, Elmer
See Masters, Edgar Lee

Chulkov, Mikhail Dmitrievich
1743-1792 .... LC 2

Churchill, Caryl 1938- .... CLC 31, 55
See also CA 102; CANR 22; DLB 13;
MTCW

Churchill, Charles 1731-1764........ LC 3
See also DLB 109

Chute, Carolyn 1947- .... CLC 39
See also CA 123

Ciardi, John (Anthony)
1916-1986 .... CLC 10, 40, 44
See also CA 5-8R; 118; CAAS 2; CANR 5,
33; CLR 19; DLB 5; DLBY 86;
MAICYA; MTCW; SATA 1, 46, 65

Cicero, Marcus Tullius
106B.C.-43B.C................ CMLC 3

Cimino, Michael 1943- .... CLC 16
See also CA 105

Cioran, E(mil) M. 1911-........... CLC 64
See also CA 25-28R

Cisneros, Sandra 1954-........... CLC 69
See also AAYA 9; CA 131; DLB 122; HW

Clair, Rene..................... CLC 20
See also Chomette, Rene Lucien

Clampitt, Amy 1920- .... CLC 32
See also CA 110; CANR 29; DLB 105

Clancy, Thomas L., Jr. 1947-
See Clancy, Tom
See also CA 125; 131; MTCW

Clancy, Tom.................... CLC 45
See also Clancy, Thomas L., Jr.
See also AAYA 9; BEST 89:1, 90:1

Clare, John 1793-1864........... NCLC 9
See also DLB 55, 96

Clarin
See Alas (y Urena), Leopoldo (Enrique
Garcia)

Clark, (Robert) Brian 1932-........ CLC 29
See also CA 41-44R

Clark, Eleanor 1913- .... CLC 5, 19
See also CA 9-12R; CANR 41; DLB 6

Clark, J. P.
See Clark, John Pepper
See also DLB 117

Clark, John Pepper 1935- .... CLC 38
See also Clark, J. P.
See also BLC 1; BW; CA 65-68; CANR 16

Clark, M. R.
See Clark, Mavis Thorpe

Clark, Mavis Thorpe 1909- .... CLC 12
See also CA 57-60; CANR 8, 37; CLR 30;
MAICYA; SAAS 5; SATA 8, 74

Clark, Walter Van Tilburg
1909-1971 .... CLC 28
See also CA 9-12R; 33-36R; DLB 9;
SATA 8

Clarke, Arthur C(harles)
1917- ...... CLC 1, 4, 13, 18, 35; SSC 3
See also AAYA 4; CA 1-4R; CANR 2, 28;
MAICYA; MTCW; SATA 13, 70

Clarke, Austin 1896-1974........ CLC 6, 9
See also CA 29-32; 49-52; CAP 2; DLB 10,
20

Clarke, Austin C(hesterfield)
1934- .... CLC 8, 53
See also BLC 1; BW; CA 25-28R;
CAAS 16; CANR 14, 32; DLB 53, 125

Clarke, Gillian 1937- .... CLC 61
See also CA 106; DLB 40

Clarke, Marcus (Andrew Hislop)
1846-1881 .... NCLC 19

Clarke, Shirley 1925-............ CLC 16

Clash, The .... CLC 30
See also Headon, (Nicky) Topper; Jones,
Mick; Simonon, Paul; Strummer, Joe

Claudel, Paul (Louis Charles Marie)
1868-1955 .... TCLC 2, 10
See also CA 104

Clavell, James (duMaresq)
1925- .... CLC 6, 25
See also CA 25-28R; CANR 26; MTCW

Cleaver, (Leroy) Eldridge 1935- .... CLC 30
See also BLC 1; BW; CA 21-24R;
CANR 16

Cleese, John (Marwood) 1939- ..... CLC 21
See also Monty Python
See also CA 112; 116; CANR 35; MTCW

Cleishbotham, Jebediah
See Scott, Walter

Cleland, John 1710-1789 .... LC 2
See also DLB 39

Clemens, Samuel Langhorne 1835-1910
See Twain, Mark
See also CA 104; 135; CDALB 1865-1917;
DA; DLB 11, 12, 23, 64, 74; MAICYA;
YABC 2

Cleophil
See Congreve, William

Clerihew, E.
See Bentley, E(dmund) C(lerihew)

Clerk, N. W.
See Lewis, C(live) S(taples)

Cliff, Jimmy..................... CLC 21
See also Chambers, James

Clifton, (Thelma) Lucille
1936- .... CLC 19, 66
See also BLC 1; BW; CA 49-52; CANR 2,
24; CLR 5; DLB 5, 41; MAICYA;
MTCW; SATA 20, 69

Clinton, Dirk
See Silverberg, Robert

Clough, Arthur Hugh 1819-1861.. NCLC 27
See also DLB 32

Clutha, Janet Paterson Frame 1924-
See Frame, Janet
See also CA 1-4R; CANR 2, 36; MTCW

Clyne, Terence
See Blatty, William Peter

Cobalt, Martin
See Mayne, William (James Carter)

Coburn, D(onald) L(ee) 1938- ...... CLC 10
See also CA 89-92

Cocteau, Jean (Maurice Eugene Clement)
1889-1963 ...... CLC 1, 8, 15, 16, 43
See also CA 25-28; CANR 40; CAP 2; DA;
DLB 65; MTCW; WLC

Codrescu, Andrei 1946- .... CLC 46
See also CA 33-36R; CANR 13, 34

Coe, Max
See Bourne, Randolph S(illiman)

Coe, Tucker
See Westlake, Donald E(dwin)

Coetzee, J(ohn) M(ichael)
1940- .... CLC 23, 33, 66
See also CA 77-80; CANR 41; MTCW

Coffey, Brian
See Koontz, Dean R(ay)

Cohen, Arthur A(llen)
1928-1986 .... CLC 7, 31
See also CA 1-4R; 120; CANR 1, 17;
DLB 28

Cohen, Leonard (Norman)
1934- .... CLC 3, 38
See also CA 21-24R; CANR 14; DLB 53;
MTCW

Cohen, Matt 1942-................ CLC 19
See also CA 61-64; CANR 40; DLB 53

Cohen-Solal, Annie 19(?)- .... CLC 50

Colegate, Isabel 1931- .... CLC 36
See also CA 17-20R; CANR 8, 22; DLB 14;
MTCW

Coleman, Emmett
See Reed, Ishmael

Coleridge, Samuel Taylor
1772-1834 .... NCLC 9
See also CDBLB 1789-1832; DA; DLB 93,
107; WLC

Coleridge, Sara 1802-1852....... NCLC 31

Coles, Don 1928- .... CLC 46
See also CA 115; CANR 38

Colette, (Sidonie-Gabrielle)
1873-1954 ...... TCLC 1, 5, 16; SSC 10
See also CA 104; 131; DLB 65; MTCW

Collett, (Jacobine) Camilla (Wergeland)
1813-1895 .... NCLC 22

Collier, Christopher 1930-........ CLC 30
See also CA 33-36R; CANR 13, 33;
MAICYA; SATA 16, 70

Cowper, William 1731-1800...... NCLC 8
See also DLB 104, 109

Cox, William Trevor 1928- ... CLC 9, 14, 71
See also Trevor, William
See also CA 9-12R; CANR 4, 37; DLB 14;
MTCW

Cozzens, James Gould
1903-1978 .... CLC 1, 4, 11
See also CA 9-12R; 81-84; CANR 19;
CDALB 1941-1968; DLB 9; DLBD 2;
DLBY 84; MTCW

Crabbe, George 1754-1832...... NCLC 26
See also DLB 93

Craig, A. A.
See Anderson, Poul (William)

Craik, Dinah Maria (Mulock)
1826-1887 .... NCLC 38
See also DLB 35; MAICYA; SATA 34

Cram, Ralph Adams 1863-1942.... TCLC 45

Crane, (Harold) Hart
1899-1932 .... TCLC 2, 5; PC 3
See also CA 104; 127; CDALB 1917-1929;
DA; DLB 4, 48; MTCW; WLC

Crane, R(onald) S(almon)
1886-1967 .... CLC 27
See also CA 85-88; DLB 63

Crane, Stephen (Townley)
1871-1900 ..... TCLC 11, 17, 32; SSC 7
See also CA 109; 140; CDALB 1865-1917;
DA; DLB 12, 54, 78; WLC; YABC 2

Crase, Douglas 1944- .... CLC 58
See also CA 106

Craven, Margaret 1901-1980...... CLC 17
See also CA 103

Crawford, F(rancis) Marion
1854-1909 .... TCLC 10
See also CA 107; DLB 71

Crawford, Isabella Valancy
1850-1887 .... NCLC 12
See also DLB 92

Crayon, Geoffrey
See Irving, Washington

Creasey, John 1908-1973.......... CLC 11
See also CA 5-8R; 41-44R; CANR 8;
DLB 77; MTCW

Crebillon, Claude Prosper Jolyot de (fils)
1707-1777 .... LC 1

Credo
See Creasey, John

Creeley, Robert (White)
1926- ..... CLC 1, 2, 4, 8, 11, 15, 36, 78
See also CA 1-4R; CAAS 10; CANR 23;
DLB 5, 16; MTCW

Crews, Harry (Eugene)
1935- .... CLC 6, 23, 49
See also AITN 1; CA 25-28R; CANR 20;
DLB 6; MTCW

Crichton, (John) Michael
1942- .... CLC 2, 6, 54
See also AAYA 10; AITN 2; CA 25-28R;
CANR 13, 40; DLBY 81; MTCW;
SATA 9

Crispin, Edmund .... CLC 22
See also Montgomery, (Robert) Bruce
See also DLB 87

Cristofer, Michael 1945(?)- .... CLC 28
See also CA 110; DLB 7

Croce, Benedetto 1866-1952 ...... TCLC 37
See also CA 120

Crockett, David 1786-1836 .... NCLC 8
See also DLB 3, 11

Crockett, Davy
See Crockett, David

Croker, John Wilson 1780-1857 .. NCLC 10
See also DLB 110

Crommelynck, Fernand 1885-1970 .. CLC 75
See also CA 89-92

Cronin, A(rchibald) J(oseph)
1896-1981 .... CLC 32
See also CA 1-4R; 102; CANR 5; SATA 25,
47

Cross, Amanda
See Heilbrun, Carolyn G(old)

Crothers, Rachel 1878(?)-1958..... TCLC 19
See also CA 113; DLB 7

Croves, Hal
See Traven, B.

Crowfield, Christopher
See Stowe, Harriet (Elizabeth) Beecher

Crowley, Aleister................. TCLC 7
See also Crowley, Edward Alexander

Crowley, Edward Alexander 1875-1947
See Crowley, Aleister
See also CA 104

Crowley, John 1942-.............. CLC 57
See also CA 61-64; DLBY 82; SATA 65

Crud
See Crumb, R(obert)

Crumarums
See Crumb, R(obert)

Crumb, R(obert) 1943-............. CLC 17
See also CA 106

Crumbum
See Crumb, R(obert)

Crumski
See Crumb, R(obert)

Crum the Bum
See Crumb, R(obert)

Crunk
See Crumb, R(obert)

Crustt
See Crumb, R(obert)

Cryer, Gretchen (Kiger) 1935-...... CLC 21
See also CA 114; 123

Csath, Geza 1887-1919.......... TCLC 13
See also CA 111

Cudlip, David 1933-............. CLC 34

Cullen, Countee 1903-1946 ..... TCLC 4, 37
See also BLC 1; BW; CA 108; 124;
CDALB 1917-1929; DA; DLB 4, 48, 51;
MTCW; SATA 18

Cum, R.
See Crumb, R(obert)

Cummings, Bruce F(rederick) 1889-1919
See Barbellion, W. N. P.
See also CA 123

Cummings, E(dward) E(stlin)
1894-1962 ...... CLC 1, 3, 8, 12, 15, 68;
PC 5
See also CA 73-76; CANR 31;
CDALB 1929-1941; DA; DLB 4, 48;
MTCW; WLC 2

Cunha, Euclides (Rodrigues Pimenta) da
1866-1909 .... TCLC 24
See also CA 123

Cunningham, E. V.
See Fast, Howard (Melvin)

Cunningham, J(ames) V(incent)
1911-1985 .... CLC 3, 31
See also CA 1-4R; 115; CANR 1; DLB 5

Cunningham, Julia (Woolfolk)
1916- .... CLC 12
See also CA 9-12R; CANR 4, 19, 36;
MAICYA; SAAS 2; SATA 1, 26

Cunningham, Michael 1952- .... CLC 34
See also CA 136

Cunninghame Graham, R(obert) B(ontine)
1852-1936 .... TCLC 19
See also Graham, R(obert) B(ontine)
Cunninghame
See also CA 119; DLB 98

Currie, Ellen 19(?)-............... CLC 44

Curtin, Philip
See Lowndes, Marie Adelaide (Belloc)

Curtis, Price
See Ellison, Harlan

Cutrate, Joe
See Spiegelman, Art

Czaczkes, Shmuel Yosef
See Agnon, S(hmuel) Y(osef Halevi)

D. P.
See Wells, H(erbert) G(eorge)

Dabrowska, Maria (Szumska)
1889-1965 .... CLC 15
See also CA 106

Dabydeen, David 1955- .... CLC 34
See also BW; CA 125

Dacey, Philip 1939- .... CLC 51
See also CA 37-40R; CAAS 17; CANR 14,
32; DLB 105

Dagerman, Stig (Halvard)
1923-1954 .... TCLC 17
See also CA 117

Dahl, Roald 1916-1990..... CLC 1, 6, 18, 79
See also CA 1-4R; 133; CANR 6, 32, 37;
CLR 1, 7; MAICYA; MTCW; SATA 1,
26, 73; SATA-Obit 65

Dahlberg, Edward 1900-1977... CLC 1, 7, 14
See also CA 9-12R; 69-72; CANR 31;
DLB 48; MTCW

Dale, Colin................... TCLC 18
See also Lawrence, T(homas) E(dward)

Dale, George E.
See Asimov, Isaac

Daly, Elizabeth 1878-1967........ CLC 52
See also CA 23-24; 25-28R; CAP 2

Daly, Maureen 1921-............. CLC 17
See also AAYA 5; CANR 37; MAICYA;
SAAS 1; SATA 2

Daniels, Brett
See Adler, Renata

De Marinis, Rick   1934- . . . .   **CLC 54**
    See also CA 57-60; CANR 9, 25

Demby, William   1922- . . . .   **CLC 53**
    See also BLC 1; BW; CA 81-84; DLB 33

Demijohn, Thom
    See Disch, Thomas M(ichael)

de Montherlant, Henry (Milon)
    See Montherlant, Henry (Milon) de

de Natale, Francine
    See Malzberg, Barry N(athaniel)

Denby, Edwin (Orr)   1903-1983 . . . . .   **CLC 48**
    See also CA 138; 110

Denis, Julio
    See Cortazar, Julio

Denmark, Harrison
    See Zelazny, Roger (Joseph)

Dennis, John   1658-1734 . . . .   **LC 11**
    See also DLB 101

Dennis, Nigel (Forbes)   1912-1989 . . . .   **CLC 8**
    See also CA 25-28R; 129; DLB 13, 15;
    MTCW

De Palma, Brian (Russell)   1940- . . . .   **CLC 20**
    See also CA 109

De Quincey, Thomas   1785-1859 . . .   **NCLC 4**
    See also CDBLB 1789-1832; DLB 110

Deren, Eleanora   1908(?)-1961
    See Deren, Maya
    See also CA 111

Deren, Maya . . . .   **CLC 16**
    See also Deren, Eleanora

Derleth, August (William)
    1909-1971 . . . .   **CLC 31**
    See also CA 1-4R; 29-32R; CANR 4;
    DLB 9; SATA 5

de Routisie, Albert
    See Aragon, Louis

Derrida, Jacques   1930- . . . .   **CLC 24**
    See also CA 124; 127

Derry Down Derry
    See Lear, Edward

Dersonnes, Jacques
    See Simenon, Georges (Jacques Christian)

Desai, Anita   1937- . . . .   **CLC 19, 37**
    See also CA 81-84; CANR 33; MTCW;
    SATA 63

de Saint-Luc, Jean
    See Glassco, John

de Saint Roman, Arnaud
    See Aragon, Louis

Descartes, Rene   1596-1650 . . . .   **LC 20**

De Sica, Vittorio   1901(?)-1974 . . . . .   **CLC 20**
    See also CA 117

Desnos, Robert   1900-1945 . . . .   **TCLC 22**
    See also CA 121

Destouches, Louis-Ferdinand
    1894-1961 . . . .   **CLC 9, 15**
    See also Celine, Louis-Ferdinand
    See also CA 85-88; CANR 28; MTCW

Deutsch, Babette   1895-1982 . . . .   **CLC 18**
    See also CA 1-4R; 108; CANR 4; DLB 45;
    SATA 1, 33

Devenant, William   1606-1649 . . . . . .   **LC 13**

Devkota, Laxmiprasad
    1909-1959 . . . .   **TCLC 23**
    See also CA 123

De Voto, Bernard (Augustine)
    1897-1955 . . . .   **TCLC 29**
    See also CA 113; DLB 9

De Vries, Peter
    1910- . . . .   **CLC 1, 2, 3, 7, 10, 28, 46**
    See also CA 17-20R; CANR 41; DLB 6;
    DLBY 82; MTCW

Dexter, Martin
    See Faust, Frederick (Schiller)

Dexter, Pete   1943- . . . .   **CLC 34, 55**
    See also BEST 89:2; CA 127; 131; MTCW

Diamano, Silmang
    See Senghor, Leopold Sedar

Diamond, Neil   1941- . . . .   **CLC 30**
    See also CA 108

di Bassetto, Corno
    See Shaw, George Bernard

Dick, Philip K(indred)
    1928-1982 . . . .   **CLC 10, 30, 72**
    See also CA 49-52; 106; CANR 2, 16;
    DLB 8; MTCW

Dickens, Charles (John Huffam)
    1812-1870 . . . .   **NCLC 3, 8, 18, 26**
    See also CDBLB 1832-1890; DA; DLB 21,
    55, 70; MAICYA; SATA 15

Dickey, James (Lafayette)
    1923- . . . .   **CLC 1, 2, 4, 7, 10, 15, 47**
    See also AITN 1, 2; CA 9-12R; CABS 2;
    CANR 10; CDALB 1968-1988; DLB 5;
    DLBD 7; DLBY 82; MTCW

Dickey, William   1928- . . . .   **CLC 3, 28**
    See also CA 9-12R; CANR 24; DLB 5

Dickinson, Charles   1951- . . . .   **CLC 49**
    See also CA 128

Dickinson, Emily (Elizabeth)
    1830-1886 . . . .   **NCLC 21; PC 1**
    See also CDALB 1865-1917; DA; DLB 1;
    SATA 29; WLC

Dickinson, Peter (Malcolm)
    1927- . . . .   **CLC 12, 35**
    See also AAYA 9; CA 41-44R; CANR 31;
    CLR 29; DLB 87; MAICYA; SATA 5, 62

Dickson, Carr
    See Carr, John Dickson

Dickson, Carter
    See Carr, John Dickson

Didion, Joan   1934- . . . . .   **CLC 1, 3, 8, 14, 32**
    See also AITN 1; CA 5-8R; CANR 14;
    CDALB 1968-1988; DLB 2; DLBY 81,
    86; MTCW

Dietrich, Robert
    See Hunt, E(verette) Howard, Jr.

Dillard, Annie   1945- . . . .   **CLC 9, 60**
    See also AAYA 6; CA 49-52; CANR 3;
    DLBY 80; MTCW; SATA 10

Dillard, R(ichard) H(enry) W(ilde)
    1937- . . . .   **CLC 5**
    See also CA 21-24R; CAAS 7; CANR 10;
    DLB 5

Dillon, Eilis   1920- . . . .   **CLC 17**
    See also CA 9-12R; CAAS 3; CANR 4, 38;
    CLR 26; MAICYA; SATA 2, 74

Dimont, Penelope
    See Mortimer, Penelope (Ruth)

Dinesen, Isak . . . .   **CLC 10, 29; SSC 7**
    See also Blixen, Karen (Christentze
    Dinesen)

Ding Ling . . . .   **CLC 68**
    See also Chiang Pin-chin

Disch, Thomas M(ichael)   1940- . . .   **CLC 7, 36**
    See also CA 21-24R; CAAS 4; CANR 17,
    36; CLR 18; DLB 8; MAICYA; MTCW;
    SAAS 15; SATA 54

Disch, Tom
    See Disch, Thomas M(ichael)

d'Isly, Georges
    See Simenon, Georges (Jacques Christian)

Disraeli, Benjamin   1804-1881 . .   **NCLC 2, 39**
    See also DLB 21, 55

Ditcum, Steve
    See Crumb, R(obert)

Dixon, Paige
    See Corcoran, Barbara

Dixon, Stephen   1936- . . . .   **CLC 52**
    See also CA 89-92; CANR 17, 40; DLB 130

Doblin, Alfred . . . .   **TCLC 13**
    See also Doeblin, Alfred

Dobrolyubov, Nikolai Alexandrovich
    1836-1861 . . . .   **NCLC 5**

Dobyns, Stephen   1941- . . . .   **CLC 37**
    See also CA 45-48; CANR 2, 18

Doctorow, E(dgar) L(aurence)
    1931- . . . . .   **CLC 6, 11, 15, 18, 37, 44, 65**
    See also AITN 2; BEST 89:3; CA 45-48;
    CANR 2, 33; CDALB 1968-1988; DLB 2,
    28; DLBY 80; MTCW

Dodgson, Charles Lutwidge   1832-1898
    See Carroll, Lewis
    See also CLR 2; DA; MAICYA; YABC 2

Dodson, Owen (Vincent)
    1914-1983 . . . .   **CLC 79**
    See also BLC 1; BW; CA 65-68; 110;
    CANR 24; DLB 76

Doeblin, Alfred   1878-1957 . . . .   **TCLC 13**
    See also Doblin, Alfred
    See also CA 110; DLB 66

Doerr, Harriet   1910- . . . .   **CLC 34**
    See also CA 117; 122

Domecq, H(onorio) Bustos
    See Bioy Casares, Adolfo; Borges, Jorge
    Luis

Domini, Rey
    See Lorde, Audre (Geraldine)

Dominique
    See Proust, (Valentin-Louis-George-Eugene-)
    Marcel

Don, A
    See Stephen, Leslie

Donaldson, Stephen R.   1947- . . . . . .   **CLC 46**
    See also CA 89-92; CANR 13

Donleavy, J(ames) P(atrick)
    1926- . . . .   **CLC 1, 4, 6, 10, 45**
    See also AITN 2; CA 9-12R; CANR 24;
    DLB 6; MTCW

Dunlap, William 1766-1839 . . . . . . NCLC 2
See also DLB 30, 37, 59

Dunn, Douglas (Eaglesham)
1942- . . . . CLC 6, 40
See also CA 45-48; CANR 2, 33; DLB 40;
MTCW

Dunn, Katherine (Karen) 1945- . . . . . CLC 71
See also CA 33-36R

Dunn, Stephen 1939- . . . . CLC 36
See also CA 33-36R; CANR 12; DLB 105

Dunne, Finley Peter 1867-1936. . . . TCLC 28
See also CA 108; DLB 11, 23

Dunne, John Gregory 1932- . . . . CLC 28
See also CA 25-28R; CANR 14; DLBY 80

**Dunsany, Edward John Moreton Drax
Plunkett** 1878-1957
See Dunsany, Lord; Lord Dunsany
See also CA 104; DLB 10

Dunsany, Lord . . . . TCLC 2
See also Dunsany, Edward John Moreton
Drax Plunkett
See also DLB 77

du Perry, Jean
See Simenon, Georges (Jacques Christian)

Durang, Christopher (Ferdinand)
1949- . . . . CLC 27, 38
See also CA 105

Duras, Marguerite
1914- . . . . . . CLC 3, 6, 11, 20, 34, 40, 68
See also CA 25-28R; DLB 83; MTCW

Durban, (Rosa) Pam 1947- . . . . CLC 39
See also CA 123

Durcan, Paul 1944- . . . . CLC 43, 70
See also CA 134

Durrell, Lawrence (George)
1912-1990 . . . . CLC 1, 4, 6, 8, 13, 27, 41
See also CA 9-12R; 132; CANR 40;
CDBLB 1945-1960; DLB 15, 27;
DLBY 90; MTCW

Durrenmatt, Friedrich
. . . . CLC 1, 4, 8, 11, 15, 43
See also Duerrenmatt, Friedrich
See also DLB 69, 124

Dutt, Toru 1856-1877. . . . . NCLC 29

Dwight, Timothy 1752-1817 . . . . . . NCLC 13
See also DLB 37

Dworkin, Andrea 1946- . . . . CLC 43
See also CA 77-80; CANR 16, 39; MTCW

Dwyer, Deanna
See Koontz, Dean R(ay)

Dwyer, K. R.
See Koontz, Dean R(ay)

Dylan, Bob 1941- . . . . . . CLC 3, 4, 6, 12, 77
See also CA 41-44R; DLB 16

Eagleton, Terence (Francis) 1943-
See Eagleton, Terry
See also CA 57-60; CANR 7, 23; MTCW

Eagleton, Terry . . . . CLC 63
See also Eagleton, Terence (Francis)

Early, Jack
See Scoppettone, Sandra

East, Michael
See West, Morris L(anglo)

Eastaway, Edward
See Thomas, (Philip) Edward

Eastlake, William (Derry) 1917- . . . . . CLC 8
See also CA 5-8R; CAAS 1; CANR 5;
DLB 6

Eberhart, Richard (Ghormley)
1904- . . . . CLC 3, 11, 19, 56
See also CA 1-4R; CANR 2;
CDALB 1941-1968; DLB 48; MTCW

Eberstadt, Fernanda 1960- . . . . CLC 39
See also CA 136

Echegaray (y Eizaguirre), Jose (Maria Waldo)
1832-1916 . . . . TCLC 4
See also CA 104; CANR 32; HW; MTCW

Echeverria, (Jose) Esteban (Antonino)
1805-1851 . . . . NCLC 18

Echo
See Proust, (Valentin-Louis-George-Eugene-)
Marcel

Eckert, Allan W. 1931- . . . . CLC 17
See also CA 13-16R; CANR 14; SATA 27,
29

Eckhart, Meister 1260(?)-1328(?) . . CMLC 9
See also DLB 115

Eckmar, F. R.
See de Hartog, Jan

Eco, Umberto 1932- . . . . CLC 28, 60
See also BEST 90:1; CA 77-80; CANR 12,
33; MTCW

Eddison, E(ric) R(ucker)
1882-1945 . . . . TCLC 15
See also CA 109

Edel, (Joseph) Leon 1907- . . . . . . CLC 29, 34
See also CA 1-4R; CANR 1, 22; DLB 103

Eden, Emily 1797-1869 . . . . NCLC 10

Edgar, David 1948- . . . . CLC 42
See also CA 57-60; CANR 12; DLB 13;
MTCW

Edgerton, Clyde (Carlyle) 1944- . . . . CLC 39
See also CA 118; 134

Edgeworth, Maria 1767-1849 . . . . . . NCLC 1
See also DLB 116; SATA 21

Edmonds, Paul
See Kuttner, Henry

Edmonds, Walter D(umaux) 1903- . . CLC 35
See also CA 5-8R; CANR 2; DLB 9;
MAICYA; SAAS 4; SATA 1, 27

Edmondson, Wallace
See Ellison, Harlan

Edson, Russell . . . . CLC 13
See also CA 33-36R

Edwards, G(erald) B(asil)
1899-1976 . . . . CLC 25
See also CA 110

Edwards, Gus 1939- . . . . CLC 43
See also CA 108

Edwards, Jonathan 1703-1758 . . . . LC 7
See also DA; DLB 24

Efron, Marina Ivanovna Tsvetaeva
See Tsvetaeva (Efron), Marina (Ivanovna)

Ehle, John (Marsden, Jr.) 1925- . . . . CLC 27
See also CA 9-12R

Ehrenbourg, Ilya (Grigoryevich)
See Ehrenburg, Ilya (Grigoryevich)

Ehrenburg, Ilya (Grigoryevich)
1891-1967 . . . . CLC 18, 34, 62
See also CA 102; 25-28R

Ehrenburg, Ilyo (Grigoryevich)
See Ehrenburg, Ilya (Grigoryevich)

Eich, Guenter 1907-1972 . . . . CLC 15
See also CA 111; 93-96; DLB 69, 124

Eichendorff, Joseph Freiherr von
1788-1857 . . . . NCLC 8
See also DLB 90

Eigner, Larry . . . . CLC 9
See also Eigner, Laurence (Joel)
See also DLB 5

Eigner, Laurence (Joel) 1927-
See Eigner, Larry
See also CA 9-12R; CANR 6

Eiseley, Loren Corey 1907-1977 . . . . . CLC 7
See also AAYA 5; CA 1-4R; 73-76;
CANR 6

Eisenstadt, Jill 1963- . . . . CLC 50
See also CA 140

Eisner, Simon
See Kornbluth, C(yril) M.

Ekeloef, (Bengt) Gunnar
1907-1968 . . . . CLC 27
See also Ekelof, (Bengt) Gunnar
See also CA 123; 25-28R

Ekelof, (Bengt) Gunnar . . . . CLC 27
See also Ekeloef, (Bengt) Gunnar

Ekwensi, C. O. D.
See Ekwensi, Cyprian (Odiatu Duaka)

Ekwensi, Cyprian (Odiatu Duaka)
1921- . . . . CLC 4
See also BLC 1; BW; CA 29-32R;
CANR 18; DLB 117; MTCW; SATA 66

Elaine . . . . TCLC 18
See also Leverson, Ada

El Crummo
See Crumb, R(obert)

Elia
See Lamb, Charles

Eliade, Mircea 1907-1986 . . . . CLC 19
See also CA 65-68; 119; CANR 30; MTCW

Eliot, A. D.
See Jewett, (Theodora) Sarah Orne

Eliot, Alice
See Jewett, (Theodora) Sarah Orne

Eliot, Dan
See Silverberg, Robert

Eliot, George
1819-1880 . . . . NCLC 4, 13, 23, 41
See also CDBLB 1832-1890; DA; DLB 21,
35, 55; WLC

Eliot, John 1604-1690 . . . . LC 5
See also DLB 24

Eliot, T(homas) S(tearns)
1888-1965 . . . . . CLC 1, 2, 3, 6, 9, 10, 13,
15, 24, 34, 41, 55, 57; PC 5
See also CA 5-8R; 25-28R; CANR 41;
CDALB 1929-1941; DA; DLB 7, 10, 45,
63; DLBY 88; MTCW; WLC 2

Elizabeth 1866-1941 . . . . TCLC 41

Elkin, Stanley L(awrence)
1930- . . . CLC 4, 6, 9, 14, 27, 51; SSC 12
See also CA 9-12R; CANR 8; DLB 2, 28;
DLBY 80; MTCW

Elledge, Scott. CLC 34

Elliott, Don
See Silverberg, Robert

Elliott, George P(aul) 1918-1980. . . . . CLC 2
See also CA 1-4R; 97-100; CANR 2

Elliott, Janice 1931- . . . . CLC 47
See also CA 13-16R; CANR 8, 29; DLB 14

Elliott, Sumner Locke 1917-1991 . . . CLC 38
See also CA 5-8R; 134; CANR 2, 21

Elliott, William
See Bradbury, Ray (Douglas)

Ellis, A. E. . . . . CLC 7

Ellis, Alice Thomas. . . . . CLC 40
See also Haycraft, Anna

Ellis, Bret Easton 1964- . . . . CLC 39, 71
See also AAYA 2; CA 118; 123

Ellis, (Henry) Havelock
1859-1939 . . . . TCLC 14
See also CA 109

Ellis, Landon
See Ellison, Harlan

Ellis, Trey 1962- . . . . CLC 55

Ellison, Harlan 1934- . . . . CLC 1, 13, 42
See also CA 5-8R; CANR 5; DLB 8;
MTCW

Ellison, Ralph (Waldo)
1914- . . . . CLC 1, 3, 11, 54
See also BLC 1; BW; CA 9-12R; CANR 24;
CDALB 1941-1968; DA; DLB 2, 76;
MTCW; WLC

Ellmann, Lucy (Elizabeth) 1956- . . . . CLC 61
See also CA 128

Ellmann, Richard (David)
1918-1987 . . . . CLC 50
See also BEST 89:2; CA 1-4R; 122;
CANR 2, 28; DLB 103; DLBY 87;
MTCW

Elman, Richard 1934- . . . . CLC 19
See also CA 17-20R; CAAS 3

Elron
See Hubbard, L(afayette) Ron(ald)

Eluard, Paul. . . . . TCLC 7, 41
See also Grindel, Eugene

Elyot, Sir Thomas 1490(?)-1546 . . . . . LC 11

Elytis, Odysseus 1911- . . . . CLC 15, 49
See also CA 102; MTCW

Emecheta, (Florence Onye) Buchi
1944- . . . . CLC 14, 48
See also BLC 2; BW; CA 81-84; CANR 27;
DLB 117; MTCW; SATA 66

Emerson, Ralph Waldo
1803-1882 . . . . NCLC 1, 38
See also CDALB 1640-1865; DA; DLB 1,
59, 73; WLC

Eminescu, Mihail 1850-1889 . . . . . NCLC 33

Empson, William
1906-1984 . . . . CLC 3, 8, 19, 33, 34
See also CA 17-20R; 112; CANR 31;
DLB 20; MTCW

Enchi Fumiko (Ueda) 1905-1986. . . . CLC 31
See also CA 129; 121

Ende, Michael (Andreas Helmuth)
1929- . . . . CLC 31
See also CA 118; 124; CANR 36; CLR 14;
DLB 75; MAICYA; SATA 42, 61

Endo, Shusaku 1923- . . . . . CLC 7, 14, 19, 54
See also CA 29-32R; CANR 21; MTCW

Engel, Marian 1933-1985. . . . . CLC 36
See also CA 25-28R; CANR 12; DLB 53

Engelhardt, Frederick
See Hubbard, L(afayette) Ron(ald)

Enright, D(ennis) J(oseph)
1920- . . . . CLC 4, 8, 31
See also CA 1-4R; CANR 1; DLB 27;
SATA 25

Enzensberger, Hans Magnus
1929- . . . . CLC 43
See also CA 116; 119

Ephron, Nora 1941- . . . . CLC 17, 31
See also AITN 2; CA 65-68; CANR 12, 39

Epsilon
See Betjeman, John

Epstein, Daniel Mark 1948- . . . . CLC 7
See also CA 49-52; CANR 2

Epstein, Jacob 1956- . . . . CLC 19
See also CA 114

Epstein, Joseph 1937-. . . . . CLC 39
See also CA 112; 119

Epstein, Leslie 1938- . . . . CLC 27
See also CA 73-76; CAAS 12; CANR 23

Equiano, Olaudah 1745(?)-1797. . . . . . LC 16
See also BLC 2; DLB 37, 50

Erasmus, Desiderius 1469(?)-1536. . . . LC 16

Erdman, Paul E(mil) 1932- . . . . CLC 25
See also AITN 1; CA 61-64; CANR 13

Erdrich, Louise 1954-. . . . . CLC 39, 54
See also AAYA 10; BEST 89:1; CA 114;
CANR 41; MTCW

Erenburg, Ilya (Grigoryevich)
See Ehrenburg, Ilya (Grigoryevich)

Erickson, Stephen Michael 1950-
See Erickson, Steve
See also CA 129

Erickson, Steve . . . . CLC 64
See also Erickson, Stephen Michael

Ericson, Walter
See Fast, Howard (Melvin)

Eriksson, Buntel
See Bergman, (Ernst) Ingmar

Eschenbach, Wolfram von
See Wolfram von Eschenbach

Eseki, Bruno
See Mphahlele, Ezekiel

Esenin, Sergei (Alexandrovich)
1895-1925 . . . . TCLC 4
See also CA 104

Eshleman, Clayton 1935-. . . . . CLC 7
See also CA 33-36R; CAAS 6; DLB 5

Espriella, Don Manuel Alvarez
See Southey, Robert

Espriu, Salvador 1913-1985. . . . . CLC 9
See also CA 115

Espronceda, Jose de 1808-1842. . . NCLC 39

Esse, James
See Stephens, James

Esterbrook, Tom
See Hubbard, L(afayette) Ron(ald)

Estleman, Loren D. 1952- . . . . CLC 48
See also CA 85-88; CANR 27; MTCW

Evan, Evin
See Faust, Frederick (Schiller)

Evans, Evan
See Faust, Frederick (Schiller)

Evans, Marian
See Eliot, George

Evans, Mary Ann
See Eliot, George

Evarts, Esther
See Benson, Sally

Everett, Percival
See Everett, Percival L.

Everett, Percival L. 1956- . . . . CLC 57
See also CA 129

Everson, R(onald) G(ilmour)
1903- . . . . CLC 27
See also CA 17-20R; DLB 88

Everson, William (Oliver)
1912- . . . . CLC 1, 5, 14
See also CA 9-12R; CANR 20; DLB 5, 16;
MTCW

Evtushenko, Evgenii Aleksandrovich
See Yevtushenko, Yevgeny (Alexandrovich)

Ewart, Gavin (Buchanan)
1916- . . . . CLC 13, 46
See also CA 89-92; CANR 17; DLB 40;
MTCW

Ewers, Hanns Heinz 1871-1943 . . . TCLC 12
See also CA 109

Ewing, Frederick R.
See Sturgeon, Theodore (Hamilton)

Exley, Frederick (Earl)
1929-1992 . . . . CLC 6, 11
See also AITN 2; CA 81-84; 138; DLBY 81

Eynhardt, Guillermo
See Quiroga, Horacio (Sylvestre)

Ezekiel, Nissim 1924-. . . . . CLC 61
See also CA 61-64

Ezekiel, Tish O'Dowd 1943- . . . . . . CLC 34
See also CA 129

Fagen, Donald 1948-. . . . . CLC 26

Fainzilberg, Ilya Arnoldovich 1897-1937
See Ilf, Ilya
See also CA 120

Fair, Ronald L. 1932-. . . . . CLC 18
See also BW; CA 69-72; CANR 25; DLB 33

Fairbairns, Zoe (Ann) 1948- . . . . . . CLC 32
See also CA 103; CANR 21

Falco, Gian
See Papini, Giovanni

Falconer, James
See Kirkup, James

Falconer, Kenneth
See Kornbluth, C(yril) M.

Falkland, Samuel
See Heijermans, Herman

Fallaci, Oriana 1930- . . . . **CLC 11**
See also CA 77-80; CANR 15; MTCW

Faludy, George 1913- . . . . **CLC 42**
See also CA 21-24R

Faludy, Gyoergy
See Faludy, George

Fanon, Frantz 1925-1961 . . . . **CLC 74**
See also BLC 2; BW; CA 116; 89-92

Fanshawe, Ann . . . . **LC 11**

Fante, John (Thomas) 1911-1983 . . . **CLC 60**
See also CA 69-72; 109; CANR 23;
DLB 130; DLBY 83

Farah, Nuruddin 1945- . . . . **CLC 53**
See also BLC 2; CA 106; DLB 125

Fargue, Leon-Paul 1876(?)-1947 . . . **TCLC 11**
See also CA 109

Farigoule, Louis
See Romains, Jules

Farina, Richard 1936(?)-1966 . . . . **CLC 9**
See also CA 81-84; 25-28R

Farley, Walter (Lorimer)
1915-1989 . . . . **CLC 17**
See also CA 17-20R; CANR 8, 29; DLB 22;
MAICYA; SATA 2, 43

Farmer, Philip Jose 1918- . . . . **CLC 1, 19**
See also CA 1-4R; CANR 4, 35; DLB 8;
MTCW

Farquhar, George 1677-1707 . . . . **LC 21**
See also DLB 84

Farrell, J(ames) G(ordon)
1935-1979 . . . . **CLC 6**
See also CA 73-76; 89-92; CANR 36;
DLB 14; MTCW

Farrell, James T(homas)
1904-1979 . . . . **CLC 1, 4, 8, 11, 66**
See also CA 5-8R; 89-92; CANR 9; DLB 4,
9, 86; DLBD 2; MTCW

Farren, Richard J.
See Betjeman, John

Farren, Richard M.
See Betjeman, John

Fassbinder, Rainer Werner
1946-1982 . . . . **CLC 20**
See also CA 93-96; 106; CANR 31

Fast, Howard (Melvin) 1914- . . . . . . **CLC 23**
See also CA 1-4R; CANR 1, 33; DLB 9;
SATA 7

Faulcon, Robert
See Holdstock, Robert P.

Faulkner, William (Cuthbert)
1897-1962 . . . . . **CLC 1, 3, 6, 8, 9, 11, 14,**
18, 28, 52, 68; SSC 1
See also AAYA 7; CA 81-84; CANR 33;
CDALB 1929-1941; DA; DLB 9, 11, 44,
102; DLBD 2; DLBY 86; MTCW; WLC

Fauset, Jessie Redmon
1884(?)-1961 . . . . **CLC 19, 54**
See also BLC 2; BW; CA 109; DLB 51

Faust, Frederick (Schiller)
1892-1944(?) . . . . **TCLC 49**
See also CA 108

Faust, Irvin 1924- . . . . **CLC 8**
See also CA 33-36R; CANR 28; DLB 2, 28;
DLBY 80

Fawkes, Guy
See Benchley, Robert (Charles)

Fearing, Kenneth (Flexner)
1902-1961 . . . . **CLC 51**
See also CA 93-96; DLB 9

Fecamps, Elise
See Creasey, John

Federman, Raymond 1928- . . . . . . **CLC 6, 47**
See also CA 17-20R; CAAS 8; CANR 10;
DLBY 80

Federspiel, J(uerg) F. 1931- . . . . **CLC 42**

Feiffer, Jules (Ralph) 1929- . . . . **CLC 2, 8, 64**
See also AAYA 3; CA 17-20R; CANR 30;
DLB 7, 44; MTCW; SATA 8, 61

Feige, Hermann Albert Otto Maximilian
See Traven, B.

Fei-Kan, Li
See Li Fei-kan

Feinberg, David B. 1956- . . . . **CLC 59**
See also CA 135

Feinstein, Elaine 1930- . . . . **CLC 36**
See also CA 69-72; CAAS 1; CANR 31;
DLB 14, 40; MTCW

Feldman, Irving (Mordecai) 1928- . . . . **CLC 7**
See also CA 1-4R; CANR 1

Fellini, Federico 1920- . . . . **CLC 16**
See also CA 65-68; CANR 33

Felsen, Henry Gregor 1916- . . . . **CLC 17**
See also CA 1-4R; CANR 1; SAAS 2;
SATA 1

Fenton, James Martin 1949- . . . . **CLC 32**
See also CA 102; DLB 40

Ferber, Edna 1887-1968 . . . . **CLC 18**
See also AITN 1; CA 5-8R; 25-28R; DLB 9,
28, 86; MTCW; SATA 7

Ferguson, Helen
See Kavan, Anna

Ferguson, Samuel 1810-1886 . . . . . **NCLC 33**
See also DLB 32

Ferling, Lawrence
See Ferlinghetti, Lawrence (Monsanto)

Ferlinghetti, Lawrence (Monsanto)
1919(?)- . . . . **CLC 2, 6, 10, 27; PC 1**
See also CA 5-8R; CANR 3, 41;
CDALB 1941-1968; DLB 5, 16; MTCW

Fernandez, Vicente Garcia Huidobro
See Huidobro Fernandez, Vicente Garcia

Ferrer, Gabriel (Francisco Victor) Miro
See Miro (Ferrer), Gabriel (Francisco
Victor)

Ferrier, Susan (Edmonstone)
1782-1854 . . . . **NCLC 8**
See also DLB 116

Ferrigno, Robert 1948(?)- . . . . **CLC 65**
See also CA 140

Feuchtwanger, Lion 1884-1958 . . . . . **TCLC 3**
See also CA 104; DLB 66

Feydeau, Georges (Leon Jules Marie)
1862-1921 . . . . **TCLC 22**
See also CA 113

Ficino, Marsilio 1433-1499 . . . . **LC 12**

Fiedler, Leslie A(aron)
1917- . . . . **CLC 4, 13, 24**
See also CA 9-12R; CANR 7; DLB 28, 67;
MTCW

Field, Andrew 1938- . . . . **CLC 44**
See also CA 97-100; CANR 25

Field, Eugene 1850-1895 . . . . **NCLC 3**
See also DLB 23, 42; MAICYA; SATA 16

Field, Gans T.
See Wellman, Manly Wade

Field, Michael . . . . **TCLC 43**

Field, Peter
See Hobson, Laura Z(ametkin)

Fielding, Henry 1707-1754 . . . . **LC 1**
See also CDBLB 1660-1789; DA; DLB 39,
84, 101; WLC

Fielding, Sarah 1710-1768 . . . . **LC 1**
See also DLB 39

Fierstein, Harvey (Forbes) 1954- . . . **CLC 33**
See also CA 123; 129

Figes, Eva 1932- . . . . **CLC 31**
See also CA 53-56; CANR 4; DLB 14

Finch, Robert (Duer Claydon)
1900- . . . . **CLC 18**
See also CA 57-60; CANR 9, 24; DLB 88

Findley, Timothy 1930- . . . . **CLC 27**
See also CA 25-28R; CANR 12; DLB 53

Fink, William
See Mencken, H(enry) L(ouis)

Firbank, Louis 1942-
See Reed, Lou
See also CA 117

Firbank, (Arthur Annesley) Ronald
1886-1926 . . . . **TCLC 1**
See also CA 104; DLB 36

Fisher, M(ary) F(rances) K(ennedy)
1908-1992 . . . . **CLC 76**
See also CA 77-80; 138

Fisher, Roy 1930- . . . . **CLC 25**
See also CA 81-84; CAAS 10; CANR 16;
DLB 40

Fisher, Rudolph 1897-1934 . . . . **TCLC 11**
See also BLC 2; BW; CA 107; 124; DLB 51,
102

Fisher, Vardis (Alvero) 1895-1968 . . . . **CLC 7**
See also CA 5-8R; 25-28R; DLB 9

Fiske, Tarleton
See Bloch, Robert (Albert)

Fitch, Clarke
See Sinclair, Upton (Beall)

Fitch, John IV
See Cormier, Robert (Edmund)

Fitgerald, Penelope 1916- . . . . **CLC 61**

Fitzgerald, Captain Hugh
See Baum, L(yman) Frank

FitzGerald, Edward 1809-1883 . . . . . **NCLC 9**
See also DLB 32

Fitzgerald, F(rancis) Scott (Key)
1896-1940 . . . . **TCLC 1, 6, 14, 28; SSC 6**
See also AITN 1; CA 110; 123;
CDALB 1917-1929; DA; DLB 4, 9, 86;
DLBD 1; DLBY 81; MTCW; WLC

Fitzgerald, Penelope 1916- . . . . . . **CLC 19, 51**
See also CA 85-88; CAAS 10; DLB 14

Fitzgerald, Robert (Stuart)
1910-1985 . . . . **CLC 39**
See also CA 1-4R; 114; CANR 1; DLBY 80

FitzGerald, Robert D(avid)
1902-1987 . . . . **CLC 19**
See also CA 17-20R

Flanagan, Thomas (James Bonner)
1923- . . . . **CLC 25, 52**
See also CA 108; DLBY 80; MTCW

Flaubert, Gustave
1821-1880 . . . . . **NCLC 2, 10, 19; SSC 11**
See also DA; DLB 119; WLC

Flecker, (Herman) James Elroy
1884-1915 . . . . **TCLC 43**
See also CA 109; DLB 10, 19

Fleming, Ian (Lancaster)
1908-1964 . . . . **CLC 3, 30**
See also CA 5-8R; CDBLB 1945-1960;
DLB 87; MTCW; SATA 9

Fleming, Thomas (James) 1927- . . . . **CLC 37**
See also CA 5-8R; CANR 10; SATA 8

Fletcher, John Gould 1886-1950 . . . **TCLC 35**
See also CA 107; DLB 4, 45

Fleur, Paul
See Pohl, Frederik

Flooglebuckle, Al
See Spiegelman, Art

Flying Officer X
See Bates, H(erbert) E(rnest)

Fo, Dario 1926- . . . . **CLC 32**
See also CA 116; 128; MTCW

Fogarty, Jonathan Titulescu Esq.
See Farrell, James T(homas)

Folke, Will
See Bloch, Robert (Albert)

Follett, Ken(neth Martin) 1949- . . . . **CLC 18**
See also AAYA 6; BEST 89:4; CA 81-84;
CANR 13, 33; DLB 87; DLBY 81;
MTCW

Fontane, Theodor 1819-1898 . . . . . **NCLC 26**
See also DLB 129

Foote, Horton 1916- . . . . **CLC 51**
See also CA 73-76; CANR 34; DLB 26

Foote, Shelby 1916- . . . . **CLC 75**
See also CA 5-8R; CANR 3; DLB 2, 17

Forbes, Esther 1891-1967 . . . . **CLC 12**
See also CA 13-14; 25-28R; CAP 1;
CLR 27; DLB 22; MAICYA; SATA 2

Forche, Carolyn (Louise) 1950- . . . . . **CLC 25**
See also CA 109; 117; DLB 5

Ford, Elbur
See Hibbert, Eleanor Alice Burford

Ford, Ford Madox
1873-1939 . . . . **TCLC 1, 15, 39**
See also CA 104; 132; CDBLB 1914-1945;
DLB 34, 98; MTCW

Ford, John 1895-1973 . . . . **CLC 16**
See also CA 45-48

Ford, Richard 1944- . . . . **CLC 46**
See also CA 69-72; CANR 11

Ford, Webster
See Masters, Edgar Lee

Foreman, Richard 1937- . . . . **CLC 50**
See also CA 65-68; CANR 32

Forester, C(ecil) S(cott)
1899-1966 . . . . **CLC 35**
See also CA 73-76; 25-28R; SATA 13

Forez
See Mauriac, Francois (Charles)

Forman, James Douglas 1932- . . . . . . **CLC 21**
See also CA 9-12R; CANR 4, 19;
MAICYA; SATA 8, 70

Fornes, Maria Irene 1930- . . . . . . **CLC 39, 61**
See also CA 25-28R; CANR 28; DLB 7;
HW; MTCW

Forrest, Leon 1937- . . . . **CLC 4**
See also BW; CA 89-92; CAAS 7;
CANR 25; DLB 33

Forster, E(dward) M(organ)
1879-1970 . . . . . **CLC 1, 2, 3, 4, 9, 10, 13,
15, 22, 45, 77**
See also AAYA 2; CA 13-14; 25-28R;
CAP 1; CDBLB 1914-1945; DA; DLB 34,
98; DLBD 10; MTCW; SATA 57; WLC

Forster, John 1812-1876 . . . . **NCLC 11**

Forsyth, Frederick 1938- . . . . . . **CLC 2, 5, 36**
See also BEST 89:4; CA 85-88; CANR 38;
DLB 87; MTCW

Forten, Charlotte L. . . . . **TCLC 16**
See also Grimke, Charlotte L(ottie) Forten
See also BLC 2; DLB 50

Foscolo, Ugo 1778-1827 . . . . **NCLC 8**

Fosse, Bob . . . . **CLC 20**
See also Fosse, Robert Louis

Fosse, Robert Louis 1927-1987
See Fosse, Bob
See also CA 110; 123

Foster, Stephen Collins
1826-1864 . . . . **NCLC 26**

Foucault, Michel
1926-1984 . . . . **CLC 31, 34, 69**
See also CA 105; 113; CANR 34; MTCW

Fouque, Friedrich (Heinrich Karl) de la Motte
1777-1843 . . . . **NCLC 2**
See also DLB 90

Fournier, Henri Alban 1886-1914
See Alain-Fournier
See also CA 104

Fournier, Pierre 1916- . . . . **CLC 11**
See also Gascar, Pierre
See also CA 89-92; CANR 16, 40

Fowles, John
1926- . . . . **CLC 1, 2, 3, 4, 6, 9, 10, 15, 33**
See also CA 5-8R; CANR 25; CDBLB 1960
to Present; DLB 14; MTCW; SATA 22

Fox, Paula 1923- . . . . **CLC 2, 8**
See also AAYA 3; CA 73-76; CANR 20,
36; CLR 1; DLB 52; MAICYA; MTCW;
SATA 17, 60

Fox, William Price (Jr.) 1926- . . . . . **CLC 22**
See also CA 17-20R; CANR 11; DLB 2;
DLBY 81

Foxe, John 1516(?)-1587 . . . . **LC 14**

Frame, Janet . . . . **CLC 2, 3, 6, 22, 66**
See also Clutha, Janet Paterson Frame

France, Anatole . . . . **TCLC 9**
See also Thibault, Jacques Anatole Francois
See also DLB 123

Francis, Claude 19(?)- . . . . **CLC 50**

Francis, Dick 1920- . . . . **CLC 2, 22, 42**
See also AAYA 5; BEST 89:3; CA 5-8R;
CANR 9; CDBLB 1960 to Present;
DLB 87; MTCW

Francis, Robert (Churchill)
1901-1987 . . . . **CLC 15**
See also CA 1-4R; 123; CANR 1

Frank, Anne(lies Marie)
1929-1945 . . . . **TCLC 17**
See also CA 113; 133; DA; MTCW;
SATA 42; WLC

Frank, Elizabeth 1945- . . . . **CLC 39**
See also CA 121; 126

Franklin, Benjamin
See Hasek, Jaroslav (Matej Frantisek)

Franklin, (Stella Maraia Sarah) Miles
1879-1954 . . . . **TCLC 7**
See also CA 104

Fraser, Antonia (Pakenham)
1932- . . . . **CLC 32**
See also CA 85-88; MTCW; SATA 32

Fraser, George MacDonald 1925- . . . . **CLC 7**
See also CA 45-48; CANR 2

Fraser, Sylvia 1935- . . . . **CLC 64**
See also CA 45-48; CANR 1, 16

Frayn, Michael 1933- . . . . . . **CLC 3, 7, 31, 47**
See also CA 5-8R; CANR 30; DLB 13, 14;
MTCW

Fraze, Candida (Merrill) 1945- . . . . . **CLC 50**
See also CA 126

Frazer, J(ames) G(eorge)
1854-1941 . . . . **TCLC 32**
See also CA 118

Frazer, Robert Caine
See Creasey, John

Frazer, Sir James George
See Frazer, J(ames) G(eorge)

Frazier, Ian 1951- . . . . **CLC 46**
See also CA 130

Frederic, Harold 1856-1898 . . . . . . **NCLC 10**
See also DLB 12, 23

Frederick, John
See Faust, Frederick (Schiller)

Frederick the Great 1712-1786 . . . . . . **LC 14**

Fredro, Aleksander 1793-1876 . . . . . **NCLC 8**

Freeling, Nicolas 1927- . . . . **CLC 38**
See also CA 49-52; CAAS 12; CANR 1, 17;
DLB 87

Freeman, Douglas Southall
1886-1953 . . . . **TCLC 11**
See also CA 109; DLB 17

Freeman, Judith 1946- . . . . **CLC 55**

Freeman, Mary Eleanor Wilkins
1852-1930 . . . . **TCLC 9; SSC 1**
See also CA 106; DLB 12, 78

Freeman, R(ichard) Austin
1862-1943 . . . . **TCLC 21**
See also CA 113; DLB 70

French, Marilyn 1929- . . . . . . **CLC 10, 18, 60**
See also CA 69-72; CANR 3, 31; MTCW

French, Paul
See Asimov, Isaac

Freneau, Philip Morin 1752-1832 . . **NCLC 1**
See also DLB 37, 43

Friedan, Betty (Naomi) 1921- ...... CLC 74
See also CA 65-68; CANR 18; MTCW

Friedman, B(ernard) H(arper)
1926- .... CLC 7
See also CA 1-4R; CANR 3

Friedman, Bruce Jay 1930-.... CLC 3, 5, 56
See also CA 9-12R; CANR 25; DLB 2, 28

Friel, Brian 1929-........... CLC 5, 42, 59
See also CA 21-24R; CANR 33; DLB 13;
MTCW

Friis-Baastad, Babbis Ellinor
1921-1970 .... CLC 12
See also CA 17-20R; 134; SATA 7

Frisch, Max (Rudolf)
1911-1991 ..... CLC 3, 9, 14, 18, 32, 44
See also CA 85-88; 134; CANR 32;
DLB 69, 124; MTCW

Fromentin, Eugene (Samuel Auguste)
1820-1876 .... NCLC 10
See also DLB 123

Frost, Frederick
See Faust, Frederick (Schiller)

Frost, Robert (Lee)
1874-1963 .... CLC 1, 3, 4, 9, 10, 13, 15,
26, 34, 44; PC 1
See also CA 89-92; CANR 33;
CDALB 1917-1929; DA; DLB 54;
DLBD 7; MTCW; SATA 14; WLC

Froy, Herald
See Waterhouse, Keith (Spencer)

Fry, Christopher 1907-...... CLC 2, 10, 14
See also CA 17-20R; CANR 9, 30; DLB 13;
MTCW; SATA 66

Frye, (Herman) Northrop
1912-1991 .... CLC 24, 70
See also CA 5-8R; 133; CANR 8, 37;
DLB 67, 68; MTCW

Fuchs, Daniel 1909-........... CLC 8, 22
See also CA 81-84; CAAS 5; CANR 40;
DLB 9, 26, 28

Fuchs, Daniel 1934-.............. CLC 34
See also CA 37-40R; CANR 14

Fuentes, Carlos
1928-...... CLC 3, 8, 10, 13, 22, 41, 60
See also AAYA 4; AITN 2; CA 69-72;
CANR 10, 32; DA; DLB 113; HW;
MTCW; WLC

Fuentes, Gregorio Lopez y
See Lopez y Fuentes, Gregorio

Fugard, (Harold) Athol
1932-....... CLC 5, 9, 14, 25, 40; DC 3
See also CA 85-88; CANR 32; MTCW

Fugard, Sheila 1932- .... CLC 48
See also CA 125

Fuller, Charles (H., Jr.)
1939- .... CLC 25; DC 1
See also BLC 2; BW; CA 108; 112; DLB 38;
MTCW

Fuller, John (Leopold) 1937-....... CLC 62
See also CA 21-24R; CANR 9; DLB 40

Fuller, Margaret .... NCLC 5
See also Ossoli, Sarah Margaret (Fuller
marchesa d')

Fuller, Roy (Broadbent)
1912-1991 .... CLC 4, 28
See also CA 5-8R; 135; CAAS 10; DLB 15,
20

Fulton, Alice 1952-.............. CLC 52
See also CA 116

Furphy, Joseph 1843-1912........ TCLC 25

Fussell, Paul 1924-.............. CLC 74
See also BEST 90:1; CA 17-20R; CANR 8,
21, 35; MTCW

Futabatei, Shimei 1864-1909 ..... TCLC 44

Futrelle, Jacques 1875-1912 ..... TCLC 19
See also CA 113

G. B. S.
See Shaw, George Bernard

Gaboriau, Emile 1835-1873 ...... NCLC 14

Gadda, Carlo Emilio 1893-1973 .... CLC 11
See also CA 89-92

Gaddis, William
1922- .... CLC 1, 3, 6, 8, 10, 19, 43
See also CA 17-20R; CANR 21; DLB 2;
MTCW

Gaines, Ernest J(ames)
1933-................... CLC 3, 11, 18
See also AITN 1; BLC 2; BW; CA 9-12R;
CANR 6, 24; CDALB 1968-1988; DLB 2,
33; DLBY 80; MTCW

Gaitskill, Mary 1954-............. CLC 69
See also CA 128

Galdos, Benito Perez
See Perez Galdos, Benito

Gale, Zona 1874-1938 .... TCLC 7
See also CA 105; DLB 9, 78

Galeano, Eduardo (Hughes) 1940-... CLC 72
See also CA 29-32R; CANR 13, 32; HW

Galiano, Juan Valera y Alcala
See Valera y Alcala-Galiano, Juan

Gallagher, Tess 1943-......... CLC 18, 63
See also CA 106; DLB 120

Gallant, Mavis
1922-......... CLC 7, 18, 38; SSC 5
See also CA 69-72; CANR 29; DLB 53;
MTCW

Gallant, Roy A(rthur) 1924- .... CLC 17
See also CA 5-8R; CANR 4, 29; CLR 30;
MAICYA; SATA 4, 68

Gallico, Paul (William) 1897-1976 ... CLC 2
See also AITN 1; CA 5-8R; 69-72;
CANR 23; DLB 9; MAICYA; SATA 13

Gallup, Ralph
See Whitemore, Hugh (John)

Galsworthy, John 1867-1933.... TCLC 1, 45
See also CA 104; CDBLB 1890-1914; DA;
DLB 10, 34, 98; WLC 2

Galt, John 1779-1839 .... NCLC 1
See also DLB 99, 116

Galvin, James 1951-.............. CLC 38
See also CA 108; CANR 26

Gamboa, Federico 1864-1939...... TCLC 36

Gann, Ernest Kellogg 1910-1991.... CLC 23
See also AITN 1; CA 1-4R; 136; CANR 1

Garcia, Christina 1959- .... CLC 76

Garcia Lorca, Federico
1898-1936 .. TCLC 1, 7, 49; DC 2; PC 3
See also CA 104; 131; DA; DLB 108; HW;
MTCW; WLC

Garcia Marquez, Gabriel (Jose)
1928- .... CLC 2, 3, 8, 10, 15, 27, 47, 55;
SSC 8
See also Marquez, Gabriel (Jose) Garcia
See also AAYA 3; BEST 89:1, 90:4;
CA 33-36R; CANR 10, 28; DA;
DLB 113; HW; MTCW; WLC

Gard, Janice
See Latham, Jean Lee

Gard, Roger Martin du
See Martin du Gard, Roger

Gardam, Jane 1928-.............. CLC 43
See also CA 49-52; CANR 2, 18, 33;
CLR 12; DLB 14; MAICYA; MTCW;
SAAS 9; SATA 28, 39

Gardner, Herb.................... CLC 44

Gardner, John (Champlin), Jr.
1933-1982 ..... CLC 2, 3, 5, 7, 8, 10, 18,
28, 34; SSC 7
See also AITN 1; CA 65-68; 107;
CANR 33; DLB 2; DLBY 82; MTCW;
SATA 31, 40

Gardner, John (Edmund) 1926-..... CLC 30
See also CA 103; CANR 15; MTCW

Gardner, Noel
See Kuttner, Henry

Gardons, S. S.
See Snodgrass, W(illiam) D(e Witt)

Garfield, Leon 1921-.............. CLC 12
See also AAYA 8; CA 17-20R; CANR 38,
41; CLR 21; MAICYA; SATA 1, 32

Garland, (Hannibal) Hamlin
1860-1940 .... TCLC 3
See also CA 104; DLB 12, 71, 78

Garneau, (Hector de) Saint-Denys
1912-1943 .... TCLC 13
See also CA 111; DLB 88

Garner, Alan 1934-.............. CLC 17
See also CA 73-76; CANR 15; CLR 20;
MAICYA; MTCW; SATA 18, 69

Garner, Hugh 1913-1979 .... CLC 13
See also CA 69-72; CANR 31; DLB 68

Garnett, David 1892-1981 .... CLC 3
See also CA 5-8R; 103; CANR 17; DLB 34

Garos, Stephanie
See Katz, Steve

Garrett, George (Palmer)
1929- .... CLC 3, 11, 51
See also CA 1-4R; CAAS 5; CANR 1;
DLB 2, 5, 130; DLBY 83

Garrick, David 1717-1779 .... LC 15
See also DLB 84

Garrigue, Jean 1914-1972 .... CLC 2, 8
See also CA 5-8R; 37-40R; CANR 20

Garrison, Frederick
See Sinclair, Upton (Beall)

Garth, Will
See Hamilton, Edmond; Kuttner, Henry

Garvey, Marcus (Moziah, Jr.)
1887-1940 .... TCLC 41
See also BLC 2; BW; CA 120; 124

Gary, Romain . . . . CLC 25
See also Kacew, Romain
See also DLB 83

Gascar, Pierre . . . . CLC 11
See also Fournier, Pierre

Gascoyne, David (Emery) 1916- . . . . CLC 45
See also CA 65-68; CANR 10, 28; DLB 20;
MTCW

Gaskell, Elizabeth Cleghorn
1810-1865 . . . . NCLC 5
See also CDBLB 1832-1890; DLB 21

Gass, William H(oward)
1924- . . . CLC 1, 2, 8, 11, 15, 39; SSC 12
See also CA 17-20R; CANR 30; DLB 2;
MTCW

Gasset, Jose Ortega y
See Ortega y Gasset, Jose

Gautier, Theophile 1811-1872 . . . . . NCLC 1
See also DLB 119

Gawsworth, John
See Bates, H(erbert) E(rnest)

Gaye, Marvin (Penze) 1939-1984 . . . CLC 26
See also CA 112

Gebler, Carlo (Ernest) 1954- . . . . CLC 39
See also CA 119; 133

Gee, Maggie (Mary) 1948- . . . . CLC 57
See also CA 130

Gee, Maurice (Gough) 1931- . . . . CLC 29
See also CA 97-100; SATA 46

Gelbart, Larry (Simon) 1923- . . . CLC 21, 61
See also CA 73-76

Gelber, Jack 1932- . . . . CLC 1, 6, 14, 79
See also CA 1-4R; CANR 2; DLB 7

Gellhorn, Martha Ellis 1908- . . . CLC 14, 60
See also CA 77-80; DLBY 82

Genet, Jean
1910-1986 . . . CLC 1, 2, 5, 10, 14, 44, 46
See also CA 13-16R; CANR 18; DLB 72;
DLBY 86; MTCW

Gent, Peter 1942- . . . . CLC 29
See also AITN 1; CA 89-92; DLBY 82

George, Jean Craighead 1919- . . . . . . CLC 35
See also AAYA 8; CA 5-8R; CANR 25;
CLR 1; DLB 52; MAICYA; SATA 2, 68

George, Stefan (Anton)
1868-1933 . . . . TCLC 2, 14
See also CA 104

Georges, Georges Martin
See Simenon, Georges (Jacques Christian)

Gerhardi, William Alexander
See Gerhardie, William Alexander

Gerhardie, William Alexander
1895-1977 . . . . CLC 5
See also CA 25-28R; 73-76; CANR 18;
DLB 36

Gerstler, Amy 1956- . . . . CLC 70

Gertler, T. . . . . CLC 34
See also CA 116; 121

Ghalib 1797-1869 . . . . NCLC 39

Ghelderode, Michel de
1898-1962 . . . . CLC 6, 11
See also CA 85-88; CANR 40

Ghiselin, Brewster 1903- . . . . CLC 23
See also CA 13-16R; CAAS 10; CANR 13

Ghose, Zulfikar 1935- . . . . CLC 42
See also CA 65-68

Ghosh, Amitav 1956- . . . . CLC 44

Giacosa, Giuseppe 1847-1906 . . . . . . TCLC 7
See also CA 104

Gibb, Lee
See Waterhouse, Keith (Spencer)

Gibbon, Lewis Grassic . . . . TCLC 4
See also Mitchell, James Leslie

Gibbons, Kaye 1960- . . . . CLC 50

Gibran, Kahlil 1883-1931 . . . . TCLC 1, 9
See also CA 104

Gibson, William 1914- . . . . CLC 23
See also CA 9-12R; CANR 9; DA; DLB 7;
SATA 66

Gibson, William (Ford) 1948- . . . CLC 39, 63
See also CA 126; 133

Gide, Andre (Paul Guillaume)
1869-1951 . . . . . TCLC 5, 12, 36; SSC 13
See also CA 104; 124; DA; DLB 65;
MTCW; WLC

Gifford, Barry (Colby) 1946- . . . . CLC 34
See also CA 65-68; CANR 9, 30, 40

Gilbert, W(illiam) S(chwenck)
1836-1911 . . . . TCLC 3
See also CA 104; SATA 36

Gilbreth, Frank B., Jr. 1911- . . . . CLC 17
See also CA 9-12R; SATA 2

Gilchrist, Ellen 1935- . . . . CLC 34, 48
See also CA 113; 116; CANR 41; DLB 130;
MTCW

Giles, Molly 1942- . . . . CLC 39
See also CA 126

Gill, Patrick
See Creasey, John

Gilliam, Terry (Vance) 1940- . . . . CLC 21
See also Monty Python
See also CA 108; 113; CANR 35

Gillian, Jerry
See Gilliam, Terry (Vance)

Gilliatt, Penelope (Ann Douglass)
1932- . . . . CLC 2, 10, 13, 53
See also AITN 2; CA 13-16R; DLB 14

Gilman, Charlotte (Anna) Perkins (Stetson)
1860-1935 . . . . TCLC 9, 37; SSC 13
See also CA 106

Gilmour, David 1949- . . . . CLC 35
See also Pink Floyd
See also CA 138

Gilpin, William 1724-1804 . . . . NCLC 30

Gilray, J. D.
See Mencken, H(enry) L(ouis)

Gilroy, Frank D(aniel) 1925- . . . . CLC 2
See also CA 81-84; CANR 32; DLB 7

Ginsberg, Allen
1926- . . . . . . CLC 1, 2, 3, 4, 6, 13, 36, 69;
PC 4
See also AITN 1; CA 1-4R; CANR 2, 41;
CDALB 1941-1968; DA; DLB 5, 16;
MTCW; WLC 3

Ginzburg, Natalia
1916-1991 . . . . CLC 5, 11, 54, 70
See also CA 85-88; 135; CANR 33; MTCW

Giono, Jean 1895-1970 . . . . CLC 4, 11
See also CA 45-48; 29-32R; CANR 2, 35;
DLB 72; MTCW

Giovanni, Nikki 1943- . . . . . CLC 2, 4, 19, 64
See also AITN 1; BLC 2; BW; CA 29-32R;
CAAS 6; CANR 18, 41; CLR 6; DA;
DLB 5, 41; MAICYA; MTCW; SATA 24

Giovene, Andrea 1904- . . . . CLC 7
See also CA 85-88

Gippius, Zinaida (Nikolayevna) 1869-1945
See Hippius, Zinaida
See also CA 106

Giraudoux, (Hippolyte) Jean
1882-1944 . . . . TCLC 2, 7
See also CA 104; DLB 65

Gironella, Jose Maria 1917- . . . . CLC 11
See also CA 101

Gissing, George (Robert)
1857-1903 . . . . TCLC 3, 24, 47
See also CA 105; DLB 18

Giurlani, Aldo
See Palazzeschi, Aldo

Gladkov, Fyodor (Vasilyevich)
1883-1958 . . . . TCLC 27

Glanville, Brian (Lester) 1931- . . . . CLC 6
See also CA 5-8R; CAAS 9; CANR 3;
DLB 15; SATA 42

Glasgow, Ellen (Anderson Gholson)
1873(?)-1945 . . . . TCLC 2, 7
See also CA 104; DLB 9, 12

Glassco, John 1909-1981 . . . . CLC 9
See also CA 13-16R; 102; CANR 15;
DLB 68

Glasscock, Amnesia
See Steinbeck, John (Ernst)

Glasser, Ronald J. 1940(?)- . . . . CLC 37

Glassman, Joyce
See Johnson, Joyce

Glendinning, Victoria 1937- . . . . CLC 50
See also CA 120; 127

Glissant, Edouard 1928- . . . . CLC 10, 68

Gloag, Julian 1930- . . . . CLC 40
See also AITN 1; CA 65-68; CANR 10

Gluck, Louise (Elisabeth)
1943- . . . . CLC 7, 22, 44
See also Glueck, Louise
See also CA 33-36R; CANR 40; DLB 5

Glueck, Louise . . . . CLC 7, 22
See also Gluck, Louise (Elisabeth)
See also DLB 5

Gobineau, Joseph Arthur (Comte) de
1816-1882 . . . . NCLC 17
See also DLB 123

Godard, Jean-Luc 1930- . . . . CLC 20
See also CA 93-96

Godden, (Margaret) Rumer 1907- . . . CLC 53
See also AAYA 6; CA 5-8R; CANR 4, 27,
36; CLR 20; MAICYA; SAAS 12;
SATA 3, 36

Godoy Alcayaga, Lucila 1889-1957
See Mistral, Gabriela
See also CA 104; 131; HW; MTCW

Gray, Thomas 1716-1771 . . . . . . LC 4; PC 2
See also CDBLB 1660-1789; DA; DLB 109;
WLC

Grayson, David
See Baker, Ray Stannard

Grayson, Richard (A.) 1951- . . . . CLC 38
See also CA 85-88; CANR 14, 31

Greeley, Andrew M(oran) 1928- . . . . CLC 28
See also CA 5-8R; CAAS 7; CANR 7;
MTCW

Green, Brian
See Card, Orson Scott

Green, Hannah . . . . CLC 3
See also CA 73-76

Green, Hannah
See Greenberg, Joanne (Goldenberg)

Green, Henry . . . . CLC 2, 13
See also Yorke, Henry Vincent
See also DLB 15

Green, Julian (Hartridge)
1900- . . . . CLC 3, 11, 77
See also CA 21-24R; CANR 33; DLB 4, 72;
MTCW

Green, Julien 1900-
See Green, Julian (Hartridge)

Green, Paul (Eliot) 1894-1981 . . . . . . CLC 25
See also AITN 1; CA 5-8R; 103; CANR 3;
DLB 7, 9; DLBY 81

Greenberg, Ivan 1908-1973
See Rahv, Philip
See also CA 85-88

Greenberg, Joanne (Goldenberg)
1932- . . . . CLC 7, 30
See also CA 5-8R; CANR 14, 32; SATA 25

Greenberg, Richard 1959(?)- . . . . CLC 57
See also CA 138

Greene, Bette 1934- . . . . CLC 30
See also AAYA 7; CA 53-56; CANR 4;
CLR 2; MAICYA; SAAS 16; SATA 8

Greene, Gael . . . . CLC 8
See also CA 13-16R; CANR 10

Greene, Graham
1904-1991 . . . . CLC 1, 3, 6, 9, 14, 18, 27,
37, 70, 72
See also AITN 2; CA 13-16R; 133;
CANR 35; CDBLB 1945-1960; DA;
DLB 13, 15, 77, 100; DLBY 91; MTCW;
SATA 20; WLC

Greer, Richard
See Silverberg, Robert

Greer, Richard
See Silverberg, Robert

Gregor, Arthur 1923- . . . . CLC 9
See also CA 25-28R; CAAS 10; CANR 11;
SATA 36

Gregor, Lee
See Pohl, Frederik

Gregory, Isabella Augusta (Persse)
1852-1932 . . . . TCLC 1
See also CA 104; DLB 10

Gregory, J. Dennis
See Williams, John A(lfred)

Grendon, Stephen
See Derleth, August (William)

Grenville, Kate 1950- . . . . CLC 61
See also CA 118

Grenville, Pelham
See Wodehouse, P(elham) G(renville)

Greve, Felix Paul (Berthold Friedrich)
1879-1948
See Grove, Frederick Philip
See also CA 104

Grey, Zane 1872-1939 . . . . TCLC 6
See also CA 104; 132; DLB 9; MTCW

Grieg, (Johan) Nordahl (Brun)
1902-1943 . . . . TCLC 10
See also CA 107

Grieve, C(hristopher) M(urray)
1892-1978 . . . . CLC 11, 19
See also MacDiarmid, Hugh
See also CA 5-8R; 85-88; CANR 33;
MTCW

Griffin, Gerald 1803-1840 . . . . NCLC 7

Griffin, John Howard 1920-1980 . . . . CLC 68
See also AITN 1; CA 1-4R; 101; CANR 2

Griffin, Peter . . . . CLC 39

Griffiths, Trevor 1935- . . . . CLC 13, 52
See also CA 97-100; DLB 13

Grigson, Geoffrey (Edward Harvey)
1905-1985 . . . . CLC 7, 39
See also CA 25-28R; 118; CANR 20, 33;
DLB 27; MTCW

Grillparzer, Franz 1791-1872 . . . . . . NCLC 1

Grimble, Reverend Charles James
See Eliot, T(homas) S(tearns)

Grimke, Charlotte L(ottie) Forten
1837(?)-1914
See Forten, Charlotte L.
See also BW; CA 117; 124

Grimm, Jacob Ludwig Karl
1785-1863 . . . . NCLC 3
See also DLB 90; MAICYA; SATA 22

Grimm, Wilhelm Karl 1786-1859 . . NCLC 3
See also DLB 90; MAICYA; SATA 22

Grimmelshausen, Johann Jakob Christoffel
von 1621-1676 . . . . LC 6

Grindel, Eugene 1895-1952
See Eluard, Paul
See also CA 104

Grossman, David 1954- . . . . CLC 67
See also CA 138

Grossman, Vasily (Semenovich)
1905-1964 . . . . CLC 41
See also CA 124; 130; MTCW

Grove, Frederick Philip . . . . TCLC 4
See also Greve, Felix Paul (Berthold
Friedrich)
See also DLB 92

Grubb
See Crumb, R(obert)

Grumbach, Doris (Isaac)
1918- . . . . CLC 13, 22, 64
See also CA 5-8R; CAAS 2; CANR 9

Grundtvig, Nicolai Frederik Severin
1783-1872 . . . . NCLC 1

Grunge
See Crumb, R(obert)

Grunwald, Lisa 1959- . . . . CLC 44
See also CA 120

Guare, John 1938- . . . . CLC 8, 14, 29, 67
See also CA 73-76; CANR 21; DLB 7;
MTCW

Gudjonsson, Halldor Kiljan 1902-
See Laxness, Halldor
See also CA 103

Guenter, Erich
See Eich, Guenter

Guest, Barbara 1920- . . . . CLC 34
See also CA 25-28R; CANR 11; DLB 5

Guest, Judith (Ann) 1936- . . . . CLC 8, 30
See also AAYA 7; CA 77-80; CANR 15;
MTCW

Guild, Nicholas M. 1944- . . . . CLC 33
See also CA 93-96

Guillemin, Jacques
See Sartre, Jean-Paul

Guillen, Jorge 1893-1984 . . . . CLC 11
See also CA 89-92; 112; DLB 108; HW

Guillen (y Batista), Nicolas (Cristobal)
1902-1989 . . . . CLC 48, 79
See also BLC 2; BW; CA 116; 125; 129;
HW

Guillevic, (Eugene) 1907- . . . . CLC 33
See also CA 93-96

Guillois
See Desnos, Robert

Guiney, Louise Imogen
1861-1920 . . . . TCLC 41
See also DLB 54

Guiraldes, Ricardo (Guillermo)
1886-1927 . . . . TCLC 39
See also CA 131; HW; MTCW

Gunn, Bill . . . . CLC 5
See also Gunn, William Harrison
See also DLB 38

Gunn, Thom(son William)
1929- . . . . CLC 3, 6, 18, 32
See also CA 17-20R; CANR 9, 33;
CDBLB 1960 to Present; DLB 27;
MTCW

Gunn, William Harrison 1934(?)-1989
See Gunn, Bill
See also AITN 1; BW; CA 13-16R; 128;
CANR 12, 25

Gunnars, Kristjana 1948- . . . . CLC 69
See also CA 113; DLB 60

Gurganus, Allan 1947- . . . . CLC 70
See also BEST 90:1; CA 135

Gurney, A(lbert) R(amsdell), Jr.
1930- . . . . CLC 32, 50, 54
See also CA 77-80; CANR 32

Gurney, Ivor (Bertie) 1890-1937 . . . TCLC 33

Gurney, Peter
See Gurney, A(lbert) R(amsdell), Jr.

Gustafson, Ralph (Barker) 1909- . . . . CLC 36
See also CA 21-24R; CANR 8; DLB 88

Gut, Gom
See Simenon, Georges (Jacques Christian)

Guthrie, A(lfred) B(ertram), Jr.
1901-1991 . . . . CLC 23
See also CA 57-60; 134; CANR 24; DLB 6;
SATA 62; SATA-Obit 67

Guthrie, Isobel
See Grieve, C(hristopher) M(urray)

Guthrie, Woodrow Wilson 1912-1967
See Guthrie, Woody
See also CA 113; 93-96

Guthrie, Woody. . . . . CLC 35
See also Guthrie, Woodrow Wilson

Guy, Rosa (Cuthbert) 1928-. . . . . . . CLC 26
See also AAYA 4; BW; CA 17-20R;
CANR 14, 34; CLR 13; DLB 33;
MAICYA; SATA 14, 62

Gwendolyn
See Bennett, (Enoch) Arnold

H. D. . . . . CLC 3, 8, 14, 31, 34, 73; PC 5
See also Doolittle, Hilda

Haavikko, Paavo Juhani
1931- . . . . CLC 18, 34
See also CA 106

Habbema, Koos
See Heijermans, Herman

Hacker, Marilyn 1942- . . . . CLC 5, 9, 23, 72
See also CA 77-80; DLB 120

Haggard, H(enry) Rider
1856-1925 . . . . TCLC 11
See also CA 108; DLB 70; SATA 16

Haig, Fenil
See Ford, Ford Madox

Haig-Brown, Roderick (Langmere)
1908-1976 . . . . CLC 21
See also CA 5-8R; 69-72; CANR 4, 38;
CLR 31; DLB 88; MAICYA; SATA 12

Hailey, Arthur 1920- . . . . CLC 5
See also AITN 2; BEST 90:3; CA 1-4R;
CANR 2, 36; DLB 88; DLBY 82; MTCW

Hailey, Elizabeth Forsythe 1938- . . . CLC 40
See also CA 93-96; CAAS 1; CANR 15

Haines, John (Meade) 1924- . . . . CLC 58
See also CA 17-20R; CANR 13, 34; DLB 5

Haldeman, Joe (William) 1943-. . . . . CLC 61
See also CA 53-56; CANR 6; DLB 8

Haley, Alex(ander Murray Palmer)
1921-1992 . . . . CLC 8, 12, 76
See also BLC 2; BW; CA 77-80; 136; DA;
DLB 38; MTCW

Haliburton, Thomas Chandler
1796-1865 . . . . NCLC 15
See also DLB 11, 99

Hall, Donald (Andrew, Jr.)
1928- . . . . CLC 1, 13, 37, 59
See also CA 5-8R; CAAS 7; CANR 2;
DLB 5; SATA 23

Hall, Frederic Sauser
See Sauser-Hall, Frederic

Hall, James
See Kuttner, Henry

Hall, James Norman 1887-1951 . . . TCLC 23
See also CA 123; SATA 21

Hall, (Marguerite) Radclyffe
1886(?)-1943 . . . . TCLC 12
See also CA 110

Hall, Rodney 1935- . . . . CLC 51
See also CA 109

Halliday, Michael
See Creasey, John

Halpern, Daniel 1945- . . . . CLC 14
See also CA 33-36R

Hamburger, Michael (Peter Leopold)
1924- . . . . CLC 5, 14
See also CA 5-8R; CAAS 4; CANR 2;
DLB 27

Hamill, Pete 1935- . . . . CLC 10
See also CA 25-28R; CANR 18

Hamilton, Clive
See Lewis, C(live) S(taples)

Hamilton, Edmond 1904-1977 . . . . . . CLC 1
See also CA 1-4R; CANR 3; DLB 8

Hamilton, Eugene (Jacob) Lee
See Lee-Hamilton, Eugene (Jacob)

Hamilton, Franklin
See Silverberg, Robert

Hamilton, Gail
See Corcoran, Barbara

Hamilton, Mollie
See Kaye, M(ary) M(argaret)

Hamilton, (Anthony Walter) Patrick
1904-1962 . . . . CLC 51
See also CA 113; DLB 10

Hamilton, Virginia 1936-. . . . . CLC 26
See also AAYA 2; BW; CA 25-28R;
CANR 20, 37; CLR 1, 11; DLB 33, 52;
MAICYA; MTCW; SATA 4, 56

Hammett, (Samuel) Dashiell
1894-1961 . . . . CLC 3, 5, 10, 19, 47
See also AITN 1; CA 81-84;
CDALB 1929-1941; DLBD 6; MTCW

Hammon, Jupiter 1711(?)-1800(?). . NCLC 5
See also BLC 2; DLB 31, 50

Hammond, Keith
See Kuttner, Henry

Hamner, Earl (Henry), Jr. 1923- . . . CLC 12
See also AITN 2; CA 73-76; DLB 6

Hampton, Christopher (James)
1946- . . . . CLC 4
See also CA 25-28R; DLB 13; MTCW

Hamsun, Knut . . . . TCLC 2, 14, 49
See also Pedersen, Knut

Handke, Peter 1942- . . CLC 5, 8, 10, 15, 38
See also CA 77-80; CANR 33; DLB 85,
124; MTCW

Hanley, James 1901-1985 . . . CLC 3, 5, 8, 13
See also CA 73-76; 117; CANR 36; MTCW

Hannah, Barry 1942-. . . . . CLC 23, 38
See also CA 108; 110; DLB 6; MTCW

Hannon, Ezra
See Hunter, Evan

Hansberry, Lorraine (Vivian)
1930-1965 . . . . CLC 17, 62; DC 2
See also BLC 2; BW; CA 109; 25-28R;
CABS 3; CDALB 1941-1968; DA;
DLB 7, 38; MTCW

Hansen, Joseph 1923-. . . . . CLC 38
See also CA 29-32R; CAAS 17; CANR 16

Hansen, Martin A. 1909-1955. . . . . TCLC 32

Hanson, Kenneth O(stlin) 1922-. . . . CLC 13
See also CA 53-56; CANR 7

Hardwick, Elizabeth 1916- . . . . CLC 13
See also CA 5-8R; CANR 3, 32; DLB 6;
MTCW

Hardy, Thomas
1840-1928 . . . . . . TCLC 4, 10, 18, 32, 48;
SSC 2
See also CA 104; 123; CDBLB 1890-1914;
DA; DLB 18, 19; MTCW; WLC

Hare, David 1947- . . . . CLC 29, 58
See also CA 97-100; CANR 39; DLB 13;
MTCW

Harford, Henry
See Hudson, W(illiam) H(enry)

Hargrave, Leonie
See Disch, Thomas M(ichael)

Harlan, Louis R(udolph) 1922- . . . . . CLC 34
See also CA 21-24R; CANR 25

Harling, Robert 1951(?)- . . . . CLC 53

Harmon, William (Ruth) 1938- . . . . . CLC 38
See also CA 33-36R; CANR 14, 32, 35;
SATA 65

Harper, F. E. W.
See Harper, Frances Ellen Watkins

Harper, Frances E. W.
See Harper, Frances Ellen Watkins

Harper, Frances E. Watkins
See Harper, Frances Ellen Watkins

Harper, Frances Ellen
See Harper, Frances Ellen Watkins

Harper, Frances Ellen Watkins
1825-1911 . . . . TCLC 14
See also BLC 2; BW; CA 111; 125; DLB 50

Harper, Michael S(teven) 1938-. . . CLC 7, 22
See also BW; CA 33-36R; CANR 24;
DLB 41

Harper, Mrs. F. E. W.
See Harper, Frances Ellen Watkins

Harris, Christie (Lucy) Irwin
1907- . . . . CLC 12
See also CA 5-8R; CANR 6; DLB 88;
MAICYA; SAAS 10; SATA 6, 74

Harris, Frank 1856(?)-1931. . . . . . . TCLC 24
See also CA 109

Harris, George Washington
1814-1869 . . . . NCLC 23
See also DLB 3, 11

Harris, Joel Chandler 1848-1908 . . . TCLC 2
See also CA 104; 137; DLB 11, 23, 42, 78,
91; MAICYA; YABC 1

Harris, John (Wyndham Parkes Lucas)
Beynon 1903-1969 . . . . CLC 19
See also CA 102; 89-92

Harris, MacDonald
See Heiney, Donald (William)

Harris, Mark 1922- . . . . CLC 19
See also CA 5-8R; CAAS 3; CANR 2;
DLB 2; DLBY 80

Harris, (Theodore) Wilson 1921-. . . . CLC 25
See also BW; CA 65-68; CAAS 16;
CANR 11, 27; DLB 117; MTCW

Harrison, Elizabeth Cavanna 1909-
See Cavanna, Betty
See also CA 9-12R; CANR 6, 27

Harrison, Harry (Max) 1925- ...... **CLC 42**
See also CA 1-4R; CANR 5, 21; DLB 8;
SATA 4

Harrison, James (Thomas) 1937-
See Harrison, Jim
See also CA 13-16R; CANR 8

Harrison, Jim .... **CLC 6, 14, 33, 66**
See also Harrison, James (Thomas)
See also DLBY 82

Harrison, Kathryn 1961- .... **CLC 70**

Harrison, Tony 1937- .... **CLC 43**
See also CA 65-68; DLB 40; MTCW

Harriss, Will(ard Irvin) 1922- ...... **CLC 34**
See also CA 111

Harson, Sley
See Ellison, Harlan

Hart, Ellis
See Ellison, Harlan

Hart, Josephine 1942(?)- .... **CLC 70**
See also CA 138

Hart, Moss 1904-1961 .... **CLC 66**
See also CA 109; 89-92; DLB 7

Harte, (Francis) Bret(t)
1836(?)-1902 .... **TCLC 1, 25; SSC 8**
See also CA 104; 140; CDALB 1865-1917;
DA; DLB 12, 64, 74, 79; SATA 26; WLC

Hartley, L(eslie) P(oles)
1895-1972 .... **CLC 2, 22**
See also CA 45-48; 37-40R; CANR 33;
DLB 15; MTCW

Hartman, Geoffrey H. 1929- .... **CLC 27**
See also CA 117; 125; DLB 67

Haruf, Kent 19(?)- .... **CLC 34**

Harwood, Ronald 1934- .... **CLC 32**
See also CA 1-4R; CANR 4; DLB 13

Hasek, Jaroslav (Matej Frantisek)
1883-1923 .... **TCLC 4**
See also CA 104; 129; MTCW

Hass, Robert 1941- .... **CLC 18, 39**
See also CA 111; CANR 30; DLB 105

Hastings, Hudson
See Kuttner, Henry

Hastings, Selina .... **CLC 44**

Hatteras, Amelia
See Mencken, H(enry) L(ouis)

Hatteras, Owen .... **TCLC 18**
See also Mencken, H(enry) L(ouis); Nathan,
George Jean

Hauptmann, Gerhart (Johann Robert)
1862-1946 .... **TCLC 4**
See also CA 104; DLB 66, 118

Havel, Vaclav 1936- .... **CLC 25, 58, 65**
See also CA 104; CANR 36; MTCW

Haviaras, Stratis .... **CLC 33**
See also Chaviaras, Strates

Hawes, Stephen 1475(?)-1523(?) ..... **LC 17**

Hawkes, John (Clendennin Burne, Jr.)
1925- ...... **CLC 1, 2, 3, 4, 7, 9, 14, 15,
27, 49**
See also CA 1-4R; CANR 2; DLB 2, 7;
DLBY 80; MTCW

Hawking, S. W.
See Hawking, Stephen W(illiam)

Hawking, Stephen W(illiam)
1942- .... **CLC 63**
See also BEST 89:1; CA 126; 129

Hawthorne, Julian 1846-1934 ..... **TCLC 25**

Hawthorne, Nathaniel
1804-1864 .... **NCLC 39; SSC 3**
See also CDALB 1640-1865; DA; DLB 1,
74; WLC; YABC 2

Haxton, Josephine Ayres 1921- .... **CLC 73**
See also CA 115; CANR 41

Hayaseca y Eizaguirre, Jorge
See Echegaray (y Eizaguirre), Jose (Maria
Waldo)

Hayashi Fumiko 1904-1951 ...... **TCLC 27**

Haycraft, Anna
See Ellis, Alice Thomas
See also CA 122

Hayden, Robert E(arl)
1913-1980 ...... **CLC 5, 9, 14, 37; PC 6**
See also BLC 2; BW; CA 69-72; 97-100;
CABS 2; CANR 24; CDALB 1941-1968;
DA; DLB 5, 76; MTCW; SATA 19, 26

Hayford, J(oseph) E(phraim) Casely
See Casely-Hayford, J(oseph) E(phraim)

Hayman, Ronald 1932- .... **CLC 44**
See also CA 25-28R; CANR 18

Haywood, Eliza (Fowler)
1693(?)-1756 .... **LC 1**

Hazlitt, William 1778-1830 ...... **NCLC 29**
See also DLB 110

Hazzard, Shirley 1931- .... **CLC 18**
See also CA 9-12R; CANR 4; DLBY 82;
MTCW

Head, Bessie 1937-1986 .... **CLC 25, 67**
See also BLC 2; BW; CA 29-32R; 119;
CANR 25; DLB 117; MTCW

Headon, (Nicky) Topper 1956(?)- ... **CLC 30**
See also Clash, The

Heaney, Seamus (Justin)
1939- .... **CLC 5, 7, 14, 25, 37, 74**
See also CA 85-88; CANR 25;
CDBLB 1960 to Present; DLB 40;
MTCW

Hearn, (Patricio) Lafcadio (Tessima Carlos)
1850-1904 .... **TCLC 9**
See also CA 105; DLB 12, 78

Hearne, Vicki 1946- .... **CLC 56**
See also CA 139

Hearon, Shelby 1931- .... **CLC 63**
See also AITN 2; CA 25-28R; CANR 18

Heat-Moon, William Least .... **CLC 29**
See also Trogdon, William (Lewis)
See also AAYA 9

Hebert, Anne 1916- .... **CLC 4, 13, 29**
See also CA 85-88; DLB 68; MTCW

Hecht, Anthony (Evan)
1923- .... **CLC 8, 13, 19**
See also CA 9-12R; CANR 6; DLB 5

Hecht, Ben 1894-1964 .... **CLC 8**
See also CA 85-88; DLB 7, 9, 25, 26, 28, 86

Hedayat, Sadeq 1903-1951 .... **TCLC 21**
See also CA 120

Heidegger, Martin 1889-1976 ...... **CLC 24**
See also CA 81-84; 65-68; CANR 34;
MTCW

Heidenstam, (Carl Gustaf) Verner von
1859-1940 .... **TCLC 5**
See also CA 104

Heifner, Jack 1946- .... **CLC 11**
See also CA 105

Heijermans, Herman 1864-1924 ... **TCLC 24**
See also CA 123

Heilbrun, Carolyn G(old) 1926- .... **CLC 25**
See also CA 45-48; CANR 1, 28

Heine, Heinrich 1797-1856 .... **NCLC 4**
See also DLB 90

Heinemann, Larry (Curtiss) 1944- .. **CLC 50**
See also CA 110; CANR 31; DLBD 9

Heiney, Donald (William) 1921- ..... **CLC 9**
See also CA 1-4R; CANR 3

Heinlein, Robert A(nson)
1907-1988 ...... **CLC 1, 3, 8, 14, 26, 55**
See also CA 1-4R; 125; CANR 1, 20;
DLB 8; MAICYA; MTCW; SATA 9, 56,
69

Helforth, John
See Doolittle, Hilda

Hellenhofferu, Vojtech Kapristian z
See Hasek, Jaroslav (Matej Frantisek)

Heller, Joseph
1923- .... **CLC 1, 3, 5, 8, 11, 36, 63**
See also AITN 1; CA 5-8R; CABS 1;
CANR 8; DA; DLB 2, 28; DLBY 80;
MTCW; WLC

Hellman, Lillian (Florence)
1906-1984 ...... **CLC 2, 4, 8, 14, 18, 34,
44, 52; DC 1**
See also AITN 1, 2; CA 13-16R; 112;
CANR 33; DLB 7; DLBY 84; MTCW

Helprin, Mark 1947- ..... **CLC 7, 10, 22, 32**
See also CA 81-84; DLBY 85; MTCW

Helyar, Jane Penelope Josephine 1933-
See Poole, Josephine
See also CA 21-24R; CANR 10, 26

Hemans, Felicia 1793-1835 ...... **NCLC 29**
See also DLB 96

Hemingway, Ernest (Miller)
1899-1961 .... **CLC 1, 3, 6, 8, 10, 13, 19,
30, 34, 39, 41, 44, 50, 61; SSC 1**
See also CA 77-80; CANR 34;
CDALB 1917-1929; DA; DLB 4, 9, 102;
DLBD 1; DLBY 81, 87; MTCW; WLC

Hempel, Amy 1951- .... **CLC 39**
See also CA 118; 137

Henderson, F. C.
See Mencken, H(enry) L(ouis)

Henderson, Sylvia
See Ashton-Warner, Sylvia (Constance)

Henley, Beth .... **CLC 23**
See also Henley, Elizabeth Becker
See also CABS 3; DLBY 86

Henley, Elizabeth Becker 1952-
See Henley, Beth
See also CA 107; CANR 32; MTCW

Henley, William Ernest
1849-1903 .... **TCLC 8**
See also CA 105; DLB 19

Hennissart, Martha
See Lathen, Emma
See also CA 85-88

Henry, O. . . . . **TCLC 1, 19; SSC 5**
See also Porter, William Sydney
See also WLC

Henryson, Robert 1430(?)-1506(?). . . . **LC 20**

Henry VIII 1491-1547 . . . . **LC 10**

Henschke, Alfred
See Klabund

Hentoff, Nat(han Irving) 1925- . . . . . **CLC 26**
See also AAYA 4; CA 1-4R; CAAS 6;
CANR 5, 25; CLR 1; MAICYA;
SATA 27, 42, 69

Heppenstall, (John) Rayner
1911-1981 . . . . **CLC 10**
See also CA 1-4R; 103; CANR 29

Herbert, Frank (Patrick)
1920-1986 . . . . **CLC 12, 23, 35, 44**
See also CA 53-56; 118; CANR 5; DLB 8;
MTCW; SATA 9, 37, 47

Herbert, George 1593-1633 . . . . **PC 4**
See also CDBLB Before 1660; DLB 126

Herbert, Zbigniew 1924- . . . . **CLC 9, 43**
See also CA 89-92; CANR 36; MTCW

Herbst, Josephine (Frey)
1897-1969 . . . . **CLC 34**
See also CA 5-8R; 25-28R; DLB 9

Hergesheimer, Joseph
1880-1954 . . . . **TCLC 11**
See also CA 109; DLB 102, 9

Herlihy, James Leo 1927- . . . . **CLC 6**
See also CA 1-4R; CANR 2

Hermogenes fl. c. 175- . . . . **CMLC 6**

Hernandez, Jose 1834-1886 . . . . . . **NCLC 17**

Herrick, Robert 1591-1674 . . . . **LC 13**
See also DA; DLB 126

Herring, Guilles
See Somerville, Edith

Herriot, James 1916- . . . . **CLC 12**
See also Wight, James Alfred
See also AAYA 1; CANR 40

Herrmann, Dorothy 1941- . . . . **CLC 44**
See also CA 107

Herrmann, Taffy
See Herrmann, Dorothy

Hersey, John (Richard)
1914-1993 . . . . **CLC 1, 2, 7, 9, 40**
See also CA 17-20R; 140; CANR 33;
DLB 6; MTCW; SATA 25

Herzen, Aleksandr Ivanovich
1812-1870 . . . . **NCLC 10**

Herzl, Theodor 1860-1904 . . . . **TCLC 36**

Herzog, Werner 1942- . . . . **CLC 16**
See also CA 89-92

Hesiod c. 8th cent. B.C.- . . . . **CMLC 5**

Hesse, Hermann
1877-1962 . . . . **CLC 1, 2, 3, 6, 11, 17, 25,
69; SSC 9**
See also CA 17-18; CAP 2; DA; DLB 66;
MTCW; SATA 50; WLC

Hewes, Cady
See De Voto, Bernard (Augustine)

Heyen, William 1940- . . . . **CLC 13, 18**
See also CA 33-36R; CAAS 9; DLB 5

Heyerdahl, Thor 1914- . . . . **CLC 26**
See also CA 5-8R; CANR 5, 22; MTCW;
SATA 2, 52

Heym, Georg (Theodor Franz Arthur)
1887-1912 . . . . **TCLC 9**
See also CA 106

Heym, Stefan 1913- . . . . **CLC 41**
See also CA 9-12R; CANR 4; DLB 69

Heyse, Paul (Johann Ludwig von)
1830-1914 . . . . **TCLC 8**
See also CA 104; DLB 129

Hibbert, Eleanor Alice Burford
1906-1993 . . . . **CLC 7**
See also BEST 90:4; CA 17-20R; CANR 9,
28; SATA 2; SATA-Obit 74

Higgins, George V(incent)
1939- . . . . **CLC 4, 7, 10, 18**
See also CA 77-80; CAAS 5; CANR 17;
DLB 2; DLBY 81; MTCW

Higginson, Thomas Wentworth
1823-1911 . . . . **TCLC 36**
See also DLB 1, 64

Highet, Helen
See MacInnes, Helen (Clark)

Highsmith, (Mary) Patricia
1921- . . . . **CLC 2, 4, 14, 42**
See also CA 1-4R; CANR 1, 20; MTCW

Highwater, Jamake (Mamake)
1942(?)- . . . . **CLC 12**
See also AAYA 7; CA 65-68; CAAS 7;
CANR 10, 34; CLR 17; DLB 52;
DLBY 85; MAICYA; SATA 30, 32, 69

Hijuelos, Oscar 1951- . . . . **CLC 65**
See also BEST 90:1; CA 123; HW

Hikmet, Nazim 1902-1963 . . . . **CLC 40**
See also CA 93-96

Hildesheimer, Wolfgang
1916-1991 . . . . **CLC 49**
See also CA 101; 135; DLB 69, 124

Hill, Geoffrey (William)
1932- . . . . **CLC 5, 8, 18, 45**
See also CA 81-84; CANR 21;
CDBLB 1960 to Present; DLB 40;
MTCW

Hill, George Roy 1921- . . . . **CLC 26**
See also CA 110; 122

Hill, John
See Koontz, Dean R(ay)

Hill, Susan (Elizabeth) 1942- . . . . **CLC 4**
See also CA 33-36R; CANR 29; DLB 14;
MTCW

Hillerman, Tony 1925- . . . . **CLC 62**
See also AAYA 6; BEST 89:1; CA 29-32R;
CANR 21; SATA 6

Hillesum, Etty 1914-1943 . . . . **TCLC 49**
See also CA 137

Hilliard, Noel (Harvey) 1929- . . . . . . **CLC 15**
See also CA 9-12R; CANR 7

Hillis, Rick 1956- . . . . **CLC 66**
See also CA 134

Hilton, James 1900-1954 . . . . **TCLC 21**
See also CA 108; DLB 34, 77; SATA 34

Himes, Chester (Bomar)
1909-1984 . . . . **CLC 2, 4, 7, 18, 58**
See also BLC 2; BW; CA 25-28R; 114;
CANR 22; DLB 2, 76; MTCW

Hinde, Thomas . . . . **CLC 6, 11**
See also Chitty, Thomas Willes

Hindin, Nathan
See Bloch, Robert (Albert)

Hine, (William) Daryl 1936- . . . . **CLC 15**
See also CA 1-4R; CAAS 15; CANR 1, 20;
DLB 60

Hinkson, Katharine Tynan
See Tynan, Katharine

Hinton, S(usan) E(loise) 1950- . . . . . **CLC 30**
See also AAYA 2; CA 81-84; CANR 32;
CLR 3, 23; DA; MAICYA; MTCW;
SATA 19, 58

Hippius, Zinaida . . . . **TCLC 9**
See also Gippius, Zinaida (Nikolayevna)

Hiraoka, Kimitake 1925-1970
See Mishima, Yukio
See also CA 97-100; 29-32R; MTCW

Hirsch, E(ric) D(onald), Jr. 1928- . . . **CLC 79**
See also CA 25-28R; CANR 27; DLB 67;
MTCW

Hirsch, Edward 1950- . . . . **CLC 31, 50**
See also CA 104; CANR 20; DLB 120

Hitchcock, Alfred (Joseph)
1899-1980 . . . . **CLC 16**
See also CA 97-100; SATA 24, 27

Hoagland, Edward 1932- . . . . **CLC 28**
See also CA 1-4R; CANR 2, 31; DLB 6;
SATA 51

Hoban, Russell (Conwell) 1925- . . **CLC 7, 25**
See also CA 5-8R; CANR 23, 37; CLR 3;
DLB 52; MAICYA; MTCW; SATA 1, 40

Hobbs, Perry
See Blackmur, R(ichard) P(almer)

Hobson, Laura Z(ametkin)
1900-1986 . . . . **CLC 7, 25**
See also CA 17-20R; 118; DLB 28;
SATA 52

Hochhuth, Rolf 1931- . . . . **CLC 4, 11, 18**
See also CA 5-8R; CANR 33; DLB 124;
MTCW

Hochman, Sandra 1936- . . . . **CLC 3, 8**
See also CA 5-8R; DLB 5

Hochwaelder, Fritz 1911-1986 . . . . . . **CLC 36**
See also Hochwalder, Fritz
See also CA 29-32R; 120; MTCW

Hochwalder, Fritz . . . . **CLC 36**
See also Hochwaelder, Fritz

Hocking, Mary (Eunice) 1921- . . . . . **CLC 13**
See also CA 101; CANR 18, 40

Hodgins, Jack 1938- . . . . **CLC 23**
See also CA 93-96; DLB 60

Hodgson, William Hope
1877(?)-1918 . . . . **TCLC 13**
See also CA 111; DLB 70

Hoffman, Alice 1952- . . . . **CLC 51**
See also CA 77-80; CANR 34; MTCW

Hoffman, Daniel (Gerard)
1923- . . . . **CLC 6, 13, 23**
See also CA 1-4R; CANR 4; DLB 5

Hoffman, Stanley 1944- . . . . CLC 5
See also CA 77-80

Hoffman, William M(oses) 1939- . . . CLC 40
See also CA 57-60; CANR 11

Hoffmann, E(rnst) T(heodor) A(madeus)
1776-1822 . . . . NCLC 2; SSC 13
See also DLB 90; SATA 27

Hofmann, Gert 1931- . . . . CLC 54
See also CA 128

Hofmannsthal, Hugo von
1874-1929 . . . . TCLC 11
See also CA 106; DLB 81, 118

Hogan, Linda 1947- . . . . CLC 73
See also CA 120

Hogarth, Charles
See Creasey, John

Hogg, James 1770-1835 . . . . NCLC 4
See also DLB 93, 116

Holbach, Paul Henri Thiry Baron
1723-1789 . . . . LC 14

Holberg, Ludvig 1684-1754 . . . . LC 6

Holden, Ursula 1921- . . . . CLC 18
See also CA 101; CAAS 8; CANR 22

Holderlin, (Johann Christian) Friedrich
1770-1843 . . . . NCLC 16; PC 4

Holdstock, Robert
See Holdstock, Robert P.

Holdstock, Robert P. 1948- . . . . CLC 39
See also CA 131

Holland, Isabelle 1920- . . . . CLC 21
See also CA 21-24R; CANR 10, 25;
MAICYA; SATA 8, 70

Holland, Marcus
See Caldwell, (Janet Miriam) Taylor
(Holland)

Hollander, John 1929- . . . . . . CLC 2, 5, 8, 14
See also CA 1-4R; CANR 1; DLB 5;
SATA 13

Hollander, Paul
See Silverberg, Robert

Holleran, Andrew 1943(?)- . . . . CLC 38

Hollinghurst, Alan 1954- . . . . CLC 55
See also CA 114

Hollis, Jim
See Summers, Hollis (Spurgeon, Jr.)

Holmes, John
See Souster, (Holmes) Raymond

Holmes, John Clellon 1926-1988 . . . . CLC 56
See also CA 9-12R; 125; CANR 4; DLB 16

Holmes, Oliver Wendell
1809-1894 . . . . NCLC 14
See also CDALB 1640-1865; DLB 1;
SATA 34

Holmes, Raymond
See Souster, (Holmes) Raymond

Holt, Victoria
See Hibbert, Eleanor Alice Burford

Holub, Miroslav 1923- . . . . CLC 4
See also CA 21-24R; CANR 10

Homer c. 8th cent. B.C.- . . . . CMLC 1
See also DA

Honig, Edwin 1919- . . . . CLC 33
See also CA 5-8R; CAAS 8; CANR 4;
DLB 5

Hood, Hugh (John Blagdon)
1928- . . . . CLC 15, 28
See also CA 49-52; CAAS 17; CANR 1, 33;
DLB 53

Hood, Thomas 1799-1845 . . . . NCLC 16
See also DLB 96

Hooker, (Peter) Jeremy 1941- . . . . . . CLC 43
See also CA 77-80; CANR 22; DLB 40

Hope, A(lec) D(erwent) 1907- . . . . CLC 3, 51
See also CA 21-24R; CANR 33; MTCW

Hope, Brian
See Creasey, John

Hope, Christopher (David Tully)
1944- . . . . CLC 52
See also CA 106; SATA 62

Hopkins, Gerard Manley
1844-1889 . . . . NCLC 17
See also CDBLB 1890-1914; DA; DLB 35,
57; WLC

Hopkins, John (Richard) 1931- . . . . . . CLC 4
See also CA 85-88

Hopkins, Pauline Elizabeth
1859-1930 . . . . TCLC 28
See also BLC 2; DLB 50

Hopley-Woolrich, Cornell George 1903-1968
See Woolrich, Cornell
See also CA 13-14; CAP 1

Horatio
See Proust, (Valentin-Louis-George-Eugene-)
Marcel

Horgan, Paul 1903- . . . . CLC 9, 53
See also CA 13-16R; CANR 9, 35;
DLB 102; DLBY 85; MTCW; SATA 13

Horn, Peter
See Kuttner, Henry

Hornem, Horace Esq.
See Byron, George Gordon (Noel)

Horovitz, Israel 1939- . . . . CLC 56
See also CA 33-36R; DLB 7

Horvath, Odon von
See Horvath, Oedoen von
See also DLB 85, 124

Horvath, Oedoen von 1901-1938 . . . TCLC 45
See also Horvath, Odon von
See also CA 118

Horwitz, Julius 1920-1986 . . . . CLC 14
See also CA 9-12R; 119; CANR 12

Hospital, Janette Turner 1942- . . . . . CLC 42
See also CA 108

Hostos, E. M. de
See Hostos (y Bonilla), Eugenio Maria de

Hostos, Eugenio M. de
See Hostos (y Bonilla), Eugenio Maria de

Hostos, Eugenio Maria
See Hostos (y Bonilla), Eugenio Maria de

Hostos (y Bonilla), Eugenio Maria de
1839-1903 . . . . TCLC 24
See also CA 123; 131; HW

Houdini
See Lovecraft, H(oward) P(hillips)

Hougan, Carolyn 1943- . . . . CLC 34
See also CA 139

Household, Geoffrey (Edward West)
1900-1988 . . . . CLC 11
See also CA 77-80; 126; DLB 87; SATA 14,
59

Housman, A(lfred) E(dward)
1859-1936 . . . . TCLC 1, 10; PC 2
See also CA 104; 125; DA; DLB 19;
MTCW

Housman, Laurence 1865-1959 . . . . . TCLC 7
See also CA 106; DLB 10; SATA 25

Howard, Elizabeth Jane 1923- . . . CLC 7, 29
See also CA 5-8R; CANR 8

Howard, Maureen 1930- . . . . . CLC 5, 14, 46
See also CA 53-56; CANR 31; DLBY 83;
MTCW

Howard, Richard 1929- . . . . CLC 7, 10, 47
See also AITN 1; CA 85-88; CANR 25;
DLB 5

Howard, Robert Ervin 1906-1936 . . . TCLC 8
See also CA 105

Howard, Warren F.
See Pohl, Frederik

Howe, Fanny 1940- . . . . CLC 47
See also CA 117; SATA 52

Howe, Julia Ward 1819-1910 . . . . . TCLC 21
See also CA 117; DLB 1

Howe, Susan 1937- . . . . CLC 72
See also DLB 120

Howe, Tina 1937- . . . . CLC 48
See also CA 109

Howell, James 1594(?)-1666 . . . . LC 13

Howells, W. D.
See Howells, William Dean

Howells, William D.
See Howells, William Dean

Howells, William Dean
1837-1920 . . . . TCLC 41, 7, 17
See also CA 104; 134; CDALB 1865-1917;
DLB 12, 64, 74, 79

Howes, Barbara 1914- . . . . CLC 15
See also CA 9-12R; CAAS 3; SATA 5

Hrabal, Bohumil 1914- . . . . CLC 13, 67
See also CA 106; CAAS 12

Hsun, Lu . . . . TCLC 3
See also Shu-Jen, Chou

Hubbard, L(afayette) Ron(ald)
1911-1986 . . . . CLC 43
See also CA 77-80; 118; CANR 22

Huch, Ricarda (Octavia)
1864-1947 . . . . TCLC 13
See also CA 111; DLB 66

Huddle, David 1942- . . . . CLC 49
See also CA 57-60; DLB 130

Hudson, Jeffrey
See Crichton, (John) Michael

Hudson, W(illiam) H(enry)
1841-1922 . . . . TCLC 29
See also CA 115; DLB 98; SATA 35

Hueffer, Ford Madox
See Ford, Ford Madox

Hughart, Barry 1934- . . . . CLC 39
See also CA 137

Hughes, Colin
See Creasey, John

Hughes, David (John) 1930- .... **CLC 48**
See also CA 116; 129; DLB 14

Hughes, (James) Langston
1902-1967 ..... **CLC 1, 5, 10, 15, 35, 44;
DC 3; PC 1; SSC 6**
See also BLC 2; BW; CA 1-4R; 25-28R;
CANR 1, 34; CDALB 1929-1941;
CLR 17; DA; DLB 4, 7, 48, 51, 86;
MAICYA; MTCW; SATA 4, 33; WLC

Hughes, Richard (Arthur Warren)
1900-1976 .... **CLC 1, 11**
See also CA 5-8R; 65-68; CANR 4;
DLB 15; MTCW; SATA 8, 25

Hughes, Ted
1930- .... **CLC 2, 4, 9, 14, 37; PC 7**
See also CA 1-4R; CANR 1, 33; CLR 3;
DLB 40; MAICYA; MTCW; SATA 27,
49

Hugo, Richard F(ranklin)
1923-1982 .... **CLC 6, 18, 32**
See also CA 49-52; 108; CANR 3; DLB 5

Hugo, Victor (Marie)
1802-1885 .... **NCLC 3, 10, 21**
See also DA; DLB 119; SATA 47; WLC

Huidobro, Vicente
See Huidobro Fernandez, Vicente Garcia

Huidobro Fernandez, Vicente Garcia
1893-1948 .... **TCLC 31**
See also CA 131; HW

Hulme, Keri 1947- .... **CLC 39**
See also CA 125

Hulme, T(homas) E(rnest)
1883-1917 .... **TCLC 21**
See also CA 117; DLB 19

Hume, David 1711-1776............. **LC 7**
See also DLB 104

Humphrey, William 1924-......... **CLC 45**
See also CA 77-80; DLB 6

Humphreys, Emyr Owen 1919-..... **CLC 47**
See also CA 5-8R; CANR 3, 24; DLB 15

Humphreys, Josephine 1945-.... **CLC 34, 57**
See also CA 121; 127

Hungerford, Pixie
See Brinsmead, H(esba) F(ay)

Hunt, E(verette) Howard, Jr.
1918- .... **CLC 3**
See also AITN 1; CA 45-48; CANR 2

Hunt, Kyle
See Creasey, John

Hunt, (James Henry) Leigh
1784-1859 .... **NCLC 1**

Hunt, Marsha 1946-.............. **CLC 70**

Hunter, E. Waldo
See Sturgeon, Theodore (Hamilton)

Hunter, Evan 1926- .... **CLC 11, 31**
See also CA 5-8R; CANR 5, 38; DLBY 82;
MTCW; SATA 25

Hunter, Kristin (Eggleston) 1931-... **CLC 35**
See also AITN 1; BW; CA 13-16R;
CANR 13; CLR 3; DLB 33; MAICYA;
SAAS 10; SATA 12

Hunter, Mollie 1922-............. **CLC 21**
See also McIlwraith, Maureen Mollie
Hunter
See also CANR 37; CLR 25; MAICYA;
SAAS 7; SATA 54

Hunter, Robert (?)-1734............. **LC 7**

Hurston, Zora Neale
1903-1960 .... **CLC 7, 30, 61; SSC 4**
See also BLC 2; BW; CA 85-88; DA;
DLB 51, 86; MTCW

Huston, John (Marcellus)
1906-1987 .... **CLC 20**
See also CA 73-76; 123; CANR 34; DLB 26

Hustvedt, Siri 1955-.............. **CLC 76**
See also CA 137

Hutten, Ulrich von 1488-1523...... **LC 16**

Huxley, Aldous (Leonard)
1894-1963 ..... **CLC 1, 3, 4, 5, 8, 11, 18,
35, 79**
See also CA 85-88; CDBLB 1914-1945; DA;
DLB 36, 100; MTCW; SATA 63; WLC

Huysmans, Charles Marie Georges
1848-1907
See Huysmans, Joris-Karl
See also CA 104

Huysmans, Joris-Karl............. **TCLC 7**
See also Huysmans, Charles Marie Georges
See also DLB 123

Hwang, David Henry 1957-........ **CLC 55**
See also CA 127; 132

Hyde, Anthony 1946-............. **CLC 42**
See also CA 136

Hyde, Margaret O(ldroyd) 1917- ... **CLC 21**
See also CA 1-4R; CANR 1, 36; CLR 23;
MAICYA; SAAS 8; SATA 1, 42

Hynes, James 1956(?)-............ **CLC 65**

Ian, Janis 1951- .... **CLC 21**
See also CA 105

Ibanez, Vicente Blasco
See Blasco Ibanez, Vicente

Ibarguengoitia, Jorge 1928-1983.... **CLC 37**
See also CA 124; 113; HW

Ibsen, Henrik (Johan)
1828-1906 ..... **TCLC 2, 8, 16, 37; DC 2**
See also CA 104; DA; WLC

Ibuse Masuji 1898-.............. **CLC 22**
See also CA 127

Ichikawa, Kon 1915-............. **CLC 20**
See also CA 121

Idle, Eric 1943-.................. **CLC 21**
See also Monty Python
See also CA 116; CANR 35

Ignatow, David 1914-...... **CLC 4, 7, 14, 40**
See also CA 9-12R; CAAS 3; CANR 31;
DLB 5

Ihimaera, Witi 1944- .... **CLC 46**
See also CA 77-80

Ilf, Ilya........................ **TCLC 21**
See also Fainzilberg, Ilya Arnoldovich

Immermann, Karl (Lebrecht)
1796-1840 .... **NCLC 4**

Inclan, Ramon (Maria) del Valle
See Valle-Inclan, Ramon (Maria) del

Infante, G(uillermo) Cabrera
See Cabrera Infante, G(uillermo)

Ingalls, Rachel (Holmes) 1940-..... **CLC 42**
See also CA 123; 127

Ingamells, Rex 1913-1955 .... **TCLC 35**

Inge, William Motter
1913-1973 .... **CLC 1, 8, 19**
See also CA 9-12R; CDALB 1941-1968;
DLB 7; MTCW

Ingelow, Jean 1820-1897 .... **NCLC 39**
See also DLB 35; SATA 33

Ingram, Willis J.
See Harris, Mark

Innaurato, Albert (F.) 1948(?)- ... **CLC 21, 60**
See also CA 115; 122

Innes, Michael
See Stewart, J(ohn) I(nnes) M(ackintosh)

Ionesco, Eugene
1912- .... **CLC 1, 4, 6, 9, 11, 15, 41**
See also CA 9-12R; DA; MTCW; SATA 7;
WLC

Iqbal, Muhammad 1873-1938 ..... **TCLC 28**

Ireland, Patrick
See O'Doherty, Brian

Irland, David
See Green, Julian (Hartridge)

Iron, Ralph
See Schreiner, Olive (Emilie Albertina)

Irving, John (Winslow)
1942- .... **CLC 13, 23, 38**
See also AAYA 8; BEST 89:3; CA 25-28R;
CANR 28; DLB 6; DLBY 82; MTCW

Irving, Washington
1783-1859 .... **NCLC 2, 19; SSC 2**
See also CDALB 1640-1865; DA; DLB 3,
11, 30, 59, 73, 74; WLC; YABC 2

Irwin, P. K.
See Page, P(atricia) K(athleen)

Isaacs, Susan 1943- .... **CLC 32**
See also BEST 89:1; CA 89-92; CANR 20,
41; MTCW

Isherwood, Christopher (William Bradshaw)
1904-1986 .... **CLC 1, 9, 11, 14, 44**
See also CA 13-16R; 117; CANR 35;
DLB 15; DLBY 86; MTCW

Ishiguro, Kazuo 1954- ...... **CLC 27, 56, 59**
See also BEST 90:2; CA 120; MTCW

Ishikawa Takuboku
1886(?)-1912 .... **TCLC 15**
See also CA 113

Iskander, Fazil 1929-............. **CLC 47**
See also CA 102

Ivan IV 1530-1584 .... **LC 17**

Ivanov, Vyacheslav Ivanovich
1866-1949 .... **TCLC 33**
See also CA 122

Ivask, Ivar Vidrik 1927-1992....... **CLC 14**
See also CA 37-40R; 139; CANR 24

Jackson, Daniel
See Wingrove, David (John)

Jackson, Jesse 1908-1983 .... **CLC 12**
See also BW; CA 25-28R; 109; CANR 27;
CLR 28; MAICYA; SATA 2, 29, 48

Jones, D(ouglas) G(ordon) 1929-.... **CLC 10**
See also CA 29-32R; CANR 13; DLB 53

Jones, David (Michael)
1895-1974 .... **CLC 2, 4, 7, 13, 42**
See also CA 9-12R; 53-56; CANR 28;
CDBLB 1945-1960; DLB 20, 100; MTCW

Jones, David Robert 1947-
See Bowie, David
See also CA 103

Jones, Diana Wynne 1934- .... **CLC 26**
See also CA 49-52; CANR 4, 26; CLR 23;
MAICYA; SAAS 7; SATA 9, 70

Jones, Edward P. 1951-.......... **CLC 76**

Jones, Gayl 1949-............... **CLC 6, 9**
See also BLC 2; BW; CA 77-80; CANR 27;
DLB 33; MTCW

Jones, James 1921-1977.... **CLC 1, 3, 10, 39**
See also AITN 1, 2; CA 1-4R; 69-72;
CANR 6; DLB 2; MTCW

Jones, John J.
See Lovecraft, H(oward) P(hillips)

Jones, LeRoi .... **CLC 1, 2, 3, 5, 10, 14**
See also Baraka, Amiri

Jones, Louis B. .... **CLC 65**

Jones, Madison (Percy, Jr.) 1925- ... **CLC 4**
See also CA 13-16R; CAAS 11; CANR 7

Jones, Mervyn 1922- .... **CLC 10, 52**
See also CA 45-48; CAAS 5; CANR 1;
MTCW

Jones, Mick 1956(?)-............. **CLC 30**
See also Clash, The

Jones, Nettie (Pearl) 1941- .... **CLC 34**
See also CA 137

Jones, Preston 1936-1979 .... **CLC 10**
See also CA 73-76; 89-92; DLB 7

Jones, Robert F(rancis) 1934-....... **CLC 7**
See also CA 49-52; CANR 2

Jones, Rod 1953- .... **CLC 50**
See also CA 128

Jones, Terence Graham Parry
1942- .... **CLC 21**
See also Jones, Terry; Monty Python
See also CA 112; 116; CANR 35; SATA 51

Jones, Terry
See Jones, Terence Graham Parry
See also SATA 67

Jong, Erica 1942-.......... **CLC 4, 6, 8, 18**
See also AITN 1; BEST 90:2; CA 73-76;
CANR 26; DLB 2, 5, 28; MTCW

Jonson, Ben(jamin) 1572(?)-1637...... **LC 6**
See also CDBLB Before 1660; DA; DLB 62,
121; WLC

Jordan, June 1936-.......... **CLC 5, 11, 23**
See also AAYA 2; BW; CA 33-36R;
CANR 25; CLR 10; DLB 38; MAICYA;
MTCW; SATA 4

Jordan, Pat(rick M.) 1941- .... **CLC 37**
See also CA 33-36R

Jorgensen, Ivar
See Ellison, Harlan

Jorgenson, Ivar
See Silverberg, Robert

Josipovici, Gabriel 1940-........ **CLC 6, 43**
See also CA 37-40R; CAAS 8; DLB 14

Joubert, Joseph 1754-1824 .... **NCLC 9**

Jouve, Pierre Jean 1887-1976...... **CLC 47**
See also CA 65-68

Joyce, James (Augustine Aloysius)
1882-1941 .... **TCLC 3, 8, 16, 35; SSC 3**
See also CA 104; 126; CDBLB 1914-1945;
DA; DLB 10, 19, 36; MTCW; WLC

Jozsef, Attila 1905-1937......... **TCLC 22**
See also CA 116

Juana Ines de la Cruz 1651(?)-1695 ... **LC 5**

Judd, Cyril
See Kornbluth, C(yril) M.; Pohl, Frederik

Julian of Norwich 1342(?)-1416(?) .... **LC 6**

Just, Ward (Swift) 1935-........ **CLC 4, 27**
See also CA 25-28R; CANR 32

Justice, Donald (Rodney) 1925- .. **CLC 6, 19**
See also CA 5-8R; CANR 26; DLBY 83

Juvenal c. 55-c. 127 .... **CMLC 8**

Juvenis
See Bourne, Randolph S(illiman)

Kacew, Romain 1914-1980
See Gary, Romain
See also CA 108; 102

Kadare, Ismail 1936- .... **CLC 52**

Kadohata, Cynthia................. **CLC 59**
See also CA 140

Kafka, Franz
1883-1924 ...... **TCLC 2, 6, 13, 29, 47;**
SSC 5
See also CA 105; 126; DA; DLB 81;
MTCW; WLC

Kahn, Roger 1927-............... **CLC 30**
See also CA 25-28R; SATA 37

Kain, Saul
See Sassoon, Siegfried (Lorraine)

Kaiser, Georg 1878-1945 .... **TCLC 9**
See also CA 106; DLB 124

Kaletski, Alexander 1946-......... **CLC 39**
See also CA 118

Kalidasa fl. c. 400- .... **CMLC 9**

Kallman, Chester (Simon)
1921-1975 .... **CLC 2**
See also CA 45-48; 53-56; CANR 3

Kaminsky, Melvin 1926-
See Brooks, Mel
See also CA 65-68; CANR 16

Kaminsky, Stuart M(elvin) 1934- ... **CLC 59**
See also CA 73-76; CANR 29

Kane, Paul
See Simon, Paul

Kane, Wilson
See Bloch, Robert (Albert)

Kanin, Garson 1912-............... **CLC 22**
See also AITN 1; CA 5-8R; CANR 7;
DLB 7

Kaniuk, Yoram 1930-............. **CLC 19**
See also CA 134

Kant, Immanuel 1724-1804 ...... **NCLC 27**
See also DLB 94

Kantor, MacKinlay 1904-1977 ...... **CLC 7**
See also CA 61-64; 73-76; DLB 9, 102

Kaplan, David Michael 1946- ...... **CLC 50**

Kaplan, James 1951- .... **CLC 59**
See also CA 135

Karageorge, Michael
See Anderson, Poul (William)

Karamzin, Nikolai Mikhailovich
1766-1826 .... **NCLC 3**

Karapanou, Margarita 1946-....... **CLC 13**
See also CA 101

Karinthy, Frigyes 1887-1938...... **TCLC 47**

Karl, Frederick R(obert) 1927-..... **CLC 34**
See also CA 5-8R; CANR 3

Kastel, Warren
See Silverberg, Robert

Kataev, Evgeny Petrovich 1903-1942
See Petrov, Evgeny
See also CA 120

Kataphusin
See Ruskin, John

Katz, Steve 1935-............... **CLC 47**
See also CA 25-28R; CAAS 14; CANR 12;
DLBY 83

Kauffman, Janet 1945-............ **CLC 42**
See also CA 117; DLBY 86

Kaufman, Bob (Garnell)
1925-1986 .... **CLC 49**
See also BW; CA 41-44R; 118; CANR 22;
DLB 16, 41

Kaufman, George S. 1889-1961..... **CLC 38**
See also CA 108; 93-96; DLB 7

Kaufman, Sue .... **CLC 3, 8**
See also Barondess, Sue K(aufman)

Kavafis, Konstantinos Petrou 1863-1933
See Cavafy, C(onstantine) P(eter)
See also CA 104

Kavan, Anna 1901-1968........ **CLC 5, 13**
See also CA 5-8R; CANR 6; MTCW

Kavanagh, Dan
See Barnes, Julian

Kavanagh, Patrick (Joseph)
1904-1967 .... **CLC 22**
See also CA 123; 25-28R; DLB 15, 20;
MTCW

Kawabata, Yasunari
1899-1972 .... **CLC 2, 5, 9, 18**
See also CA 93-96; 33-36R

Kaye, M(ary) M(argaret) 1909-..... **CLC 28**
See also CA 89-92; CANR 24; MTCW;
SATA 62

Kaye, Mollie
See Kaye, M(ary) M(argaret)

Kaye-Smith, Sheila 1887-1956..... **TCLC 20**
See also CA 118; DLB 36

Kaymor, Patrice Maguilene
See Senghor, Leopold Sedar

Kazan, Elia 1909-.......... **CLC 6, 16, 63**
See also CA 21-24R; CANR 32

Kazantzakis, Nikos
1883(?)-1957 .... **TCLC 2, 5, 33**
See also CA 105; 132; MTCW

Kazin, Alfred 1915- .... **CLC 34, 38**
See also CA 1-4R; CAAS 7; CANR 1;
DLB 67

Klein, A(braham) M(oses)
  1909-1972 . . . . CLC **19**
  See also CA 101; 37-40R; DLB 68

Klein, Norma 1938-1989 . . . . CLC **30**
  See also AAYA 2; CA 41-44R; 128;
  CANR 15, 37; CLR 2, 19; MAICYA;
  SAAS 1; SATA 7, 57

Klein, T(heodore) E(ibon) D(onald)
  1947- . . . . CLC **34**
  See also CA 119

Kleist, Heinrich von 1777-1811 . . . . NCLC **2**
  See also DLB 90

Klima, Ivan 1931- . . . . CLC **56**
  See also CA 25-28R; CANR 17

Klimentov, Andrei Platonovich 1899-1951
  See Platonov, Andrei
  See also CA 108

Klinger, Friedrich Maximilian von
  1752-1831 . . . . NCLC **1**
  See also DLB 94

Klopstock, Friedrich Gottlieb
  1724-1803 . . . . NCLC **11**
  See also DLB 97

Knebel, Fletcher 1911-1993 . . . . CLC **14**
  See also AITN 1; CA 1-4R; 140; CAAS 3;
  CANR 1, 36; SATA 36

Knickerbocker, Diedrich
  See Irving, Washington

Knight, Etheridge 1931-1991 . . . . CLC **40**
  See also BLC 2; BW; CA 21-24R; 133;
  CANR 23; DLB 41

Knight, Sarah Kemble 1666-1727 . . . . . LC **7**
  See also DLB 24

Knowles, John 1926- . . . . . . CLC **1, 4, 10, 26**
  See also AAYA 10; CA 17-20R; CANR 40;
  CDALB 1968-1988; DA; DLB 6; MTCW;
  SATA 8

Knox, Calvin M.
  See Silverberg, Robert

Knye, Cassandra
  See Disch, Thomas M(ichael)

Koch, C(hristopher) J(ohn) 1932- . . . CLC **42**
  See also CA 127

Koch, Christopher
  See Koch, C(hristopher) J(ohn)

Koch, Kenneth 1925- . . . . CLC **5, 8, 44**
  See also CA 1-4R; CANR 6, 36; DLB 5;
  SATA 65

Kochanowski, Jan 1530-1584 . . . . LC **10**

Kock, Charles Paul de
  1794-1871 . . . . NCLC **16**

Koda Shigeyuki 1867-1947
  See Rohan, Koda
  See also CA 121

Koestler, Arthur
  1905-1983 . . . . CLC **1, 3, 6, 8, 15, 33**
  See also CA 1-4R; 109; CANR 1, 33;
  CDBLB 1945-1960; DLBY 83; MTCW

Kogawa, Joy Nozomi 1935- . . . . CLC **78**
  See also CA 101; CANR 19

Kohout, Pavel 1928- . . . . CLC **13**
  See also CA 45-48; CANR 3

Koizumi, Yakumo
  See Hearn, (Patricio) Lafcadio (Tessima
  Carlos)

Kolmar, Gertrud 1894-1943 . . . . . . TCLC **40**

Konrad, George
  See Konrad, Gyoergy

Konrad, Gyoergy 1933- . . . . . . CLC **4, 10, 73**
  See also CA 85-88

Konwicki, Tadeusz 1926- . . . . . CLC **8, 28, 54**
  See also CA 101; CAAS 9; CANR 39;
  MTCW

Koontz, Dean R(ay) 1945- . . . . CLC **78**
  See also AAYA 9; BEST 89:3, 90:2;
  CA 108; CANR 19, 36; MTCW

Kopit, Arthur (Lee) 1937- . . . . CLC **1, 18, 33**
  See also AITN 1; CA 81-84; CABS 3;
  DLB 7; MTCW

Kops, Bernard 1926- . . . . CLC **4**
  See also CA 5-8R; DLB 13

Kornbluth, C(yril) M. 1923-1958 . . . . TCLC **8**
  See also CA 105; DLB 8

Korolenko, V. G.
  See Korolenko, Vladimir Galaktionovich

Korolenko, Vladimir
  See Korolenko, Vladimir Galaktionovich

Korolenko, Vladimir G.
  See Korolenko, Vladimir Galaktionovich

Korolenko, Vladimir Galaktionovich
  1853-1921 . . . . TCLC **22**
  See also CA 121

Kosinski, Jerzy (Nikodem)
  1933-1991 . . . . CLC **1, 2, 3, 6, 10, 15, 53,
  70**
  See also CA 17-20R; 134; CANR 9; DLB 2;
  DLBY 82; MTCW

Kostelanetz, Richard (Cory) 1940- . . CLC **28**
  See also CA 13-16R; CAAS 8; CANR 38

Kostrowitzki, Wilhelm Apollinaris de
  1880-1918
  See Apollinaire, Guillaume
  See also CA 104

Kotlowitz, Robert 1924- . . . . CLC **4**
  See also CA 33-36R; CANR 36

Kotzebue, August (Friedrich Ferdinand) von
  1761-1819 . . . . NCLC **25**
  See also DLB 94

Kotzwinkle, William 1938- . . . CLC **5, 14, 35**
  See also CA 45-48; CANR 3; CLR 6;
  MAICYA; SATA 24, 70

Kozol, Jonathan 1936- . . . . CLC **17**
  See also CA 61-64; CANR 16

Kozoll, Michael 1940(?)- . . . . CLC **35**

Kramer, Kathryn 19(?)- . . . . CLC **34**

Kramer, Larry 1935- . . . . CLC **42**
  See also CA 124; 126

Krasicki, Ignacy 1735-1801 . . . . NCLC **8**

Krasinski, Zygmunt 1812-1859 . . . . NCLC **4**

Kraus, Karl 1874-1936 . . . . TCLC **5**
  See also CA 104; DLB 118

Kreve (Mickevicius), Vincas
  1882-1954 . . . . TCLC **27**

Kristeva, Julia 1941- . . . . CLC **77**

Kristofferson, Kris 1936- . . . . CLC **26**
  See also CA 104

Krizanc, John 1956- . . . . CLC **57**

Krleza, Miroslav 1893-1981 . . . . CLC **8**
  See also CA 97-100; 105

Kroetsch, Robert 1927- . . . . . . CLC **5, 23, 57**
  See also CA 17-20R; CANR 8, 38; DLB 53;
  MTCW

Kroetz, Franz
  See Kroetz, Franz Xaver

Kroetz, Franz Xaver 1946- . . . . CLC **41**
  See also CA 130

Kroker, Arthur 1945- . . . . CLC **77**

Kropotkin, Peter (Aleksieevich)
  1842-1921 . . . . TCLC **36**
  See also CA 119

Krotkov, Yuri 1917- . . . . CLC **19**
  See also CA 102

Krumb
  See Crumb, R(obert)

Krumgold, Joseph (Quincy)
  1908-1980 . . . . CLC **12**
  See also CA 9-12R; 101; CANR 7;
  MAICYA; SATA 1, 23, 48

Krumwitz
  See Crumb, R(obert)

Krutch, Joseph Wood 1893-1970 . . . . CLC **24**
  See also CA 1-4R; 25-28R; CANR 4;
  DLB 63

Krutzch, Gus
  See Eliot, T(homas) S(tearns)

Krylov, Ivan Andreevich
  1768(?)-1844 . . . . NCLC **1**

Kubin, Alfred 1877-1959 . . . . TCLC **23**
  See also CA 112; DLB 81

Kubrick, Stanley 1928- . . . . CLC **16**
  See also CA 81-84; CANR 33; DLB 26

Kumin, Maxine (Winokur)
  1925- . . . . CLC **5, 13, 28**
  See also AITN 2; CA 1-4R; CAAS 8;
  CANR 1, 21; DLB 5; MTCW; SATA 12

Kundera, Milan
  1929- . . . . CLC **4, 9, 19, 32, 68**
  See also AAYA 2; CA 85-88; CANR 19;
  MTCW

Kunitz, Stanley (Jasspon)
  1905- . . . . CLC **6, 11, 14**
  See also CA 41-44R; CANR 26; DLB 48;
  MTCW

Kunze, Reiner 1933- . . . . CLC **10**
  See also CA 93-96; DLB 75

Kuprin, Aleksandr Ivanovich
  1870-1938 . . . . TCLC **5**
  See also CA 104

Kureishi, Hanif 1954(?)- . . . . CLC **64**
  See also CA 139

Kurosawa, Akira 1910- . . . . CLC **16**
  See also CA 101

Kuttner, Henry 1915-1958 . . . . TCLC **10**
  See also CA 107; DLB 8

Kuzma, Greg 1944- . . . . CLC **7**
  See also CA 33-36R

Kuzmin, Mikhail 1872(?)-1936 . . . . TCLC **40**

Kyd, Thomas 1558-1594 . . . . . . LC 22; DC 3
See also DLB 62

Kyprianos, Iossif
See Samarakis, Antonis

La Bruyere, Jean de 1645-1696 . . . . . . LC 17

Lacan, Jacques (Marie Emile)
1901-1981 . . . . CLC 75
See also CA 121; 104

**Laclos, Pierre Ambroise Francois Choderlos
de** 1741-1803 . . . . NCLC 4

La Colere, Francois
See Aragon, Louis

Lacolere, Francois
See Aragon, Louis

La Deshabilleuse
See Simenon, Georges (Jacques Christian)

Lady Gregory
See Gregory, Isabella Augusta (Persse)

Lady of Quality, A
See Bagnold, Enid

**La Fayette, Marie (Madelaine Pioche de la
Vergne Comtes** 1634-1693 . . . . . . LC 2

Lafayette, Rene
See Hubbard, L(afayette) Ron(ald)

Laforgue, Jules 1860-1887 . . . . NCLC 5

Lagerkvist, Paer (Fabian)
1891-1974 . . . . CLC 7, 10, 13, 54
See also Lagerkvist, Par
See also CA 85-88; 49-52; MTCW

Lagerkvist, Par
See Lagerkvist, Paer (Fabian)
See also SSC 12

Lagerloef, Selma (Ottiliana Lovisa)
1858-1940 . . . . TCLC 4, 36
See also Lagerlof, Selma (Ottiliana Lovisa)
See also CA 108; CLR 7; SATA 15

Lagerlof, Selma (Ottiliana Lovisa)
See Lagerloef, Selma (Ottiliana Lovisa)
See also CLR 7; SATA 15

La Guma, (Justin) Alex(ander)
1925-1985 . . . . CLC 19
See also BW; CA 49-52; 118; CANR 25;
DLB 117; MTCW

Laidlaw, A. K.
See Grieve, C(hristopher) M(urray)

Lainez, Manuel Mujica
See Mujica Lainez, Manuel
See also HW

Lamartine, Alphonse (Marie Louis Prat) de
1790-1869 . . . . NCLC 11

Lamb, Charles 1775-1834 . . . . NCLC 10
See also CDBLB 1789-1832; DA; DLB 93,
107; SATA 17; WLC

Lamb, Lady Caroline 1785-1828 . . NCLC 38
See also DLB 116

Lamming, George (William)
1927- . . . . CLC 2, 4, 66
See also BLC 2; BW; CA 85-88; CANR 26;
DLB 125; MTCW

L'Amour, Louis (Dearborn)
1908-1988 . . . . CLC 25, 55
See also AITN 2; BEST 89:2; CA 1-4R;
125; CANR 3, 25, 40; DLBY 80; MTCW

Lampedusa, Giuseppe (Tomasi) di . . . TCLC 13
See also Tomasi di Lampedusa, Giuseppe

Lampman, Archibald 1861-1899 . . NCLC 25
See also DLB 92

Lancaster, Bruce 1896-1963 . . . . CLC 36
See also CA 9-10; CAP 1; SATA 9

Landau, Mark Alexandrovich
See Aldanov, Mark (Alexandrovich)

Landau-Aldanov, Mark Alexandrovich
See Aldanov, Mark (Alexandrovich)

Landis, John 1950- . . . . CLC 26
See also CA 112; 122

Landolfi, Tommaso 1908-1979 . . . CLC 11, 49
See also CA 127; 117

Landon, Letitia Elizabeth
1802-1838 . . . . NCLC 15
See also DLB 96

Landor, Walter Savage
1775-1864 . . . . NCLC 14
See also DLB 93, 107

Landwirth, Heinz 1927-
See Lind, Jakov
See also CA 9-12R; CANR 7

Lane, Patrick 1939- . . . . CLC 25
See also CA 97-100; DLB 53

Lang, Andrew 1844-1912 . . . . TCLC 16
See also CA 114; 137; DLB 98; MAICYA;
SATA 16

Lang, Fritz 1890-1976 . . . . CLC 20
See also CA 77-80; 69-72; CANR 30

Lange, John
See Crichton, (John) Michael

Langer, Elinor 1939- . . . . CLC 34
See also CA 121

Langland, William 1330(?)-1400(?) . . . LC 19
See also DA

Langstaff, Launcelot
See Irving, Washington

Lanier, Sidney 1842-1881 . . . . NCLC 6
See also DLB 64; MAICYA; SATA 18

Lanyer, Aemilia 1569-1645 . . . . LC 10

Lao Tzu . . . . CMLC 7

Lapine, James (Elliot) 1949- . . . . CLC 39
See also CA 123; 130

Larbaud, Valery (Nicolas)
1881-1957 . . . . TCLC 9
See also CA 106

Lardner, Ring
See Lardner, Ring(gold) W(ilmer)

Lardner, Ring W., Jr.
See Lardner, Ring(gold) W(ilmer)

Lardner, Ring(gold) W(ilmer)
1885-1933 . . . . TCLC 2, 14
See also CA 104; 131; CDALB 1917-1929;
DLB 11, 25, 86; MTCW

Laredo, Betty
See Codrescu, Andrei

Larkin, Maia
See Wojciechowska, Maia (Teresa)

Larkin, Philip (Arthur)
1922-1985 . . . . CLC 3, 5, 8, 9, 13, 18, 33,
39, 64
See also CA 5-8R; 117; CANR 24;
CDBLB 1960 to Present; DLB 27;
MTCW

Larra (y Sanchez de Castro), Mariano Jose de
1809-1837 . . . . NCLC 17

Larsen, Eric 1941- . . . . CLC 55
See also CA 132

Larsen, Nella 1891-1964 . . . . CLC 37
See also BLC 2; BW; CA 125; DLB 51

Larson, Charles R(aymond) 1938- . . . CLC 31
See also CA 53-56; CANR 4

Latham, Jean Lee 1902- . . . . CLC 12
See also AITN 1; CA 5-8R; CANR 7;
MAICYA; SATA 2, 68

Latham, Mavis
See Clark, Mavis Thorpe

Lathen, Emma . . . . CLC 2
See also Hennissart, Martha; Latsis, Mary
J(ane)

Lathrop, Francis
See Leiber, Fritz (Reuter, Jr.)

Latsis, Mary J(ane)
See Lathen, Emma
See also CA 85-88

Lattimore, Richmond (Alexander)
1906-1984 . . . . CLC 3
See also CA 1-4R; 112; CANR 1

Laughlin, James 1914- . . . . CLC 49
See also CA 21-24R; CANR 9; DLB 48

Laurence, (Jean) Margaret (Wemyss)
1926-1987 . . CLC 3, 6, 13, 50, 62; SSC 7
See also CA 5-8R; 121; CANR 33; DLB 53;
MTCW; SATA 50

Laurent, Antoine 1952- . . . . CLC 50

Lauscher, Hermann
See Hesse, Hermann

Lautreamont, Comte de
1846-1870 . . . . NCLC 12

Laverty, Donald
See Blish, James (Benjamin)

Lavin, Mary 1912- . . . . . . CLC 4, 18; SSC 4
See also CA 9-12R; CANR 33; DLB 15;
MTCW

Lavond, Paul Dennis
See Kornbluth, C(yril) M.; Pohl, Frederik

Lawler, Raymond Evenor 1922- . . . . CLC 58
See also CA 103

Lawrence, D(avid) H(erbert Richards)
1885-1930 . . . . TCLC 2, 9, 16, 33, 48;
SSC 4
See also CA 104; 121; CDBLB 1914-1945;
DA; DLB 10, 19, 36, 98; MTCW; WLC

Lawrence, T(homas) E(dward)
1888-1935 . . . . TCLC 18
See also Dale, Colin
See also CA 115

Lawrence Of Arabia
See Lawrence, T(homas) E(dward)

Lawson, Henry (Archibald Hertzberg)
1867-1922 . . . . TCLC 27
See also CA 120

Lawton, Dennis
  See Faust, Frederick (Schiller)

Laxness, Halldor . . . . CLC 25
  See also Gudjonsson, Halldor Kiljan

Layamon fl. c. 1200- . . . . CMLC 10

Laye, Camara 1928-1980 . . . . CLC 4, 38
  See also BLC 2; BW; CA 85-88; 97-100;
    CANR 25; MTCW

Layton, Irving (Peter) 1912- . . . . . CLC 2, 15
  See also CA 1-4R; CANR 2, 33; DLB 88;
    MTCW

Lazarus, Emma 1849-1887 . . . . NCLC 8

Lazarus, Felix
  See Cable, George Washington

Lazarus, Henry
  See Slavitt, David R(ytman)

Lea, Joan
  See Neufeld, John (Arthur)

Leacock, Stephen (Butler)
  1869-1944 . . . . TCLC 2
  See also CA 104; DLB 92

Lear, Edward 1812-1888 . . . . NCLC 3
  See also CLR 1; DLB 32; MAICYA;
    SATA 18

Lear, Norman (Milton) 1922- . . . . . . CLC 12
  See also CA 73-76

Leavis, F(rank) R(aymond)
  1895-1978 . . . . CLC 24
  See also CA 21-24R; 77-80; MTCW

Leavitt, David 1961- . . . . CLC 34
  See also CA 116; 122; DLB 130

Leblanc, Maurice (Marie Emile)
  1864-1941 . . . . TCLC 49
  See also CA 110

Lebowitz, Fran(ces Ann)
  1951(?)- . . . . CLC 11, 36
  See also CA 81-84; CANR 14; MTCW

le Carre, John . . . . CLC 3, 5, 9, 15, 28
  See also Cornwell, David (John Moore)
  See also BEST 89:4; CDBLB 1960 to
    Present; DLB 87

Le Clezio, J(ean) M(arie) G(ustave)
  1940- . . . . CLC 31
  See also CA 116; 128; DLB 83

Leconte de Lisle, Charles-Marie-Rene
  1818-1894 . . . . NCLC 29

Le Coq, Monsieur
  See Simenon, Georges (Jacques Christian)

Leduc, Violette 1907-1972 . . . . CLC 22
  See also CA 13-14; 33-36R; CAP 1

Ledwidge, Francis 1887(?)-1917 . . . TCLC 23
  See also CA 123; DLB 20

Lee, Andrea 1953- . . . . CLC 36
  See also BLC 2; BW; CA 125

Lee, Andrew
  See Auchincloss, Louis (Stanton)

Lee, Don L. . . . . CLC 2
  See also Madhubuti, Haki R.

Lee, George W(ashington)
  1894-1976 . . . . CLC 52
  See also BLC 2; BW; CA 125; DLB 51

Lee, (Nelle) Harper 1926- . . . . . . CLC 12, 60
  See also CA 13-16R; CDALB 1941-1968;
    DA; DLB 6; MTCW; SATA 11; WLC

Lee, Julian
  See Latham, Jean Lee

Lee, Lawrence 1903- . . . . CLC 34
  See also CA 25-28R

Lee, Manfred B(ennington)
  1905-1971 . . . . CLC 11
  See also Queen, Ellery
  See also CA 1-4R; 29-32R; CANR 2

Lee, Stan 1922- . . . . CLC 17
  See also AAYA 5; CA 108; 111

Lee, Tanith 1947- . . . . CLC 46
  See also CA 37-40R; SATA 8

Lee, Vernon . . . . TCLC 5
  See also Paget, Violet
  See also DLB 57

Lee, William
  See Burroughs, William S(eward)

Lee, Willy
  See Burroughs, William S(eward)

Lee-Hamilton, Eugene (Jacob)
  1845-1907 . . . . TCLC 22
  See also CA 117

Leet, Judith 1935- . . . . CLC 11

Le Fanu, Joseph Sheridan
  1814-1873 . . . . NCLC 9
  See also DLB 21, 70

Leffland, Ella 1931- . . . . CLC 19
  See also CA 29-32R; CANR 35; DLBY 84;
    SATA 65

Leger, (Marie-Rene) Alexis Saint-Leger
  1887-1975 . . . . CLC 11
  See also Perse, St.-John
  See also CA 13-16R; 61-64; MTCW

Leger, Saintleger
  See Leger, (Marie-Rene) Alexis Saint-Leger

Le Guin, Ursula K(roeber)
  1929- . . . . CLC 8, 13, 22, 45, 71; SSC 12
  See also AAYA 9; AITN 1; CA 21-24R;
    CANR 9, 32; CDALB 1968-1988; CLR 3,
    28; DLB 8, 52; MAICYA; MTCW;
    SATA 4, 52

Lehmann, Rosamond (Nina)
  1901-1990 . . . . CLC 5
  See also CA 77-80; 131; CANR 8; DLB 15

Leiber, Fritz (Reuter, Jr.)
  1910-1992 . . . . CLC 25
  See also CA 45-48; 139; CANR 2, 40;
    DLB 8; MTCW; SATA 45;
    SATA-Obit 73

Leimbach, Martha 1963-
  See Leimbach, Marti
  See also CA 130

Leimbach, Marti . . . . CLC 65
  See also Leimbach, Martha

Leino, Eino . . . . TCLC 24
  See also Loennbohm, Armas Eino Leopold

Leiris, Michel (Julien) 1901-1990 . . . CLC 61
  See also CA 119; 128; 132

Leithauser, Brad 1953- . . . . CLC 27
  See also CA 107; CANR 27; DLB 120

Lelchuk, Alan 1938- . . . . CLC 5
  See also CA 45-48; CANR 1

Lem, Stanislaw 1921- . . . . CLC 8, 15, 40
  See also CA 105; CAAS 1; CANR 32;
    MTCW

Lemann, Nancy 1956- . . . . CLC 39
  See also CA 118; 136

Lemonnier, (Antoine Louis) Camille
  1844-1913 . . . . TCLC 22
  See also CA 121

Lenau, Nikolaus 1802-1850 . . . . . . NCLC 16

L'Engle, Madeleine (Camp Franklin)
  1918- . . . . CLC 12
  See also AAYA 1; AITN 2; CA 1-4R;
    CANR 3, 21, 39; CLR 1, 14; DLB 52;
    MAICYA; MTCW; SAAS 15; SATA 1,
    27

Lengyel, Jozsef 1896-1975 . . . . CLC 7
  See also CA 85-88; 57-60

Lennon, John (Ono)
  1940-1980 . . . . CLC 12, 35
  See also CA 102

Lennox, Charlotte Ramsay
  1729(?)-1804 . . . . NCLC 23
  See also DLB 39

Lentricchia, Frank (Jr.) 1940- . . . . . . CLC 34
  See also CA 25-28R; CANR 19

Lenz, Siegfried 1926- . . . . CLC 27
  See also CA 89-92; DLB 75

Leonard, Elmore (John, Jr.)
  1925- . . . . CLC 28, 34, 71
  See also AITN 1; BEST 89:1, 90:4;
    CA 81-84; CANR 12, 28; MTCW

Leonard, Hugh
  See Byrne, John Keyes
  See also DLB 13

**Leopardi, (Conte) Giacomo (Talegardo
    Francesco di Sales Save**
  1798-1837 . . . . NCLC 22

Le Reveler
  See Artaud, Antonin

Lerman, Eleanor 1952- . . . . CLC 9
  See also CA 85-88

Lerman, Rhoda 1936- . . . . CLC 56
  See also CA 49-52

Lermontov, Mikhail Yuryevich
  1814-1841 . . . . NCLC 5

Leroux, Gaston 1868-1927 . . . . TCLC 25
  See also CA 108; 136; SATA 65

Lesage, Alain-Rene 1668-1747 . . . . . . LC 2

Leskov, Nikolai (Semyonovich)
  1831-1895 . . . . NCLC 25

Lessing, Doris (May)
  1919- . . . . . CLC 1, 2, 3, 6, 10, 15, 22, 40;
                                          SSC 6
  See also CA 9-12R; CAAS 14; CANR 33;
    CDBLB 1960 to Present; DA; DLB 15;
    DLBY 85; MTCW

Lessing, Gotthold Ephraim
  1729-1781 . . . . LC 8
  See also DLB 97

Lester, Richard 1932- . . . . CLC 20

Lever, Charles (James)
  1806-1872 . . . . NCLC 23
  See also DLB 21

Leverson, Ada 1865(?)-1936(?) . . . . TCLC 18
  See also Elaine
  See also CA 117

Levertov, Denise
1923- . . . . . . **CLC 1, 2, 3, 5, 8, 15, 28, 66**
See also CA 1-4R; CANR 3, 29; DLB 5;
MTCW

Levi, Jonathan. . . . . **CLC 76**

Levi, Peter (Chad Tigar) 1931- . . . . . **CLC 41**
See also CA 5-8R; CANR 34; DLB 40

Levi, Primo
1919-1987 . . . . **CLC 37, 50; SSC 12**
See also CA 13-16R; 122; CANR 12, 33;
MTCW

Levin, Ira 1929- . . . . **CLC 3, 6**
See also CA 21-24R; CANR 17; MTCW;
SATA 66

Levin, Meyer 1905-1981 . . . . **CLC 7**
See also AITN 1; CA 9-12R; 104;
CANR 15; DLB 9, 28; DLBY 81;
SATA 21, 27

Levine, Norman 1924- . . . . **CLC 54**
See also CA 73-76; CANR 14; DLB 88

Levine, Philip 1928- . . **CLC 2, 4, 5, 9, 14, 33**
See also CA 9-12R; CANR 9, 37; DLB 5

Levinson, Deirdre 1931- . . . . **CLC 49**
See also CA 73-76

Levi-Strauss, Claude 1908- . . . . **CLC 38**
See also CA 1-4R; CANR 6, 32; MTCW

Levitin, Sonia (Wolff) 1934- . . . . **CLC 17**
See also CA 29-32R; CANR 14, 32;
MAICYA; SAAS 2; SATA 4, 68

Levon, O. U.
See Kesey, Ken (Elton)

Lewes, George Henry
1817-1878 . . . . **NCLC 25**
See also DLB 55

Lewis, Alun 1915-1944. . . . . **TCLC 3**
See also CA 104; DLB 20

Lewis, C. Day
See Day Lewis, C(ecil)

Lewis, C(live) S(taples)
1898-1963 . . . . **CLC 1, 3, 6, 14, 27**
See also AAYA 3; CA 81-84; CANR 33;
CDBLB 1945-1960; CLR 3, 27; DA;
DLB 15, 100; MAICYA; MTCW;
SATA 13; WLC

Lewis, Janet 1899- . . . . **CLC 41**
See also Winters, Janet Lewis
See also CA 9-12R; CANR 29; CAP 1;
DLBY 87

Lewis, Matthew Gregory
1775-1818 . . . . **NCLC 11**
See also DLB 39

Lewis, (Harry) Sinclair
1885-1951 . . . . **TCLC 4, 13, 23, 39**
See also CA 104; 133; CDALB 1917-1929;
DA; DLB 9, 102; DLBD 1; MTCW;
WLC

Lewis, (Percy) Wyndham
1884(?)-1957 . . . . **TCLC 2, 9**
See also CA 104; DLB 15

Lewisohn, Ludwig 1883-1955. . . . . . **TCLC 19**
See also CA 107; DLB 4, 9, 28, 102

Lezama Lima, Jose 1910-1976 . . . **CLC 4, 10**
See also CA 77-80; DLB 113; HW

L'Heureux, John (Clarke) 1934- . . . . **CLC 52**
See also CA 13-16R; CANR 23

Liddell, C. H.
See Kuttner, Henry

Lie, Jonas (Lauritz Idemil)
1833-1908(?) . . . . **TCLC 5**
See also CA 115

Lieber, Joel 1937-1971. . . . . **CLC 6**
See also CA 73-76; 29-32R

Lieber, Stanley Martin
See Lee, Stan

Lieberman, Laurence (James)
1935- . . . . **CLC 4, 36**
See also CA 17-20R; CANR 8, 36

Lieksman, Anders
See Haavikko, Paavo Juhani

Li Fei-kan 1904-. . . . . **CLC 18**
See also CA 105

Lifton, Robert Jay 1926-. . . . . **CLC 67**
See also CA 17-20R; CANR 27; SATA 66

Lightfoot, Gordon 1938-. . . . . **CLC 26**
See also CA 109

Ligotti, Thomas 1953- . . . . **CLC 44**
See also CA 123

Liliencron, (Friedrich Adolf Axel) Detlev von
1844-1909 . . . . **TCLC 18**
See also CA 117

Lima, Jose Lezama
See Lezama Lima, Jose

Lima Barreto, Afonso Henrique de
1881-1922 . . . . **TCLC 23**
See also CA 117

Limonov, Eduard. . . . . **CLC 67**

Lin, Frank
See Atherton, Gertrude (Franklin Horn)

Lincoln, Abraham 1809-1865. . . . . **NCLC 18**

Lind, Jakov . . . . **CLC 1, 2, 4, 27**
See also Landwirth, Heinz
See also CAAS 4

Lindsay, David 1878-1945 . . . . **TCLC 15**
See also CA 113

Lindsay, (Nicholas) Vachel
1879-1931 . . . . **TCLC 17**
See also CA 114; 135; CDALB 1865-1917;
DA; DLB 54; SATA 40; WLC

Linney, Romulus 1930- . . . . **CLC 51**
See also CA 1-4R; CANR 40

Linton, Eliza Lynn 1822-1898. . . . **NCLC 41**
See also DLB 18

Li Po 701-763. . . . . **CMLC 2**

Lipsius, Justus 1547-1606 . . . . **LC 16**

Lipsyte, Robert (Michael) 1938- . . . . **CLC 21**
See also AAYA 7; CA 17-20R; CANR 8;
CLR 23; DA; MAICYA; SATA 5, 68

Lish, Gordon (Jay) 1934-. . . . . **CLC 45**
See also CA 113; 117; DLB 130

Lispector, Clarice 1925-1977. . . . . . . **CLC 43**
See also CA 139; 116; DLB 113

Littell, Robert 1935(?)- . . . . **CLC 42**
See also CA 109; 112

Littlewit, Humphrey Gent.
See Lovecraft, H(oward) P(hillips)

Litwos
See Sienkiewicz, Henryk (Adam Alexander
Pius)

Liu E 1857-1909. . . . . **TCLC 15**
See also CA 115

Lively, Penelope (Margaret)
1933- . . . . **CLC 32, 50**
See also CA 41-44R; CANR 29; CLR 7;
DLB 14; MAICYA; MTCW; SATA 7, 60

Livesay, Dorothy (Kathleen)
1909- . . . . **CLC 4, 15, 79**
See also AITN 2; CA 25-28R; CAAS 8;
CANR 36; DLB 68; MTCW

Livy c. 59B.C.-c. 17 . . . . **CMLC 11**

Lizardi, Jose Joaquin Fernandez de
1776-1827 . . . . **NCLC 30**

Llewellyn, Richard . . . . **CLC 7**
See also Llewellyn Lloyd, Richard Dafydd
Vivian
See also DLB 15

Llewellyn Lloyd, Richard Dafydd Vivian
1906-1983
See Llewellyn, Richard
See also CA 53-56; 111; CANR 7;
SATA 11, 37

Llosa, (Jorge) Mario (Pedro) Vargas
See Vargas Llosa, (Jorge) Mario (Pedro)

Lloyd Webber, Andrew 1948-
See Webber, Andrew Lloyd
See also AAYA 1; CA 116; SATA 56

Locke, Alain (Le Roy)
1886-1954 . . . . **TCLC 43**
See also BW; CA 106; 124; DLB 51

Locke, John 1632-1704 . . . . **LC 7**
See also DLB 101

Locke-Elliott, Sumner
See Elliott, Sumner Locke

Lockhart, John Gibson
1794-1854 . . . . **NCLC 6**
See also DLB 110, 116

Lodge, David (John) 1935-. . . . . **CLC 36**
See also BEST 90:1; CA 17-20R; CANR 19;
DLB 14; MTCW

Loennbohm, Armas Eino Leopold 1878-1926
See Leino, Eino
See also CA 123

Loewinsohn, Ron(ald William)
1937- . . . . **CLC 52**
See also CA 25-28R

Logan, Jake
See Smith, Martin Cruz

Logan, John (Burton) 1923-1987. . . . . **CLC 5**
See also CA 77-80; 124; DLB 5

Lo Kuan-chung 1330(?)-1400(?). . . . . **LC 12**

Lombard, Nap
See Johnson, Pamela Hansford

London, Jack. . . . . **TCLC 9, 15, 39; SSC 4**
See also London, John Griffith
See also AITN 2; CDALB 1865-1917;
DLB 8, 12, 78; SATA 18; WLC

London, John Griffith 1876-1916
See London, Jack
See also CA 110; 119; DA; MAICYA;
MTCW

Long, Emmett
See Leonard, Elmore (John, Jr.)

Longbaugh, Harry
See Goldman, William (W.)

Longfellow, Henry Wadsworth
1807-1882 .... NCLC 2
See also CDALB 1640-1865; DA; DLB 1,
59; SATA 19

Longley, Michael 1939- .... CLC 29
See also CA 102; DLB 40

Longus fl. c. 2nd cent. - .... CMLC 7

Longway, A. Hugh
See Lang, Andrew

Lopate, Phillip 1943- .... CLC 29
See also CA 97-100; DLBY 80

Lopez Portillo (y Pacheco), Jose
1920- .... CLC 46
See also CA 129; HW

Lopez y Fuentes, Gregorio
1897(?)-1966 .... CLC 32
See also CA 131; HW

Lorca, Federico Garcia
See Garcia Lorca, Federico

Lord, Bette Bao 1938- .... CLC 23
See also BEST 90:3; CA 107; CANR 41;
SATA 58

Lord Auch
See Bataille, Georges

Lord Byron
See Byron, George Gordon (Noel)

Lord Dunsany .... TCLC 2
See also Dunsany, Edward John Moreton
Drax Plunkett

Lorde, Audre (Geraldine)
1934- .... CLC 18, 71
See also BLC 2; BW; CA 25-28R;
CANR 16, 26; DLB 41; MTCW

Lord Jeffrey
See Jeffrey, Francis

Lorenzo, Heberto Padilla
See Padilla (Lorenzo), Heberto

Loris
See Hofmannsthal, Hugo von

Loti, Pierre .... TCLC 11
See also Viaud, (Louis Marie) Julien
See also DLB 123

Louie, David Wong 1954- .... CLC 70
See also CA 139

Louis, Father M.
See Merton, Thomas

Lovecraft, H(oward) P(hillips)
1890-1937 .... TCLC 4, 22; SSC 3
See also CA 104; 133; MTCW

Lovelace, Earl 1935- .... CLC 51
See also CA 77-80; CANR 41; DLB 125;
MTCW

Lowell, Amy 1874-1925 .... TCLC 1, 8
See also CA 104; DLB 54

Lowell, James Russell 1819-1891 .. NCLC 2
See also CDALB 1640-1865; DLB 1, 11, 64,
79

Lowell, Robert (Traill Spence, Jr.)
1917-1977 ... CLC 1, 2, 3, 4, 5, 8, 9, 11,
15, 37; PC 3
See also CA 9-12R; 73-76; CABS 2;
CANR 26; DA; DLB 5; MTCW; WLC

Lowndes, Marie Adelaide (Belloc)
1868-1947 .... TCLC 12
See also CA 107; DLB 70

Lowry, (Clarence) Malcolm
1909-1957 .... TCLC 6, 40
See also CA 105; 131; CDBLB 1945-1960;
DLB 15; MTCW

Lowry, Mina Gertrude 1882-1966
See Loy, Mina
See also CA 113

Loxsmith, John
See Brunner, John (Kilian Houston)

Loy, Mina .... CLC 28
See also Lowry, Mina Gertrude
See also DLB 4, 54

Loyson-Bridet
See Schwob, (Mayer Andre) Marcel

Lucas, Craig 1951- .... CLC 64
See also CA 137

Lucas, George 1944- .... CLC 16
See also AAYA 1; CA 77-80; CANR 30;
SATA 56

Lucas, Hans
See Godard, Jean-Luc

Lucas, Victoria
See Plath, Sylvia

Ludlam, Charles 1943-1987 ..... CLC 46, 50
See also CA 85-88; 122

Ludlum, Robert 1927- .... CLC 22, 43
See also AAYA 10; BEST 89:1, 90:3;
CA 33-36R; CANR 25, 41; DLBY 82;
MTCW

Ludwig, Ken..................... CLC 60

Ludwig, Otto 1813-1865.......... NCLC 4
See also DLB 129

Lugones, Leopoldo 1874-1938 ..... TCLC 15
See also CA 116; 131; HW

Lu Hsun 1881-1936 .... TCLC 3

Lukacs, George .... CLC 24
See also Lukacs, Gyorgy (Szegeny von)

Lukacs, Gyorgy (Szegeny von) 1885-1971
See Lukacs, George
See also CA 101; 29-32R

Luke, Peter (Ambrose Cyprian)
1919- .... CLC 38
See also CA 81-84; DLB 13

Lunar, Dennis
See Mungo, Raymond

Lurie, Alison 1926- .... CLC 4, 5, 18, 39
See also CA 1-4R; CANR 2, 17; DLB 2;
MTCW; SATA 46

Lustig, Arnost 1926- .... CLC 56
See also AAYA 3; CA 69-72; SATA 56

Luther, Martin 1483-1546.......... LC 9

Luzi, Mario 1914-................ CLC 13
See also CA 61-64; CANR 9; DLB 128

Lynch, B. Suarez
See Bioy Casares, Adolfo; Borges, Jorge
Luis

Lynch, David (K.) 1946- .... CLC 66
See also CA 124; 129

Lynch, James
See Andreyev, Leonid (Nikolaevich)

Lynch Davis, B.
See Bioy Casares, Adolfo; Borges, Jorge
Luis

Lyndsay, Sir David 1490-1555 .... LC 20

Lynn, Kenneth S(chuyler) 1923- .... CLC 50
See also CA 1-4R; CANR 3, 27

Lynx
See West, Rebecca

Lyons, Marcus
See Blish, James (Benjamin)

Lyre, Pinchbeck
See Sassoon, Siegfried (Lorraine)

Lytle, Andrew (Nelson) 1902- ...... CLC 22
See also CA 9-12R; DLB 6

Lyttelton, George 1709-1773........ LC 10

Maas, Peter 1929- .... CLC 29
See also CA 93-96

Macaulay, Rose 1881-1958 ..... TCLC 7, 44
See also CA 104; DLB 36

MacBeth, George (Mann)
1932-1992 .... CLC 2, 5, 9
See also CA 25-28R; 136; DLB 40; MTCW;
SATA 4; SATA-Obit 70

MacCaig, Norman (Alexander)
1910- .... CLC 36
See also CA 9-12R; CANR 3, 34; DLB 27

MacCarthy, (Sir Charles Otto) Desmond
1877-1952 .... TCLC 36

MacDiarmid, Hugh..... CLC 2, 4, 11, 19, 63
See also Grieve, C(hristopher) M(urray)
See also CDBLB 1945-1960; DLB 20

MacDonald, Anson
See Heinlein, Robert A(nson)

Macdonald, Cynthia 1928-...... CLC 13, 19
See also CA 49-52; CANR 4; DLB 105

MacDonald, George 1824-1905 ..... TCLC 9
See also CA 106; 137; DLB 18; MAICYA;
SATA 33

Macdonald, John
See Millar, Kenneth

MacDonald, John D(ann)
1916-1986 .... CLC 3, 27, 44
See also CA 1-4R; 121; CANR 1, 19;
DLB 8; DLBY 86; MTCW

Macdonald, John Ross
See Millar, Kenneth

Macdonald, Ross..... CLC 1, 2, 3, 14, 34, 41
See also Millar, Kenneth
See also DLBD 6

MacDougal, John
See Blish, James (Benjamin)

MacEwen, Gwendolyn (Margaret)
1941-1987 .... CLC 13, 55
See also CA 9-12R; 124; CANR 7, 22;
DLB 53; SATA 50, 55

Machado (y Ruiz), Antonio
1875-1939 .... TCLC 3
See also CA 104; DLB 108

Machado de Assis, Joaquim Maria
1839-1908 .... TCLC 10
See also BLC 2; CA 107

Machen, Arthur................... TCLC 4
See also Jones, Arthur Llewellyn
See also DLB 36

Mantecon, Juan Jimenez
   See Jimenez (Mantecon), Juan Ramon

Manton, Peter
   See Creasey, John

Man Without a Spleen, A
   See Chekhov, Anton (Pavlovich)

Manzoni, Alessandro 1785-1873 . . NCLC 29

Mapu, Abraham (ben Jekutiel)
   1808-1867 . . . . NCLC 18

Mara, Sally
   See Queneau, Raymond

Marat, Jean Paul 1743-1793 . . . . LC 10

Marcel, Gabriel Honore
   1889-1973 . . . . CLC 15
   See also CA 102; 45-48; MTCW

Marchbanks, Samuel
   See Davies, (William) Robertson

Marchi, Giacomo
   See Bassani, Giorgio

Margulies, Donald. . . . . CLC 76

Marie de France c. 12th cent. -. . . . CMLC 8

Marie de l'Incarnation 1599-1672. . . . LC 10

Mariner, Scott
   See Pohl, Frederik

Marinetti, Filippo Tommaso
   1876-1944 . . . . TCLC 10
   See also CA 107; DLB 114

Marivaux, Pierre Carlet de Chamblain de
   1688-1763 . . . . LC 4

Markandaya, Kamala . . . . CLC 8, 38
   See also Taylor, Kamala (Purnaiya)

Markfield, Wallace 1926-. . . . . CLC 8
   See also CA 69-72; CAAS 3; DLB 2, 28

Markham, Edwin 1852-1940 . . . . . . TCLC 47
   See also DLB 54

Markham, Robert
   See Amis, Kingsley (William)

Marks, J
   See Highwater, Jamake (Mamake)

Marks-Highwater, J
   See Highwater, Jamake (Mamake)

Markson, David M(errill) 1927- . . . . CLC 67
   See also CA 49-52; CANR 1

Marley, Bob. CLC 17
   See also Marley, Robert Nesta

Marley, Robert Nesta 1945-1981
   See Marley, Bob
   See also CA 107; 103

Marlowe, Christopher
   1564-1593 . . . . LC 22; DC 1
   See also CDBLB Before 1660; DA; DLB 62;
   WLC

Marmontel, Jean-Francois
   1723-1799 . . . . LC 2

Marquand, John P(hillips)
   1893-1960 . . . . CLC 2, 10
   See also CA 85-88; DLB 9, 102

Marquez, Gabriel (Jose) Garcia. . . . . . CLC 68
   See also Garcia Marquez, Gabriel (Jose)

Marquis, Don(ald Robert Perry)
   1878-1937 . . . . TCLC 7
   See also CA 104; DLB 11, 25

Marric, J. J.
   See Creasey, John

Marrow, Bernard
   See Moore, Brian

Marryat, Frederick 1792-1848 . . . . NCLC 3
   See also DLB 21

Marsden, James
   See Creasey, John

Marsh, (Edith) Ngaio
   1899-1982 . . . . CLC 7, 53
   See also CA 9-12R; CANR 6; DLB 77;
   MTCW

Marshall, Garry 1934-. . . . . CLC 17
   See also AAYA 3; CA 111; SATA 60

Marshall, Paule 1929- . . CLC 27, 72; SSC 3
   See also BLC 3; BW; CA 77-80; CANR 25;
   DLB 33; MTCW

Marsten, Richard
   See Hunter, Evan

Martha, Henry
   See Harris, Mark

Martin, Ken
   See Hubbard, L(afayette) Ron(ald)

Martin, Richard
   See Creasey, John

Martin, Steve 1945-. . . . . CLC 30
   See also CA 97-100; CANR 30; MTCW

Martin, Violet Florence
   1862-1915 . . . . TCLC 51

Martin, Webber
   See Silverberg, Robert

Martin du Gard, Roger
   1881-1958 . . . . TCLC 24
   See also CA 118; DLB 65

Martineau, Harriet 1802-1876. . . . NCLC 26
   See also DLB 21, 55; YABC 2

Martines, Julia
   See O'Faolain, Julia

Martinez, Jacinto Benavente y
   See Benavente (y Martinez), Jacinto

Martinez Ruiz, Jose 1873-1967
   See Azorin; Ruiz, Jose Martinez
   See also CA 93-96; HW

Martinez Sierra, Gregorio
   1881-1947 . . . . TCLC 6
   See also CA 115

Martinez Sierra, Maria (de la O'LeJarraga)
   1874-1974 . . . . TCLC 6
   See also CA 115

Martinsen, Martin
   See Follett, Ken(neth Martin)

Martinson, Harry (Edmund)
   1904-1978 . . . . CLC 14
   See also CA 77-80; CANR 34

Marut, Ret
   See Traven, B.

Marut, Robert
   See Traven, B.

Marvell, Andrew 1621-1678. . . . . LC 4
   See also CDBLB 1660-1789; DA; DLB 131;
   WLC

Marx, Karl (Heinrich)
   1818-1883 . . . . NCLC 17
   See also DLB 129

Masaoka Shiki. . . . . TCLC 18
   See also Masaoka Tsunenori

Masaoka Tsunenori 1867-1902
   See Masaoka Shiki
   See also CA 117

Masefield, John (Edward)
   1878-1967 . . . . CLC 11, 47
   See also CA 19-20; 25-28R; CANR 33;
   CAP 2; CDBLB 1890-1914; DLB 10;
   MTCW; SATA 19

Maso, Carole 19(?)- . . . . CLC 44

Mason, Bobbie Ann
   1940- . . . . CLC 28, 43; SSC 4
   See also AAYA 5; CA 53-56; CANR 11,
   31; DLBY 87; MTCW

Mason, Ernst
   See Pohl, Frederik

Mason, Lee W.
   See Malzberg, Barry N(athaniel)

Mason, Nick 1945-. . . . . CLC 35
   See also Pink Floyd

Mason, Tally
   See Derleth, August (William)

Mass, William
   See Gibson, William

Masters, Edgar Lee
   1868-1950 . . . . TCLC 2, 25; PC 1
   See also CA 104; 133; CDALB 1865-1917;
   DA; DLB 54; MTCW

Masters, Hilary 1928-. . . . . CLC 48
   See also CA 25-28R; CANR 13

Mastrosimone, William 19(?)-. . . . . . CLC 36

Mathe, Albert
   See Camus, Albert

Matheson, Richard Burton 1926- . . . CLC 37
   See also CA 97-100; DLB 8, 44

Mathews, Harry 1930-. . . . . CLC 6, 52
   See also CA 21-24R; CAAS 6; CANR 18,
   40

Mathias, Roland (Glyn) 1915-. . . . . . CLC 45
   See also CA 97-100; CANR 19, 41; DLB 27

Matsuo Basho 1644-1694. . . . . PC 3

Mattheson, Rodney
   See Creasey, John

Matthews, Greg 1949-. . . . . CLC 45
   See also CA 135

Matthews, William 1942-. . . . . CLC 40
   See also CA 29-32R; CANR 12; DLB 5

Matthias, John (Edward) 1941-. . . . . . CLC 9
   See also CA 33-36R

Matthiessen, Peter
   1927- . . . . CLC 5, 7, 11, 32, 64
   See also AAYA 6; BEST 90:4; CA 9-12R;
   CANR 21; DLB 6; MTCW; SATA 27

Maturin, Charles Robert
   1780(?)-1824 . . . . NCLC 6

Matute (Ausejo), Ana Maria
   1925- . . . . CLC 11
   See also CA 89-92; MTCW

Maugham, W. S.
   See Maugham, W(illiam) Somerset

Maugham, W(illiam) Somerset
1874-1965 .... **CLC 1, 11, 15, 67; SSC 8**
See also CA 5-8R; 25-28R; CANR 40;
CDBLB 1914-1945; DA; DLB 10, 36, 77,
100; MTCW; SATA 54; WLC

Maugham, William Somerset
See Maugham, W(illiam) Somerset

Maupassant, (Henri Rene Albert) Guy de
1850-1893 .... **NCLC 1; SSC 1**
See also DA; DLB 123; WLC

Maurhut, Richard
See Traven, B.

Mauriac, Claude   1914- .... **CLC 9**
See also CA 89-92; DLB 83

Mauriac, Francois (Charles)
1885-1970 .... **CLC 4, 9, 56**
See also CA 25-28; CAP 2; DLB 65;
MTCW

Mavor, Osborne Henry   1888-1951
See Bridie, James
See also CA 104

Maxwell, William (Keepers, Jr.)
1908- .... **CLC 19**
See also CA 93-96; DLBY 80

May, Elaine   1932- .... **CLC 16**
See also CA 124; DLB 44

Mayakovski, Vladimir (Vladimirovich)
1893-1930 .... **TCLC 4, 18**
See also CA 104

Mayhew, Henry   1812-1887 ...... **NCLC 31**
See also DLB 18, 55

Maynard, Joyce   1953- .... **CLC 23**
See also CA 111; 129

Mayne, William (James Carter)
1928- .... **CLC 12**
See also CA 9-12R; CANR 37; CLR 25;
MAICYA; SAAS 11; SATA 6, 68

Mayo, Jim
See L'Amour, Louis (Dearborn)

Maysles, Albert   1926- .... **CLC 16**
See also CA 29-32R

Maysles, David   1932- .... **CLC 16**

Mazer, Norma Fox   1931- .... **CLC 26**
See also AAYA 5; CA 69-72; CANR 12,
32; CLR 23; MAICYA; SAAS 1;
SATA 24, 67

Mazzini, Guiseppe   1805-1872 .... **NCLC 34**

McAuley, James Phillip
1917-1976 .... **CLC 45**
See also CA 97-100

McBain, Ed
See Hunter, Evan

McBrien, William Augustine
1930- .... **CLC 44**
See also CA 107

McCaffrey, Anne (Inez)   1926- ...... **CLC 17**
See also AAYA 6; AITN 2; BEST 89:2;
CA 25-28R; CANR 15, 35; DLB 8;
MAICYA; MTCW; SAAS 11; SATA 8,
70

McCann, Arthur
See Campbell, John W(ood, Jr.)

McCann, Edson
See Pohl, Frederik

McCarthy, Cormac, Jr. .... **CLC 4, 57**
See also McCarthy, Charles, Jr.
See also DLB 6

McCarthy, Mary (Therese)
1912-1989 ... **CLC 1, 3, 5, 14, 24, 39, 59**
See also CA 5-8R; 129; CANR 16; DLB 2;
DLBY 81; MTCW

McCartney, (James) Paul
1942- .... **CLC 12, 35**

McCauley, Stephen (D.)   1955- ..... **CLC 50**

McClure, Michael (Thomas)
1932- .... **CLC 6, 10**
See also CA 21-24R; CANR 17; DLB 16

McCorkle, Jill (Collins)   1958- ...... **CLC 51**
See also CA 121; DLBY 87

McCourt, James   1941- .... **CLC 5**
See also CA 57-60

McCoy, Horace (Stanley)
1897-1955 .... **TCLC 28**
See also CA 108; DLB 9

McCrae, John   1872-1918 .... **TCLC 12**
See also CA 109; DLB 92

McCreigh, James
See Pohl, Frederik

McCullers, (Lula) Carson (Smith)
1917-1967 .. **CLC 1, 4, 10, 12, 48; SSC 9**
See also CA 5-8R; 25-28R; CABS 1, 3;
CANR 18; CDALB 1941-1968; DA;
DLB 2, 7; MTCW; SATA 27; WLC

McCulloch, John Tyler
See Burroughs, Edgar Rice

McCullough, Colleen   1938(?)- ...... **CLC 27**
See also CA 81-84; CANR 17; MTCW

McElroy, Joseph   1930- .... **CLC 5, 47**
See also CA 17-20R

McEwan, Ian (Russell)   1948- ... **CLC 13, 66**
See also BEST 90:4; CA 61-64; CANR 14,
41; DLB 14; MTCW

McFadden, David   1940- .... **CLC 48**
See also CA 104; DLB 60

McFarland, Dennis   1950- .... **CLC 65**

McGahern, John   1934- .... **CLC 5, 9, 48**
See also CA 17-20R; CANR 29; DLB 14;
MTCW

McGinley, Patrick (Anthony)
1937- .... **CLC 41**
See also CA 120; 127

McGinley, Phyllis   1905-1978 ...... **CLC 14**
See also CA 9-12R; 77-80; CANR 19;
DLB 11, 48; SATA 2, 24, 44

McGinniss, Joe   1942- .... **CLC 32**
See also AITN 2; BEST 89:2; CA 25-28R;
CANR 26

McGivern, Maureen Daly
See Daly, Maureen

McGrath, Patrick   1950- .... **CLC 55**
See also CA 136

McGrath, Thomas (Matthew)
1916-1990 .... **CLC 28, 59**
See also CA 9-12R; 132; CANR 6, 33;
MTCW; SATA 41; SATA-Obit 66

McGuane, Thomas (Francis III)
1939- .... **CLC 3, 7, 18, 45**
See also AITN 2; CA 49-52; CANR 5, 24;
DLB 2; DLBY 80; MTCW

McGuckian, Medbh   1950- .... **CLC 48**
See also DLB 40

McHale, Tom   1942(?)-1982 .... **CLC 3, 5**
See also AITN 1; CA 77-80; 106

McIlvanney, William   1936- .... **CLC 42**
See also CA 25-28R; DLB 14

McIlwraith, Maureen Mollie Hunter
See Hunter, Mollie
See also SATA 2

McInerney, Jay   1955- .... **CLC 34**
See also CA 116; 123

McIntyre, Vonda N(eel)   1948- ..... **CLC 18**
See also CA 81-84; CANR 17, 34; MTCW

McKay, Claude .... **TCLC 7, 41; PC 2**
See also McKay, Festus Claudius
See also BLC 3; DLB 4, 45, 51, 117

McKay, Festus Claudius   1889-1948
See McKay, Claude
See also BW; CA 104; 124; DA; MTCW;
WLC

McKuen, Rod   1933- .... **CLC 1, 3**
See also AITN 1; CA 41-44R; CANR 40

McLoughlin, R. B.
See Mencken, H(enry) L(ouis)

McLuhan, (Herbert) Marshall
1911-1980 .... **CLC 37**
See also CA 9-12R; 102; CANR 12, 34;
DLB 88; MTCW

McMillan, Terry (L.)   1951- ..... **CLC 50, 61**
See also CA 140

McMurtry, Larry (Jeff)
1936- .... **CLC 2, 3, 7, 11, 27, 44**
See also AITN 2; BEST 89:2; CA 5-8R;
CANR 19; CDALB 1968-1988; DLB 2;
DLBY 80, 87; MTCW

McNally, Terrence   1939- ...... **CLC 4, 7, 41**
See also CA 45-48; CANR 2; DLB 7

McNamer, Deirdre   1950- .... **CLC 70**

McNeile, Herman Cyril   1888-1937
See Sapper
See also DLB 77

McPhee, John (Angus)   1931- ...... **CLC 36**
See also BEST 90:1; CA 65-68; CANR 20;
MTCW

McPherson, James Alan
1943- .... **CLC 19, 77**
See also BW; CA 25-28R; CAAS 17;
CANR 24; DLB 38; MTCW

McPherson, William (Alexander)
1933- .... **CLC 34**
See also CA 69-72; CANR 28

McSweeney, Kerry .... **CLC 34**

Mead, Margaret   1901-1978 .... **CLC 37**
See also AITN 1; CA 1-4R; 81-84;
CANR 4; MTCW; SATA 20

Meaker, Marijane (Agnes)   1927-
See Kerr, M. E.
See also CA 107; CANR 37; MAICYA;
MTCW; SATA 20, 61

Medoff, Mark (Howard) 1940- . . . **CLC 6, 23**
See also AITN 1; CA 53-56; CANR 5;
DLB 7

Meged, Aharon
See Megged, Aharon

Meged, Aron
See Megged, Aharon

Megged, Aharon 1920- . . . . **CLC 9**
See also CA 49-52; CAAS 13; CANR 1

Mehta, Ved (Parkash) 1934- . . . . **CLC 37**
See also CA 1-4R; CANR 2, 23; MTCW

Melanter
See Blackmore, R(ichard) D(oddridge)

Melikow, Loris
See Hofmannsthal, Hugo von

Melmoth, Sebastian
See Wilde, Oscar (Fingal O'Flahertie Wills)

Meltzer, Milton 1915- . . . . **CLC 26**
See also AAYA 8; CA 13-16R; CANR 38;
CLR 13; DLB 61; MAICYA; SAAS 1;
SATA 1, 50

Melville, Herman
1819-1891 . . . . . . **NCLC 3, 12, 29; SSC 1**
See also CDALB 1640-1865; DA; DLB 3,
74; SATA 59; WLC

Menander
c. 342B.C.-c. 292B.C. . . . . **CMLC 9; DC 3**

Mencken, H(enry) L(ouis)
1880-1956 . . . . **TCLC 13**
See also CA 105; 125; CDALB 1917-1929;
DLB 11, 29, 63; MTCW

Mercer, David 1928-1980 . . . . **CLC 5**
See also CA 9-12R; 102; CANR 23;
DLB 13; MTCW

Merchant, Paul
See Ellison, Harlan

Meredith, George 1828-1909 . . . **TCLC 17, 43**
See also CA 117; CDBLB 1832-1890;
DLB 18, 35, 57

Meredith, William (Morris)
1919- . . . . **CLC 4, 13, 22, 55**
See also CA 9-12R; CAAS 14; CANR 6, 40;
DLB 5

Merezhkovsky, Dmitry Sergeyevich
1865-1941 . . . . **TCLC 29**

Merimee, Prosper
1803-1870 . . . . **NCLC 6; SSC 7**
See also DLB 119

Merkin, Daphne 1954- . . . . **CLC 44**
See also CA 123

Merlin, Arthur
See Blish, James (Benjamin)

Merrill, James (Ingram)
1926- . . . . **CLC 2, 3, 6, 8, 13, 18, 34**
See also CA 13-16R; CANR 10; DLB 5;
DLBY 85; MTCW

Merriman, Alex
See Silverberg, Robert

Merritt, E. B.
See Waddington, Miriam

Merton, Thomas
1915-1968 . . . . **CLC 1, 3, 11, 34**
See also CA 5-8R; 25-28R; CANR 22;
DLB 48; DLBY 81; MTCW

Merwin, W(illiam) S(tanley)
1927- . . . . . . **CLC 1, 2, 3, 5, 8, 13, 18, 45**
See also CA 13-16R; CANR 15; DLB 5;
MTCW

Metcalf, John 1938- . . . . **CLC 37**
See also CA 113; DLB 60

Metcalf, Suzanne
See Baum, L(yman) Frank

Mew, Charlotte (Mary)
1870-1928 . . . . **TCLC 8**
See also CA 105; DLB 19

Mewshaw, Michael 1943- . . . . **CLC 9**
See also CA 53-56; CANR 7; DLBY 80

Meyer, June
See Jordan, June

Meyer, Lynn
See Slavitt, David R(ytman)

Meyer-Meyrink, Gustav 1868-1932
See Meyrink, Gustav
See also CA 117

Meyers, Jeffrey 1939- . . . . **CLC 39**
See also CA 73-76; DLB 111

Meynell, Alice (Christina Gertrude Thompson)
1847-1922 . . . . **TCLC 6**
See also CA 104; DLB 19, 98

Meyrink, Gustav . . . . **TCLC 21**
See also Meyer-Meyrink, Gustav
See also DLB 81

Michaels, Leonard 1933- . . . . **CLC 6, 25**
See also CA 61-64; CANR 21; DLB 130;
MTCW

Michaux, Henri 1899-1984 . . . . . . **CLC 8, 19**
See also CA 85-88; 114

Michelangelo 1475-1564 . . . . **LC 12**

Michelet, Jules 1798-1874 . . . . **NCLC 31**

Michener, James A(lbert)
1907(?)- . . . . **CLC 1, 5, 11, 29, 60**
See also AITN 1; BEST 90:1; CA 5-8R;
CANR 21; DLB 6; MTCW

Mickiewicz, Adam 1798-1855 . . . . . **NCLC 3**

Middleton, Christopher 1926- . . . . . . **CLC 13**
See also CA 13-16R; CANR 29; DLB 40

Middleton, Stanley 1919- . . . . **CLC 7, 38**
See also CA 25-28R; CANR 21; DLB 14

Migueis, Jose Rodrigues 1901- . . . . . **CLC 10**

Mikszath, Kalman 1847-1910 . . . . . **TCLC 31**

Miles, Josephine
1911-1985 . . . . **CLC 1, 2, 14, 34, 39**
See also CA 1-4R; 116; CANR 2; DLB 48

Militant
See Sandburg, Carl (August)

Mill, John Stuart 1806-1873 . . . . . **NCLC 11**
See also CDBLB 1832-1890; DLB 55

Millar, Kenneth 1915-1983 . . . . **CLC 14**
See also Macdonald, Ross
See also CA 9-12R; 110; CANR 16; DLB 2;
DLBD 6; DLBY 83; MTCW

Millay, E. Vincent
See Millay, Edna St. Vincent

Millay, Edna St. Vincent
1892-1950 . . . . **TCLC 4, 49; PC 6**
See also CA 104; 130; CDALB 1917-1929;
DA; DLB 45; MTCW

Miller, Arthur
1915- . . . . **CLC 1, 2, 6, 10, 15, 26, 47, 78;
DC 1**
See also AITN 1; CA 1-4R; CABS 3;
CANR 2, 30; CDALB 1941-1968; DA;
DLB 7; MTCW; WLC

Miller, Henry (Valentine)
1891-1980 . . . . **CLC 1, 2, 4, 9, 14, 43**
See also CA 9-12R; 97-100; CANR 33;
CDALB 1929-1941; DA; DLB 4, 9;
DLBY 80; MTCW; WLC

Miller, Jason 1939(?)- . . . . **CLC 2**
See also AITN 1; CA 73-76; DLB 7

Miller, Sue 1943- . . . . **CLC 44**
See also BEST 90:3; CA 139

Miller, Walter M(ichael, Jr.)
1923- . . . . **CLC 4, 30**
See also CA 85-88; DLB 8

Millett, Kate 1934- . . . . **CLC 67**
See also AITN 1; CA 73-76; CANR 32;
MTCW

Millhauser, Steven 1943- . . . . **CLC 21, 54**
See also CA 110; 111; DLB 2

Millin, Sarah Gertrude 1889-1968 . . **CLC 49**
See also CA 102; 93-96

Milne, A(lan) A(lexander)
1882-1956 . . . . **TCLC 6**
See also CA 104; 133; CLR 1, 26; DLB 10,
77, 100; MAICYA; MTCW; YABC 1

Milner, Ron(ald) 1938- . . . . **CLC 56**
See also AITN 1; BLC 3; BW; CA 73-76;
CANR 24; DLB 38; MTCW

Milosz, Czeslaw
1911- . . . . **CLC 5, 11, 22, 31, 56**
See also CA 81-84; CANR 23; MTCW

Milton, John 1608-1674 . . . . **LC 9**
See also CDBLB 1660-1789; DA; DLB 131;
WLC

Minehaha, Cornelius
See Wedekind, (Benjamin) Frank(lin)

Miner, Valerie 1947- . . . . **CLC 40**
See also CA 97-100

Minimo, Duca
See D'Annunzio, Gabriele

Minot, Susan 1956- . . . . **CLC 44**
See also CA 134

Minus, Ed 1938- . . . . **CLC 39**

Miranda, Javier
See Bioy Casares, Adolfo

Miro (Ferrer), Gabriel (Francisco Victor)
1879-1930 . . . . **TCLC 5**
See also CA 104

Mishima, Yukio
. . . . **CLC 2, 4, 6, 9, 27; DC 1; SSC 4**
See also Hiraoka, Kimitake

Mistral, Frederic 1830-1914 . . . . . . **TCLC 51**
See also CA 122

Mistral, Gabriela . . . . **TCLC 2**
See also Godoy Alcayaga, Lucila

Mistry, Rohinton 1952- . . . . **CLC 71**

Mitchell, Clyde
See Ellison, Harlan; Silverberg, Robert

Neruda, Pablo
1904-1973 ..... **CLC 1, 2, 5, 7, 9, 28, 62;**
PC 4
See also CA 19-20; 45-48; CAP 2; DA; HW;
MTCW; WLC

Nerval, Gerard de 1808-1855..... **NCLC 1**

Nervo, (Jose) Amado (Ruiz de)
1870-1919 .... **TCLC 11**
See also CA 109; 131; HW

Nessi, Pio Baroja y
See Baroja (y Nessi), Pio

Neufeld, John (Arthur) 1938- ...... **CLC 17**
See also CA 25-28R; CANR 11, 37;
MAICYA; SAAS 3; SATA 6

Neville, Emily Cheney 1919-....... **CLC 12**
See also CA 5-8R; CANR 3, 37; MAICYA;
SAAS 2; SATA 1

Newbound, Bernard Slade 1930-
See Slade, Bernard
See also CA 81-84

Newby, P(ercy) H(oward)
1918- .... **CLC 2, 13**
See also CA 5-8R; CANR 32; DLB 15;
MTCW

Newlove, Donald 1928- .... **CLC 6**
See also CA 29-32R; CANR 25

Newlove, John (Herbert) 1938-..... **CLC 14**
See also CA 21-24R; CANR 9, 25

Newman, Charles 1938-.......... **CLC 2, 8**
See also CA 21-24R

Newman, Edwin (Harold) 1919- .... **CLC 14**
See also AITN 1; CA 69-72; CANR 5

Newman, John Henry
1801-1890 .... **NCLC 38**
See also DLB 18, 32, 55

Newton, Suzanne 1936- .... **CLC 35**
See also CA 41-44R; CANR 14; SATA 5

Nexo, Martin Andersen
1869-1954 .... **TCLC 43**

Nezval, Vitezslav 1900-1958 ...... **TCLC 44**
See also CA 123

Ngema, Mbongeni 1955- .... **CLC 57**

Ngugi, James T(hiong'o)........ **CLC 3, 7, 13**
See also Ngugi wa Thiong'o

Ngugi wa Thiong'o 1938-.......... **CLC 36**
See also Ngugi, James T(hiong'o)
See also BLC 3; BW; CA 81-84; CANR 27;
DLB 125; MTCW

Nichol, B(arrie) P(hillip)
1944-1988 .... **CLC 18**
See also CA 53-56; DLB 53; SATA 66

Nichols, John (Treadwell) 1940-.... **CLC 38**
See also CA 9-12R; CAAS 2; CANR 6;
DLBY 82

Nichols, Leigh
See Koontz, Dean R(ay)

Nichols, Peter (Richard)
1927- .... **CLC 5, 36, 65**
See also CA 104; CANR 33; DLB 13;
MTCW

Nicolas, F. R. E.
See Freeling, Nicolas

Niedecker, Lorine 1903-1970.... **CLC 10, 42**
See also CA 25-28; CAP 2; DLB 48

Nietzsche, Friedrich (Wilhelm)
1844-1900 .... **TCLC 10, 18**
See also CA 107; 121; DLB 129

Nievo, Ippolito 1831-1861 .... **NCLC 22**

Nightingale, Anne Redmon 1943-
See Redmon, Anne
See also CA 103

Nik.T.O.
See Annensky, Innokenty Fyodorovich

Nin, Anais
1903-1977 ...... **CLC 1, 4, 8, 11, 14, 60;**
SSC 10
See also AITN 2; CA 13-16R; 69-72;
CANR 22; DLB 2, 4; MTCW

Nissenson, Hugh 1933-.......... **CLC 4, 9**
See also CA 17-20R; CANR 27; DLB 28

Niven, Larry .... **CLC 8**
See also Niven, Laurence Van Cott
See also DLB 8

Niven, Laurence Van Cott 1938-
See Niven, Larry
See also CA 21-24R; CAAS 12; CANR 14;
MTCW

Nixon, Agnes Eckhardt 1927-...... **CLC 21**
See also CA 110

Nizan, Paul 1905-1940.......... **TCLC 40**
See also DLB 72

Nkosi, Lewis 1936-.............. **CLC 45**
See also BLC 3; BW; CA 65-68; CANR 27

Nodier, (Jean) Charles (Emmanuel)
1780-1844 .... **NCLC 19**
See also DLB 119

Nolan, Christopher 1965-.......... **CLC 58**
See also CA 111

Norden, Charles
See Durrell, Lawrence (George)

Nordhoff, Charles (Bernard)
1887-1947 .... **TCLC 23**
See also CA 108; DLB 9; SATA 23

Norfolk, Lawrence 1963-.......... **CLC 76**

Norman, Marsha 1947- .... **CLC 28**
See also CA 105; CABS 3; CANR 41;
DLBY 84

Norris, Benjamin Franklin, Jr.
1870-1902 .... **TCLC 24**
See also Norris, Frank
See also CA 110

Norris, Frank
See Norris, Benjamin Franklin, Jr.
See also CDALB 1865-1917; DLB 12, 71

Norris, Leslie 1921-.............. **CLC 14**
See also CA 11-12; CANR 14; CAP 1;
DLB 27

North, Andrew
See Norton, Andre

North, Anthony
See Koontz, Dean R(ay)

North, Captain George
See Stevenson, Robert Louis (Balfour)

North, Milou
See Erdrich, Louise

Northrup, B. A.
See Hubbard, L(afayette) Ron(ald)

North Staffs
See Hulme, T(homas) E(rnest)

Norton, Alice Mary
See Norton, Andre
See also MAICYA; SATA 1, 43

Norton, Andre 1912- .... **CLC 12**
See also Norton, Alice Mary
See also CA 1-4R; CANR 2, 31; DLB 8, 52;
MTCW

Norway, Nevil Shute 1899-1960
See Shute, Nevil
See also CA 102; 93-96

Norwid, Cyprian Kamil
1821-1883 .... **NCLC 17**

Nosille, Nabrah
See Ellison, Harlan

Nossack, Hans Erich 1901-1978..... **CLC 6**
See also CA 93-96; 85-88; DLB 69

Nosu, Chuji
See Ozu, Yasujiro

Nova, Craig 1945-.............. **CLC 7, 31**
See also CA 45-48; CANR 2

Novak, Joseph
See Kosinski, Jerzy (Nikodem)

Novalis 1772-1801 .... **NCLC 13**
See also DLB 90

Nowlan, Alden (Albert) 1933-1983 .. **CLC 15**
See also CA 9-12R; CANR 5; DLB 53

Noyes, Alfred 1880-1958 .... **TCLC 7**
See also CA 104; DLB 20

Nunn, Kem 19(?)-................ **CLC 34**

Nye, Robert 1939- .... **CLC 13, 42**
See also CA 33-36R; CANR 29; DLB 14;
MTCW; SATA 6

Nyro, Laura 1947- .... **CLC 17**

Oates, Joyce Carol
1938- ......**CLC 1, 2, 3, 6, 9, 11, 15, 19,**
33, 52; SSC 6
See also AITN 1; BEST 89:2; CA 5-8R;
CANR 25; CDALB 1968-1988; DA;
DLB 2, 5, 130; DLBY 81; MTCW; WLC

O'Brien, E. G.
See Clarke, Arthur C(harles)

O'Brien, Edna
1936- ... **CLC 3, 5, 8, 13, 36, 65; SSC 10**
See also CA 1-4R; CANR 6, 41;
CDBLB 1960 to Present; DLB 14;
MTCW

O'Brien, Fitz-James 1828-1862... **NCLC 21**
See also DLB 74

O'Brien, Flann....... **CLC 1, 4, 5, 7, 10, 47**
See also O Nuallain, Brian

O'Brien, Richard 1942-........... **CLC 17**
See also CA 124

O'Brien, Tim 1946-.......... **CLC 7, 19, 40**
See also CA 85-88; CANR 40; DLBD 9;
DLBY 80

Obstfelder, Sigbjoern 1866-1900... **TCLC 23**
See also CA 123

O'Casey, Sean
1880-1964 .... **CLC 1, 5, 9, 11, 15**
See also CA 89-92; CDBLB 1914-1945;
DLB 10; MTCW

O'Cathasaigh, Sean
  See O'Casey, Sean

Ochs, Phil   1940-1976............ CLC 17
  See also CA 65-68

O'Connor, Edwin (Greene)
  1918-1968 .... CLC 14
  See also CA 93-96; 25-28R

O'Connor, (Mary) Flannery
  1925-1964 .... CLC 1, 2, 3, 6, 10, 13, 15,
                       21, 66; SSC 1
  See also AAYA 7; CA 1-4R; CANR 3, 41;
    CDALB 1941-1968; DA; DLB 2;
    DLBY 80; MTCW; WLC

O'Connor, Frank.......... CLC 23; SSC 5
  See also O'Donovan, Michael John

O'Dell, Scott   1898-1989.......... CLC 30
  See also AAYA 3; CA 61-64; 129;
    CANR 12, 30; CLR 1, 16; DLB 52;
    MAICYA; SATA 12, 60

Odets, Clifford   1906-1963 .... CLC 2, 28
  See also CA 85-88; DLB 7, 26; MTCW

O'Doherty, Brian   1934-.......... CLC 76
  See also CA 105

O'Donnell, K. M.
  See Malzberg, Barry N(athaniel)

O'Donnell, Lawrence
  See Kuttner, Henry

O'Donovan, Michael John
  1903-1966 .... CLC 14
  See also O'Connor, Frank
  See also CA 93-96

Oe, Kenzaburo   1935-.......... CLC 10, 36
  See also CA 97-100; CANR 36; MTCW

O'Faolain, Julia   1932-....... CLC 6, 19, 47
  See also CA 81-84; CAAS 2; CANR 12;
    DLB 14; MTCW

O'Faolain, Sean
  1900-1991 .... CLC 1, 7, 14, 32, 70;
                     SSC 13
  See also CA 61-64; 134; CANR 12;
    DLB 15; MTCW

O'Flaherty, Liam
  1896-1984 .... CLC 5, 34; SSC 6
  See also CA 101; 113; CANR 35; DLB 36;
    DLBY 84; MTCW

Ogilvy, Gavin
  See Barrie, J(ames) M(atthew)

O'Grady, Standish James
  1846-1928 .... TCLC 5
  See also CA 104

O'Grady, Timothy   1951-......... CLC 59
  See also CA 138

O'Hara, Frank
  1926-1966 .... CLC 2, 5, 13, 78
  See also CA 9-12R; 25-28R; CANR 33;
    DLB 5, 16; MTCW

O'Hara, John (Henry)
  1905-1970 .... CLC 1, 2, 3, 6, 11, 42
  See also CA 5-8R; 25-28R; CANR 31;
    CDALB 1929-1941; DLB 9, 86; DLBD 2;
    MTCW

O Hehir, Diana   1922- .... CLC 41
  See also CA 93-96

Okigbo, Christopher (Ifenayichukwu)
  1932-1967 .... CLC 25; PC 7
  See also BLC 3; BW; CA 77-80; DLB 125;
    MTCW

Olds, Sharon   1942-........... CLC 32, 39
  See also CA 101; CANR 18, 41; DLB 120

Oldstyle, Jonathan
  See Irving, Washington

Olesha, Yuri (Karlovich)
  1899-1960 .... CLC 8
  See also CA 85-88

Oliphant, Margaret (Oliphant Wilson)
  1828-1897 .... NCLC 11
  See also DLB 18

Oliver, Mary   1935-........... CLC 19, 34
  See also CA 21-24R; CANR 9; DLB 5

Olivier, Laurence (Kerr)
  1907-1989 .... CLC 20
  See also CA 111; 129

Olsen, Tillie   1913- ..... CLC 4, 13; SSC 11
  See also CA 1-4R; CANR 1; DA; DLB 28;
    DLBY 80; MTCW

Olson, Charles (John)
  1910-1970 ..... CLC 1, 2, 5, 6, 9, 11, 29
  See also CA 13-16; 25-28R; CABS 2;
    CANR 35; CAP 1; DLB 5, 16; MTCW

Olson, Toby   1937-............... CLC 28
  See also CA 65-68; CANR 9, 31

Olyesha, Yuri
  See Olesha, Yuri (Karlovich)

Ondaatje, (Philip) Michael
  1943- .... CLC 14, 29, 51, 76
  See also CA 77-80; DLB 60

Oneal, Elizabeth   1934-
  See Oneal, Zibby
  See also CA 106; CANR 28; MAICYA;
    SATA 30

Oneal, Zibby .... CLC 30
  See also Oneal, Elizabeth
  See also AAYA 5; CLR 13

O'Neill, Eugene (Gladstone)
  1888-1953 .... TCLC 1, 6, 27, 49
  See also AITN 1; CA 110; 132;
    CDALB 1929-1941; DA; DLB 7; MTCW;
    WLC

Onetti, Juan Carlos   1909-....... CLC 7, 10
  See also CA 85-88; CANR 32; DLB 113;
    HW; MTCW

O Nuallain, Brian   1911-1966
  See O'Brien, Flann
  See also CA 21-22; 25-28R; CAP 2

Oppen, George   1908-1984 .... CLC 7, 13, 34
  See also CA 13-16R; 113; CANR 8; DLB 5

Oppenheim, E(dward) Phillips
  1866-1946 .... TCLC 45
  See also CA 111; DLB 70

Orlovitz, Gil   1918-1973 .... CLC 22
  See also CA 77-80; 45-48; DLB 2, 5

Orris
  See Ingelow, Jean

Ortega y Gasset, Jose   1883-1955 ... TCLC 9
  See also CA 106; 130; HW; MTCW

Ortiz, Simon J(oseph)   1941-....... CLC 45
  See also CA 134; DLB 120

Orton, Joe .... CLC 4, 13, 43; DC 3
  See also Orton, John Kingsley
  See also CDBLB 1960 to Present; DLB 13

Orton, John Kingsley   1933-1967
  See Orton, Joe
  See also CA 85-88; CANR 35; MTCW

Orwell, George .... TCLC 2, 6, 15, 31, 51
  See also Blair, Eric (Arthur)
  See also CDBLB 1945-1960; DLB 15, 98;
    WLC

Osborne, David
  See Silverberg, Robert

Osborne, George
  See Silverberg, Robert

Osborne, John (James)
  1929- .... CLC 1, 2, 5, 11, 45
  See also CA 13-16R; CANR 21;
    CDBLB 1945-1960; DA; DLB 13;
    MTCW; WLC

Osborne, Lawrence   1958- .... CLC 50

Oshima, Nagisa   1932-............ CLC 20
  See also CA 116; 121

Oskison, John M(ilton)
  1874-1947 .... TCLC 35

Ossoli, Sarah Margaret (Fuller marchesa d')
  1810-1850
  See Fuller, Margaret
  See also SATA 25

Ostrovsky, Alexander
  1823-1886 .... NCLC 30

Otero, Blas de   1916- .... CLC 11
  See also CA 89-92

Otto, Whitney   1955-............. CLC 70
  See also CA 140

Ouida .... TCLC 43
  See also De La Ramee, (Marie) Louise
  See also DLB 18

Ousmane, Sembene   1923- .... CLC 66
  See also BLC 3; BW; CA 117; 125; MTCW

Ovid   43B.C.-18th cent. (?)... CMLC 7; PC 2

Owen, Hugh
  See Faust, Frederick (Schiller)

Owen, Wilfred (Edward Salter)
  1893-1918 .... TCLC 5, 27
  See also CA 104; CDBLB 1914-1945; DA;
    DLB 20; WLC

Owens, Rochelle   1936-............ CLC 8
  See also CA 17-20R; CAAS 2; CANR 39

Oz, Amos   1939- ... CLC 5, 8, 11, 27, 33, 54
  See also CA 53-56; CANR 27; MTCW

Ozick, Cynthia   1928-...... CLC 3, 7, 28, 62
  See also BEST 90:1; CA 17-20R; CANR 23;
    DLB 28; DLBY 82; MTCW

Ozu, Yasujiro   1903-1963 .... CLC 16
  See also CA 112

Pacheco, C.
  See Pessoa, Fernando (Antonio Nogueira)

Pa Chin
  See Li Fei-kan

Pack, Robert   1929-.............. CLC 13
  See also CA 1-4R; CANR 3; DLB 5

Padgett, Lewis
  See Kuttner, Henry

Padilla (Lorenzo), Heberto 1932- .... **CLC 38**
See also AITN 1; CA 123; 131; HW

Page, Jimmy 1944- .... **CLC 12**

Page, Louise 1955- .... **CLC 40**
See also CA 140

Page, P(atricia) K(athleen)
1916- .... **CLC 7, 18**
See also CA 53-56; CANR 4, 22; DLB 68;
MTCW

Paget, Violet 1856-1935
See Lee, Vernon
See also CA 104

Paget-Lowe, Henry
See Lovecraft, H(oward) P(hillips)

Paglia, Camille (Anna) 1947- .... **CLC 68**
See also CA 140

Paige, Richard
See Koontz, Dean R(ay)

Pakenham, Antonia
See Fraser, Antonia (Pakenham)

Palamas, Kostes 1859-1943 .... **TCLC 5**
See also CA 105

Palazzeschi, Aldo 1885-1974 ...... **CLC 11**
See also CA 89-92; 53-56; DLB 114

Paley, Grace 1922- .... **CLC 4, 6, 37; SSC 8**
See also CA 25-28R; CANR 13; DLB 28;
MTCW

Palin, Michael (Edward) 1943- ..... **CLC 21**
See also Monty Python
See also CA 107; CANR 35; SATA 67

Palliser, Charles 1947- .... **CLC 65**
See also CA 136

Palma, Ricardo 1833-1919 .... **TCLC 29**

Pancake, Breece Dexter 1952-1979
See Pancake, Breece D'J
See also CA 123; 109

Pancake, Breece D'J .... **CLC 29**
See also Pancake, Breece Dexter
See also DLB 130

Panko, Rudy
See Gogol, Nikolai (Vasilyevich)

Papadiamantis, Alexandros
1851-1911 .... **TCLC 29**

Papadiamantopoulos, Johannes 1856-1910
See Moreas, Jean
See also CA 117

Papini, Giovanni 1881-1956 ...... **TCLC 22**
See also CA 121

Paracelsus 1493-1541 .... **LC 14**

Parasol, Peter
See Stevens, Wallace

Parfenie, Maria
See Codrescu, Andrei

Parini, Jay (Lee) 1948- .... **CLC 54**
See also CA 97-100; CAAS 16; CANR 32

Park, Jordan
See Kornbluth, C(yril) M.; Pohl, Frederik

Parker, Bert
See Ellison, Harlan

Parker, Dorothy (Rothschild)
1893-1967 .... **CLC 15, 68; SSC 2**
See also CA 19-20; 25-28R; CAP 2;
DLB 11, 45, 86; MTCW

Parker, Robert B(rown) 1932- ...... **CLC 27**
See also BEST 89:4; CA 49-52; CANR 1,
26; MTCW

Parkes, Lucas
See Harris, John (Wyndham Parkes Lucas)
Beynon

Parkin, Frank 1940- .... **CLC 43**

Parkman, Francis, Jr.
1823-1893 .... **NCLC 12**
See also DLB 1, 30

Parks, Gordon (Alexander Buchanan)
1912- .... **CLC 1, 16**
See also AITN 2; BLC 3; BW; CA 41-44R;
CANR 26; DLB 33; SATA 8

Parnell, Thomas 1679-1718 .... **LC 3**
See also DLB 94

Parra, Nicanor 1914- .... **CLC 2**
See also CA 85-88; CANR 32; HW; MTCW

Parrish, Mary Frances
See Fisher, M(ary) F(rances) K(ennedy)

Parson
See Coleridge, Samuel Taylor

Parson Lot
See Kingsley, Charles

Partridge, Anthony
See Oppenheim, E(dward) Phillips

Pascoli, Giovanni 1855-1912 ...... **TCLC 45**

Pasolini, Pier Paolo
1922-1975 .... **CLC 20, 37**
See also CA 93-96; 61-64; DLB 128;
MTCW

Pasquini
See Silone, Ignazio

Pastan, Linda (Olenik) 1932- ...... **CLC 27**
See also CA 61-64; CANR 18, 40; DLB 5

Pasternak, Boris (Leonidovich)
1890-1960 ..... **CLC 7, 10, 18, 63; PC 6**
See also CA 127; 116; DA; MTCW; WLC

Patchen, Kenneth 1911-1972 ... **CLC 1, 2, 18**
See also CA 1-4R; 33-36R; CANR 3, 35;
DLB 16, 48; MTCW

Pater, Walter (Horatio)
1839-1894 .... **NCLC 7**
See also CDBLB 1832-1890; DLB 57

Paterson, A(ndrew) B(arton)
1864-1941 .... **TCLC 32**

Paterson, Katherine (Womeldorf)
1932- .... **CLC 12, 30**
See also AAYA 1; CA 21-24R; CANR 28;
CLR 7; DLB 52; MAICYA; MTCW;
SATA 13, 53

Patmore, Coventry Kersey Dighton
1823-1896 .... **NCLC 9**
See also DLB 35, 98

Paton, Alan (Stewart)
1903-1988 .... **CLC 4, 10, 25, 55**
See also CA 13-16; 125; CANR 22; CAP 1;
DA; MTCW; SATA 11, 56; WLC

Paton Walsh, Gillian 1937-
See Walsh, Jill Paton
See also CANR 38; MAICYA; SAAS 3;
SATA 4, 72

Paulding, James Kirke 1778-1860 . . **NCLC 2**
See also DLB 3, 59, 74

Paulin, Thomas Neilson 1949-
See Paulin, Tom
See also CA 123; 128

Paulin, Tom .... **CLC 37**
See also Paulin, Thomas Neilson
See also DLB 40

Paustovsky, Konstantin (Georgievich)
1892-1968 .... **CLC 40**
See also CA 93-96; 25-28R

Pavese, Cesare 1908-1950 .... **TCLC 3**
See also CA 104; DLB 128

Pavic, Milorad 1929- .... **CLC 60**
See also CA 136

Payne, Alan
See Jakes, John (William)

Paz, Gil
See Lugones, Leopoldo

Paz, Octavio
1914- .... **CLC 3, 4, 6, 10, 19, 51, 65;
PC 1**
See also CA 73-76; CANR 32; DA;
DLBY 90; HW; MTCW; WLC

Peacock, Molly 1947- .... **CLC 60**
See also CA 103; DLB 120

Peacock, Thomas Love
1785-1866 .... **NCLC 22**
See also DLB 96, 116

Peake, Mervyn 1911-1968 .... **CLC 7, 54**
See also CA 5-8R; 25-28R; CANR 3;
DLB 15; MTCW; SATA 23

Pearce, Philippa .... **CLC 21**
See also Christie, (Ann) Philippa
See also CLR 9; MAICYA; SATA 1, 67

Pearl, Eric
See Elman, Richard

Pearson, T(homas) R(eid) 1956- .... **CLC 39**
See also CA 120; 130

Peck, John 1941- .... **CLC 3**
See also CA 49-52; CANR 3

Peck, Richard (Wayne) 1934- ...... **CLC 21**
See also AAYA 1; CA 85-88; CANR 19,
38; MAICYA; SAAS 2; SATA 18, 55

Peck, Robert Newton 1928- .... **CLC 17**
See also AAYA 3; CA 81-84; CANR 31;
DA; MAICYA; SAAS 1; SATA 21, 62

Peckinpah, (David) Sam(uel)
1925-1984 .... **CLC 20**
See also CA 109; 114

Pedersen, Knut 1859-1952
See Hamsun, Knut
See also CA 104; 119; MTCW

Peeslake, Gaffer
See Durrell, Lawrence (George)

Peguy, Charles Pierre
1873-1914 .... **TCLC 10**
See also CA 107

Pena, Ramon del Valle y
See Valle-Inclan, Ramon (Maria) del

Pendennis, Arthur Esquir
See Thackeray, William Makepeace

Pepys, Samuel 1633-1703 .... **LC 11**
See also CDBLB 1660-1789; DA; DLB 101;
WLC

Percy, Walker
     1916-1990 .... **CLC 2, 3, 6, 8, 14, 18, 47,**
                                                              65
     See also CA 1-4R; 131; CANR 1, 23;
     DLB 2; DLBY 80, 90; MTCW

Perec, Georges   1936-1982 .... **CLC 56**
     See also DLB 83

Pereda (y Sanchez de Porrua), Jose Maria de
     1833-1906 .... **TCLC 16**
     See also CA 117

Pereda y Porrua, Jose Maria de
     See Pereda (y Sanchez de Porrua), Jose
     Maria de

Peregoy, George Weems
     See Mencken, H(enry) L(ouis)

Perelman, S(idney) J(oseph)
     1904-1979 ... **CLC 3, 5, 9, 15, 23, 44, 49**
     See also AITN 1, 2; CA 73-76; 89-92;
     CANR 18; DLB 11, 44; MTCW

Peret, Benjamin   1899-1959 .... **TCLC 20**
     See also CA 117

Peretz, Isaac Loeb   1851(?)-1915... **TCLC 16**
     See also CA 109

Peretz, Yitzkhok Leibush
     See Peretz, Isaac Loeb

Perez Galdos, Benito   1843-1920... **TCLC 27**
     See also CA 125; HW

Perrault, Charles   1628-1703 .... **LC 2**
     See also MAICYA; SATA 25

Perry, Brighton
     See Sherwood, Robert E(mmet)

Perse, St.-John .... **CLC 4, 11, 46**
     See also Leger, (Marie-Rene) Alexis
     Saint-Leger

Perse, Saint-John
     See Leger, (Marie-Rene) Alexis Saint-Leger

Peseenz, Tulio F.
     See Lopez y Fuentes, Gregorio

Pesetsky, Bette   1932-............ **CLC 28**
     See also CA 133; DLB 130

Peshkov, Alexei Maximovich   1868-1936
     See Gorky, Maxim
     See also CA 105; DA

Pessoa, Fernando (Antonio Nogueira)
     1888-1935 .... **TCLC 27**
     See also CA 125

Peterkin, Julia Mood   1880-1961.... **CLC 31**
     See also CA 102; DLB 9

Peters, Joan K.   1945-............ **CLC 39**

Peters, Robert L(ouis)   1924-....... **CLC 7**
     See also CA 13-16R; CAAS 8; DLB 105

Petofi, Sandor   1823-1849........ **NCLC 21**

Petrakis, Harry Mark   1923-........ **CLC 3**
     See also CA 9-12R; CANR 4, 30

Petrov, Evgeny .... **TCLC 21**
     See also Kataev, Evgeny Petrovich

Petry, Ann (Lane)   1908- ...... **CLC 1, 7, 18**
     See also BW; CA 5-8R; CAAS 6; CANR 4;
     CLR 12; DLB 76; MAICYA; MTCW;
     SATA 5

Petursson, Halligrimur   1614-1674 .... **LC 8**

Philipson, Morris H.   1926-........ **CLC 53**
     See also CA 1-4R; CANR 4

Phillips, David Graham
     1867-1911 .... **TCLC 44**
     See also CA 108; DLB 9, 12

Phillips, Jack
     See Sandburg, Carl (August)

Phillips, Jayne Anne   1952-..... **CLC 15, 33**
     See also CA 101; CANR 24; DLBY 80;
     MTCW

Phillips, Richard
     See Dick, Philip K(indred)

Phillips, Robert (Schaeffer)   1938-... **CLC 28**
     See also CA 17-20R; CAAS 13; CANR 8;
     DLB 105

Phillips, Ward
     See Lovecraft, H(oward) P(hillips)

Piccolo, Lucio   1901-1969......... **CLC 13**
     See also CA 97-100; DLB 114

Pickthall, Marjorie L(owry) C(hristie)
     1883-1922 .... **TCLC 21**
     See also CA 107; DLB 92

Pico della Mirandola, Giovanni
     1463-1494 .... **LC 15**

Piercy, Marge
     1936-......... **CLC 3, 6, 14, 18, 27, 62**
     See also CA 21-24R; CAAS 1; CANR 13;
     DLB 120; MTCW

Piers, Robert
     See Anthony, Piers

Pieyre de Mandiargues, Andre   1909-1991
     See Mandiargues, Andre Pieyre de
     See also CA 103; 136; CANR 22

Pilnyak, Boris .... **TCLC 23**
     See also Vogau, Boris Andreyevich

Pincherle, Alberto   1907-1990... **CLC 11, 18**
     See also Moravia, Alberto
     See also CA 25-28R; 132; CANR 33;
     MTCW

Pinckney, Darryl   1953-........... **CLC 76**

Pineda, Cecile   1942-............. **CLC 39**
     See also CA 118

Pinero, Arthur Wing   1855-1934... **TCLC 32**
     See also CA 110; DLB 10

Pinero, Miguel (Antonio Gomez)
     1946-1988 .... **CLC 4, 55**
     See also CA 61-64; 125; CANR 29; HW

Pinget, Robert   1919-........ **CLC 7, 13, 37**
     See also CA 85-88; DLB 83

Pink Floyd...................... **CLC 35**
     See also Barrett, (Roger) Syd; Gilmour,
     David; Mason, Nick; Waters, Roger;
     Wright, Rick

Pinkney, Edward   1802-1828..... **NCLC 31**

Pinkwater, Daniel Manus   1941-.... **CLC 35**
     See also Pinkwater, Manus
     See also AAYA 1; CA 29-32R; CANR 12,
     38; CLR 4; MAICYA; SAAS 3; SATA 46

Pinkwater, Manus
     See Pinkwater, Daniel Manus
     See also SATA 8

Pinsky, Robert   1940-........ **CLC 9, 19, 38**
     See also CA 29-32R; CAAS 4; DLBY 82

Pinta, Harold
     See Pinter, Harold

Pinter, Harold
     1930-.. **CLC 1, 3, 6, 9, 11, 15, 27, 58, 73**
     See also CA 5-8R; CANR 33; CDBLB 1960
     to Present; DA; DLB 13; MTCW; WLC

Pirandello, Luigi   1867-1936..... **TCLC 4, 29**
     See also CA 104; DA; WLC

Pirsig, Robert M(aynard)
     1928-.................. **CLC 4, 6, 73**
     See also CA 53-56; MTCW; SATA 39

Pisarev, Dmitry Ivanovich
     1840-1868 .... **NCLC 25**

Pix, Mary (Griffith)   1666-1709....... **LC 8**
     See also DLB 80

Pixerecourt, Guilbert de
     1773-1844 .... **NCLC 39**

Plaidy, Jean
     See Hibbert, Eleanor Alice Burford

Plant, Robert   1948-.............. **CLC 12**

Plante, David (Robert)
     1940-.................. **CLC 7, 23, 38**
     See also CA 37-40R; CANR 12, 36;
     DLBY 83; MTCW

Plath, Sylvia
     1932-1963 ..... **CLC 1, 2, 3, 5, 9, 11, 14,**
                       17, 50, 51, 62; PC 1
     See also CA 19-20; CANR 34; CAP 2;
     CDALB 1941-1968; DA; DLB 5, 6;
     MTCW; WLC

Plato   428(?)B.C.-348(?)B.C....... **CMLC 8**
     See also DA

Platonov, Andrei .... **TCLC 14**
     See also Klimentov, Andrei Platonovich

Platt, Kin   1911-................. **CLC 26**
     See also CA 17-20R; CANR 11; SATA 21

Plick et Plock
     See Simenon, Georges (Jacques Christian)

Plimpton, George (Ames)   1927-..... **CLC 36**
     See also AITN 1; CA 21-24R; CANR 32;
     MTCW; SATA 10

Plomer, William Charles Franklin
     1903-1973 .... **CLC 4, 8**
     See also CA 21-22; CANR 34; CAP 2;
     DLB 20; MTCW; SATA 24

Plowman, Piers
     See Kavanagh, Patrick (Joseph)

Plum, J.
     See Wodehouse, P(elham) G(renville)

Plumly, Stanley (Ross)   1939-...... **CLC 33**
     See also CA 108; 110; DLB 5

Poe, Edgar Allan
     1809-1849... **NCLC 1, 16; PC 1; SSC 1**
     See also CDALB 1640-1865; DA; DLB 3,
     59, 73, 74; SATA 23; WLC

Poet of Titchfield Street, The
     See Pound, Ezra (Weston Loomis)

Pohl, Frederik   1919- .... **CLC 18**
     See also CA 61-64; CAAS 1; CANR 11, 37;
     DLB 8; MTCW; SATA 24

Poirier, Louis   1910-
     See Gracq, Julien
     See also CA 122; 126

Poitier, Sidney   1927-............. **CLC 26**
     See also BW; CA 117

Polanski, Roman 1933- . . . . **CLC 16**
See also CA 77-80

Poliakoff, Stephen 1952- . . . . **CLC 38**
See also CA 106; DLB 13

Police, The . . . . **CLC 26**
See also Copeland, Stewart (Armstrong);
Summers, Andrew James; Sumner,
Gordon Matthew

Pollitt, Katha 1949- . . . . **CLC 28**
See also CA 120; 122; MTCW

Pollock, (Mary) Sharon 1936- . . . . . . **CLC 50**
See also DLB 60

Pomerance, Bernard 1940- . . . . **CLC 13**
See also CA 101

Ponge, Francis (Jean Gaston Alfred)
1899-1988 . . . . **CLC 6, 18**
See also CA 85-88; 126; CANR 40

Pontoppidan, Henrik 1857-1943 . . . **TCLC 29**

Poole, Josephine . . . . **CLC 17**
See also Helyar, Jane Penelope Josephine
See also SAAS 2; SATA 5

Popa, Vasko 1922- . . . . **CLC 19**
See also CA 112

Pope, Alexander 1688-1744 . . . . **LC 3**
See also CDBLB 1660-1789; DA; DLB 95,
101; WLC

Porter, Connie 1960- . . . . **CLC 70**

Porter, Gene(va Grace) Stratton
1863(?)-1924 . . . . **TCLC 21**
See also CA 112

Porter, Katherine Anne
1890-1980 . . . . . . **CLC 1, 3, 7, 10, 13, 15,
27; SSC 4**
See also AITN 2; CA 1-4R; 101; CANR 1;
DA; DLB 4, 9, 102; DLBY 80; MTCW;
SATA 23, 39

Porter, Peter (Neville Frederick)
1929- . . . . **CLC 5, 13, 33**
See also CA 85-88; DLB 40

Porter, William Sydney 1862-1910
See Henry, O.
See also CA 104; 131; CDALB 1865-1917;
DA; DLB 12, 78, 79; MTCW; YABC 2

Portillo (y Pacheco), Jose Lopez
See Lopez Portillo (y Pacheco), Jose

Post, Melville Davisson
1869-1930 . . . . **TCLC 39**
See also CA 110

Potok, Chaim 1929- . . . . **CLC 2, 7, 14, 26**
See also AITN 1, 2; CA 17-20R; CANR 19,
35; DLB 28; MTCW; SATA 33

Potter, Beatrice
See Webb, (Martha) Beatrice (Potter)
See also MAICYA

Potter, Dennis (Christopher George)
1935- . . . . **CLC 58**
See also CA 107; CANR 33; MTCW

Pound, Ezra (Weston Loomis)
1885-1972 . . . . . . **CLC 1, 2, 3, 4, 5, 7, 10,
13, 18, 34, 48, 50; PC 4**
See also CA 5-8R; 37-40R; CANR 40;
CDALB 1917-1929; DA; DLB 4, 45, 63;
MTCW; WLC

Povod, Reinaldo 1959- . . . . **CLC 44**
See also CA 136

Powell, Anthony (Dymoke)
1905- . . . . **CLC 1, 3, 7, 9, 10, 31**
See also CA 1-4R; CANR 1, 32;
CDBLB 1945-1960; DLB 15; MTCW

Powell, Dawn 1897-1965 . . . . **CLC 66**
See also CA 5-8R

Powell, Padgett 1952- . . . . **CLC 34**
See also CA 126

Powers, J(ames) F(arl)
1917- . . . . **CLC 1, 4, 8, 57; SSC 4**
See also CA 1-4R; CANR 2; DLB 130;
MTCW

Powers, John J(ames) 1945-
See Powers, John R.
See also CA 69-72

Powers, John R. . . . . **CLC 66**
See also Powers, John J(ames)

Pownall, David 1938- . . . . **CLC 10**
See also CA 89-92; DLB 14

Powys, John Cowper
1872-1963 . . . . **CLC 7, 9, 15, 46**
See also CA 85-88; DLB 15; MTCW

Powys, T(heodore) F(rancis)
1875-1953 . . . . **TCLC 9**
See also CA 106; DLB 36

Prager, Emily 1952- . . . . **CLC 56**

Pratt, E(dwin) J(ohn)
1883(?)-1964 . . . . **CLC 19**
See also CA 93-96; DLB 92

Premchand . . . . **TCLC 21**
See also Srivastava, Dhanpat Rai

Preussler, Otfried 1923- . . . . **CLC 17**
See also CA 77-80; SATA 24

Prevert, Jacques (Henri Marie)
1900-1977 . . . . **CLC 15**
See also CA 77-80; 69-72; CANR 29;
MTCW; SATA 30

Prevost, Abbe (Antoine Francois)
1697-1763 . . . . **LC 1**

Price, (Edward) Reynolds
1933- . . . . **CLC 3, 6, 13, 43, 50, 63**
See also CA 1-4R; CANR 1, 37; DLB 2

Price, Richard 1949- . . . . **CLC 6, 12**
See also CA 49-52; CANR 3; DLBY 81

Prichard, Katharine Susannah
1883-1969 . . . . **CLC 46**
See also CA 11-12; CANR 33; CAP 1;
MTCW; SATA 66

Priestley, J(ohn) B(oynton)
1894-1984 . . . . **CLC 2, 5, 9, 34**
See also CA 9-12R; 113; CANR 33;
CDBLB 1914-1945; DLB 10, 34, 77, 100;
DLBY 84; MTCW

Prince 1958(?)- . . . . **CLC 35**

Prince, F(rank) T(empleton) 1912- . . **CLC 22**
See also CA 101; DLB 20

Prince Kropotkin
See Kropotkin, Peter (Aleksieevich)

Prior, Matthew 1664-1721 . . . . **LC 4**
See also DLB 95

Pritchard, William H(arrison)
1932- . . . . **CLC 34**
See also CA 65-68; CANR 23; DLB 111

Pritchett, V(ictor) S(awdon)
1900- . . . . **CLC 5, 13, 15, 41**
See also CA 61-64; CANR 31; DLB 15;
MTCW

Private 19022
See Manning, Frederic

Probst, Mark 1925- . . . . **CLC 59**
See also CA 130

Prokosch, Frederic 1908-1989 . . . . **CLC 4, 48**
See also CA 73-76; 128; DLB 48

Prophet, The
See Dreiser, Theodore (Herman Albert)

Prose, Francine 1947- . . . . **CLC 45**
See also CA 109; 112

Proudhon
See Cunha, Euclides (Rodrigues Pimenta) da

Proust, (Valentin-Louis-George-Eugene-)
Marcel 1871-1922 . . . . **TCLC 7, 13, 33**
See also CA 104; 120; DA; DLB 65;
MTCW; WLC

Prowler, Harley
See Masters, Edgar Lee

Prus, Boleslaw . . . . **TCLC 48**
See also Glowacki, Aleksander

Pryor, Richard (Franklin Lenox Thomas)
1940- . . . . **CLC 26**
See also CA 122

Przybyszewski, Stanislaw
1868-1927 . . . . **TCLC 36**
See also DLB 66

Pteleon
See Grieve, C(hristopher) M(urray)

Puckett, Lute
See Masters, Edgar Lee

Puig, Manuel
1932-1990 . . . . **CLC 3, 5, 10, 28, 65**
See also CA 45-48; CANR 2, 32; DLB 113;
HW; MTCW

Purdy, A(lfred) W(ellington)
1918- . . . . **CLC 3, 6, 14, 50**
See also Purdy, Al
See also CA 81-84

Purdy, Al
See Purdy, A(lfred) W(ellington)
See also CAAS 17; DLB 88

Purdy, James (Amos)
1923- . . . . **CLC 2, 4, 10, 28, 52**
See also CA 33-36R; CAAS 1; CANR 19;
DLB 2; MTCW

Pure, Simon
See Swinnerton, Frank Arthur

Pushkin, Alexander (Sergeyevich)
1799-1837 . . . . **NCLC 3, 27**
See also DA; SATA 61; WLC

P'u Sung-ling 1640-1715 . . . . **LC 3**

Putnam, Arthur Lee
See Alger, Horatio, Jr.

Puzo, Mario 1920- . . . . **CLC 1, 2, 6, 36**
See also CA 65-68; CANR 4; DLB 6;
MTCW

Pym, Barbara (Mary Crampton)
1913-1980 . . . . **CLC 13, 19, 37**
See also CA 13-14; 97-100; CANR 13, 34;
CAP 1; DLB 14; DLBY 87; MTCW

Pynchon, Thomas (Ruggles, Jr.)
1937- . . CLC **2, 3, 6, 9, 11, 18, 33, 62, 72**
See also BEST 90:2; CA 17-20R; CANR 22;
DA; DLB 2; MTCW; WLC

Qian Zhongshu
See Ch'ien Chung-shu

Qroll
See Dagerman, Stig (Halvard)

Quarrington, Paul (Lewis) 1953-.... CLC **65**
See also CA 129

Quasimodo, Salvatore 1901-1968 . . . CLC **10**
See also CA 13-16; 25-28R; CAP 1;
DLB 114; MTCW

Queen, Ellery. . . . . CLC **3, 11**
See also Dannay, Frederic; Davidson,
Avram; Lee, Manfred B(ennington);
Sturgeon, Theodore (Hamilton); Vance,
John Holbrook

Queen, Ellery, Jr.
See Dannay, Frederic; Lee, Manfred
B(ennington)

Queneau, Raymond
1903-1976 . . . . CLC **2, 5, 10, 42**
See also CA 77-80; 69-72; CANR 32;
DLB 72; MTCW

Quevedo, Francisco de 1580-1645.... LC **23**

Quin, Ann (Marie) 1936-1973 . . . . CLC **6**
See also CA 9-12R; 45-48; DLB 14

Quinn, Martin
See Smith, Martin Cruz

Quinn, Simon
See Smith, Martin Cruz

Quiroga, Horacio (Sylvestre)
1878-1937 . . . . TCLC **20**
See also CA 117; 131; HW; MTCW

Quoirez, Francoise 1935-. . . . . CLC **9**
See also Sagan, Francoise
See also CA 49-52; CANR 6, 39; MTCW

Raabe, Wilhelm 1831-1910 . . . . TCLC **45**
See also DLB 129

Rabe, David (William) 1940-. . . CLC **4, 8, 33**
See also CA 85-88; CABS 3; DLB 7

Rabelais, Francois 1483-1553 . . . . LC **5**
See also DA; WLC

Rabinovitch, Sholem 1859-1916
See Aleichem, Sholom
See also CA 104

Radcliffe, Ann (Ward) 1764-1823 . . NCLC **6**
See also DLB 39

Radiguet, Raymond 1903-1923 . . . . TCLC **29**
See also DLB 65

Radnoti, Miklos 1909-1944 . . . . . . TCLC **16**
See also CA 118

Rado, James 1939-. . . . . CLC **17**
See also CA 105

Radvanyi, Netty 1900-1983
See Seghers, Anna
See also CA 85-88; 110

Raeburn, John (Hay) 1941-. . . . . CLC **34**
See also CA 57-60

Ragni, Gerome 1942-1991 . . . . CLC **17**
See also CA 105; 134

Rahv, Philip. . . . . CLC **24**
See also Greenberg, Ivan

Raine, Craig 1944-. . . . . CLC **32**
See also CA 108; CANR 29; DLB 40

Raine, Kathleen (Jessie) 1908- . . . CLC **7, 45**
See also CA 85-88; DLB 20; MTCW

Rainis, Janis 1865-1929 . . . . TCLC **29**

Rakosi, Carl. . . . . CLC **47**
See also Rawley, Callman
See also CAAS 5

Raleigh, Richard
See Lovecraft, H(oward) P(hillips)

Rallentando, H. P.
See Sayers, Dorothy L(eigh)

Ramal, Walter
See de la Mare, Walter (John)

Ramon, Juan
See Jimenez (Mantecon), Juan Ramon

Ramos, Graciliano 1892-1953 . . . . . TCLC **32**

Rampersad, Arnold 1941-. . . . . CLC **44**
See also CA 127; 133; DLB 111

Rampling, Anne
See Rice, Anne

Ramuz, Charles-Ferdinand
1878-1947 . . . . TCLC **33**

Rand, Ayn 1905-1982. . . . . CLC **3, 30, 44, 79**
See also AAYA 10; CA 13-16R; 105;
CANR 27; DA; MTCW; WLC

Randall, Dudley (Felker) 1914-. . . . . . CLC **1**
See also BLC 3; BW; CA 25-28R;
CANR 23; DLB 41

Randall, Robert
See Silverberg, Robert

Ranger, Ken
See Creasey, John

Ransom, John Crowe
1888-1974 . . . . CLC **2, 4, 5, 11, 24**
See also CA 5-8R; 49-52; CANR 6, 34;
DLB 45, 63; MTCW

Rao, Raja 1909-. . . . . CLC **25, 56**
See also CA 73-76; MTCW

Raphael, Frederic (Michael)
1931-. CLC **2, 14**
See also CA 1-4R; CANR 1; DLB 14

Ratcliffe, James P.
See Mencken, H(enry) L(ouis)

Rathbone, Julian 1935- . . . . CLC **41**
See also CA 101; CANR 34

Rattigan, Terence (Mervyn)
1911-1977 . . . . CLC **7**
See also CA 85-88; 73-76;
CDBLB 1945-1960; DLB 13; MTCW

Ratushinskaya, Irina 1954-. . . . . CLC **54**
See also CA 129

Raven, Simon (Arthur Noel)
1927-. . . . . CLC **14**
See also CA 81-84

Rawley, Callman 1903-
See Rakosi, Carl
See also CA 21-24R; CANR 12, 32

Rawlings, Marjorie Kinnan
1896-1953 . . . . TCLC **4**
See also CA 104; 137; DLB 9, 22, 102;
MAICYA; YABC 1

Ray, Satyajit 1921-1992. . . . . . . CLC **16, 76**
See also CA 114; 137

Read, Herbert Edward 1893-1968.... CLC **4**
See also CA 85-88; 25-28R; DLB 20

Read, Piers Paul 1941- . . . . . . CLC **4, 10, 25**
See also CA 21-24R; CANR 38; DLB 14;
SATA 21

Reade, Charles 1814-1884 . . . . NCLC **2**
See also DLB 21

Reade, Hamish
See Gray, Simon (James Holliday)

Reading, Peter 1946-. . . . . CLC **47**
See also CA 103; DLB 40

Reaney, James 1926-. . . . . CLC **13**
See also CA 41-44R; CAAS 15; DLB 68;
SATA 43

Rebreanu, Liviu 1885-1944 . . . . TCLC **28**

Rechy, John (Francisco)
1934-. . . . . CLC **1, 7, 14, 18**
See also CA 5-8R; CAAS 4; CANR 6, 32;
DLB 122; DLBY 82; HW

Redcam, Tom 1870-1933 . . . . TCLC **25**

Reddin, Keith. . . . . CLC **67**

Redgrove, Peter (William)
1932-. CLC **6, 41**
See also CA 1-4R; CANR 3, 39; DLB 40

Redmon, Anne. . . . . CLC **22**
See also Nightingale, Anne Redmon
See also DLBY 86

Reed, Eliot
See Ambler, Eric

Reed, Ishmael
1938-. . . . . CLC **2, 3, 5, 6, 13, 32, 60**
See also BLC 3; BW; CA 21-24R;
CANR 25; DLB 2, 5, 33; DLBD 8;
MTCW

Reed, John (Silas) 1887-1920 . . . . . . TCLC **9**
See also CA 106

Reed, Lou. . . . . CLC **21**
See also Firbank, Louis

Reeve, Clara 1729-1807 . . . . NCLC **19**
See also DLB 39

Reid, Christopher (John) 1949-. . . . . CLC **33**
See also CA 140; DLB 40

Reid, Desmond
See Moorcock, Michael (John)

Reid Banks, Lynne 1929-
See Banks, Lynne Reid
See also CA 1-4R; CANR 6, 22, 38;
CLR 24; MAICYA; SATA 22

Reilly, William K.
See Creasey, John

Reiner, Max
See Caldwell, (Janet Miriam) Taylor
(Holland)

Reis, Ricardo
See Pessoa, Fernando (Antonio Nogueira)

Remarque, Erich Maria
1898-1970 . . . . CLC **21**
See also CA 77-80; 29-32R; DA; DLB 56;
MTCW

Remizov, A.
See Remizov, Aleksei (Mikhailovich)

Remizov, A. M.
See Remizov, Aleksei (Mikhailovich)

Remizov, Aleksei (Mikhailovich)
1877-1957 . . . . **TCLC 27**
See also CA 125; 133

Renan, Joseph Ernest
1823-1892 . . . . **NCLC 26**

Renard, Jules 1864-1910 . . . . **TCLC 17**
See also CA 117

Renault, Mary . . . . **CLC 3, 11, 17**
See also Challans, Mary
See also DLBY 83

Rendell, Ruth (Barbara) 1930- . . **CLC 28, 48**
See also Vine, Barbara
See also CA 109; CANR 32; DLB 87;
MTCW

Renoir, Jean 1894-1979 . . . . **CLC 20**
See also CA 129; 85-88

Resnais, Alain 1922- . . . . **CLC 16**

Reverdy, Pierre 1889-1960 . . . . **CLC 53**
See also CA 97-100; 89-92

Rexroth, Kenneth
1905-1982 . . . . . . **CLC 1, 2, 6, 11, 22, 49**
See also CA 5-8R; 107; CANR 14, 34;
CDALB 1941-1968; DLB 16, 48;
DLBY 82; MTCW

Reyes, Alfonso 1889-1959 . . . . **TCLC 33**
See also CA 131; HW

Reyes y Basoalto, Ricardo Eliecer Neftali
See Neruda, Pablo

Reymont, Wladyslaw (Stanislaw)
1868(?)-1925 . . . . **TCLC 5**
See also CA 104

Reynolds, Jonathan 1942- . . . . **CLC 6, 38**
See also CA 65-68; CANR 28

Reynolds, Joshua 1723-1792 . . . . **LC 15**
See also DLB 104

Reynolds, Michael Shane 1937- . . . . **CLC 44**
See also CA 65-68; CANR 9

Reznikoff, Charles 1894-1976 . . . . **CLC 9**
See also CA 33-36; 61-64; CAP 2; DLB 28,
45

Rezzori (d'Arezzo), Gregor von
1914- . . . . **CLC 25**
See also CA 122; 136

Rhine, Richard
See Silverstein, Alvin

R'hoone
See Balzac, Honore de

Rhys, Jean
1890(?)-1979 . . . . **CLC 2, 4, 6, 14, 19, 51**
See also CA 25-28R; 85-88; CANR 35;
CDBLB 1945-1960; DLB 36, 117; MTCW

Ribeiro, Darcy 1922- . . . . **CLC 34**
See also CA 33-36R

Ribeiro, Joao Ubaldo (Osorio Pimentel)
1941- . . . . **CLC 10, 67**
See also CA 81-84

Ribman, Ronald (Burt) 1932- . . . . **CLC 7**
See also CA 21-24R

Ricci, Nino 1959- . . . . **CLC 70**
See also CA 137

Rice, Anne 1941- . . . . **CLC 41**
See also AAYA 9; BEST 89:2; CA 65-68;
CANR 12, 36

Rice, Elmer (Leopold)
1892-1967 . . . . **CLC 7, 49**
See also CA 21-22; 25-28R; CAP 2; DLB 4,
7; MTCW

Rice, Tim 1944- . . . . **CLC 21**
See also CA 103

Rich, Adrienne (Cecile)
1929- . . . . **CLC 3, 6, 7, 11, 18, 36, 73, 76;**
PC 5
See also CA 9-12R; CANR 20; DLB 5, 67;
MTCW

Rich, Barbara
See Graves, Robert (von Ranke)

Rich, Robert
See Trumbo, Dalton

Richards, David Adams 1950- . . . . . . **CLC 59**
See also CA 93-96; DLB 53

Richards, I(vor) A(rmstrong)
1893-1979 . . . . **CLC 14, 24**
See also CA 41-44R; 89-92; CANR 34;
DLB 27

Richardson, Anne
See Roiphe, Anne Richardson

Richardson, Dorothy Miller
1873-1957 . . . . **TCLC 3**
See also CA 104; DLB 36

Richardson, Ethel Florence (Lindesay)
1870-1946
See Richardson, Henry Handel
See also CA 105

Richardson, Henry Handel . . . . **TCLC 4**
See also Richardson, Ethel Florence
(Lindesay)

Richardson, Samuel 1689-1761 . . . . **LC 1**
See also CDBLB 1660-1789; DA; DLB 39;
WLC

Richler, Mordecai
1931- . . . . **CLC 3, 5, 9, 13, 18, 46, 70**
See also AITN 1; CA 65-68; CANR 31;
CLR 17; DLB 53; MAICYA; MTCW;
SATA 27, 44

Richter, Conrad (Michael)
1890-1968 . . . . **CLC 30**
See also CA 5-8R; 25-28R; CANR 23;
DLB 9; MTCW; SATA 3

Riddell, J. H. 1832-1906 . . . . **TCLC 40**

Riding, Laura . . . . **CLC 3, 7**
See also Jackson, Laura (Riding)

Riefenstahl, Berta Helene Amalia 1902-
See Riefenstahl, Leni
See also CA 108

Riefenstahl, Leni . . . . **CLC 16**
See also Riefenstahl, Berta Helene Amalia

Riffe, Ernest
See Bergman, (Ernst) Ingmar

Riley, James Whitcomb
1849-1916 . . . . **TCLC 51**
See also CA 118; 137; MAICYA; SATA 17

Riley, Tex
See Creasey, John

Rilke, Rainer Maria
1875-1926 . . . . **TCLC 1, 6, 19; PC 2**
See also CA 104; 132; DLB 81; MTCW

Rimbaud, (Jean Nicolas) Arthur
1854-1891 . . . . **NCLC 4, 35; PC 3**
See also DA; WLC

Ringmaster, The
See Mencken, H(enry) L(ouis)

Ringwood, Gwen(dolyn Margaret) Pharis
1910-1984 . . . . **CLC 48**
See also CA 112; DLB 88

Rio, Michel 19(?)- . . . . **CLC 43**

Ritsos, Giannes
See Ritsos, Yannis

Ritsos, Yannis 1909-1990 . . . . . **CLC 6, 13, 31**
See also CA 77-80; 133; CANR 39; MTCW

Ritter, Erika 1948(?)- . . . . **CLC 52**

Rivera, Jose Eustasio 1889-1928 . . . **TCLC 35**
See also HW

Rivers, Conrad Kent 1933-1968 . . . . . . **CLC 1**
See also BW; CA 85-88; DLB 41

Rivers, Elfrida
See Bradley, Marion Zimmer

Riverside, John
See Heinlein, Robert A(nson)

Rizal, Jose 1861-1896 . . . . **NCLC 27**

Roa Bastos, Augusto (Antonio)
1917- . . . . **CLC 45**
See also CA 131; DLB 113; HW

Robbe-Grillet, Alain
1922- . . . . . . **CLC 1, 2, 4, 6, 8, 10, 14, 43**
See also CA 9-12R; CANR 33; DLB 83;
MTCW

Robbins, Harold 1916- . . . . **CLC 5**
See also CA 73-76; CANR 26; MTCW

Robbins, Thomas Eugene 1936-
See Robbins, Tom
See also CA 81-84; CANR 29; MTCW

Robbins, Tom . . . . **CLC 9, 32, 64**
See also Robbins, Thomas Eugene
See also BEST 90:3; DLBY 80

Robbins, Trina 1938- . . . . **CLC 21**
See also CA 128

Roberts, Charles G(eorge) D(ouglas)
1860-1943 . . . . **TCLC 8**
See also CA 105; DLB 92; SATA 29

Roberts, Kate 1891-1985 . . . . **CLC 15**
See also CA 107; 116

Roberts, Keith (John Kingston)
1935- . . . . **CLC 14**
See also CA 25-28R

Roberts, Kenneth (Lewis)
1885-1957 . . . . **TCLC 23**
See also CA 109; DLB 9

Roberts, Michele (B.) 1949- . . . . **CLC 48**
See also CA 115

Robertson, Ellis
See Ellison, Harlan; Silverberg, Robert

Robertson, Thomas William
1829-1871 . . . . **NCLC 35**

Robinson, Edwin Arlington
1869-1935 . . . . **TCLC 5; PC 1**
See also CA 104; 133; CDALB 1865-1917;
DA; DLB 54; MTCW

Robinson, Henry Crabb
1775-1867 . . . . **NCLC 15**
See also DLB 107

Robinson, Jill 1936-.............. **CLC 10**
See also CA 102

Robinson, Kim Stanley 1952- ...... **CLC 34**
See also CA 126

Robinson, Lloyd
See Silverberg, Robert

Robinson, Marilynne 1944-........ **CLC 25**
See also CA 116

Robinson, Smokey................. **CLC 21**
See also Robinson, William, Jr.

Robinson, William, Jr. 1940-
See Robinson, Smokey
See also CA 116

Robison, Mary 1949-............. **CLC 42**
See also CA 113; 116; DLB 130

Roddenberry, Eugene Wesley 1921-1991
See Roddenberry, Gene
See also CA 110; 135; CANR 37; SATA 45

Roddenberry, Gene............... **CLC 17**
See also Roddenberry, Eugene Wesley
See also AAYA 5; SATA-Obit 69

Rodgers, Mary 1931-............. **CLC 12**
See also CA 49-52; CANR 8; CLR 20;
MAICYA; SATA 8

Rodgers, W(illiam) R(obert)
1909-1969 .... **CLC 7**
See also CA 85-88; DLB 20

Rodman, Eric
See Silverberg, Robert

Rodman, Howard 1920(?)-1985..... **CLC 65**
See also CA 118

Rodman, Maia
See Wojciechowska, Maia (Teresa)

Rodriguez, Claudio 1934-......... **CLC 10**

Roelvaag, O(le) E(dvart)
1876-1931 .... **TCLC 17**
See also CA 117; DLB 9

Roethke, Theodore (Huebner)
1908-1963 ...... **CLC 1, 3, 8, 11, 19, 46**
See also CA 81-84; CABS 2;
CDALB 1941-1968; DLB 5; MTCW

Rogers, Thomas Hunton 1927-..... **CLC 57**
See also CA 89-92

Rogers, Will(iam Penn Adair)
1879-1935 .... **TCLC 8**
See also CA 105; DLB 11

Rogin, Gilbert 1929-............. **CLC 18**
See also CA 65-68; CANR 15

Rohan, Koda .... **TCLC 22**
See also Koda Shigeyuki

Rohmer, Eric................... **CLC 16**
See also Scherer, Jean-Marie Maurice

Rohmer, Sax .... **TCLC 28**
See also Ward, Arthur Henry Sarsfield
See also DLB 70

Roiphe, Anne Richardson 1935- ... **CLC 3, 9**
See also CA 89-92; DLBY 80

Rojas, Fernando de 1465-1541 ...... **LC 23**

**Rolfe, Frederick (William Serafino Austin
Lewis Mary)** 1860-1913...... **TCLC 12**
See also CA 107; DLB 34

Rolland, Romain 1866-1944....... **TCLC 23**
See also CA 118; DLB 65

Rolvaag, O(le) E(dvart)
See Roelvaag, O(le) E(dvart)

Romain Arnaud, Saint
See Aragon, Louis

Romains, Jules 1885-1972.......... **CLC 7**
See also CA 85-88; CANR 34; DLB 65;
MTCW

Romero, Jose Ruben 1890-1952 ... **TCLC 14**
See also CA 114; 131; HW

Ronsard, Pierre de 1524-1585....... **LC 6**

Rooke, Leon 1934-............. **CLC 25, 34**
See also CA 25-28R; CANR 23

Roper, William 1498-1578.......... **LC 10**

Roquelaure, A. N.
See Rice, Anne

Rosa, Joao Guimaraes 1908-1967 ... **CLC 23**
See also CA 89-92; DLB 113

Rosen, Richard (Dean) 1949-....... **CLC 39**
See also CA 77-80

Rosenberg, Isaac 1890-1918...... **TCLC 12**
See also CA 107; DLB 20

Rosenblatt, Joe .... **CLC 15**
See also Rosenblatt, Joseph

Rosenblatt, Joseph 1933-
See Rosenblatt, Joe
See also CA 89-92

Rosenfeld, Samuel 1896-1963
See Tzara, Tristan
See also CA 89-92

Rosenthal, M(acha) L(ouis) 1917-... **CLC 28**
See also CA 1-4R; CAAS 6; CANR 4;
DLB 5; SATA 59

Ross, Barnaby
See Dannay, Frederic

Ross, Bernard L.
See Follett, Ken(neth Martin)

Ross, J. H.
See Lawrence, T(homas) E(dward)

Ross, Martin
See Martin, Violet Florence

Ross, (James) Sinclair 1908-....... **CLC 13**
See also CA 73-76; DLB 88

Rossetti, Christina (Georgina)
1830-1894 .... **NCLC 2; PC 7**
See also DA; DLB 35; MAICYA;
SATA 20; WLC

Rossetti, Dante Gabriel
1828-1882 .... **NCLC 4**
See also CDBLB 1832-1890; DA; DLB 35;
WLC

Rossner, Judith (Perelman)
1935- .... **CLC 6, 9, 29**
See also AITN 2; BEST 90:3; CA 17-20R;
CANR 18; DLB 6; MTCW

Rostand, Edmond (Eugene Alexis)
1868-1918 .... **TCLC 6, 37**
See also CA 104; 126; DA; MTCW

Roth, Henry 1906-.......... **CLC 2, 6, 11**
See also CA 11-12; CANR 38; CAP 1;
DLB 28; MTCW

Roth, Joseph 1894-1939.......... **TCLC 33**
See also DLB 85

Roth, Philip (Milton)
1933-...... **CLC 1, 2, 3, 4, 6, 9, 15, 22,
31, 47, 66**
See also BEST 90:3; CA 1-4R; CANR 1, 22,
36; CDALB 1968-1988; DA; DLB 2, 28;
DLBY 82; MTCW; WLC

Rothenberg, Jerome 1931-....... **CLC 6, 57**
See also CA 45-48; CANR 1; DLB 5

Roumain, Jacques (Jean Baptiste)
1907-1944 .... **TCLC 19**
See also BLC 3; BW; CA 117; 125

Rourke, Constance (Mayfield)
1885-1941 .... **TCLC 12**
See also CA 107; YABC 1

Rousseau, Jean-Baptiste 1671-1741 ... **LC 9**

Rousseau, Jean-Jacques 1712-1778... **LC 14**
See also DA; WLC

Roussel, Raymond 1877-1933 ..... **TCLC 20**
See also CA 117

Rovit, Earl (Herbert) 1927-........ **CLC 7**
See also CA 5-8R; CANR 12

Rowe, Nicholas 1674-1718........... **LC 8**
See also DLB 84

Rowley, Ames Dorrance
See Lovecraft, H(oward) P(hillips)

Rowson, Susanna Haswell
1762(?)-1824 .... **NCLC 5**
See also DLB 37

Roy, Gabrielle 1909-1983....... **CLC 10, 14**
See also CA 53-56; 110; CANR 5; DLB 68;
MTCW

Rozewicz, Tadeusz 1921-........ **CLC 9, 23**
See also CA 108; CANR 36; MTCW

Ruark, Gibbons 1941- .... **CLC 3**
See also CA 33-36R; CANR 14, 31;
DLB 120

Rubens, Bernice (Ruth) 1923-... **CLC 19, 31**
See also CA 25-28R; CANR 33; DLB 14;
MTCW

Rudkin, (James) David 1936- ...... **CLC 14**
See also CA 89-92; DLB 13

Rudnik, Raphael 1933-............. **CLC 7**
See also CA 29-32R

Ruffian, M.
See Hasek, Jaroslav (Matej Frantisek)

Ruiz, Jose Martinez............... **CLC 11**
See also Martinez Ruiz, Jose

Rukeyser, Muriel
1913-1980 .... **CLC 6, 10, 15, 27**
See also CA 5-8R; 93-96; CANR 26;
DLB 48; MTCW; SATA 22

Rule, Jane (Vance) 1931-.......... **CLC 27**
See also CA 25-28R; CANR 12; DLB 60

Rulfo, Juan 1918-1986............. **CLC 8**
See also CA 85-88; 118; CANR 26;
DLB 113; HW; MTCW

Runeberg, Johan 1804-1877...... **NCLC 41**

Runyon, (Alfred) Damon
1884(?)-1946 .... **TCLC 10**
See also CA 107; DLB 11, 86

Rush, Norman 1933-............. **CLC 44**
See also CA 121; 126

Sarton, (Eleanor) May
1912- . . . . **CLC 4, 14, 49**
See also CA 1-4R; CANR 1, 34; DLB 48;
DLBY 81; MTCW; SATA 36

Sartre, Jean-Paul
1905-1980 . . . . **CLC 1, 4, 7, 9, 13, 18, 24,
44, 50, 52; DC 3**
See also CA 9-12R; 97-100; CANR 21; DA;
DLB 72; MTCW; WLC

Sassoon, Siegfried (Lorraine)
1886-1967 . . . . **CLC 36**
See also CA 104; 25-28R; CANR 36;
DLB 20; MTCW

Satterfield, Charles
See Pohl, Frederik

Saul, John (W. III) 1942- . . . . **CLC 46**
See also AAYA 10; BEST 90:4; CA 81-84;
CANR 16, 40

Saunders, Caleb
See Heinlein, Robert A(nson)

Saura (Atares), Carlos 1932- . . . . **CLC 20**
See also CA 114; 131; HW

Sauser-Hall, Frederic 1887-1961 . . . . **CLC 18**
See also CA 102; 93-96; CANR 36; MTCW

Saussure, Ferdinand de
1857-1913 . . . . **TCLC 49**

Savage, Catharine
See Brosman, Catharine Savage

Savage, Thomas 1915- . . . . **CLC 40**
See also CA 126; 132; CAAS 15

Savan, Glenn . . . . **CLC 50**

Saven, Glenn 19(?)- . . . . **CLC 50**

Sayers, Dorothy L(eigh)
1893-1957 . . . . **TCLC 2, 15**
See also CA 104; 119; CDBLB 1914-1945;
DLB 10, 36, 77, 100; MTCW

Sayers, Valerie 1952- . . . . **CLC 50**
See also CA 134

Sayles, John (Thomas)
1950- . . . . **CLC 7, 10, 14**
See also CA 57-60; CANR 41; DLB 44

Scammell, Michael . . . . **CLC 34**

Scannell, Vernon 1922- . . . . **CLC 49**
See also CA 5-8R; CANR 8, 24; DLB 27;
SATA 59

Scarlett, Susan
See Streatfeild, (Mary) Noel

Schaeffer, Susan Fromberg
1941- . . . . **CLC 6, 11, 22**
See also CA 49-52; CANR 18; DLB 28;
MTCW; SATA 22

Schary, Jill
See Robinson, Jill

Schell, Jonathan 1943- . . . . **CLC 35**
See also CA 73-76; CANR 12

Schelling, Friedrich Wilhelm Joseph von
1775-1854 . . . . **NCLC 30**
See also DLB 90

Scherer, Jean-Marie Maurice 1920-
See Rohmer, Eric
See also CA 110

Schevill, James (Erwin) 1920- . . . . . . **CLC 7**
See also CA 5-8R; CAAS 12

Schiller, Friedrich 1759-1805 . . . . **NCLC 39**
See also DLB 94

Schisgal, Murray (Joseph) 1926- . . . . . **CLC 6**
See also CA 21-24R

Schlee, Ann 1934- . . . . **CLC 35**
See also CA 101; CANR 29; SATA 36, 44

Schlegel, August Wilhelm von
1767-1845 . . . . **NCLC 15**
See also DLB 94

Schlegel, Johann Elias (von)
1719(?)-1749 . . . . **LC 5**

Schmidt, Arno (Otto) 1914-1979 . . . . **CLC 56**
See also CA 128; 109; DLB 69

Schmitz, Aron Hector 1861-1928
See Svevo, Italo
See also CA 104; 122; MTCW

Schnackenberg, Gjertrud 1953- . . . . . **CLC 40**
See also CA 116; DLB 120

Schneider, Leonard Alfred 1925-1966
See Bruce, Lenny
See also CA 89-92

Schnitzler, Arthur 1862-1931 . . . . . . **TCLC 4**
See also CA 104; DLB 81, 118

Schor, Sandra (M.) 1932(?)-1990 . . . **CLC 65**
See also CA 132

Schorer, Mark 1908-1977 . . . . **CLC 9**
See also CA 5-8R; 73-76; CANR 7;
DLB 103

Schrader, Paul (Joseph) 1946- . . . . . . **CLC 26**
See also CA 37-40R; CANR 41; DLB 44

Schreiner, Olive (Emilie Albertina)
1855-1920 . . . . **TCLC 9**
See also CA 105; DLB 18

Schulberg, Budd (Wilson)
1914- . . . . **CLC 7, 48**
See also CA 25-28R; CANR 19; DLB 6, 26,
28; DLBY 81

Schulz, Bruno
1892-1942 . . . . **TCLC 5, 51; SSC 13**
See also CA 115; 123

Schulz, Charles M(onroe) 1922- . . . . **CLC 12**
See also CA 9-12R; CANR 6; SATA 10

Schuyler, James Marcus
1923-1991 . . . . **CLC 5, 23**
See also CA 101; 134; DLB 5

Schwartz, Delmore (David)
1913-1966 . . . . **CLC 2, 4, 10, 45**
See also CA 17-18; 25-28R; CANR 35;
CAP 2; DLB 28, 48; MTCW

Schwartz, Ernst
See Ozu, Yasujiro

Schwartz, John Burnham 1965- . . . . **CLC 59**
See also CA 132

Schwartz, Lynne Sharon 1939- . . . . . **CLC 31**
See also CA 103

Schwartz, Muriel A.
See Eliot, T(homas) S(tearns)

Schwarz-Bart, Andre 1928- . . . . **CLC 2, 4**
See also CA 89-92

Schwarz-Bart, Simone 1938- . . . . **CLC 7**
See also CA 97-100

Schwob, (Mayer Andre) Marcel
1867-1905 . . . . **TCLC 20**
See also CA 117; DLB 123

Sciascia, Leonardo
1921-1989 . . . . **CLC 8, 9, 41**
See also CA 85-88; 130; CANR 35; MTCW

Scoppettone, Sandra 1936- . . . . **CLC 26**
See also CA 5-8R; CANR 41; SATA 9

Scorsese, Martin 1942- . . . . **CLC 20**
See also CA 110; 114

Scotland, Jay
See Jakes, John (William)

Scott, Duncan Campbell
1862-1947 . . . . **TCLC 6**
See also CA 104; DLB 92

Scott, Evelyn 1893-1963 . . . . **CLC 43**
See also CA 104; 112; DLB 9, 48

Scott, F(rancis) R(eginald)
1899-1985 . . . . **CLC 22**
See also CA 101; 114; DLB 88

Scott, Frank
See Scott, F(rancis) R(eginald)

Scott, Joanna 1960- . . . . **CLC 50**
See also CA 126

Scott, Paul (Mark) 1920-1978 . . . . **CLC 9, 60**
See also CA 81-84; 77-80; CANR 33;
DLB 14; MTCW

Scott, Walter 1771-1832 . . . . **NCLC 15**
See also CDBLB 1789-1832; DA; DLB 93,
107, 116; WLC; YABC 2

Scribe, (Augustin) Eugene
1791-1861 . . . . **NCLC 16**

Scrum, R.
See Crumb, R(obert)

Scudery, Madeleine de 1607-1701 . . . . . **LC 2**

Scum
See Crumb, R(obert)

Scumbag, Little Bobby
See Crumb, R(obert)

Seabrook, John
See Hubbard, L(afayette) Ron(ald)

Sealy, I. Allan 1951- . . . . **CLC 55**

Search, Alexander
See Pessoa, Fernando (Antonio Nogueira)

Sebastian, Lee
See Silverberg, Robert

Sebastian Owl
See Thompson, Hunter S(tockton)

Sebestyen, Ouida 1924- . . . . **CLC 30**
See also AAYA 8; CA 107; CANR 40;
CLR 17; MAICYA; SAAS 10; SATA 39

Secundus, H. Scriblerus
See Fielding, Henry

Sedges, John
See Buck, Pearl S(ydenstricker)

Sedgwick, Catharine Maria
1789-1867 . . . . **NCLC 19**
See also DLB 1, 74

Seelye, John 1931- . . . . **CLC 7**

Seferiades, Giorgos Stylianou 1900-1971
See Seferis, George
See also CA 5-8R; 33-36R; CANR 5, 36;
MTCW

Seferis, George . . . . **CLC 5, 11**
See also Seferiades, Giorgos Stylianou

Segal, Erich (Wolf) 1937- .... CLC 3, 10
See also BEST 89:1; CA 25-28R; CANR 20, 36; DLBY 86; MTCW

Seger, Bob 1945-................ CLC 35

Seghers, Anna .... CLC 7
See also Radvanyi, Netty
See also DLB 69

Seidel, Frederick (Lewis) 1936-..... CLC 18
See also CA 13-16R; CANR 8; DLBY 84

Seifert, Jaroslav 1901-1986 ..... CLC 34, 44
See also CA 127; MTCW

Sei Shonagon c. 966-1017(?) ...... CMLC 6

Selby, Hubert, Jr. 1928- ..... CLC 1, 2, 4, 8
See also CA 13-16R; CANR 33; DLB 2

Selzer, Richard 1928-............. CLC 74
See also CA 65-68; CANR 14

Sembene, Ousmane
See Ousmane, Sembene

Senancour, Etienne Pivert de
1770-1846 .... NCLC 16
See also DLB 119

Sender, Ramon (Jose) 1902-1982 .... CLC 8
See also CA 5-8R; 105; CANR 8; HW; MTCW

Seneca, Lucius Annaeus
4B.C.-65..................... CMLC 6

Senghor, Leopold Sedar 1906-...... CLC 54
See also BLC 3; BW; CA 116; 125; MTCW

Serling, (Edward) Rod(man)
1924-1975 .... CLC 30
See also AITN 1; CA 65-68; 57-60; DLB 26

Serna, Ramon Gomez de la
See Gomez de la Serna, Ramon

Serpieres
See Guillevic, (Eugene)

Service, Robert
See Service, Robert W(illiam)
See also DLB 92

Service, Robert W(illiam)
1874(?)-1958 .... TCLC 15
See also Service, Robert
See also CA 115; 140; DA; SATA 20; WLC

Seth, Vikram 1952-............... CLC 43
See also CA 121; 127; DLB 120

Seton, Cynthia Propper
1926-1982 .... CLC 27
See also CA 5-8R; 108; CANR 7

Seton, Ernest (Evan) Thompson
1860-1946 .... TCLC 31
See also CA 109; DLB 92; SATA 18

Seton-Thompson, Ernest
See Seton, Ernest (Evan) Thompson

Settle, Mary Lee 1918- .... CLC 19, 61
See also CA 89-92; CAAS 1; DLB 6

Seuphor, Michel
See Arp, Jean

Sevigne, Marie (de Rabutin-Chantal) Marquise
de 1626-1696 .... LC 11

Sexton, Anne (Harvey)
1928-1974 .... CLC 2, 4, 6, 8, 10, 15, 53;
PC 2
See also CA 1-4R; 53-56; CABS 2;
CANR 3, 36; CDALB 1941-1968; DA;
DLB 5; MTCW; SATA 10; WLC

Shaara, Michael (Joseph Jr.)
1929-1988 .... CLC 15
See also AITN 1; CA 102; DLBY 83

Shackleton, C. C.
See Aldiss, Brian W(ilson)

Shacochis, Bob .... CLC 39
See also Shacochis, Robert G.

Shacochis, Robert G. 1951-
See Shacochis, Bob
See also CA 119; 124

Shaffer, Anthony (Joshua) 1926-.... CLC 19
See also CA 110; 116; DLB 13

Shaffer, Peter (Levin)
1926- .... CLC 5, 14, 18, 37, 60
See also CA 25-28R; CANR 25;
CDBLB 1960 to Present; DLB 13;
MTCW

Shakey, Bernard
See Young, Neil

Shalamov, Varlam (Tikhonovich)
1907(?)-1982 .... CLC 18
See also CA 129; 105

Shamlu, Ahmad 1925- .... CLC 10

Shammas, Anton 1951-........... CLC 55

Shange, Ntozake
1948- .... CLC 8, 25, 38, 74; DC 3
See also AAYA 9; BLC 3; BW; CA 85-88;
CABS 3; CANR 27; DLB 38; MTCW

Shanley, John Patrick 1950-....... CLC 75
See also CA 128; 133

Shapcott, Thomas William 1935- ... CLC 38
See also CA 69-72

Shapiro, Jane.................... CLC 76

Shapiro, Karl (Jay) 1913- .. CLC 4, 8, 15, 53
See also CA 1-4R; CAAS 6; CANR 1, 36;
DLB 48; MTCW

Sharp, William 1855-1905 .... TCLC 39

Sharpe, Thomas Ridley 1928-
See Sharpe, Tom
See also CA 114; 122

Sharpe, Tom.................... CLC 36
See also Sharpe, Thomas Ridley
See also DLB 14

Shaw, Bernard................. TCLC 45
See also Shaw, George Bernard

Shaw, G. Bernard
See Shaw, George Bernard

Shaw, George Bernard
1856-1950 .... TCLC 3, 9, 21
See also Shaw, Bernard
See also CA 104; 128; CDBLB 1914-1945;
DA; DLB 10, 57; MTCW; WLC

Shaw, Henry Wheeler
1818-1885 .... NCLC 15
See also DLB 11

Shaw, Irwin 1913-1984...... CLC 7, 23, 34
See also AITN 1; CA 13-16R; 112;
CANR 21; CDALB 1941-1968; DLB 6,
102; DLBY 84; MTCW

Shaw, Robert 1927-1978 .... CLC 5
See also AITN 1; CA 1-4R; 81-84;
CANR 4; DLB 13, 14

Shaw, T. E.
See Lawrence, T(homas) E(dward)

Shawn, Wallace 1943- .... CLC 41
See also CA 112

Sheed, Wilfrid (John Joseph)
1930- .... CLC 2, 4, 10, 53
See also CA 65-68; CANR 30; DLB 6;
MTCW

Sheldon, Alice Hastings Bradley
1915(?)-1987
See Tiptree, James, Jr.
See also CA 108; 122; CANR 34; MTCW

Sheldon, John
See Bloch, Robert (Albert)

Shelley, Mary Wollstonecraft (Godwin)
1797-1851 .... NCLC 14
See also CDBLB 1789-1832; DA; DLB 110,
116; SATA 29; WLC

Shelley, Percy Bysshe
1792-1822 .... NCLC 18
See also CDBLB 1789-1832; DA; DLB 96,
110; WLC

Shepard, Jim 1956-............... CLC 36
See also CA 137

Shepard, Lucius 1947-........... CLC 34
See also CA 128

Shepard, Sam
1943- .... CLC 4, 6, 17, 34, 41, 44
See also AAYA 1; CA 69-72; CABS 3;
CANR 22; DLB 7; MTCW

Shepherd, Michael
See Ludlum, Robert

Sherburne, Zoa (Morin) 1912-...... CLC 30
See also CA 1-4R; CANR 3, 37; MAICYA;
SATA 3

Sheridan, Frances 1724-1766........ LC 7
See also DLB 39, 84

Sheridan, Richard Brinsley
1751-1816 .... NCLC 5; DC 1
See also CDBLB 1660-1789; DA; DLB 89;
WLC

Sherman, Jonathan Marc.......... CLC 55

Sherman, Martin 1941(?)-........ CLC 19
See also CA 116; 123

Sherwin, Judith Johnson 1936-... CLC 7, 15
See also CA 25-28R; CANR 34

Sherwood, Robert E(mmet)
1896-1955 .... TCLC 3
See also CA 104; DLB 7, 26

Shiel, M(atthew) P(hipps)
1865-1947 .... TCLC 8
See also CA 106

Shiga, Naoya 1883-1971.......... CLC 33
See also CA 101; 33-36R

Shimazaki Haruki 1872-1943
See Shimazaki Toson
See also CA 105; 134

Shimazaki Toson................. TCLC 5
See also Shimazaki Haruki

Sholokhov, Mikhail (Aleksandrovich)
1905-1984 .... CLC 7, 15
See also CA 101; 112; MTCW; SATA 36

Shone, Patric
See Hanley, James

Shreve, Susan Richards 1939-...... CLC 23
See also CA 49-52; CAAS 5; CANR 5, 38;
MAICYA; SATA 41, 46

Shue, Larry 1946-1985 . . . . CLC 52
See also CA 117

Shu-Jen, Chou 1881-1936
See Hsun, Lu
See also CA 104

Shulman, Alix Kates 1932- . . . . . . CLC 2, 10
See also CA 29-32R; SATA 7

Shuster, Joe 1914- . . . . CLC 21

Shute, Nevil . . . . CLC 30
See also Norway, Nevil Shute

Shuttle, Penelope (Diane) 1947- . . . . . CLC 7
See also CA 93-96; CANR 39; DLB 14, 40

Sidney, Mary 1561-1621 . . . . LC 19

Sidney, Sir Philip 1554-1586 . . . . LC 19
See also CDBLB Before 1660; DA

Siegel, Jerome 1914- . . . . CLC 21
See also CA 116

Siegel, Jerry
See Siegel, Jerome

Sienkiewicz, Henryk (Adam Alexander Pius)
1846-1916 . . . . TCLC 3
See also CA 104; 134

Sierra, Gregorio Martinez
See Martinez Sierra, Gregorio

Sierra, Maria (de la O'LeJarraga) Martinez
See Martinez Sierra, Maria (de la
O'LeJarraga)

Sigal, Clancy 1926- . . . . CLC 7
See also CA 1-4R

Sigourney, Lydia Howard (Huntley)
1791-1865 . . . . NCLC 21
See also DLB 1, 42, 73

Siguenza y Gongora, Carlos de
1645-1700 . . . . LC 8

Sigurjonsson, Johann 1880-1919 . . . TCLC 27

Sikelianos, Angelos 1884-1951 . . . . TCLC 39

Silkin, Jon 1930- . . . . CLC 2, 6, 43
See also CA 5-8R; CAAS 5; DLB 27

Silko, Leslie Marmon 1948- . . . . CLC 23, 74
See also CA 115; 122; DA

Sillanpaa, Frans Eemil 1888-1964 . . . CLC 19
See also CA 129; 93-96; MTCW

Sillitoe, Alan
1928- . . . . CLC 1, 3, 6, 10, 19, 57
See also AITN 1; CA 9-12R; CAAS 2;
CANR 8, 26; CDBLB 1960 to Present;
DLB 14; MTCW; SATA 61

Silone, Ignazio 1900-1978 . . . . CLC 4
See also CA 25-28; 81-84; CANR 34;
CAP 2; MTCW

Silver, Joan Micklin 1935- . . . . CLC 20
See also CA 114; 121

Silver, Nicholas
See Faust, Frederick (Schiller)

Silverberg, Robert 1935- . . . . CLC 7
See also CA 1-4R; CAAS 3; CANR 1, 20,
36; DLB 8; MAICYA; MTCW; SATA 13

Silverstein, Alvin 1933- . . . . CLC 17
See also CA 49-52; CANR 2; CLR 25;
MAICYA; SATA 8, 69

Silverstein, Virginia B(arbara Opshelor)
1937- . . . . CLC 17
See also CA 49-52; CANR 2; CLR 25;
MAICYA; SATA 8, 69

Sim, Georges
See Simenon, Georges (Jacques Christian)

Simak, Clifford D(onald)
1904-1988 . . . . CLC 1, 55
See also CA 1-4R; 125; CANR 1, 35;
DLB 8; MTCW; SATA 56

Simenon, Georges (Jacques Christian)
1903-1989 . . . . CLC 1, 2, 3, 8, 18, 47
See also CA 85-88; CANR 35;
DLB 72; DLBY 89; MTCW

Simic, Charles 1938- . . . CLC 6, 9, 22, 49, 68
See also CA 29-32R; CAAS 4; CANR 12,
33; DLB 105

Simmons, Charles (Paul) 1924- . . . . . CLC 57
See also CA 89-92

Simmons, Dan 1948- . . . . CLC 44
See also CA 138

Simmons, James (Stewart Alexander)
1933- . . . . CLC 43
See also CA 105; DLB 40

Simms, William Gilmore
1806-1870 . . . . NCLC 3
See also DLB 3, 30, 59, 73

Simon, Carly 1945- . . . . CLC 26
See also CA 105

Simon, Claude 1913- . . . . . . CLC 4, 9, 15, 39
See also CA 89-92; CANR 33; DLB 83;
MTCW

Simon, (Marvin) Neil
1927- . . . . CLC 6, 11, 31, 39, 70
See also AITN 1; CA 21-24R; CANR 26;
DLB 7; MTCW

Simon, Paul 1942(?)- . . . . CLC 17
See also CA 116

Simonon, Paul 1956(?)- . . . . CLC 30
See also Clash, The

Simpson, Harriette
See Arnow, Harriette (Louisa) Simpson

Simpson, Louis (Aston Marantz)
1923- . . . . CLC 4, 7, 9, 32
See also CA 1-4R; CAAS 4; CANR 1;
DLB 5; MTCW

Simpson, Mona (Elizabeth) 1957- . . . CLC 44
See also CA 122; 135

Simpson, N(orman) F(rederick)
1919- . . . . CLC 29
See also CA 13-16R; DLB 13

Sinclair, Andrew (Annandale)
1935- . . . . CLC 2, 14
See also CA 9-12R; CAAS 5; CANR 14, 38;
DLB 14; MTCW

Sinclair, Emil
See Hesse, Hermann

Sinclair, Iain 1943- . . . . CLC 76
See also CA 132

Sinclair, Iain MacGregor
See Sinclair, Iain

Sinclair, Mary Amelia St. Clair 1865(?)-1946
See Sinclair, May
See also CA 104

Sinclair, May . . . . TCLC 3, 11
See also Sinclair, Mary Amelia St. Clair
See also DLB 36

Sinclair, Upton (Beall)
1878-1968 . . . . CLC 1, 11, 15, 63
See also CA 5-8R; 25-28R; CANR 7;
CDALB 1929-1941; DA; DLB 9; MTCW;
SATA 9; WLC

Singer, Isaac
See Singer, Isaac Bashevis

Singer, Isaac Bashevis
1904-1991 . . . . CLC 1, 3, 6, 9, 11, 15, 23,
38, 69; SSC 3
See also AITN 1, 2; CA 1-4R; 134;
CANR 1, 39; CDALB 1941-1968; CLR 1;
DA; DLB 6, 28, 52; DLBY 91;
MAICYA; MTCW; SATA 3, 27;
SATA-Obit 68; WLC

Singer, Israel Joshua 1893-1944 . . . TCLC 33

Singh, Khushwant 1915- . . . . CLC 11
See also CA 9-12R; CAAS 9; CANR 6

Sinjohn, John
See Galsworthy, John

Sinyavsky, Andrei (Donatevich)
1925- . . . . CLC 8
See also CA 85-88

Sirin, V.
See Nabokov, Vladimir (Vladimirovich)

Sissman, L(ouis) E(dward)
1928-1976 . . . . CLC 9, 18
See also CA 21-24R; 65-68; CANR 13;
DLB 5

Sisson, C(harles) H(ubert) 1914- . . . . . CLC 8
See also CA 1-4R; CAAS 3; CANR 3;
DLB 27

Sitwell, Dame Edith
1887-1964 . . . . CLC 2, 9, 67; PC 3
See also CA 9-12R; CANR 35;
CDBLB 1945-1960; DLB 20; MTCW

Sjoewall, Maj 1935- . . . . CLC 7
See also CA 65-68

Sjowall, Maj
See Sjoewall, Maj

Skelton, Robin 1925- . . . . CLC 13
See also AITN 2; CA 5-8R; CAAS 5;
CANR 28; DLB 27, 53

Skolimowski, Jerzy 1938- . . . . CLC 20
See also CA 128

Skram, Amalie (Bertha)
1847-1905 . . . . TCLC 25

Skvorecky, Josef (Vaclav)
1924- . . . . CLC 15, 39, 69
See also CA 61-64; CAAS 1; CANR 10, 34;
MTCW

Slade, Bernard . . . . CLC 11, 46
See also Newbound, Bernard Slade
See also CAAS 9; DLB 53

Slaughter, Carolyn 1946- . . . . CLC 56
See also CA 85-88

Slaughter, Frank G(ill) 1908- . . . . . . CLC 29
See also AITN 2; CA 5-8R; CANR 5

Slavitt, David R(ytman) 1935- . . . . CLC 5, 14
See also CA 21-24R; CAAS 3; CANR 41;
DLB 5, 6

Slesinger, Tess 1905-1945 . . . . TCLC 10
See also CA 107; DLB 102

Slessor, Kenneth 1901-1971 . . . . CLC 14
See also CA 102; 89-92

Slowacki, Juliusz 1809-1849 . . . . . NCLC 15

Smart, Christopher 1722-1771 . . . . LC 3
See also DLB 109

Smart, Elizabeth 1913-1986 . . . . CLC 54
See also CA 81-84; 118; DLB 88

Smiley, Jane (Graves) 1949- . . . . CLC 53, 76
See also CA 104; CANR 30

Smith, A(rthur) J(ames) M(arshall)
1902-1980 . . . . CLC 15
See also CA 1-4R; 102; CANR 4; DLB 88

Smith, Betty (Wehner) 1896-1972 . . . CLC 19
See also CA 5-8R; 33-36R; DLBY 82;
SATA 6

Smith, Charlotte (Turner)
1749-1806 . . . . NCLC 23
See also DLB 39, 109

Smith, Clark Ashton 1893-1961 . . . . CLC 43

Smith, Dave . . . . CLC 22, 42
See also Smith, David (Jeddie)
See also CAAS 7; DLB 5

Smith, David (Jeddie) 1942-
See Smith, Dave
See also CA 49-52; CANR 1

Smith, Florence Margaret
1902-1971 . . . . CLC 8
See also Smith, Stevie
See also CA 17-18; 29-32R; CANR 35;
CAP 2; MTCW

Smith, Iain Crichton 1928- . . . . CLC 64
See also CA 21-24R; DLB 40

Smith, John 1580(?)-1631 . . . . LC 9

Smith, Johnston
See Crane, Stephen (Townley)

Smith, Lee 1944- . . . . CLC 25, 73
See also CA 114; 119; DLBY 83

Smith, Martin
See Smith, Martin Cruz

Smith, Martin Cruz 1942- . . . . CLC 25
See also BEST 89:4; CA 85-88; CANR 6, 23

Smith, Mary-Ann Tirone 1944- . . . . . CLC 39
See also CA 118; 136

Smith, Patti 1946- . . . . CLC 12
See also CA 93-96

Smith, Pauline (Urmson)
1882-1959 . . . . TCLC 25

Smith, Rosamond
See Oates, Joyce Carol

Smith, Sheila Kaye
See Kaye-Smith, Sheila

Smith, Stevie . . . . CLC 3, 8, 25, 44
See also Smith, Florence Margaret
See also DLB 20

Smith, Wilbur A(ddison) 1933- . . . . . CLC 33
See also CA 13-16R; CANR 7; MTCW

Smith, William Jay 1918- . . . . CLC 6
See also CA 5-8R; DLB 5; MAICYA;
SATA 2, 68

Smith, Woodrow Wilson
See Kuttner, Henry

Smolenskin, Peretz 1842-1885 . . . . NCLC 30

Smollett, Tobias (George) 1721-1771 . . LC 2
See also CDBLB 1660-1789; DLB 39, 104

Snodgrass, W(illiam) D(e Witt)
1926- . . . . CLC 2, 6, 10, 18, 68
See also CA 1-4R; CANR 6, 36; DLB 5;
MTCW

Snow, C(harles) P(ercy)
1905-1980 . . . . CLC 1, 4, 6, 9, 13, 19
See also CA 5-8R; 101; CANR 28;
CDBLB 1945-1960; DLB 15, 77; MTCW

Snow, Frances Compton
See Adams, Henry (Brooks)

Snyder, Gary (Sherman)
1930- . . . . CLC 1, 2, 5, 9, 32
See also CA 17-20R; CANR 30; DLB 5, 16

Snyder, Zilpha Keatley 1927- . . . . . . CLC 17
See also CA 9-12R; CANR 38; CLR 31;
MAICYA; SAAS 2; SATA 1, 28

Soares, Bernardo
See Pessoa, Fernando (Antonio Nogueira)

Sobh, A.
See Shamlu, Ahmad

Sobol, Joshua . . . . CLC 60

Soderberg, Hjalmar 1869-1941 . . . . TCLC 39

Sodergran, Edith (Irene)
See Soedergran, Edith (Irene)

Soedergran, Edith (Irene)
1892-1923 . . . . TCLC 31

Softly, Edgar
See Lovecraft, H(oward) P(hillips)

Softly, Edward
See Lovecraft, H(oward) P(hillips)

Sokolov, Raymond 1941- . . . . CLC 7
See also CA 85-88

Solo, Jay
See Ellison, Harlan

Sologub, Fyodor . . . . TCLC 9
See also Teternikov, Fyodor Kuzmich

Solomons, Ikey Esquir
See Thackeray, William Makepeace

Solomos, Dionysios 1798-1857 . . . NCLC 15

Solwoska, Mara
See French, Marilyn

Solzhenitsyn, Aleksandr I(sayevich)
1918- . . . . . . CLC 1, 2, 4, 7, 9, 10, 18, 26,
34, 78
See also AITN 1; CA 69-72; CANR 40;
DA; MTCW; WLC

Somers, Jane
See Lessing, Doris (May)

Somerville, Edith 1858-1949 . . . . . . TCLC 51

Sommer, Scott 1951- . . . . CLC 25
See also CA 106

Sondheim, Stephen (Joshua)
1930- . . . . CLC 30, 39
See also CA 103

Sontag, Susan 1933- . . . CLC 1, 2, 10, 13, 31
See also CA 17-20R; CANR 25; DLB 2, 67;
MTCW

Sophocles
496(?)B.C.-406(?)B.C. . . . CMLC 2; DC 1
See also DA

Sorel, Julia
See Drexler, Rosalyn

Sorrentino, Gilbert
1929- . . . . CLC 3, 7, 14, 22, 40
See also CA 77-80; CANR 14, 33; DLB 5;
DLBY 80

Soto, Gary 1952- . . . . CLC 32
See also AAYA 10; CA 119; 125; DLB 82;
HW

Soupault, Philippe 1897-1990 . . . . . . CLC 68
See also CA 116; 131

Souster, (Holmes) Raymond
1921- . . . . CLC 5, 14
See also CA 13-16R; CAAS 14; CANR 13,
29; DLB 88; SATA 63

Southern, Terry 1926- . . . . CLC 7
See also CA 1-4R; CANR 1; DLB 2

Southey, Robert 1774-1843 . . . . NCLC 8
See also DLB 93, 107; SATA 54

Southworth, Emma Dorothy Eliza Nevitte
1819-1899 . . . . NCLC 26

Souza, Ernest
See Scott, Evelyn

Soyinka, Wole
1934- . . . . CLC 3, 5, 14, 36, 44; DC 2
See also BLC 3; BW; CA 13-16R;
CANR 27, 39; DA; DLB 125; MTCW;
WLC

Spackman, W(illiam) M(ode)
1905-1990 . . . . CLC 46
See also CA 81-84; 132

Spacks, Barry 1931- . . . . CLC 14
See also CA 29-32R; CANR 33; DLB 105

Spanidou, Irini 1946- . . . . CLC 44

Spark, Muriel (Sarah)
1918- . . . . CLC 2, 3, 5, 8, 13, 18, 40;
SSC 10
See also CA 5-8R; CANR 12, 36;
CDBLB 1945-1960; DLB 15; MTCW

Spaulding, Douglas
See Bradbury, Ray (Douglas)

Spaulding, Leonard
See Bradbury, Ray (Douglas)

Spence, J. A. D.
See Eliot, T(homas) S(tearns)

Spencer, Elizabeth 1921- . . . . CLC 22
See also CA 13-16R; CANR 32; DLB 6;
MTCW; SATA 14

Spencer, Leonard G.
See Silverberg, Robert

Spencer, Scott 1945- . . . . CLC 30
See also CA 113; DLBY 86

Spender, Stephen (Harold)
1909- . . . . CLC 1, 2, 5, 10, 41
See also CA 9-12R; CANR 31;
CDBLB 1945-1960; DLB 20; MTCW

Spengler, Oswald (Arnold Gottfried)
1880-1936 . . . . TCLC 25
See also CA 118

Spenser, Edmund 1552(?)-1599 . . . . LC 5
See also CDBLB Before 1660; DA; WLC

Spicer, Jack 1925-1965 . . . . . . CLC 8, 18, 72
See also CA 85-88; DLB 5, 16

Spiegelman, Art 1948- . . . . CLC 76
See also AAYA 10; CA 125; CANR 41

Spielberg, Peter 1929- . . . . CLC 6
See also CA 5-8R; CANR 4; DLBY 81

Spielberg, Steven 1947- . . . . CLC 20
See also AAYA 8; CA 77-80; CANR 32;
SATA 32

Spillane, Frank Morrison 1918-
See Spillane, Mickey
See also CA 25-28R; CANR 28; MTCW;
SATA 66

Spillane, Mickey . . . . CLC 3, 13
See also Spillane, Frank Morrison

Spinoza, Benedictus de 1632-1677 . . . . LC 9

Spinrad, Norman (Richard) 1940- . . . CLC 46
See also CA 37-40R; CANR 20; DLB 8

Spitteler, Carl (Friedrich Georg)
1845-1924 . . . . TCLC 12
See also CA 109; DLB 129

Spivack, Kathleen (Romola Drucker)
1938- . . . . CLC 6
See also CA 49-52

Spoto, Donald 1941- . . . . CLC 39
See also CA 65-68; CANR 11

Springsteen, Bruce (F.) 1949- . . . . . . CLC 17
See also CA 111

Spurling, Hilary 1940- . . . . CLC 34
See also CA 104; CANR 25

Squires, (James) Radcliffe
1917-1993 . . . . CLC 51
See also CA 1-4R; 140; CANR 6, 21

Srivastava, Dhanpat Rai 1880(?)-1936
See Premchand
See also CA 118

Stacy, Donald
See Pohl, Frederik

Stael, Germaine de
See Stael-Holstein, Anne Louise Germaine
Necker Baronn
See also DLB 119

Stael-Holstein, Anne Louise Germaine Necker
Baronn 1766-1817 . . . . NCLC 3
See also Stael, Germaine de

Stafford, Jean 1915-1979 . . . CLC 4, 7, 19, 68
See also CA 1-4R; 85-88; CANR 3; DLB 2;
MTCW; SATA 22

Stafford, William (Edgar)
1914- . . . . CLC 4, 7, 29
See also CA 5-8R; CAAS 3; CANR 5, 22;
DLB 5

Staines, Trevor
See Brunner, John (Kilian Houston)

Stairs, Gordon
See Austin, Mary (Hunter)

Stannard, Martin . . . . CLC 44

Stanton, Maura 1946- . . . . CLC 9
See also CA 89-92; CANR 15; DLB 120

Stanton, Schuyler
See Baum, L(yman) Frank

Stapledon, (William) Olaf
1886-1950 . . . . TCLC 22
See also CA 111; DLB 15

Starbuck, George (Edwin) 1931- . . . . CLC 53
See also CA 21-24R; CANR 23

Stark, Richard
See Westlake, Donald E(dwin)

Staunton, Schuyler
See Baum, L(yman) Frank

Stead, Christina (Ellen)
1902-1983 . . . . CLC 2, 5, 8, 32
See also CA 13-16R; 109; CANR 33, 40;
MTCW

Stead, William Thomas
1849-1912 . . . . TCLC 48

Steele, Richard 1672-1729 . . . . LC 18
See also CDBLB 1660-1789; DLB 84, 101

Steele, Timothy (Reid) 1948- . . . . CLC 45
See also CA 93-96; CANR 16; DLB 120

Steffens, (Joseph) Lincoln
1866-1936 . . . . TCLC 20
See also CA 117

Stegner, Wallace (Earle) 1909- . . . CLC 9, 49
See also AITN 1; BEST 90:3; CA 1-4R;
CAAS 9; CANR 1, 21; DLB 9; MTCW

Stein, Gertrude
1874-1946 . . . . TCLC 1, 6, 28, 48
See also CA 104; 132; CDALB 1917-1929;
DA; DLB 4, 54, 86; MTCW; WLC

Steinbeck, John (Ernst)
1902-1968 . . . . . . CLC 1, 5, 9, 13, 21, 34,
45, 75; SSC 11
See also CA 1-4R; 25-28R; CANR 1, 35;
CDALB 1929-1941; DA; DLB 7, 9;
DLBD 2; MTCW; SATA 9; WLC

Steinem, Gloria 1934- . . . . CLC 63
See also CA 53-56; CANR 28; MTCW

Steiner, George 1929- . . . . CLC 24
See also CA 73-76; CANR 31; DLB 67;
MTCW; SATA 62

Steiner, Rudolf 1861-1925 . . . . TCLC 13
See also CA 107

Stendhal 1783-1842 . . . . NCLC 23
See also DA; DLB 119; WLC

Stephen, Leslie 1832-1904 . . . . TCLC 23
See also CA 123; DLB 57

Stephen, Sir Leslie
See Stephen, Leslie

Stephen, Virginia
See Woolf, (Adeline) Virginia

Stephens, James 1882(?)-1950 . . . . . . TCLC 4
See also CA 104; DLB 19

Stephens, Reed
See Donaldson, Stephen R.

Steptoe, Lydia
See Barnes, Djuna

Sterchi, Beat 1949- . . . . CLC 65

Sterling, Brett
See Bradbury, Ray (Douglas); Hamilton,
Edmond

Sterling, Bruce 1954- . . . . CLC 72
See also CA 119

Sterling, George 1869-1926 . . . . TCLC 20
See also CA 117; DLB 54

Stern, Gerald 1925- . . . . CLC 40
See also CA 81-84; CANR 28; DLB 105

Stern, Richard (Gustave) 1928- . . . CLC 4, 39
See also CA 1-4R; CANR 1, 25; DLBY 87

Sternberg, Josef von 1894-1969 . . . . . CLC 20
See also CA 81-84

Sterne, Laurence 1713-1768 . . . . LC 2
See also CDBLB 1660-1789; DA; DLB 39;
WLC

Sternheim, (William Adolf) Carl
1878-1942 . . . . TCLC 8
See also CA 105; DLB 56, 118

Stevens, Mark 1951- . . . . CLC 34
See also CA 122

Stevens, Wallace
1879-1955 . . . . TCLC 3, 12, 45; PC 6
See also CA 104; 124; CDALB 1929-1941;
DA; DLB 54; MTCW; WLC

Stevenson, Anne (Katharine)
1933- . . . . CLC 7, 33
See also CA 17-20R; CAAS 9; CANR 9, 33;
DLB 40; MTCW

Stevenson, Robert Louis (Balfour)
1850-1894 . . . . NCLC 5, 14; SSC 11
See also CDBLB 1890-1914; CLR 10, 11;
DA; DLB 18, 57; MAICYA; WLC;
YABC 2

Stewart, J(ohn) I(nnes) M(ackintosh)
1906- . . . . CLC 7, 14, 32
See also CA 85-88; CAAS 3; MTCW

Stewart, Mary (Florence Elinor)
1916- . . . . CLC 7, 35
See also CA 1-4R; CANR 1; SATA 12

Stewart, Mary Rainbow
See Stewart, Mary (Florence Elinor)

Stifter, Adalbert 1805-1868 . . . . . . NCLC 41

Still, James 1906- . . . . CLC 49
See also CA 65-68; CAAS 17; CANR 10,
26; DLB 9; SATA 29

Sting
See Sumner, Gordon Matthew

Stirling, Arthur
See Sinclair, Upton (Beall)

Stitt, Milan 1941- . . . . CLC 29
See also CA 69-72

Stockton, Francis Richard 1834-1902
See Stockton, Frank R.
See also CA 108; 137; MAICYA; SATA 44

Stockton, Frank R. . . . . TCLC 47
See also Stockton, Francis Richard
See also DLB 42, 74; SATA 32

Stoddard, Charles
See Kuttner, Henry

Stoker, Abraham 1847-1912
See Stoker, Bram
See also CA 105; DA; SATA 29

Stoker, Bram . . . . TCLC 8
See also Stoker, Abraham
See also CDBLB 1890-1914; DLB 36, 70;
WLC

Stolz, Mary (Slattery) 1920- . . . . CLC 12
See also AAYA 8; AITN 1; CA 5-8R;
CANR 13, 41; MAICYA; SAAS 3;
SATA 10, 70, 71

Stone, Irving 1903-1989 . . . . CLC 7
See also AITN 1; CA 1-4R; 129; CAAS 3;
CANR 1, 23; MTCW; SATA 3;
SATA-Obit 64

Tabori, George 1914- .... **CLC 19**
See also CA 49-52; CANR 4

Tagore, Rabindranath 1861-1941.... **TCLC 3**
See also CA 104; 120; MTCW

Taine, Hippolyte Adolphe
1828-1893 .... **NCLC 15**

Talese, Gay 1932- .... **CLC 37**
See also AITN 1; CA 1-4R; CANR 9;
MTCW

Tallent, Elizabeth (Ann) 1954- ..... **CLC 45**
See also CA 117; DLB 130

Tally, Ted 1952- .... **CLC 42**
See also CA 120; 124

Tamayo y Baus, Manuel
1829-1898 .... **NCLC 1**

Tammsaare, A(nton) H(ansen)
1878-1940 .... **TCLC 27**

Tan, Amy 1952- .... **CLC 59**
See also AAYA 9; BEST 89:3; CA 136

Tandem, Felix
See Spitteler, Carl (Friedrich Georg)

Tanizaki, Jun'ichiro
1886-1965 .... **CLC 8, 14, 28**
See also CA 93-96; 25-28R

Tanner, William
See Amis, Kingsley (William)

Tao Lao
See Storni, Alfonsina

Tarassoff, Lev
See Troyat, Henri

Tarbell, Ida M(inerva)
1857-1944 .... **TCLC 40**
See also CA 122; DLB 47

Tarkington, (Newton) Booth
1869-1946 .... **TCLC 9**
See also CA 110; DLB 9, 102; SATA 17

Tarkovsky, Andrei (Arsenyevich)
1932-1986 .... **CLC 75**
See also CA 127

Tartt, Donna 1964(?)- .... **CLC 76**

Tasso, Torquato 1544-1595 .... **LC 5**

Tate, (John Orley) Allen
1899-1979 .... **CLC 2, 4, 6, 9, 11, 14, 24**
See also CA 5-8R; 85-88; CANR 32;
DLB 4, 45, 63; MTCW

Tate, Ellalice
See Hibbert, Eleanor Alice Burford

Tate, James (Vincent) 1943- ... **CLC 2, 6, 25**
See also CA 21-24R; CANR 29; DLB 5

Tavel, Ronald 1940- .... **CLC 6**
See also CA 21-24R; CANR 33

Taylor, Cecil Philip 1929-1981 ..... **CLC 27**
See also CA 25-28R; 105

Taylor, Edward 1642(?)-1729........ **LC 11**
See also DA; DLB 24

Taylor, Eleanor Ross 1920-........ **CLC 5**
See also CA 81-84

Taylor, Elizabeth 1912-1975 ... **CLC 2, 4, 29**
See also CA 13-16R; CANR 9; MTCW;
SATA 13

Taylor, Henry (Splawn) 1942-...... **CLC 44**
See also CA 33-36R; CAAS 7; CANR 31;
DLB 5

Taylor, Kamala (Purnaiya) 1924-
See Markandaya, Kamala
See also CA 77-80

Taylor, Mildred D. .... **CLC 21**
See also AAYA 10; BW; CA 85-88;
CANR 25; CLR 9; DLB 52; MAICYA;
SAAS 5; SATA 15, 70

Taylor, Peter (Hillsman)
1917- ...... **CLC 1, 4, 18, 37, 44, 50, 71;**
SSC 10
See also CA 13-16R; CANR 9; DLBY 81;
MTCW

Taylor, Robert Lewis 1912-........ **CLC 14**
See also CA 1-4R; CANR 3; SATA 10

Tchekhov, Anton
See Chekhov, Anton (Pavlovich)

Teasdale, Sara 1884-1933......... **TCLC 4**
See also CA 104; DLB 45; SATA 32

Tegner, Esaias 1782-1846........ **NCLC 2**

Teilhard de Chardin, (Marie Joseph) Pierre
1881-1955 .... **TCLC 9**
See also CA 105

Temple, Ann
See Mortimer, Penelope (Ruth)

Tennant, Emma (Christina)
1937- .... **CLC 13, 52**
See also CA 65-68; CAAS 9; CANR 10, 38;
DLB 14

Tenneshaw, S. M.
See Silverberg, Robert

Tennyson, Alfred
1809-1892 .... **NCLC 30; PC 6**
See also CDBLB 1832-1890; DA; DLB 32;
WLC

Teran, Lisa St. Aubin de .... **CLC 36**
See also St. Aubin de Teran, Lisa

Teresa de Jesus, St. 1515-1582...... **LC 18**

Terkel, Louis 1912-
See Terkel, Studs
See also CA 57-60; CANR 18; MTCW

Terkel, Studs .... **CLC 38**
See also Terkel, Louis
See also AITN 1

Terry, C. V.
See Slaughter, Frank G(ill)

Terry, Megan 1932- .... **CLC 19**
See also CA 77-80; CABS 3; DLB 7

Tertz, Abram
See Sinyavsky, Andrei (Donatevich)

Tesich, Steve 1943(?)-......... **CLC 40, 69**
See also CA 105; DLBY 83

Teternikov, Fyodor Kuzmich 1863-1927
See Sologub, Fyodor
See also CA 104

Tevis, Walter 1928-1984 .... **CLC 42**
See also CA 113

Tey, Josephine .... **TCLC 14**
See also Mackintosh, Elizabeth
See also DLB 77

Thackeray, William Makepeace
1811-1863 .... **NCLC 5, 14, 22**
See also CDBLB 1832-1890; DA; DLB 21,
55; SATA 23; WLC

Thakura, Ravindranatha
See Tagore, Rabindranath

Tharoor, Shashi 1956- .... **CLC 70**

Thelwell, Michael Miles 1939- ..... **CLC 22**
See also CA 101

Theobald, Lewis, Jr.
See Lovecraft, H(oward) P(hillips)

The Prophet
See Dreiser, Theodore (Herman Albert)

Theriault, Yves 1915-1983......... **CLC 79**
See also CA 102; DLB 88

Theroux, Alexander (Louis)
1939- .... **CLC 2, 25**
See also CA 85-88; CANR 20

Theroux, Paul (Edward)
1941- .... **CLC 5, 8, 11, 15, 28, 46**
See also BEST 89:4; CA 33-36R; CANR 20;
DLB 2; MTCW; SATA 44

Thesen, Sharon 1946-............ **CLC 56**

Thevenin, Denis
See Duhamel, Georges

Thibault, Jacques Anatole Francois
1844-1924
See France, Anatole
See also CA 106; 127; MTCW

Thiele, Colin (Milton) 1920- .... **CLC 17**
See also CA 29-32R; CANR 12, 28;
CLR 27; MAICYA; SAAS 2; SATA 14,
72

Thomas, Audrey (Callahan)
1935-.................. **CLC 7, 13, 37**
See also AITN 2; CA 21-24R; CANR 36;
DLB 60; MTCW

Thomas, D(onald) M(ichael)
1935- .... **CLC 13, 22, 31**
See also CA 61-64; CAAS 11; CANR 17;
CDBLB 1960 to Present; DLB 40;
MTCW

Thomas, Dylan (Marlais)
1914-1953 .... **TCLC 1, 8, 45; PC 2;**
SSC 3
See also CA 104; 120; CDBLB 1945-1960;
DA; DLB 13, 20; MTCW; SATA 60;
WLC

Thomas, (Philip) Edward
1878-1917 .... **TCLC 10**
See also CA 106; DLB 19

Thomas, Joyce Carol 1938-........ **CLC 35**
See also BW; CA 113; 116; CLR 19;
DLB 33; MAICYA; MTCW; SAAS 7;
SATA 40

Thomas, Lewis 1913- .... **CLC 35**
See also CA 85-88; CANR 38; MTCW

Thomas, Paul
See Mann, (Paul) Thomas

Thomas, Piri 1928-............... **CLC 17**
See also CA 73-76; HW

Thomas, R(onald) S(tuart)
1913- .... **CLC 6, 13, 48**
See also CA 89-92; CAAS 4; CANR 30;
CDBLB 1960 to Present; DLB 27;
MTCW

Thomas, Ross (Elmore) 1926- ...... **CLC 39**
See also CA 33-36R; CANR 22

Thompson, Francis Clegg
See Mencken, H(enry) L(ouis)

Thompson, Francis Joseph
1859-1907 .... TCLC 4
See also CA 104; CDBLB 1890-1914;
DLB 19

Thompson, Hunter S(tockton)
1939- .... CLC 9, 17, 40
See also BEST 89:1; CA 17-20R; CANR 23;
MTCW

Thompson, Jim 1906-1977(?)...... CLC 69

Thompson, Judith .... CLC 39

Thomson, James 1700-1748........ LC 16

Thomson, James 1834-1882...... NCLC 18

Thoreau, Henry David
1817-1862 .... NCLC 7, 21
See also CDALB 1640-1865; DA; DLB 1;
WLC

Thornton, Hall
See Silverberg, Robert

Thurber, James (Grover)
1894-1961 .... CLC 5, 11, 25; SSC 1
See also CA 73-76; CANR 17, 39;
CDALB 1929-1941; DA; DLB 4, 11, 22,
102; MAICYA; MTCW; SATA 13

Thurman, Wallace (Henry)
1902-1934 .... TCLC 6
See also BLC 3; BW; CA 104; 124; DLB 51

Ticheburn, Cheviot
See Ainsworth, William Harrison

Tieck, (Johann) Ludwig
1773-1853 .... NCLC 5
See also DLB 90

Tiger, Derry
See Ellison, Harlan

Tilghman, Christopher 1948(?)-..... CLC 65

Tillinghast, Richard (Williford)
1940- .... CLC 29
See also CA 29-32R; CANR 26

Timrod, Henry 1828-1867 .... NCLC 25
See also DLB 3

Tindall, Gillian 1938-............. CLC 7
See also CA 21-24R; CANR 11

Tiptree, James, Jr. .... CLC 48, 50
See also Sheldon, Alice Hastings Bradley
See also DLB 8

Titmarsh, Michael Angelo
See Thackeray, William Makepeace

Tocqueville, Alexis (Charles Henri Maurice
Clerel Comte) 1805-1859..... NCLC 7

Tolkien, J(ohn) R(onald) R(euel)
1892-1973 .... CLC 1, 2, 3, 8, 12, 38
See also AAYA 10; AITN 1; CA 17-18;
45-48; CANR 36; CAP 2;
CDBLB 1914-1945; DA; DLB 15;
MAICYA; MTCW; SATA 2, 24, 32;
WLC

Toller, Ernst 1893-1939 .... TCLC 10
See also CA 107; DLB 124

Tolson, M. B.
See Tolson, Melvin B(eaunorus)

Tolson, Melvin B(eaunorus)
1898(?)-1966 .... CLC 36
See also BLC 3; BW; CA 124; 89-92;
DLB 48, 76

Tolstoi, Aleksei Nikolaevich
See Tolstoy, Alexey Nikolaevich

Tolstoy, Alexey Nikolaevich
1882-1945 .... TCLC 18
See also CA 107

Tolstoy, Count Leo
See Tolstoy, Leo (Nikolaevich)

Tolstoy, Leo (Nikolaevich)
1828-1910 ..... TCLC 4, 11, 17, 28, 44;
SSC 9
See also CA 104; 123; DA; SATA 26; WLC

Tomasi di Lampedusa, Giuseppe 1896-1957
See Lampedusa, Giuseppe (Tomasi) di
See also CA 111

Tomlin, Lily................ CLC 17
See also Tomlin, Mary Jean

Tomlin, Mary Jean 1939(?)-
See Tomlin, Lily
See also CA 117

Tomlinson, (Alfred) Charles
1927- .... CLC 2, 4, 6, 13, 45
See also CA 5-8R; CANR 33; DLB 40

Tonson, Jacob
See Bennett, (Enoch) Arnold

Toole, John Kennedy
1937-1969 .... CLC 19, 64
See also CA 104; DLBY 81

Toomer, Jean
1894-1967 ...... CLC 1, 4, 13, 22; PC 7;
SSC 1
See also BLC 3; BW; CA 85-88;
CDALB 1917-1929; DLB 45, 51; MTCW

Torley, Luke
See Blish, James (Benjamin)

Tornimparte, Alessandra
See Ginzburg, Natalia

Torre, Raoul della
See Mencken, H(enry) L(ouis)

Torrey, E(dwin) Fuller 1937-....... CLC 34
See also CA 119

Torsvan, Ben Traven
See Traven, B.

Torsvan, Benno Traven
See Traven, B.

Torsvan, Berick Traven
See Traven, B.

Torsvan, Berwick Traven
See Traven, B.

Torsvan, Bruno Traven
See Traven, B.

Torsvan, Traven
See Traven, B.

Tournier, Michel (Edouard)
1924- .... CLC 6, 23, 36
See also CA 49-52; CANR 3, 36; DLB 83;
MTCW; SATA 23

Tournimparte, Alessandra
See Ginzburg, Natalia

Towers, Ivar
See Kornbluth, C(yril) M.

Townsend, Sue 1946- .... CLC 61
See also CA 119; 127; MTCW; SATA 48,
55

Townshend, Peter (Dennis Blandford)
1945- .... CLC 17, 42
See also CA 107

Tozzi, Federigo 1883-1920....... TCLC 31

Traill, Catharine Parr
1802-1899 .... NCLC 31
See also DLB 99

Trakl, Georg 1887-1914........... TCLC 5
See also CA 104

Transtroemer, Tomas (Goesta)
1931- .... CLC 52, 65
See also CA 117; 129; CAAS 17

Transtromer, Tomas Gosta
See Transtroemer, Tomas (Goesta)

Traven, B. (?)-1969............. CLC 8, 11
See also CA 19-20; 25-28R; CAP 2; DLB 9,
56; MTCW

Treitel, Jonathan 1959- .... CLC 70

Tremain, Rose 1943-............. CLC 42
See also CA 97-100; DLB 14

Tremblay, Michel 1942-........... CLC 29
See also CA 116; 128; DLB 60; MTCW

Trevanian (a pseudonym) 1930(?)-... CLC 29
See also CA 108

Trevor, Glen
See Hilton, James

Trevor, William
1928- .... CLC 7, 9, 14, 25, 71
See also Cox, William Trevor
See also DLB 14

Trifonov, Yuri (Valentinovich)
1925-1981 .... CLC 45
See also CA 126; 103; MTCW

Trilling, Lionel 1905-1975 .... CLC 9, 11, 24
See also CA 9-12R; 61-64; CANR 10;
DLB 28, 63; MTCW

Trimball, W. H.
See Mencken, H(enry) L(ouis)

Tristan
See Gomez de la Serna, Ramon

Tristram
See Housman, A(lfred) E(dward)

Trogdon, William (Lewis) 1939-
See Heat-Moon, William Least
See also CA 115; 119

Trollope, Anthony 1815-1882 .. NCLC 6, 33
See also CDBLB 1832-1890; DA; DLB 21,
57; SATA 22; WLC

Trollope, Frances 1779-1863 ..... NCLC 30
See also DLB 21

Trotsky, Leon 1879-1940........ TCLC 22
See also CA 118

Trotter (Cockburn), Catharine
1679-1749 .... LC 8
See also DLB 84

Trout, Kilgore
See Farmer, Philip Jose

Trow, George W. S. 1943-........ CLC 52
See also CA 126

Troyat, Henri 1911-.............. CLC 23
See also CA 45-48; CANR 2, 33; MTCW

Trudeau, G(arretson) B(eekman) 1948-
See Trudeau, Garry B.
See also CA 81-84; CANR 31; SATA 35

Trudeau, Garry B................. **CLC 12**
See also Trudeau, G(arretson) B(eekman)
See also AAYA 10; AITN 2

Truffaut, Francois 1932-1984....... **CLC 20**
See also CA 81-84; 113; CANR 34

Trumbo, Dalton 1905-1976 .... **CLC 19**
See also CA 21-24R; 69-72; CANR 10;
DLB 26

Trumbull, John 1750-1831....... **NCLC 30**
See also DLB 31

Trundlett, Helen B.
See Eliot, T(homas) S(tearns)

Tryon, Thomas 1926-1991 ...... **CLC 3, 11**
See also AITN 1; CA 29-32R; 135;
CANR 32; MTCW

Tryon, Tom
See Tryon, Thomas

Ts'ao Hsueh-ch'in 1715(?)-1763....... **LC 1**

Tsushima, Shuji 1909-1948
See Dazai, Osamu
See also CA 107

Tsvetaeva (Efron), Marina (Ivanovna)
1892-1941 .... **TCLC 7, 35**
See also CA 104; 128; MTCW

Tuck, Lily 1938-................. **CLC 70**
See also CA 139

Tunis, John R(oberts) 1889-1975 ... **CLC 12**
See also CA 61-64; DLB 22; MAICYA;
SATA 30, 37

Tuohy, Frank..................... **CLC 37**
See also Tuohy, John Francis
See also DLB 14

Tuohy, John Francis 1925-
See Tuohy, Frank
See also CA 5-8R; CANR 3

Turco, Lewis (Putnam) 1934- ... **CLC 11, 63**
See also CA 13-16R; CANR 24; DLBY 84

Turgenev, Ivan
1818-1883 .... **NCLC 21; SSC 7**
See also DA; WLC

Turner, Frederick 1943-.......... **CLC 48**
See also CA 73-76; CAAS 10; CANR 12,
30; DLB 40

Tusan, Stan 1936-................. **CLC 22**
See also CA 105

Tutuola, Amos 1920- .... **CLC 5, 14, 29**
See also BLC 3; BW; CA 9-12R; CANR 27;
DLB 125; MTCW

Twain, Mark
.... **TCLC 6, 12, 19, 36, 48; SSC 6**
See also Clemens, Samuel Langhorne
See also DLB 11, 12, 23, 64, 74; WLC

Tyler, Anne
1941- .... **CLC 7, 11, 18, 28, 44, 59**
See also BEST 89:1; CA 9-12R; CANR 11,
33; DLB 6; DLBY 82; MTCW; SATA 7

Tyler, Royall 1757-1826.......... **NCLC 3**
See also DLB 37

Tynan, Katharine 1861-1931 .... **TCLC 3**
See also CA 104

Tytell, John 1939- .... **CLC 50**
See also CA 29-32R

Tyutchev, Fyodor 1803-1873..... **NCLC 34**

Tzara, Tristan .... **CLC 47**
See also Rosenfeld, Samuel

Uhry, Alfred 1936-.............. **CLC 55**
See also CA 127; 133

Ulf, Haerved
See Strindberg, (Johan) August

Ulf, Harved
See Strindberg, (Johan) August

Unamuno (y Jugo), Miguel de
1864-1936 .... **TCLC 2, 9; SSC 11**
See also CA 104; 131; DLB 108; HW;
MTCW

Undercliffe, Errol
See Campbell, (John) Ramsey

Underwood, Miles
See Glassco, John

Undset, Sigrid 1882-1949.......... **TCLC 3**
See also CA 104; 129; DA; MTCW; WLC

Ungaretti, Giuseppe
1888-1970 .... **CLC 7, 11, 15**
See also CA 19-20; 25-28R; CAP 2;
DLB 114

Unger, Douglas 1952-............. **CLC 34**
See also CA 130

Unsworth, Barry (Forster) 1930-.... **CLC 76**
See also CA 25-28R; CANR 30

Updike, John (Hoyer)
1932- ...... **CLC 1, 2, 3, 5, 7, 9, 13, 15,
23, 34, 43, 70; SSC 13**
See also CA 1-4R; CABS 1; CANR 4, 33;
CDALB 1968-1988; DA; DLB 2, 5;
DLBD 3; DLBY 80, 82; MTCW; WLC

Upshaw, Margaret Mitchell
See Mitchell, Margaret (Munnerlyn)

Upton, Mark
See Sanders, Lawrence

Urdang, Constance (Henriette)
1922- .... **CLC 47**
See also CA 21-24R; CANR 9, 24

Uriel, Henry
See Faust, Frederick (Schiller)

Uris, Leon (Marcus) 1924-....... **CLC 7, 32**
See also AITN 1, 2; BEST 89:2; CA 1-4R;
CANR 1, 40; MTCW; SATA 49

Urmuz
See Codrescu, Andrei

Ustinov, Peter (Alexander) 1921-.... **CLC 1**
See also AITN 1; CA 13-16R; CANR 25;
DLB 13

V
See Chekhov, Anton (Pavlovich)

Vaculik, Ludvik 1926- .... **CLC 7**
See also CA 53-56

Valenzuela, Luisa 1938-........... **CLC 31**
See also CA 101; CANR 32; DLB 113; HW

Valera y Alcala-Galiano, Juan
1824-1905 .... **TCLC 10**
See also CA 106

Valery, (Ambroise) Paul (Toussaint Jules)
1871-1945 .... **TCLC 4, 15**
See also CA 104; 122; MTCW

Valle-Inclan, Ramon (Maria) del
1866-1936 .... **TCLC 5**
See also CA 106

Vallejo, Antonio Buero
See Buero Vallejo, Antonio

Vallejo, Cesar (Abraham)
1892-1938 .... **TCLC 3**
See also CA 105; HW

Valle Y Pena, Ramon del
See Valle-Inclan, Ramon (Maria) del

Van Ash, Cay 1918-.............. **CLC 34**

Vanbrugh, Sir John 1664-1726 ...... **LC 21**
See also DLB 80

Van Campen, Karl
See Campbell, John W(ood, Jr.)

Vance, Gerald
See Silverberg, Robert

Vance, Jack...................... **CLC 35**
See also Vance, John Holbrook
See also DLB 8

Vance, John Holbrook 1916-
See Queen, Ellery; Vance, Jack
See also CA 29-32R; CANR 17; MTCW

**Van Den Bogarde, Derek Jules Gaspard Ulric
Niven** 1921-
See Bogarde, Dirk
See also CA 77-80

Vandenburgh, Jane .... **CLC 59**

Vanderhaeghe, Guy 1951- .... **CLC 41**
See also CA 113

van der Post, Laurens (Jan) 1906- ... **CLC 5**
See also CA 5-8R; CANR 35

van de Wetering, Janwillem 1931- .. **CLC 47**
See also CA 49-52; CANR 4

Van Dine, S. S................... **TCLC 23**
See also Wright, Willard Huntington

Van Doren, Carl (Clinton)
1885-1950 .... **TCLC 18**
See also CA 111

Van Doren, Mark 1894-1972..... **CLC 6, 10**
See also CA 1-4R; 37-40R; CANR 3;
DLB 45; MTCW

Van Druten, John (William)
1901-1957 .... **TCLC 2**
See also CA 104; DLB 10

Van Duyn, Mona (Jane)
1921-................. **CLC 3, 7, 63**
See also CA 9-12R; CANR 7, 38; DLB 5

Van Dyne, Edith
See Baum, L(yman) Frank

van Itallie, Jean-Claude 1936-....... **CLC 3**
See also CA 45-48; CAAS 2; CANR 1;
DLB 7

van Ostaijen, Paul 1896-1928 ..... **TCLC 33**

Van Peebles, Melvin 1932- ...... **CLC 2, 20**
See also BW; CA 85-88; CANR 27

Vansittart, Peter 1920-............ **CLC 42**
See also CA 1-4R; CANR 3

Van Vechten, Carl 1880-1964 ...... **CLC 33**
See also CA 89-92; DLB 4, 9, 51

Van Vogt, A(lfred) E(lton) 1912-..... **CLC 1**
See also CA 21-24R; CANR 28; DLB 8;
SATA 14

Weiss, Theodore (Russell)
1916- . . . . **CLC 3, 8, 14**
See also CA 9-12R; CAAS 2; DLB 5

Welch, (Maurice) Denton
1915-1948 . . . . **TCLC 22**
See also CA 121

Welch, James 1940- . . . . **CLC 6, 14, 52**
See also CA 85-88

Weldon, Fay
1933(?)- . . . . **CLC 6, 9, 11, 19, 36, 59**
See also CA 21-24R; CANR 16;
CDBLB 1960 to Present; DLB 14;
MTCW

Wellek, Rene 1903- . . . . **CLC 28**
See also CA 5-8R; CAAS 7; CANR 8;
DLB 63

Weller, Michael 1942- . . . . **CLC 10, 53**
See also CA 85-88

Weller, Paul 1958- . . . . **CLC 26**

Wellershoff, Dieter 1925- . . . . **CLC 46**
See also CA 89-92; CANR 16, 37

Welles, (George) Orson
1915-1985 . . . . **CLC 20**
See also CA 93-96; 117

Wellman, Mac 1945- . . . . **CLC 65**

Wellman, Manly Wade 1903-1986 . . **CLC 49**
See also CA 1-4R; 118; CANR 6, 16;
SATA 6, 47

Wells, Carolyn 1869(?)-1942 . . . . . . **TCLC 35**
See also CA 113; DLB 11

Wells, H(erbert) G(eorge)
1866-1946 . . . . . . **TCLC 6, 12, 19; SSC 6**
See also CA 110; 121; CDBLB 1914-1945;
DA; DLB 34, 70; MTCW; SATA 20;
WLC

Wells, Rosemary 1943- . . . . **CLC 12**
See also CA 85-88; CLR 16; MAICYA;
SAAS 1; SATA 18, 69

Welty, Eudora
1909- . . . . **CLC 1, 2, 5, 14, 22, 33; SSC 1**
See also CA 9-12R; CABS 1; CANR 32;
CDALB 1941-1968; DA; DLB 2, 102;
DLBY 87; MTCW; WLC

Wen I-to 1899-1946 . . . . **TCLC 28**

Wentworth, Robert
See Hamilton, Edmond

Werfel, Franz (V.) 1890-1945 . . . . . . **TCLC 8**
See also CA 104; DLB 81, 124

Wergeland, Henrik Arnold
1808-1845 . . . . **NCLC 5**

Wersba, Barbara 1932- . . . . **CLC 30**
See also AAYA 2; CA 29-32R; CANR 16,
38; CLR 3; DLB 52; MAICYA; SAAS 2;
SATA 1, 58

Wertmueller, Lina 1928- . . . . **CLC 16**
See also CA 97-100; CANR 39

Wescott, Glenway 1901-1987 . . . . **CLC 13**
See also CA 13-16R; 121; CANR 23;
DLB 4, 9, 102

Wesker, Arnold 1932- . . . . **CLC 3, 5, 42**
See also CA 1-4R; CAAS 7; CANR 1, 33;
CDBLB 1960 to Present; DLB 13;
MTCW

Wesley, Richard (Errol) 1945- . . . . **CLC 7**
See also BW; CA 57-60; CANR 27; DLB 38

Wessel, Johan Herman 1742-1785 . . . . **LC 7**

West, Anthony (Panther)
1914-1987 . . . . **CLC 50**
See also CA 45-48; 124; CANR 3, 19;
DLB 15

West, C. P.
See Wodehouse, P(elham) G(renville)

West, (Mary) Jessamyn
1902-1984 . . . . **CLC 7, 17**
See also CA 9-12R; 112; CANR 27; DLB 6;
DLBY 84; MTCW; SATA 37

West, Morris L(anglo) 1916- . . . . . **CLC 6, 33**
See also CA 5-8R; CANR 24; MTCW

West, Nathanael
1903-1940 . . . . **TCLC 1, 14, 44**
See also CA 104; 125; CDALB 1929-1941;
DLB 4, 9, 28; MTCW

West, Owen
See Koontz, Dean R(ay)

West, Paul 1930- . . . . **CLC 7, 14**
See also CA 13-16R; CAAS 7; CANR 22;
DLB 14

West, Rebecca 1892-1983 . . **CLC 7, 9, 31, 50**
See also CA 5-8R; 109; CANR 19; DLB 36;
DLBY 83; MTCW

Westall, Robert (Atkinson) 1929- . . . **CLC 17**
See also CA 69-72; CANR 18; CLR 13;
MAICYA; SAAS 2; SATA 23, 69

Westlake, Donald E(dwin)
1933- . . . . **CLC 7, 33**
See also CA 17-20R; CAAS 13; CANR 16

Westmacott, Mary
See Christie, Agatha (Mary Clarissa)

Weston, Allen
See Norton, Andre

Wetcheek, J. L.
See Feuchtwanger, Lion

Wetering, Janwillem van de
See van de Wetering, Janwillem

Wetherell, Elizabeth
See Warner, Susan (Bogert)

Whalen, Philip 1923- . . . . **CLC 6, 29**
See also CA 9-12R; CANR 5, 39; DLB 16

Wharton, Edith (Newbold Jones)
1862-1937 . . . . . . **TCLC 3, 9, 27; SSC 6**
See also CA 104; 132; CDALB 1865-1917;
DA; DLB 4, 9, 12, 78; MTCW; WLC

Wharton, James
See Mencken, H(enry) L(ouis)

Wharton, William (a pseudonym)
. . . . **CLC 18, 37**
See also CA 93-96; DLBY 80

Wheatley (Peters), Phillis
1754(?)-1784 . . . . **LC 3; PC 3**
See also BLC 3; CDALB 1640-1865; DA;
DLB 31, 50; WLC

Wheelock, John Hall 1886-1978 . . . . **CLC 14**
See also CA 13-16R; 77-80; CANR 14;
DLB 45

White, E(lwyn) B(rooks)
1899-1985 . . . . **CLC 10, 34, 39**
See also AITN 2; CA 13-16R; 116;
CANR 16, 37; CLR 1, 21; DLB 11, 22;
MAICYA; MTCW; SATA 2, 29, 44

White, Edmund (Valentine III)
1940- . . . . **CLC 27**
See also AAYA 7; CA 45-48; CANR 3, 19,
36; MTCW

White, Patrick (Victor Martindale)
1912-1990 . . **CLC 3, 4, 5, 7, 9, 18, 65, 69**
See also CA 81-84; 132; MTCW

White, Phyllis Dorothy James 1920-
See James, P. D.
See also CA 21-24R; CANR 17; MTCW

White, T(erence) H(anbury)
1906-1964 . . . . **CLC 30**
See also CA 73-76; CANR 37; MAICYA;
SATA 12

White, Terence de Vere 1912- . . . . . . **CLC 49**
See also CA 49-52; CANR 3

White, Walter F(rancis)
1893-1955 . . . . **TCLC 15**
See also White, Walter
See also CA 115; 124; DLB 51

White, William Hale 1831-1913
See Rutherford, Mark
See also CA 121

Whitehead, E(dward) A(nthony)
1933- . . . . **CLC 5**
See also CA 65-68

Whitemore, Hugh (John) 1936- . . . . . **CLC 37**
See also CA 132

Whitman, Sarah Helen (Power)
1803-1878 . . . . **NCLC 19**
See also DLB 1

Whitman, Walt(er)
1819-1892 . . . . **NCLC 4, 31; PC 3**
See also CDALB 1640-1865; DA; DLB 3,
64; SATA 20; WLC

Whitney, Phyllis A(yame) 1903- . . . . **CLC 42**
See also AITN 2; BEST 90:3; CA 1-4R;
CANR 3, 25, 38; MAICYA; SATA 1, 30

Whittemore, (Edward) Reed (Jr.)
1919- . . . . **CLC 4**
See also CA 9-12R; CAAS 8; CANR 4;
DLB 5

Whittier, John Greenleaf
1807-1892 . . . . **NCLC 8**
See also CDALB 1640-1865; DLB 1

Whittlebot, Hernia
See Coward, Noel (Peirce)

Wicker, Thomas Grey 1926-
See Wicker, Tom
See also CA 65-68; CANR 21

Wicker, Tom . . . . **CLC 7**
See also Wicker, Thomas Grey

Wideman, John Edgar
1941- . . . . **CLC 5, 34, 36, 67**
See also BLC 3; BW; CA 85-88; CANR 14;
DLB 33

Wiebe, Rudy (H.) 1934- . . . . **CLC 6, 11, 14**
See also CA 37-40R; DLB 60

Wieland, Christoph Martin
1733-1813 . . . . **NCLC 17**
See also DLB 97

Wieners, John 1934- . . . . **CLC 7**
See also CA 13-16R; DLB 16

Wiesel, Elie(zer)   1928-..... **CLC 3, 5, 11, 37**
See also AAYA 7; AITN 1; CA 5-8R;
CAAS 4; CANR 8, 40; DA; DLB 83;
DLBY 87; MTCW; SATA 56

Wiggins, Marianne   1947-......... **CLC 57**
See also BEST 89:3; CA 130

Wight, James Alfred   1916-
See Herriot, James
See also CA 77-80; SATA 44, 55

Wilbur, Richard (Purdy)
1921-............ **CLC 3, 6, 9, 14, 53**
See also CA 1-4R; CABS 2; CANR 2, 29;
DA; DLB 5; MTCW; SATA 9

Wild, Peter   1940-................ **CLC 14**
See also CA 37-40R; DLB 5

Wilde, Oscar (Fingal O'Flahertie Wills)
1854(?)-1900 .... **TCLC 1, 8, 23, 41;**
                                          SSC 11
See also CA 104; 119; CDBLB 1890-1914;
DA; DLB 10, 19, 34, 57; SATA 24; WLC

Wilder, Billy .... **CLC 20**
See also Wilder, Samuel
See also DLB 26

Wilder, Samuel   1906-
See Wilder, Billy
See also CA 89-92

Wilder, Thornton (Niven)
1897-1975 ...... **CLC 1, 5, 6, 10, 15, 35;**
                                          DC 1
See also AITN 2; CA 13-16R; 61-64;
CANR 40; DA; DLB 4, 7, 9; MTCW;
WLC

Wilding, Michael   1942-........... **CLC 73**
See also CA 104; CANR 24

Wiley, Richard   1944-............. **CLC 44**
See also CA 121; 129

Wilhelm, Kate .... **CLC 7**
See also Wilhelm, Katie Gertrude
See also CAAS 5; DLB 8

Wilhelm, Katie Gertrude   1928-
See Wilhelm, Kate
See also CA 37-40R; CANR 17, 36; MTCW

Wilkins, Mary
See Freeman, Mary Eleanor Wilkins

Willard, Nancy   1936-........... **CLC 7, 37**
See also CA 89-92; CANR 10, 39; CLR 5;
DLB 5, 52; MAICYA; MTCW;
SATA 30, 37, 71

Williams, C(harles) K(enneth)
1936-................... **CLC 33, 56**
See also CA 37-40R; DLB 5

Williams, Charles
See Collier, James L(incoln)

Williams, Charles (Walter Stansby)
1886-1945 .... **TCLC 1, 11**
See also CA 104; DLB 100

Williams, (George) Emlyn
1905-1987 .... **CLC 15**
See also CA 104; 123; CANR 36; DLB 10,
77; MTCW

Williams, Hugo   1942-............. **CLC 42**
See also CA 17-20R; DLB 40

Williams, J. Walker
See Wodehouse, P(elham) G(renville)

Williams, John A(lfred)   1925-.... **CLC 5, 13**
See also BLC 3; BW; CA 53-56; CAAS 3;
CANR 6, 26; DLB 2, 33

Williams, Jonathan (Chamberlain)
1929-....................... **CLC 13**
See also CA 9-12R; CAAS 12; CANR 8;
DLB 5

Williams, Joy   1944-.............. **CLC 31**
See also CA 41-44R; CANR 22

Williams, Norman   1952-.......... **CLC 39**
See also CA 118

Williams, Tennessee
1911-1983 ..... **CLC 1, 2, 5, 7, 8, 11, 15,**
                         19, 30, 39, 45, 71
See also AITN 1, 2; CA 5-8R; 108;
CABS 3; CANR 31; CDALB 1941-1968;
DA; DLB 7; DLBD 4; DLBY 83;
MTCW; WLC

Williams, Thomas (Alonzo)
1926-1990 .... **CLC 14**
See also CA 1-4R; 132; CANR 2

Williams, William C.
See Williams, William Carlos

Williams, William Carlos
1883-1963 .... **CLC 1, 2, 5, 9, 13, 22, 42,**
                         67; PC 7
See also CA 89-92; CANR 34;
CDALB 1917-1929; DA; DLB 4, 16, 54,
86; MTCW

Williamson, David (Keith)   1942-.... **CLC 56**
See also CA 103; CANR 41

Williamson, Jack.................. **CLC 29**
See also Williamson, John Stewart
See also CAAS 8; DLB 8

Williamson, John Stewart   1908-
See Williamson, Jack
See also CA 17-20R; CANR 23

Willie, Frederick
See Lovecraft, H(oward) P(hillips)

Willingham, Calder (Baynard, Jr.)
1922-..................... **CLC 5, 51**
See also CA 5-8R; CANR 3; DLB 2, 44;
MTCW

Willis, Charles
See Clarke, Arthur C(harles)

Willy
See Colette, (Sidonie-Gabrielle)

Willy, Colette
See Colette, (Sidonie-Gabrielle)

Wilson, A(ndrew) N(orman)   1950- .. **CLC 33**
See also CA 112; 122; DLB 14

Wilson, Angus (Frank Johnstone)
1913-1991 .... **CLC 2, 3, 5, 25, 34**
See also CA 5-8R; 134; CANR 21; DLB 15;
MTCW

Wilson, August
1945-.......... **CLC 39, 50, 63; DC 2**
See also BLC 3; BW; CA 115; 122; DA;
MTCW

Wilson, Brian   1942-.............. **CLC 12**

Wilson, Colin   1931-............. **CLC 3, 14**
See also CA 1-4R; CAAS 5; CANR 1, 22,
33; DLB 14; MTCW

Wilson, Dirk
See Pohl, Frederik

Wilson, Edmund
1895-1972 .... **CLC 1, 2, 3, 8, 24**
See also CA 1-4R; 37-40R; CANR 1;
DLB 63; MTCW

Wilson, Ethel Davis (Bryant)
1888(?)-1980 .... **CLC 13**
See also CA 102; DLB 68; MTCW

Wilson, John   1785-1854.......... **NCLC 5**

Wilson, John (Anthony) Burgess
1917-.............. **CLC 8, 10, 13**
See also Burgess, Anthony
See also CA 1-4R; CANR 2; MTCW

Wilson, Lanford   1937-........ **CLC 7, 14, 36**
See also CA 17-20R; CABS 3; DLB 7

Wilson, Robert M.   1944-......... **CLC 7, 9**
See also CA 49-52; CANR 2, 41; MTCW

Wilson, Robert McLiam   1964-..... **CLC 59**
See also CA 132

Wilson, Sloan   1920-............. **CLC 32**
See also CA 1-4R; CANR 1

Wilson, Snoo   1948-.............. **CLC 33**
See also CA 69-72

Wilson, William S(mith)   1932-..... **CLC 49**
See also CA 81-84

Winchilsea, Anne (Kingsmill) Finch Counte
1661-1720 .... **LC 3**

Windham, Basil
See Wodehouse, P(elham) G(renville)

Wingrove, David (John)   1954-...... **CLC 68**
See also CA 133

Winters, Janet Lewis .... **CLC 41**
See also Lewis, Janet
See also DLBY 87

Winters, (Arthur) Yvor
1900-1968 .... **CLC 4, 8, 32**
See also CA 11-12; 25-28R; CAP 1;
DLB 48; MTCW

Winterson, Jeanette   1959-......... **CLC 64**
See also CA 136

Wiseman, Frederick   1930-......... **CLC 20**

Wister, Owen   1860-1938 .... **TCLC 21**
See also CA 108; DLB 9, 78; SATA 62

Witkacy
See Witkiewicz, Stanislaw Ignacy

Witkiewicz, Stanislaw Ignacy
1885-1939 .... **TCLC 8**
See also CA 105

Wittig, Monique   1935(?)-.......... **CLC 22**
See also CA 116; 135; DLB 83

Wittlin, Jozef   1896-1976 .... **CLC 25**
See also CA 49-52; 65-68; CANR 3

Wodehouse, P(elham) G(renville)
1881-1975 ... **CLC 1, 2, 5, 10, 22; SSC 2**
See also AITN 2; CA 45-48; 57-60;
CANR 3, 33; CDBLB 1914-1945;
DLB 34; MTCW; SATA 22

Woiwode, L.
See Woiwode, Larry (Alfred)

Woiwode, Larry (Alfred)   1941-... **CLC 6, 10**
See also CA 73-76; CANR 16; DLB 6

Wojciechowska, Maia (Teresa)
1927-.................... **CLC 26**
See also AAYA 8; CA 9-12R; CANR 4, 41;
CLR 1; MAICYA; SAAS 1; SATA 1, 28

Zaturenska, Marya 1902-1982.... **CLC 6, 11**
See also CA 13-16R; 105; CANR 22

Zelazny, Roger (Joseph) 1937- ..... **CLC 21**
See also AAYA 7; CA 21-24R; CANR 26;
DLB 8; MTCW; SATA 39, 57

Zhdanov, Andrei A(lexandrovich)
1896-1948 .... **TCLC 18**
See also CA 117

Zhukovsky, Vasily 1783-1852 .... **NCLC 35**

Ziegenhagen, Eric .... **CLC 55**

Zimmer, Jill Schary
See Robinson, Jill

Zimmerman, Robert
See Dylan, Bob

Zindel, Paul 1936- .... **CLC 6, 26**
See also AAYA 2; CA 73-76; CANR 31;
CLR 3; DA; DLB 7, 52; MAICYA;
MTCW; SATA 16, 58

Zinov'Ev, A. A.
See Zinoviev, Alexander (Aleksandrovich)

Zinoviev, Alexander (Aleksandrovich)
1922- .... **CLC 19**
See also CA 116; 133; CAAS 10

Zoilus
See Lovecraft, H(oward) P(hillips)

Zola, Emile (Edouard Charles Antoine)
1840-1902 .... **TCLC 1, 6, 21, 41**
See also CA 104; 138; DA; DLB 123; WLC

Zoline, Pamela 1941- .... **CLC 62**

Zorrilla y Moral, Jose 1817-1893.. **NCLC 6**

Zoshchenko, Mikhail (Mikhailovich)
1895-1958 .... **TCLC 15**
See also CA 115

Zuckmayer, Carl 1896-1977....... **CLC 18**
See also CA 69-72; DLB 56, 124

Zuk, Georges
See Skelton, Robin

Zukofsky, Louis
1904-1978 ...... **CLC 1, 2, 4, 7, 11, 18**
See also CA 9-12R; 77-80; CANR 39;
DLB 5; MTCW

Zweig, Paul 1935-1984........ **CLC 34, 42**
See also CA 85-88; 113

Zweig, Stefan 1881-1942 .... **TCLC 17**
See also CA 112; DLB 81, 118

CLC Cumulative Nationality Index

Nationality Index

Nationality Index

Nationality Index

Nationality Index

Nationality Index

CLC-79 Title Index

ISBN 0-8103-4987-6